For Tutorial Review

The Accounting Transaction Tutor (ATT) reinforces your understanding of financial accounting transactions in the first four chapters of the text* by helping you review important terms and accounting procedures. Specifically, you will be able to:

- **Study more efficiently.** Built-in Diagnostic Tests identify your strengths and weaknesses and allow you to select exercises where you need the most help.

- **Learn interactively at your own pace.** Interactive exercises prompt you to discover the correct answers on your own while working at your own study speed.

- **Seek glossary help when needed.** The Tutor provides access to key accounting terms and concepts.

- **Get more out of your accounting text.** The Accounting Transaction Tutor is linked to the text's learning objectives.

*A full version of the software, including tutorials for all 16 chapters of the text, is also available. For more information consult the Houghton Mifflin web site at http://college.hmco.com.

Also, Visit the Needles Accounting Resource Center

Visit http://college.hmco.com and select "Accounting" to access the Needles Accounting Resource Center, which contains a variety of educational resources for students and instructors, including:

For Students

- **ACE,** a self-testing program that allows students to check their mastery of the topics covered in each chapter
- **Research activities** based on the material covered in each chapter
- **Toys "R" Us Annual Report Activities** that make use of the latest Toys "R" Us financial statements
- **Links** to the web sites of companies and annual reports referenced in the book
- **Business readings** from leading periodicals
- **Excel Templates** that include templates for all Problems and Alternate Problems in the text

For Instructors

- **PowerPoint slides** for classroom presentation
- **Text previews,** which detail new features and provide supplement demonstrations
- **Sample syllabi** from your colleagues
- **Accounting Instructors' Report newsletter,** which explores a wide range of contemporary teaching issues
- **Going to Distance in Accounting,** an online training program from Faculty Development Programs, which provides suggestions for integrating new technologies into accounting education
- **Electronic Solutions** that contain answers to exercises, problems, and cases from the printed Instructor's Solutions Manual

Financial Accounting

Financial Accounting

SEVENTH EDITION

Belverd E. Needles, Jr., Ph.D., C.P.A., C.M.A.
DePaul University

Marian Powers, Ph.D.
Northwestern University

Houghton Mifflin Company   Boston   New York

To Annabelle and Abigail Needles
In memory of Mr. and Mrs. Belverd E. Needles, Sr., and
* Mr. and Mrs. Benjamin E. Needles*
To Mr. and Mrs. Thomas R. Powers

Senior Sponsoring Editor: Bonnie Binkert
Associate Sponsoring Editor: Margaret E. Monahan
Senior Project Editor: Margaret M. Kearney
Senior Production/Design Coordinator: Sarah L. Ambrose
Senior Manufacturing Coordinator: Priscilla J. Bailey
Marketing Manager: Melissa Russell

Cover Design: Rebecca Fagan
Cover Image: © Theo Rudnak/SIS

PHOTO CREDITS: page 3, © 2000 PhotoDisc, Inc.; page 4, Courtesy of Intel
Corporation; page 91, © Mark Wagner/Tony Stone Images; page 133,
© Vesey/Vanderburg/International Stock; page 175, © Koopman/Envision;
page 227, © Len Mastri/StockFood America; page 279, © 2000 PhotoDisc, Inc.;
page 280, Courtesy of Office Depot, Inc.; page 327, © 2000 PhotoDisc, Inc.;
page 373, © 2000 PhotoDisc, Inc.; page 415, © Nick Gunderson/Tony Stone
Images; page 459, © 2000 PhotoDisc, Inc.; page 460, Fermilab photo; page 507,
© 2000 PhotoDisc, Inc.; page 553, © Andrew Sacks/Tony Stone Images; page 554,
Courtesy of Lotus Development Corporation; page 593, © 2000 PhotoDisc, Inc.;
page 635, © 2000 PhotoDisc, Inc.; page 637, © Ben & Jerry's Homemade
Holdings, Inc. 2000; page 689, © Z. & B. Baran/Tony Stone Images; page 731,
© Peter Dazeley/Tony Stone Images.

The Toys "R" Us Annual Report (excerpts and complete) for the year ended
January 30, 1999, which appears at the end of Chapter 1, pages 63–89, is reprinted
by permission. The cartoon characters in the margins of the Supplement to
Chapter 1: How to Read an Annual Report, pages 53–59, are reprinted by permission from the Toys "R" Us Annual Report for the year ended January 28, 1995.

This book is written to provide accurate and authoritative information concerning
the covered topics. It is not meant to take the place of professional advice.

Printed in the U.S.A.
Library of Congress Catalog Card No.: 00-104438
ISBN: 0-618-023356
123456789-VH-04 03 02 01 00

Brief Contents

Contents

4 Accounting Systems   174

5 Financial Reporting and Analysis   226

Part Two
Measuring and Reporting the Operating Cycle   277

6   Merchandising Operations and Internal Control   278

7   Short-Term Liquid Assets   326

8   Inventories   372

9   Current Liabilities and the Time Value of Money   414

Part Three
Measuring and Reporting Long-Term Assets and Long-Term Financing 457

11 Long-Term Liabilities   506

12 Contributed Capital   552

Part Four
Expanded Presentation and Analysis of Accounting Information 591

Appendix A
The Merchandising Work Sheet and Closing Entries 769

Appendix B
Special-Purpose Journals 778

Appendix C
Accounting for Unincorporated Businesses 793

Appendix D
Future Value and Present Value Tables 803

Preface

FINANCIAL ACCOUNTING, Seventh Edition, recognizes that a majority of the students who take the financial accounting course are business and management majors who will read, analyze, and interpret financial statements throughout their careers. We feel that the fundamental purpose of accounting is to provide information for decision making, and, while not neglecting topics important for accounting majors, our mission is for all students to become intelligent users of financial statements and to understand that financial information, when interpreted and analyzed, will be useful to them in making critical business decisions throughout their careers.

FINANCIAL ACCOUNTING, Seventh Edition, is a first course in financial accounting for students with no previous training in accounting or business. This textbook is intended for use at both the undergraduate and graduate level. It has proven successful in a traditional one-quarter or one-semester course and has been used equally well in a two-quarter course in financial accounting.

The revision of FINANCIAL ACCOUNTING focuses on these major themes:

- Technology for classroom and distance learning environments
- Strong user approach that features financial statements and principal business activities
- Real-world relevance
- Comprehensive and flexible assignment material

Technology for Classroom and Distance Learning Environments

New technologies are a driving force behind business growth and accounting education today. The technologies we have developed for use by students and teachers in the traditional classroom, and those we have created to aid students and educators in the distance education environment, reflect state-of-the-art software and Web-based applications as well as the most current learning approaches.

Internet Web Site

The Needles Accounting Resource Center (visit http://college.hmco.com and select "Accounting") provides a wealth of resources for instructors and students. For example, the web site contains links directly to the financial statements (not just to the home pages) of companies cited as examples in the text and assignments. An Ace It icon in the margin next to the Chapter Review section of each chapter of the text reminds students to access ACE, a self-testing program that allows them to take sample quizzes and check their mastery of the chapter material. Other student resources include relevant readings from leading business and accounting periodicals (such as *Business Week, Forbes, The Wall Street Journal,* and *The Journal of Accountancy*), which examine current business issues, the accounting profession, and career options in a broad context; research activities, which present extended investigations of topics covered in the text; Toys "R" Us annual report activities, which make use of the latest Toys "R" Us financial statements; and Excel templates, designed so that students can work homework problems electronically.

For instructors, the Needles Accounting Resource Center contains a variety of resources designed to facilitate instruction, both within the traditional classroom and outside of it. Text previews detail new features of FINANCIAL ACCOUNTING and provide demonstrations of the supplements package. Sample syllabi show how your colleagues organize and teach the financial accounting course. The Accounting Instructors' Report newsletter explores a wide range of contemporary teaching issues. Faculty Development Programs' online training provides suggestions for integrating new technologies into the classroom. PowerPoint slides contain classroom presentation materials, discussion questions, figures from the text, and supplemental material, designed to support your classroom teaching. Electronic solutions, available both on the web site and on a CD-ROM, are fully functioning Excel spreadsheets for all exercises, problems, and alternate problems in the text. These solutions are designed to allow for "what if" analyses and are intended for both classroom use and electronic distribution, should you wish to allow your students access to them.

Distance Education Support Technology

You may supplement classroom discussion with the Blackboard Course Cartridge and Web CT Courselet for financial accounting or use them as a complete distance learning solution. They include electronic versions of the chapter planning matrices, chapter overviews, check figures for in-text problems, practice quizzes, Internet exercises, PowerPoint slide presentations, links to the Needles Accounting Resource Center, and Excel templates. You may also use the cartridges and courselets to post announcements, course documents, assignments, and quizzes.

Going To Distance in Accounting is a Blackboard-based course that will teach you how to put a course online. The sessions help you learn the basics of creating an online course, experience online learning from a student's perspective, develop teaching strategies, construct learning activities, design outcome assessment, and deliver the course. Tutorials and examples of online platform tools are also included.

Other Technology Supplements

- Fingraph® Financial Analyst™ CD-ROM: This CD-ROM program contains two main components: Fingraph® Financial Analyst™ software and a database of actual corporate annual reports. The Fingraph software enables students to prepare financial analyses of real companies in a very short time, analyzing information already in the database or financial data from any other source. The software accommodates a variety of learning styles: analyses are presented in tabular, graphic, and written formats. In addition, each chapter of FINANCIAL ACCOUNTING contains a case designed to be worked in conjunction with the CD-ROM database, in which students analyze balance sheets, income statements, and statements of cash flows of real companies.

- Accounting Transaction Tutor: This easy-to-use Windows software program reinforces accounting concepts and procedures through abundant exercises keyed to Learning Objectives. It also includes an online glossary and diagnostic tests that allow students to monitor their progress through the course material.

- Windows General Ledger Software: This is a fully operational general ledger program designed to function as a commercial package, containing preliminary data for selected problems in the text. This package offers complete coverage of accounting concepts and procedures in a straightforward, user-friendly Windows environment.

■ Excel Templates: This Excel-based program contains templates for all Problems and Alternate Problems in the text. Using this program to work the assignments, students learn both accounting and the basic skills required for spreadsheet applications.

Strong User Approach Featuring Financial Statements and Principal Business Activities

We know that most instructors want to place more emphasis on the analysis and use of accounting information by management, and on decisions that management makes with the help of accounting information. There are many ways the text reflects this emphasis, including the following:

Ideal Balance of Conceptual and Technical Content

Our goal is to provide exactly the right balance between conceptual understanding and technical application and analysis. Because our focus is on the application of concepts, we have substantially revised many chapters to reduce procedural detail by deleting unnecessary topics or by placing procedures that are not essential to conceptual understanding in supplemental objectives at the end of chapters. In the end-of-chapter assignments, we have scrutinized all exercises and problems with a view to reducing the number of journal entries and the amount of posting required; this eliminates unnecessary "pencil pushing" on the part of students completing the assignments.

Management Sections

Reflecting our goal to place more emphasis throughout the book on the use and analysis of accounting information by management and on decisions that management makes using accounting, all chapters now address management's use of accounting information. In most cases, this discussion can be found in the opening Learning Objective where it focuses students' attention on the purpose of the chapter; we then expand upon these management issues in the body of the chapter.

Performance Measurement

Beginning with Chapter 1, we integrate the concept of using financial information in performance evaluation and measurement at appropriate points in the text.

Cash Flow

We emphasize the effect of business activities on cash flow throughout the text. Beginning in Chapter 1, we introduce the statement of cash flows and we point out the difference between income measurement and cash flow in various chapters while reinforcing it through assignments. Cash flow discussions are indicated by a cash flow icon in the margin.

Key Ratios

Starting in Chapter 5, we examine financial analysis ratios and integrate them in subsequent chapters at appropriate points. These ratios are usually discussed in the "management issues" section at the beginning of the chapters, and where appropriate, appear as components of the review problems. We bring all the ratios together in a comprehensive financial analysis of Sun Microsystems, Inc., in Chapter 15. Key ratio presentations are indicated by a Key Ratio icon in the margin.

Organization

The Part and Chapter organization reflects, first, an early introduction of financial statements and, second, the relationship of financial accounting to the major activities of a business. For example, we have positioned a supplement entitled "How To Read An Annual Report" (which includes the entire Toys "R" Us annual report), after Chapter 1 to facilitate the presentation, early in the course, of published financial statements. We introduce performance measurements, cash flow effects, and ratio analysis in **Part One,** making the integration of these key management techniques throughout the text possible. **Part Two** emphasizes operating activities. **Part Three** focuses on investing in long-term assets and long-term financing activities. **Part Four** discusses advanced statements and analyses.

Real-World Relevance

Our goal is to reflect business practice as it is today in a context that is relevant and exciting to students. To this end, we have taken many steps to increase the real-world emphasis of the text.

Actual Financial Statements

To enhance students' appreciation for the usefulness and relevance of accounting information, we include excerpts from annual reports of real companies and articles about them in business journals. In total, we cite more than one hundred publicly held companies in the text as illustrative examples and in the chapter assignments as well. These companies are identified either by a Hot Links to Real Companies icon or by a CD-ROM icon in the margin.

In addition to containing the complete annual report of Toys "R" Us, Chapter 1 shows the interaction of the four basic financial statements of Toys "R" Us; Chapter 5 presents the financial statements of Dell Computer Corporation in graphical form using the Fingraph® Financial Analyst™ CD-ROM software; and the comprehensive financial analysis in Chapter 15 features the financial statements of Sun Microsystems, Inc. These are only a few examples of the scores of other well-known companies we mention as examples throughout the text.

Decision Points

Every chapter begins with a Decision Point based on excerpts from a real company's annual report or from articles in the business press. Decision Points present a situation requiring a decision by management and then demonstrate how the decision can be made using accounting information.

Business Focus Boxes

Business Focus boxes contain short items related to the chapter topics that show the relevance of accounting in four areas:

- Business Focus on Practice
- Business Focus on International
- Business Focus on Technology
- Business Focus on Ethics

Real-World Graphic Illustrations

We present graphs and tables illustrating how actual business practices relate to chapter topics. Many of these illustrations are based on data from studies of 600 annual reports published in *Accounting Trends and Techniques*. Beginning with Chapter 5, most chapters display a graphic that shows selected ratios for selected industries based on Dun & Bradstreet data. Service industry examples include accounting, bookkeeping, and interstate trucking companies. Merchandising industry examples include auto, home supply, and grocery store companies. Manufacturing industry examples include pharmaceutical and tableware companies.

International Accounting

In recognition of the global economy in which all businesses operate today, we introduce international accounting examples in Chapter 1 and incorporate them throughout the text. Some examples of foreign companies we point to in the text and assignments are Takashimaya Co. (Japanese), Glaxco-Wellcome (British), Mitsubishi (Japanese), and Groupe Michelin (French).

Governmental and Not-for-Profit Organizations

Acknowledging the importance of governmental and not-for-profit organizations in our society, we include discussions and examples using governmental and not-for-profit organizations at appropriate points.

Comprehensive and Flexible Assignment Material

Our goal is to provide the most comprehensive and flexible set of assignments available involving real companies. Whether you favor more traditional assignments, or cases that enhance a broader set of student skills, or a combination of both, we provide ample assignments—clearly identified—to meet your goals.

Building Your Knowledge Foundation

This section consists of a variety of questions, exercises, and problems designed to develop basic knowledge, comprehension, and application of the concepts and techniques in the chapter.

■ Questions (Q): Fifteen to 25 review questions covering the essential topics of the chapter.

■ Short Exercises (SE): Ten very brief exercises suitable for classroom use.

■ Exercises (E): An average of 15 single topic exercises that stress application.

■ Problems (P): Five extensive applications of chapter topics, often covering more than one Learning Objective. Selected problems in each chapter contain writing components.

■ Alternate Problems (P): An alternative set of the most popular problems, which we have developed based on feedback from our study of users' syllabi.

The assignments that are most suitable for computer applications are marked with the following icons:

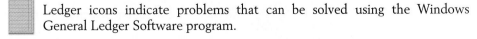 Ledger icons indicate problems that can be solved using the Windows General Ledger Software program.

Spreadsheet icons indicate problems that can be solved using the Excel Templates program.

Expanding Your Critical Thinking, Communication, and Interpersonal Skills

The Accounting Education Change Commission, the American Accounting Association, The American Institute of CPAs, and the Institute of Management accountants have all called for the development of a broader set of skills among business and accounting graduates. The assignments in this section of each chapter address this need by providing skills development (SD) cases and financial reporting analysis (FRA) cases. These sections each contain five or more cases, the majority of which are based on real companies. All of these cases require critical thinking and communication skills in the form of writing: at least one assignment in each chapter requires students to practice good business communication skills by writing a business memorandum, reporting their results and explaining their recommendations. All of the cases are suitable for development of interpersonal skills through group activities, but for those that are especially appropriate for teamwork, we provide specific instructions for applying an appropriate group teaching/learning methodology. So that you can see at a glance which content area, skills, and technological component each case addresses, we display the following icons in the margins:

 Ace It icons prompt students to visit the Needles Accounting Resource Center web site and access ACE, a self-testing quiz program.

 Cash Flow icons indicate text discussion of cash flow and assignments dealing with cash flow.

 CD-ROM icons in the text discussion identify companies whose annual reports are provided on the Fingraph® Financial Analyst™ CD-ROM. In the end-of-chapter materials, these icons indicate assignments that are designed to be worked with the CD-ROM.

 Communication icons identify assignments that are designed to help students develop their ability to understand and communicate accounting information successfully.

 Critical Thinking icons indicate assignments intended to strengthen students' critical thinking skills.

 Ethics icons identify assignments that address ethical issues.

 Group Activity icons identify assignments appropriate for groups or teamwork.

 Hot Links to Real Companies icons indicate companies whose annual reports can be accessed by direct link from the Needles Accounting Resource Center web site.

 International icons indicate international company cases.

 Internet icons designate assignments featuring use of the Internet.

K/R   Key Ratio icons indicate the presence of financial analysis ratios in the text and assignments.

Memorandum icons point to problems and cases that require students to write short business memorandums.

Each case has a specific purpose as described in the following paragraphs:

CONCEPTUAL ANALYSIS   Designed so that a written solution is appropriate, these short cases are based on real companies and address conceptual accounting issues.

ETHICAL DILEMMA   In recognition of the need for accounting and business students to be exposed to ethical considerations, every chapter contains a short case, often based on a real company, in which students must address an ethical dilemma directly related to the chapter content.

RESEARCH ACTIVITY   These exercises are designed to foster greater learning by acquainting students with business periodicals, the use of annual reports and business references, and the use of the library. Some are designed to improve students' interviewing and observation skills through field activities at actual businesses. An icon in the margin indicates which activities can be researched on the Internet.

DECISION-MAKING PRACTICE   In the role of decision maker, students are asked to extract relevant data from a case, make computations as necessary, and arrive at a decision. The decision maker may be a manager, an investor, an analyst, or a creditor.

INTERPRETING FINANCIAL REPORTS   These short cases, abstracted from business articles and annual reports of well-known corporations and organizations such as Kmart, Sears, IBM, Toys "R" Us, Chrysler, and UAL (United Airlines), require students to extract relevant data, make computations, and interpret the results.

INTERNATIONAL COMPANY   These cases involve a company from a foreign country that has had an accounting experience compatible with chapter content.

TOYS "R" US ANNUAL REPORT   The reading and analysis of the actual annual report of Toys "R" Us, contained in the Supplement to Chapter 1, forms the basis of these cases.

FINGRAPH® FINANCIAL ANALYST™   These cases make use of the Fingraph® Financial Analyst™ annual report database software. The annual reports of more than 20 well-known companies are included in the database.

INTERNET CASE   Each chapter of the text now features an Internet case, which asks students to research a topic on the Internet, answer critical and analytical thinking questions, then prepare either a written or oral report on their findings.

The Annual Report Project

Because the use of real companies' annual reports is the most rapidly growing type of term project in the financial accounting course, we provide an annual report project that we have used in our own classes for several years. Depending on how comprehensive you want the project to be, we have developed four assignment options, including the use of the Fingraph® Financial Analyst™ CD-ROM software.

Video Cases

To provide more real world opportunities to reinforce key concepts and techniques, we have integrated five videos cases into the text, indicated by the video icon on the left. These five-minute videos may be used with groups and include written critical thinking assignments:

■ Intel Corporation (Chapter 1) introduces the business goals of liquidity and profitability and the business activities of financing, investing, and operating.

■ Office Depot, Inc. (Chapter 6) discusses the merchandising company, the merchandising income statement, and the concept of the operating cycle.

■ Fermi National Accelerator Laboratory (Chapter 10) demonstrates the importance of long-term assets to a unique scientific laboratory.

■ Lotus Corporation (Chapter 12) tells the history of the company from its beginning as a small start-up through its growth to one of America's most successful companies and finally to its sale to IBM. The case analyzes Lotus's equity financing needs along the way.

■ Ben & Jerry's Homemade, Inc. (Chapter 14) examines Ben & Jerry's struggle to maintain its unique character while achieving adequate income and cash flows.

Financial Analysis Cases

Also available is a series of comprehensive financial analysis cases that may be integrated throughout the course after Chapter 5 or may be used as capstone cases for the course. The first, *General Mills, Inc., Annual Report: A Decision Case in Financial Analysis*, uses the actual financial statements of General Mills Corporation. The other cases, *Heartland Airways, Inc.* and *Richland Home Centers, Inc.*, present complete annual reports for an airline company and a home improvements retailing chain, respectively, and guide students through a complete financial analysis. These cases may be assigned individually, but also provide excellent groupwork opportunities.

Supplementary Learning Aids for Students

Study Guide
Working Papers for Exercises and Problems
NEW! Ready Notes
Fingraph® Financial Analyst™ CD-ROM
Accounting Transaction Tutor
Windows General Ledger Software
Excel Templates
Internet Web Site
NEW! Houghton Mifflin Brief Accounting Dictionary
Soft-Tec Practice Case
General Mills, Inc., Annual Report: A Decision Case in Financial Analysis
Heartland Airways, Inc.
Richland Home Centers, Inc.

Instructor's Support Materials

Instructor's Solutions manual
Electronic Solutions
Course Manual
Test Bank with Answers

Computerized Test Bank
Teaching Transparency Masters
Solutions Transparencies
PowerPoint Classroom Presentation Slides
Video Cases
Master Teacher Videos
Business Bulletin Videos
Internet Web Site
Soft-Tec Practice Case Instructor's Solutions Manual
General Mills, Inc., Annual Report: A Decision Case in Financial Analysis Instructor's Solutions Manual
Heartland Airways, Inc. Instructor's Solutions Manual
Richland Home Centers, Inc. Instructor's Solutions Manual

Readable, Accessible Text

Today's business and accounting students are learning the skills that will help them succeed in business. FINANCIAL ACCOUNTING helps students acquire and integrate these skills by combining authoritative, practical, and contemporary content with an efficient and effective pedagogical approach.

English as a Second Language Reviews

Growing numbers of students who take the financial accounting course are from foreign countries, and English is a second language for them. To meet their needs fully, we as instructors must be aware of how the complexities and nuances of English, particularly business English, might hinder these students' understanding.

Each chapter of FINANCIAL ACCOUNTING has been reviewed by Business instructors who teach English as a second language (ESL) courses and English for Special Purpose courses, as well as by students taking these courses. With their assistance and advice, as well as with our own experience of teaching classes with a high degree of cultural diversity, we have taken the following measures to ensure that the text is accessible:

- Word Choice: We replaced words and phrases that were unfamiliar to ESL students with ones they more readily recognize and understand. For instance, we substituted "raise" for "bolster," "require" for "call for," and "available" for "on hand."

- Length: Because short, direct sentences are easier to comprehend than sentences containing multiple clauses, we paid strict attention to the length and grammatical complexity of our sentences.

- Examples: Examples reinforce concepts and help to make the abstract concrete. We have added simple, straightforward examples for further clarity.

Student Annotations

In this edition of FINANCIAL ACCOUNTING we have added two types of marginal annotations to help students excel in their study of accounting.

PEDAGOGICAL ANNOTATIONS   These annotations appear in Chapter 1 only, and they introduce each pedagogical element of the text—Learning Objectives, Decision Points, Content Annotations, and Chapter Reviews, to name a few—to students. They describe the purpose of the pedagogy and provide usage suggestions so that students can derive maximum benefit when reading and studying the text.

CONTENT ANNOTATIONS These marginal annotations appear throughout the text, offering material that enriches the text discussion as well as strategies and tips for mastering text content. Content Annotations fall into the following categories:

- Key Point: Key Point annotations briefly summarize main concepts or ideas.
- Enrichment Note: These annotations offer interesting insights—such as historical perspectives—to heighten students' appreciation of the material.
- Terminology Note: Terminology Notes provide succinct definitions of key terms and concepts used in the text discussion.
- Business-World Example: These short anecdotes are drawn from real businesses and help students see the day-to-day relevance of accounting in real companies.
- Critical Thinking Question: Intended to sharpen students' critical thinking skills, these annotations pose at least one critical thinking question and provide a sample answer.
- Ethical Consideration: Ethical Consideration annotations highlight practices or behaviors that might engender ethical concern.
- Study Note: These annotations provide useful strategies and tips to help students avoid common pitfalls.

Acknowledgments

Preparing a financial accounting text is a long and demanding project that cannot really succeed without the help of one's colleagues. We are grateful to a large number of professors, other professional colleagues, and students for their many constructive comments on the text. Unfortunately, any attempt to list those who have helped means that some are slighted by omission. An attempt, however, must be made to mention those who have been so helpful.

We wish to express our deep appreciation to colleagues at DePaul University, who have been extremely supportive and encouraging.

The thoughtful and meticulous work of Edward H. Julius (California Lutheran University) is reflected not only in the Study Guide, but in many other ways as well. We would also like to thank Marion Taube (University of Pittsburgh) for her contribution to the Test Bank and the Working Papers.

Also very important to the quality of this book is the supportive collaboration of our senior sponsoring editor, Bonnie Binkert. We furthered benefited from the ideas and guidance of our associate sponsoring editor, Margaret E. Monahan; developmental editor, Jacquie Commanday; and senior project editor, Margaret M. Kearney.

Others who have been supportive and have had an impact on this book throughout their reviews, suggestions, and class testing are:

Gregory D. Barnes	Clarion University
Mohamed E. Bayou	The University of Michigan—Dearborn
Charles M. Betts	Delaware Technical & Community College
Michael C. Blue	Bloomsburg University
Gary R. Bower	Community College of Rhode Island
Lee Cannell	El Paso Community College
John D. Cunha	University of California—Berkeley
Mark W. Dawson	Duquesne University
Patricia A. Doherty	Boston University
Lizabeth England	American Language Academy
David Fetyko	Kent State University

Sue Garr	Wayne State University
Roxanne Gooch	Cameron University
Christine Uber Grosse	The American Graduate School of International Management
Dennis A. Gutting	Orange County Community College
John Hancock	University of California—Davis Graduate School of Management
Edward H. Julius	California Lutheran University
Howard A. Kanter	DePaul University
Kevin McClure	ESL Language Center
George McGowan	
Gail A. Mestas	
Michael F. Monahan	
Jenine Moscove	
Glenn Owen	Alan Hancock College
Beth Brooks Patel	University of California—Berkeley
LaVonda Ramey	Schoolcraft College
Roberta Rettner	American Ways
James B. Rosa	Queensborough Community College
Donald Shannon	DePaul University
S. Murray Simons	Northeastern University
Marion Taube	University of Pittsburgh
Kathleen Villani	Queensborough Community College
John Weber	DeVry Institute
Kay Westerfield	University of Oregon
Carol Yacht	
Glenn Allen Young	Tulsa Junior College
Marilyn J. Young	Tulsa Junior College

B.N. and M. P.

To the Student

How to Study Accounting Successfully

Whether you are majoring in accounting or in another business discipline, your introductory accounting course is one of the most important classes you will take, because it is fundamental to the business curriculum and to your success in the business world beyond college. The course has multiple purposes because its students have diverse interests, backgrounds, and purposes for taking it. What are your goals in studying accounting? Being clear about your goals can contribute to your success in this course.

Success in this class also depends on your desire to learn and your willingness to work hard. And it depends on your understanding of how the text complements the way your instructor teaches and the way you learn. A familiarity with how this text is structured will help you to study more efficiently, make better use of classroom time, and improve your performance on examinations and other assignments.

To be successful in the business world after you graduate, you will need a broad set of skills, which may be summarized as follows:

TECHNICAL/ANALYTICAL SKILLS   A major objective of your accounting course is to give you a firm grasp of the essential business and accounting terminology and techniques that you will need to succeed in a business environment. With this foundation, you then can begin to develop the higher-level perception skills that will help you to acquire further knowledge on your own.

An even more crucial objective of this course is to help you develop analytical skills that will allow you to evaluate data. Well-developed analytical and decision-making skills are among the professional skills most highly valued by employers and will serve you well throughout your academic and professional careers.

COMMUNICATION SKILLS   Another skill highly prized by employers is the ability to express oneself in a manner that is understood correctly by others. This can include writing skills, speaking skills, and presentation skills. Communication skills are developed through particular tasks and assignments and are improved through constructive criticism. Reading skills and listening skills support the direct communication skills.

INTERPERSONAL SKILLS   Effective interaction between two people requires a solid foundation of interpersonal skills. The success of such interaction depends on empathy, or the ability to identify with and understand the problems, concerns, and motives of others. Leadership, supervision, and interviewing skills also facilitate a professional's interaction with others.

PERSONAL/SELF SKILLS   Personal/self skills form the foundation for growth in the use of all other skills. To succeed, a professional must take initiative, possess self-confidence, show independence, and be ethical in all areas of life. Personal/self skills can be enhanced significantly by the formal learning process and by peers and mentors who provide models upon which you can build. Accounting is just one course in your entire curriculum, but it can play an important role in your development of the above skills. Your instructor is interested in helping you gain both a knowledge of accounting and the more general skills you will need to succeed in the business world. The following sections describe how you can get the most out of this course.

The Teaching/Learning Cycle™

Both teaching and learning have natural, parallel, and mutually compatible cycles. This teaching/learning cycle, as shown in Figure 1, interacts with the basic structure of learning objectives in this text.

THE TEACHING CYCLE   The inner (tan) circle in Figure 1 shows the steps an instructor takes in teaching a chapter. Your teacher *assigns* material, *presents* the subject in lecture, *explains* by going over assignments and answering questions, *reviews* the subject prior to an exam, and *assesses* your knowledge and understanding using examinations and other means of evaluation.

THE LEARNING CYCLE   Moving outward, the next circle (green) in Figure 1 shows the steps you should take in studying a chapter. You should *preview* the material, *read* the chapter, *apply* your understanding by working the assignments, *review* the chapter, and *recall* and *demonstrate* your knowledge and understanding of the material on examinations and other assessments.

INTEGRATED LEARNING OBJECTIVES   Your textbook supports the teaching/learning cycle through the use of integrated learning objectives. Learning objectives are simply statements of what you should be able to do after you have completed a chapter. In Figure 1, the outside (blue) circle shows how learning objectives are integrated into your text and other study aids and how they interact with the teaching/learning cycle.

1. Learning objectives appear at the beginning of the chapter, as an aid to your teacher in making assignments and as a preview of the chapter for you.

2. Each learning objective is repeated in the text at the point where that subject is covered to assist your teacher in presenting the material and to help you organize your thoughts as you read the material.

3. Every exercise, problem, and case in the chapter assignments shows the applicable learning objective(s) so you can refer to the text if you need help.

4. A summary of the key points for each learning objective, a list of new concepts and terms referenced by learning objectives, and a review problem covering key learning objectives assist you in reviewing each chapter. Your Study Guide, also organized by learning objectives, provides for additional review.

WHY STUDENTS SUCCEED   Students succeed in their accounting course when they coordinate their personal learning cycle with their instructor's cycle. Students who do a good job of previewing their assignments, reading the chapters before the instructor is ready to present them, preparing homework assignments before they are discussed in class, and reviewing carefully will ultimately achieve their potential on exams. Those who get out of phase with their instructor, for whatever reason, will do poorly or fail. To ensure that your learning cycle is synchronized with your instructor's teaching cycle, check your study habits against these suggestions.

Previewing the Chapter

1. Read the learning objectives at the beginning of the chapter. These learning objectives specifically describe what you should be able to do after completing the chapter.

Figure 1
The Teaching/Learning Cycle™ with
Integrated Learning Objectives

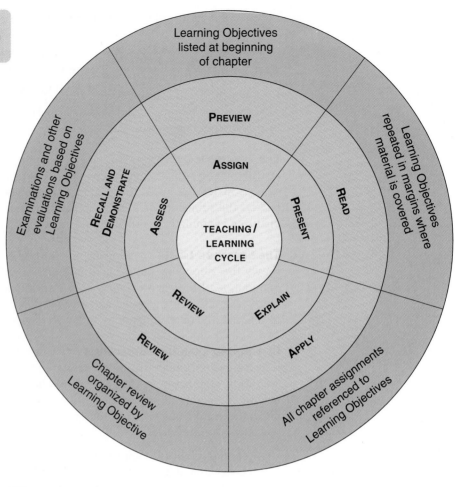

TEACHING CYCLE

LEARNING CYCLE

LEARNING OBJECTIVES STRUCTURE

2. Study your syllabus. Know where you are in the course and where you are going. Know the rules of the course.

3. Realize that in an accounting course, each assignment builds on previous ones. If you do poorly in Chapter 1, you may have difficulty in Chapter 2 and be lost in Chapter 3.

Reading the Chapter

1. As you read each chapter, be aware of the learning objectives in the margins. They will tell you why the material is relevant.

2. Allow yourself plenty of time to read the text. Accounting is a technical subject. Accounting books are so full of information that almost every sentence is important.

3. Strive to understand why as well as how each procedure is done. Accounting is logical and requires reasoning. If you understand why something is done in accounting, there is little need to memorize.

4. Relate each new topic to its learning objective and be able to explain it in your own words.

5. Be aware of colors as you read. They are designed to help you understand the text. (See the chart on the back of your textbook.)
Gold: All source documents and inputs are in gold.
Green: All accounting forms, working papers, and accounting processes are shown in green.
Purple: All financial statements, the output or final product of the accounting process, are shown in purple.
Tan: In selected tables and illustrations, tan is used to heighten contrasts and aid understanding.

6. If there is something you do not understand, prepare specific questions for your instructor. Pinpoint the topic or concept that confuses you. Some students keep a notebook of points with which they have difficulty.

Applying the Chapter

1. In addition to understanding why each procedure is done, you must be able to do it yourself by working exercises, problems, and cases. Accounting is a "do-it-yourself" course.

2. Read assignments and instructions carefully. Each assignment has a specific purpose. The wording is precise, and a clear understanding of it will save time and improve your performance. Acquaint yourself with the end-of-chapter assignment materials in this text by reading the description of them in the Preface.

3. Try to work exercises, problems, and cases without referring to their discussions in the chapter. If you cannot work an assignment without looking in the chapter, you will not be able to work a similar problem on an exam. After you have tried on your own, refer to the chapter (based on the learning objective reference) and check your answer. Try to understand any mistakes you may have made.

4. Be neat and orderly. Sloppy calculations, messy papers, and general carelessness cause most errors on accounting assignments.

5. Allow plenty of time to work the chapter assignments. You will find that assignments seem harder and that you make more errors when you are feeling pressed for time.

6. Keep up with your class. Check your work against the solutions presented in class. Find your mistakes. Be sure you understand the correct solutions.

7. Note the part of each exercise, problem, or case that causes you difficulty so you can ask for help.

8. Attend class. Most instructors design classes to help you and to answer your questions. Absence from even one class can hurt your performance.

Reviewing the Chapter

1. Read the summary of learning objectives in the chapter review. Be sure you know the definitions of all the words in the review of concepts and terminology.

2. Review all assigned exercises, problems, and cases. Know them cold. Be sure you can work the assignments without the aid of the book.

3. Determine the learning objectives for which most of the problems were assigned. They refer to topics that your instructor is most likely to emphasize

on an exam. Scan the text for such learning objectives and pay particular attention to the examples and illustrations.

4. Look for and scan other similar assignments that cover the same learning objectives. They may be helpful on an exam.

5. Review quizzes. Similar material will often appear on longer exams.

6. Attend any labs or visit any tutors your school provides, or see your instructor during office hours to get assistance. Be sure to have specific questions ready.

Taking Examinations

1. Arrive at class early so you can get the feel of the room and make a last-minute review of your notes.

2. Have plenty of sharp pencils and your calculator (if allowed) ready.

3. Review the exam quickly when it is handed out to get an overview of your task. Start with a part you know. It will give you confidence and save time.

4. Allocate your time to the various parts of the exam, and stick to your schedule. Every exam has time constraints. You need to move ahead and make sure you attempt all parts of the exam.

5. Read the questions carefully. Some may not be exactly like your homework assignments. They may approach the material from a slightly different angle to test your understanding and ability to reason, rather than your ability to memorize.

6. To avoid unnecessary errors, be neat, use good form, and show calculations.

7. Relax. If you have followed the above guidelines, your effort will be rewarded.

Preparing Other Assignments

1. Understand the assignment. Written assignments, term papers, computer projects, oral presentations, case studies, group activities, individual field trips, video critiques, and other activities are designed to enhance skills beyond your technical knowledge. It is essential to know exactly what your instructor expects. Know the purpose, audience, scope, and expected end product.

2. Allow plenty of time. "Murphy's Law" applies to such assignments: If anything can go wrong, it will.

3. Prepare an outline of each report, paper, or presentation. A project that is done well always has a logical structure.

4. Write a rough draft of each paper and report, and practice each presentation. Professionals always try out their ideas in advance and thoroughly rehearse their presentations. Good results are not accomplished by accident.

5. Make sure that each paper, report, or presentation is of professional quality. Instructors appreciate attention to detail and polish. A good rule of thumb is to ask yourself: Would I give this work to my boss?

About the Authors

BELVERD E. NEEDLES, JR., PH.D., C.P.A., C.M.A.

Belverd E. Needles, Jr. received his BBA and MBA degrees from Texas Tech University and his Ph.D. degree from the University of Illinois. Dr. Needles teaches auditing and financial accounting at DePaul University, where he is the Arthur Andersen LLP Alumni Distinguished Professor and is an internationally known expert in international auditing and accounting education. He has published in leading journals in these fields and is the author or editor of more than 20 books and monographs.

Dr. Needles is active in many academic and professional organizations. He is president of the International Association for Accounting Education and Research and past president of the Federation of Schools of Accountancy. He has served as the elected U.S. representative to the European Accounting Association and chair of the International Accounting Section of the American Accounting Association. He has served as director of Continuing Education of the American Accounting Association. He serves on the Information Technology Executive Committee of the American Institute of CPAs. For the past five years he has served as the U.S. representative on the Education Committee of the International Federation of Accountants.

Dr. Needles has received the Distinguished Alumni Award from Texas Tech University, the Illinois CPA Society Outstanding Educator Award, the Joseph A. Silvoso Faculty Award of Merit from the Federation of Schools and Accountancy, the Ledger & Quill Award of Merit, and the Ledger & Quill Teaching Excellence Award. In 1992, he was named Educator of the Year by the national honorary society Beta Alpha Psi. In 1996, he received from the American Accounting Association the award of Outstanding International Accounting Educator.

MARIAN POWERS, PH.D.

Marian Powers earned her Ph.D. in accounting from the University of Illinois at Urbana. She has served on the accounting faculty of the Kellogg Graduate School of Management at Northwestern University, the University of Illinois at Chicago, and the Lake Forest Graduate School of Management. Since 1987, she has been a professor of accounting at the Allen Center for Executive Education at Northwestern University, specializing in teaching financial reporting and analysis to executives. She is also co-author of several successful in-depth cases on financial analysis, and her research has been published in *The Accounting Review; The International Journal of Accounting; Issues in Accounting Education; The Journal of Accountancy; The Journal of Business, Finance, and Accounting;* and *Financial Management,* among others. Dr. Powers has received recognition and awards for her teaching.

Dr. Powers has been active in several professional organizations, including the Illinois CPA Society, the American Accounting Association, the European Accounting Association, the International Association of Accounting Education and Research, the American Society of Women Accountants, and the Education Foundation for Women in Accounting. She is currently serving as secretary of the Education Foundation for Women in Accounting. She is past president of the Chicago chapter and past national officer of the American Society of Women Accountants.

Check Figures

Chapter 1 Problems
P 1. Total Assets: $18,300
P 2. Total Assets: $14,060
P 3. Total Assets: $16,920
P 4. Total Assets: $115,000
P 5. Total Assets: $10,240
P 6. Total Assets: $21,640
P 7. Total Assets: $143,800
P 8. Total Assets: $97,500

Chapter 2 Problems
P 1. No check figure
P 2. Trial Balance: $42,200
P 3. Trial Balance: $7,400
P 4. Trial Balance: $21,080
P 5. Trial Balance: $61,420
P 6. No check figure
P 7. Trial Balance: $11,550
P 8. Trial Balance: $47,030

Chapter 3 Problems
P 1. No check figure
P 2. No check figure
P 3. Adjusted Trial Balance: $62,896
P 4. Adjusted Trial Balance: $34,372
P 5. Adjusted Trial Balance: $87,120
P 6. No check figure
P 7. No check figure
P 8. Adjusted Trial Balance: $218,334

Chapter 4 Problems
P 1. Net Income: 442,739
P 2. Total Assets: $6,943
P 3. Net Income for May: $431;
Net Income for June: $467
P 4. Net Income: $22,893
P 5. Net Income: $78,622
P 6. Net Income: $83,150
P 7. Total Assets: $113,616
P 8. Net Income: $6,687

Chapter 5 Problems
P 1. No check figure
P 2. Income from Operations: 20x3, $34,320;
20x2, $84,748
P 3. Total Assets, $595,600
P 4. Return on Equity: 20x3, 15.6 %; 20x2, 12.2%
P 5. Net Income: $72,260; Total Assets: $1,083,800
P 6. No check figure
P 7. Income from Operations: 20x2, $66,426;
20x1, $110,628
P 8. Return on Equity: 20x4, 25.2%; 20x3, 21.7%

Chapter 6 Problems
P 1. Net Income: $13,435
P 2. No check figure

P 3. Net Income: $2,435
P 4. No check figure
P 5. No check figure
P 6. No check figure
P 7. Net Income: $5,522
P 8. No check figure
P 9. Net Income: $18,941
P 10. No check figure

Chapter 7 Problems
P 1. Short-Term Investments (at market): June 30, 20x2, $903,875
P 2. No check figure
P 3. Amount of Adjustment: $9,533
P 4. No check figure
P 5. Adjusted Balance: $149,473.28
P 6. Short-Term Investments (at market): June 30, 20x2, $354,000
P 7. No check fugre
P 8. Amount of Adjustment: $73,413
P 9. No check figure
P 10. Adjusted Cash Balance: $54,485.60

Chapter 8 Problems
P 1. Cost of Goods Available for Sale: $10,560,000
P 2. 1. Cost of Goods Sold: June, $19,320;
July, $44,237
P 3. 1. Cost of Goods Sold: June, $19,160;
July, $43,982
P 4. Estimated Inventory Shortage: At Cost, $42,431; At Retail, $56,200
P 5. Estimated Destroyed Inventory: $730,000
P 6. 1. Cost of Goods Available for Sale: $315,960
P 7. 1. Cost of Goods Sold: March, $4,578;
April, $15,457
P 8. 1. Cost of Goods Sold: March, $4,560;
April, $15,424

Chapter 9 Problems
P 1. Total Current Liabilities: $36,988.20
P 2. No check figure
P 3. 1.b. Estimated Product Warranty Liability: $10,800
P 4. No check figure
P 5. 1. Fund balance: $116,600
P 6. No check figure
P 7. 1.b. Estimated Product Warranty Liability: $10,080
P 8. 1. Fund balance: $1,655,000

Chapter 10 Problems
P 1. Totals: Land: $426,212; Land Improvements: $166,560; Buildings: $833,940; Machinery: $1,262,640; Expense: $18,120
P 2. 1. Depreciation, Year 3: a. $54,250; b. $81,375; c. $53,407

P 3.   Total Depreciation Expense: 20x1, $71,820; 20x2, $103,092; 20x3, $84,072

P 4.   a. Gain on Sale of Computer: $6,000; b. Loss on Sale of Computer: $3,000; c. Gain on Exchange of Computer: $4,500; d. Loss on Exchange of Computer: $2,000; e. No gain recognized; f. Loss on Exchange of Computer: $2,000; g. Computer (new): $31,500; h. Computer (new): $38,000

P 5.   Part A. d. Leasehold Amortization Expense: $6,000; e. Leasehold Improvements Amortization Expense: $13,500; Part B. c. Patent Amortization Expense: $148,000; d. Loss on Write-off of Patent: $1,184,000

P 6.   Totals: Land: $723,900; Land Improvements: $142,000; Building: $1,383,600; Equipment: $210,800

P 7.   Depreciation, Year 3: a. $330,000; b. $264,000; c. $180,000

P 8.   Total Depreciation Expense: 20x2, $26,560; 20x3, $37,520; 20x4, $31,456

Chapter 11 Problems

P 1.   1. Bond Interest Expense: Nov. 30, $517,500; Dec. 31, $86,250

P 2.   1. Bond Interest Expense: Sept. 1, $377,200; Nov. 30, $188,536

P 3.   Bond Interest Expense: June 30, 20x2, $289,332; Sept. 1, 20x2, $186,580

P 4.   2. Loss on early retirement: $2,261,293

P 5.   Bond Interest Expense: Jan. 31, 20x4, $2,400,000; June 30, 20x4, $2,000,000

P 6.   1. Bond Interest Expense: Sept. 1, $374,400; Nov. 30, $187,200

P 7.   1. Bond Interest Expense: Nov. 30, $1,040,300; Dec. 31, $173,302

Chapter 12 Problems

P 1.   2. Total Stockholders' Equity: $1,488,000

P 2.   1. 20x3 Total dividends: Preferred, $420,000; Common, $380,000

P 3.   No check figure

P 4.   2. Total Stockholders' Equity: $1,446,900

P 5.   2. Total Stockholders' Equity: $330,375

P 6.   2. Total Stockholders' Equity: $351,400

P 7.   1. 20x3 Total dividends: Preferred, $120,000; Common, $68,000

P 8.   2. Total Stockholders' Equity: $475,040

Chapter 13 Problems

P 1.   2. Difference in net income: $97,600

P 2.   Income Before Extraordinary Items and Cumulative Effect of Accounting Change: $216,000

P 3.   1. Income from Continuing Operations, December 31, 20x3: $157,500

P 4.   2. Total Stockholders' Equity, December 31, 20x5: $2,964,000

P 5.   2. Retained Earnings: $250,000; Total Stockholders' Equity: $2,350,000

P 6.   2. Total Stockholders' Equity, December 31, 20x2: $2,802,800

P 7.   Income Before Extraordinary Items and Cumulative Effect of Accounting Change: $410,000

P 8.   2. Total Stockholders' Equity, December 31, 20x3: $518,500

P 9.   2. Retained Earnings: $397,000; Total Stockholders' Equity: $2,577,000

Chapter 14 Problems

P 1.   No check figure

P 2.   1. Net Cash Flows from: Operating Activities, $46,800; Investing Activities, ($14,400); Financing Activities, $102,000

P 3.   1. Net Cash Flows from: Operating Activities, ($106,000); Investing Activities, $34,000; Financing Activities, $44,000

P 4.   2. Same as **P 3**

P 5.   Net Cash Flows from Operating Activities: $47,600

P 6.   1. Net Cash Flows from: Operating Activities, $548,000; Investing Activities, $6,000; Financing Activities, ($260,000)

P 7.   No check figure

P 8.   1. Net Cash Flows from: Operating Activities, $63,300; Investing Activities, ($12,900); Financing Activities, $7,000

P 9.   2. Same as **P 8**

Chapter 15 Problems

P 1.   No check figure

P 2.   Increase: a, b, e, f, l, m

P 3.   1.c. Receivable turnover: 20x2, 14.1 times; 20x1, 14.4 times

P 4.   1.b. Quick ratio: Lewis, 1.5 times; Ramsey, 1.2 times; 2.d. Return on equity: Lewis, 8.8 %; Ramsey, 4.9 %

P 5.   Increase: d, h, I

P 6.   1.a. Current ratio: 20x2, 1.5 times; 20x1, 1.5 times; 2.c. Return on assets: 20x2, 5.0 %; 20x1, 10.7 %

Chapter 16 Problems

P 1.   No check figure

P 2.   No check figure

P 3.   2. Investment in Vivanco Company, Ending Balance: $640,000

P 4.   Total Assets, Consolidated Balance Sheet: $4,488,000

P 5.   Total Assets, Consolidated Balance Sheet: $1,280,000

P 6.   No check figure

P 7.   2. Investment in Waters Corporation, Ending Balance: $734,000

Accounting as an Information System

Accounting is an information system for measuring, processing, and communicating information that is useful in making economic decisions. **Part One** focuses on the users and uses of accounting information and presents the fundamental concepts and techniques of the basic accounting system, including the presentation and analysis of financial statements.

Chapter 1 Uses of Accounting Information and the Financial Statements explores the nature and environment of accounting, with special emphasis on the users and uses of accounting information. It introduces the four basic financial statements, the concept of accounting measurement, and the effects of business transactions on financial position. This chapter concludes with a discussion of ethical considerations in accounting and a supplement entitled "How to Read an Annual Report."

Chapter 2 Measuring Business Transactions continues the exploration of accounting measurement by focusing on the problems of recognition, valuation, and classification and how they are solved in the measuring and recording of business transactions.

Chapter 3 Measuring Business Income defines the accounting concept of business income, discusses the role of adjusting entries in the measurement of income, and demonstrates the preparation of financial statements.

Chapter 4 Accounting Systems focuses on the principles of accounting system design and computer systems and on the preparation of closing entries and the completion of the accounting cycle. The work sheet is presented as a supplemental learning objective.

Chapter 5 Financial Reporting and Analysis introduces the objectives and qualitative aspects of financial information. It demonstrates how much more useful classified financial statements are than simple financial statements in presenting information to statement users. This chapter also includes an introduction to financial statement analysis.

1 Uses of Accounting Information and the Financial Statements

LEARNING OBJECTIVES

Look to the learning objectives (LO's) as a guide to help you master the material. You will see many references to LO's throughout each chapter.

1 Define *accounting,* identify business goals and activities, and describe the role of accounting in making informed decisions.

2 Identify the many users of accounting information in society.

3 Explain the importance of business transactions, money measure, and separate entity to accounting measurement.

4 Describe the corporate form of business organization.

5 Define *financial position,* state the accounting equation, and show how they are affected by simple transactions.

6 Identify the four financial statements.

7 State the relationship of generally accepted accounting principles (GAAP) to financial statements and the independent CPA's report, and identify the organizations that influence GAAP.

8 Define *ethics* and describe the ethical responsibilities of accountants.

DECISION POINT: A USER'S FOCUS

Microsoft Corporation Microsoft Corporation, the giant software company, is considered one of the world's most successful companies. Why is Microsoft considered successful? An ordinary person sees the quality of the company's enormously successful products, such as Microsoft Windows, Microsoft Word, and Microsoft Excel; an investment company and others with a financial stake in the company evaluate Microsoft and its management in financial terms. Many Microsoft employees have become millionaires by owning a part of the company through stock ownership. This success is reflected in the Financial Highlights from the company's 1999 annual report, shown here.[1]

These Financial Highlights contain a number of terms for common financial measures of all companies, large or small. These measures are used to evaluate a company's management and to evaluate a company in comparison to other companies. It is easy to see the large increases at Microsoft over the years in such measures as revenue, net income, total assets, and stockholders' equity, but what do these terms mean? What financial knowledge do Microsoft's managers need in order to measure progress toward their financial goals? What financial knowledge does anyone who is evaluating Microsoft in relation to other companies need in order to understand these measures?

Microsoft's managers must have a thorough knowledge of accounting to understand how the operations for which they are responsible contribute to the firm's overall financial health.

A Decision Point introduces each chapter to show how leading businesses use accounting information reported in annual reports to make business decisions.

Financial Highlights

(In millions, except earnings per share)

	Year Ended June 30				
	1995	1996	1997	1998	**1999**
Revenue	$5,937	$ 8,671	$11,358	$14,484	**$19,747**
Net income	1,453	2,195	3,454	4,490	**7,785**
Earnings per share	0.58	0.86	1.32	1.67	**1.42**
Cash and short-term investments	4,750	6,940	8,966	13,927	**17,236**
Total assets	7,210	10,093	14,387	22,357	**37,156**
Stockholders' equity	5,333	6,908	10,777	16,627	**28,438**

Key Point: Management must have a good understanding of accounting to set financial goals and to make financial decisions. Management not only must understand how accounting information is compiled and processed but also must realize that accounting information is imperfect and should be interpreted with caution.

People with a financial stake in the company, such as owners, investors, creditors, employees, attorneys, and governmental regulators, must also know accounting to evaluate the financial performance of a business. Anyone who aspires to any of these roles in a business requires mastery of accounting terminology and concepts, the process of producing financial information, and how that information is interpreted and analyzed. The purpose of this course and this textbook is to assist you in acquiring that mastery.

Look in the margin for reminders of key concepts or ideas.

Video cases introduce key concepts and techniques presented in the chapter in the context of a real company.

VIDEO CASE

Intel Corporation

Objectives

- To examine the principal activities of a business enterprise: financing, investing, and operating.

- To explore the principal performance goals of a business enterprise: liquidity and profitability.

- To relate these activities and goals to the financial statements.

Background for the Case

You are probably familiar with the slogan "Intel Inside," from a marketing campaign for Intel Corporation, one of the

most successful companies in the world. In 1971, Intel introduced the world's first microprocessor. The microprocessor made possible the personal computer (PC), which has changed the world. Today, Intel supplies the computing industry with chips, boards, systems, and software. Its principal products include:

- **Microprocessors.** Also called central processing units (CPUs), these are frequently described as the "brains" of a computer because they act as the central control for the processing of data in PCs. This category includes the famous Pentium® processor.

- **Networking and Communications Products.** These products enhance the capabilities and ease of use of PC systems by allowing users to talk to each other and to share information.

- **Semiconductor Products.** Semiconductors facilitate flash memory, making possible easily reprogrammable

memory for computers, mobile phones, and many other products. Included in this category are embedded control chips that are programmed to regulate specific functions in products such as automobile engines, laser printers, disk drives, and home appliances.

Intel's customers include PC users and manufacturers of computers and computer systems, automobiles, and a wide range of industrial and telecommunications equipment.

For more information about Intel Corporation, visit the company's web site through the Needles Accounting Resource Center at:

http://college.hmco.com

Required

View the video on Intel Corporation that accompanies this book. As you are watching the video, take notes related to the following:

1. All businesses engage in three basic activities—financing, investing, and operating—but how they engage in them differs from company to company. Describe in your own words the nature of each of these activities and give as many examples as you can of how Intel engages in each activity.

2. To be successful, all businesses must achieve two performance objectives—liquidity and profitability. Describe in your own words the nature of each of these goals and describe how each applies to Intel.

3. There are four financial statements that apply to business enterprises. Which statements are most closely associated with the goal of liquidity? Which statement is most closely associated with the goal of profitability? Which statement shows the financial position of the company?

Accounting as an Information System

Today's accountant focuses on the ultimate needs of decision makers who use accounting information, whether those decision makers are inside or outside the business. **Accounting** "is not an end in itself,"[2] but is *an information system that measures, processes, and communicates financial information about an identifiable economic entity.* An economic entity is a unit that exists independently—for example, a business, a hospital, or a governmental body. The central focus of this book is on business entities and business activities, although other economic units, such as hospitals and governmental units, will be mentioned at appropriate points in the text and assignment material.

Accounting provides a vital service by supplying the information that decision makers need in order to make "reasoned choices among alternative uses of scarce resources in the conduct of business and economic activities."[3] As shown in Figure 1, accounting is a link between business activities and decision makers. First, accounting measures business activities by recording data about them for future use. Second, the data are stored until needed and then processed to become useful information. Third, the information is communicated, through reports, to decision makers. We might say that data about business activities are the input to the accounting system and that useful information for decision makers is the output.

Business Goals, Activities, and Performance Measures

A **business** is an economic unit that aims to sell goods and services to customers at prices that will provide an adequate return to its owners. For example, listed

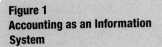

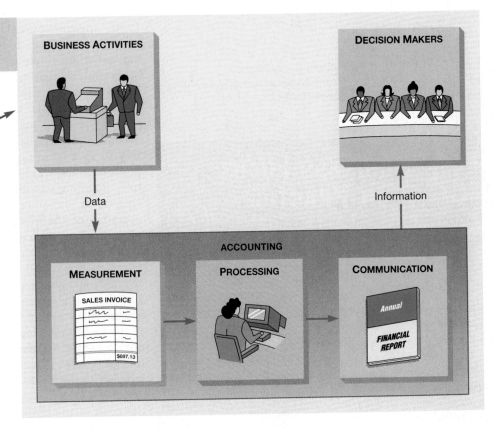

BUSINESS FOCUS ON PRACTICE

Accounting is a very old discipline. Forms of it have been essential to commerce for more than five thousand years. Accounting, in a version close to what we know today, gained widespread use in the 1400s, especially in Italy, where it was instrumental in the development of shipping, trade, construction, and other forms of commerce. This system of double-entry bookkeeping was documented by the famous Italian mathematician, scholar, and philosopher Fra Luca Pacioli. In 1494, Pacioli published his most important work, *Summa de Arithmetica, Geometrica, Proportioni et Proportionalita*, which contained a detailed description of accounting as practiced in that age. This book became the most widely read book on mathematics in Italy and firmly established Pacioli as the "Father of Accounting."

Icons are visual guides to key features of text and supporting study aids. See page 48 for a complete list of icons and their meanings.

Business Focus boxes highlight the relevance of accounting in four different areas: practice, technology, ethics, and international.

BUSINESS FOCUS ON PRACTICE

A study of chief executive officer bonus contracts shows that almost all companies use financial measures for determining annual bonuses. The most frequent measures are earnings per share, net income, operating income, return on equity, and cash flow. About one-third of the companies studied also use nonfinancial measures to determine bonuses. Examples of nonfinancial measures are customer satisfaction, product or service quality, nonfinancial strategic objectives, efficiency or productivity, and employee safety.[4]

 below are some companies and the principal goods or services they sell:

General Mills, Inc.	Food products
Reebok International Ltd.	Athletic footwear and clothing
Sony Corp.	Consumer electronics
Wendy's International Inc.	Food service
Hilton Hotels Corp.	Hotels and resorts service
Southwest Airlines Co.	Passenger airline service

Despite their differences, all these businesses have similar goals and engage in similar activities, as shown in Figure 2. Each must take in enough money from customers to pay all the costs of doing business, with enough left over as profit for the owners to want to stay in the business. This need to earn enough income to attract and hold investment capital is the goal of **profitability**. In addition, businesses must meet the goal of liquidity. **Liquidity** means having enough cash available to pay debts when they are due. For example, Toyota may meet the goal of profitability by selling many cars at a price that earns a profit, but if its customers do not pay for their cars quickly enough to enable Toyota to pay its suppliers and employees, the company may fail to meet the goal of liquidity. Both goals must be met if a company is to survive and be successful.

All businesses pursue their goals by engaging in similar activities. First, each business must engage in **financing activities** to obtain adequate funds, or capital, to begin and to continue operating. Financing activities include obtaining capital from owners and from creditors, such as banks and suppliers. They also include repaying creditors and paying a return to the owners. Second, each business must engage in **investing activities** to spend the capital it receives in ways that are productive and will help the business achieve its objectives. Investing activities include buying land, buildings, equipment, and other resources that are needed in the operation of the business, and selling these resources when they are no longer needed. Third, each business must engage in **operating activities**. In addition to the selling of goods and services to customers, operating activities include such actions as employing managers and workers, buying and producing goods and services, and paying taxes to the government.

An important function of accounting is to provide **performance measures**, which indicate whether managers are achieving their business goals and whether the business activities are well managed. It is important that these performance measures align with the goals of the business. For example, earned income

BUSINESS GOALS   BUSINESS ACTIVITIES

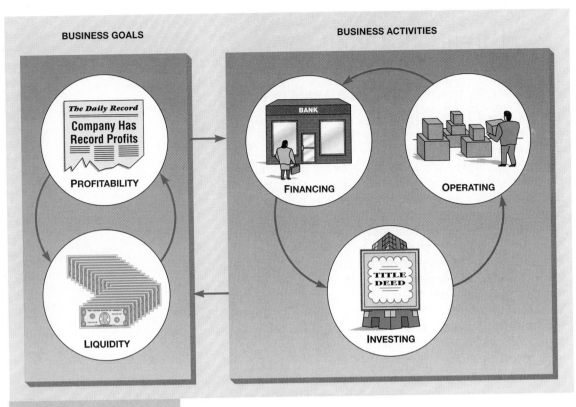

Figure 2
Business Goals and Activities

The key ratio icon highlights discussion of a measure used to evaluate the performance of a company.

Critical Thinking Question: Why would a business have more than one financial goal? **Answer:** Multiple financial goals signal that there is not just one measure of performance that is of interest to all users. For example, lenders are concerned primarily with cash flow, and owners are concerned with earnings and dividends.

Check your comprehension. Stop and ask yourself the above questions.

The hot links to real companies icon highlights hot links to the Internet through the Needles Accounting Resource Center at http://college.hmco.com.

The cash flow icon highlights discussion in the text of cash as a measure of liquidity.

is a measure of profitability and cash flow is a measure of liquidity. Ratios of accounting measures are also used as performance measures. For instance, one performance measure for operating activities might be the ratio of expenses to the revenue of the business. A performance measure for financing activities might be the ratio of money owed by the business to total resources controlled by the company. Because managers are usually evaluated on whether targeted levels of specific performance measures are achieved, they must have a knowledge of accounting to understand how they are evaluated and how they can improve their performance. Further, because managers will act to achieve the targeted performance measures, these measures must be crafted in such a way as to motivate managers to take actions that are in the best interests of the owners of the business.

Financial and Management Accounting

Accounting's role of assisting decision makers by measuring, processing, and communicating information is usually divided into the categories of management accounting and financial accounting. Although there is considerable overlap in the functions of management accounting and financial accounting, the two can be distinguished by who the principal users of their information will be. **Management accounting** provides internal decision makers who are charged with achieving the goals of profitability and liquidity with information about financing, investing, and operating activities. Managers and employees who conduct the activities of the business need information that tells them how they have done in the past and what they can expect in the future. For example, The Gap, a retail clothing business, needs an operating report on each mall outlet that tells how much was sold at

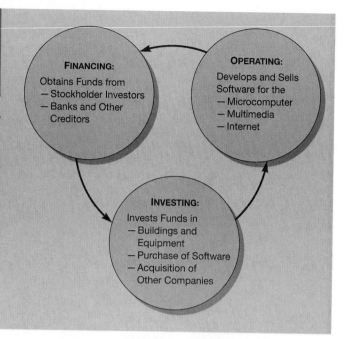

Microsoft Corporation projects its performance in meeting the major business objectives in its annual report.[5]

Liquidity: "Management believes existing cash and short-term investments together with funds generated from operations will be sufficient to meet the company's operating requirements for the next twelve months."

Profitability: "Microsoft continued to perform strongly in 1999. . . . Net income as a percent of revenue increased."

Microsoft's main business activities are shown at the right.

FINANCING:
Obtains Funds from
— Stockholder Investors
— Banks and Other Creditors

OPERATING:
Develops and Sells Software for the
— Microcomputer
— Multimedia
— Internet

INVESTING:
Invests Funds in
— Buildings and Equipment
— Purchase of Software
— Acquisition of Other Companies

---

that outlet and what costs were incurred, and it needs a budget for each outlet that projects the sales and costs for the next year. **Financial accounting** generates reports and communicates them to external decision makers so that they can evaluate how well the business has achieved its goals. These reports to external users are called **financial statements**. The Gap, for instance, will send its financial statements to its owners (called *stockholders*), its banks and other creditors, and government regulators. Financial statements report directly on the goals of profitability and liquidity and are used extensively both inside and outside a business to evaluate the business's success. It is important for every person involved with a business to understand financial statements. They are a central feature of accounting and are the primary focus of this book.

Processing Accounting Information

To avoid misunderstandings, it is important to distinguish accounting itself from the ways in which accounting information is processed by bookkeeping, the computer, and management information systems.

People often fail to understand the difference between accounting and bookkeeping. **Bookkeeping** is the process of recording financial transactions and keeping financial records. Mechanical and repetitive, bookkeeping is only a small—but important—part of accounting. Accounting, on the other hand, includes the design of an information system that meets the user's needs. The major goals of accounting are the analysis, interpretation, and use of information.

The **computer** is an electronic tool that is used to collect, organize, and communicate vast amounts of information with great speed. Accountants were among the earliest and most enthusiastic users of computers, and today they use microcomputers in all aspects of their work. It may appear that the computer is doing the accountant's job; in fact, it is only a tool that is instructed to do routine bookkeeping and to perform complex calculations.

With the widespread use of the computer today, a business's many information needs are organized into what is called a **management information system**

Key Point: Computerized accounting information is only as reliable and useful as the data input into the system. The accountant must have a thorough understanding of the concepts that underlie accounting to ensure the data's reliability and usefulness.

(MIS). A management information system consists of the interconnected subsystems that provide the information needed to run a business. The accounting information system is the most important subsystem because it plays the key role of managing the flow of economic data to all parts of a business and to interested parties outside the business.

Decision Makers: The Users of Accounting Information

The people who use accounting information to make decisions fall into three categories: (1) those who manage a business; (2) those outside a business enterprise who have a direct financial interest in the business; and (3) those people, organizations, and agencies that have an indirect financial interest in the business, as shown in Figure 3. These categories apply to government and not-for-profit organizations as well as to profit-oriented ventures.

Management

Management, collectively, is the people who have overall responsibility for operating a business and for meeting its profitability and liquidity goals. In a small business, management may include the owners. In a large business, management more often consists of people who have been hired. Managers must decide what to do, how to do it, and whether the results match their original plans. Successful managers consistently make the right decisions based on timely and valid information. To make good decisions, managers need answers to such questions as: What was the company's net income during the past quarter? Is the rate of return to the owners adequate? Does the company have enough cash? Which products are most profitable? What is the cost of manufacturing each product? Because so many key decisions are based on accounting data, management is one of the most important users of accounting information.

In carrying out its decision-making process, management performs a set of functions that are essential to the operation of the business. Although larger businesses

Key Point: Managers are internal users of accounting information.

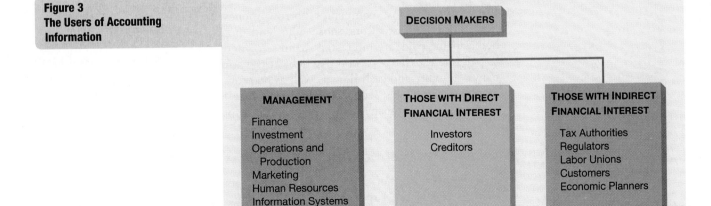

Figure 3
The Users of Accounting Information

DECISION MAKERS

MANAGEMENT	THOSE WITH DIRECT FINANCIAL INTEREST	THOSE WITH INDIRECT FINANCIAL INTEREST
Finance	Investors	Tax Authorities
Investment	Creditors	Regulators
Operations and Production		Labor Unions
Marketing		Customers
Human Resources		Economic Planners
Information Systems		
Accounting		

will have more elaborate operations, the same basic functions must be accomplished in all cases, and each requires accounting information for decision making. The basic management functions are:

Financing the business   Financial management obtains financial resources so that the company can begin and continue operating.

Investing the resources of the business   Asset management invests the financial resources of the business in productive assets that support the company's goals.

Producing goods and services   Operations and production management develops and produces products and services.

Marketing goods and services   Marketing management sells, advertises, and distributes goods and services.

Managing employees   Human resource management encompasses the hiring, evaluation, and compensation of employees.

Providing information to decision makers   Information systems management captures data about all aspects of the company's operations, organizes the data into usable information, and provides reports to internal managers and appropriate outside parties. Accounting plays a key role in this function.

Users with a Direct Financial Interest

Key Point: The primary external users of accounting information are investors and creditors.

Another group of decision makers who need accounting information are those with a direct financial interest in a business. They depend on accounting to measure and report information about how a business has performed. Most businesses periodically publish a set of general-purpose financial statements that report their success in meeting the goals of profitability and liquidity. These statements show what has happened in the past, and they are important indicators of what is going to happen in the future. Many people outside the company carefully study these financial reports. The two most important outside groups are investors and creditors.

INVESTORS   Those who invest or may invest in a business and acquire a part ownership are interested in its past success and its potential earnings. A thorough study of a company's financial statements helps potential investors judge the prospects for a profitable investment. After investing in a company, investors must continually review their commitment, again by examining the company's financial statements.

CREDITORS   Most companies borrow money for both long- and short-term operating needs. Creditors, those who lend money or deliver goods and services before being paid, are interested mainly in whether a company will have the cash to pay interest charges and repay debt at the appropriate time. They study a company's liquidity and cash flow as well as its profitability. Banks, finance companies, mortgage companies, securities firms, insurance firms, suppliers, and other lenders must analyze a company's financial position before they make a loan.

Users with an Indirect Financial Interest

In recent years, society as a whole, through government and public groups, has become one of the largest and most important users of accounting information. Users who need accounting information to make decisions on public issues include (1) tax authorities, (2) regulatory agencies, and (3) other groups.

TAX AUTHORITIES   Government at every level is financed through the collection of taxes. Under federal, state, and local laws, companies and individuals pay many kinds of taxes, including federal, state, and city income taxes; social security and other payroll taxes; excise taxes; and sales taxes. Each tax requires special tax returns, and often a complex set of records as well. Proper reporting is generally a matter of law and can be very complicated. The Internal Revenue Code, for instance, contains thousands of rules governing the preparation of the accounting information used in computing federal income taxes.

REGULATORY AGENCIES   Most companies must report periodically to one or more regulatory agencies at the federal, state, and local levels. For example, all public corporations must report periodically to the **Securities and Exchange Commission (SEC)**. This body, which was set up by Congress to protect the public, regulates the issuing, buying, and selling of stocks in the United States. Companies that are listed on a stock exchange also must meet the special reporting requirements of their exchange.

OTHER GROUPS   Labor unions study the financial statements of corporations as part of preparing for contract negotiations. A company's income and costs often play an important role in these negotiations. Those who advise investors and creditors—financial analysts and advisers, brokers, underwriters, lawyers, economists, and the financial press—also have an indirect interest in the financial performance and prospects of a business. Consumer groups, customers, and the general public have become more concerned about the financing and earnings of corporations as well as the effects that corporations have on inflation, the environment, social problems, and the quality of life. And economic planners, among them members of the President's Council of Economic Advisers and the Federal Reserve Board, use aggregated accounting information to set economic policies and to evaluate economic programs.

Government and Not-for-Profit Organizations

More than 30 percent of the U.S. economy is generated by government and not-for-profit organizations (hospitals, universities, professional organizations, and charities). The managers of these diverse entities need to understand and to use accounting information to perform the same functions as managers in businesses. They need to raise funds from investors, creditors, taxpayers, and donors, and to deploy scarce resources. They need to plan to pay for operations and repay creditors on a timely basis. Moreover, they have an obligation to report their financial performance to legislators, boards, and donors, as well as to deal with tax authorities, regulators, and labor unions. Although most of the examples throughout this text focus on business enterprises, the same basic principles apply to government and not-for-profit organizations.

Accounting Measurement

Accounting is an information system that measures, processes, and communicates financial information. In this section, you begin the study of the measurement aspects of accounting. Here you learn what accounting actually measures and study the effects of certain transactions on a company's financial position.

To make an accounting measurement, the accountant must answer four basic questions:

1. What is measured?
2. When should the measurement be made?
3. What value should be placed on what is measured?
4. How should what is measured be classified?

Terminology notes give definitions of terminology used in the text.

Terminology Note: *Measurement* means the analysis of transactions in terms of recognition, valuation, and classification. That is, it answers the question: How is this transaction best represented in the accounting records?

All these questions deal with basic assumptions and generally accepted accounting principles, and their answers establish what accounting is and what it is not. Accountants in industry, professional associations, public accounting, government, and academic circles debate the answers to these questions constantly, and the answers change as new knowledge and practice require. But the basis of today's accounting practice rests on a number of widely accepted concepts and conventions, which are described in this book. We begin by focusing on the first question: What is measured?

What Is Measured?

The world contains an unlimited number of things to measure and ways to measure them. For example, consider a machine that makes bottle caps. How many measurements of this machine could you make? You might start with size and then go on to location, weight, cost, or many other units of measurement. Some of these measurements are relevant to accounting; some are not. Every system must define what it measures, and accounting is no exception. Basically, financial accounting uses money measures to gauge the impact of business transactions on separate business entities. The concepts of business transactions, money measure, and separate entity are discussed in the next sections.

Business Transactions as the Object of Measurement

Business transactions are economic events that affect the financial position of a business entity. Business entities can have hundreds or even thousands of transactions every day. These business transactions are the raw material of accounting reports.

A transaction can be an exchange of value (a purchase, sale, payment, collection, or loan) between two or more independent parties. A transaction also can be an economic event that has the same effect as an exchange transaction but does not involve an exchange. Some examples of "nonexchange" transactions are losses from fire, flood, explosion, and theft; physical wear and tear on machinery and equipment; and the day-by-day accumulation of interest.

To be recorded, a transaction must relate directly to a business entity. For example, suppose a customer buys a shovel from Ace Hardware but has to buy a hoe from a competing store because Ace is out of hoes. The transaction in which the shovel was sold is entered in Ace's records. However, the purchase of the hoe from the competitor is not entered in Ace's records because even though it indirectly affects Ace economically, it does not involve a direct exchange of value between Ace and the customer.

Money Measure

All business transactions are recorded in terms of money. This concept is termed **money measure**. Of course, information of a nonfinancial nature may be recorded, but it is through the recording of monetary amounts that the diverse transactions and activities of a business are measured. Money is the only factor that is common to all business transactions, and thus it is the only practical unit of measure that can produce financial data that are alike and can be compared.

The monetary unit a business uses depends on the country in which the business resides. For example, in the United States, the basic unit of money is the dollar. In Japan, it is the yen; in Europe, the euro; and in the United Kingdom, the pound. If there are transactions between countries, exchange rates must be used to translate from one currency to another. An **exchange rate** is the value of one currency in terms of another. For example, a British person purchasing goods from a U.S. company and paying in U.S. dollars must exchange British pounds for U.S. dollars before making payment. In effect, the currencies are goods that can be bought and sold. Table 1 illustrates the exchange rates for several currencies in dollars. It shows the exchange rate for British pounds as $1.64 per pound on a particular date. Like the prices of most goods or services, these prices change daily according to supply and demand for the currencies. For example, a few years earlier the exchange rate for British pounds was $1.20. Although our discussion in this book focuses on dollars, selected examples and certain assignments will be in foreign currencies.

The Concept of Separate Entity

For accounting purposes, a business is a **separate entity**, distinct not only from its creditors and customers but also from its owner or owners. It should have a completely separate set of records, and its financial records and reports should refer only to its own financial affairs.

For example, the Jones Florist Company should have a bank account that is separate from the account of Kay Jones, the owner. Kay Jones may own a home, a car, and other property, and she may have personal debts, but these are not the Jones Florist Company's resources or debts. Kay Jones also may own another business, say a stationery shop. If she does, she should have a completely separate set of records for each business.

Key Point: The common unit of measurement in the United States for financial reporting purposes is the dollar.

Study notes provide useful study tips and information to avoid common pitfalls.

Study Note: There is a difference between separate *legal* entity and separate *economic* entity. Make the distinction, and note that for accounting purposes a business is *always* separate and distinct from its owners, creditors, and customers.

A table gives factual information referred to in the text.

Table 1. Partial Listing of Foreign Exchange Rates

Country	Price in $ U.S.	Country	Price in $ U.S.
Britain (pound)	1.64	Hong Kong (dollar)	0.13
Canada (dollar)	0.66	Italy (lira)	0.0006
Europe (euro)	1.13	Japan (yen)	0.009
France (franc)	0.172	Mexico (peso)	0.10
Germany (mark)	0.578	Taiwan (dollar)	0.03

Source: Data from *The Wall Street Journal*, February 2, 1999.

The Corporation as a Separate Entity

OBJECTIVE

4 Describe the corporate form of business organization

There are three basic forms of business enterprise. Besides the corporate form, there are the sole proprietorship form and the partnership form. Whichever form is used, the business should be viewed for accounting purposes as a separate entity, and all its records and reports should be developed separate and apart from those of its owners.

Corporations Differentiated from Sole Proprietorships and Partnerships

Key Point: In many ways, a sole proprietorship and a partnership are alike. A corporation, however, is very different from the other two forms of business organization.

Key Point: A key disadvantage of the partnership is the unlimited liability of its owners. Unlimited liability can be avoided by organizing the business as a corporation.

A **sole proprietorship** is a business owned by one person. The individual receives all profits or losses and is liable for all obligations of the business. Sole proprietorships represent the largest number of businesses in the United States, but typically they are the smallest in size. A **partnership** is like a sole proprietorship in most ways, but it has two or more co-owners. The partners share the profits and losses of the partnership according to an agreed-upon formula. Generally, any partner can bind the partnership to another party, and, if necessary, the personal resources of each partner can be called on to pay obligations of the partnership. A partnership must be dissolved if the ownership changes, as when a partner leaves or dies. If the business is to continue as a partnership after this occurs, a new partnership must be formed. Both the sole proprietorship and the partnership are convenient ways of separating the business owners' commercial activities from their personal activities. But legally there is no economic separation between the owners and the businesses.[7]

A **corporation**, on the other hand, is a business unit granted a charter from the state and is legally separate from its owners (the stockholders). The stockholders, whose ownership is represented by shares of stock, do not directly control the corporation's operations. Instead, they elect a board of directors to run the corporation for their benefit. In exchange for their limited involvement in the corporation's actual operations, stockholders enjoy limited liability. That is, their risk of loss is limited to the amount they paid for their shares. If they wish, stockholders can sell their shares without affecting corporate operations. Because of this limited liability, stockholders are often willing to invest in riskier, but potentially more profitable, activities. Also, because ownership can be transferred without dissolving the corporation, the life of a corporation is unlimited and not subject to the whims or health of a proprietor or a partner.

The characteristics of corporations make them very efficient in amassing capital, which enables them to grow extremely large. Even though corporations are fewer in number than sole proprietorships and partnerships, they contribute much more to the U.S. economy in monetary terms (see Figure 4). For example, in 1999, General Motors generated more revenues than all but 30 of the world's countries. Because of the economic significance of corporations, this book will emphasize accounting for the corporate form of business.

BUSINESS FOCUS ON PRACTICE

Most people think of corporations as large national or global companies whose shares of stock are held by thousands of people and institutions. Indeed, corporations can be huge and have many stockholders. However, of the approximately 4 million corporations in the United States, only about 15,000 have stock that is publicly bought and sold. The vast majority of corporations are small businesses that are privately held by a few stockholders. In Illinois alone there are more than 250,000 corporations. For this reason, the study of corporations is just as relevant to small businesses as it is to large ones.

Figure 4
Number and Receipts of U.S. Proprietorships, Partnerships, and Corporations, 1996

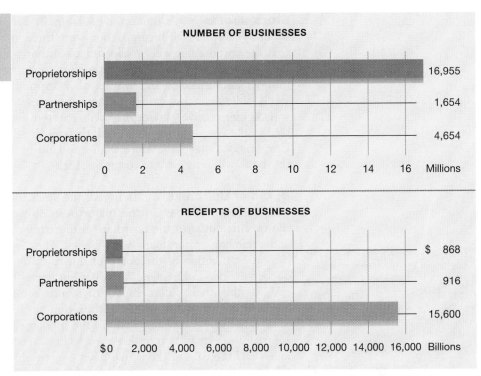

NUMBER OF BUSINESSES

Proprietorships	16,955
Partnerships	1,654
Corporations	4,654

0   2   4   6   8   10   12   14   16   Millions

RECEIPTS OF BUSINESSES

Proprietorships	$ 868
Partnerships	916
Corporations	15,600

$0   2,000   4,000   6,000   8,000   10,000   12,000   14,000   16,000   Billions

Source: U.S. Treasury Department, Internal Revenue Service, *Statistics of Income Bulletin*, Summer 1998.

Formation of a Corporation

To form a corporation, most states require individuals, called incorporators, to sign an application and file it with the proper state official. This application contains the **articles of incorporation**. If approved by the state, these articles or company charter become a contract between the state and the incorporators. The company is then authorized to do business.

Organization of a Corporation

The authority to manage the corporation is delegated by the stockholders to the board of directors and by the board of directors to the corporate officers (see Figure 5). That is, the stockholders elect the board of directors, which sets company policies and chooses the corporate officers, who in turn carry out the corporate policies by managing the business.

Figure 5
The Corporate Form of Business

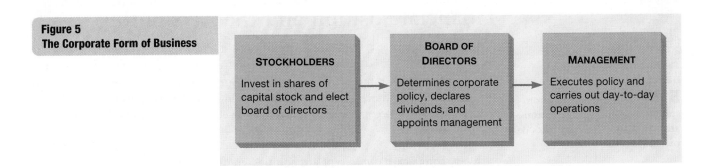

STOCKHOLDERS	**BOARD OF DIRECTORS**	**MANAGEMENT**
Invest in shares of capital stock and elect board of directors	Determines corporate policy, declares dividends, and appoints management	Executes policy and carries out day-to-day operations

STOCKHOLDERS A unit of ownership in a corporation is called a **share of stock**. The articles of incorporation state the maximum number of shares of stock that the corporation will be allowed, or authorized, to issue. The number of shares held by stockholders is the outstanding capital stock; this may be less than the number authorized in the articles of incorporation. To invest in a corporation, a stockholder transfers cash or other resources to the corporation. In return, the stockholder receives shares of stock representing a proportionate share of ownership in the corporation. Afterward, the stockholder may transfer the shares at will. Corporations may have more than one kind of capital stock, but the first part of this book will refer only to common stock.

BOARD OF DIRECTORS As noted, the stockholders elect the board of directors, which in turn decides on the major business policies of the corporation. Among the specific duties of the board are authorizing contracts, setting executive salaries, and arranging major loans with banks. The declaration of dividends is also an important function of the board of directors. Only the board has the authority to declare dividends. Dividends are distributions of resources, generally in the form of cash, to the stockholders. Paying dividends is one way of rewarding stockholders for their investment when the corporation has been successful in earning a profit. (The other way is through a rise in the market value of the stock.) Although there is usually a delay of two or three weeks between the time the board declares a dividend and the date of the actual payment, we shall assume in the early chapters of this book that declaration and payment are made on the same day.

The board of directors will vary in composition from company to company, but in most cases it will contain several officers of the corporation and several outsiders. Today, the formation of an **audit committee** with several outside directors is encouraged in order to make sure that the board will be objective in evaluating management's performance. One function of the audit committee is to engage the company's independent auditors and review their work. Another is to make sure that proper systems exist to safeguard the company's resources and ensure that reliable accounting records are kept.

MANAGEMENT The board of directors appoints managers to carry out the corporation's policies and run day-to-day operations. The management consists of the operating officers, who are generally the president, vice presidents, controller, treasurer, and secretary. Besides being responsible for running the business, management has the duty of reporting the financial results of its administration to the board of directors and the stockholders. Though management must, at a minimum, make a comprehensive annual report, it may and generally does report more often. The annual reports of large public corporations are available to the public. Excerpts from many of them will be used throughout this book.

Financial Position and the Accounting Equation

OBJECTIVE

5 Define *financial position,* state the accounting equation, and show how they are affected by simple transactions

Financial position refers to the economic resources that belong to a company and the claims against those resources at a point in time. Another term for claims is *equities.* Therefore, a company can be viewed as economic resources and equities:

Economic Resources = Equities

Every company has two types of equities, creditors' equities and owners' equity:

$$\text{Economic Resources} = \text{Creditors' Equities} + \text{Owners' Equity}$$

In accounting terminology, economic resources are called *assets* and creditors' equities are called *liabilities*. So the equation can be written like this:

$$\text{Assets} = \text{Liabilities} + \text{Owners' Equity}$$

This equation is known as the **accounting equation**. The two sides of the equation always must be equal, or "in balance." To evaluate the financial effects of business activities, it is important to understand their effects on this equation.

Assets

Assets are economic resources owned by a business that are expected to benefit future operations. Certain kinds of assets—for example, cash and money owed to the company by customers (called *accounts receivable*)—are monetary items. Other assets—inventories (goods held for sale), land, buildings, and equipment—are nonmonetary physical things. Still other assets—the rights granted by patents, trademarks, or copyrights—are nonphysical.

Liabilities

Liabilities are present obligations of a business to pay cash, transfer assets, or provide services to other entities in the future. Among these obligations are debts of the business, amounts owed to suppliers for goods or services bought on credit (called *accounts payable*), borrowed money (for example, money owed on loans payable to banks), salaries and wages owed to employees, taxes owed to the government, and services to be performed.

As debts, liabilities are claims recognized by law. That is, the law gives creditors the right to force the sale of a company's assets if the company fails to pay its debts. Creditors have rights over owners and must be paid in full before the owners receive anything, even if payment of a debt uses up all the assets of a business.

Owners' Equity

Owners' equity represents the claims by the owners of a business to the assets of the business. It equals the residual interest, or *residual equity*, in the assets of an entity that remains after deducting the entity's liabilities. Theoretically, it is what would be left over if all the liabilities were paid, and it is sometimes said to equal **net assets**. By rearranging the accounting equation, we can define owners' equity this way:

$$\text{Owners' Equity} = \text{Assets} - \text{Liabilities}$$

The owners' equity of a corporation is called **stockholders' equity**, so the accounting equation becomes

$$\text{Assets} = \text{Liabilities} + \text{Stockholders' Equity}$$

Stockholders' equity has two parts, contributed capital and retained earnings:

$$\text{Stockholders' Equity} = \text{Contributed Capital} + \text{Retained Earnings}$$

Contributed capital is the amount that is invested in the business by the stockholders. Their ownership in the business is represented by shares of capital stock. Figure 6 is a Toys "R" Us stock certificate, which represents such ownership.

Typically, contributed capital is divided between par value and additional paid-in capital. Par value is an amount per share that is entered in the corporation's capital stock account and is the minimum amount that can be reported as contributed

The CD-ROM icon indicates that data for the company in the text is available on the Fingraph® CD-ROM.

Figure 6
A Toys "R" Us Stock Certificate

Source: Courtesy of Toys "R" Us, Inc.

capital. Additional paid-in capital results when stock is issued, and the value received is greater than par value. In the initial chapters of this book, contributed capital will be shown as common stock that has been issued at par value.

Retained earnings represent the equity of the stockholders generated from the income-producing activities of the business and kept for use in the business. As you can see in Figure 7, retained earnings are affected by three kinds of transactions: revenues, expenses, and dividends.

Simply stated, **revenues** and **expenses** are the increases and decreases in stockholders' equity that result from operating a business. For example, the amount a customer pays (or agrees to pay in the future) to a company in return for a service provided by the company is a revenue to the company. The assets (cash or accounts receivable) of the company increase, and the stockholders' equity in those assets also increases. On the other hand, the amount a company pays out (or agrees to pay in the future) in the process of providing a service is an expense. In this case, the assets (cash) decrease or the liabilities (accounts payable) increase, and the stockholders' equity decreases. Generally speaking, a company is successful if its revenues exceed its expenses. When revenues exceed expenses, the difference is called **net income**; when expenses exceed revenues, the difference is called **net loss**. **Dividends** are distributions to stockholders of assets (usually cash) generated by past earnings. It is important not to confuse expenses and dividends, both of which reduce retained earnings. In summary, retained earnings is the accumulated net income (revenues − expenses) less dividends over the life of the business.

Some Illustrative Transactions

Let us now examine the effect of some of the most common business transactions on the accounting equation. Suppose that James and Jessica Shannon open a real

Figure 7
Three Types of Transactions
That Affect Retained Earnings

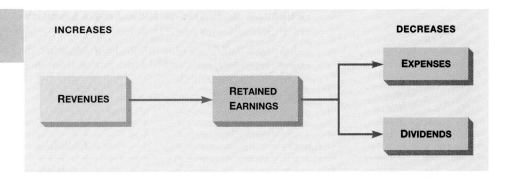

estate agency called Shannon Realty, Inc., on December 1. During December, their business engages in the transactions described in the following paragraphs.

OWNERS' INVESTMENTS   James and Jessica Shannon file articles of incorporation with the state and receive their charter. To begin their new business, they invest $50,000 in Shannon Realty, Inc., in exchange for 5,000 shares of $10 par value stock. The first balance sheet of the new company would show the asset Cash and the contributed capital (Common Stock) of the owners:

Assets	=	Stockholders' Equity (SE)	
Cash		Common Stock	Type of SE Transaction
1. $50,000		$50,000	Stockholders' Investments

At this point, the company has no liabilities, and assets equal stockholders' equity. The labels Cash and Common Stock are called **accounts**. These are used by accountants to accumulate amounts that result from similar transactions. Transactions that affect stockholders' equity are identified by type so that similar types may later be grouped together on accounting reports.

PURCHASE OF ASSETS WITH CASH   After a good location is found, the company pays cash to purchase a lot for $10,000 and a small building on the lot for $25,000. This transaction does not change the total assets, liabilities, or stockholders' equity of Shannon Realty, Inc., but it does change the composition of the assets—it decreases Cash and increases Land and Building:

	Assets			=	Stockholders' Equity	
	Cash	Land	Building		Common Stock	Type of SE Transaction
bal.	$50,000				$50,000	
2.	−35,000	+$10,000	+$25,000			
bal.	$15,000	$10,000	$25,000		$50,000	
		$50,000				

Key Point: The purchase of an asset does not affect stockholders' equity.

PURCHASE OF ASSETS BY INCURRING A LIABILITY   Assets do not always have to be purchased with cash. They may also be purchased on credit, that is, on the basis of an agreement to pay for them later. Suppose the company buys some office supplies for $500 on credit. This transaction increases the assets (Supplies) and increases the liabilities of Shannon Realty, Inc. This liability is designated by an account called Accounts Payable:

	Assets				=	Liabilities	+	Stockholders' Equity	
	Cash	Supplies	Land	Building		Accounts Payable		Common Stock	Type of SE Transaction
bal.	$15,000		$10,000	$25,000				$50,000	
3.		+$500				+$500			
bal.	$15,000	$500	$10,000	$25,000		$500		$50,000	
			$50,500				$50,500		

Notice that this transaction increases both sides of the accounting equation to $50,500.

> **Key Point:** Payment of a liability does not affect stockholders' equity or the asset purchased on credit.

PAYMENT OF A LIABILITY   If Shannon Realty, Inc., later pays $200 of the $500 owed for the supplies, both assets (Cash) and liabilities (Accounts Payable) decrease, but Supplies is unaffected:

	Assets				=	Liabilities	+	Stockholders' Equity	
	Cash	Supplies	Land	Building		Accounts Payable		Common Stock	Type of SE Transaction
bal.	$15,000	$500	$10,000	$25,000		$500		$50,000	
4.	−200					−200			
bal.	$14,800	$500	$10,000	$25,000		$300		$50,000	
			$50,300				$50,300		

Notice that both sides of the accounting equation are still equal, although now at a total of $50,300.

REVENUES   Shannon Realty, Inc., earns revenues in the form of commissions by selling houses for clients. Sometimes these commissions are paid to Shannon Realty, Inc., immediately in the form of cash, and sometimes the client agrees to pay the commission later. In either case, the commission is recorded when it is earned and Shannon Realty, Inc., has a right to a current or future receipt of cash. First, assume that Shannon Realty, Inc., sells a house and receives a commission of $1,500 in cash. This transaction increases both assets (Cash) and stockholders' equity (Retained Earnings):

	Assets				= Liabilities +	Stockholders' Equity		
	Cash	Supplies	Land	Building	Accounts Payable	Common Stock	Retained Earnings	Type of SE Transaction
bal.	$14,800	$500	$10,000	$25,000	$300	$50,000		
5.	+1,500						+$1,500	Commissions Earned
bal.	$16,300	$500	$10,000	$25,000	$300	$50,000	$1,500	

$51,800 $51,800

Key Point: Revenues are recorded when they are earned, not necessarily when payments are received.

Now assume that Shannon Realty, Inc., sells a house, in the process earning a commission of $2,000, and agrees to wait for payment of the commission. Because the commission has been earned now, a bill or invoice is sent to the client, and the transaction is recorded now. This revenue transaction increases both assets and stockholders' equity as before, but a new asset account, Accounts Receivable, shows that Shannon Realty, Inc., is awaiting receipt of the commission:

	Assets					= Liabilities +	Stockholders' Equity		
	Cash	Accounts Receivable	Supplies	Land	Building	Accounts Payable	Common Stock	Retained Earnings	Type of SE Transaction
bal.	$16,300		$500	$10,000	$25,000	$300	$50,000	$1,500	
6.		+$2,000						+2,000	Commissions Earned
bal.	$16,300	$2,000	$500	$10,000	$25,000	$300	$50,000	$3,500	

$53,800 $53,800

As you progress in your study of accounting, you will be shown the use of separate accounts for revenues, like Commissions Earned.

COLLECTION OF ACCOUNTS RECEIVABLE Let us assume that a few days later Shannon Realty, Inc., receives $1,000 from the client in transaction **6**. At that time, the asset Cash increases and the asset Accounts Receivable decreases:

	Assets					= Liabilities +	Stockholders' Equity		
	Cash	Accounts Receivable	Supplies	Land	Building	Accounts Payable	Common Stock	Retained Earnings	Type of SE Transaction
bal.	$16,300	$2,000	$500	$10,000	$25,000	$300	$50,000	$3,500	
7.	+1,000	−1,000							
bal.	$17,300	$1,000	$500	$10,000	$25,000	$300	$50,000	$3,500	

$53,800 $53,800

Notice that this transaction does not affect stockholders' equity because the commission revenue was already recorded in transaction **6**. Also, notice that the balance of Accounts Receivable is $1,000, indicating that $1,000 is still to be collected.

EXPENSES Just as revenues are recorded when they are earned, expenses are recorded when they are incurred. Expenses can be paid in cash when they occur, or they can be paid later. If payment is going to be made later, a liability—for example, Accounts Payable or Wages Payable—increases. In both cases, stockholders' equity decreases. Assume that Shannon Realty, Inc., pays $1,000 to rent some equipment for the office and $400 in wages to a part-time helper. These transactions reduce assets (Cash) and stockholders' equity (Retained Earnings):

		Assets				= Liabilities +		Stockholders' Equity	
	Cash	Accounts Receivable	Supplies	Land	Building	Accounts Payable	Common Stock	Retained Earnings	Type of SE Transaction
bal.	$17,300	$1,000	$500	$10,000	$25,000	$300	$50,000	$3,500	
8.	−1,000							−1,000	Equipment Rental Expense
9.	−400							−400	Wages Expense
bal.	$15,900	$1,000	$500	$10,000	$25,000	$300	$50,000	$2,100	

$52,400 = $52,400

Now assume that Shannon Realty, Inc., has not paid the $300 bill for utilities expense incurred for December. In this case, the effect on stockholders' equity is the same as when the expense is paid in cash, but instead of a reduction in assets, there is an increase in liabilities (Accounts Payable):

		Assets				= Liabilities +		Stockholders' Equity	
	Cash	Accounts Receivable	Supplies	Land	Building	Accounts Payable	Common Stock	Retained Earnings	Type of SE Transaction
bal.	$15,900	$1,000	$500	$10,000	$25,000	$300	$50,000	$2,100	
10.						+300		−300	Utilities Expense
bal.	$15,900	$1,000	$500	$10,000	$25,000	$600	$50,000	$1,800	

$52,400 = $52,400

As you progress in your study of accounting, you will be shown the use of separate accounts for expenses, like Equipment Rental Expense, Wages Expense, and Utilities Expense.

DIVIDENDS A dividend of $600 is declared, and it is paid by taking $600 out of the company's bank account and paying it to the stockholders for deposit in their personal bank accounts. The payment of dividends reduces assets (Cash) and stockholders' equity (Retained Earnings). Note that even though these dividends reduce retained earnings in the same way as the expenses in transactions **8, 9,** and **10,** they perform a different function. They are distributions of assets (Cash) to the stockholders, whereas the function of the expenses is to pay for services that helped produce the revenues in transactions **5** and **6.**

			Assets			= Liabilities +		Stockholders' Equity	
	Cash	Accounts Receiv- able	Supplies	Land	Building	Accounts Payable	Common Stock	Retained Earnings	Type of SE Transaction
bal.	$15,900	$1,000	$500	$10,000	$25,000	$600	$50,000	$1,800	
11.	−600							−600	Dividends
bal.	$15,300	$1,000	$500	$10,000	$25,000	$600	$50,000	$1,200	

$51,800 $51,800

SUMMARY   A summary of these 11 illustrative transactions is presented in Exhibit 1 on the next page.

Communication Through Financial Statements

Financial statements are the primary means of communicating important accounting information to users. It is helpful to think of these statements as models of the business enterprise because they show the business in financial terms. As is true of all models, however, financial statements are not perfect pictures of the real thing. Rather, they are the accountant's best effort to represent what is real. Four major financial statements are used to communicate accounting information about a business: the income statement, the statement of retained earnings, the balance sheet, and the statement of cash flows.

Exhibit 2 illustrates the relationship among the four financial statements by showing how they would appear for Shannon Realty, Inc., after the eleven sample transactions shown in Exhibit 1. It is assumed that the time period covered is the month of December 20xx. Notice that each statement is headed in a similar way. Each heading identifies the company and the kind of statement. The income statement, the statement of retained earnings, and the statement of cash flows give the time period to which they apply; the balance sheet gives the specific date to which it applies. Much of this book deals with developing, using, and interpreting more complete versions of these basic statements.

The Income Statement

The **income statement** summarizes the revenues earned and expenses incurred by a business over a period of time. Many people consider it the most important financial report because it shows whether or not a business achieved its profitability goal of earning an acceptable income. In Exhibit 2, Shannon Realty, Inc., had revenues in the form of commissions earned of $3,500 ($2,000 of revenue earned on credit and $1,500 of cash). From this amount, total expenses of $1,700 were deducted (equipment rental expense of $1,000, wages expense of $400, and utilities expense of $300), to arrive at a net income of $1,800. In order to show that

Exhibit 1
Summary of Effects of Illustrative Transactions on Financial Position

	Assets					= Liabilities +	Stockholders' Equity		
	Cash	Accounts Receivable	Supplies	Land	Building	Accounts Payable	Common Stock	Retained Earnings	Type of Stockholders' Equity Transaction
1.	$50,000						$50,000		Stockholders' Investments
2.	–35,000			+$10,000	+$25,000				
bal.	$15,000			$10,000	$25,000		$50,000		
3.			+$500			+$500			
bal.	$15,000		$500	$10,000	$25,000	$500	$50,000		
4.	–200					–200			
bal.	$14,800		$500	$10,000	$25,000	$300	$50,000		
5.	+1,500							+$1,500	Commissions Earned
bal.	$16,300		$500	$10,000	$25,000	$300	$50,000	$1,500	
6.		+$2,000						+2,000	Commissions Earned
bal.	$16,300	$2,000	$500	$10,000	$25,000	$300	$50,000	$3,500	
7.	+1,000	–1,000							
bal.	$17,300	$1,000	$500	$10,000	$25,000	$300	$50,000	$3,500	
8.	–1,000							–1,000	Equipment Rental Expense
9.	–400							–400	Wages Expense
bal.	$15,900	$1,000	$500	$10,000	$25,000	$300	$50,000	$2,100	
10.						+300		–300	Utilities Expense
bal.	$15,900	$1,000	$500	$10,000	$25,000	$600	$50,000	$1,800	
11.	–600							–600	Dividends
bal.	$15,300	$1,000	$500	$10,000	$25,000	$600	$50,000	$1,200	
	$51,800							$51,800	

Exhibit 2

Income Statement, Statement of Retained Earnings, Balance Sheet, and Statement of Cash Flows for Shannon Realty, Inc.

Shannon Realty, Inc.
Income Statement
For the Month Ended December 31, 20xx

Revenues		
Commissions Earned		$3,500
Expenses		
Equipment Rental Expense	$1,000	
Wages Expense	400	
Utilities Expense	300	
Total Expenses		1,700
Net Income		$1,800

Shannon Realty, Inc.
Statement of Retained Earnings
For the Month Ended December 31, 20xx

Retained Earnings, December 1, 20xx	$ 0
Net Income for the Month	1,800
Subtotal	$1,800
Less Dividends	600
Retained Earnings, December 31, 20xx	$1,200

Shannon Realty, Inc.
Statement of Cash Flows
For the Month Ended December 31, 20xx

Cash Flows from Operating Activities		
Net Income		$ 1,800
Adjustments to Reconcile Net Income to Net Cash Flows from Operating Activities		
Increase in Accounts Receivable	($ 1,000)*	
Increase in Supplies	(500)	
Increase in Accounts Payable	600	(900)
Net Cash Flows from Operating Activities		$ 900
Cash Flows from Investing Activities		
Purchase of Land	($10,000)	
Purchase of Building	(25,000)	
Net Cash Flows from Investing Activities		(35,000)
Cash Flows from Financing Activities		
Investments by Stockholders	$50,000	
Dividends	(600)	
Net Cash Flows from Financing Activities		49,400
Net Increase (Decrease) in Cash		$15,300
Cash at Beginning of Month		0
Cash at End of Month		$15,300

Shannon Realty, Inc.
Balance Sheet
December 31, 20xx

Assets		Liabilities	
Cash	$15,300	Accounts Payable	$ 600
Accounts Receivable	1,000		
Supplies	500	**Stockholders' Equity**	
Land	10,000	Common	
Building	25,000	Stock	$50,000
		Retained Earnings	1,200
		Total Stockholders' Equity	51,200
		Total Liabilities and Stockholders' Equity	
Total Assets	$51,800		$51,800

Key Point: Notice the sequence in which these financial statements must be prepared. The statement of retained earnings is a link between the income statement and the balance sheet, and the statement of cash flows is prepared last.

*Parentheses indicate a negative amount.

it applies to a period of time, the statement is dated "For the Month Ended December 31, 20xx."

The Statement of Retained Earnings

The **statement of retained earnings** shows the changes in retained earnings over a period of time. In Exhibit 2, the beginning retained earnings is zero because the company was started in this accounting period. During the month, the company earned an income (as shown on the income statement) of $1,800. Deducted from this amount are the dividends for the month of $600, leaving an ending balance of $1,200 of earnings retained in the business.

The Balance Sheet

Terminology Note: The balance sheet is also called the *statement of financial position*. It represents two different views of a business: The left side shows the resources of the business; the right side shows who provided those resources (the creditors and the owners).

The purpose of a **balance sheet** is to show the financial position of a business on a certain date, usually the end of the month or year. For this reason, it often is called the *statement of financial position* and is dated as of a certain date. The balance sheet presents a view of the business as the holder of resources, or assets, that are equal to the claims against those assets. The claims consist of the company's liabilities and the stockholders' equity in the company. In Exhibit 2, Shannon Realty, Inc., has several categories of assets, which total $51,800. These assets equal the total liabilities of $600 (Accounts Payable) plus the ending balance of stockholders' equity of $51,200. Notice that the Retained Earnings account on the balance sheet comes from the ending balance on the statement of retained earnings.

The Statement of Cash Flows

Key Point: The purpose of the statement of cash flows is to explain the change in cash in terms of operating, investing, and financing activities over an accounting period. It provides valuable information that cannot be determined in an examination of the other three financial statements.

Whereas the income statement focuses on a company's profitability goal, the **statement of cash flows** is directed toward the company's liquidity goal. **Cash flows** are the inflows and outflows of cash into and out of a business. Net cash flows are the difference between the inflows and outflows. The statement of cash flows shows the cash produced by operating a business as well as important investing and financing transactions that take place during an accounting period. Exhibit 2 shows the statement of cash flows for Shannon Realty, Inc. Notice that the statement explains how the Cash account changed during the period. Cash increased by $15,300. Operating activities produced net cash flows of $900, and financing activities produced net cash flows of $49,400. Investing activities used cash flows of $35,000.

This statement is related directly to the other three statements. Notice that net income comes from the income statement and that dividends come from the statement of retained earnings. The other items in the statement represent changes in the balance sheet accounts: Accounts Receivable, Supplies, Accounts Payable, Land, Building, and Common Stock. Here we focus on the importance and overall structure of the statement. Its construction and use are discussed in detail in the chapter on the statement of cash flows.

Financial Statements of Toys "R" Us, Inc.

The financial statements of Shannon Realty, Inc., are relatively simple and easy to understand. While significantly more complex, the financial statements of a large company like Toys "R" Us, Inc., are based on the same concepts and structure. The financial statements for Toys "R" Us are shown in Exhibits 3 through 6. Although there are a few terms in these statements that you will not yet understand, you can comprehend the structure and interrelationships of the statements.

Exhibit 3
Toys "R" Us Income Statements

The word *consolidated* means all companies owned by Toys "R" Us are combined.

Consolidated Statements of Earnings

Toys "R" Us's fiscal year ends on the Saturday nearest to January 31.

(In millions except per share data)	Year Ended		
	January 30, 1999	January 31, 1998	February 1, 1997
Net Sales	$11,170	$11,038	$9,932
Cost of sales	8,191	7,710	6,892
Gross Profit	2,979	3,328	3,040
Selling, advertising, general and administrative expenses	2,443	2,231	2,020
Depreciation, amortization and asset write-offs	255	253	206
Restructuring and other charges	294	—	60
Total Operating Expenses	2,992	2,484	2,286
Operating (Loss)/Income	(13)	844	754
Interest expense	102	85	98
Interest and other income	(9)	(13)	(17)
Interest Expense, Net	93	72	81
(Loss)/Earnings Before Income Taxes	(106)	772	673
Income Taxes	26	282	246
Net (Loss)/Earnings	$ (132)	$ 490	$ 427
Basic (Loss)/Earnings Per Share	$ (0.50)	$ 1.72	$ 1.56
Diluted (Loss)/Earnings Per Share	$ (0.50)	$ 1.70	$ 1.54

Taxes on income are shown separately.

Net earnings figure moves to statements of stockholders' equity.

Source: Toys "R" Us, Inc., *Annual Report,* 1999 (year ended January 30, 1999).

Many excerpts from the annual reports of leading businesses illustrate key concepts.

In these statements, either two years or three years are presented. These are called comparative financial statements because they enable the reader to compare Toys "R" Us's performance from year to year. Also note that the year-end date of Toys "R" Us's business, or the fiscal year, in these financial statements is the Saturday nearest the end of January (January 30, 1999), rather than December 31. A company usually may end its business year on any day it likes as long as it is consistent from year to year. Finally, note that the data are given in millions, so that net revenues for 1999, shown as $11,170, are actually $11,170,000,000. For purposes of readability and for showing meaningful relationships, it is not necessary for Toys "R" Us to show the last six digits of the numbers.

The income statements for Toys "R" Us, which are shown in Exhibit 3, are called Consolidated Statements of Earnings. "Earnings before income taxes" is computed before deducting "Income taxes" to arrive at "Net earnings" rather than net income being arrived at in one step, as was done in Shannon Realty, Inc.'s income statement. Because the company is a corporation, a provision is made for income taxes

Consolidated Statements of Stockholders' Equity

Each stockholders' equity account has a column that explains the change from year to year.

(In millions)	Common Stock Issued Shares	Amount	In Treasury Shares	Amount	Additional paid-in capital	Foreign currency translation adjustments	Retained earnings	Total stockholders' equity
Balance, February 3, 1996	300.4	$ 30	(27.3)	$ (846)	$ 542	$ 13	$ 3,693	$ 3,432
Net earnings for the year	—	—	—	—	—	—	427	427
Foreign currency translation adjustments	—	—	—	—	—	(73)	—	(73)
Comprehensive Income								354
Acquisition of Baby Superstore, Inc.	—	—	13.0	400	(23)	—	—	377
Exercise of stock options, net	—	—	1.7	58	(30)	—	—	28
Balance, February 1, 1997	300.4	30	(12.6)	(388)	489	(60)	4,120	4,191
Net earnings for the year	—	—	—	—	—	—	490	490
Foreign currency translation adjustments	—	—	—	—	—	(62)	—	(62)
Comprehensive Income								428
Share repurchase program	—	—	(8.2)	(253)	—	—	—	(253)
Exercise of stock options, net	—	—	2.8	84	(22)	—	—	62
Balance, January 31, 1998	300.4	30	(18.0)	(557)	467	(122)	4,610	4,428
Net loss for the year	—	—	—	—	—	—	(132)	(132)
Foreign currency translation adjustments	—	—	—	—	—	22	—	22
Comprehensive loss								(110)
Share repurchase program	—	—	(32.2)	(723)	—	—	—	(723)
Issuance of restricted stock	—	—	—	15	(2)	—	—	13
Exercise of stock options, net	—	—	4	22	(6)	—	—	16
Balance, January 30, 1999	300.4	$ 30	(49.8)	$(1,243)	$ 459	$ (100)	$ 4,478	$ 3,624

Net earnings (loss) from Income Statement

Balances of accounts to the balance sheets

Source: Toys "R" Us, Inc., *Annual Report,* 1999 (year ended January 30, 1999).

that Toys "R" Us must pay. The statements show earnings per share, the net earnings divided by the weighted-average shares outstanding.

The consolidated statements of stockholders' equity, shown in Exhibit 4, are different from Shannon Realty, Inc.'s statement of retained earnings in that they explain the changes in all the stockholders' equity accounts, including retained earnings. As for Shannon Realty, the net earnings from the consolidated statements of earnings appear in the Retained Earnings column of the statements of stockholders' equity. Under the column heading "Common Stock," "In Treasury" refers to shares of issued common stock owned by Toys "R" Us. Foreign currency translation adjustments result from the business the company does in other countries.

The ending balances of stockholders' equity accounts, including retained earnings, carry over to the stockholders' equity section of the balance sheets in Exhibit 5.

Exhibit 5
Toys "R" Us Balance Sheets

Consolidated Balance Sheets (In millions)	January 30, 1999	January 31, 1998
ASSETS		
Current Assets:		
Cash and cash equivalents	$ 410	$ 214
Accounts and other receivables	204	175
Merchandise inventories	1,902	2,464
Prepaid expenses and other current assets	81	51
Total Current Assets	2,597	2,904
Property and Equipment:		
Real estate, net	2,354	2,435
Other, net	1,872	1,777
Total Property and Equipment	4,226	4,212
Goodwill, net	347	356
Other assets	729	491
	$ 7,899	$7,963
LIABILITIES AND STOCKHOLDERS' EQUITY		
Current Liabilities:		
Short-term borrowings	$ 156	$ 134
Accounts payable	1,415	1,280
Accrued expenses and other current liabilities	696	680
Income taxes payable	224	231
Total Current Liabilities	2,491	2,325
Long-Term Debt	1,222	851
Deferred Income Taxes	333	219
Other Liabilities	229	140
Stockholders' Equity:		
Common stock	30	30
Additional paid-in capital	459	467
Retained earnings	4,478	4,610
Foreign currency translation adjustments	(100)	(122)
Treasury shares, at cost	(1,243)	(557)
Total Stockholders' Equity	3,624	4,428
	$ 7,899	$7,963

Toys "R" Us categorizes certain assets as current assets.

Toys "R" Us categorizes certain liabilities as current liabilities.

Balances from the statements of stockholders' equity.

Source: Toys "R" Us, Inc., *Annual Report,* 1999 (year ended January 30, 1999).

Toys "R" Us's balance sheets present two years of data and are structured similarly to Shannon Realty's balance sheet. The only difference is that some assets are categorized as current assets and some liabilities as current liabilities. Generally speaking, current assets are assets that will be realized as cash or used up in the next year, as opposed to property, plant, and equipment and other assets, which will benefit the company for a longer period of time. Similarly, current liabilities are

Exhibit 6
Toys "R" Us Statements of Cash Flows

Consolidated Statements of Cash Flows

(In millions)	Year Ended January 30, 1999	January 31, 1998	February 1, 1997
CASH FLOWS FROM OPERATING ACTIVITIES			
Net (loss)/earnings	$ (132)	$ 490	$ 427
Adjustments to reconcile net (loss)/earnings to net cash provided by operating activities:			
Depreciation, amortization and asset write-offs	255	253	206
Deferred income taxes	(90)	18	23
Restructuring and other charges	546	—	—
Changes in operating assets and liabilities:			
Accounts and other receivables	(43)	(40)	(14)
Merchandise inventories	233	(265)	(195)
Prepaid expenses and other operating assets	(27)	(9)	(10)
Accounts payable, accrued expenses and other liabilities	229	22	262
Income taxes payable	(7)	40	44
Net cash provided by operating activities	964	509	743
CASH FLOWS FROM INVESTING ACTIVITIES			
Capital expenditures, net	(373)	(494)	(415)
Other assets	(49)	(22)	(36)
Cash received with the acquisition of Baby Superstore	—	—	67
Net cash used in investing activities	(422)	(516)	(384)
CASH FLOWS FROM FINANCING ACTIVITIES			
Short-term borrowings, net	4	(142)	(10)
Long-term borrowings	771	11	326
Long-term debt repayments	(412)	(176)	(133)
Exercise of stock options	16	62	28
Share repurchase program	(723)	(253)	—
Net cash (used in)/provided by financing activities	(344)	(498)	211
Effect of exchange rate changes on cash and cash equivalents	(2)	(42)	(12)
CASH AND CASH EQUIVALENTS			
Increase/(decrease) during year	196	(547)	558
Beginning of year	214	761	203
End of year	$ 410	$ 214	$ 761
SUPPLEMENTAL DISCLOSURES OF CASH FLOW INFORMATION			
Income Tax Payments	$ 122	$ 192	$ 177
Interest Payments	$ 109	$ 83	$ 109

Cash flows are shown for operating activities, investing activities, and financing activities.

Cash and cash equivalents to Balance Sheets

Source: Toys "R" Us, Inc., *Annual Report,* 1999 (year ended January 30, 1999).

obligations that generally must be fulfilled within the next year, whereas long-term debt represents obligations to be paid more than one year from the balance sheet date. Toys "R" Us has deferred income taxes and other liabilities that the company will have to pay in future years, which is explained in the notes to the financial statements. From Toys "R" Us's 1999 balance sheet, the equality of the accounting equation may be proved:

$$
\begin{array}{ccc}
\text{Assets} & = & \text{Liabilities} & + \text{Stockholders' Equity} \\
\$7,899,000,000 & = & \$4,275,000,000 + & \$3,624,000,000
\end{array}
$$

Finally, Toys "R" Us's cash flow statements, shown in Exhibit 6, like those of Shannon Realty, Inc., show the changes in cash. These statements are very similar to those of Shannon Realty except that "cash" is called "cash and cash equivalents" by Toys "R" Us, which means that it includes certain accounts or securities that are very similar to cash. The totals of cash and cash equivalents carry over to the balance sheet.

Generally Accepted Accounting Principles

OBJECTIVE

7 State the relationship of generally accepted accounting principles (GAAP) to financial statements and the independent CPA's report, and identify the organizations that influence GAAP

To ensure that financial statements will be understandable to their users, a set of practices, called **generally accepted accounting principles (GAAP)**, has been developed to provide guidelines for financial accounting. Although the term has several meanings in the literature of accounting, perhaps this is the best definition: "Generally accepted accounting principles encompass the conventions, rules, and procedures necessary to define accepted accounting practice at a particular time."[8] In other words, GAAP arise from wide agreement on the theory and practice of accounting at a particular time. These "principles" are not like the unchangeable laws of nature found in chemistry or physics. They are developed by accountants and businesses to serve the needs of decision makers, and they can be altered as better methods evolve or as circumstances change.

Key Point: GAAP are constantly evolving; they are not like laws of science. They are designed to measure the performance of businesses. They can be abused to make a company look better on paper than it really is.

In this book, we present accounting practice, or GAAP, as it is today. We also try to explain the reasons or theory on which the practice is based. Both theory and practice are important to the study of accounting. However, you should realize that accounting is a discipline that is always growing, changing, and improving. Just as years of research are necessary before a new surgical method or lifesaving drug can be introduced, it may take years for research and new discoveries in accounting to be commonly implemented. As a result, you may encounter practices that seem contradictory. In some cases, we point out new directions in accounting. Your instructor also may mention certain weaknesses in current theory or practice.

Financial Statements, GAAP, and the Independent CPA's Report

Key Point: The purpose of an audit is to lend credibility to a set of financial statements. The auditor does *not* attest to the absolute accuracy of the published information or to the value of the company as an investment. All he or she renders is an opinion, based on appropriate testing, about the fairness of the presentation of the financial information.

Because financial statements are prepared by the management of a company and could be falsified for personal gain, all companies that sell ownership to the public and many companies that apply for sizable loans have their financial statements audited by an independent certified public accountant. **Certified public accountants (CPAs)** are licensed by all states for the same reason that lawyers and doctors are—to protect the public by ensuring the quality of professional service. One important attribute of CPAs is independence: They have no financial or other compromising ties with the companies they audit. This gives the public confidence in their work. The firms listed in Table 2 employ about 25 percent of all CPAs.

An independent CPA performs an **audit**, which is an examination of a company's financial statements and the accounting systems, controls, and records that produced them. The purpose of the audit is to ascertain that the financial statements

Table 2. Large International Certified Public Accounting Firms

Firm	Home Office	Some Major Clients
Arthur Andersen	Chicago	ITT, Texaco, United Airlines
Deloitte & Touche	New York	General Motors, Procter & Gamble, Sears
Ernst & Young	New York	Coca-Cola, McDonald's, Mobil
KPMG	New York	General Electric, Xerox
PricewaterhouseCoopers	New York	Du Pont, Exxon, IBM, Ford

Ethical Consideration: To lend credibility to the work of the independent auditor, the profession has developed a set of guidelines that dictate appropriate professional behavior. Known as the AICPA Code of Professional Ethics, the current guidelines were adopted in 1988 and are based on earlier standards. Learning Objective 8 covers the topic of ethics in detail.

have been prepared in accordance with generally accepted accounting principles. If the independent accountant is satisfied that this standard has been met, his or her report contains the following language:

> In our opinion, the financial statements . . . present fairly, in all material respects . . . in conformity with generally accepted accounting principles.

This wording emphasizes the fact that accounting and auditing are not exact sciences. Because the framework of GAAP provides room for interpretation and the application of GAAP necessitates the making of estimates, the auditor can render an opinion or judgment only that the financial statements *present fairly* or conform *in all material respects* to GAAP. The accountant's report does not preclude minor or immaterial errors in the financial statements. However, it does imply that on the whole, investors and creditors can rely on those statements. Historically, auditors have enjoyed a strong reputation for competence and independence. As a result, banks, investors, and creditors are willing to rely on an auditor's opinion when deciding to invest in a company or to make loans to a firm that has been audited. The independent audit is an important factor in the worldwide growth of financial markets.

Organizations That Influence Current Practice

Key Point: The FASB is the primary source of GAAP.

Key Point: The AICPA is considered the primary organization of certified public accountants.

Many organizations directly or indirectly influence GAAP and so influence much of what is in this book. The **Financial Accounting Standards Board (FASB)** is the most important body for developing and issuing rules on accounting practice. This independent body issues *Statements of Financial Accounting Standards*. The **American Institute of Certified Public Accountants (AICPA)** is the professional association of certified public accountants and influences accounting practice through the activities of its senior technical committees. The Securities and Exchange Commission (SEC) is an agency of the federal government that has the legal power to set and enforce accounting practices for companies whose securities are offered for sale to the general public. As such, it has enormous influence on accounting practice. The **Governmental Accounting Standards Board (GASB)**, which was established in 1984 under the same governing body as the Financial Accounting Standards Board, is responsible for issuing accounting standards for state and local governments.

With the growth of financial markets throughout the world, worldwide cooperation in the development of accounting principles has become a priority. The **International Accounting Standards Committee (IASC)** has approved more than 30 international standards, which have been translated into six languages.

U.S. tax laws that govern the assessment and collection of revenue for operating the federal government also influence accounting practice. Because a major source of the government's revenue is the income tax, these laws specify the rules for determining taxable income. These rules are interpreted and enforced by the **Internal Revenue Service (IRS)**. In some cases, these rules conflict with good accounting practice, but they still are an important influence on that practice. Businesses use certain accounting practices simply because they are required by the tax laws. Sometimes companies follow an accounting practice specified in the tax laws to take advantage of rules that can help them financially. Cases in which the tax laws affect accounting practice are noted throughout this book.

Professional Ethics and the Accounting Profession

OBJECTIVE

8 Define *ethics* and describe the ethical responsibilities of accountants

Ethics is a code of conduct that applies to everyday life. It addresses the question of whether actions are right or wrong. Ethical actions are the product of individual decisions. You are faced with many situations involving ethical issues every day. Some may be potentially illegal—the temptation to take office supplies from your employer to use when you do homework, for example. Others are not illegal but are equally unethical—for example, deciding not to tell a fellow student who missed class that a test has been announced for the next class meeting. When an organization is said to act ethically or unethically, it means that individuals within the organization have made a decision to act ethically or unethically. When a company uses false advertising, cheats customers, pollutes the environment, treats employees poorly, or misleads investors by presenting false financial statements, members of management and other employees have made a conscious decision to act unethically. In the same way, ethical behavior within a company is a direct result of the actions and decisions of the company's employees.

Ethical issues are discussed in each chapter; they relate to real business situations that require ethical judgments. ——▶ **Professional ethics** is a code of conduct that applies to the practice of a profession. Like the ethical conduct of a company, the ethical actions of a profession are a collection of individual actions. As members of a profession, accountants have a responsibility, not only to their employers and clients but to society as a whole, to uphold the highest ethical standards. Historically, accountants have been held in high regard. For example, a survey of over one thousand prominent people in business, education, and government ranked the accounting profession second only to the clergy as having the highest ethical standards.[9] It is the responsibility of every person who becomes an accountant to uphold the high standards of the profession, regardless of the field of accounting the individual enters.

To ensure that its members understand the responsibilities of being professional accountants, the AICPA and each state have adopted codes of professional conduct that must be followed by certified public accountants. Fundamental to these codes is responsibility to the public, including clients, creditors, investors, and anyone else who relies on the work of the certified public accountant. In resolving conflicts among these groups, the accountant must act with integrity, even to the sacrifice of personal benefit. **Integrity** means that the accountant is honest and candid, and subordinates personal gain to service and the public trust. The accountant must also be objective. **Objectivity** means that he or she is impartial and intellectually honest. Furthermore, the accountant must be independent. **Independence** means avoiding all relationships that impair or even appear to impair the accountant's objectivity.

One way in which the auditor of a company maintains independence is by having no direct financial interest in the company and by not being an employee of the company. The accountant must exercise **due care** in all activities, carrying out professional responsibilities with competence and diligence. For example, an accountant must not accept a job for which he or she is not qualified, even at the risk of losing a client to another firm, and careless work is not acceptable. These broad principles are supported by more specific rules that public accountants must follow. (For instance, with certain exceptions, client information must be kept strictly confidential.) Accountants who violate the rules can be disciplined or even suspended from practice.

A professional association, the **Institute of Management Accountants (IMA)**, has adopted the Code of Professional Conduct for Management Accountants. This ethical code emphasizes that management accountants have a responsibility to be competent in their jobs, to keep information confidential except when authorized or legally required to disclose it, to maintain integrity and avoid conflicts of interest, and to communicate information objectively and without bias.[10]

The Chapter Review restates each learning objective and its main ideas.

Chapter Review

REVIEW OF LEARNING OBJECTIVES

Ace it

Check out Ace It, an Internet quiz on chapter content, at http://college.hmco.com.

1. Define *accounting*, **identify business goals and activities, and describe the role of accounting in making informed decisions.** Accounting is an information system that measures, processes, and communicates information, primarily financial in nature, about an identifiable entity for the purpose of making economic decisions. Management accounting focuses on the preparation of information primarily for internal use by management. Financial accounting is concerned with the development and use of accounting reports that are communicated to those external to the business organization as well as to management. Accounting is not an end in itself but a tool that provides the information that is necessary to make reasoned choices among alternative uses of scarce resources in the conduct of business and economic activities.

2. Identify the many users of accounting information in society. Accounting plays a significant role in society by providing information to managers of all institutions and to individuals with a direct financial interest in those institutions, including present or potential investors or creditors. Accounting information is also important to those with an indirect financial interest in the business—for example, tax authorities, regulatory agencies, and economic planners.

3. Explain the importance of business transactions, money measure, and separate entity to accounting measurement. To make an accounting measurement, the accountant must determine what is measured, when the measurement should be made, what value should be placed on what is measured, and how what is measured should be classified. The object of accounting measurement is business transactions that are measured in terms of money and are for separate entities. Relating these concepts, financial accounting uses money measure to gauge the impact of business transactions on a separate business entity.

4. Describe the corporate form of business organization. Corporations, whose ownership is represented by shares of stock, are separate entities for both legal and accounting purposes. The stockholders own the corporation and elect the board of directors, whose duty it is to determine corporate policy. The corporate officers or management of the corporation are appointed by the board of directors and are responsible for the operation of the business in accordance with the board's policies.

5. Define *financial position*, **state the accounting equation, and show how they are affected by simple transactions.** Financial position is the

Want more review? The student study guide is a very thorough review of each learning objective, providing a detailed outline, true/false and multiple choice questions, and exercises. Answers are included. Ask for it at your bookstore.

economic resources that belong to a company and the claims against those resources at a point in time. The accounting equation shows financial position in the equation form Assets = Liabilities + Owners' Equity. For a corporation, the accounting equation is Assets = Liabilities + Stockholders' Equity. Business transactions affect financial position by decreasing or increasing assets, liabilities, or stockholders' equity in such a way that the accounting equation is always in balance.

6. **Identify the four financial statements.** Financial statements are the means by which accountants communicate the financial condition and activities of a business to those who have an interest in the business. The four basic financial statements are the income statement, the statement of retained earnings, the balance sheet, and the statement of cash flows.

7. **State the relationship of generally accepted accounting principles (GAAP) to financial statements and the independent CPA's report, and identify the organizations that influence GAAP.** Acceptable accounting practice consists of those conventions, rules, and procedures that make up generally accepted accounting principles at a particular time. GAAP are essential to the preparation and interpretation of financial statements and the independent CPA's report. Among the organizations that influence the formulation of GAAP are the Financial Accounting Standards Board, the American Institute of Certified Public Accountants, the Securities and Exchange Commission, and the Internal Revenue Service.

8. **Define *ethics* and describe the ethical responsibilities of accountants.** All accountants are required to follow a code of professional ethics, the foundation of which is responsibility to the public. Accountants must act with integrity, objectivity, and independence, and they must exercise due care in all their activities.

REVIEW OF CONCEPTS AND TERMINOLOGY

Notice that each chapter has a glossary that reviews the key concepts and terms defined in the chapter. For further discussion, see references to the LO next to each term.

The following concepts and terms were introduced in this chapter:

LO 1 **Accounting:** An information system that measures, processes, and communicates financial information about an identifiable economic entity.

LO 5 **Accounting equation:** Assets = Liabilities + Owners' Equity or, for corporations, Assets = Liabilities + Stockholders' Equity.

LO 5 **Accounts:** The labels used by accountants to accumulate the amounts produced from similar transactions.

LO 7 **American Institute of Certified Public Accountants (AICPA):** The professional association of certified public accountants.

LO 4 **Articles of incorporation:** An official document filed with and approved by a state that authorizes the incorporators to do business as a corporation.

LO 5 **Assets:** Economic resources owned by a business that are expected to benefit future operations.

LO 7 **Audit:** An examination of a company's financial statements in order to render an independent professional opinion that they have been presented fairly, in all material respects, in conformity with generally accepted accounting principles.

LO 4 **Audit committee:** A subgroup of the board of directors of a corporation that is charged with ensuring that the board will be objective in reviewing management's performance; it engages the company's independent auditors and reviews their work.

LO 6 **Balance sheet:** The financial statement that shows the assets, liabilities, and stockholders' equity of a business at a point in time. Also called a *statement of financial position*.

LO 1   **Bookkeeping:** The process of recording financial transactions and keeping financial records.

LO 1   **Business:** An economic unit that aims to sell goods and services to customers at prices that will provide an adequate return to its owners.

LO 3   **Business transactions:** Economic events that affect the financial position of a business entity.

LO 6   **Cash flows:** The inflows and outflows of cash into and out of a business.

LO 7   **Certified public accountants (CPAs):** Public accountants who have met the stringent licensing requirements set by the individual states.

LO 1   **Computer:** An electronic tool for the rapid collection, organization, and communication of large amounts of information.

LO 5   **Contributed capital:** The part of stockholders' equity that represents the amount invested in the business by the owners (stockholders).

LO 4   **Corporation:** A business unit granted a state charter recognizing it as a separate legal entity having its own rights, privileges, and liabilities distinct from those of its owners.

LO 5   **Dividends:** Distributions to stockholders of assets (usually cash) generated by past earnings.

LO 8   **Due care:** The act of carrying out professional responsibilities competently and diligently.

LO 8   **Ethics:** A code of conduct that addresses whether everyday actions are right or wrong.

LO 3   **Exchange rate:** The value of one currency in terms of another.

LO 5   **Expenses:** Decreases in stockholders' equity that result from operating a business.

LO 1   **Financial accounting:** The process of generating and communicating accounting information in the form of financial statements to those outside the organization.

LO 7   **Financial Accounting Standards Board (FASB):** The most important body for developing and issuing rules on accounting practice, called *Statements of Financial Accounting Standards.*

LO 5   **Financial position:** The economic resources that belong to a company and the claims (equities) against those resources at a point in time.

LO 1   **Financial statements:** The primary means of communicating important accounting information to users. They include the income statement, statement of retained earnings, balance sheet, and statement of cash flows.

LO 1   **Financing activities:** Activities undertaken by management to obtain adequate funds to begin and to continue operating a business.

LO 7   **Generally accepted accounting principles (GAAP):** The conventions, rules, and procedures that define accepted accounting practice at a particular time.

LO 7   **Governmental Accounting Standards Board (GASB):** The board responsible for issuing accounting standards for state and local governments.

LO 6   **Income statement:** The financial statement that summarizes the revenues earned and expenses incurred by a business over a period of time.

LO 8   **Independence:** The avoidance of all relationships that impair or appear to impair an accountant's objectivity.

LO 8   **Institute of Management Accountants (IMA):** A professional organization made up primarily of management accountants.

LO 8   **Integrity:** Honesty, candidness, and the subordination of personal gain to service and the public trust.

LO 7   **Internal Revenue Service (IRS):** The federal agency that interprets and enforces the tax laws governing the assessment and collection of revenue for operating the national government.

LO 7   **International Accounting Standards Committee (IASC):** The organization that encourages worldwide cooperation in the development of accounting principles; it has approved more than 30 international standards of accounting.

LO 1   **Investing activities:** Activities undertaken by management to spend capital in ways that are productive and will help a business achieve its objectives.

LO 5   **Liabilities:** Present obligations of a business to pay cash, transfer assets, or provide services to other entities in the future.

LO 1   **Liquidity:** Having enough cash available to pay debts when they are due.

LO 2   **Management:** Collectively, the people who have overall responsibility for operating a business and meeting its goals.

LO 1   **Management accounting:** The process of producing accounting information for the internal use of a company's management.

LO 1   **Management information system (MIS):** The interconnected subsystems that provide the information needed to run a business.

LO 3   **Money measure:** The recording of all business transactions in terms of money.

LO 5   **Net assets:** Assets minus liabilities; owners' equity or stockholders' equity.

LO 5   **Net income:** The difference between revenues and expenses when revenues exceed expenses.

LO 5   **Net loss:** The difference between expenses and revenues when expenses exceed revenues.

LO 8   **Objectivity:** Impartiality and intellectual honesty.

LO 1   **Operating activities:** Activities undertaken by management in the course of running the business.

LO 5   **Owners' equity:** The residual interest in the assets of a business entity that remains after deducting the entity's liabilities. Also called *residual equity* or, for corporations, *stockholders' equity.*

LO 4   **Partnership:** A business owned by two or more people that is not incorporated.

LO 1   **Performance measures:** Indicators of whether managers are achieving business goals and whether the business activities are well managed.

LO 8   **Professional ethics:** A code of conduct that applies to the practice of a profession.

LO 1   **Profitability:** The ability to earn enough income to attract and hold investment capital.

LO 5   **Retained earnings:** The equity of the stockholders generated from the income-producing activities of the business and kept for use in the business.

LO 5   **Revenues:** Increases in stockholders' equity that result from operating a business.

LO 2   **Securities and Exchange Commission (SEC):** An agency of the federal government set up by the U.S. Congress to protect the public by regulating the issuing, buying, and selling of stocks. It has the legal power to set and enforce accounting practices for firms whose securities are sold to the general public.

LO 3   **Separate entity:** A business that is treated as distinct from its creditors, customers, and owners.

LO 4   **Share of stock:** A unit of ownership in a corporation.

LO 4   **Sole proprietorship:** A business owned by one person that is not incorporated.

LO 6   **Statement of cash flows:** The financial statement that shows the inflows and outflows of cash from operating activities, investing activities, and financing activities over a period of time.

LO 6   **Statement of retained earnings:** The financial statement that shows the changes in retained earnings over a period of time.

LO 5   **Stockholders' equity:** The owners' equity of a corporation, consisting of contributed capital and retained earnings.

REVIEW PROBLEM

LO 5

Not sure you understood the techniques and calculations or want to check if you are ready for a chapter test? This review problem models main computations or analysis of the chapter and other problem assignments. The answer is provided for immediate feedback.

The Effect of Transactions on the Accounting Equation

Charlene Rudek finished law school in June and immediately set up her own law practice. During the first month of operation, she completed the following transactions:

a. Began the law practice by exchanging $2,000 for 1,000 shares of $2 par value common stock of the corporation.
b. Purchased a law library for $900 cash.
c. Purchased office supplies for $400 on credit.
d. Accepted $500 in cash for completing a contract.
e. Billed clients $1,950 for services rendered during the month.
f. Paid $200 of the amount owed for office supplies.
g. Received $1,250 in cash from one client who had been billed previously for services rendered.
h. Paid rent expense for the month in the amount of $1,200.
i. Declared and paid a dividend of $400.

REQUIRED

1. Show the effect of each of these transactions on the accounting equation by completing a table similar to Exhibit 1. Identify each stockholders' equity transaction.

2. Contrast the effects on cash flows of transactions **c** and **f** with transaction **b** and of transactions **e** and **g** with transaction **d**.

ANSWER TO REVIEW PROBLEM

1.

	Cash	Accounts Receivable	Office Supplies	Law Library	Accounts Payable	Common Stock	Retained Earnings	Type of SE Transaction
		Assets			**= Liabilities +**		**Stockholders' Equity (SE)**	
a.	$2,000					$2,000		Stockholders' Investment
b.	−900			+$900				
bal.	$1,100			$900		$2,000		
c.			+$400		+$400			
bal.	$1,100		$400	$900	$400	$2,000		
d.	+500						+$ 500	Legal Fees Earned
bal.	$1,600		$400	$900	$400	$2,000	$ 500	
e.		+$1,950					+1,950	Legal Fees Earned
bal.	$1,600	$1,950	$400	$900	$400	$2,000	$2,450	
f.	−200				−200			
bal.	$1,400	$1,950	$400	$900	$200	$2,000	$2,450	
g.	+1,250	−1,250						
bal.	$2,650	$ 700	$400	$900	$200	$2,000	$2,450	
h.	−1,200						−1,200	Rent Expense
bal.	$1,450	$ 700	$400	$900	$200	$2,000	$1,250	
i.	−400						−400	Dividends
bal.	$1,050	$ 700	$400	$900	$200	$2,000	$ 850	
			$3,050				$3,050	

2. Transaction **c,** a purchase on credit, enables the company to use the asset immediately and defer payment of cash until later. Cash is expended to partially pay for the asset in transaction **f.** The remainder is to be paid subsequently. This series of transactions contrasts with transaction **b,** in which cash is expended immediately for the asset. In each case, an asset is purchased, but the effects on cash flows are different.

Transaction **e,** a sale on credit, allows the customer to pay later for services provided. This payment is partially received in transaction **g,** and the remainder is to be received later. These transactions contrast with transaction **d,** in which payment is received immediately for the services performed. In each case, the revenue is earned initially, but the effect on cash flows is different.

Chapter Assignments

BUILDING YOUR KNOWLEDGE FOUNDATION

Questions review key concepts, terminology, and topics of the chapter.

QUESTIONS

1. Why is accounting considered an information system?
2. What is the role of accounting in the decision-making process, and what broad business goals and activities does it help management to achieve and manage?
3. Distinguish between management accounting and financial accounting.
4. Distinguish among these terms: *accounting, bookkeeping,* and *management information systems.*
5. Which decision makers use accounting information?
6. A business is an economic unit whose goal is to sell goods and services to customers at prices that will provide an adequate return to the business's owners. What functions must management perform to achieve that goal?
7. Why are investors and creditors interested in reviewing the financial statements of a company?
8. Among those who use accounting information are people and organizations that have an indirect interest in the business entity. Briefly describe these people and organizations.
9. Why has society, as a whole, become one of the largest users of accounting information?
10. Use the terms *business transactions, money measure,* and *separate entity* in a single sentence that demonstrates their relevance to financial accounting.
11. How do sole proprietorships, partnerships, and corporations differ?
12. In a corporation, what are the functions of stockholders, the board of directors, and management?
13. Define *assets, liabilities,* and *stockholders' equity.*
14. Arnold Smith's corporation has assets of $22,000 and liabilities of $10,000. What is the amount of the stockholders' equity?
15. What three elements affect retained earnings? How?
16. Give examples of the types of transactions that (a) increase assets and (b) increase liabilities.
17. What is the function of the statement of retained earnings?
18. Why is the balance sheet sometimes called the statement of financial position?
19. Contrast the purpose of the balance sheet with that of the income statement.
20. A statement for an accounting period that ends in June can be headed "June 30, 20xx" or "For the Year Ended June 30, 20xx." Which heading is appropriate for (a) a balance sheet and (b) an income statement?
21. How does the income statement differ from the statement of cash flows?
22. What are GAAP? Why are they important to the readers of financial statements?

Short exercises are a simple application of chapter material for a single learning objective. Notice the reference to the learning objective so you can easily refer back to the text for help.

23. What do auditors mean by the phrase *in all material respects* when they state that financial statements "present fairly, in all material respects . . . in conformity with generally accepted accounting principles"?

24. What organization has the most influence on GAAP?

25. Discuss the importance of professional ethics in the accounting profession.

SHORT EXERCISES

SE 1.
LO 3   Accounting Concepts

Tell whether each of the following words or phrases relates most closely to (a) a business transaction, (b) a separate entity, or (c) a money measure.

1. Partnership
2. U.S. dollar
3. Payment of an expense
4. Corporation
5. Sale of an asset

SE 2.
LO 5   The Accounting Equation

Determine the amount missing from each accounting equation below.

	Assets	=	Liabilities	+	Stockholders' Equity
1.	?		$25,000		$35,000
2.	$ 78,000		$42,000		?
3.	$146,000		?		$96,000

SE 3.
LO 5   The Accounting Equation

Use the accounting equation to answer each question below.

1. The assets of Cruse Company are $480,000, and the liabilities are $360,000. What is the amount of the stockholders' equity?

2. The liabilities of Nabors Company equal one-fifth of the total assets. The stockholders' equity is $80,000. What is the amount of the liabilities?

SE 4.
LO 5   The Accounting Equation

Use the accounting equation to answer each question below.

1. At the beginning of the year, Gilbert Company's assets were $180,000, and its stockholders' equity was $100,000. During the year, assets increased by $60,000 and liabilities increased by $10,000. What was the stockholders' equity at the end of the year?

2. At the beginning of the year, Sailor Company had liabilities of $50,000 and stockholders' equity of $48,000. If assets increased by $20,000 and liabilities decreased by $15,000, what was the stockholders' equity at the end of the year?

SE 5.
LO 5   The Accounting Equation and Net Income

Use the following information and the accounting equation to determine the net income for the year for each alternative below.

	Assets	Liabilities
Beginning of the year	$ 70,000	$30,000
End of the year	100,000	50,000

1. No investments were made in the business and no dividends were paid during the year.

2. Investments of $10,000 were made in the business, but no dividends were paid during the year.

3. No investments were made in the business, but dividends of $2,000 were paid during the year.

SE 6.
LO 5   The Accounting Equation and Net Income

Murillo Company had assets of $140,000 and liabilities of $60,000 at the beginning of the year, and assets of $200,000 and liabilities of $70,000 at the end of the year. During the year, there was an investment of $20,000 in the business, and dividends of $24,000 were paid. What amount of net income was earned during the year?

SE 7.
LO 5   Effect of Transactions on the Accounting Equation

On a sheet of paper, list the numbers 1 through 6, with columns labeled Assets, Liabilities, and Stockholders' Equity. In the columns, indicate whether each transaction that follows caused an increase (+), a decrease (−), or no change (NC) in assets, liabilities, and stockholders' equity.

1. Purchased equipment on credit.
2. Purchased equipment for cash.
3. Billed customers for services performed.
4. Received and immediately paid a utility bill.
5. Received payment from a previously billed customer.
6. Received an additional investment from a stockholder.

SE 8.

LO 5 Effect of Transactions on the Accounting Equation

On a sheet of paper, list the numbers 1 through 6, with columns labeled Assets, Liabilities, and Stockholders' Equity. In the columns, indicate whether each transaction below caused an increase (+), a decrease (−), or no change (NC) in assets, liabilities, and stockholders' equity.

1. Purchased supplies on credit.
2. Paid for previously purchased supplies.
3. Paid employee's weekly wages.
4. Paid a dividend to stockholders.

5. Purchased a truck with cash.
6. Received a telephone bill to be paid next month.

SE 9.

LO 6 Preparation and Completion of a Balance Sheet

Use the following accounts and balances to prepare a balance sheet for DeLay Company at June 30, 20x1, using Exhibit 2 as a model.

Accounts Receivable	$ 800
Wages Payable	250
Retained Earnings	1,750
Common Stock	12,000
Building	10,000
Cash	?

Exercises are richer applications of all chapter material referenced by LO's.

EXERCISES

E 1.

LO 1 The Nature of
LO 2 Accounting
LO 7

Match the terms on the left with the descriptions on the right.

_____ 1. Bookkeeping
_____ 2. Creditors
_____ 3. Measurement
_____ 4. Financial Accounting Standards Board (FASB)
_____ 5. Tax authorities
_____ 6. Computer
_____ 7. Communication
_____ 8. Securities and Exchange Commission (SEC)
_____ 9. Investors
_____ 10. Processing
_____ 11. Management
_____ 12. Management information system

a. Function of accounting
b. Often confused with accounting
c. User(s) of accounting information
d. Organization that influences current practice
e. Tool that facilitates the practice of accounting

E 2.

LO 3 Business Transactions

Louisa owns and operates a minimart. State which of the actions below are business transactions. Explain why any other actions are not regarded as transactions.

1. Louisa reduces the price of a gallon of milk in order to match the price offered by a competitor.
2. Louisa pays a high school student cash for cleaning up the driveway behind the market.
3. Louisa fills her son's car with gasoline in payment for restocking the vending machines and the snack food shelves.
4. Louisa pays interest to herself on a loan she made to the business three years ago.

LO 3 **Accounting Concepts**
LO 4

E 3. Financial accounting uses money measures to gauge the impact of business transactions on a separate business entity. Tell whether each of the following words or phrases relates most closely to (a) a business transaction, (b) a separate entity, or (c) a money measure.

1. Corporation
2. French franc
3. Sales of products
4. Receipt of cash
5. Sole proprietorship
6. U.S. dollar
7. Partnership
8. Stockholders' investments
9. Japanese yen
10. Purchase of supplies

LO 3 **Money Measure**

E 4. You have been asked to compare the sales and assets of four companies that make computer chips and determine which company is the largest in each category. You have gathered the following data, but they cannot be used for direct comparison because each company's sales and assets are in its own currency:

Company (Currency)	Sales	Assets
Inchip (U.S. dollar)	20,000,000	13,000,000
Chan (Taiwan dollar)	50,000,000	24,000,000
Ito (Japanese yen)	3,500,000,000	2,500,000,000
Works (German mark)	35,000,000	39,000,000

Assuming that the exchange rates in Table 1 are current and appropriate, convert all the figures to U.S. dollars and determine which company is the largest in sales and which is the largest in assets.

LO 5 **The Accounting Equation**

E 5. Use the accounting equation to answer each question that follows. Show any calculations you make.

1. The assets of Quizo Corporation are $800,000, and the stockholders' equity is $310,000. What is the amount of the liabilities?

2. The liabilities and stockholders' equity of Arthur Corporation are $72,000 and $53,000, respectively. What is the amount of the assets?

3. The liabilities of Shimon Corp. equal one-third of the total assets, and stockholders' equity is $240,000. What is the amount of the liabilities?

4. At the beginning of the year, Card Corporation's assets were $220,000 and its stockholders' equity was $120,000. During the year, assets increased $60,000 and liabilities decreased $18,000. What is the stockholders' equity at the end of the year?

LO 5 **Stockholders' Equity Transactions**

E 6. Identify the following transactions by marking each as a stockholders' investment (I), dividend (D), revenue (R), expense (E), or not a stockholders' equity transaction (NSE).

a. Received cash for providing a service.
b. Took assets out of the business for personal use.
c. Received cash from a customer previously billed for a service.
d. Transferred assets to the business from a personal account.
e. Paid a service station for gasoline for a business vehicle.
f. Performed a service and received a promise of payment.
g. Paid cash to purchase equipment.
h. Paid cash to an employee for services performed.

LO 5 **Effect of Transactions on the Accounting Equation**

E 7. During the month of April, Tybat Corporation had the following transactions:

a. Paid salaries for April, $1,800.
b. Purchased equipment on credit, $3,000.
c. Purchased supplies with cash, $100.
d. Additional investment by stockholders, $4,000.
e. Received payment for services performed, $600.
f. Made partial payment on equipment purchased in transaction b, $1,000.
g. Billed customers for services performed, $1,600.
h. Received payment from customers billed in transaction g, $300.
i. Received utility bill, $70.
j. Declared and paid dividends of $1,500.

On a sheet of paper, list the letters **a** through **j**, with columns labeled Assets, Liabilities, and Stockholders' Equity. In the columns, indicate whether each transaction caused an increase (+), a decrease (−), or no change (NC) in assets, liabilities, and stockholders' equity.

E 8.

LO 5   Examples of Transactions

For each of the categories below, describe a transaction that would have the required effect on the elements of the accounting equation.

1. Increase one asset and decrease another asset.
2. Decrease an asset and decrease a liability.
3. Increase an asset and increase a liability.
4. Increase an asset and increase stockholders' equity.
5. Decrease an asset and decrease stockholders' equity.

E 9.

LO 5   Effect of Transactions on the Accounting Equation

The total assets and liabilities at the beginning and end of the year for Continental Company are listed below.

	Assets	Liabilities
Beginning of the year	$140,000	$ 55,000
End of the year	220,000	130,000

Determine Continental Company's net income or loss for the year under each of the following alternatives:

1. The stockholders made no investments in the business and no dividends were paid during the year.
2. The stockholders made no investments in the business, but dividends of $22,000 were paid during the year.
3. The stockholders made investments of $13,000, but no dividends were paid during the year.
4. The stockholders made investments of $10,000 in the business, and dividends of $22,000 were paid during the year.

E 10.

LO 5   Identification of
LO 6   Accounts

1. Indicate whether each of the following accounts is an asset (A), a liability (L), or a part of stockholders' equity (SE).
   a. Cash
   b. Salaries Payable
   c. Accounts Receivable
   d. Common Stock
   e. Land
   f. Accounts Payable
   g. Supplies

2. Indicate whether each account below would be shown on the income statement (IS), the statement of retained earnings (RE), or the balance sheet (BS).
   a. Repair Revenue
   b. Automobile
   c. Fuel Expense
   d. Cash
   e. Rent Expense
   f. Accounts Payable
   g. Dividends

E 11.

LO 6   Preparation of a Balance Sheet

Listed in random order below are the balance sheet figures for the Falls Company as of December 31, 20xx.

Accounts Payable	$ 40,000
Building	90,000
Common Stock	100,000
Supplies	10,000
Accounts Receivable	50,000
Cash	20,000
Equipment	40,000
Retained Earnings	70,000

Sort the balances and prepare a balance sheet similar to the one in Exhibit 2.

E 12.

LO 6   Completion of Financial Statements

Determine the amounts that correspond to the letters by completing the following independent sets of financial statements. (Assume no new investments by the stockholders.)

Income Statement	Set A	Set B	Set C
Revenues	$ 550	$ g	$120
Expenses	a	2,600	m
Net Income	$ b	$ h	$ 40

Statement of Retained Earnings			
Beginning Balance	$1,450	$ 7,700	$100
Net Income	c	800	n
Less Dividends	100	i	o
Ending Balance	$1,500	$ j	$p

Balance Sheet			
Total Assets	$ d	$15,500	$q
Liabilities	$ 800	$ 2,500	$r
Stockholders' Equity			
Common Stock	1,000	5,000	50
Retained Earnings	e	k	140
Total Liabilities and Stockholders' Equity	$ f	$ l	$290

E 13.
LO 6 Preparation of Financial Statements

Valley Corporation engaged in the following activities during the year: Service Revenue, $26,400; Rent Expense, $2,400; Wages Expense, $16,540; Advertising Expense, $2,700; Utilities Expense, $1,800; and Dividends, $1,400. In addition, the year-end balances of selected accounts were as follows: Cash, $3,100; Accounts Receivable, $1,500; Supplies, $200; Land, $2,000; Accounts Payable, $900; and Common Stock, $2,000.

In proper format, prepare the income statement, statement of retained earnings, and balance sheet for Valley Corporation (assume the year ends on December 31, 20x3). (**Hint:** You must solve for the beginning and ending balances of retained earnings for 20x3.)

E 14.
LO 6 Statement of Cash Flows

Aqua Corporation began the year 20x1 with cash of $43,000. In addition to earning a net income of $25,000 and paying a cash dividend of $15,000, Aqua borrowed $60,000 from the bank and purchased equipment for $90,000 with cash. Also, Accounts Receivable increased by $6,000 and Accounts Payable increased by $9,000.

Determine the amount of cash on hand at December 31, 20x1, by preparing a statement of cash flows similar to the one in Exhibit 2.

E 15.
LO 7 Accounting Abbreviations

Identify the accounting meaning of each of the following abbreviations: AICPA, SEC, GAAP, FASB, IRS, GASB, IASC, IMA, and CPA.

PROBLEMS

P 1.
LO 5 Effect of Transactions on the Accounting Equation

Problems are comprehensive applications of chapter material often covering multiple learning objectives.

Woodframe, Inc., was started by Sam Steel in a small shopping center. In the first weeks of operation, he completed the following transactions:

a. Deposited $14,000 in an account in the name of the corporation, in exchange for 1,400 shares of $10 par value common stock of the corporation.
b. Paid the current month's rent, $1,000.
c. Purchased store equipment on credit, $7,200.
d. Purchased framing supplies for cash, $3,400.
e. Received framing revenue, $1,600.
f. Billed customers for services, $1,400.
g. Paid utilities expense, $500.
h. Received payment from customers in transaction **f**, $400.
i. Made payment on store equipment purchased in transaction **c**, $3,600.
j. Declared and paid dividends of $800.

REQUIRED

1. Arrange the following asset, liability, and stockholders' equity accounts in an equation similar to Exhibit 1: Cash, Accounts Receivable, Framing Supplies, Store Equipment, Accounts Payable, Common Stock, and Retained Earnings.

2. Show by addition and subtraction, as in Exhibit 1, the effects of the transactions on the accounting equation. Show new balances after each transaction, and identify each stockholders' equity transaction by type.

3. Contrast the effects on cash flows of transactions **c** and **i** with transaction **d** and of transactions **f** and **h** with transaction **e**.

P 2.

LO 5 **Effect of Transactions on the Accounting Equation**

All problems can be worked on Excel Template Software.

The Quality Courier Corporation was founded by Johnny Hui on March 1 and engaged in the following transactions:

a. Deposited $12,000 in cash in the name of Quality Courier Corporation, in exchange for 12,000 shares of $1 par value stock of the corporation.
b. Purchased a motorbike on credit, $3,200.
c. Purchased delivery supplies for cash, $400.
d. Billed a customer for a delivery, $200.
e. Received delivery fees in cash, $600.
f. Made a payment on the motorbike, $1,400.
g. Paid repair expense, $240.
h. Received payment from customer billed in transaction **d**, $100.
i. Declared and paid dividends of $300.

REQUIRED

1. Arrange the following asset, liability, and stockholders' equity accounts in an equation similar to Exhibit 1: Cash, Accounts Receivable, Delivery Supplies, Motorbike, Accounts Payable, Common Stock, and Retained Earnings.

2. Show by addition and subtraction, as in Exhibit 1, the effects of the transactions on the accounting equation. Show new balances after each transaction, and identify each stockholders' equity transaction by type.

P 3.

LO 5 **Effect of Transactions on the Accounting Equation**

After completing his Ph.D. in management, Wally Damato set up a consulting practice. At the end of his first month of operation, he had the following account balances: Cash, $5,860; Accounts Receivable, $2,800; Office Supplies, $540; Office Equipment, $8,400; Accounts Payable, $3,800; Common Stock, $12,000; and Retained Earnings, $1,800. Soon thereafter, the following transactions were completed:

a. Paid current month's rent, $800.
b. Made payment toward accounts payable, $900.
c. Billed clients for services performed, $1,600.
d. Received payment from clients billed last month, $2,000.
e. Purchased office supplies for cash, $160.
f. Paid secretary's salary, $1,700.
g. Paid utilities expense, $180.
h. Paid telephone expense, $100.
i. Purchased additional office equipment for cash, $800.
j. Received cash from clients for services performed, $2,400.
k. Declared and paid dividends of $1,000.

REQUIRED

Curious if you got the right answer? Look at check figures on pages xxxiv-xxxv of the text.

1. Arrange the following asset, liability, and stockholders' equity accounts in an equation similar to Exhibit 1: Cash, Accounts Receivable, Office Supplies, Office Equipment, Accounts Payable, Common Stock, and Retained Earnings.

2. Enter the beginning balances of the assets, liabilities, and stockholders' equity.

3. Show by addition and subtraction, as in Exhibit 1, the effects of the transactions on the accounting equation. Show new balances after each transaction, and identify each stockholders' equity transaction by type.

P 4.

LO 6 **Preparation of Financial Statements**

At the end of its first month of operation, June 20xx, Verdun Plumbing Corporation had the following account balances:

Cash	$58,600
Accounts Receivable	10,800
Delivery Truck	38,000
Tools	7,600
Accounts Payable	8,600

In addition, during the month of June, the following transactions affected stockholders' equity:

Initial investment by S. Verdun	$40,000
Further investment by S. Verdun	60,000
Contract revenue	23,200
Repair revenue	5,600
Salaries expense	16,600
Rent expense	1,400
Fuel expense	400
Dividends	4,000

REQUIRED

Using Exhibit 2 as a model, prepare an income statement, a statement of retained earnings, and a balance sheet for Verdun Plumbing Corporation. (**Hint:** The final balance of Stockholders' Equity is $106,400.)

P 5.

LO 5 **Effect of Transactions on the**
LO 6 **Accounting Equation and**
Preparation of Financial
Statements

Arrow Copying Service, Inc., began operations and engaged in the following transactions during August 20xx:

a. Myra Lomax deposited $10,000 in cash in the name of the corporation, in exchange for 1,000 shares of $10 par value stock of the corporation.
b. Paid current month's rent, $900.
c. Purchased copier for cash, $5,000.
d. Received copying job payments in cash, $1,780.
e. Billed copying job to major customer, $1,360.
f. Paid cash for paper and other copier supplies, $380.
g. Paid wages to part-time employees, $560.
h. Purchased additional copier supplies on credit, $280.
i. Received partial payment from customer in transaction **e**, $600.
j. Paid current month's utility bill, $180.
k. Made partial payment on supplies purchased in transaction **h**, $140.
l. Declared and paid dividends of $1,400.

REQUIRED

1. Arrange the asset, liability, and stockholders' equity accounts in an equation similar to Exhibit 1, using these account titles: Cash, Accounts Receivable, Supplies, Copier, Accounts Payable, Common Stock, and Retained Earnings.

2. Show by addition and subtraction, as in Exhibit 1, the effects of the transactions on the accounting equation. Show new balances after each transaction, and identify each stockholders' equity transaction by type.

Looking for more practice?
Alternate problems model an
earlier problem in the chapter
with the same format and
learning objectives.

3. Using Exhibit 2 as a guide, prepare an income statement, a statement of retained earnings, and a balance sheet for Arrow Copying Service, Inc.

ALTERNATE PROBLEMS

P 6.

LO 5 **Effect of Transactions on the**
Accounting Equation

Victoria Ho, after receiving her degree in computer science, started her own business, Computer Edge Corporation. She completed the following transactions soon after starting the business:

a. Invested $18,000 in cash and a systems library valued at $1,840 in exchange for 1,984 shares of $10 par value common stock in the corporation.
b. Paid current month's rent on an office, $720.
c. Purchased a computer for cash, $4,000.
d. Purchased computer supplies on credit, $1,200.
e. Received payment from a client for programming done, $1,600.
f. Billed a client on completion of a short programming project, $1,420.
g. Paid utilities, $800.
h. Received a partial payment from the client billed in transaction **f**, $160.
i. Made a partial payment on the computer supplies purchased in transaction **d**, $400.
j. Declared and paid dividends of $500.

REQUIRED

1. Arrange the asset, liability, and stockholders' equity accounts in an equation that is similar to Exhibit 1, using the following account titles: Cash, Accounts Receivable,

Computer Supplies, Equipment, Systems Library, Accounts Payable, Common Stock, and Retained Earnings.

2. Show by addition and subtraction, as in Exhibit 1, the effects of the transactions on the accounting equation. Show new balances after each transaction, and identify each stockholders' equity transaction by type.

3. Contrast the effects on cash flows of transactions **d** and **i** with transaction **c** and of transactions **f** and **h** with transaction **e**.

P 7.

LO 6 Preparation of Financial Statements

At the end of October 20xx, the Common Stock account of the Wichita Riding Club, Inc., had a balance of $60,000 and Retained Earnings had a balance of $14,600. After operating during November, the club had the following account balances:

Cash	$17,400
Accounts Receivable	2,400
Supplies	2,000
Land	42,000
Building	60,000
Horses	20,000
Accounts Payable	35,600

In addition, the following transactions affected stockholders' equity during November:

Stockholders' investment in common stock	$32,000
Riding lesson revenue	12,400
Locker rental revenue	3,400
Salaries expense	4,600
Feed expense	2,000
Utilities expense	1,200
Dividends	6,400

REQUIRED

Using Exhibit 2 as a model, prepare an income statement, a statement of retained earnings, and a balance sheet for Wichita Riding Club, Inc. (**Hint:** The final total of Stockholders' Equity is $108,200.)

P 8.

LO 5 Effect of Transactions on
LO 6 the Accounting Equation and Preparation of Financial Statements

On April 1, 20xx, AAFast Limousine Service, Inc., began operation. The company engaged in the following transactions during April:

a. Sean Derry deposited $84,000 in a bank account in the name of the corporation, in exchange for 8,400 shares of $10 par value stock in the corporation.
b. Purchased limousine for cash, $38,000.
c. Purchased auto supplies on credit, $800.
d. Received limousine fares in cash, $6,400.
e. Paid wages to part-time drivers, $1,000.
f. Purchased gasoline during month for cash, $1,600.
g. Purchased car washes during month on credit, $240.
h. Owner made a further investment in 1,000 shares, $10,000.
i. Paid part of the amount owed for the auto supplies purchased in transaction c, $400.
j. Billed major client for fares, $1,800.
k. Paid for automobile repairs, $500.
l. Declared and paid dividends of $2,000.

REQUIRED

1. Arrange the asset, liability, and stockholders' equity accounts in an equation similar to Exhibit 1, using the following account titles: Cash, Accounts Receivable, Auto Supplies, Limousine, Accounts Payable, Common Stock, and Retained Earnings.

2. Show by addition and subtraction, as in Exhibit 1, the effects of the transactions on the accounting equation. Show new balances after each transaction, and identify each stockholders' equity transaction by type.

3. Using Exhibit 2 as a guide, prepare an income statement, a statement of retained earnings, and a balance sheet for AAFast Limousine Service, Inc. (Optional: Also prepare a statement of cash flows.)

EXPANDING YOUR CRITICAL THINKING, COMMUNICATION, AND INTERPERSONAL SKILLS

These cases focus on conceptual accounting issues based on real companies and situations.

SKILLS DEVELOPMENT

Conceptual Analysis

LO 1 Business Activities and
LO 2 Management Functions

SD 1. *J.C. Penney Company, Inc.,* is America's largest department store company. According to its letter to stockholders, financial results didn't meet company expectations.

> J.C. Penney is implementing a number of strategic initiatives to ensure our competitiveness, to meet our growth objectives, and to provide a strong return on our stockholders' investment. These initiatives include: accelerated growth in our top 10 markets; expand our women's apparel and accessories business; speed merchandise to market; reduce our cost structure and enhance customer service.[11]

To achieve its strategy, J.C. Penney must organize its management into functions that relate to the principal activities of a business. Discuss the three basic activities J.C. Penney will engage in to achieve its goals, and suggest some examples of each. What is the role of J.C. Penney's management, and what functions must its management perform to accomplish these activities?

LO 2 Users of Accounting
Information

SD 2. Public companies report quarterly and annually on their success or failure in making a net income. The following item appeared in *The Wall Street Journal:* "**Coca-Cola Co.**'s fourth-quarter net income plunged 27%, a dismal end to a disappointing year, as economic weakness in several overseas markets hurt sales of soft drinks."[12]

Discuss why each of the following individuals or groups might be interested in seeing the accounting reports that support this statement.

1. The management of Coca-Cola
2. The stockholders of Coca-Cola
3. The creditors of Coca-Cola
4. Potential stockholders of Coca-Cola
5. The Internal Revenue Service
6. The Securities and Exchange Commission
7. The Teamsters' union
8. A consumers' group called Public Cause
9. An economic adviser to the President of the United States

Group Activity: Assign each user to a different group. Ask each group to discuss and present why its user needs accounting information.

LO 3 Concept of an Asset

SD 3. *Southwest Airlines Co.* is one of the most successful airlines in the United States. Its annual report contains this statement: "We are a company of People, not Planes. That is what distinguishes us from other airlines and other companies. At Southwest Airlines, People are our most important asset."[13] Are employees considered assets in the financial statements? Discuss in what sense Southwest considers its employees to be assets.

Ethical Dilemma

LO 8 Professional Ethics

Ethical dilemmas provide practice in dealing with the tough choices businesses often face.

SD 4. Discuss the ethical choices in the situations below. In each instance, determine the alternative courses of action, describe the ethical dilemma, and tell what you would do.

1. You are the payroll accountant for a small business. A friend asks you how much another employee is paid per hour.
2. As an accountant for the branch office of a wholesale supplier, you discover that several of the receipts the branch manager has submitted for reimbursement as selling expense actually stem from nights out with his spouse.

   Cash Flow   CD-ROM   Communication   Critical Thinking   Ethics   General Ledger   Group Activity   Hot Links to Real Companies   International   Internet Key Ratio Memo   Spreadsheet

3. You are an accountant in the purchasing department of a construction company. When you arrive home from work on December 22, you find a large ham in a box marked "Happy Holidays—It's a pleasure to work with you." The gift is from a supplier who has bid on a contract your employer plans to award next week.

4. As an auditor with one year's experience at a local CPA firm, you are expected to complete a certain part of an audit in 20 hours. Because of your lack of experience, you know you cannot finish the job within that time. Rather than admit this, you are thinking about working late to finish the job and not telling anyone.

5. You are a tax accountant at a local CPA firm. You help your neighbor fill out her tax return, and she pays you $200 in cash. Because there is no record of this transaction, you are considering not reporting it on your tax return.

6. The accounting firm for which you work as a CPA has just won a new client, a firm in which you own 200 shares of stock that you received as an inheritance from your grandmother. Because it is only a small number of shares and you think the company will be very successful, you are considering not disclosing the investment.

Group Activity. Assign each case to a different group to resolve and report.

You are asked to gather information from the Internet or business publications and apply it to the accounting concepts in the chapter.

Research Activity

SD 5.

LO 1 Need for Knowledge of
LO 2 Accounting

Locate an article about a company from one of the following sources: the business section of your local paper or a nearby metropolitan daily, *The Wall Street Journal, Business Week, Forbes,* or the Needles Accounting Resource Center web site at http://college.hmco.com. List all the financial and accounting terms used in the article. Bring the article to class and be prepared to discuss how a knowledge of accounting would help a reader understand the content of the article.

Decision-Making Practice

SD 6.

LO 5 Effect of Transactions on
LO 6 the Balance Sheet

What are the relevant numbers and what do they mean? Practice making business decisions based on accounting information.

Instead of hunting for a summer job after finishing her junior year in college, Beth Murphy started a lawn service business in her neighborhood. On June 1, she deposited $2,700 in a new bank account in the name of her corporation. The $2,700 consisted of a $1,000 loan from her father and $1,700 of her own money. In return for her investment, Beth issued 1,700 shares of $1 par value common stock to herself.

Using the money in this checking account, Beth rented lawn equipment, purchased supplies, and hired neighborhood high school students to mow and trim the lawns of neighbors who had agreed to pay her for the service. At the end of each month, she mailed bills to her customers.

On August 31, Beth was ready to dissolve her business and go back to school for the fall term. Because she had been so busy, she had not kept any records other than her checkbook and a list of amounts owed by customers.

Her checkbook had a balance of $3,520, and her customers owed her $875. She expected these customers to pay her during September. She planned to return unused supplies to the Lawn Care Center for a full credit of $50. When she brought back the rented lawn equipment, the Lawn Care Center also would return a deposit of $200 she had made in June. She owed the Lawn Care Center $525 for equipment rentals and supplies. In addition, she owed the students who had worked for her $100, and she still owed her father $700. Although Beth feels she did quite well, she is not sure just how successful she was.

1. Prepare one balance sheet dated June 1 and another dated August 31 for Murphy Lawn Services, Inc.

2. Compare the two balance sheets and comment on the performance of Murphy Lawn Services, Inc. Did the company have a profit or a loss? (Assume that Beth used none of the company's assets for personal purposes.)

3. If Beth wants to continue her business next summer, what kind of information from her recordkeeping system would make it easier for her to tell whether or not she is earning a profit?

FINANCIAL REPORTING AND ANALYSIS

Interpreting Financial Reports

FRA 1.

LO 1 **Uses of Accounting**
LO 2 **Information**

*Using excerpts from
business articles or annual
reports of well-known companies, you are asked to
extract relevant data, make
computations, and interpret
your results.*

The following excerpts are from an article in *The Wall Street Journal*:

For Deborah Hopkins, the new chief financial officer (CFO) at faltering Boeing Co.,
a moment of truth came earlier this month when she stepped up to a blackboard
during a company retreat.... [She] chalked out what she thought was a rehash
of simple formulas for measuring profitability.... To her astonishment, dozens of
the 280 senior Boeing executives at the retreat came up to compliment her afterward, and some even said it was the first time they had understood the concepts.

The lack of financial acumen, especially in the struggling commercial-airplane
group, has been a bit of a surprise says the plainspoken Ms. Hopkins. Until recently,
she says, some senior managers were apparently selling airplanes without understanding the profit margins (net income divided by revenues) on each jetliner.

Boeing's leaders ... [want to] instill a sense that financial performance is as important as building great airplanes. Landing Ms. Hopkins offers top management the
chance to signal to an anxious board and angry stockholders that a turnaround is
under way after two awful years of flagging share prices and factory foul-ups.

Somewhere high on her list [of assignments] is raising Boeing's return on assets
(net income divided by total assets), which in turn could raise expectations for
stock price. While Ms. Hopkins won't detail her ideas, better control of inventory
and more outsourcing of parts production are likely elements. The former has
proved difficult to some of Boeing's finest manufacturing engineers. The latter is
a touchy matter, with unions already riled by plans to cut more than 40,000 jobs
during the next two years.*

REQUIRED

Write a memo to the board of directors discussing the four factors you consider essential to a financial turnaround at Boeing. Also suggest the best source of information
about each of the factors you list. Be as specific as possible.

FRA 2.

LO 6 **Nature of Cash, Assets, and
Net Income**

Charles Schwab Corporation is a rapidly growing financial services firm. Information
for 1998 and 1997 from the company's annual report is presented below.[14] (All numbers

Charles Schwab Corporation Condensed Balance Sheets December 31, 1998 and 1997 (in thousands)		
	1998	1997
Assets		
Cash	$ 1,155,928	$ 797,447
Other Assets	21,108,462	15,684,260
Total Assets	$22,264,390	$16,481,707
Liabilities		
Total Liabilities	$20,835,768	$15,336,590
Stockholders' Equity		
Common Stock	$ 217,331	$ 244,099
Retained Earnings	1,211,291	901,018
Total Liabilities and Stockholders' Equity	$22,264,390	$16,481,707

*Republished with permission of *Wall Street Journal*, from "New Boeing CFO's Assignment: Signal
a Turnaround," January 26, 1999; permission conveyed through Copyright Clearance Center, Inc.

are in thousands.) Three students who were looking at Charles Schwab's annual report were overheard to make the following comments:

> Student A: What a great year Charles Schwab had in 1998! The company earned net income of $5,782,683,000 because its total assets increased from $16,481,707,000 to $22,264,390,000.

> Student B: But the change in total assets isn't the same as net income! The company had a net income of only $388,481,000 because cash increased from $797,447,000 to $1,155,928,000.

> Student C: I see from the annual report that Charles Schwab paid cash dividends of $43,068,000 in 1998. Don't you have to take that into consideration when analyzing the company's performance?

REQUIRED

1. Comment on the interpretations of Students A and B, and then answer Student C's question.

2. Calculate Charles Schwab's net income for 1998. (**Hint:** Reconstruct the statement of retained earnings.)

Group Activity: After discussing **1**, let groups compete to see which one can come up with the answer to **2** first.

International Company

FRA 3.

LO 1 The Goal of Profitability

Explore accounting issues facing international companies.

The celebrated Danish toy company *Lego Group* reported its first loss since the 1930s in 1998. While its bright plastic bricks are famous around the globe, Lego is rapidly losing market share to computer and video games. The company's president said, "The Lego Group is not in critical condition, but action is needed. . . . We have to acknowledge that growth and innovation are not enough. We also have to be a profitable business."[15] Discuss the meaning of *profitability.* What other goal must a business achieve? Why is the goal of profitability important to Lego's president? What is the accounting measure of profitability, and on which statement is it determined?

Toys "R" Us Annual Report

FRA 4.

LO 6 The Four Basic Financial Statements

Every chapter has a case on Toys "R" Us; the complete Toys "R" Us Annual Report for a recent year follows this chapter.

Refer to the Toys "R" Us annual report to answer the questions below. Keep in mind that every company, while following basic principles, adapts financial statements and terminology to its own special needs. Therefore, the complexity of the financial statements and the terminology in the Toys "R" Us statements will sometimes differ from those in the text. (Note that 1999 refers to the year ended January 30, 1999, and 1998 refers to the year ended January 31, 1998.)

1. What names does Toys "R" Us give its four basic financial statements? (Note that the use of the word "Consolidated" in the names of the financial statements means that these statements combine those of several companies owned by Toys "R" Us.)

2. Prove that the accounting equation works for Toys "R" Us on January 30, 1999, by finding the amounts for the following equation: Assets = Liabilities + Stockholders' Equity.

3. What were the total revenues of Toys "R" Us for the year ended January 30, 1999?

4. Was Toys "R" Us profitable in the year ended January 30, 1999? How much was net income (loss) in that year, and did it increase or decrease from the year ended January 31, 1998?

5. Did the company's cash and cash equivalents increase from January 31, 1998, to January 30, 1999? By how much? In what two places in the statements can this number be found or computed?

6. Did cash flows from operating activities, cash flows from investing activities, and cash flows from financing activities increase or decrease from 1998 to 1999?

Group Activity: Assign the above to in-class groups of three or four students. Set a time limit. The first group to answer all questions correctly wins.

Use the professional software Fingraph® to investigate annual reports and analyze financial data.

Fingraph® Financial Analyst™

FRA 5.

LO 1 Financial Statements,
LO 6 Business Activities, and
Goals

Choose any company in the Fingraph® Financial Analyst™ CD-ROM software.

1. In the company's annual report, find a description of the business. What business is the company in? How would you describe its operating activities?

2. Find and identify the company's four basic financial statements. Which statement shows the resources of the business and the various claims to those resources? From the balance sheet, prove the accounting equation by showing that the company's assets equal its liabilities plus stockholders' equity. What is the company's largest category of assets? Which statement shows changes in all or part of the company's stockholders' equity during the year? Did the company pay any dividends in the last year?

3. Which statement is most closely associated with the company's profitability goal? How much net income did the company earn in the last year? Which statement is most closely associated with the company's liquidity goal? Did cash (and cash equivalents) increase in the last year? Which provided the most positive cash flows in the last year: operating, investing, or financing activities?

4. Prepare a one-page executive summary that highlights what you have learned from parts **1**, **2**, and **3**. An executive summary is a short, easy-to-read report that emphasizes important information and conclusions by listing them by numbered paragraphs or bullet points.

Internet cases are accounting cases tailored to the Internet, based on concepts and applications from the chapter.

Internet Case

FRA 6.

LO 1 Financial Performance
LO 5 Comparison of Two High-Tech Companies

Microsoft Corporation and *Intel, Inc.,* are two of the most successful high-tech companies. Compare the two companies' financial performance first by going to the Needles Accounting Resource Center web site at http://college.hmco.com. and clicking on Intel under Chapter 1 companies. Utilizing the consolidated balance sheet and consolidated statement of income from the annual report, find the amount of total assets, revenues, and net income for the most recent year shown. Then compare these amounts to the same amounts for Microsoft shown in the first decision point of this chapter. Also compute net income to revenues and net income to total assets for both companies. Which company is larger? Which is more profitable?

ENDNOTES

1. Microsoft Corporation, *Annual Report*, 1999.
2. *Statement of Financial Accounting Concepts No. 1,* "Objectives of Financial Reporting by Business Enterprises" (Norwalk, Conn.: Financial Accounting Standards Board, 1978), par. 9.
3. Ibid.
4. Christopher D. Ittner, David F. Larcker, and Madhav V. Rajan, "The Choice of Performance Measures in Annual Bonus Contracts," *The Accounting Review*, April 1997.
5. Microsoft Corporation, *Annual Report*, 1999.
6. Kathy Williams and James Hart, "Microsoft: Tooling the Information Age," *Management Accounting*, May 1996, p. 42.
7. Accounting for sole proprietorships and partnerships is discussed in an appendix to this book.
8. *Statement of the Accounting Principles Board No. 4,* "Basic Concepts and Accounting Principles Underlying Financial Statements of Business Enterprises" (New York: American Institute of Certified Public Accountants, 1970), par. 138.
9. Touche Ross & Co., "Ethics in American Business" (New York: Touche Ross & Co., 1988), p. 7.
10. *Statement Number IC,* "Standards of Ethical Conduct for Management Accountants" (Montvale, N.J.: Institute of Management Accountants, 1983, revised 1997).
11. J.C. Penney Company, Inc., *Annual Report*, 1995.
12. Nikhil Deogun, "Coca-Cola Reports 27% Drop in Profits Hurt by Weakness in Foreign Markets," *The Wall Street Journal*, January 27, 1999.
13. Southwest Airlines Co., *Annual Report*, 1996.
14. The Charles Schwab Corporation, *Annual Report*, 1998.
15. Robert Frank, "Facing a Loss, Lego Narrates a Sad Toy Story," *The Wall Street Journal*, January 22, 1999.

SUPPLEMENT TO CHAPTER 1

How to Read an Annual Report

More than 4 million corporations are chartered in the United States. Most of these corporations are small, usually family-owned, businesses. They are called *private* or *closely held corporations* because their common stock is held by only a few people and is not available for sale to the public. Larger companies usually find it desirable to raise investment funds from many investors by issuing common stock to the public. These companies are called *public companies.* Although they are fewer in number than private companies, the total economic impact of public companies is much greater.

Public companies must register their common stock with the Securities and Exchange Commission (SEC), which regulates the issuance and subsequent trading of the stock of public companies. One important responsibility of the management of public companies under SEC rules is to report each year to the company's stockholders on the financial performance of the company. This report, called an *annual report,* contains the annual financial statements and other information about the company. Annual reports, which are a primary source of financial information about public companies, are distributed to all the company's stockholders and filed with the SEC. When filed with the SEC, the annual report is called the *S-1* because a Form S-1 is used to file the report. The general public may obtain a company's annual report by calling or writing the company. Many libraries have files of annual reports or have them available on electronic media such as *Compact Disclosure.* The annual reports of many companies can be accessed on the Internet by going to a company's home page on the World Wide Web. Also, many large companies file their S-1s electronically with the SEC. These annual reports and other filings may be accessed on the Internet at http://www.sec.gov/edgarhp.htm.

This supplement describes the major sections of the typical annual report and contains the complete annual report for one of the most successful retailers of this generation, *Toys "R" Us, Inc.* In addition to stores that sell toys and other items for children, the company has opened a chain of stores that sell children's clothes, called Kids "R" Us. The Toys "R" Us annual report should be referred to in completing the case assignments related to the company in each chapter.

The Components of an Annual Report

In addition to the financial statements, the annual report contains the notes to the financial statements, a letter to the stockholders (or shareholders), a multiyear summary of financial highlights, a description of the business, management's discussion of operating results and financial condition, a report of management's responsibility, the auditors' report, and a list of directors and officers of the company.

Letter to the Stockholders

Traditionally, at the beginning of the annual report, there is a letter in which the top officers of a corporation tell stockholders about the performance of and prospects for the company. The chief executive officer of Toys "R" Us wrote to the stockholders about the highlights of the past year, outlook for the new year, the benefits of its restructuring during 1999, and a detailed discussion of its total solutions strategy. He also discusses the company's venture into electronic commerce. The chief executive officer introduces these topics in the following way:

> [1999] was indeed a year of enormous challenge and change. We've spent the year intensively reviewing every aspect of our business and making some tough calls aimed at repositioning our worldwide business. Key elements of our strategic plan include a Total Solutions Strategy focused on our C-3 plan, which includes the reformatting and repositioning of our toy stores; development of a customer-driven culture; expanding product development; improving our customer value proposition; accelerating our supply chain management program; and expanding our channels of selling. In conjunction with these restructuring efforts, we have been proactively rebuilding and reshaping a stronger management team which will serve to build the foundation for repositioning [our] Company in the years ahead. We believe that the sum total of these efforts will serve as the springboard toward implementing our expanded vision for the future: to position Toys "R" Us as the worldwide authority on kids, families and fun.

Financial Highlights

The financial highlights section of the annual report presents key financial statistics for a ten-year period and is often accompanied by graphs. The Toys "R" Us annual report, for example, gives key figures for operations, financial position, and number of stores at year end and uses a graph to illustrate consolidated net sales for the last ten years. Other key figures are also shown graphically at appropriate points in the report. Note that the financial highlights section often includes nonfinancial data, such as number of stores.

In addition to financial highlights, an annual report will contain a detailed description of the products and divisions of the company. Some analysts tend to scoff at this section of the annual report because it often contains glossy photographs and other image-building material, but it should not be overlooked because it may provide useful information about past results and future plans.

Financial Statements

All companies present four basic financial statements. Toys "R" Us presents statements of earnings, balance sheets, statements of cash flows, and statements of stockholders' equity. Refer to the Toys "R" Us statements following this supplement during the discussion.

All of the Toys "R" Us financial statements are preceded by the word *consolidated*. A corporation issues *consolidated financial statements* when it consists of several companies and has combined their data for reporting purposes. For example, Toys "R" Us also operates Kids "R" Us and has combined that company's financial data with those of the Toys "R" Us stores.

Toys "R" Us also provides several years of data for each financial statement: two years for the balance sheet and three years for the others. Financial statements presented in this fashion are called *comparative financial statements*. Such statements are in accordance with generally accepted accounting principles and help readers to assess the company's performance over several years.

You may notice that the fiscal year for Toys "R" Us, instead of ending on the same date each year, ends on the Saturday nearest to the end of January. The reason is that Toys "R" Us is a retail company. It is common for retailers to end their fiscal years at a slow period after the busiest time of year.

In a note at the bottom of each page of the financial statements, the company reminds the reader that the accompanying notes are an integral part of the statements and must be consulted in interpreting the data.

CONSOLIDATED STATEMENTS OF EARNINGS   Toys "R" Us uses a modified single-step form of the income statement that includes all costs and expenses as a deduction from net sales to arrive at earnings before taxes on income. Income taxes are deducted in a separate step.

Net earnings is an alternative name for net income. The company also discloses the earnings per share, which is the net earnings divided by the weighted average number of shares of common stock held by stockholders during the year.

CONSOLIDATED BALANCE SHEETS   Toys "R" Us has a typical balance sheet for a merchandising company. In the assets and liabilities sections, the company separates out the current assets and the current liabilities. These are assets that will become available as cash or be used up in the next year and liabilities that will have to be paid or provided in the next year. These groupings help in understanding the company's liquidity.

Several items in the stockholders' equity section need further explanation. Common stock represents the number of shares outstanding at par value. Additional paid-in capital represents amounts invested by stockholders in excess of the par value of the common stock. Foreign currency translation adjustments occur because Toys "R" Us has foreign operations (see the chapter on international accounting and long-term investments). Treasury shares is a deduction from stockholders' equity that represents the cost of previously issued shares that have been bought back by the company.

CONSOLIDATED STATEMENTS OF CASH FLOWS   The preparation of the consolidated statement of cash flows is presented in the chapter on the statement of cash flows. Whereas the income statement reflects a company's profitability, the statement of cash flows reflects its liquidity. The statement provides information about a company's cash receipts, cash payments, and investing and financing activities during an accounting period.

Refer to the consolidated statements of cash flows in the Toys "R" Us annual report. The first section shows cash flows from operating activities. It begins with the net earnings (income) from the consolidated statements of earnings and adjusts that figure to a figure that represents the net cash flows provided by operating activities. Among the adjustments are increases for depreciation and amortization, which are expenses that do not require the use of cash, and increases and decreases for the changes in the working capital accounts. In the year ended January 30,

1999, Toys "R" Us had a net loss of $132,000,000, and its net cash inflow from operating activities was $964,000,000. Added to net income are expenses that do not require a current outlay of cash, such as depreciation, amortization and asset write-offs of $255,000,000 and restructuring and other charges of $546,000,000. Increases of $43,000,000 in accounts and other receivables and of $27,000,000 in prepaid expenses and other operating assets had a negative effect on cash flow. Also, income taxes payable had a small negative effect. Cash flow was enhanced by a decrease in merchandise inventories ($233,000,000) and by an increase of $229,000,000 in accounts payable, accrued expenses, and other liabilities. These results show how even though a company suffers a net loss, it can still generate positive cash flows.

The second major section of the consolidated statements of cash flows is cash flows from investing activities. The main item in this category is capital expenditures, net, of $373,000,000. This shows that Toys "R" Us is a growing company.

The third major section of the consolidated statements of cash flows is cash flows from financing activities. You can see here that the sources of cash from financing activities are short-term borrowings of $4,000,000, long-term borrowings of $771,000,000, and exercise of stock options of $16,000,000. Cash flows were used to make long-term debt repayments of $412,000,000 and to repurchase shares in the amount of $723,000,000. As a result, the company used $344,000,000 in financing activities during the year.

At the bottom of the consolidated statements of cash flows, the net effect of the operating, investing, and financing activities on the cash balance may be seen. Toys "R" Us had an increase in cash and cash equivalents during the year of $196,000,000 and ended the year with $410,000,000 of cash and cash equivalents on hand.

The supplemental disclosures of cash flow information show income tax and interest payments for the last three years.

CONSOLIDATED STATEMENTS OF STOCKHOLDERS' EQUITY   Instead of a simple statement of retained earnings, Toys "R" Us presents a *statement of stockholders' equity*. This statement explains the changes in five components of stockholders' equity.

Notes to Consolidated Financial Statements

To meet the requirements of full disclosure, the company must add *notes to the financial statements* to help users interpret some of the more complex items. The notes are considered an integral part of the financial statements. In recent years, the need for explanation and further details has become so great that the notes often take more space than the statements themselves. The notes to the financial statements can be put into three broad groups: summary of significant accounting policies, explanatory notes, and supplementary information notes.

SUMMARY OF SIGNIFICANT ACCOUNTING POLICIES   Generally accepted accounting principles require that the financial statements include a *summary of significant accounting policies*. In most cases, this summary is presented in the first note to the financial statements or as a separate section just before the notes. In this summary, the company tells which generally accepted accounting principles it has followed in preparing the statements. For example, in the Toys "R" Us report the company states the principles followed for property and equipment:

> Property and equipment are recorded at cost. Depreciation and amortization are provided using the straight-line method over the estimated useful lives of the assets or, where applicable, the terms of the respective leases, whichever is shorter.

Other important accounting policies listed by Toys "R" Us deal with fiscal year, principles of consolidation, cash and cash equivalents, merchandise inventories, preopening costs, financial instruments, forward foreign exchange contracts, and the use of estimates.

EXPLANATORY NOTES   Other notes explain some of the items in the financial statements. For example, Toys "R" Us showed the details of its Property and Equipment account, which is reproduced below. Other notes had to do with seasonal financing and long-term debt, leases, stockholders' equity, earnings per share, taxes on income, stock options, profit-sharing plan, segments, acquisition, restructuring and other charges, and other matters.

	Useful Life (in years)	January 30, 1999	January 31, 1998
Land		$ 829	$ 817
Buildings	45–50	1,842	1,849
Furniture and equipment	5–20	1,861	1,711
Leaseholds and leasehold improvements	12½–35	1,213	1,158
Construction in progress		42	46
Leased property under capital leases		27	29
		5,814	5,610
Less accumulated depreciation and amortization		1,588	1,398
		$4,226	$4,212

SUPPLEMENTARY INFORMATION NOTES   In recent years, the FASB and the SEC have ruled that certain supplemental information must be presented with financial statements. Examples are the quarterly reports that most companies present to their stockholders and to the Securities and Exchange Commission. These quarterly reports, which are called *interim financial statements*, are in most cases reviewed but not audited by the company's independent CPA firm. In its annual report, Toys "R" Us presented unaudited quarterly financial data from its 1998 quarterly statements, which are shown in the following table (for the year ended January 30, 1999, dollars in millions, except per share amounts):

	First Quarter	Second Quarter	Third Quarter	Fourth Quarter
1998				
Net Sales	$2,043	$2,020	$2,171	$4,936
Cost of Sales	1,417	1,390	1,831	3,553
Net Earnings/(Loss)	19	14	(475)	310
Basic Earnings/(Loss) per Share	$ .07	$ .05	$ (1.85)	$ 1.23
Diluted Earnings/(Loss) per Share	$ .07	$ .05	$ (1.85)	$ 1.23

Interim data were presented for the prior year as well. Toys "R" Us also provides supplemental information on the market price of its common stock during the years and data on its store locations.

Report of Management's Responsibilities

A statement of management's responsibility for the financial statements and the internal control structure may accompany the financial statements. The management report of Toys "R" Us acknowledges management's responsibility for the integrity and objectivity of the financial information and for the system of internal controls. It mentions the company's internal audit program and its distribution of policies to employees. It also states that the financial statements have been audited.

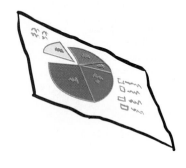

Management's Discussion and Analysis

Management also presents a discussion and analysis of financial condition and results of operations. In this section, management explains the difference from one year to the next. For example, the management of Toys "R" Us describes the company's sales performance in the following way:

> The Company's total sales increased to $11.2 billion for 1998, a 1.2% increase from total sales of $11.0 billion last year. Sales increased by 11.1% in 1997 and 5.4% in 1996. In 1998 sales were negatively impacted by the overall weakness in the worldwide toy industry which was cycling against strong sales of virtual pets, action figures and plush [toys] a year ago. In addition, sales were negatively impacted by sales of video hardware and software at lower price points as well as the deflationary effect from sales of clearance merchandise related to the Company's inventory reduction program. Comparable store sales for the Toys USA division declined 4% while the Toys International division had a 2% comparable store sales decline, in local currency. Kids "R" Us reported a 2% comparable store sales decrease in 1998. The softness in Toys and Kids was offset to some extent by an almost 20% comparable store sales gain in Babies "R" Us.

Its management of cash flows is described as follows:

> The seasonal nature of the business (approximately 45% of sales take place in the fourth quarter) typically causes cash to decline from the beginning of the year through October as inventory increases for the holiday selling season and funds are used for land purchases and construction of new stores, which usually open in the first ten months of the year. The Company has a $1 billion multi-currency unsecured committed revolving credit facility expiring in December 2002, from a syndicate of financial institutions. There were no outstanding balances under this revolver at January 1999, 1998, and 1997. Cash requirements for operations, capital expenditures, lease commitments and the share repurchase program will be met primarily through operating activities, borrowings under the revolving credit facility, issuance of short-term commercial paper and other bank borrowings for foreign subsidiaries.

Report of Certified Public Accountants

The *independent auditors' report* deals with the credibility of the financial statements. This report by independent certified public accountants gives the accountants' opinion about how fairly these statements have been presented. Using financial statements prepared by managers without an independent audit would be like having a judge hear a case in which he or she was personally involved. Management, through its internal accounting system, is logically responsible for recordkeeping because it needs similar information for its own use in operating the business. The certified public accountants, acting independently, add the necessary

REPORT OF INDEPENDENT AUDITORS

To the Board of Directors and Stockholders
Toys"R"Us, Inc.

(1) We have audited the accompanying consolidated balance sheets of Toys"R"Us, Inc. and subsidiaries as of January 30, 1999 and January 31, 1998, and the related consolidated statements of earnings, stockholders' equity and cash flows for each of the three years in the period ended January 30, 1999. These financial statements are the responsibility of the Company's management. Our responsibility is to express an opinion on these financial statements based on our audits.

(2) We conducted our audits in accordance with generally accepted auditing standards. Those standards require that we plan and perform the audit to obtain reasonable assurance about whether the financial statements are free of material misstatement. An audit includes examining, on a test basis, evidence supporting the amounts and disclosures in the financial statements. An audit also includes assessing the accounting principles used and significant estimates made by management,

as well as evaluating the overall financial statement presentation. We believe that our audits provide a reasonable basis for our opinion.

(3) In our opinion, the financial statements referred to above present fairly, in all material respects, the consolidated financial position of Toys"R"Us, Inc. and subsidiaries at January 30, 1999 and January 31, 1998, and the consolidated results of their operations and their cash flows for each of the three years in the period ended January 30, 1999, in conformity with generally accepted accounting principles.

Ernst & Young LLP

New York, New York
March 10, 1999

Figure 8
Auditors' Report for Toys "R" Us, Inc.

Source: Reprinted courtesy of Toys "R" Us, Inc. The notes to the financial statement, which are an integral part of the report, are not included.

credibility to management's figures for interested third parties. They report to the board of directors and the stockholders rather than to management.

In form and language, most auditors' reports are like the one shown in Figure 8. Usually such a report is short, but its language is very important. The report is divided into three parts.

1. The first paragraph identifies the financial statements subject to the auditors' report. This paragraph also identifies responsibilities. Company management is responsible for the financial statements, and the auditor is responsible for expressing an opinion on the financial statements based on the audit.

2. The second paragraph, or *scope section*, states that the examination was made in accordance with generally accepted auditing standards. These standards call for an acceptable level of quality in ten areas established by the American Institute of Certified Public Accountants. This paragraph also contains a brief description of the objectives and nature of the audit.

3. The third paragraph, or *opinion section*, states the results of the auditors' examination. The use of the word *opinion* is very important because the auditor does not certify or guarantee that the statements are absolutely correct. To do so would go beyond the truth, since many items, such as depreciation, are based on estimates. Instead, the auditors simply give an opinion about whether, overall, the financial statements "present fairly," in all material respects, the financial position, results of operations, and cash flows. This means that the statements are prepared in accordance with generally accepted accounting principles. If, in the auditors' opinion, the statements do not meet accepted standards, the auditors must explain why and to what extent.

The Annual Report Project

Many instructors assign a term project that requires reading and analyzing a real annual report. The Annual Report Project described here is one that has proved successful in the authors' classes. It may be used with the annual report of any company, including the Toys "R" Us Annual Report that is provided with this supplement.

The extent to which the financial analysis is required depends on the point in the course at which the Annual Report Project is assigned. Several options are provided in Instruction 3E, below.

Instructions:

1. Select an annual report of a company from those available on the Fingraph® Financial Analyst™ CD-ROM database that accompanies this text, or obtain one from the company, your library, or another source.

2. Library and Internet Research
    Go to the library or use the Web Resources at the Needles Accounting Resource Center web site (*http://college.hmco.com*) to learn about the company you have chosen and the industry in which it operates. Find at least two articles or other references to the industry and the company and summarize your findings.

    Also, access the company's Internet home page directly or through the Needles Accounting Resource Center web site. Learn about the company's products and services and find its financial information. Summarize what you have learned.

3. Your term project should consist of five or six double-spaced pages organized according to the following outline:

    A. Introduction
    - Identify your company by writing a summary that includes the following elements:
    - Name of the chief executive officer
    - Home office
    - Ending date of latest fiscal year
    - Description of the principal products or services that the company provides
    - Main geographic area of activity

- Name of the company's independent accountants (auditors). In your own words, what did the accountants say about the company's financial statements?
- The most recent price of the company's stock and its dividend per share.
- Be sure to provide the date for this information.

B. Industry Situation and Company Plans

Describe the industry and its outlook and summarize the company's future plans based on your library research and on reading the annual report. Be sure to read the letter to the stockholders and include relevant information about the company's plans from that discussion.

C. Financial Statements

Income Statement: Is the format most similar to a single-step or multi-step format? Determine gross profit, income from operations, and net income for the last two years and comment on the increases or decreases in these amounts.

Balance Sheet: Show that Assets = Liabilities + Stockholders' Equity for the past two years.

Statement of Cash Flows: Are cash flows from operations more or less than net income for the past two years? Is the company expanding through investing activities? What is the company's most important source of financing? Overall, has cash increased or decreased over the past two years?

D. Accounting Policies

What are the significant accounting policies, if any, relating to revenue recognition, cash, short-term investments, merchandise inventories, property and equipment, and preopening costs?

What are the topics of the notes to the financial statements?

E. Financial Analysis

For the past two years, calculate and discuss the significance of the following ratios:

Option (a): Basic (After Chapter 5)

Liquidity Ratios
Working capital
Current ratio

Profitability Ratios
Profit margin
Asset turnover
Return on assets
Debt to equity
Return on equity

Option (b): Basic with Enhanced Liquidity Analysis (After Chapter 7)

Liquidity Ratios
Working capital
Current ratio
Receivable turnover
Average days' sales uncollected
Inventory turnover
Average days' inventory on hand

Profitability Ratios
 Profit margin
 Asset turnover
 Return on assets
 Debt to equity
 Return on equity

Option (c): Comprehensive (After Chapter 15)

Liquidity Ratios
 Working capital
 Current ratio
 Receivable turnover
 Average days' sales uncollected
 Inventory turnover
 Average days' inventory on hand

Profitability Ratios
 Profit margin
 Asset turnover
 Return on assets
 Return on equity

Long-Term Solvency Ratios
 Debt to equity
 Interest coverage

Cash Flow Adequacy
 Cash flow yield
 Cash flows to sales
 Cash flows to assets
 Free cash flow

Market Strength Ratios
 Price/earnings per share
 Dividends yield

 Option (d): Comprehensive using Fingraph® Financial Analyst™ software on the CD-ROM that accompanies this text.

Tomorrow Begins With Us

This annual report is for the year ended January 30, 1999.
Reprinted courtesy of Toys "R" Us, Inc.

TOYS'Я'US®
Annual Report 1998

Toys"R"Us
The Worldwide
Authority on
Kids, Families
and Fun

TABLE OF CONTENTS

Financial Highlights
TOYS"R"US, INC. AND SUBSIDIARIES

(Dollars in millions except per share data)   Fiscal Year Ended

	Jan. 30, 1999*	Jan. 31, 1998	Feb.1, 1997*	Feb. 3, 1996*	Jan. 28, 1995	Jan. 29, 1994	Jan. 30, 1993	Feb. 1, 1992	Feb. 2, 1991	Jan. 28, 1990
OPERATIONS:										
Net Sales	$11,170	$11,038	$ 9,932	$ 9,427	$ 8,746	$ 7,946	$ 7,169	$ 6,124	$ 5,510	$ 4,788
Net (Loss)/Earnings	(132)	490	427	148	532	483	438	340	326	321
Basic (Loss)/Earnings Per Share	(0.50)	1.72	1.56	0.54	1.88	1.66	1.51	1.18	1.12	1.11
Diluted (Loss)/Earnings Per Share	(0.50)	1.70	1.54	0.53	1.85	1.63	1.47	1.15	1.11	1.09
FINANCIAL POSITION AT YEAR END:										
Working Capital	$ 106	$ 579	$ 619	$ 326	$ 484	$ 633	$ 797	$ 328	$ 177	$ 238
Real Estate-Net	2,354	2,435	2,411	2,336	2,271	2,036	1,877	1,751	1,433	1,142
Total Assets	7,899	7,963	8,023	6,738	6,571	6,150	5,323	4,583	3,582	3,075
Long-Term Debt	1,222	851	909	827	785	724	671	391	195	173
Stockholders' Equity	3,624	4,428	4,191	3,432	3,429	3,148	2,889	2,426	2,046	1,705
NUMBER OF STORES AT YEAR END:										
Toys"R"Us - United States	704	700	682	653	618	581	540	497	451	404
Toys"R"Us - International	452	441	396	337	293	234	167	126	97	74
Kids"R"Us - United States	212	215	212	213	204	217	211	189	164	137
Babies"R"Us - United States	113	98	82	–	–	–	–	–	–	–
Total Stores	1,481	1,454	1,372	1,203	1,115	1,032	918	812	712	615

*After restructuring and other charges.

To Our Stockholders

1998 was indeed a year of enormous challenge and change. We've spent the year intensively reviewing every aspect of our business and making some tough calls aimed at repositioning our worldwide business. Key elements of our strategic plan include a Total Solutions Strategy focused on our C-3 plan, which includes the reformatting and repositioning of our toy stores; development of a customer-driven culture; expanding product development; improving our customer value proposition; accelerating our supply chain management program; and expanding our channels of selling. In conjunction with these restructuring efforts, we have been proactively rebuilding and reshaping a stronger management team which will serve to build the foundation for repositioning your Company in the years ahead. We believe that the sum total of these efforts will serve as the springboard toward implementing our expanded vision for the future: to position Toys"R"Us as the worldwide authority on kids, families and fun.

Before outlining our strategic initiatives, let's take a quick look at 1998.

ROBERT C. NAKASONE
Chief Executive Officer

1998 Financial Summary

From a financial standpoint, 1998 was a disappointing year. Our sales totaled $11.2 billion, which represented a 1.2% increase over the $11.0 billion reported last year. Comparable store sales in our U.S. toy stores declined by 4% while our International toy store sales declined by 2%, in local currency. A key factor behind these sales declines was the much-publicized weakness in the overall worldwide toy industry which was cycling against very strong sales of virtual pets, action figures and plush a year ago. In addition, the lower sales also reflect retail price deflation in the video game hardware and software category, as well as the deflationary impact of clearance merchandise sales related to our previously-announced inventory reduction programs.

Comparable sales at Kids"R"Us were down 2%. Nonetheless, it is worth noting that comparable store apparel sales were considerably stronger in our 65 "combo" stores where we have reallocated roughly 6,000 square feet of Kids"R"Us

apparel into existing Toys"R"Us stores. We believe this underscores the important role of apparel in all our future "R"Us store configurations.

At Babies"R"Us, we're very pleased to report a record performance for 1998. Comparable store sales were up almost 20%. We now operate 118 Babies"R"Us stores nationwide and are the market share leader in the juvenile specialty category. Needless to say, we are extremely pleased with the performance of this division and plan to continue our aggressive expansion with approximately 20 new stores slated for '99.

Largely as a result of these sales trends, our net earnings, before restructuring and other charges, were $376 million or $1.41 per share. Including the restructuring and other charges of $698 million, ($508 million net of taxes) the Company incurred a net loss of $132 million or $0.50 per share for 1998.

1998 Restructuring Benefits

We ended 1998 a much healthier and vibrant company. This was attributable to some tough strategic decisions that will shape the Company's future. We recorded restructuring and other charges of $508 million net of taxes, which caused the Company to incur a net loss in 1998. The impact of making these tough calls will be evident in our future operations, growth and financial performance. These charges are the result of an exhaustive review of all our operations in 1998 from both a strategic and an Economic Value Added ("EVA®") perspective. These reviews prompted the following significant actions:

• The closing and/or downsizing of approximately 50 toy stores in the International arena, predominantly in continental Europe, and about 9 U.S. toy stores which do not meet the Company's strategic or financial objectives. This will free our management to focus on higher return opportunities;

• The conversion of 28 existing U.S. toy stores into "combo" stores, which will enable us to close 31 nearby Kids"R"Us stores. In addition to reducing operating costs and releasing working capital, this will allow us to enhance our productivity by further expanding kids' apparel into additional Toys"R"Us stores;

• The consolidation of several distribution centers and over half a dozen administrative offices. These actions will reduce administrative support functions in the U.S. and Europe, which will not only generate selling, general and administrative efficiencies, but "flatten" our organization and bring our management even closer to our stores and customers;

• The continuation of taking aggressive markdowns on clearance product to optimize inventory levels, accommodate new product offerings and accelerate our store reformatting. In conjunction with the initial stages of our supply chain re-engineering, we have already been able to reduce same store inventories in all our divisions by over $560 million or 24% at year end 1998, with roughly $480 million or 31% of this favorable swing coming from reduced inventory in the U.S. toy stores division alone. This brought us into the new year with heightened merchandise flexibility and increased "open to buy" as we begin the rollout of the initial phase of our store reformat program in 1999.

One of our other key priorities in 1998 was to build a strong executive team, and we are well on our way towards assembling a truly outstanding management team. Since the beginning of '98, more than 50 percent of our officer team has either joined the company from the outside, or has been promoted or transferred to new assignments, bringing fresh perspectives and proven skills to our business.

It is obvious our 1998 sales and earnings were not what we wanted them to be. However, we've spent a year making tough calls and hard decisions, and we're now ready to move forward stronger and more focused than ever.

Total Solutions Strategy

Our restructuring program, in September 1998, was the first step required to launch a winning strategy for Toys"R"Us – a strategy which will realign our assets, organization and thinking based on customer-driven priorities in a more competitive marketplace. In the "R"Us brand, we have one of the best-known brand names in the world: our challenge is to more effectively develop this strong customer franchise potential. Today's retail marketplace demands stores that are exciting, easy to shop and customer-friendly. While our selection is still superior to our competitors, that alone is not compelling enough to rebuild market share and brand loyalty. We must become more focused on developing greater everyday customer value in terms of price, service and the total shopping experience.

To fulfill these objectives, we are moving into the second phase of our Total Solutions Strategy in 1999.

We are rebuilding our "worlds" around theirs.

C-3 – More Than Just a Store

Over the next two years, the C-3 plan will include the implementation of new merchandise as well as customer service, store layout, price/value and supply chain improvements that provide an integrated approach to maximizing customer potential.

This has led our new management team to develop an initiative that is a **C**ustomer driven . . .**C**ost effective . . . **C**oncept delivering sustainable, long-term performance. C-3 is a total customer solution involving every facet of our Company from merchandising and replenishment to operations and people development.

In October 1998, we started our C-3 development operationally in nine stores to "stress test" a new, more customer-friendly store layout during our high sales season. We proved that our operations could handle high velocity seasonal inventory flow despite a 33% smaller backroom, and that we could maintain acceptable in-stock conditions despite an entirely new operating approach. We are encouraged by the positive customer reaction to these stores, and are experiencing positive sales trends, even though a majority of C-3 merchandise enhancements will not be implemented until mid-1999.

Based on the positive results of this initial operational phase of C-3, we are even more committed to the 1999 conversion of approximately 200 U.S. stores, which will include the development of many new merchandising "worlds." We will also retrofit the front end in an additional 125 stores this year to include the R Zone (teen electronics), promotional product and easier customer access. The C-3 Total Solutions Strategy consists of an easier-to-shop store layout, an expanded merchandise offering, a higher standard of customer service and a more effective supply chain approach that will enable us to build long-term performance improvement. Over the next few years we will align our organization, capital investments and operating approach to fully focus on the following C-3 objectives:

• Store Repositioning

Our stores must be made easier to shop and present merchandise in a more dynamic selling environment. The C-3 store layout creates wider aisles, more feature opportunities and end-caps, shops and logical category adjacencies – all designed to improve customer shopping patterns and experience. The sales floor has been expanded by 20% with a one-third reduction in the size of our backrooms.

• Customer-Driven Culture

The customer must experience a higher level of service in our stores. To accomplish this, we are streamlining our organization and operating processes to allow us to invest more in sales floor staffing, associate product knowledge training, and improving overall customer-friendly service. We are also intensifying our in-store informational graphics and product inter-activity to give our customers access to more substantial product knowledge on a "self-service" basis.

R Zone, the new "hot spot" for teens, features the newest in electronics and video.

• Product Development

We must give our customers more reasons to shop our stores. Based on the results of extensive customer research, we have created merchandise "worlds." Each "world" has a unique customer franchise from juvenile (Mom and her baby), to R Zone electronics and video products (the "cool" spot for teenage customers). Each "world" will establish its own business plan and has a complete support team to develop its business from product sourcing to customer advertising and promotion.

The "worlds" presently being developed are:

• R Zone (video, electronics, computer software, related products)

• Action and Adventure (action figures, diecast cars, etc.)

• Girls (dolls, collectibles, accessories, lifestyle products)

• Outdoor Fun (bikes, sports, playsets)

• Pre-School (toys, accessories)

• Seasonal (Christmas, Halloween, Summer, etc.)

• Juvenile (baby products and 0-4 apparel)

• Learning Center (educational and developmental products)

• Family Fun (games and puzzles)

1999 will see a majority of the new "world" product selection and merchandising included in our C-3 rollout.

In addition, emphasis on proprietary product, private label, and branded exclusives will continue to be a significant part of our product development strategy. Retail sale of proprietary, exclusive and private label merchandising was up significantly in 1998, and we are targeting to double this business over the next three years.

Families love shopping at our newest location: www.toysrus.com.

Customer Value Proposition

The "R"Us brand must take on new dimensions of significant value to our customers. We are evaluating our pricing model to assure an everyday, competitive position on key products. We are more aggressively pursuing high demand and closeout product opportunities to bring more special price values to our customers in 1999. We also see a great opportunity to further leverage our substantial "R"Us customer database through the creation of a Loyalty Marketing Program, which will be piloted in several metropolitan markets in 1999. The mandate for our new team in marketing is quite clear: sharpen our advertising, promotion and "R"Us brand-building efforts.

Supply Chain

The first step in improving our supply chain management in 1998 was to unclog slow turning inventory from our stores. Our inventory reduction program will allow us to transform our stores' physical and merchandising layout. This will be completed in 1999. These actions will allow us to create a more customer-driven product flow, improve turns, effectively manage space for product productivity and operationally have the right product …at the right place …at the right time.

E-Commerce

We are extending our presence beyond our stores by expanding our channels of selling to our customers. We will be wherever our customers are, and that includes mediums such as mail-order catalogs and electronic commerce.

1998 marked our entry into the exciting world of electronic commerce with the introduction of Internet shopping through www.toysrus.com. Following our launch on the Internet last June, traffic to our website has grown significantly. We are upgrading our capacity to meet the growing demand and we are committed to making this site a dominant force in online retailing. We are presently aligning our distribution, buying and brand strengths to more broadly impact the Internet in 1999.

"Worldwide Authority on Kids, Families and Fun" – The "R"Us Potential

Most of us grew up as Toys"R"Us kids. We strongly believe that our Company's success and growth as we proceed into the next millennium will be tied to our unique ability to delight our valued customers – past, present and future. We must captivate their imaginations and introduce them to the exciting and fun world of limitless possibilities that the "R"Us family is committed to providing: a world where they know *they* are the most important ingredient in everything we do.

These are aggressive goals that require a total commitment to our customers, dramatic cultural change in our organization and a clear, strategic vision that effectively mobilizes the substantial resources of our Company. It will take time. It will not be easy. But we believe in the strength and potential of the "R"Us customer franchise, and we most importantly believe that the people in the Toys"R"Us organization worldwide have what it takes to create a strong, successful future for all of us.

That future begins now.

Sincerely,

Robert C. Nakasone

ROBERT C. NAKASONE
Chief Executive Officer
March 29, 1999

Everyday, a new customer is born.

Management's Discussion and Analysis

RESULTS OF OPERATIONS AND FINANCIAL CONDITION

Results of Operations*

The Company's total sales increased to $11.2 billion for 1998, a 1.2% increase from total sales of $11.0 billion last year. Sales increased by 11.1% in 1997 and 5.4% in 1996. In 1998 sales were negatively impacted by the overall weakness in the worldwide toy industry which was cycling against strong sales of virtual pets, action figures and plush a year ago. In addition, sales were negatively impacted by sales of video hardware and software at lower price points as well as the deflationary effect from sales of clearance merchandise related to the Company's inventory reduction program. Comparable store sales for the Toys USA division declined 4% while the Toys International division had a 2% comparable store sales decline, in local currency. Kids"R"Us reported a 2% comparable store sales decrease in 1998. The softness in Toys and Kids was offset to some extent by an almost 20% comparable store sales gain in Babies"R"Us.

The Company's three-year sales growth is primarily attributable to the acquisition of Baby Superstore and the Company's continued store expansion. The Company opened 56 new U.S.A. toy stores, 133 international toy stores, including franchise and joint venture stores, 10 children's clothing stores, 40 baby specialty stores, and acquired 76 baby specialty stores during the three year period. The Company closed 23 stores from 1996 through 1998 and terminated a franchise agreement in Italy for 14 stores. These closures did not have a significant impact on the Company's financial position.

Cost of sales as a percentage of sales increased to 73.3% in 1998 from 69.8% in 1997. Cost of sales was negatively impacted by clearance markdowns of $253 million, markdowns related to strategic initiatives of $29 million, and inventory system refinements and changes in accounting estimates of $63 million. Before the impact of these charges, cost of sales as a percentage of sales was 70.2%. Excluding these charges, the Toys USA division reported cost of sales as a percentage of sales of 71.0% in 1998 and 70.5% in 1997. The Toys International division, also excluding the charges, reported cost of sales as a percentage of sales of 69.1% in 1998 and 68.8% in 1997. These increases were due to a change in the sales mix consisting of a decrease in sales of higher margin action figures and virtual pets, as well as higher sales of lower margin video software merchandise. Consolidated cost of sales as a percentage of sales increased by 0.4% in 1997 from 69.4% in 1996 as a result of higher costs related to the Company's promotional holiday selling program, higher than historical inventory shrinkage and the continued strengthening of the Company's lower margin video business.

Selling, advertising, general and administrative expenses (SG&A) as a percentage of sales were 21.9% in 1998, 20.2% in 1997, and 20.3% in 1996. SG&A for 1998 includes $59 million of changes in accounting estimates and provisions for legal settlements discussed below. Before the impact of these charges, SG&A as a percentage of sales for 1998 was 21.3%. Excluding these charges, the Toys USA division reported SG&A as a percentage of sales of 18.6% in 1998 and 17.5% in 1997, while Toys International's SG&A as a percentage of sales was 23.6% in 1998 and 23.1% in 1997. These increases were the result of the implementation of strategic initiatives and store expansion, not offset by sales leveraging. The slight decrease in consolidated SG&A in 1997 was primarily due to expense control and sales leveraging, partially offset by additional distribution and handling costs related to higher than planned inventory levels.

Depreciation, amortization and asset write-offs were $255 million, $253 million and $206 million in 1998, 1997 and 1996, respectively. The increase in 1997 included $19 million in asset write-offs for store conversions.

During 1998 the Company announced strategic initiatives to reposition its worldwide business and other charges including the customer-focused reformatting of its toy stores into the new C-3 format, as well as the restructuring of its International operations which resulted in a charge of $353 million ($279 million net of tax benefits, or $1.05 per share). The strategic initiatives resulted in a restructuring charge of $294 million. The other charges of $59 million primarily consist of changes in accounting estimates and provisions for legal settlements. The Company is closing and/or downsizing underperforming stores and consolidating distribution centers and administrative offices. As a result, approximately 2,600 employees will be terminated worldwide. Stores expected to be closed had aggregate store sales and net operating losses of approximately $322 million and $5 million, respectively, for the year ended January 30, 1999. The write-down of property, plant and equipment relating to the above mentioned closures and downsizings were based on both internal and independent appraisals. Unused reserves at January 30, 1999, should be utilized in 1999, with the exception of long-term lease commitments, which will be utilized in 1999 and thereafter. Details on the components of the charges are described in the Notes to the Consolidated Financial Statements and are as follows:

---

*References to 1998, 1997 and 1996, are for the 52 weeks ended January 30, 1999, January 31, 1998 and February 1, 1997.

Management's Discussion and Analysis

RESULTS OF OPERATIONS AND FINANCIAL CONDITION

Description	Charge	Utilized	Reserve Balance @1/30/99
Closings/Downsizings:			
Lease commitments	$ 81	$ –	$ 81
Severance and other closing costs	29	4	25
Write-down of property, plant & equipment	155	155	–
Other	29	5	24
Total Restructuring	$ 294	$164	$130
Changes in accounting estimates and provisions for legal settlements	$ 59	$ 20	$ 39

In 1998 the Company also announced markdowns and other charges of $345 million ($229 million net of tax benefits, or $.86 per share). Of this charge, $253 million relates to markdowns required to clear excess inventory from stores. These markdowns should enable the Company to achieve its optimal inventory assortment and streamline systems so that it can proceed with the C-3 conversions on an accelerated basis. The Company's objective with its new C-3 concept is to provide customers with a better shopping experience leading to increased sales and higher inventory turns. In addition, the Company recorded $29 million in markdowns related to the store closings discussed previously. The Company also recorded charges to cost of sales of $63 million related to inventory system refinements and changes in accounting estimates. Unused reserves at January 30, 1999 are expected to be utilized in 1999. Details of the markdowns and other charges are as follows:

Description	Charge	Utilized	Reserve Balance @1/30/99
Markdowns			
Clear excess inventory	$253	$179	$ 74
Store closings	29	2	27
Change in accounting estimates and other	63	57	6
Total Cost of Sales	$345	$238	$107

The strategic initiatives, markdowns and other charges described above are expected to improve the Company's free cash flow and increase operating earnings.

The Company's 1996 results were impacted by a charge of $60 million ($38 million net of tax benefits, or $.14 cents per share), relating to an arbitration award rendered against the Company involving a dispute over a 1982 franchise agreement to operate stores in the Middle East.

At January 30, 1999, the Company had approximately $45 million of reserves remaining from its restructuring program announced in 1995, primarily relating to long-term lease obligations. The Company believes these reserves are adequate to complete the restructuring program.

Interest expense increased by $17 million in 1998, as compared to 1997, primarily due to higher borrowings throughout the year as a result of the Company's share repurchase programs. Also included in 1998 interest expense is $6 million for the early extinguishment of long-term debt. Interest expense decreased in 1997 as compared to 1996 primarily due to lower average short-term borrowings and to a $325 million medium-term financing which replaced borrowings carrying higher interest rates.

The Company's effective tax rate for 1998 was unfavorably affected by the restructuring and other charges recorded in the third quarter of 1998. Excluding the impact of these charges, the Company's effective tax rate was 36.5% in 1998, as well as in 1997 and 1996.

International sales were unfavorably impacted by the translation of local currency results into U.S. dollars by approximately $30 million, $250 million and $150 million in 1998, 1997 and 1996, respectively. Neither the translation of local currency results into U.S. dollars nor inflation had a material effect on the Company's operating results for the last three years.

Liquidity & Capital Resources

The Company's cash flows from operations increased to $964 million in 1998 from $509 million in 1997 primarily due to a significant reduction in inventories during 1998 as well as higher accounts payable, accrued expenses and other liabilities at January 30, 1999. Cash flows from operations decreased by $234 million in 1997 compared with 1996 primarily due to higher inventories.

Cash flows used for investing activities decreased by $94 million in 1998, primarily due to fewer new store openings in 1998, as well as fewer store conversions in 1998 compared with 1997. Store conversions were the primary factor in the $79 million capital expenditure increase in 1997.

Cash flows used for financing activities decreased to $344 million in 1998 from $498 million in 1997 primarily due to repayment of a $115 million Baby Superstore obligation in 1997. The Company repurchased over 32 million shares of its stock for $723 million in 1998, which was the primary reason for the increase in total borrowings net of cash of

Management's Discussion and Analysis
RESULTS OF OPERATIONS AND FINANCIAL CONDITION

$200 million in 1998 as compared with 1997. Cash flows used for financing activities increased by $709 million in 1997 compared with 1996 primarily due to the $325 million medium term financing in 1996, as well as $253 million expended for the Company's stock repurchase program in 1997.

On February 3, 1997, the Company acquired Baby Superstore, Inc. for 13 million treasury shares of the Company's common stock valued at approximately $376 million. This acquisition was accounted for as a purchase as of February 1, 1997, and the excess of purchase price over net assets acquired in the amount of $365 million has been recorded as goodwill and is being amortized over 40 years.

In 1999, the Company plans to open approximately 10 toy stores in the United States and approximately 25 international toy stores, including 10 franchise stores. Our newest division, Babies"R"Us, will open approximately 20 stores in the United States.

For 1999, capital requirements for real estate, store and warehouse fixtures and equipment, leasehold improvements and other additions to property and equipment are estimated at approximately $550 million. These plans include the full conversion of approximately 200 toy stores and the partial conversion of an additional 125 toy stores in the United States to the C-3 format.

In 1998 the Company repurchased over 32 million shares of its common stock through its share repurchase programs for a total of $723 million. In 1998 the Company completed its $1 billion share repurchase program announced in January 1994, and has $330 million remaining in its $1 billion share repurchase program announced in January 1998.

The seasonal nature of the business (approximately 45% of sales take place in the fourth quarter) typically causes cash to decline from the beginning of the year through October as inventory increases for the holiday selling season and funds are used for land purchases and construction of new stores, which usually open in the first ten months of the year. The Company has a $1 billion multi-currency unsecured committed revolving credit facility expiring in December 2002, from a syndicate of financial institutions. There were no outstanding balances under this revolver at January 1999, 1998, and 1997. Cash requirements for operations, capital expenditures, lease commitments and the share repurchase program will be met primarily through operating activities, borrowings under the revolving credit facility, issuance of commercial paper and/or other bank borrowings for foreign subsidiaries.

Quantitative and Qualitative Disclosures About Market Risks

The Company is exposed to market risk from potential changes in interest rates and foreign exchange rates. The Company regularly evaluates these risks and has taken the following measures to mitigate these risks: the countries in which the Company owns assets and operates stores are politically stable; the Company's foreign exchange risk management objectives are to stabilize cash flow from the effects of foreign currency fluctuations; the Company will, whenever practical, offset local investments in foreign currencies with borrowings denominated in the same currencies; the Company also enters into foreign exchange contracts or purchases options to eliminate specific transaction risk. The market risk related to these derivative contracts is offset by the changes in value of the underlying items being hedged. Approximately half of the Company's long-term debt is at fixed interest rates and therefore, the fair value is affected by changes in market interest rates. The Company believes the amount of risk and the use of derivative financial instruments described above are not material to the Company's financial condition or results of operations.

Impact of Year 2000

Year 2000 issues are those related to the inability of certain computer systems to properly recognize and process date-sensitive information relative to the year 2000 and beyond. The Company's Year 2000 project which began in 1997, includes four major elements: 1) information technology (IT) systems, 2) non-IT systems, 3) relationships with key business partners and 4) contingency planning. The Company has substantially completed the required coding conversions and testing on IT and non-IT systems as of January 30, 1999. The Company will continue to perform full integrated testing in 1999. The Company has utilized both internal and external resources to implement the conversion of its systems for Year 2000 compliance.

The total estimated cost to achieve Year 2000 compliance is approximately $25 million, which is being expensed as incurred. These estimates exclude internal labor and related costs. Approximately $20 million of these costs have been incurred as of January 30, 1999. All of these costs are being funded through cash flows from operations. The Company has identified significant business partners and is working closely with them to understand their Year 2000 compliance status. The Company anticipates minimal business interruption to occur as a result of Year 2000 issues within its control. However, possible consequences include, but are not limited to, loss of communication links with store locations, loss of electric power, delayed product deliveries from major suppliers, and

Management's Discussion and Analysis
RESULTS OF OPERATIONS AND FINANCIAL CONDITION

the inability to process transactions or engage in similar normal business activities. In addition, not all customer situations can be anticipated. The Company may experience an increase of sales returns of products containing hardware or software components. Such returns, if they occur, are likely to be the responsibility of the manufacturers and are not expected to be material to the Company's financial condition or results of operations. The Company believes the readiness of third parties is the most significant area of risk to the Company related to Year 2000. However, the Company also believes that ongoing communication with and assessment of readiness of these third parties will minimize this risk. The Company has begun to develop but has not yet finalized a contingency plan for possible Year 2000 issues. Contingency plans are expected to be in place by the end of the second quarter of 1999.

The total cost of the Year 2000 project is not expected to have a material effect on the Company's financial condition or results of operations. The costs of conversion and the completion dates for the project are management's best estimates.

Recent Accounting Pronouncements

In June 1997, the Financial Accounting Standards Board issued SFAS No. 130 - Reporting Comprehensive Income, which requires the separate reporting of all changes to stockholders' equity, and SFAS No. 131 - Disclosures About Segments of an Enterprise and Related Information, which revises existing guidelines about the level of financial disclosure of a Company's operations. In March 1998, the Accounting Standards Executive Committee issued Statement of Position 98-1, Accounting for Computer Software Developed for Internal Use, which requires capitalization of certain costs to develop internal use computer software. These statements were adopted by the Company in fiscal 1998 and did not have a material effect on the consolidated financial position, results of operations or cash flows of the Company.

In June 1998, the Financial Accounting Standards Board issued Statement No. 133 - Accounting for Derivative Instruments and Hedging Activities, which the Company is required to adopt in its fiscal year beginning February 2000. SFAS No. 133 requires that all derivative instruments be recorded on the balance sheet at fair value. Changes in the fair value of derivatives are recorded each period in current earnings or other comprehensive income, depending on whether a derivative is designated as part of a hedge transaction and the type of hedge transaction. The ineffective portion of all hedges will be recognized in earnings.

While not expected to be material, the Company is in the process of determining the impact that the adoption of SFAS No. 133 will have on the consolidated financial position, results of operations and cash flows of the Company.

Euro Conversion

The Company has developed a plan to ensure business and systems continuity during the introduction of the Euro currency in certain of the Company's European operations. The initial phase of this plan was implemented prior to the January 1, 1999 (Phase 1) introduction of the Euro. Further implementation of this plan is scheduled to coincide with the transition phases (Phases 2 and 3) of completely converting from local denominated currencies to the Euro (the "Euro conversion"). Total costs for the entire Euro conversion program are not expected to be material. Based on the actions taken to date, the Company does not expect the Euro conversion to have a material effect on the consolidated financial position, results of operations or cash flows of the Company.

Forward Looking Statements

This annual report contains "forward looking" statements which are intended to be covered by the safe harbors created thereby. All statements that are not historical facts, including statements about the Company's beliefs or expectations, are forward-looking statements. Such statements involve risks and uncertainties that exist in the Company's operations and business environment that could render actual outcomes and results materially different than predicted. The Company's forward-looking statements are based on assumptions about many factors, including, but not limited to, ongoing competitive pressures in the retail industry, changes in consumer spending, general economic conditions in the United States and other jurisdictions in which the Company conducts business (such as interest rates and consumer confidence) and normal business uncertainty. While the Company believes that its assumptions are reasonable at the time forward-looking statements were made, it cautions that it is impossible to predict the actual outcome of numerous factors and, therefore, readers should not place undue reliance on such statements. Forward-looking statements speak only as of the date they are made, and the Company undertakes no obligation to update such statements in light of new information or future events that involve inherent risks and uncertainties. Actual results may differ materially from those contained in any forward looking statement.

Consolidated Statements of Earnings

TOYS"R"US, INC. AND SUBSIDIARIES

(In millions except per share data)	January 30, 1999	January 31, 1998	Year Ended February 1, 1997
Net Sales	$11,170	$11,038	$ 9,932
Cost of sales	8,191	7,710	6,892
Gross Profit	2,979	3,328	3,040
Selling, advertising, general and administrative expenses	2,443	2,231	2,020
Depreciation, amortization and asset write-offs	255	253	206
Restructuring and other charges	294	–	60
Total Operating Expenses	2,992	2,484	2,286
Operating (Loss)/Income	(13)	844	754
Interest expense	102	85	98
Interest and other income	(9)	(13)	(17)
Interest Expense, Net	93	72	81
(Loss)/Earnings Before Income Taxes	(106)	772	673
Income Taxes	26	282	246
Net (Loss)/Earnings	$ (132)	$ 490	$ 427
Basic (Loss)/Earnings Per Share	$ (0.50)	$ 1.72	$ 1.56
Diluted (Loss)/Earnings Per Share	$ (0.50)	$ 1.70	$ 1.54

See notes to consolidated financial statements.

The "R"Us brand has
successfully captured
young imaginations
and a significant
market share.

Consolidated Balance Sheets

TOYS"R"US, INC. AND SUBSIDIARIES

Our ever-expanding outdoor and sports headquarters features everything fun under the sun.

(In millions)	January 30, 1999	January 31, 1998
ASSETS		
Current Assets:		
Cash and cash equivalents	$ 410	$ 214
Accounts and other receivables	204	175
Merchandise inventories	1,902	2,464
Prepaid expenses and other current assets	81	51
Total Current Assets	2,597	2,904
Property and Equipment:		
Real estate, net	2,354	2,435
Other, net	1,872	1,777
Total Property and Equipment	4,226	4,212
Goodwill, net	347	356
Other assets	729	491
	$ 7,899	$ 7,963
LIABILITIES AND STOCKHOLDERS' EQUITY		
Current Liabilities:		
Short-term borrowings	$ 156	$ 134
Accounts payable	1,415	1,280
Accrued expenses and other current liabilities	696	680
Income taxes payable	224	231
Total Current Liabilities	2,491	2,325
Long-Term Debt	1,222	851
Deferred Income Taxes	333	219
Other Liabilities	229	140
Stockholders' Equity:		
Common stock	30	30
Additional paid-in capital	459	467
Retained earnings	4,478	4,610
Foreign currency translation adjustments	(100)	(122)
Treasury shares, at cost	(1,243)	(557)
Total Stockholders' Equity	3,624	4,428
	$ 7,899	$ 7,963

See notes to consolidated financial statements.

Consolidated Statements of Cash Flows

TOYS"R"US, INC. AND SUBSIDIARIES

(In millions)	January 30, 1999	January 31, 1998	Year Ended February 1, 1997
CASH FLOWS FROM OPERATING ACTIVITIES			
Net (loss)/earnings	$ (132)	$ 490	$ 427
Adjustments to reconcile net (loss)/earnings to net cash provided by operating activities:			
Depreciation, amortization and asset write-offs	255	253	206
Deferred income taxes	(90)	18	23
Restructuring and other charges	546	–	–
Changes in operating assets and liabilities:			
Accounts and other receivables	(43)	(40)	(14)
Merchandise inventories	233	(265)	(195)
Prepaid expenses and other operating assets	(27)	(9)	(10)
Accounts payable, accrued expenses and other liabilities	229	22	262
Income taxes payable	(7)	40	44
Net cash provided by operating activities	964	509	743
CASH FLOWS FROM INVESTING ACTIVITIES			
Capital expenditures, net	(373)	(494)	(415)
Other assets	(49)	(22)	(36)
Cash received with the acquisition of Baby Superstore	–	–	67
Net cash used in investing activities	(422)	(516)	(384)
CASH FLOWS FROM FINANCING ACTIVITIES			
Short-term borrowings, net	4	(142)	(10)
Long-term borrowings	771	11	326
Long-term debt repayments	(412)	(176)	(133)
Exercise of stock options	16	62	28
Share repurchase program	(723)	(253)	–
Net cash (used in)/provided by financing activities	(344)	(498)	211
Effect of exchange rate changes on cash and cash equivalents	(2)	(42)	(12)
CASH AND CASH EQUIVALENTS			
Increase/(decrease) during year	196	(547)	558
Beginning of year	214	761	203
End of year	$ 410	$ 214	$ 761
SUPPLEMENTAL DISCLOSURES OF CASH FLOW INFORMATION			
Income Tax Payments	$ 122	$ 192	$ 177
Interest Payments	$ 109	$ 83	$ 109

See notes to consolidated financial statements.

Consolidated Statements of Stockholders' Equity

TOYS"R"US, INC. AND SUBSIDIARIES

(In millions)	Common Stock Issued Shares	Common Stock Issued Amount	In Treasury Shares	In Treasury Amount	Additional paid-in capital	Foreign currency translation adjustments	Retained earnings	Total stockholders' equity
Balance, February 3, 1996	300.4	$ 30	(27.3)	$ (846)	$ 542	$ 13	$ 3,693	$ 3,432
Net earnings for the year	–	–	–	–	–	–	427	427
Foreign currency translation adjustments	–	–	–	–	–	(73)	–	(73)
Comprehensive Income								354
Acquisition of Baby Superstore, Inc.	–	–	13.0	400	(23)	–	–	377
Exercise of stock options, net	–	–	1.7	58	(30)	–	–	28
Balance, February 1, 1997	300.4	30	(12.6)	(388)	489	(60)	4,120	4,191
Net earnings for the year	–	–	–	–	–	–	490	490
Foreign currency translation adjustments	–	–	–	–	–	(62)	–	(62)
Comprehensive Income								428
Share repurchase program	–	–	(8.2)	(253)	–	–	–	(253)
Exercise of stock options, net	–	–	2.8	84	(22)	–	–	62
Balance, January 31, 1998	300.4	30	(18.0)	(557)	467	(122)	4,610	4,428
Net loss for the year	–	–	–	–	–	–	(132)	(132)
Foreign currency translation adjustments	–	–	–	–	–	22	–	22
Comprehensive loss								(110)
Share repurchase program	–	–	(32.2)	(723)	–	–	–	(723)
Issuance of restricted stock	–	–	–	15	(2)	–	–	13
Exercise of stock options, net	–	–	.4	22	(6)	–	–	16
Balance, January 30, 1999	**300.4**	**$ 30**	**(49.8)**	**$(1,243)**	**$ 459**	**$ (100)**	**$ 4,478**	**$ 3,624**

See notes to consolidated financial statements.

#1 for Family Fun!
For generations Toys"R"Us
has given families ways to
spend quality time together.

Notes to Consolidated Financial Statements

TOYS"R"US, INC. AND SUBSIDIARIES

(Amounts in millions except per share data)
SUMMARY OF SIGNIFICANT ACCOUNTING POLICIES

Fiscal Year

The Company's fiscal year ends on the Saturday nearest to January 31. Reference to 1998, 1997 and 1996 are for the 52 weeks ended January 30, 1999, January 31, 1998, and February 1, 1997, respectively.

Principles of Consolidation

The consolidated financial statements include the accounts of the Company and its subsidiaries. The 1996 consolidated statement of cash flows also reflects the acquisition of Baby Superstore, Inc. All material intercompany balances and transactions have been eliminated. Assets and liabilities of foreign operations are translated at current rates of exchange at the balance sheet date while results of operations are translated at average rates in effect for the period. Translation gains or losses are shown as a separate component of stockholders' equity.

Cash and Cash Equivalents

The Company considers its highly liquid investments with original maturities of less than three months to be cash equivalents.

Merchandise Inventories

Merchandise inventories for the U.S.A. toy store operations, which represent approximately 60% of total inventories, are stated at the lower of LIFO (last-in, first-out) cost or market, as determined by the retail inventory method. If inventories had been valued at the lower of FIFO (first-in, first-out) cost or market, inventories would show no change at January 30, 1999 or January 31, 1998. All other merchandise inventories are stated at the lower of FIFO cost or market as determined by the retail inventory method.

Property and Equipment

Property and equipment are recorded at cost. Depreciation and amortization are provided using the straight-line method over the estimated useful lives of the assets or, where applicable, the terms of the respective leases, whichever is shorter. The Company evaluates the need to recognize impairment losses relating to long-lived assets based on several factors including, but not limited to, management's plans for future operations, recent operating results and projected cash flows.

Preopening Costs

Preopening costs, which consist primarily of advertising, occupancy and payroll expenses, are amortized over expected sales to the end of the fiscal year in which the store opens.

Financial Instruments

The carrying amounts reported in the balance sheets for cash and cash equivalents and short-term borrowings approximate their fair market values.

Forward Foreign Exchange Contracts

The Company enters into forward foreign exchange contracts to eliminate the risk associated with currency movement relating to its short-term intercompany loan program with foreign subsidiaries and inventory purchases denominated in foreign currency. Gains and losses, which offset the movement in the underlying transactions, are recognized as part of such transactions. Gross deferred unrealized gains and losses on the forward contracts were not material at either January 30, 1999 or January 31, 1998. The related receivable, payable and deferred gain or loss are included on a net basis in the balance sheet. The Company had $209 and $439 of short term outstanding forward contracts at January 30, 1999 and January 31, 1998, maturing in 1999 and 1998, respectively. These contracts are entered into with counterparties that have high credit ratings and with which the Company has the contractual right to net forward currency settlements. In addition, the Company had a $342 currency swap obligation outstanding at January 30, 1999 related to its 475 Swiss franc note payable due 2004.

Use of Estimates

The preparation of financial statements in conformity with generally accepted accounting principles requires management to make estimates and assumptions that affect the amounts reported in the consolidated financial statements and accompanying notes. Actual results could differ from those estimates.

PROPERTY AND EQUIPMENT

	Useful Life (in years)	January 30, 1999	January 31, 1998
Land		$ 829	$ 817
Buildings	45-50	1,842	1,849
Furniture and equipment	5-20	1,861	1,711
Leaseholds and leasehold improvements	12^1/2-35	1,213	1,158
Construction in progress		42	46
Leased property under capital leases		27	29
		5,814	5,610
Less accumulated depreciation and amortization		1,588	1,398
		$ 4,226	$ 4,212

SEASONAL FINANCING AND LONG-TERM DEBT

	January 30, 1999	January 31, 1998
Commercial Paper interest rates from 4.87% to 4.89%	$ 368	$ –
475 Swiss franc note payable, due 2004[a]	342	–
8 3/4% debentures, due 2021, net of expenses	198	198
Japanese yen loans with interest payable at annual rates from 1.49% to 6.47%, due in varying amounts through 2012	198	123
Industrial revenue bonds, net of expenses [b]	60	60
7% British pound sterling loan payable, due quarterly through 2001[c]	33	49
8 1/4% sinking fund debentures, due 2017, net of discounts	24	89
Mortgage notes payable at annual interest rates from 10.16% to 11.00% [d]	11	14
Obligations under capital leases	11	14
5.78% 200 British pound sterling note payable [e]	–	325
	1,245	872
Less current portion [f]	23	21
	$ 1,222	$ 851

(a) Supported by a 406 Swiss franc bank letter of credit. This note has been converted by an interest rate and currency swap to a floating rate, US dollar obligation at 3 month LIBOR less approximately 107 basis points.

(b) Bank letters of credit of $41, expiring in 2000, support certain of these industrial revenue bonds. The Company expects that the bank letters of credit will be renewed. The bonds have fixed or variable interest rates with an average rate of 3.6% at January 30, 1999.

(c) Collateralized by property with a carrying value of $160 at January 30, 1999.

(d) Collateralized by property and equipment with an aggregate carrying value of $15 at January 30, 1999.

(e) Supported by a 200 British pound sterling bank letter of credit. This note was redeemed on January 29, 1999.

(f) Included in accrued expenses and other current liabilities on the consolidated balance sheets.

The fair market value of the Company's long-term debt at January 30, 1999, exclusive of commercial paper, and January 31, 1998 were approximately $980 and $1,004, respectively. The fair market value was estimated using quoted market rates for publicly traded debt and estimated interest rates for non-public debt.

The Company has a $1 billion unsecured committed revolving credit facility expiring in December 2002. This multi-currency facility permits the Company to borrow at the lower of LIBOR plus a fixed spread or a rate set by competitive auction. The facility is available to support domestic commercial paper borrowings and to meet worldwide cash requirements.

Commercial paper is classified as long-term debt at January 30, 1999 as the company maintains long-term committed credit agreements, as described above, to support these borrowings and intends to refinance them on a long-term basis through continued commercial paper borrowings. Commercial paper of $70 at January 31, 1998 was included in short-term borrowings.

Additionally, the Company also has lines of credit with various banks to meet the short-term financing needs of its foreign subsidiaries.

The weighted average interest rate on short-term borrowings outstanding at January 30, 1999 and January 31, 1998 was 3.8% and 5.0%, respectively.

The annual maturities of long-term debt at January 30, 1999, excluding commercial paper of $368, are as follows:

1999	$ 23
2000	65
2001	7
2002	8
2003	7
2004 and subsequent	767
	$ 877

LEASES

The Company leases a portion of the real estate used in its operations. Most leases require the Company to pay real estate taxes and other expenses; some require additional amounts based on percentages of sales.

Minimum rental commitments under noncancelable operating leases having a term of more than one year as of January 30, 1999 are as follows:

	Gross minimum rentals	Sublease income	Net minimum rentals
1999	$ 355	$ 20	$ 335
2000	352	18	334
2001	346	15	331
2002	339	13	326
2003	338	11	327
2004 and subsequent	2,964	60	2,904
	$ 4,694	$ 137	$ 4,557

Total rent expense, net of sublease income was $334, $309 and $282 in 1998, 1997 and 1996, respectively.

STOCKHOLDERS' EQUITY

The common shares of the Company, par value $.10 per share, were as follows:

	January 30, 1999	January 31, 1998
Authorized shares	650.0	650.0
Issued shares	300.4	300.4
Treasury shares	49.8	18.0
Issued and outstanding shares	250.6	282.4

EARNINGS PER SHARE

The following table sets forth the computation of basic and diluted earnings per share:

	1998	1997	1996
Numerator:			
Net(loss)/income available to common stockholders	$ (132)	$ 490	$ 427
Denominator for basic earnings per share - weighted average shares	265.4	285.3	274.0
Effect of diluted securities: Stock options, etc.	–	3.1	3.5
Denominator for diluted earnings per share - adjusted weighted average shares	265.4	288.4	277.5
Basic (Loss)/Earnings per share	$ (0.50)	$ 1.72	$ 1.56
Diluted (Loss)/Earnings per share	$ (0.50)	$ 1.70	$ 1.54

Options to purchase approximately 25.0 shares of common stock were outstanding during 1998, but were not included in the computation of diluted loss per share as the effect would be antidilutive.

TAXES ON INCOME

The provisions for income taxes consist of the following:

	1998	1997	1996
Current:			
Federal	$ 78	$ 199	$ 136
Foreign	18	35	57
State	20	30	30
	116	264	223
Deferred:			
Federal	(64)	32	58
Foreign	(9)	(17)	(39)
State	(17)	3	4
	(90)	18	23
Total tax provision	$ 26	$ 282	$ 246

The tax effects of temporary differences and carry forwards that give rise to significant portions of deferred tax assets and liabilities consist of the following:

	January 30, 1999	January 31, 1998
Deferred tax assets:		
Foreign net operating loss carryforwards	$ 311	$ 214
Restructuring	92	20
Other	27	42
Gross deferred tax assets	430	276
Valuation allowance related to net operating losses	(141)	(43)
	$ 289	$ 233
Deferred tax liabilities:		
Property, plant and equipment	281	277
LIFO inventory	50	88
Other tax	–	–
Gross deferred tax liabilities	$ 331	$ 365
Net deferred tax liability	$ 42	$ 132

A reconciliation of the federal statutory tax rate with the effective tax rate follows:

	1998	1997	1996
Statutory tax rate	35.0%	35.0%	35.0%
State income taxes, net of federal income tax benefit	(4.2)	3.2	3.7
Foreign taxes, net of valuation allowances	(52.3)	(2.3)	(2.3)
Subpart F income	(8.5)	–	–
Foreign tax credits	6.8	–	–
Amortization of goodwill	(3.0)	0.4	–
Other, net	1.7	0.2	0.1
Effective tax rate	(24.5)%	36.5%	36.5%

Certain foreign tax benefits have been offset by valuation allowances related to net operating losses due in part to the restructuring and other charges recorded in 1998. Deferred income taxes are not provided on unremitted earnings of foreign subsidiaries that are intended to be indefinitely invested. Exclusive of amounts, that if remitted would result in little or no tax under current U.S. tax laws, unremitted earnings were approximately $515 at January 30, 1999. Net income taxes of approximately $139 would be due if these earnings were to be remitted.

STOCK OPTIONS

The Company has Stock Option Plans (the "Plans") which provide for the granting of options to purchase the Company's common stock. The plans cover substantially all employees and non-employee directors of the Company and provide for the issuance of non-qualified options, incentive stock options, performance share options, performance units, stock appreciation rights, restricted shares, restricted units and unrestricted shares. Of the total number of shares reserved for the Plans, 3.0 shares of Company stock have been reserved for the issuance of restricted shares, restricted units, performance units, and unrestricted shares. The Plans provide for a variety of vesting dates with the majority of the options vesting approximately five years from the date of grant. The options granted to non-employee directors are exercisable 20% each year on a cumulative basis commencing one year from the date of grant.

In addition to the aforementioned plans, 1.0 stock options were granted to certain senior executives during the period from 1993 to 1996 pursuant to stockholder approved individual plans. Of this total, 0.5 options vest 20% each year on a cumulative basis commencing one year from the date of grant with the balance of the options vesting five years from the date of grant.

The exercise price per share of all options granted has been the average of the high and low market price of the Company's common stock on the date of grant. All options must be exercised within ten years from the date of grant.

At January 30, 1999, an aggregate of 46.3 shares of authorized common stock were reserved for all of the Plans noted above, of which 9.5 were available for future grants. All outstanding options expire at dates ranging from July 5, 1999 to November 30, 2008.

Stock option transactions are summarized as follows:

	Shares	Weighted-Average Exercise Price
Outstanding January 31, 1998	24.1	$ 29.12
Granted	17.7	22.18
Exercised	(0.7)	17.99
Canceled	(4.3)	28.89
Outstanding January 30, 1999	**36.8**	**$ 26.02**
Options exercisable at January 30, 1999	**10.8**	**$ 28.25**

The Company utilizes a restoration feature to encourage the early exercise of certain options and retention of shares, thereby promoting increased employee ownership. This feature provides for the grant of new options when previously owned shares of Company stock are used to exercise existing options. Restoration option grants are non-dilutive as they do not increase the combined number of shares of Company stock and options held by an employee prior to exercise. The new options are granted at a price equal to the fair market value on the date of the new grant, and generally expire on the same date as the original options that were exercised.

The Company has adopted the disclosure only provisions of SFAS No. 123, Accounting for Stock-Based Compensation, issued in October 1995. In accordance with the provisions of SFAS No. 123, the Company applies APB Opinion 25 and related interpretations in accounting for its stock option plans and, accordingly, does not recognize compensation cost. If the Company had elected to recognize compensation cost based on the fair value of the options granted at grant date as prescribed by SFAS No. 123, net income and earnings per share would have been reduced to the pro forma amounts indicated in the table below:

	1998	1997	1996
Net (loss)/income – as reported	$ (132)	$ 490	$ 427
Net (loss)/income – pro forma	(162)	470	411
Basic (loss)/earnings per share – as reported	(0.50)	1.72	1.56
Basic (loss)/earnings per share – pro forma	(0.61)	1.65	1.50
Diluted (loss)/earnings per share – as reported	(0.50)	1.70	1.54
Diluted (loss)/earnings per share – pro forma	(0.61)	1.63	1.48

The weighted-average fair value at date of grant for options granted in 1998, 1997 and 1996 were $5.31, $7.66 and $7.35, respectively. The fair value of each option grant is estimated on the date of grant using the Black-Scholes option pricing model. As there were a number of options granted during the years of 1996 through 1998, a range of assumptions are provided below:

	1998	1997	1996
Expected stock price volatility	.283 - .347	.294 - .334	.284 - .328
Risk-free interest rate	4.7% - 5.8%	5.0% - 6.9%	5.0% - 6.8%
Weighted average expected life of options	6 years	6 years	6 years

The effects of applying SFAS No. 123 and the results obtained through the use of the Black-Scholes option pricing model are not necessarily indicative of future values.

PROFIT SHARING PLAN

The Company has a profit sharing plan with a 401(k) salary deferral feature for eligible domestic employees. The terms of the plan call for annual contributions by the Company as determined by the Board of Directors, subject to certain limitations. The profit sharing plan may be terminated at the Company's discretion. Provisions of $41, $39 and $31 have been charged to earnings in 1998, 1997, and 1996, respectively.

SEGMENTS

As a result of the adoption of SFAS No. 131 – Disclosures About Segments of an Enterprise and Related Information, segment information for 1997 and 1996 has been restated to conform to the 1998 presentation.

The Company's reportable segments are Toys"R"Us - United States and Toys"R"Us - International. Divisions that do not meet quantitative reportable thresholds are included in the category classified as Other. This category is comprised of the Kids"R"Us and Babies"R"Us divisions. Toys"R"Us - United States operates toy stores in 49 states and Puerto Rico and Toys"R"Us - International operates or franchises toy stores in 26 countries outside the United States. Information on segments and a reconciliation to (loss)/income before income taxes, are as follows:

		Year ended	
	January 30, 1999	January 31, 1998	February 1, 1997
Sales			
Toys"R"Us - USA	**$ 6,581**	$ 6,814	$ 6,336
Toys"R"Us - International	**2,996**	2,867	2,781
Other	**1,593**	1,357	815
Total	**$11,170**	$ 11,038	$ 9,932
Operating Profit			
Toys"R"Us - USA	**$501**	$ 654	$650
Toys"R"Us - International	**146**	165	126
Other	**59**	41	48
General corporate expenses	**(21)**	(16)	(10)
Interest expense, net	**(93)**	(72)	(81)
Restructuring & other charges	**(698)**[(a)]	–	(60)[(b)]
(Loss)/earnings before taxes on income	**$ (106)**	$ 772	$ 673
Identifiable Assets			
Toys"R"Us - USA	**$ 5,075**	$ 5,193	$ 3,889
Toys"R"Us - International	**2,095**	2,282	2,346
Other	**303**	243	993
Corporate[(c)]	**426**	245	795
Total	**$ 7,899**	$ 7,963	$ 8,023

(a) The Company recorded charges of $698 ($508 net of tax benefits) for restructuring and other charges.

(b) Arbitration award charge of $60 ($38 net of tax benefits).

(c) Consists primarily of cash and cash equivalents.

ACQUISITION

On February 3, 1997, the Company acquired all of the outstanding common shares of Baby Superstore, Inc. ("Baby Superstore") for 13 shares of its treasury stock valued at approximately $376. This acquisition was accounted for as a purchase as at February 1, 1997. The excess of purchase price over net assets acquired of $365 has been recorded as goodwill and is being amortized on a straight-line basis over 40 years.

RESTRUCTURING AND OTHER CHARGES

On September 16, 1998, the Company announced strategic initiatives to reposition its worldwide business. The cost to implement these initiatives, as well as other charges resulted in a total charge of $333 ($266 net of tax benefits, or $1.00 per share). The Company determined that the strategic initiatives required a restructuring charge of $294 to close and/or downsize stores, distribution centers and administrative functions. This worldwide plan includes the closing of 50 toy stores in the International division, predominately in continental Europe, and 9 in the United States that do not meet the Company's return on investment objectives. The Company will also close 31 Kids"R"Us stores and convert 28 nearby US toy stores into combination stores in the new C-3 format discussed below. Combination stores include toys and an apparel selling space of approximately 5,000 square feet. Other charges consist primarily of changes in accounting estimates and provisions for legal settlements of $39 recorded in selling, general and administrative expenses. Of the total restructuring and other charges, $149 relates to domestic operations and $184 relates to International operations. Remaining reserves of $149 should be utilized in 1999, with the exception of long-term lease commitments, which will be utilized in 1999 and thereafter.

Also on September 16, 1998, the Company announced markdowns and other charges to cost of sales of $345 ($229 net of tax benefits, or $.86 per share). The Company has designed a new store format called C-3. The Company plans to convert approximately 200 US toy stores to the new C-3 format in 1999. Of this charge, $253 related to markdowns required to clear excess inventory from its stores so the Company can proceed with its new C-3 store format on an accelerated basis. Another component of the charge was inventory markdowns of $29 related to the closing and/or downsizing of stores discussed above. The Company also recorded charges to cost of sales of $63 related to inventory system refinements and changes in accounting estimates. Of these charges, $288 relate to domestic operations and $57 relate to International operations. Remaining reserves of $107 are expected to be utilized in 1999.

Additionally, in the fourth quarter of 1998 the Company recorded a charge of $20 ($13 net of tax benefits, or $.05 per share), related to the resolution of third party claims asserted from allegations made by the Federal Trade Commission. This charge was in addition to a $15 charge relating to the same matter, included in the charges mentioned above. (See Other Matters).

At January 30, 1999, the Company had approximately $45 of liabilities remaining for its restructuring program announced in 1995 primarily relating to long-term lease obligations.

The Company believes that reserves are adequate to complete the restructuring and other programs described previously.

On July 12, 1996, an arbitrator rendered an award against the Company in connection with a dispute involving rights under a 1982 license agreement for toy store operations in the Middle East. Accordingly, the Company recorded a provision of $60 during 1996, ($38 net of tax benefits, or $.14 cents per share), representing all costs in connection with this matter.

OTHER MATTERS

On May 22, 1996, the Staff of the Federal Trade Commission (the "FTC") filed an administrative complaint against the Company alleging that the Company is in violation of Section 5 of the Federal Trade Commission Act for its practices relating to warehouse clubs. The complaint alleges that the Company reached understandings with various suppliers that such suppliers not sell to the clubs the same items that they sell to the Company. The complaint also alleges that the Company "facilitated understandings" among the manufacturers that such manufacturers not sell to clubs. The complaint seeks an order that the Company cease and desist from this practice. The matter was tried before an administrative law judge in the period from March through May of 1997. On September 30, 1997, the administrative law judge filed an Initial Decision upholding the FTC's complaint against the Company. On October 13, 1998, the FTC issued a final order and opinion upholding the FTC's complaint against the Company.

The Company has appealed the FTC's decision to the United States Court of Appeals for the Seventh Circuit.

After the filing of the FTC complaint, several class action suits were filed against the Company in State courts in Alabama and California, alleging that the Company has violated certain state competition laws as a consequence of the behavior alleged in the FTC complaint. After the Initial Decision was handed down, more than thirty purported class actions were filed in federal and state courts in various jurisdictions alleging that the Company has violated the federal antitrust laws as a consequence of the behavior alleged in the FTC complaint. In addition, the attorneys general of forty-four states, the

District of Columbia and Puerto Rico have filed a suit against the Company in their capacity as representatives of the consumers of their states, alleging that the Company has violated federal and state antitrust laws as a consequence of the behavior alleged in the FTC complaint. These suits seek damages in unspecified amounts and other relief under state and/or federal law.

The Company believes that it has always acted fairly and in the best interests of its customers and that both its policy and its conduct in connection with the foregoing have been and are within the law. However, to avoid the cost and uncertainty of protracted litigation the Company has reached an agreement in principle to settle all of the class action and attorney general lawsuits in a manner which will not have a material adverse effect on its financial condition, results of operations or cash flow. The Company has accrued all anticipated costs relating to this matter as of January 30, 1999.

Some of the most popular electronic systems, video games and computer software are seen first at Toys"R"Us!

REPORT OF MANAGEMENT

Responsibility for the integrity and objectivity of the financial information presented in this Annual Report rests with the management of Toys"R"Us. The accompanying financial statements have been prepared from accounting records which management believes fairly and accurately reflect the operations and financial position of the Company. Management has established a system of internal controls to provide reasonable assurance that assets are maintained and accounted for in accordance with its policies and that transactions are recorded accurately on the Company's books and records.

The Company's comprehensive internal audit program provides for constant evaluation of the adequacy of the adherence to management's established policies and procedures. The Company has distributed to key employees its policies for conducting business affairs in a lawful and ethical manner.

The Audit Committee of the Board of Directors, which is comprised solely of outside directors, provides oversight to the financial reporting process through periodic meetings with our independent auditors, internal auditors and management.

The financial statements of the Company have been audited by Ernst & Young LLP, independent auditors, in accordance with generally accepted auditing standards, including a review of financial reporting matters and internal controls to the extent necessary to express an opinion on the consolidated financial statements.

Robert C. Nakasone
Chief Executive Officer

Louis Lipschitz
Executive Vice President
and Chief Financial Officer

REPORT OF INDEPENDENT AUDITORS

The Board of Directors and Stockholders
Toys"R"Us, Inc.

We have audited the accompanying consolidated balance sheets of Toys"R"Us, Inc. and subsidiaries as of January 30, 1999 and January 31, 1998, and the related consolidated statements of earnings, stockholders' equity and cash flows for each of the three years in the period ended January 30, 1999. These financial statements are the responsibility of the Company's management. Our responsibility is to express an opinion on these financial statements based on our audits.

We conducted our audits in accordance with generally accepted auditing standards. Those standards require that we plan and perform the audit to obtain reasonable assurance about whether the financial statements are free of material misstatement. An audit includes examining, on a test basis, evidence supporting the amounts and disclosures in the financial statements. An audit also includes assessing the accounting principles used and significant estimates made by management, as well as evaluating the overall financial statement presentation. We believe that our audits provide a reasonable basis for our opinion.

In our opinion, the financial statements referred to above present fairly, in all material respects, the consolidated financial position of Toys"R"Us, Inc. and subsidiaries at January 30, 1999 and January 31, 1998, and the consolidated results of their operations and their cash flows for each of the three years in the period ended January 30, 1999, in conformity with generally accepted accounting principles.

Ernst & Young LLP

New York, New York
March 10, 1999

Directors and Officers

Directors

CHARLES LAZARUS
Chairman Emeritus of the Company

MICHAEL GOLDSTEIN
Chairman of the Board of the Company

ROBERT A. BERNHARD
Real Estate Developer

ROANN COSTIN
President, Reservoir Capital
Management, Inc.

CALVIN HILL
Consultant

SHIRLEY STRUM KENNY
President, State University of
New York at Stony Brook

NORMAN S. MATTHEWS
Consultant

HOWARD W. MOORE
Consultant

ROBERT C. NAKASONE
Chief Executive Officer
of the Company

ARTHUR B. NEWMAN
Senior Managing Director,
Blackstone Group

Corporate and Administrative

ROBERT C. NAKASONE
Chief Executive Officer

LOUIS LIPSCHITZ
Executive Vice President
and Chief Financial Officer

MICHAEL G. SHANNON
Executive Vice President and
President U.S. Toy Stores

FRANCESCA L. BROCKETT
Senior Vice President -
Strategic Planning/Business
Development

ROGER C. GASTON
Senior Vice President -
Human Resources

JOHN HOLOHAN
Senior Vice President -
Chief Information Officer

RAYMOND L. ARTHUR
Vice President - Corporate Controller

DAN BOOHER
Vice President -
Architecture and Construction

KRISTOPHER M. BROWN
Vice President - Distribution and Traffic

REBECCA A. CARUSO
Vice President -
Corporate Communications

MICHAEL J. CORRIGAN
Vice President -
Compensation and Benefits

RICHARD N. CUDRIN
Vice President -
Associate Relations

EILEEN C. GABRIEL
Vice President - Information Systems

ELIZABETH S. JORDAN
Vice President -
Organizational Development

JON W. KIMMINS
Vice President - Treasurer

DION C. ROONEY
Vice President - Systems Development

MICHAEL L. TUMOLO
Vice President - Counsel

PETER W. WEISS
Vice President - Taxes

ROBERT S. ZARRA
Vice President - Internal Audit

DENNIS J. BLOCK
Secretary
Partner-Cadwalader, Wickersham & Taft

Toys"R"Us United States

MICHAEL G. SHANNON
President

MICHAEL J. MADDEN
President - Store Operations

KEITH C. VAN BEEK
President -
Merchandising and Marketing

JAMES E. FELDT
Executive Vice President -
Merchandising

WARREN F. KORNBLUM
Senior Vice President -
Chief Marketing Officer

ROBERT J. WEINBERG
Senior Vice President -
General Merchandise Manager

JOEL D. ANDERSON
Vice President - Toys"R"Us Direct

DAVID M. BREWI
Vice President - World Leader

THOMAS F. DELUCA
Vice President - Imports, Product
Development and Safety Assurance

BARBARA A. FITZGERALD
Vice President - People Development

PHILIP S. FOUSSEKIS
Vice President - Loss Prevention

ANDREW R. GATTO
Vice President -
Product Development

DANIEL D. HLAVATY
Vice President - Business Reengineering

JEREL G. HOLLENS
Vice President -
Merchandising Planning

MARIANITA HOWARD
Vice President -
Creative Services

FREDERICK L. HURLEY
Vice President - World Leader

JOSEPH J. LOMBARDI
Vice President - Controller

MITCHELL B. LOUKOTA
Vice President - World Leader

CHARLENE MADY
Vice President -
Area Merchandise Planning

GERALD S. PARKER
Vice President -
Customer Support and Administration

DAVID P. PICOT
Vice President - Real Estate

DEBRA M. ROOD
Vice President -
Toys"R"Us Direct Fulfillment

TIMOTHY J. SLADE
Vice President - Store Planning

WILLIAM A. STEPHENSON
Vice President -
Merchandise Planning and Allocation

JOHN P. SULLIVAN
Vice President - World Leader

GREGG TREADWAY
Vice President - C-3 Development

DENNIS J. WILLIAMS
Vice President - Sales

THOMAS A. DRUGAN
Regional Vice President - Midwest

HARVEY J. FINKEL
Regional Vice President - Northeast

TRUVILLUS HALL
Regional Vice President - Northwest

MICHAEL K. HEFFNER
Regional Vice President - Gulf States

SAMUEL M. MARTIN
Regional Vice President - West

JOHN J. PRAWLOCKI
Regional Vice President - Southeast

EDWARD F. SIEGLER
Regional Vice President - Mid-Atlantic

KEVIN VANDERGRIEND
Regional Vice President - Ohio Valley

Toys"R"US International

GREGORY R. STALEY
President

BRUNO A. ROQUEPLO
Senior Vice President -
Finance and Administration

ERNEST V. SPERANZA
Senior Vice President - Marketing

JOAN W. DONOVAN
Vice President -
General Merchandise Manager

JEFF HANDLER
Vice President - Advertising

*Country Management

LARRY S. JOHNSON
Vice President - Franchise Markets

MICHAEL C. TAYLOR
Vice President - Franchising/Logistics

DAVID RURKA
Managing Director -
Toys"R"Us United Kingdom and
Chairman of the European
Management Board

JOHANNES DERCKS
President -
Toys"R"Us Central Europe

JACQUES LEFOLL
President -
Toys"R"Us France/Belgium

ROBERT F. MORAN
President - Toys "R" Us (Canada) Ltd.

JOHN SCHRYVER
Managing Director -
Toys"R"Us Australia

MANABU TAZAKI
President -
Toys"R"Us Japan

ANTONIO URCELAY
Managing Director -
Toys"R"Us Iberia

LARRY D. GARDNER
Vice President -
Toys"R"Us Asia

SCOTT W.K. CHEN*
General Manager -
Toys"R"Us Taiwan

JOE TANG*
General Manager -
Toys"R"Us Hong Kong

MICHAEL S.M. YEO*
General Manager -
Toys"R"Us Singapore

Kids"R"Us/Babies"R"Us*

RICHARD L. MARKEE
President -
Kids"R"Us and Babies"R"Us

JAMES G. PARROS
Senior Vice President -
Stores and Distribution Center Operations

MARTIN E. FOGELMAN
Vice President -
World Leader Juvenile Products

*Kids"R"Us Officer, unless otherwise indicated.

LAURA J. FREEMAN
Vice President - Divisional
Merchandise Manager

JONATHAN M. FRIEDMAN
Vice President - Chief Financial Officer -
Kids"R"Us and Babies"R"Us

JAMES L. EASTON
Vice President -
General Merchandise Manager

VINCENT A. SCARFONE
Vice President -
Human Resources

CHRISTOPHER M. SCHERM
Vice President -
Divisional Merchandise Manager

DAVID E. SCHOENBECK
Vice President -
Operations - Babies "R" Us

SANDEE A. SPRINGER
Vice President- Divisional
Merchandise Manager

DAVID S. WALKER
Vice President - Advertising

PAMELA B. WALLACK
Vice President - Product Development

Parents and children
discover amazing
ways to play and
learn in our
Learning Center.

25

Quarterly Financial Data and Market Information

TOYS"R"US, INC. AND SUBSIDIARIES

Quarterly Financial Data

(In millions except per share data)

The following table sets forth certain unaudited quarterly financial information.

	First Quarter	Second Quarter	Third Quarter	Fourth Quarter
1998				
Net Sales	$ 2,043	$ 2,020	$ 2,171	$ 4,936
Cost of Sales	1,417	1,390	1,831	3,553
Net Earnings/(Loss)	19	14	(475)[a]	310[b]
Basic Earnings/(Loss) per Share	$ .07	$ .05	$ (1.85)	$ 1.23
Diluted Earnings/(Loss) per Share	$ .07	$ .05	$ (1.85)	$ 1.23
1997				
Net Sales	$ 1,924	$ 1,989	$ 2,142	$ 4,983
Cost of Sales	1,326	1,355	1,455	3,574
Net Earnings	29	37	46	378
Basic Earnings per Share	$ 0.10	$ 0.13	$ 0.16	$ 1.33
Diluted Earnings per Share	$ 0.10	$ 0.13	$ 0.16	$ 1.32

(a) Third quarter results include restructuring and other charges of $678 ($495 net of tax benefits, or $1.86 per share).

(b) Fourth quarter results include provisions for legal settlements of $20 ($13 net of tax benefits, or $.05 per share).

Market Information

The Company's common stock is listed on the New York Stock Exchange. The following table reflects the high and low prices (rounded to the nearest one-sixteenth) based on New York Stock Exchange trading since February 1, 1997.

The Company has not paid any cash dividends, however, the Board of Directors of the Company reviews this policy annually.

The Company had approximately 31,200 Stockholders of Record on March 9, 1999.

			High	Low
1997	1st	Quarter	29 7/8	24 1/2
	2nd	Quarter	34 13/16	28 1/4
	3rd	Quarter	37 1/8	29 1/8
	4th	Quarter	35 7/16	24 7/8
1998	1st	Quarter	30 7/8	25 7/8
	2nd	Quarter	29 1/2	22 5/16
	3rd	Quarter	23 13/16	15 5/8
	4th	Quarter	21 1/2	14 7/16

Store Locations

Stores Across the United States

	Toys	Kids	Babies
Alabama	8	1	2
Alaska	1	–	–
Arizona	11	–	2
Arkansas	4	–	–
California	87	23	8
Colorado	11	–	2
Connecticut	11	6	–
Delaware	2	1	1
Florida	47	10	10
Georgia	18	4	6
Hawaii	1	–	–
Idaho	2	–	–
Illinois	34	19	5
Indiana	13	7	2
Iowa	8	1	–
Kansas	5	1	1
Kentucky	8	–	1
Louisiana	11	–	1
Maine	2	1	1
Maryland	19	9	3
Massachusetts	19	6	1
Michigan	25	13	5
Minnesota	12	2	1
Mississippi	5	–	–
Missouri	13	5	3
Montana	1	–	–

	Toys	Kids	Babies
Nebraska	3	1	–
Nevada	4	–	2
New Hampshire	5	2	–
New Jersey	26	18	7
New Mexico	4	–	–
New York	46	23	3
North Carolina	16	1	5
North Dakota	1	–	–
Ohio	33	18	6
Oklahoma	5	–	1
Oregon	8	–	1
Pennsylvania	33	15	3
Rhode Island	1	1	1
South Carolina	9	–	3
South Dakota	2	–	–
Tennessee	14	2	4
Texas	54	9	13
Utah	6	3	1
Vermont	1	–	–
Virginia	22	7	7
Washington	14	–	1
West Virginia	5	–	–
Wisconsin	10	3	–
Puerto Rico	4	–	–
	704	212	113

TOYS"R"US International – 452

Australia - 24	Netherlands - 9[a]
Austria - 8	Portugal - 6
Belgium - 3	Saudi Arabia - 3[a]
Canada - 64	Singapore - 4
Denmark - 10[a]	South Africa - 8[a]
France - 44	Spain - 29
Germany - 59	Sweden - 5
Hong Kong - 5[a]	Switzerland - 5
Indonesia - 3[a]	Taiwan - 6[a]
Israel - 5[a]	Turkey - 5[a]
Japan - 76[b]	United Arab
Luxembourg - 1	Emirates - 4[a]
Malaysia - 5[a]	United Kingdom - 61

(a) Franchise or joint venture.

(b) 80 % owned.

Corporate Data and Citizenship

TOYS"R"US, INC. AND SUBSIDIARIES

Annual Meeting

The Annual Meeting of the Stockholders of Toys"R"Us will be held at the Westin Hotel Atlanta North at Perimeter, 7 Concourse Parkway in Atlanta, Georgia, on June 9, 1999 at 10:00 A.M.

The Offices of The Company are Located at

461 From Road
Paramus, New Jersey 07652
Telephone: 201-262-7800

225 Summit Avenue
Montvale, New Jersey 07645
Telephone: 201-802-5000

General Counsel

Cadwalader, Wickersham & Taft
100 Maiden Lane
New York, New York 10036

Independent Auditors

Ernst & Young LLP
787 Seventh Avenue
New York, New York 10019

Registrar and Transfer Agent

American Stock Transfer and
Trust Company
40 Wall Street,
New York, New York 10005
Telephone: 718-921-8200

Common Stock Listed

New York Stock Exchange, Symbol: TOY

Stockholder Information

The Company will supply to any owner of Common Stock, upon written request to Mr. Louis Lipschitz of the Company at the above address and without charge, a copy of the Annual Report on Form 10-K for the year ended January 30, 1999, which has been filed with the Securities and Exchange Commission.

Stockholder information, including quarterly earnings and other corporate news releases, can be obtained by calling 800-785-TOYS, or at our web site on the internet at www.toysrus.com

Significant news releases are anticipated to be available as follows:

Call after...	For the following...
May 17, 1999	1st Quarter Results
Aug. 16, 1999	2nd Quarter Results
Nov. 15, 1999	3rd Quarter Results
Jan. 6, 2000	Holiday Sales Results
Mar. 8, 2000	1999 Results

Corporate Citizenship

Toys"R"Us maintains a company-wide giving program focused on improving the health care needs of children by supporting many national and regional children's health care organizations. The Counsel on Economic Priority awarded Toys"R"Us the Pioneer Award in Global Ethics. This award was the direct result of the implementation of our Code of Conduct for suppliers which outlines the Company's position against child labor and unsafe working conditions. In order for a vendor's product to be sold in any of our stores, they must comply with our Code of Conduct. If you would like to receive more information on Toys"R"Us' corporate citizenship please write to Mr. Roger Gaston of the Company at the Company's address.

Visit us on the internet at www.toysrus.com.

Undoubtedly, the brand kids love most!

2

Measuring Business Transactions

1 Explain, in simple terms, the generally accepted ways of solving the measurement issues of recognition, valuation, and classification.

2 Describe the chart of accounts and recognize commonly used accounts.

3 Define *double-entry system* and state the rules for double entry.

4 Apply the steps for transaction analysis and processing to simple transactions.

5 Prepare a trial balance and describe its value and limitations.

6 Record transactions in the general journal.

7 Post transactions from the general journal to the ledger.

Delta Air Lines, Inc. & The Boeing Co.

In December 1998, Delta Air Lines, Inc., announced that it had ordered 49 Boeing jetliners, including 737, 757, 767, and 777 aircraft.[1] The $3 billion order was part of an exclusive agreement Boeing negotiated with Delta. This exclusive 20-year agreement to purchase only Boeing aircraft was Boeing's fourth such agreement with a major airline and positioned the company favorably against Airbus, its European competitor. How should this important order have been recorded, if at all, in the records of Delta and Boeing? When should the purchase and sale that result from this order be recorded in the companies' records?

The order obviously was an important event, one with long-term consequences for both companies. But, as you will see in this chapter, it was not recorded in the accounting records of either company. At the time the order was placed, the aircraft were yet to be manufactured and would not begin to be delivered for several years. Even for "firm" orders, Boeing has cautioned that "an economic downturn could result in airline equipment requirements less than currently anticipated resulting in requests to negotiate the rescheduling or possible cancellation of firm orders."[2] The aircraft were not assets of Delta, and the company had not incurred a liability. No aircraft had been delivered or even built, so Delta was not obligated to pay at that point. And Boeing could not record any revenue until the aircraft were manufactured and delivered to Delta, and title to the aircraft shifted from Boeing to Delta. In fact, Boeing later experienced cancellation or extension of large previously firm orders from China because of the economic slowdown in Asia.[3]

To understand and use financial statements, it is important to know how to analyze events in order to determine the extent of their impact on those statements.

Measurement Issues

OBJECTIVE

1 Explain, in simple terms, the generally accepted ways of solving the measurement issues of recognition, valuation, and classification

Business transactions are economic events that affect the financial position of a business entity. To measure a business transaction, the accountant must decide when the transaction occurred (the recognition issue), what value to place on the transaction (the valuation issue), and how the components of the transaction should be categorized (the classification issue).

These three issues—recognition, valuation, and classification—underlie almost every major decision in financial accounting today. They lie at the heart of accounting for pension plans, for mergers of giant companies, and for international transactions. In discussing the three basic issues, we follow generally accepted accounting principles and use an approach that promotes an understanding of the basic ideas of accounting. Keep in mind, however, that controversy does exist, and that solutions to some problems are not as cut-and-dried as they appear.

The Recognition Issue

Terminology Note: *Recognize* here means to record a transaction or event.

The **recognition** issue refers to the difficulty of deciding when a business transaction should be recorded. Often the facts of a situation are known, but there is disagreement about *when* the event should be recorded. Suppose, for instance, that a company orders, receives, and pays for an office desk. Which of the following actions constitutes a recordable event?

Key Point: A purchase should not be recognized (recorded) before title is transferred because, until that point, the vendor has not fulfilled its contractual obligation and the buyer has no liability.

1. An employee sends a purchase requisition to the purchasing department.
2. The purchasing department sends a purchase order to the supplier.
3. The supplier ships the desk.
4. The company receives the desk.
5. The company receives the bill from the supplier.
6. The company pays the bill.

BUSINESS FOCUS ON PRACTICE

Many companies include information on the recognition rules followed by the company in the "Summary of Significant Accounting Policies" section of their annual reports. For instance, Sun Microsystems Inc., the large supplier of networked workstations, servers, and other computer software and hardware, describes its revenue recognition rules as follows:

Sun generally recognizes revenues from hardware and software sales at the time of shipment. Service revenues are recognized ratably over the contractual period or as the services are provided.[4]

The answer to this question is important because amounts in the financial statements are affected by the date on which a purchase is recorded. According to accounting tradition, the transaction is recorded when title to the desk passes from the supplier to the purchaser, creating an obligation to pay. Thus, depending on the details of the shipping agreement, the transaction is recognized (recorded) at the time of either action **3** or action **4**. This is the guideline that we generally use in this book. However, in many small businesses that have simple accounting systems, the transaction is not recorded until the bill is received (action **5**) or paid (action **6**) because these are the implied points of title transfer. The predetermined time at which a transaction should be recorded is the **recognition point**.

The recognition issue is not always easy to solve. Consider the case of an advertising agency that is asked by a client to prepare a major advertising campaign. People may work on the campaign several hours a day for a number of weeks. Value is added to the plan as the employees develop it. Should this added value be recognized as the campaign is being produced or at the time it is completed? Normally, the increase in value is recorded at the time the plan is finished and the client is billed for it. However, if a plan is going to take a long period to develop, the agency and the client may agree that the client will be billed at key points during its development. A transaction is recorded at each billing.

The Valuation Issue

Enrichment Note: The value of a transaction usually is based on a business document—a canceled check or an invoice. In general, appraisals or other subjective amounts are not recorded.

Valuation is perhaps the most controversial issue in accounting. The **valuation** issue focuses on assigning a monetary value to a business transaction. Generally accepted accounting principles state that the appropriate value to assign to all business transactions—and therefore to all assets, liabilities, and components of stockholders' equity, including revenues and expenses, recorded by a business—is the original cost (often called *historical cost*).

Cost is defined here as the exchange price associated with a business transaction at the point of recognition. According to this guideline, the purpose of accounting is not to account for value in terms of worth, which can change after a transaction occurs, but to account for value in terms of cost at the time of the transaction. For example, the cost of an asset is recorded when the asset is acquired, and the value is held at that level until the asset is sold, expires, or is consumed. In this context, *value* means the cost at the time of the transaction. The practice of recording transactions at cost is referred to as the **cost principle**.

Suppose that a person offers a building for sale at $120,000. It may be valued for real estate taxes at $75,000, and it may be insured for $90,000. One prospective buyer may offer $100,000 for the building, and another may offer $105,000. At this point, several different, unverifiable opinions of value have been expressed. Finally, suppose the seller and a buyer settle on a price and complete the sale for $110,000. All of these figures are values of one kind or another, but only the last is sufficiently reliable to be used in the records. The market value of the building may vary over the years, but the building will remain on the new buyer's records at $110,000 until it is sold again. At that point, the accountant will record the new transaction at the new exchange price, and a profit or loss will be recognized.

The cost principle is used because the cost is verifiable. It results from the actions of independent buyers and sellers who come to an agreement on price. An exchange price is an objective price that can be verified by evidence created at the time of the transaction. It is this final price, verified by agreement of the two parties, at which the transaction is recorded.

Business Focus on Practice

With many aspects of accounting, there are sometimes exceptions to the general rules. For instance, the cost principle is not followed in all parts of the financial statements. Investments, for example, are often accounted for at fair or market value because these investments are available for sale. The fair or market value is the best measure of the potential benefit to the company. Intel Corp., the large microprocessor company, states in its annual report:

A substantial majority of the company's marketable investments are classified as available-for-sale as of the balance sheet date and are reported at fair value.[5]

The Classification Issue

The **classification** issue has to do with assigning all the transactions in which a business engages to appropriate categories, or accounts. For example, a company's ability to borrow money can be affected by the way in which its debts are categorized. Or a company's income can be affected by whether purchases of small items such as tools are considered repair expenses (a component of stockholders' equity) or equipment (assets).

Key Point: Assets, liabilities, and the components of owners' equity are not accounts, but account *classifications*. For example, Cash is a type of asset account, and Accounts Payable is a type of liability account.

Proper classification depends not only on correctly analyzing the effect of each transaction on the business but also on maintaining a system of accounts that reflects that effect. The rest of this chapter explains the classification of accounts and the analysis and recording of transactions.

Accounts and the Chart of Accounts

OBJECTIVE

2 Describe the chart of accounts and recognize commonly used accounts

In the measurement of business transactions, large amounts of data are gathered. These data require a method of storage. Businesspeople should be able to retrieve transaction data quickly and in usable form. In other words, there should be a filing system to sort out or classify all the transactions that occur in a business. This filing system consists of accounts. Recall that accounts are the basic storage units for accounting data and are used to accumulate amounts from similar transactions. An accounting system has a separate account for each asset, each liability, and each component of stockholders' equity, including revenues and expenses. Whether a company keeps records by hand or by computer, management must be able to refer to accounts so that it can study the company's financial history and plan for the future. A very small company may need only a few dozen accounts; a multinational corporation may need thousands.

In a manual accounting system, each account is kept on a separate page or card. These pages or cards are placed together in a book or file called the **general ledger**. In the computerized systems that most companies have today, accounts are maintained on magnetic tapes or disks. However, as a matter of convenience, accountants still refer to the group of company accounts as the *general ledger*, or simply the *ledger*.

Key Point: A chart of accounts is a table of contents for the ledger. The accounts typically are listed in the same order as they appear in the ledger, and the numbering scheme should allow for some flexibility.

To help identify accounts in the ledger and to make them easy to find, the accountant often numbers them. A list of these numbers with the corresponding account names is called a **chart of accounts**. A very simple chart of accounts appears in Exhibit 1. Notice that the first digit refers to the major financial statement classification. An account number that begins with the digit 1 represents an asset, an account number that begins with a 2 represents a liability, and so forth. The second and third digits refer to individual accounts. Notice the gaps in the sequence of numbers. These gaps allow the accountant to expand the number of accounts. The accounts that are listed in Exhibit 1 will be used in this chapter and in the next two chapters, through the sample case of the Joan Miller Advertising Agency, Inc.

Stockholders' Equity Accounts

In the chart of accounts shown in Exhibit 1, the revenue accounts and the expense accounts are separated from the stockholders' equity accounts. The relationships of these accounts to each other and to the financial statements are illustrated in Figure 1. The distinctions among them are important for legal and financial reporting purposes.

First, the stockholders' equity accounts represent legal claims by the stockholders against the assets of the company. Common Stock is a capital stock account (corporations may have more than one type of capital stock) that represents stockholders' claims arising from their investments in the company, and Retained Earnings represents stockholders' claims arising from profitable operations. Both are claims against the general assets of the company, not against specific assets.

Exhibit 1
Chart of Accounts for a Small Business

Account Number	Account Name	Description
		Assets
111	Cash	Money and any medium of exchange, including coins, currency, checks, postal and express money orders, and money on deposit in a bank
112	Notes Receivable	Amounts due from others in the form of promissory notes (written promises to pay definite sums of money at fixed future dates)
113	Accounts Receivable	Amounts due from others for revenues or sale on credit (sales on account)
114	Fees Receivable	Amounts arising from services performed but not yet billed to customers
115	Art Supplies	Prepaid expense; art supplies purchased and not used
116	Office Supplies	Prepaid expense; office supplies purchased and not used
117	Prepaid Rent	Prepaid expense; rent paid in advance and not used
118	Prepaid Insurance	Prepaid expense; insurance purchased and not expired; unexpired insurance
141	Land	Property owned for use in the business
142	Buildings	Structures owned for use in the business
143	Accumulated Depreciation, Buildings	Sum of the periodic allocation of the cost of buildings to expense
144	Art Equipment	Art equipment owned for use in the business
145	Accumulated Depreciation, Art Equipment	Sum of the periodic allocation of the cost of art equipment to expense
146	Office Equipment	Office equipment owned for use in the business
147	Accumulated Depreciation, Office Equipment	Sum of the periodic allocation of the cost of office equipment to expense
		Liabilities
211	Notes Payable	Amounts due to others in the form of promissory notes
212	Accounts Payable	Amounts due to others for purchases on credit
213	Unearned Art Fees	Unearned revenue; advance deposits for artwork to be provided in the future
214	Wages Payable	Amounts due to employees for wages earned and not paid
215	Income Taxes Payable	Amounts due to government for income taxes owed and not paid
221	Mortgage Payable	Amounts due on loans that are backed by the company's property and buildings

(continued)

Key Point: Account names must be both concise and descriptive. Although some account names, such as Cash and Land, generally are fixed, others are not.

Key Point: Accounts are usually listed in the order in which they appear on the financial statements.

Exhibit 1
Chart of Accounts for a Small Business (continued)

Account Number	Account Name	Description
		Stockholders' Equity
311	Common Stock	Stockholders' investments in a corporation for which they receive shares of capital stock
312	Retained Earnings	Stockholders' claims against company assets derived from profitable operations
313	Dividends	Distributions of assets (usually cash) that reduce retained earnings
314	Income Summary	Temporary account used at the end of the accounting period to summarize the revenues and expenses for the period
		Revenues
411	Advertising Fees Earned	Revenues derived from performing advertising services
412	Art Fees Earned	Revenues derived from performing art services
		Expenses
511	Wages Expense	Amounts earned by employees
512	Utilities Expense	Amounts of utilities, such as water, electricity, and gas, used
513	Telephone Expense	Amounts of telephone services used
514	Rent Expense	Amounts of rent on property and buildings used
515	Insurance Expense	Amounts for insurance expired
516	Art Supplies Expense	Amounts for art supplies used
517	Office Supplies Expense	Amounts for office supplies used
518	Depreciation Expense, Buildings	Amount of buildings' cost allocated to expense
519	Depreciation Expense, Art Equipment	Amount of art equipment costs allocated to expense
520	Depreciation Expense, Office Equipment	Amount of office equipment costs allocated to expense
521	Interest Expense	Amount of interest on debts

Key Point: Although dividends are a component of stockholders' equity, they normally appear only in the statement of retained earnings, not in the stockholders' equity section of the balance sheet. In addition, they do not appear as an expense on the income statement.

Key Point: Although revenues and expenses are components of stockholders' equity, they appear on the income statement, *not* on the stockholders' equity section of the balance sheet. Figure 1 illustrates this point.

They do not represent pools of funds that have been set aside. Dividends are included among the stockholders' equity accounts because they are distributions of assets that reduce stockholders' claims on retained earnings and are shown on the statement of retained earnings.

Second, the law requires that capital investments and dividends be separated from revenues and expenses for income tax reporting, financial reporting, and other purposes.

Third, management needs a detailed breakdown of revenues and expenses for budgeting and operating purposes. From these accounts, which are included on the income statement, management can identify the sources of all revenues and the nature of all expenses. In this way, accounting gives management information about whether it has achieved its primary goal of earning a net income.

Figure 1
Relationships of Stockholders' Equity Accounts

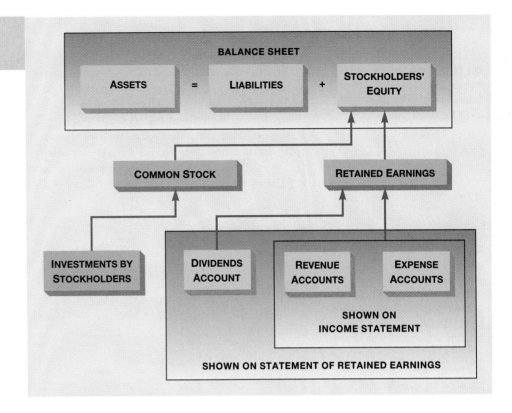

Account Titles

The names of accounts often confuse beginning accounting students because some of the words are new or have technical meanings. Also, the same asset, liability, or stockholders' equity account can have different names in different companies. (Actually, this is not so strange. People, too, often are called different names by their friends, families, and associates.) For example, Fixed Assets, Plant and Equipment, Capital Assets, and Long-Lived Assets are all names for long-term asset accounts. Even the most acceptable names change over time, and, out of habit, some companies continue to use names that are out of date.

In general, an account title should describe what is recorded in the account. When you come across an account title that you do not recognize, you should examine the context of the name—whether it is classified as an asset, liability, or stockholders' equity component, including revenue or expense, on the financial statements—and look for the kind of transaction that gave rise to the account.

The Double-Entry System: The Basic Method of Accounting

OBJECTIVE

3 Define *double-entry system* and state the rules for double entry

The double-entry system, the backbone of accounting, evolved during the Renaissance. As noted previously, the first systematic description of double-entry bookkeeping appeared in 1494, two years after Columbus discovered America, in a mathematics book written by Fra Luca Pacioli. Goethe, the famous German poet and dramatist, referred to double-entry bookkeeping as "one of the finest discoveries of the human intellect." And Werner Sombart, an eminent economist-sociologist, believed that "double-entry bookkeeping is born of the same spirit as the system of Galileo and Newton."

What is the significance of the double-entry system? The system is based on the *principle of duality*, which means that every economic event has two aspects—effort and reward, sacrifice and benefit, source and use—that offset or balance each other. In the **double-entry system**, each transaction must be recorded with at least one debit and one credit, so that the total dollar amount of debits and the total dollar amount of credits equal each other. Because of the way it is designed, the whole system is always in balance. All accounting systems, no matter how sophisticated, are based on the principle of duality.

> **Key Point:** Each transaction must include at least one debit and one credit, and the debit totals must equal the credit totals.

The T Account

> **Key Point:** A T account is simply an abbreviated version of a ledger account. T accounts are used by accountants, instructors, students, and textbooks to quickly analyze a set of transactions; ledger accounts are used in the accounting records.

> **Key Point:** Many students have preconceived ideas about what *debit* and *credit* mean. They think that *debit* means "decrease" (or implies something bad) and that *credit* means "increase" (or implies something good). It is important that they realize that *debit* simply means "left side" and *credit* simply means "right side."

The T account is a good place to begin the study of the double-entry system. In its simplest form, an account has three parts: (1) a title, which describes the asset, the liability, or the stockholders' equity account; (2) a left side, which is called the **debit** side; and (3) a right side, which is called the **credit** side. This form of an account, called a **T account** because it resembles the letter *T*, is used to analyze transactions. It looks like this:

Title of Account	
Debit (left) side	Credit (right) side

Any entry made on the left side of the account is a debit, or debit entry; and any entry made on the right side of the account is a credit, or credit entry. The terms *debit* (abbreviated Dr., from the Latin *debere*) and *credit* (abbreviated Cr., from the Latin *credere*) are simply the accountant's words for "left" and "right" (not for "increase" or "decrease"). We present a more formal version of the T account, the ledger account form, later in this chapter.

The T Account Illustrated

In the chapter on uses of accounting information and the financial statements, Shannon Realty, Inc., had several transactions that involved the receipt or payment of cash. These transactions can be summarized in the Cash account by recording receipts on the left (debit) side of the account and payments on the right (credit) side:

	Cash			
(1)	50,000	(2)	35,000
(5)	1,500	(4)	200
(7)	1,000	(8)	1,000
		(9)	400
		(11)	600
	52,500		37,200
Bal.	15,300		

The cash receipts on the left total $52,500. (The total is written in small figures so that it cannot be confused with an actual debit entry.) The cash payments on the right side total $37,200. These totals are simply working totals, or **footings**. Footings, which are calculated at the end of each month, are an easy way to determine cash on hand. The difference in dollars between the total debit footing and the total credit footing is called the **balance**, or *account balance.* If the balance is a debit, it is written on the left side. If it is a credit, it is written on the right side. Notice that Shannon Realty, Inc.'s Cash account has a debit balance of $15,300 ($52,500 − $37,200). This is the amount of cash the business has on hand at the end of the month.

Analyzing and Processing Transactions

The two rules of double-entry bookkeeping are that every transaction affects at least two accounts and that total debits must equal total credits. In other words, for every transaction, one or more accounts must be debited and one or more accounts must be credited, and the total dollar amount of the debits must equal the total dollar amount of the credits.

Look again at the accounting equation:

$$\text{Assets} = \text{Liabilities} + \text{Stockholders' Equity}$$

You can see that if a debit increases assets, then a credit must be used to increase liabilities or stockholders' equity because they are on opposite sides of the equal sign. Likewise, if a credit decreases assets, then a debit must be used to decrease liabilities or stockholders' equity. These rules can be shown as follows:

Assets		=	Liabilities		+	Stockholders' Equity	
Debit for increases (+)	Credit for decreases (−)		Debit for decreases (−)	Credit for increases (+)		Debit for decreases (−)	Credit for increases (+)

1. Increases in assets are debited to asset accounts. Decreases in assets are credited to asset accounts.
2. Increases in liabilities and stockholders' equity are credited to liability and stockholders' equity accounts. Decreases in liabilities and stockholders' equity are debited to liability and stockholders' equity accounts.

One of the more difficult points to understand is the application of double-entry rules to the stockholders' equity components. The key is to remember that dividends and expenses are deductions from stockholders' equity. Thus, transactions that *increase* dividends or expenses *decrease* stockholders' equity. Consider this expanded version of the accounting equation:

Stockholders' Equity

$$\text{Assets} = \text{Liabilities} + \underbrace{\text{Common Stock} + \text{Retained Earnings} - \text{Dividends} + \text{Revenues} - \text{Expenses}}$$

This equation may be rearranged by shifting dividends and expenses to the left side, as follows:

Assets		+	Dividends		+	Expenses		=	Liabilities		+	Common Stock		+	Retained Earnings		+	Revenues	
+ (debits)	− (credits)		+ (debits)	− (credits)		+ (debits)	− (credits)		− (debits)	+ (credits)		− (debits)	+ (credits)		− (debits)	+ (credits)		− (debits)	+ (credits)

Note that the rules for double entry for all the accounts on the left of the equal sign are just the opposite of the rules for all the accounts on the right of the equal

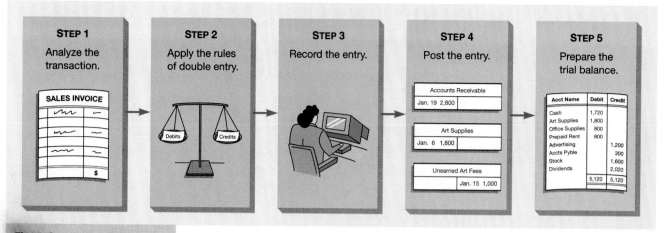

Figure 2
Analyzing and Processing Transactions

sign. Assets, dividends, and expenses are increased by debits and decreased by credits. Liabilities, common stock, retained earnings, and revenues are increased by credits and decreased by debits.

With this basic information about double entry, it is possible to analyze and process transactions by following the five steps illustrated in Figure 2. To show how the steps are applied, assume that on June 1, Koenig Art Supplies borrows $100,000 from its bank on a promissory note. The transaction is analyzed and processed as follows:

1. *Analyze the transaction to determine its effect on assets, liabilities, and stockholders' equity.* In this case, both an asset (Cash) and a liability (Notes Payable) increase. A transaction is usually supported by some kind of **source document**—an invoice, a receipt, a check, or a contract. Here, a copy of the signed note would be the source document.

2. *Apply the rules of double entry.* Increases in assets are recorded by debits. Increases in liabilities are recorded by credits.

3. *Record the entry.* Transactions are recorded in chronological order in a journal. In one form of journal, which is explained in more detail later in this chapter, the date, debit account, and debit amount are recorded on one line and the credit account and credit amount, indented, on the next line, as follows:

		Dr.	Cr.
A = L + OE	June 1 Cash	100,000	
+ +	Notes Payable		100,000

This form is referred to as **journal form** and carries an explanation immediately following the entry. If more than one account is debited or credited, additional lines are used.

4. *Post the entry.* The entry is posted to the general ledger by transferring the date and amounts to the proper accounts. The T account is one form of ledger account.

Cash		**Notes Payable**	
June 1 100,000			June 1 100,000

In formal records, step **3** is never omitted. However, for purposes of analysis, accountants often bypass step **3** and record entries directly in T accounts because doing so clearly and quickly shows the effects of transactions on the accounts. Some of the assignments in this chapter use the same approach to emphasize the analytical aspects of double entry.

5. *Prepare the trial balance to confirm the balance of the accounts.* Periodically, accountants prepare a trial balance to confirm that the accounts are still in balance after the recording and posting of transactions. Preparation of the trial balance is explained later in this chapter.

Transaction Analysis Illustrated

OBJECTIVE

4 Apply the steps for transaction analysis and processing to simple transactions

In the next few pages, we examine the transactions for Joan Miller Advertising Agency, Inc., during the month of January. In the discussion, we illustrate the principle of duality and show how transactions are recorded in the accounts.

January 1: Joan Miller obtains a charter from the state and invests $10,000 in her own advertising agency in exchange for 10,000 shares of $1 par value common stock.

A = L + OE
+   +

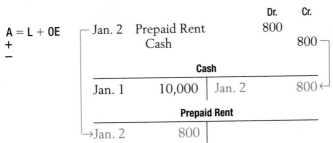

		Dr.	Cr.
Jan. 1	Cash	10,000	
	Common Stock		10,000

Cash

Jan. 1 | 10,000 |

Common Stock

| Jan. 1 | 10,000 |

Transaction: Investment in business.

Analysis: Assets increase. Stockholders' equity increases.

Rules: Increases in assets are recorded by debits. Increases in stockholders' equity are recorded by credits.

Entry: The increase in assets is recorded by a debit to Cash. The increase in stockholders' equity is recorded by a credit to Common Stock.

Key Point: For this transaction, many students incorrectly credit Stockholders' Equity rather than Common Stock. Stockholders' equity is an account *classification*, not an account title.

Analysis: If Joan Miller had invested assets other than cash in the business, the appropriate asset accounts would be debited.

January 2: Rents an office, paying two months' rent, $800, in advance.

A = L + OE
+
–

		Dr.	Cr.
Jan. 2	Prepaid Rent	800	
	Cash		800

Cash

| Jan. 1 | 10,000 | Jan. 2 | 800 |

Prepaid Rent

| Jan. 2 | 800 |

Transaction: Rent paid in advance.

Analysis: Assets increase. Assets decrease.

Rules: Increases in assets are recorded by debits. Decreases in assets are recorded by credits.

Entry: The increase in assets is recorded by a debit to Prepaid Rent. The decrease in assets is recorded by a credit to Cash.

January 3: Orders art supplies, $1,800, and office supplies, $800.

Analysis: No entry is made because no transaction has occurred. According to the recognition issue, there is no liability until the supplies are shipped or received and there is an obligation to pay for them.

January 4: Purchases art equipment, $4,200, with cash.

A = L + OE
+
–

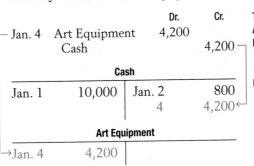

		Dr.	Cr.
Jan. 4	Art Equipment	4,200	
	Cash		4,200

Cash

| Jan. 1 | 10,000 | Jan. 2 | 800 |
| | | 4 | 4,200 |

Art Equipment

| Jan. 4 | 4,200 |

Transaction: Purchase of equipment.

Analysis: Assets increase. Assets decrease.

Rules: Increases in assets are recorded by debits. Decreases in assets are recorded by credits.

Entry: The increase in assets is recorded by a debit to Art Equipment. The decrease in assets is recorded by a credit to Cash.

Key Point: Terms such as *Cash Paid* and *Art Equipment Purchased* are not acceptable account names. *Cash* and *Art Equipment* are the correct account names.

January 5: Purchases office equipment, $3,000, from Morgan Equipment; pays $1,500 in cash and agrees to pay the rest next month.

A = L + OE
+ +
−

Key Point: Office equipment is recorded at the full $3,000, even though only half of it has been paid for.

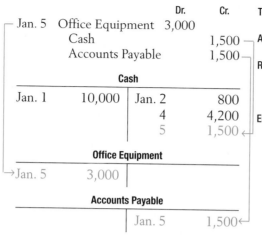

		Dr.	Cr.
Jan. 5	Office Equipment	3,000	
	Cash		1,500
	Accounts Payable		1,500

Cash

Jan. 1	10,000	Jan. 2	800
		4	4,200
		5	1,500

Office Equipment

Jan. 5	3,000	

Accounts Payable

		Jan. 5	1,500

Transaction: Purchase of equipment and partial payment.
Analysis: Assets increase. Assets decrease. Liabilities increase.
Rules: Increases in assets are recorded by debits. Decreases in assets are recorded by credits. Increases in liabilities are recorded by credits.
Entry: The increase in assets is recorded by a debit to Office Equipment. The decrease in assets is recorded by a credit to Cash. The increase in liabilities is recorded by a credit to Accounts Payable.

January 6: Purchases art supplies, $1,800, and office supplies, $800, from Taylor Supply Company, on credit.

A = L + OE
+ +
+

Key Point: Accounts Payable is used when there is a delay between purchase and payment.

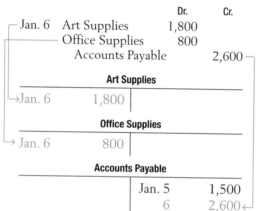

		Dr.	Cr.
Jan. 6	Art Supplies	1,800	
	Office Supplies	800	
	Accounts Payable		2,600

Art Supplies

Jan. 6	1,800	

Office Supplies

Jan. 6	800	

Accounts Payable

		Jan. 5	1,500
		6	2,600

Transaction: Purchase of supplies on credit.
Analysis: Assets increase. Liabilities increase.
Rules: Increases in assets are recorded by debits. Increases in liabilities are recorded by credits.
Entry: The increase in assets is recorded by debits to Art Supplies and Office Supplies. The increase in liabilities is recorded by a credit to Accounts Payable.

BUSINESS FOCUS ON ETHICS

Not only are the accounting solutions related to recognition (when a transaction occurred), valuation (what value to place on the transaction), and classification (how the components of the transaction should be categorized) important for good financial reporting, but they are also designed to help a company's management fulfill its responsibilities to the owners and the public. Informix Corporation was one of the most successful software companies and was a serious challenger in the market for large corporate databases. However, when the public discovered that the company was using a questionable application of the recognition principle, its stock price plummeted, the NASDAQ stock market began actions to delist the company, and some questioned whether it would ultimately survive. Its problems occurred when management disclosed that a substantial portion of the company's revenue came from shipments to resellers that had not been sold to the final user, bringing into question whether sales had actually occurred.[6]

January 8: Pays for a one-year life insurance policy, $480, with coverage effective January 1.

A = L + OE
+
−

		Dr.	Cr.
Jan. 8	Prepaid Insurance	480	
	Cash		480

Cash

Jan. 1	10,000	Jan. 2	800
		4	4,200
		5	1,500
		8	480

Prepaid Insurance

Jan. 8	480	

Transaction: Insurance purchased in advance.
Analysis: Assets increase. Assets decrease.
Rules: Increases in assets are recorded by debits. Decreases in assets are recorded by credits.
Entry: The increase in assets is recorded by a debit to Prepaid Insurance. The decrease in assets is recorded by a credit to Cash.

January 9: Pays Taylor Supply Company $1,000 of the amount owed.

A = L + OE
−   −

Key Point: Accounts Payable, not Art Supplies or Office Supplies, is debited. Also, a liability usually is credited before it can be debited.

		Dr.	Cr.
Jan. 9	Accounts Payable	1,000	
	Cash		1,000

Cash

Jan. 1	10,000	Jan. 2	800
		4	4,200
		5	1,500
		8	480
		9	1,000

Accounts Payable

Jan. 9	1,000	Jan. 5	1,500
		6	2,600

Transaction: Partial payment on a liability.
Analysis: Assets decrease. Liabilities decrease.
Rules: Decreases in liabilities are recorded by debits. Decreases in assets are recorded by credits.
Entry: The decrease in liabilities is recorded by a debit to Accounts Payable. The decrease in assets is recorded by a credit to Cash.

January 10: Performs a service for an automobile dealer by placing advertisements in the newspaper and collects a fee, $1,400.

A = L + OE
+   +

		Dr.	Cr.
Jan. 10	Cash	1,400	
	Advertising Fees Earned		1,400

Cash

Jan.	1	10,000	Jan.	2	800
	10	1,400		4	4,200
				5	1,500
				8	480
				9	1,000

Advertising Fees Earned

		Jan. 10	1,400

Transaction: Revenue earned and cash collected.
Analysis: Assets increase. Stockholders' equity increases.
Rules: Increases in assets are recorded by debits. Increases in stockholders' equity are recorded by credits.
Entry: The increase in assets is recorded by a debit to Cash. The increase in stockholders' equity is recorded by a credit to Advertising Fees Earned.

January 12: Pays the secretary two weeks' wages, $600.

A = L + OE
−   −

			Dr.	Cr.
Jan. 12	Wages Expense		600	
	Cash			600

Cash

Jan.	1	10,000	Jan.	2	800
	10	1,400		4	4,200
				5	1,500
				8	480
				9	1,000
				12	600

Wages Expense

Jan. 12	600	

Transaction: Payment of wages expense.
Analysis: Assets decrease. Stockholders' equity decreases.
Rules: Decreases in stockholders' equity are recorded by debits. Decreases in assets are recorded by credits.
Entry: The decrease in stockholders' equity is recorded by a debit to Wages Expense. The decrease in assets is recorded by a credit to Cash.

January 15: Accepts an advance fee, $1,000, for artwork to be done for another agency.

A = L + OE
+   +

			Dr.	Cr.
Jan. 15	Cash		1,000	
	Unearned Art Fees			1,000

Cash

Jan.	1	10,000	Jan.	2	800
	10	1,400		4	4,200
	15	1,000		5	1,500
				8	480
				9	1,000
				12	600

Unearned Art Fees

		Jan. 15	1,000

Transaction: Payment received for future services.
Analysis: Assets increase. Liabilities increase.
Rules: Increases in assets are recorded by debits. Increases in liabilities are recorded by credits.
Entry: The increase in assets is recorded by a debit to Cash. The increase in liabilities is recorded by a credit to Unearned Art Fees.

January 19: Performs a service by placing several major advertisements for Ward Department Stores. The fee, $2,800, is billed now but will be collected next month.

A = L + OE
+   +

			Dr.	Cr.
Jan. 19	Accounts Receivable		2,800	
	Advertising Fees Earned			2,800

Accounts Receivable

Jan. 19	2,800	

Advertising Fees Earned

		Jan. 10	1,400
		19	2,800

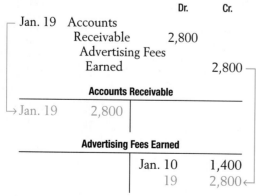

Key Point: Revenue is recognized even though payment has not been received yet. Accounts Receivable is used when there is a delay between the sale of services or merchandise and payment.

Transaction: Revenue earned, to be received later.
Analysis: Assets increase. Stockholders' equity increases.
Rules: Increases in assets are recorded by debits. Increases in stockholders' equity are recorded by credits.
Entry: The increase in assets is recorded by a debit to Accounts Receivable. The increase in stockholders' equity is recorded by a credit to Advertising Fees Earned.

January 26: Pays the secretary two more weeks' wages, $600.

A = L + OE
−   −

		Dr.	Cr.
Jan. 26	Wages Expense	600	
	Cash		600

Cash

Jan.	1	10,000	Jan.	2	800
	10	1,400		4	4,200
	15	1,000		5	1,500
				8	480
				9	1,000
				12	600
				26	600

Wages Expense

Jan.	12	600	
	26	600	

Transaction: Payment of wages expense.
Analysis: Assets decrease. Stockholders' equity decreases.
Rules: Decreases in stockholders' equity are recorded by debits. Decreases in assets are recorded by credits.
Entry: The decrease in stockholders' equity is recorded by a debit to Wages Expense. The decrease in assets is recorded by a credit to Cash.

January 29: Receives and pays the utility bill, $100.

A = L + OE
−   −

		Dr.	Cr.
Jan. 29	Utilities Expense	100	
	Cash		100

Cash

Jan.	1	10,000	Jan.	2	800
	10	1,400		4	4,200
	15	1,000		5	1,500
				8	480
				9	1,000
				12	600
				26	600
				29	100

Utilities Expense

Jan. 29	100	

Transaction: Payment of utilities expense.
Analysis: Assets decrease. Stockholders' equity decreases.
Rules: Decreases in stockholders' equity are recorded by debits. Decreases in assets are recorded by credits.
Entry: The decrease in stockholders' equity is recorded by a debit to Utilities Expense. The decrease in assets is recorded by a credit to Cash.

January 30: Receives (but does not pay) the telephone bill, $70.

A = L + OE
+   −

Key Point: The expense and liability are recognized at this point, even though payment has not yet been made, because an expense has been incurred. Telephone services have been used, and the obligation to pay exists.

		Dr.	Cr.
Jan. 30	Telephone Expense	70	
	Accounts Payable		70

Accounts Payable

Jan.	9	1,000	Jan.	5	1,500
				6	2,600
				30	70

Telephone Expense

Jan. 30	70	

Transaction: Expense incurred, to be paid later.
Analysis: Liabilities increase. Stockholders' equity decreases.
Rules: Decreases in stockholders' equity are recorded by debits. Increases in liabilities are recorded by credits.
Entry: The decrease in stockholders' equity is recorded by a debit to Telephone Expense. The increase in liabilities is recorded by a credit to Accounts Payable.

January 31: Declared and paid a dividend of $1,400.

$$A = L + OE$$
$$- \quad -$$

		Dr.	Cr.
Jan. 31	Dividends	1,400	
	Cash		1,400

Key Point: Dividends are not considered expenses. Expenses are costs of operating a business, but dividends are assets distributed to the stockholders of the business.

Cash

Jan. 1	10,000	Jan. 2	800
10	1,400	4	4,200
15	1,000	5	1,500
		8	480
		9	1,000
		12	600
		26	600
		29	100
		31	1,400

Transaction: Declaration and payment of dividends.

Analysis: Assets decrease. Stockholders' equity decreases.

Rules: Decreases in stockholders' equity are recorded by debits. Decreases in assets are recorded by credits.

Entry: The decrease in stockholders' equity is recorded by a debit to Dividends. The decrease in assets is recorded by a credit to Cash.

Dividends

Jan. 31	1,400	

Summary of Transactions

In Exhibit 2 the transactions for January are shown in their accounts and in relation to the accounting equation. Note that all transactions have been recorded on the date they are recognized. Most of these transactions involve either the receipt or payment of cash as may be seen in the Cash account. There are important exceptions, however. For instance, on January 19 Advertising Fees were earned, but receipt of cash for these fees will come later. Also, on January 5, 6, and 30 there were transactions recognized that totaled $4,170 in Accounts Payable. This means the company can wait to pay. At the end of the month, only the $1,000 recorded on January 9 had been paid. These lags between recognition of transactions and the subsequent cash inflows or outflows impact achieving the goal of liquidity.

The Trial Balance

OBJECTIVE

5 Prepare a trial balance and describe its value and limitations

For every amount debited, an equal amount must be credited. This means that the total of debits and credits in the T accounts must be equal. To test this, the accountant periodically prepares a **trial balance**. Exhibit 3 shows a trial balance for Joan Miller Advertising Agency, Inc. It was prepared from the accounts in Exhibit 2.

A trial balance may be prepared at any time but is usually prepared on the last day of the month. Here are the steps in preparing a trial balance:

1. List each T account that has a balance, with debit balances in the left column and credit balances in the right column. Accounts are listed in the order in which they appear in the ledger.

2. Add each column.

3. Compare the totals of the columns.

Key Point: The trial balance is prepared at the end of the accounting period. It is an initial check that the ledger is in balance.

In accounts in which increases are recorded by debits, the **normal balance** (the usual balance) is a debit balance; in accounts in which increases are recorded by credits, the normal balance is a credit balance. Table 1 summarizes the normal account balances of the major account categories. According to the table, the T

Exhibit 2
Summary of Transactions for Joan Miller Advertising Agency, Inc.

Assets	=	Liabilities	+	Stockholders' Equity

Cash

Jan.	1	10,000	Jan.	2	800
	10	1,400		4	4,200
	15	1,000		5	1,500
				8	480
				9	1,000
				12	600
				26	600
				29	100
				31	1,400
		12,400			10,680
Bal.		1,720			

Accounts Receivable

Jan. 19	2,800	

Art Supplies

Jan. 6	1,800	

Office Supplies

Jan. 6	800	

Prepaid Rent

Jan. 2	800	

Prepaid Insurance

Jan. 8	480	

Art Equipment

Jan. 4	4,200	

Office Equipment

Jan. 5	3,000	

Accounts Payable

Jan. 9	1,000	Jan. 5	1,500
		6	2,600
		30	70
	1,000		4,170
		Bal.	3,170

Unearned Art Fees

		Jan. 15	1,000

This account links to the statement of cash flows.

Common Stock

	Jan. 1	10,000

Dividends

Jan. 31	1,400	

Advertising Fees Earned

	Jan. 10	1,400
	19	2,800
	Bal.	4,200

Wages Expense

Jan. 12	600	
26	600	
Bal.	1,200	

Utilities Expense

Jan. 29	100	

Telephone Expense

Jan. 30	70	

These accounts link to the income statement.

account Accounts Payable (a liability) typically has a credit balance and is copied into the trial balance as a credit balance.

Once in a while, a transaction leaves an account with a balance that is not "normal." For example, when a company overdraws its account at the bank, its Cash account (an asset) will show a credit balance instead of a debit balance. The "abnormal" balance should be copied into the trial balance columns as it stands, as a debit or a credit.

The trial balance proves whether or not the ledger is in balance. *In balance* means that the total of all debits recorded equals the total of all credits recorded.

Joan Miller Advertising Agency, Inc.
Trial Balance
January 31, 20xx

Key Point: The accounts are listed in the same order as in the ledger. At this point, the Retained Earnings account does not reflect any revenues, expenses, or dividends for the period.

	Debit	Credit
Cash	$ 1,720	
Accounts Receivable	2,800	
Art Supplies	1,800	
Office Supplies	800	
Prepaid Rent	800	
Prepaid Insurance	480	
Art Equipment	4,200	
Office Equipment	3,000	
Accounts Payable		$ 3,170
Unearned Art Fees		1,000
Common Stock		10,000
Dividends	1,400	
Advertising Fees Earned		4,200
Wages Expense	1,200	
Utilities Expense	100	
Telephone Expense	70	
	$18,370	$18,370

But the trial balance does not prove that the transactions were analyzed correctly or recorded in the proper accounts. For example, there is no way of determining from the trial balance that a debit should have been made in the Art Equipment account rather than the Office Equipment account. And the trial balance does not detect whether transactions have been omitted, because equal debits and credits will have been omitted. Also, if an error of the same amount is made in both a debit and a credit, it will not be discovered by the trial balance. The trial balance proves only that the debits and credits in the accounts are in balance.

If the debit and credit columns of the trial balance are not equal, look for one or more of the following errors: (1) a debit was entered in an account as a credit, or vice versa; (2) the balance of an account was computed incorrectly; (3) an error

Table 1. Normal Account Balances of Major Account Categories

	Increases Recorded by		Normal Balance	
Account Category	**Debit**	**Credit**	**Debit**	**Credit**
Assets	x		x	
Liabilities		x		x
Stockholders' Equity:				
Common Stock		x		x
Retained Earnings		x		x
Dividends	x		x	
Revenues		x		x
Expenses	x		x	

was made in carrying the account balance to the trial balance; or (4) the trial balance was summed incorrectly.

Other than simply incorrectly adding the columns, the two most common mistakes in preparing a trial balance are (1) recording an account with a debit balance as a credit, or vice versa, and (2) transposing two numbers when transferring an amount to the trial balance (for example, entering $23,459 as $23,549). The first of these mistakes causes the trial balance to be out of balance by an amount divisible by 2. The second causes the trial balance to be out of balance by a number divisible by 9. Thus, if a trial balance is out of balance and the addition has been verified, determine the amount by which the trial balance is out of balance and divide it first by 2 and then by 9. If the amount is divisible by 2, look in the trial balance for an amount equal to the quotient. If you find such an amount, it is probably in the wrong column. If the amount is divisible by 9, trace each amount to the ledger account balance, checking carefully for a transposition error. If neither of these techniques identifies the error, first recompute the balance of each account in the ledger, then, if the error still has not been found, retrace each posting from the journal to the ledger.

Some Notes on Presentation

A ruled line appears in financial reports before each subtotal or total to indicate that the amounts above are added or subtracted. It is common practice to use a double line under a final total to show that it has been checked, or verified.

Dollar signs ($) are required in all financial statements, including the balance sheet and income statement, and in the trial balance and other schedules. On these statements, a dollar sign should be placed before the first amount in each column and before the first amount in a column following a ruled line. Dollar signs in the same column are aligned. Dollar signs are not used in journals and ledgers.

On unruled paper, commas and decimal points are used in dollar amounts. On paper with ruled columns—like the paper in journals and ledgers—commas and decimal points are not needed. In this book, because most problems and illustrations are in whole dollar amounts, the cents column usually is omitted. When accountants deal with whole dollars, they often use a dash in the cents column to indicate whole dollars rather than take the time to write zeros.

BUSINESS FOCUS ON INTERNATIONAL

Determining the dollar amount or valuation of a sale or purchase transaction is often not difficult because it equals the amount of cash that changes hands. However, in some areas of the world it is not so easy to determine. In a country where the currency is declining in value and there is high inflation, companies often are forced to resort to barter transactions, in which one good or service is traded for another. In Russia, for example, perhaps as many as two-thirds of all transactions are barter-type transactions. It is not uncommon for companies often to end up with piles of goods stacked around their offices and warehouses. In one case, an electric utility company provided a textile-machinery plant with electricity in exchange for wool blankets, which the plant had received in exchange for equipment sold to another company. Determining the value can be difficult in this case because it becomes a matter of determining the fair value of the goods being traded.[7]

Recording and Posting Transactions

Let us now take a look at the formal process of recording transactions in the general journal and posting them to the ledger.

The General Journal

Key Point: The journal is a chronological record of events. Only the general journal is discussed in this chapter.

As you have seen, transactions can be entered directly into the accounts. But this method makes identifying individual transactions or finding errors very difficult because the debit is recorded in one account and the credit in another. The solution is to record all transactions chronologically in a **journal**. The journal is sometimes called the *book of original entry* because it is where transactions first enter the accounting records. Later, the debit and credit portions of each transaction can be transferred to the appropriate accounts in the ledger. A separate **journal entry** is used to record each transaction, and the process of recording transactions is called **journalizing**.

Most businesses have more than one kind of journal. Several types of journals are discussed in the appendix on special-purpose journals. The simplest and most flexible type is the **general journal**, the one we focus on in this chapter. Entries in the general journal include the following information about each transaction:

1. The date
2. The names of the accounts debited and the dollar amounts on the same lines in the debit column
3. The names of the accounts credited and the dollar amounts on the same lines in the credit column
4. An explanation of the transaction
5. The account identification numbers, if appropriate

Exhibit 4 displays two of the earlier transactions for Joan Miller Advertising Agency, Inc. The procedure for recording transactions in the general journal is as follows:

1. Record the date by writing the year in small figures on the first line at the top of the first column, the month on the next line of the first column, and the

Exhibit 4
The General Journal

	General Journal			Page 1
Date	**Description**	**Post. Ref.**	**Debit**	**Credit**
20xx Jan. 6	Art Supplies		1,800	
	Office Supplies		800	
	Accounts Payable			2,600
	Purchase of art and office supplies on credit			
8	Prepaid Insurance		480	
	Cash			480
	Paid one-year life insurance premium			

A = L + OE
+   +
+

A = L + OE
+
−

day in the second column opposite the month. For subsequent entries on the same page for the same month and year, the month and year can be omitted.

2. Write the exact names of the accounts debited and credited in the Description column. Starting on the same line as the date, write the name(s) of the account(s) debited next to the left margin and indent the name(s) of the account(s) credited. The explanation is placed on the next line and further indented. The explanation should be brief but sufficient to explain and identify the transaction. A transaction can have more than one debit or credit entry; this is called a **compound entry**. In a compound entry, all debit accounts are listed before any credit accounts. (The January 6 transaction of Joan Miller Advertising Agency, Inc., in Exhibit 4 is an example of a compound entry.)

3. Write the debit amounts in the Debit column opposite the accounts to be debited, and write the credit amounts in the Credit column opposite the accounts to be credited.

4. At the time the transactions are recorded, nothing is placed in the Post. Ref. (posting reference) column. (This column is sometimes called *LP* or *Folio.*) Later, if the company uses account numbers to identify accounts in the ledger, fill in the account numbers to provide a convenient cross-reference from the general journal to the ledger and to indicate that the entry has been posted to the ledger. If the accounts are not numbered, use a checkmark (✓).

5. It is customary to skip a line after each journal entry.

The General Ledger

SUPPLEMENTAL OBJECTIVE

7 Post transactions from the general journal to the ledger

The general journal is used to record the details of each transaction. The general ledger is used to update each account.

THE LEDGER ACCOUNT FORM   The T account is a simple, direct means of recording transactions. In practice, a somewhat more complicated form of the account is needed in order to record more information. The **ledger account form**, which contains four columns for dollar amounts, is illustrated in Exhibit 5.

The account title and number appear at the top of the account form. The date of the transaction appears in the first two columns as it does in the journal. The Item column is used only rarely to identify transactions, because explanations already appear in the journal. The Post. Ref. column is used to note the journal page where the original entry for the transaction can be found. The dollar amount of the entry is entered in the appropriate Debit or Credit column, and a new

Exhibit 5
Accounts Payable in the General Ledger

General Ledger

| Accounts Payable | | | | | | | Account No. 212 |

						Balance	
Date		Item	Post. Ref.	Debit	Credit	Debit	Credit
20xx Jan.	5		J1		1,500		1,500
	6		J1		2,600		4,100
	9		J1	1,000			3,100
	30		J2		70		3,170

account balance is computed in the final two columns after each entry. The advantage of this form of account over the T account is that the current balance of the account is readily available.

POSTING TO THE LEDGER   After transactions have been entered in the journal, they must be transferred to the ledger. The process of transferring journal entry information from the journal to the ledger is called **posting**. Posting is usually done after several entries have been made—for example, at the end of each day or less frequently, depending on the number of transactions. As shown in Exhibit 6, through posting, each amount in the Debit column of the journal is transferred into the Debit column of the appropriate account in the ledger, and each amount in the Credit column of the journal is transferred into the Credit column of the

Exhibit 6
Posting from the General Journal to the Ledger

A = L + OE
+   −

General Journal   ② Page 2

Date		Description	Post. Ref.	Debit	Credit
20xx Jan.	② 30	① Telephone Expense	⑤ 513	⑤ 70	③
		Accounts Payable	212		70
		Received bill for			
		telephone expense			

General Ledger

Accounts Payable   Account No. 212

Date		Item	Post. Ref.	Debit	Credit	Balance Debit	Balance Credit
20xx Jan.	5		J1		1,500		1,500
	6		J1		2,600		4,100
	9		J1	1,000			3,100
	30		J2		70		3,170

General Ledger

Telephone Expense   Account No. 513

Date		Item	Post. Ref.	Debit	Credit	Balance Debit	Balance Credit
20xx Jan.	30		J2	70		④ 70	

BUSINESS FOCUS ON TECHNOLOGY

In computerized accounting systems, posting is done automatically and the trial balance can be easily prepared as often as needed. Any accounts with abnormal balances are highlighted for investigation. Some general ledger software packages for small businesses list the trial balance amounts in a single column, with credit balances shown as minuses. In such cases, the trial balance is in balance if the total is zero.

appropriate account in the ledger. The steps in the posting process are as follows:

1. In the ledger, locate the debit account named in the journal entry.
2. Enter the date of the transaction and, in the Post. Ref. column of the ledger, the journal page number from which the entry comes.
3. Enter in the Debit column of the ledger account the amount of the debit as it appears in the journal.
4. Calculate the account balance and enter it in the appropriate Balance column.
5. Enter in the Post. Ref. column of the journal the account number to which the amount has been posted.
6. Repeat the same five steps for the credit side of the journal entry.

Notice that step **5** is the last step in the posting process for each debit and credit. In addition to serving as an easy reference between the journal entry and the ledger account, this entry in the Post. Ref. column of the journal indicates that all steps for the transaction have been completed. This allows accountants who have been called away from their work to easily find where they were before the interruption.

Chapter Review

REVIEW OF LEARNING OBJECTIVES

Ace *it*

1. **Explain, in simple terms, the generally accepted ways of solving the measurement issues of recognition, valuation, and classification.** To measure a business transaction, the accountant determines when the transaction occurred (the recognition issue), what value should be placed on the transaction (the valuation issue), and how the components of the transaction should be categorized (the classification issue). In general, recognition occurs when title passes, and a transaction is valued at the exchange price, the cost at the time the transaction is recognized. Classification refers to the categorizing of transactions according to a system of accounts.

2. **Describe the chart of accounts and recognize commonly used accounts.** An account is a device for storing data from transactions. There is one account for each asset, liability, and component of stockholders' equity, including revenues and expenses. The ledger is a book or file containing all of a company's accounts, arranged according to a chart of accounts. Commonly used asset accounts are Cash, Notes Receivable, Accounts Receivable, Prepaid Expenses, Land, Buildings, and Equipment. Common liability accounts are Notes Payable, Accounts Payable, Wages Payable, and Mortgage Payable. Common stockholders' equity accounts are Common Stock, Retained Earnings, Dividends, and revenue and expense accounts.

3. **Define *double-entry system* and state the rules for double entry.** In the double-entry system, each transaction must be recorded with at least one debit and one credit so that the total dollar amount of the debits equals the

total dollar amount of the credits. The rules for double entry are (1) increases in assets are debited to asset accounts; decreases in assets are credited to asset accounts; and (2) increases in liabilities and stockholders' equity are credited to those accounts; decreases in liabilities and stockholders' equity are debited to those accounts.

4. **Apply the steps for transaction analysis and processing to simple transactions.** The procedure for analyzing transactions is (1) analyze the effect of the transaction on assets, liabilities, and stockholders' equity; (2) apply the appropriate double-entry rule; (3) record the entry; (4) post the entry; and (5) prepare a trial balance.

5. **Prepare a trial balance and describe its value and limitations.** A trial balance is used to check that the debit and credit balances are equal. It is prepared by listing each account with its balance in the Debit or Credit column. Then the two columns are added and the totals compared to test the balances. The major limitation of the trial balance is that even if debit and credit balances are equal, this does not guarantee that the transactions were analyzed correctly or recorded in the proper accounts.

SUPPLEMENTAL OBJECTIVES

6. **Record transactions in the general journal.** The general journal is a chronological record of all transactions. That record contains the date of each transaction, the names of the accounts and the dollar amounts debited and credited, an explanation of each entry, and the account numbers to which postings have been made.

7. **Post transactions from the general journal to the ledger.** After transactions have been entered in the general journal, they are posted to the ledger. Posting is done by transferring each amount in the Debit column of the general journal to the Debit column of the appropriate account in the ledger, and transferring each amount in the Credit column of the general journal to the Credit column of the appropriate account in the ledger. After each entry is posted, a new balance is entered in the appropriate Balance column.

REVIEW OF CONCEPTS AND TERMINOLOGY

The following concepts and terms were introduced in this chapter:

LO 3   **Balance:** The difference in dollars between the total debit footing and the total credit footing of an account. Also called *account balance.*

LO 2   **Chart of accounts:** A scheme that assigns a unique number to each account to facilitate finding the account in the ledger; also, the list of account numbers and titles.

LO 1   **Classification:** The process of assigning transactions to the appropriate accounts.

SO 6   **Compound entry:** An entry that has more than one debit or credit entry.

LO 1   **Cost:** The exchange price associated with a business transaction at the point of recognition.

LO 1   **Cost principle:** The practice of recording a transaction at cost.

LO 3   **Credit:** The right side of an account.

LO 3   **Debit:** The left side of an account.

LO 3   **Double-entry system:** The accounting system in which each transaction is recorded with at least one debit and one credit so that the total dollar amount of debits and the total dollar amount of credits equal each other.

LO 3   **Footings:** Working totals of columns of numbers. *To foot* means to total a column of numbers.

SO 6 **General journal:** The simplest and most flexible type of journal.

LO 2 **General ledger:** The book or file that contains all of the company's accounts, arranged in the order of the chart of accounts. Also called *ledger.*

SO 6 **Journal:** A chronological record of all transactions; the place where transactions first enter the accounting records. Also called *book of original entry.*

SO 6 **Journal entry:** The notations in the journal that are used to record a single transaction.

LO 3 **Journal form:** A form of journal in which the date, the debit account, and the debit amount of a transaction are recorded on one line and the credit account and credit amount on the next line.

SO 6 **Journalizing:** The process of recording transactions in a journal.

SO 7 **Ledger account form:** The form of account that has four dollar amount columns: one column for debit entries, one column for credit entries, and two columns (debit and credit) for showing the balance of the account.

LO 5 **Normal balance:** The usual balance of an account; also the side (debit or credit) that increases the account.

SO 7 **Posting:** The process of transferring journal entry information from the journal to the ledger.

LO 1 **Recognition:** The determination of when a business transaction should be recorded.

LO 1 **Recognition point:** The predetermined time at which a transaction should be recorded; usually, the point at which title passes to the buyer.

LO 3 **Source document:** An invoice, check, receipt, or other document that supports a transaction.

LO 3 **T account:** The simplest form of an account, used to analyze transactions.

LO 5 **Trial balance:** A comparison of the total of debit and credit balances in the accounts to check that they are equal.

LO 1 **Valuation:** The process of assigning a monetary value to a business transaction.

REVIEW PROBLEM

LO 4
LO 5

Transaction Analysis, Journalizing, T Accounts, and Trial Balance

After graduation from veterinary school, Laura Cox entered private practice. The transactions of the business through May 27 are as follows:

20xx
May 1 Laura Cox invested $2,000 in 2,000 shares of $1 par value common stock of her newly chartered company, Pet Clinic, Inc.
3 Paid $300 for two months' rent in advance for an office.
9 Purchased medical supplies for $200 in cash.
12 Purchased $400 of equipment on credit, making a 25 percent down payment.
15 Delivered a calf for a fee of $35 on credit.
18 Made a partial payment of $50 on the equipment purchased May 12.
27 Paid a utility bill of $40.

REQUIRED

1. Record these transactions in journal form.

2. Post the transactions to the following T accounts: Cash; Accounts Receivable; Medical Supplies; Prepaid Rent; Equipment; Accounts Payable; Common Stock; Veterinary Fees Earned; and Utilities Expense.

3. Prepare a trial balance as of May 31.

4. How does the transaction of May 15 relate to recognition and cash flows? Also compare the transactions of May 9 and May 27 with regard to classification.

ANSWER TO REVIEW PROBLEM

1. Record the transactions in journal form.

May	1	Cash	2,000	
		Common Stock		2,000
		Invested $2,000 in 2,000 shares of $1 par value common stock		
	3	Prepaid Rent	300	
		Cash		300
		Paid two months' rent in advance for an office		
	9	Medical Supplies	200	
		Cash		200
		Purchased medical supplies for cash		
	12	Equipment	400	
		Accounts Payable		300
		Cash		100
		Purchased equipment on credit, paying 25 percent down		
	15	Accounts Receivable	35	
		Veterinary Fees Earned		35
		Fee on credit for delivery of a calf		
	18	Accounts Payable	50	
		Cash		50
		Partial payment for equipment purchased May 12		
	27	Utilities Expense	40	
		Cash		40
		Paid utility bill		

2. Set up T accounts and post the transactions in the accounts.

Cash

May 1	2,000	May 3	300
		9	200
		12	100
		18	50
		27	40
	2,000		690
Bal.	1,310		

Accounts Receivable

May 15	35

Medical Supplies

May 9	200

Prepaid Rent

May 3	300

Equipment

May 12	400

Accounts Payable

May 18	50	May 12	300
		Bal.	250

Common Stock

May 1	2,000

Veterinary Fees Earned

May 15	35

Utilities Expense

May 27	40

3. Complete the trial balance.

Pet Clinic, Inc. Trial Balance May 31, 20xx		
Cash	$1,310	
Accounts Receivable	35	
Medical Supplies	200	
Prepaid Rent	300	
Equipment	400	
Accounts Payable		$ 250
Common Stock		2,000
Veterinary Fees Earned		35
Utilities Expense	40	
	$2,285	$2,285

4. The transaction is recorded, or recognized, on May 15, even though no cash is received. The revenue is earned because the service was provided to and accepted by the buyer. The customer now has an obligation to pay the seller. It is recorded as an accounts receivable because the customer has been allowed to pay later. The transaction on May 9 is classified as an asset, Medical Supplies, because these supplies will benefit the company in the future. The transaction on May 27 is classified as an expense, Utilities Expense, because the utilities have already been used and will not benefit the company in the future.

Chapter Assignments

BUILDING YOUR
KNOWLEDGE
FOUNDATION

QUESTIONS

1. What three issues underlie most accounting measurement decisions?
2. Why is recognition an issue for accountants?
3. A customer asks the owner of a store to save an item for him and says that he will pick it up and pay for it next week. The owner agrees to hold it. Should this transaction be recorded as a sale? Explain your answer.
4. Why is it practical for accountants to rely on original cost for valuation purposes?
5. Under the cost principle, changes in value after a transaction is recorded are not usually recognized in the accounts. Comment on this possible limitation of using original cost in accounting measurements.
6. What is an account, and how is it related to the ledger?
7. Tell whether each of the following accounts is an asset account, a liability account, or a stockholders' equity account:
   a. Notes Receivable
   b. Land
   c. Dividends
   d. Mortgage Payable
   e. Prepaid Rent
   f. Insurance Expense
   g. Service Revenue
8. In the stockholders' equity accounts, why do accountants maintain separate accounts for revenues and expenses rather than using the Retained Earnings account?
9. Why is the system of recording entries called the double-entry system? What is significant about this system?

10. "Double-entry accounting refers to entering a transaction in both the journal and the ledger." Comment on this statement.

11. "Debits are bad; credits are good." Comment on this statement.

12. What are the rules of double entry for (a) assets, (b) liabilities, and (c) stockholders' equity?

13. Why are the rules of double entry the same for liabilities and stockholders' equity?

14. What is the meaning of the statement, "The Cash account has a debit balance of $500"?

15. Explain why debits, which decrease stockholders' equity, also increase expenses, which are a component of stockholders' equity.

16. What are the five steps in analyzing and processing a transaction?

17. What does a trial balance prove?

18. What is the normal balance of Accounts Payable? Under what conditions could Accounts Payable have a debit balance?

19. Can errors be present even though a trial balance balances? Explain your answer.

20. Is it a good idea to forgo the journal and enter a transaction directly into the ledger? Explain your answer.

21. In recording entries in a journal, which is written first, the debit or the credit? How is indentation used in the journal?

22. What is the relationship between the journal and the ledger?

23. Describe each of the following:
    a. Account
    b. Journal
    c. Ledger
    d. Book of original entry
    e. Post. Ref. column
    f. Journalizing
    g. Posting
    h. Footings
    i. Compound entry

24. List the following six items in sequence to illustrate the flow of events through the accounting system:
    a. Analysis of the transaction
    b. Debits and credits posted from the journal to the ledger
    c. Occurrence of the business transaction
    d. Preparation of the financial statements
    e. Entry made in the journal
    f. Preparation of the trial balance

SHORT EXERCISES

LO 1   Recognition

SE 1. Which of the following events would be recognized and entered in the accounting records of Hawthorne Corporation? Why?

Jan. 10   Hawthorne Corporation places an order for office supplies.
Feb. 15   Hawthorne Corporation receives the office supplies and a bill for them.
Mar. 1   Hawthorne Corporation pays for the office supplies.

LO 2   Classification of Accounts

SE 2. Tell whether each of the following accounts is an asset, a liability, a revenue, an expense, or none of these.

a. Accounts Payable
b. Supplies
c. Dividends
d. Fees Earned
e. Supplies Expense
f. Accounts Receivable
g. Unearned Revenue
h. Equipment

LO 5   Normal Balances

SE 3. Tell whether the normal balance of each account in **SE 2** is a debit or a credit.

LO 4   Transaction Analysis

SE 4. For each transaction below, tell which account is debited and which account is credited.

May 2   Joe Hurley started a computer programming business, Hurley's Programming Service, Inc., by investing $5,000 in exchange for common stock.
      5   Purchased a computer for $2,500 in cash.

May 7 Purchased supplies on credit for $300.
19 Received cash for programming services performed, $500.
22 Received cash for programming services to be performed, $600.
25 Paid the rent for May, $650.
31 Billed a customer for programming services performed, $250.

SE 5.
LO 4 Recording Transactions in T Accounts

Set up T accounts and record each transaction in **SE 4.** Determine the balance of each account.

SE 6.
LO 5 Preparing a Trial Balance

From the T accounts created in **SE 5,** prepare a trial balance dated May 31, 20x1.

SE 7.
LO 5 Correcting Errors in a Trial Balance

The trial balance that follows is out of balance. Assuming all balances are normal, place the accounts in proper order and correct the trial balance so that debits equal credits.

Sanders Boating Service, Inc.
Trial Balance
January 31, 20x1

Cash	$2,000	
Accounts Payable	400	
Fuel Expense	800	
Unearned Service Revenue	250	
Accounts Receivable		$1,300
Prepaid Rent		150
Common Stock		1,500
Service Revenue	1,750	
Wages Expense		300
Retained Earnings	650	
	$5,850	$3,250

SE 8.
SO 6 Recording Transactions in the General Journal

Prepare a general journal form like the one in Exhibit 4 and label it Page 4. Record the following transactions in the journal.

Sept. 6 Billed a customer for services performed, $1,900.
16 Received partial payment from the customer billed on Sept. 6, $900.

SE 9.
SO 7 Posting to the Ledger Accounts

Prepare ledger account forms like the ones in Exhibit 5 for the following accounts: Cash (111), Accounts Receivable (113), and Service Revenue (411). Post the transactions that are recorded in **SE 8** to the ledger accounts, at the same time making proper posting references.

EXERCISES

E 1.
LO 1 Recognition

Which of the following events would be recognized and recorded in the accounting records of the Sula Corporation on the date indicated?

Jan. 15 Sula Corporation offers to purchase a tract of land for $140,000. There is a high likelihood that the offer will be accepted.
Feb. 2 Sula Corporation receives notice that its rent will be increased from $500 per month to $600 per month effective March 1.
Mar. 29 Sula Corporation receives its utility bill for the month of March. The bill is not due until April 9.
June 10 Sula Corporation places a firm order for new office equipment costing $21,000.
July 6 The office equipment ordered on June 10 arrives. Payment is not due until August 1.

E 2.

LO 1 **Application of Recognition Point**

Fleider's Parts Shop, Inc., uses a large amount of supplies in its business. The following table summarizes selected transaction data for orders of supplies purchased:

Order	Date Shipped	Date Received	Amount
a	June 26	July 5	$ 600
b	July 10	15	1,500
c	16	22	800
d	23	30	1,200
e	27	Aug. 1	1,500
f	Aug. 3	7	1,000

Determine the total purchases of supplies for July alone under each of the following assumptions:

1. Fleider's Parts Shop, Inc., recognizes purchases when orders are shipped.

2. Fleider's Parts Shop, Inc., recognizes purchases when orders are received.

E 3.

LO 2 **Classification of**
LO 5 **Accounts**

The following ledger accounts are for the Vishna Service Corporation:

a. Cash
b. Wages Expense
c. Accounts Receivable
d. Common Stock
e. Service Revenue
f. Prepaid Rent
g. Accounts Payable
h. Investments in Securities
i. Income Taxes Payable
j. Income Taxes Expense
k. Land
l. Supplies Expense
m. Prepaid Insurance
n. Utilities Expense
o. Fees Earned
p. Dividends
q. Wages Payable
r. Unearned Revenue
s. Office Equipment
t. Rent Payable
u. Notes Receivable
v. Interest Expense
w. Notes Payable
x. Supplies
y. Interest Receivable
z. Rent Expense

Complete the following table, using Xs to indicate each account's classification and normal balance (whether a debit or credit increases the account).

Type of Account

Item	Asset	Liability	Common Stock	Dividends	Revenue	Expense	Debit	Credit
a.	X						X	

(Header spanning: **Stockholders' Equity** over Common Stock, Dividends, Revenue, Expense; **Retained Earnings** over Dividends, Revenue, Expense. **Normal Balance (increases balance)** over Debit, Credit.)

E 4.

LO 4 **Transaction Analysis**

Analyze transactions **a–g,** following the example below.

a. Oscar Wyatt established Best Barber Shop, Inc., by incorporating and investing $1,200 for 120 shares of $10 par value common stock.
b. Paid two months' rent in advance, $840.
c. Purchased supplies on credit, $60.
d. Received cash for barbering services, $300.
e. Paid for supplies purchased in **c.**
f. Paid utility bill, $36.
g. Declared and paid a dividend of $50.

Example:

a. The asset Cash was increased. Increases in assets are recorded by debits. Debit Cash $1,200. A component of stockholders' equity, Common Stock, was increased. Increases in stockholders' equity are recorded by credits. Credit Common Stock $1,200.

E 5.

LO 4 Recording Transactions in T Accounts

Open the following T accounts: Cash; Repair Supplies; Repair Equipment; Accounts Payable; Common Stock; Dividends; Repair Fees Earned; Salaries Expense; and Rent Expense. Record the following transactions for the month of June directly in the T accounts; use the letters to identify the transactions in your T accounts. Determine the balance in each account.

a. Dora Amonti opened Glass & China Repair Service, Inc., by investing $4,300 in cash and $1,600 in repair equipment in return for 5,900 shares of the company's $1 par value common stock.
b. Paid $400 for the current month's rent.
c. Purchased repair supplies on credit, $500.
d. Purchased additional repair equipment for cash, $300.
e. Paid salary to a helper, $450.
f. Paid $200 of amount purchased on credit in **c**.
g. Accepted cash for repairs completed, $1,860.
h. Declared and paid a dividend of $600.

E 6.

LO 5 Trial Balance

After recording the transactions in **E 5**, prepare a trial balance in proper sequence for Glass & China Repair Service, Inc., as of June 30, 20xx.

E 7.

LO 4 Analysis of Transactions

Explain each transaction (**a–h**) entered in the following T accounts:

Cash			
a.	60,000	b.	15,000
g.	1,500	e.	3,000
h.	900	f.	4,500

Accounts Receivable			
c.	6,000	g.	1,500

Equipment			
b.	15,000	h.	900
d.	9,000		

Accounts Payable			
f.	4,500	d.	9,000

Common Stock		
	a.	60,000

Service Revenue		
	c.	6,000

Wages Expense	
e.	3,000

E 8.

LO 5 Preparing a Trial Balance

The accounts of the Hanu Metal Corporation as of March 31, 20xx, are listed below in alphabetical order. The amount of Accounts Payable is omitted.

Accounts Payable	?
Accounts Receivable	$ 3,000
Building	34,000
Cash	9,000
Common Stock	20,000
Equipment	12,000
Land	5,200
Notes Payable	20,000
Prepaid Insurance	1,100
Retained Earnings	11,450

Prepare a trial balance with the proper heading (see Exhibit 3) and with the accounts listed in the chart of accounts sequence (see Exhibit 1). Compute the balance of Accounts Payable.

E 9.

LO 5 Effects of Errors on a Trial Balance

Which of the following errors would cause a trial balance to have unequal totals? Explain your answers.

a. A payment to a creditor was recorded as a debit to Accounts Payable for $86 and a credit to Cash for $68.
b. A payment of $100 to a creditor for an account payable was debited to Accounts Receivable and credited to Cash.
c. A purchase of office supplies of $280 was recorded as a debit to Office Supplies for $28 and a credit to Cash for $28.
d. A purchase of equipment for $300 was recorded as a debit to Supplies for $300 and a credit to Cash for $300.

E 10.

This was the trial balance for Feinglass Services, Inc., at the end of July:

Feinglass Services, Inc. Trial Balance July 31, 20xx		
Cash	$ 1,920	
Accounts Receivable	2,830	
Supplies	60	
Prepaid Insurance	90	
Equipment	4,200	
Accounts Payable		$ 2,270
Common Stock		2,000
Retained Earnings		3,780
Dividends		350
Revenues		2,960
Salaries Expense	1,300	
Rent Expense	300	
Advertising Expense	170	
Utilities Expense	13	
	$10,883	$11,360

The trial balance does not balance because of a number of errors. Feinglass's accountant compared the amounts in the trial balance with the ledger, recomputed the account balances, and compared the postings. He found the following errors:

a. The balance of Cash was understated by $200.
b. A cash payment of $210 was credited to Cash for $120.
c. A debit of $60 to Accounts Receivable was not posted.
d. Supplies purchased for $30 were posted as a credit to Supplies.
e. A debit of $90 to Prepaid Insurance was not posted.
f. The Accounts Payable account had debits of $2,660 and credits of $4,590.
g. The Notes Payable account, with a credit balance of $1,200, was not included on the trial balance.
h. The debit balance of Dividends was listed in the trial balance as a credit.
i. A $100 debit to Dividends was posted as a credit.
j. The actual balance of Utilities Expense, $130, was listed as $13 in the trial balance.

Prepare a corrected trial balance.

E 11.

The Peron Construction Corporation builds foundations for buildings and parking lots. The following alphabetical list shows the account balances as of April 30, 20xx:

Accounts Payable	$ 3,900	Office Trailer	$ 2,200
Accounts Receivable	10,120	Prepaid Insurance	4,600
Cash	?	Retained Earnings	10,000
Common Stock	30,000	Revenue Earned	17,400
Construction Supplies	1,900	Revenue Earned	17,400
Dividends	7,800	Utilities Expense	420
Equipment	24,500	Wages Expense	8,800
Notes Payable	20,000		

Prepare a trial balance for the company with the proper heading and with the accounts in balance sheet sequence. Determine the correct balance for the Cash account on April 30, 20xx.

E 12.

Managers and accountants often encounter transactions with which they are unfamiliar. Use your analytical skills to analyze and record in journal form the transactions that follow, which have not yet been discussed in the text.

May 1 Purchased merchandise inventory on account, $2,400.
2 Purchased marketable securities for cash, $5,600.
3 Returned part of merchandise inventory purchased in **a** for full credit, $500.
4 Sold merchandise inventory on account, $1,600 (record sale only).
5 Purchased land and a building for $600,000. Payment is $120,000 cash and a thirty-year mortgage for the remainder. The purchase price is allocated $200,000 to the land and $400,000 to the building.
6 Received an order for $24,000 in services to be provided. With the order was a deposit of $8,000.

E 13.

SO 6 Recording Transactions
SO 7 in the General Journal and Posting to the Ledger Accounts

Open a general journal form like the one in Exhibit 4, and label it Page 10. After opening the form, record the following transactions in the journal.

Dec. 14 Purchased an item of equipment for $6,000, paying $2,000 as a cash down payment.
28 Paid $3,000 of the amount owed on the equipment.

Prepare three ledger account forms like the one shown in Exhibit 5. Use the following account numbers: Cash, 111; Equipment, 144; and Accounts Payable, 212. Then post the two transactions from the general journal to the ledger accounts, being sure to make proper posting references.

Assume that the Cash account has a debit balance of $8,000 on the day prior to the first transaction.

PROBLEMS

P 1.

LO 4 Transaction Analysis

The following accounts are applicable to Green Life Services, Inc., a company that maintains indoor plants:

1. Cash
2. Accounts Receivable
3. Supplies
4. Prepaid Insurance
5. Equipment
6. Accounts Payable
7. Common Stock
8. Retained Earnings
9. Dividends
10. Plant Services Revenue
11. Wages Expense
12. Rent Expense
13. Utilities Expense

Green Life Services, Inc., completed the following transactions:

	Debit	Credit
a. Received cash from customers billed last month.	1	2
b. Made a payment on accounts payable.		
c. Purchased a new one-year insurance policy in advance.		
d. Purchased supplies on credit.		
e. Billed a client for plant services.		
f. Made a rent payment for the current month.		
g. Received cash from customers for plant services.		
h. Paid wages for the staff.		
i. Ordered equipment.		
j. Paid the current month's utility bill.		
k. Received and paid for the equipment ordered in **i**.		
l. Returned for full credit some of the supplies purchased in **d** because they were defective.		
m. Paid for supplies purchased in **d**, less the return in **l**.		
n. Declared and paid a dividend.		

REQUIRED

Analyze each transaction and show the accounts affected by entering the corresponding numbers in the appropriate debit or credit columns as shown in transaction **a**. Indicate no entry, if appropriate.

LO 4 **Transaction Analysis,**
LO 5 **T Accounts, and Trial
       Balance**

P 2. Elena Garcia established a small business, Garcia Training Center, Inc., to teach individuals how to use spreadsheet analysis, word processing, and other techniques on microcomputers. She completed the following transactions.

a. Garcia began by transferring the following assets to the business in exchange for 39,200 shares of $1 par value common stock:

Cash	$18,400
Furniture	6,200
Microcomputer	14,600

b. Paid the first month's rent on a small storefront, $560.

c. Purchased computer software on credit, $1,500.

d. Paid for an advertisement in the local newspaper, $200.

e. Received enrollment applications from five students for a five-day course to start next week. Each student will pay $400 if he or she actually begins the course.

f. Paid wages to a part-time helper, $300.

g. Received cash payments from three of the students enrolled in **e,** $1,200.

h. Billed the two other students in **e,** who attended but did not pay in cash, $800.

i. Paid the utility bill for the current month, $220.

j. Made a payment on the software purchased in **c,** $500.

k. Received payment from one student billed in **h,** $400.

l. Purchased a second microcomputer for cash, $9,400.

m. Declared and paid a dividend of $600.

REQUIRED

1. Set up the following T accounts: Cash; Accounts Receivable; Software; Furniture; Microcomputers; Accounts Payable; Common Stock; Dividends; Tuition Revenue; Wages Expense; Utilities Expense; Rent Expense; and Advertising Expense.

2. Record the transactions directly in the T accounts, using the transaction letter to identify each debit and credit.

3. Prepare a trial balance using today's date.

4. Contrast the effects on cash flows of transactions **c** and **j** with transaction **d** and of transactions **h** and **k** with transaction **g.**

LO 4 **Transaction Analysis,**
LO 5 **T Accounts, and Trial
       Balance**

P 3. Simon Ing began an apartment-cleaning business on October 1 and engaged in the following transactions during the month:

Oct.	1	Began business by depositing $6,000 in a bank account in the name of the corporation in exchange for 6,000 shares of $1 par value common stock.
	2	Ordered cleaning supplies, $500.
	3	Purchased cleaning equipment for cash, $1,400.
	4	Leased a van by making two months' lease payment in advance, $600.
	7	Received the cleaning supplies ordered on October 2 and agreed to pay half the amount in 10 days and the rest in 30 days.
	9	Paid for repairs on the van with cash, $40.
	12	Received cash for cleaning apartments, $480.
	17	Paid half of the amount owed on supplies purchased on October 7, $250.
	21	Billed customers for cleaning apartments, $670.
	24	Paid cash for additional repairs on the van, $40.
	27	Received $300 from the customers billed on October 21.
	31	Declared and paid a dividend of $350.

REQUIRED

1. Set up the following T accounts: Cash; Accounts Receivable; Cleaning Supplies; Prepaid Lease; Cleaning Equipment; Accounts Payable; Common Stock; Dividends; Cleaning Revenue; and Repair Expense.

2. Record transactions directly in the T accounts. Identify each entry by date.

3. Prepare a trial balance for Ing's Dust-Busters Service, Inc., as of October 31, 20xx.

LO 1 **Transaction Analysis,**
LO 4 **Journal Form,**
LO 5 **T Accounts, and Trial Balance**

P 4. Ed Ludovic won a concession to rent bicycles in the local park during the summer. During the month of June, Ed completed the following transactions for his bicycle rental business:

June 2 Began business by placing $14,400 in a business checking account in the name of the corporation in exchange for 14,400 shares of $1 par value common stock.

3 Purchased supplies on account for $300.

4 Purchased 10 bicycles for $5,000, paying $2,400 down and agreeing to pay the rest in 30 days.

5 Paid $5,800 in cash for a small shed to store the bicycles and use for other operations.

6 Received $940 in cash for rentals during the first week of operation.

8 Paid $800 in cash for shipping and installation costs (considered an addition to the cost of the shed) to place the shed at the park entrance.

9 Hired a part-time assistant to help out on weekends at $8 per hour.

10 Paid a maintenance person $150 to clean the grounds.

13 Received $1,000 in cash for rentals during the second week of operation.

15 Paid the assistant $160 for a weekend's work.

17 Paid $300 for the supplies purchased on June 3.

18 Paid a $110 repair bill on bicycles.

20 Received $1,100 in cash for rentals during the third week of operation.

22 Paid the assistant $160 for a weekend's work.

23 Billed a company $220 for bicycle rentals for an employee outing.

25 Paid the $200 fee for June to the Park District for the right to the bicycle concession.

27 Received $820 in cash for rentals during the week.

29 Paid the assistant $160 for a weekend's work.

30 Declared and paid a dividend of $1,000.

REQUIRED

1. Prepare entries to record these transactions in journal form.

2. Set up the following T accounts and post all the journal entries: Cash; Accounts Receivable; Supplies; Shed; Bicycles; Accounts Payable; Common Stock; Dividends; Rental Revenue; Wages Expense; Maintenance Expense; Repair Expense; and Concession Fee Expense.

3. Prepare a trial balance for Ludovic Rentals, Inc., as of June 30, 20xx.

4. Compare how recognition applies to the transactions of June 23 and 27 and their effects on cash flow and how classification applies to the transactions of June 8 and 10.

LO 4 **Transaction Analysis,**
LO 5 **General Journal,**
SO 6 **Ledger Accounts, and**
SO 7 **Trial Balance**

P 5. Capitol Communications Corporation is a marketing firm. On September 30, 20xx, the company's trial balance was as shown below.

Capitol Communications Corporation Trial Balance September 30, 20xx		
Cash (111)	$20,400	
Accounts Receivable (113)	11,000	
Supplies (115)	1,220	
Office Equipment (141)	8,400	
Accounts Payable (212)		$ 5,200
Common Stock (311)		24,000
Retained Earnings (312)		11,820
	$41,020	$41,020

During the month of October, the company completed the following transactions:

Oct. 2 Paid rent for October, $1,300.
3 Received cash from customers on account, $4,600.
7 Ordered supplies, $760.
10 Billed customers for services provided, $5,600.
12 Made a payment on accounts payable, $2,200.
14 Received the supplies ordered on October 7 and agreed to pay for them in 30 days, $760.
15 Paid salaries for the first half of October, $3,800.
17 Discovered some of the supplies were not as ordered and returned them for full credit, $160.
19 Received cash from a customer for services provided, $9,600.
24 Paid the utility bill for October, $320.
25 Paid the telephone bill for October, $240.
26 Received a bill, to be paid in November, for ads placed in the local newspaper during October to promote Capitol Communications Corporation, $1,400.
29 Billed a customer for services provided, $5,400.
30 Paid salaries for the last half of October, $3,800.
31 Declared and paid a dividend of $2,400.

REQUIRED

1. Open accounts in the ledger for the accounts in the trial balance plus the following accounts: Dividends (313); Marketing Fees (411); Salaries Expense (511); Rent Expense (512); Utilities Expense (513); Telephone Expense (514); and Advertising Expense (515).

2. Enter the September 30, 20xx, account balances from the trial balance.

3. Enter the above transactions in the general journal (Pages 22 and 23).

4. Post the journal entries to the ledger.

5. Prepare a trial balance as of October 31, 20xx.

ALTERNATE PROBLEMS

P 6.

LO 4 Transaction Analysis

The following accounts are applicable to Thomas Tiles, Inc.:

1. Cash	6. Notes Payable	11. Service Revenue
2. Accounts Receivable	7. Accounts Payable	12. Rent Expense
3. Supplies	8. Common Stock	13. Repair Expense
4. Prepaid Insurance	9. Retained Earnings	
5. Equipment	10. Dividends	

Thomas Tiles, Inc., completed the following transactions:

	Debit	Credit
a. Paid for supplies purchased on credit last month.	7	1
b. Billed customers for services performed.		
c. Paid the current month's rent.		
d. Purchased supplies on credit.		
e. Received cash from customers for services performed but not yet billed.		
f. Purchased equipment on account.		
g. Received a bill for repairs.		
h. Returned part of the equipment purchased in f for a credit.		
i. Received payments from customers previously billed.		
j. Paid the bill received in **g**.		
k. Received an order for services to be performed.		
l. Paid for repairs with cash.		
m. Made a payment to reduce the principal of the note payable.		
n. Declared and paid a dividend.		

REQUIRED

Analyze each transaction and show the accounts affected by entering the corresponding numbers in the appropriate debit or credit column as shown in transaction **a**. Indicate no entry, if appropriate.

P 7. Jack White Eyes is a house painter. During the month of June, he completed the following transactions:

June 2   Began his business by contributing equipment valued at $1,230 and depositing $7,100 in a checking account in the name of the corporation in exchange for 833 shares of $10 par value common stock of the corporation.

3   Purchased a used truck costing $1,900. Paid $500 cash and signed a note for the balance.

4   Purchased supplies on account for $320.

5   Completed a painting job and billed the customer $480.

7   Received $150 in cash for painting two rooms.

8   Hired an assistant at $6 per hour.

10   Purchased supplies for $160 in cash.

11   Received a $480 check from the customer billed on June 5.

12   Paid $400 for an insurance policy for 18 months' coverage.

13   Billed a customer $620 for a painting job.

14   Paid the assistant $150 for 25 hours' work.

15   Paid $40 for a tune-up for the truck.

18   Paid for the supplies purchased on June 4.

20   Purchased a new ladder (equipment) for $60 and supplies for $290, on account.

22   Received a telephone bill for $60, due next month.

23   Received $330 in cash from the customer billed on June 13.

25   Received $360 in cash for painting a five-room apartment.

27   Paid $200 on the note signed for the truck.

29   Paid the assistant $180 for 30 hours' work.

30   Declared and paid a dividend of $300.

REQUIRED

1. Prepare journal entries to record the above transactions in journal form. Use the accounts listed below.

2. Set up the following T accounts and post all the journal entries: Cash; Accounts Receivable; Supplies; Prepaid Insurance; Equipment; Truck; Notes Payable; Accounts Payable; Common Stock; Dividends; Painting Fees Earned; Wages Expense; Telephone Expense; and Repair Expense.

3. Prepare a trial balance for White Eyes Painting Service, Inc., as of June 30, 20xx.

4. Compare how recognition applies to the transactions of June 5 and 7 and their effects on cash flows and how classification applies to the transactions of June 12 and 14.

P 8. The Nanny-Care Corporation provides baby-sitting and child-care programs. On July 31, 20xx, the company had a trial balance as shown below.

Nanny-Care Corporation Trial Balance July 31, 20xx		
Cash (111)	$ 3,740	
Accounts Receivable (113)	3,400	
Equipment (141)	2,080	
Buses (143)	34,800	
Notes Payable (211)		$30,000
Accounts Payable (212)		3,280
Common Stock (311)		8,000
Retained Earnings (312)		2,740
	$44,020	$44,020

During the month of August, the company completed the following transactions:

Aug. 2 Paid this month's rent, $540.
3 Received fees for this month's services, $1,300.
4 Purchased supplies on account, $170.
5 Reimbursed the bus driver for gas expenses, $80.
6 Ordered playground equipment, $2,000.
7 Paid part-time assistants for two weeks' services, $460.
8 Made a payment on account, $340.
9 Received payments from customers on account, $2,400.
10 Billed customers who had not yet paid for this month's services, $1,400.
11 Paid for the supplies purchased on August 4.
13 Purchased playground equipment for cash, $2,000.
17 Purchased equipment on account, $580.
19 Paid this month's utility bill, $290.
21 Paid part-time assistants for two weeks' services, $460.
22 Received payment for one month's services from customers previously billed, $1,000.
27 Purchased gas and oil for the bus on account, $70.
29 Paid for a one-year insurance policy, $580.
31 Declared and paid a dividend of $220.

REQUIRED

1. Open accounts in the ledger for the accounts in the trial balance plus the following ones: Supplies (115); Prepaid Insurance (116); Dividends (313); Service Revenue (411); Rent Expense (511); Gas and Oil Expense (512); Wages Expense (513); and Utilities Expense (514).

2. Enter the July 31, 20xx, account balances from the trial balance.

3. Enter the above transactions in the general journal (Pages 17, 18, and 19).

4. Post the entries to the ledger accounts. Be sure to make the appropriate posting references in the journal and ledger as you post.

5. Prepare a trial balance as of August 31, 20xx.

EXPANDING YOUR CRITICAL THINKING, COMMUNICATION, AND INTERPERSONAL SKILLS

SKILLS DEVELOPMENT

Conceptual Analysis

SD 1.
LO 1 **Valuation Issue**

Nike, Inc., manufactures athletic shoes and related products. In one of its annual reports, Nike made this statement: "Property, plant, and equipment are recorded at cost."[8] Given that the property, plant, and equipment undoubtedly were purchased over several years and that the current value of those assets was likely to be very different from their original cost, tell what authoritative basis there is for carrying the assets at cost. Does accounting generally recognize changes in value subsequent to the purchase of property, plant, and equipment? Assume you are a Nike accountant. Write a memo to management explaining the rationale underlying Nike's approach.

SD 2.
LO 1 **Recognition, Valuation,**
LO 4 **and Classification Issues**

Chambers Development, a landfill development company, announced a change in its accounting practices. The company said the change would result in a restatement of its prior year's earnings. News of the accounting change caused the stock price to drop

Cash Flow | CD-ROM | Communication | Critical Thinking | Ethics | General Ledger | Group Activity | Hot Links to Real Companies | International | Internet | Key Ratio | Memo | Spreadsheet

from $30½ to $11⅛ in one day, and it continued to decline to a low of $1⅞ two years later. According to one account,

> At the core of the problem was how Chambers accounted for millions of dollars it was spending to develop landfills. The company's choice: charge the costs in the year in which they were incurred or over the life of the landfill. The first method would increase operating costs, thereby depressing current earnings. On the other hand, writing off the costs gradually—"capitalizing" them in accounting parlance—would boost current earnings.[9]

Chambers initially chose to capitalize these costs (as an asset) and expense them gradually over future years. The change to immediate expensing led to a reduction of prior years' earnings of $362 million. The SEC required the restatement of Chambers' financial statements back to the year the company went public. The SEC determined that the amounts capitalized exceeded the reported pretax earnings. Instead of earning profits, the company had actually incurred losses.

The SEC discovered that management would set a target earnings level and back into the amount of costs to be capitalized to achieve the earnings target. The SEC investigation concluded "that the accounting practices that created millions of dollars in false profits were well outside the general bounds of generally accepted accounting practices. They were based on queered mathematics and an overzealous desire to please Wall Street, not an uncommon cause of corporate accounting scandals."[10]

1. Prepare the journal entry that Chambers made to record landfill costs as an asset (prepaid landfill costs). Prepare the journal entry to reduce its prepaid landfill costs by $362 million.

2. Three issues that must be addressed when recording a transaction are recognition, valuation, and classification. Which of these issues were of most concern to the SEC in the Chambers case? Explain how each applies to the transactions in part **1**.

Group Activity: Students work in groups to complete part **1**. Discuss part **2** as a class.

Ethical Dilemma

LO 1 **Recognition Point and Ethical Considerations**

SD 3. One of ***Penn Office Supplies Corporation***'s sales representatives, Jerry Hasbrow, is compensated on a commission basis and receives a substantial bonus for meeting his annual sales goal. The company's recognition point for sales is the day of shipment. On December 31, Jerry realizes that he needs sales of $2,000 to reach his sales goal and receive the bonus. He calls a purchaser for a local insurance company, whom he knows well, and asks him to buy $2,000 worth of copier paper today. The purchaser says, "But Jerry, that's more than a year's supply for us." Jerry says, "Buy it today. If you decide it's too much, you can return however much you want for full credit next month." The purchaser says, "Okay, ship it." The paper is shipped on December 31 and recorded as a sale. On January 15, the purchaser returns $1,750 worth of paper for full credit (okayed by Jerry) against the bill. Should the shipment on December 31 be recorded as a sale? Discuss the ethics of Jerry's action.

Group Activity: Divide the class into informal groups to discuss and report on the ethical issues of this case.

Research Activity

LO 4 **Transactions in a Business Article**

SD 4. Locate an article on a company you recognize or on a company in a business that interests you in one of the following sources: a recent issue of a business journal (such as *Barron's, Fortune, The Wall Street Journal, Business Week,* or *Forbes*), or the Needles Accounting Resource Center web site at http://college.hmco.com. Read the article carefully, noting any references to transactions in which the company engages. These may be normal transactions (sales, purchases) or unusual transactions (a merger, the purchase of another company). Bring a copy of the article to class and be prepared to describe how you would analyze and record the transactions you have noted.

Decision-Making Practice

SD 5.
LO 4 Transaction Analysis and
LO 5 Evaluation of a Trial Balance

Luis Ruiz hired an attorney to help him start Ruiz Repair Service Corporation. On March 1, Luis deposited $11,500 cash in a bank account in the name of the corporation in exchange for 1,150 shares of $10 par value common stock. When he paid the attorney's bill of $700, the attorney advised him to hire an accountant to keep his records. Luis was so busy that it was March 31 before he asked you to straighten out his records. Your first task is to develop a trial balance based on the March transactions.

After investing in his business and paying his attorney, Luis borrowed $5,000 from the bank. He later paid $260, including interest of $60, on this loan. He also purchased a used pickup truck in the company's name, paying $2,500 down and financing $7,400. The first payment on the truck is due April 15. Luis then rented an office and paid three months' rent, $900, in advance. Credit purchases of office equipment of $800 and repair tools of $500 must be paid by April 10.

In March, Ruiz Repair Service completed repairs of $1,300, of which $400 were cash transactions. Of the credit transactions, $300 were collected during March, and $600 remained to be collected at the end of March. Wages of $450 were paid to employees. On March 31, the company received a $75 bill for the March utilities expense and a $50 check from a customer for work to be completed in April.

1. Record the March transactions in journal form. Label each entry alphabetically.

2. Set up T accounts. Then post the entries to the T accounts. Identify each posting with the letter corresponding to the transaction.

3. Determine the balance of each account.

4. Prepare a trial balance for Ruiz Repair Service Corporation as of March 31.

5. Luis Ruiz is unsure how to evaluate the trial balance. His Cash account balance is $12,440, which exceeds his original investment of $11,500 by $940. Did he make a profit of $940? Explain why the Cash account is not an indicator of business earnings. Cite specific examples to show why it is difficult to determine net income by looking solely at figures in the trial balance.

FINANCIAL REPORTING AND ANALYSIS

Interpreting Financial Reports

FRA 1.
LO 2 Interpreting a Bank's
LO 4 Financial Statements

First Chicago NBD Corp. is a large midwestern bank holding company. Selected accounts from the company's 1997 annual report are as follows (in millions):[11]

| Cash and Due from Banks | $ 7,223 | Investment Securities | $ 9,330 |
| Loans to Customers | 68,724 | Deposits by Customers | 68,489 |

REQUIRED

1. Indicate whether each of the accounts just listed is an asset, a liability, or a component of stockholders' equity on First Chicago NBD's balance sheet.

2. Assume that you are in a position to do business with First Chicago NBD. Prepare the entry on the bank's books in journal form to record each of the following transactions:
   a. You sell securities in the amount of $2,000 to the bank.
   b. You deposit the $2,000 received in step **a** in the bank.
   c. You borrow $5,000 from the bank.

International Company

FRA 2.
LO 4 Transaction Analysis

Ajinomoto Company, a Japanese company with operations in 22 countries, is primarily engaged in the manufacture and sale of food products. The following selected aggregate cash transactions were reported in the statement of cash flows in Ajinomoto's 1998 annual report (amounts in millions of yen):[12]

Dividends paid	¥ 6,491
Purchase of property, plant, and equipment	47,845
Proceeds from issuance of long-term debt	67,419
Repayment of long-term debt	85,130

REQUIRED

Prepare entries in journal form to record the above transactions.

Toys "R" Us Annual Report

FRA 3.

LO 4 **Transaction Analysis**

Refer to the balance sheet in the Toys "R" Us annual report. Prepare T accounts for the accounts Cash and Cash Equivalents, Accounts and Other Receivables, Prepaid Expenses and Other Current Assets, Accounts Payable, and Income Taxes Payable. Properly place the balance of the account at January 30, 1999, in the T accounts. Below are some typical transactions in which Toys "R" Us would engage. Analyze each transaction, enter it in the T accounts, and determine the balance of each account. Assume all entries are in thousands.

a. Paid cash in advance for certain expenses, $20,000.
b. Received cash from customers billed previously, $35,000.
c. Paid cash for income taxes previously owed, $70,000.
d. Paid cash to suppliers for amounts owed, $120,000.

Fingraph® Financial Analyst™

FRA 4.

LO 1 **Transaction**
LO 3 **Identification**
LO 4

Choose any company in the Fingraph® Financial Analyst™ CD-ROM software.

1. From the company's annual report, determine the industry(ies) in which the company operates.

2. Find the summary of significant accounting policies that appears following the financial statements. In these policies, find examples of the application of recognition, valuation, and classification.

3. Identify six types of transactions that your company would commonly engage in. Are any of these transactions more common in the industry in which your company operates than in other industries? For each transaction, tell what account would typically be debited and what account would be credited.

4. Prepare a one-page executive summary that highlights what you have learned from parts **1, 2,** and **3.**

Internet Case

FRA 5.

LO 2 **Comparison of Contrasting**
LO 4 **Companies**

Sun Microsystems and *Oracle Corporation* are leading computer and software companies. Compare and contrast the balance sheets of the two companies by first going to the Needles Accounting Resource Center web site at http://college.hmco.com. After choosing your textbook, click on "Chapter Resources" for Chapter 2. Then click on "Links to Companies in Text." Both companies are here. For each company, find its balance sheet. First, what differences and similarities do you find in the account titles used by Sun Microsystems and those used by Oracle? What differences and similarities do you find in the account titles used by the two companies and those used in your text? Second, although the companies are in the same general industry, their businesses differ. How are these differences reflected on the balance sheets? What types of transactions resulted in the differences?

ENDNOTES

1. "Delta Air Lines Orders 49 Planes from Boeing," *Morning News Tribune*, December 23, 1998.
2. The Boeing Co., *Annual Report*, 1994.
3. Craig S. Smith, "China Halts New Purchases of Jets," *The Wall Street Journal*, February 9, 1999.
4. Sun Microsystems Inc., *Annual Report*, 1998.
5. Intel Corp., *Annual Report*, 1998.
6. David Bank, "Informix Says Accounting Problems Were More Serious Than First Disclosed," *The Wall Street Journal*, September 23, 1997.
7. Patricia Kranz, "Rubles? Who Needs Rubles?" *Business Week*, April 13, 1998; Andrew Higgins, "Lacking Money to Pay, Russian Firms Survive on Deft Barter System," *The Wall Street Journal*, August 27, 1998.
8. Nike, Inc., *Annual Report*, 1998.
9. Len Boselovic, "A Look at How the SEC Disposed of Chambers' Claims," *Pittsburgh Post-Gazette*, May 14, 1995.
10. Ibid.
11. First Chicago NBD Corp., *Annual Report*, 1997.
12. Ajinomoto Company, *Annual Report*, 1998.

3

Measuring Business Income

DECISION POINT: A USER'S FOCUS

Southwest Airlines Co. Southwest Airlines Co. has become one of the most successful airlines by providing low-fare service between city pairs that are relatively close together. During any given year, Southwest incurs various operating expenses that are recorded as expenses when they are paid. However, at the end of the year, some expenses—including, for example, the wages of employees during the last days before the end of the year—will have been incurred but will not be paid until the next year. If these expenses are not accounted for correctly, they will appear in the wrong year—the year in which they are paid instead of the year in which Southwest benefited from them. The result is a misstatement of the company's income, a key profitability performance measure. How is this problem avoided?

According to the concepts of accrual accounting and the matching rule, which you will learn in this chapter, the amount of expenses that have been incurred but not paid must be determined and then recorded as expenses of the current year with corresponding liabilities to be paid the next year. The accompanying figure shows the liabilities, called *accrued liabilities*, that resulted from this process at Southwest Airlines.[1] Accrued liabilities for aircraft rentals, employee profit sharing and savings plans, vacation pay, and other were $368,625,000 in 1996 and $426,950,000 in 1997. If these items had not been recorded in their respective years, income would have been misstated by a significant amount and the readers would have been misled.

Financial Highlights: Notes to the Financial Statements

3. ACCRUED LIABILITIES

(in thousands)	1997	1996
Aircraft rentals	$123,669	$121,384
Employee profitsharing and savings plans (Note 8)	92,857	61,286
Vacation pay	50,812	44,763
Other	159,612	141,192
	$426,950	$368,625

Profitability Measurement: The Role of Business Income

Profitability is one of the two major goals of a business (the other being liquidity). For a business to succeed, or even to survive, it must earn a profit. The word **profit**, though, has many meanings. One is the increase in stockholders' equity that results from business operations. However, even this definition can be interpreted differently by economists, lawyers, businesspeople, and the public. Because the word *profit* has more than one meaning, accountants prefer to use the term *net income*, which can be precisely defined from an accounting point of view. Net income is reported on the income statement and is a performance measure used by management, stockholders, and others to monitor a business's progress in meeting the goal of profitability. Readers of income statements need to understand how the accountant defines net income and to be aware of its strengths and weaknesses as a measure of company performance.

Net Income

Net income is the net increase in stockholders' equity that results from the operations of a company and is accumulated in the Retained Earnings account. Net income, in its simplest form, is measured by the difference between revenues and expenses when revenues exceed expenses:

$$\text{Net Income} = \text{Revenues} - \text{Expenses}$$

When expenses exceed revenues, a **net loss** occurs.

REVENUES   **Revenues** are increases in stockholders' equity resulting from selling goods, rendering services, or performing other business activities. In the simplest case, revenues equal the price of goods sold and services rendered over a specific period of time. When a business delivers a product or provides a service to a customer, it usually receives either cash or a promise to pay cash in the near future. The promise to pay is recorded in either Accounts Receivable or Notes Receivable. The revenue for a given period equals the total of cash and receivables from goods and services provided to customers during that period.

Liabilities generally are not affected by revenues, and some transactions that increase cash and other assets are not revenues. For example, a bank loan increases liabilities and cash but does not produce revenue. The collection of accounts receivable, which increases cash and decreases accounts receivable, does not produce revenue either. Remember that when a sale on credit takes place, the asset account Accounts Receivable increases; at the same time, a stockholders' equity revenue account increases. So counting the collection of the receivable as revenue later would be counting the same sale twice.

Not all increases in stockholders' equity arise from revenues. Stockholders' investments increase stockholders' equity but are not revenue.

EXPENSES   **Expenses** are decreases in stockholders' equity resulting from the costs of selling goods, rendering services, or performing other business activities. In other words, expenses are the costs of the goods and services used up in the course of earning revenues. Often called the *cost of doing business*, expenses include the costs of goods sold, the costs of activities necessary to carry on a business, and the costs of attracting and serving customers. Other examples are salaries, rent, advertising, telephone service, and depreciation (allocation of cost) of a building or office equipment.

Business-World Example: Income measurement is difficult in many industries because of the uncertainties associated with their revenues and expenses. For example, in the period of the sale, cereal companies must recognize the expense associated with boxtops and coupons expected to be redeemed ultimately. And construction companies must estimate their revenues based upon a project's percentage of completion.

Just as not all cash receipts are revenues, not all cash payments are expenses. A cash payment to reduce a liability does not result in an expense. The liability, however, may have come from incurring a previous expense, such as advertising, that is to be paid later. There may also be two steps before an expenditure of cash becomes an expense. For example, prepaid expenses and plant assets (such as machinery and equipment) are recorded as assets when they are acquired. Later, as their usefulness expires in the operation of the business, their cost is allocated to expenses. In fact, expenses sometimes are called *expired costs*.

Not all decreases in stockholders' equity arise from expenses. Dividends decrease stockholders' equity, but they are not expenses.

The Accounting Period Issue

OBJECTIVE

2a Explain the difficulties of income measurement caused by the accounting period issue

The **accounting period issue** addresses the difficulty of assigning revenues and expenses to a short period of time, such as a month or a year. Not all transactions can be easily assigned to specific time periods. Purchases of buildings and equipment, for example, have effects that extend over many years. Accountants solve this problem by estimating the number of years the buildings or equipment will be in use and the cost that should be assigned to each year. In the process, they make an assumption about **periodicity**: that the net income for any period of time less than the life of the business, although tentative, is still a useful estimate of the entity's profitability for the period.

Key Point: Accounting periods must be of equal length so that one period can be compared to the next.

Generally, to make comparisons easier, the time periods are of equal length. Financial statements may be prepared for any time period. Accounting periods of less than one year—for example, a month or a quarter—are called *interim periods*. The 12-month accounting period used by an organization is called its **fiscal year**. Many organizations use the calendar year, January 1 to December 31, for their fiscal year. Others find it convenient to choose a fiscal year that ends during a slack season rather than a peak season. In this case, the fiscal year corresponds to the yearly cycle of business activity. The time period should always be noted in the financial statements.

The Continuity Issue

OBJECTIVE

2b Explain the difficulties of income measurement caused by the continuity issue

The process of measuring business income requires that certain expense and revenue transactions be allocated over several accounting periods. The number of accounting periods raises the **continuity issue**. How long will the business entity last? Many businesses last less than five years; in any given year, thousands of businesses go bankrupt. To prepare financial statements for an accounting period, the accountant must make an assumption about the ability of the business to survive. Specifically, unless there is evidence to the contrary, the accountant assumes that

BUSINESS FOCUS ON PRACTICE

The table on the right shows the diverse fiscal years used by some well-known companies. Many governmental and educational units use fiscal years that end June 30 or September 30.

Company	Last Month of Fiscal Year
American Greetings Corp.	February
Caesars World Inc.	July
The Walt Disney Company	September
Eastman Kodak Company	December
Fleetwood Enterprises Inc.	April
Lorimar Syndication	March
Mattel Inc.	December
MGM-UA Communications Co.	August
Polaroid Corp.	December

the business will continue to operate indefinitely, that the business is a **going concern**. Justification for all the techniques of income measurement rests on the assumption of continuity. For example, this assumption allows the cost of certain assets to be held on the balance sheet until a future year, when it will become an expense on the income statement.

Another example has to do with the value of assets on the balance sheet. The accountant records assets at cost and does not record subsequent changes in their value. But the value of assets to a going concern is much higher than the value of assets to a firm facing bankruptcy. In the latter case, the accountant may be asked to set aside the assumption of continuity and to prepare financial statements based on the assumption that the firm will go out of business and sell all of its assets at liquidation value—that is, for what they will bring in cash.

Business-World Example: The continuity assumption is set aside when an organization is formed for a limited venture, such as a World's Fair or an Olympics.

The Matching Issue

OBJECTIVE

2c Explain the difficulties of income measurement caused by the matching issue

Key Point: Although the cash basis often is used for tax purposes, it seldom produces an accurate measurement of a business's performance for financial reporting purposes.

Revenues and expenses can be accounted for on a cash received and cash paid basis. This practice is known as the **cash basis of accounting**. Individuals and some businesses may use the cash basis of accounting for income tax purposes. Under this method, revenues are reported in the period in which cash is received, and expenses are reported in the period in which cash is paid. Taxable income, therefore, is calculated as the difference between cash receipts from revenues and cash payments for expenses.

Although the cash basis of accounting works well for some small businesses and many individuals, it does not meet the needs of most businesses. As explained above, revenues can be earned in a period other than the one in which cash is received, and expenses can be incurred in a period other than the one in which cash is paid. To measure net income adequately, revenues and expenses must be assigned to the appropriate accounting period. The accountant solves this problem by applying the **matching rule**:

Revenues must be assigned to the accounting period in which the goods are sold or the services performed, and expenses must be assigned to the accounting period in which they are used to produce revenue.

Direct cause-and-effect relationships seldom can be demonstrated for certain, but many costs appear to be related to particular revenues. The accountant recognizes these expenses and the related revenues in the same accounting period. Examples are the costs of goods sold and sales commissions. When there is no direct means of connecting expenses and revenues, the accountant tries to allocate

BUSINESS FOCUS ON ETHICS

Accounting practices are meant to inform the readers of financial statements, not to deceive them. Accounting assumptions and rules, such as the periodicity assumption and the matching rule, should not be applied in a way that will distort or obscure financial results. In recent years, Securities and Exchange Commission Chairman Arthur Levitt has been waging a public cam-

paign against corporate accounting practices that arise when companies manage or manipulate their earnings to meet Wall Street analysts' expectations. Management in these cases is fearful that a shortfall will trigger a big decline in its company's stock price. Companies, for instance, may increase expenses, inappropriately applying the matching rule and periodicity assumption by reducing earnings in a year of unusually high income and boosting income in subsequent years by reducing expenses. The SEC has challenged the accounting of many companies, including Sunbeam-Oster Company, Inc., and Cisco Systems.[2]

costs in a systematic way among the accounting periods that benefit from the costs. For example, a building is converted from an asset to an expense by allocating its cost over the years that the company benefits from its use.

Accrual Accounting

OBJECTIVE

3 Define *accrual accounting* and explain two broad ways of accomplishing it

To apply the matching rule, accountants have developed accrual accounting. **Accrual accounting** "attempts to record the financial effects on an enterprise of transactions and other events and circumstances . . . in the periods in which those transactions, events, and circumstances occur rather than only in the periods in which cash is received or paid by the enterprise."[3] That is, accrual accounting consists of all the techniques developed by accountants to apply the matching rule. It is done in two general ways: (1) by recording revenues when earned and expenses when incurred and (2) by adjusting the accounts.

Recognizing Revenues When Earned and Expenses When Incurred

The first application of accrual accounting is the recognition of revenues when earned and expenses when incurred. For example, when Joan Miller Advertising Agency, Inc., makes a sale on credit by placing advertisements for a client, revenue is recorded at the time of the sale by debiting Accounts Receivable and crediting Advertising Fees Earned. This is how the accountant recognizes the revenue from a credit sale before the cash is collected. Accounts Receivable serves as a holding account until payment is received. The process of determining when revenue is earned, and consequently when it should be recorded, is called **revenue recognition**.

When Joan Miller Advertising Agency receives its telephone bill, the expense is recognized both as having been incurred and as helping to produce revenue. The transaction is recorded by debiting Telephone Expense and crediting Accounts Payable. Until the bill is paid, Accounts Payable serves as a holding account. Notice that recognition of the expense does not depend on the payment of cash.

Adjusting the Accounts

Enrichment Note: The accountant waits until the end of an accounting period to update certain revenues and expenses even though the revenues and expenses theoretically have changed during the period. There usually is no need to adjust them until the end of the period, when the financial statements are prepared. In fact, it would be impractical, even impossible, to adjust the accounts each time they are affected.

The second application of accrual accounting is adjusting the accounts. Adjustments are necessary because the accounting period, by definition, ends on a particular day. The balance sheet must list all assets and liabilities as of the end of that day, and the income statement must contain all revenues and expenses applicable to the period ending on that day. Although operating a business is a continuous process, there must be a cutoff point for the periodic reports. Some transactions invariably span the cutoff point; thus, some accounts need adjustment.

For example, some of the accounts in the end-of-the-period trial balance for Joan Miller Advertising Agency (Exhibit 1) do not show the correct balances for preparing the financial statements. The January 31 trial balance lists prepaid rent of $800. At $400 per month, this represents rent for the months of January and February. So on January 31, one-half of the $800, or $400, represents rent expense for January; the remaining $400 represents an asset that will be used in February. An adjustment is needed to reflect the $400 balance in the Prepaid Rent account on the balance sheet and the $400 rent expense on the income statement. As you will see on the following pages, several other accounts in the Joan Miller Advertising Agency trial balance do not reflect their correct balances. Like the Prepaid Rent account, they need to be adjusted.

Joan Miller Advertising Agency, Inc.
Trial Balance
January 31, 20xx

Cash	$ 1,720	
Accounts Receivable	2,800	
Art Supplies	1,800	
Office Supplies	800	
Prepaid Rent	800	
Prepaid Insurance	480	
Art Equipment	4,200	
Office Equipment	3,000	
Accounts Payable		$ 3,170
Unearned Art Fees		1,000
Common Stock		10,000
Dividends	1,400	
Advertising Fees Earned		4,200
Wages Expense	1,200	
Utilities Expense	100	
Telephone Expense	70	
	$18,370	$18,370

Accrual Accounting and Performance Measures

Accrual accounting can be difficult to understand. The related adjustments take time to calculate and enter in the records. Also, adjusting entries do not affect cash flows in the current period because they never involve the Cash account. You might ask, "Why go to all the trouble of making them? Why worry about them?" The Securities and Exchange Commission, in fact, has identified issues related to accrual accounting and adjustments to be an area of utmost importance because of the potential for abuse and misrepresentation.[4]

All adjustments are important because they are necessary to measure key profitability performance measures. Adjusting entries affect net income on the income statement, and they affect profitability comparisons from one accounting period to the next. Adjusting entries also affect assets and liabilities on the balance sheet and thus provide information about a company's *future* cash inflows and outflows. This information is needed to assess management's short-term goal of achieving sufficient liquidity to meet its needs for cash to pay ongoing obligations. The potential for abuse arises from the fact that considerable judgment underlies the application of adjusting entries. Misuse of this judgment can result in misleading measures of performance.

The Adjustment Process

OBJECTIVE

4 State four principal situations that require adjusting entries

Accountants use **adjusting entries** to apply accrual accounting to transactions that span more than one accounting period. There are four situations in which adjusting entries are required, as illustrated in Figure 1. As shown, each situation affects one balance sheet account and one income statement account. Adjusting

**Figure 1
The Four Types of Adjustments**

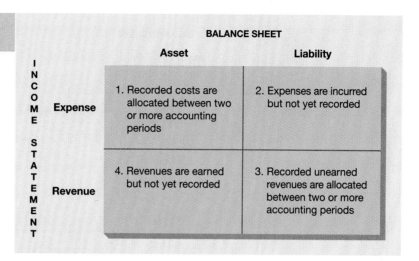

entries never involve the Cash account. The four types of adjusting entries may be stated as follows:

Key Point: Each adjusting entry must include at least one balance sheet account and one income statement account. By definition, it cannot include a debit or a credit to Cash.

1. Costs have been recorded that must be allocated between two or more accounting periods. Examples are prepaid rent, prepaid insurance, supplies, and costs of a building. The adjusting entry in this case involves an asset account and an expense account.

2. Expenses have been incurred but are not yet recorded. Examples are the wages earned by employees in the current accounting period but after the last pay period. The adjusting entry involves an expense account and a liability account.

3. Revenues have been recorded that must be allocated between two or more accounting periods. An example is payments collected for services yet to be rendered. The adjusting entry involves a liability account and a revenue account.

Key Point: If adjustments are not made, the type of operating performance measure you would have more closely resembles cash flows (cash receipts minus cash disbursements). Adjusting entries never affect cash.

4. Revenues have been earned but not yet recorded. An example is fees earned but not yet collected or billed to customers. The adjusting entry involves an asset account and a revenue account.

Accountants often refer to adjusting entries as deferrals or accruals. A **deferral** is the postponement of the recognition of an expense already paid (Type 1 adjustment) or of a revenue received in advance (Type 3 adjustment). Recording of the receipt or payment of cash precedes the adjusting entry. An **accrual** is the recognition of a revenue (Type 4 adjustment) or expense (Type 2 adjustment) that has arisen but has not yet been recorded. No cash was received or paid prior to the adjusting entry; this will occur in a future accounting period. Once again, we use Joan Miller Advertising Agency, Inc., to illustrate the kinds of adjusting entries that most businesses make.

Type 1: Allocating Recorded Costs Between Two or More Accounting Periods (Deferred Expenses)

OBJECTIVE

5 Prepare typical adjusting entries

Companies often make expenditures that benefit more than one period. These expenditures are usually debited to an asset account. At the end of the accounting period, the amount that has been used is transferred from the asset account to an expense account. Two of the more important kinds of adjustments are those for prepaid expenses and the depreciation of plant and equipment.

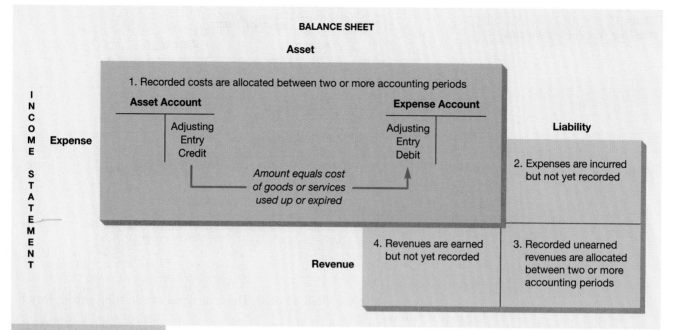

Figure 2
Adjustment for Prepaid (Deferred) Expenses

Key Point: The expired portion of a prepayment is converted to an expense; the unexpired portion remains an asset.

PREPAID EXPENSES Some expenses customarily are paid in advance. These expenditures are called **prepaid expenses**. Among them are rent, insurance, and supplies. At the end of an accounting period, a portion (or all) of these goods or services will have been used up or will have expired. An adjusting entry reducing the asset and increasing the expense, as shown in Figure 2, is always required. The amount of the adjustment equals the cost of the goods or services used up or expired. If adjusting entries for prepaid expenses are not made at the end of the period, both the balance sheet and the income statement will present incorrect information: The assets of the company will be overstated, and the expenses of the company will be understated. This means that stockholders' equity on the balance sheet and net income on the income statement will be overstated.

At the beginning of the month, Joan Miller Advertising Agency paid two months' rent in advance. This expenditure resulted in an asset consisting of the right to occupy the office for two months. As each day in the month passed, part of the asset's cost expired and became an expense. By January 31, one-half had expired and should be treated as an expense. Here is the analysis of this economic event:

Prepaid Rent (Adjustment a)

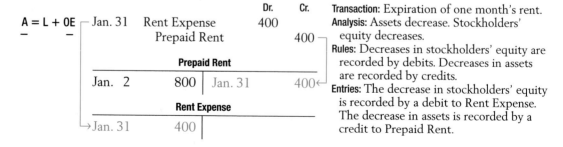

The Prepaid Rent account now has a balance of $400, which represents one month's rent paid in advance. The Rent Expense account reflects the $400 expense for the month of January.

Besides rent, Joan Miller Advertising Agency prepaid expenses for insurance, art supplies, and office supplies, all of which call for adjusting entries.

On January 8, the agency purchased a one-year life insurance policy, paying for it in advance. Like prepaid rent, prepaid insurance offers benefits (in this case, protection) that expire day by day. By the end of the month, one-twelfth of the protection had expired. The adjustment is analyzed and recorded like this:

Prepaid Insurance (Adjustment b)

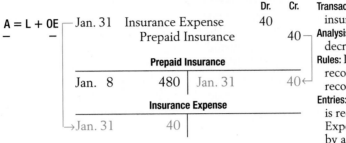

Transaction: Expiration of one month's life insurance.
Analysis: Assets decrease. Stockholders' equity decreases.
Rules: Decreases in stockholders' equity are recorded by debits. Decreases in assets are recorded by credits.
Entries: The decrease in stockholders' equity is recorded by a debit to Insurance Expense. The decrease in assets is recorded by a credit to Prepaid Insurance.

The Prepaid Insurance account now shows the correct balance, $440, and Insurance Expense reflects the expired cost, $40 for the month of January.

Early in the month, Joan Miller Advertising Agency, Inc., purchased art supplies and office supplies. As Joan Miller prepared advertising designs for various clients, art supplies were consumed, and her secretary used office supplies. There is no need to account for these supplies every day because the financial statements are not prepared until the end of the month and the recordkeeping would involve too much work. Instead, Joan Miller makes a careful inventory of the art and office supplies at the end of the month. This inventory records the number and cost of those supplies that are still assets of the company—that are yet to be consumed.

Key Point: Notice that the cost of supplies consumed is inferred, not observed.

Suppose the inventory shows that art supplies costing $1,300 and office supplies costing $600 are still on hand. This means that of the $1,800 of art supplies originally purchased, $500 worth were used up (became an expense) in January. Of the original $800 of office supplies, $200 worth were consumed. These transactions are analyzed and recorded as follows:

Art Supplies and Office Supplies (Adjustments c and d)

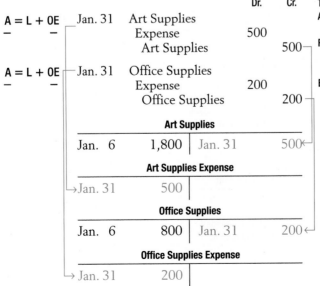

Transaction: Consumption of supplies.
Analysis: Assets decrease. Stockholders' equity decreases.
Rules: Decreases in stockholders' equity are recorded by debits. Decreases in assets are recorded by credits.
Entries: The decreases in stockholders' equity are recorded by debits to Art Supplies Expense and Office Supplies Expense. The decreases in assets are recorded by credits to Art Supplies and Office Supplies.

The asset accounts Art Supplies and Office Supplies now reflect the correct balances, $1,300 and $600, respectively, of supplies that are yet to be consumed. In addition, the amount of art supplies used up during the month of January is shown as $500, and the amount of office supplies used up is shown as $200.

Key Point: In accounting, depreciation refers only to the *allocation* of an asset's cost, not to the decline in its value.

Key Point: The difficulty in estimating an asset's useful life is further evidence that the bottom-line figure is, at best, an estimate.

DEPRECIATION OF PLANT AND EQUIPMENT When a company buys a long-term asset—a building, trucks, computers, store fixtures, or furniture—it is, in effect, prepaying for the usefulness of that asset for as long as it benefits the company. Because a long-term asset is a deferral of an expense, the accountant must allocate the cost of the asset over its estimated useful life. The amount allocated to any one accounting period is called **depreciation** or *depreciation expense*. Depreciation, like other expenses, is incurred during an accounting period to produce revenue.

It is often impossible to tell how long an asset will last or how much of the asset is used in any one period. For this reason, depreciation must be estimated. Accountants have developed a number of methods for estimating depreciation and for dealing with the related complex problems. Here we look at the simplest case, depreciation on the art and office equipment for Joan Miller Advertising Agency, Inc.

Art Equipment and Office Equipment (Adjustments e and f)

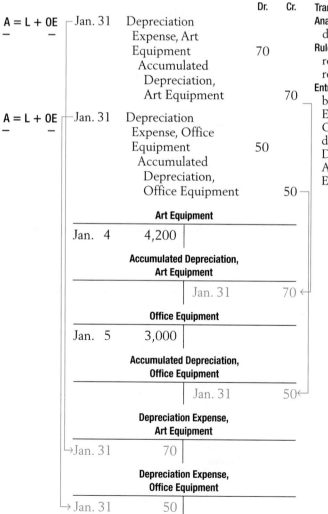

Transaction: Recording depreciation expense.
Analysis: Assets decrease. Stockholders' equity decreases.
Rules: Decreases in stockholders' equity are recorded by debits. Decreases in assets are recorded by credits.
Entries: The stockholders' equity is decreased by debits to Depreciation Expense, Art Equipment and Depreciation Expense, Office Equipment. The assets are decreased by credits to Accumulated Depreciation, Art Equipment and Accumulated Depreciation, Office Equipment.

Suppose, for example, that Joan Miller estimates that the art equipment and office equipment for which she paid $4,200 and $3,000, respectively, will last five years (60 months) and will have zero value at the end of that time. The monthly depreciation of art equipment and office equipment is $70 ($4,200 ÷ 60 months) and $50 ($3,000 ÷ 60 months), respectively. These amounts represent the costs allocated to January, and they are the amounts by which the asset accounts must be reduced and the expense accounts increased (reducing stockholders' equity).

ACCUMULATED DEPRECIATION—A CONTRA ACCOUNT   Notice that in the previous analysis, the asset accounts are not credited directly. Instead, as shown in Figure 3, new accounts—Accumulated Depreciation, Art Equipment and Accumulated Depreciation, Office Equipment—are credited. These **accumulated**

Figure 3
Adjustment for Depreciation

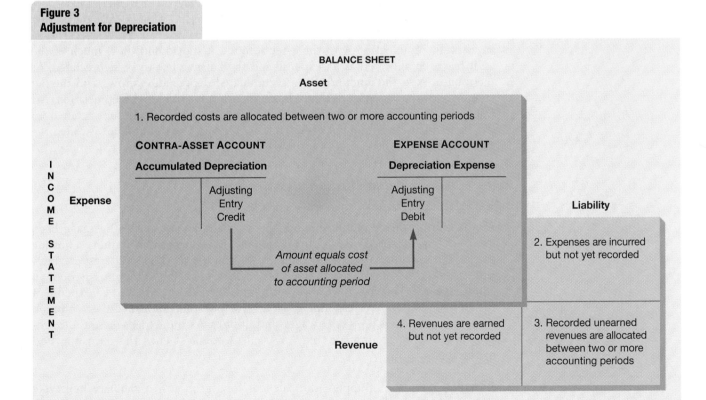

Exhibit 2
Plant and Equipment Section of the Balance Sheet

Joan Miller Advertising Agency, Inc.
Partial Balance Sheet
January 31, 20xx

Plant and Equipment		
Art Equipment	$4,200	
Less Accumulated Depreciation	70	$4,130
Office Equipment	$3,000	
Less Accumulated Depreciation	50	2,950
Total Plant and Equipment		$7,080

depreciation accounts are contra-asset accounts used to total the past depreciation expense on specific long-term assets. A **contra account** is a separate account that is paired with a related account—in this case an asset account. The balance of the contra account is shown on the financial statement as a deduction from the related account.

There are several types of contra accounts. In this case, the balance of Accumulated Depreciation, Art Equipment is shown on the balance sheet as a deduction from the associated account Art Equipment. Likewise, Accumulated Depreciation, Office Equipment is a deduction from Office Equipment. Exhibit 2 shows the plant and equipment section of the balance sheet for Joan Miller Advertising Agency, Inc., after these adjusting entries have been made.

A contra account is used for two very good reasons. First, it recognizes that depreciation is an estimate. Second, a contra account preserves the original cost of an asset: In combination with the asset account, it shows both how much of the asset has been allocated as an expense and the balance left to be depreciated. As the months pass, the amount of the accumulated depreciation grows, and the net amount shown as an asset declines. In six months, Accumulated Depreciation, Art Equipment will show a balance of $420; when this amount is subtracted from Art Equipment, a net amount of $3,780 will remain. The net amount is called the **carrying value**, or *book value*, of the asset.

Type 2: Recognizing Unrecorded Expenses (Accrued Expenses)

At the end of an accounting period, there usually are expenses that have been incurred but not recorded in the accounts. These expenses require adjusting entries. One such case is interest on borrowed money. Each day, interest accumulates on the debt. As shown in Figure 4, at the end of the accounting period, an adjusting entry is made to record this accumulated interest, which is an expense of the period, and the corresponding liability to pay the interest. Other common unrecorded expenses are taxes, wages, and utilities. As the expense and the corresponding liability accumulate, they are said to *accrue*—hence the term **accrued expenses**.

ACCRUED WAGES   Suppose the calendar for the month of January looks like the calendar that follows.

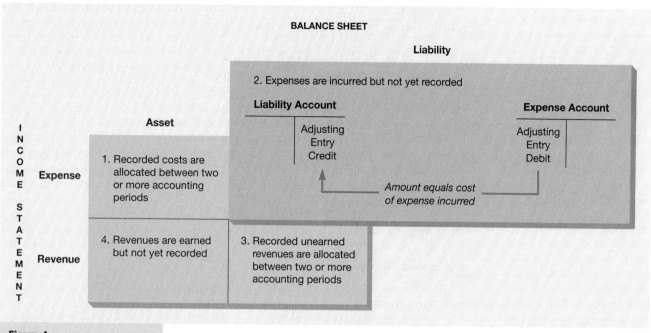

Figure 4
Adjustment for Unrecorded (Accrued) Expenses

January

Su	M	T	W	Th	F	Sa
	1	2	3	4	5	6
7	8	9	10	11	12	13
14	15	16	17	18	19	20
21	22	23	24	25	26	27
28	29	30	31			

By the end of business on January 31, the secretary at Joan Miller Advertising Agency, Inc., will have worked three days (Monday, Tuesday, and Wednesday) beyond the last biweekly pay period, which ended on January 26. The employee has earned the wages for these days, but she will not be paid until the regular payday in February. The wages for these three days are rightfully an expense for January, and the liabilities should reflect the fact that the company owes the secretary for those days. Because the secretary's wage rate is $600 every two weeks, or $60 per day ($600 ÷ 10 working days), the expense is $180 ($60 × 3 days).

Accrued Wages (Adjustment g)

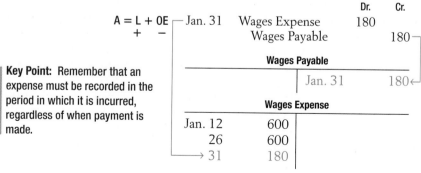

Key Point: Remember that an expense must be recorded in the period in which it is incurred, regardless of when payment is made.

Transaction: Accrual of unrecorded expense.
Analysis: Liabilities increase. Stockholders' equity decreases.
Rules: Decreases in stockholders' equity are recorded by debits. Increases in liabilities are recorded by credits.
Entries: The decrease in stockholders' equity is recorded by a debit to Wages Expense. The increase in liabilities is recorded by a credit to Wages Payable.

The liability of $180 is now reflected correctly in the Wages Payable account. The actual expense incurred for wages during January, $1,380, is also correct.

ESTIMATED INCOME TAXES   As a corporation, Joan Miller Advertising Agency, Inc., is subject to federal income taxes. Although the actual amount owed cannot be determined until after net income is computed at the end of the fiscal year, each month should bear its part of the total year's expense, in accordance with the matching concept. Therefore, the amount of income taxes expense for the current month must be estimated. Assume that after analyzing the first month's operations and conferring with her CPA, Joan Miller estimates January's share of federal income taxes for the year to be $400. This estimated expense can be analyzed and recorded as shown below.

Estimated Income Taxes (Adjustment h)

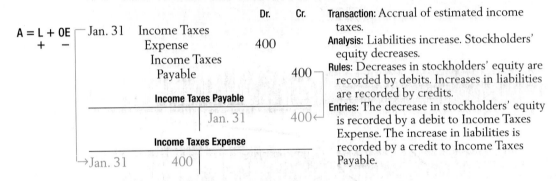

Expenses for January will now reflect the estimated income taxes attributable to that month, and the liability for these estimated income taxes will appear on the balance sheet.

Type 3: Allocating Recorded Unearned Revenues Between Two or More Accounting Periods (Deferred Revenues)

Key Point: Unearned Revenue is a liability because there is an obligation either to deliver goods or perform a service, or to return the payment. Once the goods have been delivered or the service performed, the liability is converted into revenue.

Just as expenses can be paid before they are used, revenues can be received before they are earned. When revenues are received in advance, the company has an obligation to deliver goods or perform services. Therefore, **unearned revenues** are shown in a liability account. For example, publishing companies usually receive payment in advance for magazine subscriptions. These receipts are recorded in a liability account. If the company fails to deliver the magazines, subscribers are entitled to their money back. As the company delivers each issue of the magazine, it earns a part of the advance payments. This earned portion must be transferred from the Unearned Subscriptions account to the Subscription Revenue account, as shown in Figure 5.

During the month of January, Joan Miller Advertising Agency received $1,000 as an advance payment for advertising designs to be prepared for another agency. Assume that by the end of the month, $400 of the design was completed and accepted by the other agency. Here is the transaction analysis:

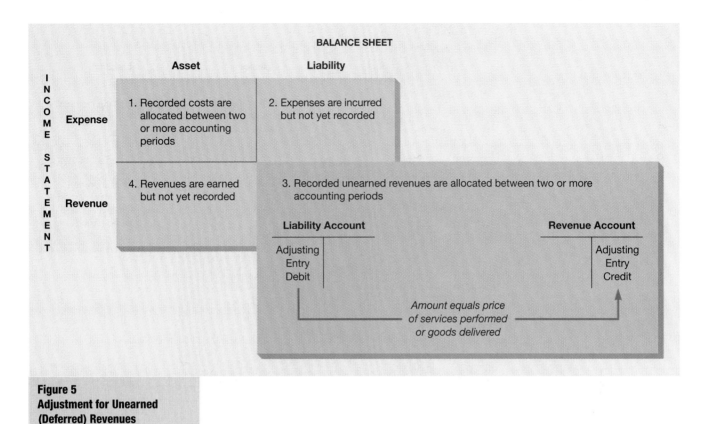

Figure 5
Adjustment for Unearned (Deferred) Revenues

Unearned Art Fees (Adjustment i)

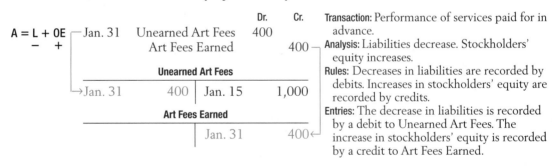

The liability account Unearned Art Fees now reflects the amount of work still to be performed, $600. The revenue account Art Fees Earned reflects the services performed and the revenue earned for them during January, $400.

Type 4: Recognizing Unrecorded Revenues (Accrued Revenues)

Accrued revenues are revenues for which a service has been performed or goods delivered but for which no entry has been recorded. Any revenues that have been earned but not recorded during the accounting period call for an adjusting entry that debits an asset account and credits a revenue account, as shown in Figure 6. For example, the interest on a note receivable is earned day by day but may not be received until another accounting period. Interest Receivable should be debited

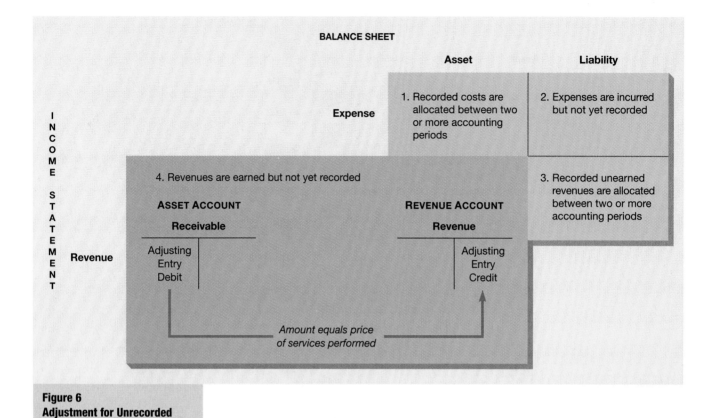

BALANCE SHEET

Figure 6
Adjustment for Unrecorded (Accrued) Revenues

and Interest Income should be credited for the interest accrued at the end of the current period.

Suppose that Joan Miller Advertising Agency, Inc., has agreed to place a series of advertisements for Marsh Tire Company and that the first appears on January 31, the last day of the month. The fee of $200 for this advertisement, which has been earned but not recorded, should be recorded this way:

Accrued Advertising Fees (Adjustment j)

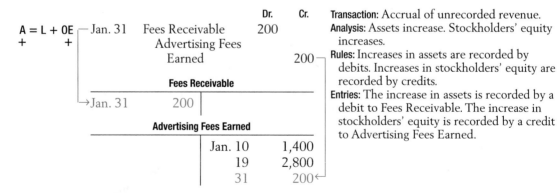

Now both the asset and the revenue accounts show the correct balance: The $200 in Fees Receivable is owed to the company, and the $4,400 in Advertising Fees Earned has been earned by the company during January. Marsh Tire Company will be billed for the series of advertisements when they are completed.

BUSINESS FOCUS ON TECHNOLOGY

By now, everyone has heard of the "Y2K Bug" or Y2K issue. Why did it arise? In the accounting records, most accountants abbreviate the year by using the last two digits of the year, and most computer systems are programmed to handle dates the same way. For example, the year 1997 is written 97. But what happens after the year 2000? What will 04 represent? Is it 1904 or 2004?

Most computer systems assume it is 1904. If a debt is due in 04, the computer cannot figure out how long it is until it is due because 1904 minus 1997 gives a non-sense answer. Most companies worried about compliance with Y2K. In fact, the American Institute of CPAs had identified the Y2K issue as the number-one technology issue on its Top Ten Technologies list. Companies spent huge amounts of money, estimated to be $600 billion, to solve the problem.[5] In the end, Y2K turned out not to be a major problem because of the precautions taken.

A Note About Journal Entries

Thus far we have presented a full analysis of each journal entry. The analyses showed you the thought process behind each entry. By now, you should be fully aware of the effects of transactions on the accounting equation and the rules of debit and credit. For this reason, in the rest of the book, journal entries are presented without full analysis.

Using the Adjusted Trial Balance to Prepare Financial Statements

OBJECTIVE

6 Prepare financial statements from an adjusted trial balance

After adjusting entries have been recorded and posted, an **adjusted trial balance** is prepared by listing all accounts and their balances. If the adjusting entries have been posted to the accounts correctly, the adjusted trial balance should have equal debit and credit totals.

The adjusted trial balance for Joan Miller Advertising Agency, Inc., is shown on the left side of Exhibit 3. Notice that some accounts, such as Cash and Accounts Receivable, have the same balances they have in the trial balance (see Exhibit 1) because no adjusting entries affected them. Some new accounts, such as Fees Receivable, depreciation accounts, and Wages Payable, appear in the adjusted trial balance, and other accounts, such as Art Supplies, Office Supplies, Prepaid Rent, and Prepaid Insurance, have balances different from those in the trial balance because adjusting entries did affect them.

Key Point: The adjusted trial balance is a second check that the ledger is still in balance. Because it reflects updated information from the adjusting entries, it may be used to prepare the formal financial statements.

From the adjusted trial balance, the financial statements can be easily prepared. The income statement is prepared from the revenue and expense accounts, as shown in Exhibit 3. Then, as shown in Exhibit 4, the statement of retained earnings and the balance sheet are prepared. Notice that the net income from the income statement is combined with dividends on the statement of retained earnings to give the net change in Joan Miller Advertising Agency's Retained Earnings account. The resulting balance of Retained Earnings at January 31 is used on the balance sheet, as are the asset and liability accounts.

Exhibit 3
Relationship of Adjusted Trial Balance to Income Statement

Joan Miller Advertising Agency, Inc. Adjusted Trial Balance January 31, 20xx		
Cash	$ 1,720	
Accounts Receivable	2,800	
Fees Receivable	200	
Art Supplies	1,300	
Office Supplies	600	
Prepaid Rent	400	
Prepaid Insurance	440	
Art Equipment	4,200	
Accumulated Depreciation, Art Equipment		$ 70
Office Equipment	3,000	
Accumulated Depreciation, Office Equipment		50
Accounts Payable		3,170
Unearned Art Fees		600
Wages Payable		180
Income Taxes Payable		400
Common Stock		10,000
Dividends	1,400	
Advertising Fees Earned		4,400
Art Fees Earned		400
Wages Expense	1,380	
Utilities Expense	100	
Telephone Expense	70	
Rent Expense	400	
Insurance Expense	40	
Art Supplies Expense	500	
Office Supplies Expense	200	
Depreciation Expense, Art Equipment	70	
Depreciation Expense, Office Equipment	50	
Income Taxes Expense	400	
	$19,270	$19,270

Joan Miller Advertising Agency, Inc. Income Statement For the Month Ended January 31, 20xx		
Revenues		
Advertising Fees Earned		$4,400
Art Fees Earned		400
Total Revenues		$4,800
Expenses		
Wages Expense	$1,380	
Utilities Expense	100	
Telephone Expense	70	
Rent Expense	400	
Insurance Expense	40	
Art Supplies Expense	500	
Office Supplies Expense	200	
Depreciation Expense, Art Equipment	70	
Depreciation Expense, Office Equipment	50	
Income Taxes Expense	400	
Total Expenses		3,210
Net Income		$1,590

Key Point: The income statement is prepared before the statement of retained earnings, and that statement before the balance sheet, because the net income figure is needed to prepare the statement of retained earnings and the bottom-line figure of the statement of retained earnings is needed to prepare the balance sheet.

Cash Flows from Accrual-Based Information

SUPPLEMENTAL OBJECTIVE

7 Analyze cash flows from accrual-based information

Management has the short-range goal of achieving sufficient liquidity to meet its needs for cash to pay its ongoing obligations. It is important for managers to be able to use accrual-based financial information to analyze cash flows in order to plan payments to creditors and assess the need for short-term borrowing.

Every revenue or expense account on the income statement has one or more related accounts on the balance sheet. For instance, Supplies Expense is related to

Exhibit 4

Relationship of Adjusted Trial Balance to Balance Sheet and Statement of Retained Earnings

Joan Miller Advertising Agency, Inc.
Adjusted Trial Balance
January 31, 20xx

Cash	$ 1,720	
Accounts Receivable	2,800	
Fees Receivable	200	
Art Supplies	1,300	
Office Supplies	600	
Prepaid Rent	400	
Prepaid Insurance	440	
Art Equipment	4,200	
Accumulated Depreciation, Art Equipment		$ 70
Office Equipment	3,000	
Accumulated Depreciation, Office Equipment		50
Accounts Payable		3,170
Unearned Art Fees		600
Wages Payable		180
Income Taxes Payable		400
Common Stock		10,000
Dividends	1,400	
Advertising Fees Earned		4,400
Art Fees Earned		400
Wages Expense	1,380	
Utilities Expense	100	
Telephone Expense	70	
Rent Expense	400	
Insurance Expense	40	
Art Supplies Expense	500	
Office Supplies Expense	200	
Depreciation Expense, Art Equipment	70	
Depreciation Expense, Office Equipment	50	
Income Taxes Expense	400	
	$19,270	$19,270

Joan Miller Advertising Agency, Inc.
Balance Sheet
January 31, 20xx

Assets

Cash		$ 1,720
Accounts Receivable		2,800
Fees Receivable		200
Art Supplies		1,300
Office Supplies		600
Prepaid Rent		400
Prepaid Insurance		440
Art Equipment	$ 4,200	
Less Accumulated Depreciation	70	4,130
Office Equipment	$ 3,000	
Less Accumulated Depreciation	50	2,950
Total Assets		$14,540

Liabilities

Accounts Payable	$ 3,170
Unearned Art Fees	600
Wages Payable	180
Income Taxes Payable	400
Total Liabilities	$ 4,350

Stockholders' Equity

Common Stock	$10,000	
Retained Earnings	190	
Total Stockholders' Equity		10,190
Total Liabilities and Stockholders' Equity		$14,540

Joan Miller Advertising Agency, Inc.
Statement of Retained Earnings
For the Month Ended January 31, 20xx

Retained Earnings, January 1, 20xx	—
Net Income	$1,590
Subtotal	$1,590
Less Dividends	1,400
Retained Earnings, January 31, 20xx	$ 190

From Income Statement in Exhibit 3

Key Point: Notice that the adjusted trial balance figure for Retained Earnings does not reflect net income or dividends during the period. The balance is updated when the closing entries are prepared.

Supplies, Wages Expense to Wages Payable, and Art Fees Earned to Unearned Art Fees. As shown in this chapter, these accounts are related through adjusting entries whose purpose is to apply the matching rule in the measurement of net income. The cash flows generated or paid by company operations may also be determined by analyzing these relationships. For example, suppose that after receiving the financial statements in Exhibits 3 and 4, management wants to know how much cash was expended for art supplies. On the income statement, Art Supplies Expense is $500, and on the balance sheet, Art Supplies is $1,300. Because January was the first month of operation for the company, there was no prior balance of art supplies, so the amount of cash expended for art supplies during the month was $1,800. The cash flow used to purchase art supplies ($1,800) was much greater than the amount expensed in determining income ($500). In planning for February, management can anticipate that the cash needed may be less than the amount expensed because, given the large inventory of art supplies, it will probably not be necessary to buy art supplies for more than a month. Understanding these cash flow effects enables management to better predict the business's need for cash during February.

The general rule for determining the cash flow received from any revenue or paid for any expense (except depreciation, which is a special case not covered here) is to determine the potential cash payments or cash receipts and deduct the amount not paid or received. The application of the general rule varies with the type of asset or liability account, which is shown as follows:

Type of Account	Potential Payment or Receipt	Not Paid or Received	Result
Prepaid Expense	Ending Balance + Expense for the Period	− Beginning Balance	= Cash Payments for Expenses
Unearned Revenue	Ending Balance + Revenue for the Period	− Beginning Balance	= Cash Receipts from Revenues
Accrued Payable	Beginning Balance + Expense for the Period	− Ending Balance	= Cash Payments for Expenses
Accrued Receivable	Beginning Balance + Revenue for the Period	− Ending Balance	= Cash Receipts from Revenues

For instance, assume that on May 31 a company had a balance of $480 in Prepaid Insurance and that on June 30 the balance was $670. If the insurance expense during June was $120, the amount of cash expended on insurance during June can be computed as follows:

Prepaid Insurance at June 30	$670
Insurance Expense during June	120
Potential cash payments for insurance	$790
Less Prepaid Insurance at May 31	480
Cash payments for insurance during June	$310

The beginning balance is deducted because it was paid in a prior accounting period. Note that the cash payments equal the expense plus the increase in the balance of the Prepaid Insurance account [$120 + ($670 − $480) = $310]. In this case, the cash paid was almost three times the amount of insurance expense. In future months, cash payments are likely to be less than the expense.

Chapter Review

REVIEW OF LEARNING OBJECTIVES

1. **Define *net income* and its two major components, *revenues* and *expenses*.** Net income is the net increase in stockholders' equity that results from the operations of a company. Net income equals revenues minus expenses, unless expenses exceed revenues, in which case a net loss results. Revenues

equal the price of goods sold and services rendered during a specific period. Expenses are the costs of goods and services used up in the process of producing revenues.

2. **Explain the difficulties of income measurement caused by (a) the accounting period issue, (b) the continuity issue, and (c) the matching issue.** The accounting period issue recognizes that net income measurements for short periods of time are necessarily tentative. The continuity issue recognizes that even though businesses face an uncertain future, without evidence to the contrary, accountants must assume that a business will continue indefinitely. The matching issue has to do with the difficulty of assigning revenues and expenses to a period of time. It is addressed by applying the matching rule: Revenues must be assigned to the accounting period in which the goods are sold or the services performed, and expenses must be assigned to the accounting period in which they are used to produce revenue.

3. **Define *accrual accounting* and explain two broad ways of accomplishing it.** Accrual accounting consists of all the techniques developed by accountants to apply the matching rule. The two general ways of accomplishing accrual accounting are (1) by recognizing revenues when earned and expenses when incurred and (2) by adjusting the accounts.

4. **State four principal situations that require adjusting entries.** Adjusting entries are required (1) when recorded costs have to be allocated between two or more accounting periods, (2) when unrecorded expenses exist, (3) when recorded unearned revenues must be allocated between two or more accounting periods, and (4) when unrecorded revenues exist.

5. **Prepare typical adjusting entries.** The preparation of adjusting entries is summarized in the following table:

Type of Adjusting Entry	Type of Account		Balance Sheet Account Examples
	Debited	Credited	
1. Allocating recorded costs (previously paid, expired)	Expense	Asset (or contra-asset)	Prepaid Rent Prepaid Insurance Supplies Accumulated Depreciation, Buildings Accumulated Depreciation, Equipment
2. Accrued expenses (incurred, not paid)	Expense	Liability	Wages Payable Income Taxes Payable
3. Allocating recorded unearned revenues (previously received, earned)	Liability	Revenue	Unearned Art Fees
4. Accrued revenues (earned, not received)	Asset	Revenue	Fees Receivable Interest Receivable

6. **Prepare financial statements from an adjusted trial balance.** An adjusted trial balance is prepared after adjusting entries have been posted to the accounts. Its purpose is to test whether the adjusting entries are posted correctly

before the financial statements are prepared. The income statement is prepared from the revenue and expense accounts in the adjusted trial balance. The balance sheet is prepared from the asset and liability accounts in the adjusted trial balance and from the statement of retained earnings.

SUPPLEMENTAL OBJECTIVE

7. Analyze cash flows from accrual-based information. Cash flow information bears on management's liquidity goal. The general rule for determining the cash flow effect of any revenue or expense (except depreciation, which is a special case not covered here) is to determine the potential cash payments or cash receipts and deduct the amount not paid or received.

REVIEW OF CONCEPTS AND TERMINOLOGY

The following concepts and terms were introduced in this chapter:

LO 2   **Accounting period issue:** The difficulty of assigning revenues and expenses to a short period of time.

LO 4   **Accrual:** The recognition of an expense or revenue that has arisen but has not yet been recorded.

LO 3   **Accrual accounting:** The attempt to record the financial effects of transactions and other events in the periods in which those transactions or events occur, rather than only in the periods in which cash is received or paid by the business; all the techniques developed by accountants to apply the matching rule.

LO 5   **Accrued expenses:** Expenses that have been incurred but are not recognized in the accounts; unrecorded expenses.

LO 5   **Accrued revenues:** Revenues for which a service has been performed or goods delivered but for which no entry has been made; unrecorded revenues.

LO 5   **Accumulated depreciation accounts:** Contra-asset accounts used to accumulate the depreciation expense of specific long-lived assets.

LO 6   **Adjusted trial balance:** A trial balance prepared after all adjusting entries have been recorded and posted to the accounts.

LO 4   **Adjusting entries:** Entries made to apply accrual accounting to transactions that span more than one accounting period.

LO 5   **Carrying value:** The unexpired portion of the cost of an asset. Also called *book value.*

LO 2   **Cash basis of accounting:** Accounting for revenues and expenses on a cash received and cash paid basis.

LO 2   **Continuity issue:** The difficulty associated with not knowing how long a business entity will survive.

LO 5   **Contra account:** An account whose balance is subtracted from an associated account in the financial statements.

LO 4   **Deferral:** The postponement of the recognition of an expense that already has been paid or of a revenue that already has been received.

LO 5   **Depreciation:** The portion of the cost of a tangible long-term asset allocated to any one accounting period. Also called *depreciation expense.*

LO 1   **Expenses:** Decreases in stockholders' equity resulting from the costs of goods and services used up in the course of earning revenues. Also called *cost of doing business* or *expired costs.*

LO 2   **Fiscal year:** Any 12-month accounting period used by an economic entity.

LO 2   **Going concern:** The assumption, unless there is evidence to the contrary, that a business entity will continue to operate indefinitely.

LO 2   **Matching rule:** Revenues must be assigned to the accounting period in which the goods are sold or the services performed, and expenses must be assigned to the accounting period in which they are used to produce revenue.

LO 1   **Net income:** The net increase in stockholders' equity that results from business operations and is accumulated in the Retained Earnings account; revenues less expenses when revenues exceed expenses.

LO 1   **Net loss:** The net decrease in stockholders' equity that results from business operations when expenses exceed revenues. It is accumulated in the Retained Earnings account.

LO 2   **Periodicity:** The recognition that net income for any period less than the life of the business, although tentative, is still a useful measure.

LO 5   **Prepaid expenses:** Expenses paid in advance that have not yet expired; an asset account.

LO 1   **Profit:** The increase in stockholders' equity that results from business operations.

LO 3   **Revenue recognition:** In accrual accounting, the process of determining when revenue is earned.

LO 1   **Revenues:** Increases in stockholders' equity resulting from selling goods, rendering services, or performing other business activities.

LO 5   **Unearned revenues:** Revenues received in advance for which the goods have not yet been delivered or the services performed; a liability account.

REVIEW PROBLEM

Determining Adjusting Entries, Posting to T Accounts, Preparing Adjusted Trial Balance, and Preparing Financial Statements

LO 5
LO 6   The following is the unadjusted trial balance for Certified Answering Service, Inc., on December 31, 20x2:

Certified Answering Service, Inc.
Trial Balance
December 31, 20x2

Cash	$2,160	
Accounts Receivable	1,250	
Office Supplies	180	
Prepaid Insurance	240	
Office Equipment	3,400	
Accumulated Depreciation, Office Equipment		$ 600
Accounts Payable		700
Unearned Revenue		460
Common Stock		2,000
Retained Earnings		2,870
Dividends	400	
Answering Service Revenue		2,900
Wages Expense	1,500	
Rent Expense	400	
	$9,530	$9,530

The following information is also available:

a. Insurance that expired during December amounted to $40.
b. Office supplies on hand at the end of December totaled $75.
c. Depreciation for the month of December totaled $100.
d. Accrued wages at the end of December totaled $120.
e. Revenues earned for services performed in December but not yet billed on December 31 totaled $300.

f. Revenues earned in December for services performed that were paid in advance totaled $160.

g. Income taxes for December are estimated to be $250.

1. Prepare T accounts for the accounts in the trial balance and enter the balances.

2. Determine the required adjusting entries and record them directly to the T accounts. Open new T accounts as needed.

3. Prepare an adjusted trial balance.

4. Prepare an income statement, a statement of retained earnings, and a balance sheet for the month ended December 31, 20x2.

ANSWER TO REVIEW PROBLEM

1. T accounts set up and amounts from trial balance entered

2. Adjusting entries recorded

Cash			Accounts Receivable			Service Revenue Receivable		
Bal.	2,160		Bal.	1,250		(e)	300	

Office Supplies			Prepaid Insurance			Office Equipment		
Bal.	180	(b) 105	Bal.	240	(a) 40	Bal.	3,400	
Bal.	75		Bal.	200				

Accumulated Depreciation, Office Equipment			Accounts Payable			Unearned Revenue		
		Bal. 600			Bal. 700	(f)	160	Bal. 460
		(c) 100						Bal. 300
		Bal. 700						

Wages Payable			Income Taxes Payable			Common Stock		
		(d) 120			(g) 250			Bal. 2,000

Retained Earnings			Dividends			Answering Service Revenue		
		Bal. 2,870	Bal.	400				Bal. 2,900
								(e) 300
								(f) 160
								Bal. 3,360

Wages Expense			Rent Expense			Insurance Expense		
Bal.	1,500		Bal.	400		(a)	40	
(d)	120							
Bal.	1,620							

Office Supplies Expense			Depreciation Expense, Office Equipment			Income Taxes Expense		
(b)	105		(c)	100		(g)	250	

3. Adjusted trial balance prepared

Certified Answering Service, Inc. Adjusted Trial Balance December 31, 20x2		
Cash	$ 2,160	
Accounts Receivable	1,250	
Service Revenue Receivable	300	
Office Supplies	75	
Prepaid Insurance	200	
Office Equipment	3,400	
Accumulated Depreciation, Office Equipment		$ 700
Accounts Payable		700
Unearned Revenue		300
Wages Payable		120
Income Taxes Payable		250
Common Stock		2,000
Retained Earnings		2,870
Dividends	400	
Answering Service Revenue		3,360
Wages Expense	1,620	
Rent Expense	400	
Insurance Expense	40	
Office Supplies Expense	105	
Depreciation Expense, Office Equipment	100	
Income Taxes Expense	250	
	$10,300	$10,300

4. Financial statements prepared

Certified Answering Service, Inc. Income Statement For the Month Ended December 31, 20x2		
Revenues		
Answering Service Revenue		$3,360
Expenses		
Wages Expense	$1,620	
Rent Expense	400	
Insurance Expense	40	
Office Supplies Expense	105	
Depreciation Expense, Office Equipment	100	
Income Taxes Expense	250	
Total Expenses		2,515
Net Income		$ 845

Certified Answering Service, Inc.
Statement of Retained Earnings
For the Month Ended December 31, 20x2

Retained Earnings, November 30, 20x2	$2,870
Net Income	845
Subtotal	$3,715
Less Dividends	400
Retained Earnings, December 31, 20x2	$3,315

Certified Answering Service, Inc.
Balance Sheet
December 31, 20x2

Assets

Cash		$2,160
Accounts Receivable		1,250
Service Revenue Receivable		300
Office Supplies		75
Prepaid Insurance		200
Office Equipment	$3,400	
Less Accumulated Depreciation	700	2,700
Total Assets		$6,685

Liabilities

Accounts Payable	$ 700
Unearned Revenue	300
Wages Payable	120
Income Taxes Payable	250
Total Liabilities	$1,370

Stockholders' Equity

Common Stock	$2,000	
Retained Earnings	3,315	
Total Stockholders' Equity		5,315
Total Liabilities and Stockholders' Equity		$6,685

Chapter Assignments

BUILDING YOUR KNOWLEDGE FOUNDATION

QUESTIONS

1. Why does the accountant use the term *net income* instead of *profit*?
2. Define the terms *revenues* and *expenses*.
3. Why does the need for an accounting period cause problems?
4. What is the significance of the continuity assumption?

5. "The matching rule is the most significant concept in accounting." Do you agree with this statement? Explain your answer.

6. What is the difference between the cash basis and the accrual basis of accounting?

7. In what two ways is accrual accounting accomplished?

8. Why are adjusting entries necessary?

9. What are the four situations that require adjusting entries? Give an example of each.

10. "Some assets are expenses that have not expired." Explain this statement.

11. What do plant and equipment, office supplies, and prepaid insurance have in common?

12. What is the difference between accumulated depreciation and depreciation expense?

13. What is a contra account? Give an example.

14. Why are contra accounts used to record depreciation?

15. How does unearned revenue arise? Give an example.

16. Where does unearned revenue appear in the financial statements?

17. What accounting problem does a magazine publisher who sells three-year subscriptions have?

18. Under what circumstances does a company have accrued revenues? Give an example. What asset arises when the adjustment is made?

19. What is an accrued expense? Give two examples.

20. "Why worry about adjustments? Doesn't it all come out in the wash?" Discuss these questions.

21. Why is the income statement usually the first statement prepared from the adjusted trial balance?

22. To what management goals do the measurements of net income and cash flow relate?

SHORT EXERCISES

SE 1.

LO 2 **Accrual Accounting**
LO 3 **Concepts**

Match the concepts of accrual accounting on the right with the assumptions or actions on the left.

1. Assumes expenses can be assigned to the accounting period in which they are used to produce revenues
2. Assumes a business will last indefinitely
3. Assumes revenues are earned at a point in time
4. Assumes net income measured for a short period of time, such as one quarter, is a useful measure

a. Periodicity
b. Going concern
c. Matching rule
d. Revenue recognition

SE 2.

LO 5 **Adjustment for Prepaid Insurance**

The Prepaid Insurance account began the year with a balance of $230. During the year, insurance in the amount of $570 was purchased. At the end of the year (December 31), the amount of insurance still unexpired was $350. Make the year-end entry in journal form to record the adjustment for insurance expense for the year.

SE 3.

LO 5 **Adjustment for Supplies**

The Supplies account began the year with a balance of $190. During the year, supplies in the amount of $490 were purchased. At the end of the year (December 31), the inventory of supplies on hand was $220. Make the year-end entry in journal form to record the adjustment for supplies expense for the year.

SE 4.

LO 5 **Adjustment for Depreciation**

The depreciation expense on office equipment for the month of March is $50. This is the third month that the office equipment, which cost $950, has been owned. Prepare the adjusting entry in journal form to record depreciation for March and show the balance sheet presentation for office equipment and related accounts after the adjustment.

SE 5.

LO 5 **Adjustment for Accrued Wages**

Wages are paid each Saturday for a six-day work week. Wages are currently running $690 per week. Make the adjusting entry required on June 30, assuming July 1 falls on a Tuesday.

SE 6.

LO 5 Adjustment for Unearned Revenue

During the month of August, deposits in the amount of $550 were received for services to be performed. By the end of the month, services in the amount of $380 had been performed. Prepare the necessary adjustment for Service Revenue at the end of the month.

SE 7.

LO 6 Preparation of an Income Statement from an Adjusted Trial Balance

The adjusted trial balance for Heller Company on December 31, 20x1, contains the following accounts and balances: Retained Earnings, $4,300; Dividends, $350; Service Revenue, $2,600; Rent Expense, $400; Wages Expense, $900; Utilities Expense, $200; Telephone Expense, $50; and Income Taxes Expense, $350. Prepare an income statement in proper form for the month of December.

SE 8.

LO 6 Preparation of a Statement of Retained Earnings

Using the data in **SE 7**, prepare a statement of retained earnings for Heller Company.

SE 9.

SO 7 Determination of Cash Flows

Wages Payable was $590 at the end of May and $920 at the end of June. Wages Expense for June was $2,300. How much cash was paid for wages during June?

SE 10.

SO 7 Determination of Cash Flows

Unearned Revenue was $1,300 at the end of November and $900 at the end of December. Service Revenue was $5,100 for the month of December. How much cash was received for services provided during December?

EXERCISES

E 1.

LO 2 Applications of
LO 3 Accounting Concepts
LO 4 Related to Accrual Accounting

The accountant for Pivar Company makes the assumptions or performs the activities listed below. Tell which of the following concepts of accrual accounting most directly relates to each assumption or action: (a) periodicity, (b) going concern, (c) matching rule, (d) revenue recognition, (e) deferral, and (f) accrual.

1. In estimating the life of a building, assumes that the business will last indefinitely.
2. Records a sale when the customer is billed.
3. Postpones the recognition of a one-year insurance policy as an expense by initially recording the expenditure as an asset.
4. Recognizes the usefulness of financial statements prepared on a monthly basis even though they are based on estimates.
5. Recognizes, by making an adjusting entry, wages expense that has been incurred but not yet recorded.
6. Prepares an income statement that shows the revenues earned and the expenses incurred during the accounting period.

E 2.

LO 5 Adjusting Entry for Unearned Revenue

AboutTown Company of Canton, Ohio, publishes a monthly magazine featuring local restaurant reviews and upcoming social, cultural, and sporting events. Subscribers pay for subscriptions either one year or two years in advance. Cash received from subscribers is credited to an account called Magazine Subscriptions Received in Advance. On December 31, 20x3, the end of the company's fiscal year, the balance of this account was $1,000,000. Expiration of subscriptions revenue is as follows:

During 20x3	$200,000
During 20x4	500,000
During 20x5	300,000

Prepare the adjusting entry in journal form for December 31, 20x3.

E 3.

LO 5 Adjusting Entries for Prepaid Insurance

An examination of the Prepaid Insurance account shows a balance of $4,112 at the end of an accounting period, before adjustment. Prepare entries in journal form to record the insurance expense for the period under the independent assumptions that follow.

1. An examination of the insurance policies shows unexpired insurance that cost $1,974 at the end of the period.

2. An examination of the insurance policies shows that insurance that cost $694 has expired during the period.

E 4.

LO 5 **Supplies Account: Missing Data**

Each column below represents a Supplies account:

	a	b	c	d
Supplies on hand at July 1	$132	$217	$98	$?
Supplies purchased during the month	26	?	87	964
Supplies consumed during the month	97	486	?	816
Supplies on hand at July 31	?	218	28	594

1. Determine the amounts indicated by the question marks in the columns.

2. Make the adjusting entry for column **a,** assuming supplies purchased are debited to an asset account.

E 5.

LO 5 **Adjusting Entry for Accrued Salaries**

Discus has a five-day work week and pays salaries of $35,000 each Friday.

1. Make the adjusting entry required on May 31, assuming that June 1 falls on a Wednesday.

2. Make the entry to pay the salaries on June 3.

E 6.

LO 5 **Revenue and Expense Recognition**

Freestyle Company produces computer software that is sold by Hunan Comp, Inc. Freestyle receives a royalty of 15 percent of sales. Royalties are paid by Hunan Comp and received by Freestyle semiannually on May 1 for sales made in July through December of the previous year and on November 1 for sales made in January through June of the current year. Royalty expense for Hunan Comp and royalty income for Freestyle in the amount of $12,000 were accrued on December 31, 20x2. Cash in the amounts of $12,000 and $20,000 was paid and received on May 1 and November 1, 20x3, respectively. Software sales during the July to December 20x3 period totaled $300,000.

1. Calculate the amount of royalty expense for Hunan Comp and royalty income for Freestyle during 20x3.

2. Record the appropriate adjusting entry made by each company on December 31, 20x3.

E 7.

LO 5 **Adjusting Entries**

Prepare year-end adjusting entries for each of the following:

1. Office Supplies had a balance of $84 on January 1. Purchases debited to Office Supplies during the year amount to $415. A year-end inventory reveals supplies of $285 on hand.

2. Depreciation of office equipment is estimated to be $2,130 for the year.

3. Property taxes for six months, estimated at $875, have accrued but have not been recorded.

4. Unrecorded interest receivable on U.S. government bonds is $850.

5. Unearned Revenue has a balance of $900. Services for $300 received in advance have now been performed.

6. Services totaling $200 have been performed; the customer has not yet been billed.

E 8.

LO 5 **Accounting for Revenue Received in Advance**

Saraj Haseem, a lawyer, was paid $24,000 on October 1 to represent a client in real estate negotiations over the next 12 months.

1. Record the entries required in Haseem's records on October 1 and at the end of the fiscal year, December 31.

2. How would this transaction be reflected on the income statement and balance sheet on December 31?

E 9.

LO 6 **Preparation of Financial Statements**

Prepare the monthly income statement, statement of retained earnings, and balance sheet for We Scrubit Service, Inc., from the data provided in the following adjusted trial balance:

We Scrubit Service, Inc. Adjusted Trial Balance August 31, 20xx		
Cash	$ 2,295	
Accounts Receivable	1,296	
Prepaid Insurance	190	
Prepaid Rent	100	
Cleaning Supplies	76	
Cleaning Equipment	1,600	
Accumulated Depreciation, Cleaning Equipment		$ 160
Truck	3,600	
Accumulated Depreciation, Truck		360
Accounts Payable		210
Wages Payable		40
Unearned Janitorial Revenue		460
Income Taxes Payable		400
Common Stock		2,000
Retained Earnings		5,517
Dividends	1,000	
Janitorial Revenue		7,310
Wages Expense	2,840	
Rent Expense	600	
Gas, Oil, and Other Truck Expenses	290	
Insurance Expense	190	
Supplies Expense	1,460	
Depreciation Expense, Cleaning Equipment	160	
Depreciation Expense, Truck	360	
Income Taxes Expense	400	
	$16,457	$16,457

E 10.

SO 7 **Determination of Cash Flows**

After adjusting entries had been made, the balance sheets of Oslo Company showed the following asset and liability amounts at the end of 20x3 and 20x4:

	20x4	20x3
Prepaid Insurance	$2,400	$2,900
Wages Payable	1,200	2,200
Unearned Fees	4,200	1,900

The following amounts were taken from the 20x4 income statement:

Insurance Expense	$ 3,800
Wages Expense	19,500
Fees Earned	8,900

Calculate the amount of cash paid for insurance and wages and the amount of cash received for fees during 20x4.

E 11.

The income statement for Libra Company included the following expenses for 20xx:

Rent Expense	$ 2,600
Interest Expense	3,900
Salaries Expense	41,500

Listed below are the related balance sheet account balances at year end for last year and this year.

	Last Year	This Year
Prepaid Rent	—	$ 450
Interest Payable	$ 600	—
Salaries Payable	2,500	4,800

1. Compute the cash paid for rent during the year.
2. Compute the cash paid for interest during the year.
3. Compute the cash paid for salaries during the year.

PROBLEMS

P 1.

At the end of the first three months of operation, the trial balance of Citywide Answering Service, Inc., appears below. Sudi Patel, the owner of Citywide, has hired an accountant to prepare financial statements to determine how well the company is doing after three months. Upon examining the accounting records, the accountant finds the following items of interest:

Citywide Answering Service, Inc.
Trial Balance
March 31, 20x2

Cash	$ 6,964	
Accounts Receivable	8,472	
Office Supplies	1,806	
Prepaid Rent	1,600	
Equipment	9,400	
Accounts Payable		$ 5,346
Unearned Answering Service Revenue		1,776
Common Stock		11,866
Dividends	4,260	
Answering Service Revenue		18,004
Wages Expense	3,800	
Office Cleaning Expense	690	
	$36,992	$36,992

a. An inventory of office supplies reveals supplies on hand of $266.
b. The Prepaid Rent account includes the rent for the first three months plus a deposit for April's rent.
c. Depreciation on the equipment for the first three months is $416.
d. The balance of the Unearned Answering Service Revenue account represents a 12-month service contract paid in advance on February 1.
e. On March 31, accrued wages total $160.
f. Federal income taxes for the three months are estimated to be $3,000.

The balance of the Common Stock account represents investments by Sudi Patel.

All adjustments affect one balance sheet account and one income statement account. For each of the above situations, show the accounts affected, the amount of the adjustment (using a + or − to indicate an increase or decrease), and the balance of the account after the adjustment in the following format:

Balance Sheet Account	Amount of Adjustment (+ or −)	Balance after Adjustment	Income Statement Account	Amount of Adjustment (+ or −)	Balance after Adjustment

P 2.
LO 5 Preparing Adjusting Entries

On November 30, the end of the current fiscal year, the following information was available to assist Chase Corporation's accountants in making adjusting entries:

a. The Supplies account showed a beginning balance of $4,348. Purchases during the year were $9,052. The end-of-year inventory revealed supplies on hand of $2,794.

b. The Prepaid Insurance account showed the following on November 30:

Beginning balance	$ 7,160
July 1	8,400
October 1	14,544

The beginning balance represents the unexpired portion of a one-year policy purchased the previous year. The July 1 entry represents a new one-year policy, and the October 1 entry represents additional coverage in the form of a three-year policy.

c. The following table contains the cost and annual depreciation for buildings and equipment, all of which were purchased before the current year:

Account	Cost	Annual Depreciation
Buildings	$572,000	$29,000
Equipment	748,000	70,800

d. On September 1, the company completed negotiations with a client and accepted a payment of $33,600, which represented one year's services paid in advance. The $33,600 was credited to Unearned Services Revenue.

e. The company calculated that as of November 30, it had earned $8,000 on a $22,000 contract that would be completed and billed in January.

f. Among the liabilities of the company is a note payable in the amount of $600,000. On November 30, the accrued interest on this note amounted to $30,000.

g. On Saturday, December 2, the company, which is on a six-day work week, will pay its regular salaried employees $24,600.

h. On November 29, the company completed negotiations and signed a contract to provide services to a new client at an annual rate of $35,000.

i. Management estimates income taxes for the year to be $50,000.

Prepare adjusting entries in journal form for each item listed above.

P 3.
LO 5 Determining Adjusting Entries, Posting to T Accounts, and Preparing an Adjusted Trial Balance

The trial balance for Smythe Financial Services, Inc., on December 31 is presented on the next page. The following information is also available:

a. Ending inventory of office supplies, $132.

b. Prepaid rent expired, $220.

c. Depreciation of office equipment for the period, $330.

d. Accrued interest expense at the end of the period, $275.

e. Accrued salaries at the end of the period, $165.

f. Fees still unearned at the end of the period, $583.

g. Fees earned but unrecorded, $1,100.

h. Estimated income taxes for the period, $2,000.

1. Open T accounts for the accounts in the trial balance plus the following: Fees Receivable; Interest Payable; Salaries Payable; Income Taxes Payable; Office Supplies Expense; Depreciation Expense, Office Equipment; Interest Expense; and Income Taxes Expense. Enter the balances shown on the trial balance.

Smythe Financial Services, Inc.
Trial Balance
December 31, 20xx

Cash	$ 8,250	
Accounts Receivable	4,125	
Office Supplies	1,331	
Prepaid Rent	660	
Office Equipment	4,620	
Accumulated Depreciation, Office Equipment		$ 770
Accounts Payable		2,970
Notes Payable		5,500
Unearned Fees		1,485
Common Stock		5,000
Retained Earnings		7,001
Dividends	11,000	
Fees Revenue		36,300
Salaries Expense	24,700	
Rent Expense	2,200	
Utilities Expense	2,140	
	$59,026	$59,026

2. Determine the adjusting entries and post them directly to the T accounts.

3. Prepare an adjusted trial balance.

P 4.

LO 5 **Determining Adjusting**
LO 6 **Entries and Tracing Their**
Effects to Financial
Statements

The Foremost Janitorial Service, Inc., is owned by Ron Hudson. After six months of operations, the September 30, 20xx, trial balance for the company was prepared as shown below.

Foremost Janitorial Service, Inc.
Trial Balance
September 30, 20xx

Cash	$ 4,524	
Accounts Receivable	3,828	
Prepaid Insurance	760	
Prepaid Rent	1,400	
Cleaning Supplies	2,792	
Cleaning Equipment	3,480	
Truck	7,200	
Accounts Payable		$ 340
Unearned Janitorial Fees		960
Common Stock		14,190
Dividends	1,000	
Janitorial Fees		14,974
Wages Expense	4,800	
Gas, Oil, and Other Truck Expenses	680	
	$30,464	$30,464

The balance of the Common Stock account reflects investments made by Ron Hudson. The following information is also available:

a. Cleaning supplies of $234 are on hand.
b. Prepaid Insurance represents the cost of a one-year policy purchased on April 1.
c. Prepaid Rent represents a $200 payment made on April 1 toward the last month's rent of a three-year lease plus $200 rent per month for each of the past six months.
d. The cleaning equipment and trucks are depreciated at the rate of 20 percent per year (10 percent for each six-month period).
e. The unearned revenue represents a six-month payment in advance made by a customer on August 1.
f. During the last week of September, Ron completed the first stage of work on a project that will not be billed until the contract is completed. The price of this stage is $800.
g. On Saturday, October 3, Ron will owe his employees $1,080 for one week's work (six-day work week).
h. Federal income taxes for the six months are estimated to be $1,500.

REQUIRED

1. Open T accounts for the accounts in the trial balance plus the following: Fees Receivable; Accumulated Depreciation, Cleaning Equipment; Accumulated Depreciation, Truck; Wages Payable; Income Taxes Payable; Rent Expense; Insurance Expense; Cleaning Supplies Expense; Depreciation Expense, Cleaning Equipment; Depreciation Expense, Truck; and Income Taxes Expense.

2. Determine the adjusting entries and post them directly to the T accounts.

3. Prepare an adjusted trial balance, an income statement, a statement of retained earnings, and a balance sheet.

P 5.

LO 5 Determining
LO 6 Adjusting Entries and Tracing Their Effects to Financial Statements

The trial balance for Century Dance School, Inc., at the end of its current fiscal year appears as follows:

Century Dance School, Inc. Trial Balance July 31, 20x2		
Cash (111)	$ 5,084	
Accounts Receivable (112)	3,551	
Supplies (115)	510	
Prepaid Rent (116)	1,200	
Prepaid Insurance (117)	1,080	
Equipment (141)	18,300	
Accumulated Depreciation, Equipment (142)		$ 1,200
Accounts Payable (211)		1,140
Unearned Dance Fees (213)		2,700
Common Stock (311)		4,500
Retained Earnings (312)		3,000
Dividends (313)	26,000	
Dance Fees (411)		62,985
Wages Expense (511)	9,600	
Rent Expense (512)	6,600	
Utilities Expense (515)	3,600	
	$75,525	$75,525

Loretta Harper, the owner, made no investments in the business during the year. The following information is available to help in the preparation of adjusting entries:

a. An inventory of supplies reveals $276 still on hand.
b. Prepaid Rent reflects the rent for July plus the rent for the last month of the lease.
c. Prepaid Insurance consists of a two-year policy purchased on February 1, 20x2.
d. Depreciation on equipment is estimated at $2,400.
e. Accrued wages are $195 on July 31.
f. Two-thirds of the unearned dance fees had been earned by July 31.
g. Management estimates federal income taxes for the year to be $9,000.

REQUIRED

1. Record the adjusting entries in the general journal (Pages 53 and 54).

2. Open ledger accounts for the accounts in the trial balance plus the following: Wages Payable (212); Income Taxes Payable (214); Supplies Expense (513); Insurance Expense (514); Depreciation Expense, Equipment (516); and Income Taxes Expense (520). Record the balances shown in the trial balance.

3. Post the adjusting entries from the general journal to the ledger accounts, showing the correct references.

4. Prepare an adjusted trial balance, an income statement, a statement of retained earnings, and a balance sheet.

ALTERNATE PROBLEMS

P 6.

LO 5   Determining Adjustments

At the end of its fiscal year, the trial balance for Harlem Cleaners, Inc., appears as follows:

<table>
<tr><td colspan="3" align="center">**Harlem Cleaners, Inc.**
Trial Balance
September 30, 20x2</td></tr>
<tr><td>Cash</td><td>$ 5,894</td><td></td></tr>
<tr><td>Accounts Receivable</td><td>13,247</td><td></td></tr>
<tr><td>Prepaid Insurance</td><td>1,700</td><td></td></tr>
<tr><td>Cleaning Supplies</td><td>3,687</td><td></td></tr>
<tr><td>Land</td><td>9,000</td><td></td></tr>
<tr><td>Building</td><td>92,500</td><td></td></tr>
<tr><td>Accumulated Depreciation, Building</td><td></td><td>$ 22,800</td></tr>
<tr><td>Accounts Payable</td><td></td><td>10,200</td></tr>
<tr><td>Unearned Dry Cleaning Revenue</td><td></td><td>800</td></tr>
<tr><td>Mortgage Payable</td><td></td><td>55,000</td></tr>
<tr><td>Common Stock</td><td></td><td>20,000</td></tr>
<tr><td>Retained Earnings</td><td></td><td>8,280</td></tr>
<tr><td>Dividends</td><td>5,000</td><td></td></tr>
<tr><td>Dry Cleaning Revenue</td><td></td><td>60,167</td></tr>
<tr><td>Laundry Revenue</td><td></td><td>18,650</td></tr>
<tr><td>Wages Expense</td><td>50,665</td><td></td></tr>
<tr><td>Cleaning Equipment Rent Expense</td><td>3,000</td><td></td></tr>
<tr><td>Delivery Truck Expense</td><td>2,187</td><td></td></tr>
<tr><td>Interest Expense</td><td>5,500</td><td></td></tr>
<tr><td>Other Expenses</td><td>3,517</td><td></td></tr>
<tr><td></td><td>$195,897</td><td>$195,897</td></tr>
</table>

The following information is also available:

a. A study of insurance policies shows that $340 is unexpired at the end of the year.

b. An inventory of cleaning supplies shows $622 on hand.

c. Estimated depreciation on the building for the year is $6,400.

d. Accrued interest on the mortgage payable amounts to $500.

e. On September 1, the company signed a contract, effective immediately, with Kings County Hospital to dry clean, for a fixed monthly charge of $200, the uniforms used by doctors in surgery. The hospital paid for four months' service in advance.

f. Sales and delivery wages are paid on Saturday. The weekly payroll is $1,260. September 30 falls on a Thursday and the company has a six-day pay week.

g. Federal income taxes for the period are estimated to be $1,000.

REQUIRED

All adjustments affect one balance sheet account and one income statement account. For each of the above situations, show the accounts affected, the amount of the adjustment (using a + or − to indicate an increase or decrease), and the balance of the account after the adjustment in the following format:

Balance Sheet Account	Amount of Adjustment (+ or −)	Balance after Adjustment	Income Statement Account	Amount of Adjustment (+ or −)	Balance after Adjustment

P 7.

LO 5 Preparing Adjusting Entries

On September 30, the end of the current fiscal year, the following information was available to aid the Dilworth Company's accountants in making adjusting entries:

a. Among the liabilities of the company is a mortgage payable in the amount of $48,000. On September 30, the accrued interest on this mortgage amounted to $24,000.

b. On Friday, October 2, the company, which is on a five-day work week and pays employees weekly, will pay its regular salaried employees $38,400.

c. On September 29, the company completed negotiations and signed a contract to provide services to a new client at an annual rate of $7,200.

d. The Supplies account showed a beginning balance of $3,230 and purchases during the year of $7,532. The end-of-year inventory revealed supplies on hand of $2,372.

e. The Prepaid Insurance account showed the following entries on September 30:

Beginning balance	$3,060
April 1	5,800
August 1	6,732

The beginning balance represents the unexpired portion of a one-year policy purchased the previous year. The April 1 entry represents a new one-year policy, and the August 1 entry represents the additional coverage of a three-year policy.

f. The following table contains the cost and annual depreciation for buildings and equipment, all of which were purchased before the current year:

Account	Cost	Annual Depreciation
Buildings	$370,000	$14,600
Equipment	436,000	43,600

g. On September 1, the company completed negotiations with another client and accepted a payment of $42,000, representing one year's services paid in advance. The $42,000 was credited to Services Collected in Advance.

h. The company calculated that as of September 30 it had earned $7,000 on a $15,000 contract that would be completed and billed in November.

i. Federal income taxes for the year are estimated to be $15,000.

REQUIRED

Prepare adjusting entries in journal form for each item listed above.

P 8.

LO 5 Determining Adjusting Entries, Posting to T Accounts, and Preparing an Adjusted Trial Balance

The following schedule presents the trial balance for the Pi Consultants Corporation on August 31, 20x2:

Pi Consultants Corporation Trial Balance August 31, 20x2		
Cash	$ 25,572	
Accounts Receivable	49,680	
Office Supplies	1,982	
Prepaid Rent	2,800	
Office Equipment	13,400	
Accumulated Depreciation, Office Equipment		$ 3,200
Accounts Payable		3,640
Notes Payable		20,000
Unearned Fees		5,720
Common Stock		20,000
Retained Earnings		38,774
Dividends	30,000	
Fees Revenue		117,000
Salaries Expense	66,000	
Utilities Expense	3,500	
Rent Expense	15,400	
	$208,334	$208,334

The following information is also available:

a. Ending inventory of office supplies, $172.
b. Prepaid rent expired, $1,400.
c. Depreciation of office equipment for the period, $1,200.
d. Interest accrued on the note payable, $1,200.
e. Salaries accrued at the end of the period, $400.
f. Fees still unearned at the end of the period, $2,820.
g. Fees earned but not billed, $1,200.
h. Estimated federal income taxes for the period, $6,000.

REQUIRED

1. Open T accounts for the accounts in the trial balance plus the following: Fees Receivable; Interest Payable; Salaries Payable; Income Taxes Payable; Office Supplies Expense; Depreciation Expense, Office Equipment; Interest Expense; and Income Taxes Expense. Enter the account balances.

2. Determine the adjusting entries and post them directly to the T accounts.

3. Prepare an adjusted trial balance.

EXPANDING YOUR CRITICAL THINKING, COMMUNICATION, AND INTERPERSONAL SKILLS

SKILLS DEVELOPMENT

Conceptual Analysis

SD 1.

LO 2
LO 3 **Importance of Adjustments**
LO 4

Never Flake Company, which operated in the northeastern part of the United States, provided a rust-prevention coating for the underside of new automobiles. The company advertised widely and offered its services through new car dealers. When a dealer sold a new car, the salesperson attempted to sell the rust-prevention coating as an option. The protective coating was supposed to make cars last longer in the severe northeastern winters. A key selling point was Never Flake's warranty, which stated that it would repair any damage due to rust at no charge for as long as the buyer owned the car.

During the 1980s and most of the 1990s, Never Flake was very successful in generating enough cash to continue operations. But in 1998 the company suddenly declared bankruptcy. Company officials said that the firm had only $5.5 million in assets against liabilities of $32.9 million. Most of the liabilities represented potential claims under the company's lifetime warranty. It seemed that owners were keeping their cars longer in the 1990s than they had in the 1980s. Therefore, more damage was being attributed to rust. Discuss what accounting decisions could have helped Never Flake to survive under these circumstances.

Group Activity: Divide the class into groups to discuss this case. Then debrief as a class by asking a person from each group to comment.

SD 2.

LO 3 **Application of Accrual**
LO 4 **Accounting**

The *Lyric Opera of Chicago* is one of the largest and best-managed opera companies in the United States. Managing opera productions requires advance planning, including the development of scenery, costumes, and stage properties and the sale of tickets. To measure how well the company is operating in any given year, accrual accounting must be applied to these and other transactions. At year end, April 30, 1998, Lyric Opera of Chicago's balance sheet showed Deferred Production Costs of $1,535,185 and Deferred Ticket Revenue of $16,842,887.[6] Be prepared to discuss what accounting policies and adjusting entries are applicable to these accounts. Why are they important to Lyric Opera's management?

Ethical Dilemma

SD 3.

LO 2
LO 3 **Importance of Adjustments**
LO 4

Central Appliance Service Co., Inc., has achieved fast growth in the St. Louis area by selling service contracts on large appliances, such as washers, dryers, and refrigerators. For a fee, Central Appliance agrees to provide all parts and labor on an appliance after the regular warranty runs out. For example, by paying a fee of $200, a person who buys a dishwasher can add two years (years 2 and 3) to the regular one-year (year 1) warranty on the appliance. In 2000, the company sold service contracts in the amount of $1.8 million, all of which applied to future years. Management wanted all the sales recorded as revenues in 2000, contending that the amount of the contracts could be determined and the cash had been received. Discuss whether or not you agree with this logic. How would you record the cash receipts? What assumptions do you think should be made? Would you consider it unethical to follow management's recommendation? Who might be hurt or helped by this action?

| Cash Flow | CD-ROM | Communication | Critical Thinking | Ethics | General Ledger | Group Activity | Hot Links to Real Companies | International | Internet | Key Ratio | Memo | Spreadsheet |

Research Activity

SD 4.

LO 4 **Real-World Observation of Business Activities**

Choose a company with which you are familiar. Visit the company and observe its operations. For example, it can be where you work, where you eat, or where you buy things. Identify at least two sources of revenue for the company and six types of expenses. For each type of revenue and each type of expense, determine whether it is probable that an adjusting entry is required at the end of the accounting period and specify the adjusting entry as a deferred revenue, deferred expense, accrued revenue, or accrued expense.

Decision-Making Practice

SD 5.

LO 1 **Adjusting Entries,**
LO 5 **Dividend Performance Evaluation, and Dividend Policy**

Karen Jamison, the owner of a newsletter for managers of hotels and restaurants, has prepared the following condensed amounts from the financial statements for 20x3:

Revenues	$346,000
Expenses	282,000
Net Income	$ 64,000
Total Assets	$172,000
Liabilities	$ 48,000
Stockholders' Equity	124,000
Total Liabilities and Stockholders' Equity	$172,000

Given these figures, Jamison is planning a cash dividend of $50,000. However, Jamison's accountant has found that the following items were overlooked:

a. Although the balance of the Printing Supplies account is $32,000, only $14,000 in supplies is on hand at the end of the year.
b. Depreciation of $20,000 on equipment has not been recorded.
c. Wages of $9,400 have been earned by Jamison's employees but not recognized in the accounts.
d. No provision has been made for estimated income taxes payable of $10,800.
e. A liability account called Unearned Subscriptions has a balance of $16,200, although it has been determined that one-third of these subscriptions have been mailed to subscribers.

1. Prepare the necessary adjusting entries.
2. Recast the condensed financial statement figures after you have made the necessary adjustments.
3. Discuss the performance of Jamison's business after the adjustments have been made. (**Hint:** Compare net income to revenues and total assets before and after the adjustments.) Do you think that paying the dividend is advisable?

FINANCIAL REPORTING AND ANALYSIS

Interpreting Financial Reports

FRA 1.

LO 2 **Analysis of an Asset**
LO 5 **Account**

REQUIRED

The Walt Disney Company is engaged in the financing, production, and distribution of motion pictures and television programming. In Disney's 1997 annual report, the balance sheet contains an asset called Film and Television Costs. Film and Television Costs, which consist of the cost associated with producing films and television programs less the amount expensed, were $4,401,000,000. The statement of cash flows reveals that the amount of film and television costs expensed (amortized) during the year was $3,781,000,000. The amount spent for new film productions was $5,054,000,000.[7]

1. What are Film and Television Costs and why would they be classified as an asset?
2. Prepare an entry in journal form to record the amount spent on new film and television production during 1997 (assume all expenditures are paid for in cash).

3. Prepare the adjusting entry that would be made to record the expense for film and television productions in 1997.

4. Can you suggest a method by which The Walt Disney Company might have determined the amount of the expense in **3** in accordance with the matching rule?

FRA 2.

LO 5 Identification of Accruals

H.J. Heinz Company, a major food company, had a net income in 1998 of $801,566,000 and had the following current liabilities at the end of 1998:[8]

Current Liabilities (in thousands):	1998
Short-term debt	$ 301,028
Portion of long-term debt due within one year	38,598
Accounts payable	978,365
Salaries and wages	66,473
Accrued marketing	163,405
Accrued restructuring costs	94,400
Other accrued liabilities	360,608
Income taxes	161,396
Total current liabilities	$2,164,273

REQUIRED

1. Which of the current liabilities definitely arose as the result of an adjusting entry at the end of the year? Which ones may partially have arisen from an adjusting entry? Which ones probably did not arise from an adjusting entry?

2. What effect do adjustments that create new liabilities have on net income or loss? Based on your answer in **1**, what percentage of current liabilities was definitely the result of an adjusting entry? Assuming the adjusting entries for these items had not been performed, what would have been Heinz's net income or loss?

International Company

FRA 3.

LO 2 Account Identification
LO 3 and Accrual Accounting

Takashimaya Company, Limited, is Japan's largest department store chain. An account on Takashimaya's balance sheet called Gift Certificates contains ¥45,370 million ($433 million).[9] Is this account an asset or a liability? What transaction gives rise to the account? How is this account an example of the application of accrual accounting? Explain the conceptual issues that must be resolved for an adjusting entry to be valid.

Toys "R" Us Annual Report

FRA 4.

LO 4 Analysis of Balance Sheet
and Adjusting Entries

Refer to the balance sheet in the Toys "R" Us annual report. Examine the accounts listed in the current assets, property and equipment, and current liabilities sections. Which accounts are most likely to have had year-end adjusting entries? Tell the nature of the adjusting entries. For more information about the property and equipment section, refer to the notes to the consolidated financial statements.

Fingraph® Financial Analyst™

FRA 5.

LO 1 Income Measurement
LO 2 and Adjustments
LO 4

Choose any company in the Fingraph® Financial Analyst™ CD-ROM software.

1. Does the company have a calendar year end or other fiscal year? Do you think the year end corresponds to the company's natural business year?

2. Find the company's balance sheet. From the asset accounts and liability accounts, find four examples of accounts that might have been related to an adjusting entry at the end of the year. For each example, tell whether it is a deferral or an accrual and suggest an income statement account that might be associated with it.

3. Find the summary of significant accounting policies that appears following the financial statements. In these policies, find examples of the application of going concern and accrual accounting. Explain your choices of examples.

4. Prepare a one-page executive summary that highlights what you have learned from parts **1, 2,** and **3**.

Internet Case

FRA 6.

LO 4 Comparison of Accrued Expenses

How important are accrued expenses? Randomly choose the annual reports of four different companies from the Needles Accounting Resource Center web site at http:// college.hmco.com. For each company, find the section of the balance sheet labeled "Current Liabilities" and identify the current liabilities that are accrued expenses (sometimes called *accrued liabilities*). More than one account may be involved. On a pad, write the information you find in four columns: name of company, total current liabilities, total accrued liabilities, and total accrued liabilities as a percentage of total current liabilities. Write a memorandum to your instructor listing the companies you chose, telling how you obtained their reports, reporting the data you have gathered in the form of a table, and stating a conclusion, with reasons, as to the importance of accrued expenses to the companies you studied. (**Hint:** Compute the average percentage of total accrued expenses for the four companies you chose.)

ENDNOTES

1. Southwest Airlines Co., *Annual Report*, 1997.
2. Elizabeth MacDonald, "SEC Says Earnings Scrutiny Goes Too Far," *The Wall Street Journal*, February 1, 1999.
3. *Statement of Financial Accounting Concepts No. 1*, "Objectives of Financial Reporting by Business Enterprises" (Norwalk, Conn.: Financial Accounting Standards Board, 1978), par. 44.
4. Michael Schroeder and Elizabeth MacDonald, "SEC Expects More Big Cases on Accounting," *The Wall Street Journal*, December 24, 1998.
5. "Y2K Tops List of Technology Issues for CPAs," *AICPA InfoTech Update*, November/December 1998.
6. Lyric Opera of Chicago, *Annual Report*, 1998.
7. The Walt Disney Company, *Annual Report*, 1997.
8. H.J. Heinz Company, *Annual Report*, 1998.
9. Takashimaya Company, Limited, *Annual Report*, 1996.

4 Accounting Systems

DECISION POINT: A USER'S FOCUS

Hershey Foods Corp. Hershey Foods Corp. is a large multinational company that is well known for its chocolate products. As a company whose shares are traded on the New York Stock Exchange, Hershey is required to prepare both annual and quarterly financial statements for its stockholders. Note the interim income statement from Hershey's quarterly report filed with the Securities and Exchange Commission that appears here.[1] This statement shows that Hershey's net sales for the three months ended October 4, 1998, were greater than those for the same period of the preceding year and that net income increased by approximately 6.8 percent from $100,673,000 to $107,533,000 for the same period.

Whether required by law or not, the preparation of *interim financial statements* every quarter, or even every month, is a good idea for all businesses because such reports give management an ongoing view of a company's financial performance. What are the costs and time involved in preparing interim financial statements?

The preparation of interim financial statements throughout the year requires more effort than the preparation of a single set of financial statements for the entire year. Each time the financial statements are prepared, adjusting entries must be determined, prepared, and recorded. Also, the ledger accounts must be prepared to begin the next accounting period. These procedures are time-consuming

Financial Highlights: Interim Income Statement

(Unaudited—in thousands)

	For the Three Months Ended	
	October 4, 1998	September 28, 1997
Net Sales	$1,217,237	$1,151,610
Costs and Expenses:		
Cost of sales	706,605	672,604
Selling, marketing and administrative	311,658	292,593
Total costs and expenses	1,018,263	965,197
Income Before Interest and Income Taxes	198,974	186,413
Interest expense, net	22,691	20,558
Income Before Income Taxes	176,283	165,855
Provision for income taxes	68,750	65,182
Net Income	$ 107,533	$ 100,673

and costly. However, the advantages of preparing interim financial statements, even when they are not required, usually outweigh the costs, because such statements give management timely information for making decisions that will improve operations. This chapter explains the accounting systems used to process data and prepare financial statements at the end of an accounting period, whether that period is a month, a quarter, or a year.

Principles of Accounting Systems Design

OBJECTIVE

1 Identify the principles of accounting systems design

Accounting systems summarize financial data about a business and organize the data into useful forms. Accountants communicate the results to management. The means by which an accounting system accomplishes these objectives is called **data processing**. Management uses the resulting information to make a variety of business decisions.

As businesses have grown larger and more complex, the role of accounting systems has also grown. Today, the need for a total information system with accounting as its base is more pressing. For this reason, accountants must understand all phases of their company's operations as well as the latest developments in systems design and technology.

Key Point: To work effectively with a computerized accounting system, students must understand how a manual accounting system works. A computerized system functions exactly like a manual system, except that it processes information at lightning speed.

Most businesses use computerized accounting systems. Computerized accounting systems can be set up, monitored, and operated by accountants. However, their primary role is to provide timely accounting information to decision makers. Computer use does not eliminate the need to understand the accounting process. In fact, it is impossible to use accounting software without a basic knowledge of accounting. The opposite is also true: An accountant must have a basic knowledge of computer systems.

Analysis of computer system choices begins with the four general principles of accounting systems design: (1) cost-benefit principle, (2) control principle, (3) compatibility principle, and (4) flexibility principle.

Cost-Benefit Principle

Key Point: The cost of making a wrong decision is an intangible cost that can easily be overlooked in designing an accounting system. It is the systems analyst's job to strike the optimal balance between expected benefits and costs.

The most important systems principle, the **cost-benefit principle**, holds that the benefits derived from an accounting system and the information it generates must be equal to or greater than the system's cost. In addition to performing certain routine tasks—preparing payroll and tax reports and financial statements, and maintaining internal control—the accounting system may be called upon to provide other information that management wants or needs. The benefits from that information must be weighed against both the tangible and the intangible costs of gathering it.

Among the tangible costs are those for personnel, forms, and equipment. One of the intangible costs is the cost of wrong decisions stemming from the lack of good information. For instance, wrong decisions can lead to loss of sales, production stoppages, or inventory losses. Some companies have spent thousands of dollars on computer systems that do not offer enough benefits. On the other hand, some managers have failed to realize the important benefits that could be gained from investing in more advanced systems. It is the job of the accountant and the systems designer or analyst to weigh the costs and benefits.

Control Principle

Key Point: An accounting system should help protect the company's assets and provide reliable data.

The **control principle** requires that an accounting system provide all the features of internal control needed to protect the firm's assets and ensure that data are reliable. For example, before expenditures are made, they should be approved by a responsible member of management.

Compatibility Principle

Key Point: A systems analyst must carefully consider a business's activities, objectives, and performance measures as well as the behavioral characteristics of its employees.

The **compatibility principle** holds that the design of an accounting system must be in harmony with the organizational and human factors of the business. The organizational factors have to do with the nature of a company's business and the formal roles its units play in meeting business objectives. For example, a company can organize its marketing efforts by region or by product. If a company is organized by region, its accounting system should report revenues and expenses by region. If a company is organized by product, its system should report revenues and expenses first by product and then by region.

The human factors of business have to do with the people within the organization and their abilities, behaviors, and personalities. The interest, support, and competence of a company's employees are very important to the success or failure of systems design. In changing systems or installing new ones, the accountant must deal with the people who are carrying out or supervising existing procedures. Such people must understand, accept, and, in many cases, be trained in the new procedures. The new system cannot succeed unless the system and the people in the organization are compatible.

Flexibility Principle

The **flexibility principle** holds that an accounting system must be flexible enough to allow the volume of transactions to grow and organizational changes to be made. Businesses do not stay the same. They grow, offer new products, add new branch offices, sell existing divisions, or make other changes that require adjustments in the accounting system. A carefully designed accounting system allows a business to grow and change without having to make major alterations in the system. For example, the chart of accounts should be designed to allow the addition of new asset, liability, stockholders' equity, revenue, and expense accounts.

Overview of the Accounting Cycle

OBJECTIVE

2 State all the steps in the accounting cycle

The **accounting cycle** is a series of steps in the accounting system whose purpose is to measure business activities in the form of transactions and to transform these transactions into financial statements that will communicate useful information to decision makers. The steps in the accounting cycle, as illustrated in Figure 1, are as follows:

1. *Analyze* business transactions from source documents.
2. *Record* the entries in the journal.
3. *Post* the entries to the ledger and prepare a trial balance.
4. *Adjust* the accounts and prepare an adjusted trial balance.
5. *Close* the accounts and prepare a post-closing trial balance.
6. *Prepare* financial statements.

Figure 1
Overview of the Accounting Cycle

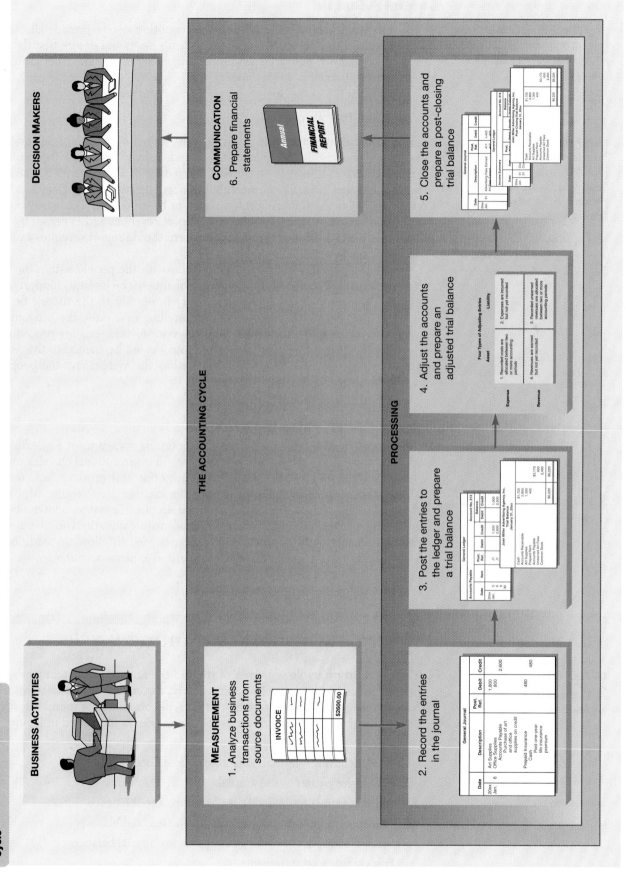

You are already familiar with steps 1 through 4 and 6. Step 5 is covered in this chapter. The order of these steps can vary to some extent depending on the system in place. For instance, the financial statements (step 6) may be completed before the closing entries are prepared (step 5). In fact, in a computerized system, step 6 usually must be performed before step 5. The point is that all these steps must be accomplished to complete the accounting cycle. At key points in the accounting cycle, trial balances are prepared to ensure that the ledger remains in balance.

Computer Software for Accounting

OBJECTIVE

3 Describe how general ledger software and spreadsheet software are used in accounting

Accountants use a variety of software programs to assist them in performing their jobs. Two of the most important types of programs are general ledger software and spreadsheet software.

General Ledger Software

General ledger software is the term commonly used to identify the group of integrated software programs that an accountant uses to perform major functions such as accounting for sales and accounts receivable, purchases and accounts payable, and payroll.

Today, most general ledger software is written using the Windows® operating system. Windows® has a **graphical user interface (GUI)**. A graphical user interface employs common symbols called **icons** to represent common operations. Examples of icons include a file folder, eraser, hourglass, and magnifying glass. The keyboard can be used in the traditional way, or a *mouse* or *trackball* may be used. When a program uses Windows® as its graphical user interface, the program is termed *Windows®-compatible*. The visual format and the ability to use a mouse or trackball make Windows®-compatible software easy to use.

Figure 2 shows how Peachtree Complete Accounting™ for Windows® (PCW) uses a combination of text and icons. It is an example of what a graphical user interface looks like on your computer.

One of the benefits of Windows®-compatible software is the use of standardized terms and operations within software programs. Once you know how to use Peachtree Complete, you can use other Windows®-compatible applications, as they are similar.

Three software programs available for this book are (1) General Ledger Software, (2) Peachtree Complete Accounting™ for Windows®, and (3) Quickbooks®. General Ledger Software is used to supplement end-of-chapter problems. It is designed for educational use and cannot be purchased commercially. Peachtree Complete and Quickbooks® can be purchased through retail stores. They can also be used with selected end-of-chapter problems.

Spreadsheet Software

Accountants use spreadsheet software in addition to general ledger software. General ledger software is effective for transactions that require double-entry accounting. Spreadsheets are used to analyze data. A **spreadsheet** is a grid made up of columns and rows into which are placed data or formulas used for financial planning, cost estimating, and other accounting tasks. Windows® Excel and Lotus are popular commercial spreadsheet programs used for financial analysis and other purposes.

Figure 2
Graphical User Interface

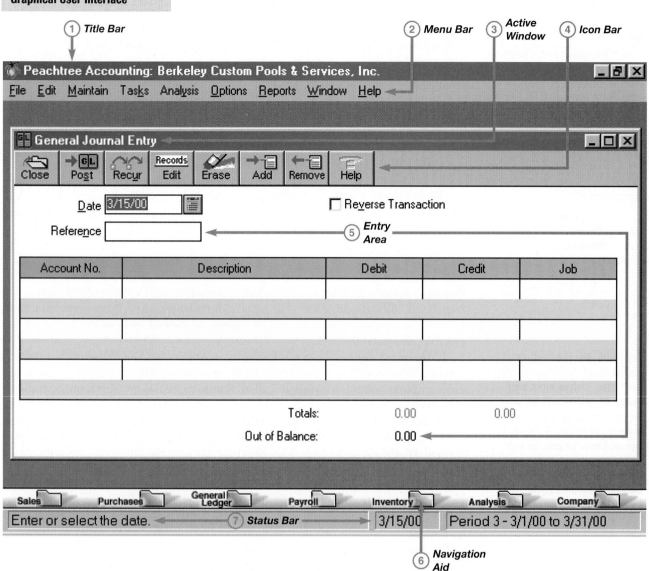

(1) **Title Bar:** The title bar is the bar at the top of your screen. When you enter the program, the name of the company is displayed on the title bar with Peachtree Accounting.

(2) **Menu Bar:** When you click on one of the menu bar headings, a submenu of options is pulled down or opened. These options are selected with a mouse or by holding down the <Alt> key and pressing the letter that is underlined in the desired menu bar option.

(3) **Active Window:** The "General Journal Entry" window has been chosen here in order to record an entry. This bar shows what window is open or "active."

(4) **Icon Bar:** The icon bar shows visual images that pertain to the window. Some icons are common to all windows, whereas other

icons are specific to a particular window. You click on an icon to perform that function.

(5) **Entry Area:** This part of the screen is where information is entered for the journal entry.

(6) **Navigation Aid:** The navigation aid offers a graphical supplement to the menu bar. The major functions of the program are represented as icons or pictures that show you how tasks flow through the system.

(7) **Status Bar:** The gray bar (screen colors may vary) at the bottom of the window shows "help" information about the window, the current date, and the current accounting period.

Computerized Accounting Systems

OBJECTIVE

4 Identify the basic elements of computer systems, and describe microcomputer accounting systems

Most businesses use computerized accounting systems. The parts of such systems may be put together in many different ways, and companies use their computers for many different purposes. A company's overall goal is to meet all its computing needs at the lowest possible cost. The computer system is the nerve center of the company. Large, multinational companies have vast computer resources and use very powerful computers that are linked together to provide communication and data transfer around the world. However, even in these large companies and in most small companies, the PC or microcomputer system has become a critical element in the processing of information. This will become even more critical as Internet growth continues and companies expand usage of the Internet to communicate and transact business directly with vendors, suppliers, and clients.

Elements of a Computer System

Key Point: *Hardware* is another term for "computer equipment." Examples of hardware are disk drives, printers, terminals, and keyboards.

HARDWARE Hardware is the equipment needed to operate a computer system. The computer system includes components that are used to input data through the keyboard, the central processing unit (CPU) or network server for processing and storing data, and the printer or plotter for output. PCs allow accountants to process data using general ledger software and spreadsheet software. The day's transactions can be entered through the keyboard, observed on the monitor, then saved on the hard drive or floppy disk drive. Printed reports can be generated from the general ledger or spreadsheet program.

Key Point: *Software* is another term for "computer programs." Currently available software packages can accomplish a variety of accounting tasks.

SOFTWARE A program is a set of instructions and steps that bring about the desired results in a computer system. Programs are known collectively as software. As mentioned earlier in the chapter, accounting tasks are performed by commercially available software programs such as Peachtree Complete Accounting™ for Windows®, Quickbooks®, Lotus, and Excel.

Often businesses link their computers together in a network environment. Networks can be configured as local area networks (LANs) or wide area networks (WANs). In a LAN, two or more computers in one location are networked. Computers that are networked in a classroom are an example of a LAN. Computers in different cities or around the world that are networked form a WAN. A large corporation's networked computers in different locations around the world are an example of a WAN.

BUSINESS FOCUS ON TECHNOLOGY

Many businesses achieve the computing power of mainframes (large computers) by linking many microcomputers in a network. In a daisy chain network, the microcomputers are linked in a type of circle, or daisy chain. With this network, a person may have to go through several other microcomputers to reach a file or communicate with a person at another computer. In a home base, or star, network, all microcomputers are linked to a central switching point, or home base. A separate microcomputer called a *server* contains all the common data files, such as the accounting records, and is also linked to the home base. All users can access accounting records and other data files by going through the home base. This type of network is faster and more efficient than the daisy chain network.

PERSONNEL   The key personnel involved with a computer system are the systems analyst, the programmer, and the computer operator. The **systems analyst** designs the system on the basis of the organization's information needs, the **programmer** writes instructions for the computer, and the **computer operator** uses the computer to complete job-related tasks. In large organizations, the accountant works closely with the systems analyst to make sure that the accounting system is designed in accordance with the specific needs of the users of financial information. In smaller organizations, the company's owners or management often works with the certified public accounting firm to purchase and install commercial software that meets the company's needs.

Microcomputer Accounting Systems

Most small businesses purchase commercial accounting software that is already programmed to perform accounting functions. Most of these programs are organized so that each module performs a major task of the accounting system. A typical configuration of general ledger software is shown in Figure 3. Note that there is a software module, or feature, for each major accounting function—sales/accounts receivable, purchases/accounts payable, cash receipts, cash disbursements, payroll, and general journal. When these features interact with one another, the software is called an *integrated program*.

Each transaction entered into the accounting system should be supported by **source documents**, or written evidence. Source documents verify that a transaction occurred and provide the details of the transaction. For example, a customer's invoice should support each sale on account, and a vendor's invoice should support each purchase. Even though the transactions are recorded by the computer in a file

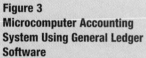

**Figure 3
Microcomputer Accounting
System Using General Ledger
Software**

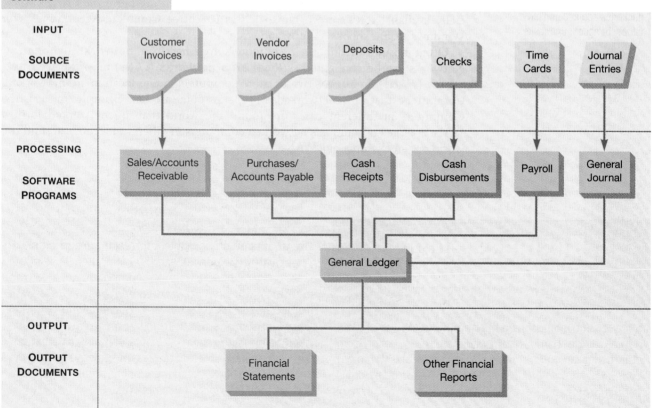

(on floppy disks or hard disks), the documents should be kept so that they can be examined at a later date if a question arises about the accuracy of the accounting records.

After transactions are processed, a procedure is followed to post them to and update the ledgers and to prepare the trial balance. Finally, the financial statements and other accounting reports are printed.

Peachtree Complete Accounting™ for Windows® general ledger program allows either batch posting or real-time posting. In a batch posting system, source documents are recorded in the appropriate journal and saved. Posting is done at the end of the day, week, or month. In a real-time posting system, documents are posted as they are recorded in the journal. The basic goal of general ledger software is to computerize existing accounting tasks to make them less time-consuming and more accurate and dependable. However, it is important to understand, in principle, just what the computer is accomplishing. Knowledge of the underlying accounting process helps ensure that the accounting records are accurate, helps protect the assets of the business, and aids in the analysis of financial statements.

Accountants and the Internet

OBJECTIVE

5 Explain how accountants use the Internet

The **Internet** is the world's largest computer network. The Internet allows any computer on the network to communicate with any other computer on the network. Internet usage is the fastest-growing part of the computer revolution. To access the Internet, a computer needs a modem that connects it to a phone line. A subscription to an Internet service provider (ISP) is usually necessary. Some ISPs are America Online (AOL), MCI World Com, and AT&T. Local Internet providers are also available.

The Internet has many capabilities, including the following:

■ **Electronic mail** **Electronic mail (E-mail)** is the sending and receiving of communications over a computer network. *Electronic mailing lists* are subscriptions to organizations that share a common interest.

■ **World Wide Web** The **World Wide Web** is a repository that provides access to enormous amounts of information over the Internet. It can be compared to the biggest library in the world. When people type in a World Wide Web address, they may not only access the material at that location, but they may also "surf

BUSINESS FOCUS ON TECHNOLOGY

Accountants use the Internet for E-mail and for information retrieval. To find your way around the Internet, you use your browser and a *search engine*. Search engines are organized by subject, similar to the Yellow Pages or a library's catalog, and allow the user to find sources of information. Some popular search engines are Excite, Lycos, and Yahoo! There are many other features of the Internet that are also of interest to accountants.

Newspapers and magazines such as *The New York Times*, *The Washington Post*, *Money*, and *Forbes* have web sites. Many government agencies, such as the IRS, maintain web sites. There is an *Electronic Accountant Newswire* available at Faulkner & Gray's web site, http://www.faulknergray.com. Articles of interest to accountants are updated daily at this web site. The public accounting firm Arthur Andersen has a web subscription service called Knowledge-Space™. Arthur Andersen says KnowledgeSpace™ will sift, sort, and interpret current news and relevant Arthur Andersen resources to help subscribers improve their business performance.

the Web." The software used to navigate the Web is known as a *browser.* The most popular browsers today are Netscape Navigator and Microsoft Internet Explorer.

■ **Information retrieval Information retrieval** is the downloading of files from the Internet to an individual's computer. Companies sometimes offer upgrades of their software this way. Sometimes the information is free and sometimes there is a charge.

■ **Bulletin boards Bulletin boards** allow people who have common interests to share information with one another over the Internet. Many hardware and software companies offer bulletin boards for technical support and troubleshooting.

■ **Electronic commerce** Businesses and consumers increasingly are using the Internet for such activities as selling books, buying stocks, or paying bills. These practices and others using computers to conduct business transactions are called **electronic commerce** and provide new challenges for accountants in terms of keeping records of transactions and maintaining good internal controls.

Closing Entries

OBJECTIVE

6 Explain the purposes of closing entries and prepare required closing entries

Balance sheet accounts are considered to be **permanent accounts**, or *real accounts,* because they carry their end-of-period balances into the next accounting period. On the other hand, revenue and expense accounts are **temporary accounts**, or *nominal accounts,* because they begin each accounting period with a zero balance, accumulate a balance during the period, and are then cleared by means of closing entries.

Closing entries are journal entries made at the end of an accounting period. They have two purposes. First, closing entries set the stage for the next accounting period by clearing revenue, expense, and dividend accounts of their balances. Remember that the income statement reports net income (or loss) for a single accounting period and shows revenues and expenses for that period only. For the income statement to present the activity of a single accounting period, the revenue and expense accounts must begin each new period with zero balances. The zero balances are obtained by using closing entries to clear the balances in the revenue and expense accounts at the end of each accounting period. The Dividends account is closed in a similar manner.

Second, closing entries summarize a period's revenues and expenses. This is done by transferring the balances of revenue and expense accounts to the **Income Summary** account. This temporary account, which appears in the chart of accounts between the Dividends account and the first revenue account, provides a

BUSINESS FOCUS ON PRACTICE

Performing routine accounting functions for other companies has become big business. The practice of managing a customer's information systems for a fixed fee is a form of *outsourcing.* If it leaves the information systems operations to an outside company, management can devote its attention to income-earning activities. Electronic Data Systems, Inc., founded by H. Ross Perot in 1962 and the source of his fortune, is the largest company in this business (it was owned for several years by General Motors until 1997 and now is a separate company again). Major competitors of EDS are Andersen Consulting and SAP, the large German software company.

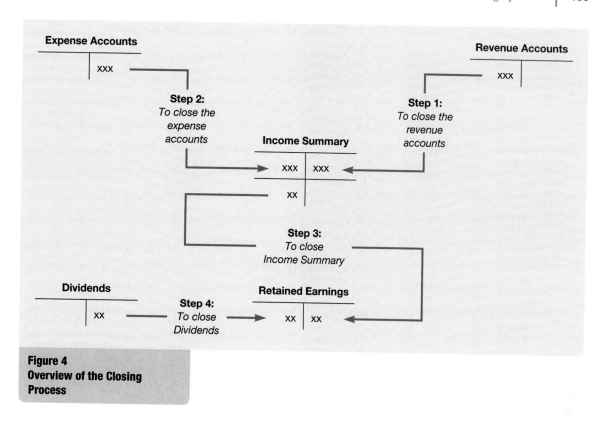

Figure 4
Overview of the Closing Process

place to summarize all revenues and expenses. It is used only in the closing process and never appears in the financial statements.

The balance of the Income Summary account equals the net income or loss reported on the income statement. The net income or loss is then transferred to the Retained Earnings account. This is done because even though revenues and expenses are recorded in revenue and expense accounts, they actually represent increases and decreases in stockholders' equity. Closing entries transfer the net effect of increases (revenues) and decreases (expenses) to stockholders' equity. An overview of the closing process is illustrated in Figure 4.

Required Closing Entries

There are four important steps in closing the accounts:

1. Closing the credit balances from income statement accounts to the Income Summary account

2. Closing the debit balances from income statement accounts to the Income Summary account

3. Closing the Income Summary account balance to the Retained Earnings account

4. Closing the Dividends account balance to the Retained Earnings account

Each step is accomplished by a closing entry. All the data needed to record the closing entries are found in the adjusted trial balance. The relationships of the four kinds of entries to the adjusted trial balance are shown in Exhibit 1.

Enrichment Note: It is not absolutely necessary to use the Income Summary account when preparing closing entries. However, it does simplify the procedure. The Income Summary account is opened and closed with the preparation of closing entries.

STEP 1: CLOSING THE CREDIT BALANCES FROM INCOME STATEMENT ACCOUNTS TO THE INCOME SUMMARY ACCOUNT On the credit side of the adjusted trial balance in Exhibit 1, two revenue accounts show balances: Advertising Fees Earned and Art Fees Earned. To close these two accounts, a journal

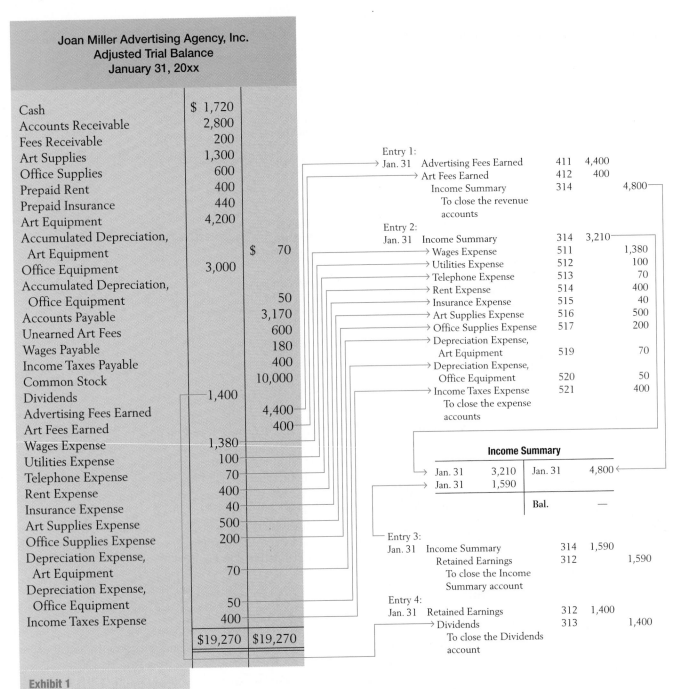

Exhibit 1

Preparing Closing Entries from the Adjusted Trial Balance

entry must be made debiting each account in the amount of its balance and crediting the total to the Income Summary account. The effect of posting the entry is illustrated in Exhibit 2. Notice that the entry (1) sets the balances of the revenue accounts to zero and (2) transfers the total revenues to the credit side of the Income Summary account.

STEP 2: CLOSING THE DEBIT BALANCES FROM INCOME STATEMENT ACCOUNTS TO THE INCOME SUMMARY ACCOUNT

Several expense accounts show balances on the debit side of the adjusted trial balance in Exhibit 1. A compound entry is needed to credit each of these expense accounts for its balance and to debit the Income Summary account for the total. The effect of posting the closing entry is shown in Exhibit 3. Notice how the entry (1) reduces the

Key Point: The Income Summary account now reflects the account balances that the revenue accounts contained before they were closed.

Exhibit 2

Posting the Closing Entry of the Credit Balances from the Income Statement Accounts to the Income Summary Account

Advertising Fees Earned — Account No. 411

Date	Item	Post. Ref.	Debit	Credit	Balance Debit	Balance Credit
Jan. 10		J2		1,400		1,400
19		J2		2,800		4,200
31	Adj. (j)	J3		200		4,400
31	Closing	J4	4,400			—

Income Summary — Account No. 314

Date	Item	Post. Ref.	Debit	Credit	Balance Debit	Balance Credit
Jan. 31	Closing	J4		4,800		4,800

4,400
400
4,800

Art Fees Earned — Account No. 412

Date	Item	Post. Ref.	Debit	Credit	Balance Debit	Balance Credit
Jan. 31	Adj. (i)	J3		400		400
31	Closing	J4	400			—

expense account balances to zero and (2) transfers the total of the account balances to the debit side of the Income Summary account.

STEP 3: CLOSING THE INCOME SUMMARY ACCOUNT BALANCE TO THE RETAINED EARNINGS ACCOUNT

After the entries closing the revenue and expense accounts have been posted, the balance of the Income Summary account equals the net income or loss for the period. Since revenues are represented by the credit to Income Summary and expenses are represented by the debit to Income Summary, a net income is indicated by a credit balance (where revenues exceed expenses) and a net loss by a debit balance (where expenses exceed revenues). At this point, the Income Summary account balance, whatever its nature, must be closed to the Retained Earnings account, as shown in Exhibit 1. The effect of posting the closing entry when the company has a net income is shown in Exhibit 4. Notice the dual effect of (1) closing the Income Summary account and (2) transferring the balance, net income in this case, to Retained Earnings.

Key Point: In a net loss situation, debit the Retained Earnings account (to reduce it) and credit Income Summary (to close it).

STEP 4: CLOSING THE DIVIDENDS ACCOUNT BALANCE TO THE RETAINED EARNINGS ACCOUNT

The Dividends account shows the amount by which retained earnings is reduced during the period by cash dividends. The debit balance of the Dividends account is closed to the Retained Earnings account, as shown in Exhibit 1. The effect of this closing entry, as shown in Exhibit 5, is to (1) close the Dividends account and (2) transfer the balance to the Retained Earnings account.

Key Point: Notice that the Dividends account is closed to the Retained Earnings account, not to the Income Summary account.

The Accounts After Closing

After all the steps in the closing process have been completed and all closing entries have been posted to the accounts, everything is ready for the next accounting period. The ledger accounts of Joan Miller Advertising Agency, Inc., as they appear at this point, are shown in Exhibit 6. The revenue, expense, and Dividends accounts (temporary accounts) have zero balances. Retained Earnings has been increased to reflect the agency's net income and decreased for dividends. The balance sheet accounts (permanent accounts) show the correct balances, which are carried forward to the next period.

Exhibit 3

Posting the Closing Entry of the Debit Balances from the Income Statement Accounts to the Income Summary Account

Wages Expense — Account No. 511

Date	Item	Post. Ref.	Debit	Credit	Balance Debit	Balance Credit
Jan. 12		J2	600		600	
26		J2	600		1,200	
31	Adj. (g)	J3	180		1,380	
31	Closing	J4		1,380	—	

Utilities Expense — Account No. 512

Date	Item	Post. Ref.	Debit	Credit	Balance Debit	Balance Credit
Jan. 29		J2	100		100	
31	Closing	J4		100	—	

Telephone Expense — Account No. 513

Date	Item	Post. Ref.	Debit	Credit	Balance Debit	Balance Credit
Jan. 30		J2	70		70	
31	Closing	J4		70	—	

Rent Expense — Account No. 514

Date	Item	Post. Ref.	Debit	Credit	Balance Debit	Balance Credit
Jan. 31	Adj. (a)	J3	400		400	
31	Closing	J4		400	—	

Insurance Expense — Account No. 515

Date	Item	Post. Ref.	Debit	Credit	Balance Debit	Balance Credit
Jan. 31	Adj. (b)	J3	40		40	
31	Closing	J4		40	—	

Art Supplies Expense — Account No. 516

Date	Item	Post. Ref.	Debit	Credit	Balance Debit	Balance Credit
Jan. 31	Adj. (c)	J3	500		500	
31	Closing	J4		500	—	

Office Supplies Expense — Account No. 517

Date	Item	Post. Ref.	Debit	Credit	Balance Debit	Balance Credit
Jan. 31	Adj. (d)	J3	200		200	
31	Closing	J4		200	—	

Income Summary — Account No. 314

Date	Item	Post. Ref.	Debit	Credit	Balance Debit	Balance Credit
Jan. 31	Closing	J4		4,800		4,800
31	Closing	J4	3,210			1,590

1,380
100
70
400
40
500
200
400
50
70
3,210

Depreciation Expense, Art Equipment — Account No. 519

Date	Item	Post. Ref.	Debit	Credit	Balance Debit	Balance Credit
Jan. 31	Adj. (e)	J3	70		70	
31	Closing	J4		70	—	

Depreciation Expense, Office Equipment — Account No. 520

Date	Item	Post. Ref.	Debit	Credit	Balance Debit	Balance Credit
Jan. 31	Adj. (f)	J3	50		50	
31	Closing	J4		50	—	

Income Taxes Expense — Account No. 521

Date	Item	Post. Ref.	Debit	Credit	Balance Debit	Balance Credit
Jan. 31	Adj. (h)	J3	400		400	
31	Closing	J4		400	—	

Key Point: The credit balance of the Income Summary account at this point ($1,590) represents the key performance measure of net income.

Exhibit 4
Posting the Closing Entry of the Income Summary Account Balance to the Retained Earnings Account

Income Summary — Account No. 314

Date	Item	Post. Ref.	Debit	Credit	Balance Debit	Balance Credit
Jan. 31	Closing	J4		4,800		4,800
31	Closing	J4	3,210			1,590
31	Closing	J4	1,590			—

Retained Earnings — Account No. 312

Date	Item	Post. Ref.	Debit	Credit	Balance Debit	Balance Credit
Jan. 31	Closing	J4		1,590		1,590

Exhibit 5
Posting the Closing Entry of the Dividends Account Balance to the Retained Earnings Account

Dividends — Account No. 313

Date	Item	Post. Ref.	Debit	Credit	Balance Debit	Balance Credit
Jan. 31		J2	1,400		1,400	
31	Closing	J4		1,400	—	

Retained Earnings — Account No. 312

Date	Item	Post. Ref.	Debit	Credit	Balance Debit	Balance Credit
Jan. 31	Closing	J4		1,590		1,590
31	Closing	J4	1,400			190

Exhibit 6
The Accounts After Closing Entries Are Posted

Cash — Account No. 111

Date	Item	Post. Ref.	Debit	Credit	Balance Debit	Balance Credit
Jan. 1		J1	10,000		10,000	
2		J1		800	9,200	
4		J1		4,200	5,000	
5		J1		1,500	3,500	
8		J1		480	3,020	
9		J1		1,000	2,020	
10		J2	1,400		3,420	
12		J2		600	2,820	
15		J2	1,000		3,820	
26		J2		600	3,220	
29		J2		100	3,120	
31		J2		1,400	1,720	

Accounts Receivable — Account No. 113

Date	Item	Post. Ref.	Debit	Credit	Balance Debit	Balance Credit
Jan. 19		J2	2,800		2,800	

Fees Receivable — Account No. 114

Date	Item	Post. Ref.	Debit	Credit	Balance Debit	Balance Credit
Jan. 31	Adj. (j)	J3	200		200	

Art Supplies — Account No. 115

Date	Item	Post. Ref.	Debit	Credit	Balance Debit	Balance Credit
Jan. 6		J1	1,800		1,800	
31	Adj. (c)	J3		500	1,300	

Office Supplies — Account No. 116

Date	Item	Post. Ref.	Debit	Credit	Balance Debit	Balance Credit
Jan. 6		J1	800		800	
31	Adj. (d)	J3		200	600	

Prepaid Rent — Account No. 117

Date	Item	Post. Ref.	Debit	Credit	Balance Debit	Balance Credit
Jan. 2		J1	800		800	
31	Adj. (a)	J3		400	400	

Prepaid Insurance — Account No. 118

Date	Item	Post. Ref.	Debit	Credit	Balance Debit	Balance Credit
Jan. 8		J1	480		480	
31	Adj. (b)	J3		40	440	

(continued)

Exhibit 6

The Accounts After Closing Entries Are Posted *(continued)*

Art Equipment — Account No. 144

Date	Item	Post. Ref.	Debit	Credit	Balance Debit	Balance Credit
Jan. 4		J1	4,200		4,200	

Accumulated Depreciation, Art Equipment — Account No. 145

Date	Item	Post. Ref.	Debit	Credit	Balance Debit	Balance Credit
Jan. 31	Adj. (e)	J3		70		70

Office Equipment — Account No. 146

Date	Item	Post. Ref.	Debit	Credit	Balance Debit	Balance Credit
Jan. 5		J1	3,000		3,000	

Accumulated Depreciation, Office Equipment — Account No. 147

Date	Item	Post. Ref.	Debit	Credit	Balance Debit	Balance Credit
Jan. 31	Adj. (f)	J3		50		50

Accounts Payable — Account No. 212

Date	Item	Post. Ref.	Debit	Credit	Balance Debit	Balance Credit
Jan. 5		J1		1,500		1,500
6		J1		2,600		4,100
9		J1	1,000			3,100
30		J2		70		3,170

Unearned Art Fees — Account No. 213

Date	Item	Post. Ref.	Debit	Credit	Balance Debit	Balance Credit
Jan. 15		J2		1,000		1,000
31	Adj. (i)	J3	400			600

Wages Payable — Account No. 214

Date	Item	Post. Ref.	Debit	Credit	Balance Debit	Balance Credit
Jan. 31	Adj. (g)	J3		180		180

Income Taxes Payable — Account No. 215

Date	Item	Post. Ref.	Debit	Credit	Balance Debit	Balance Credit
Jan. 31	Adj. (h)	J3		400		400

Common Stock — Account No. 311

Date	Item	Post. Ref.	Debit	Credit	Balance Debit	Balance Credit
Jan. 1		J1		10,000		10,000

Retained Earnings — Account No. 312

Date	Item	Post. Ref.	Debit	Credit	Balance Debit	Balance Credit
Jan. 31	Closing	J4		1,590		1,590
31	Closing	J4	1,400			190

Dividends — Account No. 313

Date	Item	Post. Ref.	Debit	Credit	Balance Debit	Balance Credit
Jan. 31		J2	1,400		1,400	
31	Closing	J4		1,400	—	

Income Summary — Account No. 314

Date	Item	Post. Ref.	Debit	Credit	Balance Debit	Balance Credit
Jan. 31	Closing	J4		4,800		4,800
31	Closing	J4	3,210			1,590
31	Closing	J4	1,590			—

Advertising Fees Earned — Account No. 411

Date	Item	Post. Ref.	Debit	Credit	Balance Debit	Balance Credit
Jan. 10		J2		1,400		1,400
19		J2		2,800		4,200
31	Adj. (j)	J3		200		4,400
31	Closing	J4	4,400			—

Art Fees Earned — Account No. 412

Date	Item	Post. Ref.	Debit	Credit	Balance Debit	Balance Credit
Jan. 31	Adj. (i)	J3		400		400
31	Closing	J4	400			—

Wages Expense — Account No. 511

Date	Item	Post. Ref.	Debit	Credit	Balance Debit	Balance Credit
Jan. 12		J2	600		600	
26		J2	600		1,200	
31	Adj. (g)	J3	180		1,380	
31	Closing	J4		1,380	—	

Utilities Expense — Account No. 512

Date	Item	Post. Ref.	Debit	Credit	Balance Debit	Balance Credit
Jan. 29		J2	100		100	
31	Closing	J4		100	—	

(continued)

Exhibit 6
The Accounts After Closing Entries Are Posted *(continued)*

Telephone Expense						Account No. 513
		Post. Ref.	Debit	Credit	Balance Debit	Balance Credit
Date	Item					
Jan. 30		J2	70		70	
31	Closing	J4		70	—	

Office Supplies Expense						Account No. 517
		Post. Ref.	Debit	Credit	Balance Debit	Balance Credit
Date	Item					
Jan. 31	Adj. (d)	J3	200		200	
31	Closing	J4		200	—	

Rent Expense						Account No. 514
		Post. Ref.	Debit	Credit	Balance Debit	Balance Credit
Date	Item					
Jan. 31	Adj. (a)	J3	400		400	
31	Closing	J4		400	—	

Depreciation Expense, Art Equipment						Account No. 519
		Post. Ref.	Debit	Credit	Balance Debit	Balance Credit
Date	Item					
Jan. 31	Adj. (e)	J3	70		70	
31	Closing	J4		70	—	

Insurance Expense						Account No. 515
		Post. Ref.	Debit	Credit	Balance Debit	Balance Credit
Date	Item					
Jan. 31	Adj. (b)	J3	40		40	
31	Closing	J4		40	—	

Depreciation Expense, Office Equipment						Account No. 520
		Post. Ref.	Debit	Credit	Balance Debit	Balance Credit
Date	Item					
Jan. 31	Adj. (f)	J3	50		50	
31	Closing	J4		50	—	

Art Supplies Expense						Account No. 516
		Post. Ref.	Debit	Credit	Balance Debit	Balance Credit
Date	Item					
Jan. 31	Adj. (c)	J3	500		500	
31	Closing	J4		500	—	

Income Taxes Expense						Account No. 521
		Post. Ref.	Debit	Credit	Balance Debit	Balance Credit
Date	Item					
Jan. 31	Adj. (h)	J3	400		400	
31	Closing	J4		400	—	

The Post-Closing Trial Balance

OBJECTIVE

7 Prepare the post-closing trial balance

Because it is possible to make errors in posting the closing entries to the ledger accounts, it is necessary to determine that all temporary accounts have zero balances and to double-check that total debits equal total credits by preparing a new trial balance. This final trial balance, called the **post-closing trial balance**, is shown in Exhibit 7 for Joan Miller Advertising Agency, Inc. Notice that only the balance sheet accounts show balances because the income statement accounts and the Dividends account have all been closed.

BUSINESS FOCUS ON TECHNOLOGY

When General Mills needed to speed up its year-end closing procedures, it selected a team from its Financial Reporting and Information Services Division to design an automated fiscal year-end accounting package. The team put together a system using software spreadsheets like Lotus and Microsoft Excel to record and consolidate annual results. Not only did this accelerate the process, increase accuracy, reduce outside help and overtime, and provide flexibility, but its cost was very low because it used PCs and software that the company already owned. The whole process was reduced from nine weeks to just six work days.[2]

Joan Miller Advertising Agency, Inc.
Post-Closing Trial Balance
January 31, 20xx

Cash	$ 1,720	
Accounts Receivable	2,800	
Fees Receivable	200	
Art Supplies	1,300	
Office Supplies	600	
Prepaid Rent	400	
Prepaid Insurance	440	
Art Equipment	4,200	
Accumulated Depreciation, Art Equipment		$ 70
Office Equipment	3,000	
Accumulated Depreciation, Office Equipment		50
Accounts Payable		3,170
Unearned Art Fees		600
Wages Payable		180
Income Taxes Payable		400
Common Stock		10,000
Retained Earnings		190
	$14,660	$14,660

Key Point: Notice that Retained Earnings now reflects the correct month-end balance, $190.

Reversing Entries: The Optional First Step in the Next Accounting Period

SUPPLEMENTAL OBJECTIVE

8 Prepare reversing entries as appropriate

Key Point: Reversing entries are the opposite of adjusting entries and are dated the first day of the new period. They apply to only certain adjusting entries and are never required.

At the end of each accounting period, adjusting entries are made to bring revenues and expenses into conformity with the matching rule. A **reversing entry** is a general journal entry made on the first day of a new accounting period that is the exact reverse of an adjusting entry made at the end of the previous period. Reversing entries are optional. They simplify the bookkeeping process for transactions involving certain types of adjustments. Not all adjusting entries can be reversed. For the recording system used in this book, only adjustments for accruals (accrued revenues and accrued expenses) can be reversed. Deferrals cannot be reversed because such reversals would not simplify the bookkeeping process in future accounting periods.

To see how reversing entries can be helpful, consider the adjusting entry made in the records of Joan Miller Advertising Agency, Inc., to accrue wages expense:

A = L + OE
+ −

Jan. 31	Wages Expense	180	
	Wages Payable		180
	To accrue unrecorded wages		

When the secretary is paid on the next regular payday, the accountant would make this entry:

A = L + OE
− − −

Feb. 9	Wages Payable	180	
	Wages Expense	420	
	Cash		600
	Payment of two weeks' wages to secretary, $180 of which accrued in the previous period		

Notice that when the payment is made, if there is no reversing entry, the accountant must look in the records to find out how much of the $600 applies to the current accounting period and how much is applicable to the previous period. This may seem easy in our example, but think how difficult and time-consuming it would be if a company had hundreds of employees working on different schedules. A reversing entry helps solve the problem of applying revenues and expenses to the correct accounting period. It is exactly what its name implies: a reversal made by debiting the credits and crediting the debits of a previously made adjusting entry.

For example, notice the following sequence of entries and their effects on the ledger account Wages Expense:

1. Adjusting Entry
Jan. 31 Wages Expense   180
     Wages Payable   180

2. Closing Entry
Jan. 31 Income Summary   1,380
     Wages Expense   1,380

3. Reversing Entry
Feb. 1 Wages Payable   180
     Wages Expense   180

4. Payment Entry
Feb. 9 Wages Expense   600
     Cash   600

Wages Expense				Account No. 511	
				Balance	
Date	Post. Ref.	Debit	Credit	Debit	Credit
Jan. 12	J2	600		600	
26	J2	600		1,200	
31	J3	180		1,380	
31	J4		1,380	—	
Feb. 1	J5		180		180
9	J6	600		420	

Key Point: Notice the abnormal credit balance as of February 1. This situation is "corrected" with the February 9 entry, an entry the bookkeeper can make easily.

Entry 1 adjusted Wages Expense to accrue $180 in the January accounting period.

Entry 2 closed the $1,380 in Wages Expense for January to Income Summary, leaving a zero balance.

Entry 3, the reversing entry, set up a credit balance of $180 on February 1 in Wages Expense, which is the expense recognized through the adjusting entry in January (and also reduced the liability account Wages Payable to a zero balance). The reversing entry always sets up an abnormal balance in the income statement account and produces a zero balance in the balance sheet account.

Entry 4 recorded the $600 payment of two weeks' wages as a debit to Wages Expense, automatically leaving a balance of $420, which represents the correct wages expense to date in February.

The reversing entry simplified the process of making the payment entry on February 9.

Reversing entries apply to any accrued expenses or revenues. In the case of Joan Miller Advertising Agency, Inc., Income Taxes Expense is also an accrued expense that can be reversed. In addition, the asset Fees Receivable was created as a result of the adjusting entry made to accrue fees earned but not yet billed. The adjusting entry for this accrued revenue can be reversed as well. The two additional reversing entries are as follows:

A = L + OE − +	Feb. 1	Income Taxes Payable	400	
		Income Taxes Expense		400
		To reverse adjusting entry for estimated income taxes		
A = L + OE − −	1	Advertising Fees Earned	200	
		Fees Receivable		200
		To reverse adjusting entry for accrued fees receivable		

When the series of advertisements is finished, the company can credit all the proceeds to Advertising Fees Earned without regard to the amount accrued in the previous period. The credit will automatically be reduced to the amount earned during February by the $200 debit in the account.

As noted earlier, under the system of recording used in this book, reversing entries apply only to accruals. Reversing entries do not apply to deferrals, such as the entries that involve supplies, prepaid rent, prepaid insurance, depreciation, and unearned art fees.

The Work Sheet: An Accountant's Tool

SUPPLEMENTAL OBJECTIVE
9 Prepare a work sheet

As seen earlier, the flow of information that affects a business does not stop arbitrarily at the end of an accounting period. In preparing financial reports, accountants must collect relevant data to determine what should be included. For example, they need to examine insurance policies to see how much prepaid insurance has expired, examine plant and equipment records to determine depreciation, take an inventory of supplies on hand, and calculate the amount of accrued wages. These calculations, together with other computations, analyses, and preliminary drafts of statements, make up the accountants' **working papers**. Working papers are important for two reasons. First, they help accountants organize their work and thus avoid omitting important data or steps that affect the financial statements. Second, they provide evidence of past work so that accountants or auditors can retrace their steps and support the information in the financial statements.

A special kind of working paper is the **work sheet**. The work sheet is often used as a preliminary step in the preparation of financial statements. Using a work sheet lessens the possibility of leaving out an adjustment, helps the accountant check the arithmetical accuracy of the accounts, and facilitates the preparation of financial statements. The work sheet is never published and is rarely seen by management. It is a tool for the accountant. Because preparing a work sheet is a very mechanical process, many accountants use a microcomputer. In some cases, accountants use a spreadsheet program to prepare the work sheet. In other cases, they use general ledger software to prepare financial statements from the adjusted trial balance.

Key Point: The work sheet is extremely useful when an accountant must prepare numerous adjustments. It is not a financial statement, it is not required, and it is not made public.

Preparing the Work Sheet

So far, adjusting entries have been entered directly in the journal and posted to the ledger, and the financial statements have been prepared from the adjusted trial balance. The process has been relatively simple because Joan Miller Advertising Agency, Inc., is a small company. For larger companies, which may require many adjusting entries, a work sheet is essential. To illustrate the preparation of the work sheet, we continue with the Joan Miller Advertising Agency example.

A common form of work sheet has one column for account names and/or numbers and ten more columns with the headings shown in Exhibit 8. Notice that the work sheet is identified by a heading that consists of (1) the name of the company, (2) the title "Work Sheet," and (3) the period of time covered (as on the income statement).

Preparation of a work sheet involves the following five steps:

Key Point: The work sheet Trial Balance columns take the place of the "traditional" trial balance.

1. **Enter and total the account balances in the Trial Balance columns.** The titles and balances of the accounts as of January 31 are copied directly from the ledger into the Trial Balance columns, as shown in Exhibit 8. When a work sheet is used, the accountant does not have to prepare a separate trial balance.

Exhibit 8
Entering the Account Balances in the Trial Balance Columns

Joan Miller Advertising Agency, Inc.
Work Sheet
For the Month Ended January 31, 20xx

Account Name	Trial Balance Debit	Trial Balance Credit	Adjustments Debit	Adjustments Credit	Adjusted Trial Balance Debit	Adjusted Trial Balance Credit	Income Statement Debit	Income Statement Credit	Balance Sheet Debit	Balance Sheet Credit
Cash	1,720									
Accounts Receivable	2,800									
Art Supplies	1,800									
Office Supplies	800									
Prepaid Rent	800									
Prepaid Insurance	480									
Art Equipment	4,200									
Accumulated Depreciation, Art Equipment										
Office Equipment	3,000									
Accumulated Depreciation, Office Equipment										
Accounts Payable		3,170								
Unearned Art Fees		1,000								
Common Stock		10,000								
Dividends	1,400									
Advertising Fees Earned		4,200								
Wages Expense	1,200									
Utilities Expense	100									
Telephone Expense	70									
	18,370	18,370								

Joan Miller Advertising Agency, Inc.
Work Sheet
For the Month Ended January 31, 20xx

Account Name	Trial Balance		Adjustments		Adjusted Trial Balance		Income Statement		Balance Sheet	
	Debit	Credit	Debit	Credit	Debit	Credit	Debit	Credit	Debit	Credit
Cash	1,720									
Accounts Receivable	2,800									
Art Supplies	1,800			(c) 500						
Office Supplies	800			(d) 200						
Prepaid Rent	800			(a) 400						
Prepaid Insurance	480			(b) 40						
Art Equipment	4,200									
Accumulated Depreciation, Art Equipment				(e) 70						
Office Equipment	3,000									
Accumulated Depreciation, Office Equipment				(f) 50						
Accounts Payable		3,170								
Unearned Art Fees		1,000	(i) 400							
Common Stock		10,000								
Dividends	1,400									
Advertising Fees Earned		4,200		(j) 200						
Wages Expense	1,200		(g) 180							
Utilities Expense	100									
Telephone Expense	70									
	18,370	18,370								
Rent Expense			(a) 400							
Insurance Expense			(b) 40							
Art Supplies Expense			(c) 500							
Office Supplies Expense			(d) 200							
Depreciation Expense, Art Equipment			(e) 70							
Depreciation Expense, Office Equipment			(f) 50							
Wages Payable				(g) 180						
Income Taxes Expense			(h) 400							
Income Taxes Payable				(h) 400						
Art Fees Earned				(i) 400						
Fees Receivable			(j) 200							
			2,440	2,440						

Exhibit 9
Entries in the Adjustments Columns

2. **Enter and total the adjustments in the Adjustments columns.** The required adjustments for Joan Miller Advertising Agency, Inc., are entered in the Adjustments columns of the work sheet as shown in Exhibit 9. As each adjustment is entered, a letter is used to identify its debit and credit parts. The first adjustment, identified by the letter **a,** is to recognize rent expense, which results in a debit to Rent Expense and a credit to Prepaid Rent. In practice, this letter may be used to reference supporting computations or documentation underlying the adjusting entry and may simplify the recording of adjusting entries in the general journal.

   If an adjustment calls for an account that has not been used in the trial balance, the new account is added below the accounts listed in the trial balance. The trial balance includes only those accounts that have balances. For example, Rent Expense has been added in Exhibit 9. The only exception to this rule is the Accumulated Depreciation accounts, which have a zero balance only in the initial period of operation. Accumulated Depreciation accounts are listed immediately after their associated asset accounts.

   When all the adjustments have been made, the two Adjustments columns must be totaled. This step proves that the debits and credits of the adjustments are equal and generally reduces errors in the preparation of the work sheet.

3. **Enter and total the adjusted account balances in the Adjusted Trial Balance columns.** Exhibit 10 shows the adjusted trial balance. It is prepared by combining the amount of each account in the original Trial Balance columns with the corresponding amount in the Adjustments columns and entering each result in the Adjusted Trial Balance columns.

   Some examples from Exhibit 10 illustrate **crossfooting**, or adding and subtracting a group of numbers horizontally. The first line shows Cash with a debit balance of $1,720. Because there are no adjustments to the Cash account, $1,720 is entered in the debit column of the Adjusted Trial Balance columns. The second line is Accounts Receivable, which shows a debit of $2,800 in the Trial Balance columns. Because there are no adjustments to Accounts Receivable, the $2,800 balance is carried over to the debit column of the Adjusted Trial Balance columns. The next line is Art Supplies, which shows a debit of $1,800 in the Trial Balance columns and a credit of $500 from adjustment c in the Adjustments columns. Subtracting $500 from $1,800 results in a $1,300 debit balance in the Adjusted Trial Balance columns. This process is followed for all the accounts, including those added below the trial balance totals. The Adjusted Trial Balance columns are then footed (totaled) to check the accuracy of the crossfooting.

4. **Extend the account balances from the Adjusted Trial Balance columns to the Income Statement columns or the Balance Sheet columns.** Every account in the adjusted trial balance is either a balance sheet account or an income statement account. Each account is extended to its proper place as a debit or credit in either the Income Statement columns or the Balance Sheet columns. The result of extending the accounts is shown in Exhibit 11. Revenue and expense accounts are copied to the Income Statement columns. Assets, liabilities, and the Common Stock and Dividends accounts are extended to the Balance Sheet columns. To avoid overlooking an account, extend the accounts line by line, beginning with the first line (which is Cash) and not omitting any subsequent lines. For instance, the Cash debit balance of $1,720 is extended to the debit column of the Balance Sheet columns; the Accounts Receivable debit balance of $2,800 is extended to the same debit column, and so forth. Each amount is carried across to only one column.

Joan Miller Advertising Agency, Inc.
Work Sheet
For the Month Ended January 31, 20xx

Account Name	Trial Balance Debit	Trial Balance Credit	Adjustments Debit	Adjustments Credit	Adjusted Trial Balance Debit	Adjusted Trial Balance Credit	Income Statement Debit	Income Statement Credit	Balance Sheet Debit	Balance Sheet Credit
Cash	1,720				1,720					
Accounts Receivable	2,800				2,800					
Art Supplies	1,800			(c) 500	1,300					
Office Supplies	800			(d) 200	600					
Prepaid Rent	800			(a) 400	400					
Prepaid Insurance	480			(b) 40	440					
Art Equipment	4,200				4,200					
Accumulated Depreciation, Art Equipment				(e) 70		70				
Office Equipment	3,000				3,000					
Accumulated Depreciation, Office Equipment				(f) 50		50				
Accounts Payable		3,170				3,170				
Unearned Art Fees		1,000	(i) 400			600				
Common Stock		10,000				10,000				
Dividends	1,400				1,400					
Advertising Fees Earned		4,200		(j) 200		4,400				
Wages Expense	1,200		(g) 180		1,380					
Utilities Expense	100				100					
Telephone Expense	70				70					
	18,370	18,370								
Rent Expense			(a) 400		400					
Insurance Expense			(b) 40		40					
Art Supplies Expense			(c) 500		500					
Office Supplies Expense			(d) 200		200					
Depreciation Expense, Art Equipment			(e) 70		70					
Depreciation Expense, Office Equipment			(f) 50		50					
Wages Payable				(g) 180		180				
Income Taxes Expense			(h) 400		400					
Income Taxes Payable				(h) 400		400				
Art Fees Earned				(i) 400		400				
Fees Receivable			(j) 200		200					
			2,440	2,440	19,270	19,270				

Exhibit 10
Entries in the Adjusted Trial Balance Columns

Joan Miller Advertising Agency, Inc.
Work Sheet
For the Month Ended January 31, 20xx

Account Name	Trial Balance Debit	Trial Balance Credit	Adjustments Debit	Adjustments Credit	Adjusted Trial Balance Debit	Adjusted Trial Balance Credit	Income Statement Debit	Income Statement Credit	Balance Sheet Debit	Balance Sheet Credit
Cash	1,720				1,720				1,720	
Accounts Receivable	2,800				2,800				2,800	
Art Supplies	1,800			(c) 500	1,300				1,300	
Office Supplies	800			(d) 200	600				600	
Prepaid Rent	800			(a) 400	400				400	
Prepaid Insurance	480			(b) 40	440				440	
Art Equipment	4,200				4,200				4,200	
Accumulated Depreciation, Art Equipment				(e) 70		70				70
Office Equipment	3,000				3,000				3,000	
Accumulated Depreciation, Office Equipment				(f) 50		50				50
Accounts Payable		3,170				3,170				3,170
Unearned Art Fees		1,000	(i) 400			600				600
Common Stock		10,000				10,000				10,000
Dividends	1,400				1,400				1,400	
Advertising Fees Earned		4,200		(j) 200		4,400		4,400		
Wages Expense	1,200		(g) 180		1,380		1,380			
Utilities Expense	100				100		100			
Telephone Expense	70				70		70			
	18,370	18,370								
Rent Expense			(a) 400		400		400			
Insurance Expense			(b) 40		40		40			
Art Supplies Expense			(c) 500		500		500			
Office Supplies Expense			(d) 200		200		200			
Depreciation Expense, Art Equipment			(e) 70		70		70			
Depreciation Expense, Office Equipment			(f) 50		50		50			
Wages Payable				(g) 180		180				180
Income Taxes Expense			(h) 400		400		400			
Income Taxes Payable				(h) 400		400				400
Art Fees Earned				(i) 400		400		400		
Fees Receivable			(j) 200		200				200	
			2,440	2,440	19,270	19,270				

Exhibit 11
Extensions to the Income Statement and Balance Sheet Columns

Joan Miller Advertising Agency, Inc.
Work Sheet
For the Month Ended January 31, 20xx

Account Name	Trial Balance Debit	Trial Balance Credit	Adjustments Debit	Adjustments Credit	Adjusted Trial Balance Debit	Adjusted Trial Balance Credit	Income Statement Debit	Income Statement Credit	Balance Sheet Debit	Balance Sheet Credit
Cash	1,720				1,720				1,720	
Accounts Receivable	2,800				2,800				2,800	
Art Supplies	1,800			(c) 500	1,300				1,300	
Office Supplies	800			(d) 200	600				600	
Prepaid Rent	800			(a) 400	400				400	
Prepaid Insurance	480			(b) 40	440				440	
Art Equipment	4,200				4,200				4,200	
Accumulated Depreciation, Art Equipment				(e) 70		70				70
Office Equipment	3,000				3,000				3,000	
Accumulated Depreciation, Office Equipment				(f) 50		50				50
Accounts Payable		3,170				3,170				3,170
Unearned Art Fees		1,000	(i) 400			600				600
Common Stock		10,000				10,000				10,000
Dividends	1,400				1,400				1,400	
Advertising Fees Earned		4,200		(j) 200		4,400		4,400		
Wages Expense	1,200		(g) 180		1,380		1,380			
Utilities Expense	100				100		100			
Telephone Expense	70				70		70			
	18,370	18,370								
Rent Expense			(a) 400		400		400			
Insurance Expense			(b) 40		40		40			
Art Supplies Expense			(c) 500		500		500			
Office Supplies Expense			(d) 200		200		200			
Depreciation Expense, Art Equipment			(e) 70		70		70			
Depreciation Expense, Office Equipment			(f) 50		50		50			
Wages Payable				(g) 180		180				180
Income Taxes Expense			(h) 400		400		400			
Income Taxes Payable				(h) 400		400				400
Art Fees Earned				(i) 400		400		400		
Fees Receivable			(j) 200		200				200	
			2,440	2,440	19,270	19,270	3,210	4,800	16,060	14,470
Net Income							1,590			1,590
							4,800	4,800	16,060	16,060

Exhibit 12
Totals of the Income Statement and Balance Sheet Columns and Net Income

5. **Total the Income Statement columns and the Balance Sheet columns. Enter the net income or net loss in both pairs of columns as a balancing figure, and recompute the column totals.** This last step, as shown in Exhibit 12, is necessary in order to compute net income or net loss and to prove the arithmetical accuracy of the work sheet.

Net income (or net loss) is equal to the difference between the total debits and credits of the Income Statement columns. It also equals the difference between the total debits and credits of the Balance Sheet columns:

Revenues (Income Statement credit column total)	$4,800
Expenses (Income Statement debit column total)	(3,210)
Net Income	$1,590

In this case, revenues (credit column) exceed expenses (debit column). Consequently, the company has a net income of $1,590. The same difference is shown between the total debits and credits of the Balance Sheet columns.

The $1,590 is entered in the debit side of the Income Statement columns to balance the columns, and it is entered in the credit side of the Balance Sheet columns to balance the columns. Remember that the excess of revenues over expenses (net income) increases stockholders' equity and that increases in stockholders' equity are recorded by credits.

When a net loss occurs, the opposite rule applies. The excess of expenses over revenues—net loss—is placed in the credit side of the Income Statement columns as a balancing figure. It is then placed in the debit side of the Balance Sheet columns because a net loss decreases stockholders' equity, and decreases in stockholders' equity are recorded by debits.

As a final check, the four columns are totaled again. If the Income Statement columns and the Balance Sheet columns do not balance, an account may have been extended or sorted to the wrong column, or an error may have been made in adding the columns. Of course, equal totals in the two pairs of columns are not absolute proof of accuracy. If an asset has been carried to the Income Statement debit column (or an expense has been carried to the Balance Sheet debit column) or a similar error with revenues or liabilities has been made, the work sheet will still balance, but the net income figure will be wrong.

Using the Work Sheet

The completed work sheet assists the accountant in three principal tasks: (1) recording the adjusting entries, (2) recording the closing entries in the general journal to prepare the records for the beginning of the next period, and (3) preparing the financial statements.

Study Note: Theoretically, the formal adjusting entries can be prepared before the formal financial statements, or even before the work sheet itself is completed. However, they always precede the preparation of formal closing entries. It is in the preparation of formal adjusting entries that the value of identification letters becomes apparent.

RECORDING THE ADJUSTING ENTRIES For Joan Miller Advertising Agency, Inc., the adjustments were determined while completing the work sheet because they are essential to the preparation of the financial statements. The adjusting entries could have been recorded in the general journal at that point. However, in a manual system it is often convenient to delay recording the adjusting entries until after the work sheet and the financial statements have been prepared because this task can be accomplished at the same time the closing entries are recorded, a process described earlier in this chapter.

Recording the adjusting entries with appropriate explanations in the general journal, as shown in Exhibit 13, is an easy step. The information can be copied from the work sheet. Adjusting entries are then posted to the general ledger.

		General Journal			Page 3
Date		Description	Post. Ref.	Debit	Credit

20xx Jan.	31	Rent Expense
		    Prepaid Rent
		        To recognize expiration of one month's rent
			514
			117
				400	400

	31	Insurance Expense
		    Prepaid Insurance
		        To recognize expiration of one month's insurance
			515
			118
				40	40

	31	Art Supplies Expense
		    Art Supplies
		        To recognize art supplies used during the month
			516
			115
				500	500

	31	Office Supplies Expense
		    Office Supplies
		        To recognize office supplies used during the month
			517
			116
				200	200

	31	Depreciation Expense, Art Equipment
		    Accumulated Depreciation, Art Equipment
		        To record depreciation of art equipment for a month
			519
			145
				70	70

	31	Depreciation Expense, Office Equipment
		    Accumulated Depreciation, Office Equipment
		        To record depreciation of office equipment for a month
			520
			147
				50	50

	31	Wages Expense
		    Wages Payable
		        To accrue unrecorded wages
			511
			214
				180	180

	31	Income Taxes Expense
		    Income Taxes Payable
		        To accrue estimated income taxes
			521
			215
				400	400

	31	Unearned Art Fees
		    Art Fees Earned
		        To recognize performance of services paid for in advance
			213
			412
				400	400

	31	Fees Receivable
		    Advertising Fees Earned
		        To accrue advertising fees earned but unrecorded
			114
			411
				200	200

Exhibit 13
Adjustments from Work Sheet Entered in the General Journal

RECORDING THE CLOSING ENTRIES The four closing entries for Joan Miller Advertising Agency, Inc., are entered in the journal and posted to the ledger as shown in Exhibits 1 through 5. All accounts that need to be closed, except for Dividends, may be found in the Income Statement columns of the work sheet.

PREPARING THE FINANCIAL STATEMENTS Once the work sheet has been completed, preparing the financial statements shown in Exhibit 14 is simple because the account balances have been sorted into Income Statement and Balance Sheet columns. The income statement shown was prepared from the account balances in the Income Statement columns of Exhibit 12. The account balances for the statement of retained earnings and the balance sheet are drawn from the Balance Sheet columns of the work sheet shown in Exhibit 12. Notice that the total assets and the total liabilities and stockholders' equity in the balance sheet are not the same as the totals of the Balance Sheet columns in the work sheet. The reason is that the Accumulated Depreciation and Dividends accounts have normal balances that appear in different columns from their associated accounts on the balance sheet. In addition, the Retained Earnings account on the balance sheet is the amount determined on the statement of retained earnings. At this point, the financial statements have been prepared from the work sheet, not from the ledger accounts. For the ledger accounts to show the correct balances, the adjusting entries must be journalized and posted to the ledger.

Exhibit 14
Financial Statements for Joan Miller Advertising Agency, Inc.

Joan Miller Advertising Agency, Inc.
Income Statement
For the Month Ended January 31, 20xx

Revenues		
Advertising Fees Earned		$4,400
Art Fees Earned		400
Total Revenues		$4,800
Expenses		
Wages Expense	$1,380	
Utilities Expense	100	
Telephone Expense	70	
Rent Expense	400	
Insurance Expense	40	
Art Supplies Expense	500	
Office Supplies Expense	200	
Depreciation Expense, Art Equipment	70	
Depreciation Expense, Office Equipment	50	
Income Taxes Expense	400	
Total Expenses		3,210
Net Income		**$1,590**

Joan Miller Advertising Agency, Inc.
Statement of Retained Earnings
For the Month Ended January 31, 20xx

Retained Earnings, January 1, 20xx	$ —
Net Income	1,590
Subtotal	$1,590
Less Dividends	1,400
Retained Earnings, January 31, 20xx	$ 190

(continued)

Joan Miller Advertising Agency, Inc.
Balance Sheet
January 31, 20xx

Assets

Cash		$ 1,720
Accounts Receivable		2,800
Fees Receivable		200
Art Supplies		1,300
Office Supplies		600
Prepaid Rent		400
Prepaid Insurance		440
Art Equipment	$ 4,200	
Less Accumulated Depreciation	70	4,130
Office Equipment	$ 3,000	
Less Accumulated Depreciation	50	2,950
Total Assets		$14,540

Liabilities

Accounts Payable	$ 3,170	
Unearned Art Fees	600	
Wages Payable	180	
Income Taxes Payable	400	
Total Liabilities		$ 4,350

Stockholders' Equity

Common Stock	$10,000	
Retained Earnings	190 ←	
Total Stockholders' Equity		10,190
Total Liabilities and Stockholders' Equity		$14,540

Chapter Review

REVIEW OF LEARNING OBJECTIVES

Ace it

1. **Identify the principles of accounting systems design.** The developers of an accounting system must keep in mind the four principles of systems design: the cost-benefit principle, the control principle, the compatibility principle, and the flexibility principle.

2. **State all the steps in the accounting cycle.** The steps in the accounting cycle are (1) analyze business transactions from source documents, (2) record the entries in the journal, (3) post the entries to the ledger and prepare a trial balance, (4) adjust the accounts and prepare an adjusted trial balance, (5) close the accounts and prepare a post-closing trial balance, and (6) prepare the financial statements.

3. **Describe how general ledger software and spreadsheet software are used in accounting.** General ledger software is a group of integrated software programs that perform major accounting functions such as general ledger, purchases and accounts payable, sales and accounts receivable, payroll, and others in an integrated fashion. Some software uses icons in a graphical user interface to easily guide the accountant through the tasks. Spreadsheet software is also used widely by accountants for analysis.

4. **Identify the basic elements of computer systems, and describe microcomputer accounting systems.** Computerized accounting systems, regardless of their size, consist of the hardware or equipment, the programs or software, and the personnel to run the system. Most small companies use microcomputer accounting systems that use general ledger software to perform the major accounting functions.

5. **Explain how accountants use the Internet.** Accountants are increasingly using the Internet for electronic mail, for obtaining information or help on many issues via the World Wide Web and information retrieval, and for exchanging information on bulletin boards. Businesses are using the Internet for electronic commerce, which provides new challenges to the accountant.

6. **Explain the purposes of closing entries and prepare required closing entries.** Closing entries have two purposes. First, they clear the balances of all temporary accounts (revenue and expense accounts and Dividends) so that they have zero balances at the beginning of the next accounting period. Second, they summarize a period's revenues and expenses in the Income Summary account so that the net income or loss for the period can be transferred as a total to Retained Earnings. In preparing closing entries, first the revenue and expense account balances are transferred to the Income Summary account. Then the balance of the Income Summary account is transferred to the Retained Earnings account. And, finally, the balance of the Dividends account is transferred to the Retained Earnings account.

7. **Prepare the post-closing trial balance.** As a final check on the balance of the ledger and to ensure that all temporary (nominal) accounts have been closed, a post-closing trial balance is prepared after the closing entries are posted to the ledger accounts.

SUPPLEMENTAL OBJECTIVES

8. **Prepare reversing entries as appropriate.** Reversing entries are optional entries made on the first day of a new accounting period in order to simplify routine bookkeeping procedures. They reverse certain adjusting entries made in the previous period. Under the system used in this text, they apply only to accruals.

9. **Prepare a work sheet.** There are five steps in the preparation of a work sheet: (1) Enter and total the account balances in the Trial Balance columns; (2) enter and total the adjustments in the Adjustments columns; (3) enter and total the adjusted account balances in the Adjusted Trial Balance columns; (4) extend the account balances from the Adjusted Trial Balance columns to the Income Statement or Balance Sheet columns; and (5) total the Income Statement and Balance Sheet columns, enter the net income or net loss in both pairs of columns as a balancing figure, and recompute the column totals.

10. **Use a work sheet for three different purposes.** A work sheet is useful in (1) recording the adjusting entries, (2) recording the closing entries, and (3) preparing the financial statements. Adjusting entries can be recorded in the general journal directly from the Adjustments columns of the work sheet.

Closing entries may be prepared from the Income Statement columns, except for Dividends, which is found in the Balance Sheet columns. The balance sheet and income statement can be prepared directly from the Balance Sheet and Income Statement columns of the completed work sheet. The statement of retained earnings is prepared using Dividends, net income, and the beginning balance of Retained Earnings. Notice that the ending balance of Retained Earnings does not appear on the work sheet.

REVIEW OF CONCEPTS AND TERMINOLOGY

The following concepts and terms were introduced in this chapter.

LO 2   **Accounting cycle:** The sequence of steps followed in the accounting system to measure business transactions and transform them into financial statements; it includes analyzing and recording transactions, posting entries, adjusting and closing the accounts, and preparing financial statements.

LO 1   **Accounting systems:** The processes that gather data, put them into useful form, and communicate the results to management.

LO 5   **Bulletin boards:** A method for individuals with common interests to share information over the Internet.

LO 6   **Closing entries:** Journal entries made at the end of an accounting period that set the stage for the next accounting period by clearing the temporary accounts of their balances and that summarize a period's revenues and expenses.

LO 1   **Compatibility principle:** The principle that holds that the design of an accounting system must be in harmony with the organizational and human factors of the business.

LO 4   **Computer operator:** A person who uses a computer to complete job-related tasks.

LO 1   **Control principle:** The principle that holds that an accounting system must provide all the features of internal control needed to protect the firm's assets and ensure that data are reliable.

LO 1   **Cost-benefit principle:** The principle that holds that the benefits derived from an accounting system and the information it generates must be equal to or greater than its cost.

SO 9   **Crossfooting:** Adding and subtracting numbers across a row.

LO 1   **Data processing:** The means by which an accounting system gathers data, organizes them into useful forms, and issues the resulting information to users.

LO 5   **Electronic commerce:** The conducting of business transactions on computer networks, including the Internet.

LO 5   **Electronic mail (E-mail):** The sending and receiving of communications over a network.

LO 1   **Flexibility principle:** The principle that holds that an accounting system must be flexible enough to allow the volume of transactions to grow and organizational changes to be made.

LO 3   **General ledger software:** A group of integrated software programs that an accountant uses to direct the computer to carry out the major accounting functions.

LO 3   **Graphical user interface (GUI):** The employment of symbols, called *icons*, to represent common operations, making software easier to use.

LO 4   **Hardware:** The equipment needed to operate a computer system.

LO 3   **Icons:** Symbols representing common operations that appear on the screen as part of a graphical user interface.

LO 6 **Income Summary:** A temporary account used during the closing process that holds a summary of all revenues and expenses before the net income or loss is transferred to the Retained Earnings account.

LO 5 **Information retrieval:** The downloading of files from the Internet to a computer.

LO 5 **Internet:** The world's largest computer network; it allows communication among computers of individuals and organizations around the world.

LO 4 **Local area networks (LANs):** Networks of two or more computers in one location.

LO 4 **Network:** The linking of two or more microcomputers to enable them to communicate with one another.

LO 6 **Permanent accounts:** Balance sheet accounts; accounts whose balances can extend past the end of an accounting period. Also called *real accounts*.

LO 7 **Post-closing trial balance:** A trial balance prepared at the end of the accounting period after all adjusting and closing entries have been posted; a final check on the balance of the ledger to ensure that all temporary accounts have zero balances and that total debits equal total credits.

LO 4 **Program:** A set of instructions and steps that bring about a desired result in a computer system.

LO 4 **Programmer:** A person who writes instructions for a computer.

SO 8 **Reversing entry:** A journal entry dated on the first day of a new accounting period that is the exact opposite of an adjusting entry made on the last day of the prior accounting period.

LO 4 **Software:** The programs in a computer system.

LO 4 **Source documents:** The written evidence that supports each accounting transaction for each major accounting function.

LO 3 **Spreadsheet:** A computerized grid of columns and rows into which are placed data or formulas used for financial planning, cost estimating, and other accounting tasks.

LO 4 **Systems analyst:** A person who designs a computer system on the basis of an organization's information needs.

LO 6 **Temporary accounts:** Accounts that show the accumulation of revenues and expenses over one accounting period; at the end of the accounting period, these account balances are transferred to stockholders' equity. Also called *nominal accounts*.

LO 4 **Wide area networks (WANs):** Networks of two or more computers in widely separated locations.

SO 9 **Working papers:** Documents used by accountants to organize their work and to support the information in the financial statements.

SO 9 **Work sheet:** A type of working paper used as a preliminary step in recording adjusting and closing entries and in the preparation of financial statements.

LO 5 **World Wide Web:** The repository of vast amounts of information on the Internet.

REVIEW PROBLEM

Preparation of Closing Entries

LO 6 At the end of the current fiscal year, the adjusted trial balance for Westwood Movers, Inc., appears as shown on the next page.

REQUIRED

Prepare the necessary closing entries.

Westwood Movers, Inc.
Adjusted Trial Balance
June 30, 20xx

Cash	$ 14,200	
Accounts Receivable	18,600	
Packing Supplies	4,200	
Prepaid Insurance	7,900	
Land	4,000	
Building	80,000	
Accumulated Depreciation, Building		$ 7,500
Trucks	106,000	
Accumulated Depreciation, Trucks		27,500
Accounts Payable		7,650
Unearned Storage Fees		5,400
Income Taxes Payable		9,000
Mortgage Payable		70,000
Common Stock		80,000
Retained Earnings		24,740
Dividends	18,000	
Moving Services Earned		159,000
Storage Fees Earned		26,400
Driver Wages Expense	88,900	
Fuel Expense	19,000	
Wages Expense	14,400	
Packing Supplies Expense	6,200	
Office Equipment Rental Expense	3,000	
Utilities Expense	4,450	
Insurance Expense	4,200	
Interest Expense	5,100	
Depreciation Expense, Building	4,000	
Depreciation Expense, Trucks	6,040	
Income Taxes Expense	9,000	
	$417,190	$417,190

ANSWER TO REVIEW PROBLEM

June 30	Moving Services Earned	159,000	
	Storage Fees Earned	26,400	
	Income Summary		185,400
	To close the revenue accounts		
30	Income Summary	164,290	
	Driver Wages Expense		88,900
	Fuel Expense		19,000
	Wages Expense		14,400
	Packing Supplies Expense		6,200
	Office Equipment Rental Expense		3,000
	Utilities Expense		4,450
	Insurance Expense		4,200
	Interest Expense		5,100
	Depreciation Expense, Building		4,000
	Depreciation Expense, Trucks		6,040
	Income Taxes Expense		9,000
	To close the expense accounts		

June 30	Income Summary		21,110	
	Retained Earnings			21,110
	To close the Income Summary account			
30	Retained Earnings		18,000	
	Dividends			18,000
	To close the Dividends account			

Chapter Assignments

BUILDING YOUR KNOWLEDGE FOUNDATION

QUESTIONS

1. What is the relationship of accounting systems to data processing?

2. Describe the four principles of accounting systems design.

3. Resequence the following activities **a** through **f** to indicate the correct order of the accounting cycle:
   a. The transactions are entered in the journal.
   b. The financial statements are prepared.
   c. The transactions are analyzed from the source documents.
   d. The adjusting entries are prepared.
   e. The closing entries are prepared.
   f. The transactions are posted to the ledger.

4. What are two common types of software used by accountants, and how do they differ in terms of their use?

5. Why is a graphical user interface important to the successful use of general ledger software?

6. Describe the three basic elements of a computer system.

7. Data are the raw material of a computer system. Trace the flow of data through the different parts of a microcomputer accounting system.

8. How does a microcomputer accounting system using general ledger software relate to the major accounting functions?

9. In what ways can the Internet assist an individual in performing a job?

10. What are the two purposes of closing entries?

11. What is the difference between adjusting entries and closing entries?

12. What is the purpose of the Income Summary account?

13. Which of the following accounts do not show a balance after the closing entries are prepared and posted?
   a. Insurance Expense
   b. Accounts Receivable
   c. Commission Revenue
   d. Prepaid Insurance
   e. Dividends
   f. Supplies
   g. Supplies Expense
   h. Retained Earnings

14. What is the significance of the post-closing trial balance?

15. Which of the following accounts would you expect to find in the post-closing trial balance?
   a. Insurance Expense
   b. Accounts Receivable
   c. Commission Revenue
   d. Prepaid Insurance
   e. Dividends
   f. Supplies
   g. Supplies Expense
   h. Retained Earnings

16. How do reversing entries simplify the bookkeeping process?

17. To what types of adjustments do reversing entries apply? To what types do they not apply?

18. Why are working papers important to accountants?

19. Why are work sheets never published and rarely seen by management?

20. Can the work sheet be used as a substitute for the financial statements? Explain your answer.

21. What is the normal balance (debit or credit) of the following accounts?
    a. Cash
    b. Accounts Payable
    c. Prepaid Rent
    d. Common Stock
    e. Commission Revenue
    f. Dividends
    g. Rent Expense
    h. Accumulated Depreciation, Office Equipment
    i. Office Equipment

22. Why should the Adjusted Trial Balance columns of the work sheet be totaled before the adjusted amounts are carried to the Income Statement and Balance Sheet columns?

23. What sequence should be followed in extending the amounts in the Adjusted Trial Balance columns to the Income Statement and Balance Sheet columns? Discuss your answer.

24. Do the Income Statement columns and the Balance Sheet columns of the work sheet balance after the amounts from the Adjusted Trial Balance columns are extended?

25. Do the totals of the Balance Sheet columns of the work sheet agree with the totals on the balance sheet? Explain your answer.

26. Should adjusting entries be posted to the ledger accounts before or after the closing entries? Explain your answer.

27. At the end of the accounting period, does the posting of adjusting entries to the ledger precede or follow the preparation of the work sheet?

SHORT EXERCISES

SE 1.
LO 1 Principles of Accounting Information System Design

Indicate whether each of the following statements concerning a newly installed accounting information system is most closely related to the (a) cost-benefit principle, (b) control principle, (c) compatibility principle, or (d) flexibility principle.

1. Procedures are put in place to ensure that the data entered into the system are reliable.

2. The system allows for growth in the number and types of transactions entered into by the company.

3. The system was installed after careful consideration of the additional costs in relation to the improved decision making that will result.

4. The system takes into account the various operations of the business and the capabilities of the people who will interact with the system.

SE 2.
LO 2 Accounting Cycle

Resequence the following activities to indicate the usual order of the accounting cycle.

a. Close the accounts.
b. Analyze the transactions.
c. Post the entries to the ledger.
d. Prepare the financial statements.
e. Adjust the accounts.
f. Record the transactions in the journal.
g. Prepare the post-closing trial balance.
h. Prepare the initial trial balance.
i. Prepare the adjusted trial balance.

SE 3.
LO 4 Elements of a Computer System

Indicate whether each of these elements in a newly installed accounting information system is most properly identified as (a) hardware, (b) software, or (c) personnel.

1. The computer program that instructs the computer to record and post transactions

2. The programmer who writes instructions for the computer

3. The devices that process and store data

SE 4.
LO 4 Microcomputer Accounting System

Assuming that a company uses a general ledger package for a microcomputer accounting system, indicate whether each source document listed would provide input to (a) sales/accounts receivable, (b) purchases/accounts payable, (c) cash receipts, (d) cash disbursements, (e) payroll, or (f) the general journal.

1. Deposit slips
2. Time cards
3. Vendor invoices
4. Checks issued
5. Customer invoices
6. Documents for other journal entries

SE 5.

LO 6 Closing Revenue and Expense Accounts

Assuming credit balances at the end of the accounting period of $3,400 in Patient Services Revenues and $1,800 in Laboratory Fees Revenues and debit balances at the end of the accounting period of $1,400 in Rent Expense, $1,100 in Wages Expense, and $500 in Other Expenses, prepare the required entries to close the revenue and expense accounts. The accounting period ends December 31.

SE 6.

LO 6 Closing the Income Summary Account

Assuming that total revenues were $5,200 and total expenses were $3,000, prepare the entry in journal form to close the Income Summary account. The accounting period ends December 31.

SE 7.

LO 6 Closing the Dividends Account

Assuming that dividends during the accounting period were $800, prepare the entry in journal form to close the Dividends account. The accounting period ends December 31.

SE 8.

LO 6 Posting Closing Entries

Show the effects of the transactions in **SE 5, SE 6,** and **SE 7** by entering beginning balances in appropriate T accounts and recording the transactions. Assume that Retained Earnings has a beginning balance of $1,300.

SE 9.

SO 8 Preparation of Reversing Entries

Below, indicated by letters, are the adjusting entries at the end of March. Prepare the required reversing entries.

Account Name	Debit	Credit
Prepaid Insurance		(a) 180
Accumulated Depreciation, Office Equipment		(b) 1,050
Salaries Expense	(c) 360	
Insurance Expense	(a) 180	
Depreciation Expense, Office Equipment	(b) 1,050	
Salaries Payable		(c) 360
Income Taxes Expense	(d) 470	
Income Taxes Payable		(d) 470
	2,060	2,060

SE 10.

LO 6 Preparing Closing
SO 10 Entries from a Work Sheet

Prepare the required closing entries for the year ended December 31, using the following items from the Income Statement columns of a work sheet and assuming that dividends were $6,000:

Account Name	Income Statement	
	Debit	Credit
Repair Revenue		36,860
Wages Expense	12,260	
Rent Expense	1,800	
Supplies Expense	6,390	
Insurance Expense	1,370	
Depreciation Expense, Repair Equipment	2,020	
Income Taxes Expense	4,000	
	27,840	36,860
Net Income	9,020	
	36,860	36,860

EXERCISES

E 1. The adjusted trial balance for the Schwab Consultant Corporation at the end of its fiscal year is shown below.

Schwab Consultant Corporation Adjusted Trial Balance December 31, 20xx		
Cash	$ 7,275	
Accounts Receivable	2,325	
Prepaid Insurance	585	
Office Supplies	440	
Office Equipment	6,300	
Accumulated Depreciation, Office Equipment		$ 765
Automobile	6,750	
Accumulated Depreciation, Automobile		750
Accounts Payable		1,700
Unearned Consulting Fees		1,500
Income Taxes Payable		3,000
Common Stock		10,000
Retained Earnings		4,535
Dividends	7,000	
Consulting Fees Earned		31,700
Office Salaries Expense	13,500	
Advertising Expense	2,525	
Rent Expense	2,650	
Telephone Expense	1,600	
Income Taxes Expense	3,000	
	$53,950	$53,950

Prepare the required closing entries.

E 2. The Retained Earnings, Dividends, and Income Summary accounts for Jamie's Hair Shop, Inc., are shown in T account form below. The closing entries have been recorded for the year ended December 31, 20x1.

Retained Earnings				
12/31/x1	9,000	12/31/x0	26,000
		12/31/x1	19,000
		Bal.	36,000

Income Summary				
12/31/x1	43,000	12/31/x1	62,000
12/31/x1	19,000		
Bal.	—		

Dividends			
4/1/x1	3,000	12/31/x1	9,000
7/1/x1	3,000		
10/1/x1	3,000		
Bal.	—		

Prepare a statement of retained earnings for Jamie's Hair Shop, Inc.

SO 8 **Reversing Entries**

E 3. Selected T accounts for Clinton Corporation are presented below.

Supplies			
12/1 Bal.	430	12/31 Adjust.	640
Dec. purchases	470		
Bal.	260		

Supplies Expense			
12/31 Adjust.	640	12/31 Closing	640
Bal.	—		

Wages Payable			
		12/31 Adjust.	320
		Bal.	320

Wages Expense			
Dec. wages	1,970	12/31 Closing	2,290
12/31 Adjust.	320		
Bal.	—		

1. In which of the accounts would a reversing entry be helpful? Why?
2. Prepare the appropriate reversing entry.
3. Prepare the entry to record the payment on January 5 for wages totaling $1,570. How much of this amount represents wages expense for January?

SO 9 **Preparation of a Trial Balance**

E 4. The following alphabetical list presents the accounts and balances for Esme Realty, Inc., on December 31, 20xx. All the accounts have normal balances.

Accounts Payable	$ 5,140
Accounts Receivable	2,550
Accumulated Depreciation, Office Equipment	450
Advertising Expense	600
Cash	2,545
Common Stock	5,000
Dividends	9,000
Office Equipment	5,170
Prepaid Insurance	560
Rent Expense	2,400
Retained Earnings	5,210
Revenue from Commissions	19,300
Supplies	275
Wages Expense	12,000

Prepare the trial balance by listing the accounts in the correct order for work sheet preparation, with the balances in the appropriate debit or credit column.

SO 9 **Completion of a Work Sheet**

E 5. The following is a highly simplified alphabetical list of trial balance accounts and their normal balances for the month ended October 31, 20xx.

Trial Balance Accounts and Balances

Accounts Payable	$ 4
Accounts Receivable	7
Accumulated Depreciation, Office Equipment	1
Cash	4
Common Stock	5
Dividends	6
Office Equipment	8
Prepaid Insurance	2
Retained Earnings	7
Service Revenue	23
Supplies	4
Unearned Revenues	3
Utilities Expense	2
Wages Expense	10

1. Prepare a work sheet, entering the trial balance accounts in the order in which they would normally appear and entering the balances in the correct debit or credit column.

2. Complete the work sheet using the following information:
   a. Expired insurance, $1.
   b. Of the unearned revenues balance, $2 has been earned by the end of the month.
   c. Estimated depreciation on office equipment, $1.
   d. Accrued wages, $1.
   e. Unused supplies on hand, $1.
   f. Estimated federal income taxes, $1.

E 6.

SO 10 Derivation of Adjusting Entries and Preparation of a Balance Sheet

Below is a partial work sheet of Tsang Corporation at June 30, 20x1, in which the Trial Balance and Income Statement columns have been completed. All amounts shown are in dollars.

Account Name	Trial Balance		Income Statement	
	Debit	Credit	Debit	Credit
Cash	8			
Accounts Receivable	12			
Supplies	11			
Prepaid Insurance	8			
Building	25			
Accumulated Depreciation, Building		8		
Accounts Payable		4		
Unearned Revenues		2		
Common Stock		20		
Retained Earnings		12		
Revenues		45		47
Wages Expense	27		30	
	91	91		
Insurance Expense			4	
Supplies Expense			8	
Depreciation Expense, Building			2	
Wages Payable				
Income Taxes Expense			1	
Income Taxes Payable				
			45	47
Net Income			2	
			47	47

1. Show the adjustments that have been made in journal form without explanation.
2. Prepare a balance sheet.

E 7.

SO 8 Preparation of Adjusting
SO 10 and Reversing Entries from Work Sheet Columns

The items at the top of the next page are from the Adjustments columns of a work sheet dated June 30, 20xx.

1. Prepare the adjusting entries.
2. Where required, prepare appropriate reversing entries.

Account Name	Adjustments Debit	Adjustments Credit
Prepaid Insurance		(a) 120
Office Supplies		(b) 315
Accumulated Depreciation, Office Equipment		(c) 700
Accumulated Depreciation, Store Equipment		(d) 1,100
Office Salaries Expense	(e) 120	
Store Salaries Expense	(e) 240	
Insurance Expense	(a) 120	
Office Supplies Expense	(b) 315	
Depreciation Expense, Office Equipment	(c) 700	
Depreciation Expense, Store Equipment	(d) 1,100	
Salaries Payable		(e) 360
Income Taxes Expense	(f) 400	
Income Taxes Payable		(f) 400
	2,995	2,995

E 8.

LO 6 Preparation of Closing
SO 10 Entries from the Work
Sheet

The items below are from the Income Statement columns of the work sheet for Rondo Repair Shop, Inc., for the year ended December 31, 20xx. Prepare entries to close the revenue, expense, Income Summary, and Dividends accounts. Dividends of $5,000 were paid during the year.

Account Name	Income Statement Debit	Income Statement Credit
Repair Revenue		25,620
Wages Expense	8,110	
Rent Expense	1,200	
Supplies Expense	4,260	
Insurance Expense	915	
Depreciation Expense, Repair Equipment	1,345	
Income Taxes Expense	1,000	
	16,830	25,620
Net Income	8,790	
	25,620	25,620

PROBLEMS

P 1.

LO 6 Closing Entries Using
T Accounts and Preparation
of Financial Statements

The adjusted trial balance for Zoom Carts, Inc., at the end of the company's fiscal year appears at the top of the next page.

REQUIRED

1. Prepare T accounts and enter the balances for Retained Earnings, Dividends, Income Summary, and all revenue and expense accounts.

Zoom Carts, Inc.
Adjusted Trial Balance
December 31, 20x2

Cash	$ 16,214	
Accounts Receivable	7,388	
Supplies	156	
Prepaid Insurance	300	
Land	5,000	
Building	100,000	
Accumulated Depreciation, Building		$ 27,200
Equipment	125,000	
Accumulated Depreciation, Equipment		33,000
Accounts Payable		15,044
Notes Payable		70,000
Unearned Revenues		300
Wages Payable		3,962
Property Taxes Payable		10,000
Income Taxes Payable		15,000
Common Stock		20,000
Retained Earnings		40,813
Dividends	24,000	
Revenues		618,263
Wages Expense	381,076	
Advertising Expense	15,200	
Maintenance Expense	84,100	
Supplies Expense	1,148	
Insurance Expense	1,500	
Depreciation Expense, Building	4,800	
Depreciation Expense, Equipment	11,000	
Utilities Expense	42,200	
Miscellaneous Expense	9,500	
Property Taxes Expense	10,000	
Income Taxes Expense	15,000	
	$853,582	$853,582

2. Enter in the T accounts the four required closing entries, labeling the components *a*, *b*, *c*, and *d* as appropriate.
3. Prepare an income statement, a statement of retained earnings, and a balance sheet.

P 2.

LO 6 Closing Entries and Preparation of Financial Statements

Tempo Trailer Rental, Inc., owns 30 small trailers that are rented by the day for local moving jobs. The adjusted trial balance for Tempo Trailer Rental, Inc., for the year ended June 30, 20x2, which is the end of the current fiscal year, is shown at the top of the next page.

REQUIRED

1. From the information given, record closing entries in journal form.
2. Prepare an income statement, a statement of retained earnings, and a balance sheet.

Tempo Trailer Rental, Inc. Adjusted Trial Balance June 30, 20x2		
Cash	$ 692	
Accounts Receivable	972	
Supplies	119	
Prepaid Insurance	360	
Trailers	12,000	
Accumulated Depreciation, Trailers		$ 7,200
Accounts Payable		271
Wages Payable		200
Income Taxes Payable		2,000
Common Stock		1,000
Retained Earnings		4,694
Dividends	7,200	
Trailer Rentals Revenue		45,546
Wages Expense	23,400	
Insurance Expense	720	
Supplies Expense	266	
Depreciation Expense, Trailers	2,400	
Other Expenses	10,782	
Income Taxes Expense	2,000	
	$60,911	$60,911

P 3.

LO 2 **The Complete**
LO 6 **Accounting Cycle**
LO 7 **Without a Work Sheet:**
Two Months (second month
optional)

On May 1, 20xx, Elsa Suarez opened Suarez Repair Service, Inc. During the month, she completed the following transactions for the company:

May 1 Began business by depositing $5,000 in a bank account in the name of the company in exchange for 500 shares of $10 par value common stock.

1 Paid the rent for a store for current month, $425.

1 Paid the premium on a one-year insurance policy, $480.

2 Purchased repair equipment from Essa Company for $4,200. The terms were $600 down and $300 per month for one year. The first payment is due on June 1.

5 Purchased repair supplies from Don Company on credit, $468.

8 Paid cash for an advertisement in a local newspaper, $60.

15 Received cash repair revenue for the first half of the month, $400.

21 Paid Don Company on account, $225.

31 Received cash repair revenue for the second half of May, $975.

31 Declared and paid a cash dividend, $300.

REQUIRED FOR MAY

1. Prepare journal entries to record the May transactions.

2. Open the following accounts: Cash (111); Prepaid Insurance (117); Repair Supplies (119); Repair Equipment (144); Accumulated Depreciation, Repair Equipment (145); Accounts Payable (212); Income Taxes Payable (213); Common Stock (311); Retained Earnings (312); Dividends (313); Income Summary (314); Repair Revenue (411); Store Rent Expense (511); Advertising Expense (512); Insurance Expense (513); Repair Supplies Expense (514); Depreciation Expense, Repair Equipment (515); and Income Taxes Expense (516). Post the May journal entries to the ledger accounts.

3. Using the information that follows, record adjusting entries in the general journal and post to the ledger accounts.

a. One month's insurance has expired.
b. The remaining inventory of unused repair supplies is $169.
c. The estimated depreciation on repair equipment is $70.
d. Estimated income taxes are $50.

4. From the accounts in the ledger, prepare an adjusted trial balance. (Note: Normally a trial balance is prepared before adjustments but is omitted here to save time.)

5. From the adjusted trial balance, prepare an income statement, a statement of retained earnings, and a balance sheet for May.

6. Prepare and post closing entries.

7. Prepare a post-closing trial balance.

(Optional)   During June, Elsa Suarez completed these transactions for Suarez Repair Service, Inc.:

June 1   Paid the monthly rent, $425.
       1   Made the monthly payment to Essa Company, $300.
       6   Purchased additional repair supplies on credit from Don Company, $863.
      15   Received cash repair revenue for the first half of the month, $914.
      20   Paid cash for an advertisement in the local newspaper, $60.
      23   Paid Don Company on account, $600.
      30   Received cash repair revenue for the last half of the month, $817.
      30   Declared and paid a cash dividend, $300.

REQUIRED FOR JUNE

8. Prepare and post journal entries to record the June transactions.

9. Using the following information, record adjusting entries in the general journal and post to the ledger accounts:
a. One month's insurance has expired.
b. The inventory of unused repair supplies is $413.
c. The estimated depreciation on repair equipment is $70.
d. Estimated income taxes are $50.

10. From the accounts in the ledger, prepare an adjusted trial balance.

11. From the adjusted trial balance, prepare the June income statement, statement of retained earnings, and balance sheet.

12. Prepare and post closing entries.

13. Prepare a post-closing trial balance.

P 4.

LO 6   **Preparation of a**
SO 8   **Work Sheet; Financial**
SO 9   **Statements; and**
SO 10   **Adjusting, Closing, and**
           Reversing Entries

Donald Leung began his consulting practice immediately after earning his MBA. To help him get started, several clients paid him retainers (payments in advance) for future services. Other clients paid when service was provided. The firm's trial balance after one year appears below.

Donald Leung, Consultant, Inc.
Trial Balance
June 30, 20x3

Cash	$ 9,750	
Accounts Receivable	8,127	
Office Supplies	1,146	
Office Equipment	11,265	
Accounts Payable		$ 3,888
Unearned Retainers		15,000
Common Stock		12,000
Dividends	18,000	
Consulting Fees		54,525
Rent Expense	5,400	
Utilities Expense	2,151	
Wages Expense	29,574	
	$85,413	$85,413

1. Enter the trial balance amounts in the Trial Balance columns of a work sheet. Remember that accumulated depreciation is listed with its asset account. Complete the work sheet using the following information:
   a. Inventory of unused office supplies, $174.
   b. Estimated depreciation on office equipment, $1,800.
   c. Services rendered during the month but not yet billed, $2,175.
   d. Services rendered that should be applied against unearned retainers, $9,450.
   e. Wages earned by employees but not yet paid, $360.
   f. Estimated income taxes for the year, $3,000.

2. Prepare an income statement, a statement of retained earnings, and a balance sheet.

3. Prepare adjusting, closing, and, if required, reversing entries.

4. How would you evaluate Donald Leung's first year in practice?

P 5.

LO 6 **Preparation of a**
SO 8 **Work Sheet; Financial**
SO 9 **Statements; and**
SO 10 **Adjusting, Closing, and**
 Reversing Entries

At the end of the current fiscal year, this was the trial balance of the Drexel Theater Corporation:

Drexel Theater Corporation Trial Balance June 30, 20x2		
Cash	$ 31,800	
Accounts Receivable	18,544	
Prepaid Insurance	19,600	
Office Supplies	780	
Cleaning Supplies	3,590	
Land	20,000	
Building	400,000	
Accumulated Depreciation, Building		$ 39,400
Theater Furnishings	370,000	
Accumulated Depreciation, Theater Furnishings		65,000
Office Equipment	31,600	
Accumulated Depreciation, Office Equipment		15,560
Accounts Payable		45,506
Gift Books Liability		41,900
Mortgage Payable		300,000
Common Stock		200,000
Retained Earnings		112,648
Dividends	60,000	
Ticket Sales Revenue		411,400
Theater Rental Revenue		45,200
Usher Wages Expense	157,000	
Office Wages Expense	24,000	
Utilities Expense	112,700	
Interest Expense	27,000	
	$1,276,614	$1,276,614

1. Enter the trial balance amounts in the Trial Balance columns of a work sheet, and complete the work sheet using the following information:
   a. Expired insurance, $17,400.
   b. Inventory of unused office supplies, $244.
   c. Inventory of unused cleaning supplies, $468.
   d. Estimated depreciation on the building, $14,000.
   e. Estimated depreciation on the theater furnishings, $36,000.
   f. Estimated depreciation on the office equipment, $3,160.

g. The company credits all gift books sold during the year to the Gift Books Liability account. A gift book is a booklet of ticket coupons that is purchased in advance as a gift. The recipient redeems the coupons at some point in the future. On June 30 it was estimated that $37,800 worth of the gift books had been redeemed.

h. Accrued but unpaid usher wages at the end of the accounting period, $860.

i. Estimated federal income taxes, $20,000.

2. Prepare an income statement, a statement of retained earnings, and a balance sheet.

3. Prepare adjusting, closing, and, if required, reversing entries.

ALTERNATE PROBLEMS

P 6.

LO 6   Closing Entries Using T Accounts and Preparation of Financial Statements

The adjusted trial balance for Wolf Path Tennis Club, Inc., at the end of the company's fiscal year appears below.

Wolf Path Tennis Club, Inc. Adjusted Trial Balance June 30, 20x2		
Cash	$ 26,200	
Prepaid Advertising	9,600	
Supplies	1,200	
Land	100,000	
Building	645,200	
Accumulated Depreciation, Building		$ 260,000
Equipment	156,000	
Accumulated Depreciation, Equipment		50,400
Accounts Payable		73,000
Wages Payable		9,000
Property Taxes Payable		22,500
Unearned Revenues, Locker Fees		3,000
Income Taxes Payable		20,000
Common Stock		200,000
Retained Earnings		271,150
Dividends	54,000	
Revenues from Court Fees		678,100
Revenues from Locker Fees		9,600
Wages Expense	351,000	
Maintenance Expense	51,600	
Advertising Expense	39,750	
Utilities Expense	64,800	
Supplies Expense	6,000	
Depreciation Expense, Building	30,000	
Depreciation Expense, Equipment	12,000	
Property Taxes Expense	22,500	
Miscellaneous Expense	6,900	
Income Taxes Expense	20,000	
	$1,596,750	$1,596,750

REQUIRED

1. Prepare T accounts and enter the balances for Retained Earnings, Dividends, Income Summary, and all revenue and expense accounts.

2. Enter the four required closing entries in the T accounts, labeling the components *a*, *b*, *c*, and *d*, as appropriate.

3. Prepare an income statement, a statement of retained earnings, and a balance sheet.

P 7.

LO 6 Closing Entries Using Journal Form and Preparation of Financial Statements

Raccoon Campgrounds, Inc., rents out campsites in a wooded park. The adjusted trial balance for Raccoon Campgrounds on March 31, 20x1, the end of the current fiscal year, is as follows:

Raccoon Campgrounds, Inc. Adjusted Trial Balance March 31, 20x1		
Cash	$ 4,080	
Accounts Receivable	7,320	
Supplies	228	
Prepaid Insurance	1,188	
Land	30,000	
Building	91,800	
Accumulated Depreciation, Building		$ 21,000
Accounts Payable		3,450
Wages Payable		1,650
Income Taxes Payable		10,000
Common Stock		40,000
Retained Earnings		53,070
Dividends	36,000	
Campsite Rentals		88,200
Wages Expense	23,850	
Insurance Expense	3,784	
Utilities Expense	1,800	
Supplies Expense	1,320	
Depreciation Expense, Building	6,000	
Income Taxes Expense	10,000	
	$217,370	$217,370

REQUIRED

1. Record the closing entries in journal form.

2. From the information given, prepare an income statement, a statement of retained earnings, and a balance sheet.

P 8.

LO 6 Preparation of a Work
SO 8 Sheet; Financial
SO 9 Statements; and
SO 10 Adjusting, Closing, and Reversing Entries

Leo Jones opened his executive search service on July 1, 20x1. Some customers paid for his services after they were rendered, and others paid in advance for one year of service. After six months of operation, Jones wanted to know how his business stood. The trial balance on December 31 appears on the next page.

REQUIRED

1. Enter the trial balance amounts in the Trial Balance columns of the work sheet. Remember that accumulated depreciation is listed with its asset account. Complete the work sheet using the following information:
   a. One year's rent had been paid in advance when Jones began business.
   b. Inventory of unused office supplies, $75.
   c. One-half year's depreciation on office equipment, $900.
   d. Service rendered that had been paid for in advance, $863.
   e. Executive search services rendered during the month but not yet billed, $270.

Jones Executive Search Service, Inc. Trial Balance December 31, 20x1		
Cash	$ 1,713	
Prepaid Rent	1,800	
Office Supplies	413	
Office Equipment	15,750	
Accounts Payable		$ 3,173
Unearned Revenue		1,823
Common Stock		10,000
Dividends	5,200	
Search Revenue		20,140
Utilities Expense	1,260	
Wages Expense	9,000	
	$35,136	$35,136

f. Wages earned by employees but not yet paid, $188.

g. Estimated income taxes for the half-year, $2,000.

2. From the work sheet, prepare an income statement, a statement of retained earnings, and a balance sheet.

3. From the work sheet, prepare adjusting and closing entries and, if required, reversing entries.

4. What is your evaluation of Jones's first six months in business?

EXPANDING YOUR CRITICAL THINKING, COMMUNICATION, AND INTERPERSONAL SKILLS

SKILLS DEVELOPMENT

Conceptual Analysis

LO 2 Interim Financial Statements

SD 1. *Ocean Oil Services Corporation* provides services for drilling operations off the coast of Louisiana. The company has a significant amount of debt to River National Bank in Baton Rouge. The bank requires the company to provide it with financial statements every quarter. Explain what is involved in preparing financial statements every quarter.

SO 8 Accounting Efficiency

SD 2. *Way Heaters, Inc.,* located just outside Milwaukee, Wisconsin, is a small, successful manufacturer of industrial heaters. The company's heaters are used, for instance, by candy manufacturers to heat chocolate. The company sells its heaters to some of its customers on credit with generous terms. The terms usually specify payment six months after purchase and an interest rate based on current bank rates. Because the interest on the loans accrues a little bit every day but is not paid until the due date of the note, it is necessary to make an adjusting entry at the end of each accounting period to debit Interest Receivable and credit Interest Income for the amount of the interest accrued but not paid to date. The company prepares financial statements every month. Keeping track of what has been accrued in the past is time-consuming because the

| Cash Flow | CD-ROM | Communication | Critical Thinking | Ethics | General Ledger | Group Activity | Hot Links to Real Companies | International | Internet | Key Ratio | Memo | Spreadsheet |

notes carry different dates and interest rates. Discuss what the accountant can do to simplify the process of making the adjusting entry for accrued interest each month.

Ethical Dilemma

SD 3.

LO 2   Ethics and Time Pressure

Jay Wheeler, an accountant for *WB, Inc.,* has made adjusting entries and is preparing the adjusted trial balance for the first six months of the year. Financial statements must be delivered to the bank by 5 o'clock to support a critical loan agreement. By noon, Jay cannot balance the adjusted trial balance. The figures are off by $1,320, so he increases the balance of the Retained Earnings account by $1,320. He closes the accounts, prepares the statements, and sends them to the bank on time. Jay hopes that no one will notice the problem and believes that he can find the error and correct it by the end of next month. Are Jay's actions ethical? Why or why not? Did Jay have other alternatives?

Research Activity

SD 4.

LO 2   Interview of a Local
LO 6   Businessperson
SO 8
SO 9

Arrange to spend about an hour interviewing the owner, manager, or accountant of a local service or retail business. Your goal is to learn as much as you can about the accounting cycle of the person's business. Ask the interviewee to show you his or her accounting records and to tell you how such transactions as sales, purchases, payments, and payroll are handled. Examine the documents used to support the transactions. Look at any journals, ledgers, or work sheets. Does the business use a computer? Does it use its own accounting system, or does it use an outside or centralized service? Does it use the cash or the accrual basis of accounting? When does it prepare adjusting entries? When does it prepare closing entries? How often does it prepare financial statements? Does it prepare reversing entries? How do its procedures differ from those described in the text? When the interview is finished, organize and write up your findings and be prepared to present them to your class.

Group Activity: Divide the class into groups and assign each group to a different type of business, such as shoe store, fast-food, grocery, hardware, records, and others. Have the groups give presentations in class.

Decision-Making Practice

SD 5.

LO 2   Conversion from Accrual to
Cash Statement

Adele's Secretarial Service, Inc., is a very simple business. Adele provides typing services for students at the local university. Her accountant prepared the income statement that appears below for the year ended June 30, 20x4.

Adele's Secretarial Service, Inc. Income Statement For the Year Ended June 30, 20x4		
Revenues		
Typing Services		$20,980
Expenses		
Rent Expense	$2,400	
Depreciation Expense, Office Equipment	2,200	
Supplies Expense	960	
Other Expenses	1,240	
Total Expenses		6,800
Net Income		$14,180

In reviewing this statement, Adele is puzzled. She knows the company paid cash dividends of $15,600 to her, the sole stockholder, yet the cash balance in the company's bank account increased from $460 to $3,100 from last June 30 to this June 30. She wants to know how her net income could be less than the cash dividends she took out of the business if there is an increase in the cash balance.

Her accountant has completed the closing entries and shows her the balance sheets for June 30, 20x4, and June 30, 20x3. She explains that besides the change in the cash balance, accounts receivable from customers decreased by $1,480 and accounts payable increased by $380 (supplies are the only items Adele buys on credit). The only other asset or liability account that changed during the year was Accumulated Depreciation, Office Equipment, which increased by $2,200.

1. Verify the cash balance increase by preparing a statement that lists the receipts of cash and the expenditures of cash during the year.

2. Write a memorandum to Adele explaining why the accountant is pointing out year-to-year changes in the balance sheet. Include an explanation of your treatment of depreciation expense, giving your reasons for the treatment.

FINANCIAL REPORTING AND ANALYSIS

Interpreting Financial Reports

FRA 1.

LO 6   Closing Entries

H&R Block, Inc., is the world's largest tax preparation service firm. Adapted information from the statement of earnings (in thousands, without earnings per share information) from its annual report for the year ended April 30, 1998, is shown below.[3]

Revenues

Service Revenues	$1,083,985
Product Sales	103,717
Royalties	111,142
Investment Income	24,916
Other Revenues	7,941
Total Revenues	$1,331,701

Expenses

Employee Compensation and Benefits	$ 487,956
Occupancy and Equipment Expense	195,549
Marketing and Advertising Expense	75,567
Supplies, Freight, and Postage Expense	51,733
Interest Expense	52,252
Other Operating Expenses	187,753
Total Expenses	$1,050,810
Earnings Before Income Taxes	$ 280,891
Income Taxes	106,739
Net Earnings	$ 174,152

In its statement of retained earnings, the company reported cash dividends in the amount of $83,635,000 to the owners in 1998.

1. Prepare, in journal form, the closing entries that would have been made by H&R Block on April 30, 1998.

2. Based on the way you handled expenses and cash distributions in 1 and their ultimate effect on stockholders' equity, what theoretical reason can you give for not including expenses and cash distributions in the same closing entry?

FRA 2.

LO 1   Identification of
LO 2   Adjusting Entries
LO 6   and Closing Entries

Halliburton Company is one of the world's larger and more diversified oil field services and engineering/construction organizations. The following items appeared on the company's December 31, 1997, balance sheet (in millions).[4] The contracts referred to are agreements to perform services for engineering/construction clients.

Among the assets:
  Unbilled Work on Uncompleted Contracts $390.0

Among the liabilities:
  Advance Billings on Uncompleted Contracts $303.7

Contained in Note 1: Unbilled work on uncompleted contracts generally represents work currently billable, and such work is usually billed during normal billing processes in the next month.

1. Which of the two accounts above arises from an adjusting entry? What would be the debit and credit accounts of the entry?

2. Which of the two accounts above would normally require an adjusting entry at the end of the accounting period? What are the debit and credit accounts of the entry?

3. How does the accounting policy described in Note 1 differ from the general rule covered in this text? Why does it differ?

4. Of the four accounts you mentioned in the adjusting entries in **1** and **2** above, which require closing at the end of the year?

International Company

FRA 3.

LO 2 **Accounting Cycle and**
LO 6 **Closing Entries**

Nestlé S.A., maker of such well-known products as Nescafé, Lean Cuisine, and Perrier, is one of the largest and most internationally diverse companies in the world. Only 2 percent of its $60.5 billion in revenues comes from its home country of Switzerland, with the rest coming from sales in almost every other country of the world. Nestlé has over 220,000 employees in 70 countries[5] and is highly decentralized; that is, many of its divisions operate as separate companies in their countries. Managing the accounting operations of such a vast empire is a tremendous challenge. In what ways do you think the accounting cycle, including the closing process, would be the same for Nestlé as it is for Joan Miller Advertising Agency, Inc., and in what ways would it be different?

Toys "R" Us Annual Report

FRA 4.

LO 2 **Fiscal Year, Closing Process, and Interim Reports**

Refer to the Notes to Consolidated Financial Statements in the Toys "R" Us annual report. When does Toys "R" Us end its fiscal year? What reasons can you give for the company's having chosen this date? From the standpoint of completing the accounting cycle, what advantages does this date have? Does Toys "R" Us prepare interim financial statements? What are the implications of interim financial statements for the accounting cycle?

Fingraph® Financial Analyst™

This activity is not applicable to this chapter.

Internet Case

FRA 5.

LO 1 **Comparison of Accounting**
LO 5 **Systems and the Y2K Problem**

The Y2K problem, or the "millennium bug," was a major cost and a major risk for companies. This problem, in which computers are unable to recognize the year digits of "00" as the year 2000, was so important that the Securities and Exchange Commission required management to address in its annual report the extent of the risk to the company, what the company was doing about the problem, and how much the solution would cost the company. Go to the Needles Accounting Resource Center at http://college.hmco.com. Under web links, find the annual reports on the web sites for *H&R Block, Inc.,* and *Ford Motor Co.* In the annual reports look for the "Management's Discussion and Analysis" for the discussion of the Y2K problem. Compare how the two companies approached the problem. For which company was the problem more complex from the standpoint of the accounting design systems principle of compatibility? Which company seems to have had more control of the situation and which seems to have faced more risk?

ENDNOTES

1. Hershey Foods Corporation, Form 10-Q, October 4, 1998.
2. Earl E. Robertson and Dean Lockwood, "Tapping the Power of the PC at General Mills," *Management Accounting,* August 1994.
3. Adapted from H&R Block, Inc., *Annual Report,* 1998.
4. Halliburton Company, *Annual Report,* 1997.
5. Nestlé S.A., *Annual Report,* 1996.

5

Financial Reporting and Analysis

LEARNING OBJECTIVES

1 State the objectives of financial reporting.

2 State the qualitative characteristics of accounting information and describe their interrelationships.

3 Define and describe the use of the conventions of *comparability* and *consistency, materiality, conservatism, full disclosure,* and *cost-benefit.*

4 Explain management's responsibility for ethical financial reporting and define *fraudulent financial reporting.*

5 Identify and describe the basic components of a classified balance sheet.

6 Prepare multistep and single-step classified income statements.

7 Evaluate liquidity and profitability using classified financial statements.

General Mills, Inc. The management of a corporation is judged by the company's financial performance. This financial performance is reported to stockholders and others outside the business in the company's published annual report, which includes the company's financial statements and other relevant information. Performance measures are usually based on the relationships of key data in the financial statements and are communicated by management to the reader. For large companies, this often means condensing a tremendous amount of information to a few numbers considered important by management. For example, what key measures does the management of General Mills, Inc., a successful food products company with brands such as Cheerios, Wheaties, Hamburger Helper, and Fruit Roll-ups, choose to focus on as its goals?

In its letter to shareholders, General Mills states its financial goals as follows:

> *General Mills' objective for 1999 is to deliver superior performance, consistent with our long-term goals. Those goals are: to achieve a 12 percent average annual growth in earnings per share; to generate a minimum 25 percent return on [assets].*[1]

General Mills has chosen to highlight earnings growth and return on assets and has set benchmarks of 12 percent and 25 percent, respectively.

Of course, investors and creditors will want to do their own analysis of General Mills as well. This will require reading and interpretation of the financial statements and the calculation of other ratios. However, this analysis will be meaningless unless the reader understands financial statements and generally accepted accounting principles, on which the statements are based. Also important to learning how to read and interpret financial statements is a comprehension of the categories and classifications used in balance sheets and income statements. Key financial ratios used in

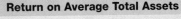

Return on Average Total Assets

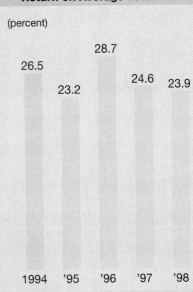

(percent)

26.5   23.2   28.7   24.6   23.9

1994   '95   '96   '97   '98

financial statement analysis are based on those categories. The chapter begins by describing the objectives, characteristics, and conventions that underlie the preparation of financial statements.

Objectives of Financial Information

The United States has a highly developed exchange economy. In this kind of economy, most goods and services are exchanged for money or claims to money instead of being used or bartered by their producers. Most business is carried on through corporations, including many extremely large firms that buy, sell, and obtain financing in U.S. and world markets.

By issuing stocks and bonds that are traded in financial markets, businesses can raise capital for production and marketing activities. Investors are interested mainly in returns from dividends and increases in the market price of their investments. Creditors want to know if the business can repay a loan plus interest in accordance with required terms. Thus, investors and creditors both need to know if a company can generate adequate cash flows. Financial statements are important to both groups in making that judgment. They offer valuable information that helps investors and creditors judge a company's ability to pay dividends and repay debts with interest. In this way, the market puts scarce resources to work in the companies that can use them most efficiently.

The information needs of users and the general business environment are the basis for the Financial Accounting Standards Board's (FASB) three objectives of financial reporting:[2]

| **Key Point:** Although people reading reports need some understanding of business, they do not need the skills required of a CPA.

1. *To furnish information that is useful in making investment and credit decisions.* Financial reporting should offer information that can help present and potential investors and creditors make rational investment and credit decisions. The reports should be in a form that makes sense to those who have some understanding of business and are willing to study the information carefully.

2. *To provide information useful in assessing cash flow prospects.* Financial reporting should supply information to help present and potential investors and creditors judge the amounts, timing, and risk of expected cash receipts from dividends or interest and the proceeds from the sale, redemption, or maturity of stocks or loans.

3. *To provide information about business resources, claims to those resources, and changes in them.* Financial reporting should give information about the company's assets, liabilities, and stockholders' equity, and the effects of transactions on the company's assets, liabilities, and stockholders' equity.

Financial statements are the most important way of periodically presenting to parties outside the business the information that has been gathered and processed in the accounting system. For this reason, the financial statements—the balance sheet, the income statement, the statement of retained earnings, and the statement of cash flows—are the most important output of the accounting system. These financial statements are "general purpose" because of their wide audience. They are "external" because their users are outside the business. Because of a potential conflict of interest between managers, who must prepare the statements, and investors or creditors, who invest in or lend money to the business, these statements often are audited by outside accountants to increase confidence in their reliability.

Qualitative Characteristics of Accounting Information

OBJECTIVE

2 State the qualitative characteristics of accounting information and describe their interrelationships

Key Point: Financial statements should be free of material misstatements.

It is easy for students in their first accounting course to get the idea that accounting is 100 percent accurate. This idea is reinforced by the fact that all the problems in this and other introductory books can be solved. The numbers all add up; what is supposed to equal something else does. Accounting seems very much like mathematics in its precision. In this course, the basics of accounting are presented in a simple form to help you understand them. In practice, however, accounting information is neither simple nor precise, and it rarely satisfies all criteria. The FASB emphasizes this fact in the following statement:

> The information provided by financial reporting often results from approximate, rather than exact, measures. The measures commonly involve numerous estimates, classifications, summarizations, judgments and allocations. The outcome of economic activity in a dynamic economy is uncertain and results from combinations of many factors. Thus, despite the aura of precision that may seem to surround financial reporting in general and financial statements in particular, with few exceptions the measures are approximations, which may be based on rules and conventions, rather than exact amounts.[3]

The goal of accounting information—to provide the basic data that different users need to make informed decisions—is an ideal. The gap between the ideal and the actual provides much of the interest and controversy in accounting. To facilitate interpretation, the FASB has described the **qualitative characteristics** of accounting information, which are standards for judging that information. In addition, there are generally accepted conventions for recording and reporting that simplify interpretation. The relationships among these concepts are shown in Figure 1.

Figure 1
Qualitative Characteristics and the Conventions of Accounting Information

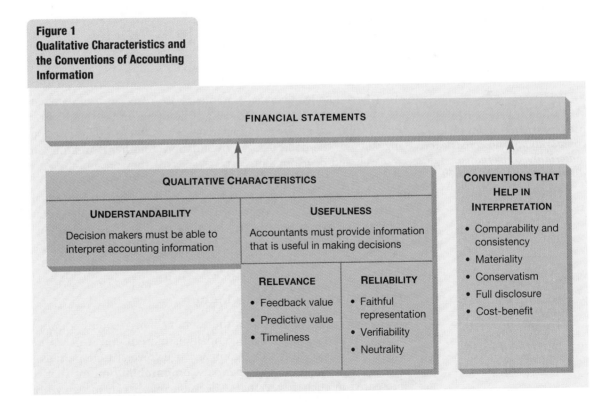

The most important qualitative characteristics are understandability and usefulness. **Understandability** depends on both the accountant and the decision maker. The accountant prepares the financial statements in accordance with accepted practices, generating important information that is believed to be understandable. But the decision maker must interpret the information and use it in making decisions. The decision maker must judge what information to use, how to use it, and what it means.

For accounting information to meet the standard of **usefulness**, it must have two major qualitative characteristics: relevance and reliability. **Relevance** means that the information can affect the outcome of a decision. In other words, a different decision would be made if the relevant information were not available. To be relevant, information must provide feedback, help predict future conditions, and be timely. For example, the income statement provides information about how a company performed over the past year (feedback), and it helps in planning for the next year (prediction). In order to be useful, however, it also must be communicated soon enough after the end of the accounting period to enable the reader to make decisions (timeliness).

In addition to being relevant, accounting information must have **reliability**. In other words, the user must be able to depend on the information. It must represent what it is meant to represent. It must be credible and verifiable by independent parties using the same methods of measuring. It also must be neutral. Accounting should convey information about business activity as faithfully as possible without influencing anyone in a specific direction. For example, the balance sheet should represent the economic resources, obligations, and stockholders' equity of a business as faithfully as possible in accordance with generally accepted accounting principles, and this balance sheet should be verifiable by an auditor.

Conventions That Help in the Interpretation of Financial Information

OBJECTIVE

3 Define and describe the use of the conventions of *comparability* and *consistency, materiality, conservatism, full disclosure,* and *cost-benefit*

To a large extent, financial statements are based on estimates and application of accounting rules for recognition and allocation. In this book, we point out a number of difficulties with financial statements. One is failing to recognize the changing value of the dollar caused by inflation. Another is treating intangibles, such as research and development costs, as assets if they are purchased outside the company and as expenses if they are developed within the company. Such problems do not mean that financial statements are useless; they are essential. However, users must know how to interpret them. To help in this interpretation, accountants depend on five **conventions**, or rules of thumb, in recording transactions and preparing financial statements: (1) comparability and consistency, (2) materiality, (3) conservatism, (4) full disclosure, and (5) cost-benefit.

Comparability and Consistency

A characteristic that increases the usefulness of accounting information is comparability. Information about a company is more useful if it can be compared with similar facts about the same company over several time periods or about another company for the same time period. **Comparability** means that the information is presented in such a way that a decision maker can recognize similarities, differences, and trends over different time periods or between different companies.

Consistent use of accounting measures and procedures is important in achieving comparability. The **consistency** convention requires that an accounting procedure, once adopted by a company, remain in use from one period to the next unless users are informed of the change. Thus, without a note to the contrary, users of financial statements can assume that there has been no arbitrary change in the treatment of a particular transaction, account, or item that would affect the interpretation of the statements.

If management decides that a certain procedure is no longer appropriate and should be changed, generally accepted accounting principles require that the change and its dollar effect be described in the notes to the financial statements:

> The nature of and justification for a change in accounting principle and its effect on income should be disclosed in the financial statements of the period in which the change is made. The justification for the change should explain clearly why the newly adopted accounting principle is preferable.[4]

 For example, in its 1997 annual report, Fruit of the Loom Inc. stated that it changed its method of accounting for inventories because management felt the new method improved the matching of revenues and costs.

Materiality

The term **materiality** refers to the relative importance of an item or event. If an item or event is material, it is probably relevant to the user of financial statements. In other words, an item is material if users would have done something differently if they had not known about the item. The accountant is often faced with decisions about small items or events that make little difference to users no matter how they are handled. For example, a large company may decide that expenditures for durable items of less than $500 should be charged as expenses rather than recorded as long-term assets and depreciated.

In general, an item is material if there is a reasonable expectation that knowing about it would influence the decisions of users of financial statements. The materiality of an item normally is determined by relating its dollar value to an element of the financial statements, such as net income or total assets. Some accountants feel that when an item is 5 percent or more of net income, it is material. However, materiality also depends on the nature of the item, not just its value. For example, in a multimillion-dollar company, a mistake of $5,000 in recording an item may not be important, but the discovery of a $5,000 bribe or theft can be very important. Also, many small errors can combine into a material amount. Accountants judge the materiality of many things, and the users of financial statements depend on their judgments being fair and accurate. The SEC has recently questioned companies' judgment about materiality to avoid showing certain items in the financial statements.

Conservatism

Accountants try to base their decisions on logic and evidence that lead to the fairest report of what happened. In judging and estimating, however, accountants often are faced with uncertainties. In these cases, they look to the convention of **conservatism**. This convention means that when accountants face major uncertainties about which accounting procedure to use, they generally choose the one that is least likely to overstate assets and income.

One of the most common applications of the conservatism convention is the use of the lower-of-cost-or-market method in accounting for inventories. Under this method, if an item's market value is greater than its cost, the more conservative cost figure is used. If the market value falls below the cost, the more conservative market value is used. The latter situation often occurs in the computer industry.

Key Point: Expensing a long-term asset in the period of purchase is not a GAAP alternative.

Conservatism can be a useful tool in doubtful cases, but its abuse leads to incorrect and misleading financial statements. Suppose that someone incorrectly applies the conservatism convention by expensing a long-term asset of material cost in the period of purchase. In this case, there is no uncertainty. Income and assets for the current period would be understated, and income in future periods would be overstated. For this reason, accountants depend on the conservatism convention only when there is uncertainty about which accounting procedure to use.

Full Disclosure

The convention of **full disclosure** requires that financial statements and their notes present all information that is relevant to the users' understanding of the statements. That is, the statements should offer any explanation that is needed to keep them from being misleading. Explanatory notes are considered an integral part of the financial statements. For instance, a change from one accounting procedure to another should be reported. In general, the form of the financial statements can affect their usefulness in making certain decisions. Also, certain items, such as the amount of depreciation expense on the income statement and the accumulated depreciation on the balance sheet, are essential to the readers of financial statements.

Enrichment Note: Significant events arising after the balance sheet date must be disclosed in the statements. Suppose a firm purchased a piece of land for a future subdivision. Shortly after the end of its fiscal year, the firm is served papers to halt construction because the Environmental Protection Agency asserts that the land was once a toxic waste dump. This information, which obviously affects the users of the financial statements, must be disclosed in the statements for the just-ended fiscal year.

Other examples of disclosures required by the Financial Accounting Standards Board and other official bodies are the accounting procedures used in preparing the statements, important terms of the company's debt, commitments and contingencies, and important events taking place after the date of the statements. However, there is a point at which the statements become so cluttered that notes impede rather than help understanding. Beyond required disclosures, the application of the full-disclosure convention is based on the judgment of management and of the accountants who prepare the financial statements.

In recent years, the principle of full disclosure also has been influenced by users of accounting information. To protect investors and creditors, independent auditors, the stock exchanges, and the SEC have made more demands for disclosure by publicly owned companies. The SEC has been pushing especially hard for the enforcement of full disclosure. As a result, more and better information about corporations is available to the public today than ever before.

BUSINESS FOCUS ON PRACTICE

When is "full disclosure" too much? When does the cost exceed the benefits? The big-five accounting firm of Ernst & Young reports that over a 20-year period the total number of pages in the annual reports of 25 large, well-known companies increased an average of 84 percent and the number of pages of notes increased 325 percent—from 4 pages to 17 pages. Management's discussion and analysis increased 300 percent, from 3 pages to 12.[5] Because some people feel that "these documents are so daunting that people don't read them at all," the Securities and Exchange Commission (SEC) allows companies to issue "summary reports" to the public that would eliminate many of the current notes. These reports would be more accessible and less costly. This is a controversial action because many analysts feel that it is in the notes that one gets the detailed information necessary to understand complex business operations. One analyst remarked, "To banish the notes for fear they will turn off readers would be like eliminating fractions from math books on the theory that the average student prefers to work with whole numbers."[6] Where this controversy will end, nobody knows. Detailed reports still must be filed with the SEC, but more and more companies are providing summary reports to the public.

Cost-Benefit

The **cost-benefit** convention underlies all the qualitative characteristics and conventions. It holds that the benefits to be gained from providing accounting information should be greater than the costs of providing it. Of course, minimum levels of relevance and reliability must be reached if accounting information is to be useful. Beyond the minimum levels, however, it is up to the FASB and the SEC, which require the information, and the accountant, who provides the information, to judge the costs and benefits in each case. Most of the costs of providing information fall at first on the preparers; the benefits are reaped by both preparers and users. Finally, both the costs and the benefits are passed on to society in the form of prices and social benefits from more efficient allocation of resources.

The costs and benefits of a particular requirement for accounting disclosure are both direct and indirect, immediate and deferred. For example, it is hard to judge the final costs and benefits of a far-reaching and costly regulation. The FASB, for instance, allows certain large companies to make a supplemental disclosure in their financial statements of the effects of changes in current costs. Most companies choose not to present this information because they believe the costs of producing and providing it exceed its benefits to the readers of their financial statements. Cost-benefit is a question faced by all regulators, including the FASB and the SEC. Even though there are no definitive ways of measuring costs and benefits, much of an accountant's work deals with these concepts.

Management's Responsibility for Ethical Reporting

The users of financial statements depend on the good faith of those who prepare these statements. This dependence places a duty on a company's management and its accountants to act ethically in the reporting process. That duty is often expressed in the report of management that accompanies financial statements. For example, the report of the management of Quaker Oats Co., a company known for strong financial reporting and controls, states:

> Management is responsible for the preparation and integrity of the Company's financial statements. The financial statements have been prepared in accordance with generally accepted accounting principles and necessarily include some amounts that are based on management's estimates and judgment.[7]

Quaker Oats' management also tells how it meets this responsibility:

> To fulfill its responsibility, management's goal is to maintain strong systems of internal controls, supported by formal policies and procedures that are communicated throughout the Company. Management regularly evaluates its systems of internal control with an eye toward improvement. Management also maintains a staff of internal auditors who evaluate the adequacy of and investigate the adherence to these controls, policies, and procedures.[8]

The intentional preparation of misleading financial statements is called **fraudulent financial reporting**.[9] It can result from the distortion of records (the manipulation of inventory records), falsified transactions (fictitious sales or orders), or the misapplication of accounting principles (treating as an asset an item that should be expensed). There are a number of possible motives for fraudulent reporting—for instance, to obtain a higher price when a company is sold, to meet the expectations

of stockholders, or to obtain a loan. Other times, the incentive is personal gain, such as additional compensation, promotion, or avoidance of penalties for poor performance. The personal costs of such actions can be high—individuals who authorize or prepare fraudulent financial statements may face criminal penalties and financial loss. Others, including investors and lenders to the company, employees, and customers, suffer from fraudulent financial reporting as well.

Incentives for fraudulent financial reporting exist to some extent in every company. It is management's responsibility to insist on honest financial reporting, but it is also the company accountants' responsibility to maintain high ethical standards. Ethical reporting demands that accountants apply financial accounting concepts to present a fair view of the company's operations and financial position and to avoid misleading readers of the financial statements.

Classified Balance Sheet

The balance sheets you have seen in the chapters thus far categorize accounts as assets, liabilities, and stockholders' equity. Because even a fairly small company can have hundreds of accounts, simply listing accounts in these broad categories is not particularly helpful to a statement user. Setting up subcategories within the major categories often makes financial statements much more useful. Investors and creditors study and evaluate the relationships among the subcategories. General-purpose external financial statements that are divided into useful subcategories are called **classified financial statements**.

The balance sheet presents the financial position of a company at a particular time. The subdivisions of the classified balance sheet shown in Exhibit 1 are typical of most companies in the United States. The subdivisions under owners' or stockholders' equity, of course, depend on the form of business.

Assets

A company's assets are often divided into four categories: (1) current assets; (2) investments; (3) property, plant, and equipment; and (4) intangible assets. For simplicity, some companies group investments, intangible assets, and other miscellaneous assets into a category called "other assets." These categories are listed in the order of their presumed ease of conversion into cash. For example, current assets are usually more easily converted to cash than are property, plant, and equipment.

Exhibit 1
Classified Balance Sheet for Shafer Auto Parts Corporation

Shafer Auto Parts Corporation
Balance Sheet
December 31, 20x2

Assets

Current Assets

Cash	$10,360	
Short-Term Investments	2,000	
Notes Receivable	8,000	
Accounts Receivable	35,300	
Merchandise Inventory	60,400	
Prepaid Insurance	6,600	
Store Supplies	1,060	
Office Supplies	636	
Total Current Assets		$124,356

Investments

Land Held for Future Use		5,000

Property, Plant, and Equipment

Land		$ 4,500	
Building	$20,650		
Less Accumulated Depreciation	8,640	12,010	
Delivery Equipment	$18,400		
Less Accumulated Depreciation	9,450	8,950	
Office Equipment	$ 8,600		
Less Accumulated Depreciation	5,000	3,600	
Total Property, Plant, and Equipment			29,060

Intangible Assets

Trademark		500
Total Assets		$158,916

Liabilities

Current Liabilities

Notes Payable	$15,000	
Accounts Payable	25,683	
Salaries Payable	2,000	
Total Current Liabilities		$ 42,683

Long-Term Liabilities

Mortgage Payable		17,800
Total Liabilities		$ 60,483

Stockholders' Equity

Contributed Capital

Common Stock, $10 par value, 5,000 shares authorized, issued, and outstanding	$50,000	
Additional Paid-in Capital	10,000	
Total Contributed Capital	$60,000	
Retained Earnings	38,433	
Total Stockholders' Equity		98,433
Total Liabilities and Stockholders' Equity		$158,916

CURRENT ASSETS **Current assets** are cash and other assets that are reasonably expected to be converted to cash, sold, or consumed within one year or within the normal operating cycle of the business, whichever is longer. The normal operating cycle of a company is the average time needed to go from cash to cash. For example, cash is used to buy merchandise inventory, which is sold for cash, or for a promise of cash if the sale is made on account. If a sale is made on account, the resulting receivable must be collected before the cycle is completed.

Key Point: Use one year as the current period unless the normal operating cycle happens to be longer.

The normal operating cycle for most companies is less than one year, but there are exceptions. Tobacco companies, for example, must age their tobacco for two or three years before it can be sold. The tobacco inventory is nonetheless considered a current asset because it will be sold within the normal operating cycle. Another example is a company that sells on the installment basis. The payments for a television set or a refrigerator can be extended over 24 or 36 months, but these receivables are still considered current assets.

Cash is obviously a current asset. Temporary investments, notes and accounts receivable, and inventory are also current assets because they are expected to be converted to cash within the next year or during the normal operating cycle. On the balance sheet, they are listed in the order of their ease of conversion into cash.

Prepaid expenses, such as rent and insurance paid for in advance, and inventories of supplies bought for use rather than for sale also should be classified as current assets. These kinds of assets are current in the sense that if they had not been bought earlier, a current outlay of cash would be needed to obtain them.[11]

Key Point: For an investment to be classified as current, management must intend to sell it within the next year or the current operating cycle, and it must be readily marketable.

In deciding whether an asset is current or noncurrent, the idea of "reasonable expectation" is important. For example, Short-Term Investments is an account used for temporary investments of idle cash, or cash that is not immediately required for operating purposes. Management can reasonably expect to sell these securities as cash needs arise over the next year or operating cycle. Investments in securities that management does not expect to sell within the next year and that do not involve the temporary use of idle cash should be shown in the investments category of a classified balance sheet.

INVESTMENTS The **investments** category includes assets, usually long term, that are not used in the normal operation of the business and that management does not plan to convert to cash within the next year. Items in this category are securities held for long-term investment, long-term notes receivable, land held for future use, plant or equipment not used in the business, and special funds established to pay off a debt or buy a building. Also included are large permanent investments in another company for the purpose of controlling that company.

PROPERTY, PLANT, AND EQUIPMENT The category **property, plant, and equipment** includes long-term assets used in the continuing operation of the business. They represent a place to operate (land and buildings) and equipment to produce, sell, deliver, and service the company's goods. Consequently, they may also be called *operating assets* or, sometimes, *fixed assets, tangible assets, long-lived assets,* or *plant assets.* Through depreciation, the costs of these assets (except land) are spread over the periods they benefit. Past depreciation is recorded in the Accumulated Depreciation accounts. The order in which property, plant, and equipment are listed on the balance sheet is not the same everywhere. In practice, accounts are often combined to make the financial statements less cluttered. For example:

Property, Plant, and Equipment

Land		$ 4,500
Buildings and Equipment	$47,650	
Less Accumulated Depreciation	23,090	24,560
Total Property, Plant, and Equipment		$29,060

Many companies simply show a single line with a total for property, plant, and equipment and provide the details in a note to the financial statements.

Property, plant, and equipment also includes natural resources owned by the company, such as forest lands, oil and gas properties, and coal mines. Assets that are not used in the regular course of business are listed in the investments category, as noted above.

INTANGIBLE ASSETS   **Intangible assets** are long-term assets that have no physical substance but have a value based on the rights or privileges that belong to their owner. Examples are patents, copyrights, goodwill, franchises, and trademarks. These assets are recorded at cost, which is spread over the expected life of the right or privilege.

OTHER ASSETS   Some companies use the category **other assets** to group all owned assets other than current assets and property, plant, and equipment. Other assets can include investments and intangible assets.

Liabilities

Liabilities are divided into two categories, based on when the liabilities fall due: current liabilities and long-term liabilities.

Business-World Example: The portion of a mortgage, which is paid monthly for 120 months, due during the next year or the current operating cycle would be classified as a current liability; the portion due after the next year or the current operating cycle would be classified as a long-term liability.

CURRENT LIABILITIES   The category **current liabilities** consists of obligations due to be paid or performed within one year or within the normal operating cycle of the business, whichever is longer. Current liabilities are typically paid from current assets or by incurring new short-term liabilities. They include notes payable, accounts payable, the current portion of long-term debt, salaries and wages payable, taxes payable, and customer advances (unearned revenues).

LONG-TERM LIABILITIES   The debts of a business that fall due more than one year in the future or beyond the normal operating cycle, or that are to be paid out of noncurrent assets, are **long-term liabilities**. Mortgages payable, long-term notes, bonds payable, employee pension obligations, and long-term lease liabilities generally fall into the category of long-term liabilities. Deferred income taxes are often disclosed as a separate category in the long-term liability section of the balance sheet of publicly held corporations. This liability arises because the rules for measuring income for tax purposes differ from those for financial reporting. The cumulative annual difference between the income taxes payable to governments and the income taxes expense reported on the income statement is included in the account Deferred Income Taxes.

Stockholders' Equity

The stockholders' equity section for a corporation would appear as shown in the balance sheet for Shafer Auto Parts Corporation. As you learned earlier, corporations are separate legal entities that are owned by their stockholders. The stockholders' equity section of a balance sheet has two parts: contributed or paid-in capital and retained earnings. Generally, contributed capital is shown on corporate balance sheets by two amounts: (1) the par value of the issued stock and (2) the amounts paid in or contributed in excess of the par value per share.

Other Forms of Business Organization

The accounting treatment of assets and liabilities is not usually affected by the form of business organization. However, the equity section of the balance sheet for a business that is organized as a sole proprietorship or a partnership is very different from that for a corporation.

SOLE PROPRIETORSHIP   The equity section for a sole proprietorship simply shows the capital in the owner's name at an amount equal to the net assets of the company. The equity section of a sole proprietorship might appear as follows:

Owner's Equity

Hershell Serton, Capital	$57,390

Because there is no legal separation between an owner and his or her sole proprietorship, there is no need for contributed capital to be separated from earnings retained for use in a business. This capital account is increased by both the owner's investments and net income. It is decreased by net losses and withdrawals of assets from the business for personal use by the owner. In this kind of business, the formality of declaring and paying dividends is not required.

In fact, the terms *owner's equity*, *proprietorship*, *capital*, and *net worth* are used interchangeably. They all stand for the owner's interest in the company. The first three terms are preferred to *net worth* because most assets are recorded at original cost rather than at current value. For this reason, the ownership section will not represent "worth." It is really a claim against the assets of the company.

Key Point: The only difference in equity between a sole proprietorship and a partnership is in the number of capital accounts.

PARTNERSHIP   The equity section of the balance sheet for a partnership is called *partners' equity* and is much like that for the sole proprietorship. It might appear as follows:

Partners' Equity

A. J. Martin, Capital	$21,666	
R. C. Moore, Capital	35,724	
Total Partners' Equity		$57,390

Reading and Graphing Real Company Balance Sheets

Although financial statements usually follow the same general form as illustrated for Shafer Auto Parts Corporation, no two companies will have statements that are exactly alike. In Exhibit 2, the balance sheet of Dell Computer Corp., the world's leading direct computer systems company, is a good example. Note that two years of data are provided so that the change from one year to the next can be evaluated. Also note that the major classifications are similar but not identical to those for Shafer Auto Parts Corporation. For instance, the assets of Shafer Auto Parts Corporation include investments and intangible assets categories, whereas Dell Computer Corp. has an asset category called "Other Assets," which is a very small amount of its total assets. Also notice that there is a category called "Other Liabilities." Because this category appears after long-term debt, it represents longer-term liabilities, due more than one year from the balance sheet dates.

We may also observe that Dell's stockholders' equity section differs from the stockholders' equity section of Shafer Auto Parts Corporation because it contains a category called "Other Equity," which is subtracted from common stock and retained earnings. However, it is possible to look at the total stockholders' equity and know that this amount relates to the claims by the stockholders on the company.

When we look at columns of numbers, it is sometimes difficult to see the patterns. Graphical presentation of the statements is helpful in visualizing the changes

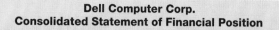

Exhibit 2
Balance Sheet for Dell Computer Corp.

Dell Computer Corp.
Consolidated Statement of Financial Position

(In millions)

	Jan. 29, 1999	Feb. 1, 1998
ASSETS		
CURRENT ASSETS:		
Cash	$ 520	$ 320
Marketable securities	2,661	1,524
Accounts receivable, net	2,094	1,486
Inventories	273	233
Other	791	349
Total current assets	6,339	3,912
PROPERTY, PLANT, AND EQUIPMENT:		
Land and buildings	172	137
Computer equipment	205	135
Equipment and other	398	237
Total	775	509
Less accumulated depreciation	252	167
Property, plant, and equipment, net	523	342
OTHER ASSETS	15	14
TOTAL ASSETS	$6,877	$4,268
LIABILITIES AND STOCKHOLDERS' EQUITY		
CURRENT LIABILITIES:		
Accounts payable	$2,397	$1,643
Accrued and other	1,298	1,054
Total current liabilities	3,695	2,697
LONG-TERM DEBT	512	17
OTHER LIABILITIES	349	261
TOTAL LIABILITIES	4,556	2,975
STOCKHOLDERS' EQUITY:		
Common stock	1,781	747
Retained earnings	606	607
Less other equity	66	61
STOCKHOLDERS' EQUITY	2,321	1,293
TOTAL LIABILITIES AND EQUITY	$6,877	$4,268

that are taking place in a company's financial position. For example, Dell's balance sheet from Exhibit 2 is presented graphically in Figure 2 using the Fingraph® Financial Analyst™ CD-ROM software that accompanies this text. In the graph, total assets and its components are graphed on the left side, and total liabilities and its components, together with total stockholders' equity, are on the right side. The composition of the assets and liabilities, their relation to stockholders' equity, and the changes in them from 1998 to 1999 are clearly seen. These graphs show that overall there was significant growth in both totals and components for Dell from

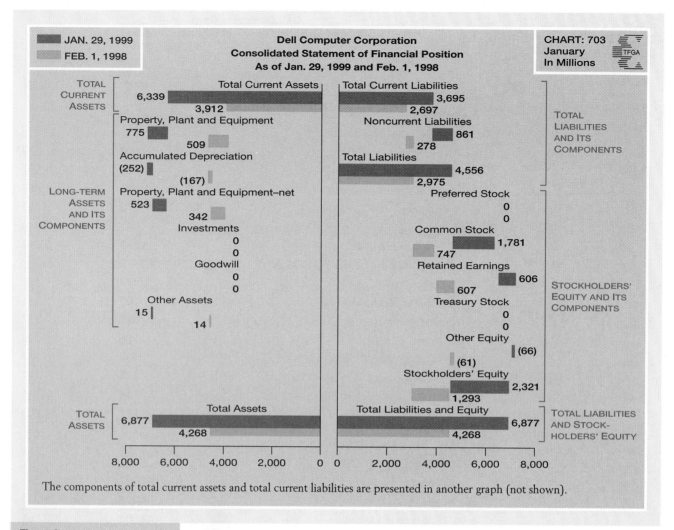

Figure 2
Graphical Presentation of Dell Computer Corp.'s Balance Sheets

1998 to 1999. Also note that showing the balance sheet visually reduces the detailed clutter of the statement. For instance, all current assets are combined and represented by a single component line.

Multistep Income Statement

OBJECTIVE

6 Prepare multistep and single-step classified income statements

Thus far in this text, all income statements have been presented in a simple single-step form in which all expenses are deducted from revenues to arrive at net income. In practice, many companies use some form of a **multistep income statement**, which goes through a series of steps, or subtotals, to arrive at net income. The multistep income statement for service companies is compared with that for **merchandising companies**, which buy and sell products, and **manufacturing companies**, which make and sell products, in Figure 3. Note that in the multistep income statement for service companies, the operating expenses are deducted from revenues in a single step to arrive at income from operations. In

Figure 3
The Components of Multistep Income Statements for Service and Merchandising or Manufacturing Companies

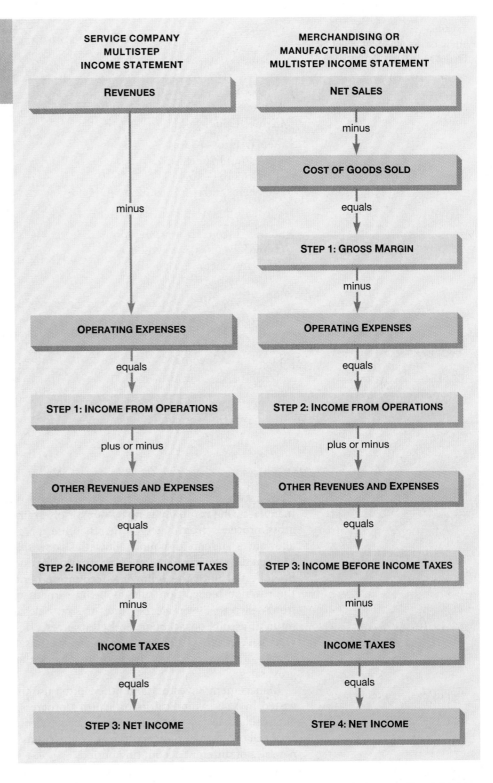

SERVICE COMPANY MULTISTEP INCOME STATEMENT

REVENUES

minus

OPERATING EXPENSES

equals

STEP 1: INCOME FROM OPERATIONS

plus or minus

OTHER REVENUES AND EXPENSES

equals

STEP 2: INCOME BEFORE INCOME TAXES

minus

INCOME TAXES

equals

STEP 3: NET INCOME

MERCHANDISING OR MANUFACTURING COMPANY MULTISTEP INCOME STATEMENT

NET SALES

minus

COST OF GOODS SOLD

equals

STEP 1: GROSS MARGIN

minus

OPERATING EXPENSES

equals

STEP 2: INCOME FROM OPERATIONS

plus or minus

OTHER REVENUES AND EXPENSES

equals

STEP 3: INCOME BEFORE INCOME TAXES

minus

INCOME TAXES

equals

STEP 4: NET INCOME

Business-World Example: The multistep income statement is a valuable analytical tool that is often overlooked. Analysts will frequently convert a single-step statement into a multistep one because the latter separates operating from nonoperating sources of net income. Investors want net income to result primarily from operations, not from one-time gains or losses.

contrast, because manufacturing and merchandising companies make or buy goods for sale, they must include an additional step in the multistep income statement for the cost of these goods that are sold. In the following discussion of these components, the income statement for Shafer Auto Parts Corporation, a merchandising company, presented in Exhibit 3, will serve as an example of a multistep income statement.

Exhibit 3

Multistep Income Statement for Shafer Auto Parts Corporation

Shafer Auto Parts Corporation
Income Statement
For the Year Ended December 31, 20x2

Net Sales		$289,656
Cost of Goods Sold		181,260
Step 1: Gross Margin		$108,396
Operating Expenses		
Selling Expenses	$54,780	
General and Administrative Expenses	34,504	
Total Operating Expenses		89,284
Step 2: Income from Operations		$ 19,112
Other Revenues and Expenses		
Interest Income	$ 1,400	
Less Interest Expense	2,631	
Excess of Other Expenses over Other Revenues		1,231
Step 3: Income Before Income Taxes		$ 17,881
Income Taxes		3,381
Step 4: Net Income		$ 14,500
Earnings per share		$ 2.90

Net Sales

The first major part of the multistep income statement for a merchandising or manufacturing company is **net sales**, or often simply *sales*. Net sales consist of the gross proceeds from sales of merchandise, or gross sales, less sales returns and allowances and any discounts allowed. **Gross sales** consist of total cash sales and total credit sales during a given accounting period. Even though the cash may not be collected until the following accounting period, revenue is recognized, under the revenue recognition rule, as being earned when title for merchandise passes from seller to buyer at the time of sale. Sales returns and allowances are cash refunds, credits on account, and allowances off selling prices made to customers who have received defective or otherwise unsatisfactory products. If other discounts or allowances are given to customers, they also should be deducted from gross sales.

Management, investors, and others often use the amount of sales and trends suggested by sales as indicators of a firm's progress. Increasing sales suggest growth; decreasing sales indicate the possibility of decreased future earnings and other financial problems. To detect trends, comparisons are frequently made between the net sales of different accounting periods.

Key Point: The cost of goods sold (also called the *cost of sales*) is an expense.

Key Point: The matching rule precludes the cost of inventory from being expensed until the inventory has been sold.

Cost of Goods Sold

Cost of goods sold, or simply *cost of sales*, which is the amount a merchandiser paid for the merchandise that was sold during an accounting period or the cost to a manufacturer of manufacturing the products that were sold during an accounting period, is the second part of the multistep income statement for a merchandiser or manufacturer.

Gross Margin

The third major part of the multistep income statement for a merchandiser or manufacturer is **gross margin**, or *gross profit*, which is the difference between net sales and cost of goods sold. To be successful, companies must achieve a gross margin that is sufficient to cover operating expenses and provide an adequate after-tax income.

Management is interested in both the amount and the percentage of gross margin. The percentage of gross margin is computed by dividing the amount of gross margin by net sales. In the case of Shafer Auto Parts Corporation, the amount of gross margin is $108,396 and the percentage of gross margin is 37.4 percent ($108,396 ÷ $289,656). This information is useful in planning business operations. For instance, management may try to increase total sales dollars by reducing the selling price. This strategy reduces the percentage of gross margin, but it will work if the total of items sold increases enough to raise the absolute amount of gross margin. This is the strategy followed by a discount warehouse store like Sam's Clubs. On the other hand, management may decide to keep a high gross margin from sales and attempt to increase sales and the amount of gross margin by increasing operating expenses such as advertising. This is the strategy followed by upscale specialty stores like Neiman Marcus. Other strategies to increase gross margin from sales, such as reducing cost of goods sold by better purchasing methods, can also be explored.

Operating Expenses

The next major area of the multistep income statement consists of **operating expenses**, which are the expenses other than cost of goods sold that are incurred in running a business. They are similar to the expenses of a service company. It is customary to group operating expenses into categories, such as selling expenses and general and administrative expenses. Selling expenses include the costs of storing goods and preparing them for sale; preparing displays, advertising, and otherwise promoting sales; making sales; and delivering goods to the buyer, if the seller pays the cost of delivery. The latter cost is often called **freight out expense**, or *delivery expense*. Among general and administrative expenses are general office expenses, which include expenses for accounting, personnel, and credit and collections, and any other expenses that apply to overall operations. Although general occupancy expenses, such as rent expense, insurance expense, and utilities expense, are often classified as general and administrative expenses, they may also be allocated between the selling and the general and administrative categories. Careful planning and control of operating expenses can improve a company's profitability.

Income from Operations

Income from operations, or simply *operating income*, is the difference between gross margin and operating expenses and represents the income from a company's normal, or main, business. Because companies may have significant other revenues and expenses and different income tax rates, income from operations is often used to compare the profitability of two or more companies or divisions within a company.

Other Revenues and Expenses

Other revenues and expenses, or *nonoperating revenues and expenses*, are not part of a company's operating activities. This section includes revenues or income from investments (such as dividends and interest on stocks, bonds, and savings accounts) and interest earned on credit or notes extended to customers. It also includes interest expense and other expenses that result from borrowing money or from credit extended to the company. If the company has revenues and expenses other than interest and dividends that are not related to the company's normal business operations, they too are included in this part of the income statement. An analyst who wants to compare two companies independent of their financing methods—that is, before considering other revenues and expenses—would focus on income from operations.

Income Before Income Taxes

Income before income taxes is the amount the company has earned from all activities—operating and nonoperating—before taking into account the amount of income taxes the company incurred. Because companies may be subject to different income tax rates, income before income taxes is also used to compare the profitability of two or more companies or divisions within a company.

Income Taxes

Income taxes, also called *provision for income taxes*, represent the expense for federal, state, and local taxes on corporate income. The Income Taxes account is shown as a separate item on the income statement. Usually the word *expense* is not used. This account would not appear on the income statements of sole proprietorships and partnerships because they are not tax-paying units. The individuals who own these businesses are the tax-paying units, and they pay income taxes on their share of the business income. Corporations, however, must report and pay income taxes on earnings. Because federal, state, and local income taxes for corporations are substantial, they have a significant effect on business decisions. Current federal income tax rates for corporations can vary from 15 percent to 38 percent depending on the amount of income before income taxes and other factors. Most other taxes, such as property taxes, employment taxes, licenses, and fees, are shown among the operating expenses.

Net Income

Net income, the final figure, or "bottom line," of the income statement, is what remains of the gross margin after operating expenses are deducted, other revenues and expenses are added or deducted, and income taxes are deducted. It is an important performance measure because it represents the amount of business earnings that accrue to stockholders. It is the amount that is transferred to retained earnings from all the income-generating activities during the year. Both management and investors often use net income to measure whether a business has been operating successfully during the past accounting period.

Earnings per Share

Enrichment Note: Earnings per share is the most commonly cited performance measure in the business press because it is a shorthand measure of profitability.

Earnings per share, often called *net income per share*, of common stock is also unique to corporate reporting. Ownership in corporations is represented by shares of stock, and the net income per share is reported immediately below net income on the income statement. In the simplest case, it is computed by dividing the net income by the average number of shares of common stock outstanding during the year. For example, Shafer's earnings per share of $2.90 was computed by dividing the net income of $14,500 by the 5,000 shares of common stock outstanding, as reported in the stockholders' equity section of the balance sheet (Exhibit 1). Investors find the figure useful as a quick way of assessing both a company's profit-earning success and its earnings in relation to the market price of its stock.

Reading and Graphing Real Company Income Statements

As with the presentation of balance sheets, you will rarely find income statements that are exactly like the one for Shafer Auto Parts Corporation. You will encounter terms and structure that differ, such as those on the multistep income statement for Dell Computer Corp. in Exhibit 4, where management provides three years of data for comparison purposes. Sometimes there may be components in the income statement that are not covered in this chapter. If this occurs, refer to the index at the end of the book to find the topic and read about it.

Using the Fingraph® Financial Analyst™ CD-ROM software that accompanies this text to graphically present Dell's income from operations, as shown in Figure 4, helps to show the company's progress in meeting its profitability objectives. On the left side of the graph are the components of income from operations, beginning with total revenues at the top and ending with income from operations at the bottom. On the right side, the changes in the components are graphed. Increases are shown on the right of the vertical column, and decreases are shown on the left. Operating income increased by $730 million because gross margin increased by $1,384 million while operating expenses increased by only $586 million.

A separate graphical presentation (not shown) is used to show the remainder of the income statement. The income statement shows annual increases in net income similar to increases in income from operations.

Exhibit 4
Income Statement for Dell Computer Corp.

Dell Computer Corp.
Consolidated Statements of Income

(In millions)

	Fiscal Year Ended		
	Jan. 29, 1999	Feb. 1, 1998	Feb. 2, 1997
Net revenues	$18,243	$12,327	$7,759
Cost of revenue	14,137	9,605	6,093
Gross margin	4,106	2,722	1,666
Operating expenses:			
Selling, general and administrative	1,788	1,202	826
Research and development	272	204	126
Total operating expenses	2,060	1,406	952
Operating income	2,046	1,316	714
Financing and other income	38	52	33
Income before income taxes	2,084	1,368	747
Provision for income taxes	624	424	216
Income before extraordinary loss	1,460	944	531
Extraordinary loss, net of taxes			(13)
Net income	1,460	944	518

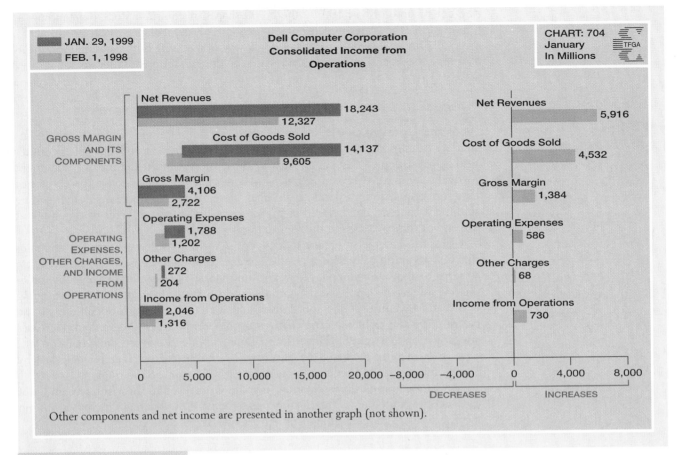

JAN. 29, 1999
FEB. 1, 1998

**Dell Computer Corporation
Consolidated Income from
Operations**

CHART: 704
January
In Millions

GROSS MARGIN
AND ITS
COMPONENTS

Net Revenues
18,243
12,327

Cost of Goods Sold
14,137
9,605

Gross Margin
4,106
2,722

OPERATING
EXPENSES,
OTHER CHARGES,
AND INCOME
FROM
OPERATIONS

Operating Expenses
1,788
1,202

Other Charges
272
204

Income from Operations
2,046
1,316

Net Revenues
5,916

Cost of Goods Sold
4,532

Gross Margin
1,384

Operating Expenses
586

Other Charges
68

Income from Operations
730

0   5,000   10,000   15,000   20,000   −8,000   −4,000   0   4,000   8,000

DECREASES   INCREASES

Other components and net income are presented in another graph (not shown).

**Figure 4
Graphical Presentation of
Dell Computer Corp.'s Income
Statement**

Single-Step Income Statement

The **single-step income statement**, which is illustrated for Shafer Auto Parts Corporation in Exhibit 5, derives income before income taxes in a single step by putting the major categories of revenues in the first part of the statement and the major categories of costs and expenses in the second part of the statement. Income taxes are shown as a separate item, as on the multistep income statement. The multistep form and the single-step form each have advantages. For example, the multistep form shows the components used in deriving net income, and the single-step form has the advantage of simplicity.

When a company uses the single-step form, as Nike, Inc., the footwear company, does in Exhibit 6, most analysts will still calculate gross margin and income from operations and each component's percentages of revenues (as shown on the next left page for Nike, Inc.):

Exhibit 5
Single-Step Income Statement for Shafer Auto Parts Corporation

Shafer Auto Parts Corporation
Income Statement
For the Year Ended December 31, 20x2

Revenues		
Net Sales		$289,656
Interest Income		1,400
Total Revenues		$291,056
Costs and Expenses		
Cost of Goods Sold	$181,260	
Selling Expenses	54,780	
General and Administrative Expenses	34,504	
Interest Expense	2,631	
Total Costs and Expenses		273,175
Income Before Income Taxes		$ 17,881
Income Taxes		3,381
Net Income		$ 14,500
Earnings per share		$ 2.90

Exhibit 6
Single-Step Income Statement for Nike, Inc.

Nike. Inc.
Consolidated Statements of Income

(In millions, except per share data)

	Year Ended May 31		
	1998	1997	1996
Revenues	**$9,553.1**	$9,186.5	$6,470.6
Costs and expenses:			
Costs of sales	**6,065.5**	5,503.0	3,906.7
Selling and administrative	**2,623.8**	2,303.7	1,588.6
Interest expense	**60.0**	52.3	39.5
Other (income)/expense, net	**20.9**	32.2	36.7
Restructuring charge	**129.9**	—	—
	8,900.1	7,891.3	5,571.5
Income before income taxes	**653.0**	1,295.2	899.1
Income taxes	**253.4**	499.4	345.9
Net income	**399.6**	$ 795.8	$ 553.2
Basic income per common share	**$ 1.38**	$ 2.76	$ 1.93

The accompanying notes to consolidated financial statements are an integral part of this statement.

Source: Nike, Inc., *Annual Report,* 1998.

	1998	Percent	1997	Percent
Revenues	$9,553.1	100.0	$9,186.5	100.0
Cost of Sales	6,065.5	63.5	5,503.0	59.9
Gross Margin	$3,487.6	36.5	$3,683.5	40.1
Selling and Administrative	2,623.8	27.5	2,303.7	25.1
Income from Operations	$ 863.8	9.0	$1,379.8	15.0

From this analysis, it may be seen that Nike was not able to maintain its profitability as measured by income from operations even though sales increased 4 percent. Cost of sales and selling and administrative expenses grew faster than revenues resulting in declining amounts and percentages of gross margins and income from operations. This type of analysis is often performed because a majority of public companies use some form of the single-step income statement.

Using Classified Financial Statements

OBJECTIVE

7 Evaluate liquidity and profitability using classified financial statements

Earlier in this chapter, you learned that financial reporting, according to the Financial Accounting Standards Board, seeks to provide information that is useful in making investment and credit decisions, in judging cash flow prospects, and in understanding business resources, claims to those resources, and changes in them. These objectives are related to two of the more important goals of management—maintaining adequate liquidity and achieving satisfactory profitability—because investors and creditors base their decisions largely on their assessment of a company's potential liquidity and profitability. The following analysis focuses on these two important goals.

In this section, a series of charts shows average ratios for six industries based on data obtained from *Industry Norms and Key Business Ratios*, a publication of Dun & Bradstreet. There are two examples from service industries, advertising agencies and interstate trucking; two examples from merchandising industries, auto and home supply and grocery stores; and two examples from manufacturing industries, pharmaceuticals and computers. Shafer Auto Parts Corporation, the example used in this chapter, falls into the auto and home supply industry.

Evaluation of Liquidity

Liquidity means having enough money on hand to pay bills when they are due and to take care of unexpected needs for cash. Two measures of liquidity are working capital and the current ratio.

Key Point: It is imperative that accounts be classified correctly before the ratios are computed. If accounts are not classified correctly, the ratios will not be correct.

WORKING CAPITAL The first measure, **working capital**, is the amount by which total current assets exceed total current liabilities. This is an important measure of liquidity because current liabilities are debts that must be paid or obligations that must be performed within one year, and current assets are assets that will be realized in cash or used up within one year or one operating cycle, whichever is longer. By definition, current liabilities are paid out of current assets. So the excess of current assets over current liabilities is the net current assets on hand to continue business operations. It is the working capital that can be used to buy inventory, obtain credit, and finance expanded sales. Lack of working capital can lead to a company's failure.

For Shafer Auto Parts Corporation, working capital is computed as follows:

Current assets	$124,356
Less current liabilities	42,683
Working capital	$ 81,673

CURRENT RATIO   The second measure of liquidity, the current ratio, is closely related to working capital and is believed by many bankers and other creditors to be a good indicator of a company's ability to pay its bills and to repay outstanding loans. The **current ratio** is the ratio of current assets to current liabilities. For Shafer Auto Parts Corporation, it would be computed like this:

$$\text{Current Ratio} = \frac{\text{Current Assets}}{\text{Current Liabilities}} = \frac{\$124{,}356}{\$42{,}683} = 2.9$$

Business-World Example: Some successful companies, such as McDonald's, manage to have very low current ratios by carefully planning their cash flows.

Enrichment Note: It is inadvisable to have too high a current ratio because the firm could probably use the excess funds more effectively to increase its overall profit.

Thus, Shafer has $2.90 of current assets for each $1.00 of current liabilities. Is that good or bad? The answer requires the comparison of this year's ratio with ratios for earlier years and with similar measures for successful companies in the same industry. The average current ratio varies widely from industry to industry, as shown in Figure 5. For advertising agencies, which have no merchandise inventory, the current ratio is 1.4. In contrast, auto and home supply companies, which carry large merchandise inventories, have an average current ratio of 2.1. The current ratio for Shafer Auto Parts Corporation, 2.9, exceeds the average for its industry. A very low current ratio, of course, can be unfavorable, but so can a very high one. The latter may indicate that the company is not using its assets effectively.

Evaluation of Profitability

Just as important as paying bills on time is **profitability**—the ability to earn a satisfactory income. As a goal, profitability competes with liquidity for managerial attention because liquid assets, although important, are not the best profit-producing resources. Cash, for example, means purchasing power, but a satisfactory profit can be made only if purchasing power is used to buy profit-producing (and less liquid) assets, such as inventory and long-term assets.

Among the common measures of a company's ability to earn income are (1) profit margin, (2) asset turnover, (3) return on assets, (4) debt to equity, and (5) return on equity. To evaluate a company meaningfully, one must relate its profit performance to its past performance and prospects for the future as well as to the averages for other companies in the same industry.

Figure 5
Average Current Ratio for Selected Industries

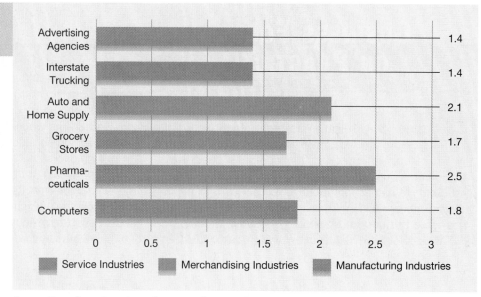

Source: Data from Dun & Bradstreet, *Industry Norms and Key Business Ratios,* 1997–98.

 PROFIT MARGIN   The **profit margin** shows the percentage of each sales dollar that results in net income. It is figured by dividing net income by net sales. It should not be confused with gross margin, which is not a ratio but rather the amount by which revenues exceed the cost of goods sold.

Shafer Auto Parts Corporation has a profit margin of 5.0 percent:

$$\text{Profit Margin} = \frac{\text{Net Income}}{\text{Net Sales}} = \frac{\$14,500}{\$289,656} = .050\ (5.0\%)$$

On each dollar of net sales, Shafer Auto Parts Corporation made 5.0 cents. A difference of 1 or 2 percent in a company's profit margin can mean the difference between a fair year and a very profitable one.

ASSET TURNOVER   **Asset turnover** measures how efficiently assets are used to produce sales. Computed by dividing net sales by average total assets, it shows how many dollars of sales were generated by each dollar of assets. A company with a higher asset turnover uses its assets more productively than one with a lower asset turnover. Average total assets is computed by adding total assets at the beginning of the year to total assets at the end of the year and dividing by 2.

Key Point: Average total assets equals assets at the beginning of the year plus assets at the end of the year, divided by 2.

Assuming that total assets for Shafer Auto Parts Corporation were $148,620 at the beginning of the year, its asset turnover is computed as follows:

$$\text{Asset Turnover} = \frac{\text{Net Sales}}{\text{Average Total Assets}}$$

$$= \frac{\$289,656}{(\$158,916 + \$148,620) \div 2} = \frac{\$289,656}{\$153,768} = 1.9 \text{ times}$$

Shafer Auto Parts Corporation produces $1.90 in sales for each $1.00 invested in average total assets. This ratio shows a meaningful relationship between an income statement figure and a balance sheet figure.

RETURN ON ASSETS   Both the profit margin and the asset turnover ratios have some limitations. The profit margin ratio does not take into consideration the assets necessary to produce income, and the asset turnover ratio does not take into account the amount of income produced. The **return on assets** ratio overcomes these deficiencies by relating net income to average total assets. It is computed like this:

K/R

$$\text{Return on Assets} = \frac{\text{Net Income}}{\text{Average Total Assets}}$$

$$= \frac{\$14,500}{(\$158,916 + \$148,620) \div 2} = \frac{\$14,500}{\$153,768} = .094 \text{ (or 9.4\%)}$$

For each dollar invested, Shafer Auto Parts Corporation's assets generated 9.4 cents of net income. This ratio indicates the income-generating strength (profit margin) of the company's resources and how efficiently the company is using all its assets (asset turnover).

Key Point: Return on assets is one of the most widely used measures of profitability because it reflects both the profit margin and asset turnover.

Return on assets, then, combines profit margin and asset turnover:

$$\frac{\text{Net Income}}{\text{Net Sales}} \times \frac{\text{Net Sales}}{\text{Average Total Assets}} = \frac{\text{Net Income}}{\text{Average Total Assets}}$$

Profit Margin	×	Asset Turnover	=	Return on Assets
5.0%	×	1.9 times	=	9.5%*

*The slight difference between 9.4 and 9.5 is due to rounding.

Thus, a company's management can improve overall profitability by increasing the profit margin, the asset turnover, or both. Similarly, in evaluating a company's overall profitability, the financial statement user must consider the interaction of both ratios to produce return on assets.

Careful study of Figures 6, 7, and 8 shows the different ways in which the selected industries combine profit margin and asset turnover to produce return on assets. For instance, compare the return on assets for grocery stores and computers, and see how they achieve it in very different ways. Grocery stores have a smaller profit margin, 1.7 percent, which when multiplied by a higher asset turnover, 5.3 times, gives a return on assets of 9.0 percent. Computers, on the other hand, have a higher profit margin, 2.6 percent, and a lower asset turnover, 2.8 times, and produce a return on assets of 7.3 percent.

Shafer Auto Parts Corporation's profit margin of 5.0 percent is well above the auto and home supply industry average of 2.8 percent, but its asset turnover of 1.9 times lags behind the industry average of 2.8 times. Shafer is sacrificing asset turnover to achieve a high profit margin. It is clear that this strategy is working, because Shafer's return on assets of 9.4 percent exceeds the industry average of 7.8 percent.

Key Point: A company with a low debt to equity ratio has a better chance of surviving in rough times. Debt requires additional expenses (interest) that must be paid.

DEBT TO EQUITY Another useful measure is the **debt to equity** ratio, which shows the proportion of the company financed by creditors in comparison to that financed by stockholders. This ratio is computed by dividing total liabilities by stockholders' equity. Since the balance sheets of most public companies do not show total liabilities, a short way of determining total liabilities is to deduct the total stockholders' equity from total assets. A debt to equity ratio of 1.0 means that total liabilities equal stockholders' equity—that half of the company's assets are financed by creditors. A ratio of .5 would mean that one-third of the assets are financed by creditors. A company with a high debt to equity ratio is riskier in poor economic times because it must continue to repay creditors. Stockholders' investments, on the other hand, do not have to be repaid, and dividends can be deferred if the company is suffering because of a poor economy.

Figure 6
Average Profit Margin for Selected Industries

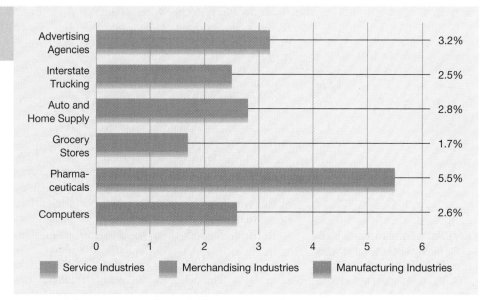

Source: Data from Dun & Bradstreet, *Industry Norms and Key Business Ratios*, 1997–98.

Shafer Auto Parts Corporation's debt to equity ratio is computed as follows:

$$\text{Debt to Equity} = \frac{\text{Total Liabilities}}{\text{Stockholders' Equity}} = \frac{\$60,483}{\$98,433} = .614 \text{ (or } 61.4\%)$$

A debt to equity ratio of 61.4 percent, which is less than 100 percent, means that Shafer Auto Parts Corporation receives less than half its financing from creditors and more than half from its investors.

The debt to equity ratio does not fit neatly into either the liquidity or the profitability category. It is clearly very important to liquidity analysis because it relates to debt and its repayment. However, the debt to equity ratio is also relevant to

Figure 7
Asset Turnover for Selected Industries

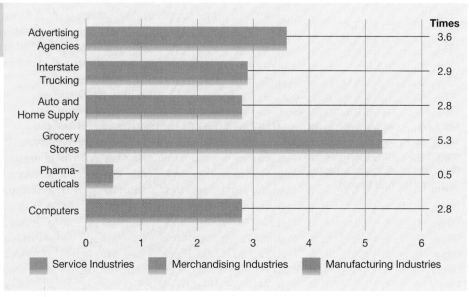

Source: Data from Dun & Bradstreet, *Industry Norms and Key Business Ratios*, 1997–98.

Figure 8
Return on Assets for Selected Industries

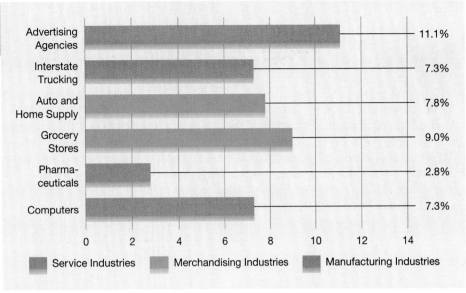

Source: Data from Dun & Bradstreet, *Industry Norms and Key Business Ratios,* 1997–98.

profitability for two reasons. First, creditors are interested in the proportion of the business that is debt financed because the more debt a company has, the more profit it must earn to protect the payment of interest to its creditors. Second, stockholders are interested in the proportion of the business that is debt financed because the amount of interest that must be paid on the debt affects the amount of profit that is left to provide a return on stockholders' investments. The debt to equity ratio also shows how much expansion is possible by borrowing additional long-term funds. Figure 9 shows that the debt to equity ratio in our selected industries varies from a low of 66.9 percent in the pharmaceutical industry to a high of 158.7 percent in interstate trucking.

Figure 9
Average Debt to Equity for Selected Industries

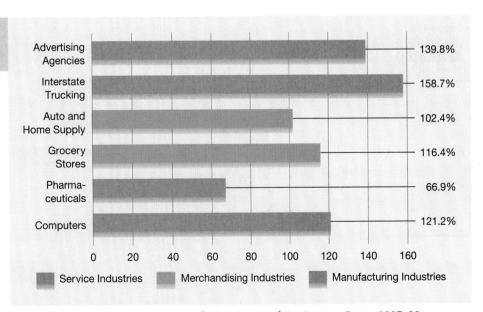

Source: Data from Dun & Bradstreet, *Industry Norms and Key Business Ratios,* 1997–98.

BUSINESS FOCUS ON PRACTICE

To what level of profitability should a company aspire? At one time, a company earning a 20 percent return on equity was considered among the elite. Walt Disney, and ⬭ Wal-Mart, ⬭ Coca-Cola, and a few other companies were able to achieve this level of profitability. However, *The Wall Street Journal* reports that in the first quarter of 1995, for the first time, the average company of the Standard & Poor's 500 companies made a return on equity of 20.12 percent. It says that this performance is "akin to the average ball player hitting .350."[13] This means that stockholders' equity will double every four years.

Why did this happen? First, a good business environment and cost cutting led to more profitable operations. Second, special charges and other accounting transactions reduced the amount of stockholders' equity for many companies.

The number of companies with a return on equity of 20 percent or more has continued to increase as profits have grown through the end of the decade.

RETURN ON EQUITY   Of course, stockholders are interested in how much they have earned on their investment in the business. Their **return on equity** is measured by the ratio of net income to average stockholders' equity. Taking the ending stockholders' equity from the balance sheet and assuming that beginning stockholders' equity is $100,553, Shafer's return on equity is computed as follows:

$$\text{Return on Equity} = \frac{\text{Net Income}}{\text{Average Stockholders' Equity}}$$

$$= \frac{\$14,500}{(\$100,553 + \$98,433) \div 2} = \frac{\$14,500}{\$99,493} = .146 \text{ (or 14.6\%)}$$

In 20x2, Shafer Auto Parts Corporation earned 14.6 cents for every dollar invested by stockholders.

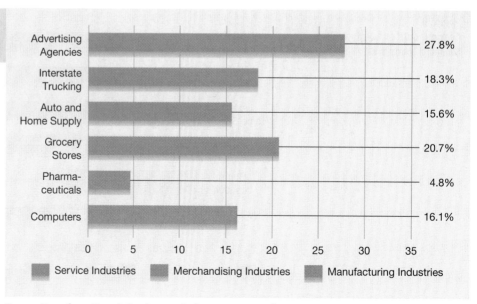

Figure 10
Average Return on Equity for Selected Industries

Advertising Agencies — 27.8%
Interstate Trucking — 18.3%
Auto and Home Supply — 15.6%
Grocery Stores — 20.7%
Pharmaceuticals — 4.8%
Computers — 16.1%

0   5   10   15   20   25   30   35

■ Service Industries   ■ Merchandising Industries   ■ Manufacturing Industries

Source: Data from Dun & Bradstreet, *Industry Norms and Key Business Ratios,* 1997–98.

Whether or not this is an acceptable return depends on several factors, such as how much the company earned in prior years and how much other companies in the same industry earned. As measured by return on equity (Figure 10), advertising agencies are the most profitable of our sample industries, with a return on equity of 27.8 percent. Shafer Auto Parts Corporation's average return on equity of 14.6 percent is less than the average of 15.6 percent for the auto and home supply industry.

GRAPHING RATIO ANALYSIS   Using the Fingraph® Financial Analyst™ CD-ROM software that accompanies this text to graphically present Dell Computer Corp.'s profitability ratios involving net income, shown in Figure 11, helps us visualize the progress of the company in meeting its profitability objectives. On the left of the figure are the components of the ratios. On the right of the figure are the ratios for the past two years. It may be seen that the changes in return on equity and return on assets are linked to changes in profit margin or asset turnover. The Fingraph® Financial Analyst™ CD-ROM software graphs all the ratios used in this book and provides narrative analysis. The asset turnover ratio is shown graphically with the balance sheet analysis.

Figure 11
Graphical Presentation of Dell Computer Corp.'s Profitability Ratios

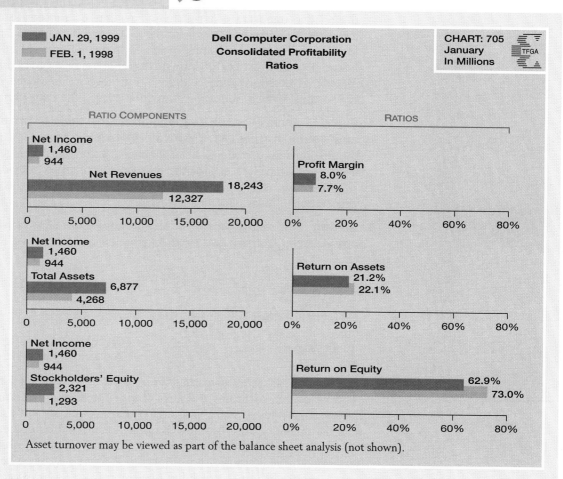

Chapter Review

1. State the objectives of financial reporting. The objectives of financial reporting are (1) to furnish information that is useful in making investment and credit decisions, (2) to provide information that can be used to assess cash flow prospects, and (3) to provide information about business resources, claims to those resources, and changes in them.

2. State the qualitative characteristics of accounting information and describe their interrelationships. Understandability depends on the knowledge of the user and the ability of the accountant to provide useful information. Usefulness is a function of two primary characteristics, relevance and reliability. Information is relevant when it affects the outcome of a decision. Information that is relevant has feedback value and predictive value, and is timely. To be reliable, information must represent what it is supposed to represent, must be verifiable, and must be neutral.

3. Define and describe the use of the conventions of *comparability* and *consistency, materiality, conservatism, full disclosure,* and *cost-benefit*. Because accountants' measurements are not exact, certain conventions have come to be applied in current practice to help users interpret financial statements. One of these conventions is consistency, which requires the use of the same accounting procedures from period to period and enhances the comparability of financial statements. The second is materiality, which has to do with the relative importance of an item. The third is conservatism, which entails using the procedure that is least likely to overstate assets and income. The fourth is full disclosure, which means including all relevant information in the financial statements. The fifth is cost-benefit, which suggests that above a minimum level of information, additional information should be provided only if the benefits derived from the information exceed the costs of providing it.

4. Explain management's responsibility for ethical financial reporting and define *fraudulent financial reporting*. Management is responsible for the preparation of financial statements in accordance with generally accepted accounting principles and for the internal controls that provide assurance that this objective is achieved. Fraudulent financial reporting is the intentional preparation of misleading financial statements.

5. Identify and describe the basic components of a classified balance sheet. The classified balance sheet is subdivided as follows:

Assets	Liabilities
Current Assets	Current Liabilities
Investments	Long-Term Liabilities
Property, Plant, and Equipment	**Stockholders' Equity**
Intangible Assets	
(Other Assets)	Contributed Capital
	Retained Earnings

A current asset is an asset that can reasonably be expected to be realized in cash or consumed during the next year or the normal operating cycle, whichever is longer. Investments are long-term assets that are not usually used in the normal operation of a business. Property, plant, and equipment are long-term assets that are used in day-to-day operations. Intangible assets are long-term assets whose value stems from the rights or privileges they extend to stockholders. A current liability is a liability that can reasonably be expected to be paid or performed during the next year or the normal operating cycle, whichever is longer. Long-term liabilities are debts that fall due more than one year in the future or beyond the normal operating cycle. The equity section of the balance sheet for a corporation differs from that for a proprietorship or partnership in that it has subdivisions of contributed capital (the value of assets invested by stockholders) and retained earnings (stockholders' claim to assets earned from operations and reinvested in operations).

6. **Prepare multistep and single-step classified income statements.** Classified income statements for external reporting can be in multistep or in single-step form. The multistep form arrives at income before income taxes through a series of steps; the single-step form arrives at income before income taxes in a single step. There is usually a separate section in the multistep form for other revenues and expenses.

7. **Evaluate liquidity and profitability using classified financial statements.** One important use of classified financial statements is to evaluate a company's liquidity and profitability. Two simple measures of liquidity are working capital and the current ratio. Five simple measures of profitability are profit margin, asset turnover, return on assets, debt to equity, and return on equity.

REVIEW OF CONCEPTS AND TERMINOLOGY

The following concepts and terms were introduced in this chapter.

LO 7 **Asset turnover:** A measure of profitability that shows how efficiently assets are used to produce sales; net sales divided by average total assets.

LO 5 **Classified financial statements:** General-purpose external financial statements that are divided into subcategories.

LO 3 **Comparability:** The convention of presenting information in a way that enables decision makers to recognize similarities, differences, and trends over different time periods or between different companies.

LO 3 **Conservatism:** The convention mandating that, when faced with two equally acceptable alternatives, the accountant must choose the one least likely to overstate assets and income.

LO 3 **Consistency:** The convention requiring that an accounting procedure, once it is adopted, not be changed from one period to another unless users are informed of the change.

LO 3 **Conventions:** Rules of thumb or customary ways of recording transactions or preparing financial statements.

LO 3 **Cost-benefit:** The convention holding that benefits which are gained from providing accounting information should be greater than the costs of providing that information.

LO 6 **Cost of goods sold:** The amount a merchandiser paid for the merchandise that was sold during an accounting period or the cost to a manufacturer of manufacturing the products that were sold during an accounting period. Also called *cost of sales.*

LO 5 **Current assets:** Cash and other assets that are reasonably expected to be converted to cash, sold, or consumed within one year or within a normal operating cycle, whichever is longer.

LO 5 **Current liabilities:** Obligations due to be paid or performed within one year or within the normal operating cycle, whichever is longer.

LO 7 **Current ratio:** A measure of liquidity; current assets divided by current liabilities.

LO 7 **Debt to equity:** A ratio that measures the relationship of assets financed by creditors to those financed by stockholders; total liabilities divided by stockholders' equity.

LO 6 **Earnings per share:** Net income earned on each share of common stock; net income divided by the average number of common shares outstanding during the year. Also called *net income per share* or *net earnings per share*.

LO 4 **Fraudulent financial reporting:** The intentional preparation of misleading financial statements.

LO 6 **Freight out expense:** The cost to the seller of shipping sold goods to the customer. Also called *delivery expense*.

LO 3 **Full disclosure:** The convention requiring that a company's financial statements and their notes present all information relevant to the users' understanding of the statements.

LO 6 **Gross margin:** The difference between net sales and cost of goods sold. Also called *gross profit*.

LO 6 **Gross sales:** Total sales for cash and on credit occurring during an accounting period.

LO 6 **Income before income taxes:** The amount the company has earned from all activities—operating and nonoperating—before taking into account the amount of income taxes the company incurred.

LO 6 **Income from operations:** Gross margin less operating expenses. Also called *operating income*.

LO 6 **Income taxes:** Represent the expense for federal, state, and local taxes on corporate income; the Income Taxes account appears only on income statements of corporations. Also called *provision for income taxes*.

LO 5 **Intangible assets:** Long-term assets that have no physical substance but have a value based on the rights or privileges that belong to their owner.

LO 5 **Investments:** Assets, usually long-term assets, that are not used in the normal operation of a business and that management does not intend to convert to cash within the next year.

LO 7 **Liquidity:** Having enough money on hand to pay bills when they are due and to take care of unexpected needs for cash.

LO 5 **Long-term liabilities:** Debts that fall due more than one year in the future or beyond the normal operating cycle; debts to be paid out of noncurrent assets.

LO 6 **Manufacturing companies:** Companies that make and sell products.

LO 3 **Materiality:** The convention that refers to the relative importance of an item or event in a financial statement and its influence on the decisions of the users of financial statements.

LO 6 **Merchandising companies:** Companies that buy and sell products. Includes wholesalers and retailers.

LO 6 **Multistep income statement:** A form of income statement that arrives at income before income taxes in steps. Also called *multistep form*.

LO 6 **Net income:** On the income statement, what remains of the gross margin after operating expenses are deducted, other revenues and expenses are added or deducted, and income taxes are deducted. Referred to as *the bottom line*.

LO 6 **Net sales:** The gross proceeds from sales of merchandise, or gross sales, less sales returns and allowances and any discounts allowed.

LO 6 **Operating expenses:** The expenses other than cost of goods sold that are incurred in running a business.

LO 5 **Other assets:** A balance sheet category that may include various types of assets other than current assets and property, plant, and equipment.

LO 6 **Other revenues and expenses:** The section of a multistep income statement that includes nonoperating revenues and expenses.

LO 7 **Profitability:** The ability of a business to earn a satisfactory income.

LO 7 **Profit margin:** A measure of profitability that shows the percentage of each sales dollar that results in net income; net income divided by net sales.

LO 5 **Property, plant, and equipment:** Tangible long-term assets used in the continuing operation of a business. Also called *operating assets, fixed assets, tangible assets, long-lived assets,* or *plant assets.*

LO 2 **Qualitative characteristics:** Standards for judging the information that accountants give to decision makers.

LO 2 **Relevance:** The qualitative characteristic of information bearing directly on the outcome of a decision.

LO 2 **Reliability:** The qualitative characteristic of information being representationally faithful, verifiable, and neutral.

LO 7 **Return on assets:** A measure of profitability that shows how efficiently a company uses its assets to produce income; net income divided by average total assets.

LO 7 **Return on equity:** A measure of profitability that relates the amount earned by a business to the stockholders' investment in the business; net income divided by average stockholders' equity.

LO 6 **Single-step income statement:** A form of income statement that arrives at income before income taxes in a single step. Also called *single-step form.*

LO 2 **Understandability:** The qualitative characteristic of information communicating an intended meaning.

LO 2 **Usefulness:** The qualitative characteristic of information being relevant and reliable.

LO 7 **Working capital:** A measure of liquidity that shows the net current assets on hand to continue business operations; total current assets minus total current liabilities.

REVIEW PROBLEM

Analyzing Liquidity and Profitability Using Ratios

LO 7 Flavin Shirt Company has faced increased competition from overseas shirtmakers in recent years. Presented below is summary information for the last two years:

	20x2	20x1
Current Assets	$ 200,000	$ 170,000
Total Assets	880,000	710,000
Current Liabilities	90,000	50,000
Long-Term Liabilities	150,000	50,000
Stockholders' Equity	640,000	610,000
Sales	1,200,000	1,050,000
Net Income	60,000	80,000

Total assets and stockholders' equity at the beginning of 20x1 were $690,000 and $590,000, respectively.

REQUIRED

Use (1) liquidity analysis and (2) profitability analysis to document the declining financial position of Flavin Shirt Company.

ANSWER TO REVIEW PROBLEM

1. Liquidity analysis

	Current Assets	Current Liabilities	Working Capital	Current Ratio
20x1	$170,000	$50,000	$120,000	3.40
20x2	200,000	90,000	110,000	2.22
Decrease in working capital			$ 10,000	
Decrease in current ratio				1.18

Both working capital and the current ratio declined because, although current assets increased by $30,000 ($200,000 − $170,000), current liabilities increased by a greater amount, $40,000 ($90,000 − $50,000), from 20x1 to 20x2.

K/R 2. Profitability analysis

	Net Income	Sales	Profit Margin	Average Total Assets	Asset Turnover	Return on Assets	Average Stock- holders' Equity	Return on Equity
20x1	$80,000	$1,050,000	7.6%	$700,000[1]	1.50	11.4%	$600,000[3]	13.3%
20x2	60,000	1,200,000	5.0%	795,000[2]	1.51	7.5%	625,000[4]	9.6%
Increase (decrease)	($20,000)	$ 150,000	(2.6)%	$ 95,000	0.01	(3.9)%	$ 25,000	(3.7)%

[1]($690,000 + $710,000) ÷ 2   [3]($590,000 + $610,000) ÷ 2
[2]($710,000 + $880,000) ÷ 2   [4]($610,000 + $640,000) ÷ 2

Net income decreased by $20,000 despite an increase in sales of $150,000 and an increase in average total assets of $95,000. The results were decreases in profit margin from 7.6 percent to 5.0 percent and in return on assets from 11.4 percent to 7.5 percent. Asset turnover showed almost no change, and so did not contribute to the decline in profitability. The decrease in return on equity, from 13.3 percent to 9.6 percent, was not as great as the decrease in return on assets because the growth in total assets was financed mainly by debt instead of by stockholders' equity, as shown by the capital structure analysis below.

	Total Liabilities	Stockholders' Equity	Debt to Equity Ratio
20x1	$100,000	$610,000	16.4%
20x2	240,000	640,000	37.5%
Increase	$140,000	$ 30,000	21.1%

Total liabilities increased by $140,000, while stockholders' equity increased by $30,000. As a result, the amount of the business financed by debt in relation to the amount of the business financed by stockholders' equity increased from 20x1 to 20x2.

Chapter Assignments

BUILDING YOUR KNOWLEDGE FOUNDATION

QUESTIONS

1. What are the three objectives of financial reporting?
2. What are the qualitative characteristics of accounting information, and what is their significance?
3. What are the accounting conventions? How does each help in the interpretation of financial information?

4. Who is responsible for the preparation of reliable financial statements, and what is a principal way of achieving this objective?

5. What is the purpose of classified financial statements?

6. What are four common categories of assets?

7. What criteria must an asset meet to be classified as current? Under what condition is an asset considered current even though it will not be realized as cash within a year? What are two examples of assets that fall into this category?

8. In what order should current assets be listed?

9. What is the difference between a short-term investment in the current assets section of the balance sheet and a security in the investments section?

10. What is an intangible asset? Give at least three examples.

11. Name the two major categories of liabilities.

12. What are the primary differences between the equity section of the balance sheet for a sole proprietorship or partnership and the corresponding section for a corporation?

13. What is the primary difference between the operations of a merchandising business and those of a service business, and how is it reflected on the income statement?

14. Define *gross margin*. Why is it important?

15. During its first year in operation, Kumler Nursery had a cost of goods sold of $64,000 and a gross margin equal to 40 percent of sales. What was the dollar amount of the company's sales?

16. Could Kumler Nursery (in Question 15) have a net loss for the year? Explain your answer.

17. Explain how the multistep form of income statement differs from the single-step form. What are the relative merits of each?

18. Why are other revenues and expenses separated from operating revenues and expenses in the multistep income statement?

19. What are some of the differences between the income statement for a sole proprietorship and that for a corporation?

20. Explain earnings per share and indicate how this figure appears on the income statement.

21. Define *liquidity* and name two measures of liquidity.

22. How is the current ratio computed, and why is it important?

23. Which is the more important goal, liquidity or profitability? Explain your answer.

24. Name five measures of profitability.

25. "Return on assets is a better measure of profitability than profit margin." Evaluate this statement.

SHORT EXERCISES

SE 1.

LO 3 Accounting Conventions

State which of the accounting conventions—comparability and consistency, materiality, conservatism, full disclosure, or cost-benefit—is being followed in each case below.

1. Management provides detailed information about the company's long-term debt in the notes to the financial statements.

2. A company does not account separately for discounts received for prompt payment of accounts payable because few of these transactions occur and the total amount of the discounts is small.

3. Management eliminates a weekly report on property, plant, and equipment acquisitions and disposals because no one finds it useful.

4. A company follows the policy of recognizing a loss on inventory when the market value of an item falls below its cost but does nothing if the market value rises.

5. When several accounting methods are acceptable, management chooses a single method and follows that method from year to year.

SE 2.

LO 5 Classification of Accounts: Balance Sheet

Tell whether each of the following accounts is a current asset; an investment; property, plant, and equipment; an intangible asset; a current liability; a long-term liability; stockholders' equity; or not on the balance sheet.

1. Delivery Trucks
2. Accounts Payable
3. Note Payable (due in 90 days)
4. Delivery Expense
5. Common Stock
6. Prepaid Insurance
7. Trademark
8. Investment to Be Held Six Months
9. Income Taxes Payable
10. Factory Not Used in Business

SE 3.

LO 5 Classified Balance Sheet

Using the following accounts, prepare a classified balance sheet at year end, May 31, 20xx: Accounts Payable, $400; Accounts Receivable, $550; Accumulated Depreciation, Equipment, $350; Cash, $100; Common Stock, $500; Equipment, $2,000; Franchise, $100; Investments (long-term), $250; Merchandise Inventory, $300; Notes Payable (long-term), $200; Retained Earnings, ?; Wages Payable, $50.

SE 4.

LO 6 Classification of Accounts: Income Statement

Tell whether each of the following accounts is part of net sales, cost of goods sold, operating expenses, or other revenues and expenses, or is not on the income statement.

1. Delivery Expense
2. Interest Expense
3. Unearned Revenue
4. Sales Returns and Allowances
5. Cost of Goods Sold
6. Depreciation Expense
7. Investment Income
8. Retained Earnings

SE 5.

LO 6 Single-Step Income Statement

Using the following accounts, prepare a single-step income statement at year end, May 31, 20xx: Cost of Goods Sold, $280; General Expenses, $150; Income Taxes, $35; Interest Expense, $70; Interest Income, $30; Net Sales, $800; Selling Expenses, $185. Ignore earnings per share.

SE 6.

LO 6 Multistep Income Statement

Using the accounts presented in **SE 5,** prepare a multistep income statement.

SE 7.

LO 7 Liquidity Ratios

Using the following accounts and balances taken from a year-end balance sheet, compute working capital and the current ratio:

Accounts Payable	$ 7,000
Accounts Receivable	10,000
Cash	4,000
Common Stock	20,000
Marketable Securities	2,000
Merchandise Inventory	12,000
Notes Payable in Three Years	13,000
Property, Plant, and Equipment	40,000
Retained Earnings	28,000

SE 8.

LO 7 Profitability Ratios

Using the following information from a balance sheet and an income statement, compute the (1) profit margin, (2) asset turnover, (3) return on assets, (4) debt to equity, and (5) return on equity. (The previous year's total assets were $100,000 and stockholders' equity was $70,000.)

Total Assets	$120,000
Total Liabilities	30,000
Total Stockholders' Equity	90,000
Net Sales	130,000
Cost of Goods Sold	70,000
Operating Expenses	40,000
Income Taxes	5,000

SE 9.

LO 7 Relationship of Profitability Ratios

Assume that a company has a profit margin of 6.0 percent, an asset turnover of 3.2 times, and a debt to equity ratio of .5 times. What are the company's return on assets and return on equity?

EXERCISES

E 1.

LO 3 Accounting Concepts and Conventions

Each of the statements below violates a convention in accounting. State which of the following accounting conventions is violated: comparability and consistency, materiality, conservatism, full disclosure, or cost-benefit.

1. A series of reports that are time-consuming and expensive to prepare is presented to the board of directors each month even though the reports are never used.
2. A company changes its method of accounting for depreciation.
3. The company in **2** does not indicate in the financial statements that the method of depreciation was changed, nor does it specify the effect of the change on net income.
4. A new office building next to the factory is debited to the Factory account because it represents a fairly small dollar amount in relation to the factory.
5. The asset account for a pickup truck still used in the business is written down to what the truck could be sold for even though the carrying value under conventional depreciation methods is higher.

E 2.

LO 1 Financial Accounting
LO 2 Concepts
LO 3

The lettered items below represent a classification scheme for the concepts of financial accounting. Match each numbered term with the letter of the category in which it belongs.

a. Decision makers (users of accounting information)
b. Business activities or entities relevant to accounting measurement
c. Objectives of accounting information
d. Accounting measurement considerations
e. Accounting processing considerations
f. Qualitative characteristics
g. Accounting conventions
h. Financial statements

1. Conservatism
2. Verifiability
3. Statement of cash flows
4. Materiality
5. Reliability
6. Recognition
7. Cost-benefit
8. Understandability
9. Business transactions
10. Consistency
11. Full disclosure
12. Furnishing information that is useful to investors and creditors
13. Specific business entities
14. Classification
15. Management
16. Neutrality
17. Internal accounting control
18. Valuation
19. Investors
20. Timeliness
21. Relevance
22. Furnishing information that is useful in assessing cash flow prospects

E 3.

LO 5 **Classification of Accounts: Balance Sheet**

The lettered items below represent a classification scheme for a balance sheet, and the numbered items are account titles. Match each account with the letter of the category in which it belongs.

a. Current assets
b. Investments
c. Property, plant, and equipment
d. Intangible assets
e. Current liabilities
f. Long-term liabilities
g. Stockholders' equity
h. Not on balance sheet

1. Patent
2. Building Held for Sale
3. Prepaid Rent
4. Wages Payable
5. Note Payable in Five Years
6. Building Used in Operations
7. Fund Held to Pay Off Long-Term Debt
8. Inventory

9. Prepaid Insurance
10. Depreciation Expense
11. Accounts Receivable
12. Interest Expense
13. Unearned Revenue
14. Short-Term Investments
15. Accumulated Depreciation
16. Retained Earnings

E 4.

LO 5 **Classified Balance Sheet Preparation**

The following data pertain to BUR, Inc.: Accounts Payable, $51,000; Accounts Receivable, $38,000; Accumulated Depreciation, Building, $14,000; Accumulated Depreciation, Equipment, $17,000; Bonds Payable, $60,000; Building, $70,000; Cash, $31,200; Common Stock, $10 par, 10,000 shares authorized, issued, and outstanding, $100,000; Copyright, $6,200; Equipment, $152,000; Inventory, $40,000; Investment in Corporate Securities (long-term), $20,000; Investment in Six-Month Government Securities, $16,400; Land, $8,000; Paid-in Capital in Excess of Par Value, $50,000; Prepaid Rent, $1,200; Retained Earnings, $88,200; and Revenue Received in Advance, $2,800.

Prepare a classified balance sheet at December 31, 20xx.

E 5.

LO 6 **Classification of Accounts: Income Statement**

Using the classification scheme below for a multistep income statement, match each account with the letter of the category in which it belongs.

a. Net sales
b. Cost of goods sold
c. Selling expenses
d. General and administrative expenses
e. Other revenues and expenses
f. Not on income statement

1. Sales Discounts
2. Cost of Goods Sold
3. Dividend Income
4. Advertising Expense
5. Office Salaries Expense
6. Freight Out Expense
7. Prepaid Insurance

8. Utilities Expense
9. Sales Salaries Expense
10. Rent Expense
11. Depreciation Expense, Delivery Equipment
12. Taxes Payable
13. Interest Expense

E 6.

LO 6 **Preparation of Income Statements**

The following data pertain to a corporation: Net Sales, $810,000; Cost of Goods Sold, $440,000; Selling Expenses, $180,000; General and Administrative Expenses, $120,000; Income Taxes, $15,000; Interest Expense, $8,000; Interest Income, $6,000; and Common Stock Outstanding, 100,000 shares.

1. Prepare a single-step income statement.
2. Prepare a multistep income statement.

E 7.
LO 6 Multistep Income Statement

A single-step income statement appears below. Present the information in a multistep income statement, and tell what insights can be obtained from the multistep form as opposed to the single-step form.

Wingo Linens Corporation
Income Statement
For the Year Ended December 31, 20xx

Revenues		
Net Sales		$598,566
Interest Income		2,860
Total Revenues		$601,426
Costs and Expenses		
Cost of Goods Sold	$388,540	
Selling Expenses	101,870	
General and Administrative Expenses	50,344	
Interest Expense	6,780	
Total Costs and Expenses		547,534
Income Before Income Taxes		$ 53,892
Income Taxes		12,000
Net Income		$ 41,892
Earnings per share		$ 4.19

E 8.
LO 7 Liquidity Ratios

The following accounts and balances are taken from the general ledger of Northern Corporation:

Accounts Payable	$16,600
Accounts Receivable	10,200
Cash	1,500
Current Portion of Long-Term Debt	10,000
Long-Term Investments	10,400
Marketable Securities	12,600
Merchandise Inventory	25,400
Notes Payable, 90 days	15,000
Notes Payable, 2 years	20,000
Notes Receivable, 90 days	26,000
Notes Receivable, 2 years	10,000
Prepaid Insurance	400
Property, Plant, and Equipment	60,000
Property Taxes Payable	1,250
Retained Earnings	28,300
Salaries Payable	850
Supplies	350
Unearned Revenue	750

Compute the (1) working capital and (2) current ratio.

E 9.
LO 7 Profitability Ratios

The following end-of-year amounts are taken from the financial statements of Gomez Corporation: Total Assets, $426,000; Total Liabilities, $172,000; Stockholders' Equity, $254,000; Net Sales, $782,000; Cost of Goods Sold, $486,000; Operating Expenses, $178,000; Income Taxes, $24,000; and Dividends, $40,000. During the past year, total assets increased by $75,000. Total stockholders' equity was affected only by net income and dividends. Compute the (1) profit margin, (2) asset turnover, (3) return on assets, (4) debt to equity, and (5) return on equity.

E 10. The simplified balance sheet and income statement for a corporation appear below.

LO 7 Computation of Ratios

Balance Sheet December 31, 20xx				
Assets		**Liabilities**		
Current Assets	$100,000	Current Liabilities	$ 40,000	
Investments	20,000	Long-Term Liabilities	60,000	
Property, Plant, and Equipment	293,000	Total Liabilities	$100,000	
Intangible Assets	27,000	**Stockholders' Equity**		
		Common Stock	$200,000	
		Retained Earnings	140,000	
		Total Stockholders' Equity	$340,000	
Total Assets	$440,000	Total Liabilities and Stockholders' Equity	$440,000	

Income Statement For the Year Ended December 31, 20xx	
Net Sales	$820,000
Cost of Goods Sold	500,000
Gross Margin	$320,000
Operating Expenses	260,000
Income Before Income Taxes	$ 60,000
Income Taxes	10,000
Net Income	$ 50,000

Total assets and stockholders' equity at the beginning of 20xx were $360,000 and $280,000, respectively.

1. Compute the following liquidity measures: (a) working capital and (b) current ratio.
2. Compute the following profitability measures: (a) profit margin, (b) asset turnover, (c) return on assets, (d) debt to equity, and (e) return on equity.

PROBLEMS

P 1. In each case below, accounting conventions *may* have been violated.

LO 3 Accounting Conventions

1. After careful study, Kipling Company, which has offices in 40 states, has determined that its method of depreciating office furniture should be changed. The new method is adopted for the current year, and the change is noted in the financial statements.
2. In the past, Cortes Corporation has recorded operating expenses in general accounts for each classification (for example, Salaries Expense, Depreciation Expense, and Utilities Expense). Management has determined that despite the additional record-

keeping costs, the company's income statement should break down each operating expense into its components of selling expense and administrative expense.

3. Amber Hews, the auditor of Fitz Corporation, discovered that an official of the company had authorized the payment of an $800 bribe to a local official. Management argued that because the item was so small in relation to the size of the company ($1,500,000 in sales), the illegal payment should not be disclosed.

4. Glowacki's Bookstore built a small addition to its main building to house a new computer games section. Because no one could be sure that the computer games section would succeed, the accountant took a conservative approach and recorded the addition as an expense.

5. Since its origin ten years ago, Xu Company has used the same generally accepted inventory method. Because there has been no change in the inventory method, the company does not disclose in its financial statements what inventory method it uses.

REQUIRED

In each case, state the convention that applies, tell whether or not the treatment is in accord with the convention and generally accepted accounting principles, and briefly explain why.

P 2.

LO 6 Forms of the Income Statement

The income statements that follow are for Loury Hardware Corporation.

Loury Hardware Corporation Income Statements For the Years Ended July 31, 20x3 and 20x2		
	20x3	**20x2**
Revenues		
Net Sales	$464,200	$388,466
Interest Income	420	500
Total Revenues	$464,620	$388,966
Costs and Expenses		
Cost of Goods Sold	$243,880	$198,788
Selling Expenses	95,160	55,644
General and Administrative Expenses	90,840	49,286
Interest Expense	5,600	1,100
Total Costs and Expenses	$435,480	$304,818
Income Before Income Taxes	$ 29,140	$ 84,148
Income Taxes	7,000	21,000
Net Income	$ 22,140	$ 63,148
Earnings per share	$ 2.21	$ 6.31

REQUIRED

1. From the information provided, prepare a multistep income statement for 20x2 and 20x3 showing percentages of net sales for each component.

2. Did income from operations increase or decrease from 20x2 to 20x3? Write a short analysis explaining why this change occurred.

3. What effect did other revenues and expenses have on the change in income before income taxes? What action by management probably accounted for this change?

P 3.

LO 5   Classified Balance Sheet

Accounts from the July 31, 20x3, post-closing trial balance of Kissell Hardware Corporation appear below.

Account Name	Debit	Credit
Cash	$ 31,000	
Short-Term Investments	33,000	
Notes Receivable	10,000	
Accounts Receivable	276,000	
Merchandise Inventory	145,000	
Prepaid Rent	1,600	
Prepaid Insurance	4,800	
Sales Supplies	1,280	
Office Supplies	440	
Deposit for Future Advertising	3,680	
Building, Not in Use	49,600	
Land	22,400	
Delivery Equipment	41,200	
Accumulated Depreciation, Delivery Equipment		$ 28,400
Franchise Fee	4,000	
Accounts Payable		114,600
Salaries Payable		5,200
Interest Payable		840
Long-Term Notes Payable		80,000
Common Stock, $1 par value		20,000
Paid-in Capital in Excess of Par Value		160,000
Retained Earnings		214,960

REQUIRED

From the information provided, prepare a classified balance sheet.

P 4.

**LO 7   Ratio Analysis: Liquidity and
Profitability**

Rollins Products Corporation has had poor operating results for the past two years. As the accountant for the company, you have the following information available to you:

	20x3	20x2
Current Assets	$ 45,000	$ 35,000
Total Assets	145,000	110,000
Current Liabilities	20,000	10,000
Long-Term Liabilities	20,000	—
Stockholders' Equity	105,000	100,000
Net Sales	262,000	200,000
Net Income	16,000	11,000

Total assets and stockholders' equity at the beginning of 20x2 were $90,000 and $80,000, respectively.

REQUIRED

1. Compute the following measures of liquidity for 20x2 and 20x3: (a) working capital and (b) current ratio. Comment on the differences between the years.

2. Compute the following measures of profitability for 20x2 and 20x3: (a) profit margin, (b) asset turnover, (c) return on assets, (d) debt to equity, and (e) return on equity. Comment on the change in performance from 20x2 to 20x3.

P 5.

**LO 5   Classified Financial
LO 6   Statement
LO 7   Preparation and Evaluation**

Wu Corporation sells outdoor sports equipment. At the December 31, 20x2, year end, the following financial information was available from the income statement: Administrative Expenses, $161,600; Cost of Goods Sold, $700,840; Income Taxes, $14,000; Interest Expense, $45,280; Interest Income, $5,600; Net Sales, $1,428,780; and Selling Expenses, $440,400.

The following information was available from the balance sheet (after closing entries were made): Accounts Payable, $65,200; Accounts Receivable, $209,600; Accumulated Depreciation, Delivery Equipment, $34,200; Accumulated Depreciation, Store Fixtures, $84,440; Cash, $56,800; Common Stock, $1 par value, 20,000 shares authorized, issued, and outstanding, $20,000; Delivery Equipment, $177,000; Dividends, $120,000; Inventory, $273,080; Investment in Securities (long-term), $112,000; Investment in U.S. Government Securities (short-term), $79,200; Long-Term Notes Payable, $200,000; Paid-in Capital in Excess of Par Value, $180,000; Retained Earnings, $518,600 (ending balance); Notes Payable (short-term), $100,000; Prepaid Expenses (short-term), $11,520; and Store Fixtures, $283,240.

Total assets and total stockholders' equity at December 31, 20x1, were $1,048,800 and $766,340, respectively.

REQUIRED

1. From the information above, prepare (a) an income statement in single-step form, (b) a statement of retained earnings, and (c) a classified balance sheet.

2. From the statements you have prepared, compute the following measures: (a) working capital and current ratio (for liquidity); and (b) profit margin, asset turnover, return on assets, debt to equity, and return on equity (for profitability).

ALTERNATE PROBLEMS

P 6.

LO 3   Accounting Conventions

In each case below, accounting conventions *may* have been violated.

1. Hastings Manufacturing Company uses the cost method for computing the balance sheet amount of inventory unless the market value of the inventory is less than the cost, in which case the market value is used. At the end of the current year, the market value is $154,000 and the cost is $160,000. Hastings uses the $154,000 figure to compute current assets because management feels it is the more cautious approach.

2. Gormanus Company has annual sales of $20,000,000. It follows the practice of recording any items costing less than $500 as expenses in the year purchased. During the current year, it purchased several chairs for the executive conference rooms at $490 each, including freight. Although the chairs were expected to last for at least ten years, they were recorded as an expense in accordance with company policy.

3. Nogel Company closed its books on October 31, 20x2, before preparing its annual report. On October 30, 20x2, a fire destroyed one of the company's two factories. Although the company had fire insurance and would not suffer a loss on the building, a significant decrease in sales in 20x3 was expected because of the fire. The fire damage was not reported in the 20x2 financial statements because the operations for that year were not affected by the fire.

4. Ex-Act Drug Company spends a substantial portion of its profits on research and development. The company has been reporting its $5,000,000 expenditure for research and development as a lump sum, but management recently decided to begin classifying the expenditures by project even though the recordkeeping costs will increase.

5. During the current year, RBI Company changed from one generally accepted method of accounting for inventories to another method.

REQUIRED

In each case, state the convention that applies, tell whether or not the treatment is in accord with the convention and generally accepted accounting principles, and briefly explain why.

P 7.

LO 6   Forms of the Income Statement

The single-step income statements of Ramos Nursery Corporation for the years ended April 30, 20x2 and 20x1, appear on the next page. The company had 20,000 shares of common stock outstanding during each year.

Ramos Nursery Corporation Income Statements For the Years Ended April 30, 20x2 and 20x1		
	20x2	**20x1**
Revenues		
Net Sales	$525,932	$475,264
Interest Income	800	700
Total Revenues	$526,732	$475,964
Costs and Expenses		
Cost of Goods Sold	$234,948	$171,850
Selling Expenses	161,692	150,700
General and Administrative Expenses	62,866	42,086
Interest Expense	3,600	850
Total Costs and Expenses	$463,106	$365,486
Income Before Income Taxes	$ 63,626	$110,478
Income Taxes	15,000	27,600
Net Income	$ 48,626	$ 82,878
Earnings per share	$ 2.43	$ 4.14

REQUIRED

1. From the information provided, prepare multistep income statements for 20x1 and 20x2 showing percentages of net sales for each component.

2. Did income from operations increase or decrease from 20x1 to 20x2? Write a short analysis explaining why this change occurred.

3. What effect did other revenues and expenses have on the change in income before income taxes? What action by management probably caused this change?

P 8.

LO 7 Ratio Analysis: Liquidity and Profitability

Below is a summary of data taken from the income statements and balance sheets for Okumura Construction Supply, Inc., for the past two years.

	20x4	20x3
Current Assets	$ 366,000	$ 310,000
Total Assets	2,320,000	1,740,000
Current Liabilities	180,000	120,000
Long-Term Liabilities	800,000	580,000
Stockholders' Equity	1,340,000	1,040,000
Net Sales	4,600,000	3,480,000
Net Income	300,000	204,000

Total assets and stockholders' equity at the beginning of 20x3 were $1,360,000 and $840,000, respectively.

REQUIRED

1. Compute the following liquidity measures for 20x3 and 20x4: (a) working capital and (b) current ratio. Comment on the differences between the years.

2. Compute the following measures of profitability for 20x3 and 20x4: (a) profit margin, (b) asset turnover, (c) return on assets, (d) debt to equity, and (e) return on equity. Comment on the change in performance from 20x3 to 20x4.

EXPANDING YOUR CRITICAL THINKING, COMMUNICATION, AND INTERPERSONAL SKILLS

SKILLS DEVELOPMENT

Conceptual Analysis

LO 3 Accounting Conventions

SD 1. *Mason Parking,* which operates a seven-story parking building in downtown Chicago, has a calendar year end. It serves daily and hourly parkers, as well as monthly parkers who pay a fixed monthly rate in advance. The company traditionally has recorded all cash receipts as revenues when received. Most monthly parkers pay in full during the month prior to that in which they have the right to park. The company's auditors have said that beginning in 2000, the company should consider recording the cash receipts from monthly parking on an accrual basis, crediting Unearned Revenues. Total cash receipts for 2000 were $2,500,000, and the cash receipts received in 2000 and applicable to January 2001 were $125,000. Discuss the relevance of the accounting conventions of consistency, materiality, and full disclosure to the decision to record the monthly parking revenues on an accrual basis.

LO 3 Materiality

SD 2. *Mackey Electronics, Inc.,* operates a chain of consumer electronics stores in the Atlanta area. This year the company achieved annual sales of $50 million, on which it earned a net income of $2 million. At the beginning of the year, management implemented a new inventory system that enabled it to track all purchases and sales. At the end of the year, a physical inventory revealed that the actual inventory was $80,000 below what the new system indicated it should be. The inventory loss, which probably resulted from shoplifting, is reflected in a higher cost of goods sold. The problem concerns management but seems to be less important to the company's auditors. What is materiality? Why might the inventory loss concern management more than it does the auditors? Do you think the amount is material?

Ethical Dilemma

LO 4 Ethics and Financial Reporting

SD 3. *Salem Software,* located outside Boston, develops computer software and licenses it to financial institutions. The firm uses an aggressive accounting method that records revenues from the software it has developed on a percentage of completion basis. Consequently, revenue for partially completed projects is recognized based on the proportion of the project that is completed. If a project is 50 percent completed, then 50 percent of the contracted revenue is recognized. In 20x2, preliminary estimates for a $5 million project are that the project is 75 percent complete. Because the estimate of completion is a matter of judgment, management asks for a new report showing the project to be 90 percent complete. The change will enable senior managers to meet their financial goals for the year and thus receive substantial year-end bonuses. Do you think management's action is ethical? If you were the company controller and were asked to prepare the new report, would you do it? What action would you take?

 Group Activity: Use in-class groups to debate the ethics of the action.

LO 4 Ethics and Financial Reporting

SD 4. *Treon Microsystems, Inc.,* a Silicon Valley manufacturer of microchips for personal computers, has just completed its year-end physical inventory in advance of preparing financial statements. To celebrate, the entire accounting department goes out for a New Year's Eve party at a local establishment. As senior accountant, you join the fun. At the party, you fall into conversation with an employee of one of your main competitors. After a while, the employee reveals that the competitor plans to introduce a new product in 60 days that will make Treon's principal product obsolete.

| Cash Flow | CD-ROM | Communication | Critical Thinking | Ethics | General Ledger | Group Activity | Hot Links to Real Companies | International | Internet | Key Ratio | Memo | Spreadsheet |

On Monday morning, you go to the financial vice president with this information, stating that the inventory may have to be written down and net income reduced. To your surprise, the financial vice president says that you were right to come to her, but urges you to say nothing about the problem. She says, "It is probably a rumor, and even if it is true, there will be plenty of time to write down the inventory in 60 days." You wonder if this is the appropriate thing to do. You feel confident that your source knew what he was talking about. You know that the salaries of all top managers, including the financial vice president, are tied to net income. What is fraudulent financial reporting? Is this an example of fraudulent financial reporting? What action would you take?

Research Activity

SD 5.

LO 4 Accounting and Fraud

Most university and public libraries have access to indexes of leading newspapers such as *The Wall Street Journal* and *The New York Times* on CD-ROM. Go to a library and do a search for a recent year using the key words "accounting and fraud," "accounting and restatement," or "accounting and irregularities." Choose one of the articles you find and read it. What company is involved and how is accounting connected with the fraud, restatement, or irregularity? Describe the situation. Does it involve an apparently legal or illegal activity? Does it involve fraudulent financial reporting? Explain your answer and be prepared to discuss it in class.

Decision-Making Practice

SD 6.

LO 7 Financial Analysis for Loan Decision

Steve Sulong was recently promoted to loan officer at **First National Bank.** He has authority to issue loans up to $50,000 without approval from a higher bank official. This week two small companies, Handy Harvey, Inc., and Sheila's Fashions, Inc., have each submitted a proposal for a six-month $50,000 loan. To prepare financial analyses of the two companies, Steve has obtained the information summarized below.

Handy Harvey, Inc., is a local lumber and home improvement company. Because sales have increased so much during the past two years, Handy Harvey has had to raise additional working capital, especially as represented by receivables and inventory. The $50,000 loan is needed to assure the company of enough working capital for the next year. Handy Harvey began the year with total assets of $740,000 and stockholders' equity of $260,000. During the past year the company had a net income of $40,000 on net sales of $760,000. The company's current unclassified balance sheet appears as follows:

Assets		Liabilities and Stockholders' Equity	
Cash	$ 30,000	Accounts Payable	$200,000
Accounts Receivable (net)	150,000	Notes Payable (short term)	100,000
Inventory	250,000	Notes Payable (long term)	200,000
Land	50,000	Common Stock	250,000
Buildings (net)	250,000	Retained Earnings	50,000
Equipment (net)	70,000	Total Liabilities and	
Total Assets	$800,000	Stockholders' Equity	$800,000

Sheila's Fashions, Inc., has for three years been a successful clothing store for young professional women. The leased store is located in the downtown financial district. Sheila's loan proposal asks for $50,000 to pay for stocking a new line of women's suits during the coming season. At the beginning of the year, the company had total assets of $200,000 and total stockholders' equity of $114,000. Over the past year, the company earned a net income of $36,000 on net sales of $480,000. The firm's unclassified balance sheet at the current date appears as follows:

Assets		Liabilities and Stockholders' Equity	
Cash	$ 10,000	Accounts Payable	$ 80,000
Accounts Receivable (net)	50,000	Accrued Liabilities	10,000
Inventory	135,000	Common Stock	50,000
Prepaid Expenses	5,000	Retained Earnings	100,000
Equipment (net)	40,000	Total Liabilities and	
Total Assets	$240,000	Stockholders' Equity	$240,000

1. Prepare a financial analysis of each company's liquidity before and after receiving the proposed loan. Also compute profitability ratios before and after, as appropriate. Write a brief summary of the effect of the proposed loan on each company's financial position.

2. Assume you are Steve and you can make a loan to only one of these companies. Write a memorandum to the bank's vice president naming the company to which you would recommend loaning $50,000. Be sure to state what positive and negative factors could affect each company's ability to pay back the loan in the next year. Also indicate what other information of a financial or nonfinancial nature would be helpful in making a final decision.

FINANCIAL REPORTING AND ANALYSIS

Interpreting Financial Reports

FRA 1.
LO 7 Comparison of Profitability

Two of the largest chains of grocery/drugstores in the United States are **Albertson's Inc.** and **Giant Food Inc.** In its fiscal year ended January 28, 1998, Albertson's had a net income of $567.2 million, and in its fiscal year ended February 28, 1998, Giant had a net income of $71.2 million. It is difficult to judge which company is more profitable from those figures alone because they do not take into account the relative sales, sizes, and investments of the companies. Data (in millions) to complete a financial analysis of the two companies follow:[14]

	Albertson's	Giant Food
Net Sales	$16,005.1	$4,230.6
Beginning Total Assets	5,218.6	1,503.5
Ending Total Assets	6,234.0	1,521.9
Beginning Total Liabilities	2,799.1	629.8
Ending Total Liabilities	3,423.5	619.3
Beginning Stockholders' Equity	2,419.5	873.7
Ending Stockholders' Equity	2,810.5	902.6

REQUIRED

1. Determine which company was more profitable by computing profit margin, asset turnover, return on assets, debt to equity, and return on equity for the two companies. Comment on the relative profitability of the two companies.

2. What do the ratios tell you about the factors that go into achieving an adequate return on assets in the grocery industry? For industry data, refer to Figures 6 through 10.

3. How would you characterize the use of debt financing in the grocery industry and the use of debt by the two companies?

Group Activity: Assign each ratio or company to a group and hold a class discussion.

FRA 2.
LO 7 Evaluation of Profitability

Carla Cruz is the principal stockholder and president of **Cruz Tapestries, Inc.,** which wholesales fine tapestries to retail stores. Because Cruz was not satisfied with the company earnings in 20x3, she raised prices in 20x4, increasing gross margin from sales from 30 percent in 20x3 to 35 percent in 20x4. Cruz is pleased that net income did go up from 20x3 to 20x4, as shown in the following comparative income statements:

	20x4	20x3
Revenues		
Net Sales	$611,300	$693,200
Costs and Expenses		
Cost of Goods Sold	$397,345	$485,240
Selling and Administrative Expenses	154,199	152,504
Total Costs and Expenses	$551,544	$637,744
Income Before Income Taxes	$ 59,756	$ 55,456
Income Taxes	15,000	14,000
Net Income	$ 44,756	$ 41,456

Total assets for Cruz Tapestries, Inc., at year end for 20x2, 20x3, and 20x4 were $623,390, $693,405, and $768,455, respectively. Has Cruz Tapestries' profitability really improved? (*Hint:* Compute profit margin and return on assets, and comment.) What factors has Cruz overlooked in evaluating the profitability of the company? (*Hint:* Compute asset turnover and comment on the role it plays in profitability.)

FRA 3.

LO 7   Financial Analysis with Industry Comparison

Exhibits 2 and 4 in this chapter contain the comparative balance sheet and income statement for **Dell Computer Corp.** Assume you are the chief financial officer.

REQUIRED

1. Compute liquidity ratios (working capital and current ratio) and profitability ratios (profit margin, asset turnover, return on assets, debt to equity, and return on equity) for 1998 and 1999 and show the industry ratios (except working capital) from Figures 5 to 10 in the chapter. Use income from continuing operations and end-of-year assets and stockholders' equity to compute the ratios.

2. Write a short memorandum to the board of directors in executive summary form summarizing changes in Dell's liquidity and profitability performance from 1998 to 1999 compared with the industry averages.

International Company

FRA 4.

LO 5   Interpretation and
LO 7   Analysis of British Financial Statements

On the opposite page are the classified balance sheets for the British company **Glaxo Wellcome plc,** a pharmaceutical firm with marketing and manufacturing operations in 57 countries.[15]

In the United Kingdom, the format used for classified financial statements is usually different from that used in the United States. To compare the financial statements of companies in different countries, it is important to develop the ability to interpret a variety of formats.

REQUIRED

1. For each line on Glaxo Wellcome plc's balance sheet, indicate the corresponding term that would be found on a U.S. balance sheet. (For this exercise, consider Provisions for Liabilities and Charges to be long-term liabilities.) What is the focus or rationale behind the format of the U.K. balance sheet?

2. Assuming that Glaxo Wellcome plc earned a net income of £2,488 million and £2,822 million in 1998 and 1997, respectively, compute the current ratio, debt to equity, return on assets, and return on equity for 1998 and 1997. (Use year-end amounts to compute ratios.)

Toys "R" Us Annual Report

FRA 5.

LO 5   Reading and Analyzing
LO 6   an Annual Report
LO 7

Refer to the Toys "R" Us annual report to answer the following questions. (Note that 1999 refers to the year ended January 30, 1999, and 1998 refers to the year ended January 31, 1998.)

1. Consolidated balance sheets: (a) Did the amount of working capital increase or decrease from 1998 to 1999? By how much? (b) Did the current ratio improve from 1998 to 1999? (c) Does the company have long-term investments or intangible assets? (d) Did the debt to equity ratio of Toys "R" Us change from 1998 to 1999? (e) What is the contributed capital for 1999? How does it compare with retained earnings?

2. Consolidated statements of earnings: (a) Does Toys "R" Us use a multistep or a single-step form of income statement? (b) Is it a comparative statement? (c) What is the trend of net earnings? (d) How significant are income taxes for Toys "R" Us? (e) Did the profit margin increase from 1998 to 1999? (f) Did asset turnover improve from 1998 to 1999? (g) Did the return on assets increase from 1998 to 1999? (h) Did the return on equity increase from 1998 to 1999? Total assets and total stockholders' equity for 1997 may be obtained from the financial highlights.

Glaxo Wellcome plc and Subsidiaries
Consolidated Balance Sheets

	At 30.6.98 £m	At 30.6.97 £m
Fixed assets		
Tangible assets	3,529	3,811
Investments and other	229	100
	3,758	3,911
Current assets		
Stocks	948	844
Debtors	2,387	2,478
Liquid investments	1,196	1,012
Cash at bank	214	196
	4,745	4,530
Creditors: amounts due within one year		
Loans and overdrafts	1,251	1,080
Other creditors	2,288	2,039
	3,532	3,119
Net current (liabilities)/assets	1,213	1,411
Total assets less current liabilities	4,971	5,322
Creditors: amounts due after one year		
Loans	1,795	1,874
Convertible bonds	—	88
Other creditors	216	585
	2,011	2,547
Provisions for liabilities and charges	654	961
Net assets	2,306	1,814
Capital and reserves		
Called up share capital	899	891
Share premium account	954	738
Goodwill reserve	—	4,863
Other reserves	395	4,992
Equity shareholders' funds	2,248	1,758
Equity minority interests	58	56
Capital employed	2,306	1,814

3. Multistep income statement: In Toys "R" Us's 1987 annual report, management stated that the company's "[operating] expense levels were among the best controlled in retailing [at] 18.8 percent. . . . We were able to operate with lower merchandise margins and still increase our earnings and return on sales."[16] Prepare a multistep income statement for Toys "R" Us down to income from operations for 1998 and 1999, excluding the restructuring and other charges, and compute the ratios of gross margin, operating expenses, and income from operations to net sales. Comment on whether the company continued, as of 1999, to maintain the level of performance indicated by management in 1987. In 1987, gross margin was 31.2 percent and income from operations was 12.4 percent of net sales.

Fingraph® Financial Analyst™

Choose one or both of the following analyses:

1. *Alternative to FRA 3:* Analyze Dell Computer Corp.'s balance sheet and income statement using Fingraph® Financial Analyst™ CD-ROM software. To do this assignment, you will need to enter the data from Dell's financial statements shown in this chapter. Complete part 1 of **FRA 3.** Prepare the memorandum required in part 2 of **FRA 3** separately.

2. *Alternative to FRA 5:* Analyze the Toys "R" Us balance sheet and income statement using Fingraph® Financial Analyst™ CD-ROM software. The CD-ROM contains both the 1999 Toys "R" Us annual report that appears in this textbook and the 2000 annual report. Your instructor will specify which year to analyze. Complete requirements 1, 2, and 3 of **FRA 5.**

Internet Case

Obtain the annual report for a large, well-known company from either your college's library or the Needles Accounting Resource Center web site at http://college.hmco.com. Companies in this chapter include General Mills, Dell Computer, Nike, and Quaker Oats. In the annual report, identify the four basic financial statements and the notes to the financial statements. Perform a liquidity analysis, including the calculation of working capital and the current ratio. Perform a profitability analysis, calculating profit margin, asset turnover, return on assets, debt to equity, and return on equity. Be prepared to present your findings in class.

ENDNOTES

1. General Mills, Inc., *Annual Report*, 1998.
2. "Objectives of Financial Reporting by Business Enterprises," *Statement of Financial Accounting Concepts No. 1* (Norwalk, Conn.: Financial Accounting Standards Board, 1978), pars. 32–54.
3. "Qualitative Characteristics of Accounting Information," *Statement of Financial Accounting Concepts No. 1* (Norwalk, Conn.: Financial Accounting Standards Board, 1980), par. 20.
4. Accounting Principles Board, "Accounting Changes," *Opinion No. 20* (New York: American Institute of Certified Public Accountants, 1971), par. 17.
5. Ray J. Groves, "Here's the Annual Report. Got a Few Hours?" *The Wall Street Journal Europe*, August 26–27, 1994.
6. Roger Lowenstein, "Investors Will Fish for Footnotes in 'Abbreviated' Annual Reports," *The Wall Street Journal*, September 14, 1995.
7. Quaker Oats Co., *Annual Report*, 1998.
8. Ibid.
9. National Commission on Fraudulent Financial Reporting, *Report of the National Commission on Fraudulent Financial Reporting* (Washington, D.C., 1987), p. 2.
10. Arthur Levitt, "The Numbers Game," NYU Center for Law and Business, September 28, 1998.
11. *Accounting Research and Terminology Bulletin*, final ed. (New York: American Institute of Certified Public Accountants, 1961), p. 20.
12. Roger Lowenstein, "Lenders' Stampede Tramples Caldor," *The Wall Street Journal*, October 26, 1995.
13. Roger Lowenstein, "The '20% Club' No Longer Is Exclusive," *The Wall Street Journal*, May 4, 1995.
14. Albertson's Inc. and Giant Food Inc., *Annual Reports*, January 28, 1998, and February 28, 1998, respectively.
15. Glaxo Wellcome plc, *Half-Year Report*, 1998.
16. Toys "R" Us, *Annual Report*, 1987.

Measuring and Reporting the Operating Cycle

Accounting, as you have seen, is an information system that measures, processes, and communicates information for decision-making purposes. **Part One** presented the basic concepts, principles, and techniques of accounting, financial reporting, and analysis. **Part Two** focuses on the relevance of financial accounting to the management of the operating cycle, which is the cycle of purchasing and paying for merchandise, selling merchandise, and collecting from customers, and to the measurement and reporting of the assets and liabilities associated with the operating cycle. Special attention is given to management choices in accounting measurements and their effects on financial reporting.

Chapter 6 Merchandising Operations and Internal Control
Chapter 6 introduces the operating cycle and other management issues associated with operating merchandising and manufacturing businesses. The periodic and perpetual inventory systems receive equal treatment. Internal control for merchandising businesses is the final topic of the chapter.

Chapter 7 Short-Term Liquid Assets
Chapter 7 focuses on the management of and accounting for four types of short-term assets: cash and cash equivalents, short-term investments, accounts receivable, and notes receivable.

Chapter 8 Inventories
Chapter 8 presents the management issues associated with inventories, including a detailed discussion of the costing of inventories for financial reporting.

Chapter 9 Current Liabilities and the Time Value of Money
Chapter 9 presents the management issues associated with current liabilities. The basic concepts and techniques of the time value of money are presented, with emphasis on their applications to accounting.

6 Merchandising Operations and Internal Control

DECISION POINT: A USER'S FOCUS

Target Stores The management of merchandising businesses has two key decisions to make: the price at which merchandise is sold and the level of service the company provides. For example, a department store can set the price of its merchandise at a relatively high level and provide a great deal of service. A discount store, on the other hand, may price its merchandise at a relatively low level and provide limited service. The following figures show that Target Stores, a division of Target Corp., is successful.[1] What decisions did Target Stores' management make about pricing and service to achieve this success?

Target distinguishes itself from other discounters by providing its guests with quality, trend-right merchandise, superior service, a convenient shopping experience, and competitive prices. In other words, Target emphasizes high-quality, name-brand merchandise that might be sold at full price in specialty stores, but sells it at discount prices that are competitive with the prices of other discount stores that sell less well known merchandise. Target's chief executive officer says, "At the core of our strong financial results and consistent store growth is Target's clearly differentiated strategy. Target also benefited from our continued focus on expense reduction."[2]

Business-World Example: In terms of sales dollars, the largest retailers in 1999 were Wal-Mart, Sears, and Kmart.

Financial Highlights

(Millions of dollars, except stores and square feet)

	1998	1997	1996
Revenues	$23,056	$20,368	$17,853
Operating profit	$ 1,578	$ 1,287	$ 1,042
Stores	881	796	736
Retail square feet*	94,553	87,158	79,360

*In thousands, reflects total square feet, less office, warehouse, and vacant space.

Management Issues in Merchandising Businesses

OBJECTIVE

1 Identify the management issues related to merchandising businesses

A **merchandising business** earns income by buying and selling products or merchandise. Such a company, whether wholesale or retail, uses the same basic accounting methods as do service companies, but the buying and selling of merchandise adds to the complexity of the process. As a foundation for discussing the accounting issues of merchandising businesses, we must first identify the management issues involved in running such a business. It is also important to note that analyses, systems, and controls for merchandising businesses are equally relevant to manufacturing companies.

VIDEO CASE

Office Depot, Inc.

Objectives

- To become familiar with the nature of merchandising operations.
- To identify the management issues associated with a merchandising business.
- To show how gross margin and operating expenses affect the business goal of profitability.

Background for the Case

All retailing companies are merchandising companies. Office Depot, Inc., is the world's largest office products

retailer and one of the fastest-growing retailing companies in the world. Through its chain of office products superstores and delivery warehouses, the company serves the growing market of small and medium-size businesses, home offices, and individual consumers. A typical Office Depot store is 25,000 to 30,000 square feet in size and features over 6,000 name-brand products at prices that are generally 60 percent below manufacturers' suggested retail or catalogue prices. Office Depot's merchandise assortment includes office supplies, business electronics, state-of-the-art computer hardware and software, office furniture, and a complete business service center. The company operates a national network of Customer Service Centers where customers can pick up purchases or have them delivered. The delivery business represents more than

30 percent of the company's total sales. Office Depot is expanding by opening megastores of approximately 50,000 square feet, free-standing furniture stores, and copying and publishing services outlets. The company is faced with intense competition from companies such as OfficeMax, Inc., and Staples, Inc.

For more information about Office Depot, Inc., visit the company's web site through the Needles Accounting Resource Center web site at:
http://college.hmco.com

Required

▶️ View the video on Office Depot, Inc., that accompanies this book. As you are watching the video, take notes related to the following questions:

1. All merchandising companies have inventories and need to control these inventories. In your own words, what is inventory, and why is it important to implement controls over it? Identify the types of products that Office Depot typically has in inventory and some ways in which the company might control its inventory.

2. All merchandising companies have an operating cycle. Describe the operating cycle and explain how it applies to Office Depot.

3. All merchandising companies try to achieve the goal of profitability by producing a satisfactory gross margin and maintaining acceptable levels of operating expenses. What is gross margin, and how does it relate to operating expenses? Describe how Office Depot's operations affect gross margin and operating expenses in a way that enables the company to achieve superior profitability.

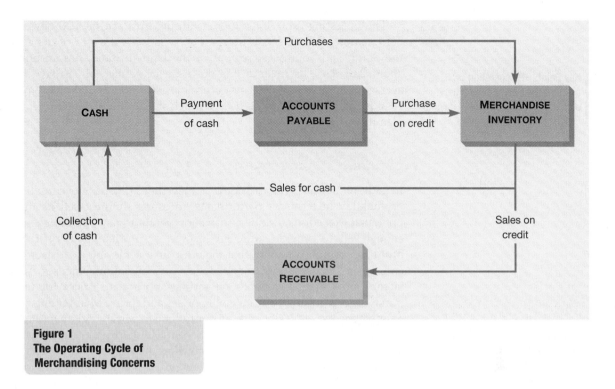

Figure 1
The Operating Cycle of Merchandising Concerns

Cash Flow Management

 Merchandising businesses differ from service businesses in that they have goods on hand for sale to customers, called **merchandise inventory**, and they engage in a series of transactions called the **operating cycle**, as shown in Figure 1. The transactions in the operating cycle consist of (1) purchase of merchandise inventory for cash or on credit, (2) payment for purchases made on credit, (3) sales of merchandise inventory for cash or on credit, and (4) collection of cash from credit sales. Purchases of merchandise are usually made on credit, so the merchandiser has a period of time before payment is due, but this period is generally less than the time it takes to sell the merchandise. Therefore, management will have to plan for cash flows from within the company or from borrowing to finance the inventory until it is sold and the resulting revenue is collected.

In the case of cash sales, the cash is collected immediately. Sales on bank credit cards, such as Visa or MasterCard, are considered cash sales because funds from these sales are available to the merchandiser immediately. In the case of credit sales, the company must wait a period of time before receiving the cash. Some very small retail stores may have mostly cash or credit card sales and very few credit sales, whereas large wholesale concerns may have almost all credit sales. Most merchandising concerns, however, have a combination of cash and credit sales.

Regardless of the relationships of purchases, payments, cash and credit sales, and collections, the operators of a merchandising business must carefully manage cash flow, or liquidity. Such **cash flow management** involves planning the company's receipts and payments of cash. If a company is not able to pay its bills when they are due, it may be forced out of business. As mentioned above, merchandise that is purchased must often be paid for before it is sold and the cash from its sale collected. For example, if a retail business must pay for its purchases in 30 days, it must have cash available or arrange for borrowing if it cannot sell and collect payment for the merchandise in 30 days.

Key Point: A sale takes place when title to the goods transfers to the buyer.

Key Point: The operating cycle is average day's inventory on hand plus the average number of days to collect credit sales.

The operating cycle for a merchandising firm can be 120 days, or even longer. For example, Dillard Dept. Stores, Inc., a successful chain of department stores in the South and Southwest regions of the United States, has an operating cycle of about 218 days. Its inventory is on hand an average of 78 days, and it takes, on average, 140 days to collect its receivables. Because the company pays for its merchandise in an average of 66 days, a much shorter time, management must carefully plan its cash flow.

Profitability Management

In addition to managing cash flow, management must achieve a satisfactory level of profitability in terms of performance measures. It must sell its merchandise at a price that exceeds its cost by a sufficient margin to pay operating expenses and have enough left to provide sufficient income, or profitability. **Profitability management** is a complex activity that includes, first, achieving a satisfactory gross margin and, second, maintaining acceptable levels of operating expenses. Achieving a satisfactory gross margin depends on setting appropriate prices for merchandise and purchasing merchandise at favorable prices and terms. Maintaining acceptable levels of operating expenses depends on controlling expenses and operating efficiently.

Key Point: An operating budget is a financial plan for achieving the goal of profitability.

One of the more effective ways of controlling expenses is to use operating budgets. An **operating budget** reflects management's operating plans and consists of detailed listings of projected selling and general and administrative expenses for a company. At key times during the year and at the end of the year, management should compare the budget with actual expenses and make adjustments to operations as appropriate. An example of an operating budget for Fenwick Fashions Corporation is shown in Exhibit 1. Total selling expenses exceeded the budget by only $80, but four of the expense categories exceeded the budget by a total of $2,080. Management should investigate the possibility that underspending in advertising of $2,000 hid inefficiencies and waste in other areas. Also, sales may have been penalized by not spending the budgeted amount on advertising. Total general and administrative expenses exceed the budget by $6,904. Management should determine why large differences occurred for office salaries expense, insurance expense, and office supplies expense. The amount of insurance expense is usually set by the insurance company; thus an error in the initial budgeting of insurance expense may have caused the unfavorable result. The operating budget has helped management focus on the specific areas that need attention.

Choice of Inventory System

Another issue the management of a merchandising business must address is the choice of inventory system. Management must choose the system or combination of systems that is best for achieving the company's goals. There are two basic systems of accounting for the many items in the merchandise inventory: the perpetual inventory system and the periodic inventory system.

Key Point: Under the perpetual inventory system, the Merchandise Inventory account and the Cost of Goods Sold account are updated with every sale.

Under the **perpetual inventory system** continuous records are kept of the quantity and, usually, the cost of individual items as they are bought and sold. The detailed data available under the perpetual inventory system enable management to respond to customers' inquiries about product availability, to order inventory more effectively and thus avoid running out of stock, and to control the financial costs associated with investments in inventory. Under this system, the cost of each item is recorded in the Merchandise Inventory account when it is purchased. As merchandise is sold, its cost is transferred from the Merchandise Inventory account to the Cost of Goods Sold account. Thus, at all times the balance of the

Exhibit 1
An Example of an Operating Budget

Fenwick Fashions Corporation
Operating Budget
For the Year Ended December 31, 20x2

Operating Expenses	Budget	Actual	Difference Under (Over) Budget
Selling Expenses			
Sales Salaries Expense	$22,000	$22,500	($ 500)
Freight Out Expense	5,500	5,740	(240)
Advertising Expense	12,000	10,000	2,000
Insurance Expense, Selling	800	1,600	(800)
Store Supplies Expense	1,000	1,540	(540)
Total Selling Expenses	$41,300	$41,380	($ 80)
General and Administrative Expenses			
Office Salaries Expense	$23,000	$26,900	($3,900)
Insurance Expense, General	2,100	4,200	(2,100)
Office Supplies Expense	500	1,204	(704)
Depreciation Expense, Building	2,600	2,600	—
Depreciation Expense, Office Equipment	2,000	2,200	(200)
Total General and Administrative Expenses	$30,200	$37,104	($6,904)
Total Operating Expenses	$71,500	$78,484	($6,984)

Key Point: The valuation of ending inventory on the balance sheet is determined by multiplying the quantity of each inventory item by its unit cost.

Key Point: Although computerization has made the perpetual inventory system more popular in recent years, a physical count still should be made periodically to ensure that the actual number of goods on hand matches the quantity indicated by the computer records.

Merchandise Inventory account equals the cost of goods on hand, and the balance in Cost of Goods Sold equals the cost of merchandise sold to customers.

Under the **periodic inventory system**, the inventory not yet sold, or on hand, is counted periodically, usually at the end of the accounting period. No detailed records of the actual inventory on hand are maintained during the accounting period. The figure for inventory on hand is accurate only on the balance sheet date. As soon as any purchases or sales are made, the figure becomes a historical amount, and it remains so until the new ending inventory amount is entered at the end of the next accounting period.

Some retail and wholesale businesses use periodic inventory systems in order to reduce the amount of clerical work. If a business is fairly small, management can maintain control over its inventory simply through observation or by the use of an off-line system of cards or computer records. On the other hand, for larger businesses, the lack of detailed records could lead to either lost sales or high operating costs.

Traditionally, the periodic inventory system has been used by companies that sell items of low value in high volume because of the difficulty and expense of accounting for the purchase and sale of each item. Examples of such companies are drugstores, automobile parts stores, department stores, discount stores, and grain companies. In contrast, companies that sell items of high unit value, such as

BUSINESS FOCUS ON TECHNOLOGY

Many grocery stores, which traditionally used the periodic inventory system, now employ bar coding to update the physical inventory as items are sold. At the checkout counter, the cashier scans the electronic marking on each product, called a *bar code* or *universal product code* (UPC), into the cash register, which is linked to a computer. The price of the item appears on the cash register, and its sale is recorded by the computer. Bar coding has become common in all types of retail companies, and in manufacturing firms and hospitals as well. Some retail businesses now use the perpetual system for keeping track of the physical flow of inventory and the periodic system for preparing the financial statements.

appliances or automobiles, tend to use the perpetual inventory system. This distinction between high and low unit value for inventory systems has blurred considerably in recent years because of the widespread use of computers. Although use of the periodic inventory system is still widespread, use of the perpetual inventory system has increased greatly.

Control of Merchandising Operations

The principal transactions of merchandising businesses, such as buying and selling, involve assets—cash, accounts receivable, and merchandise inventory—that are vulnerable to theft and embezzlement. One reason for this vulnerability is that cash and inventory are fairly easy to steal. Another is that these assets are usually involved in a large number of transactions, such as cash receipts, receipts on account, payments for purchases, and receipts and shipments of inventory, which can become difficult to monitor. If a merchandising company does not take steps to protect its assets, it can have high losses of cash and inventory. Management's responsibility is to establish an environment, accounting systems, and control procedures that will protect the company's assets. These systems and procedures are called *internal controls*.

Maintaining control over merchandise inventory is facilitated by taking a **physical inventory**. This process involves an actual count of all merchandise on hand. It can be a difficult task because it is easy to accidentally omit items or to count them twice. A physical inventory must be taken under both the periodic and the perpetual inventory systems.

Merchandise inventory includes all goods intended for sale that are owned by a concern, regardless of where they are located—on shelves, in storerooms, in warehouses, or in trucks between warehouses and stores. It also includes goods in transit from suppliers if title to the goods has passed to the merchant. Ending inventory does not include merchandise that has been sold but has not yet been delivered to customers or goods that cannot be sold because they are damaged or obsolete. If the damaged or obsolete goods can be sold at a reduced price, however, they should be included in ending inventory at their reduced value.

The actual count is usually taken after the close of business on the last day of the fiscal year. To facilitate taking the physical inventory, many companies end their fiscal year in a slow season, when inventories are at relatively low levels. Retail department stores often end their fiscal year in January or February, for example. After hours, at night, or on the weekend, employees count all items and record the results on numbered inventory tickets or sheets, following procedures to make sure that no items are missed. Sometimes a store closes for all or part of a day for inventory taking. The use of bar coding to take inventory electronically has greatly facilitated the taking of a physical inventory in many companies.

Terms of Sale

Key Point: A trade discount applies to the list or catalogue price. A sales discount applies to the sales price.

Enrichment Note: Early collection also has the advantage of reducing to zero the probability of a customer's defaulting.

When goods are sold on credit, both parties should understand the amount and timing of payment as well as other terms of the purchase, such as who pays delivery or freight charges and what warranties or rights of return apply. Sellers quote prices in different ways. Many merchants quote the price at which they expect to sell their goods. Others, particularly manufacturers and wholesalers, provide a price list or catalogue and quote prices as a percentage (usually 30 percent or more) off the list or catalogue prices. Such a reduction of the list price is called a **trade discount**. For example, if an article was listed at $1,000 with a trade discount of 40 percent, or $400, the seller would record the sale at $600 and the buyer would record the purchase at $600. If the seller wishes to change the selling price, the trade discount can be raised or lowered. At times the trade discount may vary depending on the quantity purchased. The list price and related trade discount are used only to arrive at the agreed-upon price; they do not appear in the accounting records.

The terms of sale are usually printed on the sales invoice and thus constitute part of the sales agreement. Customary terms differ from industry to industry. In some industries, payment is expected in a short period of time, such as 10 or 30 days. In these cases, the invoice is marked "n/10" or "n/30" (read as "net 10" or "net 30"), meaning that the amount of the invoice is due either 10 days or 30 days after the invoice date. If the invoice is due 10 days after the end of the month, it is marked "n/10 eom."

In some industries it is customary to give a discount for early payment. This discount, called a **sales discount**, is intended to increase the seller's liquidity by reducing the amount of money tied up in accounts receivable. An invoice that offers a sales discount might be labeled "2/10, n/30," which means that the buyer either can pay the invoice within 10 days of the invoice date and take a 2 percent discount or can wait 30 days and then pay the full amount of the invoice. It is almost always advantageous for a buyer to take the discount because the saving of 2 percent over a period of 20 days (from the eleventh day to the thirtieth day) represents an effective annual rate of 36 percent (365 days ÷ 20 days × 2% = 36.5%). Most companies would be better off borrowing money to take the discount. The practice of giving sales discounts has been declining because it is costly to the seller and because, from the buyer's viewpoint, the amount of the discount is usually very small in relation to the price of the purchase. Accounting for sales discounts is covered in supplemental objective 8.

BUSINESS FOCUS ON TECHNOLOGY

An increasing percentage of merchandising transactions are conducted electronically. Credit cards have long been in use, but debit, purchase, and Smart cards are becoming integral parts of the so-called cashless society. The debit card allows consumers to access their bank accounts for ATM transactions or with any seller that accepts major credit cards. The price of the sale is withdrawn immediately from the customer's account when purchases are made at grocery stores, drugstores, gas stations, dry cleaners, or hardware stores. The purchase card, the business equivalent of a debit card, allows employees to purchase merchandise for their business. Smart cards have an embedded integrated circuit that stores information, such as prepaid amounts from which purchases are deducted at the point of purchase.

In some industries, it is customary for the seller to pay transportation costs and to charge a price that includes those costs. In other industries, it is customary for the purchaser to pay transportation charges on merchandise. Special terms designate whether the seller or the purchaser pays the freight charges. **FOB shipping point** means that the seller places the merchandise "free on board" at the point of origin, and the buyer bears the shipping costs. The title to the merchandise passes to the buyer at that point. For example, when the sales agreement for the purchase of a car says "FOB factory," the buyer must pay the freight from where the car was made to wherever he or she is located, and the buyer owns the car from the time it leaves the factory.

On the other hand, **FOB destination** means that the seller bears the transportation costs to the place where the merchandise is delivered. The seller retains title until the merchandise reaches its destination and usually prepays the shipping costs, in which case the buyer makes no accounting entry for freight. The effects of these special shipping terms are summarized as follows:

Shipping Term	Where Title Passes	Who Pays the Cost of Transportation
FOB shipping point	At origin	Buyer
FOB destination	At destination	Seller

Applying the Perpetual Inventory System

OBJECTIVE

3 Prepare an income statement and record merchandising transactions under the perpetual inventory system

The income statement for Fenwick Fashions Corporation under the perpetual inventory system is shown in Exhibit 2. The focal point of this income statement is cost of goods sold, which is deducted from net sales to arrive at gross margin. Under the perpetual inventory system, this account is continually updated during the accounting period as purchases, sales, and other inventory transactions take place. The Merchandise Inventory account on the balance sheet is updated at the same time. In Exhibit 2, freight in is included in cost of goods sold. Theoretically,

Exhibit 2
Income Statement Under the Perpetual Inventory System

Fenwick Fashions Corporation Income Statement For the Year Ended December 31, 20x2		
Net Sales		$239,325
Cost of Goods Sold*		131,360
Gross Margin		$107,965
Operating Expenses		
Selling Expenses	$41,380	
General and Administrative Expenses	37,104	
Total Operating Expenses		78,484
Income Before Income Taxes		$ 29,481
Income Taxes		5,000
Net Income		$ 24,481

*Freight in has been included in Cost of Goods Sold.

freight in should be allocated between ending inventory and cost of goods sold, but most companies choose to include the cost of freight in cost of goods sold on the income statement because it is a relatively small amount.

Transactions Related to Purchases of Merchandise

The recording of typical transactions related to purchases of merchandise under the perpetual inventory system is illustrated in the following sections.

Purchases of Merchandise on Credit

Key Point: The Merchandise Inventory account is increased when a purchase is made.

A = L + OE
+ +

Oct. 3   Received merchandise purchased on credit from Neebok Company, invoice dated October 1, terms n/10, FOB shipping point, $4,890.

Oct. 3	Merchandise Inventory	4,890	
	Accounts Payable		4,890
	Purchased merchandise from Neebok Company, terms n/10, FOB shipping point, invoice dated Oct. 1		

Under the perpetual inventory system, the cost of merchandise purchased is placed in the Merchandise Inventory account at the time of purchase.

Transportation Costs on Purchases

Key Point: Freight In appears within the cost of goods sold section of the income statement, and Freight Out Expense appears as an operating expense.

A = L + OE
+ −

Oct. 4   Received bill from Transfer Freight Company for transportation costs on October 3 shipment, invoice dated October 1, terms n/10, $160.

Oct. 4	Freight In	160	
	Accounts Payable		160
	Transportation charges on Oct. 3 purchase, Transfer Freight Company, terms n/10, invoice dated Oct. 1		

Freight in, also called *transportation in*, is the transportation cost of receiving merchandise. Transportation costs are accumulated in a Freight In account because most shipments contain multiple items. It is usually not practical to identify the specific cost of shipping each item of inventory.

In some cases, the seller pays the freight charges and bills them to the buyer as a separate item on the invoice. When this occurs, the entries are the same as in the October 3 example, except that an additional debit is made to Freight In for the amount of the freight charges and Accounts Payable is increased by a like amount.

Purchases Returns and Allowances

A = L + OE
− −

Oct. 6   Returned merchandise received from Neebok Company on October 3 for credit, $480.

Oct. 6	Accounts Payable	480	
	Merchandise Inventory		480
	Merchandise from purchase of Oct. 3 returned to Neebok Company for full credit		

If a seller sends the wrong product or one that is otherwise unsatisfactory, the buyer may be allowed to return the item for a cash refund or credit on account, or the buyer may be given an allowance off the sales price. Under the perpetual inventory system, the returned merchandise is removed from the Merchandise Inventory account.

Payments on Account

Oct. 10   Paid in full the amount due to Neebok Company for the purchase of October 3, part of which was returned on October 6.

A = L + OE   Oct. 10 Accounts Payable   4,410
−   −   Cash   4,410
                                Made payment on account to
                                Neebok Company
                                $4,890 − $480 = $4,410

Transactions Related to Sales of Merchandise

Under the perpetual inventory system, at the time of a sale, the cost of the merchandise is transferred from the Merchandise Inventory account to the Cost of Goods Sold account. In the case of a return of sold merchandise, the cost of the merchandise is transferred from Cost of Goods Sold back to Merchandise Inventory. Transactions related to sales made by Fenwick Fashions Corporation follow.

Key Point: The Cost of Goods Sold account is increased and the Merchandise Inventory account is decreased when a sale is made.

Sales of Merchandise on Credit

Oct. 7   Sold merchandise on credit to Gonzales Distributors, terms n/30, FOB destination, $1,200; the cost of the merchandise was $720.

A = L + OE   Oct. 7 Accounts Receivable   1,200
+   +   Sales   1,200
                                Sale of merchandise to Gonzales
                                Distributors, terms n/30, FOB destination

A = L + OE   Cost of Goods Sold   720
−   −   Merchandise Inventory   720
                                To transfer cost of merchandise inventory
                                sold to Cost of Goods Sold account

Under the perpetual inventory system, two entries are necessary. First, the sale is recorded. Second, Cost of Goods Sold is updated by a transfer from Merchandise Inventory. In the case of cash sales, Cash rather than Accounts Receivable is debited for the amount of the sale.

Payment of Delivery Costs

Oct. 8   Paid transportation costs for the sale on October 7, $78.

A = L + OE   Oct. 8 Freight Out Expense   78
−   −   Cash   78
                                Delivery costs on Oct. 7 sale

A seller will often absorb delivery or freight out costs in the belief that doing so will facilitate the sale of its products. These costs are accumulated in an account called **Freight Out Expense**, or *Delivery Expense*, which is shown as a selling expense on the income statement.

Returns of Merchandise Sold

Oct. 9   Merchandise sold on October 7 accepted back from Gonzales Distributors for full credit and returned to merchandise inventory, $300; the cost of the merchandise was $180.

$A = L + OE$
$-$ $-$

Oct. 9   Sales Returns and Allowances   300
      Accounts Receivable   300
       Return of merchandise from
       Gonzales Distributors

$A = L + OE$
$+$ $+$

      Merchandise Inventory   180
       Cost of Goods Sold   180
       To transfer cost of merchandise returned
       to the Merchandise Inventory account

Key Point: Because the Sales account is established with a credit, its contra account, Sales Returns and Allowances, is established with a debit.

Because returns and allowances to customers for wrong or unsatisfactory merchandise are often an indicator of customer dissatisfaction, such amounts are accumulated in a **Sales Returns and Allowances** account. This account is a contra-revenue account with a normal debit balance and is deducted from Sales on the income statement. Under the perpetual inventory system, the cost of the merchandise must also be transferred from the Cost of Goods Sold account back into the Merchandise Inventory account. If an allowance is made instead of accepting a return, or if the merchandise cannot be returned to inventory and resold, this transfer is not made.

Receipts on Account

Nov. 5   Received payment in full from Gonzales Distributors for sale of merchandise on October 7, less the return on October 9.

$A = L + OE$
$+$
$-$

Nov. 5   Cash   900
      Accounts Receivable   900
       Receipt on account from
       Gonzales Distributors
       \$1,200 − \$300 = \$900

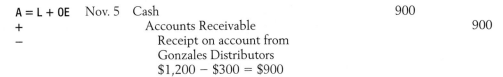

Applying the Periodic Inventory System

OBJECTIVE

4 Prepare an income statement and record merchandising transactions under the periodic inventory system

The income statement for Fenwick Fashions Corporation under the periodic inventory system is shown in Exhibit 3 and illustrated in Figure 2. A major feature of this income statement is the computation of cost of goods sold. Cost of goods sold must be computed because it is not updated for purchases, sales, and other transactions during the accounting period as it is under the perpetual inventory system.

To calculate cost of goods sold, the **goods available for sale** must first be determined. The goods available for sale during the year is the sum of two factors, beginning inventory and the net cost of purchases during the year. In this case, the goods available for sale is \$179,660 (\$52,800 + \$126,860).

If a company sold all the goods available for sale during an accounting period, the cost of goods sold would equal the goods available for sale. In most businesses, however, some merchandise will remain unsold and on hand at the end of the period. This merchandise, or ending inventory, must be deducted from the goods available for sale to determine the cost of goods sold. In the case of Fenwick Fashions Corporation, the ending inventory on December 31, 20x2, is \$48,300. Thus, the cost of goods sold is \$131,360 (\$179,660 − \$48,300).

An important component of the cost of goods sold section is **net cost of purchases**, which consists of net purchases plus any freight charges on the purchases. **Net purchases** equals total purchases less any deductions, such as purchases returns and allowances and any discounts allowed by suppliers for early payment

Exhibit 3
Income Statement Under the Periodic Inventory System

Enrichment Note: Most published financial statements are condensed, eliminating much of the detail shown here.

Fenwick Fashions Corporation
Income Statement
For the Year Ended December 31, 20x2

Net Sales			$239,325
Cost of Goods Sold			
Merchandise Inventory, December 31, 20x1		$ 52,800	
Purchases	$126,400		
Less Purchases Returns and Allowances	7,776		
Net Purchases	$118,624		
Freight In	8,236		
Net Cost of Purchases		126,860	
Goods Available for Sale		$179,660	
Less Merchandise Inventory, December 31, 20x2		48,300	
Cost of Goods Sold			131,360
Gross Margin			$107,965
Operating Expenses			
Selling Expenses		$ 41,380	
General and Administrative Expenses		37,104	
Total Operating Expenses			78,484
Income Before Income Taxes			$ 29,481
Income Taxes			5,000
Net Income			$ 24,481

Figure 2
The Components of Cost of Goods Sold

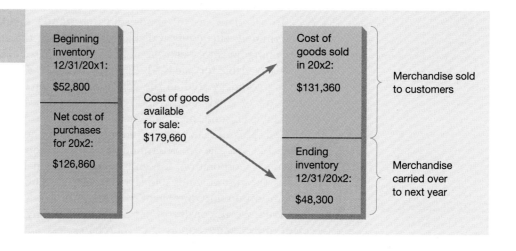

(see supplemental objective 8). Because transportation charges, or freight in, are a necessary cost of receiving merchandise for sale, they are added to net purchases to arrive at the net cost of purchases, as shown in Exhibit 3.

Transactions Related to Purchases of Merchandise

The primary difference in accounting between the perpetual and the periodic inventory systems is that under the perpetual inventory system, the Merchandise Inventory account is continuously adjusted because purchases, sales, and other inventory transactions are entered in the account as they occur. Under the periodic inventory system, on the other hand, the Merchandise Inventory account stays at its beginning balance until the physical inventory is recorded at the end of the period. A Purchases account is used to accumulate the purchases of merchandise during the accounting period, and a Purchases Returns and Allowances account is used to accumulate returns of and allowances on purchases.

To illustrate the periodic inventory system, purchase transactions made by Fenwick Fashions Corporation follow.

Key Point: The Purchases account is increased when a purchase is made under the periodic inventory system.

Purchases of Merchandise on Credit

Oct. 3   Received merchandise purchased on credit from Neebok Company, invoice dated October 1, terms n/10, FOB shipping point, $4,890.

A = L + OE
   +   −

Oct. 3	Purchases	4,890	
	Accounts Payable		4,890
	Purchased merchandise from Neebok		
	Company, terms n/10, FOB shipping		
	point, invoice dated Oct. 1		

Under the periodic inventory system, **Purchases** is a temporary account. Its sole purpose is to accumulate the total cost of merchandise purchased for resale during an accounting period. (Purchases of other assets, such as equipment, are recorded in the appropriate asset account, not in the Purchases account.) The Purchases account does not indicate whether merchandise has been sold or is still on hand.

Transportation Costs on Purchases

Oct. 4   Received bill from Transfer Freight Company for transportation costs on October 3 shipment, invoice dated October 1, terms n/10, $160.

A = L + OE
   +   −

Oct. 4	Freight In	160	
	Accounts Payable		160
	Transportation charges on Oct. 3 purchase,		
	Transfer Freight Company, terms n/10,		
	invoice dated Oct. 1		

Transportation costs on purchases are usually accumulated in a Freight In account. In some cases, the seller pays the freight charges and bills them to the buyer as a separate item on the invoice. When this occurs, the entries are the same as in the October 3 example, except that an additional debit is made to Freight In for the amount of the freight charges and Accounts Payable is increased by a like amount.

Enrichment Note: Accounts such as Purchases and Purchases Returns and Allowances are used only in conjunction with a periodic inventory system.

Purchases Returns and Allowances

Oct. 6   Returned merchandise received from Neebok Company on October 3 for credit, $480.

A = L + OE	Oct. 6 Accounts Payable	480	
− +	Purchases Returns and Allowances		480
	Merchandise from purchase of Oct. 3		
	returned to Neebok Company for		
	full credit		

Key Point: Because the Purchases account is established with a debit, its contra account, Purchases Returns and Allowances, is established with a credit.

If a seller sends the wrong product or one that is otherwise unsatisfactory, the buyer may be allowed to return the item for a cash refund or credit on account, or the buyer may be given an allowance off the sales price. Under the periodic inventory system, the amount of the return or allowance is recorded in the **Purchases Returns and Allowances** account. This account is a contra-purchases account with a normal credit balance, and it is deducted from Purchases on the income statement.

Payments on Account

Oct. 10   Paid in full the amount due to Neebok Company for the purchase of October 3, part of which was returned on October 6.

A = L + OE	Oct. 10 Accounts Payable	4,410	
− −	Cash		4,410
	Made payment on account to		
	Neebok Company		
	$4,890 − $480 = $4,410		

Transactions Related to Sales of Merchandise

The Cost of Goods Sold account, which is updated for sales and returns under the perpetual inventory system, is not used under the periodic inventory system because the Merchandise Inventory account is not updated until the end of the accounting period. Transactions related to sales made by Fenwick Fashions Corporation follow.

Sales of Merchandise on Credit

Oct. 7   Sold merchandise on credit to Gonzales Distributors, terms n/30, FOB destination, $1,200; the cost of the merchandise was $720.

A = L + OE	Oct. 7 Accounts Receivable	1,200	
+ +	Sales		1,200
	Sale of merchandise to		
	Gonzales Distributors, terms n/30,		
	FOB destination		

In the case of cash sales, Cash rather than Accounts Receivable is debited for the amount of the sale.

Payment of Delivery Costs

Oct. 8   Paid transportation costs for the sale on October 7, $78.

A = L + OE	Oct. 8 Freight Out Expense	78	
− −	Cash		78
	Delivery costs on Oct. 7 sale		

Delivery or freight out costs are accumulated in the Freight Out Expense (also called Delivery Expense) account. This account is shown as a selling expense on the income statement.

Returns of Merchandise Sold

Oct. 9   Merchandise sold on October 7 accepted back from Gonzales Distributors for full credit and returned to merchandise inventory.

A = L + OE
–   –

Oct. 9	Sales Returns and Allowances	300	
	Accounts Receivable		300
	Return of merchandise from Gonzales Distributors		

Returns and allowances to customers for wrong or unsatisfactory merchandise are accumulated in the Sales Returns and Allowances account. This account is a contra-revenue account with a normal debit balance and is deducted from Sales on the income statement.

Receipts on Account

Nov. 5   Received payment in full from Gonzales Distributors for sale of merchandise on October 7, less the return on October 9.

A = L + OE
+
–

Nov. 5	Cash	900	
	Accounts Receivable		900
	Receipt on account from Gonzales Distributors		
	$1,200 − $300 = $900		

Credit Card Sales

Many retailers allow customers to charge their purchases to a third-party company that the customer will pay later. These transactions are normally handled with credit cards. Five of the most widely used credit cards are American Express, Discover Card, Diners Club, MasterCard, and Visa. The customer establishes credit with the lender (the credit card issuer) and receives a plastic card to use in making charge purchases. If the seller accepts the card, an invoice is prepared and signed by the customer at the time of the sale. The seller then deposits the invoice in the bank and receives cash. Because the seller does not have to establish the customer's credit, collect from the customer, or tie money up in accounts receivable, the seller receives an economic benefit provided by the lender. As payment, the lender takes a discount of 2 to 6 percent on the credit card sales invoices rather than paying 100 percent of their total amount. The discount is a selling expense for the merchandiser. For example, assume that a restaurant made sales of $1,000 on Visa credit cards and that Visa takes a 4 percent discount on the sales. Assume also that the sales invoices are deposited in a special Visa bank account in the name of the company, in much the same way that checks from cash sales are deposited. The sales are recorded as follows:

A = L + OE
+   –
+

	Cash	960	
	Credit Card Discount Expense	40	
	Sales		1,000
	Sales on Visa cards		

Inventory Losses

Enrichment Note: Inventory shortages could result from honest mistakes. That is, inventory could have been tagged with the wrong number.

Most companies experience losses of merchandise inventory from spoilage, shoplifting, and theft by employees. When such losses occur, the periodic inventory system provides no means of identifying them because the costs are automatically included in the cost of goods sold. For example, assume that a company has lost $1,250 in stolen merchandise during an accounting period. When the physical inventory is taken, the missing items are not in stock, so they cannot be counted. Because the ending inventory does not contain these items, the amount subtracted from goods available for sale is less than it would be if the goods were in stock. The cost of goods sold, then, is overstated by $1,250. In a sense, the cost of goods sold is inflated by the amount of merchandise that has been lost.

The perpetual inventory system makes it easier to identify such losses. Because the Merchandise Inventory account is continuously updated for sales, purchases, and returns, the loss will show up as the difference between the inventory records and the physical inventory taken at the end of the accounting period. Once the amount of the loss has been identified, the ending inventory is updated by crediting the Merchandise Inventory account. The offsetting debit is usually an increase in Cost of Goods Sold because the loss is considered a cost that reduces the company's gross margin.

Key Point: An adjustment to the Merchandise Inventory account will be needed if the physical inventory reveals a difference between the actual inventory and the amount in the records.

Internal Control: Basic Components and Control Activities

OBJECTIVE

5 Define *internal control*, identify the five components of internal control, and explain seven examples of control activities

A merchandising company can have inaccurate accounting records as well as high losses of cash and inventory if it does not take steps to protect its assets. The best way to do this is to set up and maintain a good system of internal control.

Management's Responsibility for Internal Control

Management is responsible for establishing a satisfactory system of internal control. **Internal control** is defined as all the policies and procedures management uses to ensure the reliability of financial reporting, compliance with laws and regulations, and the effectiveness and efficiency of operations. In other words, management must safeguard the firm's assets and have reliable accounting records. It must ensure that employees comply with legal requirements and operate the company in the best way possible.

Management comments on its responsibility and effectiveness in achieving the goals of internal control in the "Report of Management" in the company's annual report to stockholders. For example, a portion of this statement from the annual report of Circuit City Stores, Inc., follows:

> Management is responsible for maintaining an internal control structure designed to provide reasonable assurance that the books and records reflect the transactions of the Company and that the Company's established policies and procedures are carefully followed. Because of inherent limitations in any system, there can be no absolute assurance that errors or irregularities will not occur. Nevertheless, management believes that the internal control structure provides reasonable assurance that assets are safeguarded and that financial information is objective and reliable.[3]

Components of Internal Control

To accomplish the objectives of internal control, management must establish five interrelated components of internal control:[4]

1. *Control environment* The **control environment** is created by the overall attitude, awareness, and actions of management. It includes management's integrity

and ethics, philosophy and operating style, organizational structure, method of assigning authority and responsibility, and personnel policies and practices. Personnel should be qualified to handle responsibilities, which means that employees must be trained and informed. For example, the manager of a retail store should train employees to follow prescribed procedures for handling cash sales, credit card sales, and returns and refunds.

2. *Risk assessment*   **Risk assessment** is the identification of areas where risks of loss of assets or inaccuracies in the accounting records are high so that adequate controls can be implemented. For example, among the greater risks in a retail store are the risks that employees will take cash or that customers will shoplift merchandise.

3. *Information and communication*   **Information and communication** relates to the accounting systems established by management to identify, assemble, analyze, classify, record, and report a company's transactions. Management should establish clear communication of individual responsibilities in achieving these functions.

4. *Control activities*   **Control activities** are the policies and procedures management puts in place to see that its directives are carried out. Control activities are discussed in more detail below.

5. *Monitoring*   **Monitoring** involves management's regular assessment of the quality of internal control including periodic review of compliance with all policies and procedures. For example, large companies often have a staff of internal auditors who review the company's system of internal control to determine if it is working properly and if procedures are being followed. In smaller businesses, owners and managers should conduct these reviews.

Control Activities

Control activities are a principal way in which internal control is implemented in the accounting system. They safeguard a company's assets and ensure the reliability of accounting records. These control activities include the following:

1. *Authorization*   All transactions and activities should be properly authorized by management. In a retail store, for example, some transactions, such as normal cash sales, are authorized routinely; others, such as issuing a refund, may require a manager's approval.

2. *Recording transactions*   To facilitate preparation of financial statements and to establish accountability for assets, all transactions should be recorded. In a retail store, for example, the cash register records sales, refunds, and other transactions internally on a paper tape or computer disk so that the cashier can be held responsible for the cash received and the merchandise removed during his or her shift.

3. *Documents and records*   The design and use of adequate documents help ensure the proper recording of transactions. For example, to ensure that all transactions are recorded, invoices and other documents should be prenumbered and all numbers should be accounted for.

4. *Physical controls*   Physical controls permit access to assets only with management's authorization. For example, retail stores should use cash registers, and only the cashier responsible for the cash in a register should have access to it. Other employees should not be able to open the cash drawer if the cashier is not present. Likewise, warehouses and storerooms should be accessible only to authorized personnel. Access to accounting records, including company computers, should also be controlled.

5. *Periodic checks* The records should be checked against the assets by someone other than the persons responsible for those records and assets. For example, at the end of each shift or day, the owner or store manager should count the cash in the cash drawer and compare the amount to the amounts recorded on the tape or computer disk in the cash register. Other examples of independent verification are the monthly bank reconciliation and periodic counts of physical inventory.

6. *Separation of duties* The organizational plan should separate functional responsibilities. Within a department, no one person should be in charge of authorizing transactions, operating the department, handling assets, and keeping records of assets. For example, in a stereo store, each employee should oversee only a single part of a transaction. A sales employee takes the order and creates an invoice. Another employee receives the customer's cash or credit card payment and issues a receipt. Once the customer has a paid receipt, and only then, a third employee obtains the item from the warehouse and gives it to the customer. A person in the accounting department subsequently records the sales from the tape in the cash register, comparing them with the sales invoices and updating the inventory in the records. The separation of duties means that a mistake, careless or not, cannot be made without being seen by at least one other person.

Key Point: No control procedure can guarantee the prevention of theft. However, the more procedures there are in place, the less the likelihood of a theft occurring.

7. *Sound personnel procedures* Sound practices should be followed in managing the people who carry out the functions of each department. Among those practices are supervision, rotation of key people among different jobs, insistence that employees take vacations, and bonding of personnel who handle cash or inventories. **Bonding** is the process of carefully checking an employee's background and insuring the company against theft by that person. Bonding does not guarantee against theft, but it does prevent or reduce economic loss if theft occurs. Prudent personnel procedures help to ensure that employees know their jobs, are honest, and will find it difficult to carry out and conceal embezzlement over time.

Limitations of Internal Control

OBJECTIVE
6 Describe the inherent limitations of internal control

No system of internal control is without weaknesses. As long as control procedures are performed by people, the internal control system is vulnerable to human error. Errors may arise from misunderstandings, mistakes in judgment, carelessness, distraction, or fatigue. Separation of duties can be defeated through collusion by employees who secretly agree to deceive the company. Also, established procedures may be ineffective against employees' errors or dishonesty, or controls that

A survey of 5,000 large U.S. businesses disclosed that 21 percent suffered frauds in excess of $1 million. Common frauds were credit card frauds, check frauds, inventory theft, false invoices and phantom vendors, and expense account abuse. The most common ways in which the frauds were allowed to take place were through poor internal controls, management override of internal controls, and collusion. The frauds were most commonly detected by notification by an employee, internal controls, internal auditor review, notification by a customer, and by accident. Companies successful in preventing fraud have a good system of internal control and a formal code of ethics with a program to monitor compliance. The company routinely communicates the existence of the program to employees, which includes a system to report incidents of fraud.[5]

were initially effective may become ineffective because conditions have changed.[6] In some cases, the costs of establishing and maintaining elaborate systems may exceed the benefits. In a small business, for example, active involvement by the owner can be a practical substitute for the separation of some duties.

Internal Control over Merchandising Transactions

Key Point: The separation of duties *can* be defeated through the collusion of two or more people.

Key Point: Maintaining internal control is especially complex and difficult for a merchandiser. Management must not only establish controls for cash sales receipts, purchases, and cash payments, but also go to great lengths to manage and protect its inventory.

Sound internal control activities are needed in all aspects of a business, but particularly when assets are involved. Assets are especially vulnerable when they enter or leave a business. When sales are made, for example, cash or other assets enter the business, and goods or services leave the business. Activities must be set up to prevent theft during those transactions.

Likewise, purchases of assets and payments of liabilities must be controlled. The majority of those transactions can be safeguarded by adequate purchasing and payment systems. In addition, assets on hand, such as cash, investments, inventory, plant, and equipment, must be protected.

In this section, you will see how internal control activities are applied to such merchandising transactions as cash sales, receipts, purchases, and cash payments. Similar activities are applicable to service and manufacturing businesses.

Internal Control and Management Goals

When a system of internal control is applied effectively to merchandising transactions, it can achieve important management goals. For example, two key goals for the success of a merchandising business are:

1. To prevent losses of cash or inventory owing to theft or fraud
2. To provide accurate records of merchandising transactions and account balances

Three broader goals for management are:

1. To keep enough inventory on hand to sell to customers without overstocking
2. To keep enough cash on hand to pay for purchases in time to receive discounts
3. To keep credit losses as low as possible by making credit sales only to customers who are likely to pay on time

 One control used in meeting broad management goals is the cash budget, which projects future cash receipts and disbursements. By maintaining adequate cash balances, a company is able to take advantage of discounts on purchases, prepare to borrow money when necessary, and avoid the damaging effects of being unable to pay bills when they are due. By investing excess cash, the company can earn interest until the cash is needed.

A more specific accounting control is the separation of duties that involve the handling of cash. Such separation makes theft without detection extremely unlikely, unless two or more employees conspire. The separation of duties is easier in large businesses than in small ones, where one person may have to carry out several duties. The effectiveness of internal control over cash varies, based on the size and nature of the company. Most firms, however, should use the following procedures:

1. Separate the functions of authorization, recordkeeping, and custodianship of cash.
2. Limit the number of people who have access to cash.

3. Designate specific people who are responsible for handling cash.

4. Use banking facilities as much as possible, and keep the amount of cash on hand to a minimum.

5. Bond all employees who have access to cash.

6. Physically protect cash on hand by using cash registers, cashiers' cages, and safes.

7. Have a person who does not handle or record cash make unannounced audits of the cash on hand.

8. Record all cash receipts promptly.

9. Deposit all cash receipts promptly.

10. Make payments by check rather than by currency.

11. Have a person who does not authorize, handle, or record cash transactions reconcile the Cash account.

Notice that each of the foregoing procedures helps to safeguard cash by making it more difficult for any one individual who has access to cash to steal or misuse it without being detected.

Control of Cash Sales Receipts

 Cash payments for sales of goods and services can be received by mail or over the counter in the form of checks or currency. Whatever the source of the payments, cash should be recorded immediately upon receipt. This is usually done by making an entry in a cash receipts journal. Such a journal establishes a written record of cash receipts that should prevent errors and make theft more difficult.

CONTROL OF CASH RECEIVED THROUGH THE MAIL   Cash receipts that arrive by mail are vulnerable to theft by the employees who handle them. Payment by mail is increasing because of the expansion of mail-order sales. Therefore, to control mailed receipts, customers should be urged to pay by check or credit card instead of with currency.

Cash that comes in through the mail should be handled by two or more employees. The employee who opens the mail should make a list in triplicate of the money received. The list should contain each payer's name, the purpose for which the money was sent, and the amount. One copy goes with the cash to the cashier, who deposits the money. The second copy goes to the accounting department for recording. The third copy is kept by the person who opens the mail. Errors can be easily caught because the amount deposited by the cashier must agree with the amount received and the amount recorded in the cash receipts journal.

Key Point: The cashier should not be allowed to remove the cash register tape or to record the day's cash receipts.

CONTROL OF CASH RECEIVED OVER THE COUNTER   Two common tools for controlling cash sales receipts are cash registers and prenumbered sales tickets. The amount of a cash sale should be rung up on a cash register at the time of the sale. The cash register should be placed so that the customer can see the amount recorded. Each cash register should have a locked-in tape on which it prints the day's transactions. At the end of the day, the cashier counts the cash in the cash register and turns it in to the cashier's office. Another employee takes the tape out of the cash register and records the cash receipts for the day in the cash receipts journal. The amount of cash turned in and the amount recorded on the tape should agree; if not, any differences must be explained. Large retail chains commonly monitor cash receipts by having each cash register tied directly into a computer that records each transaction as it occurs. Whether the elements are performed manually or by computer, separating responsibility for cash receipts, cash deposits, and recordkeeping is necessary to ensure good internal control.

In some stores, internal control is further strengthened by the use of prenumbered sales tickets and a central cash register or cashier's office, where all sales are rung up and collected by a person who does not participate in the sale. The salesperson completes a prenumbered sales ticket at the time of the sale, giving one copy to the customer and keeping a copy. At the end of the day, all sales tickets must be accounted for, and the sales total computed from the sales tickets should equal the total sales recorded on the cash register.

Control of Purchases and Cash Disbursements

Cash disbursements are particularly vulnerable to fraud and embezzlement. In one recent case, the treasurer of one of the nation's largest jewelry retailers was charged with having stolen over $500,000 by systematically overpaying federal income taxes and keeping the refund checks as they came back to the company.

To avoid such theft, cash should be paid only after the receipt of specific authorization supported by documents that establish the validity and amount of the claim. In addition, maximum possible use should be made of the principle of separation of duties in the purchase of goods and services and the payment for them. The degree of separation of duties varies, depending on the size of the business. Figure 3 shows how separation of duties can be maximized in large companies. In the figure, five internal units (the requesting department, the purchasing department, the accounting department, the receiving department, and the treasurer) and two external contacts (the supplier and the banking system) all play a role in

Figure 3
Internal Control for Purchasing and Paying for Goods and Services

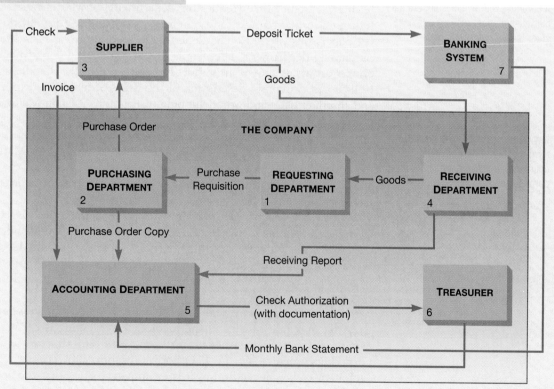

BUSINESS FOCUS ON TECHNOLOGY

One of the more difficult challenges facing computer programmers is to build good internal controls into computerized accounting programs. Such computer programs must include controls that prevent unintentional errors as well as unauthorized access and tampering. The programs prevent errors through reasonableness checks that, for example, may allow no transactions over a specified amount, mathematical checks that verify the arithmetic of transactions, and sequence checks that require documents and transactions to be in proper order. They typically use passwords and questions about randomly selected personal data to prevent unauthorized access to computer records. With unauthorized Internet access easily available in many systems, data encryption and firewalls are important. Data encryption is a way of coding data so that if they are stolen, they are useless to the thief. A firewall is a strong electronic barrier to access from outside a computer system.

the internal control plan. Notice that business documents are also crucial components of the plan.

As shown in Figure 4 (pages 302–303), every action is documented and verified by at least one other person. For instance, the requesting department cannot work out a kickback scheme to make illegal payments to the supplier because the receiving department independently records receipts and the accounting department verifies prices. The receiving department cannot steal goods because the receiving report must equal the invoice. For the same reason, the supplier cannot bill for more goods than it ships. The accounting department's work is verified by the treasurer, and the treasurer ultimately is checked by the accounting department.

Using the forms shown with Figure 4, follow the typical sequence of documents used in this internal control plan for the purchase of 20 boxes of fax paper rolls. To begin, the credit office (requesting department) of Martin Maintenance Company fills out a formal request for a purchase, or **purchase requisition**, for 20 boxes of fax paper rolls (item 1). The department head approves it and forwards it to the purchasing department. The people in the purchasing department prepare a **purchase order**, as shown in item 2. The purchase order is addressed to the vendor (seller) and contains a description of the items ordered; the expected price, terms, and shipping date; and other shipping instructions. Martin Maintenance Company does not pay any bill that is not accompanied by a purchase order number.

After receiving the purchase order, the vendor, Henderson Supply Company, ships the goods and sends an **invoice** or bill (item 3) to Martin Maintenance Company. The invoice gives the quantity and description of the goods delivered and the terms of payment. If goods cannot all be shipped immediately, the estimated date for shipment of the remainder is indicated.

When the goods reach the receiving department of Martin Maintenance Company, an employee writes the description, quantity, and condition of the goods on a form called a **receiving report** (item 4). The receiving department does not receive a copy of the purchase order or the invoice, so its employees do not know what should be received or its value. Thus, they are not tempted to steal any excess that may be delivered.

The receiving report is sent to the accounting department, where it is compared with the purchase order and the invoice. If everything is correct, the accounting department completes a **check authorization** and attaches it to the three supporting documents. The check authorization form shown in item 5 has a space for each item to be checked off as it is examined. Notice that the accounting department has all the documentary evidence for the transaction but does not have

Key Point: A purchase requisition is not the same as a purchase order. A purchase requisition is sent to the purchasing department; a purchase order is sent to the vendor.

Key Point: *Invoice* is the business term for "bill." Every business document must have a number for purposes of reference.

access to the assets purchased. Nor does it write the check for payment. This means that the people performing the accounting function cannot gain by falsifying documents in an effort to conceal fraud.

Finally, the treasurer examines all the documents and issues an order to the bank for payment, called a **check** (item 6), for the amount of the invoice less any appropriate discount. In some systems, the accounting department fills out the check so that all the treasurer has to do is inspect and sign it. The check is then sent to the supplier, with a remittance advice that shows what the check is for. A supplier who is not paid the proper amount will complain, of course, thus providing a form of outside control over the payment. Using a deposit ticket, the supplier deposits the check in the bank, which returns the canceled check with Martin Maintenance Company's next bank statement (item 7). If the treasurer has made the check out for the wrong amount (or altered a pre-filled-in check), the problem will show up in the bank reconciliation.

There are many variations of the system just described. This example is offered as a simple system that provides adequate internal control.

Accounting for Discounts

Sales Discounts

SUPPLEMENTAL OBJECTIVE

8 Apply sales and purchases discounts to merchandising transactions

As mentioned earlier, some industries give sales discounts for early payment. Because it usually is not possible to know at the time of the sale whether the customer will pay in time to take advantage of sales discounts, the discounts are recorded only at the time the customer pays. For example, assume that Fenwick Fashions Corporation sells merchandise to a customer on September 20 for $300, on terms of 2/10, n/60. This is the entry at the time of the sale:

A = L + OE
+   +

Sept. 20	Accounts Receivable	300	
	Sales		300
	Sold merchandise on credit, terms 2/10, n/60		

Key Point: Accounts Receivable must be credited for the full $300 even though only $294 has been received.

The customer can take advantage of the sales discount any time on or before September 30, ten days after the date of the invoice. If the customer pays on September 29, the entry in Fenwick's records would look like this:

A = L + OE
+   −
−

Sept. 29	Cash	294	
	Sales Discounts	6	
	Accounts Receivable		300
	Received payment for Sept. 20 sale; discount taken		

If the customer does not take advantage of the sales discount but waits until November 19 to pay for the merchandise, the entry would be as follows:

A = L + OE
+
−

Nov. 19	Cash	300	
	Accounts Receivable		300
	Received payment for Sept. 20 sale; no discount taken		

At the end of the accounting period, the Sales Discounts account has accumulated all the sales discounts taken during the period. Because sales discounts reduce revenues from sales, Sales Discounts is a contra-revenue account with a normal debit balance that is deducted from gross sales on the income statement.

Figure 4
Internal Control Plan for Purchases and Cash Disbursements

① PURCHASE REQUISITION No. 7077

Martin Maintenance Company

From: Credit Office   Date: September 6, 20xx

To: Purchasing Department   Suggested Vendor: Henderson Supply Company

Please purchase the following items:

Quantity	Number	Description
20 boxes	X 144	FAX paper rolls

Reason for Request
Six months' supply for office

To be filled in by Purchasing Department

Date ordered 9/8/20xx   P.O. No. J 102

Approved J.P.

② PURCHASE ORDER No. J 102

Martin Maintenance Company
8428 Rocky Island Avenue
Chicago, Illinois 60643

To: Henderson Supply Company   Date: September 8, 20xx
2525 25th Street   FOB: Destination
Mesa, Illinois 61611
    Ship by: September 12, 20xx
Ship to: Martin Maintenance Company
Above Address   Terms: 2/10, n/30

Please ship the following:

Quantity	✓	Number	Description	Price	Per	Amount
20 boxes		X 144	FAX paper rolls	12.00	box	$240.00

Purchase order number must appear on all shipments and invoices.

Ordered by Marsha Owen

③ INVOICE No. 0468

Henderson Supply Company   Date: September 12, 20xx
2525 25th Street
Mesa, Illinois 61611   Your Order No.: J 102

Sold to: Ship to:

Martin Maintenance Company   Same
8428 Rocky Island Avenue
Chicago, Illinois 60643

Sales Representative: Joe Jacobs

Quantity Ordered	Quantity Shipped	Description	Price	Per	Amount
20	20	X 144 FAX paper rolls	12.00	box	$240.00

FOB Destination | Terms: 2/10, n/30 | Date Shipped: 9/12/20xx Via: Self

④ RECEIVING REPORT No. JR065

Martin Maintenance Company
8428 Rocky Island Avenue
Chicago, Illinois 60643

Date: September 12, 20xx

Quantity	Number	Description	Condition
20 boxes	X 144	FAX paper rolls	O.K.

Received by B.M.

⑤ CHECK AUTHORIZATION

	NO.	CHECK
Purchase Order	J 102	✓
Receiving Report	JR 065	✓
INVOICE	0468	✓
Price		✓
Calculations		✓
Terms		✓

Approved for Payment J Joseph

⑥

Martin Maintenance Company   NO. 2570
8428 Rocky Island Avenue   61-153/313
Chicago, Illinois 60643

9/21 20xx

PAY TO THE ORDER OF Henderson Supply Company $ 235.20

Two hundred thirty-five and 20/100 — — — — — — — — — Dollars

THE LAKE PARK NATIONAL BANK   Martin Maintenance Company
Chicago, Illinois

⑈031301532⑈ ⑆8030 647 4⑈   by Arthur Martin

Remittance Advice

Date	P.O. No.	DESCRIPTION	AMOUNT
9/21/20xx	J 102	20 X 144 FAX paper rolls	
		Supplier Inv. No. 0468	$240.00
		Less 2% discount	4.80
		Net	$235.20
		Martin Maintenance Company	

Business Document	Prepared by	Sent to	Verification and Related Procedures
① Purchase requisition	Requesting department	Purchasing department	Purchasing verifies authorization.
② Purchase order	Purchasing department	Supplier	Supplier sends goods or services in accordance with purchase order.
③ Invoice	Supplier	Accounting department	Accounting receives invoice from supplier.
④ Receiving report	Receiving department	Accounting department	Accounting compares invoice, purchase order, and receiving report. Accounting verifies prices.
⑤ Check authorization	Accounting department	Treasurer	Accounting attaches check authorization to invoice, purchase order, and receiving report.
⑥ Check	Treasurer	Supplier	Treasurer verifies all documents before preparing check.
⑦ Bank statement	Buyer's bank	Accounting department	Accounting compares amount and payee's name on returned check with check authorization.

⑦

Statement of Account with
THE LAKE PARK NATIONAL BANK
Chicago, Illinois

Martin Maintenance Company
8428 Rocky Island Avenue
Chicago, Illinois 60643

Checking Acct No
8030-647-4
Period covered
Sept.30-Oct.31,20xx

Previous Balance	Checks/Debits—No.	Deposits/Credits—No.	S.C.	Current Balance
$2,645.78	$4,319.33 --16	$5,157.12 --7	$12.50	$3,471.07

CHECKS/DEBITS			DEPOSITS/CREDITS		DAILY BALANCES	
Posting Date	Check No.	Amount	Posting Date	Amount	Date	Amount
					09/30	2,645.78
10/01	2564	100.00	10/01	586.00	10/01	2,881.78
10/01	2565	250.00	10/05	1,500.00	10/04	2,825.60
10/04	2567	56.18	10/06	300.00	10/05	3,900.46
10/05	2566	425.14	10/16	1,845.50	10/06	4,183.34
10/06	2568	17.12	10/21	600.00	10/12	2,242.34
10/12	2569	1,705.80	10/24	300.00CM	10/16	3,687.84
10/12	2570	235.20	10/31	25.62IN	10/17	3,589.09
10/16	2571	400.00			10/21	4,189.09
10/17	2572	29.75			10/24	3,745.59
10/17	2573	69.00			10/25	3,586.09
10/24	2574	738.50			10/28	3,457.95
10/24		5.00DM			10/31	3,471.07
10/25	2575	7.50				
10/25	2577	152.00				
10/28		118.14NSF				
10/28		10.00DM				
10/31		12.50SC				

Explanation of Symbols:

CM – Credit Memo   SC – Service Charge   The last amount
DM – Debit Memo   EC – Error Correction   in this column
NSF – Non-Sufficient Funds   OD – Overdraft   is your balance.
    IN – Interest on Average Balance

Please examine; if no errors are reported within ten (10) days, the account will be considered to be correct.

Purchases Discounts

Merchandise purchases are usually made on credit and sometimes involve **purchases discounts** for early payment. Purchases discounts are discounts taken for early payment for merchandise purchased for resale. They are to the buyer what sales discounts are to the seller. The amount of discounts taken is recorded in a separate account. Assume that Fenwick made a credit purchase of merchandise on November 12 for $1,500 with terms of 2/10, n/30 and returned $200 in merchandise on November 14. When payment is made within the discount period, Fenwick's journal entry looks like this:

A = L + OE
– – +

Key Point: Accounts Payable must be debited for the full $1,300 even though only $1,274 has been paid.

Nov. 22	Accounts Payable		1,300	
	Purchases Discounts			26
	Cash			1,274
	Paid the invoice of Nov. 12			

Purchase Nov. 12	$1,500	
Less return Nov. 14	200	
Net purchase	$1,300	
Discount: 2%	26	
Cash paid	$1,274	

If the purchase is not paid for within the discount period, this is the entry:

A = L + OE
– –

Dec. 12	Accounts Payable	1,300	
	Cash		1,300
	Paid the invoice of Nov. 12, less the return, on due date; no discount taken		

Like Purchases Returns and Allowances, Purchases Discounts is a contra-purchases account with a normal credit balance that is deducted from Purchases on the income statement. If a company makes only a partial payment on an invoice, most creditors allow the company to take the discount applicable to the partial payment. The discount usually does not apply to freight, postage, taxes, or other charges that might appear on the invoice.

Chapter Review

REVIEW OF LEARNING OBJECTIVES

Ace it

1. **Identify the management issues related to merchandising businesses.** Merchandising companies differ from service companies in that they earn income by buying and selling products or merchandise. The buying and selling of merchandise adds to the complexity of the business and raises four issues that management must address. First, the series of transactions in which merchandising companies engage (the operating cycle) requires careful cash flow management. Second, profitability management requires the company to price goods and control operating costs and expenses by using budgets to ensure the earning of an adequate income after operating expenses and income taxes have been paid. Third, the company must choose whether to use the periodic or the perpetual inventory system. Fourth, management must establish an internal control structure that protects the assets cash, merchandise inventory, and accounts receivable.

2. **Define and distinguish the terms of sale for merchandising transactions.** Trade discounts are a reduction from the catalogue or list price of a product. A sales discount is a discount given for early payment of a sale on

credit. FOB shipping point means the buyer bears the cost of transportation, and title to the goods passes to the buyer at the shipping origin. FOB destination means that the seller bears the cost of transportation, and title does not pass to the buyer until the goods reach their destination.

3. **Prepare an income statement and record merchandising transactions under the perpetual inventory system.** Under the perpetual inventory system, records of the quantity and, usually, the cost of individual items of inventory are kept throughout the year. The cost of goods sold is recorded as goods are transferred to customers, and the inventory balance is kept current throughout the year as items are bought and sold. The main advantage of the perpetual inventory system is that it provides management with timely information about the status of the inventory. The main disadvantages are that it is more difficult to maintain and more costly than a periodic inventory system. A physical inventory, or physical count, is taken at the end of the accounting period to establish a basis for accuracy and detect possible inventory losses under the perpetual inventory system. The Merchandise Inventory account is continuously adjusted by entering purchases, sales, and other inventory transactions as they occur. Purchases increase the Merchandise Inventory account, and purchases returns decrease it. As goods are sold, their cost is transferred from the Merchandise Inventory account to the Cost of Goods Sold account.

4. **Prepare an income statement and record merchandising transactions under the periodic inventory system.** Under the periodic inventory system, no detailed records of the actual inventory on hand are maintained during the accounting period. A physical count of inventory is made at the end of the accounting period to update the Inventory account and to determine cost of goods sold. The main advantages of the periodic inventory system are that it is simpler and less costly than the perpetual inventory system. The main disadvantage of the periodic inventory system is that the lack of detailed records may lead to inefficiencies, lost sales, and higher operating costs. When the periodic inventory system is used, the income statement must include a cost of goods sold section that includes the following elements:

$$\text{Gross Purchases} - \text{Purchases Returns and Allowances} + \text{Freight In} = \text{Net Cost of Purchases}$$

$$\text{Beginning Merchandise Inventory} + \text{Net Cost of Purchases} = \text{Goods Available for Sale}$$

$$\text{Goods Available for Sale} - \text{Ending Merchandise Inventory} = \text{Cost of Goods Sold}$$

Under the periodic inventory system, the Merchandise Inventory account stays at the beginning level until the physical inventory is recorded at the end of the period. A Purchases account is used to accumulate purchases of merchandise during the accounting period, and a Purchases Returns and Allowances account is used to accumulate returns of and allowances on purchases.

5. **Define *internal control*, identify the five components of internal control, and explain seven examples of control activities.** Internal control is the policies and procedures management uses to protect the organization's assets and to ensure the accuracy and reliability of accounting records. It also works to maintain efficient operations and compliance with management's policies. Internal control consists of five components: the control environment, risk assessment, information and communication, control activities, and monitoring. Examples of control activities are proper authorization of transactions; recording transactions to facilitate preparation of financial statements and to establish

accountability for assets; use of well-designed documents and records; physical controls; periodic checks of records and assets; separation of duties into the functions of authorization, operations, custody of assets, and recordkeeping; and use of sound personnel policies.

6. **Describe the inherent limitations of internal control.** A system of internal control relies on the people who implement it. Thus, the effectiveness of internal control is limited by the people involved. Human error, collusion, and failure to recognize changed conditions all can contribute to a system's failure.

7. **Apply internal control activities to common merchandising transactions.** Certain procedures strengthen internal control over sales, cash receipts, purchases, and cash disbursements. First, the functions of authorization, recordkeeping, and custody should be kept separate. Second, the accounting system should provide for physical protection of assets (especially cash and merchandise inventory), use of banking services, prompt recording and deposit of cash receipts, and payment by check. Third, the people who have access to cash and merchandise inventory should be specifically designated and their number limited. Fourth, employees who have access to cash or merchandise inventory should be bonded. Fifth, the Cash account should be reconciled each month, and unannounced audits of cash on hand should be made by an individual who does not authorize, handle, or record cash transactions.

SUPPLEMENTAL OBJECTIVE

8. **Apply sales and purchases discounts to merchandising transactions.** Sales discounts are discounts for early payment. Terms of 2/10, n/30 mean that the buyer can take a 2 percent discount if the invoice is paid within ten days of the invoice date. Otherwise, the buyer is obligated to pay the full amount in 30 days. Discounts on sales are recorded in the Sales Discounts account, and discounts on purchases are recorded in the Purchases Discounts account.

REVIEW OF CONCEPTS AND TERMINOLOGY

The following concepts and terms were introduced in this chapter.

LO 5   **Bonding:** The process of carefully checking an employee's background and insuring the company against theft by that person.

LO 1   **Cash flow management:** The planning of a company's receipts and payments of cash.

LO 7   **Check:** A written order to a bank to pay the amount specified from funds on deposit.

LO 7   **Check authorization:** A form prepared by the accounting department after it has compared the receiving report for goods received with the purchase order and the invoice. It permits the issuance of a check to pay the invoice.

LO 5   **Control activities:** Procedures and policies established by management to ensure that the objectives of internal control are met.

LO 5   **Control environment:** The overall attitude, awareness, and actions of the owners and management of a business, as reflected in philosophy and operating style, organizational structure, methods of assigning authority and responsibility, and personnel policies and practices.

LO 2   **FOB destination:** A shipping term that means that the seller bears transportation costs to the place of delivery.

LO 2   **FOB shipping point:** A shipping term that means that the buyer bears transportation costs from the point of origin.

LO 3   **Freight in:** Transportation charges on merchandise purchased for resale. Also called *transportation in*.

LO 3 **Freight Out Expense:** The account that accumulates transportation charges on merchandise sold, which are shown as a selling expense. Also called *Delivery Expense.*

LO 4 **Goods available for sale:** The sum of beginning inventory and the net cost of purchases during the period; the total goods available for sale to customers during an accounting period.

LO 5 **Information and communication:** The accounting system established by management and the communication of responsibilities with regard to the accounting system.

LO 5 **Internal control:** All the policies and procedures a company uses to ensure the reliability of financial reporting, compliance with laws and regulations, and the effectiveness and efficiency of operations.

LO 7 **Invoice:** A form sent to the purchaser by the vendor that describes the quantity and price of the goods or services delivered and the terms of payment.

LO 1 **Merchandise inventory:** The goods on hand at any one time that are available for sale to customers.

LO 1 **Merchandising business:** A business that earns income by buying and selling products or merchandise.

LO 5 **Monitoring:** Management's regular assessment of the quality of internal control.

LO 4 **Net cost of purchases:** Net purchases plus any freight charges on the purchases.

LO 4 **Net purchases:** Total purchases less any deductions, such as purchases returns and allowances and purchases discounts.

LO 1 **Operating budget:** Management's operating plans as reflected by detailed listings of projected selling and general and administrative expenses.

LO 1 **Operating cycle:** A series of transactions that includes purchases of merchandise inventory for cash or on credit, payment for purchases made on credit, sales of merchandise inventory for cash or on credit, and collection of cash from the sales.

LO 1 **Periodic inventory system:** A system for determining inventory on hand by a physical count at the end of an accounting period.

LO 1 **Perpetual inventory system:** A system for determining inventory on hand by keeping continuous records of the quantity and, usually, the cost of individual items as they are bought and sold.

LO 1 **Physical inventory:** An actual count of all merchandise on hand at the end of an accounting period.

LO 1 **Profitability management:** The process of achieving a satisfactory gross margin—by setting appropriate prices for merchandise and purchasing merchandise at favorable prices and terms—and maintaining acceptable levels of operating expenses.

LO 7 **Purchase order:** A form prepared by a company's purchasing department and sent to a vendor; it describes the items ordered; their expected price, terms, and shipping date; and other shipping instructions.

LO 7 **Purchase requisition:** A formal written request for a purchase, prepared by the requesting department in an organization and sent to the purchasing department.

LO 4 **Purchases:** A temporary account used under the periodic inventory system to accumulate the total cost of all merchandise purchased for resale during an accounting period.

SO 8 **Purchases discounts:** Discounts taken for prompt payment for merchandise purchased for resale; the Purchases Discounts account is a contra-purchases account.

LO 4 **Purchases Returns and Allowances:** A contra-purchases account used under the periodic inventory system to accumulate cash refunds, credits on account, and other allowances made by suppliers on merchandise originally purchased for resale.

LO 7 **Receiving report:** A form prepared by the receiving department of a company; describes the quantity and condition of goods received.

LO 5 **Risk assessment:** The identification of areas where risks of loss of assets or inaccuracies in the accounting records are high.

LO 2 **Sales discount:** A discount given to a buyer for early payment of a sale made on credit; the Sales Discounts account is a contra-revenue account.

LO 3 **Sales Returns and Allowances:** A contra-revenue account used to accumulate cash refunds, credits on account, and other allowances made to customers who have received defective or otherwise unsatisfactory products.

LO 2 **Trade discount:** A deduction (usually 30 percent or more) off a list or catalogue price that is not recorded in the accounting records.

REVIEW PROBLEM

Merchandising Transactions: Periodic and Perpetual Inventory Systems

LO 3
LO 4

Dawkins Company engaged in the following transactions during October.

Oct. 1 Sold merchandise to Ernie Devlin on credit, terms n/30, FOB shipping point, $1,050 (cost, $630).

2 Purchased merchandise on credit from Ruland Company, terms n/30, FOB shipping point, $1,900.

2 Paid Custom Freight $145 for freight charges on merchandise received.

6 Purchased store supplies on credit from Arizin Supply House, terms n/30, $318.

9 Purchased merchandise on credit from LNP Company, terms n/30, FOB shipping point, $1,800, including $100 freight costs paid by LNP Company.

11 Accepted from Ernie Devlin a return of merchandise, which was returned to inventory, $150 (cost, $90).

14 Returned for credit $300 of merchandise received on October 2.

15 Returned for credit $100 of store supplies purchased on October 6.

16 Sold merchandise for cash, $500 (cost, $300).

22 Paid Ruland Company for purchase of October 2 less return of October 14.

23 Received full payment from Ernie Devlin for his October 1 purchase, less return on October 11.

REQUIRED

1. Prepare entries in journal form to record the transactions, assuming the periodic inventory system is used.

2. Prepare entries in journal form to record the transactions, assuming the perpetual inventory system is used.

ANSWER TO REVIEW PROBLEM

Note: Accounts that differ under the two systems are highlighted.

1. Periodic Inventory System

Oct. 1	Accounts Receivable	1,050	
	Sales		1,050
	Sale on account to Ernie Devlin, terms n/30, FOB shipping point		
2	Purchases	1,900	
	Accounts Payable		1,900
	Purchase on account from Ruland Company, terms n/30, FOB shipping point		

2. Perpetual Inventory System

Accounts Receivable	1,050	
Sales		1,050
Sale on account to Ernie Devlin, terms n/30, FOB shipping point		
Cost of Goods Sold	630	
Merchandise Inventory		630
To transfer cost of merchandise sold to Cost of Goods Sold account		
Merchandise Inventory	1,900	
Accounts Payable		1,900
Purchase on account from Ruland Company, terms n/30, FOB shipping point		

	1. Periodic Inventory System			2. Perpetual Inventory System		
Oct. 2	Freight In	145		Freight In	145	
	Cash		145	Cash		145
	Freight on previous purchase			Freight on previous purchase		
6	Store Supplies	318		Store Supplies	318	
	Accounts Payable		318	Accounts Payable		318
	Purchase of store supplies on account from Arizin Supply House, terms n/30			Purchase of store supplies on account from Arizin Supply House, terms n/30		
9	Purchases	1,700		Merchandise Inventory	1,700	
	Freight In	100		Freight In	100	
	Accounts Payable		1,800	Accounts Payable		1,800
	Purchase on account from LNP Company, terms n/30, FOB shipping point, freight paid by supplier			Purchase on account from LNP Company, terms n/30, FOB shipping point, freight paid by supplier		
11	Sales Returns and Allowances	150		Sales Returns and Allowances	150	
	Accounts Receivable		150	Accounts Receivable		150
	Return of merchandise from Ernie Devlin			Return of merchandise from Ernie Devlin		
				Merchandise Inventory	90	
				Cost of Goods Sold		90
				To transfer cost of merchandise returned to Merchandise Inventory account		
14	Accounts Payable	300		Accounts Payable	300	
	Purchases Returns and Allowances		300	Merchandise Inventory		300
	Return of portion of merchandise purchased from Ruland Company			Return of portion of merchandise purchased from Ruland Company		
15	Accounts Payable	100		Accounts Payable	100	
	Store Supplies		100	Store Supplies		100
	Return of store supplies (not merchandise) purchased on October 6 for credit			Return of store supplies (not merchandise) purchased on October 6 for credit		
16	Cash	500		Cash	500	
	Sales		500	Sales		500
	Sale of merchandise for cash			Sale of merchandise for cash		
				Cost of Goods Sold	300	
				Merchandise Inventory		300
				To transfer cost of merchandise sold to Cost of Goods Sold account		
22	Accounts Payable	1,600		Accounts Payable	1,600	
	Cash		1,600	Cash		1,600
	Payment on account to Ruland Company $1,900 − $300 = $1,600			Payment on account to Ruland Company $1,900 − $300 = $1,600		
23	Cash	900		Cash	900	
	Accounts Receivable		900	Accounts Receivable		900
	Receipt on account of Ernie Devlin $1,050 − $150 = $900			Receipt on account of Ernie Devlin $1,050 − $150 = $900		

Chapter Assignments

QUESTIONS

1. What four issues must be faced by managers of merchandising businesses?
2. What is the operating cycle of a merchandising business, and why is it important?
3. What are two important elements in achieving a satisfactory profit in a merchandising business?
4. What is an operating budget, and how does it help management improve profitability?
5. What is the difference between a trade discount and a sales discount?
6. Two companies quoted the following prices and terms on 50 units of product:

	Price	Terms
Supplier A	$20 per unit	FOB shipping point
Supplier B	$21 per unit	FOB destination

   Which supplier is quoting the better deal? Explain your answer.
7. Under which inventory system is a Cost of Goods Sold account maintained? Explain why.
8. Discuss this statement: "The perpetual inventory system is the best system because management always needs to know how much inventory it has."
9. Why is it advisable to maintain a Sales Returns and Allowances account when the same result could be obtained by debiting each return or allowance to the Sales account?
10. Is freight in an operating expense? Explain your answer.
11. Under the periodic inventory system, goods available for sale is an important figure in computing cost of goods sold. What are the two main components of goods available for sale, and what is the relationship of ending inventory to goods available for sale?
12. Under the periodic inventory system, how must the amount of inventory at the end of the year be determined?
13. Hornberger Hardware purchased the following items: (a) a delivery truck, (b) two dozen hammers, (c) supplies for its office workers, and (d) a broom for the janitor. Which items should be debited to the Purchases account under the periodic inventory system?
14. What is the difference between the periodic inventory system and the perpetual inventory system?
15. What are the principal differences in the handling of merchandise inventory in the accounting records under the periodic inventory system and the perpetual inventory system?
16. Why are merchants willing to pay a fee to credit card companies to gain the ability to accept their cards from customers?
17. Most people think of internal control as a means of making fraud harder to commit and easier to detect. Can you think of some other important purposes of internal control?
18. What are the five components of internal control?
19. What are some examples of control activities?
20. Why is the separation of duties necessary to ensure sound internal control? What does this principle assume about the relationships of employees in a company and the possibility of two or more of them stealing from the company?
21. In a small business, it is sometimes impossible to separate duties completely. What are three other practices that a small business can follow to achieve the objectives of internal control over cash?

22. At Thrifty Variety Store, each sales clerk counts the cash in his or her cash drawer at the end of the day, then removes the cash register tape and prepares a daily cash form, noting any discrepancies. This information is checked by an employee in the cashier's office, who counts the cash, compares the total with the form, and then gives the cash to the cashier. What is the weakness in this system of internal control?

23. How does a movie theater control cash receipts?

24. Is the normal balance of the Sales Discounts account a debit or a credit balance? Is it an asset, liability, expense, or contra-revenue account?

SHORT EXERCISES

SE 1.

LO 1 Identification of Management Issues

Identify each of the following decisions as most directly related to (a) cash flow management, (b) profitability management, (c) choice of inventory system, or (d) control of merchandising operations.

1. Determination of how to protect cash from theft or embezzlement
2. Determination of the selling price of goods for sale
3. Determination of policies governing sales of merchandise on credit
4. Determination of whether to use the periodic or the perpetual inventory system

SE 2.

LO 2 Terms of Sale

A machine tool dealer buys machines from a manufacturer and resells them to its customers.

a. The manufacturer sets a list or catalogue price of $6,000 for a machine. The manufacturer offers its dealers a 40 percent trade discount.
b. The manufacturer sells the machine under terms of FOB shipping point. The cost of shipping is $350.
c. The manufacturer offers a sales discount of 2/10, n/30. The sales discount does not apply to shipping costs.

What is the net cost of the machine tool to the dealer, assuming it is paid for within ten days of purchase?

SE 3.

LO 3 Purchases of Merchandise: Perpetual Inventory System

Record in journal form each of the following transactions, assuming the perpetual inventory system is used.

Aug. 2 Purchased merchandise on credit from Gear Company, invoice dated August 1, terms n/10, FOB shipping point, $2,300.
    3 Received bill from State Shipping Company for transportation costs on August 2 shipment, invoice dated August 1, terms n/30, $210.
    7 Returned damaged merchandise received from Gear Company on August 2 for credit, $360.
   10 Paid in full the amount due to Gear Company for the purchase of August 2, part of which was returned on August 7.

SE 4.

LO 4 Purchases of Merchandise: Periodic Inventory System

Record in journal form the transactions in **SE 3** above, assuming the periodic inventory system is used.

SE 5.

LO 4 Cost of Goods Sold: Periodic Inventory System

Using the following data and assuming cost of goods sold is $230,000, prepare the cost of goods sold section of a merchandising income statement (periodic inventory system), including computation of the amount of purchases for the month of October.

Freight In	$12,000
Merchandise Inventory, Sept. 30, 20xx	33,000
Merchandise Inventory, Oct. 31, 20xx	44,000
Purchases	?
Purchases Returns and Allowances	9,000

SE 6.

LO 4 **Sales of Merchandise: Periodic Inventory System**

Record in journal form the following transactions, assuming the periodic inventory system is used.

Aug. 4 Sold merchandise on credit to Kwai Corporation, terms n/30, FOB destination, $1,200.
   5 Paid transportation costs for sale of August 4, $110.
   9 Part of the merchandise sold on August 4 was accepted back from Kwai Corporation for full credit and returned to the merchandise inventory, $350.
Sept. 3 Received payment in full from Kwai Corporation for merchandise sold on August 4, less the return on August 9.

SE 7.

LO 4 **Credit Card Sales Transaction**

Record in journal form the following transaction for Jenny's Novelties Store.

Apr. 19 A tabulation of invoices at the end of the day showed $400 in Visa invoices, which are deposited in a special bank account at full value less 5 percent discount.

SE 8.

LO 5 **Internal Control**
LO 7 **Activities**

Match each of the control activities to the appropriate checkwriting policies for a small business listed below.

a. Authorization
b. Recording transactions
c. Documents and records
d. Physical controls
e. Periodic independent check
f. Separation of duties
g. Sound personnel policies

1. The person who writes the checks to pay bills is different from the persons who authorize the payments and who keep the records of the payments.
2. The checks are kept in a locked drawer. The only person who has the key is the person who writes the checks.
3. The person who writes the checks is bonded.
4. Once each month the owner compares and reconciles the amount of money shown in the accounting records with the amount in the bank account.
5. Each check is approved by the owner of the business before it is mailed.
6. A check stub recording pertinent information is completed for each check.
7. Every day, all checks are recorded in the accounting records, using the information on the check stubs.

SE 9.

LO 6 **Limitations of Internal Control**

Internal control is subject to several inherent limitations. Indicate whether each of the following situations is an example of (a) human error, (b) collusion, (c) changed conditions, or (d) cost-benefit considerations.

1. Effective separation of duties in a restaurant is impractical because the business is too small.
2. The cashier and the manager of a retail shoe store work together to circumvent the internal controls for the purpose of embezzling funds.
3. The cashier in a pizza shop does not understand the procedures for operating the cash register and thus fails to ring up all sales and to count the cash at the end of the day.
4. At a law firm, computer supplies were mistakenly delivered to the reception area instead of the receiving area because the supplier began using a different means of shipment. As a result, the receipt of supplies was not recorded.

SE 10.

SO 8 **Sales and Purchases Discounts**

On April 15, Sural Company sold merchandise to Astor Company for $1,500 on terms of 2/10, n/30. Record the entries in both Sural's and Astor's records for (1) the sale, (2) a return of merchandise on April 20 of $300, and (3) payment in full on April 25. Assume both companies use the periodic inventory system.

EXERCISES

E 1.

LO 1 **Management Issues and Decisions**

The decisions and actions that follow were undertaken by the management of Rugged Denim Company. Indicate whether each action pertains primarily to (a) cash flow management, (b) profitability management, (c) choice of inventory system, or (d) control of merchandise operations.

1. Decided to mark each item of inventory with a magnetic tag that sets off an alarm if the tag is removed from the store before being deactivated.
2. Decided to reduce the credit terms offered to customers from 30 days to 20 days to speed up collection of accounts.
3. Decided that the benefits of keeping track of each item of inventory as it is bought and sold would exceed the costs of such a system and acted to implement the decision.
4. Decided to raise the price of each item of inventory to achieve a higher gross margin to offset an increase in rent expense.
5. Decided to purchase a new type of cash register that can be operated only by a person who knows a predetermined code.
6. Decided to switch to a new cleaning service that will provide the same service at a lower cost.

E 2.

LO 1   Operating Budget

The operating budget and actual performance for the six months ended June 30, 20x1, for Levy's Hardware Corporation appear below.

	Budget	Actual
Selling Expenses		
Sales Salaries Expense	$ 90,000	$102,030
Sales Supplies Expense	2,000	1,642
Rent Expense, Selling Space	18,000	18,000
Utilities Expense, Selling Space	12,000	11,256
Advertising Expense	15,000	21,986
Depreciation Expense, Selling Fixtures	6,500	6,778
Total Selling Expenses	$143,500	$161,692
General and Administrative Expenses		
Office Salaries Expense	$ 50,000	$ 47,912
Office Supplies Expense	1,000	782
Rent Expense, Office Space	4,000	4,000
Depreciation Expense, Office Equipment	3,000	3,251
Utilities Expense, Office Space	3,000	3,114
Postage Expense	500	626
Insurance Expense	2,000	2,700
Miscellaneous Expense	500	481
Total General and Administrative Expenses	$ 64,000	$ 62,866
Total Operating Expenses	$207,500	$224,558

1. Prepare an operating report that shows budget, actual, and difference.
2. Discuss the results, including identifying which differences most likely should be investigated by management.

E 3.

LO 2   Terms of Sale

A household appliance dealer buys refrigerators from a manufacturer and resells them to its customers.

a. The manufacturer sets a list or catalogue price of $1,000 for a refrigerator. The manufacturer offers its dealers a 30 percent trade discount.
b. The manufacturer sells the machine under terms of FOB destination. The cost of shipping is $100.
c. The manufacturer offers a sales discount of 2/10, n/30. Sales discounts do not apply to shipping costs.

What is the net cost of the refrigerator to the dealer, assuming it is paid for within ten days of purchase?

E 4.

LO 3 **Preparation of the Income Statement: Perpetual Inventory System**

Using the selected account balances at December 31, 20xx, for Tents, Etc. that follow, prepare an income statement for the year ended December 31, 20xx. Show detail of net sales. The company uses the perpetual inventory system, and Freight In has not been included in Cost of Goods Sold.

Account Name	Debit	Credit
Sales		$237,500
Sales Returns and Allowances	$ 11,750	
Cost of Goods Sold	140,000	
Freight In	6,750	
Selling Expenses	21,500	
General and Administrative Expenses	43,500	
Income Taxes	5,000	

E 5.

LO 3 **Recording Purchases: Perpetual Inventory System**

Give the entries to record each of the following transactions under the perpetual inventory system:

a. Purchased merchandise on credit, terms n/30, FOB shipping point, $2,500.
b. Paid freight on the shipment in transaction **a,** $135.
c. Purchased merchandise on credit, terms n/30, FOB destination, $1,400.
d. Purchased merchandise on credit, terms n/30, FOB shipping point, $2,600, which includes freight paid by the supplier of $200.
e. Returned part of the merchandise purchased in transaction **c,** $500.
f. Paid the amount owed on the purchase in transaction **a.**
g. Paid the amount owed on the purchase in transaction **d.**
h. Paid the amount owed on the purchase in transaction **c** less the return in **e.**

E 6.

LO 3 **Recording Sales: Perpetual Inventory System**

On June 15, Vega Company sold merchandise for $1,300 on terms of n/30 to Whist Company. On June 20, Whist Company returned some of the merchandise for a credit of $300, and on June 25, Whist paid the balance owed. Give Vega's entries to record the sale, return, and receipt of payment under the perpetual inventory system. The cost of the merchandise sold on June 15 was $750, and the cost of the merchandise returned to inventory on June 20 was $175.

E 7.

LO 4 **Preparation of the Income Statement: Periodic Inventory System**

Using the selected year-end account balances at December 31, 20x2, for the Boston General Store shown below, prepare a 20x2 income statement. Show detail of net sales. The company uses the periodic inventory system. Beginning merchandise inventory was $52,000; ending merchandise inventory is $44,000.

Account Name	Debit	Credit
Sales		$594,000
Sales Returns and Allowances	$ 30,400	
Purchases	229,600	
Purchases Returns and Allowances		8,000
Freight In	11,200	
Selling Expenses	97,000	
General and Administrative Expenses	74,400	
Income Taxes	30,000	

E 8.

LO 4 **Merchandising Income Statement: Missing Data, Multiple Years**

Determine the missing data for each letter in the following three income statements for Leseur Wholesale Paper Company (in thousands):

	20x3	20x2	20x1
Gross Sales	$ p	$ h	$286
Sales Returns and Allowances	24	19	a
Net Sales	q	317	b
Merchandise Inventory, Beginning	r	i	38
Purchases	192	169	c
Purchases Returns and Allowances	31	j	17
Freight In	s	29	22
Net Cost of Purchases	189	k	d
Goods Available for Sale	222	212	182
Merchandise Inventory, Ending	39	l	42
Cost of Goods Sold	t	179	e
Gross Margin	142	m	126
Selling Expenses	u	78	f
General and Administrative Expenses	39	n	33
Total Operating Expenses	130	128	g
Income Before Income Taxes	v	o	27
Income Taxes	3	2	5
Net Income	w	8	22

E 9.

LO 4 **Recording Purchases: Periodic Inventory System**

Using the data in **E 5,** give the entries to record each of the transactions under the periodic inventory system.

E 10.

LO 4 **Recording Sales: Periodic Inventory System**

Using the relevant data in **E 6,** give the entries to record each of the transactions under the periodic inventory system.

E 11.

LO 5 **Use of Accounting Records in Internal Control**

Careful scrutiny of accounting records and financial statements can lead to the discovery of fraud or embezzlement. Each of the following situations may indicate a breakdown in internal control. Indicate the nature of the possible fraud or embezzlement in each of these situations.

1. Wages expense for a branch office was 30 percent higher in 20x2 than in 20x1, even though the office was authorized to employ only the same four employees and raises were only 5 percent in 20x2.

2. Sales returns and allowances increased from 5 percent to 20 percent of sales in the first two months of 20x2, after record sales in 20x1 resulted in large bonuses being paid to the sales staff.

3. Gross margin decreased from 40 percent of net sales in 20x1 to 30 percent in 20x2, even though there was no change in pricing. Ending inventory was 50 percent less at the end of 20x2 than it was at the beginning of the year. There is no immediate explanation for the decrease in inventory.

4. A review of daily records of cash register receipts shows that one cashier consistently accepts more discount coupons for purchases than do the other cashiers.

E 12.

LO 5 **Control Procedures**
LO 7

Ben Choudoury, who operates a small grocery store, has established the following policies with regard to the checkout cashiers.

1. Each cashier has his or her own cash drawer, to which no one else has access.

2. Each cashier may accept checks for purchases under $50 with proper identification. Checks over $50 must be approved by Choudoury before they are accepted.

3. Every sale must be rung up on the cash register and a receipt given to the customer. Each sale is recorded on a tape inside the cash register.

4. At the end of each day, Choudoury counts the cash in the drawer and compares it to the amount on the tape inside the cash register.

Identify by letter which of the following conditions for internal control applies to each of the policies listed above.

a. Transactions are executed in accordance with management's general or specific authorization.
b. Transactions are recorded as necessary to permit preparation of financial statements and maintain accountability for assets.
c. Access to assets is permitted only as allowed by management.
d. At reasonable intervals, the records of assets are compared with the existing assets.

E 13.

LO 5   Internal Control Procedures

Paglicci Video Store maintains the following policies with regard to purchases of new videotapes at each of its branch stores.

1. Employees are required to take vacations, and the duties of employees are rotated periodically.
2. Once each month a person from the home office visits each branch to examine the receiving records and to compare the inventory of tapes with the accounting records.
3. Purchases of new tapes must be authorized by purchase order in the home office and paid for by the treasurer in the home office. Receiving reports are prepared in each branch and sent to the home office.
4. All new personnel receive one hour of training in how to receive and catalogue new tapes.
5. The company maintains a perpetual inventory system that keeps track of all tapes purchased, sold, and on hand.

Indicate by letter which of the following control procedures apply to each of the above policies. (Some may have several answers.)

a. Authorization
b. Recording transactions
c. Documents and records
d. Limited access

e. Periodic independent verification
f. Separation of duties
g. Sound personnel policies

E 14.

SO 8   Sales Involving Discounts

Give the entries to record the following transactions engaged in by Amal Company, which uses the periodic inventory system.

Mar. 1   Sold merchandise on credit to Lin Company, terms 2/10, n/30, FOB shipping point, $1,000.
      3   Accepted a return from Lin Company for full credit, $400.
     10   Received payment from Lin Company for the sale, less the return and discount.
     11   Sold merchandise on credit to Lin Company, terms 2/10, n/30, FOB shipping point, $1,600.
     31   Received payment for amount due from Lin Company for the sale of March 11.

E 15.

SO 8   Purchases Involving Discounts

Give the entries to record the following transactions engaged in by Walton Company, which uses the periodic inventory system.

July 2   Purchased merchandise on credit from Iqbal Company, terms 2/10, n/30, FOB destination, invoice dated July 1, $1,600.
      6   Returned some merchandise to Iqbal Company for full credit, $200.
     11   Paid Iqbal Company for purchase of July 2 less return and discount.
     14   Purchased merchandise on credit from Iqbal Company, terms 2/10, n/30, FOB destination, invoice dated July 12, $1,800.
     31   Paid amount owed Iqbal Company for purchase of July 14.

E 16.

SO 8   Purchases and Sales Involving Discounts

Pinsky Company purchased $4,600 of merchandise, terms 2/10, n/30, from A&G Company and paid for the merchandise within the discount period. Give the entries (1) by Pinsky Company to record the purchase and payment and (2) by A&G Company to record the sale and receipt of payment. Both companies use the periodic inventory system.

PROBLEMS

LO 1 Merchandising Income
LO 3 Statement: Perpetual
        Inventory System

P 1. At the end of the fiscal year, August 31, 20x2, selected accounts from the adjusted trial balance for Alan's Accessories, Inc., appeared as follows:

Alan's Accessories, Inc. Partial Adjusted Trial Balance August 31, 20x2		
Sales		$162,000
Sales Returns and Allowances	$ 2,000	
Cost of Goods Sold	61,400	
Freight In	2,300	
Store Salaries Expense	32,625	
Office Salaries Expense	12,875	
Advertising Expense	24,300	
Rent Expense	2,400	
Insurance Expense	1,200	
Utilities Expense	1,560	
Store Supplies Expense	2,880	
Office Supplies Expense	1,175	
Depreciation Expense, Store Equipment	1,050	
Depreciation Expense, Office Equipment	800	
Income Taxes	2,000	

REQUIRED

1. Using the information given, prepare an income statement for Alan's Accessories, Inc. Combine Freight In with Cost of Goods Sold. Store Salaries Expense; Advertising Expense; Store Supplies Expense; and Depreciation Expense, Store Equipment are selling expenses. The other expenses are general and administrative expenses. The company uses the perpetual inventory system. Show details of net sales and operating expenses.

2. Based on your knowledge to this point in the course, how would you use the income statement for Alan's Accessories, Inc., to evaluate the company's profitability? What other financial statement should be considered and why?

P 2. Tattle Company engaged in the following transactions in October 20xx.

LO 3 Merchandising Transactions:
        Perpetual Inventory System

Oct. 7   Sold merchandise on credit to Lina Ortiz, terms n/30, FOB shipping point, $6,000 (cost, $3,600).

8   Purchased merchandise on credit from Ruff Company, terms n/30, FOB shipping point, $12,000.

9   Paid Curry Company for shipping charges on merchandise purchased on October 8, $508.

10   Purchased merchandise on credit from Sewall Company, terms n/30, FOB shipping point, $19,200, including $1,200 freight costs paid by Sewall.

13   Purchased office supplies on credit from Door Company, terms n/30, $4,800.

14   Sold merchandise on credit to Peter Watts, terms n/30, FOB shipping point, $4,800 (cost, $2,880).

14   Returned damaged merchandise received from Ruff Company on October 8 for credit, $1,200.

17   Received check from Lina Ortiz for her purchase of October 7.

18   Returned a portion of the office supplies received on October 13 for credit because the wrong items were sent, $800.

19   Sold merchandise for cash, $3,600 (cost, $2,160).

20   Paid Sewall Company for purchase of October 10.

Oct. 21   Paid Ruff Company the balance from the transactions of October 8 and October 14.

      24   Accepted from Peter Watts a return of merchandise, which was put back in inventory, $400 (cost, $240).

REQUIRED

Prepare entries in journal form to record the transactions, assuming the perpetual inventory system is used.

P 3.

LO 1   **Merchandising Income**
LO 4   **Statement: Periodic**
         Inventory System

Selected accounts from the adjusted trial balance for Carol's Kitchen Shop, Inc., as of March 31, 20x4, the end of the fiscal year, are shown below. The merchandise inventory for Carol's Kitchen Shop, Inc., was $38,200 at the beginning of the year and $29,400 at the end of the year.

Carol's Kitchen Shop, Inc. Partial Adjusted Trial Balance March 31, 20x4		
Sales		$165,000
Sales Returns and Allowances	$ 2,000	
Purchases	70,200	
Purchases Returns and Allowances		2,600
Freight In	2,300	
Store Salaries Expense	32,625	
Office Salaries Expense	12,875	
Advertising Expense	24,300	
Rent Expense	2,400	
Insurance Expense	1,200	
Utilities Expense	1,560	
Store Supplies Expense	2,880	
Office Supplies Expense	1,175	
Depreciation Expense, Store Equipment	1,050	
Depreciation Expense, Office Equipment	800	
Income Taxes	1,000	

REQUIRED

1. Using the information given, prepare an income statement for Carol's Kitchen Shop, Inc. Store Salaries Expense; Advertising Expense; Store Supplies Expense; and Depreciation Expense, Store Equipment are selling expenses. The other expenses are general and administrative expenses. The company uses the periodic inventory system. Show detail of net sales and operating expenses.

2. Based on your knowledge at this point in the course, how would you use the income statement for Carol's Kitchen Shop, Inc., to evaluate the company's profitability? What other financial statements should be considered and why?

P 4.

LO 4   **Merchandising Transactions:**
         Periodic Inventory System

Use the data in **P 2** for this problem.

REQUIRED

Prepare entries in journal form to record the transactions, assuming the periodic inventory system is used.

P 5.

LO 5   **Internal Control**
LO 6   **Evaluation**
LO 7

Industrial Services Company provides maintenance services to factories in the West Bend, Wisconsin, area. The company, which buys a large amount of cleaning supplies, consistently has been over budget in its expenditures for these items. In the past, supplies were left open in the warehouse to be taken each evening as needed by the on-site supervisors. A clerk in the accounting department periodically ordered additional supplies from a long-time supplier. No records were maintained other than to record purchases. Once a year, an inventory of supplies was made for the preparation of the financial statements.

To solve the budgetary problem, management implemented a new system for controlling and purchasing supplies. A supplies clerk was put in charge of a secured storeroom for cleaning supplies. Supplies are requested with a purchase requisition by the supervisors for the jobs they oversee. Each job receives a predetermined amount of supplies based on a study of its needs. In the storeroom, the supplies clerk notes the levels of supplies and completes a purchase requisition when supplies are needed. The purchase requisition goes to the purchasing clerk, a new position, who is solely responsible for authorizing purchases and who prepares the purchase orders. Supplier prices are monitored constantly to ensure that the lowest price is obtained. When supplies are received, the supplies clerk checks them in and prepares a receiving report, which is sent to accounting, where each payment to a supplier is documented by the purchase requisition, the purchase order, and the receiving report. The accounting department also maintains a record of supplies inventory, supplies requisitioned by supervisors, and supplies received. Once each month, a physical inventory of cleaning supplies in the storeroom is made by the warehouse manager and compared against the supplies inventory records maintained by the accounting department.

REQUIRED

Show how the new system applies or does not apply to the seven control activities described in this chapter. Is each new control activity better than the old system?

P 6.

LO 4   Merchandising
SO 8   Transactions, Including Discounts: Periodic Inventory System

The following is a list of transactions for Attention Promotions, Inc., for the month of March 20xx:

Mar. 1 Sold merchandise on credit to M. Gaberman, terms 2/10, n/60, FOB shipping point, $2,200.
    3 Purchased merchandise on credit from King Company, terms 2/10, n/30, FOB shipping point, $12,800.
    4 Received freight bill for shipment received on March 3, $900.
    6 Sold merchandise for cash, $1,100.
    7 Sold merchandise on credit to B. Gomez, terms 2/10, n/60, $2,400.
    9 Purchased merchandise from Armstrong Company, terms 1/10, n/30, FOB shipping point, $6,180, which includes freight charges of $400.
    10 Sold merchandise on credit to G. Horn, terms 2/10, n/20, $4,400.
    10 Received check from M. Gaberman for payment in full for sale of March 1.
    11 Purchased merchandise from King Company, terms 2/10, n/30, FOB shipping point, $16,400.
    12 Received freight bill for shipment of March 11, $1,460.
    13 Paid King Company for purchase of March 3.
    14 Returned merchandise from the March 9 shipment that was the wrong size and color, for credit, $580.
    16 G. Horn returned some of the merchandise sold to him on March 10 for credit, $400.
    17 Received payment from B. Gomez for half of his purchase on March 7. A discount is allowed on partial payment.
    18 Paid Armstrong Company balance due on account from transactions on March 9 and 14.
    20 In checking the purchase of March 11 from King Company, the accounting department found an overcharge of $800. King agreed to issue a credit.
    21 Paid freight company for freight charges of March 4 and 12.
    23 Purchased cleaning supplies on credit from Moon Company, terms n/5, $500.
    24 Discovered that some of the cleaning supplies purchased on March 23 had not been ordered. Returned them to Moon Company for credit, $100.
    25 Sold merchandise for cash, $1,600.
    27 Paid Moon Company for the March 23 purchase less the March 24 return.
    28 Received payment in full from G. Horn for transactions on March 10 and 16.
    29 Paid King Company for purchase of March 11 less allowance of March 20.
    31 Received payment for balance of amount owed from B. Gomez from transactions of March 7 and 17.

REQUIRED

Prepare entries in journal form to record the transactions, assuming that the periodic inventory system is used.

ALTERNATE PROBLEMS

LO 1 **Merchandising Income**
LO 3 **Statement: Perpetual Inventory System**

P 7. At the end of the fiscal year, June 30, 20x3, selected accounts from the adjusted trial balance for Hans' Video Store, Inc., appeared as shown below.

Hans' Video Store, Inc. Partial Adjusted Trial Balance June 30, 20x3		
Sales		$867,824
Sales Returns and Allowances	$ 22,500	
Cost of Goods Sold	442,370	
Freight In	20,156	
Store Salaries Expense	215,100	
Office Salaries Expense	53,000	
Advertising Expense	36,400	
Rent Expense	28,800	
Insurance Expense	5,600	
Utilities Expense	17,520	
Store Supplies Expense	4,928	
Office Supplies Expense	3,628	
Depreciation Expense, Store Equipment	3,600	
Depreciation Expense, Office Equipment	3,700	
Income Taxes	5,000	

REQUIRED

1. Prepare a multistep income statement for Hans' Video Store, Inc. Freight In should be combined with Cost of Goods Sold. Store Salaries Expense; Advertising Expense; Store Supplies Expense; and Depreciation Expense, Store Equipment are selling expenses. The other expenses are general and administrative expenses. The company uses the perpetual inventory system. Show detail of net sales and operating expenses.

2. Based on your knowledge to this point in the course, how would you use the income statement for Hans' Video Store, Inc., to evaluate the company's profitability? What other financial statement should be considered and why?

P 8. Tonia Company engaged in the following transactions in July 20xx:

LO 3 **Merchandising Transactions: Perpetual Inventory System**

July 1 Sold merchandise to Su Long on credit, terms n/30, FOB shipping point, $4,200 (cost, $2,520).
   3 Purchased merchandise on credit from Angier Company, terms n/30, FOB shipping point, $7,600.
   5 Paid Mix Freight for freight charges on merchandise received, $580.
   6 Purchased store supplies on credit from Exto Supply Company, terms n/20, $1,272.
   8 Purchased merchandise on credit from Ginn Company, terms n/30, FOB shipping point, $7,200, which includes $400 freight costs paid by Ginn Company.
   12 Returned some of the merchandise received on July 3 for credit, $1,200.
   15 Sold merchandise on credit to Pete Smith, terms n/30, FOB shipping point, $2,400 (cost, $1,440).
   16 Returned some of the store supplies purchased on July 6 for credit, $400.
   17 Sold merchandise for cash, $2,000 (cost, $1,200).
   18 Accepted for full credit a return from Su Long and returned merchandise to inventory, $400 (cost, $240).
   24 Paid Angier Company for purchase of July 3 less return of July 12.
   25 Received full payment from Su Long for her July 1 purchase less the return on July 18.

REQUIRED

Prepare entries in journal form to record the transactions, assuming use of the perpetual inventory system.

P 9.

LO 1   Merchandising Income
LO 4   Statement: Periodic
Inventory System

The data below come from Dan's Sports Equipment, Inc.'s adjusted trial balance as of September 30, 20x5, the fiscal year end. The company's beginning merchandise inventory was $81,222 and ending merchandise inventory is $76,664 for the period.

Dan's Sports Equipment, Inc. Partial Adjusted Trial Balance September 30, 20x5		
Sales		$433,912
Sales Returns and Allowances	$ 11,250	
Purchases	221,185	
Purchases Returns and Allowances		30,238
Freight In	10,078	
Store Salaries Expense	107,550	
Office Salaries Expense	26,500	
Advertising Expense	18,200	
Rent Expense	14,400	
Insurance Expense	2,800	
Utilities Expense	18,760	
Store Supplies Expense	464	
Office Supplies Expense	814	
Depreciation Expense, Store Equipment	1,800	
Depreciation Expense, Office Equipment	1,850	
Income Taxes	5,000	

REQUIRED

1. Prepare a multistep income statement for Dan's Sports Equipment, Inc. Store Salaries Expense; Advertising Expense; Store Supplies Expense; and Depreciation Expense, Store Equipment are selling expenses. The other expenses are general and administrative expenses. The company uses the periodic inventory system. Show detail of net sales and operating expenses.

2. Based on your knowledge at this point in the course, how would you use the income statement for Dan's Sports Equipment, Inc., to evaluate the company's profitability? What other financial statements should be considered and why?

P 10.

LO 4   Merchandising Transactions:
Periodic Inventory System

REQUIRED

Use the data in **P 8** for this problem.

Prepare entries in journal form to record the transactions, assuming the periodic inventory system is used.

EXPANDING YOUR CRITICAL THINKING, COMMUNICATION, AND INTERPERSONAL SKILLS

SKILLS DEVELOPMENT

Conceptual Analysis

SD 1. *Village TV* and *TV Warehouse* sell television sets and other video equipment in the Phoenix area. Village TV gives each customer individual attention, with employees explaining the features, advantages, and disadvantages of each video component. When

Cash Flow

CD-ROM

Communication

Critical Thinking

Ethics

General Ledger

Group Activity

Hot Links to Real Companies

International

Internet

Key Ratio

Memo

Spreadsheet

LO 1 **Merchandising Income**
LO 3 **Statement**
LO 4

a customer buys a television set or video system, Village provides free delivery, installs and adjusts the equipment, and teaches the family how to use it. TV Warehouse sells the same video components through showroom display. If a customer wants to buy a video component or a system, he or she fills out a form and takes it to the cashier for payment. After paying, the customer drives to the back of the warehouse to pick up the component, which he or she then takes home and installs. Village TV charges higher prices than TV Warehouse for the same components. Discuss how you would expect the income statements of Village TV and TV Warehouse to differ. Is it possible to tell which approach is more profitable?

SD 2.

LO 1 **Periodic versus Perpetual**
      Inventory Systems

The Book Nook is a well-established chain of 20 bookstores in eastern Michigan. In recent years the company has grown rapidly, adding five new stores in regional malls. Management has relied on the manager of each store to place orders keyed to the market in his or her neighborhood, selected from a master list of available titles provided by the central office. Every six months, a physical inventory is taken, and financial statements are prepared using the periodic inventory system. At that time, books that have not sold well are placed on sale or, whenever possible, returned to the publisher. As a result of the company's fast growth, there are many new store managers, who management has found do not have the same ability to judge the market as do managers of the older, established stores. Thus, management is considering a recommendation to implement a perpetual inventory system and carefully monitor sales from the central office. Do you think The Book Nook should switch to the perpetual inventory system or stay with the periodic inventory system? Discuss the advantages and disadvantages of each system.

Ethical Dilemma

SD 3.

SO 8 **Ethics and Purchases**
      Discounts

The purchasing power of some customers is such that they can exert pressure on suppliers to go beyond the suppliers' customary allowances. For example, ***Wal-Mart*** represents more than 10 percent of annual sales for many suppliers, such as Fruit of the Loom, Rubbermaid, Sunbeam, and Coleman. *Forbes* magazine reports that while many of these suppliers allow a 2 percent discount if bills are paid within 15 days, "Wal-Mart routinely pays its bills closer to 30 days and takes the 2 percent discount anyway on the gross amount of the invoice, not the net amount, which deducts for [trade] discounts and things like freight costs."[7] Identify two ways in which Wal-Mart's practice benefits Wal-Mart. Do you think this practice is unethical, or is it just good cash management on the part of Wal-Mart? Are the suppliers harmed by it?

Research Activity

SD 4.

LO 1 **Inventory Systems and**
LO 3 **Internal Controls**
LO 4
LO 5
LO 7

Identify a retail business in your local shopping area or a local shopping mall, such as a bookstore, a clothing shop, a gift shop, a grocery, a hardware store, or a car dealership. Ask to speak to someone who is knowledgeable about the store's inventory methods. Find out the answers to the following questions and be prepared to discuss your findings in class.

1. *Inventory systems* How is each item of inventory identified? Does the business have a computerized or a manual inventory system? Which inventory system, periodic or perpetual, is used? How often do employees take a physical inventory? What procedures are followed in taking a physical inventory? What kinds of inventory reports are prepared or received?

2. *Internal control structure* How does the company protect against inventory theft and loss? What control activities, including authorization, recording transactions, documents and records, physical controls, periodic checks, separation of duties, and sound personnel policies, does the company use? Can you see these control procedures in use?

Group Activity: Assign teams to carry out the above assignments.

Decision-Making Practice

SD 5.

LO 3 **Analysis of**
LO 4 **Merchandising Income**
Statement

In 20x1 Mark Fischer opened a small retail store in a suburban mall. Called *Fischer Garb Company,* the shop sold designer jeans. Mark worked 14 hours a day and controlled all aspects of the operation. All sales were for cash or bank credit card. The business was such a success that in 20x2 Mark decided to open a second store in another mall. Because the new shop needed his attention, he hired a manager to work in the original store with two sales clerks. During 20x2 the new store was successful, but the operations of the original store did not match the first year's performance.

Concerned about this turn of events, Mark compared the two years' results for the original store. The figures are as follows:

	20x2	20x1
Net Sales	$325,000	$350,000
Cost of Goods Sold	225,000	225,000
Gross Margin	$100,000	$125,000
Operating Expenses	75,000	50,000
Income Before Income Taxes	$ 25,000	$ 75,000

In addition, Mark's analysis revealed that the cost and selling price of jeans were about the same in both years and that the level of operating expenses was roughly the same in both years, except for the new manager's $25,000 salary. Sales returns and allowances were insignificant amounts in both years.

Studying the situation further, Mark discovered the following facts about the cost of goods sold:

	20x2	20x1
Gross purchases	$200,000	$271,000
Total purchases allowances	15,000	20,000
Freight in	19,000	27,000
Physical inventory, end of year	32,000	53,000

Still not satisfied, Mark went through all the individual sales and purchase records for the year. Both sales and purchases were verified. However, the 20x2 ending inventory should have been $57,000, given the unit purchases and sales during the year. After puzzling over all this information, Mark comes to you for accounting help.

1. Using Mark's new information, recompute the cost of goods sold for 20x1 and 20x2, and account for the difference in income before income taxes between 20x1 and 20x2.

2. Suggest at least two reasons for the discrepancy in the 20x2 ending inventory. How might Mark improve the management of the original store?

FINANCIAL REPORTING AND ANALYSIS

Interpreting Financial Reports

FRA 1.

LO 1 **Comparison of Operating**
LO 3 **Philosophies and Income**
LO 4 **Statements**

Wal-Mart Stores, Inc., and *Kmart Corp.,* two of the largest retailers in the United States, have different approaches to retailing. Their success has been different also. At one time, Kmart was larger than Wal-Mart. Today, Wal-Mart is almost three times as large. You can see the difference by analyzing their respective income statements and merchandise inventories. Selected information from their annual reports for the year ended January 31, 1999, is presented below. (All amounts are in millions.)

Wal-Mart: Net Sales, $137,634; Cost of Goods Sold, $108,725; Operating Expenses, $22,363; Ending Inventory, $17,076[8]

Kmart: Net Sales, $33,674; Cost of Goods Sold, $26,319; Operating Expenses, $6,245; Ending Inventory, $6,536[9]

REQUIRED

1. Prepare a schedule computing the gross margin and income from operations for both companies as dollar amounts and as percentages of net sales. Also, compute inventory as a percentage of the cost of goods sold.

2. From what you know about the different retailing approaches of these two companies, do the gross margins and incomes from operations you computed in 1 seem compatible with these approaches? What is it about the nature of Wal-Mart's operations that produces lower gross margin and lower operating expenses in percentages in comparison to Kmart? Which company's approach was more successful in the fiscal year ending January 31, 1999? Explain your answer.

3. Both companies have chosen a fiscal year that ends on January 31. Why do you suppose they made this choice? How realistic do you think the inventory figures are as indicators of inventory levels during the rest of the year?

FRA 2.

LO 1 **Business Objectives and**
LO 3 **Income Statements**

Superior Products, Inc., is one of the nation's largest discount retailers, operating 216 stores in 30 states. In a letter to stockholders in the 1999 annual report (fiscal year ended January 31, 2000), the chairman and chief executive officer of the company stated, "Our operating plan for fiscal 2000 (year ended January 30, 2001) calls for moderate sales increases, continued improvement in gross margins, and a continuation of aggressive expense reduction programs." The following data are taken from the income statements presented in the 2000 annual report (dated January 30, 2001) (in millions):

	Year Ended		
	January 30, 2001	January 31, 2000	February 1, 1999
Net Sales	$2,067	$2,142	$2,235
Cost of Goods Sold	1,500	1,593	1,685
Operating Expenses	466	486	502

REQUIRED

Did Superior Products, Inc., achieve the objective stated by its chairman? (*Hint:* Prepare an income statement for each year and compute gross margin and operating expenses as percentages of net sales.)

FRA 3.

LO 5 **Classic Internal Control**
LO 7 **Lapse**

J. Walter Thompson Co. (JWT) is one of the world's largest advertising agencies, with more than $1 billion in billings per year. One of its smaller units is a television syndication unit that acquires rights to distribute television programming and sells those rights to local television stations, receiving in exchange advertising time that it sells to the agency's clients. Cash rarely changes hands between the unit and the television station, but the unit is supposed to recognize revenue when the television programs are exchanged for advertising time that later will be used by clients.

The Wall Street Journal reported on February 17, 1982, that the company "had discovered 'fictitious' accounting entries that inflated revenue at the television program syndication unit."[10] The article went on to say that "the syndication unit booked revenue of $29.3 million over a five-year period, but that $24.5 million of that amount was fictitious" and that "the accounting irregularities didn't involve an outlay of cash . . . and its [JWT's] advertising clients weren't improperly billed. . . . The fictitious sales were recorded in such a manner as to prevent the issuance of billings to advertising clients. The sole effect of these transactions was to overstate the degree to which the unit was achieving its revenue and profit objectives."

The chief financial officer of JWT indicated that "the discrepancies began to surface . . . when the company reorganized so that all accounting functions reported to the chief financial officer's central office. Previously, he said, 'we had been decentralized in accounting,' with the unit keeping its own books."

REQUIRED

1. Show an example entry to recognize revenue from the exchange of the right to televise a show for advertising time and an example entry to bill a client for using the advertising time. Explain how the fraud was accomplished.

2. What would motivate the head of the syndication unit to perpetrate this fraud if no cash or other assets were stolen?

3. What principles of internal control were violated that would allow this fraud to exist for five years? How did correction of the weaknesses in internal control allow the fraud to be discovered?

International Company

FRA 4.

LO 3 **Terminology for**
LO 4 **Merchandising Transactions in England**

Marks & Spencer is a large English retailer with department stores throughout England and in other European countries, especially France. The company also owns Brooks Brothers, the business clothing store, in the United States. Merchandising terms in England differ from those in the United States. For instance, in England, the income statement is called the profit and loss account, sales is called turnover, merchandise inventory is called stocks, accounts receivable is called debtors, and accounts payable is called creditors. Of course, the amounts are stated in terms of pounds (£). In today's business world, it is important to use terminology employed by professionals from other countries. Explain in your own words why the English may use the terms *profit and loss account, turnover, stocks, debtors,* and *creditors* in place of the American terms.

Toys "R" Us Annual Report

FRA 5.

LO 1 **Operating Cycle**

Refer to the Toys "R" Us annual report and to Figure 1 in this chapter. Write a memorandum to your instructor on the subject of the Toys "R" Us operating cycle. This memorandum should identify the most common transactions in the operating cycle as it applies to Toys "R" Us and should support the answer by referring to the importance of accounts receivable, accounts payable, and merchandise inventory in the Toys "R" Us financial statements. Complete the memorandum by explaining why this operating cycle is favorable to Toys "R" Us.

Fingraph® Financial Analyst™

FRA 6.

LO 1 **Income Statement Analysis**
LO 3

Choose any retail company from the Fingraph® Financial Analyst™ CD-ROM software and display the Income Statements Analysis: Income from Operations in tabular and graphical form for the company. Write an executive summary that analyzes the change in the company's income from operations from the first to the second year. In preparing your response, focus on the reasons the change occurred by answering the following questions: Did the company's income from operations improve or decline from the first to the second year? What was the relationship of the change to the change in net sales? Was the change in income from operations primarily due to a change in gross margin or to a change in operating expenses? Suggest some possible reasons for the change in gross margin or operating expenses. Use percentages to support your answer.

Internet Case

FRA 7.

LO 5 **Comparison of Reports of Management on Internal Control**

Go to the Needles Accounting Resource Center at http://college.hmco.com. Clicking on "Companies" under "Web Links," go to the annual reports in the web sites for *Tandy Corporation* and *Circuit City Stores, Inc.* Find the "Report of Management on Internal Accounting Controls" in the case of Tandy and "Management's Report" in the case of Circuit City in the companies' respective annual reports. A portion of the Circuit City's report is quoted in the text. Compare management statements. What similarities do you find in the content? What is a difference in the reports? Which, in your opinion, does a better job of explaining what management has done to fulfill its responsibility of internal control?

ENDNOTES

1. Dayton-Hudson Corp., *Annual Report*, 1998.
2. Ibid.
3. Circuit City Stores, *Annual Report*, 1998.
4. *Professional Standards*, Vol. 1 (New York: American Institute of Certified Public Accountants, June 1, 1999), Sec. AU 322.07.
5. "1998 Fraud Survey," KPMG Peat Marwick, 1998.
6. *Professional Standards*, Vol. 1 (New York: American Institute of Certified Public Accountants, June 1, 1999), Sec. AU 325.16.
7. Matthew Schifrin, "The Big Squeeze," *Forbes*, March 11, 1996.
8. Wal-Mart Stores, Inc., *Annual Report*, 1999.
9. Kmart Corp., *Annual Report*, 1999.
10. Paul Blustein, "JWT Sees Pretax Write-Off of $18 Million; Fictitious Accounting Entries at Unit Cited," *The Wall Street Journal*, February 17, 1982, p. 16.

7

Short-Term Liquid Assets

LEARNING OBJECTIVES

1 Identify and explain the management issues related to short-term liquid assets.

2 Explain *cash*, *cash equivalents*, and the importance of electronic funds transfer.

3 Account for short-term investments.

4 Define *accounts receivable* and apply the allowance method of accounting for uncollectible accounts, using both the percentage of net sales method and the accounts receivable aging method.

5 Define and describe a *promissory note*, and make calculations and journal entries involving promissory notes.

SUPPLEMENTAL OBJECTIVE

6 Prepare a bank reconciliation.

Pioneer Electronic Corporation A company must use its assets to maximize income earned while maintaining liquidity. Pioneer Electronic Corporation, a leading provider of electronics for home, commerce, and industry, manages about $1.4 billion in short-term liquid assets. Short-term liquid assets are financial assets that arise from cash transactions, the investment of cash, and the extension of credit. What is the composition of these assets? Why are they important to Pioneer's management?

Pioneer's short-term liquid assets (in millions), as reported on the balance sheet in this Japanese company's 1998 annual report, are shown here.[1] These assets make up almost one-third of Pioneer's total assets, and they are very important to the company's strategy for meeting its goals. Effective asset management techniques ensure that these assets remain liquid and usable for the company's operations.

A commonly used ratio for measuring the adequacy of short-term liquid assets is the quick ratio. The quick ratio is the ratio of short-term liquid assets to current liabilities. Because Pioneer's current liabilities are (in millions) ¥178,897 ($1,355.0), its quick ratio is 1.01, which is computed as follows:

K/R $$\text{Quick Ratio} = \frac{\text{Short-Term Liquid Assets}}{\text{Current Liabilities}} = \frac{\$1,367,900,000}{\$1,355,000,000} = 1.01$$

A quick ratio of about 1.0 is a common benchmark, but it is more important to look at industry characteristics and at the trends for a particular company to see if the ratio is improving or not. A lower ratio may mean that a company is a very good manager of its short-term liquid assets. Pioneer has maintained a quick ratio of about 1.0 over several years.

Financial Highlights

(In millions)

	Yen	Dollars
Cash and Cash Equivalents	¥ 90,910	$ 688.7
Short-Term Investments	141	1.1
Accounts Receivable, Net of Allowances of ¥5,511 ($41.8)	82,801	627.2
Notes Receivable	6,726	50.9
Total Short-Term Liquid Assets	¥180,578	$1,367.9

Through good cash management, the company has not tied up excess funds in quick assets relative to current liabilities. This chapter emphasizes management of, and accounting for, short-term liquid assets to achieve liquidity.

Management Issues Related to Short-Term Liquid Assets

OBJECTIVE

1 Identify and explain the management issues related to short-term liquid assets

The management of short-term liquid assets is critical to the goal of providing adequate liquidity. In dealing with short-term liquid assets, management must address three key issues: managing cash needs during seasonal cycles, setting credit policies, and financing receivables.

Managing Cash Needs During Seasonal Cycles

Most companies experience seasonal cycles of business activity during the year. These cycles involve some periods when sales are weak and other periods when sales are strong. There are also periods when expenditures are greater and periods when expenditures are smaller. In some companies, such as toy companies, college publishers, amusement parks, construction companies, and sports equipment companies, the cycles are dramatic, but all companies experience them to some degree.

Seasonal cycles require careful planning of cash inflows, cash outflows, borrowing, and investing. For example, Figure 1 might represent the seasonal cycles for a home improvement company like The Home Depot, Inc. As you can see, cash receipts from sales are highest in the late spring, summer, and fall because that is when most people make home improvements. Sales are relatively low in the winter months. On the other hand, cash expenditures are highest in late winter and spring as the company builds up inventory for spring and summer selling. During the late summer, fall, and winter, the company has excess cash on hand that it needs to invest in a way that will earn a return, but still permit access as needed. During the late spring and early summer, the company needs to plan for short-term borrowing to tide it over until cash receipts pick up later in the year. The discussion in this

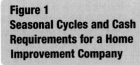

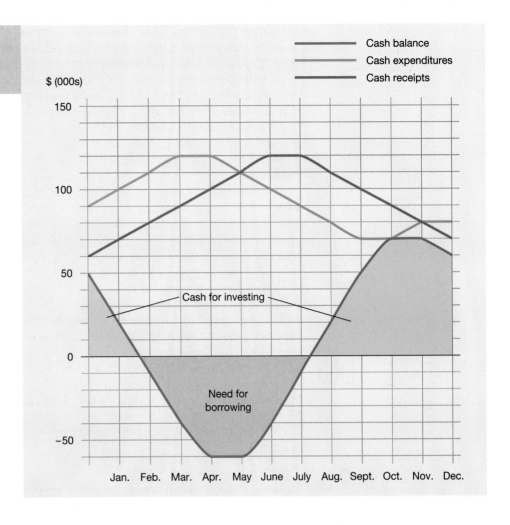

chapter of accounting for cash, cash equivalents, and short-term investments is directly related to managing for the seasonal cycles of a business.

Setting Credit Policies

Companies that sell on credit do so in order to be competitive and to increase sales. In setting credit terms, management must keep in mind both the terms the company's competitors are offering and the needs of its customers. Obviously,

BUSINESS FOCUS ON PRACTICE

To be profitable, not only must a company sell goods and services, it also must generate cash flows by collecting on those sales. When Bally Total Fitness, the nation's largest health-club chain, announced a successful new membership program that generated $100 million in new revenue, the stock market responded by pushing up the price of the company's stock. Under the new membership program, a $1,300 three-year membership could be paid in monthly installments. It quickly became apparent, however, that as much as 40 percent of the memberships were not paid or were canceled. The memberships were not profitable and the company's stock dropped by half. The Securities and Exchange Commission (SEC) has now told health clubs to stop recognizing memberships as revenue until payments are received.[3]

companies that sell on credit want to have customers who will pay the debts they incur. To increase the likelihood of selling only to customers who will pay on time, most companies develop control procedures and maintain a credit department. The credit department's responsibilities include the examination of each person or company that applies for credit and the approval or rejection of a credit sale to that customer. Typically, the credit department will ask for information about the customer's financial resources and debts. It may also check personal references and credit bureaus for further information. Then, based on the information it has gathered, the credit department will decide whether or not to extend credit to the customer.

Two common measures of the effect of a company's credit policies are **receivable turnover** and **average days' sales uncollected**. The receivable turnover reflects the relative size of a company's accounts receivable and the success of its credit and collection policies. It may also be affected by external factors, such as seasonal conditions and interest rates. It shows how many times, on average, the receivables were turned into cash during the accounting period. The average days' sales uncollected is a related measure that shows, on average, how long it takes to collect accounts receivable.

Turnover ratios usually consist of one balance sheet account and one income statement account. The receivable turnover is computed by dividing net sales by average net accounts receivable. Theoretically, the numerator should be net credit sales, but the amount of net credit sales is rarely made available in public reports, so total net sales is used. American Greetings Corp. is the second largest producer of greeting cards in the United States. The company's net sales in 1998 were $2,198,765,000, and its net trade accounts receivable in 1998 and 1997 were $373,594,000 and $375,324,000, respectively.[4] Its receivable turnover is computed as follows:

$$\text{Receivable Turnover} = \frac{\text{Net Sales}}{\text{Average Net Accounts Receivable}}$$

$$= \frac{\$2,198,765,000}{(\$373,594,000 + \$375,324,000) \div 2}$$

$$= \frac{\$2,198,765,000}{\$374,459,000} = 5.9 \text{ times}$$

To find the average days' sales uncollected, the number of days in a year is divided by the receivable turnover, as follows:

$$\text{Average Days' Sales Uncollected} = \frac{365 \text{ days}}{\text{Receivable Turnover}} = \frac{365 \text{ days}}{5.9} = 61.9 \text{ days}$$

American Greetings turns its receivables 5.9 times a year, for an average of every 61.9 days. While this turnover period is longer than those of many companies, it is not unusual for greeting card companies because their credit terms allow retail outlets to receive and sell cards for various holidays, such as Easter, Thanksgiving, and Christmas, before paying for them. This example demonstrates the need to interpret ratios in light of the specific industry's practice.

As may be seen from Figure 2, the receivable turnover ratio varies substantially from industry to industry. Grocery stores, for example, have a high turnover because that type of business has few receivables; the turnover in interstate trucking is 10.4 times because the typical credit terms in that industry are 30 days. The turnover in the pharmaceutical industry is lower because that industry tends to have longer credit terms.

Business-World Example: For many businesses with seasonal sales activity, such as Nordstrom, Dillard, Marshall Field's, and Macy's, the fourth quarter produces more than 25 percent of annual sales. For such businesses, receivables are highest at the balance sheet date, resulting in an artificially low receivable turnover and high average days' sales uncollected.

Figure 2
Receivable Turnover for Selected Industries

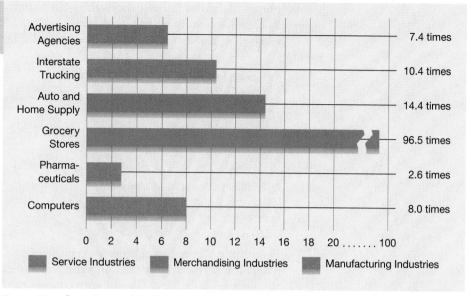

Industry	Turnover
Advertising Agencies	7.4 times
Interstate Trucking	10.4 times
Auto and Home Supply	14.4 times
Grocery Stores	96.5 times
Pharmaceuticals	2.6 times
Computers	8.0 times

■ Service Industries   ■ Merchandising Industries   ■ Manufacturing Industries

Source: Data from Dun and Bradstreet, *Industry Norms and Key Business Ratios,* 1997–1998.

Financing Receivables

Financial flexibility is important to most companies. Companies that have significant amounts of assets tied up in accounts receivable may be unwilling or unable to wait until the receivables are collected to receive the cash they represent. Many companies have set up finance companies to help their customers finance the purchase of their products. For example, Ford Motor Co. has Ford Motor Credit Co. (FMCC), General Motors Corp. has General Motors Acceptance Corp. (GMAC), and Sears, Roebuck and Co. has Sears Roebuck Acceptance Corp. (SRAC). Some companies borrow funds by pledging their accounts receivable as collateral. If a company does not pay back its loan, the creditor can take the collateral, in this case the accounts receivable, and convert it to cash to satisfy the loan.

Companies can also raise funds by selling or transferring accounts receivable to another entity, called a **factor**. The sale or transfer of accounts receivable, called **factoring**, can be done with or without recourse. *Without recourse* means that the factor that buys the accounts receivable bears any losses from uncollectible accounts. A company's acceptance of credit cards like Visa, MasterCard, or American Express is an example of factoring without recourse because the credit card issuers accept the risk of nonpayment.

Key Point: The receivable turnover and average days' sales uncollected will appear better for a company that factors receivables than for a company that does not factor.

With recourse means that the seller of the receivables is liable to the purchaser if the receivable is not collected. The factor, of course, charges a fee for its service. The fee for sales with recourse is usually about 1 percent of the accounts receivable. The fee is higher for sales without recourse because the factor's risk is greater. In accounting terminology, the seller of the receivables with recourse is said to be contingently liable. A **contingent liability** is a potential liability that can develop into a real liability if a possible subsequent event occurs. In this case, the subsequent event would be nonpayment of the receivable by the customer.

Circuit City Stores, Inc., is one of the nation's largest electronics, appliance, and car retailers. To sell its products, the company offers its customers generous terms through its installment programs, under which customers pay over a number of months. The company is growing rapidly and needs the cash from these installment receivables sooner than the customers have agreed to pay. To generate cash immediately from these receivables, the company sells them. After generating $123 million from selling receivables in 1998, the cumulative total amount of receivables sold but not yet collected was $2.75 billion, as follows:[5]

Financial Highlights	
(Amounts in thousands)	1998
Securitized receivables	$2,749,793
Interest retained by company	(248,543)
Net receivables sold	$2,501,250
Net receivables sold with recourse	726,000
Net receivables sold without recourse	$1,775,250

Securitized receivables are those receivables sold both with and without recourse. The interest retained by the company is in effect a provision or allowance for customers who do not pay. The finance charges paid by customers on the accounts go to the buyers of the receivables to cover interest costs, uncollectible accounts, and servicing fees. The net receivables sold with recourse represents a contingent liability for the company. If the receivables are paid as expected, Circuit City will have no further liability.

Another method of financing receivables is through the **discounting**, or selling, of promissory notes held as notes receivable. Selling notes receivable is called discounting because the bank deducts the interest from the maturity value of the note to determine the proceeds. The holder of the note (usually the payee) endorses the note and delivers it to the bank. The bank expects to collect the maturity value of the note (principal plus interest) on the maturity date but also has recourse against the endorser or seller of the note. If the maker fails to pay, the endorser is liable to the bank for payment. The endorser has a contingent liability in the amount of the discounted notes plus interest that must be disclosed in the notes to the financial statements.

Cash and Cash Equivalents

OBJECTIVE

2 Explain *cash, cash equivalents,* and the importance of electronic funds transfer

The annual report of Pioneer Electronic Corporation refers to *cash and cash equivalents.* Of the two terms, *cash* is the easier to understand. It is the most liquid of all assets and the most readily available to pay debts. On the balance sheet, **cash** normally consists of coins and currency on hand, checks and money orders from customers, and deposits in bank checking accounts. Cash may also include a **compensating balance**, an amount that is not entirely free to be spent. A compensating balance is a minimum amount that a bank requires a company to keep in its bank account as part of a credit-granting arrangement. Such an arrangement restricts cash and may reduce a company's liquidity. Therefore, the SEC requires companies to disclose the amount of any compensating balances in a note to the financial statements.

The term *cash equivalents* is a little harder to understand. At times a company may find that it has more cash on hand than it needs to pay current obligations. Excess cash should not remain idle, especially during periods of high interest rates. Thus, management may periodically invest idle funds in time deposits or certificates of deposit at banks and other financial institutions, in government securities such as U.S. Treasury notes, or in other securities. Such actions are rightfully called investments. However, if the investments have a term of 90 days or less when they are purchased, they are called **cash equivalents** because the funds revert to cash so quickly that they are regarded as cash on the balance sheet. For example, Bell Atlantic Corp. follows this practice. Its policy is stated as follows: "The Company considers all highly liquid investments with a maturity of 90 days or less when purchased to be cash equivalents. Cash equivalents are stated at cost, which approximates market value."[6] A survey of the practices of 600 large U.S. corporations found that 56 of them, or 9 percent, used the term *cash* as the balance sheet caption and 501, or 84 percent, used the phrase *cash and cash equivalents* or *cash and equivalents*. Thirty-two companies, or 5 percent, combined cash with marketable securities.[7] The average amount of cash held can also vary by industry.

Most companies need to keep some currency and coins on hand. Currency and coins are needed for cash registers and for paying expenses that are impractical to pay by check. A company may need to advance cash to sales representatives for travel expenses, to divisions to cover their payrolls, and to individual employees to cash their paychecks.

One way to control a cash fund or cash advances is through the use of an **imprest system**. A common form of imprest system is a petty cash fund, which is established at a fixed amount. Each cash payment from the fund is documented by a receipt. Then the fund is periodically reimbursed, based on the documented expenditures, by the exact amount necessary to restore its original cash balance. The person responsible for the petty cash fund must always be able to account for its contents by having cash and receipts whose total equals the originally fixed amount.

Banking and Electronic Funds Transfer

Enrichment Note: Periodically, banks detect individuals who are *kiting*. Kiting is the illegal issuing of checks when there is not enough money to cover them. Before one kited check clears the bank, a kited check from another account is deposited to cover it, making an endless circle.

Banks greatly help businesses to control both cash receipts and cash disbursements. Banks serve as safe depositories for cash, negotiable instruments, and other valuable business documents, such as stocks and bonds. The checking accounts that banks provide improve control by minimizing the amount of currency a company needs to keep on hand and by supplying permanent records of all cash payments. Banks can also serve as agents in a variety of transactions, such as the collection and payment of certain kinds of debts and the exchange of foreign currencies.

Many companies commonly conduct transactions through a means of electronic communication called **electronic funds transfer (EFT)**. Instead of writing checks to pay for purchases or to repay loans, the company arranges to have cash transferred electronically from its bank to another company's bank. Wal-Mart Stores,

BUSINESS FOCUS ON ETHICS

To combat the laundering of money by drug dealers, U.S. law requires banks to report cash transactions in excess of $10,000. Not to be deterred, money launderers began to sidestep the regulation by electronically transferring funds from overseas to banks, money exchanges, and brokerage firms. In response, the Treasury Department set up rules that require those institutions to keep records about the sources and recipients of all electronic transfers. Given the widespread use of electronic transfers in today's business world, it is questionable how much effect this action will have in the ongoing battle against drugs. Looking for drug money by combing the millions of transfers that occur every day is "like looking for a needle in a haystack."[8]

Inc., for example, operates the largest electronic funds network in the retail industry and makes 75 percent of its payments to suppliers by this method. The actual cash, of course, is not transferred. For the banks, an electronic transfer is simply a bookkeeping entry.

In serving customers, banks may also offer automated teller machines (ATMs) for making deposits, withdrawing cash, transferring funds among accounts, and paying bills. Large consumer banks like Citibank, BankOne, and NationsBank will process hundreds of thousands of ATM transactions each week. Many banks also give customers the option of paying bills over the telephone and with *debit cards.* When a customer makes a retail purchase using a debit card, the amount of the purchase is deducted directly from the buyer's bank account. The bank usually documents debit card transactions for the retailer, but the retailer must develop new internal controls to ensure that the transactions are recorded properly and that unauthorized transfers are not permitted. It is expected that within a few years 25 percent of all retail activity will be handled electronically.

Short-Term Investments

OBJECTIVE

3 Account for short-term investments

When investments have a maturity of more than 90 days but are intended to be held only until cash is needed for current operations, they are called **short-term investments** or **marketable securities**.

Investments that are intended to be held for more than one year are called *long-term investments.* Long-term investments are reported in an investments section of the balance sheet, not in the current assets section. Although long-term investments may be just as marketable as short-term assets, management intends to hold them for an indefinite period of time.

Securities that may be held as short-term or long-term investments fall into three categories, as specified by the Financial Accounting Standards Board: held-to-maturity securities, trading securities, and available-for-sale securities.[9] Trading securities are classified as short-term investments. Held-to-maturity securities and available-for-sale securities, depending on their length to maturity or management's intent to hold them, may be classified as either short-term or long-term investments. The three categories of securities when held as short-term investments are discussed here.

Held-to-Maturity Securities

Key Point: Any broker costs or taxes paid to acquire securities are part of the cost of the securities.

Held-to-maturity securities are debt securities that management intends to hold to their maturity date and whose cash value is not needed until that date. Such securities are recorded at cost and valued on the balance sheet at cost adjusted for the effects of interest. For example, suppose that on December 1, 20x1, Lowes Company pays $97,000 for U.S. Treasury bills, which are short-term debt of the federal government. The bills will mature in 120 days at $100,000. The following entry would be made by Lowes:

20x1			
Dec. 1	Short-Term Investments	97,000	
	Cash		97,000
	Purchase of U.S. Treasury bills that mature in 120 days		

A = L + OE
+
−

At Lowes' year end on December 31, the entry to accrue the interest income earned to date would be as follows:

A = L + OE
+   +

20x1
Dec. 31   Short-Term Investments   750
              Interest Income   750
                  Accrual of interest on U.S. Treasury bills
                  $3,000 × 30/120 = $750

On December 31, the U.S. Treasury bills would be shown on the balance sheet as a short-term investment at their amortized cost of $97,750 ($97,000 + $750). When Lowes receives the maturity value on March 31, 20x2, the entry is as follows:

A = L + OE
+   +
–

20x2
Mar. 31   Cash   100,000
              Short-Term Investments   97,750
              Interest Income   2,250
                  Receipt of cash at maturity of
                  U.S. Treasury bills and recognition
                  of related income

Trading Securities

Trading securities are debt and equity securities bought and held principally for the purpose of being sold in the near term. Such securities are frequently bought and sold to generate profits on short-term changes in their prices. Trading securities are classified as current assets on the balance sheet and valued at fair value, which is usually the same as market value—for example, when securities are traded on a stock exchange or in the over-the-counter market.

An increase or decrease in the total trading portfolio (the group of securities held for trading purposes) is included in net income in the accounting period in which the increase or decrease occurs. For example, assume that Franklin Company purchases 10,000 shares of Exxon Mobil Corporation for $900,000 ($90 per share) and 5,000 shares of Texaco Inc. for $300,000 ($60 per share) on October 25, 20x1. The purchase is made for trading purposes; that is, management intends to realize a gain by holding the shares for only a short period. The entry to record the investment at cost follows:

A = L + OE
+
–

20x1
Oct. 25   Short-Term Investments   1,200,000
              Cash   1,200,000
                  Investment in stocks for trading
                  ($900,000 + $300,000 = $1,200,000)

Assume that at year end Exxon Mobil's stock price has decreased to $80 per share and Texaco's has risen to $64 per share. The trading portfolio may now be valued at $1,120,000:

Security	Cost	Market Value
Exxon Mobil (10,000 shares)	$ 900,000	$ 800,000
Texaco (5,000 shares)	300,000	320,000
Totals	$1,200,000	$1,120,000

Because the current fair value of the portfolio is $80,000 less than the original cost of $1,200,000, an adjusting entry is needed, as follows:

A = L + OE
–   –

20x1
Dec. 31   Unrealized Loss on Investments   80,000
              Allowance to Adjust Short-Term
              Investments to Market   80,000
                  Recognition of unrealized loss
                  on trading portfolio

The unrealized loss will appear on the income statement as a reduction in income. (The loss is unrealized because the securities have not been sold.) The Allowance to Adjust Short-Term Investments to Market account appears on the balance sheet as a contra-asset, as follows:

Short-Term Investments (at cost)	$1,200,000
Less Allowance to Adjust Short-Term Investments to Market	80,000
Short-Term Investments (at market)	$1,120,000

Key Point: The Allowance to Adjust Short-Term Investments to Market account is never changed when securities are sold. It changes only with an adjusting entry at year end.

or more simply,

Short-Term Investments (at market value, cost is $1,200,000)	$1,120,000

If Franklin sells its 5,000 shares of Texaco for $70 per share on March 2, 20x2, a realized gain on trading securities is recorded as follows:

A = L + OE
+   +
−

20x2			
Mar. 2	Cash	350,000	
	Short-Term Investments		300,000
	Realized Gain on Investments		50,000
	Sale of 5,000 shares of Texaco		
	for $70 per share; cost was $60 per share		

The realized gain will appear on the income statement. Note that the realized gain is unaffected by the adjustment for the unrealized loss at the end of 20x1. The two transactions are treated independently. If the stock had been sold for less than cost, a realized loss on investments would have been recorded. Realized losses also appear on the income statement.

Let's assume that during 20x2 Franklin buys 2,000 shares of BP Amoco Corporation at $64 per share and has no transactions involving Exxon Mobil. Also assume that by December 31, 20x2, the price of Exxon Mobil's stock has risen to $95 per share, or $5 per share more than the original cost, and that BP Amoco's stock price has fallen to $58, or $6 less than the original cost. The trading portfolio now can be analyzed as follows:

Security	Cost	Market Value
Exxon Mobil (10,000 shares)	$ 900,000	$ 950,000
BP Amoco (2,000 shares)	128,000	116,000
Totals	$1,028,000	$1,066,000

Key Point: The entry to Allowance to Adjust Short-Term Investments to Market is equal to the change in the market value. Compute the new allowance and then compute the amount needed to change the account. The unrealized loss or gain is the other half of the entry.

The market value of the portfolio now exceeds the cost by $38,000 ($1,066,000 − $1,028,000). This amount represents the targeted ending balance for the Allowance to Adjust Short-Term Investments to Market account. Recall that at the end of 20x1, that account had a credit balance of $80,000, meaning that the market value of the trading portfolio was less than the cost. The account has no entries during 20x2 and thus retains its balance until adjusting entries are made at the end of the year. The adjustment for 20x2 must be $118,000—enough to result in a debit balance of $38,000 in the allowance account.

A = L + OE
+   +

20x2			
Dec. 31	Allowance to Adjust Short-Term		
	Investments to Market	118,000	
	Unrealized Gain on Investments		118,000
	Recognition of unrealized gain		
	on trading portfolio		
	($80,000 + $38,000 = $118,000)		

The 20x2 ending balance of the allowance account may be determined as follows:

Allowance to Adjust Short-Term Investments to Market

Dec. 31, 20x2 adj.	118,000	Dec. 31, 20x1 bal.	80,000
Dec. 31, 20x2 bal.	**38,000**		

The balance sheet presentation of short-term investment is as follows:

Short-Term Investments (at cost)	$1,028,000
Allowance to Adjust Short-Term Investments to Market	38,000
Short-Term Investments (at market)	$1,066,000

or, more simply,

Short-Term Investments (at market value, cost is $1,028,000)	$1,066,000

If the company also holds held-to-maturity securities, they are included in short-term investments at cost adjusted for the effects of interest.

Available-for-Sale Securities

Available-for-sale securities are debt and equity securities that do not meet the criteria for either held-to-maturity or trading securities. They are accounted for in exactly the same way as trading securities, except that the unrealized gain or loss is not reported on the income statement, but is reported as a special item in the stockholders' equity section of the balance sheet. For example, Pioneer Electronic states in its annual report that "all debt securities and marketable equity securities held by the Company are classified as available-for-sale securities, and are carried at their fair values with unrealized gains and losses reported as a component of shareholders' equity."[10] This latter component is called Accumulated Other Comprehensive Income.

Dividend and Interest Income

Dividend and interest income for all three categories of investments is shown in the Other Income and Expenses section of the income statement.

Accounts Receivable

OBJECTIVE

4 Define *accounts receivable* and apply the allowance method of accounting for uncollectible accounts, using both the percentage of net sales method and the accounts receivable aging method

The other major types of short-term liquid assets are accounts receivable and notes receivable. Both result from credit sales to customers. Retail companies such as Sears, Roebuck and Co. have made credit available to nearly every responsible person in the United States. Every field of retail trade has expanded by allowing customers to make payments a month or more after the date of sale. What is not so apparent is that credit has expanded even more in the wholesale and manufacturing industries than at the retail level. The levels of accounts receivable in several industries are shown in Figure 3.

Accounts receivable are short-term liquid assets that arise from sales on credit to customers by wholesalers or retailers. This type of credit is often called **trade credit**. Terms on trade credit usually range from five to 60 days, depending on industry practice. For some companies that sell to consumers, **installment accounts receivable** constitute a significant portion of accounts receivable. Installment accounts receivable arise from the sale of goods on terms that allow the buyer to make a series of time payments. Department stores, appliance stores,

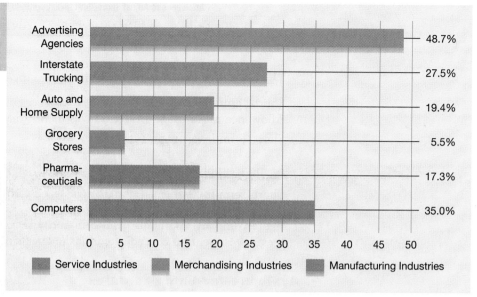

Figure 3
Accounts Receivable as a
Percentage of Total Assets for
Selected Industries

Source: Data from Dun and Bradstreet, *Industry Norms and Key Business Ratios*, 1997–1998.

furniture stores, used car companies, and other retail businesses often offer installment credit. Retailers such as J.C. Penney Company, Inc., and Sears, Roebuck and Co. have millions of dollars in installment accounts receivable. Although the payment period may be 24 months or more, installment accounts receivable are classified as current assets if such credit policies are customary in the industry.

On the balance sheet, the title Accounts Receivable is used for amounts arising from sales made to customers in the ordinary course of business. If loans or sales that do not fall into this category are made to employees, officers of the corporation, or owners, they should be shown separately with an asset title such as Receivables from Employees.

Normally, individual customer accounts receivable have debit balances, but sometimes customers overpay their accounts either by mistake or in anticipation of future purchases. When individual customer accounts show credit balances, the total of the credits should be shown on the balance sheet as a current liability because the amounts must be refunded if future sales are not made to those customers.

Uncollectible Accounts and the Direct Charge-off Method

A company will always have some customers who cannot or will not pay their debts. The accounts owed by such customers are called **uncollectible accounts**, or *bad debts*, and are a loss or an expense of selling on credit. Why does a company sell on credit if it expects that some of its accounts will not be paid? The answer is that the company expects to sell much more than it would if it did not sell on credit, thereby increasing its earnings.

Key Point: The direct charge-off method does not conform to the matching rule.

Some companies recognize the loss from an uncollectible account receivable at the time it is determined to be uncollectible by reducing Accounts Receivable directly and increasing Uncollectible Accounts Expense. Many small companies use this method because it is required in computing taxable income under federal tax regulations. However, companies that follow generally accepted accounting principles do not use the **direct charge-off method** in their financial statements because it makes no attempt to match revenues and expenses. They prefer the allowance method, which is explained in the next section.

Uncollectible Accounts and the Allowance Method

Key Point: The allowance method relies on an estimate of uncollectible accounts but is in accord with the matching rule.

Under the **allowance method** of accounting for uncollectible accounts, bad debt losses are matched against the sales they help to produce. As mentioned earlier, when management extends credit to increase sales, it knows that it will incur some losses from uncollectible accounts. Those losses are expenses that occur at the time sales on credit are made and should be matched to the revenues they help to generate. Of course, at the time the sales are made, management cannot identify which customers will not pay their debts, nor can it predict the exact amount of money that will be lost. Therefore, to observe the matching rule, losses from uncollectible accounts must be estimated, and the estimate becomes an expense in the fiscal year in which the sales are made.

For example, let us assume that Cottage Sales Company made most of its sales on credit during its first year of operation, 20x2. At the end of the year, accounts receivable amounted to $100,000. On December 31, 20x2, management reviewed the collectible status of the accounts receivable. Approximately $6,000 of the $100,000 of accounts receivable were estimated to be uncollectible. Therefore, the uncollectible accounts expense for the first year of operation was estimated to be $6,000. The following adjusting entry would be made on December 31 of that year:

$A = L + OE$
$-\quad\ \ -$

20x2			
Dec. 31	Uncollectible Accounts Expense	6,000	
	Allowance for Uncollectible Accounts		6,000
	To record the estimated uncollectible		
	accounts expense for the year		

Uncollectible Accounts Expense appears on the income statement as an operating expense. **Allowance for Uncollectible Accounts** appears on the balance sheet as a contra account that is deducted from Accounts Receivable.* It reduces the accounts receivable to the amount expected to be realized, or collected in cash, as follows:

Current Assets		
Cash		$ 10,000
Short-Term Investments		15,000
Accounts Receivable	$100,000	
Less Allowance for Uncollectible Accounts	6,000	94,000
Inventory		56,000
Total Current Assets		$175,000

Accounts receivable may also be shown on the balance sheet as follows:

Accounts Receivable (net of allowance for uncollectible	
accounts of $6,000)	$94,000

Or they may be shown at "net," with the amount of the allowance for uncollectible accounts identified in a note to the financial statements. The estimated uncollectible amount cannot be identified with any particular customer; therefore, it is credited to a separate contra-asset account—Allowance for Uncollectible Accounts.

---

*The purpose of Allowance for Uncollectible Accounts is to reduce the gross accounts receivable to the amount estimated to be collectible (net realizable value). The purpose of another contra account, Accumulated Depreciation, is *not* to reduce the gross plant and equipment accounts to realizable value. Rather, its purpose is to show how much of the cost of the plant and equipment has been allocated as an expense to previous accounting periods.

The allowance account will often have other titles, such as *Allowance for Doubtful Accounts* or *Allowance for Bad Debts*. Once in a while, the older phrase *Reserve for Bad Debts* will be seen, but in modern practice it should not be used. *Bad Debts Expense* is another title often used for Uncollectible Accounts Expense.

Estimating Uncollectible Accounts Expense

As noted, it is necessary to estimate the expense to cover the expected losses for the year. Of course, estimates can vary widely. If management takes an optimistic view and projects a small loss from uncollectible accounts, the resulting net accounts receivable will be larger than if management takes a pessimistic view. The net income will also be larger under the optimistic view because the estimated expense will be smaller. The company's accountant makes an estimate based on past experience and current economic conditions. For example, losses from uncollectible accounts are normally expected to be greater in a recession than during a period of economic growth. The final decision, made by management, on the amount of the expense will depend on objective information, such as the accountant's analyses, and on certain qualitative factors, such as how investors, bankers, creditors, and others may view the performance of the company. Regardless of the qualitative considerations, the estimated losses from uncollectible accounts should be realistic.

The accountant may choose from two common methods for estimating uncollectible accounts expense for an accounting period: the percentage of net sales method and the accounts receivable aging method.

Key Point: The percentage of net sales method can be described as the income statement method to emphasize that the percentage of the net sales calculated is the amount expensed. That is, any previous balance in the allowance account is irrelevant in preparing the adjustment.

PERCENTAGE OF NET SALES METHOD   The **percentage of net sales method** asks, How much of this year's net sales will not be collected? The answer determines the amount of uncollectible accounts expense for the year. For example, the following balances represent the ending figures for Hassel Company for the year 20x9:

Sales		Sales Returns and Allowances	
	Dec. 31 645,000	Dec. 31 40,000	

Sales Discounts		Allowance for Uncollectible Accounts	
Dec. 31 5,000			Dec. 31 3,600

Below are the actual losses from uncollectible accounts for the past three years:

Year	Net Sales	Losses from Uncollectible Accounts	Percentage
20x6	$ 520,000	$10,200	1.96
20x7	595,000	13,900	2.34
20x8	585,000	9,900	1.69
Total	$1,700,000	$34,000	2.00

In many businesses, net sales is understood to approximate net credit sales. If there are substantial cash sales, then net credit sales should be used. Management believes that uncollectible accounts will continue to average about 2 percent of net sales. The uncollectible accounts expense for the year 20x9 is therefore estimated to be

$$.02 \times (\$645,000 - \$40,000 - \$5,000) = .02 \times \$600,000 = \$12,000$$

BUSINESS FOCUS ON INTERNATIONAL

Companies in emerging economies do not always follow the accounting practices accepted in the United States. The Shanghai Stock Exchange is one of the fastest-growing stock markets in the world. Few Chinese companies acknowledge that uncollected receivables are not worth full value even though many receivables have been outstanding for a year or more. It is common practice in the United States to write off receivables more than six months old. Now that Chinese companies like Shanghai Steel Tube and Shanghai Industrial Sewing Machine are making their shares of stock available to outsiders, they must estimate uncollectible accounts in accordance with international accounting standards. Recognition of this expense could easily wipe out annual earnings.[11]

The entry to record this estimate is

$$A = L + OE$$
$$\overline{} \quad \overline{}$$

20x9			
Dec. 31	Uncollectible Accounts Expense	12,000	
	Allowance for Uncollectible Accounts		12,000
	To record uncollectible accounts expense		
	at 2 percent of $600,000 net sales		

After the above entry is posted, Allowance for Uncollectible Accounts will have a balance of $15,600.

Allowance for Uncollectible Accounts

	Dec. 31	3,600	
	Dec. 31 adj.	12,000	
	Dec. 31 bal.	15,600	

The balance consists of the $12,000 estimated uncollectible accounts receivable from 20x9 sales and the $3,600 estimated uncollectible accounts receivable from previous years.

Enrichment Note: The aging method is often superior to the percentage of net sales method during changing economic times. For example, during a recession, more bad debts occur. The aging method automatically reflects the economic change as accounts receivable age because customers are unable to pay. A company using the percentage of net sales method must anticipate the change and modify the percentage it uses.

ACCOUNTS RECEIVABLE AGING METHOD The **accounts receivable aging method** asks the question, How much of the year-end balance of accounts receivable will not be collected? Under this method, the year-end balance of Allowance for Uncollectible Accounts is determined directly by an analysis of accounts receivable. The difference between the amount determined to be uncollectible and the actual balance of Allowance for Uncollectible Accounts is the expense for the year. In theory, this method should produce the same result as the percentage of net sales method, but in practice it rarely does.

The **aging of accounts receivable** is the process of listing each customer's receivable account according to the due date of the account. If the customer's account is past due, there is a possibility that the account will not be paid. And the further past due an account is, the greater that possibility. The aging of accounts receivable helps management evaluate its credit and collection policies and alerts it to possible problems.

The aging of accounts receivable for Myer Company is illustrated in Exhibit 1. Each account receivable is classified as being not yet due or as 1–30 days, 31–60 days, 61–90 days, or over 90 days past due. The estimated percentage uncollectible in each category is multiplied by the amount in each category in order to determine the estimated, or target, balance of Allowance for Uncollectible Accounts. In total, it is estimated that $2,459 of the $44,400 accounts receivable will not be collected.

| | | | 1–30 | 31–60 | 61–90 | Over |
| | | Not | Days | Days | Days | 90 Days |
Customer	Total	Yet Due	Past Due	Past Due	Past Due	Past Due
				Myer Company		
			Analysis of Accounts Receivable by Age			
			December 31, 20xx			
A. Arnold	$ 150		$ 150			
M. Benoit	400			$ 400		
J. Connolly	1,000	$ 900	100			
R. Deering	250				$ 250	
Others	42,600	21,000	14,000	3,800	2,200	$1,600
Totals	$44,400	$21,900	$14,250	$4,200	$2,450	$1,600
Estimated percentage uncollectible		1.0	2.0	10.0	30.0	50.0
Allowance for Uncollectible Accounts	$ 2,459	$ 219	$ 285	$ 420	$ 735	$ 800

Exhibit 1
Analysis of Accounts Receivable by Age

Once the target balance for Allowance for Uncollectible Accounts has been found, it is necessary to determine how much the adjustment is. The amount of the adjustment depends on the current balance of the allowance account. Let us assume two cases for the December 31 balance of Myer Company's Allowance for Uncollectible Accounts: (1) a credit balance of $800 and (2) a debit balance of $800.

In the first case, an adjustment of $1,659 is needed to bring the balance of the allowance account to $2,459, calculated as follows:

Targeted Balance for Allowance for Uncollectible Accounts	$2,459
Less Current Credit Balance of Allowance for Uncollectible Accounts	800
Uncollectible Accounts Expense	$1,659

Key Point: When the write-offs in an accounting period exceed the amount of the allowance, a debit balance in the Allowance for Uncollectible Accounts account results.

The uncollectible accounts expense is recorded as follows:

A = L + OE
−   −

20x2
Dec. 31   Uncollectible Accounts Expense   1,659
             Allowance for Uncollectible Accounts   1,659
             To bring the allowance for
             uncollectible accounts to the
             level of estimated losses

The resulting balance of Allowance for Uncollectible Accounts is $2,459, as follows:

Allowance for Uncollectible Accounts

	Dec. 31	800
	Dec. 31 adj.	1,659
	Dec. 31 bal.	**2,459**

In the second case, because Allowance for Uncollectible Accounts has a debit balance of $800, the estimated uncollectible accounts expense for the year will have to be $3,259 to reach the targeted balance of $2,459. This calculation is as follows:

Targeted Balance for Allowance for Uncollectible Accounts	$2,459
Plus Current Debit Balance of Allowance for Uncollectible Accounts	800
Uncollectible Accounts Expense	$3,259

The uncollectible accounts expense is recorded as follows:

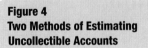

20x2
Dec. 31 Uncollectible Accounts Expense 3,259
      Allowance for Uncollectible Accounts 3,259
        To bring the allowance for
        uncollectible accounts to the
        level of estimated losses

Key Point: Describing the aging method as the balance sheet method emphasizes that the computation is based on ending accounts receivable, rather than on net sales for the period.

After this entry, Allowance for Uncollectible Accounts has a credit balance of $2,459, as shown below:

Allowance for Uncollectible Accounts			
Dec. 31	800	Dec. 31 adj.	3,259
		Dec. 31 bal.	2,459

COMPARISON OF THE TWO METHODS   Both the percentage of net sales method and the accounts receivable aging method estimate the uncollectible accounts expense in accordance with the matching rule, but as shown in Figure 4, they do so in different ways. The percentage of net sales method is an income statement approach. It assumes that a certain proportion of sales will not be collected, and this proportion is the *amount of Uncollectible Accounts Expense* for the accounting period. The accounts receivable aging method is a balance sheet approach. It assumes that a certain proportion of accounts receivable outstanding will not be collected. This proportion is the *targeted balance of the Allowance for Uncollectible*

Figure 4
Two Methods of Estimating Uncollectible Accounts

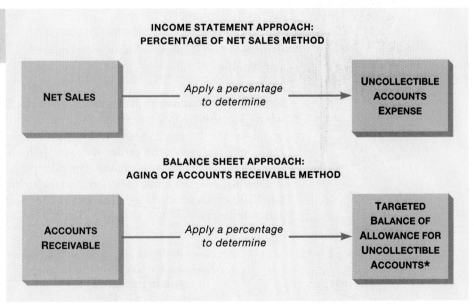

*Add current debit balance or subtract current credit balance to determine uncollectible accounts expense.

Accounts account. The expense for the accounting period is the difference between the targeted balance and the current balance of the allowance account.

WHY ACCOUNTS WRITTEN OFF WILL DIFFER FROM ESTIMATES   Regardless of the method used to estimate uncollectible accounts, the total of accounts receivable written off in any given year will rarely equal the estimated uncollectible amount. The allowance account will show a credit balance when the total of accounts written off is less than the estimated uncollectible amount. The allowance account will show a debit balance when the total of accounts written off is greater than the estimated uncollectible amount.

Writing Off an Uncollectible Account

When it becomes clear that a specific account receivable will not be collected, the amount should be written off to Allowance for Uncollectible Accounts. Remember that the uncollectible amount was already accounted for as an expense when the allowance was established. For example, assume that on January 15, 20x3, R. Deering, who owes Myer Company $250, is declared bankrupt by a federal court. The entry to *write off* this account is as follows:

	20x3			
A = L + OE	Jan. 15	Allowance for Uncollectible Accounts	250	
+		Accounts Receivable		250
−		To write off receivable from		
		R. Deering as uncollectible;		
		Deering declared bankrupt		
		on January 15		

Key Point: When writing off an individual account, debit Allowance for Uncollectible Accounts, not Uncollectible Accounts Expense.

Although the write-off removes the uncollectible amount from Accounts Receivable, it does not affect the estimated net realizable value of accounts receivable. The write-off simply reduces R. Deering's account to zero and reduces Allowance for Uncollectible Accounts by a similar amount, as shown below:

	Balances Before Write-off	Balances After Write-off
Accounts Receivable	$44,400	$44,150
Less Allowance for Uncollectible Accounts	2,459	2,209
Estimated Net Realizable Value of Accounts Receivable	$41,941	$41,941

RECOVERY OF ACCOUNTS RECEIVABLE WRITTEN OFF   Occasionally, a customer whose account has been written off as uncollectible will later be able to pay some or all of the amount owed. When this happens, two journal entries must be made: one to reverse the earlier write-off (which is now incorrect) and another to show the collection of the account. For example, assume that on September 1, 20x3, R. Deering, after his bankruptcy on January 15, notified the company that he could pay $100 of his account and sent a check for $50. The entries to record this transaction follow:

	20x3			
A = L + OE	Sept. 1	Accounts Receivable	100	
+		Allowance for Uncollectible Accounts		100
+		To reinstate the portion of		
		the account of R. Deering		
		now considered collectible;		
		originally written off January 15		

A = L + OE
+
–

	Sept. 1	Cash	50	
		Accounts Receivable		50
		Collection from R. Deering		

The collectible portion of R. Deering's account must be restored to his account and credited to Allowance for Uncollectible Accounts for two reasons. First, it turned out to be wrong to write off the full $250 on January 15 because only $150 was actually uncollectible. Second, the accounts receivable subsidiary account for R. Deering should reflect his ability to pay a portion of the money he owed despite his declaration of bankruptcy. Documentation of this action will give a clear picture of R. Deering's credit record for future credit action.

Notes Receivable

OBJECTIVE

5 Define and describe a *promissory note*, and make calculations and journal entries involving promissory notes

A **promissory note** is an unconditional promise to pay a definite sum of money on demand or at a future date. The entity who signs the note and thereby promises to pay is called the *maker* of the note. The entity to whom payment is to be made is called the *payee*.

The promissory note illustrated in Figure 5 is dated May 20, 20x1, and is an unconditional promise by the maker, Samuel Mason, to pay a definite sum, or principal ($1,000), to the payee, Cook County Bank & Trust Company, at the future date of August 18, 20x1. The promissory note bears an interest rate of 8 percent. The payee regards all promissory notes it holds that are due in less than one year as **notes receivable** in the current assets section of the balance sheet. The maker regards them as **notes payable** in the current liabilities section of the balance sheet.

This portion of the chapter is concerned primarily with notes received from customers. The nature of a business generally determines how frequently promissory notes are received from customers. Firms selling durable goods of high value,

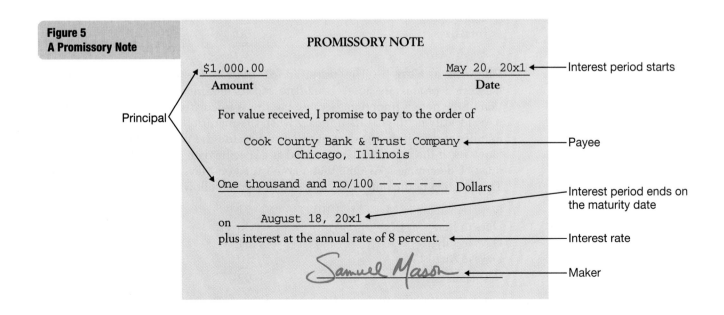

Figure 5
A Promissory Note

PROMISSORY NOTE

$1,000.00   May 20, 20x1 ◄——— Interest period starts
Amount   **Date**

Principal

For value received, I promise to pay to the order of

Cook County Bank & Trust Company ◄——————— Payee
Chicago, Illinois

One thousand and no/100 – – – – – Dollars
————————————————————————— Interest period ends on
                                                            the maturity date
on ———— August 18, 20x1 ————————

plus interest at the annual rate of 8 percent. ◄——— Interest rate

Samuel Mason ◄——————— Maker

such as farm machinery and automobiles, will often accept promissory notes. Among the advantages of promissory notes are that they produce interest income and represent a stronger legal claim against a debtor than do accounts receivable. In addition, selling or discounting promissory notes to banks is a common financing method. Almost all companies will occasionally receive a note, and many companies obtain notes receivable in settlement of past-due accounts.

Computations for Promissory Notes

In accounting for promissory notes, the following terms are important to remember: (1) maturity date, (2) duration of note, (3) interest and interest rate, and (4) maturity value.

Study Note: Another way to compute the duration of notes is to begin with the interest period, as follows:

90	Interest period
−11	days remaining in May (31 − 20)
79	
−30	days in June
49	
−31	days in July
18	due date in August

MATURITY DATE The **maturity date** is the date on which the note must be paid. This date must either be stated on the promissory note or be determinable from the facts stated on the note. Among the most common statements of maturity date are the following:

1. A specific date, such as "November 14, 20xx"
2. A specific number of months after the date of the note, for example, "3 months after date"
3. A specific number of days after the date of the note, for example, "60 days after date"

The maturity date is obvious when a specific date is stated. And when the maturity date is a number of months from the date of the note, one simply uses the same day in the appropriate future month. For example, a note that is dated January 20 and that is due in two months would be due on March 20.

When the maturity date is a specific number of days from the date of the note, however, the exact maturity date must be determined. In computing the maturity date, it is important to exclude the date of the note. For example, a note dated May 20 and due in 90 days would be due on August 18, computed as follows:

Days remaining in May (31 − 20)	11
Days in June	30
Days in July	31
Days in August	18
Total days	90

DURATION OF NOTE The **duration of note** is the length of time in days between a promissory note's issue date and its maturity date. Knowing the duration of the note is important because interest is calculated for the exact number of days. Identifying the duration is easy when the maturity date is stated as a specific number of days from the date of the note because the two numbers are the same. However, if the maturity date is stated as a specific date, the exact number of days must be determined. Assume that a note issued on May 10 matures on August 10. The duration of the note is 92 days, determined as follows:

Days remaining in May (31 − 10)	21
Days in June	30
Days in July	31
Days in August	10
Total days	92

Practice as to the computation of interest varies. Most banks use a 365-day year for all loans, but some use a 360-day year for commercial loans. The brokerage firm of May Financial Corporation of Dallas, Texas, states in its customer loan agreement, "Interest is calculated on a 360-day basis." In Europe, use of a 360-day year is common. Financial institutions that use the 360-day basis earn slightly more interest than those that use the 365-day basis. In this book, we use a 360-day year to keep the computations simple.

INTEREST AND INTEREST RATE   The **interest** is the cost of borrowing money or the return for lending money, depending on whether one is the borrower or the lender. The amount of interest is based on three factors: the principal (the amount of money borrowed or lent), the rate of interest, and the loan's length of time. The formula used in computing interest is as follows:

$$\text{Principal} \times \text{Rate of Interest} \times \text{Time} = \text{Interest}$$

Interest rates are usually stated on an annual basis. For example, the interest on a $1,000, one-year, 8 percent note would be $80 ($1,000 × 8/100 × 1 = $80). If the term, or time period, of the note were three months instead of a year, the interest charge would be $20 ($1,000 × 8/100 × 3/12 = $20).

When the term of a note is expressed in days, the exact number of days must be used in computing the interest. To keep the computation simple, let us compute interest on the basis of 360 days per year. Therefore, if the term of the above note were 45 days, the interest would be $10, computed as follows: $1,000 × 8/100 × 45/360 = $10.

MATURITY VALUE   The **maturity value** is the total proceeds of a note at the maturity date. The maturity value is the face value of the note plus interest. The maturity value of a 90-day, 8 percent, $1,000 note is computed as follows:

$$
\begin{aligned}
\text{Maturity Value} &= \text{Principal} + \text{Interest} \\
&= \$1,000 + (\$1,000 \times 8/100 \times 90/360) \\
&= \$1,000 + \$20 \\
&= \$1,020
\end{aligned}
$$

There are also so-called non-interest-bearing notes. The maturity value is the face value, or principal amount. In this case, the principal includes an implied interest cost.

Illustrative Accounting Entries

Key Point: The entry to record receipt of a note does not include interest because no interest has yet been earned.

The accounting entries for promissory notes receivable fall into these four groups: (1) recording receipt of a note, (2) recording collection on a note, (3) recording a dishonored note, and (4) recording adjusting entries.

RECORDING RECEIPT OF A NOTE   Assume that on June 1 a 30-day, 12 percent note is received from a customer, J. Halsted, in settlement of an existing account receivable of $4,000. The entry for this transaction is as follows:

A = L + OE
\+
\-

June 1   Notes Receivable   4,000
                 Accounts Receivable   4,000
                 Received 30-day, 12 percent note in
                 payment of account of J. Halsted

RECORDING COLLECTION ON A NOTE

When the note plus interest is collected 30 days later, the entry is as follows:

A = L + OE
\+   \+
\-

July 1   Cash   4,040
                 Notes Receivable   4,000
                 Interest Income   40
                 Collected 30-day, 12 percent
                 note from J. Halsted

Study Note: Dishonored notes are, in effect, not written off. The amounts are merely transferred to accounts receivable, which can be written off later.

RECORDING A DISHONORED NOTE

When the maker of a note does not pay the note at maturity, the note is said to be dishonored. The holder, or payee, of a **dishonored note** should make an entry to transfer the total amount due from Notes Receivable to an account receivable from the debtor. If J. Halsted dishonors her note on July 1, the following entry would be made.

A = L + OE
\+   \+
\-

July 1   Accounts Receivable   4,040
                 Notes Receivable   4,000
                 Interest Income   40
                 30-day, 12 percent note
                 dishonored by J. Halsted

The interest earned is recorded because, although J. Halsted did not pay the note, she is still obligated to pay both the principal and the interest.

Two things are accomplished by transferring a dishonored note receivable into an Accounts Receivable account. First, this leaves the Notes Receivable account with only notes that have not matured and are presumably negotiable and collectible. Second, it establishes a record in the borrower's accounts receivable account that he or she has dishonored a note receivable. Such information may be helpful in deciding whether to extend future credit to the customer.

RECORDING ADJUSTING ENTRIES

A promissory note received in one period may not be due until a following accounting period. Because the interest on a note accrues by a small amount each day of the note's duration, it is necessary, according to the matching rule, to apportion the interest earned to the periods in which it belongs. For example, assume that on August 31 a 60-day, 8 percent, $2,000 note was received and that the company prepares financial statements monthly. The following adjusting entry is necessary on September 30 to show how the interest earned for September has accrued.

A = L + OE
\+   \+

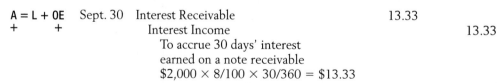

Sept. 30   Interest Receivable   13.33
                   Interest Income   13.33
                   To accrue 30 days' interest
                   earned on a note receivable
                   $2,000 × 8/100 × 30/360 = $13.33

The account Interest Receivable is a current asset on the balance sheet. When payment of the note plus interest is received on October 30, the following entry is made:*

*Some firms may follow the practice of reversing the September 30 adjusting entry. Here we assume that a reversing entry is not made.

A = L + OE	Oct. 30	Cash	2,026.67	
+ +		Notes Receivable		2,000.00
–		Interest Receivable		13.33
		Interest Income		13.34
		Receipt of note receivable		
		plus interest		

As seen from these transactions, both September and October receive the benefit of one-half the interest earned.

Preparing a Bank Reconciliation

SUPPLEMENTAL OBJECTIVE

6 Prepare a bank reconciliation

Rarely will the balance of a company's Cash account exactly equal the cash balance shown on the bank statement. Certain transactions shown in the company's records may not have been recorded by the bank, and certain bank transactions may not appear in the company's records. Therefore, a necessary step in internal control is to prove both the balance shown on the bank statement and the balance of Cash in the accounting records. A **bank reconciliation** is the process of accounting for the differences between the balance appearing on the bank statement and the balance of Cash according to the company's records. This process involves making additions to and subtractions from both balances to arrive at the adjusted cash balance.

The most common examples of transactions shown in the company's records but not entered in the bank's records are the following:

1. **Outstanding checks** These are checks that have been issued and recorded by the company, but do not yet appear on the bank statement.

2. **Deposits in transit** These are deposits that were mailed or taken to the bank but were not received in time to be recorded on the bank statement.

Transactions that may appear on the bank statement but that have not been recorded by the company include the following:

1. **Service charges (SC)** Banks often charge a fee, or service charge, for the use of a checking account. Many banks base the service charge on a number of factors, such as the average balance of the account during the month or the number of checks drawn.

2. **NSF (nonsufficient funds) checks** An NSF check is a check deposited by the company that is not paid when the company's bank presents it to the maker's bank. The bank charges the company's account and returns the check so that the company can try to collect the amount due. If the bank has deducted the NSF check from the bank statement but the company has not deducted it from its book balance, an adjustment must be made in the bank reconciliation. The depositor usually reclassifies the NSF check from Cash to Accounts Receivable because the company must now collect from the person or company that wrote the check.

3. **Interest income** It is very common for banks to pay interest on a company's average balance. These accounts are sometimes called NOW or money market accounts, but they can take other forms. Such interest is reported on the bank statement.

4. **Miscellaneous charges and credits** Banks also charge for other services, such as collection and payment of promissory notes, stopping payment on checks,

and printing checks. The bank notifies the depositor of each deduction by including a debit memorandum with the monthly statement. A bank will sometimes serve as an agent in collecting on promissory notes for the depositor. In such a case, a credit memorandum will be included.

An error by either the bank or the depositor will, of course, require immediate correction.

Key Point: The ending bank statement balance does not represent the amount that should appear on the balance sheet for cash. There are events and items, such as deposits in transit and outstanding checks, that the bank is unaware of at the cutoff date. This is why a bank reconciliation must be prepared.

ILLUSTRATION OF A BANK RECONCILIATION   Assume that the October bank statement for Martin Maintenance Company indicates a balance on October 31 of $3,471.07, and that in its records, Martin Maintenance Company has a cash balance on October 31 of $2,415.91. The purpose of a bank reconciliation is to identify the items that make up the difference between these amounts and to determine the correct cash balance. The bank reconciliation for Martin Maintenance is given in Exhibit 2. The numbered items in the exhibit refer to the following:

1. A deposit in the amount of $276.00 was mailed to the bank on October 31 and has not been recorded by the bank.

2. Five checks issued in October or prior months have not yet been paid by the bank, as follows:

Check No.	Date	Amount
551	Sept. 14	$150.00
576	Oct. 30	40.68
578	Oct. 31	500.00
579	Oct. 31	370.00
580	Oct. 31	130.50

3. The deposit for cash sales of October 6 was incorrectly recorded in Martin Maintenance Company's records as $330.00. The bank correctly recorded the deposit as $300.00.

Study Note: A credit memorandum means that an amount was *added* to the bank balance; a debit memorandum means that an amount was *deducted*.

4. Among the returned checks was a credit memorandum showing that the bank had collected a promissory note from A. Jacobs in the amount of $280.00, plus $20.00 in interest on the note. A debit memorandum was also enclosed for the $5.00 collection fee. No entry had been made on Martin Maintenance Company's records.

5. Also returned with the bank statement was an NSF check for $128.14. This check had been received from a customer named Arthur Clubb. The NSF check from Clubb was not reflected in the company's accounting records.

6. A debit memorandum was enclosed for the regular monthly service charge of $12.50. This charge had not yet been recorded by Martin Maintenance Company.

7. Interest earned by the company on the average balance was reported as $15.62.

Note in Exhibit 2 that, starting from their separate balances, both the bank and book amounts are adjusted to the amount of $2,555.89. This adjusted balance is the amount of cash owned by the company on October 31 and thus is the amount that should appear on its October 31 balance sheet.

Key Point: Notice that only those transactions the company has not recorded before receiving the bank statement are recorded.

RECORDING TRANSACTIONS AFTER RECONCILIATION   The adjusted balance of cash differs from both the bank statement and Martin Maintenance Company's records. The bank balance will automatically become correct when outstanding checks are presented for payment and the deposit in transit is received and recorded

Exhibit 2
Bank Reconciliation

Martin Maintenance Company
Bank Reconciliation
October 31, 20xx

Balance per bank, October 31		$3,471.07
① Add deposit of October 31 in transit		276.00
		$3,747.07
② Less outstanding checks:		
No. 551	$150.00	
No. 576	40.68	
No. 578	500.00	
No. 579	370.00	
No. 580	130.50	1,191.18
Adjusted bank balance, October 31		**$2,555.89** ←
Balance per books, October 31		$2,415.91
Add:		
④ Note receivable collected by bank	$280.00	
④ Interest income on note	20.00	
⑦ Interest income	15.62	315.62
		$2,731.53
Less:		
③ Overstatement of deposit of October 6	$ 30.00	
④ Collection fee	5.00	
⑤ NSF check of Arthur Clubb	128.14	
⑥ Service charge	12.50	175.64
Adjusted book balance, October 31		**$2,555.89** ←

Note: The circled numbers refer to the items listed in the text on the opposite page.

Key Point: Even though the September 14 check was deducted on the September 30 reconciliation, it must be deducted again in each subsequent month in which it remains outstanding.

Study Note: It is possible to place an item in the wrong section of a bank reconciliation and still have it balance. The *correct* adjusted balance must be obtained.

by the bank. Entries must be made, however, for the transactions necessary to update the book balance. All the items reported by the bank but not yet recorded by the company must be recorded in the general journal by means of the following entries:

Oct. 31	Cash	300.00	
	Notes Receivable		280.00
	Interest Income		20.00
	Note receivable of $280.00 and interest of $20.00 collected by bank from A. Jacobs		
31	Cash	15.62	
	Interest Income		15.62
	Interest on average bank account balance		
31	Sales	30.00	
	Cash		30.00
	Correction of error in recording a $300.00 deposit as $330.00		

Oct. 31	Accounts Receivable	128.14	
	Cash		128.14
	NSF check of Arthur Clubb returned by bank		
31	Bank Service Charges Expense	17.50	
	Cash		17.50
	Bank service charge ($12.50) and collection fee ($5.00) for October		

It is acceptable to record these entries in one or two compound entries to save time and space.

Chapter Review

REVIEW OF LEARNING OBJECTIVES

Ace it

1. **Identify and explain the management issues related to short-term liquid assets.** In managing short-term liquid assets, management must (1) consider the effects of seasonal cycles on the need for short-term investing and borrowing as the business's balance of cash fluctuates, (2) establish credit policies that balance the need for sales with the ability to collect, and (3) assess the need for additional cash flows through the financing of receivables.

2. **Explain** *cash, cash equivalents,* **and the importance of electronic funds transfer.** Cash consists of coins and currency on hand, checks and money orders received from customers, and deposits in bank accounts. Cash equivalents are investments that have a term of 90 days or less. Conducting transactions through electronic communication or electronic funds transfer is important because of its efficiency: Much of the paperwork associated with traditional recordkeeping is eliminated.

3. **Account for short-term investments.** Short-term investments may be classified as held-to-maturity securities, trading securities, or available-for-sale securities. Held-to-maturity securities are debt securities that management intends to hold to the maturity date; they are valued on the balance sheet at cost adjusted for the effects of interest. Trading securities are debt and equity securities bought and held principally for the purpose of being sold in the near term; they are valued at fair value or at market value. Unrealized gains or losses on trading securities appear on the income statement. Available-for-sale securities are debt and equity securities that do not meet the criteria for either held-to-maturity or trading securities. They are accounted for in the same way as trading securities, except that an unrealized gain or loss is reported as a special item in the stockholders' equity section of the balance sheet.

4. **Define** *accounts receivable* **and apply the allowance method of accounting for uncollectible accounts, using both the percentage of net sales method and the accounts receivable aging method.** Accounts receivable are amounts still to be collected from credit sales to customers. Because credit is offered to increase sales, uncollectible accounts associated with credit sales should be charged as expenses in the period in which the

sales are made. However, because of the time lag between the sales and the time the accounts are judged uncollectible, the accountant must estimate the amount of bad debts in any given period.

Uncollectible accounts expense is estimated by either the percentage of net sales method or the accounts receivable aging method. When the first method is used, bad debts are judged to be a certain percentage of sales during the period. When the second method is used, certain percentages are applied to groups of accounts receivable that have been arranged by due dates.

Allowance for Uncollectible Accounts is a contra-asset account to Accounts Receivable. The estimate of uncollectible accounts is debited to Uncollectible Accounts Expense and credited to the allowance account. When an individual account is determined to be uncollectible, it is removed from Accounts Receivable by debiting the allowance account and crediting Accounts Receivable. If the written-off account should later be collected, the earlier entry should be reversed and the collection recorded in the normal way.

5. **Define and describe a *promissory note*, and make calculations and journal entries involving promissory notes.** A promissory note is an unconditional promise to pay a definite sum of money on demand or at a future date. Companies selling durable goods of high value, such as farm machinery and automobiles, often accept promissory notes, which can be sold to banks as a financing method.

In accounting for promissory notes, it is important to know how to calculate the maturity date, duration of note, interest and interest rate, and maturity value. The accounting entries for promissory notes receivable fall into four groups: recording receipt of a note, recording collection on a note, recording a dishonored note, and recording adjusting entries.

SUPPLEMENTAL OBJECTIVE

6. **Prepare a bank reconciliation.** A bank reconciliation accounts for the difference between the balance that appears on the bank statement and the balance in the company's Cash account. It involves adjusting both balances to arrive at the adjusted cash balance. The bank balance is adjusted for outstanding checks and deposits in transit. The depositor's book balance is adjusted for service charges, NSF checks, interest earned, and miscellaneous debits and credits.

REVIEW OF CONCEPTS AND TERMINOLOGY

The following concepts and terms were introduced in this chapter:

LO 4 Accounts receivable: Short-term liquid assets that arise from sales on credit at the wholesale or retail level.

LO 4 Accounts receivable aging method: A method of estimating uncollectible accounts based on the assumption that a predictable proportion of each dollar of accounts receivable outstanding will not be collected.

LO 4 Aging of accounts receivable: The process of listing each customer's receivable account according to the due date of the account.

LO 4 Allowance for Uncollectible Accounts: A contra-asset account that reduces accounts receivable to the amount that is expected to be collected in cash; also called *Allowance for Bad Debts*.

LO 4 Allowance method: A method of accounting for uncollectible accounts by expensing estimated uncollectible accounts in the period in which the related sales take place.

LO 3 **Available-for-sale securities:** Debt and equity securities that do not meet the criteria for either held-to-maturity or trading securities.

LO 1 **Average days' sales uncollected:** A ratio that shows on average how long it takes to collect accounts receivable; 365 days divided by receivable turnover.

SO 6 **Bank reconciliation:** The process of accounting for the difference between the balance appearing on the bank statement and the balance of cash according to the company's records.

LO 2 **Cash:** Coins and currency on hand, checks and money orders from customers, and deposits in bank checking accounts.

LO 2 **Cash equivalents:** Short-term investments that will revert to cash in 90 days or less from when they are purchased.

LO 2 **Compensating balance:** A minimum amount that a bank requires a company to keep in its account as part of a credit-granting arrangement.

LO 1 **Contingent liability:** A potential liability that can develop into a real liability if a possible subsequent event occurs.

LO 4 **Direct charge-off method:** A method of accounting for uncollectible accounts by directly debiting an expense account when bad debts are discovered instead of using the allowance method; this method violates the matching rule but is required for federal income tax computations.

LO 1 **Discounting:** A method of selling notes receivable in which the bank deducts the interest from the maturity value of the note to determine the proceeds.

LO 5 **Dishonored note:** A promissory note that the maker cannot or will not pay at the maturity date.

LO 5 **Duration of note:** The length of time in days between a promissory note's issue date and its maturity date.

LO 2 **Electronic funds transfer (EFT):** The transfer of funds from one bank to another through electronic communication.

LO 1 **Factor:** An entity that buys accounts receivable.

LO 1 **Factoring:** The selling or transferring of accounts receivable.

LO 3 **Held-to-maturity securities:** Debt securities that management intends to hold to their maturity or payment date and whose cash value is not needed until that date.

LO 2 **Imprest system:** A system for controlling small cash disbursements by establishing a fund at a fixed amount and periodically reimbursing the fund by the amount necessary to restore its original cash balance.

LO 4 **Installment accounts receivable:** Accounts receivable that are payable in a series of time payments.

LO 5 **Interest:** The cost of borrowing money or the return for lending money, depending on whether one is the borrower or the lender.

LO 3 **Marketable securities:** Short-term investments intended to be held until needed to pay current obligations. Also called *short-term investments.*

LO 5 **Maturity date:** The date on which a promissory note must be paid.

LO 5 **Maturity value:** The total proceeds of a promissory note, including principal and interest, at the maturity date.

LO 5 **Notes payable:** Collective term for promissory notes owed by the entity (maker) who promises payment to other entities.

LO 5 **Notes receivable:** Collective term for promissory notes held by the entity to whom payment is promised (payee).

LO 4 **Percentage of net sales method:** A method of estimating uncollectible accounts based on the assumption that a predictable proportion of each dollar of sales will not be collected.

LO 5 **Promissory note:** An unconditional promise to pay a definite sum of money on demand or at a future date.

LO 1 **Quick ratio:** A ratio for measuring the adequacy of short-term liquid assets; short-term liquid assets divided by current liabilities.

LO 1 **Receivable turnover:** A ratio for measuring the average number of times receivables were turned into cash during an accounting period; net sales divided by average net accounts receivable.

LO 3 **Short-term investments:** Temporary investments of excess cash, intended to be held until needed to pay current obligations. Also called *marketable securities*.

LO 1 **Short-term liquid assets:** Financial assets that arise from cash transactions, the investment of cash, and the extension of credit.

LO 4 **Trade credit:** Credit granted to customers by wholesalers or retailers.

LO 3 **Trading securities:** Debt and equity securities bought and held principally for the purpose of being sold in the near term.

LO 4 **Uncollectible accounts:** Accounts receivable owed by customers who cannot or will not pay. Also called *bad debts*.

REVIEW PROBLEM

Estimating Uncollectible Accounts, Receivables Analysis, and Notes Receivable Transactions

LO 1
LO 4
LO 5

The Farm Implement Company sells merchandise on credit and also accepts notes for payment. During the year ended June 30, the company had net sales of $1,200,000, and at the end of the year it had Accounts Receivable of $400,000 and a debit balance in Allowance for Uncollectible Accounts of $2,100. In the past, approximately 1.5 percent of net sales have proved uncollectible. Also, an aging analysis of accounts receivable reveals that $17,000 in accounts receivable appears to be uncollectible.

The Farm Implement Company sold a tractor to R. C. Sims. Payment was received in the form of a $15,000, 90-day, 9 percent note dated March 16. On June 14, Sims dishonored the note. On June 29, the company received payment in full from Sims plus additional interest from the date of the dishonored note.

REQUIRED

1. Compute Uncollectible Accounts Expense and determine the ending balance of Allowance for Uncollectible Accounts and Accounts Receivable, Net under (a) the percentage of net sales method and (b) the accounts receivable aging method.

2. Compute the receivable turnover and average days' sales uncollected using the data from the accounts receivable aging method in **1** and assuming that the prior year's net accounts receivable were $353,000.

3. Prepare entries in journal form relating to the note received from R. C. Sims.

ANSWER TO REVIEW PROBLEM

1. Uncollectible Accounts Expense computed and balances determined
   a. Percentage of net sales method:

   Uncollectible Accounts Expense = 1.5 percent × $1,200,000 = $18,000

   Allowance for Uncollectible Accounts = $18,000 − $2,100 = $15,900

   Accounts Receivable, Net = $400,000 − $15,900 = $384,100

   b. Accounts receivable aging method:

   Uncollectible Accounts Expense = $2,100 + $17,000 = $19,100

   Allowance for Uncollectible Accounts = $17,000

   Accounts Receivable, Net = $400,000 − $17,000 = $383,000

2. Receivable turnover and average days' sales uncollected computed

$$\text{Receivable Turnover} = \frac{\$1,200,000}{(\$383,000 + \$353,000) \div 2} = 3.3 \text{ times}$$

$$\text{Average Days' Sales Uncollected} = \frac{365 \text{ days}}{3.3} = 110.6 \text{ days}$$

3. Journal entries related to the note prepared

Mar. 16	Notes Receivable	15,000.00	
	Sales		15,000.00
	Tractor sold to R. C. Sims; terms of note: 90 days, 9 percent		
June 14	Accounts Receivable	15,337.50	
	Notes Receivable		15,000.00
	Interest Income		337.50
	The note was dishonored by R. C. Sims Maturity value: $15,000 + (\$15,000 \times 9/100 \times 90/360) = \$15,337.50$		
29	Cash	15,395.02	
	Accounts Receivable		15,337.50
	Interest Income		57.52
	Received payment in full from R. C. Sims $15,337.50 + (\$15,337.50 \times 9/100 \times 15/360)$ $\$15,337.50 + \$57.52 = \$15,395.02$		

Chapter Assignments

BUILDING YOUR KNOWLEDGE FOUNDATION

QUESTIONS

1. Why does a business need short-term liquid assets? What three issues does management face in managing short-term liquid assets?
2. What is a factor, and what do the terms *factoring with recourse* and *factoring without recourse* mean?
3. What items are included in the Cash account? What is a compensating balance?
4. How do cash equivalents differ from cash? From short-term investments?
5. What are the three kinds of securities held as short-term investments, and how are they valued at the balance sheet date?
6. What are unrealized gains and losses on trading securities? On what statement are they reported?
7. Which of the following lettered items should be in Accounts Receivable? If an item does not belong in Accounts Receivable, tell where on the balance sheet it does belong: (a) installment accounts receivable from regular customers, due monthly for three years; (b) debit balances in customers' accounts; (c) receivables from employees; (d) credit balances in customers' accounts; (e) receivables from officers of the company.
8. Why does a company sell on credit if it expects that some of the accounts will not be paid? What role does a credit department play in selling on credit?

9. What accounting rule is violated by the direct charge-off method of recognizing uncollectible accounts? Why?

10. According to generally accepted accounting principles, at what point in the cycle of selling and collecting does a loss on an uncollectible account occur?

11. Are the following terms different in any way: allowance for bad debts, allowance for doubtful accounts, allowance for uncollectible accounts?

12. What is the effect on net income of management's taking an optimistic versus a pessimistic view of estimated uncollectible accounts?

13. In what ways is Allowance for Uncollectible Accounts similar to Accumulated Depreciation? In what ways is it different?

14. What is the reasoning behind the percentage of net sales method and the accounts receivable aging method of estimating uncollectible accounts?

15. What procedure for estimating uncollectible accounts also gives management a view of the status of collections and the overall quality of accounts receivable?

16. After adjusting and closing the accounts at the end of the year, suppose that Accounts Receivable is $176,000 and Allowance for Uncollectible Accounts is $14,500. (a) What is the collectible value of Accounts Receivable? (b) If the $450 account of a bankrupt customer is written off in the first month of the new year, what will be the resulting collectible value of Accounts Receivable?

17. Why should an account that has been written off as uncollectible be reinstated if the amount owed is subsequently collected?

18. What is a promissory note? Who is the maker? Who is the payee?

19. What are the maturity dates of the following notes: (a) a three-month note dated August 16, (b) a 90-day note dated August 16, and (c) a 60-day note dated March 25?

SHORT EXERCISES

SE 1.
LO 1 Management Issues

Indicate whether each of the actions below is related to (a) managing cash needs during seasonal cycles, (b) setting credit policies, or (c) financing receivables.

1. Selling accounts receivable to a factor
2. Borrowing funds for short-term needs during slow periods
3. Conducting thorough checks of new customers' ability to pay
4. Investing cash that is not currently needed for operations

SE 2.
LO 1 Short-Term Liquidity Ratios

Slater Company has cash of $20,000, short-term investments of $25,000, net accounts receivable of $45,000, inventory of $44,000, accounts payable of $60,000, and net sales of $360,000. Last year's net accounts receivable were $35,000. Compute the following ratios: quick ratio, receivable turnover, and average days' sales uncollected. Assume there are no current liabilities other than accounts payable.

SE 3.
LO 2 Cash and Cash Equivalents

Compute the amount of cash and cash equivalents on Quay Company's balance sheet if, on the balance sheet date, it has coins and currency on hand of $500, deposits in checking accounts of $3,000, U.S. Treasury bills due in 80 days of $30,000, and U.S. Treasury bonds due in 200 days of $50,000.

SE 4.
LO 3 Held-to-Maturity Securities

On May 31, Renata Company invested $49,000 in U.S. Treasury bills. The bills mature in 120 days at $50,000. Prepare entries to record the purchase on May 31; the adjustment to accrue interest on June 30, which is the end of the fiscal year; and the receipt of cash at the maturity date of September 28.

SE 5.
LO 3 Trading Securities

Monika Corporation began investing in trading securities this year. At the end of 20x1, the following trading portfolio existed:

Security	Cost	Market Value
Sara Lee (10,000 shares)	$220,000	$330,000
Skyline (5,000 shares)	100,000	75,000
Totals	$320,000	$405,000

Prepare the necessary year-end adjusting entry on December 31 and the entry for the sale of all the Skyline shares on the following March 23 for $95,000.

SE 6.
LO 4 **Percentage of Net Sales Method**

At the end of October, Mafa Company management estimates the uncollectible accounts expense to be 1 percent of net sales of $2,770,000. Give the entry to record the uncollectible accounts expense, assuming that the Allowance for Uncollectible Accounts has a debit balance of $14,000.

SE 7.
LO 4 **Accounts Receivable Aging Method**

An aging analysis on June 30 of the accounts receivable of Texbar Corporation indicates uncollectible accounts of $43,000. Give the entry to record uncollectible accounts expense under each of the following independent assumptions: (a) Allowance for Uncollectible Accounts has a credit balance of $9,000 before adjustment, and (b) Allowance for Uncollectible Accounts has a debit balance of $7,000 before adjustment.

SE 8.
LO 4 **Write-off of Accounts Receivable**

Key Company, which uses the allowance method, has an account receivable from Sandy Burgess of $4,400 that it deems to be uncollectible. Prepare the entries on May 31 to write off the account and on August 13 to record an unexpected receipt of $1,000 from Burgess. The company does not expect to collect more from Burgess.

SE 9.
LO 5 **Notes Receivable Entries**

On August 25, Rostin Company received a 90-day, 9 percent note in settlement of an account receivable in the amount of $10,000. Record the receipt of the note, the accrual of interest at fiscal year end on September 30, and collection of the note on the due date.

SE 10.
SO 6 **Bank Reconciliation**

Prepare a bank reconciliation from the following information:

a. Balance per bank statement as of June 30, $2,586.58
b. Balance per books as of June 30, $1,318.87
c. Deposits in transit, $348.00
d. Outstanding checks, $1,611.11
e. Interest on average balance, $4.60

EXERCISES

E 1.
LO 1 **Management Issues**

Indicate whether each of the following actions is primarily related to (a) managing cash needs during seasonal cycles, (b) setting credit policies, or (c) financing receivables.

1. Buying a U.S. Treasury bill with cash that is not needed for a few months
2. Comparing receivable turnovers for two years
3. Setting policy on which customers may buy on credit
4. Selling notes receivable to a financing company
5. Borrowing funds for short-term needs during the period of the year when sales are low
6. Changing the terms for credit sales in an effort to reduce the average days' sales uncollected
7. Using a factor to provide operating funds
8. Establishing a department whose responsibility is to approve customers' credit

E 2.
LO 1 **Short-Term Liquidity Ratios**

Using the following information selected from the financial statements of Phillipi Company, compute the quick ratio, the receivable turnover, and the average days' sales uncollected.

Current Assets	
Cash	$ 70,000
Short-Term Investments	170,000
Notes Receivable	240,000
Accounts Receivable, Net	200,000
Inventory	500,000
Prepaid Assets	50,000
Total Current Assets	$1,230,000
Current Liabilities	
Notes Payable	$ 300,000
Accounts Payable	150,000
Accrued Liabilities	20,000
Total Current Liabilities	$ 470,000
Net Sales	$1,600,000
Last Period's Accounts Receivable, Net	$ 180,000

E 3.

LO 2 Cash and Cash Equivalents

At year end, Burkes Company had coins and currency in cash registers of $2,800, money orders from customers of $5,000, deposits in checking accounts of $32,000, U.S. Treasury bills due in 80 days of $90,000, certificates of deposits at the bank that mature in six months of $100,000, and U.S. Treasury bonds due in one year of $50,000. Calculate the amount of cash and cash equivalents that will be shown on the company's year-end balance sheet.

E 4.

LO 3 Held-to-Maturity Securities

Isak Company experiences heavy sales in the summer and early fall, after which time it has excess cash to invest until the next spring. On November 1, 20x1, the company invested $194,000 in U.S. Treasury bills. The bills mature in 180 days at $200,000. Prepare entries to record the purchase on November 1; the adjustment to accrue interest on December 31, which is the end of the fiscal year; and the receipt of cash at the maturity date of April 30.

E 5.

LO 3 Trading Securities

Vida Corporation began investing in trading securities and engaged in the following transactions:

Jan. 6   Purchased 7,000 shares of Quaker Oats stock, $30 per share.
Feb. 15   Purchased 9,000 shares of EG&G, $22 per share.

At June 30 year end, Quaker Oats was trading at $40 per share and EG&G was trading at $18 per share. Record the entries for the purchases. Then record the necessary year-end adjusting entry. (Include a schedule of the trading portfolio cost and market in the explanation.) Also record the entry for the sale of all the EG&G shares on August 20 for $16 per share. Is the last entry affected by the June 30 adjustment?

E 6.

LO 4 Percentage of Net Sales Method

At the end of the year, Nassis Enterprises estimates the uncollectible accounts expense to be .7 percent of net sales of $30,300,000. The current credit balance of Allowance for Uncollectible Accounts is $51,600. Prepare the entry in journal form to record the uncollectible accounts expense. What is the balance of Allowance for Uncollectible Accounts after this adjustment?

E 7.

LO 4 Accounts Receivable Aging Method

Accounts Receivable of Cho Company shows a debit balance of $52,000 at the end of the year. An aging analysis of the individual accounts indicates estimated uncollectible accounts to be $3,350.

Prepare the entry in journal form to record the uncollectible accounts expense under each of the following independent assumptions: (a) Allowance for Uncollectible Accounts has a credit balance of $400 before adjustment, and (b) Allowance for Uncollectible Accounts has a debit balance of $400 before adjustment. What is the balance of Allowance for Uncollectible Accounts after this adjustment?

E 8.

LO 4 **Aging Method and Net Sales Method Contrasted**

At the beginning of 20xx, the balances for Accounts Receivable and Allowance for Uncollectible Accounts were $430,000 and $31,400, respectively. During the current year, credit sales were $3,200,000 and collections on account were $2,950,000. In addition, $35,000 in uncollectible accounts were written off.

Using T accounts, determine the year-end balances of Accounts Receivable and Allowance for Uncollectible Accounts. Then make the year-end adjusting entry to record the uncollectible accounts expense, and show the year-end balance sheet presentation of Accounts Receivable and Allowance for Uncollectible Accounts under each of the following conditions:

a. Management estimates the percentage of uncollectible credit sales to be 1.2 percent of total credit sales.

b. Based on an aging of accounts receivable, management estimates the end-of-year uncollectible accounts receivable to be $38,700.

Post the results of each entry to the T account for Allowance for Uncollectible Accounts.

E 9.

LO 4 **Aging Method and Net Sales Method Contrasted**

During 20x1, Days Supply Company had net sales of $2,850,000. Most of the sales were on credit. At the end of 20x1, the balance of Accounts Receivable was $350,000 and Allowance for Uncollectible Accounts had a debit balance of $12,000. Management has two methods of estimating uncollectible accounts expense: (a) The percentage of uncollectible sales is 1.5 percent, and (b) based on an aging of accounts receivable, the end-of-year uncollectible accounts total $35,000. Make the end-of-year adjusting entry to record the uncollectible accounts expense under each method, and tell what the balance of Allowance for Uncollectible Accounts will be after each adjustment. Why are the results different, and which method is likely to be more reliable?

E 10.

LO 4 **Aging Method and Net Sales Method Contrasted**

The Washington Parts Company sells merchandise on credit. During the fiscal year ended July 31, the company had net sales of $4,600,000. At the end of the year, it had Accounts Receivable of $1,200,000 and a debit balance in Allowance for Uncollectible Accounts of $6,800. In the past, approximately 1.4 percent of net sales have proved uncollectible. Also, an aging analysis of accounts receivable reveals that $60,000 of the receivables appear to be uncollectible. Prepare entries in journal form to record uncollectible accounts expense using: (a) the percentage of net sales method and (b) the accounts receivable aging method.

What is the resulting balance of Allowance for Uncollectible Accounts under each method? How would your answers under each method change if Allowance for Uncollectible Accounts had a credit balance of $6,800 instead of a debit balance? Why do the methods result in different balances?

E 11.

LO 4 **Accounts Receivable Transactions**

Assuming that the allowance method is being used, prepare entries in journal form to record the following transactions:

July 12, 20x4   Sold merchandise to Bea Scorboy for $1,800, terms n/10.
Oct. 18, 20x4   Received $600 from Bea Scorboy on account.
May 8, 20x5   Wrote off as uncollectible the balance of the Bea Scorboy account when she declared bankruptcy.
June 22, 20x5   Unexpectedly received a check for $200 from Bea Scorboy.

E 12.

LO 5 **Interest Computations**

Determine the interest on the following notes:

a. $22,800 at 10 percent for 90 days
b. $16,000 at 12 percent for 60 days
c. $18,000 at 9 percent for 30 days
d. $30,000 at 15 percent for 120 days
e. $10,800 at 6 percent for 60 days

E 13.

LO 5 **Notes Receivable Transactions**

Prepare entries in journal form to record the following transactions:

Jan. 16   Sold merchandise to Katz Corporation on account for $36,000, terms n/30.
Feb. 15   Accepted a $36,000, 90-day, 10 percent note from Katz Corporation in lieu of payment of account.

May 16 Katz Corporation dishonored the note.
June 15 Received payment in full from Katz Corporation, including interest at 10 percent from the date the note was dishonored.

E 14.

LO 5 Adjusting Entries: Interest Income

Prepare entries in journal form (assuming reversing entries were not made) to record the following:

Dec. 1 Received a 90-day, 12 percent note for $10,000 from a customer for a sale of merchandise.
     31 Made end-of-year adjustment for interest income.
Mar. 1 Received payment in full for note and interest.

E 15.

LO 5 Notes Receivable Transactions

Prepare entries in journal form to record these transactions:

Jan. 5 Accepted a $4,800, 60-day, 10 percent note dated this day in granting a time extension on the past-due account of S. Lavelle.
Mar. 6 S. Lavelle paid the maturity value of his $4,800 note.
      9 Accepted a $3,000, 60-day, 12 percent note dated this day in granting a time extension on the past-due account of R. Tamayo.
May   8 When asked for payment, R. Tamayo dishonored his note.
June 7 R. Tamayo paid in full the maturity value of the note plus interest at 12 percent for the period since May 8.

E 16.

SO 6 Bank Reconciliation

Prepare a bank reconciliation from the following information:

a. Balance per bank statement as of May 31, $8,454.54
b. Balance per books as of May 31, $6,138.04
c. Deposits in transit, $1,134.42
d. Outstanding checks, $3,455.92
e. Bank service charge, $5.00

PROBLEMS

P 1.

LO 3 Held-to-Maturity and Trading Securities

During certain periods, Weller Company invests its excess cash until it is needed. During 20x1 and 20x2, the company engaged in the following transactions:

20x1
Jan. 16 Invested $146,000 in 120-day U.S. Treasury bills that had a maturity value of $150,000.
Apr. 15 Purchased 10,000 shares of Rani Tools common stock at $40 per share and 5,000 shares of Soder Gas common stock at $30 per share as trading securities.
May 16 Received maturity value of U.S. Treasury bills in cash.
June 2 Received dividends of $2.00 per share from Rani Tools and $1.50 per share from Soder Gas.
     30 Made year-end adjusting entry for trading securities. Market price of Rani Tools shares is $32 per share and of Soder Gas shares is $35 per share.
Nov. 14 Sold all the shares of Rani Tools for $42 per share.

20x2
Feb. 15 Purchased 9,000 shares of MKD Communications for $50 per share.
Apr. 1 Invested $195,500 in 120-day U.S. Treasury bills that had a maturity value of $200,000.
June 1 Received dividends of $2.20 per share from Soder Gas.
     30 Made year-end adjusting entry for held-to-maturity securities.
     30 Made year-end adjusting entry for trading securities. Market price of Soder Gas shares is $33 per share and of MKD Communications shares is $60 per share.

REQUIRED

1. Prepare entries in journal form to record the preceding transactions, assuming that Weller Company's fiscal year ends on June 30.
2. Show the balance sheet presentation of short-term investments on June 30, 20x2.

P 2.

LO 1 Methods of Estimating
LO 4 Uncollectible Accounts and
Receivables Analysis

REQUIRED

On December 31 of last year, the balance sheet of Vaslor Company had Accounts Receivable of $298,000 and a credit balance in Allowance for Uncollectible Accounts of $20,300. During the current year, the company's records included the following selected activities: (a) sales on account, $1,195,000; (b) sales returns and allowances, $73,000; (c) collections from customers, $1,150,000; (d) accounts written off as worthless, $16,000. In the past, the company had found that 1.6 percent of net sales would not be collected.

1. Prepare T accounts for Accounts Receivable and Allowance for Uncollectible Accounts. Enter the beginning balances, and show the effects on these accounts of the items listed above, summarizing the year's activity. Determine the ending balance of each account.

2. Compute Uncollectible Accounts Expense and determine the ending balance of Allowance for Uncollectible Accounts under (a) the percentage of net sales method and (b) the accounts receivable aging method, assuming an aging of the accounts receivable shows that $20,000 may be uncollectible.

3. Compute the receivable turnover and average days' sales uncollected, using the data from the accounts receivable aging method in **2**.

4. How do you explain the fact that the two methods in **2** result in different amounts for Uncollectible Accounts Expense? What rationale underlies each method?

P 3.

LO 4 Accounts Receivable Aging
Method

Thant Company uses the accounts receivable aging method to estimate uncollectible accounts. The Accounts Receivable account had a debit balance of $88,430 and Allowance for Uncollectible Accounts had a credit balance of $7,200 at the beginning of the year. During the year, the company had sales on account of $473,000, sales returns and allowances of $4,200, worthless accounts written off of $7,900, and collections from customers of $450,730. At the end of the year (December 31), a junior accountant for the company was preparing an aging analysis of accounts receivable. At the top of page 6 of the report, the following totals appeared:

Customer Account	Total	Not Yet Due	1–30 Days Past Due	31–60 Days Past Due	61–90 Days Past Due	Over 90 Days Past Due
Balance Forward	$89,640	$49,030	$24,110	$9,210	$3,990	$3,300

The following accounts remained to be classified to finish the analysis:

Account	Amount	Due Date
B. Singh	$ 930	Jan. 14 (next year)
L. Wells	620	Dec. 24
A. Roc	1,955	Sept. 28
T. Cila	2,100	Aug. 16
M. Mix	375	Dec. 14
S. Price	2,685	Jan. 23 (next year)
J. Wendt	295	Nov. 5
	$8,960	

From past experience, the company has found that the following rates are realistic to estimate uncollectible accounts:

Time	Percentage Considered Uncollectible
Not yet due	2
1–30 days past due	4
31–60 days past due	20
61–90 days past due	30
Over 90 days past due	50

REQUIRED

1. Complete the aging analysis of accounts receivable.

2. Determine the end-of-year balances (before adjustments) of Accounts Receivable and Allowance for Uncollectible Accounts.

3. Prepare an analysis computing the estimated uncollectible accounts.

4. Prepare the entry in journal form to record the estimated uncollectible accounts expense for the year (round the adjustment to the nearest whole dollar).

P 4.

LO 5   Notes Receivable Transactions

Abraham Manufacturing Company sells engines. The company engaged in the following transactions involving promissory notes:

Jan. 10   Sold engines to Anton Company for $60,000, terms n/10.
      20   Accepted a 90-day, 12 percent promissory note in settlement of the account from Anton.
Apr. 20   Received payment from Anton Company for the note and interest.
May   5   Sold engines to Yu Company for $40,000, terms n/10.
      15   Received $8,000 cash and a 60-day, 13 percent note for $32,000 in settlement of the Yu account.
July 14   When asked to pay, Yu dishonored the note.
Aug. 2   Wrote off the Yu account as uncollectible after receiving news that the company declared bankruptcy.
      5   Received a 90-day, 11 percent note for $30,000 from Vila Company in settlement of an account receivable.
Nov. 3   When asked to pay, Vila dishonored the note.
      9   Received payment in full from Vila, including 15 percent interest for the 6 days since the note was dishonored.

REQUIRED

Prepare entries in journal form to record the preceding transactions.

P 5.

SO 6   Bank Reconciliation

The following information is available for Rosemary Company as of April 30, 20xx:

a. Cash on the books as of April 30 amounted to $114,175.28. Cash on the bank statement for the same date was $141,717.08.

b. A deposit of $14,249.84, representing cash receipts of April 30, did not appear on the bank statement.

c. Outstanding checks totaled $7,293.64.

d. A check for $2,420.00 returned with the statement was recorded as $2,024.00. The check was for advertising.

e. The bank service charge for April amounted to $26.00.

f. The bank collected $36,400.00 for Rosemary Company on a note. The face value of the note was $36,000.00

g. An NSF check for $1,140.00 from a customer, Chad Altier, was returned with the statement.

h. The bank mistakenly deducted a check for $800.00 drawn by Fox Corporation.

i. The bank reported a credit of $460.00 for interest on the average balance.

REQUIRED

1. Prepare a bank reconciliation for Rosemary Company as of April 30, 20xx.

2. Prepare the necessary entries in journal form from the reconciliation.

3. State the amount of cash that should appear on the balance sheet as of April 30.

ALTERNATE PROBLEMS

P 6.

LO 3   Held-to-Maturity and Trading Securities

Smitty Distributions follows a policy of investing excess cash until it is needed. During 20x1 and 20x2, the company engaged in the following transactions:

20x1
Feb.   1   Invested $97,000 in 120-day U.S. Treasury bills that had a maturity value of $100,000.
Mar. 30   Purchased 20,000 shares of Files Company common stock at $16 per share and 12,000 shares of Sun's Fruit, Inc., common stock at $10 per share as trading securities.
June   1   Received maturity value of U.S. Treasury bills in cash.

June 10   Received dividends of $.50 per share from Files Company and $.25 per share from Sun's Fruit, Inc.

30   Made year-end adjusting entry for trading securities. Market price of Files Company shares is $13 per share and of Sun's Fruit, Inc., shares is $12 per share.

Dec.   3   Sold all the shares of Files Company for $12 per share.

20x2

Mar. 17   Purchased 15,000 shares of Bytes, Inc., for $9 per share.

May 31   Invested $116,000 in 120-day U.S. Treasury bills that had a maturity value of $120,000.

June 10   Received dividends of $.30 per share from Sun's Fruit, Inc.

30   Made year-end adjusting entry for held-to-maturity securities.

30   Made year-end adjusting entry for trading securities. Market price of Sun's Fruit, Inc., shares is $6 per share and of Bytes, Inc., shares is $11 per share.

REQUIRED

1. Prepare entries in journal form to record these transactions, assuming that Smitty Distributions' fiscal year ends on June 30.

2. Show the balance sheet presentation of short-term investments on June 30, 20x2.

P 7.

LO 1   Methods of Estimating
LO 4   Uncollectible Accounts and Receivables Analysis

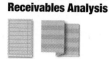

Hernandez Company had an Accounts Receivable balance of $320,000 and a credit balance in Allowance for Uncollectible Accounts of $16,700 at January 1, 20xx. During the year, the company recorded the following transactions:

a. Sales on account, $1,052,000
b. Sales returns and allowances by credit customers, $53,400
c. Collections from customers, $993,000
d. Worthless accounts written off, $19,800

The company's past history indicates that 2.5 percent of its net credit sales will not be collected.

REQUIRED

1. Prepare T accounts for Accounts Receivable and Allowance for Uncollectible Accounts. Enter the beginning balances, and show the effects on these accounts of the items listed above, summarizing the year's activity. Determine the ending balance of each account.

2. Compute Uncollectible Accounts Expense and determine the ending balance of Allowance for Uncollectible Accounts under (a) the percentage of net sales method and (b) the accounts receivable aging method, assuming an aging of the accounts receivable shows that $24,000 may be uncollectible.

3. Compute the receivable turnover and average days' sales uncollected, using the data from the accounts receivable aging method in **2**.

4. How do you explain the fact that the two methods in **2** result in different amounts for Uncollectible Accounts Expense? What rationale underlies each method?

P 8.

LO 4   Accounts Receivable Aging Method

The Forsell Fashions Store uses the accounts receivable aging method to estimate uncollectible accounts. The balance of the Accounts Receivable account was a debit of $446,341 and the balance of Allowance for Uncollectible Accounts was a credit of $43,000 at February 1, 20x1. During the year, the store had sales on account of $3,724,000, sales returns and allowances of $63,000, worthless accounts written off of $44,300, and collections from customers of $3,214,000. As part of the end-of-year (January 31, 20x2) procedures, an aging analysis of accounts receivable is prepared. The totals of the analysis, which is partially complete, follow:

Customer Account	Total	Not Yet Due	1–30 Days Past Due	31–60 Days Past Due	61–90 Days Past Due	Over 90 Days Past Due
Balance Forward	$793,791	$438,933	$149,614	$106,400	$57,442	$41,402

The following accounts remain to be classified to finish the analysis:

Account	Amount	Due Date
J. Curtis	$10,977	January 15
T. Dawson	9,314	February 15 (next fiscal year)
L. Zapata	8,664	December 20
R. Copa	780	October 1
E. Land	14,810	January 4
S. Qadri	6,316	November 15
A. Rosenthal	4,389	March 1 (next fiscal year)
	$55,250	

From past experience, the company has found that the following rates are realistic to estimate uncollectible accounts:

Time	Percentage Considered Uncollectible
Not yet due	2
1–30 days past due	5
31–60 days past due	15
61–90 days past due	25
Over 90 days past due	50

REQUIRED

1. Complete the aging analysis of accounts receivable.
2. Determine the end-of-year balances (before adjustments) of Accounts Receivable and Allowance for Uncollectible Accounts.
3. Prepare an analysis computing the estimated uncollectible accounts.
4. Prepare the entry in journal form to record the estimated uncollectible accounts expense for the year (round the adjustment to the nearest whole dollar).

P 9.

LO 5   Notes Receivable Transactions

Ault Importing Company engaged in the following transactions involving promissory notes:

Jan. 14 Sold merchandise to Riordan Company for $37,000, terms n/30.
Feb. 13 Received $8,400 in cash from Riordan Company and received a 90-day, 8 percent promissory note for the balance of the account.
May 14 Received payment in full from Riordan Company.
   15 Received a 60-day, 12 percent note from Calvin Eng Company in payment of a past-due account, $12,000.
July 14 When asked to pay, Calvin Eng Company dishonored the note.
   20 Received a check from Calvin Eng Company for payment of the maturity value of the note and interest at 12 percent for the six days beyond maturity.
   25 Sold merchandise to Leona Fancy Company for $36,000, with payment of $6,000 cash down and the remainder on account.
   31 Received a $30,000, 45-day, 10 percent promissory note from Leona Fancy Company for the outstanding account receivable.
Sept. 14 When asked to pay, Leona Fancy Company dishonored the note.
   25 Wrote off the Leona Fancy Company account as uncollectible following news that the company had declared bankruptcy.

REQUIRED   Prepare entries in journal form to record the preceding transactions.

P 10.

SO 6   Bank Reconciliation

The following information is available for Abdul Saleem Company as of May 31, 20xx:

a. Cash on the books as of May 31 amounted to $42,754.16. Cash on the bank statement for the same date was $52,351.46.
b. A deposit of $5,220.94, representing cash receipts of May 31, did not appear on the bank statement.
c. Outstanding checks totaled $3,936.80.
d. A check for $1,920.00 returned with the statement was recorded incorrectly in the check register as $1,380.00. The check was for a cash purchase of merchandise.
e. The bank service charge for May amounted to $25.

f. The bank collected $12,240.00 for Abdul Saleem Company on a note. The face value of the note was $12,000.00.

g. An NSF check for $183.56 from a customer, Ann Greeno, was returned with the statement.

h. The bank mistakenly charged to the company account a check for $850.00 drawn by another company.

i. The bank reported that it had credited the account for $240.00 in interest on the average balance for May.

REQUIRED

1. Prepare a bank reconciliation for Abdul Saleem Company as of May 31, 20xx.

2. Prepare the entries in journal form necessary to adjust the accounts.

3. State the amount that should appear on the balance sheet as of May 31.

EXPANDING YOUR CRITICAL THINKING, COMMUNICATION, AND INTERPERSONAL SKILLS

SKILLS DEVELOPMENT

Conceptual Analysis

LO 1 **Management of Cash**
LO 2
LO 3

SD 1. *Academia Publishing Company* publishes college textbooks in the sciences and humanities. More than 50 percent of the company's sales occur in July, August, and December. Its cash balances are largest in August, September, and January. During the rest of the year, its cash receipts are low. The corporate treasurer keeps the cash in a bank checking account earning little or no interest and pays bills from this account as they come due. To survive, the company has borrowed money during some slow sales months. The loans were repaid in the months when cash receipts were largest. A management consultant has suggested that the company institute a new cash management plan under which cash would be invested in marketable securities as it is received and securities would be sold when the funds are needed. In this way, the company will earn income on the cash and may realize a gain through an increase in the value of the securities, thus reducing the need for borrowing. The president of the company has asked you to assess the plan. Write a memorandum to the president that lays out the accounting implications of this cash management plan for cash and cash equivalents and for the three types of marketable securities. Include an assessment of the plan and any disadvantages to it.

LO 1 **Role of Credit Sales**
LO 4

SD 2. *Mitsubishi Corp.,*[12] a broadly diversified Japanese corporation, instituted a credit plan called Three Diamonds for customers who buy its major electronic products, such as large-screen televisions and videotape recorders, from specified retail dealers. Under the plan, approved customers who make purchases in July of one year do not have to make any payments until September of the next year and pay no interest for the intervening months. Mitsubishi pays the dealer the full amount less a small fee, sends the customer

| Cash Flow | CD-ROM | Communication | Critical Thinking | Ethics | General Ledger | Group Activity | Hot Links to Real Companies | International | Internet | Key Ratio | Memo | Spreadsheet |

a Mitsubishi credit card, and collects from the customer at the specified time. What was Mitsubishi's motivation for establishing such generous credit terms? What costs are involved? What are the accounting implications?

SD 3.

LO 1 Receivables Financing

Siegel Appliances, Inc., is a small manufacturer of washing machines and dryers located in central Michigan. Siegel sells most of its appliances to large, established discount retail companies that market the appliances under their own names. Siegel sells the appliances on trade credit terms of n/60. If a customer wants a longer term, however, Siegel will accept a note with a term of up to nine months. At present, the company is having cash flow troubles and needs $5 million immediately. Its cash balance is $200,000, its accounts receivable balance is $2.3 million, and its notes receivable balance is $3.7 million. How might Siegel's management use its accounts receivable and notes receivable to raise the cash it needs? What are the company's prospects for raising the needed cash?

Group Activity: Assign to in-class groups and debrief.

SD 4.

LO 4 Estimation of Percentage of Uncollectible Accounts Receivable

All companies that sell on credit face the risk of bad debt losses. For example, in 1996, *L.A. Gear Inc.,* a well-known maker of athletic footwear, had an allowance for uncollectible accounts of $4.1 million on gross accounts receivable of $28.1 million. Its 1996 sales were $196.4 million.[13] The percentage of uncollectible accounts receivable for 1996 was 15 percent of gross accounts receivable. What factors would determine the percentage uncollectible used by L.A. Gear Inc.? If actual collections of 1996 year-end receivables were less than $24.0 million ($28.1 − $4.1), how would the financial statements for 1996 and 1997 be affected?

Ethical Dilemma

SD 5.

LO 1 Ethics, Uncollectible
LO 4 Accounts, and Short-Term Objectives

Fitzsimmons Designs, a successful retail furniture company, is located in an affluent suburb where a major insurance company has just announced a restructuring that will lay off 4,000 employees. Fitzsimmons sells quality furniture, usually on credit. Accounts Receivable represents one of the major assets of the company and, although the company's annual uncollectible accounts losses are not out of line, they represent a sizable amount. The company depends on bank loans for its financing. Sales and net income have declined in the past year, and some customers are falling behind in paying their accounts. George Fitzsimmons, owner of the business, knows that the bank's loan officer likes to see a steady performance. Therefore, he has instructed the controller to underestimate the uncollectible accounts this year to show a small growth in earnings. Fitzsimmons believes the short-term action is justified because future successful years will average out the losses, and since the company has a history of success, the adjustments are meaningless accounting measures anyway. Are Fitzsimmons's actions ethical? Would any parties be harmed by his actions? How important is it to try to be accurate in estimating losses from uncollectible accounts?

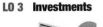

Group Activity: Assign to in-class groups and debate the ethical issues.

Research Activity

SD 6.

LO 1 Stock and Treasury
LO 3 Investments

Find a recent issue of *The Wall Street Journal* in your school library. Turn to the third, or C, section, entitled "Money & Investing." From the index at the top of the page, locate the listing of New York Stock Exchange (NYSE) stocks and turn to that page. From the listing of stocks, find five companies you have heard of, such as IBM, Deere, McDonald's, or Ford. Copy down the range of each company's stock price for the last year and the current closing price. Also copy down the dividend, if any, per share. How much did the market values of the common stocks you picked vary in the last year? Do these data demonstrate the need to value short-term investments of this type at market? How does accounting for short-term investments in these common stocks differ from accounting for short-term investments in U.S. Treasury bills? How are dividends received on investments in these common stocks accounted for? Be prepared to hand in your notes and to discuss the results of your investigation in class.

Decision-Making Practice

SD 7.

LO 3 Accounting for Short-Term Investments

Norman Christmas Tree Company's business—the growing and selling of Christmas trees—is seasonal. By January 1, after its heavy selling season, the company has cash on hand that will not be needed for several months. The company has minimal expenses from January to October and heavy expenses during the harvest and shipping months of November and December. The company's management follows the practice of investing the idle cash in marketable securities, which can be sold as the funds are needed for operations. The company's fiscal year ends on June 30. On January 10 of the current year, the company has cash of $597,300 on hand. It keeps $20,000 on hand for operating expenses and invests the rest as follows:

$100,000 3-month Treasury bills	$ 97,800
1,000 shares of Ford Motor Co. ($50 per share)	50,000
2,500 shares of McDonald's ($50 per share)	125,000
2,100 shares of IBM ($145 per share)	304,500
Total short-term investments	$577,300

During the next few months, the company receives two quarterly cash dividends from each company (assume February 10 and May 10): $.50 per share from Ford, $.05 per share from McDonald's, and $.25 per share from IBM. The Treasury bills are redeemed at face value on April 10. On June 1 management sells 500 shares of McDonald's at $55 per share. On June 30 the market values of the investments are:

Ford Motor Co.	$61 per share
McDonald's	$46 per share
IBM	$140 per share

Another quarterly dividend is received from each company (assume August 10). All the remaining shares are sold on November 1 at the following prices:

Ford Motor Co.	$55 per share
McDonald's	$44 per share
IBM	$160 per share

1. Record the investment transactions that occurred on January 10, February 10, April 10, May 10, and June 1. The Treasury bills are accounted for as held-to-maturity securities, and the stocks are trading securities. Prepare the required adjusting entry on June 30, and record the investment transactions on August 10 and November 1.

2. Explain how the short-term investments would be shown on the balance sheet on June 30.

3. After November 1, what is the balance of Allowance to Adjust Short-Term Investments to Market, and what will happen to this account next June?

4. What is your assessment of Norman Christmas Tree Company's strategy with regard to idle cash?

FINANCIAL REPORTING AND ANALYSIS

Interpreting Financial Reports

FRA 1.

LO 1 Unbilled Accounts
LO 4 Receivable, Estimate of Uncollectibles, and Financial Ratios

Systems & Computer Technology Corporation (SCT Corp) derives revenue primarily from outsourcing services contracts, software sales and services, and maintenance and enhancements. The information that follows is excerpted from the consolidated statements of operations for SCT Corporation.

Revenues (in thousands)	Year Ended September 30,	
	1998	1997
Outsourcing services	$125,554	$ 97,677
Software sales	97,844	76,948
Maintenance and enhancements	63,297	52,109
Software services	111,559	62,694
Other, primarily interest	5,414	618
	$403,668	$290,046

Fees from outsourcing services are typically based on multiyear contracts ranging from five to ten years and provide a recurring revenue stream throughout the term of the contract. For a typical outsourcing services contract, services are performed and expenses are incurred by the company at a greater rate during the first several years than in the later years of the contract. Billings usually remain constant over the term of the contract. Revenue is recorded as work is performed; therefore, revenues usually exceed billings in the early years of the contract. The resulting excess is reflected on the company's balance sheet as unbilled accounts receivable as shown:

Current Assets (in thousands)	September 30,	
	1998	1997
Cash and short-term investments	$ 78,306	$ 29,809
Receivables, including $66,158 and $59,311 of earned revenues in excess of billings, net of allowance for doubtful accounts of $4,033 and $4,098	130,457	100,543
Prepaid expenses and other receivables	13,861	8,473
Total Current Assets	$222,624	$138,825

Of the unbilled receivables (earned revenues in excess of billings) at September 30, 1998, 99 percent will be billed within the normal 12-month business cycle, although unbilled receivables will continue to build. Total assets were $333 million and $210 million in 1998 and 1997, respectively.[14]

REQUIRED

1. Compute the ratio of receivables to total assets, the ratio of unbilled receivables to total receivables, and the ratio of unbilled receivables to outsourcing revenues for both 1998 and 1997. Discuss how SCT's revenue recognition policy affects net income and cash flows.

2. Compute the percentage of gross receivables that the allowance for doubtful accounts represents. What does the change in the allowance imply?

3. Compute the 1998 receivable turnover. Exclude interest and other revenue from the computation. Discuss the impact of unbilled receivables on this ratio.

FRA 2.

LO 4 Accounting for Accounts Receivable

Bex Co. is a major consumer goods company that sells over three thousand products in 135 countries. The company's annual report to the Securities and Exchange Commission presented the following data (in thousands) pertaining to net sales and accounts related to accounts receivable for 1999, 2000, and 2001.

	2001	2000	1999
Net Sales	$4,910,000	$4,865,000	$4,888,000
Accounts Receivable	523,000	524,000	504,000
Allowance for Uncollectible Accounts	18,600	21,200	24,500
Uncollectible Accounts Expense	15,000	16,700	15,800
Uncollectible Accounts Written Off	19,300	20,100	17,700
Recoveries of Accounts Previously Written Off	1,700	100	1,000

REQUIRED

1. Compute the ratios of Uncollectible Accounts Expense to Net Sales and to Gross Accounts Receivable and of Allowance for Uncollectible Accounts to Gross Accounts Receivable for 1999, 2000, and 2001.

2. Compute the receivable turnover and average days' sales uncollected for each year, assuming 1998 net accounts receivable are $465,000,000.

3. What is your interpretation of the ratios? What appears to be management's attitude with respect to the collectibility of accounts receivable over the three-year period?

International Company

FRA 3.

LO 1 **Comparison and Interpretation of Ratios**

Philips Electronics, N.V., and *Heineken N.V.* are two of the most famous Dutch companies. Philips is a large, diversified electronics, music, and media company, and Heineken makes a popular beer. Philips is about four times bigger than Heineken, with 1997 revenues of 76 billion guilders versus 10 billion guilders for Heineken. Ratios can help in comparing and understanding the companies. For example, the receivable turnovers for the companies for two past years are as follows:

	1997	1996
Philips	6.0 times	6.1 times
Heineken	8.0 times	8.3 times

What do the ratios tell you about the credit policies of the two companies? How long does it take each on average to collect a receivable? What do the ratios tell about the companies' relative needs for capital to finance receivables? Can you tell which company has a better credit policy? Explain your answers.

Toys "R" Us Annual Report

FRA 4.

LO 1 **Analysis of Short-Term**
LO 2 **Liquid Assets**
LO 4

Refer to the Toys "R" Us annual report to answer the following questions.

1. How much cash and cash equivalents did Toys "R" Us have in 1999? Do you suppose most of that amount is cash in the bank or cash equivalents?

2. Toys "R" Us does not disclose an allowance for uncollectible accounts. How do you explain the lack of disclosure?

3. Compute the quick ratios for 1998 and 1999 and comment on them.

4. Compute receivable turnover and average days' sales uncollected for 1998 and 1999 and comment on Toys "R" Us credit policies. Accounts Receivable in 1997 were $135,000,000.

Fingraph® Financial Analyst™

FRA 5.

LO 1 **Comparison and Analysis of Short-Term Liquid Assets**

Choose any two companies from the same industry in the Fingraph® Financial Analyst™ CD-ROM software. The industry chosen should be one in which accounts receivable is likely to be an important current asset. Suggested industries from which to choose are manufacturing, consumer products, consumer food and beverage, and computers.

1. Find and read in the annual reports for the companies you have selected any reference to cash and cash equivalents, short-term or marketable securities, and accounts receivable in the summary of significant accounting policies or notes to the financial statements.

2. Display and print for the companies you have selected (a) the Current Assets and Current Liabilities Analysis page and (b) the Liquidity and Asset Utilization Analysis page in tabular and graphical form. Prepare a table that compares the quick ratio, receivable turnover, and average days' receivable for both companies for two years.

3. Find and read the liquidity analysis section of management's discussion and analysis in each annual report.

4. Write a one-page executive summary that highlights the accounting policies for short-term liquid assets and compares the short-term liquidity position of the two companies. Include your assessment of the companies' relative liquidity and make reference to management's assessment. Include the Fingraph® pages and your table as an attachment to your report.

Internet Case

FRA 6.

LO 4 Comparison of J.C. Penney and Sears

Go to the Needles Accounting Resource Center at http://college.hmco.com. Under web links, go to the annual reports on the web sites for *J.C. Penney Company, Inc.,* and *Sears, Roebuck and Co.* Find the accounts receivable and marketable securities (if any) on each company's balance sheet and the notes related to these accounts in the notes to the financial statements. If either company has marketable securities, what is the cost and what is the market value of the securities? Does the company currently have a gain or loss on the securities? Which company has the most accounts receivable as a percentage of total assets? What is the percentage of the allowance account to gross accounts receivable for each company? Which company experienced the highest loss rate on its receivables? Why do you think there is a difference? Do the companies finance their receivables? Be prepared to discuss your findings in class.

ENDNOTES

1. Pioneer Electronic Corporation, *Annual Report*, 1998.
2. Michael Selz, "Big Customers' Late Bills Choke Small Suppliers," *The Wall Street Journal*, June 22, 1994.
3. Linda Sandler, "Bally Total Fitness's Accounting Procedures Are Getting Some Skeptical Investors Exercised," *The Wall Street Journal*, August 28, 1998.
4. American Greetings Corp., *Annual Report*, 1998.
5. Adapted from Circuit City Stores, Inc., *Annual Report*, 1998.
6. Bell Atlantic Corp., *Annual Report*, 1998.
7. *Accounting Trends & Techniques* (New York: American Institute of CPAs, 1998), p. 157.
8. Jeffrey Taylor, "Rules on Electronic Transfers of Money Are Being Tightened by U.S. Treasury," *The Wall Street Journal*, September 26, 1994.
9. *Statement of Financial Accounting Standards No. 115*, "Accounting for Certain Investments in Debt and Equity Securities" (Norwalk, Conn.: Financial Accounting Standards Board, 1993).
10. Pioneer Electronic Corporation, *Annual Report*, 1999.
11. Craig S. Smith, "Chinese Companies Writing Off Old Debt," *The Wall Street Journal*, December 28, 1995.
12. Information based on promotional brochures received from Mitsubishi Electric Corp.
13. L.A. Gear Inc., *Annual Report*, 1996.
14. Systems & Computer Technology Corporation, *Annual Report*, 1998.

8 Inventories

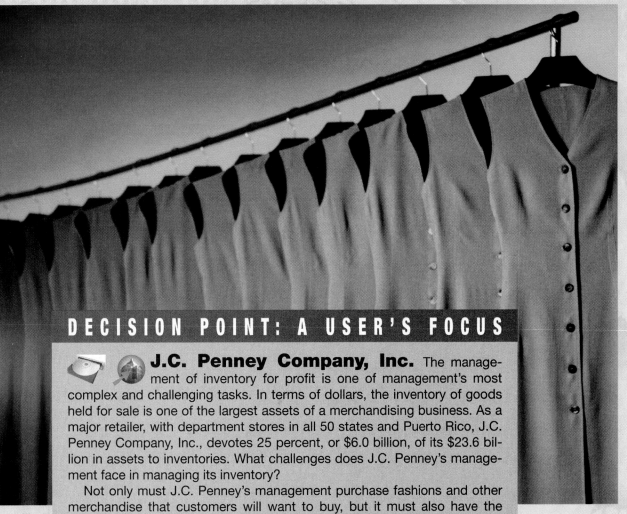

DECISION POINT: A USER'S FOCUS

J.C. Penney Company, Inc. The management of inventory for profit is one of management's most complex and challenging tasks. In terms of dollars, the inventory of goods held for sale is one of the largest assets of a merchandising business. As a major retailer, with department stores in all 50 states and Puerto Rico, J.C. Penney Company, Inc., devotes 25 percent, or $6.0 billion, of its $23.6 billion in assets to inventories. What challenges does J.C. Penney's management face in managing its inventory?

Not only must J.C. Penney's management purchase fashions and other merchandise that customers will want to buy, but it must also have the merchandise available in the right locations at the times when customers want to buy it. It also must try to minimize the cost of inventory while maintaining quality. To these ends, J.C. Penney maintains purchasing offices throughout the world, including Hong Kong, Taipei, Osaka, Seoul, Bangkok, Singapore, Bombay, and Florence. Quality assurance experts operate out of 22 domestic and 14 international offices. Further, the amount of money tied up in inventory must be controlled because of the high cost of borrowing funds and storing inventory. Important accounting decisions include what assumptions to make about the flow of inventory costs, what prices to put on inventory, what inventory systems to use, and how to protect inventory against loss. Proper management of inventory helped J.C. Penney earn net income of $594 million in 1998, but small variations in any inventory decision can mean the difference between a net profit and a net loss.

After three years of steady or increasing profits, J.C. Penney's 1999 net income was down 43 percent to $336 million. Gross margin percentage was lower on higher net sales. J.C. Penney's chairman said, "Improving the profitability of our core department store and drug store business is our top priority." The company announced its plans to close underperforming stores and liquidate certain inventories in the coming year.[1]

Management Issues Associated with Accounting for Inventories

Inventory is considered a current asset because it will normally be sold within a year's time or within a company's operating cycle. For a merchandising business like J.C. Penney or Toys "R" Us, **merchandise inventory** consists of all goods owned and held for sale in the regular course of business.

Inventories are also important for manufacturing companies. Because manufacturers are engaged in the actual making of products, they have three kinds of inventory: raw materials to be used in the production of goods, partially completed products (often called *work in process*), and finished goods ready for sale. For example, in its 1998 annual report, Illinois Tool Works, Inc., disclosed the following inventories (in thousands):

Financial Highlights		
	1998	1997
Inventories		
Raw materials	$163,868	$145,851
Work in process	72,254	67,956
Finished goods	345,633	309,189
Total inventories	$581,755	$522,996

In manufacturing operations, the costs of the work in process and the finished goods inventories include not only the cost of the raw materials that go into the product, but also the cost of the labor used to convert the raw materials to finished goods and the overhead costs that support the production process. Included in this latter category are such costs as indirect materials (for example, paint, glue, and nails), indirect labor (such as the salaries of supervisors), factory rent, depreciation of plant assets, utilities costs, and insurance costs. The methods for maintaining and pricing inventory explained in this chapter are applicable to manufactured goods, but because the details of accounting for manufacturing companies are usually covered as a management accounting topic, this chapter focuses on accounting for merchandising firms.

Applying the Matching Rule to Inventories

The American Institute of Certified Public Accountants states, "A major objective of accounting for inventories is the proper determination of income through the process of matching appropriate costs against revenues."[2] Note that the objective is the proper determination of income through the matching of costs and revenues, not the determination of the most realistic inventory value. These two objectives are sometimes incompatible, in which case the objective of income determination takes precedence.

The reason inventory accounting is so important to income measurement is linked to the way income is measured on the merchandising income statement. Recall that gross margin is computed as the difference between net sales and cost of goods sold and that cost of goods sold is dependent on the cost assigned to inventory or goods not sold. Because of those relationships, the higher the cost of ending inventory, the lower the cost of goods sold and the higher the resulting gross margin. Conversely, the lower the value assigned to ending inventory, the higher the cost of goods sold and the lower the gross margin. Because the amount of gross margin has a direct effect on the amount of net income, the amount assigned to ending inventory directly affects the amount of net income. *In effect, the value assigned to the ending inventory determines what portion of the cost of goods available for sale is assigned to cost of goods sold and what portion is assigned to the balance sheet as inventory to be carried over into the next accounting period.*

Assessing the Impact of Inventory Decisions

Figure 1 summarizes the management choices with regard to inventory systems and methods. The decisions usually result in different amounts of reported net income and, as a result, affect both the external evaluation of the company by investors and creditors and such internal evaluations as performance reviews, bonuses, and executive compensation. Because income is affected, the valuation of inventory may also have a considerable effect on the amount of income taxes paid. Federal income tax authorities have, therefore, been interested in the effects of various inventory valuation methods and have specific regulations about the acceptability of different methods. As a result, management is sometimes faced with the problem of balancing the goal of proper income determination with that of minimizing income taxes. Another consideration is that since the choice of inventory valuation method affects the amount of income taxes paid, it also affects a company's cash flows.

**Figure 1
Management Choices in
Accounting for Inventories**

Enrichment Note: Management considers the behavior of inventory prices over time when selecting inventory costing methods.

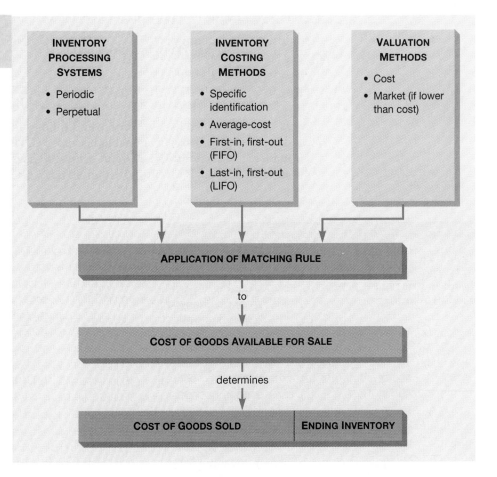

Evaluating the Level of Inventory

The level of inventory has important economic consequences for a company. Ideally, management wants to have a great variety and quantity on hand so that customers have a large choice and do not have to wait. Such an inventory policy is not costless, however. The cost of handling and storage and the interest cost of the funds necessary to maintain high inventory levels are usually substantial. On the other hand, the maintenance of low inventory levels may result in lost sales and disgruntled customers. Common measures used in the evaluation of inventory levels are inventory turnover and its related measure, average days' inventory on hand. **Inventory turnover** is a measure similar to receivable turnover. It indicates the number of times a company's average inventory is sold during an accounting period. Inventory turnover is computed by dividing cost of goods sold by average inventory. For example, J.C. Penney's cost of goods sold was $21,761 billion in 1998, and its merchandise inventory was $6,031 billion at the end of 1998 and $6,162 billion at the end of 1997. Its inventory turnover is computed as follows:

$$\text{Inventory Turnover} = \frac{\text{Cost of Goods Sold}}{\text{Average Inventory}}$$

$$= \frac{\$21,761,000,000}{(\$6,031,000,000 + \$6,162,000,000) \div 2}$$

$$= \frac{\$21,761,000,000}{\$6,096,500,000} = 3.6 \text{ times}$$

The **average days' inventory on hand** indicates the average number of days required to sell the inventory on hand. It is found by dividing the number of days in a year by the inventory turnover, as follows:

$$\text{Average Days' Inventory on Hand} = \frac{\text{Number of Days in a Year}}{\text{Inventory Turnover}}$$

$$= \frac{365 \text{ days}}{3.6 \text{ times}} = 101.4 \text{ days}$$

J.C. Penney turned its inventory over 3.6 times in 1998, or on average every 101.4 days. These figures are reasonable because J.C. Penney is in a business where fashions change every season, or about every 100 days. Management would want to sell all of each season's inventory within 90 days, even while making purchases for the

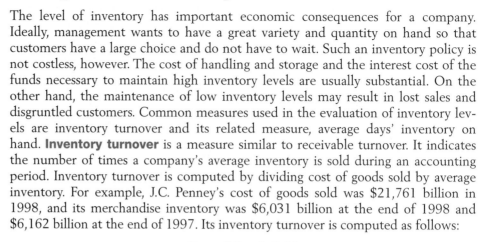

BUSINESS FOCUS ON TECHNOLOGY

Computer maker Dell Computer Corp. has long been a model of excellent inventory management with high inventory turnover ratios and keen cost controls. The use of computer technology has been critical to its success in these areas. Dell's speed from order to delivery sets the industry standard. Consider that a computer ordered by 9 A.M. can be delivered the next day by 9 P.M. How can Dell do this when it doesn't start ordering components and assembling computers until an order is booked? First, Dell's suppliers keep components warehoused just minutes from Dell's factories, making possible efficient, just-in-time operations. Another time and money saver is the handling of monitors. Dell sends an E-mail message to a shipper such as United Parcel Service. The shipper pulls a computer monitor from supplier stocks and schedules it to arrive with the PC. Monitors are no longer shipped first to Dell and then on to buyers. In addition to contributing to a high inventory turnover, this practice saves Dell about $30 per monitor in freight costs. Dell is showing the world how to run a business in the cyber age by selling more than $1 million worth of computers a day on its web site.[3]

**Figure 2
Inventory Turnover for Selected Industries**

Enrichment Note: Inventory turnover will be systematically higher if year-end inventory levels are low. For example, Toys "R" Us inventory levels on January 30 are at their lowest point of the year.

Source: Data from Dun & Bradstreet, *Industry Norms and Key Business Ratios,* 1997–98.

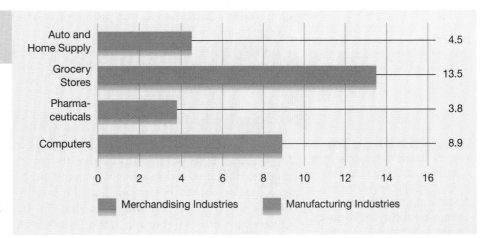

**Figure 3
Average Days' Inventory on Hand for Selected Industries**

Source: Data from Dun & Bradstreet, *Industry Norms and Key Business Ratios,* 1997–98.

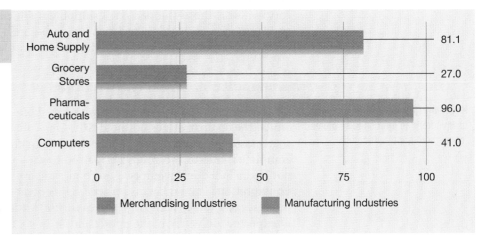

next season. There are natural levels of inventory in every industry, as shown for selected merchandising and manufacturing industries in Figures 2 and 3. However, companies that are able to maintain their inventories at lower levels and still satisfy customer needs are the most successful.

Merchandising and manufacturing companies are attempting to reduce their levels of inventory by changing to a **just-in-time operating environment**. In such an environment, rather than stockpiling inventories for later use, companies work closely with suppliers to coordinate and schedule shipments so that goods arrive just at the time they are needed. Less money is tied up in inventories, and the costs associated with carrying inventories are reduced. For example, Pacific Bell was able to close six warehouses by implementing just-in-time inventory management.

Pricing Inventory Under the Periodic Inventory System

OBJECTIVE

2 Define *inventory cost* and relate it to goods flow and cost flow

According to the AICPA, "The primary basis of accounting for inventories is cost, which has been defined generally as the price paid or consideration given to acquire an asset."[4] This definition of **inventory cost** has generally been interpreted to include the following costs: (1) invoice price less purchases discounts; (2) freight or transportation in, including insurance in transit; and (3) applicable taxes and tariffs. There are other costs—for ordering, receiving, and storing—that should in principle also be included in inventory cost. In practice, however, it is so difficult to allocate such costs to specific inventory items that they are usually considered expenses of the accounting period instead of inventory costs.

Merchandise in Transit

Business-World Example: When a customer orders merchandise from a catalogue company, he or she pays not only the price listed in the catalogue, but also such charges as shipping and insurance. Consequently, the cost is greater than the catalogue price.

Because merchandise inventory includes all items owned by a company and held for sale, the status of any merchandise in transit, whether it is being sold or being purchased by the inventorying company, must be examined to determine if the merchandise should be included in the inventory count. As Figure 4 illustrates, neither the customer nor the buyer has physical possession of the merchandise. Ownership of these goods in transit is determined by the terms of the shipping agreement, which indicate whether title has passed. Outgoing goods shipped FOB (free on board) destination would be included in the seller's merchandise inventory, whereas those shipped FOB shipping point would not. Conversely, incoming goods shipped FOB shipping point would be included in the buyer's merchandise inventory, but those shipped FOB destination would not.

Merchandise on Hand Not Included in Inventory

Key Point: The consignor will count as inventory all merchandise placed (consigned) at other locations.

At the time a physical inventory is taken, there may be merchandise on hand to which the company does not hold title. One category of such goods is merchandise that has been sold and is awaiting delivery to the buyer. Since the sale has been completed, title to the goods has passed to the buyer, and the merchandise should not be included in inventory. A second category is goods held on consignment. A **consignment** is merchandise placed by its owner (known as the *consignor*) on the premises of another company (the *consignee*) with the understanding that payment is expected only when the merchandise is sold and that unsold items may be returned to the consignor. Title to consigned goods remains with the consignor until the consignee sells the goods. Consigned goods should not be included in the physical inventory of the consignee because they still belong to the consignor.

Methods of Pricing Inventory at Cost

The prices of most kinds of merchandise vary during the year. Identical lots of merchandise may have been purchased at different prices. Also, when identical items

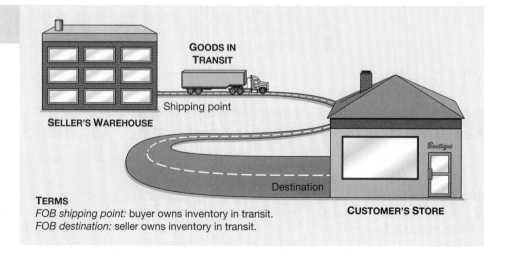

**Figure 4
Merchandise in Transit**

GOODS IN TRANSIT

Shipping point

SELLER'S WAREHOUSE

Destination

CUSTOMER'S STORE

TERMS
FOB shipping point: buyer owns inventory in transit.
FOB destination: seller owns inventory in transit.

are bought and sold, it is often impossible to tell which have been sold and which are still in inventory. For this reason, it is necessary to make an assumption about the order in which items have been sold. Because the assumed order of sale may or may not be the same as the actual order of sale, the assumption is really about the *flow of costs* rather than the *flow of physical inventory.*

The term **goods flow** refers to the actual physical movement of goods in the operations of a company, and the term **cost flow** refers to the association of costs with their *assumed* flow in the operations of a company. The assumed cost flow may or may not be the same as the actual goods flow. The possibility of a difference between cost flow and goods flow may seem strange at first, but it arises because several choices of assumed cost flow are available under generally accepted accounting principles. In fact, it is sometimes preferable to use an assumed cost flow that bears no relationship to goods flow because it gives a better estimate of income, which is the main goal of inventory valuation.

Accountants usually price inventory by using one of the following generally accepted methods, each based on a different assumption of cost flow: (1) specific identification method; (2) average-cost method; (3) first-in, first-out (FIFO) method; and (4) last-in, first-out (LIFO) method. The choice of method depends on the nature of the business, the financial effects of the methods, and the costs of implementing the methods.

To illustrate the four methods under the periodic inventory system, the following data for the month of June will be used.

Key Point: The assumed flow of costs for inventory pricing does not have to correspond to the natural flow of goods.

Inventory Data—June 30

June				
	1	Inventory	50 units @ $1.00	$ 50
	6	Purchase	50 units @ $1.10	55
	13	Purchase	150 units @ $1.20	180
	20	Purchase	100 units @ $1.30	130
	25	Purchase	150 units @ $1.40	210
Goods Available for Sale			500 units	$625
Sales			280 units	
On hand June 30			220 units	

Notice that there is a total of 500 units available for sale at a total cost of $625. Stated simply, the problem of inventory pricing is to divide the $625 between the 280 units sold and the 220 units on hand. Recall that under the periodic inventory system, the inventory is not updated after each purchase and sale. Thus it is not necessary to know when the individual sales take place.

SPECIFIC IDENTIFICATION METHOD   If the units in the ending inventory can be identified as coming from specific purchases, the **specific identification method** may be used to price the inventory by identifying the cost of each item in ending inventory. For instance, assume that the June 30 inventory consisted of 50 units from the June 1 inventory, 100 units from the purchase of June 13, and 70 units from the purchase of June 25. The cost assigned to the inventory under the specific identification method would be $268, determined as follows:

OBJECTIVE

3a Calculate the pricing of inventory, using the cost basis under the periodic inventory system, according to the specific identification method

Periodic Inventory System—Specific Identification Method

50 units @ $1.00	$ 50	Cost of Goods Available		
100 units @ $1.20	120	for Sale		$625
70 units @ $1.40	98	Less June 30 Inventory		268
220 units at a cost of	$268	Cost of Goods Sold		$357

Business-World Example: Even if it were possible to track each individual inventory item, a company would not do so because it would be excessively expensive to track which items were left in inventory. The cost would clearly exceed the benefit.

The specific identification method might be used in the purchase and sale of high-priced articles, such as automobiles, heavy equipment, and works of art. Although this method may appear logical, it is not used by many companies because it has two definite disadvantages. First, in many cases, it is difficult and impractical to keep track of the purchase and sale of individual items. Second, when a company deals in items that are identical but were purchased at different costs, deciding which items are sold becomes arbitrary; thus the company can raise or lower income by choosing to sell the lower- or higher-cost items.

OBJECTIVE

3b Calculate the pricing of inventory, using the cost basis under the periodic inventory system, according to the average-cost method

AVERAGE-COST METHOD Under the **average-cost method**, inventory is priced at the average cost of the goods available for sale during the period. Average cost is computed by dividing the total cost of goods available for sale by the total units available for sale. This gives an average unit cost that is applied to the units in ending inventory. In our illustration, the ending inventory would be $275, or $1.25 per unit, determined as follows:

Periodic Inventory System—Average-Cost Method

$$\text{Cost of Goods Available for Sale} \div \text{Units Available for Sale} = \text{Average Unit Cost}$$
$$\$625 \div 500 \text{ units} = \$1.25$$

→ Ending Inventory: 220 units @ $1.25 =	$275
Cost of Goods Available for Sale	$625
→ Less June 30 Inventory	275
Cost of Goods Sold	$350

The average-cost method tends to level out the effects of cost increases and decreases because the cost for the ending inventory calculated under this method is influenced by all the prices paid during the year and by the beginning inventory price. Some, however, criticize the average-cost method because they believe that recent costs are more relevant for income measurement and decision making.

Business-World Example: The physical flow of goods sometimes may seem to dictate a particular method, such as in a milk producer's operations in which the perishable nature of the product requires a *physical flow* of FIFO. However, the milk producer's management can choose an inventory method based on an assumed *cost flow* that differs from FIFO, such as average-cost or LIFO.

OBJECTIVE

3c Calculate the pricing of inventory, using the cost basis under the periodic inventory system, according to the first-in, first-out (FIFO) method

FIRST-IN, FIRST-OUT (FIFO) METHOD The **first-in, first-out (FIFO) method** is based on the assumption that the costs of the first items acquired should be assigned to the first items sold. The costs of the goods on hand at the end of a period are assumed to be from the most recent purchases, and the costs assigned to goods that have been sold are assumed to be from the earliest purchases. The FIFO method of determining inventory cost may be adopted by any business, regardless of the actual physical flow of goods, because the assumption is made regarding the flow of costs and not the flow of goods.

In our illustration, the June 30 inventory would be $301 when the FIFO method is used. It is computed as follows:

Periodic Inventory System—First-In, First-Out Method

150 units @ $1.40 from purchase of June 25	$210
70 units @ $1.30 from purchase of June 20	91
→ 220 units at a cost of	$301
Cost of Goods Available for Sale	$625
→ Less June 30 Inventory	301
Cost of Goods Sold	$324

Enrichment Note: When you make a FIFO cost flow assumption, you use it even if you can prove that one of the first-purchased items is still in inventory. Let's say that for the first week of January, perfume was packaged in blue boxes, and then the company changed to red packaging. When you price inventory using the FIFO method, you assume the blue boxes (the older merchandise) were sold, even if you have some of them left in inventory.

The effect of the FIFO method is to value the ending inventory at the most recent costs and include earlier costs in cost of goods sold. During periods of consistently rising prices, the FIFO method yields the highest possible amount of net income, since cost of goods sold will show costs closer to the price level at the time the goods were purchased. Another reason for this result is that businesses tend to increase selling prices as costs rise, even when inventories were purchased before the price rise. The reverse effect occurs in periods of price decreases. Consequently, a major criticism of FIFO is that it magnifies the effects of the business cycle on income.

LAST-IN, FIRST-OUT (LIFO) METHOD   The **last-in, first-out (LIFO) method** of costing inventories is based on the assumption that the costs of the last items purchased should be assigned to the first items sold and that the cost of ending inventory reflects the cost of the merchandise purchased earliest.

Under this method, the June 30 inventory would be $249, computed as follows:

OBJECTIVE

3d Calculate the pricing of inventory, using the cost basis under the periodic inventory system, according to the last-in, first-out (LIFO) method

Business-World Example: An example of physical flow under LIFO would be a gravel pile. As gravel on top is sold, more is purchased and added on top. The gravel on the bottom may never be sold. Despite this LIFO physical flow, any acceptable cost flow assumption may be made.

Periodic Inventory System—Last-In, First-Out Method

50 units @ $1.00 from June 1 inventory	$ 50
50 units @ $1.10 from purchase of June 6	55
120 units @ $1.20 from purchase of June 13	144
220 units at a cost of	$249
Cost of Goods Available for Sale	$625
Less June 30 Inventory	249
Cost of Goods Sold	$376

The effect of LIFO is to value inventory at the earliest prices and to include in cost of goods sold the cost of the most recently purchased goods. This assumption, of course, does not agree with the actual physical movement of goods in most businesses.

There is, however, a strong logical argument to support LIFO, based on the fact that a certain size inventory is necessary in a going concern. When inventory is sold, it must be replaced with more goods. The supporters of LIFO reason that the fairest determination of income occurs if the current costs of merchandise are matched against current sales prices, regardless of which physical units of merchandise are sold. When prices are moving either upward or downward, the cost of goods sold will, under LIFO, show costs closer to the price level at the time the goods were sold. As a result, the LIFO method tends to show a smaller net income during inflationary times and a larger net income during deflationary times than other methods of inventory valuation. The peaks and valleys of the business cycle tend to be smoothed out. In inventory valuation, the flow of costs, and hence income determination, is more important than the physical movement of goods and balance sheet valuation.

An argument may also be made against the LIFO method. Because the inventory valuation on the balance sheet reflects earlier prices, it often gives an unrealistic picture of the current value of the inventory. Such balance sheet measures as working capital and current ratio may be distorted and must be interpreted carefully.

BUSINESS FOCUS ON PRACTICE

A new type of retail business called the "category killer" seems to ignore the tenets of good inventory management. These retailers, such as The Home Depot, Inc., in home improvements, Barnes & Noble Inc. in bookstores, Wal-Mart Stores, Inc., in groceries and dry goods, Toys "R" Us, Inc., in toys, and Blockbuster Entertainment Corp. in videos, maintain huge inventories at such low prices that smaller competitors find it hard to compete. Although these companies have a large amount of money tied up in inventories, they maintain very sophisticated just-in-time operating environments that require suppliers to meet demanding standards for delivery of products and reduction of inventory costs. Some suppliers are required to stock the shelves and keep track of inventory levels. By minimizing handling and overhead costs and buying at favorably low prices, the category killers achieve great success.

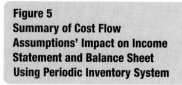

Figure 5
Summary of Cost Flow
Assumptions' Impact on Income
Statement and Balance Sheet
Using Periodic Inventory System

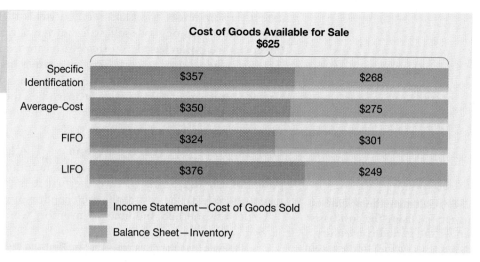

Figure 5 summarizes the impact of the four inventory cost allocation methods on the cost of goods sold as reported on the income statement and on inventory as reported on the balance sheet when a company uses the periodic inventory system. In periods of rising prices, the FIFO method yields the highest inventory valuation, the lowest cost of goods sold, and hence a higher net income. The LIFO method yields the lowest inventory valuation, the highest cost of goods sold, and thus a lower net income.

Pricing Inventory Under the Perpetual Inventory System

OBJECTIVE

4 Apply the perpetual inventory system to the pricing of inventories at cost

The pricing of inventories under the perpetual inventory system differs from pricing under the periodic inventory system. The difference occurs because under the perpetual inventory system, a continuous record of quantities and costs of merchandise is maintained as purchases and sales are made. Under the periodic inventory system, only the ending inventory is counted and priced. Cost of goods sold is determined by deducting the cost of the ending inventory from the cost of goods available for sale. Under the perpetual inventory system, cost of goods sold is accumulated as sales are made and costs are transferred from the Inventory account to Cost of Goods Sold. The cost of the ending inventory is the balance of the Inventory account. To illustrate pricing methods under the perpetual inventory system, the same data will be used as before, but specific sales dates and amounts will be added, as follows:

Inventory Data—June 30

June	1	Inventory	50 units @ $1.00
	6	Purchase	50 units @ $1.10
	10	Sale	70 units
	13	Purchase	150 units @ $1.20
	20	Purchase	100 units @ $1.30
	25	Purchase	150 units @ $1.40
	30	Sale	210 units
	30	Inventory	220 units

Pricing the inventory and cost of goods sold using the specific identification method is the same under the perpetual system as it was under the periodic system because cost of goods sold and ending inventory are based on the cost of the identified items sold and on hand. The perpetual system facilitates the use of the specific identification method because detailed records of purchases and sales are maintained.

Pricing the inventory and cost of goods sold using the average-cost method differs when the perpetual system is used. Under the periodic system, the average cost is computed for all goods available for sale during the month. Under the perpetual system, a moving average is computed after each purchase or series of purchases preceding the next sale, as follows:

Enrichment Note: An automated perpetual system still has considerable costs. These include the cost of automating the system, the cost of maintaining the system, and the cost of taking a physical inventory to check against the perpetual records.

Perpetual Inventory System—Average-Cost Method

June	1	Inventory	50 units @ $1.00	$ 50.00
	6	Purchase	50 units @ $1.10	55.00
	6	Balance	100 units @ $1.05	$105.00
	10	Sale	70 units @ $1.05	(73.50)
	10	Balance	30 units @ $1.05	$ 31.50
	13	Purchase	150 units @ $1.20	180.00
	20	Purchase	100 units @ $1.30	130.00
	25	Purchase	150 units @ $1.40	210.00
	25	Balance	430 units @ $1.28*	$551.50
	30	Sale	210 units @ $1.28	(268.80)
	30	Inventory	220 units @ $1.29*	$282.70
Cost of Goods Sold			$73.50 + $268.80	$342.30

*Rounded

The sum of the costs applied to sales becomes the cost of goods sold, $342.30. The ending inventory is the balance, or $282.70.

When pricing the inventory using the FIFO and LIFO methods, it is necessary to keep track of the components of inventory at each step of the way because as sales are made, the costs must be assigned in the proper order. To apply the FIFO method, the approach is as follows:

Perpetual Inventory System—FIFO Method

June	1	Inventory	50 units @ $1.00		$ 50.00
	6	Purchase	50 units @ $1.10		55.00
	10	Sale	50 units @ $1.00	($ 50.00)	
			20 units @ $1.10	(22.00)	(72.00)
	10	Balance	30 units @ $1.10		$ 33.00
	13	Purchase	150 units @ $1.20		180.00
	20	Purchase	100 units @ $1.30		130.00
	25	Purchase	150 units @ $1.40		210.00
	30	Sale	30 units @ $1.10	($ 33.00)	
			150 units @ $1.20	(180.00)	
			30 units @ $1.30	(39.00)	(252.00)
	30	Inventory	70 units @ $1.30	$ 91.00	
			150 units @ $1.40	210.00	$301.00
Cost of Goods Sold			$72.00 + $252.00		$324.00

BUSINESS FOCUS ON TECHNOLOGY

Using the LIFO method under the perpetual inventory system is a very tedious process, especially if done manually. However, the development of faster and less expensive computer systems has made it easier for many companies to switch to LIFO and still use the perpetual inventory system. The availability of better technology may partially account for the increasing use of LIFO in the United States and may enable more companies to enjoy LIFO's economic benefits.

Note that the ending inventory of $301 and the cost of goods sold of $324 are the same as the figures computed earlier under the periodic inventory system. This will always occur because the ending inventory under both systems will always consist of the last items purchased—in this case, the entire purchase of June 25 and 70 units from the purchase of June 20.

To apply the LIFO method, the approach is as follows:

Perpetual Inventory System—LIFO Method

June 1	Inventory	50 units @ $1.00		$ 50.00
6	Purchase	50 units @ $1.10		55.00
10	Sale	50 units @ $1.10	($ 55.00)	
		20 units @ $1.00	(20.00)	(75.00)
10	Balance	30 units @ $1.00		$ 30.00
13	Purchase	150 units @ $1.20		180.00
20	Purchase	100 units @ $1.30		130.00
25	Purchase	150 units @ $1.40		210.00
30	Sale	150 units @ $1.40	($210.00)	
		60 units @ $1.30	(78.00)	(288.00)
30	Inventory	30 units @ $1.00	$ 30.00	
		150 units @ $1.20	180.00	
		40 units @ $1.30	52.00	$262.00
Cost of Goods Sold		$75.00 + $288.00		$363.00

Notice that the ending inventory of $262 includes 30 units from the beginning inventory, all the units from the purchase of June 13, and 40 units from the purchase of June 20.

Figure 6
Summary of Cost Flow Assumptions' Impact on Income Statement and Balance Sheet Using Perpetual Inventory System

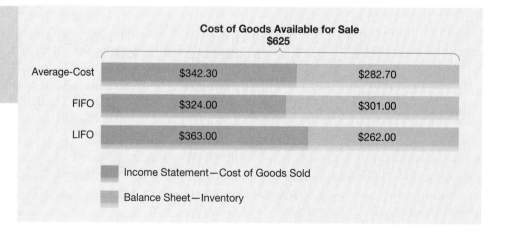

A comparison of the three cost flow assumptions or methods using a perpetual inventory system is shown in Figure 6. The relative relationship of the methods is the same as their relationship under the periodic inventory system, but some amounts have changed. For example, LIFO has the lowest inventory valuation regardless of the inventory system used, but the amount is $262 using the perpetual system versus $249 using the periodic system.

Comparison and Impact of Inventory Decisions and Misstatements

OBJECTIVE

5 State the effects of inventory methods and misstatements of inventory on income determination, income taxes, and cash flows

The specific identification, average-cost, FIFO, and LIFO methods of pricing inventory under both the periodic and the perpetual inventory systems have now been illustrated. The effects of the four methods on gross margin are shown in Exhibit 1, using the same data as before and assuming June sales of $500. Because the specific identification method is based on actual cost, it is the same under both systems.

Keeping in mind that June was a period of rising prices, we can see that LIFO, which charges the most recent, and, in this case, the highest, prices to cost of goods sold, resulted in the lowest gross margin under both systems. Conversely, FIFO, which charges the earliest, and, in this case, the lowest, prices to cost of goods sold, produced the highest gross margin. The gross margin under the average-cost method is somewhere between those under LIFO and FIFO. Thus, it is clear that the average-cost method has a less pronounced effect. Note that ending inventory and gross margin under FIFO are always the same under both the periodic and the perpetual inventory systems.

During a period of declining prices, the reverse would occur. The LIFO method would produce a higher gross margin than the FIFO method. It is apparent that

Exhibit 1
Effects of Inventory Systems and Methods Computed

	Specific Identification Method	Periodic Inventory System			Perpetual Inventory System*		
		Average-Cost Method	First-In, First-Out Method	Last-In, First-Out Method	Average-Cost Method	First-In, First-Out Method	Last-In, First-Out Method
Sales	$500	$500	$500	$500	$500	$500	$500
Cost of Goods Sold							
Beginning Inventory	$ 50	$ 50	$ 50	$ 50			
Purchases	575	575	575	575			
Cost of Goods Available for Sale	$625	$625	$625	$625			
Less Ending Inventory	268	275	301	249	$283†	$301	$262
Cost of Goods Sold	$357	$350	$324	$376	$342†	$324	$363
Gross Margin	$143	$150	$176	$124	$158	$176	$137

*Ending inventory under the perpetual inventory system is provided for comparison only. It is not used in the computation of cost of goods sold.
†Rounded.

the method of inventory valuation has the greatest importance during prolonged periods of price changes in one direction, either up or down.

Because the specific identification method depends on the particular items sold, no generalization can be made about the effect of changing prices.

Effects on the Financial Statements

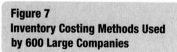

Key Point: The assumption of inventory cost flows is necessary because of changes in merchandise prices.

Each of the four methods of inventory pricing is acceptable for use in published financial statements. The FIFO, LIFO, and average-cost methods are widely used, as can be seen in Figure 7, which shows the inventory costing methods used by 600 large companies. Each has its advantages and disadvantages, and none can be considered best or perfect. The factors that should be considered in choosing an inventory method are the trend of prices and the effects of each method on financial statements, income taxes, and management decisions.

A basic problem in determining the best inventory measure for a particular company stems from the fact that inventory affects both the balance sheet and the income statement. As we have seen, the LIFO method is best suited for the income statement because it matches revenues and cost of goods sold. But it is not the best measure of the current balance sheet value of inventory, particularly during a prolonged period of price increases or decreases. The FIFO method, on the other hand, is best suited to the balance sheet because the ending inventory is closest to current values and thus gives a more realistic view of the current financial assets of a business. Readers of financial statements must be alert to inventory methods and be able to assess their effects.

Effects on Income Taxes

The Internal Revenue Service has developed several rules for valuing inventories for federal income tax purposes. A company has a wide choice of methods, including specific identification, average-cost, FIFO, and LIFO, as well as lower-of-cost-or-market. But once a method has been chosen, it must be used consistently from one year to the next. The IRS must approve any change in the inventory valuation method for income tax purposes.[5] This requirement agrees with the rule of consistency in accounting, since changes in inventory method may cause income to fluc-

Figure 7
Inventory Costing Methods Used by 600 Large Companies

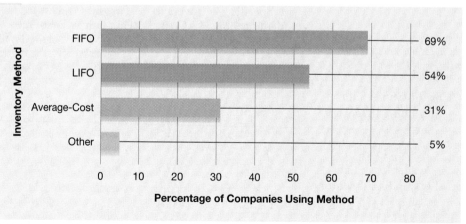

Total percentage exceeds 100 because some companies used different methods for different types of inventory.

Source: Reprinted with permission from *Accounting Trends & Techniques.* Copyright © 1998 by the American Institute of Certified Public Accountants, Inc.

BUSINESS FOCUS ON PRACTICE

Does the accounting method a company uses affect management's operating decisions? It certainly does when taxes are involved! Recent research shows that among firms that use the LIFO inventory method, those with high tax rates are more likely to buy extra inventory at year end than those with low tax rates.[6] This behavior is predictable because LIFO deducts the most recent purchases, which are likely to have higher costs than earlier purchases, in determining taxable income. This action will result in lower income taxes.

Key Point: In periods of rising prices, LIFO results in lower net income and thus lower taxes.

tuate too much and would make income statements hard to interpret from year to year. A company may change its inventory method if there is a good reason for doing so. The nature and effect of the change must be shown on the company's financial statements.

Many accountants believe that the use of the FIFO and average-cost methods in periods of rising prices causes businesses to report more than their true profit, resulting in the payment of excess income taxes. The profit is overstated because cost of goods sold is understated, relative to current prices. The company must buy replacement inventory at higher prices, but additional funds are also needed to pay income taxes. During the rapid inflation of 1979 to 1982, billions of dollars reported as profits and paid in income taxes were believed to be the result of poor matching of current costs and revenues under the FIFO and average-cost methods. Consequently, many companies, encouraged by the belief that prices will continue to rise, have since switched to the LIFO inventory method.

If a company uses the LIFO method in reporting income for tax purposes, the IRS requires that the same method be used in the accounting records. Also, the IRS will not allow the use of the lower-of-cost-or-market rule if LIFO is used to determine inventory cost. In such a case, only the LIFO cost can be used. This rule, however, does not preclude a company from using lower-of-LIFO-cost-or-market for financial reporting purposes (discussed later in this chapter).

Over a period of rising prices, a business that uses the LIFO method may find that for balance sheet purposes, its inventory is valued at a cost figure far below what it currently pays for the same items. Management must monitor this situation carefully, because if it should let the inventory quantity at year end fall below the beginning-of-the-year level, the company will find itself paying higher income taxes. Higher income before taxes results because the company would expense historical costs of inventory, which are below current costs. When this occurs, it is called a **LIFO liquidation** because sales have reduced inventories below the levels established in prior years.

A LIFO liquidation may be prevented by making enough purchases prior to year end to restore the desired inventory level. Sometimes a LIFO liquidation cannot be avoided because products are discontinued or supplies are interrupted, as in the case of a strike. In a recent year, 28 of 600 large companies reported a LIFO liquidation in which net income was increased because of the matching of older historical cost with present sales dollars.[7]

Effects of Misstatements in Inventory Measurement

The basic problem of separating goods available for sale into two components—goods sold and goods not sold—is that of assigning a cost to the goods not sold, the ending inventory. The portion of the goods available for sale not assigned to the ending inventory is used to determine the cost of goods sold.

Because the figures for ending inventory and cost of goods sold are related, a misstatement in the inventory figure at the end of the period will cause an equal misstatement in gross margin and income before income taxes in the income statement. The amount of assets and owners' equity on the balance sheet will also be misstated by the same amount. The consequences of overstatement and understatement of inventory are illustrated in the three simplified examples that follow. In each case, beginning inventory, net purchases, and cost of goods available for sale have been stated correctly. In the first example, ending inventory has been stated correctly. In the second example, ending inventory is overstated by $6,000; in the third example, ending inventory is understated by $6,000.

Example 1. Ending Inventory Correctly Stated at $10,000

Cost of Goods Sold for the Year		Income Statement for the Year	
Beginning Inventory	$12,000	Net Sales	$100,000
Net Cost of Purchases	58,000	Cost of Goods Sold	60,000
Cost of Goods Available for Sale	$70,000	Gross Margin	$ 40,000
Ending Inventory	10,000	Operating Expenses	32,000
Cost of Goods Sold	$60,000	Income Before Income Taxes	$ 8,000

Key Point: A misstatement in inventory affects not only the current year but also has the opposite effect on the next year.

Example 2. Ending Inventory Overstated by $6,000

Cost of Goods Sold for the Year		Income Statement for the Year	
Beginning Inventory	$12,000	Net Sales	$100,000
Net Cost of Purchases	58,000	Cost of Goods Sold	54,000
Cost of Goods Available for Sale	$70,000	Gross Margin	$ 46,000
Ending Inventory	16,000	Operating Expenses	32,000
Cost of Goods Sold	$54,000	Income Before Income Taxes	$ 14,000

Example 3. Ending Inventory Understated by $6,000

Cost of Goods Sold for the Year		Income Statement for the Year	
Beginning Inventory	$12,000	Net Sales	$100,000
Net Cost of Purchases	58,000	Cost of Goods Sold	66,000
Cost of Goods Available for Sale	$70,000	Gross Margin	$ 34,000
Ending Inventory	4,000	Operating Expenses	32,000
Cost of Goods Sold	$66,000	Income Before Income Taxes	$ 2,000

In all three examples, the total cost of goods available for sale was $70,000. The difference in income before income taxes resulted from how this $70,000 was divided between ending inventory and cost of goods sold.

Because the ending inventory in one period becomes the beginning inventory in the following period, it is important to recognize that a misstatement in inventory valuation affects not only the current period but also the following period. Over a two-year period, the errors in income before income taxes will offset, or counterbalance, each other. In Example **2** above, for instance, the overstatement of ending

inventory in 20x1 caused a $6,000 overstatement of beginning inventory in the following year, resulting in an understatement of income by $6,000 in the second year. This offsetting effect is illustrated in Table 1.

Because the total income before income taxes for the two years is the same, it may appear that one need not worry about inventory misstatements. However, the misstatements violate the matching rule. In addition, management, creditors, and investors make many decisions on an annual basis and depend on the accountant's determination of net income. The accountant has an obligation to make the net income figure for each year as useful as possible.

The effects of misstatements in inventory on income before income taxes are as follows:

Year 1	Year 2
Ending inventory overstated	**Beginning inventory overstated**
Cost of goods sold understated	Cost of goods sold overstated
Income before income taxes overstated	Income before income taxes understated
Ending inventory understated	**Beginning inventory understated**
Cost of goods sold overstated	Cost of goods sold understated
Income before income taxes understated	Income before income taxes overstated

A misstatement in inventory results in a misstatement in income before income taxes of the same amount. Thus the measurement of inventory is important.

Key Point: Inventory errors will correct (counterbalance) themselves over a two-year period.

Table 1. Ending Inventory Overstated by $6,000

	With Inventory Correctly Stated	With Inventory at Dec. 31, 20x1, Overstated	
		Reported Income Before Income Taxes Will Be	Reported Income Before Income Taxes Will Be Overstated (Understated)
Income Before Income Taxes for 20x1	$ 8,000	$14,000	$6,000
Income Before Income Taxes for 20x2	15,000	9,000	(6,000)
Total Income Before Income Taxes for Two Years	$23,000	$23,000	—

Inventory Measurement and Cash Flows

A company's inventory methods affect not only its reported profitability but also its reported liquidity and cash flows. In the case of a large company like International Paper Co., these effects can be complex and material. In a note on inventories, International Paper provides more detail on these effects:

> The company uses the last-in, first-out inventory method to value substantially all of its domestic inventories. Approximately 74% of the company's total raw materials and finished products inventories were valued using this method. If the first-in, first-out method had been used, it would have increased total inventory balances by approximately $253 million, $228 million and $227 million at December 31, 1997, 1996, and 1995, respectively.[9]

By using LIFO, the company usually reports a lower income before taxes. This will have a favorable effect on cash flows because of the lower amount of income taxes to be paid. The reader of the financial statements may determine what International Paper's inventory value would have been if it were valued at current prices under FIFO rather than older prices under LIFO. More realistic comparison of the company's liquidity ratios may be made. For example, the more realistic FIFO figure would show a better short-term liquidity position as measured by the current ratio than the reported LIFO figures on the face of the balance sheet would seem to indicate. However, the company's inventory turnover and average days' inventory on hand will be adversely affected if the more realistic figures are used.

Valuing Inventory at the Lower of Cost or Market (LCM)

OBJECTIVE

6 Apply the lower-of-cost-or-market (LCM) rule to inventory valuation

Although cost is usually the most appropriate basis for valuation of inventory, there are times when inventory may properly be shown in the financial statements at less than its cost. If by reason of physical deterioration, obsolescence, or decline in price level the market value of inventory falls below its cost, a loss has occurred. This loss may be recognized by writing the inventory down to **market** or current replacement cost of inventory. For a merchandising company, market is the amount that the company would pay at the present time for the same goods, purchased from the usual suppliers and in the usual quantities. The **lower-of-cost-or-market (LCM) rule** requires that when the replacement cost of inventory falls below historical cost, the inventory is written down to the lower value and a loss is recorded. This rule is an example of the application of the convention of conservatism because the loss is recognized before an actual transaction takes place. Under historical cost accounting, the inventory remains at cost until it is sold. It may help in applying the LCM rule to think of it as the "lower-of-cost-or-replacement-cost" rule.[10] Approximately 90 percent of 600 large companies report applying the LCM rule to their inventories.[11]

Key Point: The accounting convention of conservatism supports the lower-of-cost-or-market rule.

Study Note: Cost must first be determined by the specific identification, FIFO, LIFO, or average-cost method before it can be compared with market cost.

There are two basic methods of valuing inventories at the lower of cost or market accepted both by GAAP and for federal income tax purposes: (1) the item-by-item method and (2) the major category method. For example, a stereo shop could determine lower of cost or market for each kind of speaker, receiver, and turntable (item by item) or for all speakers, all receivers, and all turntables (major categories).

Table 2. Lower of Cost or Market with Item-by-Item Method

	Quantity	Per Unit Cost	Per Unit Market	Lower of Cost or Market
Category I				
Item a	200	$1.50	$1.70	$ 300
Item b	100	2.00	1.80	180
Item c	100	2.50	2.60	250
Category II				
Item d	300	5.00	4.50	1,350
Item e	200	4.00	4.10	800
Inventory at the lower of cost or market				$2,880

Item-by-Item Method

When the **item-by-item method** is used, cost and market values are compared for each item in inventory. Each individual item is then valued at its lower price (see Table 2).

Major Category Method

Under the **major category method**, the total cost and total market values for each category of items are compared. Each category is then valued at its lower amount (see Table 3).

Table 3. Lower of Cost or Market with Major Category Method

	Quantity	Per Unit Cost	Per Unit Market	Total Cost	Total Market	Lower of Cost or Market
Category I						
Item a	200	$1.50	$1.70	$ 300	$ 340	
Item b	100	2.00	1.80	200	180	
Item c	100	2.50	2.60	250	260	
Totals				$ 750	$ 780	$ 750
Category II						
Item d	300	5.00	4.50	$1,500	$1,350	
Item e	200	4.00	4.10	800	820	
Totals				$2,300	$2,170	2,170
Inventory at the lower of cost or market						$2,920

Valuing Inventory by Estimation

It is sometimes necessary or desirable to estimate the value of ending inventory. The methods most commonly used for this purpose are the retail method and the gross profit method.

Retail Method of Inventory Estimation

SUPPLEMENTAL OBJECTIVE

7a Estimate the cost of ending inventory using the retail inventory method

The **retail method**, as its name implies, is used in retail merchandising businesses to estimate the cost of ending inventory by using the ratio of cost to retail price. There are two principal reasons for its use. First, management usually requires that financial statements be prepared at least once a month. As taking a physical inventory is time-consuming and expensive, the retail method is used instead to estimate the value of inventory on hand. Second, because items in a retail store normally have a price tag or a universal product code, it is a common practice to take the physical inventory at retail from these price tags and codes and reduce the total value to cost through use of the retail method. The term *at retail* means the amount of the inventory at the marked selling prices of the inventory items.

Key Point: When estimating inventory by the retail method, the inventory need not be counted.

When the retail method is used to estimate ending inventory, the records must show the beginning inventory at cost and at retail. The records must also show the amount of goods purchased during the period both at cost and at retail. The net sales at retail is, of course, the balance of the Sales account less returns and allowances. A simple example of the retail method is shown in Table 4.

Goods available for sale is determined both at cost and at retail by listing beginning inventory and net purchases for the period at cost and at their expected selling price, adding freight to the cost column, and totaling. The ratio of these two amounts (cost to retail price) provides an estimate of the cost of each dollar of retail sales value. The estimated ending inventory at retail is then determined by deducting sales for the period from the retail price of the goods that were available for sale during the period. The inventory at retail is then converted to cost on the basis of the ratio of cost to retail.

Study Note: Freight In is not placed under the Retail column when using the retail method of inventory valuation because businesses automatically price their goods high enough to cover freight charges.

Table 4. Retail Method of Inventory Valuation

	Cost	Retail
Beginning Inventory	$ 40,000	$ 55,000
Net Purchases for the Period (excluding Freight In)	107,000	145,000
Freight In	3,000	
Merchandise Available for Sale	$150,000	$200,000
Ratio of Cost to Retail Price: $\dfrac{\$150,000}{\$200,000} = 75\%$		
Net Sales During the Period		160,000
Estimated Ending Inventory at Retail		$ 40,000
Ratio of Cost to Retail	75%	
Estimated Cost of Ending Inventory	$ 30,000	

Table 5. Gross Profit Method of Inventory Valuation

1. Beginning Inventory at Cost		$ 50,000
Purchases at Cost (including Freight In)		290,000
Cost of Goods Available for Sale		$340,000
2. Less Estimated Cost of Goods Sold		
Sales at Selling Price	$400,000	
Less Estimated Gross Margin of 30%	120,000	
Estimated Cost of Goods Sold		280,000
3. Estimated Cost of Ending Inventory		$ 60,000

The cost of ending inventory may also be estimated by applying the ratio of cost to retail price to the total retail value of the physical count of the ending inventory. Applying the retail method in practice is often more difficult than this simple example because of such complications as changes in retail price during the year, different markups on different types of merchandise, and varying volumes of sales for different types of merchandise.

Gross Profit Method of Inventory Estimation

SUPPLEMENTAL OBJECTIVE

7b Estimate the cost of ending inventory using the gross profit method

Terminology Note: The gross profit method is also known as the *gross margin method.*

Business-World Example: It is highly desirable to maintain financial records off site. If records were destroyed, it would be difficult, if not impossible, to reconstruct the data necessary for an insurance claim.

The **gross profit method** assumes that the ratio of gross margin for a business remains relatively stable from year to year. The gross profit method is used in place of the retail method when records of the retail prices of beginning inventory and purchases are not kept. It is considered acceptable for estimating the cost of inventory for interim reports, but it is not acceptable for valuing inventory in the annual financial statements. It is also useful in estimating the amount of inventory lost or destroyed by theft, fire, or other hazards. Insurance companies often use this method to verify loss claims.

The gross profit method is simple to use. First, figure the cost of goods available for sale in the usual way (add purchases to beginning inventory). Second, estimate the cost of goods sold by deducting the estimated gross margin from sales. Finally, deduct the estimated cost of goods sold from the goods available for sale to arrive at the estimated cost of ending inventory. This method is shown in Table 5.

Chapter Review

REVIEW OF LEARNING OBJECTIVES

Ace it

1. Identify and explain the management issues associated with accounting for inventories. Included in inventory are goods owned, whether produced or purchased, that are held for sale in the normal course of business. Manufacturing companies also include raw materials and work in process. Among the issues management must face in accounting for inventories are allocating the cost of inventories in accordance with the matching rule, assessing the impact of inventory decisions, and evaluating the levels of inventory. The objective of accounting for inventories is the proper determination of income through the matching of costs and revenues, not the determination of the most realistic inventory value. Because the valuation of inventory has a direct effect on a company's net income, the choice of inventory systems and methods affects not only the amount of income taxes and cash flows but also the external and internal evaluation of the company. The level of inventory as measured by the inventory turnover and its related measure, average days' inventory on hand, is important to managing the amount of investment needed by a company.

2. **Define *inventory cost* and relate it to goods flow and cost flow.** The cost of inventory includes (1) invoice price less purchases discounts; (2) freight or transportation in, including insurance in transit; and (3) applicable taxes and tariffs. Goods flow relates to the actual physical flow of merchandise, whereas cost flow refers to the assumed flow of costs in the operations of the business.

3. **Calculate the pricing of inventory, using the cost basis under the periodic inventory system, according to the (a) specific identification method; (b) average-cost method; (c) first-in, first-out (FIFO) method; and (d) last-in, first-out (LIFO) method.** The value assigned to ending inventory is the result of two measurements: quantity and price. Quantity is determined by taking a physical inventory. The pricing of inventory is usually based on the assumed cost flow of the goods as they are bought and sold. One of four assumptions is usually made regarding cost flow. These assumptions are represented by four inventory methods. Inventory pricing can be determined by the specific identification method, which associates the actual cost with each item of inventory, but this method is rarely used. The average-cost method assumes that the cost of inventory is the average cost of goods available for sale during the period. The first-in, first-out (FIFO) method assumes that the costs of the first items acquired should be assigned to the first items sold. The last-in, first-out (LIFO) method assumes that the costs of the last items acquired should be assigned to the first items sold. The inventory method chosen may or may not be equivalent to the actual physical flow of goods.

4. **Apply the perpetual inventory system to the pricing of inventories at cost.** The pricing of inventories under the perpetual inventory system differs from pricing under the periodic system because under the perpetual system a continuous record of quantities and costs of merchandise is maintained as purchases and sales are made. Cost of goods sold is accumulated as sales are made and costs are transferred from the Inventory account to Cost of Goods Sold. The cost of the ending inventory is the balance of the Inventory account. Under the perpetual inventory system, the specific identification method and the FIFO method will produce the same results as under the periodic method. The results will differ for the average-cost method because a moving average is calculated prior to each sale rather than at the end of the accounting period, and for the LIFO method because the cost components of inventory change constantly as goods are bought and sold.

5. **State the effects of inventory methods and misstatements of inventory on income determination, income taxes, and cash flows.** During periods of rising prices, the LIFO method will show the lowest net income; FIFO, the highest; and average cost, in between. The opposite effects occur in periods of falling prices. No generalization can be made regarding the specific identification method. The Internal Revenue Service requires that if LIFO is used for tax purposes, it must also be used for financial statement purposes, and that the lower-of-cost-or-market rule cannot be applied to the LIFO method. If the value of ending inventory is understated or overstated, a corresponding error—dollar for dollar—will be made in income before income taxes. Furthermore, because the ending inventory of one period is the beginning inventory of the

next, the misstatement affects two accounting periods, although the effects are opposite.

6. **Apply the lower-of-cost-or-market (LCM) rule to inventory valuation.** The lower-of-cost-or-market rule can be applied to the above methods of determining inventory at cost. This rule states that if the replacement cost (market) of the inventory is lower than the inventory cost, the lower figure should be used. Valuation can be determined on an item-by-item or major category basis.

SUPPLEMENTAL OBJECTIVE

7. **Estimate the cost of ending inventory using the (a) retail inventory method and (b) gross profit method.** Two methods of estimating the value of inventory are the retail inventory method and the gross profit method. Under the retail inventory method, inventory is determined at retail prices and is then reduced to estimated cost by applying a ratio of cost to retail price. Under the gross profit method, cost of goods sold is estimated by reducing sales by estimated gross margin. The estimated cost of goods sold is then deducted from the cost of goods available for sale to estimate the inventory.

REVIEW OF CONCEPTS AND TERMINOLOGY

The following concepts and terms were introduced in this chapter:

LO 3 **Average-cost method:** An inventory costing method in which inventory is priced at the average cost of the goods available for sale during the period.

LO 1 **Average days' inventory on hand:** The average number of days required to sell the inventory on hand; number of days in a year divided by inventory turnover.

LO 2 **Consignment:** Merchandise placed by its owner (the *consignor*) on the premises of another company (the *consignee*) with the understanding that payment is expected only when the merchandise is sold and that unsold items may be returned to the consignor.

LO 2 **Cost flow:** The association of costs with their assumed flow in the operations of a company.

LO 3 **First-in, first-out (FIFO) method:** An inventory costing method based on the assumption that the costs of the first items acquired should be assigned to the first items sold.

LO 2 **Goods flow:** The actual physical movement of goods in the operations of a company.

SO 7 **Gross profit method:** A method of inventory estimation based on the assumption that the ratio of gross margin for a business remains relatively stable from year to year.

LO 2 **Inventory cost:** The price paid or consideration given to acquire an asset; includes invoice price less purchases discounts, plus freight or transportation in, and plus applicable taxes and tariffs.

LO 1 **Inventory turnover:** A ratio indicating the number of times a company's average inventory is sold during an accounting period; cost of goods sold divided by average inventory.

LO 6 **Item-by-item method:** A lower-of-cost-or-market method of valuing inventory in which cost and market values are compared for each item in inventory, with each item then valued at its lower price.

LO 1 **Just-in-time operating environment:** An inventory management system in which companies seek to reduce their levels of inventory by working closely with suppliers to coordinate and schedule deliveries so that goods arrive just at the time they are needed.

LO 3 **Last-in, first-out (LIFO) method:** An inventory costing method based on the assumption that the costs of the last items purchased should be assigned to the first items sold.

LO 5 **LIFO liquidation:** The reduction of inventory below previous levels so that income is increased by the amount by which current prices exceed the historical cost of the inventory under LIFO.

LO 6 **Lower-of-cost-or-market (LCM) rule:** A method of valuing inventory at an amount below cost if the replacement (market) value is less than cost.

LO 6 **Major category method:** A lower-of-cost-or-market method of valuing inventory in which the total cost and total market values for each category of items are compared, with each category then valued at its lower amount.

LO 6 **Market:** Current replacement cost of inventory.

LO 1 **Merchandise inventory:** All goods owned and held for sale in the regular course of business.

SO 7 **Retail method:** A method of inventory estimation, used in retail merchandising businesses, under which inventory at retail value is reduced by the ratio of cost to retail price.

LO 3 **Specific identification method:** An inventory costing method in which the price of inventory is computed by identifying the cost of each item in ending inventory as coming from a specific purchase.

REVIEW PROBLEM

Periodic and Perpetual Inventory Systems

LO 1
LO 3
LO 4

The table below summarizes the beginning inventory, purchases, and sales of Psi Company's single product during January.

	Beginning Inventory and Purchases			
Date	Units	Cost	Total	Sales Units
Jan. 1 Inventory	1,400	$19	$26,600	
4 Sale				300
8 Purchase	600	20	12,000	
10 Sale				1,300
12 Purchase	900	21	18,900	
15 Sale				150
18 Purchase	500	22	11,000	
24 Purchase	800	23	18,400	
31 Sale				1,350
Totals	4,200		$86,900	3,100

REQUIRED

1. Assuming that the company uses the periodic inventory system, compute the cost that should be assigned to ending inventory and to cost of goods sold using (a) the average-cost method, (b) the FIFO method, and (c) the LIFO method.

2. Assuming that the company uses the perpetual inventory system, compute the cost that should be assigned to ending inventory and to cost of goods sold using (a) the average-cost method, (b) the FIFO method, and (c) the LIFO method.

3. Compute inventory turnover and average days' inventory on hand under each of the inventory cost flow assumptions in **1.** What conclusion can be made from this comparison?

	Units	Amount
Beginning Inventory	1,400	$26,600
Purchases	2,800	60,300
Available for Sale	4,200	$86,900
Sales	3,100	
Ending Inventory	1,100	

ANSWER TO REVIEW PROBLEM

1. Periodic inventory system:
   a. Average-cost method

Cost of goods available for sale	$86,900
Less Ending inventory consists of 1,100 units at $20.69*	22,759
Cost of goods sold	$64,141

   *$86,900 ÷ 4,200 = $20.69 (rounded)

   b. FIFO method

Cost of goods available for sale		$86,900
Less Ending inventory consists of		
January 24 purchase (800 × $23)	$18,400	
January 18 purchase (300 × $22)	6,600	25,000
Cost of goods sold		$61,900

   c. LIFO method

Cost of goods available for sale	$86,900
Less Ending inventory consists of Beginning inventory (1,100 × $19)	20,900
Cost of goods sold	$66,000

2. Perpetual inventory system:
   a. Average-cost method

Date		Units	Cost*	Amount*
Jan. 1	Inventory	1,400	$19.00	$26,600
4	Sale	(300)	19.00	(5,700)
4	Balance	1,100	19.00	$20,900
8	Purchase	600	20.00	12,000
8	Balance	1,700	19.35	$32,900
10	Sale	(1,300)	19.35	(25,155)
10	Balance	400	19.36	$ 7,745
12	Purchase	900	21.00	18,900
12	Balance	1,300	20.50	$26,645
15	Sale	(150)	20.50	(3,075)
15	Balance	1,150	20.50	$23,570
18	Purchase	500	22.00	11,000
24	Purchase	800	23.00	18,400
24	Balance	2,450	21.62	$52,970
31	Sale	(1,350)	21.62	(29,187)
31	Inventory	1,100	21.62	$23,783

   Cost of Goods Sold: $5,700 + $25,155 + $3,075 + $29,187 = $63,117

   *Rounded

b. FIFO method

Date		Units	Cost*	Amount*
Jan. 1	Inventory	1,400	$19	$26,600
4	Sale	(300)	19	(5,700)
4	Balance	1,100	19	$20,900
8	Purchase	600	20	12,000
8	Balance	1,100	19	
		600	20	$32,900
10	Sale	(1,100)	19	
		(200)	20	(24,900)
10	Balance	400	20	$ 8,000
12	Purchase	900	21	18,900
12	Balance	400	20	
		900	21	$26,900
15	Sale	(150)	20	(3,000)
15	Balance	250	20	
		900	21	$23,900
18	Purchase	500	22	11,000
24	Purchase	800	23	18,400
24	Balance	250	20	
		900	21	
		500	22	
		800	23	$53,300
31	Sale	(250)	20	
		(900)	21	
		(200)	22	(28,300)
31	Inventory	300	22	
		800	23	$25,000

Cost of Goods Sold: $5,700 + $24,900 + $3,000 + $28,300 = $61,900

c. LIFO method

Date		Units	Cost*	Amount*
Jan. 1	Inventory	1,400	$19	$26,600
4	Sale	(300)	19	(5,700)
4	Balance	1,100	19	$20,900
8	Purchase	600	20	12,000
8	Balance	1,100	19	
		600	20	$32,900
10	Sale	(600)	20	
		(700)	19	(25,300)
10	Balance	400	19	$ 7,600
12	Purchase	900	21	18,900
12	Balance	400	19	
		900	21	$26,500
15	Sale	(150)	21	(3,150)
15	Balance	400	19	
		750	21	$23,350
18	Purchase	500	22	11,000
24	Purchase	800	23	18,400

*Rounded

Jan. 24	Balance	400	19		
		750	21		
		500	22		
		800	23	$52,750	
31	Sale	(800)	23		
		(500)	22		
		(50)	21	(30,450)	
31	Inventory	400	19		
		700	21	$22,300	

Cost of Goods Sold: $5,700 + $25,300 + $3,150 + $30,450 = $64,600

3. Ratios computed:

	Average-Cost	FIFO	LIFO
Cost of goods sold	$64,141	$61,900	$66,000
Average inventory	$24,680*	$25,800	$23,750
	($22,759 + $26,600) ÷ 2	($25,000 + $26,600) ÷ 2	($20,900 + $26,600) ÷ 2
Inventory turnover	2.6 times	2.4 times	2.8 times
	($64,141 ÷ $24,680)	($61,900 ÷ $25,800)	($66,000 ÷ $23,750)
Average days' inventory on hand	140.4 days	152.1 days	130.4 days
	(365 days ÷ 2.6 times)	(365 days ÷ 2.4 times)	(365 days ÷ 2.8 times)

In periods of rising prices, the LIFO method will always result in a higher inventory turnover and lower average days' inventory on hand. When comparing inventory ratios for two or more companies, the inventory methods used by the companies should be considered.

*Rounded

Chapter Assignments

BUILDING YOUR KNOWLEDGE FOUNDATION

QUESTIONS

1. What is merchandise inventory, and what is the primary objective of inventory measurement?
2. How does inventory for a manufacturing company differ from that for a merchandising company?
3. Why is the level of inventory important, and what are two common measures of inventory level?
4. What items should be included in the cost of inventory?
5. Fargo Sales Company is very busy at the end of its fiscal year on June 30. There is an order for 130 units of product in the warehouse. Although the shipping department tries, it cannot ship the product by June 30, and title has not yet passed. Should the 130 units be included in the year-end count of inventory? Why or why not?
6. What is the difference between goods flow and cost flow?
7. Do the FIFO and LIFO inventory methods result in different quantities of ending inventory?
8. Under which method of cost flow are (a) the earliest costs assigned to inventory, (b) the latest costs assigned to inventory, and (c) the average costs assigned to inventory?

9. What are the relative advantages and disadvantages of FIFO and LIFO from management's point of view?

10. Why do you think it is more expensive to maintain a perpetual inventory system?

11. In periods of steadily rising prices, which inventory method—average-cost, FIFO, or LIFO—will give the (a) highest ending inventory cost, (b) lowest ending inventory cost, (c) highest net income, and (d) lowest net income?

12. May a company change its inventory cost method from year to year? Explain.

13. What is the relationship between income tax rules and inventory valuation methods?

14. If the merchandise inventory is mistakenly overstated at the end of 20x0, what is the effect on the (a) 20x0 net income, (b) 20x0 year-end balance sheet value, (c) 20x1 net income, and (d) 20x1 year-end balance sheet value?

15. In the phrase *lower of cost or market*, what is meant by the word *market*?

16. What methods can be used to determine the lower of cost or market?

17. Does using the retail inventory method mean that inventories are measured at retail value on the balance sheet? Explain.

18. For what reasons might management use the gross profit method of estimating inventory?

19. Which of the following inventory systems or methods do not require the taking of a physical inventory: (a) perpetual, (b) periodic, (c) retail, and (d) gross profit?

SHORT EXERCISES

SE 1.
LO 1   Management Issues

Indicate whether each item listed below is associated with (a) allocating the cost of inventories in accordance with the matching rule, (b) assessing the impact of inventory decisions, or (c) evaluating the level of inventory.

1. Calculating the average days' inventory on hand
2. Ordering a supply of inventory to satisfy customer needs
3. Calculating the income tax effect of an inventory method
4. Deciding the cost to place on ending inventory

SE 2.
LO 1   Inventory Turnover and Average Days' Inventory on Hand

During 20x1, Certeen Clothiers had beginning inventory of $240,000, ending inventory of $280,000, and cost of goods sold of $1,100,000. Compute the inventory turnover and average days' inventory on hand.

SE 3.
LO 3   Specific Identification Method

Assume the following data with regard to inventory for Alexis Company:

Aug. 1 Inventory	80 units @ $10 per unit	$ 800
8 Purchase	100 units @ $11 per unit	1,100
22 Purchase	70 units @ $12 per unit	840
Goods Available for Sale	250 units	$2,740
Aug. 15 Sale	90 units	
28 Sale	50 units	
Inventory, August 31	110 units	

Assuming that the inventory consists of 60 units from the August 8 purchase and 50 units from the purchase of August 22, calculate the cost of ending inventory and cost of goods sold.

SE 4.
LO 3   Average-Cost Method— Periodic Inventory System

Using the data in **SE 3,** calculate the cost of ending inventory and cost of goods sold according to the average-cost method under the periodic inventory system.

SE 5. **LO 3** FIFO Method—Periodic Inventory System	Using the data in **SE 3,** calculate the cost of ending inventory and cost of goods sold according to the FIFO method under the periodic inventory system.
SE 6. **LO 3** LIFO Method—Periodic Inventory System	Using the data in **SE 3,** calculate the cost of ending inventory and cost of goods sold according to the LIFO method under the periodic inventory system.
SE 7. **LO 4** Average-Cost Method— Perpetual Inventory System	Using the data in **SE 3,** calculate the cost of ending inventory and cost of goods sold according to the average-cost method under the perpetual inventory system.
SE 8. **LO 4** FIFO Method—Perpetual Inventory System	Using the data in **SE 3,** calculate the cost of ending inventory and cost of goods sold according to the FIFO method under the perpetual inventory system.
SE 9. **LO 4** LIFO Method—Perpetual Inventory System	Using the data in **SE 3,** calculate the cost of ending inventory and cost of goods sold according to the LIFO method under the perpetual inventory system.
SE 10. **LO 5** Effects of Methods and Changing Prices	Following the pattern of Exhibit 1, prepare a table with seven columns that shows the ending inventory and cost of goods sold for each of the results from your calculations in **SE 3** through **SE 9.** Comment on the results, including the effects of the different prices at which the merchandise was purchased. Which method(s) would result in the lowest income taxes?

SE 11.

LO 6 Lower of Cost or Market

The following schedule is based on a physical inventory and replacement costs for one product line of men's shirts:

Item	Quantity	Cost per Unit	Market per Unit
Short sleeve	280	$24	$20
Long sleeve	190	28	29
Extra-long sleeve	80	34	35

Determine the value of this category of inventory at the lower of cost or market using (1) the item-by-item method and (2) the major category method.

EXERCISES

E 1.

LO 1 Management Issues Related
to Inventory

Indicate whether each item listed below is associated with (a) allocating the cost of inventories in accordance with the matching rule, (b) assessing the impact of inventory decisions, or (c) evaluating the level of inventory.

1. Computing inventory turnover
2. Application of the just-in-time operating environment
3. Determining the effects of inventory decisions on cash flows
4. Apportioning the cost of goods available for sale to ending inventory and cost of goods sold
5. Determining the effects of inventory methods on income taxes
6. Determining the assumption about the flow of costs into and out of the company

E 2.

LO 1 Inventory Ratios

Dollar Discount Stores is assessing its levels of inventory for 20x2 and 20x3 and has gathered the following data:

	20x3	20x2	20x1
Ending inventory	$128,000	$108,000	$92,000
Cost of goods sold	640,000	600,000	

Compute the inventory turnover and average days' inventory on hand for 20x2 and 20x3 and comment on the results.

E 3.

LO 3 Periodic Inventory System and Inventory Costing Methods

Ray's Farm Store recorded the following purchases and sales of fertilizer during the year:

Jan. 1	Beginning Inventory	250 cases @ $23	$ 5,750
Feb. 25	Purchased	100 cases @ $26	2,600
June 15	Purchased	400 cases @ $28	11,200
Aug. 15	Purchased	100 cases @ $26	2,600
Oct. 15	Purchased	300 cases @ $28	8,400
Dec. 15	Purchased	200 cases @ $30	6,000
	Total Goods Available for Sale	1,350	$36,550
	Total Sales	1,000 cases	
Dec. 31	Ending Inventory	350 cases	

Assume that all of the June 15 purchase and 200 cases each from the January 1 beginning inventory, the October 15 purchase, and the December 15 purchase were sold.

Determine the costs that should be assigned to ending inventory and cost of goods sold under each of the following assumptions: (1) costs are assigned by the specific identification method; (2) costs are assigned by the average-cost method; (3) costs are assigned by the FIFO method; (4) costs are assigned by the LIFO method. What conclusions can be drawn about the effect of each method on the income statement and the balance sheet of Ray's Farm Store? Round your answers to the nearest whole number and assume the periodic inventory system.

E 4.

LO 3 Periodic Inventory System and Inventory Costing Methods

During its first year of operation, Bellows Company purchased 5,600 units of a product at $21 per unit. During the second year, it purchased 6,000 units of the same product at $24 per unit. During the third year, it purchased 5,000 units at $30 per unit. Bellows Company managed to have an ending inventory each year of 1,000 units. The company uses the periodic inventory system.

Prepare cost of goods sold statements that compare the value of ending inventory and the cost of goods sold for each of the three years using (1) the FIFO method and (2) the LIFO method. From the resulting data, what conclusions can you draw about the relationships between changes in unit price and changes in the value of ending inventory?

E 5.

LO 3 Periodic Inventory System and Inventory Costing Methods

In chronological order, the inventory, purchases, and sales of a single product for a recent month are as follows:

		Units	Amount per Unit
June 1	Beginning Inventory	300	$30
4	Purchase	800	33
8	Sale	400	60
12	Purchase	1,000	36
16	Sale	700	60
20	Sale	500	66
24	Purchase	1,200	39
28	Sale	600	66
29	Sale	400	66

Using the periodic inventory system, compute the cost of ending inventory, cost of goods sold, and gross margin. Use the average-cost, FIFO, and LIFO inventory costing methods. Explain the differences in gross margin produced by the three methods. Round unit costs to cents and totals to dollars.

E 6.

**LO 4 Perpetual Inventory System
and Inventory Costing
Methods**

Using the data provided in **E 5** and assuming the perpetual inventory system, compute the cost of ending inventory, cost of goods sold, and gross margin. Use the average-cost, FIFO, and LIFO inventory costing methods. Explain the reasons for the differences in gross margin produced by the three methods. Round unit costs to cents and totals to dollars.

E 7.

**LO 3 Inventory Costing
LO 4 Methods: Periodic and
Perpetual Systems**

During July 20x1, Toan, Inc., sold 250 units of its product Velt for $4,000. The following units were available:

	Units	Cost
Beginning Inventory	100	$ 2
Purchase 1	40	4
Purchase 2	60	6
Purchase 3	70	8
Purchase 4	80	10
Purchase 5	90	12

A sale of 100 units was made after purchase 1, and a sale of 150 units was made after purchase 4. Of the units sold, 100 came from beginning inventory and 150 from purchases 3 and 4.

Determine cost of goods available for sale and ending inventory in units. Then determine the costs that should be assigned to cost of goods sold and ending inventory under each of the following assumptions: (1) Costs are assigned under the periodic inventory system using (a) the specific identification method, (b) the average-cost method, (c) the FIFO method, and (d) the LIFO method. (2) Costs are assigned under the perpetual inventory system using (a) the average-cost method, (b) the FIFO method, and (c) the LIFO method. For each alternative, show the gross margin. Round unit costs to cents and totals to dollars.

E 8.

**LO 5 Effects of Inventory Methods
on Cash Flows**

Won Products, Inc., sold 120,000 cases of glue at $40 per case during 20x1. Its beginning inventory consisted of 20,000 cases at a cost of $24 per case. During 20x1, it purchased 60,000 cases at $28 per case and later 50,000 cases at $30 per case. Operating expenses were $1,100,000, and the applicable income tax rate was 30 percent.

Using the periodic inventory system, compute net income using the FIFO method and the LIFO method for costing inventory. Which alternative produces the larger cash flow? The company is considering a purchase of 10,000 cases at $30 per case just before the year end. What effect on net income and on cash flow will this proposed purchase have under each method? (**Hint:** What are the income tax consequences?)

E 9.

**LO 3 Inventory Costing
LO 5 Method Characteristics**

The lettered items in the list below represent inventory costing methods. Write the letter of the method that each of the following statements *best* describes.

a. Specific identification
b. Average-cost
c. First-in, first-out (FIFO)
d. Last-in, first-out (LIFO)

1. Matches recent costs with recent revenues
2. Assumes that each item of inventory is identifiable
3. Results in the most realistic balance sheet valuation
4. Results in the lowest net income in periods of deflation
5. Results in the lowest net income in periods of inflation
6. Matches the oldest costs with recent revenues
7. Results in the highest net income in periods of inflation
8. Results in the highest net income in periods of deflation
9. Tends to level out the effects of inflation
10. Is unpredictable as to the effects of inflation

E 10.

LO 5 Effects of Inventory Errors

Condensed income statements for Elan Company for two years are shown below.

	20x4	20x3
Sales	$126,000	$105,000
Cost of Goods Sold	75,000	54,000
Gross Margin	$ 51,000	$ 51,000
Operating Expenses	30,000	30,000
Income Before Income Taxes	$ 21,000	$ 21,000

After the end of 20x4, the company discovered that an error had resulted in a $9,000 understatement of the 20x3 ending inventory.

Compute the corrected income before income taxes for 20x3 and 20x4. What effect will the error have on income before income taxes and owners' equity for 20x5?

E 11.

LO 6 Lower-of-Cost-or-Market Rule

Rumore Company values its inventory, shown below, at the lower of cost or market. Compute Rumore's inventory value using (1) the item-by-item method and (2) the major category method.

		Per Unit	
	Quantity	Cost	Market
Category I			
Item aa	200	$ 2.00	$ 1.80
Item bb	240	4.00	4.40
Item cc	400	8.00	7.50
Category II			
Item dd	300	12.00	13.00
Item ee	400	18.00	18.20

E 12.

SO 7 Retail Inventory Method

Irene's Dress Shop had net retail sales of $500,000 during the current year. The following additional information was obtained from the accounting records:

	At Cost	At Retail
Beginning Inventory	$ 80,000	$120,000
Net Purchases (excluding Freight In)	280,000	440,000
Freight In	20,800	

1. Using the retail method, estimate the company's ending inventory at cost.

2. Assume that a physical inventory taken at year end revealed an inventory on hand of $36,000 at retail value. What is the estimated amount of inventory shrinkage (loss due to theft, damage, and so forth) at cost using the retail method?

E 13.

SO 7 Gross Profit Method

Lind Bales was at home watching television when he received a call from the fire department. His business was a total loss from fire. The insurance company asked him to prove his inventory loss. For the year, until the date of the fire, Lind's company had sales of $450,000 and purchases of $280,000. Freight in amounted to $13,700, and the beginning inventory was $45,000. It was Lind's custom to price goods to achieve a gross margin of 40 percent.

Compute Lind's estimated inventory loss.

PROBLEMS

P 1.

LO 1 Periodic Inventory
LO 3 System and Inventory Costing Methods

Lobo Company merchandises a single product called Piel. The following data represent beginning inventory and purchases of Piel during the past year: January 1 inventory, 68,000 units at $11.00; February purchases, 80,000 units at $12.00; March purchases, 160,000 units at $12.40; May purchases, 120,000 units at $12.60; July purchases,

200,000 units at $12.80; September purchases, 160,000 units at $12.60; and November purchases, 60,000 units at $13.00. Sales of Piel totaled 786,000 units at $20 per unit. Selling and administrative expenses totaled $5,102,000 for the year, and Lobo Company uses a periodic inventory system.

REQUIRED

1. Prepare a schedule to compute the cost of goods available for sale.

2. Compute income before income taxes under each of the following inventory cost flow assumptions: (a) the average-cost method; (b) the FIFO method; and (c) the LIFO method.

3. Compute inventory turnover and average days' inventory on hand under each of the inventory cost flow assumptions in **2.** What conclusion can be made from this comparison?

P 2.

LO 3 Periodic Inventory System and Inventory Methods

The inventory of Product EL and data on purchases and sales for a two-month period follow. The company closes its books at the end of each month. It uses a periodic inventory system.

June	1	Inventory	50 units @ $204
	5	Sale	30 units
	10	Purchase	100 units @ $220
	17	Sale	60 units
	30	Inventory	60 units
July	2	Purchase	100 units @ $216
	8	Sale	110 units
	14	Purchase	50 units @ $224
	18	Sale	40 units
	22	Purchase	60 units @ $234
	26	Sale	30 units
	30	Sale	20 units
	31	Inventory	70 units

REQUIRED

1. Compute the cost of ending inventory of Product EL on June 30 and July 31 using the average-cost method. In addition, determine cost of goods sold for June and July. Round unit costs to cents and totals to dollars.

2. Compute the cost of the ending inventory on June 30 and July 31 using the FIFO method. In addition, determine cost of goods sold for June and July.

3. Compute the cost of the ending inventory on June 30 and July 31 using the LIFO method. In addition, determine cost of goods sold for June and July.

P 3.

LO 4 Perpetual Inventory System and Inventory Methods

Use the data provided in **P 2,** but assume that the company uses the perpetual inventory system. (**Hint:** In preparing the solutions required below, it is helpful to determine the balance of inventory after each transaction, as shown in the Review Problem for this chapter.)

REQUIRED

1. Determine the cost of ending inventory and cost of goods sold for June and July using the average-cost method. Round unit costs to cents and totals to dollars.

2. Determine the cost of ending inventory and cost of goods sold for June and July using the FIFO method.

3. Determine the cost of ending inventory and cost of goods sold for June and July using the LIFO method.

P 4.

SO 7 Retail Inventory Method

Overland Company switched recently to the retail inventory method to estimate the cost of ending inventory. To test this method, the company took a physical inventory one month after its implementation. Cost, retail, and the physical inventory data are presented at the top of the next page.

	At Cost	At Retail
July 1 Beginning Inventory	$472,132	$ 622,800
Purchases	750,000	1,008,400
Purchases Returns and Allowances	(25,200)	(34,800)
Freight In	8,350	
Sales		1,060,000
Sales Returns and Allowances		(28,000)
July 31 Physical Inventory		508,200

REQUIRED

1. Prepare a schedule to estimate the dollar amount of Overland's July 31 inventory using the retail method.

2. Use Overland's cost ratio to reduce the retail value of the physical inventory to cost.

3. Calculate the estimated amount of inventory shortage at cost and at retail.

P 5.

SO 7   Gross Profit Method

Brandon Oil Products stores its oil field products in a West Texas warehouse. The warehouse and most of its inventory were completely destroyed by a tornado on April 27. The company found some of its records, but it does not keep perpetual inventory records. The warehouse manager must estimate the amount of the loss. He found the following information in the records:

Beginning Inventory, January 1	$1,320,000
Purchases, January 2 to April 27	780,000
Purchases Returns, January 2 to April 27	(30,000)
Freight In since January 2	16,000
Sales, January 2 to April 27	1,840,000
Sales Returns, January 2 to April 27	(40,000)

Inventory costing $420,000 was recovered and could be sold. The manager remembers that the average gross margin on oil field products is 48 percent.

REQUIRED

Prepare a schedule to estimate the inventory destroyed by the tornado.

ALTERNATE PROBLEMS

P 6.

LO 1   Periodic Inventory
LO 3   System and Inventory
Costing Methods

The Knapp Door Company sold 2,200 doors during 20x2 at $320 per door. Its beginning inventory on January 1 was 130 doors at $112. Purchases made during the year were as follows:

February	225 doors @ $124
April	350 doors @ $130
June	700 doors @ $140
August	300 doors @ $132
October	400 doors @ $136
November	250 doors @ $144

The company's selling and administrative expenses for the year were $202,000, and the company uses the periodic inventory system.

REQUIRED

1. Prepare a schedule to compute the cost of goods available for sale.

2. Compute income before income taxes under each of the following inventory cost flow assumptions: (a) the average-cost method; (b) the FIFO method; and (c) the LIFO method.

3. Compute inventory turnover and average days' inventory on hand under each of the inventory cost flow assumptions in **2.** What conclusion can be drawn from this comparison?

P 7.

LO 3   Periodic Inventory System
and Inventory Methods

The inventory, purchases, and sales of Product ISO for March and April follow. The company closes its books at the end of each month and uses a periodic inventory system.

Mar.	1	Inventory	60 units @ $49
	7	Sale	20 units
	10	Purchase	100 units @ $52
	19	Sale	70 units
	31	Inventory	70 units
Apr.	4	Purchase	120 units @ $53
	11	Sale	110 units
	15	Purchase	50 units @ $54
	23	Sale	80 units
	25	Purchase	100 units @ $55
	27	Sale	100 units
	30	Inventory	50 units

REQUIRED

1. Compute the cost of the ending inventory on March 31 and April 30 using the average-cost method. In addition, determine cost of goods sold for March and April. Round unit costs to cents and totals to dollars.

2. Compute the cost of the ending inventory on March 31 and April 30 using the FIFO method. In addition, determine cost of goods sold for March and April.

3. Compute the cost of the ending inventory on March 31 and April 30 using the LIFO method. In addition, determine cost of goods sold for March and April.

P 8.

LO 4   Perpetual Inventory System and Inventory Methods

Use the data provided in **P 7**, but assume that the company uses the perpetual inventory system. (**Hint:** In preparing the solutions required, it is helpful to determine the balance of inventory after each transaction, as shown in the Review Problem for this chapter.)

REQUIRED

1. Determine the cost of ending inventory and cost of goods sold for March and April using the average-cost method. Round unit costs to cents and totals to dollars.

2. Determine the cost of ending inventory and cost of goods sold for March and April using the FIFO method.

3. Determine the cost of ending inventory and cost of goods sold for March and April using the LIFO method.

EXPANDING YOUR CRITICAL THINKING, COMMUNICATION, AND INTERPERSONAL SKILLS

SKILLS DEVELOPMENT

Conceptual Analysis

SD 1.

LO 1   Evaluation of Inventory Levels

The Gap Inc. is one of the most important retailers of casual clothing for all members of the family. *Business Week* reports, "The Gap Inc. is hell-bent on becoming to apparel what McDonald's is to food." With more than 1,100 stores already open, the company plans to open about 150 new stores per year for the next half decade. How does the company stay ahead of the competition? "One way is through frequent replenishment

| Cash Flow | CD-ROM | Communication | Critical Thinking | Ethics | General Ledger | Group Activity | Hot Links to Real Companies | International | Internet | Key Ratio | Memo | Spreadsheet |

of mix-and-match inventory. That enables the company to clear out unpopular items fast—which prompts shoppers to check in on the new selections more often." The Gap replaces inventory 6.1 times a year.[12] That compares with 3.5 times at other specialty apparel stores. One way in which The Gap controls inventory is by applying a just-in-time operating environment. How many days of inventory does The Gap have on hand on average compared to the competition? Discuss why those comparisons are important to The Gap. (Think of as many business and financial reasons as you can.) What is a just-in-time operating environment? Why is it important to achieving a favorable inventory turnover?

SD 2.

LO 5 LIFO Inventory Method

Eighty-nine percent of paper companies use the LIFO inventory method for the costing of inventories, whereas only 10 percent of computer equipment companies use LIFO.[13] Describe the LIFO inventory method. What effects does it have on reported income, cash flows, and income taxes during periods of price changes? Discuss why the paper industry would use LIFO but most of the computer industry would not.

SD 3.

LO 5 Lower of Cost or Market
LO 6 and Conservatism

Mobil (now Exxon Mobil) Corporation adopted the LIFO inventory method for its U.S. operations in 1957, when crude oil prices were only about $3 per barrel, but it did not adopt LIFO for its international operations until 1982, when crude oil prices were more than $30 per barrel. In 1994, the company adopted the lower-of-LIFO-cost-or-market method and, as a result, took a $250 million charge to earnings when crude oil prices dropped precipitously to less than $20 per barrel. In 1998, when crude oil prices dropped to an average year-end price of $12.29 per barrel, the result was a $270 million inventory revaluation adjustment that lowered Mobil's reported earnings.[14] Explain why in this situation the lower-of-LIFO-cost-or-market method would result in the $270 million charge. Explain whether Mobil's domestic or international inventories would be more closely valued to market after the charge. Define the accounting convention of conservatism and tell how it explains the inconsistency between valuation of domestic and international inventories. In 2000, the price of oil recovered to more than $30 per barrel. What is the likely effect on inventory valuation and cost of goods sold under LIFO?

Ethical Dilemma

SD 4.

LO 1 Inventories, Income
LO 5 Determination, and Ethics

Flare, Inc., which has a December 31 year end, designs and sells fashions for young professional women. Sandra Mason, president of the company, feared that the forecasted 20x1 profitability goals would not be reached. She was pleased when Flare received a large order on December 30 from The Executive Woman, a retail chain of upscale stores for businesswomen. Mason immediately directed the controller to record the sale, which represented 13 percent of Flare's annual sales, but directed the inventory control department not to separate the goods for shipment until after January 1. Separated goods are not included in inventory because they have been sold. On December 31, the company's auditors arrived to observe the year-end taking of the physical inventory under the periodic inventory system. What will be the effect of Mason's action on Flare's 20x1 profitability? What will be the effect on 20x2 profitability? Was Mason's action ethical?

Research Activity

SD 5.

LO 2 Retail Business
LO 4 Inventories

Make an appointment to visit a local retail business—a grocery, clothing, book, music, or appliance store, for example—and interview the manager for 30 minutes about the company's inventory accounting system. The store may be a branch of a larger company. Find out answers to the following questions, summarize your findings in a paper to be handed in, and be prepared to discuss your results in class.

What is the physical flow of merchandise into the store, and what documents are used in connection with this flow?

What documents are prepared when merchandise is sold?

Does the store keep perpetual inventory records? If so, does it keep the records in units only, or does it keep track of cost as well? If not, what system does the store use?

How often does the company take a physical inventory?

How are financial statements generated for the store?

What method does the company use to cost its inventory for financial statements?

Group Activity: Assign teams to various types of businesses in your community.

Decision-Making Practice

SD 6.

LO 5 **Inventory Methods, Income Taxes, and Cash Flows**

The ***Osaka Trading Company*** began business in 20x1 for the purpose of importing and marketing an electronic component used widely in digital appliances. It is now December 20, 20x1, and management is considering its options. Among its considerations is which inventory method to choose. It has decided to choose either the FIFO or the LIFO method. Under the periodic inventory system, the effects on net income of using the two methods are as follows:

	FIFO Method	LIFO Method
Sales: 500,000 units × $12	$6,000,000	$6,000,000
Cost of Goods Sold		
Purchases		
200,000 × $4	$ 800,000	$ 800,000
400,000 × $6	2,400,000	2,400,000
Total Purchases	$3,200,000	$3,200,000
Less Ending Inventory		
FIFO: 100,000 × $6	(600,000)	
LIFO: 100,000 × $4		(400,000)
Cost of Goods Sold	$2,600,000	$2,800,000
Gross Margin	$3,400,000	$3,200,000
Operating Expenses	2,400,000	2,400,000
Income Before Income Taxes	$1,000,000	$ 800,000
Income Taxes	300,000	240,000
Net Income	$ 700,000	$ 560,000

Also, management has an option to purchase an additional 100,000 units of inventory before year end at a price of $8 per unit, the price that is expected to prevail during 20x2. The income tax rate applicable to the company in 20x1 is 30 percent.

Business conditions are expected to be favorable in 20x2, as they were in 20x1. Management has asked you for advice. Analyze the effects of making the additional purchase. Then prepare a memorandum to Osaka management in which you compare cash outcomes under the four alternatives and advise management which inventory method to choose and whether to order the additional inventory. Be prepared to discuss your recommendations.

SD 7.

LO 3 **FIFO versus LIFO**
LO 5 **Analysis**

Refrigerated Truck Sales Company (RTS Company) buys large refrigerated trucks from the manufacturer and sells them to companies and independent truckers who haul perishable goods for long distances. RTS has been successful in this specialized niche of the industry because it provides a unique product and service. Because of the high cost of the trucks and of financing inventory, RTS tries to maintain as small an inventory as possible. In fact, at the beginning of July the company had no inventory or liabilities, as shown by the balance sheet at the top of the next page.

On July 9, RTS takes delivery of a truck at a price of $300,000. On July 19, an identical truck is delivered to the company at a price of $320,000. On July 28, the company sells one of the trucks for $390,000. During July, expenses totaled $30,000. All transactions were paid in cash.

		RTS Company		
		Balance Sheet		
		July 1, 20xx		

Assets		**Stockholders' Equity**	
Cash	$800,000	Common Stock	$800,000
Total Assets	$800,000	Total Stockholders' Equity	$800,000

REQUIRED

1. Prepare income statements and balance sheets for RTS on July 31 using (a) the FIFO method of inventory valuation and (b) the LIFO method of inventory valuation. Assume an income tax rate of 40 percent. Explain the effects of each method on the financial statements.

2. Assume that the management of RTS Company follows the policy of declaring a cash dividend each period that is exactly equal to net income. What effects does this action have on each balance sheet prepared in **1,** and how do the resulting balance sheets compare with the balance sheet at the beginning of the month? Which inventory method, if either, do you feel is more realistic in representing RTS's income?

3. Assume that RTS receives notice of another price increase of $20,000 on refrigerated trucks, to take effect on August 1. How does this information relate to management's dividend policy, and how will it affect next month's operations?

FINANCIAL REPORTING AND ANALYSIS

Interpreting Financial Reports

FRA 1.

LO 1 LIFO, FIFO, and Income
LO 2 Taxes
LO 5

Hershey Foods Corp. is famous for its chocolate and confectionary products. A portion of the company's income statements for 1998 and 1997 follows (in thousands):[15]

	1998	1997
Net Sales	$4,435,615	$4,302,236
Cost of Goods Sold	2,625,057	2,488,896
Gross Margin	$1,810,558	$1,813,340
Selling, General, and Administrative Expenses	1,167,895	1,183,130
Income from Operations	$ 642,663	$ 630,210
Interest Expense, Net	85,657	76,255
Income Before Income Taxes	$ 557,006	$ 553,955
Provision for Income Taxes	216,118	217,704
Net Income	$ 340,888	$ 336,251

In a note on supplemental balance sheet information, Hershey indicated that most of its inventories are maintained using the last-in, first-out (LIFO) method. The company also reported that inventories (in thousands) using the LIFO method were $493,249 in 1998 and $505,525 in 1997. In addition, it reported that if valued using the first-in, first-out (FIFO) method, inventories (in thousands) would have been $583,973 in 1998 and $594,356 in 1997. In other words, inventory (in thousands) valued under FIFO would have been higher than the values under LIFO by $90,724 in 1998 and $88,831 in 1997.

REQUIRED

1. Prepare a schedule comparing net income for 1998 under the LIFO method with what it would have been under FIFO. Use a corporate income tax rate of 38.8 percent (Hershey's average tax rate in 1998).

2. Why do you suppose Hershey's management chooses to use the LIFO inventory method? On what economic conditions, if any, do those reasons depend? Given your calculations in **1,** do you believe the economic conditions relevant to Hershey were advantageous for using LIFO in 1998? Explain your answer.

3. Compute inventory turnover and average days' inventory on hand under each of the cost flow assumptions in **1.** What conclusion can be made from this comparison?

FRA 2.
LO 5   Misstatement of Inventory

The Wall Street Journal reported that **Crazy Eddie Inc.,** a discount consumer electronics chain, seemed to be missing $45 million in merchandise inventory. "It was a shock," Elias Zinn, the new president and chief executive officer, was quoted as saying.[16]

The article went on to say that Mr. Zinn headed a management team that had taken control of Crazy Eddie after a new board of directors was elected at a shareholders' meeting. A count turned up only $75 million in inventory, compared with $126.7 million reported by the old management. Net sales could account for only $6.7 million of the difference. Mr. Zinn said he didn't know whether bookkeeping errors in prior years or an actual physical loss created the shortfall, although at least one store manager felt it was a bookkeeping error, because security is strong. "It would be hard for someone to steal anything," he said.

REQUIRED

1. What has been the effect of the misstatement of inventory on Crazy Eddie's reported earnings in prior accounting periods?

2. Is this a situation you would expect in a company that is experiencing financial difficulty? Explain.

FRA 3.
LO 5   LIFO Liquidation

At December 31, 1997, and 1996, **RJR Nabisco, Inc.,** reported approximately $592 million and $194 million, respectively, of domestic tobacco inventories valued under the LIFO method. As explained in the annual report,

The current cost of LIFO inventories at December 31, 1997, and 1996, was greater than the amount at which these inventories were carried on the Consolidated Balance Sheets by $151 million and $166 million respectively. For the years ended December 31, 1997, 1996, and 1995, net income was increased by approximately $14 million, $35 million, and $29 million respectively, as a result of LIFO inventory liquidations. The LIFO liquidations resulted from programs to reduce domestic leaf durations consistent with forecasts of future operating requirements.[17]

RJR Nabisco's average income tax rates for 1997 and 1996 were 52 percent and 49 percent, respectively.

REQUIRED

1. Explain why a reduction in the quantity of inventory resulted in an increase in net income. Would the same result have occurred if RJR Nabisco had used the FIFO method to value inventory? Explain your answer.

2. What is the income tax effect of the LIFO liquidation? Is this a favorable outcome?

International Company

FRA 4.
LO 1   Comparison of
LO 5   Inventory Levels and
Methods

Two large Japanese diversified electronics companies are **Pioneer Electronic Corporation** and **Yamaha Motor Co., Ltd.** Both companies use the average-cost method and the lower-of-cost-or-market rule to account for inventories. The following data are for their 1998 fiscal years (in millions of yen):[18]

	Pioneer	Yamaha
Beginning Inventory	¥108,175	¥120,014
Ending Inventory	116,081	137,628
Cost of Goods Sold	386,313	606,445

Compare the inventory efficiency of Pioneer and Yamaha by computing the inventory turnover and average days' inventory on hand for both companies in 1998. Comment on the results. Most companies in the United States use the LIFO inventory method. How would inventory method affect your evaluation if you were to compare Pioneer and Yamaha to a U.S. company? What could you do to make the results comparable?

Toys "R" Us Annual Report

FRA 5.

LO 1 **Retail Inventory Method**
LO 5 **and Inventory Ratios**
LO 6
SO 7

Refer to the note related to inventories in the Toys "R" Us annual report to answer the following questions: What inventory method(s) does Toys "R" Us use? Why do you think that if LIFO inventories had been valued at FIFO, there would be no difference? Do you think many of the company's inventories are valued at market? Even though few companies use the retail inventory method, why do you think Toys "R" Us uses this method? Compute and compare the inventory turnover and average days' inventory on hand for Toys "R" Us for 1998 and 1999. Beginning 1997 inventory was $2,215 million.

Fingraph® Financial Analyst™

FRA 6.

LO 1 **Comparative Analysis of Inventories and Operating Cycle**

Select any two companies from the same industry on the Fingraph® Financial Analyst™ CD-ROM software. Choose an industry, such as manufacturing, consumer products, consumer food and beverage, or computers, in which inventory is likely to be an important current asset.

1. In the annual reports for the companies you have selected, read any reference to inventories in the summary of significant accounting policies or notes to the financial statements. What inventory method does the company use? What are the changes in and relative importance of raw materials, work in process, and finished goods inventories?

2. Display and print in tabular and graphical form the Liquidity and Asset Utilization Analysis page. Prepare a table that compares the inventory turnover and average days' inventory on hand for both companies for two years. Also include in your table the operating cycle by combining average days' inventory on hand with average days' sales uncollected.

3. Find and read references to inventories in the liquidity analysis section of management's discussion and analysis in each annual report.

4. Write a one-page executive summary that highlights the accounting policies for inventories, the relative importance and changes in raw materials, work in process, and finished goods, and compares the inventory utilization of the two companies, including reference to management's assessment. Comment specifically on the financing implications of the companies' relative operating cycles. Include the Fingraph® page and your table as an attachment to your report.

Internet Case

FRA 7.

LO 5 **Effect of LIFO on Income and Cash Flows**

Maytag Corporation, an appliance manufacturer, uses the LIFO inventory method. Go to www.maytagcorp.com and select "About Maytag." Then select "Financial Center." After finding the income statement and inventory note, calculate what net income would have been had the company used FIFO. Calculate how much cash the company saved for the year and cumulatively by using LIFO. What is the difference between the LIFO and FIFO gross margin and profit margin results? Which reporting alternative is better for the company?

ENDNOTES

1. J.C. Penney Company, Inc., *Annual Report,* 1999.
2. American Institute of Certified Public Accountants, *Accounting Research Bulletin No. 43* (New York: AICPA, 1953), ch. 4.
3. Gary McWilliams, "Whirlwind on the Web," *Business Week,* April 7, 1997.
4. American Institute of Certified Public Accountants, *Accounting Research Bulletin No. 43* (New York: AICPA, 1953), ch. 4.
5. A single exception to this rule is that taxpayers must notify the IRS of a change to LIFO from another method, but they do not need to have advance IRS approval.
6. Micah Frankel and Robert Trezevant, "The Year-End LIFO Inventory Purchasing Decision: An Empirical Test," *The Accounting Review,* April 1994.
7. American Institute of Certified Public Accountants, *Accounting Trends & Techniques* (New York: AICPA, 1998).

8. Teri Agins, "Report Is Said to Show Pervasive Fraud at Leslie" and "Leslie Fay Co.'s Profits Restated for Past 3 Years," *The Wall Street Journal*, September 27 and 30, 1993.

9. International Paper Company, *Annual Report*, 1997.

10. In some cases, *market value* is determined by the *realizable value* of the inventory—the amount for which the goods can be sold—rather than by the amount for which the goods can be replaced. The circumstances in which realizable value determines market value are encountered in practice only occasionally, and the valuation procedures are technical enough to be addressed in a more advanced accounting course.

11. American Institute of Certified Public Accountants, *Accounting Trends & Techniques* (New York: AICPA, 1998).

12. "Everybody's Falling into The Gap," *Business Week*, September 23, 1991, p. 36; and The Gap, Inc., *Annual Report*, 1998.

13. American Institute of Certified Public Accountants, *Accounting Trends & Techniques* (New York: AICPA, 1998).

14. Allanna Sullivan, "Accounting Change at Mobil Makes First-Quarter Profit a $145 Million Loss," *The Wall Street Journal*, August 1, 1994; and Mobil Corporation, *Annual Report*, 1998.

15. Adapted from Hershey Foods Corp., *Annual Report*, 1998.

16. Based on Ann Hagedorn, "Crazy Eddie Says About $45 Million of Goods Missing," *The Wall Street Journal*, November 20, 1987, p. 47.

17. RJR Nabisco, Inc., *Annual Report*, 1997.

18. Pioneer Electronic Corporation, *Annual Report*, 1998; and Yamaha Motor Co. Ltd., *Annual Report*, 1998.

9

Current Liabilities and the Time Value of Money

US Airways, Inc. Liabilities are one of the three major parts of the balance sheet. They are legal obligations for the future payment of assets or the future performance of services that result from past transactions. For example, the current and long-term liabilities of US Airways, Inc., which has total assets of more than $6.9 billion, are shown here.[1] Current Maturities of Long-Term Debt; Accounts Payable; Accrued Aircraft Rent; Accrued Salaries, Wages, and Vacation; and Other Accrued Expenses for the most part will require an outlay of cash in the next year. Traffic Balances Payable will require payments to other airlines, but those may be partially offset by amounts owed from other airlines. Unused Tickets are tickets already paid for by passengers and represent services that must be performed. Long-Term Debt will require cash outlays in future years. Altogether these liabilities represent over 61 percent of total assets. How does the decision of US Airways' management to incur so much debt relate to the goals of the business?

Liabilities are important because they are closely related to the goals of profitability and liquidity. Liabilities are sources of cash for operating and financing activities when they are incurred, but they are also obligations that use cash when they are paid as required. Achieving the appropriate level of liabilities is critical to business success. A company that has too few liabilities may not be earning up to its potential. A company that has too many liabilities, however, may be incurring excessive risks. This chapter focuses on the management and accounting issues involving current liabilities, including payroll liabilities and contingent liabilities.

Financial Highlights

(In millions)

Current Liabilities	1998	1997
Current Maturities of Long-Term Debt	$ 71	$ 186
Accounts Payable	430	323
Traffic Balances Payable and Unused Tickets	752	707
Accrued Aircraft Rent	166	187
Accrued Salaries, Wages and Vacation	329	311
Other Accrued Expenses	521	492
Total Current Liabilities	$2,269	$2,206
Long-Term Debt, Net of Current Maturities	**$1,955**	**$2,426**

Management Issues Related to Accounting for Current Liabilities

OBJECTIVE

1 Identify the management issues related to recognition, valuation, classification, and disclosure of current liabilities

The primary reason for incurring current liabilities is to meet needs for cash during the operating cycle. The proper identification and management of current liabilities also requires an understanding of how they are recognized, valued, classified, and disclosed.

Managing Liquidity and Cash Flows

The operating cycle is the process of converting cash to purchases, to sales, to accounts receivable, and back to cash. Most current liabilities arise in support of this cycle, as when accounts payable arise from purchases of inventory, accrued expenses arise from operating costs, and unearned revenues arise from customers' advance payments. Short-term debt is used to raise cash during periods of inventory buildup or while waiting for collection of receivables. Cash is used to pay current maturities of long-term debt and to pay off liabilities arising from operations.

Failure to manage the cash flows related to current liabilities can have serious consequences for a business. For instance, if suppliers are not paid on time, they may withhold shipments that are vital to a company's operations. Continued failure to pay current liabilities can lead to bankruptcy. To evaluate a company's ability to pay its current liabilities, three measures of liquidity—working capital, the current ratio, and the quick ratio—are often used. Current liabilities are a key component of each of these measures. They typically equal from 25 to 50 percent of total assets.

US Airways' short-term liquidity as measured by working capital has deteriorated from 1997 to 1998 (in millions):

	Current Assets	−	Current Liabilities	=	Working Capital
1998	$2,364	−	$2,269	=	$ 95
1997	$2,777	−	$2,206	=	$571

Enrichment Note: Unused tickets are often a significant liability for airlines. Like all service providers, airlines earn revenue by providing a service. The receipt of cash is usually incidental to revenue recognition.

This measure highlights the need for US Airways' management to focus on the management of short-term liquidity. It is common for airlines to have low or negative working capital because unearned ticket revenue is a current liability, but the cash from these ticket sales is quickly consumed in operations. On the assumption that only a small portion of unearned ticket revenues will be repaid to customers, unearned ticket revenue might be excluded from current liabilities for purposes of analysis. The healthiest airlines have positive working capital when unearned ticket revenue is excluded.

Another consideration with managing a company's liquidity position and cash flows is the amount of time its creditors are willing to give it to pay its accounts payable. Common measures of this time are the **payables turnover** and the **average days' payable**. The payables turnover is the number of times on average that accounts payable are paid in an accounting period and shows the relative size of a company's accounts payable. The average days' payable shows how long, on average, a company takes to pay its accounts payables.

For example, Tandy Corporation, which operates more than 7,000 Radio Shack electronics retail locations, must carefully plan its purchases and payables. It had average accounts payable of $206.4 million in 1998 and $325.2 million in 1999. Its purchases are determined by cost of goods sold adjusted for the change in inventory. An increase in inventory means purchases were more than cost of goods sold and a decrease in inventory means that purchases were less than cost of goods

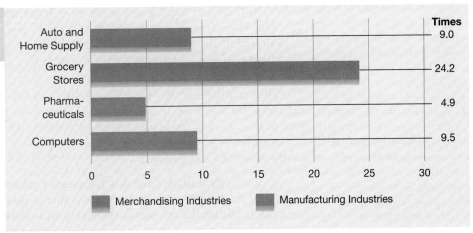

**Figure 1
Payables Turnover for Selected Industries**

Source: Data from Dun & Bradstreet, *Industry Norms and Key Business Ratios,* 1997–98.

sold. Tandy's cost of goods sold was $2,783.5 million and its inventory decreased by $293.1 million.[2] Its payables turnover is computed as follows:

$$\text{Payables Turnover} = \frac{\text{Cost of Goods Sold} \pm \text{Change in Merchandise Inventory}}{\text{Average Accounts Payable}}$$

$$= \frac{\$2,783.5 - \$293.1}{(\$325.2 + \$206.4) \div 2}$$

$$= \frac{\$2,490.4}{\$265.8} = 9.4 \text{ times}$$

To find the average days' payable, the number of days in a year is divided by the payables turnover:

$$\text{Average Days' Payable} = \frac{365 \text{ days}}{\text{Payables Turnover}} = \frac{365 \text{ days}}{9.4} = 38.8 \text{ days}$$

The payables turnover of 9.4 times and the resulting average days' payable of 38.8 days are consistent with customary 30-day credit terms.

The chart in Figure 1 shows the payables turnover for various other industries. The payables turnover should be considered in relation to the inventory turnover and the receivables turnover to get a full picture of a company's operating cycle and liquidity position.

Recognition of Liabilities

Timing is important in the recognition of liabilities. Failure to record a liability in an accounting period very often goes along with failure to record an expense. The two errors lead to an understatement of expense and an overstatement of income.

A liability is recorded when an obligation occurs. This rule is harder to apply than it might appear. When a transaction obligates a company to make future payments, a liability arises and is recognized, as when goods are bought on credit. However, current liabilities often are not represented by direct transactions. One of the key reasons for making adjusting entries at the end of an accounting period is to recognize unrecorded liabilities. Among these accrued liabilities are salaries payable and interest payable. Other liabilities that can only be estimated, such as taxes payable, must also be recognized through adjusting entries.

On the other hand, companies often enter into agreements for future transactions. For instance, a company may agree to pay an executive $50,000 a year for a period of three years, or a public utility may agree to buy an unspecified quantity of coal at a certain price over the next five years. Such contracts, though they are definite commitments, are not considered liabilities because they are for future—not past—transactions. As there is no current obligation, no liability is recognized.

Valuation of Liabilities

On the balance sheet, a liability is generally valued at the amount of money needed to pay the debt or at the fair market value of goods or services to be delivered. For most liabilities the amount is definitely known, but for some it must be estimated. For example, an automobile dealer who sells a car with a one-year warranty must provide parts and service during the year. The obligation is definite because the sale of the car has occurred, but the amount of the obligation can only be estimated. Such estimates are usually based on past experience and anticipated changes in the business environment. Additional disclosures of the fair value of liabilities may be required in the notes to the financial statements, as explained below.

Classification of Liabilities

The classification of liabilities directly matches the classification of assets. **Current liabilities** are debts and obligations expected to be satisfied within one year or within the normal operating cycle, whichever is longer. Such liabilities are normally paid out of current assets or with cash generated from operations. **Long-term liabilities**, which are liabilities due beyond one year or beyond the normal operating cycle, have a different purpose. They are used to finance long-term assets, such as aircraft in the case of US Airways. The distinction between current and long-term liabilities is important because it affects the evaluation of a company's liquidity.

Disclosure of Liabilities

To explain some accounts, supplemental disclosure in the notes to the financial statements may be required. For example, if a company has a large amount of notes payable, an explanatory note may disclose the balances, maturities, interest rates, and other features of the debts. Any special credit arrangements, such as issues of commercial paper and lines of credit, should also be disclosed. For example, The Goodyear Tire & Rubber Company, which manufactures and sells tires, vehicle components, industrial rubber products, and rubber-related chemicals, disclosed its credit arrangements in the notes to the financial statements. Excerpts from that note follow:

> **Enrichment Note:** Financial liabilities, such as loans, notes, and other borrowings, are considered financial instruments. The market value of financial instruments is reported in the notes to the financial statements.

Note 7A. Short-Term Debt and Financing Arrangements

At December 31, 1998, the Company had short-term uncommitted credit arrangements totaling $1.4 billion, of which $.4 billion were unused. These arrangements are available to the Company or certain of its international subsidiaries through various international banks at quoted market interest rates. There are no commitment fees or compensating balances associated with these arrangements.

The company had outstanding short-term debt amounting to $964.3 million at December 31, 1998. Domestic short-term debt represented $485.6

million of this total with a weighted average interest rate of 5.1% at December 31, 1998. . . . The remaining $478.7 million was international subsidiary short-term debt with a weighted average interest rate of 7.31% at December 31, 1998.[3]

This type of disclosure is helpful in assessing whether a company has additional borrowing power, because unused lines of credit allow a company to borrow on short notice, up to the agreed credit limit, with little or no negotiations.

Common Categories of Current Liabilities

Current liabilities fall into two major groups: (1) definitely determinable liabilities and (2) estimated liabilities.

Definitely Determinable Liabilities

OBJECTIVE

2 Identify, compute, and record definitely determinable and estimated current liabilities

Current liabilities that are set by contract or by statute and can be measured exactly are called **definitely determinable liabilities**. The related accounting problems are to determine the existence and amount of each such liability and to see that it is recorded properly. Definitely determinable liabilities include accounts payable, bank loans and commercial paper, notes payable, accrued liabilities, dividends payable, sales and excise taxes payable, current portions of long-term debt, payroll liabilities, and unearned or deferred revenues.

ACCOUNTS PAYABLE Accounts payable, sometimes called trade accounts payable, are short-term obligations to suppliers for goods and services. The amount in the Accounts Payable account is generally supported by an accounts payable subsidiary ledger, which contains an individual account for each person or company to which money is owed.

Key Point: On the balance sheet, the order of presentation for current liabilities is not as strict as for current assets. Generally, Accounts Payable or Notes Payable appears first, and the rest follow.

BANK LOANS AND COMMERCIAL PAPER Management will often establish a **line of credit** from a bank; this arrangement allows the company to borrow funds when they are needed to finance current operations. For example, Lowe's Companies, Inc., a large home improvement center and consumer durables company, reported in its 1998 annual report that "the company entered into a $300 million revolving credit facility with a syndicate of 11 banks expiring November 2001. This facility is used to support the company's commercial paper program and for short term borrowing. . . . There were no borrowings outstanding under this revolving credit facility."[4] A promissory note for the full amount of the line of credit is signed when the credit is granted, but the company has great flexibility in using the available funds. The company can increase its borrowing up to the limit when it needs cash and reduce the amount borrowed when it generates enough cash of its own. Both the amount borrowed and the interest rate charged by the bank may change daily. The bank may require the company to meet certain financial goals (such as maintaining specific profit margins, current ratios, or debt to equity ratios) to retain the line of credit.

Figure 2
Two Promissory Notes:
One with Interest Stated
Separately; One with Interest
in Face Amount

CASE 1: INTEREST STATED SEPARATELY

Chicago, Illinois   August 31, 20xx

Sixty days after date I promise to pay First Federal Bank
the sum of $5,000 with interest at the rate of 12% per
annum.

Sandra Caron
Caron Corporation

CASE 2: INTEREST IN FACE AMOUNT

Chicago, Illinois   August 31, 20xx

Sixty days after date I promise to pay First Federal Bank
the sum of $5,000.

Sandra Caron
Caron Corporation

Clarification Note: Only the used portion of the line of credit is recognized as a liability in the financial statements.

Companies with excellent credit ratings may borrow short-term funds by issuing **commercial paper**, unsecured loans that are sold to the public, usually through professionally managed investment firms. The portion of a line of credit currently borrowed and the amount of commercial paper issued are usually combined with notes payable in the current liabilities section of the balance sheet. Details are disclosed in a note to the financial statements.

NOTES PAYABLE   Short-term notes payable, which also arise out of the ordinary course of business, are obligations represented by promissory notes. These notes may be used to secure bank loans, to pay suppliers for goods and services, and to secure credit from other sources.

The interest may be stated separately on the face of the note (Case 1 in Figure 2), or it may be deducted in advance by discounting it from the face value of the note (Case 2 in Figure 2). The entries to record the note in each case follow.

Case 1—Interest Stated Separately			Case 2—Interest in Face Amount		

Case 1
A = L + OE
+   +

Aug. 31 | Cash | 5,000 |
| Notes Payable | | 5,000 |
| Issued 60-day, |
| 12% promissory |
| note with interest |
| stated separately |

Case 2
A = L + OE
+   −
+

Aug. 31 | Cash | 4,900 |
| Discount on Notes Payable | 100 |
| Notes Payable | | 5,000 |
| Issued 60-day |
| promissory note with |
| $100 interest included |
| in face amount |

Key Point: The effective interest rate on the loan in Case 2 is 12.24% ($100/$4,900 × 360/60). Note: For ease of computation 360 days are used to compute interest on notes.

Note that in Case 1 the money received equaled the face value of the note, whereas in Case 2 the money received ($4,900) was less than the face value ($5,000) of the note. The amount of the discount equals the amount of the interest for 60 days. Although the dollar amount of interest on each of these notes is the same, the effective interest rate is slightly higher in Case 2 because the amount received is slightly less ($4,900 in Case 2 versus $5,000 in Case 1). Discount on

Notes Payable is a contra account to Notes Payable and is deducted from Notes Payable on the balance sheet.

On October 30, when the note is paid, each alternative is recorded as follows:

Case 1—Interest Stated Separately

Case 1
A = L + OE
−   −   −

Oct. 30	Notes Payable	5,000	
	Interest Expense	100	
	Cash		5,100
	Payment of note		
	with interest stated		
	separately		

$$\$5,000 \times \frac{60}{360} \times .12 = \$100$$

Case 2—Interest in Face Amount

Case 2
A = L + OE
−   −

A = L + OE
+   −

Oct. 30	Notes Payable	5,000	
	Cash		5,000
	Payment of note		
	with interest included		
	in face amount		
30	Interest Expense	100	
	Discount on Notes		
	Payable		100
	Interest expense on		
	note payable		

ACCRUED LIABILITIES   A key reason for making adjusting entries at the end of an accounting period is to recognize and record liabilities that are not already in the accounting records. This practice applies to any type of liability. As you will see, accrued liabilities can include estimated liabilities.

Here the focus is on interest payable, a definitely determinable liability. Interest accrues daily on interest-bearing notes. At the end of the accounting period, an adjusting entry should be made in accordance with the matching rule to record the interest obligation up to that point in time. Let us again use the example of the two notes presented above. If we assume that the accounting period ends on September 30, or 30 days after the issuance of the 60-day notes, the adjusting entries for each case would be as follows:

Case 1—Interest Stated Separately

Case 1
A = L + OE
+   −

Sept. 30	Interest Expense	50	
	Interest Payable		50
	To record interest		
	expense for 30 days on		
	note with interest		
	stated separately		

$$\$5,000 \times \frac{30}{360} \times .12 = \$50$$

Case 2—Interest in Face Amount

Case 2
A = L + OE
+   −

Sept. 30	Interest Expense	50	
	Discount on Notes Payable		50
	To record interest expense		
	for 30 days on note with		
	interest included in face		
	amount		

$$\$100 \times \frac{30}{60} = \$50$$

Key Point: Both of the above entries have exactly the same impact on the financial statements.

In Case 2, Discount on Notes Payable will now have a debit balance of $50, which will become interest expense during the next 30 days.

DIVIDENDS PAYABLE   Cash dividends are a distribution of earnings by a corporation. The payment of dividends is solely the decision of the corporation's board of directors. A liability does not exist until the board declares the dividends. There is usually a short time between the date of declaration and the date of payment of dividends. During that short time, the dividends declared are considered current liabilities of the corporation.

Key Point: Try to compute sales tax on the basis of sales rather than total cash collections.

SALES AND EXCISE TAXES PAYABLE   Most states and many cities levy a sales tax on retail transactions. There is a federal excise tax on some products, such as automobile tires. A merchant who sells goods subject to these taxes must collect the taxes and forward them periodically to the appropriate government agency. The amount of tax collected represents a current liability until it is remitted to the government. For example, assume that a merchant makes a $100 sale that is subject to a 5 percent sales tax and a 10 percent excise tax. Assuming that the sale takes place on June 1, the entry to record the sale is as follows:

A = L + OE				
+ + +	June 1	Cash	115	
+		Sales		100
		Sales Tax Payable		5
		Excise Tax Payable		10
		Sale of merchandise and collection of sales and excise taxes		

The sale is properly recorded at $100, and the taxes collected are recorded as liabilities to be remitted at the proper times to the appropriate government agencies.

Enrichment Note: Liabilities such as bank loans, notes payable, and current portions of long-term debt are considered financial instruments.

CURRENT PORTIONS OF LONG-TERM DEBT If a portion of long-term debt is due within the next year and is to be paid from current assets, then that current portion is properly classified as a current liability. For example, suppose that a $500,000 debt is to be paid in installments of $100,000 per year for the next five years. The $100,000 installment due in the current year should be classified as a current liability. The remaining $400,000 should be classified as a long-term liability. Note that no journal entry is necessary. The total debt of $500,000 is simply reclassified when the financial statements are prepared, as follows:

Current Liabilities	
Current Portion of Long-Term Debt	$100,000
Long-Term Liabilities	
Long-Term Debt	400,000

PAYROLL LIABILITIES For most organizations, the cost of labor and related payroll taxes is a major expense. In some industries, such as banking and airlines, payroll costs represent more than half of all operating costs. Payroll accounting is important because complex laws and significant liabilities are involved. The employer is liable to employees for wages and salaries and to various agencies for amounts withheld from wages and salaries and for related taxes. The term **wages** refers to payment for the services of employees at an hourly rate. The term **salaries** refers to the compensation of employees who are paid at a monthly or yearly rate.

Because payroll accounting applies only to the employees of an organization, it is therefore important to distinguish between employees and independent contractors. Employees are paid a wage or salary by the organization and are under its direct supervision and control. Independent contractors are not employees of the organization, so they are not accounted for under the payroll system. They offer services to the organization for a fee, but they are not under its direct control or supervision. Some examples of independent contractors are certified public accountants, advertising agencies, and lawyers.

Figure 3 provides an illustration of payroll liabilities and their relationship to employee earnings and employer taxes and other costs. Two important observations may be made. First, the amount payable to employees is less than the amount of earnings. This occurs because employers are required by law or are requested by employees to withhold certain amounts from wages and send them directly to government agencies or other organizations. Second, the total employer liabilities exceed employee earnings because the employer must pay additional taxes and make other contributions, such as for pensions and medical care, that increase the cost and liabilities. The most common withholdings, taxes, and other payroll costs are described on page 424.

Figure 3
Illustration of Payroll Liabilities

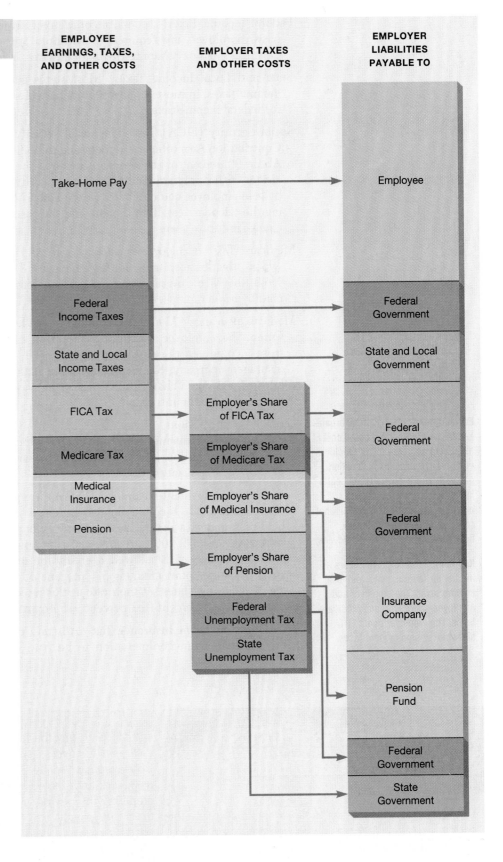

Federal Income Taxes   Federal income taxes are collected on a "pay as you go" basis. Employers are required to withhold appropriate taxes from employees' paychecks and pay them to the United States Treasury.

State and Local Income Taxes   Most states and some local governments have income taxes. In most cases, the procedures for withholding are similar to those for federal income taxes.

Social Security (FICA) Tax   The social security program (the Federal Insurance Contribution Act) offers retirement and disability benefits and survivor's benefits. About 90 percent of the people working in the United States fall under the provisions of this program. The 1999 social security tax rate of 6.20 percent was paid by *both* employee and employer on the first $72,600 earned by an employee during the calendar year. Both the rate and the base to which it applies are subject to change in future years.

Medicare Tax   A major extension of the social security program is Medicare, which provides hospitalization and medical insurance for persons over age 65. In 1999, the Medicare tax rate was 1.45 percent of gross income, with no limit, paid by *both* employee and employer.

Medical Insurance   Many organizations provide medical benefits to employees. Often, the employee contributes a portion of the cost through withholdings from income and the employer pays the rest, usually a greater amount, to the insurance company. Some proposals for national health-care reform, if they become law, could change substantially the way medical insurance is funded and provided in this country.

Pension Contributions   Many organizations also provide pension benefits to employees. In a manner similar to that for medical insurance, a portion of the pension contribution is withheld from the employee's income and the rest is paid by the organization to the pension fund.

Federal Unemployment Insurance (FUTA) Tax   This tax, referred to as FUTA after the Federal Unemployment Tax Act, is intended to pay for programs to help unemployed workers. It is paid *only* by employers and recently was 6.2 percent of the first $9,000 earned by each employee. Against this federal tax, however, the employer is allowed a credit for unemployment taxes paid to the state. The maximum credit is 5.4 percent of the first $7,000 earned by each employee. Most states set their rate at this maximum. Thus, the FUTA tax most often paid is .8 percent (6.2 percent − 5.4 percent) of the taxable wages.

State Unemployment Insurance Tax   All state unemployment programs provide for unemployment compensation to be paid to eligible unemployed workers.

Enrichment Note: For many organizations, a large portion of the cost of labor is not reflected in employees' regular paychecks. Vacation pay, sick pay, personal days, health insurance, life insurance, and pensions are some of the additional costs that may be negotiated between employers and employees.

Key Point: The employee bears all the tax for federal, state, and local income taxes. The employer and employee share FICA and Medicare taxes. The employer bears FUTA and state unemployment taxes.

BUSINESS FOCUS ON TECHNOLOGY

The processing of payroll is an ideal application for computers because it is a very routine and complex procedure that must be done with absolute accuracy: Employees want to be paid exactly what they are owed, and failure to pay the taxes and other costs as required can result in severe penalties and high interest charges. Consequently, many companies purchase carefully designed and tested computer software for use in preparing the payroll. Other companies do not process their own payroll but rely on outside businesses that specialize in providing such services. Many of these service suppliers, such as Automatic Data Processing, Inc., are successful and fast growing.

This compensation is paid out of the fund provided by the 5.4 percent of the first $7,000 (varies in some states) earned by each employee. In some states, employers with favorable employment records may be entitled to pay less than 5.4 percent.

To illustrate the recording of the payroll, assume that on February 15 total employee wages are $32,500, with withholdings of $5,400 for federal income taxes, $1,200 for state income taxes, $2,015 for social security tax, $471 for Medicare tax, $900 for medical insurance, and $1,300 for pension contributions. The entry to record this payroll follows:

A = L + OE				
+ −	Feb. 15	Wages Expense	32,500	
+		Employees' Federal Income Taxes Payable		5,400
+		Employees' State Income Taxes Payable		1,200
+		Social Security Tax Payable		2,015
+		Medicare Tax Payable		471
+		Medical Insurance Payable		900
+		Pension Contributions Payable		1,300
		Wages Payable		21,214
		To record payroll		

Note that the employees' take-home pay is only $21,214, although $32,500 was earned.

Using the same data, the additional employer taxes and other benefits costs would be recorded as follows, assuming that the payroll taxes correspond to the discussion above and that the employer pays 80 percent of the medical insurance premiums and half of the pension contributions:

A = L + OE				
+ −	Feb. 15	Payroll Taxes and Benefits Expense	9,401	
+		Social Security Tax Payable		2,015
+		Medicare Tax Payable		471
+		Medical Insurance Payable		3,600
+		Pension Contributions Payable		1,300
+		Federal Unemployment Tax Payable		260
		State Unemployment Tax Payable		1,755
		To record payroll taxes and other costs		

Note that the payroll taxes and benefits increase the total cost of the payroll to $41,901 ($9,401 + $32,500), which exceeds by almost 29 percent the amount earned by employees. This is a typical situation.

UNEARNED REVENUES   **Unearned revenues** represent obligations for goods or services that the company must provide or deliver in a future accounting period in return for an advance payment from a customer. For example, a publisher of a monthly magazine who receives annual subscriptions totaling $240 would make the following entry:

A = L + OE			
+ +	Cash	240	
	Unearned Subscriptions		240
	Receipt of annual subscriptions in advance		

The publisher now has a liability of $240 that will be reduced gradually as monthly issues of the magazine are mailed.

A = L + OE			
− +	Unearned Subscriptions	20	
	Subscription Revenues		20
	Delivery of monthly magazine issues		

BUSINESS FOCUS ON PRACTICE

Many companies promote their products by issuing coupons that offer "cents off" or other enticements for purchasers. Since four out of five shoppers use coupons, companies are forced by competition to distribute them. The total value of unredeemed coupons, each of which represents a potential liability for the issuing company, is truly staggering. NCH Promotional Services, a company owned by Dun & Bradstreet, estimates that almost 300 billion coupons are issued annually. Of course, the liability depends on how many of the coupons will actually be redeemed. NCH estimates that number at approximately 6 billion, or about 2 percent. That is not a large percentage, but the value of the redeemed coupons is estimated to be more than $4 billion.[5]

Many businesses, such as repair companies, construction companies, and special-order firms, ask for a deposit or advance from a customer before they will begin work. Such advances are also current liabilities until the goods or services are actually delivered.

Estimated Liabilities

> **Key Point:** Estimated liabilities are recorded and presented on the financial statements in the same way as definitely determinable liabilities. The only difference is that estimated liabilities involve some uncertainty in their computation.

Estimated liabilities are definite debts or obligations of which the exact dollar amount cannot be known until a later date. Since there is no doubt about the existence of the legal obligation, the primary accounting problem is to estimate and record the amount of the liability. Examples of estimated liabilities are income taxes, property taxes, product warranties, and vacation pay.

INCOME TAXES   The income of a corporation is taxed by the federal government, most state governments, and some cities and towns. The amount of income taxes liability depends on the results of operations. Often the results are not known until after the end of the year. However, because income taxes are an expense in the year in which income is earned, an adjusting entry is necessary to record the estimated tax liability. The entry is as follows:

A = L + OE
  +   −

Dec. 31	Income Taxes Expense	53,000	
	Estimated Income Taxes Payable		53,000
	To record estimated federal income taxes		

Sole proprietorships and partnerships do *not* pay income taxes. Their owners must report their share of the firm's income on their individual tax returns.

> **Enrichment Note:** The process of accruing property tax each month could be applied to income taxes if a company desires monthly financial statements.

PROPERTY TAX PAYABLE   Property taxes are levied on real property, such as land and buildings, and on personal property, such as inventory and equipment. Property taxes are a main source of revenue for local governments. They are usually assessed annually against the property involved. Because the fiscal years of local governments and their assessment dates rarely correspond to a firm's fiscal year, it is necessary to estimate the amount of property tax that applies to each month of the year. Assume, for instance, that a local government has a fiscal year of July 1 to June 30, that its assessment date is November 1 for the current fiscal year, and that its payment date is December 15. Assume also that on July 1, Janis Corporation estimates that its property tax assessment for the coming year will be $24,000. The adjusting entry to be made on July 31, which would be repeated on August 31, September 30, and October 31, would be as follows:

A = L + OE
+   −

July 31   Property Tax Expense   2,000

                Estimated Property Tax Payable   2,000

                     To record estimated property tax
expense for the month
$24,000 ÷ 12 months = $2,000

On November 1, the firm receives a property tax bill for $24,720. The estimate that was made in July was too low. The charge should have been $2,060 per month. Because the difference between the actual assessment and the estimate is small, the company decides to absorb in November the amount undercharged in the previous four months. Therefore, the property tax expense for November is $2,300 [$2,060 + 4($60)] and is recorded as follows:

A = L + OE
+   −

Nov. 30   Property Tax Expense   2,300

               Estimated Property Tax Payable   2,300

                    To record estimated property tax

The Estimated Property Tax Payable account now has a balance of $10,300. The entry to record payment on December 15 would be as follows:

A = L + OE
+   −
−

Dec. 15   Estimated Property Tax Payable   10,300

              Prepaid Property Tax   14,420

                  Cash   24,720

                    Payment of property tax

Beginning December 31 and each month afterward until June 30, property tax expense is recorded by a debit to Property Tax Expense and a credit to Prepaid Property Tax in the amount of $2,060. The total of these seven entries will reduce the Prepaid Property Tax account to zero on June 30.

Key Point: Recording product warranty expense in the year of the sale follows the matching rule.

PRODUCT WARRANTY LIABILITY   When a firm places a warranty or guarantee on its product at the time of sale, a liability exists for the length of the warranty. The cost of the warranty is properly debited to an expense account in the period of sale because it is a feature of the product or service sold and thus is included in the price paid by the customer for the product. On the basis of experience, it should be possible to estimate the amount the warranty will cost in the future. Some products or services will require little warranty service; others may require much. Thus, there will be an average cost per product or service.

For example, assume that a muffler company guarantees that it will replace free of charge any muffler it sells that fails during the time the buyer owns the car. The company charges a small service fee for replacing the muffler. This guarantee is an important selling feature for the firm's mufflers. In the past, 6 percent of the mufflers sold have been returned for replacement under the guarantee. The average cost of a muffler is $25. Assume that during July, 350 mufflers were sold. The accrued liability would be recorded as an adjustment at the end of July as shown below:

A = L + OE
+   −

July 31   Product Warranty Expense   525

               Estimated Product Warranty Liability   525

                    To record estimated product
warranty expense:

Number of units sold	350
Rate of replacement under warranty	× .06
Estimated units to be replaced	21
Estimated cost per unit	×$ 25
Estimated liability for product warranty	$525

When a muffler is returned for replacement under the warranty, the cost of the muffler is charged against the Estimated Product Warranty Liability account. For example, assume that on December 5 a customer returns with a defective muffler and pays a $10 service fee to have the muffler replaced. Assume that this particular muffler cost $20. The entry is as follows:

A = L + OE					
+ − +	Dec. 5	Cash		10	
−		Estimated Product Warranty Liability		20	
		Service Revenue			10
		Merchandise Inventory			20
		Replacement of muffler under warranty			

VACATION PAY LIABILITY   In most companies, employees earn the right to paid vacation days or weeks as they work during the year. For example, an employee may earn two weeks of paid vacation for each 50 weeks of work. Therefore, the person is paid 52 weeks' salary for 50 weeks' work. Theoretically, the cost of the two weeks' vacation should be allocated as an expense over the whole year so that month-to-month costs will not be distorted. The vacation pay represents 4 percent (two weeks' vacation divided by 50 weeks) of a worker's pay. Every week worked earns the employee a small fraction (4 percent) for vacation pay.

Vacation pay liability can amount to a substantial amount of money. For example, in its annual report Delta Air Lines, Inc., reported at its 1998 year end a vacation pay liability of $553 million.[6]

Suppose that a company with a vacation policy of two weeks of paid vacation for each 50 weeks of work has a payroll of $21,000, of which $1,000 was paid to employees on vacation for the week ended April 20. Because of turnover and rules regarding term of employment, not every employee in the company will collect vacation pay, and so it is assumed that 75 percent of employees will ultimately collect vacation pay. The computation of vacation pay expense based on the payroll of employees not on vacation ($21,000 − $1,000) is as follows: $20,000 × 4 percent × 75 percent = $600. The entry to record vacation pay expense for the week ended April 20 is as follows:

A = L + OE				
+ −	Apr. 20	Vacation Pay Expense	600	
		Estimated Liability for Vacation Pay		600
		Estimated vacation pay expense		

At the time employees receive their vacation pay, an entry is made debiting Estimated Liability for Vacation Pay and crediting Cash or Wages Payable. For

BUSINESS FOCUS ON PRACTICE

In the early 1980s, American Airlines, Inc., developed a frequent-flier program that gave free trips and other awards to customers based on the number of miles they flew on the airline. Since then, the number of similar programs by other airlines has mushroomed, and it is estimated that 38 million people now belong to airlines' frequent-flier programs. Today, U.S. airlines have more than 3 trillion miles outstanding. Seven to eight percent of all passengers are traveling on free tickets. Estimated liabilities for these tickets have become an important consideration in evaluating an airline's financial position. Complicating the estimate is that almost half the "miles" have been earned on purchases from hotel, car rental, and telephone companies and from the use of credit cards. In the latter cases, the companies giving the miles must pay the airlines at the rate of $.02 per mile. Thus, a free ticket obtained with 25,000 miles provides revenue to the airline of $500.[7]

example, the entry to record the $1,000 paid to employees on vacation during August is as follows:

$$A^* = L + OE$$
$$- \quad -$$

*assumes cash paid

Aug. 31	Estimated Liability for Vacation Pay	1,000	
	Cash (or Wages Payable)		1,000
	Wages of employees on vacation		

The treatment of vacation pay presented in this example may also be applied to other payroll costs, such as bonus plans and contributions to pension plans.

Contingent Liabilities

A **contingent liability** is not an existing liability. Rather, it is a potential liability because it depends on a future event arising out of a past transaction. For instance, a construction company that built a bridge may have been sued by the state for using poor materials. The past transaction is the building of the bridge under contract. The future event is the outcome of the lawsuit, which is not yet known.

Two conditions have been established by the FASB for determining when a contingency should be entered in the accounting records: (1) the liability must be probable and (2) it must be reasonably estimated.[8] Estimated liabilities such as the estimated income taxes liability, warranty liability, and vacation pay liability that were described earlier meet those conditions. Therefore, they are accrued in the accounting records. Potential liabilities that do not meet both conditions (probable and reasonably estimated) are reported in the notes to the financial statements. Losses from such potential liabilities are recorded when the conditions set by the FASB are met.

According to a survey of 600 large companies, the most common types of contingencies reported were litigation, which can involve many different issues, and environmental concerns.[9] The following example of contingent liabilities comes from the notes in the annual report of General Motors Corp., the world's largest automobile manufacturer:

> GM is subject to potential liability under government regulations and various claims and legal actions which are pending or may be asserted against them. Some of the pending actions purport to be class actions. The aggregate ultimate liability of GM under these government regulations and under these claims and actions, was not determinable at December 31, 1998. After discussion with counsel, it is the opinion of management that such liability is not expected to have a material adverse effect on the Corporation's consolidated financial statements.[10]

The Time Value of Money

Interest is the cost associated with the use of money for a specific period of time. It is an important cost to the debtor and an important revenue to the creditor. Because interest is a cost associated with time, and "time is money," it is also an important consideration in any business decision. For example, an individual who holds $100 for one year without putting that $100 in a savings account has forgone the interest that could have been earned. Thus, there is a cost associated with holding this money equal to the interest that could have been earned. Similarly, a business person who accepts a non-interest-bearing note instead of cash for the sale of merchandise is not forgoing the interest that could have been earned on that money but is including the interest implicitly in the price of the merchandise. These examples illustrate the point that the timing of the receipt and payment of cash must be considered in making business decisions.

Simple Interest and Compound Interest

> **Key Point:** Compound interest is the most useful concept of interest in business practice.

Simple interest is the interest cost for one or more periods if we assume that the amount on which the interest is computed stays the same from period to period. **Compound interest** is the interest cost for two or more periods if we assume that after each period the interest of that period is added to the amount on which interest is computed in future periods. In other words, compound interest is interest earned on a principal sum that is increased at the end of each period by the interest of that period.

EXAMPLE: SIMPLE INTEREST Joe Sanchez accepts an 8 percent, $30,000 note due in 90 days. How much will he receive in total at that time? Remember that the formula for calculating simple interest is as follows:

$$\begin{aligned} \text{Interest} &= \text{Principal} \times \text{Rate} \times \text{Time} \\ &= \$30{,}000 \times 8/100 \times 90/360 \\ &= \$600 \end{aligned}$$

Therefore, the total that Sanchez will receive is calculated as follows:

$$\begin{aligned} \text{Total} &= \text{Principal} + \text{Interest} \\ &= \$30{,}000 + \$600 \\ &= \$30{,}600 \end{aligned}$$

EXAMPLE: COMPOUND INTEREST Ann Clary deposits $5,000 in a savings account that pays 6 percent interest. She expects to leave the principal and accumulated interest in the account for three years. How much will her account total at the end of three years? Assume that the interest is paid at the end of the year and is added to the principal at that time, and that this total in turn earns interest. The amount at the end of three years is computed as follows:

(1) Year	(2) Principal Amount at Beginning of Year	(3) Annual Amount of Interest (Col. 2 × 6%)	(4) Accumulated Amount at End of Year (Col. 2 + Col. 3)
1	$5,000.00	$300.00	$5,300.00
2	5,300.00	318.00	5,618.00
3	5,618.00	337.08	5,955.08

At the end of three years, Clary will have $5,955.08 in her savings account. Note that the annual amount of interest increases each year by the interest rate times the interest of the previous year. For example, between year 1 and year 2, the interest increased by $18 ($318 − $300), which equals 6 percent times $300.

Future Value of a Single Invested Sum at Compound Interest

> **OBJECTIVE**
> **5** Use compound interest tables to compute the future value of a single invested sum at compound interest and of an ordinary annuity

Another way to ask the question in the example of compound interest above is, What is the future value of a single sum ($5,000) at compound interest (6 percent) for three years? **Future value** is the amount that an investment will be worth at a future date if invested at compound interest. A businessperson often wants to

Table 1. Future Value of $1 After a Given Number of Time Periods

Periods	1%	2%	3%	4%	5%	6%	7%	8%	9%	10%	12%	14%	15%
1	1.010	1.020	1.030	1.040	1.050	1.060	1.070	1.080	1.090	1.100	1.120	1.140	1.150
2	1.020	1.040	1.061	1.082	1.103	1.124	1.145	1.166	1.188	1.210	1.254	1.300	1.323
3	1.030	1.061	1.093	1.125	1.158	1.191	1.225	1.260	1.295	1.331	1.405	1.482	1.521
4	1.041	1.082	1.126	1.170	1.216	1.262	1.311	1.360	1.412	1.464	1.574	1.689	1.749
5	1.051	1.104	1.159	1.217	1.276	1.338	1.403	1.469	1.539	1.611	1.762	1.925	2.011
6	1.062	1.126	1.194	1.265	1.340	1.419	1.501	1.587	1.677	1.772	1.974	2.195	2.313
7	1.072	1.149	1.230	1.316	1.407	1.504	1.606	1.714	1.828	1.949	2.211	2.502	2.660
8	1.083	1.172	1.267	1.369	1.477	1.594	1.718	1.851	1.993	2.144	2.476	2.853	3.059
9	1.094	1.195	1.305	1.423	1.551	1.689	1.838	1.999	2.172	2.358	2.773	3.252	3.518
10	1.105	1.219	1.344	1.480	1.629	1.791	1.967	2.159	2.367	2.594	3.106	3.707	4.046

Source: Excerpt from Table 1 in the appendix on future value and present value tables.

know future value, but the method of computing the future value just illustrated is too time-consuming in practice. Imagine how tedious the calculation would be if the example were ten years instead of three. Fortunately, there are tables that simplify solving problems involving compound interest. Table 1, which shows the future value of $1 after a given number of time periods, is an example. This table is actually part of a larger table, Table 1 in the appendix on future value and present value tables.

 Suppose that we want to solve the problem of Clary's savings account above. We simply look down the 6 percent column in Table 1 until we reach the line for 3 periods and find the factor 1.191. This factor, when multiplied by $1, gives the future value of that $1 at compound interest of 6 percent for three periods (years in this case). Thus, we solve the problem as follows:

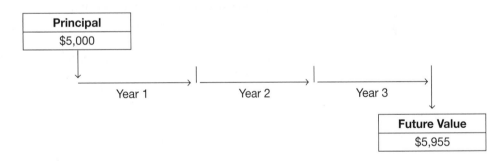

$$\text{Principal} \times \text{Factor} = \text{Future Value}$$
$$\$5{,}000 \times 1.191 = \$5{,}955$$

Except for a rounding difference of $.08, the answer is exactly the same as that calculated earlier.

Future Value of an Ordinary Annuity

Another common problem involves an **ordinary annuity**, which is a series of equal payments made at the end of equal intervals of time, with compound interest on these payments.

The following example shows how to find the future value of an ordinary annuity. Assume that Ben Katz makes a $200 payment at the end of each of the next

Table 2. Future Value of an Ordinary Annuity of $1 Paid in Each Period for a Given Number of Time Periods

Periods	1%	2%	3%	4%	5%	6%	7%	8%	9%	10%	12%	14%	15%
1	1.000	1.000	1.000	1.000	1.000	1.000	1.000	1.000	1.000	1.000	1.000	1.000	1.000
2	2.010	2.020	2.030	2.040	2.050	2.060	2.070	2.080	2.090	2.100	2.120	2.140	2.150
3	3.030	3.060	3.091	3.122	3.153	3.184	3.215	3.246	3.278	3.310	3.374	3.440	3.473
4	4.060	4.122	4.184	4.246	4.310	4.375	4.440	4.506	4.573	4.641	4.779	4.921	4.993
5	5.101	5.204	5.309	5.416	5.526	5.637	5.751	5.867	5.985	6.105	6.353	6.610	6.742
6	6.152	6.308	6.468	6.633	6.802	6.975	7.153	7.336	7.523	7.716	8.115	8.536	8.754
7	7.214	7.434	7.662	7.898	8.142	8.394	8.654	8.923	9.200	9.487	10.09	10.73	11.07
8	8.286	8.583	8.892	9.214	9.549	9.897	10.26	10.64	11.03	11.44	12.30	13.23	13.73
9	9.369	9.755	10.16	10.58	11.03	11.49	11.98	12.49	13.02	13.58	14.78	16.09	16.79
10	10.46	10.95	11.46	12.01	12.58	13.18	13.82	14.49	15.19	15.94	17.55	19.34	20.30

Source: Excerpt from Table 2 in the appendix on future value and present value tables.

three years into a savings account that pays 5 percent interest. How much money will he have in his account at the end of the three years? One way of computing the amount is shown in the following table:

(1) Year	(2) Beginning Balance	(3) Interest Earned (5% × Col. 2)	(4) Periodic Payment	(5) Accumulated at End of Period (Col. 2 + Col. 3 + Col. 4)
1	—	—	$200	$200.00
2	$200.00	$10.00	200	410.00
3	410.00	20.50	200	630.50

Katz would have $630.50 in his account at the end of three years, consisting of $600.00 in periodic payments and $30.50 in interest.

This calculation can also be simplified by using Table 2. We look down the 5 percent column until we reach 3 periods and find the factor 3.153. This factor, when multiplied by $1, gives the future value of a series of three $1 payments at compound interest of 5 percent. Thus, we solve the problem as shown below.

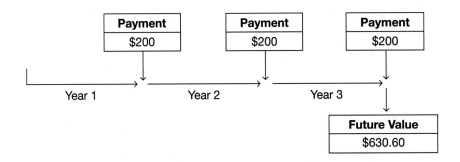

$$\text{Periodic Payment} \times \text{Factor} = \text{Future Value}$$
$$\$200.00 \quad \times \ 3.153 \ = \quad \$630.60$$

Except for a rounding difference of $.10, this result is the same as the one calculated earlier.

Present Value

OBJECTIVE

6 Use compound interest tables to compute the present value of a single sum due in the future and of an ordinary annuity

Key Point: Present value is a method of valuing future cash flows.

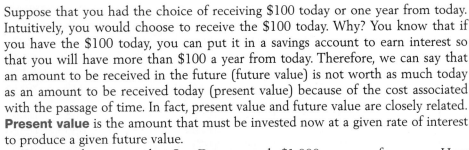

Suppose that you had the choice of receiving $100 today or one year from today. Intuitively, you would choose to receive the $100 today. Why? You know that if you have the $100 today, you can put it in a savings account to earn interest so that you will have more than $100 a year from today. Therefore, we can say that an amount to be received in the future (future value) is not worth as much today as an amount to be received today (present value) because of the cost associated with the passage of time. In fact, present value and future value are closely related. **Present value** is the amount that must be invested now at a given rate of interest to produce a given future value.

For example, assume that Sue Dapper needs $1,000 one year from now. How much should she invest today to achieve that goal if the interest rate is 5 percent? From earlier examples, the following equation may be established:

$$\begin{aligned}
\text{Present Value} \times (1.0 + \text{Interest Rate}) &= \text{Future Value} \\
\text{Present Value} \times \qquad 1.05 &= \$1,000.00 \\
\text{Present Value} &= \$1,000.00 \div 1.05 \\
\text{Present Value} &= \$952.38
\end{aligned}$$

Thus, to achieve a future value of $1,000.00, a present value of $952.38 must be invested. Interest of 5 percent on $952.38 for one year equals $47.62, and these two amounts added together equal $1,000.00.

Present Value of a Single Sum Due in the Future

When more than one time period is involved, the calculation of present value is more complicated. Consider the following example. Don Riley wants to be sure of having $4,000 at the end of three years. How much must he invest today in a 5 percent savings account to achieve this goal? Adapting the above equation, we compute the present value of $4,000 at compound interest of 5 percent for three years in the future.

Year	Amount at End of Year	Divide by		Present Value at Beginning of Year
3	$4,000.00	÷	1.05 =	$3,809.52
2	3,809.52	÷	1.05 =	3,628.11
1	3,628.11	÷	1.05 =	3,455.34

Riley must invest a present value of $3,455.34 to achieve a future value of $4,000.00 in three years. This calculation is again made much easier by using the appropriate table. In Table 3 (on the next page), we look down the 5 percent column until we reach 3 periods and find the factor .864. This factor, when multiplied by $1, gives the present value of $1 to be received three years from now at 5 percent interest. Thus, we solve the problem as shown below.

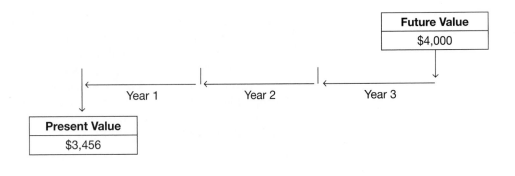

Table 3. Present Value of $1 to Be Received at the End of a Given Number of Time Periods

Periods	1%	2%	3%	4%	5%	6%	7%	8%	9%	10%
1	0.990	0.980	0.971	0.962	0.952	0.943	0.935	0.926	0.917	0.909
2	0.980	0.961	0.943	0.925	0.907	0.890	0.873	0.857	0.842	0.826
3	0.971	0.942	0.915	0.889	0.864	0.840	0.816	0.794	0.772	0.751
4	0.961	0.924	0.888	0.855	0.823	0.792	0.763	0.735	0.708	0.683
5	0.951	0.906	0.863	0.822	0.784	0.747	0.713	0.681	0.650	0.621
6	0.942	0.888	0.837	0.790	0.746	0.705	0.666	0.630	0.596	0.564
7	0.933	0.871	0.813	0.760	0.711	0.665	0.623	0.583	0.547	0.513
8	0.923	0.853	0.789	0.731	0.677	0.627	0.582	0.540	0.502	0.467
9	0.914	0.837	0.766	0.703	0.645	0.592	0.544	0.500	0.460	0.424
10	0.905	0.820	0.744	0.676	0.614	0.558	0.508	0.463	0.422	0.386

Source: Excerpt from Table 3 in the appendix on future value and present value tables.

$$\text{Future Value} \times \text{Factor} = \text{Present Value}$$
$$\$4,000 \times .864 = \$3,456$$

Except for a rounding difference of $.66, this result is the same as the one computed earlier.

Present Value of an Ordinary Annuity

Enrichment Note: Present value is one of the most common techniques used by financial analysts to determine the value today of potential investments.

It is often necessary to compute the present value of a series of receipts or payments. When we calculate the present value of equal amounts equally spaced over a period of time, we are computing the present value of an ordinary annuity.

For example, assume that Kathy Foster has sold a piece of property and is to receive $15,000 in three equal annual payments of $5,000, beginning one year from today. What is the present value of this sale, assuming a current interest rate of 5 percent? This present value may be computed by calculating a separate present value for each of the three payments (using Table 3) and summing the results, as shown in the table below.

Future Receipts (Annuity)				Present Value Factor at 5 Percent (from Table 3)		Present Value
Year 1	Year 2	Year 3				
$5,000			×	.952	=	$ 4,760
	$5,000		×	.907	=	4,535
		$5,000	×	.864	=	4,320
Total Present Value						$13,615

The present value of this sale is $13,615. Thus, there is an implied interest cost (given the 5 percent rate) of $1,385 associated with the payment plan that allows the purchaser to pay in three installments.

We can make this calculation more easily by using Table 4. We look down the 5 percent column until we reach 3 periods and find the factor 2.723. This factor, when multiplied by $1, gives the present value of a series of three $1 payments (spaced one year apart) at compound interest of 5 percent. Thus, we solve the problem as shown next.

Table 4. Present Value of an Ordinary Annuity of $1 Received Each Period for a Given Number of Time Periods

Periods	1%	2%	3%	4%	5%	6%	7%	8%	9%	10%
1	0.990	0.980	0.971	0.962	0.952	0.943	0.935	0.926	0.917	0.909
2	1.970	1.942	1.913	1.886	1.859	1.833	1.808	1.783	1.759	1.736
3	2.941	2.884	2.829	2.775	2.723	2.673	2.624	2.577	2.531	2.487
4	3.902	3.808	3.717	3.630	3.546	3.465	3.387	3.312	3.240	3.170
5	4.853	4.713	4.580	4.452	4.329	4.212	4.100	3.993	3.890	3.791
6	5.795	5.601	5.417	5.242	5.076	4.917	4.767	4.623	4.486	4.355
7	6.728	6.472	6.230	6.002	5.786	5.582	5.389	5.206	5.033	4.868
8	7.652	7.325	7.020	6.733	6.463	6.210	5.971	5.747	5.535	5.335
9	8.566	8.162	7.786	7.435	7.108	6.802	6.515	6.247	5.995	5.759
10	9.471	8.983	8.530	8.111	7.722	7.360	7.024	6.710	6.418	6.145

Source: Excerpt from Table 4 in the appendix on future value and present value tables.

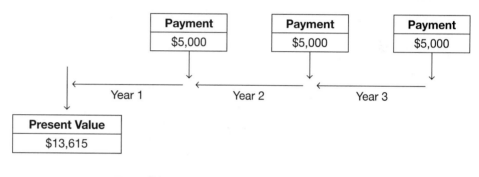

Periodic Payment × Factor = Present Value
$5,000 × 2.723 = $13,615

This result is the same as the one computed earlier.

Time Periods

Key Point: The interest rate used when compounding less than one year is the annual rate divided by the number of periods in a year.

In all of the previous examples, and in most other cases, the compounding period is one year, and the interest rate is stated on an annual basis. However, in each of the four tables, the left-hand column refers not to years but to periods. This wording is intended to accommodate compounding periods of less than one year. Savings accounts that record interest quarterly and bonds that pay interest semiannually are cases in which the compounding period is less than one year. To use the tables in such cases, it is necessary to (1) divide the annual interest rate by the number of periods in the year, and (2) multiply the number of periods in one year by the number of years.

For example, assume that a $6,000 note is to be paid in two years and carries an annual interest rate of 8 percent. Compute the maturity (future) value of the note, assuming that the compounding period is semiannual. Before using the table, it is necessary to compute the interest rate that applies to each compounding period and the total number of compounding periods. First, the interest rate to use is 4 percent (8% annual rate ÷ 2 periods per year). Second, the total number of compounding periods is 4 (2 periods per year × 2 years). From Table 1, therefore, the maturity value of the note is computed as follows:

$$\text{Principal} \times \text{Factor} = \text{Future Value}$$
$$\$6,000 \times 1.170 = \$7,020$$

The note will be worth $7,020 in two years.

This procedure for determining the interest rate and the number of periods when the compounding period is less than one year may be used with all four tables.

Applications of Present Value to Accounting

OBJECTIVE

7 Apply the concept of present value to simple accounting situations

The concept of present value is widely applicable in the discipline of accounting. Here, the purpose is to demonstrate its usefulness in some simple applications. In-depth study of present value is deferred to more advanced courses.

Imputing Interest on Non-Interest-Bearing Notes

Clearly there is no such thing as an interest-free debt, regardless of whether the interest rate is explicitly stated. The Accounting Principles Board has declared that when a long-term note does not explicitly state an interest rate (or if the interest rate is unreasonably low), a rate based on the normal interest cost of the company in question should be assigned, or imputed.[11]

Key Point: There are many applications of the time value of money. Each is based on the fact that there is an interest income or cost associated with the passage of time.

The following example applies this principle. On January 1, 20x0, Gato purchased merchandise from Haines by issuing an $8,000 non-interest-bearing note due in two years. Gato can borrow money from the bank at 9 percent interest. Gato paid the note in full after two years.

Note that the $8,000 note represents partly a payment for merchandise and partly a payment of interest for two years. In recording the purchase and sale, it is necessary to use Table 3 to determine the present value of the note. The calculation follows.

$$\text{Future Payment} \times \text{Present Value Factor (9\%, 2 years)} = \text{Present Value}$$
$$\$8,000 \times .842 = \$6,736$$

The imputed interest cost is $1,264 ($8,000 − $6,736) and is recorded as a discount on notes payable in Gato's records and as a discount on notes receivable in Haines's records. The entries necessary to record the purchase in Gato's records and the sale in Haines's records are as follows:

	Gato Journal			Haines Journal			
A = L + OE	Purchases	6,736		Notes Receivable	8,000		A = L + OE
− −	Discount on Notes			Discount on Notes			+ +
+	Payable	1,264		Receivable		1,264	−
	Notes Payable		8,000	Sales		6,736	

On December 31, 20x0, the adjustments to recognize the interest expense and interest income are as follows:

Gato Journal

A = L + OE			
+			
−			

Interest Expense   606.24
  Discount on
    Notes Payable   606.24

Haines Journal

Discount on
  Notes Receivable   606.24
    Interest Income   606.24

A = L + OE
+ +

The interest is calculated by multiplying the amount of the original purchase by the interest rate for one year ($6,736.00 × .09 = $606.24). When payment is made on December 31, 20x0, the following entries are made in the respective journals:

Gato Journal

A = L + OE		
−	+	−
	−	

Interest Expense   657.76
Notes Payable   8,000.00
  Discount on
    Notes Payable   657.76
  Cash   8,000.00

Haines Journal

Discount on
  Notes Receivable   657.76
Cash   8,000.00
    Interest Income   657.76
    Notes Receivable   8,000.00

A = L + OE	
+	+
+	
−	

The interest entries represent the remaining interest to be expensed or realized ($1,264 − $606.24 = $657.76). This amount approximates (because of rounding differences in the table) the interest for one year on the purchase plus last year's interest [($6,736 + $606.24) × .09 = $660.80].

Valuing an Asset

An asset is recorded because it will provide future benefits to the company that owns it. These future benefits are the basis for the definition of an asset. Usually, the purchase price of the asset represents the present value of these future benefits. It is possible to evaluate a proposed purchase price for an asset by comparing that price with the present value of the asset to the company.

For example, Sam Hurst is thinking of buying a new machine that will reduce his annual labor cost by $700 per year. The machine will last eight years. The interest rate that Hurst assumes for making managerial decisions is 10 percent. What is the maximum amount (present value) that Hurst should pay for the machine?

The present value of the machine to Hurst is equal to the present value of an ordinary annuity of $700 per year for eight years at compound interest of 10 percent. Using the factor from Table 4, we compute the value as follows:

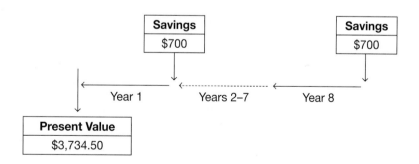

Periodic Savings × Factor = Present Value
  $700.00   × 5.335 = $3,734.50

Hurst should not pay more than $3,734.50 for the new machine because this amount equals the present value of the benefits that will be received from owning the machine.

Deferred Payment

A seller will sometimes agree to defer payment for a sale in order to encourage the buyer to make the purchase. This practice is common, for example, in the farm implement industry, where the farmer needs the equipment in the spring but cannot pay for it until the fall crop is in. Assume that Plains Implement Corporation sells a tractor to Dana Washington for $50,000 on February 1, agreeing to take payment ten months later, on December 1. When this type of agreement is made, the future payment includes not only the sales price of the tractor but also an implied (imputed) interest cost. If the prevailing annual interest rate for such transactions is 12 percent compounded monthly, the actual sale (purchase) price of the tractor would be the present value of the future payment, computed using the factor from Table 3 (10 periods, 1 percent), as follows:

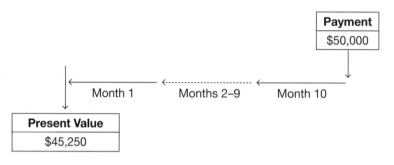

Future Payment × Factor = Present Value
$50,000 × .905 = $45,250

The purchase in Washington's records and the sale in Plains's records are recorded at the present value, $45,250. The balance consists of interest expense or interest income. The entries necessary to record the purchase in Washington's records and the sale in Plains's records are as follows:

		Washington Journal			Plains Journal			
A = L + OE	Feb. 1	Tractor	45,250		Accounts Receivable	45,250		A = L + OE
+ +		Accounts Payable		45,250	Sales		45,250	+ +
		Purchase of tractor			Sale of tractor			

When Washington pays for the tractor, the entries are as follows:

		Washington Journal			Plains Journal			
A = L + OE	Dec. 1	Accounts Payable	45,250		Cash	50,000		A = L + OE
− − −		Interest Expense	4,750		Accounts Receivable		45,250	+ +
		Cash		50,000	Interest Income		4,750	−
		Payment on account, including imputed interest expense			Receipt on account from Washington, including imputed interest earned			

Investment of Idle Cash

Childware Corporation, a toy manufacturer, has just completed a successful fall selling season and has $10,000,000 in cash to invest for six months. The company places the cash in a money market account that is expected to pay 12 percent annual interest. Interest is compounded monthly and credited to the company's account each month. How much cash will the company have at the end of six months, and what entries will be made to record the investment and the monthly interest? The future value factor from Table 1 is based on six monthly periods of 1 percent (12 percent divided by 12 months), and the future value is computed as follows:

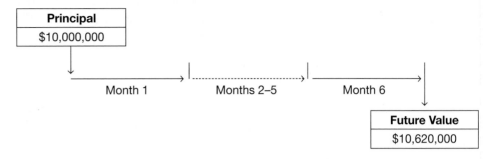

$$\begin{aligned}\text{Investment} \times \text{Factor} &= \text{Future Value}\\ \$10,000,000 \times 1.062 &= \$10,620,000\end{aligned}$$

When the investment is made, the following entry is made:

A = L + OE
\+
–

Short-Term Investments	10,000,000	
Cash		10,000,000
Investment of cash		

After the first month, the interest is recorded by increasing the Short-Term Investments account.

A = L + OE
\+   +

Short-Term Investments	100,000	
Interest Income		100,000
One month's interest income		
$10,000,000 × .01 = $100,000		

After the second month, the interest is earned on the new balance of the Short-Term Investments account.

A = L + OE
\+   +

Short-Term Investments	101,000	
Interest Income		101,000
One month's interest income		
$10,100,000 × .01 = $101,000		

Entries would continue in a similar manner for four more months, at which time the balance of Short-Term Investments would be about $10,620,000. The actual amount accumulated may vary from this total because the interest rate paid on money market accounts can vary over time as a result of changes in market conditions.

Accumulation of a Fund

When a company owes a large fixed amount due in several years, management would be wise to accumulate a fund with which to pay off the debt at maturity. Sometimes creditors, when they agree to provide a loan, require that such a fund be established. In establishing the fund, management must determine how much cash to set aside each period in order to pay the debt. The amount will depend on the estimated rate of interest the investments will earn. Assume that Vason Corporation agrees with a creditor to set aside cash at the end of each year to accumulate enough to pay off a $100,000 note due in five years. Since the first contribution to the fund will be made in one year, five annual contributions will be made by the time the note is due. Assume also that the fund is projected to earn 8 percent, compounded annually. The amount of each annual payment is calculated using Table 2 (5 periods, 8 percent), as follows:

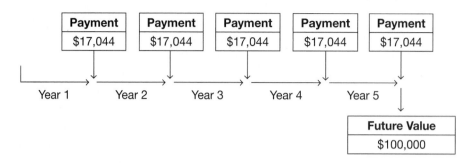

$$\text{Future Value of Fund} \div \text{Factor} = \text{Annual Investment}$$
$$\$100,000 \div 5.867 = \$17,044 \text{ (rounded)}$$

Each year's contribution to the fund is $17,044. This contribution is recorded as follows:

A = L + OE   Loan Repayment Fund   17,044
+
−   Cash   17,044
                 Annual contribution to loan repayment fund

Other Accounting Applications

There are many other applications of present value in accounting, including accounting for installment notes, valuing a bond, and recording lease obligations. Present value is also applied in such areas as pension obligations; premium and discount on debt; depreciation of property, plant, and equipment; capital expenditure decisions; and generally any problem in which time is a factor.

Chapter Review

REVIEW OF LEARNING OBJECTIVES

Ace it

1. **Identify the management issues related to recognition, valuation, classification, and disclosure of current liabilities.** Liabilities represent present legal obligations for future payment of assets or future performance of services. They result from past transactions and should be recognized when there is a transaction that obligates the company to make future payments. Liabilities are valued at the amount of money necessary to satisfy the obligation or the fair value of goods or services that must be delivered. Liabilities are classified as current or long term. Supplemental disclosure is required when the nature or details of the obligations would help in understanding the liability. Liabilities are an important consideration in assessing a company's liquidity. Key measures are working capital, payables turnover, and average days' payable.

2. **Identify, compute, and record definitely determinable and estimated current liabilities.** Two principal categories of current liabilities are definitely determinable liabilities and estimated liabilities. Although definitely determinable liabilities, such as accounts payable, notes payable, dividends

payable, accrued liabilities, and the current portion of long-term debt, can be measured exactly, the accountant must still be careful not to overlook existing liabilities in these categories. Estimated liabilities, such as liabilities for income taxes, property taxes, and product warranties, definitely exist, but the amounts must be estimated and recorded properly.

3. **Define *contingent liability.*** A contingent liability is a potential liability arising from a past transaction and dependent on a future event. Examples are lawsuits, income tax disputes, discounted notes receivable, guarantees of debt, and failure to follow government regulations.

4. **Define *interest* and distinguish between simple and compound interest.** Interest is the cost of using money for a period of time. In computing simple interest, the amount on which the interest is computed stays the same from period to period. However, in computing compound interest, the interest for a period is added to the principal amount before the interest for the next period is computed.

5. **Use compound interest tables to compute the future value of a single invested sum at compound interest and of an ordinary annuity.** Future value is the amount that an investment will be worth at a future date if invested at compound interest. An ordinary annuity is a series of equal payments made at the end of equal intervals of time, with compound interest on the payments. Use Table 1 in the appendix on future value and present value tables to compute the future value of a single sum and Table 2 in the same appendix to compute the future value of an ordinary annuity.

6. **Use compound interest tables to compute the present value of a single sum due in the future and of an ordinary annuity.** Present value is the amount that must be invested now at a given rate of interest to produce a given future value. The present value of an ordinary annuity is the present value of a series of payments. Use Table 3 in the appendix on future value and present value tables to compute the present value of a single sum and Table 4 in the same appendix to compute the present value of an ordinary annuity.

7. **Apply the concept of present value to simple accounting situations.** Present value may be used to compute interest on non-interest-bearing notes, to value a bond or other asset, to compute the present value of deferred payments, to determine a bargaining range in negotiating the sale of a business, to determine the future value of an investment of idle cash or the accumulation of a fund, to record lease obligations, and in other accounting situations.

REVIEW OF CONCEPTS AND TERMINOLOGY

The following concepts and terms were introduced in this chapter:

LO 1   **Average days' payable:** How long, on average, a company takes to pay its accounts payable; 365 days divided by payables turnover.

LO 2   **Commercial paper:** A means of borrowing short-term funds by using unsecured loans that are sold directly to the public, usually through professionally managed investment firms.

LO 4   **Compound interest:** The interest cost for two or more periods if we assume that after each period the interest of that period is added to the amount on which interest is computed in future periods.

LO 3   **Contingent liability:** A potential liability that depends on a future event arising out of a past transaction.

LO 1   **Current liabilities:** Debts and obligations expected to be satisfied within one year or within the normal operating cycle, whichever is longer.

LO 2 **Definitely determinable liabilities:** Current liabilities that are set by contract or by statute and can be measured exactly.

LO 2 **Estimated liabilities:** Definite debts or obligations of which the exact amounts cannot be known until a later date.

LO 5 **Future value:** The amount that an investment will be worth at a future date if invested at compound interest.

LO 4 **Interest:** The cost associated with the use of money for a specific period of time.

LO 1 **Liabilities:** Legal obligations for the future payment of assets or the future performance of services that result from past transactions.

LO 2 **Line of credit:** A preapproved arrangement with a commercial bank that allows a company to borrow funds as needed.

LO 1 **Long-term liabilities:** Debts or obligations due beyond one year or beyond the normal operating cycle.

LO 5 **Ordinary annuity:** A series of equal payments made at the end of equal intervals of time, with compound interest on the payments.

LO 1 **Payables turnover:** Number of times on average that accounts payable are paid in an accounting period; cost of goods sold plus (or minus) change in merchandise inventory divided by average accounts payable.

LO 6 **Present value:** The amount that must be invested now at a given rate of interest to produce a given future value.

LO 2 **Salaries:** Compensation to employees who are paid at a monthly or yearly rate.

LO 4 **Simple interest:** The interest cost for one or more periods if we assume that the amount on which the interest is computed stays the same from period to period.

LO 2 **Unearned revenues:** Revenues received in advance for which the goods will not be delivered or the services performed during the current accounting period.

LO 2 **Wages:** Payment for services of employees at an hourly rate.

REVIEW PROBLEM

LO 2

Notes Payable Transactions and End-of-Period Entries

McLaughlin, Inc., whose fiscal year ends June 30, 20xx, completed the following transactions involving notes payable:

May 11 Purchased a small crane by issuing a 60-day, 12 percent note for $54,000. The face of the note does not include interest.

16 Obtained a $40,000 bank loan to finance a temporary increase in receivables by signing a 90-day, 10 percent note. The face value includes interest.

June 30 Made the end-of-year adjusting entry to accrue interest expense.

30 Made the end-of-year adjusting entry to recognize interest expired on the note.

30 Made the end-of-year closing entry pertaining to interest expense.

July 10 Paid the note plus interest on the crane purchase.

Aug. 14 Paid off the note to the bank.

REQUIRED

Prepare entries in journal form for the above transactions.

ANSWER TO REVIEW PROBLEM

20xx

May 11	Equipment	54,000	
	Notes Payable		54,000
	Purchase of crane with 60-day, 12% note		

May 16	Cash		39,000	
	Discount on Notes Payable		1,000	
	Notes Payable			40,000
	Loan from bank obtained by signing			
	90-day, 10% note; discount equals			
	$40,000 × .10 × 90/360 = $1,000			
June 30	Interest Expense		900	
	Interest Payable			900
	To accrue interest expense			
	$54,000 × .12 × 50/360 = $900			
30	Interest Expense		500	
	Discount on Notes Payable			500
	To recognize interest on note			
	$1,000 × 45/90 = $500			
30	Income Summary		1,400	
	Interest Expense			1,400
	To close interest expense			
July 10	Notes Payable		54,000	
	Interest Payable		900	
	Interest Expense		180	
	Cash			55,080
	Payment of note on equipment			
	$54,000 × .12 × 60/360 = $1,080			
Aug. 14	Notes Payable		40,000	
	Cash			40,000
	Payment of bank loan			
14	Interest Expense		500	
	Discount on Notes Payable			500
	Interest expense on matured note			
	$1,000 − $500 = $500			

Chapter Assignments

BUILDING YOUR KNOWLEDGE FOUNDATION

QUESTIONS

1. What are liabilities?
2. Why is the timing of liability recognition important in accounting?
3. At the end of the accounting period, Janson Company had a legal obligation to accept delivery of and pay for a truckload of hospital supplies the following week. Is this legal obligation a liability?
4. Ned Johnson, a star college basketball player, received a contract from the Midwest Blazers to play professional basketball. The contract calls for a salary of $300,000 a year for four years, dependent on his making the team in each of those years. Should this contract be considered a liability and recorded on the books of the basketball team?
5. What is the rule for classifying a liability as current?
6. What are a line of credit and commercial paper? Where do they appear on the balance sheet?
7. A bank is offering Diane Wedge two alternatives for borrowing $2,000. The first alternative is a $2,000, 12 percent, 30-day note. The second alternative is a $2,000, 30-day note discounted at 12 percent. (a) What entries are required by Diane Wedge to record the two loans? (b) What entries are needed by Wedge to record the payment of the two loans? (c) Which alternative favors Wedge, and why?

8. Where should the Discount on Notes Payable account appear on the balance sheet?

9. When can a portion of long-term debt be classified as a current liability?

10. What are three types of employer-related payroll liabilities?

11. How does an employee differ from an independent contractor?

12. Who pays social security and Medicare taxes?

13. Why are unearned revenues classified as liabilities?

14. What is definite about an estimated liability?

15. Why are income taxes payable considered to be estimated liabilities?

16. When does a company incur a liability for a product warranty?

17. What is a contingent liability, and how does it differ from an estimated liability?

18. What are some examples of contingent liabilities? For what reason is each a contingent liability?

19. What is the difference between simple and compound interest?

20. What is an ordinary annuity?

21. What is the key variable that distinguishes present value from future value?

22. How does the use of a compounding period of less than one year affect the computation of present value?

23. Why is present value important to accounting? (Illustrate your answer by giving concrete examples of applications in accounting.)

SHORT EXERCISES

SE 1.
LO 1   Issues in Accounting for Liabilities

Indicate whether each of the following actions relates to (a) managing liquidity and cash flow, (b) recognition of liabilities, (c) valuation of liabilities, (d) classification of liabilities, or (e) disclosure of liabilities.

1. Determining that a liability will be paid in less than one year

2. Estimating the amount of a liability

3. Providing information about when liabilities are due and the interest rate that they carry

4. Determining when a liability arises

5. Assessing working capital and payables turnover

SE 2.
LO 1   Measuring Short-Term Liquidity

Turnbow Company has current assets of $130,000 and current liabilities of $80,000, of which accounts payable are $70,000. Turnbow's cost of goods sold is $460,000, its merchandise inventory increased by $20,000, and accounts payable were $50,000 the prior year. Calculate Turnbow's working capital, payables turnover, and average days' payable.

SE 3.
LO 2   Types of Liabilities
LO 3

Indicate whether each of the following is (a) a definitely determinable liability, (b) an estimated liability, or (c) a contingent liability.

1. Dividends Payable

2. Pending litigation

3. Income Taxes Payable

4. Current portion of long-term debt

5. Vacation Pay Liability

6. Guaranteed loans of another company

SE 4.
LO 2   Interest Expense: Interest Not Included in Face Value of Note

On the last day of August, Gross Company borrowed $60,000 on a bank note for 60 days at 10 percent interest. Assume that interest is stated separately. Prepare the following entries in journal form: (1) August 31, recording of note; and (2) October 30, payment of note plus interest.

SE 5.

LO 2 **Interest Expense: Interest Included in Face Value of Note**

Assume the same facts as in **SE 4,** except that interest of $1,000 is included in the face amount of the note and the note is discounted at the bank on August 31. Prepare the following entries in journal form: (1) August 31, recording of note; and (2) October 30, payment of note and recording of interest expense.

SE 6.

LO 2 **Payroll Entries**

The following payroll totals for the month of April were taken from the payroll register of Coover Corporation: salaries, $223,000.00; federal income taxes withheld, $31,440.00; social security tax withheld, $13,826.00; Medicare tax withheld, $3,233.50; medical insurance deductions, $6,580.00; and salaries subject to unemployment taxes, $156,600.00. Prepare journal entries to record (1) the monthly payroll and (2) employer's payroll expense, assuming social security and Medicare taxes equal to the amounts for employees, a federal unemployment insurance tax of .8 percent, a state unemployment tax of 5.4 percent, and medical insurance premiums for which the employer pays 80 percent of the cost.

SE 7.

LO 2 **Product Warranty Liability**

Rainbow Corp. manufactures and sells travel clocks. Each clock costs $25 to produce and sells for $50. In addition, each clock carries a warranty that provides for free replacement if it fails during the two years following the sale. In the past, 5 percent of the clocks sold have had to be replaced under the warranty. During October, Rainbow sold 52,000 clocks, and 2,800 clocks were replaced under the warranty. Prepare journal entries to record the estimated liability for product warranties during the month and the clocks replaced under warranty during the month.

SE 8.

LO 4 **Simple and Compound**
LO 5 **Interest**

Naber Motors, Inc., receives a one-year note that carries a 12 percent annual interest rate on $1,500 for the sale of a used car. Compute the maturity value under each of the following assumptions: (1) Simple interest is charged. (2) The interest is compounded semiannually. (3) The interest is compounded quarterly. (4) The interest is compounded monthly.

SE 9.

LO 5 **Future Value Calculations**

Find the future value of (1) a single payment of $10,000 at 7 percent for ten years, (2) ten annual payments of $1,000 at 7 percent, (3) a single payment of $3,000 at 9 percent for seven years, and (4) seven annual payments of $3,000 at 9 percent.

SE 10.

LO 6 **Present Value Calculations**

Find the present value of (1) a single payment of $12,000 at 6 percent for 12 years, (2) 12 annual payments of $1,000 at 6 percent, (3) a single payment of $2,500 at 9 percent for five years, and (4) five annual payments of $2,500 at 9 percent.

SE 11.

LO 7 **Valuing an Asset for the Purpose of Making a Purchasing Decision**

Masa owns a machine shop and has the opportunity to purchase a new machine for $15,000. After carefully studying projected costs and revenues, Masa estimates that the new machine will produce a net cash flow of $3,600 annually and will last for eight years. Masa feels that an interest rate of 10 percent is adequate for his business.

Calculate the present value of the machine to Masa. Does the purchase appear to be a correct business decision?

EXERCISES

E 1.

LO 1 **Issues in Accounting for Liabilities**

Indicate whether each of the following actions relates to (a) managing liquidity and cash flows, (b) recognition of liabilities, (c) valuation of liabilities, (d) classification of liabilities, or (e) disclosure of liabilities.

1. Setting a liability at the fair market value of goods to be delivered
2. Relating the payment date of a liability to the length of the operating cycle
3. Recording a liability in accordance with the matching rule
4. Providing information about financial instruments on the balance sheet
5. Estimating the amount of "cents-off" coupons that will be redeemed
6. Categorizing a liability as long-term debt
7. Measuring working capital
8. Comparing average days' payable with last year

LO 1   Measuring Short-Term Liquidity

E 2. In 20x1, Rady Company had current assets of $310,000 and current liabilities of $200,000, of which accounts payable were $130,000. Cost of goods sold was $850,000, merchandise inventory increased by $40,000, and accounts payable were $110,000 in the prior year. In 20x2, Rady Company had current assets of $420,000 and current liabilities of $320,000, of which accounts payable were $150,000. Cost of goods sold was $950,000 and merchandise inventory decreased by $30,000. Calculate Rady's working capital, payables turnover, and average days' payable for 20x1 and 20x2. Assess Rady's liquidity and cash flows in relation to the change in payables turnover from 20x1 to 20x2.

LO 2   Interest Expense: Interest Not Included in Face Value of Note

E 3. On the last day of October, Thespian Company borrows $30,000 on a bank note for 60 days at 12 percent interest. Assume that interest is not included in the face amount. Prepare the following entries in journal form: (1) October 31, recording of note; (2) November 30, accrual of interest expense; and (3) December 30, payment of note plus interest.

LO 2   Interest Expense: Interest Included in Face Value of Note

E 4. Assume the same facts as in **E 3,** except that interest is included in the face amount of the note and the note is discounted at the bank on October 31. Prepare the following entries in journal form: (1) October 31, recording of note; (2) November 30, recognition of interest accrued on note; and (3) December 30, payment of note and recording of interest expense.

LO 2   Sales and Excise Taxes

E 5. Quick Dial Service billed its customers a total of $980,400 for the month of August, including 9 percent federal excise tax and 5 percent sales tax.

1. Determine the proper amount of service revenue to report for the month.

2. Prepare an entry in journal form to record the revenue and related liabilities for the month.

LO 2   Payroll Entries

E 6. At the end of October, the payroll register for Echo Tool and Die Corporation contained the following totals: wages, $185,500; federal income taxes withheld, $47,442; state income taxes withheld, $7,818; social security tax withheld, $11,501; Medicare tax withheld, $2,689.75; medical insurance deductions, $6,435; and wages subject to unemployment taxes, $28,620.

Prepare entries in journal form to record the (1) monthly payroll and (2) employer payroll expenses, assuming social security and Medicare taxes equal to the amount for employees, a federal unemployment insurance tax of .8 percent, a state unemployment tax of 5.4 percent, and medical insurance premiums for which the employer pays 80 percent of the cost.

LO 2   Product Warranty Liability

E 7. Ziggy Company manufactures and sells electronic games. Each game costs $25 to produce and sells for $45. In addition, each game carries a warranty that provides for free replacement if it fails during the two years following the sale. In the past, 7 percent of the games sold had to be replaced under the warranty. During July, Ziggy sold 26,000 games and 2,800 games were replaced under the warranty.

1. Prepare an entry in journal form to record the estimated liability for product warranties during the month.

2. Prepare an entry in journal form to record the games replaced under warranty during the month.

LO 2   Vacation Pay Liability

E 8. Rochester Corporation currently allows each employee who has worked at the company for one year three weeks' paid vacation. Based on studies of employee turnover and previous experience, management estimates that 65 percent of the employees will qualify for vacation pay this year.

1. Assume that Rochester's July payroll is $600,000, of which $40,000 is paid to employees on vacation. Figure the estimated employee vacation benefit for the month.

2. Prepare an entry in journal form to record the employee benefit for July.

3. Prepare an entry in journal form to record the pay to employees on vacation.

E 9.

LO 2 Property Tax Liability

Sarro Corporation prepares monthly financial statements and ends its fiscal year on June 30, the same as the local government. In July 20x1, your first month as accountant for the company, you find that the company has not previously accrued estimated liabilities. In the past, the company, which has a large property tax bill, has charged the property tax to the month in which the bill is paid. The tax bill for the year ended June 30, 20x1, was $72,000, and it is estimated that the tax will increase by 8 percent for the year ending June 30, 20x2. The tax bill is usually received on September 1, to be paid November 1.

Figure the proper monthly charge to property tax expense and prepare entries in journal form for the following:

July 31 Accrual of property tax expense
Aug. 31 Accrual of property tax expense
Sept. 30 Accrual of property tax expense (assume the actual bill is $81,720)
Oct. 31 Accrual of property tax expense
Nov. 1 Payment of property tax
      30 Recording of monthly property tax expense

Note: Tables 1 to 4 in the appendix on future value and present value tables may be used where appropriate to solve Exercises **E 10** through **E 23**.

E 10.

LO 5 Future Value Calculations

Wieland receives a one-year note for $3,000 that carries a 12 percent annual interest rate for the sale of a used car. Compute the maturity value under each of the following assumptions: (1) The interest is simple interest. (2) The interest is compounded semiannually. (3) The interest is compounded quarterly. (4) The interest is compounded monthly.

E 11.

LO 5 Future Value Calculations

Find the future value of (1) a single payment of $20,000 at 7 percent for ten years, (2) ten annual payments of $2,000 at 7 percent, (3) a single payment of $6,000 at 9 percent for seven years, and (4) seven annual payments of $6,000 at 9 percent.

E 12.

LO 5 Future Value Calculations

Assume that $40,000 is invested today. Compute the amount that would accumulate at the end of seven years when the interest rate is (1) 8 percent compounded annually, (2) 8 percent compounded semiannually, and (3) 8 percent compounded quarterly.

E 13.

LO 5 Working Backward from a
LO 7 Future Value

Ruby Santhapur has a debt of $90,000 due in four years. She wants to save enough money to pay it off by making annual deposits, starting at the end of the first year, in an investment account that earns 8 percent annual interest. Calculate the amount she must deposit each year to reach her goal. (*Hint:* Use Table 2 in the appendix on future value and present value tables; then make a calculation.)

E 14.

LO 6 Determining an Advance
LO 7 Payment

Lydia Lafin is contemplating paying five years' rent in advance. Her annual rent is $9,600. Calculate the single sum that would have to be paid now for the advance rent, if we assume compound interest of 8 percent.

E 15.

LO 6 Present Value Calculations

Find the present value of (1) a single payment of $24,000 at 6 percent for 12 years, (2) 12 annual payments of $2,000 at 6 percent, (3) a single payment of $5,000 at 9 percent for five years, and (4) five annual payments of $5,000 at 9 percent.

E 16.

LO 6 Present Value of a
LO 7 Lump-Sum Contract

A contract calls for a lump-sum payment of $60,000. Find the present value of the contract, assuming that (1) the payment is due in five years, and the current interest rate is 9 percent; (2) the payment is due in ten years, and the current interest rate is 9 percent; (3) the payment is due in five years, and the current interest rate is 5 percent; and (4) the payment is due in ten years, and the current interest rate is 5 percent.

E 17.

LO 6 Present Value of an
LO 7 Annuity Contract

A contract calls for annual payments of $1,200. Find the present value of the contract, assuming that (1) the number of payments is seven, and the current interest rate is 6 percent; (2) the number of payments is 14, and the current interest rate is 6 percent; (3) the number of payments is seven, and the current interest rate is 8 percent; and (4) the number of payments is 14, and the current interest rate is 8 percent.

LO 6 **Non-Interest-Bearing**
LO 7 **Note**

E 18. On January 1, 20x0, Koltin purchased a machine from McGee by signing a two-year, non-interest-bearing $32,000 note. Koltin currently pays 12 percent interest to borrow money at the bank.

Prepare entries in Koltin's and McGee's journals to (1) record the purchase and the note, (2) adjust the accounts after one year, and (3) record payment of the note after two years (on December 31, 20x2).

LO 6 **Valuing an Asset for the**
LO 7 **Purpose of Making a**
Purchasing Decision

E 19. Phil owns a service station and has the opportunity to purchase a car wash machine for $30,000. After carefully studying projected costs and revenues, Phil estimates that the car wash machine will produce a net cash flow of $5,200 annually and will last for eight years. Phil feels that an interest rate of 14 percent is adequate for his business. Calculate the present value of the machine to Phil. Does the purchase appear to be a correct business decision?

LO 6 **Deferred Payment**
LO 7

E 20. Jun Equipment Corporation sold a precision tool machine with computer controls to Cruz Corporation for $800,000 on January 1, agreeing to take payment nine months later, on October 1. Assuming that the prevailing annual interest rate for such a transaction is 16 percent compounded quarterly, what is the actual sale (purchase) price of the machine tool, and what journal entries will be made at the time of the purchase (sale) and at the time of the payment (receipt) on the records of both Cruz and Jun?

LO 5 **Investment of Idle Cash**
LO 7

E 21. Black Paper Publishing Company, a publisher of college books, has just completed a successful fall selling season and has $5,000,000 in cash to invest for nine months, beginning on January 1. The company placed the cash in a money market account that is expected to pay 12 percent annual interest compounded monthly. Interest is credited to the company's account each month. How much cash will the company have at the end of nine months, and what entries are made to record the investment and the first two monthly (February 1 and March 1) interest amounts?

LO 5 **Accumulation of a Fund**
LO 7

E 22. Loretto Corporation borrowed $3,000,000 from an insurance company on a five-year note. Management agreed to set aside enough cash at the end of each year to accumulate the amount needed to pay off the note at maturity. Since the first contribution to the fund will be made in one year, four annual contributions are needed. Assuming that the fund will earn 10 percent compounded annually, how much will the annual contribution to the fund be (round to nearest dollar), and what will be the journal entry for the first contribution?

LO 6 **Negotiating the Sale**
LO 7 **of a Business**

E 23. Steve Heckle is attempting to sell his business to Vassoria Dobey. The company has assets of $900,000, liabilities of $800,000, and owners' equity of $100,000. Both parties agree that the proper rate of return to expect is 12 percent; however, they differ on other assumptions. Heckle believes that the business will generate at least $100,000 per year of cash flows for 20 years. Dobey thinks that $80,000 in cash flows per year is more reasonable and that only ten years in the future should be considered. Using Table 4 in the appendix on future value and present value tables, determine the range for negotiation by computing the present value of Heckle's offer to sell and of Dobey's offer to buy.

PROBLEMS

LO 1 **Identification of Current**
LO 2 **Liabilities**

P 1. Jerry Highland opened a small television repair shop, Highland Television Repair, on January 2, 20x0. He also sold a small line of television sets. In January 20x1, Highland realized that he had failed to file any tax reports for his business since its inception and therefore probably owed a considerable amount of taxes. Since Highland has limited experience in running a business, he has brought all his business records to you for help. The records include a checkbook, canceled checks, deposit slips, invoices from his suppliers, a notice of annual property taxes of $4,620 due to the city, and a promissory note to his father-in-law for $5,000. He wants you to determine what his business owes the government and other parties.

You analyze all his records and determine the following as of December 31, 20x0:

Unpaid invoices for televisions	$ 18,000
Television sales (excluding sales tax)	88,540
Cost of Televisions Sold	62,250
Workers' salaries	20,400
Repair revenues	120,600
Current assets	32,600
Television inventory	23,500

You learn that the company has deducted $952 from the two employees' salaries for federal income taxes owed to the government. The current social security tax is 6.2 percent on maximum earnings of $72,600 for each employee, and the current Medicare tax is 1.45 percent (no maximum earnings). The FUTA tax is 5.4 percent to the state and .8 percent to the federal government on the first $7,000 earned by each employee, and each employee earned more than $7,000. Highland has not filed a sales tax report to the state (5 percent of sales).

REQUIRED

1. Given these limited facts, determine Highland Television Repair's current liabilities as of December 31, 20x0.

2. What additional information would you want from Highland to satisfy yourself that all current liabilities have been identified?

3. Evaluate Highland's liquidity by calculating working capital, payables turnover, and average days' payable. Comment on the results. (Assume average accounts payable were the same as year-end accounts payable.)

P 2.
LO 2 Notes Payable Transactions and End-of-Period Entries

Botjen Corporation, whose fiscal year ends June 30, completed the following transactions involving notes payable:

May 11 Signed a 90-day, 12 percent, $66,000 note payable to Shire Bank for a working capital loan. The face value included interest. Proceeds received were $64,020.

21 Obtained a 60-day extension on an $18,000 trade account payable owed to a supplier by signing a 60-day, $18,000 note. Interest is in addition to the face value, at the rate of 14 percent.

June 30 Made end-of-year adjusting entry to accrue interest expense on supplier note.

30 Made end-of-year adjusting entry to recognize interest accrued on bank note.

July 20 Paid off the note plus interest due the supplier.

Aug. 9 Paid amount due to the bank on the 90-day note.

REQUIRED

Prepare entries in journal form for the notes payable transactions.

P 3.
LO 2 Product Warranty Liability

Maide Company is engaged in the retail sale of washing machines. Each machine has a 24-month warranty on parts. If a repair under warranty is required, a charge for the labor is made. Management has found that 20 percent of the machines sold require some work before the warranty expires. Furthermore, the average cost of replacement parts has been $120 per repair. At the beginning of June, the account for the estimated liability for product warranties had a credit balance of $28,600. During June, 112 machines were returned under the warranty. The cost of the parts used in repairing the machines was $17,530, and $18,884 was collected as service revenue for the labor involved. During the month, Maide Company sold 450 new machines.

REQUIRED

1. Prepare entries in journal form to record each of the following: (a) the warranty work completed during the month, including related revenue; (b) the estimated liability for product warranties for machines sold during the month.

2. Compute the balance of the Estimated Product Warranty Liability account at the end of the month.

P 4.

LO 2 **Non-Interest-Bearing**
LO 6 **Note and Valuing an**
LO 7 **Asset for the Purpose of**
Making a Purchasing
Decision

REQUIRED

Part A: Munro, Inc., provides heavy-duty industrial cleaning services to manufacturing companies. On July 1, 20x1, Munro, Inc., purchased a new truck from Lake Corporation by signing a two-year, non-interest-bearing $24,000 note. Lake currently pays 15 percent interest to borrow money at the bank.

Prepare journal entries in Munro's and Lake's records to (1) record the purchase and the note, (2) adjust the accounts after one year (assuming June 30 year end), and (3) record payment of the note after two years (on June 30, 20x3). (Reversing entries are not made by either company.)

Part B: Becker Corporation is in the lawn-care business. Management is considering the purchase of a special type of spraying machine for $38,000. After carefully studying projected costs and revenues, management estimates that the machine will produce an annual net cash flow of $10,500 for the next seven years. Management also believes that an interest rate of 18 percent is appropriate for this analysis.

REQUIRED

Calculate the present value of the machine to Becker Corporation. Does the purchase appear to be a correct business decision?

P 5.

LO 5 **Time Value of Money**
LO 6 **Applications**
LO 7

Effective January 1, 20x1, the board of directors of Riordan, Inc., approved the following actions, each of which is an application of the time value of money:

a. Established in a single payment of $100,000 a contingency fund for the possible settlement of a lawsuit. The suit is expected to be settled in two years.
b. Asked for another fund to be established by a single payment to accumulate to $300,000 in four years.
c. Approved purchase of a parcel of land for future plant expansion. Payments are to start January 1, 20x2, at $200,000 per year for 5 years.
d. Determined that a new building to be built on the property in **c** would cost $1,600,000 and authorized five annual payments to be paid starting January 1, 20x2, into a fund for its construction.
e. Purchased Riordan common stock from a stockholder who wanted to be bought out by issuing a four-year, non-interest-bearing note for $800,000.

REQUIRED

Assuming an annual interest rate of 8 percent and using Tables 1, 2, 3, and 4, answer the following questions:

1. In action **a,** how much will the fund accumulate to in two years?
2. In action **b,** how much will need to be deposited initially to accumulate the desired amount?
3. In action **c,** what is the purchase price (present value) of the land?
4. In action **d,** how much would the equal annual payments need to be to accumulate enough money to build the building?
5. In action **e,** assuming semiannual compounding of interest, what is the actual purchase price of the stock (present value of the note)?

ALTERNATE PROBLEMS

P 6.

LO 2 **Notes Payable Transactions**
and End-of-Period Entries

Csizczak Plywood Company, whose fiscal year ends December 31, completed the following transactions involving notes payable:

20x1
Nov. 25   Purchased a new loading cart by issuing a 60-day, 10 percent note for $21,600.

Dec. 16 Borrowed $25,000 from the bank to finance inventory by signing a 90-day note. The face value of the note includes interest of $750. Proceeds received were $24,250.

  31 Made the end-of-year adjusting entry to accrue interest expense on cart note.

  31 Made the end-of-year adjusting entry to recognize the interest accrued on the note to the bank.

20x2

Jan. 24 Paid off the loading cart note.

Mar. 16 Paid off the inventory note to the bank.

REQUIRED

Prepare entries in journal form for these transactions.

P 7.

LO 2   Product Warranty Liability

The Whirling Company manufactures and sells food processors. The company guarantees the processors for five years. If a processor fails, it is replaced free, but the customer is charged a service fee for handling. In the past, management has found that only 3 percent of the processors sold required replacement under the warranty. The average food processor costs the company $120. At the beginning of September, the account for estimated liability for product warranties had a credit balance of $104,000. During September, 250 processors were returned under the warranty. Service fees of $4,930 were collected for handling. During the month, the company sold 2,800 food processors.

REQUIRED

1. Prepare entries in journal form to record (a) the cost of food processors replaced under warranty and (b) the estimated liability for product warranties for processors sold during the month.

2. Compute the balance of the Estimated Product Warranty Liability account at the end of the month.

P 8.

LO 5   Time Value of Money
LO 6   Applications
LO 7

Wellstone Corporation's management took several actions, each of which was to be effective on January 1, 20x1, and each of which involved an application of the time value of money:

a. Established a new retirement plan to take effect in three years and authorized three annual payments of $500,000 starting January 1, 20x2, to establish the retirement fund.

b. Approved plans for a new distribution center to be built for $1,000,000 and authorized five annual payments, starting January 1, 20x2, to accumulate the funds for the new center.

c. Bought out the contract of a member of top management for a payment of $50,000 per year for four years beginning January 1, 20x2.

d. Accepted a two-year, non-interest-bearing note for $100,000 as payment for equipment that the company sold.

e. Set aside $300,000 for possible losses from lawsuits over a defective product. The lawsuits are not expected to be settled for three years.

REQUIRED

Assuming an annual interest rate of 10 percent and using Tables 1, 2, 3, and 4, answer the following questions:

1. In action **a,** how much will the retirement fund accumulate in three years?

2. In action **b,** how much must the annual payment be to reach the goal?

3. In action **c,** what is the cost (present value) of the buyout?

4. In action **d,** assuming that interest is compounded semiannually, what is the selling price (present value) of the equipment?

5. In action **e,** how much will the fund accumulate to in three years?

EXPANDING YOUR CRITICAL THINKING, COMMUNICATION, AND INTERPERSONAL SKILLS

SKILLS DEVELOPMENT

Conceptual Analysis

LO 2 Frequent-Flier Plan

SD 1. *America South Airways* instituted a frequent-flier program under which passengers accumulate points based on the number of miles they fly on the airline. One point is awarded for each mile flown, with a minimum of 750 miles given for any flight. Because of competition in 2001, the company began a triple mileage bonus plan under which passengers received triple the normal mileage points. In the past, about 1.5 percent of passenger miles were flown by passengers who had converted points to free flights. With the triple mileage program, it is expected that a 2.5 percent rate will be more appropriate for future years. During 2001 the company had passenger revenues of $966.3 million and passenger transportation operating expenses of $802.8 million before depreciation and amortization. Operating income was $86.1 million. What is the appropriate rate to use to estimate free miles? What would be the effect of the estimated liability for free travel by frequent fliers on 2001 net income? Describe several ways to estimate the amount of this liability. Be prepared to discuss the arguments for and against recognizing this liability.

LO 2 Nature and Recognition of
LO 3 an Estimated Liability

SD 2. Sometimes the decision to recognize and record a liability is a matter of judgment. People who use *General Motors* credit cards earn rebates toward the purchase of new cars in relation to the amount of purchases made using their cards. General Motors chooses to discuss these outstanding rebates as "Commitments" in the notes to the financial statements in the following way:

> GM sponsors a credit card program, entitled the GM Card program, that offers rebates that can be applied against the purchase or lease of GM vehicles. The amount of rebates available to qualified cardholders at December 31, 1997 and 1996 was $3.5 billion and $3.2 billion, respectively. Provisions for GM Card rebates are recorded as reductions in revenues at the time of vehicle sale.[12]

Using the two criteria established by the FASB for recognizing and recording a contingency, what reasoning do you think General Motors management uses to show this commitment in the notes, where it will likely receive less attention by analysts, rather than on the income statement as an expense and on the balance sheet as an estimated liability? Do you agree with this position? (*Hint:* Apply the matching rule.)

LO 7 Evaluation of Auto Lease

SD 3. *Ford Credit* ran an advertisement offering three alternatives for a 24-month lease on a new Lincoln automobile. The three alternatives were zero dollars down and $587 per month for 24 months, $1,975 down and $499 per month for 24 months, or $12,283 down and no payments for 24 months.[13] Assuming that you have enough cash to accept any of the three alternatives and that you determine that a 12 percent annual return compounded monthly is the relevant interest rate for you, use Table 4 in the appendix on future value and present value tables to determine which is the best deal. How would your answer change if the interest rate were higher? If it were lower?

Cash Flow

CD-ROM

Communication

Critical Thinking

Ethics

General Ledger

Group Activity

Hot Links to Real Companies

International

Internet

Key Ratio

Memo

Spreadsheet

Ethical Dilemma

SD 4.

LO 2 Known Legal Violations

Tower Restaurant is a large seafood restaurant in the suburbs of Chicago. Joe Murray, an accounting student at a nearby college, recently secured a full-time accounting job at the restaurant. Joe felt fortunate to have a good job that accommodated his class schedule because the local economy was very bad. After a few weeks on the job, Joe realized that his boss, the owner of the business, was paying the kitchen workers in cash and was not withholding federal and state income taxes or social security and Medicare taxes. Joe understands that federal and state laws require these taxes to be withheld and paid to the appropriate agency in a timely manner. Joe also realizes that if he raises this issue, he may lose his job. What alternatives are available to Joe? What action would you take if you were in Joe's position? Why did you make this choice?

Group Activity: Use in class groups. Debrief by asking each group for an alternative. Then debate the ethics of each alternative.

Research Activity

SD 5.

LO 2 Basic Research Skills
LO 3

Indexes for business periodicals, in which you can look up topics of interest, are available in your school library. Three of the most important of these indexes are the *Business Periodicals Index*, *The Wall Street Journal Index*, and the *Accountants' Index*. Using one or more of these indexes, locate and photocopy two articles related to bank financing, commercial paper, product warranties, airline frequent-flier plans, or contingent liabilities. Keep in mind that you may have to look under related topics to find an article. For example, to find articles about contingent liabilities, you might look under litigation, debt guarantees, environmental losses, or other topics. For each of the two articles, write a short summary of the situation and tell how it relates to accounting for the topic as described in the text. Be prepared to discuss your results in class.

Decision-Making Practice

SD 6.

LO 6 Basketball Contract
LO 7

The *Cleveland Barons'* fifth-year forward Reggie Simpson made the All-Star team in 2001. Simpson has three years left on a contract that is to pay him $2.4 million a year. He wants to renegotiate his contract because other players who have equally outstanding records (although they also have more experience) are receiving as much as $10.5 million per year for five years. Management has a policy of never renegotiating a current contract but is willing to consider extending the contract to additional years. In fact, the Barons have offered Simpson an additional three years at $6.0 million, $9.0 million, and $12.0 million, respectively. In addition, they have added an option year at $15.0 million. Management points out that this package is worth $42.0 million, or $10.5 million per year on average. Simpson is considering this offer and is also considering asking for a bonus to be paid upon the signing of the contract. Write a memorandum to Simpson that comments on management's position and evaluates the offer, assuming a current prime (best bank rate) interest rate of 10 percent. (*Hint:* Use present values.) Propose a range for the signing bonus. Finally, include other considerations that may affect the value of the offer.

FINANCIAL REPORTING AND ANALYSIS

Interpreting Financial Reports

FRA 1.

LO 1 Comparison of Two Companies with Industry Ratios

Two computer companies are *Sun Microsystems Inc.* and *Cisco Systems.* The following data are for their 1998 fiscal year ends (amounts are in thousands):[14]

	Sun	Cisco
Accounts Payable	$ 495,603	$ 248,872
Cost of Goods Sold	3,972,283	2,917,617
Increase (Decrease) Inventory	(91,532)	107,309

Compare the payables turnover ratio and average days' payable for both companies in 1998. Comment on the results. How are cash flows affected by average days' payable? How do Sun Microsystems and Cisco Systems compare to the 1998 industry result shown in Figure 1 of this chapter? (Use year-end amounts for ratios.)

FRA 2.

LO 3 Contingent Liabilities

Texaco, Inc., one of the largest integrated oil companies in the world, reported its loss in the largest damage judgment in history in its 1986 annual report as follows:[15]

Note 17. Contingent Liabilities
Pennzoil Litigation

State Court Action. On December 10, 1985, the 151st District Court of Harris County, Texas, entered judgment for Pennzoil Company of $7.5 billion actual damages, $3 billion punitive damages, and approximately $600 million prejudgment interest in *Pennzoil Company v. Texaco, Inc.,* an action in which Pennzoil claims that Texaco, Inc., tortiously interfered with Pennzoil's alleged contract to acquire a ⅗ths interest in Getty. Interest began accruing on the judgment at the simple rate of 10% per annum from the date of judgment. Texaco, Inc., believes that there is no legal basis for the judgment, which it believes is contrary to the evidence and applicable law. Texaco, Inc., is pursuing all available remedies to set aside or to reverse the judgment.

* * *

The outcome of the appeal on the preliminary injunction and the ultimate outcome of the Pennzoil litigation are not presently determinable, but could have a material adverse effect on the consolidated financial position and the results of the consolidated operations of Texaco, Inc.

At December 31, 1986, Texaco's retained earnings were $12.882 billion, and its cash and marketable securities totaled $3.0 billion. The company's net income for 1986 was $.725 billion.

After a series of court reversals and filing for bankruptcy in 1987, Texaco announced in December 1987 an out-of-court settlement with Pennzoil for $3.0 billion. Although less than the original amount, it is still the largest damage payment in history.

REQUIRED

1. The FASB has established two conditions that a contingent liability must meet before it is recorded in the accounting records. What are the two conditions? Does the situation described in "Note 17. Contingent Liabilities" meet those conditions? Explain your answer.

2. Do the events of 1987 change your answer to 1? Explain your response.

3. What will be the effect of the settlement on Texaco's retained earnings, cash and marketable securities, and net income?

International Company

FRA 3.

LO 1 Classification and
LO 2 Disclosure of Current
LO 3 Liabilities and Contingent
Liabilities

The German company **Man Nutzfahrzeuge Aktiengesellschaft** is one of the largest truck companies in the world. Accounting in Germany differs in some respects from that in the United States. A good example of the difference is the placement and classification of liabilities. On the balance sheet, Man places liabilities below a detailed stockholders' equity section. Man does not distinguish between current and long-term liabilities; however, a note to the financial statements does disclose the amount of the liabilities due within one year. Those liabilities are primarily what we call *definitely determinable liabilities,* such as loans and accounts and notes payable. Estimated liabilities do not seem to appear in this category. In contrast, there is an asset category called *current assets,* which is similar to that found in the United States. In another note to the financial statements, the company lists what it calls *contingent liabilities,* which have not been recorded and do not appear on the balance sheet. These include liabilities for hire and leasing contracts, guarantees of loans of other companies, and warranties on trucks.[16] What do you think of the idea of combining all liabilities, whether short-term or long-term, as a single item on the balance sheet? Do you think any of the contingent liabilities should be recorded and shown on the balance sheet?

Toys "R" Us Annual Report

FRA 4.

LO 1 Short-Term Liabilities and Seasonality

Refer to the balance sheet and the liquidity and capital resources section of Management's Discussion—Results of Operations and Financial Condition in the Toys "R" Us annual report. Compute the payables turnover for 1999 for Toys "R" Us. How does this ratio compare to that in other industries, as represented by Figure 1? Toys "R" Us is a seasonal business. Would you expect short-term borrowings and accounts payable to be unusually high or unusually low at the balance sheet date of January 30, 1999? How does management use short-term financing to meet its needs for cash during the year?

Fingraph® Financial Analyst™

FRA 5.

LO 1 Comparison of
LO 2 Current Liabilities and
LO 3 Working Capital

Choose any two companies from the same industry in the Fingraph® Financial Analyst™ CD-ROM software. The industry chosen should be one in which current liabilities are likely to be important. Choose an industry such as airlines, manufacturing, consumer products, consumer food and beverage, or computers.

1. In the annual reports for the companies you have selected, read the current liability section of the balance sheet and any reference to any current liabilities in the summary of significant accounting policies or notes to the financial statements. What are the most important current liabilities for each company? Are there any current liabilities that appear to be characteristic of the industry? Which current liabilities are definitely determinable and which appear to be accrued liabilities?

2. Display and print in tabular and graphical form the Current Assets and Current Liabilities Analysis page. Prepare a table that compares the current ratio and working capital for both companies for two years.

3. Find and read references to current liabilities in the liquidity analysis section of management's discussion and analysis in each annual report.

4. Write a one-page executive summary that highlights the most important types of current liabilities for this industry and compares the current ratio and working capital trends of the two companies, including reference to management's assessment. Include the Fingraph® page and your table as an attachment to your report.

Internet Case

FRA 6.

LO 3 Investigation of Status of Famous Contingencies

The *Texaco* case in **FRA 2** involves one of the most famous contingent liabilities in history, but there are other famous ones as well. Others include the suits against tobacco companies such as ***RJR Nabisco, Inc.,*** and ***Philip Morris Incorporated*** and the *Valdez* oil spill case against ***Exxon Corporation.*** Investigate the current status of any one of these cases, including Texaco, by first going to the Needles Accounting Resource Center web site http://college.hmco.com. and clicking on one of these companies' web links. Then find the company's latest annual report and look in the notes to the financial statements under "Contingencies." Report what you find about the case, including the possibility that the case has been settled or is no longer reported.

ENDNOTES

1. US Airways, Inc., *Annual Report*, 1998.
2. Tandy Corporation, *Annual Report*, 1998.
3. The Goodyear Tire & Rubber Company, *Annual Report*, 1998.
4. Lowe's Companies, Inc., *Annual Report*, 1998.

5. Raju Narisetti, "P&G Ad Chief Plots Demise of the Coupon," *The Wall Street Journal*, April 17, 1996.

6. Delta Air Lines, Inc., *Annual Report*, 1998.

7. Scott McCartney, "Free Airline Miles Become a Potent Tool for Selling Everything," *The Wall Street Journal*, April 16, 1996.

8. *Statement of Financial Accounting Standards No. 5*, "Accounting for Contingencies" (Norwalk, Conn.: Financial Accounting Standards Board, 1975).

9. American Institute of Certified Public Accountants, *Accounting Trends & Techniques*, 1998, p. 73.

10. General Motors Corp., *Annual Report*, 1998.

11. Accounting Principles Board, *Opinion No. 21*, "Interest on Receivables and Payables" (New York: American Institute of Certified Public Accountants, 1971), par. 13.

12. General Motors Corp., *Annual Report*, 1998.

13. Advertisement, *Chicago Tribune*, February 15, 1994.

14. Sun Microsystems Inc., *Annual Report*, 1998; Cisco Systems, *Annual Report*, 1998.

15. Texaco, Inc., *Annual Report*, 1986.

16. Man Nutzfahrzeuge Aktiengesellschaft, *Annual Report*, 1997.

Measuring and Reporting Long-Term Assets and Long-Term Financing

In addition to operating activities, which were covered in **Part Two**, the other two principal business activities are investing in long-term assets and long-term financing with debt and equity. These are covered in **Part Three.**

Chapter 10 Long-Term Assets explores the management issues associated with the acquisition, operation, and disposal of property, plant, and equipment, natural resources, and intangible assets, as well as the concepts and techniques of depreciation, depletion, and amortization.

Chapter 11 Long-Term Liabilities covers the management issues related to the long-term financing of the corporation. The most important source of long-term financing, bond liabilities, is emphasized, but attention is also paid to other sources, such as leasing, mortgages, and installment notes, and to post-retirement benefits.

Chapter 12 Contributed Capital focuses on long-term equity financing, including the types of equity securities and transactions affecting the stockholders' equity section of the balance sheet, such as stock issues, dividends, and treasury stock purchases.

10 Long-Term Assets

LEARNING OBJECTIVES

1 Identify the types of long-term assets and explain the management issues related to accounting for them.

2 Distinguish between capital and revenue expenditures, and account for the cost of property, plant, and equipment.

3 Define *depreciation*, state the factors that affect its computation, and show how to record it.

4 Compute periodic depreciation under the (a) straight-line method, (b) production method, and (c) declining-balance method.

5 Account for the disposal of depreciable assets not involving exchanges.

6 Account for the disposal of depreciable assets involving exchanges.

7 Identify the issues related to accounting for natural resources and compute depletion.

8 Apply the matching rule to intangible assets, including research and development costs and goodwill.

SUPPLEMENTAL OBJECTIVE

9 Apply depreciation methods to problems of partial years, revised rates, groups of similar items, special types of capital expenditures, and cost recovery.

DECISION POINT: A USER'S FOCUS

H. J. Heinz Company The effects of management's decisions regarding long-term assets are most apparent in the areas of reported total assets and net income. How does one learn about the significance of those items to a company? An idea of the extent of a company's long-term assets and their importance can be gained from the financial statements. For example, this list of assets (in thousands of dollars) is taken from the annual report of H. J. Heinz Company, one of the world's largest food companies. Of the company's almost $8.0 billion in total assets, about 30 percent consists of property, plant, and equipment, and another 37 percent is goodwill and other intangibles. On the income statement, depreciation and amortization expenses associated with those assets are more than $313 million, or about 39 percent of net income. On the statement of cash flows, more than $374 million was spent on new long-term assets.[1] This chapter deals with long-term assets: property, plant, and equipment and intangible assets.

Financial Highlights

(In thousands)

	1998	1997
Property, Plant, and Equipment:		
Land	$ 51,129	$ 55,992
Buildings and leasehold improvements	806,299	871,417
Equipment, furniture, and other	3,210,695	3,453,189
	4,068,123	4,380,598
Less accumulated depreciation	1,673,461	1,901,378
Total property, plant, and equipment, net	$2,394,662	$2,479,220
Other Noncurrent Assets:		
Goodwill (net of amortization: 1998—$297,868 and 1997—$259,019)	$1,764,574	$1,803,552
Trademarks (net of amortization: 1998—$67,791 and 1997—$57,186)	416,918	416,990
Other intangibles (net of amortization: 1998—$112,768 and 1997—$106,046)	194,560	210,106
Other noncurrent assets	566,188	514,813
Total other noncurrent assets	$2,942,240	$2,945,461

Management Issues Related to Accounting for Long-Term Assets

Long-term assets are assets that (1) have a useful life of more than one year, (2) are acquired for use in the operation of a business, and (3) are not intended for resale to customers. For many years, it was common to refer to long-term assets as *fixed assets*, but use of this term is declining because the word *fixed* implies that they last forever. The relative importance of long-term assets to various industries is shown in Figure 1. Long-term assets range from 18.9 percent of total assets in computers to 55.4 percent in interstate trucking.

VIDEO CASE

 # Fermi National Accelerator Laboratory

Objectives

- To describe the characteristics of long-term assets.

- To identify the four issues that must be addressed in applying the matching rule to long-term assets.

- To define depreciation and state the principal causes of depreciation.

- To identify the issues related to intangible assets, including research and development.

Background for the Case

Fermi National Accelerator Laboratory (Fermilab), located 30 miles west of Chicago, is a U.S. Department of Energy

national laboratory. Its primary mission is to advance the understanding of the fundamental nature of matter and energy.

Fermilab operates the world's highest-energy particle accelerator, the Trevatron, or "atom-smasher."

Circling through rings of magnets four miles in circumference, particle beams generate experimental conditions equivalent to those that existed in the first quadrillionth of a second after the birth of the universe. This capability to recreate such high energy levels places Fermilab at the frontier of global physics research. It provides leadership and resources for qualified experimenters to conduct basic research at the leading edge of high-energy physics and related disciplines. In the year 2000, with Collider Run II, Fermilab begins probing the smallest dimensions that humans have ever examined. These scientists have the

best opportunity to make important discoveries that could answer some of today's questions in particle physics.

Although a unit of the U.S. government, Fermilab is a financially independent non-profit corporation with a governing body consisting of the Presidents of 87 member research universities. With annual revenues of about $300,000,000, consisting mostly of government contracts, and annual expenses of about $260,000,000, Fermilab faces the same management challenges that a for-profit corporation faces. It must make huge investments in long-term assets. Other than salaries, depreciation is the lab's largest expense. In addition, Fermilab creates intellectual capital through basic research that it shares cooperatively with U.S. industry to encourage economic development.

For more information about Fermi National Accelerator Laboratory, visit the laboratory's web site through the Needles Accounting Resource Center at:

http://college.hmco.com

Required

View the video on Fermi National Accelerator Laboratory that accompanies this book. As you are watching the video, take notes related to the following questions:

1. What are the characteristics that distinguish long-term assets? What are some examples of long-term assets at Fermilab?

2. What four issues must be addressed in applying the matching rule to long-term assets?

3. What is depreciation and what are the two major causes of depreciation?

4. What are research and development costs and how does Fermilab account for them? How might this method understate the assets of Fermilab?

Figure 1
Long-Term Assets as a Percentage of Total Assets for Selected Industries

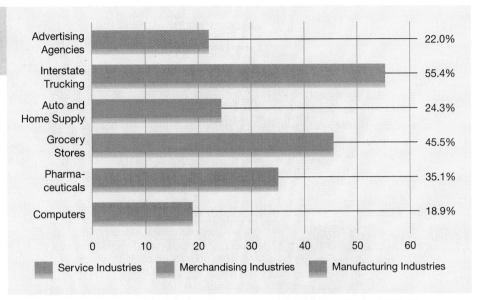

Source: Data from Dun & Bradstreet, *Industry Norms and Key Business Ratios*, 1997–98.

Study Note: For an asset to be classified as property, plant, and equipment, it must be "put in use." This means that it is available for its intended purpose. An emergency generator is "put in use" when it is available for emergencies, even if it is never used.

Key Point: A computer used in the office would be considered plant and equipment, whereas an identical computer held for sale to customers would be considered inventory.

Although there is no strict minimum useful life an asset must have to be classified as long term, the most common criterion is that the asset must be capable of repeated use for a period of at least a year. Included in this category is equipment used only in peak or emergency periods, such as generators.

Assets that are not used in the normal course of business should not be included in this category. Thus, land held for speculative reasons or buildings no longer used in ordinary business operations should not be included in the property, plant, and equipment category. Instead, they should be classified as long-term investments.

Finally, if an item is held for resale to customers, it should be classified as inventory—not plant and equipment—no matter how durable it is. For example, a printing press that is held for sale by a printing press manufacturer would be considered inventory, whereas the same printing press would be considered plant and equipment for a printing company that buys it for use in operations.

Long-term assets differ from current assets in that they support the operating cycle instead of being a part of it. They are also expected to benefit the business for a longer period than do current assets. Current assets are expected to be used up or converted to cash within one year or during the operating cycle, whichever is longer. Long-term assets are expected to last beyond that period. Long-term assets and their related expenses are summarized in Figure 2.

Generally, long-lived assets are reported at carrying value, as presented in Figure 3. **Carrying value** is the unexpired part of the cost of an asset, not its market value; it is also called *book value*. If a long-lived asset loses some or all of its revenue-generating potential prior to the end of its useful life, the asset may be deemed impaired and its carrying value reduced. **Asset impairment** occurs when the sum of the expected cash flows from the asset is less than the carrying value of the asset.[2] Reducing carrying value to fair value, as measured by the present value of future cash flows, is an application of conservatism. All long-term assets are subject to an asset impairment evaluation. A reduction in carrying value as a result of impairment is recorded as a loss.

Facing deregulation and competition for the first time, six of the seven Baby Bell regional telephone companies, including Pacific Telesis, Bell South, and NYNEX, took writedowns in the billions of dollars. In the past, the cost of old equipment

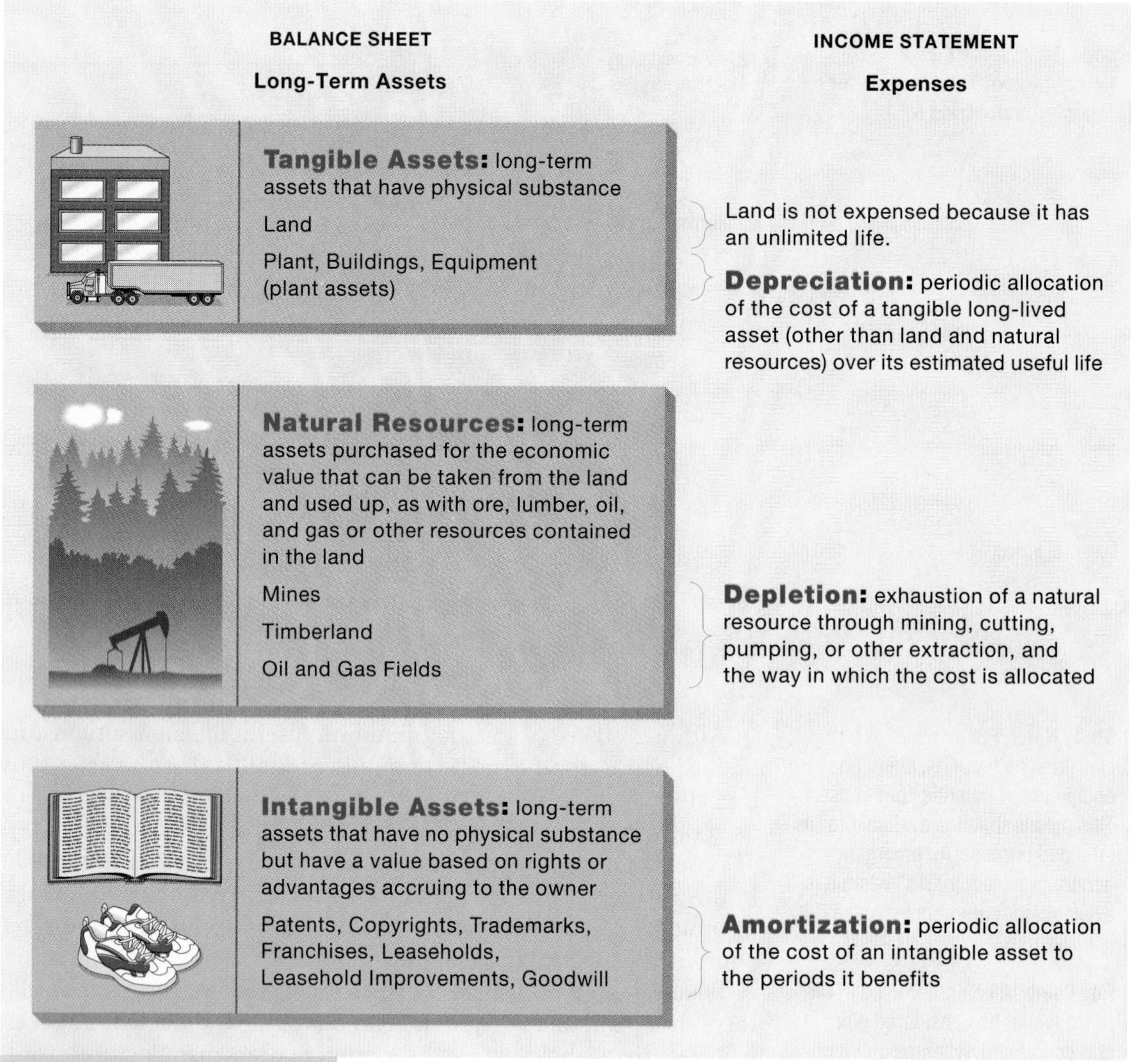

BALANCE SHEET

Long-Term Assets

INCOME STATEMENT

Expenses

Tangible Assets: long-term assets that have physical substance

Land

Plant, Buildings, Equipment (plant assets)

Land is not expensed because it has an unlimited life.

Depreciation: periodic allocation of the cost of a tangible long-lived asset (other than land and natural resources) over its estimated useful life

Natural Resources: long-term assets purchased for the economic value that can be taken from the land and used up, as with ore, lumber, oil, and gas or other resources contained in the land

Mines

Timberland

Oil and Gas Fields

Depletion: exhaustion of a natural resource through mining, cutting, pumping, or other extraction, and the way in which the cost is allocated

Intangible Assets: long-term assets that have no physical substance but have a value based on rights or advantages accruing to the owner

Patents, Copyrights, Trademarks, Franchises, Leaseholds, Leasehold Improvements, Goodwill

Amortization: periodic allocation of the cost of an intangible asset to the periods it benefits

Figure 2
Classification of Long-Term Assets and Corresponding Expenses

could be passed on to consumers through regulated rate increases, but with competition, rates are decreasing, not increasing. As a result, the future cash flows cannot justify the recorded asset carrying values of aging copper telephone lines, switching gear, and other equipment. Estimated useful lives for these assets have been reduced by 50 percent or more. The writedowns have caused the companies to report operating losses.[3]

Deciding to Acquire Long-Term Assets

The decision to acquire a long-term asset involves a complex process. Methods of evaluating data to make rational decisions in this area are grouped under a topic called capital budgeting, which is usually covered as a managerial accounting topic. However, an awareness of the general nature of the problem is helpful in understanding the accounting issues related to long-term assets. To illustrate the acquisi-

Plant Assets	Natural Resources	Intangible Assets
Less Accumulated Depreciation	Less Accumulated Depletion	Less Accumulated Amortization
Carrying Value	Carrying Value	Carrying Value

Figure 3
Carrying Value of Long-Term
Assets on Balance Sheet

tion decision, let us assume that Irena Markova, M.D., is considering the purchase of a $5,000 computer for her office. She estimates that if she purchases the computer, she can reduce the hours of a part-time employee sufficiently to save net cash flows of $2,000 per year for four years and that the computer will be worth $1,000 at the end of that period. These data are summarized as follows:

	20x1	20x2	20x3	20x4
Acquisition cost	($5,000)			
Net annual savings in cash flows	$2,000	$2,000	$2,000	$2,000
Disposal price				1,000
Net cash flows	($3,000)	$2,000	$2,000	$3,000

To place the cash flows on a comparable basis, it is helpful to use present value tables such as Tables 3 and 4 in the appendix on future value and present value tables. Assuming that the appropriate interest rate is 10 percent compounded annually, the purchase may be evaluated as follows:

		Present Value
Acquisition cost	Present value factor = 1.000 1.000 × $5,000	($5,000)
Net annual savings in cash flows	Present value factor = 3.170 (Table 4: 4 periods, 10%) 3.170 × $2,000	6,340
Disposal price	Present value factor = .683 (Table 3: 4 periods, 10%) .683 × $1,000	683
Net present value		$2,023

As long as the net present value is positive, Dr. Markova will earn at least 10 percent on the investment. In this case, the return is greater than 10 percent because the net present value is a positive $2,023. Based on this analysis, Dr. Markova makes the decision to purchase. However, there are other important considerations that have to be taken into account, such as the costs of training and maintenance, and the possibility that, because of unforeseen circumstances, the savings may not be as great as expected. In Dr. Markova's case, the decision to purchase is likely to be a good one because the net present value is both positive and large relative to the investment.

Information about a company's acquisitions of long-term assets may be found under investing activities in the statement of cash flows. For example, in referring to this section of its annual report, the management of Ford Motor Company, a manufacturer of automobiles, makes the following statement:

> Automotive capital expenditures totaled $8.1 billion in 1997, down $67 million from 1996. Capital expenditures were 6.6 percent of sales in 1997, down 4/10 percent of a point from 1996. Ford's spending in 1998 for product change is expected to be at lower levels.[4]

Financing Long-Term Assets

In addition to deciding whether or not to acquire a long-term asset, management must decide how to finance the asset if it is acquired. Some companies are profitable enough to pay for long-term assets out of cash flows from operations, but when financing is needed, some form of long-term arrangement related to the life of the asset is usually most appropriate. For example, an automobile loan generally spans four or five years, whereas a mortgage loan on a house may span as many as 30 years.

For a major long-term acquisition, a company may issue capital stock, long-term notes, or bonds. A good place to study a company's long-term financing is in the financing activities section of the statement of cash flows. For instance, in dis-

cussing this section, Ford Motor Company's management states, "Automotive debt at December 31, 1997 totaled $8.1 billion, which was 21 percent of total capitalization (stockholders' equity and Automotive debt), down from 23 percent of total capitalization a year ago."[5]

Applying the Matching Rule to Long-Term Assets

Accounting for long-term assets requires the proper application of the matching rule through the resolution of two important issues. The first is how much of the total cost to allocate to expense in the current accounting period. The second is how much to retain on the balance sheet as an asset to benefit future periods. To resolve these issues, four important questions about the acquisition, use, and disposal of each long-term asset, as illustrated in Figure 4, must be answered.

1. How is the cost of the long-term asset determined?
2. How should the expired portion of the cost of the long-term asset be allocated against revenues over time?
3. How should subsequent expenditures, such as repairs and additions, be treated?
4. How should disposal of the long-term asset be recorded?

Study Note: Useful life is measured by the service units a business expects to receive from an asset. It should not be confused with physical life, which is often much longer. If the management of a new business is having difficulty determining an asset's estimated useful life, it may obtain help from trade magazines. Nearly every industry has at least one.

Because of the long life of long-term assets and the complexity of the transactions involving them, management has many choices and estimates to make. For example, acquisition cost may be complicated by group purchases, trade-ins, or construction costs. In addition, to allocate the cost of the asset to future periods effectively, management must estimate how long the asset will last and what it will be worth at the end of its use. In making such estimates, it is helpful to think of a long-term asset as a bundle of services to be used in the operation of the business over a period of years. A delivery truck may provide 100,000 miles of service over its life. A piece of equipment may have the potential to produce 500,000 parts. A building may provide shelter for 50 years. As each of those assets is purchased, the company is paying in advance for 100,000 miles, the capacity to produce 500,000 parts, or 50 years of service. In essence, each asset is a type of long-term prepaid expense. The accounting problem is to spread the cost of the services over the

Figure 4
Issues of Accounting for Long-Term Assets

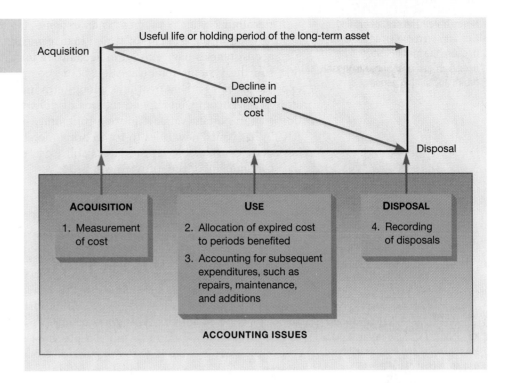

useful life of the asset. As the services benefit the company over the years, the cost becomes an expense rather than an asset.

Acquisition Cost of Property, Plant, and Equipment

OBJECTIVE
2 Distinguish between capital and revenue expenditures, and account for the cost of property, plant, and equipment

Study Note: Although dyeing a carpet may make it look almost new, it is not considered a capital expenditure because, even though the carpet looks better, its fibers are not stronger, and it probably will not last significantly longer than it would have before the color was changed.

The term **expenditure** refers to a payment or an obligation to make future payment for an asset, such as a truck, or a service, such as a repair. Expenditures may be classified as capital expenditures or revenue expenditures. A **capital expenditure** is an expenditure for the purchase or expansion of a long-term asset. Capital expenditures are recorded in the asset accounts because they benefit several future accounting periods. A **revenue expenditure** is an expenditure related to the repair, maintenance, and operation of a long-term asset. Revenue expenditures are recorded in the expense accounts because their benefits are realized in the current period.

Careful distinction between capital and revenue expenditures is important to the proper application of the matching rule. For example, if the purchase of an automobile is mistakenly recorded as a revenue expenditure, the total cost of the automobile is recorded as an expense on the income statement. As a result, current net income is reported at a lower amount (understated), and in future periods net income will be reported at a higher amount. If, on the other hand, a revenue expenditure, such as the painting of a building, were charged to an asset account, the expense of the current period would be understated. Current net income would be overstated by the same amount, and the net income of future periods would be understated.

Study Note: The cost of mailing lists may be recorded as an asset because the mailing lists will be used over and over and will benefit future accounting periods.

Determining when a payment is an expense and when it is an asset is a matter of judgment, in the exercise of which management takes a leading role. For example, inconsistencies have existed in accounting for the costs of computer programs that run the systems for businesses. Some companies immediately write off the expense, whereas others treat it as a long-term intangible asset and amortize it year after year. As companies spend billions of dollars a year on this type of software, this is an important variable in the profitability of many companies. Although the AICPA has issued new rules to try to bring more standardization to these accounting issues, considerable latitude does still exist, such as in determining how long the economic life of the software will be.[6]

General Approach to Acquisition Costs

The acquisition cost of property, plant, and equipment includes all expenditures reasonable and necessary to get the asset in place and ready for use. For example, the cost of installing and testing a machine is a legitimate cost of the machine. However, if the machine is damaged during installation, the cost of repairs is an operating expense and not an acquisition cost.

Key Point: Expenditures necessary to prepare an asset for its intended use are a cost of the asset.

Cost is easiest to determine when a purchase is made for cash. In that case, the cost of the asset is equal to the cash paid for the asset plus expenditures for freight, insurance while in transit, installation, and other necessary related costs. If a debt is incurred in the purchase of the asset, the interest charges are not a cost of the asset but a cost of borrowing the money to buy the asset. They are therefore an operating expense. An exception to this principle is that interest costs incurred during the construction of an asset are properly included as a cost of the asset.[7]

Expenditures such as freight, insurance while in transit, and installation are included in the cost of the asset because they are necessary if the asset is to function. Following the matching rule, they are allocated to the useful life of the asset rather than charged as expenses in the current period.

For practical purposes, many companies establish policies defining when an expenditure should be recorded as an expense or as an asset. For example, small expenditures for items that would normally be treated as assets may be treated as expenses because the amounts involved are not material in relation to net income. Thus, a wastebasket, which might last for years, would be recorded as a supplies expense rather than as a depreciable asset.

Some of the problems of determining the cost of a long-lived asset are demonstrated in the illustrations for land, land improvements, buildings, equipment, and group purchases presented in the next few sections.

Key Point: Many costs may be incurred to prepare land for its intended use and condition. All such costs are a cost of land.

LAND   There are often expenditures in addition to the purchase price of land that should be debited to the Land account. Some examples are commissions to real estate agents; lawyers' fees; accrued taxes paid by the purchaser; costs of preparing the land to build on, such as draining, tearing down old buildings, clearing, and grading; and assessments for local improvements, such as streets and sewage systems. The cost of landscaping is usually debited to the Land account because such improvements are relatively permanent. Land is not subject to depreciation because it does not have a limited useful life.

Enrichment Note: While the costs of tearing down existing buildings can be minor, they can also be major. For example, companies spend millions of dollars imploding buildings to remove them and build new ones.

Let us assume that a company buys land for a new retail operation. It pays a net purchase price of $170,000, pays brokerage fees of $6,000 and legal fees of $2,000, pays $10,000 to have an old building on the site torn down, receives $4,000 salvage from the old building, and pays $1,000 to have the site graded. The cost of the land will be $185,000.

Net purchase price		$170,000
Brokerage fees		6,000
Legal fees		2,000
Tearing down old building	$10,000	
Less salvage	4,000	6,000
Grading		1,000
Total cost		$185,000

LAND IMPROVEMENTS   Improvements to real estate, such as driveways, parking lots, and fences, have a limited life and are thus subject to depreciation. They should be recorded in an account called Land Improvements rather than in the Land account.

BUILDINGS   When an existing building is purchased, its cost includes the purchase price plus all repairs and other expenditures required to put it in usable condition. Buildings are subject to depreciation because they have a limited useful life. When a business constructs its own building, the cost includes all reasonable and necessary expenditures, such as those for materials, labor, part of the overhead and other indirect costs, architects' fees, insurance during construction, interest on construction loans during the period of construction, lawyers' fees, and building permits. If outside contractors are used in the construction, the net contract price plus other expenditures necessary to put the building in usable condition are included.

Enrichment Note: The electrical wiring and plumbing of a dental chair are included in the cost of the asset since they are a necessary cost of preparing the asset for use.

EQUIPMENT   The cost of equipment includes all expenditures connected with purchasing the equipment and preparing it for use. Those expenditures include the invoice price less cash discounts; freight or transportation, including insurance; excise taxes and tariffs; buying expenses; installation costs; and test runs to ready the equipment for operation. Equipment is subject to depreciation.

GROUP PURCHASES   Sometimes land and other assets are purchased for a lump sum. Because land is a nondepreciable asset that has an unlimited life, it must have

BUSINESS FOCUS ON ETHICS

Determining the acquisition price of a long-term asset is not always as clear-cut as some might imagine, especially in the case of constructed assets. Management has considerable leeway, but if choices are questioned, the results can sometimes be costly. *The Wall Street Journal* reported that Chambers Development Co., a waste-disposal company, wrote off nearly $50 million when it decided to stop deferring costs related to the development of landfills. Previously, Chambers had been including certain indirect costs, such as executives' salaries and travel, legal, and public relations fees, as capital expenditures to be written off over the life of the landfill. *The Wall Street Journal* reported that Chambers portrayed the accounting change as the outcome of a theoretical debate about good accounting practice, but SEC investigators concluded that the accounting practices created fictitious profit beyond generally accepted accounting practices. Further write-offs may follow because of the large amount of interest the company is capitalizing as a cost of the landfill. On news of the accounting change, the company's stock price dropped 63 percent in one day.[8] After straightening out its accounting, Chambers was acquired by USA Waste for $424 million.

a separate ledger account, and the lump-sum purchase price must be apportioned between the land and the other assets. For example, assume that a building and the land on which it is situated are purchased for a lump-sum payment of $85,000. The apportionment can be made by determining the price of each if purchased separately and applying the appropriate percentages to the lump-sum price. Assume that appraisals yield estimates of $10,000 for the land and $90,000 for the building, if purchased separately. In that case, 10 percent of the lump-sum price, or $8,500, would be allocated to the land and 90 percent, or $76,500, would be allocated to the building, as follows:

	Appraisal	Percentage	Apportionment
Land	$ 10,000	10% ($10,000 ÷ $100,000)	$ 8,500 ($85,000 × 10%)
Building	90,000	90% ($90,000 ÷ $100,000)	76,500 ($85,000 × 90%)
Totals	$100,000	100%	$85,000

Accounting for Depreciation

OBJECTIVE

3 Define *depreciation*, state the factors that affect its computation, and show how to record it

Depreciation accounting is described by the AICPA as follows:

> The cost of a productive facility is one of the costs of the services it renders during its useful economic life. Generally accepted accounting principles require that this cost be spread over the expected useful life of the facility in such a way as to allocate it as equitably as possible to the periods during which services are obtained from the use of the facility. This procedure is known as depreciation accounting, a system of accounting which aims to distribute the cost or other basic value of tangible capital assets, less salvage (if any), over the estimated useful life of the unit . . . in a systematic and rational manner. It is a process of allocation, not of valuation.[9]

Parenthetical Note: An older computer may be functioning as well as it did on the day of purchase, but it has become obsolete because much faster, more efficient computers are now available.

This description contains several important points. First, all tangible assets except land have a limited useful life. Because of this limited useful life, the costs of these assets must be distributed as expenses over the years they benefit. Physical deterioration and obsolescence are the major causes of the limited useful life of a depreciable asset. The **physical deterioration** of tangible assets results from use and from exposure to the elements, such as wind and sun. Periodic repairs and a sound maintenance policy may keep buildings and equipment in good operating order and extract the maximum useful life from them, but every machine or building at some point must be discarded. The need for depreciation is not eliminated by repairs. **Obsolescence** is the process of becoming out of date. Because of fast-changing technology and fast-changing demands, machinery and even buildings often become obsolete before they wear out. Accountants do not distinguish between physical deterioration and obsolescence because they are interested in the length of an asset's useful life regardless of what limits that useful life.

Second, the term *depreciation*, as used in accounting, does not refer to an asset's physical deterioration or decrease in market value over time. Depreciation means the allocation of the cost of a plant asset to the periods that benefit from the services of that asset. The term is used to describe the gradual conversion of the cost of the asset into an expense.

Third, depreciation is not a process of valuation. Accounting records are kept in accordance with the cost principle; they are not indicators of changing price levels.

Key Point: Depreciation is the allocation of the acquisition cost of an asset, and any similarity between undepreciated cost and current market value is pure coincidence.

It is possible that, because of an advantageous purchase and specific market conditions, the market value of a building may rise. Nevertheless, depreciation must continue to be recorded because it is the result of an allocation, not a valuation, process. Eventually the building will wear out or become obsolete regardless of interim fluctuations in market value.

Factors That Affect the Computation of Depreciation

Four factors affect the computation of depreciation: (1) cost, (2) residual value, (3) depreciable cost, and (4) estimated useful life.

COST As explained earlier in the chapter, cost is the net purchase price plus all reasonable and necessary expenditures to get the asset in place and ready for use.

Key Point: Residual value is the portion of an asset's acquisition cost expected to be recovered at the asset's disposal date.

RESIDUAL VALUE The **residual value** of an asset is its estimated net scrap, salvage, or trade-in value as of the estimated date of disposal. Other terms often used to describe residual value are *salvage value* and *disposal value.*

Key Point: It is depreciable cost, not acquisition cost, that is allocated over the useful life of a plant asset.

DEPRECIABLE COST The **depreciable cost** of an asset is its cost less its residual value. For example, a truck that costs $12,000 and has a residual value of $3,000 would have a depreciable cost of $9,000. Depreciable cost must be allocated over the useful life of the asset.

ESTIMATED USEFUL LIFE **Estimated useful life** is the total number of service units expected from a long-term asset. Service units may be measured in terms of years the asset is expected to be used, units expected to be produced, miles expected to be driven, or similar measures. In computing the estimated useful life of an asset, an accountant should consider all relevant information, including (1) past experience with similar assets, (2) the asset's present condition, (3) the company's repair and maintenance policy, (4) current technological and industry trends, and (5) local conditions such as weather.

Depreciation is recorded at the end of the accounting period by an adjusting entry that takes the following form:

A = L + OE
− −

Depreciation Expense, Asset Name	xxx	
Accumulated Depreciation, Asset Name		xxx
To record depreciation for the period		

BUSINESS FOCUS ON PRACTICE

Most airlines depreciate airplanes over an estimated useful life of 10 to 20 years. But how long will a properly maintained airplane really last? In July 1968 Western Airlines paid $3.3 million for a new Boeing 737. More than 78,000 flights and 30 years later this aircraft was still flying for a no-frills airline named Vanguard Airlines. During the course of its life, the owners of this aircraft have included Piedmont, Delta, US Airways, and other airlines. Virtually every part of the plane has been replaced over the years. Boeing believes the plane could theoretically make double the number of flights before it is retired.

The useful lives of many types of assets can be extended indefinitely if the assets are correctly maintained, but proper accounting in accordance with the matching rule would require depreciation over a "reasonable" useful life. Each airline that owned the plane would have accounted for the plane in this way.

Methods of Computing Depreciation

Many methods are used to allocate the cost of plant assets to accounting periods through depreciation. Each is proper for certain circumstances. The most common methods are (1) the straight-line method, (2) the production method, and (3) an accelerated method known as the declining-balance method.

OBJECTIVE

4a Compute periodic depreciation under the straight-line method

STRAIGHT-LINE METHOD   When the **straight-line method** is used to calculate depreciation, the depreciable cost of the asset is spread evenly over the estimated useful life of the asset. The straight-line method is based on the assumption that depreciation depends only on the passage of time. The depreciation expense for each period is computed by dividing the depreciable cost (cost of the depreciating asset less its estimated residual value) by the number of accounting periods in the asset's estimated useful life. The rate of depreciation is the same in each year. Suppose, for example, that a delivery truck costs $10,000 and has an estimated residual value of $1,000 at the end of its estimated useful life of five years. The annual depreciation would be $1,800 under the straight-line method, calculated as follows:

Clarification Note: The straight-line depreciation method should be used when approximately equal asset benefit is obtained each year.

Key Point: Residual value and useful life are, at best, educated guesses.

$$\frac{\text{Cost} - \text{Residual Value}}{\text{Estimated Useful Life}} = \frac{\$10,000 - \$1,000}{5 \text{ years}} = \$1,800 \text{ per year}$$

The depreciation for the five years would be as follows:

Depreciation Schedule, Straight-Line Method

	Cost	Yearly Depreciation	Accumulated Depreciation	Carrying Value
Date of purchase	$10,000	—	—	$10,000
End of first year	10,000	$1,800	$1,800	8,200
End of second year	10,000	1,800	3,600	6,400
End of third year	10,000	1,800	5,400	4,600
End of fourth year	10,000	1,800	7,200	2,800
End of fifth year	10,000	1,800	9,000	1,000

There are three important points to note from the depreciation schedule for the straight-line depreciation method. First, the depreciation is the same each year. Second, the accumulated depreciation increases uniformly. Third, the carrying value decreases uniformly until it reaches the estimated residual value.

OBJECTIVE

4b Compute periodic depreciation under the production method

PRODUCTION METHOD   The **production method** of depreciation is based on the assumption that depreciation is solely the result of use and that the passage of time plays no role in the depreciation process. If we assume that the delivery truck from the previous example has an estimated useful life of 90,000 miles, the depreciation cost per mile would be determined as follows:

$$\frac{\text{Cost} - \text{Residual Value}}{\text{Estimated Units of Useful Life}} = \frac{\$10,000 - \$1,000}{90,000 \text{ miles}} = \$.10 \text{ per mile}$$

If we assume that the use of the truck was 20,000 miles for the first year, 30,000 miles for the second, 10,000 miles for the third, 20,000 miles for the fourth, and 10,000 miles for the fifth, the depreciation schedule for the delivery truck would appear as follows.

Depreciation Schedule, Production Method

	Cost	Miles	Yearly Depreciation	Accumulated Depreciation	Carrying Value
Date of purchase	$10,000	—	—	—	$10,000
End of first year	10,000	20,000	$2,000	$2,000	8,000
End of second year	10,000	30,000	3,000	5,000	5,000
End of third year	10,000	10,000	1,000	6,000	4,000
End of fourth year	10,000	20,000	2,000	8,000	2,000
End of fifth year	10,000	10,000	1,000	9,000	1,000

There is a direct relation between the amount of depreciation each year and the units of output or use. Also, the accumulated depreciation increases each year in direct relation to units of output or use. Finally, the carrying value decreases each year in direct relation to units of output or use until it reaches the estimated residual value.

Under the production method, the unit of output or use employed to measure the estimated useful life of each asset should be appropriate for that asset. For example, the number of items produced may be an appropriate measure for one machine, but the number of hours of use may be a better measure for another. The production method should be used only when the output of an asset over its useful life can be estimated with reasonable accuracy.

OBJECTIVE

4c Compute periodic depreciation under the declining-balance method

DECLINING-BALANCE METHOD An **accelerated method** of depreciation results in relatively large amounts of depreciation in the early years of an asset's life and smaller amounts in later years. Such a method, which is based on the passage of time, assumes that many kinds of plant assets are most efficient when new, and so provide more and better service in the early years of their useful life. It is consistent with the matching rule to allocate more depreciation to earlier years than to later years if the benefits or services received in the earlier years are greater.

An accelerated method also recognizes that changing technologies make some equipment lose service value rapidly. Thus, it is realistic to allocate more to depreciation in earlier years than in later years. New inventions and products result in obsolescence of equipment bought earlier, making it necessary to replace equipment sooner than if technology changed more slowly. Another argument in favor of an accelerated method is that repair expense is likely to be greater in later years than in earlier years. Thus, the total of repair and depreciation expense remains fairly constant over a period of years. This result naturally assumes that the services received from the asset are roughly equal from year to year.

The **declining-balance method** is the most common accelerated method of depreciation. Under this method, depreciation is computed by applying a fixed rate to the carrying value (the declining balance) of a tangible long-lived asset, resulting in higher depreciation charges during the early years of the asset's life. Though any fixed rate can be used, the most common rate is a percentage equal to twice the straight-line percentage. When twice the straight-line rate is used, the method is usually called the **double-declining-balance method**.

In our earlier example, the delivery truck had an estimated useful life of five years. Consequently, under the straight-line method, the depreciation rate for each year was 20 percent (100 percent ÷ 5 years).

Under the double-declining-balance method, the fixed rate is 40 percent (2 × 20 percent). This fixed rate is applied to the *remaining carrying value* at the end of each year. Estimated residual value is not taken into account in figuring depreciation except in a year when calculated depreciation exceeds the amount necessary to bring the carrying value down to the estimated residual value. The depreciation schedule for this method is as follows:

Depreciation Schedule, Double-Declining-Balance Method

	Cost	Yearly Depreciation		Accumulated Depreciation	Carrying Value
Date of purchase	$10,000	—		—	$10,000
End of first year	10,000	(40% × $10,000)	$4,000	$4,000	6,000
End of second year	10,000	(40% × $6,000)	2,400	6,400	3,600
End of third year	10,000	(40% × $3,600)	1,440	7,840	2,160
End of fourth year	10,000	(40% × $2,160)	864	8,704	1,296
End of fifth year	10,000		296*	9,000	1,000

*Depreciation limited to amount necessary to reduce carrying value to residual value:
$296 = $1,296 (previous carrying value) − $1,000 (residual value).

Parenthetical Note: An asset remains on the books as long as it is in use. Even if the asset is fully depreciated, the company should not remove it from the books until it is taken out of service.

Note that the fixed rate is always applied to the carrying value at the end of the previous year. The depreciation is greatest in the first year and declines each year after that. Finally, the depreciation in the last year is limited to the amount necessary to reduce carrying value to residual value.

COMPARING THE THREE METHODS   A visual comparison may provide a better understanding of the three depreciation methods described above. Figure 5 compares yearly depreciation and carrying value under the three methods. In the left-hand graph, which shows yearly depreciation, straight-line depreciation is uniform at $1,800 per year over the five-year period. However, the double-declining-balance method begins at an amount greater than straight-line ($4,000) and decreases each year to amounts that are less than straight-line (ultimately, $296). The production method does not generate a regular pattern because of the random fluctuation of the depreciation from year to year. The three yearly depreciation patterns are reflected in the graph of carrying value. In that graph, each method starts in the same place (cost of $10,000) and ends at the same place (residual value of $1,000). It is the patterns during the useful life of the asset that differ for each method. For instance, the carrying value under the straight-line method is always greater than that under the double-declining-balance method, except at the beginning and end of useful life.

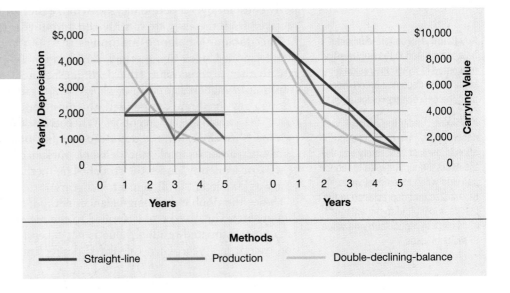

Figure 5
Graphical Comparison of Three Methods of Determining Depreciation

BUSINESS FOCUS ON PRACTICE

Most companies choose the straight-line method of depreciation for financial reporting purposes, as shown in Figure 6. Only about 14 percent use some type of accelerated method and 7 percent use the production method. These figures tend to be misleading about the importance of accelerated depreciation methods, how-ever, especially when it comes to income taxes. Federal income tax laws allow either the straight-line method or an accelerated method, and for tax purposes, according to *Accounting Trends & Techniques,* about 75 percent of the 600 large companies studied preferred an accelerated method. Companies use different methods of depreci-ation for good reason. The straight-line method can be advantageous for financial reporting because it can pro-duce the highest net income, and an accelerated method can be beneficial for tax purposes because it can result in lower income taxes.

**Figure 6
Depreciation Methods Used by
600 Large Companies**

Clarification Note: There are con-flicting objectives here. For financial reporting purposes, the objective is to accurately measure performance. For tax purposes, the objective is to minimize tax liability.

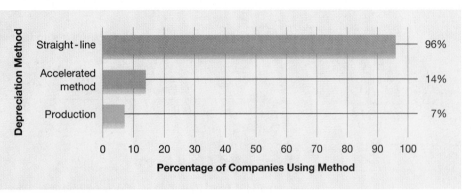

Total percentage exceeds 100 because some companies used different methods for different types of depreciable assets.

Source: Reprinted with permission from *Accounting Trends & Techniques,* Copyright © 1998 by the American Institute of Certified Public Accountants, Inc.

Disposal of Depreciable Assets

OBJECTIVE

5 Account for the disposal of depreciable assets not involving exchanges

Enrichment Note: Plant assets may also be disposed of by involuntary conversion (e.g., fire, theft, mud slide, flood) or condemnation by a governmental authority. For finan-cial reporting purposes, involuntary conversions are treated in the same way as if the assets were discarded or sold.

When plant assets are no longer useful because they are worn out or obsolete, they may be discarded, sold, or traded in on the purchase of new plant and equipment. For accounting purposes, a plant asset may be disposed of in three different ways: It may be (1) discarded, (2) sold for cash, or (3) exchanged for another asset. To illustrate how each of these cases is recorded, assume that MGC Company pur-chased a machine on January 1, 20x0, for $6,500 and planned to depreciate it on a straight-line basis over an estimated useful life of ten years. The residual value at the end of ten years was estimated to be $500. On January 1, 20x7, the balances of the relevant accounts in the plant asset ledger appear as follows:

Machinery	Accumulated Depreciation, Machinery
6,500	4,200

On September 30, 20x7, management disposes of the asset. The next few sec-tions illustrate the accounting treatment to record depreciation for the partial year and the disposal under several assumptions.

Depreciation for Partial Year

When a plant asset is discarded or disposed of in some other way, it is first necessary to record depreciation expense for the partial year up to the date of disposal. This step is required because the asset was used until that date and, under the matching rule, the accounting period should receive the proper allocation of depreciation expense.

In this illustration, MGC Company disposes of the machinery on September 30. The entry to record the depreciation for the first nine months of 20x7 (nine-twelfths of a year) is as follows:

A = L + OE
−   −

Sept. 30	Depreciation Expense, Machinery	450	
	Accumulated Depreciation, Machinery		450
	To record depreciation up to date of		
	disposal		

$$\frac{\$6,500 - \$500}{10} \times \frac{9}{12} = \$450$$

The relevant accounts in the plant asset ledger appear as follows after the entry is posted:

Machinery		Accumulated Depreciation, Machinery	
6,500			4,650

Discarded Plant Assets

A plant asset rarely lasts exactly as long as its estimated life. If it lasts longer than its estimated life, it is not depreciated past the point at which its carrying value equals its residual value. The purpose of depreciation is to spread the depreciable cost of an asset over the estimated life of the asset. Thus, the total accumulated depreciation should never exceed the total depreciable cost. If an asset remains in use beyond the end of its estimated life, its cost and accumulated depreciation remain in the ledger accounts. Proper records will thus be available for maintaining control over plant assets. If the residual value is zero, the carrying value of a fully depreciated asset is zero until the asset is disposed of. If such an asset is discarded, no gain or loss results.

In the illustration, however, the discarded equipment has a carrying value of $1,850 at the time of its disposal. The carrying value is computed from the ledger accounts above as machinery of $6,500 less accumulated depreciation of $4,650. A loss equal to the carrying value should be recorded when the machine is discarded.

A = L + OE
+   −
−

Sept. 30	Accumulated Depreciation, Machinery	4,650	
	Loss on Disposal of Machinery	1,850	
	Machinery		6,500
	Discarded machine no longer used		
	in the business		

Gains and losses on disposals of plant assets are classified as other revenues and expenses on the income statement.

Plant Assets Sold for Cash

The entry to record a plant asset sold for cash is similar to the one just illustrated except that the receipt of cash should also be recorded. The following entries show how to record the sale of a machine under three assumptions about the selling price. In the first case, the $1,850 cash received is exactly equal to the $1,850 carrying value of the machine; therefore, no gain or loss results.

A = L + OE	Sept. 30	Cash	1,850	
+		Accumulated Depreciation, Machinery	4,650	
+		Machinery		6,500
–		Sale of machine for carrying value;		
		no gain or loss		

In the second case, the $1,000 cash received is less than the carrying value of $1,850, so a loss of $850 is recorded.

A = L + OE	Sept. 30	Cash	1,000	
+ –		Accumulated Depreciation, Machinery	4,650	
+		Loss on Sale of Machinery	850	
–		Machinery		6,500
		Sale of machine at less than carrying		
		value; loss of $850 ($1,850 – $1,000)		
		recorded		

In the third case, the $2,000 cash received exceeds the carrying value of $1,850, so a gain of $150 is recorded.

A = L + OE	Sept. 30	Cash	2,000	
+ +		Accumulated Depreciation, Machinery	4,650	
+		Gain on Sale of Machinery		150
–		Machinery		6,500
		Sale of machine at more than the		
		carrying value; gain of $150		
		($2,000 – $1,850) recorded		

Exchanges of Plant Assets

OBJECTIVE

6 Account for the disposal of depreciable assets involving exchanges

Businesses also dispose of plant assets by trading them in on the purchase of other plant assets. Exchanges may involve similar assets, such as an old machine traded in on a newer model, or dissimilar assets, such as a machine traded in on a truck. In either case, the purchase price is reduced by the amount of the trade-in allowance.

The basic accounting for exchanges of plant assets is similar to accounting for sales of plant assets for cash. If the trade-in allowance received is greater than the carrying value of the asset surrendered, there has been a gain. If the allowance is less, there has been a loss. There are special rules for recognizing these gains and losses, depending on the nature of the assets exchanged.

Clarification Note: For assets to be similar, they must be used for similar purposes. A typewriter, for example, is similar to a word processor. Dissimilar assets, such as a pickup truck and a cement mixer, are not used for similar purposes.

Exchange	Losses Recognized	Gains Recognized
For financial accounting purposes		
Of dissimilar assets	Yes	Yes
Of similar assets	Yes	No
For income tax purposes		
Of dissimilar assets	Yes	Yes
Of similar assets	No	No

Both gains and losses are recognized when a company exchanges dissimilar assets. Assets are dissimilar when they perform different functions or do not meet specific monetary and type of business criteria for being considered similar assets. For financial accounting purposes, most exchanges are considered to be exchanges of dissimilar assets. In rare cases, when exchanges meet the specific criteria for them to be considered exchanges of similar assets, the gains are not recognized. In these cases, you could think of the trade-in as an extension of the life and usefulness of the original machine. Instead of recognizing a gain at the time of the exchange, the company records the new machine at the sum of the carrying value of the older machine plus any cash paid.[10]

For income tax purposes, similar assets are defined as those performing the same function. Neither gains nor losses on exchanges of these assets are recognized in computing a company's income tax liability. Thus, in practice, accountants face cases where both gains and losses are recognized (exchanges of dissimilar assets), cases where losses are recognized and gains are not recognized (exchanges of similar assets), and cases where neither gains nor losses are recognized (exchanges of similar assets for income tax purposes). Since all these options are used in practice, they are all illustrated in the following paragraphs.

LOSS RECOGNIZED ON THE EXCHANGE   A loss is recognized for financial accounting purposes on all exchanges in which a material loss occurs. To illustrate the recognition of a loss, let us assume that the firm in our example exchanges the machine for a newer, more modern machine on the following terms:

List price of new machine	$12,000
Trade-in allowance for old machine	(1,000)
Cash payment required	$11,000

In this case the trade-in allowance ($1,000) is less than the carrying value ($1,850) of the old machine. The loss on the exchange is $850 ($1,850 − $1,000). The following journal entry records this transaction under the assumption that the loss is to be recognized.

A = L + OE
+   −
+
−
−

Sept. 30	Machinery (new)	12,000	
	Accumulated Depreciation, Machinery	4,650	
	Loss on Exchange of Machinery	850	
	Machinery (old)		6,500
	Cash		11,000
	Exchange of machines		

LOSS NOT RECOGNIZED ON THE EXCHANGE   In the previous example, in which a loss was recognized, the new asset was recorded at the purchase price of $12,000 and a loss of $850 was recorded. If the transaction involves similar assets and is to be recorded for income tax purposes, the loss should not be recognized. In this case, the cost basis of the new asset will reflect the effect of the unrecorded loss. The cost basis is computed by adding the cash payment to the carrying value of the old asset:

Carrying value of old machine	$ 1,850
Cash paid	11,000
Cost basis of new machine	$12,850

Note that no loss is recognized in the entry to record this transaction.

A = L + OE
+
+
−
−

Sept. 30	Machinery (new)	12,850	
	Accumulated Depreciation, Machinery	4,650	
	Machinery (old)		6,500
	Cash		11,000
	Exchange of machines		

Note that the new machinery is reported at the purchase price of $12,000 plus the unrecognized loss of $850. The nonrecognition of the loss on the exchange is, in effect, a postponement of the loss. Since depreciation of the new machine will be computed based on a cost of $12,850 instead of $12,000, the "unrecognized" loss results in more depreciation each year on the new machine than if the loss had been recognized.

GAIN RECOGNIZED ON THE EXCHANGE   Gains on exchanges are recognized for accounting purposes when dissimilar assets are involved. To illustrate the recognition of a gain, we continue with our example, assuming the following terms and assuming the machines being exchanged serve different functions:

List price of new machine	$12,000
Trade-in allowance for old machine	(3,000)
Cash payment required	$ 9,000

Here the trade-in allowance ($3,000) exceeds the carrying value ($1,850) of the old machine by $1,150. Thus, there is a gain on the exchange, assuming that the price of the new machine has not been inflated to allow for an excessive trade-in value. In other words, a gain exists if the trade-in allowance represents the fair market value of the old machine. Assuming that this condition is true, the entry to record the transaction is as follows:

A = L + OE
+   +
+
−
−

Sept. 30	Machinery (new)	12,000	
	Accumulated Depreciation, Machinery	4,650	
	Gain on Exchange of Machinery		1,150
	Machinery (old)		6,500
	Cash		9,000
	Exchange of machines		

GAIN NOT RECOGNIZED ON THE EXCHANGE   When assets meeting the criteria for similar assets are exchanged, gains are not recognized for accounting or income tax purposes. The cost basis of the new machine must reflect the effect of the unrecorded gain. This cost basis is computed by adding the cash payment to the carrying value of the old asset.

Carrying value of old machine	$ 1,850
Cash paid	9,000
Cost basis of new machine	$10,850

The entry to record the transaction is as follows:

A = L + OE
+
+
−
−

Sept. 30	Machinery (new)	10,850	
	Accumulated Depreciation, Machinery	4,650	
	Machinery (old)		6,500
	Cash		9,000
	Exchange of machines		

As with the nonrecognition of losses, the nonrecognition of the gain on an exchange is, in effect, a postponement of the gain. In this illustration, when the new machine is eventually discarded or sold, its cost basis will be $10,850 instead of its original price of $12,000. Since depreciation will be computed on the cost basis of $10,850, the "unrecognized" gain is reflected in lower depreciation each year on the new machine than if the gain had been recognized.

Accounting for Natural Resources

OBJECTIVE

7 Identify the issues related to accounting for natural resources and compute depletion

Natural resources are shown on the balance sheet as long-term assets with such descriptive titles as Timberlands, Oil and Gas Reserves, and Mineral Deposits. The distinguishing characteristic of these assets is that they are converted into inventory by cutting, pumping, or mining. In terms of two of our examples, an oil field is a reservoir of unpumped oil, and a coal mine is a deposit of unmined coal. When the timber is cut, the oil is pumped, or the coal is mined, it becomes an inventory of the product to be sold. Natural resources are recorded at acquisition cost, which may also include some costs of development. As the resource is converted through the process of cutting, pumping, or mining, the asset account must be proportionally reduced. The carrying value of oil reserves on the balance sheet, for example, is reduced by a small amount for each barrel of oil pumped. As a result, the original cost of the oil reserves is gradually reduced, and depletion is recognized in the amount of the decrease.

Depletion

Clarification Note: Natural resources are not intangible assets. Natural resources are correctly classified as components of property, plant, and equipment.

Enrichment Note: When determining the total units available for depletion, management uses only the total units that are economically feasible to extract. This follows the cost-benefit principle. That is, when the cost of extracting a mineral is greater than the expected profit from the sale of the mineral, the company stops extracting it.

The term *depletion* is used to describe not only the exhaustion of a natural resource but also the proportional allocation of the cost of a natural resource to the units extracted. The costs are allocated in a way that is much like the production method used to calculate depreciation. When a natural resource is purchased or developed, there must be an estimate of the total units that will be available, such as barrels of oil, tons of coal, or board-feet of lumber. The depletion cost per unit is determined by dividing the cost of the natural resource (less residual value, if any) by the estimated number of units available. The amount of the depletion cost for each accounting period is then computed by multiplying the depletion cost per unit by the number of units pumped, mined, or cut and sold. For example, for a mine having an estimated 1,500,000 tons of coal, a cost of $1,800,000, and an estimated residual value of $300,000, the depletion charge per ton of coal is $1. Thus, if 115,000 tons of coal are mined and sold during the first year, the depletion charge for the year is $115,000. This charge is recorded as follows:

$A = L + OE$
$-$ $-$

Dec. 31	Depletion Expense, Coal Deposits	115,000	
	Accumulated Depletion, Coal Deposits		115,000
	To record depletion of coal mine:		
	$1 per ton for 115,000 tons mined		
	and sold		

Key Point: The matching rule dictates that the extracted resource be treated as an asset until it is sold. At that point, the asset cost is converted into an expense.

On the balance sheet, the mine would be presented as follows:

Coal Deposits	$1,800,000	
Less Accumulated Depletion	115,000	$1,685,000

Sometimes a natural resource that is extracted in one year is not sold until a later year. It is important to note that it would then be recorded as a depletion *expense* in the year it is *sold*. The part not sold is considered inventory.

Depreciation of Closely Related Plant Assets

Parenthetical Note: A company may abandon equipment that is still in good working condition. It may cost the company more to dismantle the equipment and move it to another site than to abandon it.

Natural resources often require special on-site buildings and equipment, such as conveyors, roads, tracks, and drilling and pumping devices that are necessary to extract the resource. If the useful life of those assets is longer than the estimated time it will take to deplete the resource, a special problem arises. Because such long-term assets are often abandoned and have no useful purpose once all the resources have been extracted, they should be depreciated on the same basis as the depletion is computed. For example, if machinery with a useful life of ten years is installed on an oil field that is expected to be depleted in eight years, the machinery should be depreciated over the eight-year period, using the production method. That way, each year's depreciation will be proportional to the year's depletion. If one-sixth of the oil field's total reserves is pumped in one year, then the depreciation should be one-sixth of the machinery's cost minus the residual value. If the useful life of a long-term asset is less than the expected life of the depleting asset, the shorter life should be used to compute depreciation. In such cases, or when an asset will not be abandoned once the reserves have been fully depleted, other depreciation methods, such as straight-line or declining-balance, are appropriate.

Development and Exploration Costs in the Oil and Gas Industry

The costs of exploration and development of oil and gas resources can be accounted for under either of two methods. Under **successful efforts accounting**, successful exploration—for example, the cost of a producing oil well—is a cost of the resource. This cost should be recorded as an asset and depleted over the estimated life of the resource. An unsuccessful exploration—such as the cost of a dry well—is written off immediately as a loss. Because of these immediate write-offs, successful efforts accounting is considered the more conservative method and is used by most large oil companies.

Exploration-minded independent oil companies, on the other hand, argue that the cost of dry wells is part of the overall cost of the systematic development of an oil field and thus a part of the cost of producing wells. Under this **full-costing** method, all costs, including the cost of dry wells, are recorded as assets and depleted over the estimated life of the producing resources. This method tends to improve earnings performance in the early years for companies using it. Either method is permitted by the Financial Accounting Standards Board.[11]

Accounting for Intangible Assets

OBJECTIVE

8 Apply the matching rule to intangible assets, including research and development costs and goodwill

The purchase of an intangible asset is a special kind of capital expenditure. An intangible asset is long term, but it has no physical substance. Its value comes from the long-term rights or advantages it offers to its owner. The most common examples—patents, copyrights, leaseholds, leasehold improvements, trademarks and brand names, franchises, licenses, and goodwill—are described in Table 1. Some current assets, such as accounts receivable and certain prepaid expenses, have no physical substance, but they are not classified as intangible assets because they are short term. Intangible assets are both long term and nonphysical.

Intangible assets are accounted for at acquisition cost—that is, the amount that was paid for them. Some intangible assets, such as goodwill and trademarks, may be acquired at little or no cost. Even though they may have great value and be needed for profitable operations, they should not appear on the balance sheet unless they have been purchased from another party at a price established in the marketplace.

Key Point: Generally, intangible assets, including goodwill, are recorded only when purchased. An exception is the cost of internally developed computer software after a working prototype has been developed.

The accounting issues connected with intangible assets are the same as those connected with other long-lived assets. The Accounting Principles Board, in its *Opinion No. 17*, lists them as follows:

1. Determining an initial carrying amount

2. Accounting for that amount after acquisition under normal business conditions —that is, through periodic write-off or amortization—in a manner similar to depreciation.

3. Accounting for that amount if the value declines substantially and permanently.[12]

Table 1. Accounting for Intangible Assets

Type	Description	Accounting Treatment
Patent	An exclusive right granted by the federal government for a period of 17 years to make a particular product or use a specific process.	The cost of successfully defending a patent in a patent infringement suit is added to the acquisition cost of the patent. Amortize over the useful life, which may be less than the legal life of 17 years.
Copyright	An exclusive right granted by the federal government to the possessor to publish and sell literary, musical, or other artistic materials for a period of the author's life plus 50 years; includes computer programs.	Record at acquisition cost and amortize over the useful life, which is often much shorter than the legal life, but not to exceed 40 years. For example, the cost of paperback rights to a popular novel would typically be amortized over a useful life of two to four years.
Leasehold	A right to occupy land or buildings under a long-term rental contract. For example, Company A, which owns but does not want to use a prime retail location, sells or subleases Company B the right to use it for ten years in return for one or more rental payments. Company B has purchased a leasehold.	Debit Leasehold for the amount of the rental payment, and amortize it over the remaining life of the lease. Payments to the lessor during the life of the lease should be debited to Lease Expense.
Leasehold improvements	Improvements to leased property that become the property of the lessor (the person who owns the property) at the end of the lease.	Debit Leasehold Improvements for the cost of improvements, and amortize the cost of the improvements over the remaining life of the lease.
Trademark, brand name	A registered symbol or name that can be used only by its owner to identify a product or service.	Debit Trademark or Brand Name for the acquisition cost, and amortize it over a reasonable life, not to exceed 40 years.
Franchise, license	A right to an exclusive territory or market, or the right to use a formula, technique, process, or design.	Debit Franchise or License for the acquisition cost, and amortize it over a reasonable life, not to exceed 40 years.
Goodwill	The excess of the cost of a group of assets (usually a business) over the fair market value of the net assets if purchased individually.	Debit Goodwill for the acquisition cost, and amortize it over a reasonable life, not to exceed 40 years.[13]

Clarification Note: Useful life refers to how long an intangible asset will be contributing income to a firm.

Key Point: Intangible assets should never be amortized over more than 40 years.

Besides these three problems, an intangible asset has no physical substance and, in some cases, may be impossible to identify. For these reasons, its value and its useful life may be quite hard to estimate.

The Accounting Principles Board has decided that a company should record as assets the costs of intangible assets acquired from others. However, the company should record as expenses the costs of developing intangible assets. Also, intangible assets that have a determinable useful life, such as patents, copyrights, and lease-holds, should be written off through periodic amortization over that useful life in

BUSINESS FOCUS ON PRACTICE

One of the most valuable intangible assets some companies have is a list of subscribers. For example, the Newark Morning Ledger Co., a newspaper chain, purchased a chain of Michigan newspapers whose list of 460,000 subscribers was valued at $68 million. In a 1993 decision, the U.S. Supreme Court upheld the company's right to amortize the value of the subscribers list because the company showed that the list had a limited useful life. The Internal Revenue Service had argued that the list had an indefinite life and therefore could not provide tax deductions through amortization. This ruling will benefit other types of businesses that purchase everything from bank deposits to pharmacy prescription files.[14]

much the same way that plant assets are depreciated. Even though some intangible assets, such as goodwill and trademarks, have no measurable limit on their lives, they should still be amortized over a reasonable length of time (not to exceed 40 years but see endnote 13 on page 505).

To illustrate these procedures, assume that Soda Bottling Company purchases a patent on a unique bottle cap for $18,000. The entry to record the patent would include $18,000 in the asset account Patents. Note that if Soda Bottling Company had developed the bottle cap internally instead of purchasing it from others, the costs of developing the cap, such as salaries of researchers, supplies used in testing, and costs of equipment, would have been expensed as incurred.

Assume now that Soda's management determines that, although the patent for the bottle cap will last for 17 years, the product using the cap will be sold only for the next six years. The entry to record the annual amortization expense would be for $3,000 ($18,000 ÷ 6 years). Note that the Patents account is reduced directly by the amount of the amortization expense. This is in contrast to the treatment of other long-term asset accounts, for which depreciation or depletion is accumulated in separate contra accounts.

If the patent becomes worthless before it is fully amortized, the remaining carrying value is written off as a loss by removing it from the Patents account.

Research and Development Costs

Most successful companies carry out activities, possibly within a separate department, involving research and development. Among these activities are development of new products, testing of existing and proposed products, and pure research. In the past, some companies would record as assets those costs of research and development that could be directly traced to the development of specific patents, formulas, or other rights. Other costs, such as those for testing and pure research, were treated as expenses of the accounting period and deducted from income.

The Financial Accounting Standards Board has stated that all research and development costs should be treated as revenue expenditures and charged to expense in the period when incurred.[15] The board argues that it is too hard to trace specific costs to specific profitable developments. Also, the costs of research and development are continuous and necessary for the success of a business and so should be treated as current expenses. To support this conclusion, the board cites studies showing that 30 to 90 percent of all new products fail and that three-fourths of new-product expenses go to unsuccessful products. Thus, their costs do not represent future benefits.

Computer Software Costs

Many companies develop computer programs or software to be sold or leased to individuals and companies. The costs incurred in creating a computer software product are considered research and development costs until the product has been proved to be technologically feasible. As a result, costs incurred before that point in the process should be charged to expense as incurred. A product is deemed to

BUSINESS FOCUS ON PRACTICE

Research and development expenditures are substantial expenditures for many companies. For example, in a recent year General Motors spent $7.9 billion on research and development or about 5 percent of its revenues.[16] Research and development costs can be even costlier in high-tech fields like pharmaceuticals. Two examples are Abbott Laboratories, which spent $1.2 billion or almost 10 percent of revenues, and Roche Group, which spent $3.4 billion or 14 percent of revenues.[17] Which of these costs are capitalized and amortized and which must be expensed immediately are obviously important questions for both the management and the stockholders of these companies.

be technologically feasible when a detailed working program has been designed. After the working program has been developed, all software production costs are recorded as assets and amortized over the estimated economic life of the product using the straight-line method. If at any time the company cannot expect to realize from a software product the amount of its unamortized costs on the balance sheet, the asset should be written down to the amount expected to be realized.[18] Under new rules developed by the AICPA, software programs developed for internal use by a company may be capitalized and amortized over their estimated economic life. However, software costs associated with resolving Y2K problems must be expensed immediately.

Goodwill

Enrichment Note: A company may spend thousands of dollars on goodwill because the company is paying for anticipated superior earnings and feels it will more than recoup the goodwill purchased.

The term *goodwill* is widely used by businesspeople, lawyers, and the public to mean different things. In most cases goodwill is taken to mean the good reputation of a company. From an accounting standpoint, goodwill exists when a purchaser pays more for a business than the fair market value of the net assets if purchased separately. Because the purchaser has paid more than the fair market value of the physical assets, there must be intangible assets. If the company being purchased does not have patents, copyrights, trademarks, or other identifiable intangible assets of value, the excess payment is assumed to be for goodwill. Goodwill exists because most businesses are worth more as going concerns than as collections of assets. Goodwill reflects all the factors that allow a company to earn a higher-than-market rate of return on its assets, including customer satisfaction, good management, manufacturing efficiency, the advantages of holding a monopoly, good locations, and good employee relations. The payment above and beyond the fair market value of the tangible assets and other specific intangible assets is properly recorded in the Goodwill account.

In *Opinion No. 17*, the Accounting Principles Board states that the benefits arising from purchased goodwill will in time disappear. It is hard for a company to keep having above-average earnings unless new factors of goodwill replace the old ones. For this reason, goodwill should be amortized or written off by systematic charges to income over a reasonable number of future time periods. The total time period should in no case be more than 40 years.[19]

Key Point: Goodwill equals purchase price minus adjusted net asset value.

Goodwill, as stated, should not be recorded unless it is paid for in connection with the purchase of a whole business. The amount to be recorded as goodwill can be determined by writing the identifiable net assets up to their fair market values at the time of purchase and subtracting the total from the purchase price. For example, assume that the owners of Company A agree to sell the company for $11,400,000. If the net assets (total assets − total liabilities) are fairly valued at

$10,000,000, then the amount of the goodwill is $1,400,000 ($11,400,000 − $10,000,000). If the fair market value of the net assets is later determined to be more or less than $10,000,000, an entry is made in the accounting records to adjust the assets to the fair market value. The goodwill would then represent the difference between the adjusted net assets and the purchase price of $11,400,000.

Special Problems of Depreciating Plant Assets

SUPPLEMENTAL OBJECTIVE

9 Apply depreciation methods to problems of partial years, revised rates, groups of similar items, special types of capital expenditures, and cost recovery

The illustrations used so far in this chapter have been simplified to explain the concepts and methods of depreciation. In actual business practice, there is often a need to (1) calculate depreciation for partial years, (2) revise depreciation rates based on new estimates of useful life or residual value, (3) group like items when calculating depreciation, (4) account for special types of capital expenditures, and (5) use the accelerated cost recovery method for tax purposes. The next sections discuss these five cases.

Depreciation for Partial Years

So far, the illustrations of depreciation methods have assumed that plant assets were purchased at the beginning or end of an accounting period. In most cases, however, businesses buy assets when they are needed and sell or discard them when they are no longer useful or needed. The time of year is normally not a factor in the decision. Consequently, it is often necessary to calculate depreciation for partial years.

For example, assume that a piece of equipment is purchased for $3,600 and that it has an estimated useful life of six years and an estimated residual value of $600. Assume also that it is purchased on September 5 and that the yearly accounting period ends on December 31. Depreciation must be recorded for four months, September through December, or four-twelfths of the year. This factor is applied to the calculated depreciation for the entire year. The four months' depreciation under the straight-line method is calculated as follows:

$$\frac{\$3,600 - \$600}{6 \text{ years}} \times 4/12 = \$167$$

For the other depreciation methods, most companies will compute the first year's depreciation and then multiply by the partial year factor. For example, if the company used the double-declining-balance method on the preceding equipment, the depreciation on the asset would be computed as follows:

$$\$3,600 \times 1/3 \times 4/12 = \$400$$

Typically, the depreciation calculation is rounded off to the nearest whole month because a partial month's depreciation is rarely material and the calculation is easier. In this case, depreciation was recorded from the beginning of September even though the purchase was made on September 5.

For all methods, the remainder (eight-twelfths) of the first year's depreciation is recorded in the next annual accounting period together with four-twelfths of the second year's depreciation.

Revision of Depreciation Rates

Because a depreciation rate is based on an estimate of an asset's useful life, the periodic depreciation charge is seldom precise. Sometimes it is very inadequate or excessive. This situation may result from an underestimate or overestimate of the asset's useful life or from a wrong estimate of the residual value. What action should be taken when it is found, after several years of use, that a piece of equipment will last less time—or longer—than originally thought? Sometimes it is necessary to revise the estimate of useful life so that the periodic depreciation expense increases or decreases. Then, to reflect the revised situation, the remaining depreciable cost of the asset is spread over the remaining years of useful life.

With this technique, the annual depreciation expense is increased or decreased to reduce the asset's carrying value to its residual value at the end of its remaining useful life. To illustrate, assume that a delivery truck was purchased for $7,000 and has a residual value of $1,000. At the time of the purchase, the truck was expected to last six years, and it was depreciated on the straight-line basis. However, after two years of intensive use, it is determined that the truck will last only two more years, but that its estimated residual value at the end of the two years will still be $1,000. In other words, at the end of the second year, the truck's estimated useful life is reduced from six years to four years. At that time, the asset account and its related accumulated depreciation account would appear as follows:

Delivery Truck		Accumulated Depreciation, Delivery Truck	
Cost 7,000		Depreciation, year 1	1,000
		Depreciation, year 2	1,000

The remaining depreciable cost is computed as follows:

Cost minus Depreciation Already Taken minus Residual Value

$7,000 − $2,000 − $1,000 = $4,000

The new annual periodic depreciation charge is computed by dividing the remaining depreciable cost of $4,000 by the remaining useful life of two years. Therefore, the new periodic depreciation charge is $2,000. The annual adjusting entry for depreciation for the next two years would be as follows:

$$A = L + OE$$
$$-\quad\quad -$$

Dec. 31	Depreciation Expense, Delivery Truck	2,000	
	Accumulated Depreciation, Delivery Truck		2,000
	To record depreciation expense for the year		

This method of revising depreciation is used widely in industry. It is also supported by the Accounting Principles Board of the AICPA in Accounting Principles Board *Opinion No. 9* and *Opinion No. 20*.

Group Depreciation

To say that the estimated useful life of an asset, such as a piece of equipment, is six years means that the average piece of equipment of that type is expected to last six years. In reality, some pieces may last only two or three years, and others may last eight or nine years, or longer. For this reason, and for reasons of convenience, large companies will group similar items, such as trucks, power lines, office equipment, or transformers, to calculate depreciation. This method is called **group depreciation**. Group depreciation is widely used in all fields of industry and business. A survey of large businesses indicated that 65 percent used group depreciation for all or part of their plant assets.[20]

Special Types of Capital Expenditures

Enrichment Note: Other examples of betterments would include replacing stairs with an escalator in a department store and paving a gravel parking lot.

In addition to the acquisition of plant assets, natural resources, and intangible assets, capital expenditures also include additions and betterments. An **addition** is an enlargement to the physical layout of a plant asset. As an example, if a new wing is added to a building, the benefits from the expenditure will be received over several years, and the amount paid for it should be debited to the asset account. A **betterment** is an improvement that does not add to the physical layout of a plant asset. Installation of an air-conditioning system is an example of a betterment that will offer benefits over a period of years; therefore, its cost should be charged to an asset account.

Among the more usual kinds of revenue expenditures for plant equipment are the repairs, maintenance, lubrication, cleaning, and inspection necessary to keep an asset in good working condition. Repairs fall into two categories: ordinary repairs and extraordinary repairs. **Ordinary repairs** are expenditures that are necessary to maintain an asset in good operating condition. Trucks must have periodic tune-ups, their tires and batteries must be regularly replaced, and other routine repairs must be made. Offices and halls must be painted regularly, and broken tiles or woodwork must be replaced. Such repairs are a current expense.

Enrichment Note: More examples of extraordinary repairs would be putting a new motor in a cement mixer and replacing the roof on a building, thereby extending its life.

Extraordinary repairs are repairs of a more significant nature—they affect the estimated residual value or estimated useful life of an asset. For example, a boiler for heating a building may be given a complete overhaul, at a cost of several thousand dollars, that will extend its useful life by five years. Typically, extraordinary repairs are recorded by debiting the Accumulated Depreciation account, under the assumption that some of the depreciation previously recorded has now been eliminated. The effect of this reduction in the Accumulated Depreciation account is to increase the carrying value of the asset by the cost of the extraordinary repair. Consequently, the new carrying value of the asset should be depreciated over the new estimated useful life.

Let us assume that a machine that cost $10,000 had no estimated residual value and an original estimated useful life of ten years. After eight years, the accumulated depreciation under the straight-line method was $8,000, and the carrying value was $2,000 ($10,000 − $8,000). At that point, the machine was given a major overhaul costing $1,500. This expenditure extended the machine's useful life three years beyond the original ten years. The entry for the extraordinary repair would be as follows:

A = L + OE
+
−

Jan. 4	Accumulated Depreciation, Machinery	1,500	
	Cash		1,500
	Extraordinary repair to machinery		

The annual periodic depreciation for each of the five years remaining in the machine's useful life would be calculated as follows:

Carrying value before extraordinary repairs	$2,000
Extraordinary repairs	1,500
Total	$3,500

$$\text{Annual periodic depreciation} = \frac{\$3,500}{5 \text{ years}} = \$700$$

If the machine remains in use for the five years expected after the major overhaul, the total of the five annual depreciation charges of $700 will exactly equal the new carrying value, including the cost of the extraordinary repair.

Cost Recovery for Federal Income Tax Purposes

In 1986, Congress passed the Tax Reform Act of 1986, arguably the most sweeping revision of federal tax laws since the original enactment of the Internal Revenue Code in 1913. First, a company may elect to expense the first $17,500 (which increases to $25,000 by tax year 2003) of equipment expenditures rather than recording them as an asset. Second, a new method for writing off expenditures recorded as assets, the **Modified Accelerated Cost Recovery System (MACRS)**, may be elected. MACRS discards the concepts of estimated useful life and residual value. Instead, it requires that a cost recovery allowance be computed (1) on the unadjusted cost of property being recovered, and (2) over a period of years prescribed by the law for all property of similar types. The accelerated method prescribed under MACRS for most property other than real estate is 200 percent declining balance with a half-year convention (only one half-year's depreciation is allowed in the year of purchase, and one half-year's depreciation is taken in the last year). In addition, the period over which the cost may be recovered is specified. Recovery of the cost of property placed in service after December 31, 1986, is calculated as prescribed in the 1986 law.

Congress hoped that MACRS would encourage businesses to invest in new plant and equipment by allowing them to write off such assets rapidly. MACRS accelerates the write-off of these investments in two ways. First, the prescribed recovery periods are often shorter than the estimated useful lives used for calculating depreciation for the financial statements. Second, the accelerated method allowed under the new law enables businesses to recover most of the cost of their investments early in the depreciation process.

Clarification Note: MACRS depreciation is used for tax purposes only. It cannot be used for financial reporting.

Tax methods of depreciation are not usually acceptable for financial reporting under generally accepted accounting principles because the recovery periods are shorter than the depreciable assets' estimated useful lives.

Chapter Review

REVIEW OF LEARNING OBJECTIVES

Ace it

1. **Identify the types of long-term assets and explain the management issues related to accounting for them.** Long-term assets are assets that are used in the operation of a business, are not intended for resale, and have a useful life of more than one year. Long-term assets are either tangible or intangible. In the former category are land, plant assets, and natural resources. In the latter are trademarks, patents, franchises, goodwill, and other rights. The accounting issues associated with long-term assets relate to the decision to acquire the assets, the means of financing the assets, and the methods of accounting for the assets.

2. **Distinguish between capital and revenue expenditures, and account for the cost of property, plant, and equipment.** It is important to distinguish between capital expenditures, which are recorded as assets, and revenue expenditures, which are recorded as expenses. The error of classifying one as the other will have an important effect on net income. The acquisition cost of property, plant, and equipment includes all expenditures that are reasonable

and necessary to get such an asset in place and ready for use. Among these expenditures are purchase price, installation cost, freight charges, and insurance during transit.

3. **Define *depreciation*, state the factors that affect its computation, and show how to record it.** Depreciation is the periodic allocation of the cost of a plant asset over its estimated useful life. It is recorded by debiting Depreciation Expense and crediting a related contra-asset account called Accumulated Depreciation. Factors that affect the computation of depreciation are cost, residual value, depreciable cost, and estimated useful life.

4. **Compute periodic depreciation under the (a) straight-line method, (b) production method, and (c) declining-balance method.** Depreciation is commonly computed by the straight-line method, the production method, or an accelerated method. The straight-line method is related directly to the passage of time, whereas the production method is related directly to use. An accelerated method, which results in relatively large amounts of depreciation in earlier years and reduced amounts in later years, is based on the assumption that plant assets provide greater economic benefit in their earlier years than in later years. The most common accelerated method is the declining-balance method.

5. **Account for the disposal of depreciable assets not involving exchanges.** Long-term depreciable assets may be disposed of by being discarded, sold, or exchanged. When long-term assets are disposed of, it is necessary to record the depreciation up to the date of disposal and to remove the carrying value from the accounts by removing the cost from the asset account and the depreciation to date from the accumulated depreciation account. If a long-term asset is sold at a price that differs from its carrying value, there is a gain or loss that should be recorded and reported on the income statement.

6. **Account for the disposal of depreciable assets involving exchanges.** In recording exchanges of similar plant assets, a gain or loss may arise. According to the Accounting Principles Board, losses, but not gains, should be recognized at the time of the exchange. When a gain is not recognized, the new asset is recorded at the carrying value of the old asset plus any cash paid. For income tax purposes, neither gains nor losses are recognized in the exchange of similar assets. When dissimilar assets are exchanged, gains and losses are recognized under both accounting and income tax rules.

7. **Identify the issues related to accounting for natural resources and compute depletion.** Natural resources are wasting assets that are converted to inventory by cutting, pumping, mining, or other forms of extraction. Natural resources are recorded at cost as long-term assets. They are allocated as expenses through depletion charges as the resources are sold. The depletion charge is based on the ratio of the resource extracted to the total estimated resource. A major issue related to this subject is accounting for oil and gas reserves.

8. **Apply the matching rule to intangible assets, including research and development costs and goodwill.** The purchase of an intangible asset should be treated as a capital expenditure and recorded at acquisition cost, which in turn should be amortized over the useful life of the asset. The FASB requires that research and development costs be treated as revenue expenditures and charged as expenses in the periods of expenditure. Software costs are treated as research and development costs and expensed until a feasible working program is developed, after which time the costs may be capitalized and amortized over a reasonable estimated life. Goodwill is the excess of the amount paid for the purchase of a business over the fair market value of the net

assets and is usually related to the superior earning potential of the business. It should be recorded only if paid for in connection with the purchase of a business, and it should be amortized over a period not to exceed 40 years.

9. Apply depreciation methods to problems of partial years, revised rates, groups of similar items, special types of capital expenditures, and cost recovery. In actual business practice, many factors affect depreciation calculations. It may be necessary to calculate depreciation for partial years because assets are bought and sold throughout the year, or to revise depreciation rates because of changed conditions. Because it is often difficult to estimate the useful life of a single item, and because it is more convenient, many large businesses group similar items for purposes of depreciation. Companies must also consider certain special capital expenditures when calculating depreciation. For example, expenditures for additions and betterments are capital expenditures. Extraordinary repairs, which increase the residual value or extend the life of an asset, are also treated as capital expenditures, but ordinary repairs are revenue expenditures. For income tax purposes, rapid write-offs of depreciable assets are allowed through the Modified Accelerated Cost Recovery System. Such rapid write-offs are not usually acceptable for financial accounting because the shortened recovery periods violate the matching rule.

The following concepts and terms were introduced in this chapter.

LO 4 **Accelerated method:** A method of depreciation that allocates relatively large amounts of the depreciable cost of an asset to earlier years and reduced amounts to later years.

SO 9 **Addition:** An enlargement to the physical layout of a plant asset.

LO 1 **Amortization:** The periodic allocation of the cost of an intangible asset to the periods it benefits.

LO 1 **Asset impairment:** Loss of revenue-generating potential of a long-lived asset prior to the end of its useful life. The loss is computed as the difference between the asset's carrying value and its fair value, as measured by the present value of the expected cash flows.

SO 9 **Betterment:** An improvement that does not add to the physical layout of a plant asset.

LO 8 **Brand name:** A registered name that can be used only by its owner to identify a product or service.

LO 2 **Capital expenditure:** An expenditure for the purchase or expansion of a long-term asset, recorded in an asset account.

LO 1 **Carrying value:** The unexpired part of the cost of an asset, not its market value; also called *book value.*

LO 8 **Copyright:** An exclusive right granted by the federal government to the possessor to publish and sell literary, musical, or other artistic materials for a period of the author's life plus 50 years; includes computer programs.

LO 4 **Declining-balance method:** An accelerated method of depreciation in which depreciation is computed by applying a fixed rate to the carrying value (the declining balance) of a tangible long-lived asset.

LO 1 **Depletion:** The exhaustion of a natural resource through mining, cutting, pumping, or other extraction, and the way in which the cost is allocated.

LO 3 **Depreciable cost:** The cost of an asset less its residual value.

LO 1 **Depreciation:** The periodic allocation of the cost of a tangible long-lived asset (other than land and natural resources) over its estimated useful life.

LO 4   **Double-declining-balance method:** An accelerated method of depreciation in which a fixed rate equal to twice the straight-line percentage is applied to the carrying value (the declining balance) of a tangible long-lived asset.

LO 3   **Estimated useful life:** The total number of service units expected from a long-term asset.

LO 2   **Expenditure:** A payment or an obligation to make future payment for an asset or a service.

SO 9   **Extraordinary repairs:** Repairs that affect the estimated residual value or estimated useful life of an asset, whereby the carrying value of the asset is increased.

LO 8   **Franchise:** The right or license to an exclusive territory or market.

LO 7   **Full-costing:** A method of accounting for the costs of exploration and development of oil and gas resources in which all costs are recorded as assets and depleted over the estimated life of the producing resources.

LO 8   **Goodwill:** The excess of the cost of a group of assets (usually a business) over the fair market value of the net assets if purchased individually.

SO 9   **Group depreciation:** The grouping of similar items to calculate depreciation.

LO 1   **Intangible assets:** Long-term assets that have no physical substance but have a value based on rights or advantages accruing to the owner.

LO 8   **Leasehold:** A right to occupy land or buildings under a long-term rental contract.

LO 8   **Leasehold improvements:** Improvements to leased property that become the property of the lessor at the end of the lease.

LO 8   **License:** The right to use a formula, technique, process, or design.

LO 1   **Long-term assets:** Assets that (1) have a useful life of more than one year, (2) are acquired for use in the operation of a business, and (3) are not intended for resale to customers; less commonly called *fixed assets*.

SO 9   **Modified Accelerated Cost Recovery System (MACRS):** A mandatory system of depreciation for income tax purposes, enacted by Congress in 1986, that requires a cost recovery allowance to be computed (1) on the unadjusted cost of property being recovered, and (2) over a period of years prescribed by the law for all property of similar types.

LO 1   **Natural resources:** Long-term assets purchased for the economic value that can be taken from the land and used up rather than for the value associated with the land's location.

LO 3   **Obsolescence:** The process of becoming out of date; a contributor, with physical deterioration, to the limited useful life of tangible assets.

SO 9   **Ordinary repairs:** Expenditures, usually of a recurring nature, that are recorded as current period expenses. They are necessary to maintain an asset in good operating condition in order to attain its originally intended useful life.

LO 8   **Patent:** An exclusive right granted by the federal government for a period of 17 years to make a particular product or use a specific process.

LO 3   **Physical deterioration:** Limitations on the useful life of a depreciable asset resulting from use and from exposure to the elements.

LO 4   **Production method:** A method of depreciation that assumes that depreciation is solely the result of use and that the passage of time plays no role in the depreciation process; it allocates depreciation based on the units of output or use during each period of an asset's useful life.

LO 3   **Residual value:** The estimated net scrap, salvage, or trade-in value of a tangible asset at the estimated date of disposal; also called *salvage value* or *disposal value*.

LO 2   **Revenue expenditure:** An expenditure for repairs, maintenance, or other services needed to maintain or operate a plant asset, recorded by a debit to an expense account.

LO 4 **Straight-line method:** A method of depreciation that assumes that depreciation depends only on the passage of time and that allocates an equal amount of depreciation to each accounting period in an asset's useful life.

LO 7 **Successful efforts accounting:** A method of accounting for oil and gas resources in which successful exploration is recorded as an asset and depleted over the estimated life of the resource and all unsuccessful efforts are immediately written off as losses.

LO 1 **Tangible assets:** Long-term assets that have physical substance.

LO 8 **Trademark:** A registered symbol or brand name that can be used only by its owner to identify a product or service.

REVIEW PROBLEM

LO 3
LO 4

Comparison of Depreciation Methods

Norton Construction Company purchased a cement mixer on January 1, 20x1, for $14,500. The mixer was expected to have a useful life of five years and a residual value of $1,000. The company engineers estimated that the mixer would have a useful life of 7,500 hours. It was used 1,500 hours in 20x1, 2,625 hours in 20x2, 2,250 hours in 20x3, 750 hours in 20x4, and 375 hours in 20x5. The company's year end is December 31.

REQUIRED

1. Compute the depreciation expense and carrying value for 20x1 to 20x5, using the following three methods: (a) straight-line, (b) production, and (c) double-declining-balance.

2. Prepare the adjusting entry to record the depreciation for 20x1 calculated in **1(a)**.

3. Show the balance sheet presentation for the cement mixer after the entry in **2** on December 31, 20x1.

4. What conclusions can you draw from the patterns of yearly depreciation?

ANSWER TO REVIEW PROBLEM

1. Depreciation computed:

Depreciation Method	Year	Computation	Depreciation	Carrying Value
a. Straight-line	20x1	$13,500 × 1/5	$2,700	$11,800
	20x2	13,500 × 1/5	2,700	9,100
	20x3	13,500 × 1/5	2,700	6,400
	20x4	13,500 × 1/5	2,700	3,700
	20x5	13,500 × 1/5	2,700	1,000
b. Production	20x1	$13,500 × $\frac{1,500}{7,500}$	$2,700	$11,800
	20x2	13,500 × $\frac{2,625}{7,500}$	4,725	7,075
	20x3	13,500 × $\frac{2,250}{7,500}$	4,050	3,025
	20x4	13,500 × $\frac{750}{7,500}$	1,350	1,675
	20x5	13,500 × $\frac{375}{7,500}$	675	1,000
c. Double-declining-balance	20x1	$14,500 × .4	$5,800	$ 8,700
	20x2	8,700 × .4	3,480	5,220
	20x3	5,220 × .4	2,088	3,132
	20x4	3,132 × .4	1,253*	1,879
	20x5		879*†	1,000

*Rounded.
†Remaining depreciation to reduce carrying value to residual value ($1,879 − $1,000 = $879).

2. Adjusting entry prepared—straight-line method:

20x1
Dec. 31   Depreciation Expense, Cement Mixer   2,700
              Accumulated Depreciation, Cement Mixer   2,700
                 To record depreciation expense,
                 straight-line method

3. Balance sheet presentation for 20x1 shown:

Property, Plant, and Equipment
   Cement Mixer $14,500
   Less Accumulated Depreciation   2,700
                                                   $11,800

4. Conclusions drawn from depreciation patterns: The pattern of depreciation for the straight-line method differs significantly from that for the double-declining-balance method. In the earlier years, the amount of depreciation under the double-declining-balance method is significantly greater than the amount under the straight-line method. In the later years, the opposite is true. The carrying value under the straight-line method is greater than that under the double-declining-balance method at the end of all years except the fifth year. Depreciation under the production method differs from that under the other methods in that it follows no regular pattern. It varies with the amount of use. Consequently, depreciation is greatest in 20x2 and 20x3, which are the years of greatest use. Use declined significantly in the last two years.

Chapter Assignments

BUILDING YOUR KNOWLEDGE FOUNDATION

QUESTIONS

1. What are the characteristics of long-term assets?
2. Which of the following items would be classified as plant assets on the balance sheet? (a) A truck held for sale by a truck dealer, (b) an office building that was once the company headquarters but is now to be sold, (c) a typewriter used by a secretary of the company, (d) a machine that is used in manufacturing operations but is now fully depreciated, (e) pollution-control equipment that does not reduce the cost or improve the efficiency of a factory, (f) a parking lot for company employees.
3. Why is land different from other long-term assets?
4. What do accountants mean by the term *depreciation*, and what is its relationship to depletion and amortization?
5. What is asset impairment, and how does it affect the valuation of long-term assets?
6. How do cash flows relate to the decision to acquire a long-term asset, and how does the useful life of an asset relate to the means of financing it?
7. Why is it useful to think of a plant asset as a bundle of services?
8. What is the distinction between revenue expenditures and capital expenditures, why is it important, and what in general is included in the cost of a long-term asset?
9. Which of the following expenditures stemming from the purchase of a computer system would be charged to the asset account? (a) The purchase price of the equipment, (b) interest on the debt incurred to purchase the equipment, (c) freight charges, (d) installation charges, (e) the cost of special communications outlets at

the computer site, (f) the cost of repairing a door that was damaged during installation, (g) the cost of adjustments to the system during the first month of operation.

10. Hale's Grocery obtained bids on the construction of a receiving dock at the back of its store. The lowest bid was $22,000. The company decided to build the dock itself, however, and was able to do so for $20,000, which it borrowed. The activity was recorded as a debit to Buildings for $22,000 and credits to Notes Payable for $20,000 and Gain on Construction for $2,000. Do you agree with the entry?

11. A firm buys technical equipment that is expected to last twelve years. Why might the equipment have to be depreciated over a shorter period of time?

12. A company purchased a building five years ago. The market value of the building is now greater than it was when the building was purchased. Explain why the company should continue depreciating the building.

13. Evaluate the following statement: "A parking lot should not be depreciated because adequate repairs will make it last forever."

14. Is the purpose of depreciation to determine the value of equipment? Explain your answer.

15. Contrast the assumptions underlying the straight-line depreciation method with the assumptions underlying the production depreciation method.

16. What is the principal argument supporting an accelerated depreciation method?

17. If a plant asset is sold during the year, why should depreciation be computed for the partial year prior to the date of the sale?

18. If a plant asset is discarded before the end of its useful life, how is the amount of loss measured?

19. When similar assets are exchanged, at what amount is the new asset recorded for federal income tax purposes?

20. When an exchange of similar assets occurs in which there is an unrecorded loss, is the taxpayer ever able to deduct or receive federal income tax credit for the loss?

21. Old Stake Mining Company computes the depletion rate of ore to be $2 per ton. During 20xx the company mined 400,000 tons of ore and sold 370,000 tons. What is the total depletion expense for the year?

22. Under what circumstances can a mining company depreciate its plant assets over a period of time that is less than their useful lives?

23. Because accounts receivable have no physical substance, can they be classified as intangible assets?

24. Under what circumstances can a company have intangible assets that do not appear on the balance sheet?

25. When the Accounting Principles Board indicates that accounting for intangible assets involves the same issues as accounting for tangible assets, what issues is it referring to?

26. How does the Financial Accounting Standards Board recommend that research and development costs be treated?

27. After spending three years developing a new software program for designing office buildings, Archi Draw Company recently completed the detailed working program. How does accounting for the costs of software development differ before and after the completion of a successful working program?

28. How is accounting for software development costs similar to and different from accounting for research and development costs?

29. Under what conditions should goodwill be recorded? Should it remain in the records permanently once it is recorded?

30. What basic procedure should be followed in revising a depreciation rate?

31. On what basis can depreciation be taken on a group of assets rather than on individual items?

32. What will be the effect on future years' income of charging an addition to a building to repair expense?

33. In what ways do an addition, a betterment, and an extraordinary repair differ?

34. How does an extraordinary repair differ from an ordinary repair? What is the accounting treatment for each?

35. What is the difference between depreciation for accounting purposes and the Modified Accelerated Cost Recovery System for income tax purposes?

SHORT EXERCISES

SE 1.

LO 1 Management Issues

Indicate whether each of the following actions is primarily related to (a) acquisition of long-term assets, (b) financing of long-term assets, or (c) choosing methods and estimates related to long-term assets.

1. Deciding between common stock and long-term notes for the raising of funds

2. Relating the acquisition cost of a long-term asset to cash flows generated by the asset

3. Determining how long an asset will benefit the company

4. Deciding to use cash flows from operations to purchase long-term assets

5. Determining how much an asset will sell for when it is no longer useful to the company

SE 2.

LO 2 Determining Cost of Long-Term Assets

Denecker Auto purchased a neighboring lot for a new building and parking lot. Indicate whether each of the following expenditures is properly charged to (a) Land, (b) Land Improvements, or (c) Buildings.

1. Paving costs
2. Architects' fee for building design
3. Cost of clearing the property
4. Cost of the property
5. Building construction costs
6. Lights around the property
7. Building permit
8. Interest on the construction loan

SE 3.

LO 2 Group Purchase

Altshuler Company purchased property with a warehouse and parking lot for $750,000. An appraiser valued the components of the property if purchased separately as follows:

Land	$200,000
Land improvements	100,000
Building	500,000
Total	$800,000

Determine the cost to be assigned to each component.

SE 4.

LO 4 Straight-Line Method

Vermont Sun Fitness Center purchased a new step machine for $5,500. The apparatus is expected to last four years and have a residual value of $500. What will be the depreciation expense for each year under the straight-line method?

SE 5.

LO 4 Production Method

Assuming that the step machine in **SE 4** has an estimated useful life of 8,000 hours and was used for 2,400 hours in year 1, for 2,000 hours in year 2, for 2,200 hours in year 3, and for 1,400 hours in year 4, how much would depreciation expense be in each year?

SE 6.

LO 4 Double-Declining-Balance Method

Assuming that the step machine in **SE 4** is depreciated using the declining-balance method at double the straight-line rate, how much would depreciation expense be in each year?

SE 7.

LO 5 Disposal of Plant Assets: No Trade-In

New England Printing had a piece of equipment that cost $8,100 and on which $4,500 of accumulated depreciation had been recorded. The equipment was disposed of on January 4, the first day of business of the current year. Prepare the entries in journal form to record the disposal under each of the following assumptions:

1. It was discarded as having no value.

2. It was sold for $1,500 cash.

3. It was sold for $4,000 cash.

LO 6 Disposal of Plant Assets: Trade-In

SE 8. Prepare the entries in journal form to record the disposal referred to in **SE 7** under each of the following assumptions:

1. The equipment was traded in on dissimilar equipment that had a list price of $12,000. A $3,800 trade-in was allowed, and the balance was paid in cash. Gains and losses are to be recognized.

2. The equipment was traded in on dissimilar equipment that had a list price of $12,000. A $1,750 trade-in was allowed, and the balance was paid in cash. Gains and losses are to be recognized.

3. Same as **2**, with the exception that the items are similar and gains and losses are not to be recognized.

LO 7 Natural Resources

SE 9. Lincoln Hills Company purchased land containing an estimated 4,000,000 tons of ore for $8,000,000. The land will be worth $1,200,000 without the ore after eight years of active mining. Although the equipment needed for the mining will have a useful life of 20 years, it is not expected to be usable and will have no value after the mining on this site is complete. Compute the depletion charge per ton and the amount of depletion expense for the first year of operation, assuming that 600,000 tons of ore were mined and sold. Also, compute the first-year depreciation on the mining equipment using the production method, assuming a cost of $9,600,000 with no residual value.

LO 8 Intangible Assets: Computer Software

SE 10. Alpha-Links created a new software application for PCs. Its costs during research and development were $500,000, and its costs after the working program was developed were $350,000. Although its copyright may be amortized over 40 years, management believes that the product will be viable for only five years. How should the costs be accounted for? At what value will the software appear on the balance sheet after one year?

EXERCISES

LO 1 Management Issues

E 1. Indicate whether each of the following actions is primarily related to (a) acquisition of long-term assets, (b) financing of long-term assets, or (c) choosing methods and estimates related to long-term assets.

1. Deciding to use the production method of depreciation
2. Allocating costs on a group purchase
3. Determining the total units a machine will produce
4. Deciding to borrow funds to purchase equipment
5. Estimating the savings a new machine will produce and comparing the amount to cost
6. Deciding whether to rent or buy a piece of equipment

LO 1 Purchase Decision—Present Value Analysis

E 2. Management is considering the purchase of a new machine for a cost of $12,000. It is estimated that the machine will generate positive net cash flows of $3,000 per year for five years and will have a disposal price at the end of that time of $1,000. Assuming an interest rate of 9 percent, determine if management should purchase the machine. Use Tables 3 and 4 in the appendix on future value and present value tables to determine the net present value of the new machine.

LO 2 Determining Cost of Long-Term Assets

E 3. Winkle Manufacturing purchased land next to its factory to be used as a parking lot. Expenditures incurred by the company were as follows: purchase price, $150,000; broker's fees, $12,000; title search and other fees, $1,100; demolition of a shack on the property, $4,000; general grading of property, $2,100; paving parking lots, $20,000; lighting for parking lots, $16,000; and signs for parking lots, $3,200. Determine the amounts that should be debited to the Land account and the Land Improvements account.

LO 2 Group Purchase

E 4. Nikki Hopper purchased a car wash for $480,000. If purchased separately, the land would have cost $120,000, the building $270,000, and the equipment $210,000.

Determine the amount that should be recorded in the new business's records for land, building, and equipment.

E 5.

LO 2 Cost of Long-Term Asset
LO 4 and Depreciation

Ed Ruzicka purchased a used tractor for $35,000. Before the tractor could be used, it required new tires, which cost $2,200, and an overhaul, which cost $2,800. Its first tank of fuel cost $150. The tractor is expected to last six years and have a residual value of $4,000. Determine the cost and depreciable cost of the tractor and calculate the first year's depreciation under the straight-line method.

E 6.

LO 3 Depreciation Methods
LO 4

Trujillo Oil Company purchased a drilling truck for $90,000. The company expected the truck to last five years or 200,000 miles, with an estimated residual value of $15,000 at the end of that time. During 20x5, the truck was driven 48,000 miles. The company's year end is December 31. Compute the depreciation for 20x5 under each of the following methods, assuming that the truck was purchased on January 13, 20x4: (1) straight-line, (2) production, and (3) double-declining-balance. Using the amount computed in **3,** prepare the entry in journal form to record depreciation expense for the second year and show how the Drilling Truck account would appear on the balance sheet.

E 7.

LO 4 Declining-Balance Method

Irgan Burglar Alarm Systems Company purchased a word processor for $2,240. It has an estimated useful life of four years and an estimated residual value of $240. Compute the depreciation charge for each of the four years using the double-declining-balance method.

E 8.

LO 5 Disposal of Plant Assets
LO 6

A piece of equipment that cost $32,400 and on which $18,000 of accumulated depreciation had been recorded was disposed of on January 2, the first day of business of the current year. Prepare entries in journal form to record the disposal under each of the following assumptions:

1. It was discarded as having no value.
2. It was sold for $6,000 cash.
3. It was sold for $18,000 cash.
4. It was traded in on dissimilar equipment having a list price of $48,000. A $16,200 trade-in was allowed, and the balance was paid in cash. Gains and losses are to be recognized.
5. It was traded in on dissimilar equipment having a list price of $48,000. A $7,500 trade-in was allowed, and the balance was paid in cash. Gains and losses are to be recognized.
6. Same as **5,** with the exception that the items are similar and gains and losses are not to be recognized.

E 9.

LO 5 Disposal of Plant Assets
LO 6

A microcomputer was purchased by Aristotle Company on January 1, 20x1, at a cost of $5,000. It is expected to have a useful life of five years and a residual value of $500. Assuming that the computer is disposed of on July 1, 20x4, record the partial year's depreciation for 20x4 using the straight-line method, and record the disposal under each of the following assumptions:

1. The microcomputer is discarded.
2. The microcomputer is sold for $800.
3. The microcomputer is sold for $2,200.
4. The microcomputer is exchanged for a new microcomputer with a list price of $9,000. A $1,200 trade-in is allowed on the cash purchase. The accounting approach to gains and losses is followed.
5. Same as **4,** except a $2,400 trade-in is allowed.
6. Same as **4,** except the income tax approach is followed.
7. Same as **5,** except the income tax approach is followed.
8. Same as **4,** except the microcomputer is exchanged for dissimilar office equipment.
9. Same as **5,** except the microcomputer is exchanged for dissimilar office equipment.

E 10.

LO 7 **Natural Resource Depletion and Depreciation of Related Plant Assets**

Loess Mining Company purchased land containing an estimated 10 million tons of ore for a cost of $8,800,000. The land without the ore is estimated to be worth $1,600,000. The company expects that all the usable ore can be mined in ten years. Buildings costing $800,000 with an estimated useful life of 30 years were erected on the site. Equipment costing $960,000 with an estimated useful life of ten years was installed. Because of the remote location, neither the buildings nor the equipment has an estimated residual value. During its first year of operation, the company mined and sold 800,000 tons of ore.

1. Compute the depletion charge per ton.
2. Compute the depletion expense that Loess Mining should record for the year.
3. Determine the depreciation expense for the year for the buildings, making it proportional to the depletion.
4. Determine the depreciation expense for the year for the equipment under two alternatives: (a) making the expense proportional to the depletion and (b) using the straight-line method.

E 11.

LO 8 **Amortization of Copyrights and Trademarks**

1. Okumura Publishing Company purchased the copyright to a basic computer textbook for $20,000. The usual life of a textbook is about four years. However, the copyright will remain in effect for another 50 years. Calculate the annual amortization of the copyright.

2. Austin Company purchased a trademark from a well-known supermarket for $160,000. The management of the company argued that because the trademark's value would last forever and might even increase, no amortization should be charged. Calculate the minimum amount of annual amortization that should be charged, according to guidelines of the appropriate Accounting Principles Board opinion.

E 12.

SO 9 **Depreciation Methods: Partial Years**

Using the data given for Trujillo Oil Company in **E 6,** compute the depreciation for calendar year 20x4 under each of the following methods, assuming that the truck was purchased on July 1, 20x4, and was driven 20,000 miles during 20x4: (1) straight-line, (2) production, and (3) double-declining-balance.

E 13.

SO 9 **Revision of Depreciation Rates**

Exmoor Hospital purchased a special x-ray machine for its operating room. The machine, which cost $311,560, was expected to last ten years, with an estimated residual value of $31,560. After two years of operation (and depreciation charges using the straight-line method), it became evident that the x-ray machine would last a total of only seven years. The estimated residual value, however, would remain the same. Given this information, determine the new depreciation charge for the third year on the basis of the revised estimated useful life.

E 14.

LO 2 **Special Types of Capital**
SO 9 **Expenditures**

Tell whether each of the following transactions related to an office building is a revenue expenditure (RE) or a capital expenditure (CE). In addition, indicate whether each transaction is an ordinary repair (OR), an extraordinary repair (ER), an addition (A), a betterment (B), or none of these (N).

1. The hallways and ceilings in the building are repainted at a cost of $8,300.
2. The hallways, which have tile floors, are carpeted at a cost of $28,000.
3. A new wing is added to the building at a cost of $175,000.
4. Furniture is purchased for the entrance to the building at a cost of $16,500.
5. The air-conditioning system is overhauled at a cost of $28,500. The overhaul extends the useful life of the air-conditioning system by ten years.
6. A cleaning firm is paid $200 per week to clean the newly installed carpets.

E 15.

SO 9 **Extraordinary Repairs**

Collinson Manufacturing has an incinerator that originally cost $187,200 and now has accumulated depreciation of $132,800. The incinerator has completed its fifteenth year of service in an estimated useful life of 20 years. At the beginning of the sixteenth year, the company spent $42,800 repairing and modernizing the incinerator to comply with pollution-control standards. Therefore, the incinerator is now expected to last ten more years instead of five more years. It will not, however, have more capacity than it did in the past or a residual value at the end of its useful life.

1. Prepare the entry to record the cost of the repair.
2. Compute the carrying value of the incinerator after the entry.
3. Prepare the entry to record straight-line depreciation for the current year.

PROBLEMS

P 1.
LO 2 Determining Cost of Assets

Oslo Company began operation on January 1 of the current year. At the end of the year, the company's auditor discovered that all expenditures involving long-term assets had been debited to an account called Fixed Assets. An analysis of the account, which had a year-end balance of $2,644,972, disclosed that it contained the items presented below.

Cost of land	$ 316,600
Surveying costs	4,100
Transfer of title and other fees required by the county	920
Broker's fees for land	21,144
Attorney's fees associated with land acquisition	7,048
Cost of removing unusable timber from land	50,400
Cost of grading land	4,200
Cost of digging building foundation	34,600
Architect's fee for building and land improvements (80 percent building)	64,800
Cost of building construction	710,000
Cost of sidewalks	11,400
Cost of parking lots	54,400
Cost of lighting for grounds	80,300
Cost of landscaping	11,800
Cost of machinery	989,000
Shipping cost on machinery	55,300
Cost of installing machinery	176,200
Cost of testing machinery	22,100
Cost of changes in building to comply with safety regulations pertaining to machinery	12,540
Cost of repairing building that was damaged in the installation of machinery	8,900
Cost of medical bill for injury received by employee while installing machinery	2,400
Cost of water damage to building during heavy rains prior to opening the plant for operation	6,820
Account balance	$2,644,972

The timber that was cleared from the land was sold to a firewood dealer for $5,000. This amount was credited to Miscellaneous Income. During the construction period, two supervisors devoted their full time to the construction project. They earn annual salaries of $48,000 and $42,000, respectively. They spent two months on the purchase and preparation of the land, six months on the construction of the building (approximately one-sixth of which was devoted to improvements on the grounds), and one month on machinery installation. The plant began operation on October 1, and the supervisors returned to their regular duties. Their salaries were debited to Factory Salaries Expense.

REQUIRED

Prepare a schedule with the following column headings: Land, Land Improvements, Buildings, Machinery, and Expense. List the items and place each in the proper account. Negative amounts should be shown in parentheses. Total the columns.

LO 3 Comparison of
LO 4 Depreciation Methods

REQUIRED

P 2. Myles Construction Company purchased a new crane for $360,500 at the beginning of year 1. The crane has an estimated residual value of $35,000 and an estimated useful life of six years. The crane is expected to last 10,000 hours. It was used 1,800 hours in year 1; 2,000 in year 2; 2,500 in year 3; 1,500 in year 4; 1,200 in year 5; and 1,000 in year 6.

1. Compute the annual depreciation and carrying value for the new crane for each of the six years (round to nearest dollar where necessary) under each of the following methods: (a) straight-line, (b) production, and (c) double-declining-balance.
2. Prepare the adjusting entry that would be made each year to record the depreciation calculated under the straight-line method.
3. Show the balance sheet presentation for the crane after the adjusting entry in year 2 using the straight-line method.
4. What conclusions can you draw from the patterns of yearly depreciation and carrying value in 1?

LO 4 Depreciation Methods
SO 9 and Partial Years

P 3. Chen Company operates three types of equipment. Because of the equipment's varied functions, company accounting policy requires the application of three different depreciation methods. Data on this equipment are summarized in the table below. Equipment 3 was used 2,000 hours in 20x1; 4,200 hours in 20x2; and 3,200 hours in 20x3.

Equipment	Date Purchased	Cost	Installation Cost	Estimated Residual Value	Estimated Life	Depreciation Method
1	1/12/x1	$171,000	$ 9,000	$18,000	10 years	Double-declining-balance
2	7/9/x1	191,100	15,900	21,000	10 years	Straight-line
3	10/2/x1	290,700	8,100	33,600	20,000 hours	Production

REQUIRED

Assuming that the fiscal year ends December 31, compute the depreciation expense on each type of equipment and the total depreciation expense for 20x1, 20x2, and 20x3 by filling in a table with the headings shown below.

Equipment No.	Computations	Depreciation		
		20x1	20x2	20x3

LO 5 Recording Disposals
LO 6

REQUIRED

P 4. Laughlin Designs, Inc., purchased a computer that will assist it in designing factory lay-outs. The cost of the computer was $23,500. Its expected useful life is six years. The company can probably sell the computer for $2,500 at the end of six years.

Prepare journal entries to record the disposal of the computer at the end of the third year, after the depreciation is recorded, assuming that it was depreciated using the straight-line method and making the following assumptions:

a. The computer is sold for $19,000.
b. It is sold for $10,000.
c. It is traded in on a dissimilar item (equipment) costing $36,000, a trade-in allowance of $17,500 is given, the balance is paid in cash, and gains and losses are recognized.
d. Same as c except the trade-in allowance is $11,000.
e. Same as c except it is traded for a similar computer and APB accounting rules are followed with regard to the recognition of gains or losses.
f. Same as d except it is traded for a similar computer and APB accounting rules are followed with regard to the recognition of gains or losses.
g. Same as c except it is traded for a similar computer and gains and losses are not recognized (income tax method).
h. Same as d except it is traded for a similar computer and gains and losses are not recognized (income tax method).

LO 8 Leasehold, Leasehold
Improvements, and
Amortization of Patent

P 5. **Part A:** At the beginning of the fiscal year, Chang Company purchased an eight-year leasehold or sublease on a warehouse in Peoria for $48,000. Chang will also pay rent of $1,000 a month. The warehouse needs the following improvements to meet Chang's needs:

Lighting fixtures	$18,000	Heating system	$30,000
Replacement of a wall	25,000	Break room	12,200
Office carpet	14,400	Loading dock	8,400

The expected life of the loading dock and carpet is eight years. The other items are expected to last ten years. None of the improvements will have a residual value.

REQUIRED

Prepare entries in journal form to record the following: (a) payment for the leasehold; (b) first-year lease expense payment; (c) payments for the improvements; (d) amortization of the leasehold for the year; (e) leasehold improvement amortization for the year.

Part B: At the beginning of the fiscal year, Ricks Company purchased for $1,030,000 a patent that applies to the manufacture of a unique tamper-proof lid for medicine bottles. Ricks incurred legal costs of $450,000 in successfully defending the patent against use of the lid by a competitor. Ricks estimated that the patent would be valuable for at least ten years. During the first two years of operation, Ricks successfully marketed the lid. At the beginning of the third year, a study appeared in a consumers' magazine showing that the lid could, in fact, be removed by children. As a result, all orders for the lids were canceled, and the patent was rendered worthless.

REQUIRED

Prepare entries in journal form to record the following: (a) purchase of the patent; (b) successful defense of the patent; (c) amortization expense for the first year; and (d) write-off of the patent as worthless.

ALTERNATE PROBLEMS

P 6.

LO 2 Determining Cost of Assets

Georgakis Computers constructed a new training center in 20x2. You have been hired to manage the training center. A review of the accounting records lists the following expenditures debited to an asset account titled "Training Center."

Attorney's fee, land acquisition	$ 34,900
Cost of land	598,000
Architect's fee, building design	102,000
Building	1,020,000
Parking lot and sidewalk	135,600
Electrical wiring, building	164,000
Landscaping	55,000
Cost of surveying land	9,200
Training equipment, tables, and chairs	136,400
Installation of training equipment	68,000
Cost of grading the land	14,000
Cost of changes in building to soundproof rooms	59,200
Total account balance	$2,396,300

During the center's construction, someone from Georgakis Computers worked full time on the project. He spent two months on the purchase and preparation of the site, six months on the construction, one month on land improvements, and one month on equipment installation and training room furniture purchase and setup. His salary of $64,000 during this ten-month period was charged to Administrative Expense. The training center was placed in operation on November 1.

REQUIRED

Prepare a schedule with the following four column (Account) headings: Land, Land Improvements, Building, and Equipment. Place each of the expenditures above in the appropriate column. Total the columns.

P 7.

LO 3 Comparison of
LO 4 Depreciation Methods

Gent Manufacturing Company purchased a robot for $1,440,000 at the beginning of year 1. The robot has an estimated useful life of four years and an estimated residual value of $120,000. The robot, which should last 20,000 hours, was operated 6,000 hours in year 1; 8,000 hours in year 2; 4,000 hours in year 3; and 2,000 hours in year 4.

REQUIRED

1. Compute the annual depreciation and carrying value for the robot for each year assuming the following depreciation methods: (a) straight-line, (b) production, and (c) double-declining-balance.

2. Prepare the adjusting entry that would be made each year to record the depreciation calculated under the straight-line method.

3. Show the balance sheet presentation for the robot after the adjusting entry in year 2 using the straight-line method.

4. What conclusions can you draw from the patterns of yearly depreciation and carrying value in 1?

P 8.

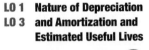

LO 4 Depreciation Methods
SO 9 and Partial Years

Rita Montes purchased a laundry company. In addition to the washing machines, Montes installed a tanning machine and a refreshment center. Because each type of asset performs a different function, she has decided to use different depreciation methods. Data on each type of asset are summarized in the table below. The tanning machine was operated 2,100 hours in 20x2, 3,000 hours in 20x3, and 2,400 hours in 20x4.

Asset	Date Purchased	Cost	Installation Cost	Residual Value	Estimated Life	Depreciation Method
Washing machines	3/5/x2	$30,000	$4,000	$5,200	4 years	Straight-line
Tanning machine	4/1/x2	68,000	6,000	2,000	7,500 hours	Production
Refreshment center	10/1/x2	6,800	1,200	1,200	10 years	Double-declining-balance

REQUIRED

Assume the fiscal year ends December 31. Compute the depreciation expense for each item and the total depreciation expense for 20x2, 20x3, and 20x4. Round your answers to the nearest dollar and present them in a table with the headings shown below.

		Depreciation		
Asset	Computations	20x2	20x3	20x4

EXPANDING YOUR CRITICAL THINKING, COMMUNICATION, AND INTERPERSONAL SKILLS

SKILLS DEVELOPMENT

Conceptual Analysis

SD 1.

LO 1 Nature of Depreciation
LO 3 and Amortization and
Estimated Useful Lives

A change in the estimated useful lives of long-term assets can have a significant effect. For instance, *General Motors Corp.* states,

> In the third quarter of 1987, the Corporation revised the estimated service lives of its plants and equipment and special tools retroactive to January 1, 1987. These revisions, which were based on 1987 studies of actual useful lives and periods of use, recognized current estimates of service lives of the assets and had the effect of reducing 1987 depreciation and amortization charges by $1,236.6 million or $2.53 per share of $1⅔ par value common stock.[21]

General Motors' income before income taxes for the year was $2,005.4 million. Discuss the purpose of depreciation and amortization. What is the estimated service life, and on what basis did General Motors change the estimates of the service lives of plants and equipment and special tools? What was the effect of this change on the corporation's income before income taxes? Is it likely that the company is in better condition economically as a result of the change? Does the company have more cash at the end of the year as a result? (Ignore income tax effects.)

| Cash Flow | CD-ROM | Communication | Critical Thinking | Ethics | General Ledger | Group Activity | Hot Links to Real Companies | International | Internet | Key Ratio | Memo | Spreadsheet |

SD 2.

LO 3 **Change of Depreciation**
LO 4 **Method**

Polaroid Corporation, a manufacturer of instant cameras and films, changed from an accelerated depreciation method for financial reporting purposes to the straight-line method for assets acquired after January 1, 1997. As noted in Polaroid's 1997 annual report:

> The company changed its method of depreciation for financial reporting for the cost of buildings, machinery, and equipment acquired on or after January 1, 1997, from primarily accelerated method to the straight-line method.[22]

What reasons can you give for Polaroid's choosing to switch to a straight-line method of depreciation? Discuss which of the two depreciation methods is more conservative. How does the change of depreciation method for financial reporting affect the company's cash flows?

SD 3.

LO 8 **Trademarks**

America Online (AOL), America's largest online Internet service, filed a trademark-infringement lawsuit against *AT&T*'s WorldNet Service seeking to block its use of such terms and phrases as "You Have Mail" and "You've Got Mail." A district court judge denied AOL's request for a temporary restraining order against AT&T's using these phrases saying it was not clear that AOL owned them. AOL claims these terms are historically associated with its service, but AT&T says they are common Internet phrases available to all. The Internet community is watching this case and others closely because the Internet is a relatively new medium in which it is not clear what rules apply. Whatever the outcome, it can have significant financial effects.[23]

What is a trademark, and why is it considered an intangible asset? Why does a trademark have value? For whom does a trademark have value? Be prepared to discuss how your answers apply to the case of AOL's use of "You Have Mail" or "You've Got Mail."

Ethical Dilemma

SD 4.

LO 2 **Ethics and Allocation of Acquisition Costs**

Signal Company has purchased land and a warehouse for $18,000,000. The warehouse is expected to last 20 years and to have a salvage value equal to 10 percent of its cost. The chief financial officer (CFO) and the controller are discussing the allocation of the purchase price. The CFO believes that the largest amount possible should be assigned to the land because this action will improve reported net income in the future. Depreciation expense will be lower because land is not depreciated. He suggests allocating one-third, or $6,000,000, of the cost to the land. This results in depreciation expense each year of $540,000 [($12,000,000 − $1,200,000) ÷ 20 years]. The controller disagrees, arguing that the smallest amount possible, say one-fifth of the purchase price, should be allocated to the land, thereby saving income taxes, since the depreciation, which is tax deductible, will be greater. Under this plan, annual depreciation would be $648,000 [($14,400,000 − $1,440,000) ÷ 20 years]. The annual tax savings at a 30 percent tax rate is $32,400 [($648,000 − $540,000) × .30]. How will this decision affect the company's cash flows? Ethically speaking, how should the purchase cost be allocated? Who will be affected by the decision?

Group Activity: Have each group develop the position of one of the two roles for presentation and debate.

SD 5.

LO 2 **Ethics of Aggressive**
LO 8 **Accounting Policies**

Is it ethical to choose aggressive accounting practices to advance a company's business? *America Online* (AOL), the largest on-line service and Internet service provider in the United States, is one of the hottest stocks on Wall Street. From its initial stock offering in 1992, its stock price was up several thousand percent. Accounting is very important to AOL because earnings enable it to sell shares of stock and raise more cash to fund its phenomenal growth. In its early years, AOL was one of the most aggressive companies in its choice of accounting principles. AOL's strategy called for building the largest customer base in the industry. Consequently, it spent many millions of dollars each year marketing its services to new customers. Such costs are usually recognized as operating expenses in the year in which they are incurred. However, AOL treated these costs as long-term assets, called "deferred subscriber acquisition costs," and expensed them over several years, because the company said the average customer was going to stay with the company for three years or more. The company also recorded research and development costs as "product development costs" and amortized them over five years. Both of these practices are justifiable theoretically, but they are not common practice. If the standard or more conservative practice had been followed, the company would have had a net loss in every year it has been in business.[24] This result would have greatly limited AOL's ability to raise money and grow as it has. Explain in your own words management's rationale for adopting the accounting policies that it did. What could go wrong with management's plan? How would you evaluate the ethics of AOL's actions? Who benefits from the actions? Who is harmed by the actions? Have you seen any developments about AOL in the news?

Research Activity

SD 6.

LO 1 **Individual Field Trip**
LO 2
LO 8

Visit a fast-food restaurant. Make a list of all the intangible and property, plant, and equipment assets you can identify. For each one, identify one management issue that relates to that asset. In addition, identify at least one capital expenditure and one revenue expenditure that is applicable to property, plant, and equipment assets (not to each one on your list). Bring your list to class for discussion.

Decision-Making Practice

SD 7.

LO 1 **Purchase Decision and Time Value of Money Application**

Morningside Machine Works has successfully obtained a subcontract to manufacture parts for a new military aircraft. The parts are to be delivered over the next five years, and Morningside will be paid as the parts are delivered. To make the parts, new equipment will have to be purchased. Two types of equipment are available. Type A is conventional equipment that can be put into service immediately, and Type B requires one year to be put into service but is more efficient. Type A requires an immediate cash investment of $1,000,000 and will produce enough parts to provide net cash receipts of $340,000 each year for the five years. Type B may be purchased by signing a two-year non-interest-bearing note for $1,346,000. It is projected that Type B will produce net cash receipts of zero in year 1, $500,000 in year 2, $600,000 in year 3, $600,000 in year 4, and $200,000 in year 5. Neither type of equipment can be used on other contracts or will have any useful life remaining at the end of the contract. Morningside currently pays an interest rate of 16 percent to borrow money.

1. What is the present value of the investment required for each type of equipment? (Use Table 3 in the appendix on future value and present value tables.)

2. Compute the net present value of each type of equipment based on your answer in **1** and the present value of the net cash receipts projected to be received. (Use Tables 3 and 4 in the appendix on future value and present value tables.)

3. Write a memorandum to the board of directors that recommends the option that appears to be best for Morningside based on your analysis (include **1** and **2** as attachments) and that explains why.

FINANCIAL REPORTING AND ANALYSIS

Interpreting Financial Reports

FRA 1.

LO 3 **Effects of Change in**
LO 4 **Accounting Method**
SO 9

Depreciation expense is a significant expense for companies in which plant assets are a high proportion of assets. The amount of depreciation expense in a given year is affected by estimates of useful life and choice of depreciation method. In 2000, *Century Steelworks Company,* a major integrated steel producer, changed the estimated useful lives for its major production assets. It also changed the method of depreciation for other steel-making assets from straight-line to the production method.

The company's 2000 annual report states, "A recent study conducted by management shows that actual years-in-service figures for our major production equipment and machinery are, in most cases, higher than the estimated useful lives assigned to these assets. We have recast the depreciable lives of such assets so that equipment previously assigned a useful life of 8 to 26 years now has an extended depreciable life of 10 to 32 years." The report goes on to explain that the new production method of depreciation "recognizes that depreciation of production equipment and machinery correlates directly to both physical wear and tear and the passage of time. The production method of depreciation, which we have now initiated, more closely allocates the cost of these assets to the periods in which products are manufactured."

The report summarized the effects of both actions on the year 2000 as follows:

Incremental Increase in Net Income	In Millions	Per Share
Lengthened lives	$11.0	$ .80
Production method		
Current year	7.3	.53
Prior years	2.8	.20
Total increase	$21.1	$1.53

During 2000, Century Steelworks reported a net loss of $83,156,500 ($6.03 per share). Depreciation expense for 2000 was $87,707,200.

In explaining the changes, the controller of Century Steelworks was quoted in an article in *Business Journal* as follows: "There is no reason for Century Steelworks to continue to depreciate our assets more conservatively than our competitors do." But the article quotes an industry analyst who argues that by slowing its method of depreciation, Century Steelworks could be viewed as reporting lower-quality earnings.

REQUIRED

1. Explain the accounting treatment when there is a change in the estimated lives of depreciable assets. What circumstances must exist for the production method to produce the effect it did in relation to the straight-line method? What would Century Steelworks' net income or loss have been if the changes had not been made? What may have motivated management to make the changes?

2. What does the controller of Century Steelworks mean when he says that Century had been depreciating "more conservatively than our competitors do"? Why might the changes at Century Steelworks indicate, as the analyst asserts, "lower-quality earnings"? What risks might Century face as a result of its decision to use the production method of depreciation?

International Company

FRA 2.
LO 8 Accounting for Trademarks and Goodwill: U.S. and British Rules

When the British company **Grand Metropolitan** (Grand Met) purchased **Pillsbury,** it adopted British accounting policies with regard to intangibles. Many analysts felt this gave British companies advantages over U.S. companies, especially in buyout situations.[25] At this time there are two major differences in accounting for intangibles between U.S. accounting standards and British accounting standards. First, under the U.S. rules, as discussed in this chapter, intangible assets such as trademarks are recorded at their acquisition cost, which is often nominal, and the cost is amortized over a reasonable life. Under British accounting standards, on the other hand, firms are able to record the value of trademarks for the purpose of increasing the total assets on their balance sheets. Further, they do not have to amortize the value if management can show that the value can be preserved through extensive brand support. Grand Met, therefore, elected to record such famous Pillsbury trademarks as the Pillsbury Doughboy, Green Giant vegetables, Häagen Dazs ice cream, and Van de Kamp fish at an estimated value and not to amortize them. Second, when one company purchases another company for more than the market value of the assets if purchased individually, under U.S. rules the excess is recorded as the asset Goodwill, which must be amortized over a period not to exceed 40 years. Under existing British accounting rules, any goodwill resulting from a purchase lowers stockholders' equity directly, rather than being recorded as an asset and lowering net income through amortization over a number of years. Analysts say that these two rules made Pillsbury more valuable to Grand Met than to Pillsbury stockholders and thus led to Pillsbury's being bought by the British firm. Write a one-page paper that addresses the following questions: What is the rationale behind the argument that the British company has an advantage due to the differences between U.S. and British accounting principles? Do you agree with U.S. or British accounting rules regarding intangibles and goodwill? Defend your answers.

Toys "R" Us Annual Report

FRA 3.

LO 1 **Long-Term Assets**
LO 2
LO 3
LO 4
LO 8

1. Refer to the consolidated balance sheets and to the note on property and equipment in the notes to consolidated financial statements in the Toys "R" Us annual report to answer the following questions: What percentage of total assets in 1999 was property and equipment? What is the most significant type of property and equipment? Does Toys "R" Us have a significant investment in land? What other kinds of things are included in the property and equipment category? (Ignore leased property under capital leases for now.)

2. Refer to the summary of significant accounting policies and to the note on property and equipment in the Toys "R" Us annual report. What method of depreciation does Toys "R" Us use? How long does management estimate its buildings to last as compared to furniture and equipment? What does this say about Toys "R" Us's need to remodel its stores?

3. Refer to the statement of cash flows in the Toys "R" Us annual report. How much did Toys "R" Us spend on property and equipment (capital expenditures, net) during 1999? Is this an increase or a decrease from prior years?

4. Refer again to the note on property and equipment. What are leaseholds and leasehold improvements? How significant are these items and what are their effects on the earnings of the company?

Fingraph® Financial Analyst™

FRA 4.

LO 1 **Comparison of Long-Term**
LO 4 **Assets**
LO 7
LO 8

Choose any two companies from the same industry in the Fingraph® Financial Analyst™ CD-ROM software. The industry chosen should be one in which long-term assets are likely to be important. Choose an industry such as airlines, manufacturing, consumer products, consumer food and beverage, or computers.

1. In the annual reports for the companies you have selected, read the long-term asset section of the balance sheet and any reference to any long-term assets in the summary of significant accounting policies or notes to the financial statements. What are the most important long-term assets for each company? What depreciation methods do the companies use? Are there any long-term assets that appear to be characteristic of the industry? What intangible assets do the companies have, and how important are they?

2. Display and print in tabular and graphical form the Balance Sheet Analysis page. Prepare a table that compares the gross and net property, plant, and equipment.

3. Locate the statements of cash flows in the two companies' annual reports. Prepare another table that compares depreciation (and amortization) expense from the operating activities section with the net purchases of property, plant, and equipment (net capital expenditures) from the investing activities section for two years. Does depreciation (and amortization) expense exceed replacement of long-term assets? Are the companies expanding or reducing their property, plant, and equipment?

4. Find and read references to long-term assets and capital expenditures in management's discussion and analysis in each annual report.

5. Write a one-page executive summary that highlights the most important long-term assets and the accounting policies for long-term assets, and compares the investing activities of the two companies, including reference to management's assessment. Include the Fingraph® page and your tables as attachments to your report.

Internet Case

FRA 5.

LO 4 **SEC and Forms 10-K**
LO 5
LO 8

Public corporations are required not only to communicate with their stockholders by means of an annual report, but also to submit an annual report to the Securities and Exchange Commission (SEC). The annual report to the SEC is called a Form 10-K and is a source of the latest information about a company. Through the Needles Accounting Resource Center web site at http://college.hmco.com, access the SEC's EDGAR files to locate either H. J. Heinz Company's or Ford Motor Company's Form 10-K. Find the financial statements and the notes to the financial statements. Scan through the notes to the financial statements and prepare a list of information you find related to long-term assets, including intangibles. For instance, what depreciation methods does the company use? What are the useful lives of its property, plant, and equipment? What intangible assets does the company have? Does the company have goodwill? How much does the company spend on research and development? In the statement of cash flows, how much did the company spend on new property, plant, and equipment (capital expenditures)? Summarize your results and be prepared to discuss them as well as your experience in using the SEC's EDGAR database.

Group Activity: Divide students into groups according to the company researched and have each group compile a comprehensive list of information about its company.

ENDNOTES

1. H. J. Heinz Company, *Annual Report*, 1998.
2. "Accounting for the Impairment of Long-Lived Assets and for Long-Lived Assets to Be Disposed Of," *Statement of Financial Accounting Standards No. 121* (Norwalk, Conn.: Financial Accounting Standards Board, 1995).
3. Leslie Canley, "Pacific Telesis Plans a Charge of $3.3 Billion," *The Wall Street Journal*, September 8, 1995.
4. Ford Motor Company, *Annual Report*, 1997.
5. Ibid.
6. *Statement of Position No. 98-1*, "Accounting for the Costs of Computer Software Developed or Planned for Internal Use" (New York: American Institute of Certified Public Accountants, 1996).
7. "Capitalization of Interest Cost," *Statement of Financial Accounting Standards No. 34* (Norwalk, Conn.: Financial Accounting Standards Board, 1979), par. 9–11.
8. Len Boselovic, "A Look at How the SEC Disposed of Chambers' Claims," *Pittsburgh Post-Gazette*, May 14, 1995.
9. *Financial Accounting Standards: Original Pronouncements as of July 1, 1977* (Norwalk, Conn.: Financial Accounting Standards Board, 1977), ARB No. 43, Ch. 9, Sec. C, par. 5.
10. Accounting Principles Board, *Opinion No. 29*, "Accounting for Nonmonetary Transactions" (New York: American Institute of Certified Public Accountants, 1973) and Emerging Issues Task Force, *EITF Issue Summary 86-29*, "Nonmonetary Transactions: Magnitude of Boot and the Exceptions to the Use of Fair Value" (Norwalk, Conn.: Financial Accounting Standards Board, 1986). The specific criteria for similar assets are the subject of more advanced courses.
11. *Statement of Financial Accounting Standards No. 25*, "Suspension of Certain Accounting Requirements for Oil and Gas Producing Companies" (Norwalk, Conn.: Financial Accounting Standards Board, 1979).
12. Adapted from Accounting Principles Board, *Opinion No. 17*, "Intangible Assets" (New York: American Institute of Certified Public Accountants, 1970), par. 2.
13. The FASB is considering shortening the amortization period for goodwill.
14. "What's in a Name?" *Time*, May 3, 1993.
15. *Statement of Financial Accounting Standards No. 2*, "Accounting for Research and Development Costs" (Norwalk, Conn.: Financial Accounting Standards Board, 1974), par. 12.
16. General Motors, *Annual Report*, 1998.
17. Abbott Laboratories, *Annual Report*, 1998; and Roche Group, *Annual Report*, 1998.
18. *Statement of Financial Accounting Standards No. 86*, "Accounting for the Costs of Computer Software to be Sold, Leased, or Otherwise Marketed" (Norwalk, Conn.: Financial Accounting Standards Board, 1985).
19. Accounting Principles Board, *Opinion No. 17*, par. 29. See note 13 above.
20. Edward P. McTague, "Accounting for Trade-Ins of Operational Assets," *National Public Accountant* (January 1986), p. 39.
21. General Motors Corp., *Annual Report*, 1987.
22. Polaroid Corporation, *Annual Report*, 1997.
23. "AOL Loses Round in AT&T Suit," Times Mirror Company web site, January 5, 1999.
24. "Stock Gives Case the Funds He Needs to Buy New Technology," *Business Week*, April 15, 1996.
25. Joanne Lipman, "British Value Brand Names—Literally," *The Wall Street Journal*, February 9, 1989, p. B4; and "Brand Name Policy Boosts Assets," *Accountancy*, October 1988, pp. 38–39.

Long-Term Liabilities

LEARNING OBJECTIVES

1 Identify the management issues related to issuing long-term debt.

2 Identify and contrast the major characteristics of bonds.

3 Record the issuance of bonds at face value and at a discount or premium.

4 Use present values to determine the value of bonds.

5 Use the straight-line and effective interest methods to amortize (a) bond discounts and (b) bond premiums.

6 Account for bonds issued between interest dates and make year-end adjustments.

7 Account for the retirement of bonds and the conversion of bonds into stock.

8 Explain the basic features of mortgages payable, installment notes payable, long-term leases, and pensions and other postretirement benefits as long-term liabilities.

AT&T Corporation Long-term liabilities, or long-term debt, are obligations of a business that are due to be paid after one year or beyond the operating cycle, whichever is longer. Decisions related to the issuance of long-term debt are among the most important that management has to make because, next to the success or failure of a company's operations, how the company finances its operations is the most important factor in the company's long-term viability. AT&T Corporation is a company that has a large amount of long-term debt, as shown by the following figures for 1998 in the Financial Highlights.[1] Total liabilities are greater than stockholders' equity, and the debt to equity ratio is 1.3 ($34,028 ÷ $25,522). What factors might have influenced AT&T's management to incur such a large amount of debt?

In the past, AT&T was the nation's long-distance telephone company. The investments in power lines, transformers, computers, and other types of property, plant, and equipment required for this business are enormous. These are mostly long-term assets, and the most sensible way to finance them is through long-term financing. When the business was protected from competition, management could reasonably predict sufficient earnings and cash flow to meet the debt and interest obligations. Also, over the years, AT&T has been very generous to employees in promising benefits that will be paid after the employees retire. Now that AT&T is facing open competition for its markets, the company must reassess not only the kind of business it is but also the amount and kinds of debt it carries. The amount and

Key Point: Pension obligations are recorded as an expense and liability now even though they will not be paid for many years, because under accrual accounting, the benefits to the company accrue while the employee is working.

Financial Highlights

(In millions)

Liabilities	
Total current liabilities	$15,442
Long-term debt	$ 5,556
Long-term benefit-related liabilities	4,255
Deferred income taxes	5,453
Other long-term liabilities and deferred credits	3,322
Total long-term liabilities	$18,586
Total liabilities	$34,028
Stockholders' equity	25,522
Total liabilities and stockholders' equity	$59,550

type of debt a company incurs will depend on many factors, including the nature of the business, its competitive environment, the state of the financial markets, and the predictability of its earnings.

Management Issues Related to Issuing Long-Term Debt

OBJECTIVE

1 Identify the management issues related to issuing long-term debt

Profitable operations and short-term credit are seldom sufficient for a growing business that must invest in long-term assets and in research and development and other activities that will produce income in future years. For such assets and activities, the company requires funds that will be available for longer periods of time. Two key sources of long-term funds are the issuance of capital stock and the issuance of long-term debt in the form of bonds, notes, mortgages, and leases. The management issues related to issuing long-term debt are (1) whether or not to have long-term debt, (2) how much long-term debt to have, and (3) what types of long-term debt to have.

The Decision to Issue Long-Term Debt

A key decision faced by management is whether to rely solely on stockholders' equity—capital stock issued and retained earnings—for long-term funds for the business or to rely partially on long-term debt for those funds.

Since long-term debts represent financial commitments that must be paid at maturity and interest or other payments that must be paid periodically, common stock would seem to have two advantages over long-term debt: It does not have to be paid back, and dividends on common stock are usually paid only if the company earns sufficient income. Long-term debt does, however, have some advantages over common stock:

1. **Stockholder control.** Since bondholders and other creditors do not have voting rights, common stockholders do not relinquish any control of the company.

2. **Tax effects.** The interest on debt is tax deductible, whereas dividends on common stock are not. For example, if a corporation pays $100,000 in interest and the income tax rate is 30 percent, the net cost to the corporation is $70,000 because it will save $30,000 on its income taxes. To pay $100,000 in dividends, the company would have to earn $142,857 before taxes ($100,000 ÷ .70).

3. **Financial leverage.** If a corporation is able to earn more on its assets than it pays in interest on debt, all of the excess will increase its earnings for stockholders. This concept is called **financial leverage** or *trading on the equity*. For example, if a company is able to earn 12 percent, or $120,000, on a $1,000,000 investment financed by long-term 10 percent notes, it will earn $20,000 before taxes ($120,000 − $100,000). Financial leverage makes heavily debt-financed investments in office buildings and shopping centers attractive to investors: They hope to earn a return that exceeds the cost of the interest on the underlying debt. The debt to equity ratio is considered an overall measure of the financial leverage of a company.

Key Point: Although carrying a lot of debt is risky, there *are* some advantages to issuing bonds instead of stock. First, bond interest expense is tax-deductible for the issuing corporation, whereas dividends paid on stock are not. Second, issuing bonds is a way to raise capital without diluting ownership of the corporation. The challenge is to determine the optimal balance between stocks and bonds so that the advantages of each can be enjoyed.

Despite these advantages, using debt financing is not always in a company's best interest. First, since cash is required to make periodic interest payments and to pay back the principal amount of the debt at the maturity date, a company whose plans for earnings do not pan out, whose operations are subject to ups and downs, or whose cash flow is weak can be in danger. If the company fails to meet its obligations, it can be forced into bankruptcy by creditors. In other words, a company may become overcommitted. Consider, for example, the heavily debt-financed airline industry. Companies such as TWA and Continental Airlines became bankrupt because they could not make payments on their long-term debt and other liabilities. Second, financial leverage can work against a company if the earnings from its investments do not exceed its interest payments. This happened during the savings and loan crisis when long-term debt was used to finance the construction of office buildings that subsequently could not be leased for enough money to cover interest payments. In recent years, the good economy has enabled airlines to take advantage of their high financial leverage to improve earnings.

How Much Debt

Although some companies carry amounts of total debt that exceed 100 percent of their stockholders' equity, many companies carry less, as can be seen from Figure 1, which shows the average debt to equity for selected industries. The range is from about 66 percent to 148 percent of equity. Clearly the use of debt financing varies widely across industries. Firms that own a high percentage of long-term assets would be looking to long-term financing as an option. We saw previously that AT&T has a high debt to equity ratio of 1.3 times. Financial leverage makes it advantageous to have long-term debt so long as the company earns a satisfactory income and is able to make interest payments and repay the debt at maturity. Since failure to make timely interest payments could possibly force a company into bankruptcy, it is important for companies to assess the risk of default or nonpayment of interest or principal.

A common measure of how much risk a company is undertaking with its debt is the **interest coverage ratio**. It measures the degree of protection a company has

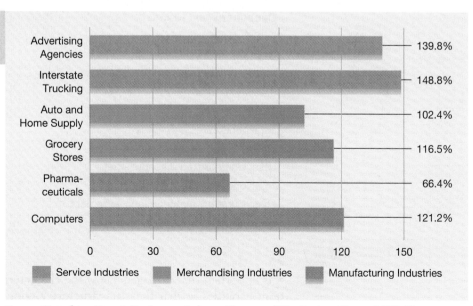

**Figure 1
Average Debt to Equity for
Selected Industries**

Industry	Percent
Advertising Agencies	139.8%
Interstate Trucking	148.8%
Auto and Home Supply	102.4%
Grocery Stores	116.5%
Pharmaceuticals	66.4%
Computers	121.2%

Service Industries Merchandising Industries Manufacturing Industries

Source: Data from Dun & Bradstreet, *Industry Norms and Key Business Ratios,* 1997–98.

from default on interest payments. This measure can help to assess the safety of AT&T in light of its huge amount of debt. This ratio for AT&T, which in 1998 had income before taxes of $3,326 million and interest expense of $427 million, is computed as follows:

$$\text{Interest Coverage Ratio} = \frac{\text{Income Before Taxes} + \text{Interest Expense}}{\text{Interest Expense}}$$

$$= \frac{\$3,326,000,000 + \$427,000,000}{\$427,000,000}$$

$$= 8.8 \text{ times}$$

This ratio shows that the interest expense for AT&T is covered 8.8 times. The coverage ratio for AT&T is in line with previous years and shows that AT&T has adequate interest coverage in spite of its large amount of debt.

What Types of Long-Term Debt

The most common type of long-term debt is long-term bonds (most of which are also called debentures). These can have many different characteristics, including the time until repayment, the amount of interest, whether or not the company can elect to repay early, and whether the bonds can be converted into other securities like common stock. However, there are many other types of long-term debt. Some examples are long-term notes, mortgages, and long-term leases. AT&T, for example, has a mixture of long-term obligations, as shown by the following excerpt from its 1998 annual report (in millions):

Financial Highlights: Long-Term Obligations

(This table shows the outstanding long-term debt obligations at December 31.)

Interest Rates (b)	Maturities	1998
Debentures and Notes		
4.38%–5.63%	1999–2001	$ 900
6.00%–7.75%	1999–2025	2,759
8.00%–8.85%	1999–2031	2,754
9.60%–11.13%	1999–2007	52
Variable rate	1999–2054	98
Total debentures and notes		6,563
Other		94
Less: Unamortized discount—net		18
Total long-term obligations		6,639
Less: Currently maturing long-term debt		1,083
Net long-term obligations		$5,556

It is important that managers know the characteristics of the various types of long-term liabilities so that they can structure a company's long-term financing to the best advantage of the company.

BUSINESS FOCUS ON PRACTICE

Missing interest payments on debt is serious business for companies. On March 3, 1995, Trans World Airlines, Inc. (TWA) reached the end of a 30-day grace period on the payment of $255 million of interest on its long-term notes. Standard & Poor's lowered the company's debt rating to D, its lowest category. If TWA had not paid by the end of the day, any group representing at least 25 percent of its noteholders could have forced the company into bankruptcy by invoking an acceleration notice that would make all the loans due immediately.[2] This action would have been unfortunate because the company was recovering after many years of losses. The company was able to meet the interest payment and continue its recovery. The booming economy of the late 1990s enabled the company to return to profitability.

The Nature of Bonds

OBJECTIVE

2 Identify and contrast the major characteristics of bonds

Enrichment Note: An investor who purchases debt securities, such as bonds or notes, is a creditor of the organization, not an owner. Debt securities normally carry a maturity date and require the organization to make periodic interest payments.

Terminology Note: Do not confuse the terms *indenture* and *debenture.* They sound alike, but an indenture is a bond contract, whereas a debenture is an unsecured bond.

Study Note: Bonds are quoted as a percentage of face value; stocks are quoted as a dollar amount.

A **bond** is a security, usually long term, representing money borrowed from the investing public by a corporation or some other entity. (Bonds are also issued by the U.S. government, state and local governments, and foreign companies and countries to raise money.) A bond must be repaid at a specified time and requires periodic payments of interest.[3] Interest is usually paid semiannually (twice a year). Bonds must not be confused with stocks. Because stocks are shares of ownership, stockholders are owners. Bondholders are creditors. Bonds are promises to repay the amount borrowed, called the *principal,* and interest at a specified rate on specified future dates.

Often a bondholder receives a **bond certificate** as evidence of the organization's debt. In most cases, the face value (denomination) of the bond is $1,000 or some multiple of $1,000. A **bond issue** is the total number of bonds issued at one time. For example, a $1,000,000 bond issue could consist of a thousand $1,000 bonds. Because a bond issue can be bought and held by many investors, the organization usually enters into a supplementary agreement called a **bond indenture**. The bond indenture defines the rights, privileges, and limitations of the bondholders. It generally describes such things as the maturity date of the bonds, interest payment dates, interest rate, and other characteristics of the bonds. Repayment plans and restrictions also may be covered.

The prices of bonds are stated in terms of a percentage of face value. A bond issue quoted at 103½ means that a $1,000 bond costs $1,035 ($1,000 × 1.035). When a bond sells at exactly 100, it is said to sell at face or par value. When it sells above 100, it is said to sell at a premium; below 100, at a discount. A $1,000 bond quoted at 87.62 would be selling at a discount and would cost the buyer $876.20.

A bond indenture can be written to fit the financing needs of an individual organization. As a result, the bonds being issued in today's financial markets have many different features. Several of the more important ones are described in the following paragraphs.

Secured or Unsecured Bonds

Study Note: A debenture of a solid company actually might be a less risky investment than a secured bond of an unstable company.

Bonds can be either secured or unsecured. If issued on the general credit of the organization, they are **unsecured bonds** (also called *debenture bonds*). **Secured bonds** give the bondholders a pledge of certain assets as a guarantee of repayment.

BUSINESS FOCUS ON INTERNATIONAL

When U.S. companies need cash, one ready source is a bond issue, but this source of funds is not available in many other countries. For instance, surprising as it may seem, Japan, the world's second largest economy and financial system, has only a fledgling corporate bond market. Whereas regular corporate bonds account for

31 percent of U.S. corporate debt, only 57, or 2 percent, of the 2,500 publicly listed companies in Japan have any domestic bonds outstanding. Japanese companies have traditionally relied on loans from big Japanese banks when they need cash. This caused problems for Japanese companies in the 1990s because Japanese banks did not have the funds to lend them as a result of the collapse of the real estate industry in Japan.[4] Similar problems have occurred more recently in other Asian countries.

The security identified by a secured bond can be any specific asset of the organization or a general category of asset, such as property, plant, or equipment.

Term or Serial Bonds

Study Note: An advantage of issuing serial bonds is that the organization retires the bonds over a period of years, rather than all at once.

When all the bonds of an issue mature at the same time, they are called **term bonds**. For instance, an organization may decide to issue $1,000,000 worth of bonds, all due 20 years from the date of issue. If the bonds in an issue mature on several different dates, the bonds are **serial bonds**. An example of serial bonds would be a $1,000,000 issue that calls for retiring $200,000 of the principal every five years. This arrangement means that after the first $200,000 payment is made, $800,000 of the bonds would remain outstanding for the next five years. In other words, $1,000,000 is outstanding for the first five years, $800,000 for the second five years, and so on. An organization may issue serial bonds to ease the task of retiring its debt.

Registered or Coupon Bonds

Most bonds issued today are **registered bonds**. The names and addresses of the owners of such bonds must be recorded with the issuing organization. The organization keeps a register of the owners and pays interest by check to the bondholders of record on the interest payment date. **Coupon bonds** generally are not registered with the organization; instead, they bear interest coupons stating the amount of interest due and the payment date. The bondholder removes the coupons from the bonds on the interest payment dates and presents them at a bank for collection.

Accounting for Bonds Payable

OBJECTIVE

3 Record the issuance of bonds at face value and at a discount or premium

When the board of directors of a corporation decides to issue bonds, it customarily presents the proposal to the stockholders. If the stockholders agree to the issue, the company prints the certificates and draws up an appropriate legal document. The bonds are then authorized for issuance. It is not necessary to make a journal entry for the authorization, but most companies prepare a memorandum in the Bonds Payable account describing the issue. This note lists the number and value of bonds authorized, the interest rate, the interest payment dates, and the life of the bonds.

Once the bonds are issued, the corporation must pay interest to the bondholders over the life of the bonds (in most cases, semiannually) and the principal of the bonds at maturity.

Balance Sheet Disclosure of Bonds

Key Point: Bonds payable are presented on the balance sheet as either a current or a long-term liability, depending on the maturity date and method of retiring the bonds.

Bonds payable and unamortized discounts or premiums (which we explain later) are typically shown on a company's balance sheet as long-term liabilities. However, if the maturity date of the bond issue is one year or less and the bonds will be retired using current assets, Bonds Payable should be listed as a current liability. If the issue is to be paid with segregated assets or replaced by another bond issue, the bonds should still be shown as a long-term liability.

Important provisions of the bond indenture are reported in the notes to the financial statements, as illustrated by the earlier excerpt from the AT&T annual report. Often reported with them is a list of all bond issues, the kinds of bonds, interest rates, any securities connected with the bonds, interest payment dates, maturity dates, and effective interest rates.

Bonds Issued at Face Value

Suppose that the Vason Corporation has authorized the issuance of $100,000 of 9 percent, five-year bonds on January 1, 20x0. According to the bond indenture, interest is to be paid on January 1 and July 1 of each year. Assume that the bonds are sold on January 1, 20x0, for their face value. The entry to record the issuance is as follows:

20x0

A = L + OE
+   +

Jan. 1	Cash	100,000	
	Bonds Payable		100,000
	Sold $100,000 of 9%, 5-year bonds		
	at face value		

Study Note: When calculating semiannual interest, do not use the annual rate (9 percent in this case) by mistake. Rather, use half the annual rate.

As stated above, interest is paid on January 1 and July 1 of each year. Therefore, the corporation would owe the bondholders $4,500 interest on July 1, 20x0:

$$\text{Interest} = \text{Principal} \times \text{Rate} \times \text{Time}$$
$$= \$100,000 \times .09 \times \frac{6}{12} \text{ year}$$
$$= \$4,500$$

The interest paid to the bondholders on each semiannual interest payment date (January 1 or July 1) would be recorded as follows:

A* = L + OE
−   −

*assumes cash paid

Bond Interest Expense	4,500	
Cash (or Interest Payable)		4,500
Paid (or accrued) semiannual interest		
to bondholders of 9%, 5-year bonds		

Face Interest Rate and Market Interest Rate

Key Point: A bond sells at face value when the face interest rate of the bond is identical to the market interest rate for similar bonds on the date of issue.

When issuing bonds, most organizations try to set the face interest rate as close as possible to the market interest rate. The **face interest rate** is the rate of interest paid to bondholders based on the face value, or principal, of the bonds. The rate and amount are fixed over the life of the bond. An organization must decide in advance what the face interest rate will be to allow time to file with regulatory bodies, publicize the issue, and print the certificates.

BUSINESS FOCUS ON PRACTICE

The price for many bonds may be found daily in business publications like *The Wall Street Journal*. For instance, shown to the right are the quotations for a number of AT&T Corporation bonds.[5] The first quoted bond is an AT&T bond with a face interest rate of 6¾ percent that is due in 2004. The current yield is 6.5 percent based on the closing price of 103½. One hundred forty-five $1,000 bonds were traded (volume), and the last sale was up by ⅛ point from the previous day's last sales.

(Republished with permission of *Wall Street Journal*, May 21, 1999; permission conveyed through Copyright Clearance Center, Inc.)

New York Exchange Bonds

Corporation Bonds
(Volume) $12,742,000

Bonds	Cur Yld	Vol	Close	Net Chg
ATT 6¾04	6.5	145	103½	+ ⅛
ATT 8.2s05	8.0	90	102½	...
ATT 7½06	7.0	10	107	− ⅜
ATT 6s09	6.1	210	97⅝	− ¼
ATT 8⅛22	7.6	50	106⅝	...
ATT 8⅛24	7.6	12	107½	+ 1¼
ATT 6½29	6.8	345	95⅝	...
ATT 8⅝31	7.9	5	109⅛	− ⅝

Key Point: When bonds with an interest rate different from the market rate are issued, they sell at a discount or premium. The discount or premium acts as an equalizing factor.

The **market interest rate** is the rate of interest paid in the market on bonds of similar risk. It is also referred to as the *effective interest rate*. The market interest rate fluctuates daily. Because an organization has no control over the market interest rate, there is often a difference between the market interest rate and the face interest rate on the issue date. The result is that the issue price of the bonds does not always equal their face value. If the market interest rate is higher than the face interest rate, the issue price will be less than the face value and the bonds are said to be issued at a **discount**. The discount equals the excess of the face value over the issue price. On the other hand, if the market interest rate is lower than the face interest rate, the issue price will be more than the face value and the bonds are said to be issued at a **premium**. The premium equals the excess of the issue price over the face value.

Bonds Issued at a Discount

Key Point: The carrying amount is always the face value of the bonds plus the unamortized premium or less the unamortized discount. The carrying amount always approaches the face value over the life of the bond.

Suppose that the Vason Corporation issues $100,000 of 9 percent, five-year bonds at 96.149 on January 1, 20x0, when the market interest rate is 10 percent. In this case, the bonds are being issued at a discount because the market interest rate exceeds the face interest rate. The following entry records the issuance of the bonds at a discount.

A = L + OE
+   +
    −

20x0			
Jan. 1	Cash	96,149	
	Unamortized Bond Discount	3,851	
	Bonds Payable		100,000
	Sold $100,000 of 9%, 5-year		
	bonds at 96.149		

Face amount of bonds	$100,000
Less purchase price of bonds	
($100,000 × .96149)	96,149
Unamortized bond discount	$ 3,851

In the entry, Cash is debited for the amount received ($96,149), Bonds Payable is credited for the face amount ($100,000) of the bond liability, and the difference ($3,851) is debited to Unamortized Bond Discount. If a balance sheet is prepared right after the bonds are issued at a discount, the liability for bonds payable is reported as follows:

> **Key Point:** The unamortized bond discount is subtracted from Bonds Payable on the balance sheet. The carrying value will be below the face value until the maturity date.

Long-Term Liabilities

9% Bonds Payable, due 1/1/x5	$100,000	
Less Unamortized Bond Discount	3,851	$96,149

Unamortized Bond Discount is a contra-liability account: Its balance is deducted from the face amount of the bonds to arrive at the carrying value, or present value, of the bonds. The bond discount is described as unamortized because it will be amortized (written off) over the life of the bonds.

Bonds Issued at a Premium

When bonds have a face interest rate above the market rate for similar investments, they are issued at a price above the face value, or at a premium. For example, assume that the Vason Corporation issues $100,000 of 9 percent, five-year bonds for $104,100 on January 1, 20x0, when the market interest rate is 8 percent. This means that investors will purchase the bonds at 104.1 percent of their face value. The issuance would be recorded as follows:

A = L + OE
+ +
　 +

20x0			
Jan. 1	Cash	104,100	
	Unamortized Bond Premium		4,100
	Bonds Payable		100,000
	Sold $100,000 of 9%, 5-year bonds		
	at 104.1 ($100,000 × 1.041)		

Right after this entry is made, bonds payable would be presented on the balance sheet as follows:

> **Key Point:** The unamortized bond premium is *added* to Bonds Payable on the balance sheet. The carrying value will be above the face value until the maturity date.

Long-Term Liabilities

9% Bonds Payable, due 1/1/x5	$100,000	
Unamortized Bond Premium	4,100	$104,100

The carrying value of the bonds payable is $104,100, which equals the face value of the bonds plus the unamortized bond premium. The cash received from the bond issue is also $104,100. This means that the purchasers were willing to pay a premium of $4,100 to buy these bonds because their face interest rate was higher than the market interest rate.

Bond Issue Costs

> **Key Point:** A separate Bond Issue Costs account is usually established and amortized over the life of the issue.

Most bonds are sold through underwriters, who receive a fee for taking care of the details of marketing the issue or for taking a chance on receiving the selling price. Such costs are connected with the issuance of bonds. Because bond issue costs benefit the whole life of a bond issue, it makes sense to spread the costs over that period. It is generally accepted practice to establish a separate account for bond issue costs and to amortize them over the life of the bonds. However, issue costs decrease the amount of money a company receives from a bond issue. They have the effect, then, of raising the discount or lowering the premium on the issue. As a result, bond issue costs can be spread over the life of the bonds through the amortization of a discount or premium. Because this method simplifies recordkeeping, we assume in the text and problems of this book that all bond issue costs increase the discounts or decrease the premiums of bond issues.

BUSINESS FOCUS ON PRACTICE

In 1993, interest rates on long-term debt were at historically low levels, which induced some companies to attempt to lock in those low costs for long periods. One of the most aggressive companies in that regard was The Walt Disney Company, which issued $150 million of 100-year bonds at a yield of only 7.5 percent. It was the first time since 1954 that 100-year bonds had been issued. Some analysts wondered if even Mickey Mouse could survive 100 years. Investors who purchase these bonds are taking a financial risk because if interest rates rise, which they are likely to do, then the market value of the bonds will decrease. Since then, other companies, including The Coca-Cola Company, Columbia HCA Healthcare, IBM, Bell South, and even the People's Republic of China, have followed suit with 100-year bonds.[6]

Using Present Value to Value a Bond

OBJECTIVE

4 Use present values to determine the value of bonds

Study Note: The amount buyers are willing to pay for an investment is normally based on what they expect to receive in return, taken at present value. In the case of a bond, the theoretical value equals the present value of the periodic interest payments plus the present value of the maturity value. The discount rate is set at the market rate (what investors are looking for), not at the face rate.

Present value is relevant to the study of bonds because the value of a bond is based on the present value of two components of cash flow: (1) a series of fixed interest payments and (2) a single payment at maturity.[7] The amount of interest a bond pays is fixed over its life. However, the market interest rate varies from day to day. Thus, the amount investors are willing to pay for a bond changes as well.

Assume, for example, that a particular bond has a face value of $10,000 and pays fixed interest of $450 every six months (a 9 percent annual rate). The bond is due in five years. If the market interest rate today is 14 percent, what is the present value of the bond?

To determine the present value of the bond, we use Table 4 in the appendix on future value and present value tables to calculate the present value of the periodic interest payments of $450, and we use Table 3 in the same appendix to calculate the present value of the single payment of $10,000 at maturity. Since interest payments are made every six months, the compounding period is half a year. Because of this, it is necessary to convert the annual rate to a semiannual rate of 7 percent (14 percent divided by two six-month periods per year) and to use ten periods (five years multiplied by two six-month periods per year). Using this information, we compute the present value of the bond.

Present value of 10 periodic payments at 7% (from Table 4 in the appendix on future value and present value tables): $450 × 7.024	$3,160.80
Present value of a single payment at the end of 10 periods at 7% (from Table 3 in the appendix on future value and present value tables): $10,000 × .508	5,080.00
Present value of $10,000 bond	$8,240.80

The market interest rate has increased so much since the bond was issued (from 9 percent to 14 percent) that the value of the bond is only $8,240.80 today. That amount is all investors would be willing to pay at this time for a bond that provides income of $450 every six months and a return of the $10,000 principal in five years.

If the market interest rate falls below the face interest rate, say to 8 percent (4 percent semiannually), the present value of the bond will be greater than the face value of $10,000.

Present value of 10 periodic payments at 4% (from Table 4 in the appendix on future value and present value tables): $450 × 8.111	$ 3,649.95
Present value of a single payment at the end of 10 periods at 4% (from Table 3 in the appendix on future value and present value tables): $10,000 × .676	6,760.00
Present value of $10,000 bond	$10,409.95

Amortizing a Bond Discount

In the example on page 514, Vason Corporation issued $100,000 of five-year bonds at a discount because the market interest rate of 10 percent exceeded the face interest rate of 9 percent. The bonds were sold for $96,149, resulting in an unamortized bond discount of $3,851. Because this discount affects interest expense in each year of the bond issue, the bond discount should be amortized (reduced gradually) over the life of the issue. This means that the unamortized bond discount will decrease gradually over time, and that the carrying value of the bond issue (face value less unamortized discount) will increase gradually. By the maturity date of the bond, the carrying value of the issue will equal its face value, and the unamortized bond discount will be zero.

Calculation of Total Interest Cost

Key Point: A bond discount is considered a component of total interest cost because a bond discount represents the amount in excess of the issue price that must be paid by the corporation at the time of maturity.

When bonds are issued at a discount, the effective interest rate paid by the company is greater than the face interest rate on the bonds. The reason is that the interest cost to the company is the stated interest payments *plus* the amount of the bond discount. That is, although the company does not receive the full face value of the bonds on issue, it still must pay back the full face value at maturity. The difference between the issue price and the face value must be added to the total interest payments to arrive at the actual interest expense. The full cost to the corporation of issuing the bonds at a discount is as follows:

Cash to be paid to bondholders	
Face value at maturity	$100,000
Interest payments ($100,000 × .09 × 5 years)	45,000
Total cash paid to bondholders	$145,000
Less cash received from bondholders	96,149
Total interest cost	$ 48,851
Or, alternatively:	
Interest payments ($100,000 × .09 × 5 years)	$ 45,000
Bond discount	3,851
Total interest cost	$ 48,851

The total interest cost of $48,851 is made up of $45,000 in interest payments and the $3,851 bond discount, so the bond discount increases the interest paid on the bonds from the stated interest rate to the effective interest rate. The *effective interest rate* is the real interest cost of the bond over its life.

Key Point: The discount on a zero coupon bond represents the interest that will be paid (in its entirety) on the maturity date.

For each year's interest expense to reflect the effective interest rate, the discount must be allocated over the remaining life of the bonds as an increase in the interest expense each period. The process of allocation is called *amortization of the bond discount*. Thus, interest expense for each period will exceed the actual payment of interest by the amount of the bond discount amortized over the period.

Some companies and governmental units issue bonds that do not require periodic interest payments. These bonds, called **zero coupon bonds**, are simply a promise to pay a fixed amount at the maturity date. They are issued at a large discount because the only interest earned by the buyer or paid by the issuer is the discount. For example, a five-year, $100,000 zero coupon bond issued at a time when the market rate is 14 percent, compounded semiannually, would sell for only $50,800. That amount is the present value of a single payment of $100,000 at the end of five years. The discount of $49,200 ($100,000 − $50,800) is the total interest cost; it is amortized over the life of the bond.

Methods of Amortizing a Bond Discount

There are two ways of amortizing bond discounts or premiums: the straight-line method and the effective interest method.

STRAIGHT-LINE METHOD The **straight-line method** is the easier of the two, with equal amortization of the discount for each interest period. Suppose that the interest payment dates for the Vason Corporation bond issue are January 1 and July 1. The amount of the bond discount amortized and the interest cost for each semiannual period are calculated in four steps.

1. Total Interest Payments = Interest Payments per Year × Life of Bonds
$$= 2 \times 5 = 10$$

2. Amortization of Bond Discount per Interest Period $= \dfrac{\text{Bond Discount}}{\text{Total Interest Payments}}$

$$= \frac{\$3,851}{10} = \$385*$$

   *Rounded.

3. Cash Interest Payment = Face Value × Face Interest Rate × Time
$$= \$100,000 \times .09 \times 6/12 = \$4,500$$

4. Interest Cost per Interest Period = Interest Payment + Amortization of Bond Discount
$$= \$4,500 + \$385 = \$4,885$$

On July 1, 20x0, the first semiannual interest date, the entry would be as follows:

A* = L + OE
– + –
*assumes cash paid

20x0			
July 1	Bond Interest Expense	4,885	
	Unamortized Bond Discount		385
	Cash (or Interest Payable)		4,500
	Paid (or accrued) semiannual interest to bondholders and amortized the discount on 9%, 5-year bonds		

Notice that the bond interest expense is $4,885, but the amount paid to the bondholders is the $4,500 face interest payment. The difference of $385 is the credit to Unamortized Bond Discount. This lowers the debit balance of the Unamortized Bond Discount account and raises the carrying value of the bonds

Enrichment Note: Although the straight-line method of amortization is easier to apply than the effective interest method, it is theoretically inferior because it does not apply a uniform rate of interest (as does the effective interest method). It can be used, however, if the amount does not differ materially from the effective interest amount. (The amounts are material if they affect a decision or the evaluation of the company.)

payable by $385 each interest period. Assuming that no changes occur in the bond issue, this entry will be made every six months for the life of the bonds. When the bond issue matures, there will be no balance in the Unamortized Bond Discount account, and the carrying value of the bonds will be $100,000—exactly equal to the amount due the bondholders.

The straight-line method has long been used, but it has a certain weakness. Because the carrying value goes up each period and the bond interest expense stays the same, the rate of interest falls over time. Conversely, when the straight-line method is used to amortize a premium, the rate of interest rises over time. Therefore, the Accounting Principles Board has ruled that the straight-line method can be used only when it does not lead to a material difference from the effective interest method.[8]

EFFECTIVE INTEREST METHOD To compute the interest and amortization of a bond discount for each interest period under the **effective interest method**, a constant interest rate is applied to the carrying value of the bonds at the beginning of the interest period. This constant rate equals the market rate, or effective rate, at the time the bonds are issued. The amount to be amortized each period is the difference between the interest computed by using the effective rate and the actual interest paid to bondholders.

As an example, we use the same facts presented earlier—a $100,000 bond issue at 9 percent, with a five-year maturity and interest to be paid twice a year. The market, or effective, interest rate at the time the bonds were issued was 10 percent. The bonds were sold for $96,149, a discount of $3,851. The interest and amortization of the bond discount are shown in Table 1.

Table 1. Interest and Amortization of a Bond Discount: Effective Interest Method

	A	B	C	D	E	F
Semiannual Interest Period	Carrying Value at Beginning of Period	Semiannual Interest Expense at 10% to Be Recorded* (5% × A)	Semiannual Interest to Be Paid to Bondholders (4½% × $100,000)	Amortization of Bond Discount (B − C)	Unamortized Bond Discount at End of Period (E − D)	Carrying Value at End of Period (A + D)
0					$3,851	$ 96,149
1	$96,149	$4,807	$4,500	$307	3,544	96,456
2	96,456	4,823	4,500	323	3,221	96,779
3	96,779	4,839	4,500	339	2,882	97,118
4	97,118	4,856	4,500	356	2,526	97,474
5	97,474	4,874	4,500	374	2,152	97,848
6	97,848	4,892	4,500	392	1,760	98,240
7	98,240	4,912	4,500	412	1,348	98,652
8	98,652	4,933	4,500	433	915	99,085
9	99,085	4,954	4,500	454	461	99,539
10	99,539	4,961†	4,500	461	—	100,000

*Rounded to the nearest dollar.
†Last period's interest expense equals $4,961 ($4,500 + $461); it does not equal $4,977 ($99,539 × .05) because of the cumulative effect of rounding.

The amounts in the table (using period 1) were computed as follows:

Column A: The carrying value of the bonds is their face value less the unamortized bond discount ($100,000 − $3,851 = $96,149).

Column B: The interest expense to be recorded is the effective interest. It is found by multiplying the carrying value of the bonds by the effective interest rate for one-half year ($96,149 × .10 × $\frac{6}{12}$ = $4,807).

Column C: The interest paid in the period is a constant amount computed by multiplying the face value of the bonds by their face interest rate by the interest time period ($100,000 × .09 × $\frac{6}{12}$ = $4,500).

Column D: The discount amortized is the difference between the effective interest expense to be recorded and the interest to be paid on the interest payment date ($4,807 − $4,500 = $307).

Column E: The unamortized bond discount is the balance of the bond discount at the beginning of the period less the current period amortization of the discount ($3,851 − $307 = $3,544). The unamortized discount decreases each interest payment period because it is amortized as a portion of interest expense.

Column F: The carrying value of the bonds at the end of the period is the carrying value at the beginning of the period plus the amortization during the period ($96,149 + $307 = $96,456). Notice that the sum of the carrying value and the unamortized discount (Column F + Column E) always equals the face value of the bonds ($96,456 + $3,544 = $100,000).

Key Point: The bond interest expense recorded exceeds the amount of interest paid because of the amortization of the bond discount. The matching rule dictates that the discount be amortized over the life of the bond.

The entry to record the interest expense is exactly like the one used when the straight-line method is applied. However, the amounts debited and credited to the various accounts are different. Using the effective interest method, the entry for July 1, 20x0, would be as follows:

$$A^* = L + OE$$
$$- \quad + \quad -$$
*assumes cash paid

20x0			
July 1	Bond Interest Expense	4,807	
	Unamortized Bond Discount		307
	Cash (or Interest Payable)		4,500
	Paid (or accrued) semiannual interest to bondholders and amortized the discount on 9%, 5-year bonds		

Notice that it is not necessary to prepare an interest and amortization table to determine the amortization of a discount for any one interest payment period. It is necessary only to multiply the carrying value by the effective interest rate and subtract the interest payment from the result. For example, the amount of discount to be amortized in the seventh interest payment period is $412, calculated as follows: ($98,240 × .05) − $4,500.

VISUAL SUMMARY OF THE EFFECTIVE INTEREST METHOD   The effect on carrying value and interest expense of the amortization of a bond discount using the effective interest method can be seen in Figure 2 (which is based on the data from Table 1). Notice that initially the carrying value (the issue price) is less than the face value, but that it gradually increases toward the face value over the life of the bond issue. Notice also that interest expense exceeds interest payments by the amount of the bond discount amortized. Interest expense increases gradually over the life of the bond because it is based on the gradually increasing carrying value (multiplied by the market interest rate).

**Figure 2
Carrying Value and Interest
Expense—Bonds Issued at
a Discount**

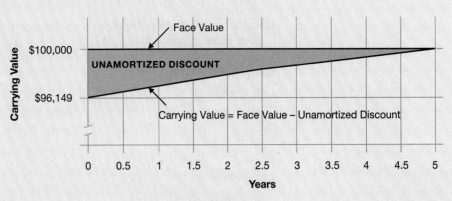

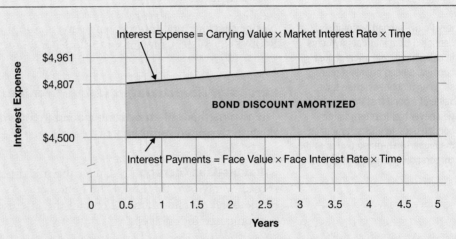

Key Point: The bond interest
expense *increases* each period
because the carrying value of the
bonds (the principal on which the
interest is calculated) increases
each period.

Amortizing a Bond Premium

OBJECTIVE

5b Use the straight-line and
effective interest methods to
amortize bond premiums

In our example on page 515, Vason Corporation issued $100,000 of five-year
bonds at a premium because the market interest rate of 8 percent was less than the
face interest rate of 9 percent. The bonds were sold for $104,100, which resulted
in an unamortized premium of $4,100. Like a discount, a premium must be amor-
tized over the life of the bonds so that it can be matched to its effects on interest
expense during that period. In the following sections, the total interest cost is calculated and the bond premium is amortized using the straight-line and the effective interest methods.

Calculation of Total Interest Cost

Because the bondholders paid more than face value for the bonds, the premium of
$4,100 ($104,100 − $100,000) represents an amount that the bondholders will
not receive at maturity. The premium is in effect a reduction, in advance, of the
total interest paid on the bonds over the life of the bond issue.

The total interest cost over the issue's life can be computed as follows:

Cash to be paid to bondholders		
Face value at maturity		$100,000
Interest payments ($100,000 × .09 × 5 years)		45,000
Total cash paid to bondholders		$145,000
Less cash received from bondholders		104,100
Total interest cost		$ 40,900

Or, alternatively:

Interest payments ($100,000 × .09 × 5 years)		$ 45,000
Less bond premium		4,100
Total interest cost		$ 40,900

Key Point: A bond premium is deducted from interest payments in calculating total interest cost because a bond premium represents an amount over the face value of a bond that the corporation never has to return to the bondholders. In effect, it reduces the higher-than-market interest the corporation is paying on the bond.

Notice that the total interest payments of $45,000 exceed the total interest cost of $40,900 by $4,100, the amount of the bond premium.

Methods of Amortizing a Bond Premium

The two methods of amortizing a bond premium are the straight-line method and the effective interest method.

STRAIGHT-LINE METHOD   Under the straight-line method, the bond premium is spread evenly over the life of the bond issue. As with bond discounts, the amount of the bond premium amortized and the interest cost for each semiannual period are computed in four steps.

1. Total Interest Payments = Interest Payments per Year × Life of Bonds
$$= 2 \times 5 = 10$$

Key Point: The bond interest expense recorded is less than the amount of the interest paid because of the amortization of the bond premium. The matching rule dictates that the premium be amortized over the life of the bond.

2. Amortization of Bond Premium per Interest Period $= \dfrac{\text{Bond Premium}}{\text{Total Interest Payments}}$

$$= \frac{\$4,100}{10} = \$410$$

3. Cash Interest Payment = Face Value × Face Interest Rate × Time
$$= \$100,000 \times .09 \times \%_2 = \$4,500$$

4. Interest Cost per Interest Period = Interest Payment − Amortization of Bond Premium

$$= \$4,500 - \$410 = \$4,090$$

On July 1, 20x0, the first semiannual interest date, the entry would be:

A* = L + OE

– – –

*assumes cash paid

20x0			
July 1	Bond Interest Expense	4,090	
	Unamortized Bond Premium	410	
	Cash (or Interest Payable)		4,500
	Paid (or accrued) semiannual interest to bondholders and amortized the premium on 9%, 5-year bonds		

Study Note: Whether a bond is originally sold at a discount or a premium, on the maturity date its carrying value will equal its face value.

Notice that the bond interest expense is $4,090, but the amount received by the bondholders is the $4,500 face interest payment. The difference of $410 is the debit to Unamortized Bond Premium. This lowers the credit balance of the Unamortized Bond Premium account and the carrying value of the bonds payable by $410 each interest period. Assuming that the bond issue remains unchanged, the same entry will be made on every semiannual interest date over the life of the bond issue. When the bond issue matures, there will be no balance in the Unamortized Bond Premium account, and the carrying value of the bonds payable will be $100,000, exactly equal to the amount due the bondholders.

As noted earlier in this chapter, the straight-line method should be used only when it does not lead to a material difference from the effective interest method.

EFFECTIVE INTEREST METHOD Under the straight-line method, the effective interest rate changes constantly, even though the interest expense is fixed, because the effective interest rate is determined by comparing the fixed interest expense with a carrying value that changes as a result of amortizing the discount or premium. To apply a fixed interest rate over the life of the bonds based on the actual market rate at the time of the bond issue requires the use of the effective interest method. Under this method, the interest expense decreases slightly each period (see Table 2, Column B) because the amount of the bond premium amortized increases slightly (Column D). This occurs because a fixed rate is applied each period to the gradually decreasing carrying value (Column A).

The first interest payment is recorded as follows:

		20x0			
$A^* = L + OE$		July 1	Bond Interest Expense	4,164	
$-$ $-$ $-$			Unamortized Bond Premium	336	
*assumes cash paid			Cash (or Interest Payable)		4,500
			Paid (or accrued) semiannual interest to bondholders and amortized the premium on 9%, 5-year bonds		

Table 2. Interest and Amortization of a Bond Premium: Effective Interest Method

	A	B	C	D	E	F
Semiannual Interest Period	Carrying Value at Beginning of Period	Semiannual Interest Expense at 8% to Be Recorded* (4% × A)	Semiannual Interest to Be Paid to Bondholders (4½% × $100,000)	Amortization of Bond Premium (C − B)	Unamortized Bond Premium at End of Period (E − D)	Carrying Value at End of Period (A − D)
0					$4,100	$104,100
1	$104,100	$4,164	$4,500	$336	3,764	103,764
2	103,764	4,151	4,500	349	3,415	103,415
3	103,415	4,137	4,500	363	3,052	103,052
4	103,052	4,122	4,500	378	2,674	102,674
5	102,674	4,107	4,500	393	2,281	102,281
6	102,281	4,091	4,500	409	1,872	101,872
7	101,872	4,075	4,500	425	1,447	101,447
8	101,447	4,058	4,500	442	1,005	101,005
9	101,005	4,040	4,500	460	545	100,545
10	100,545	3,955†	4,500	545	—	100,000

*Rounded to the nearest dollar.
†Last period's interest expense equals $3,955 ($4,500 − $545); it does not equal $4,022 ($100,545 × .04) because of the cumulative effect of rounding.

BUSINESS FOCUS ON TECHNOLOGY

Interest and amortization tables like those in Tables 1 and 2 are ideal applications for computer spreadsheet soft-

ware such as Lotus and Microsoft Excel. Once the tables have been constructed with the proper formula in each cell, only five variables must be entered to produce the entire table. The five variables are the face value of the bonds, the selling price, the life of the bonds, the face interest rate, and the effective interest rate.

Notice that the unamortized bond premium (Column E) decreases gradually to zero as the carrying value decreases to the face value (Column F). To find the amount of premium amortized in any one interest payment period, subtract the effective interest expense (the carrying value times the effective interest rate, Column B) from the interest payment (Column C). In semiannual interest period 5, for example, the amortization of premium is $393, calculated as follows: $4,500 − ($102,674 × .04).

VISUAL SUMMARY OF THE EFFECTIVE INTEREST METHOD   The effect of the amortization of a bond premium using the effective interest method on carrying value and interest expense can be seen in Figure 3 (based on data from Table 2).

Figure 3
Carrying Value and Interest Expense—Bonds Issued at a Premium

Key Point: Over the life of a bond, the premium or discount amortized increases each period.

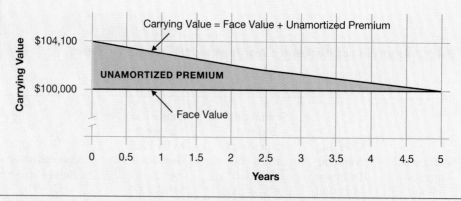

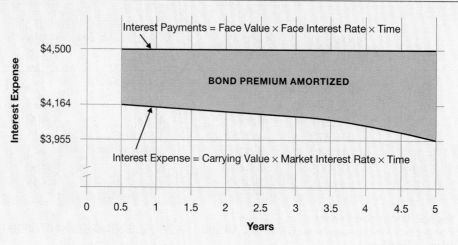

Notice that initially the carrying value (issue price) is greater than the face value, but that it gradually decreases toward the face value over the life of the bond issue. Notice also that interest payments exceed interest expense by the amount of the premium amortized, and that interest expense decreases gradually over the life of the bond because it is based on the gradually decreasing carrying value (multiplied by the market interest rate).

Other Bonds Payable Issues

OBJECTIVE

6 Account for bonds issued between interest dates and make year-end adjustments

Several other issues arise in accounting for bonds payable. Among them are the sale of bonds between interest payment dates, the year-end accrual of bond interest expense, the retirement of bonds, and the conversion of bonds into common stock.

Sale of Bonds Between Interest Dates

Bonds may be issued on an interest payment date, as in the previous examples, but they are often issued between interest payment dates. The generally accepted method of handling bonds issued in this manner is to collect from investors the interest that would have accrued for the partial period preceding the issue date. Then, when the first interest period is completed, the corporation pays investors the interest for the entire period. Thus, the interest collected when bonds are sold is returned to investors on the next interest payment date.

There are two reasons for following this procedure. The first is a practical one. If a company issued bonds on several different days and did not collect the accrued interest, records would have to be maintained for each bondholder and date of purchase. In such a case, the interest due each bondholder would have to be computed on the basis of a different time period. Clearly, large bookkeeping costs would be incurred under this kind of system. On the other hand, if accrued interest is collected when the bonds are sold, on the interest payment date the corporation can pay the interest due for the entire period, eliminating the extra computations and costs.

The second reason for collecting accrued interest in advance is that when that amount is netted against the full interest paid on the interest payment date, the resulting interest expense represents the amount for the time the money was borrowed. For example, assume that the Vason Corporation sold $100,000 of 9 percent, five-year bonds for face value on May 1, 20x0, rather than on January 1, 20x0, the issue date. The entry to record the sale of the bonds is as follows:

$A = L + OE$
$+ \quad + \quad +$

20x0				
May 1	Cash		103,000	
	Bond Interest Expense			3,000
	Bonds Payable			100,000
	Sold 9%, 5-year bonds at face value plus 4 months' accrued interest $100,000 \times .09 \times \frac{4}{12} = \$3,000$			

Enrichment Point: This is one of the few times an expense account is credited (other than when it is closed). Refer to the ledger account, which demonstrates that the net effect is the recording of two months' interest (May and June).

As shown, Cash is debited for the amount received, $103,000 (the face value of the $100,000 plus four months' accrued interest of $3,000). Bond Interest Expense is credited for the $3,000 of accrued interest, and Bonds Payable is credited for the face value of $100,000.

When the first semiannual interest payment date arrives, the entry that follows is made.

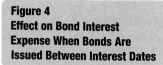

Figure 4
Effect on Bond Interest
Expense When Bonds Are
Issued Between Interest Dates

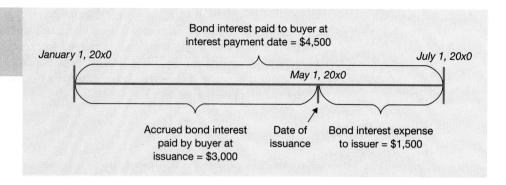

20x0

A* = L + OE
–   –

*assumes cash paid

	July 1	Bond Interest Expense	4,500	
		Cash (or Interest Payable)		4,500
		Paid (or accrued) semiannual interest		
		$100,000 \times .09 \times \%_{12} = \$4,500$		

Notice that the entire half-year interest is both debited to Bond Interest Expense and credited to Cash because the corporation pays bond interest only once every six months, in full six-month amounts. This process is illustrated in Figure 4. The actual interest expense for the two months that the bonds were outstanding is $1,500. This amount is the net balance of the $4,500 debit to Bond Interest Expense on July 1 less the $3,000 credit to Bond Interest Expense on May 1. You can see these steps clearly in the T account for Bond Interest Expense below.

Bond Interest Expense

Bal.	0	May 1	3,000
July 1	4,500		
Bal.	1,500		

Year-End Accrual for Bond Interest Expense

Bond interest payment dates rarely correspond with a company's fiscal year. Therefore, an adjustment must be made at the end of the accounting period to accrue the interest expense on the bonds from the last payment date to the end of the fiscal year. Further, if there is any discount or premium on the bonds, it must also be amortized for the fractional period.

Remember that in an earlier example, Vason Corporation issued $100,000 in bonds on January 1, 20x0, at 104.1 (see page 515). Suppose the company's fiscal year ends on September 30, 20x0. In the period since the interest payment and amortization of the premium on July 1, three months' worth of interest has accrued, and the following adjusting entry under the effective interest method must be made.

20x0

A = L + OE
     +   –
          –

	Sept. 30	Bond Interest Expense	2,075.50	
		Unamortized Bond Premium	174.50	
		Interest Payable		2,250.00
		To record accrual of interest on 9% bonds		
		payable for 3 months and amortization		
		of one-half of the premium for the		
		second interest payment period		

This entry covers one-half of the second interest period. Unamortized Bond Premium is debited for $174.50, which is one-half of $349, the amortization of the

Clarification Note: The matching rule dictates that both the accrued interest and the amortization of a premium or discount be recorded at year end. Refer to Table 2 for premium-amortization figures.

premium for the second period from Table 2. Interest Payable is credited for $2,250, three months' interest on the face value of the bonds ($100,000 × .09 × $\frac{3}{12}$). The net debit figure of $2,075.50 ($2,250.00 − $174.50) is the bond interest expense for the three-month period.

When the January 1, 20x1, payment date arrives, the entry to pay the bond-holders and amortize the premium is as follows:

20x1

A = L + OE
‒ ‒ ‒
   ‒

Jan. 1	Bond Interest Expense	2,075.50	
	Interest Payable	2,250.00	
	Unamortized Bond Premium	174.50	
	Cash		4,500.00
	Paid semiannual interest including interest previously accrued, and amortized the premium for the period since the end of the fiscal year		

As shown here, one-half ($2,250) of the amount paid ($4,500) was accrued on September 30. Unamortized Bond Premium is debited for $174.50, the remaining amount to be amortized for the period ($349.00 − $174.50). The resulting bond interest expense is the amount that applies to the three-month period from October 1 to December 31.

Bond discounts are recorded at year end in the same way as bond premiums. The difference is that the amortization of a bond discount increases interest expense instead of decreasing it, as a premium does.

Retirement of Bonds

OBJECTIVE

7 Account for the retirement of bonds and the conversion of bonds into stock

Most bond issues give the company a chance to buy back and retire the bonds at a specified **call price**, usually above face value, before maturity. Such bonds are known as **callable bonds**, and give the company flexibility in financing its operations. For example, if bond interest rates drop, the company can call its bonds and reissue debt at a lower interest rate. A company might also call its bonds if it has earned enough to pay off the debt, the reason for having the debt no longer exists, or it wants to restructure its debt to equity ratio. The bond indenture states the time period and the prices at which the bonds can be redeemed. The retirement of a bond issue before its maturity date is called **early extinguishment of debt**.

Let's assume that Vason Corporation can call or retire the $100,000 of bonds issued at a premium (page 515) at 105, and that it decides to do so on July 1, 20x3. (To simplify the example, the retirement is made on an interest payment date.) Because the bonds were issued on January 1, 20x0, the retirement takes place on the seventh interest payment date. Assume that the entry for the required interest payment and the amortization of the premium has been made. The entry to retire the bonds is as follows:

20x3

A = L + OE
‒ ‒ ‒
   ‒

July 1	Bonds Payable	100,000	
	Unamortized Bond Premium	1,447	
	Loss on Retirement of Bonds	3,553 .	
	Cash		105,000
	Retired 9% bonds at 105		

In this entry, the cash paid is the face value times the call price ($100,000 × 1.05 = $105,000). The unamortized bond premium can be found in Column E of Table 2. The loss on retirement of bonds occurs because the call price of the bonds is greater than the carrying value ($105,000 − $101,447 = $3,553). The loss, if material, is presented as an extraordinary item on the income statement.

A = L + OE
− − +
−

Sometimes a rise in the market interest rate can cause the market value of bonds to fall considerably below their face value. If it has the cash to do so, the company may find it advantageous to purchase the bonds on the open market and retire them, rather than wait and pay them off at face value. An extraordinary gain is recognized for the difference between the purchase price of the bonds and the carrying value of the retired bonds. For example, assume that because of a rise in interest rates, Vason Corporation is able to purchase the $100,000 bond issue on the open market at 85, making it unnecessary to call the bonds at the higher price of 105. Then, the entry would be as follows:

20x3			
July 1	Bonds Payable	100,000	
	Unamortized Bond Premium	1,447	
	Cash		85,000
	Gain on Retirement of Bonds		16,447
	Purchased and retired		
	9% bonds at 85		

Conversion of Bonds into Common Stock

Bonds that can be exchanged for other securities of the corporation (in most cases, common stock) are called **convertible bonds**. Convertibility enables an investor to make more money if the market price of the common stock rises, because the value of the bonds then rises. However, if the common stock price does not rise, the investor still holds the bonds and receives both the periodic interest payments and the principal at the maturity date.

Several factors related to the issuance of convertible bonds are favorable to the company. First, the interest rate is usually less than the company would have to offer if the bonds were not convertible. An investor is willing to give up some current interest for the prospect that the value of the stock will increase, and therefore the value of the bonds will also increase. Another advantage is that management will not have to give up any current control of the company. Unlike stockholders, bondholders do not have voting rights. A third benefit is tax savings. Interest paid on bonds is fully deductible for income tax purposes, whereas cash dividends on common stock are not. Fourth, the company's income will be affected favorably if the company earns a return that exceeds the interest cost of the debentures. Finally, the convertible feature offers financial flexibility. If the market value of the stock rises to a level at which the bond is worth more than face value, management can avoid repaying the bonds by calling them for redemption, thereby forcing the bondholders to convert their bonds into common stock. The bondholders will agree to convert because the common stock they will receive will be worth more than they would receive if the bonds were redeemed.

One major disadvantage of debentures is that interest must be paid semiannually. Inability to make an interest payment could force the company into bankruptcy. Common stock dividends are declared and paid only when the board of directors decides to do so. Another disadvantage is that when the bonds are converted, they become new outstanding common stock. These new shares give stockholders' rights to the bondholders and reduce the proportional ownership of the existing stockholders.

When a bondholder wishes to convert bonds into common stock, the common stock is recorded at the carrying value of the bonds. The bond liability and the associated unamortized discount or premium are written off the books. For this reason, no gain or loss on the transaction is recorded. For example, suppose that Vason Corporation's bonds are not called on July 1, 20x3. Instead, the corporation's bondholders decide to convert all the bonds to $8 par value common stock under a convertible provision of 40 shares of common stock for each $1,000 bond. The entry would be as follows:

$$A = L + OE$$
$$- \quad +$$
$$- \quad +$$

20x3			
July 1	Bonds Payable	100,000	
	Unamortized Bond Premium	1,447	
	Common Stock		32,000
	Paid-in Capital in Excess of Par		
	Value, Common		69,447
	Converted 9% bonds payable into		
	$8 par value common stock at a rate		
	of 40 shares for each $1,000 bond		

Study Point: The credits to the contributed capital accounts are based on the carrying value of the bonds converted. As a result, no gain or loss is recognized. If only a portion of the bonds had been converted, proportionate shares of the balances in Bonds Payable and Unamortized Bond Premium would be eliminated.

The unamortized bond premium is found in Column E of Table 2. At a rate of 40 shares for each $1,000 bond, 4,000 shares will be issued, with a total par value of $32,000 (4,000 × $8). The Common Stock account is credited for the amount of the par value of the stock issued. In addition, Paid-in Capital in Excess of Par Value, Common is credited for the difference between the carrying value of the bonds and the par value of the stock issued ($101,447 − $32,000 = $69,447). No gain or loss is recorded.

Other Long-Term Liabilities

OBJECTIVE

8 Explain the basic features of mortgages payable, installment notes payable, long-term leases, and pensions and other postretirement benefits as long-term liabilities

A company may have other long-term liabilities besides bonds. The most common are mortgages payable, installment notes payable, long-term leases, and pensions and other postretirement benefits.

Mortgages Payable

A **mortgage** is a long-term debt secured by real property. It is usually paid in equal monthly installments. Each monthly payment includes interest on the debt and a reduction in the debt. Table 3 shows the first three monthly payments on a $50,000, 12 percent mortgage. The mortgage was obtained on June 1, and the

Table 3. Monthly Payment Schedule on a $50,000, 12 Percent Mortgage					
	A	B	C	D	E
Payment Date	Unpaid Balance at Beginning of Period	Monthly Payment	Interest for 1 Month at 1% on Unpaid Balance* (1% × A)	Reduction in Debt (B − C)	Unpaid Balance at End of Period (A − D)
June 1					$50,000
July 1	$50,000	$800	$500	$300	49,700
Aug. 1	49,700	800	497	303	49,397
Sept. 1	49,397	800	494	306	49,091

*Rounded to the nearest dollar.

monthly payments are $800. According to the table, the entry to record the July 1 payment would be as follows:

A = L + OE
 − − −

	July 1	Mortgage Payable	300	
		Mortgage Interest Expense	500	
		Cash		800
		Made monthly mortgage payment		

Notice from the entry and from Table 3 that the July 1 payment represents interest expense of $500 ($50,000 × .12 × ½) and a reduction in the debt of $300 ($800 − $500). Therefore, the unpaid balance is reduced to $49,700 by the July payment. August's interest expense is slightly less than July's because of the decrease in the debt.

Installment Notes Payable

Enrichment Note: Although both mortgages payable and installment notes payable involve a series of payments, mortgages are used to finance real estate, whereas installment notes are used to finance other types of assets.

A long-term note can be paid at its maturity date by making a lump-sum payment that includes the amount borrowed plus the interest. Often, however, the terms of a note will call for a series of periodic payments. Such a note is called an **installment note payable** because each payment includes the interest to date plus a repayment of part of the amount that was borrowed. For example, let's assume that on December 31, 20x1, $100,000 is borrowed on a 15 percent installment note, to be paid annually over five years. The entry to record the note is as follows:

A = L + OE
 +   +

20x1				
Dec. 31	Cash		100,000	
	Notes Payable			100,000
	Borrowed $100,000 at 15%			
	on a 5-year installment note			

PAYMENTS OF ACCRUED INTEREST PLUS EQUAL AMOUNTS OF PRINCIPAL Installment notes most often call for payments consisting of accrued interest plus equal amounts of principal repayment. The amount of each installment decreases because the amount of principal on which the accrued interest is owed decreases by the amount of the previous principal payment. Banks use installment notes to finance equipment purchases by businesses; such notes are also common for other kinds of purchases when payment is spread over several years. They can be set up on a revolving basis whereby the borrower can borrow additional funds as the installments are paid. Moreover, the interest rate charged on installment notes may be adjusted periodically as market interest rates change.

Key Point: The only way to set up equal principal payments each period is to vary the total payment made. That is, the total payment equals the uniform principal payment plus a decreasing interest payment.

On our sample installment note for $100,000, the principal declines by an equal amount each year for five years, or by $20,000 per year ($100,000 ÷ 5 years). The interest is calculated on the balance of the note that remains each year. Because the balance of the note declines each year, the amount of interest also declines. For example, the entries for the first two payments of the installment note follow:

A = L + OE
 − − −

20x2				
Dec. 31	Notes Payable		20,000	
	Interest Expense		15,000	
	Cash			35,000
	Made first installment payment on note			
	$100,000 × .15 = $15,000			

A = L + OE
 − − −

20x3				
Dec. 31	Notes Payable		20,000	
	Interest Expense		12,000	
	Cash			32,000
	Made second installment payment on note			
	$80,000 × .15 = $12,000			

Notice that the amount of the payment decreases from $35,000 to $32,000 because the amount of interest accrued on the note has decreased from $15,000 to $12,000. The difference of $3,000 is the interest on the $20,000 that was repaid in 20x2. Each subsequent payment decreases by $3,000, as the note itself decreases by $20,000 each year until it is fully paid. This example assumes that the repayment of principal and the interest rate remain the same from year to year.

Payments of Accrued Interest Plus Increasing Amounts of Principal

Less commonly, the terms of an installment note, like those used for leasing equipment, may call for equal periodic (monthly or yearly) payments. Under this method, the interest is deducted from the equal payments to determine the amount by which the principal will be reduced each year.

This procedure, presented in Table 4, is very similar to that for mortgages, shown in Table 3. Each equal payment of $29,833 is allocated between interest and principal reduction. Each year the interest is calculated on the remaining principal. As the principal decreases, the annual interest also decreases, and because the payment remains the same, the amount by which the principal decreases becomes larger each year. The entries for the first two years, with data taken from Table 4, follow:

Key Point: This situation, unlike the previous one, is exactly the same as a typical mortgage payment plan.

20x2

$A = L + OE$
$-\quad-\quad-$

Dec. 31	Notes Payable	14,833	
	Interest Expense	15,000	
	Cash		29,833
	Made first installment payment on note		

20x3

$A = L + OE$
$-\quad-\quad-$

Dec. 31	Notes Payable	17,058	
	Interest Expense	12,775	
	Cash		29,833
	Made second installment payment on note		

Similar entries will be made for the next three years.

How is the equal annual payment calculated? Because the $100,000 borrowed is the present value of the five equal annual payments at 15 percent interest, it is

Table 4. Payment Schedule on a $100,000, 15 Percent Installment Note

Payment Date	A Unpaid Principal at Beginning of Period	B Equal Annual Payment	C Interest for 1 Year at 15% on Unpaid Principal* (15% × A)	D Reduction in Principal (B − C)	E Unpaid Principal at End of Period (A − D)
					$100,000
20x2	$100,000	$29,833	$15,000	$14,833	85,167
20x3	85,167	29,833	12,775	17,058	68,109
20x4	68,109	29,833	10,216	19,617	48,492
20x5	48,492	29,833	7,274	22,559	25,933
20x6	25,933	29,833	3,900†	25,933	—

*Rounded to the nearest dollar.
†The last year's interest equals $3,900 ($29,833 − $25,933); it does not exactly equal $3,890 ($25,933 × .15) because of the cumulative effect of rounding.

possible to use present value tables to calculate the annual payments. Using Table 4 from the appendix on future value and present value tables, the calculation is made as shown below:

Periodic Payment × Factor (Table 4 in the appendix on future value and present value tables: 15%, 5 periods) = Present Value

Periodic Payment × 3.352   = $100,000

Periodic Payment = $100,000 ÷ 3.352 = $29,833

Table 4 shows that five equal annual payments of $29,833 at 15 percent will reduce the principal balance to zero (except for the discrepancy due to rounding).

Long-Term Leases

There are several ways for a company to obtain new operating assets. One way is to borrow money and buy the asset. Another is to rent the equipment on a short-term lease. A third way is to obtain the equipment on a long-term lease. The first two methods do not create accounting problems. In the first case, the asset and liability are recorded at the amount paid, and the asset is subject to periodic depreciation. In the second case, the lease is short term in relation to the useful life of the asset, and the risks of ownership remain with the lessor. This type of agreement is called an **operating lease**. It is proper accounting procedure to treat operating lease payments as an expense and to debit the amount of each monthly payment to Rent Expense.

> **Terminology Note:** From the lessee's point of view, a lease is treated as either an operating lease or a capital lease. An operating lease is a true lease and is treated as such. A capital lease, however, is in substance an installment purchase, and the leased asset and related liability must be recognized at their present value.

The third alternative, a long-term lease, is one of the fastest-growing ways of financing operating equipment in the United States today. It has several advantages. For instance, a long-term lease requires no immediate cash payment, the rental payment is deducted in full for tax purposes, and it costs less than a short-term lease. Acquiring the use of plant assets under long-term leases does cause several accounting challenges, however. Often, such leases cannot be canceled. Also, their duration may be about the same as the useful life of the asset. Finally, they may provide for the lessee to buy the asset at a nominal price at the end of the lease. The lease is much like an installment purchase because the risks of ownership are transferred to the lessee. Both the lessee's available assets and its legal obligations (liabilities) increase because the lessee must make a number of payments over the life of the asset.

The Financial Accounting Standards Board has described this kind of long-term lease as a **capital lease**. The term reflects the provisions of such a lease, which make the transaction more like a purchase or sale on installment. The FASB has ruled that in the case of a capital lease, the lessee must record an asset and a long-term liability equal to the present value of the total lease payments during the lease term. In doing so, the lessee must use the present value at the beginning of the lease.[9] Much like a mortgage payment, each lease payment consists partly of interest expense and partly of repayment of debt. Further, depreciation expense is figured on the asset and entered on the records of the lessee.

> **Key Point:** Under a capital lease, depreciation must be recorded by the lessee, using any allowable method. Depreciation is *not* recorded under an operating lease, however, because the leased asset is not recognized on the lessee's books.

Suppose, for example, that Isaacs Company enters into a long-term lease for a machine used in its manufacturing operations. The lease terms call for an annual payment of $4,000 for six years, which approximates the useful life of the machine (see Table 5). At the end of the lease period, the title to the machine passes to Isaacs. This lease is clearly a capital lease and should be recorded as an asset and a liability according to FASB *Statement No. 13*.

A lease is a periodic payment for the right to use an asset or assets. Present value techniques can be used to place a value on the asset and on the corresponding liability associated with a capital lease. If Isaac's interest cost is 16 percent, the present value of the lease payments can be computed as follows:

Table 5. Payment Schedule on a 16 Percent Capital Lease

Year	A Lease Payment	B Interest (16%) on Unpaid Obligation* (D × 16%)	C Reduction of Lease Obligation (A − B)	D Balance of Lease Obligation (D − C)
Beginning				$14,740
1	$ 4,000	$2,358	$ 1,642	13,098
2	4,000	2,096	1,904	11,194
3	4,000	1,791	2,209	8,985
4	4,000	1,438	2,562	6,423
5	4,000	1,028	2,972	3,451
6	4,000	549†	3,451	—
	$24,000	$9,260	$14,740	

*Computations are rounded to the nearest dollar.
†The last year's interest equals $549 ($4,000 − $3,451); it does not exactly equal $552 ($3,451 × .16) because of the cumulative effect of rounding.

Periodic Payment × Factor (Table 4 in the appendix on future value and present value tables: 16%, 6 periods) = Present Value

$4,000 × 3.685   = $14,740

The entry to record the lease contract is as follows:

A = L + OE
+   +

Equipment Under Capital Lease	14,740	
Obligations Under Capital Lease		14,740
To record capital lease on machinery		

Equipment Under Capital Lease is classified as a long-term asset; Obligations Under Capital Lease is classified as a long-term liability. Each year, Isaacs must record depreciation on the leased asset. Using straight-line depreciation, a six-year life, and no salvage value, the following entry would record the depreciation:

A = L + OE
−   −

Depreciation Expense, Equipment Under Capital Lease	2,457	
Accumulated Depreciation, Equipment Under Capital Lease		2,457
To record depreciation expense on capital lease		

The interest expense for each year is computed by multiplying the interest rate (16 percent) by the amount of the remaining lease obligation. Table 5 shows these calculations. Using the data in the table, the first lease payment would be recorded as follows:

A = L + OE
−   −   −

Interest Expense (Column B)	2,358	
Obligations Under Capital Lease (Column C)	1,642	
Cash		4,000
Made payment on capital lease		

Pensions

Most employees who work for medium- and large-sized companies are covered by some sort of pension plan. A **pension plan** is a contract between a company and its employees in which the company agrees to pay benefits to the employees after they retire. Many companies contribute the full cost of the pension, but frequently the employees also pay part of their salary or wages toward their pension. The contributions from both parties are typically paid into a **pension fund**, from which benefits are paid to retirees. In most cases, pension benefits consist of monthly payments to retired employees and other payments upon disability or death.

There are two kinds of pension plans. Under a *defined contribution plan*, the employer is required to contribute an annual amount specified by an agreement between the company and its employees or by a resolution of the board of directors. Retirement payments depend on the amount of pension payments the accumulated contributions can support. Under a *defined benefit plan*, the employer's annual contribution is the amount required to fund pension liabilities arising from employment in the current year, but the exact amount will not be determined until the retirement and death of the current employees. Under a defined benefit plan, the amount of future benefits is fixed, but the annual contributions vary depending on assumptions about how much the pension fund will earn. Under a defined contribution plan, each year's contribution is fixed, but the benefits vary depending on how much the pension fund earns.

Accounting for annual pension expense under a defined contribution plan is simple. After the required contribution is determined, Pension Expense is debited and a liability (or Cash) is credited.

Accounting for annual expense under a defined benefit plan is one of the most complex topics in accounting; thus, the intricacies are reserved for advanced courses. In concept, however, the procedure is simple. First, the amount of pension expense is determined. Then, if the amount of cash contributed to the fund is less than the pension expense, a liability results, which is reported on the balance sheet. If the amount of cash paid to the pension plan exceeds the pension expense, a prepaid expense arises and appears on the asset side of the balance sheet. For example, the annual report for Philip Morris Companies, Inc. includes among assets on the balance sheet a prepaid pension of $814 million.[10]

In accordance with the FASB's *Statement No. 87*, all companies should use the same actuarial method to compute pension expense.[11] However, because of the need to estimate many factors, such as the average remaining service life of active employees, the expected long-run return on pension plan assets, and expected future salary increases, the computation of pension expense is not simple. In addition, actuarial terminology further complicates pension accounting. In nontechnical terms, the pension expense for the year includes not only the cost of the benefits earned by people working during the year but interest costs on the total pension obligation (which are calculated on the present value of future benefits to be paid) and other adjustments. Those costs are reduced by the expected return on the pension fund assets.

Since 1989, all employers whose pension plans do not have sufficient assets to cover the present value of their pension benefit obligations (on a termination basis) must record the amount of the shortfall as a liability on their balance sheets. The investor no longer has to read the notes to the financial statements to learn whether or not the pension plan is fully funded. However, if a pension plan does have sufficient assets to cover its obligations, then no balance sheet reporting is required or permitted.

Other Postretirement Benefits

In addition to pensions, many companies provide health care and other benefits to employees after retirement. In the past, these **other postretirement benefits** were accounted for on a cash basis; that is, they were expensed when the benefits were paid, after an employee had retired. The FASB has concluded, however, that

---

Enrichment Note: Accounting for a defined benefit plan is far more complex than accounting for a defined contribution plan. Fortunately, accountants can rely on the calculations of professional actuaries, whose expertise includes the mathematics of pension plans.

those benefits are earned by the employee, and that, in accordance with the matching rule, they should be estimated and accrued during the period of time the employee is working.[12]

The estimates must take into account assumptions about retirement age, mortality, and, most significantly, future trends in health care benefits. Like pension benefits, such future benefits should be discounted to the current period. In a field test conducted by the Financial Executives Research Foundation, it was determined that the change to accrual accounting increased postretirement benefits by two to seven times the amount recognized on a cash basis.

Chapter Review

REVIEW OF LEARNING OBJECTIVES

Ace it

1. **Identify the management issues related to issuing long-term debt.** Long-term debt is used to finance long-term assets and business activities that have long-term earnings potential, such as property, plant, and equipment and research and development. In issuing long-term debt, management must decide (1) whether or not to have long-term debt, (2) how much long-term debt to have, and (3) what types of long-term debt to have. Among the advantages of long-term debt financing are that (1) common stockholders do not relinquish any control, (2) interest on debt is tax deductible, and (3) financial leverage may increase earnings. Disadvantages of long-term financing are that (1) interest and principal must be repaid on schedule, and (2) financial leverage can work against a company if a project is not successful.

2. **Identify and contrast the major characteristics of bonds.** A bond is a security that represents money borrowed from the investing public. When a corporation issues bonds, it enters into a contract, called a bond indenture, with the bondholders. The bond indenture identifies the major conditions of the bonds. A corporation can issue several types of bonds, each having different characteristics. For example, a bond issue may or may not require security (secured versus unsecured bonds). It may be payable at a single time (term bonds) or at several times (serial bonds). And the holder may receive interest automatically (registered bonds) or may have to return coupons to receive interest payable (coupon bonds).

3. **Record the issuance of bonds at face value and at a discount or premium.** When bonds are issued, the bondholders pay an amount equal to, less than, or greater than the bonds' face value. Bondholders pay face value for bonds when the interest rate on the bonds approximates the market rate for similar investments. The issuing corporation records the bond issue at face value as a long-term liability in the Bonds Payable account.

Bonds are issued at an amount less than face value when their face interest rate is lower than the market rate for similar investments. The difference between the face value and the issue price is called a discount and is debited to Unamortized Bond Discount.

When the face interest rate on bonds is greater than the market interest rate on similar investments, investors are willing to pay more than face value for the bonds. The difference between the issue price and the face value is called a premium and is credited to Unamortized Bond Premium.

4. **Use present values to determine the value of bonds.** The value of a bond is determined by summing the present values of (a) the series of fixed interest payments of the bond issue and (b) the single payment of the face

value at maturity. Tables 3 and 4 in the appendix on future value and present value tables should be used in making these computations.

5. Use the straight-line and effective interest methods to amortize (a) bond discounts and (b) bond premiums. When bonds are sold at a discount or a premium, the interest rate is adjusted from the face rate to an effective rate that is close to the market rate when the bonds were issued. Therefore, bond discounts or premiums have the effect of increasing or decreasing the interest expense on the bonds over their life. Under these conditions, it is necessary to amortize the discount or premium over the life of the bonds by using either the straight-line method or the effective interest method.

The straight-line method allocates a fixed portion of the bond discount or premium each interest period to adjust the interest payment to interest expense. The effective interest method, which is used when the effects of amortization are material, results in a constant rate of interest on the carrying value of the bonds. To find interest and the amortization of discounts or premiums, the effective interest rate is applied to the carrying value of the bonds (face value minus the discount or plus the premium) at the beginning of the interest period. The amount of the discount or premium to be amortized is the difference between the interest figured by using the effective rate and that obtained by using the face rate. The results of using the effective interest method on bonds issued at a discount or a premium are summarized below and compared with issuance at face value.

	Bonds Issued At		
	Face Value	Discount	Premium
Trend in carrying value over bond term	Constant	Increasing	Decreasing
Trend in interest expense over bond term	Constant	Increasing	Decreasing
Interest expense versus interest payments	Interest expense = interest payments	Interest expense > interest payments	Interest expense < interest payments
Classification of bond discount or premium	Not applicable	Contra-liability (deducted from Bonds Payable)	Liability (added to Bonds Payable)

6. Account for bonds issued between interest dates and make year-end adjustments. When bonds are sold on dates between the interest payment dates, the issuing corporation collects from investors the interest that has accrued since the last interest payment date. When the next interest payment date arrives, the corporation pays the bondholders interest for the entire interest period.

When the end of a corporation's fiscal year does not fall on an interest payment date, the corporation must accrue bond interest expense from the last interest payment date to the end of the company's fiscal year. This accrual results in the inclusion of the interest expense in the year incurred.

7. Account for the retirement of bonds and the conversion of bonds into stock. Callable bonds can be retired before maturity at the option of the issuing corporation. The call price is usually an amount greater than the face value of the bonds, so the corporation usually recognizes a loss on the retirement of bonds. An extraordinary gain can be recognized on the early extinguishment of debt when a company purchases its bonds on the open market at a price below carrying value. This happens when a rise in the market interest rate causes the market value of the bonds to fall.

Convertible bonds allow the bondholder to convert bonds to stock in the issuing corporation. In this case, the common stock issued is recorded at the carrying value of the bonds being converted. No gain or loss is recognized.

8. **Explain the basic features of mortgages payable, installment notes payable, long-term leases, and pensions and other postretirement benefits as long-term liabilities.** A mortgage is a long-term debt secured by real property. It usually is paid in equal monthly installments. Each payment is partly interest expense and partly debt repayment. Installment notes payable are long-term notes that are paid in a series of payments. Part of each payment is interest, and part is repayment of principal. If a long-term lease is a capital lease, the risks of ownership lie with the lessee. Like a mortgage payment, each lease payment is partly interest and partly a reduction of debt. For a capital lease, both an asset and a long-term liability should be recorded. The liability should be equal to the present value at the beginning of the lease of the total lease payments over the lease term. The recorded asset is subject to depreciation. Pension expense must be recorded in the current period. Other postretirement benefits should be estimated and accrued while the employee is still working.

REVIEW OF CONCEPTS AND TERMINOLOGY

The following concepts and terms were introduced in this chapter.

LO 2 **Bond:** A security, usually long term, representing money borrowed from the investing public by a corporation or some other entity.

LO 2 **Bond certificate:** Evidence of an organization's debt to a bondholder.

LO 2 **Bond indenture:** A supplementary agreement to a bond issue that defines the rights, privileges, and limitations of bondholders.

LO 2 **Bond issue:** The total value of bonds issued at one time.

LO 7 **Callable bonds:** Bonds that an organization can buy back and retire at a call price before maturity.

LO 7 **Call price:** A specified price, usually above face value, at which a corporation may, at its option, buy back and retire bonds before maturity.

LO 8 **Capital lease:** A long-term lease in which the risk of ownership lies with the lessee and whose terms resemble a purchase or sale on installment.

LO 7 **Convertible bonds:** Bonds that can be exchanged for other securities of the corporation, usually its common stock.

LO 2 **Coupon bonds:** Bonds that are usually not registered with the issuing organization but instead bear interest coupons stating the amount of interest due and the payment date.

LO 3 **Discount:** The amount by which the face value of a bond exceeds the issue price; occurs when the market interest rate is higher than the face interest rate.

LO 7 **Early extinguishment of debt:** The retirement of a bond issue before its maturity date.

LO 5 **Effective interest method:** A method of amortizing bond discounts or premiums that applies a constant interest rate, the market rate at the time the bonds were issued, to the carrying value of the bonds at the beginning of each interest period.

LO 3 **Face interest rate:** The rate of interest paid to bondholders based on the face value of the bonds.

LO 1 **Financial leverage:** The ability to increase earnings for stockholders by earning more on assets than is paid in interest on debt incurred to finance the assets; also called *trading on the equity.*

LO 8 **Installment note payable:** A long-term note paid off in a series of payments, of which part is interest and part is repayment of principal.

LO 1 **Interest coverage ratio:** A measure of the degree of protection a company has from default on interest payments; income before taxes and interest expense divided by interest expense.

LO 3 **Market interest rate:** The rate of interest paid in the market on bonds of similar risk; also called *effective interest rate.*

LO 8 **Mortgage:** A long-term debt secured by real property; usually paid in equal monthly installments, of which part is interest and part is repayment of principal.

LO 8 **Operating lease:** A short-term or cancelable lease in which the risks of ownership lie with the lessor, and whose payments are recorded as a rent expense.

LO 8 **Other postretirement benefits:** Health care and other nonpension benefits paid to a worker after retirement but earned while the employee is still working.

LO 8 **Pension fund:** A fund established through contributions from an employer (and, sometimes, employees) from which payments are made to employees after retirement or on disability or death.

LO 8 **Pension plan:** A contract between a company and its employees under which the company agrees to pay benefits to the employees after they retire.

LO 3 **Premium:** The amount by which the issue price of a bond exceeds its face value; occurs when the market interest rate is lower than the face interest rate.

LO 2 **Registered bonds:** Bonds for which the names and addresses of bondholders are recorded with the issuing organization.

LO 2 **Secured bonds:** Bonds that give the bondholders a pledge of certain assets as a guarantee of repayment.

LO 2 **Serial bonds:** A bond issue with several different maturity dates.

LO 5 **Straight-line method:** A method of amortizing bond discounts or premiums that allocates the discount or premium equally over each interest period of the life of a bond.

LO 2 **Term bonds:** Bonds of a bond issue that all mature at the same time.

LO 2 **Unsecured bonds:** Bonds issued on the general credit of an organization; also called *debenture bonds.*

LO 5 **Zero coupon bonds:** Bonds that do not pay periodic interest but that promise to pay a fixed amount on the maturity date.

REVIEW PROBLEM

Interest and Amortization of a Bond Discount, Bond Retirement, and Bond Conversion

LO 3
LO 5
LO 7
When the Merrill Manufacturing Company was expanding its metal window division, it did not have enough capital to finance the expansion. So, management sought and received approval from the board of directors to issue bonds. The company planned to issue $5,000,000 of 8 percent, five-year bonds in 20x1. Interest would be paid on June 30 and December 31 of each year. The bonds would be callable at 104, and each $1,000 bond would be convertible into 30 shares of $10 par value common stock.

On January 1, 20x1, the bonds were sold at 96 because the market rate of interest for similar investments was 9 percent. The company decided to amortize the bond discount by using the effective interest method. On July 1, 20x3, management called and retired half the bonds, and investors converted the other half into common stock.

REQUIRED

1. Prepare an interest and amortization schedule for the first five interest periods.
2. Prepare the journal entries to record the sale of the bonds, the first two interest payments, the bond retirement, and the bond conversion.

ANSWER TO REVIEW PROBLEM

1. Prepare a schedule for the first five interest periods.

Interest and Amortization of Bond Discount

Semiannual Interest Payment Date	Carrying Value at Beginning of Period	Semiannual Interest Expense* (9% × ½)	Semiannual Interest Paid per Period (8% × ½)	Amortiza- tion of Discount	Unamortized Bond Discount at End of Period	Carrying Value at End of Period
Jan. 1, 20x1					$200,000	$4,800,000
June 30, 20x1	$4,800,000	$216,000	$200,000	$16,000	184,000	4,816,000
Dec. 31, 20x1	4,816,000	216,720	200,000	16,720	167,280	4,832,720
June 30, 20x2	4,832,720	217,472	200,000	17,472	149,808	4,850,192
Dec. 31, 20x2	4,850,192	218,259	200,000	18,259	131,549	4,868,451
June 30, 20x3	4,868,451	219,080	200,000	19,080	112,469	4,887,531

*Rounded to the nearest dollar.

2. Prepare the journal entries.

20x1

Jan.	1	Cash	4,800,000	
		Unamortized Bond Discount	200,000	
		Bonds Payable		5,000,000
		Sold $5,000,000 of 8%, 5-year bonds at 96		

June 30		Bond Interest Expense	216,000	
		Unamortized Bond Discount		16,000
		Cash		200,000
		Paid semiannual interest and amortized the discount on 8%, 5-year bonds		

Dec. 31		Bond Interest Expense	216,720	
		Unamortized Bond Discount		16,720
		Cash		200,000
		Paid semiannual interest and amortized the discount on 8%, 5-year bonds		

20x3

July	1	Bonds Payable	2,500,000	
		Loss on Retirement of Bonds	156,235	
		Unamortized Bond Discount		56,235
		Cash		2,600,000
		Called $2,500,000 of 8% bonds and retired them at 104 $112,469 × ½ = $56,235*		

	1	Bonds Payable	2,500,000	
		Unamortized Bond Discount		56,234
		Common Stock		750,000
		Paid-in Capital in Excess of Par Value, Common		1,693,766
		Converted $2,500,000 of 8% bonds into common stock: 2,500 × 30 shares = 75,000 shares 75,000 shares × $10 = $750,000 $112,469 − $56,235 = $56,234 $2,500,000 − ($56,234 + $750,000) = $1,693,766		

*Rounded.

Chapter Assignments

**BUILDING YOUR
KNOWLEDGE
FOUNDATION**

QUESTIONS

1. What are the advantages and disadvantages of issuing long-term debt?
2. What are a bond certificate, a bond issue, and a bond indenture? What information is found in a bond indenture?
3. What are the essential differences between (a) secured and debenture bonds, (b) term and serial bonds, and (c) registered and coupon bonds?
4. Napier Corporation sold $500,000 of 5 percent $1,000 bonds on the interest payment date. What would the proceeds from the sale be if the bonds were issued at 95, at 100, and at 102?
5. If you were about to buy bonds on which the face interest rate was less than the market interest rate, would you expect to pay more or less than par value for the bonds?
6. Why does the amortization of a bond discount increase interest expense to an amount greater than interest paid? Why does the amortization of a premium have the opposite effect?
7. When the effective interest method of amortizing a bond discount or premium is used, why does the amount of interest expense change from period to period?
8. When bonds are issued between interest dates, why is it necessary for the issuer to collect an amount equal to accrued interest from the buyer?
9. Why would a company want to exercise the call provision of a bond when it can wait to pay off the debt?
10. What are the advantages of convertible bonds to the company issuing them and to the investor?
11. What are the two components of a uniform monthly mortgage payment?
12. What are the two methods of repaying an installment note?
13. Under what conditions is a long-term lease called a capital lease? Why should an accountant record both an asset and a liability in connection with this type of lease? What items should appear on the income statement as the result of a capital lease?
14. What is a pension plan? What is a pension fund?
15. What is the difference between a defined contribution plan and a defined benefit plan? In general, how is expense determined under each plan? What assumptions must be made to account for the expenses of such a plan?
16. What are other postretirement benefits, and how is the matching rule applied?

SHORT EXERCISES

SE 1.

LO 1 Bond Versus Common Stock Financing

Indicate whether each of the following is an advantage or a disadvantage of using long-term bond financing rather than issuing common stock.

1. Interest paid on bonds is tax deductible.
2. Sometimes projects are not as successful as planned.
3. Financial leverage can have a negative effect when investments do not earn as much as the interest payments on the related debt.
4. Bondholders do not have voting rights in a corporation.
5. Positive financial leverage may be achieved.

SE 2.

**LO 3 Journal Entries for
LO 5 Interest Using the Straight-
Line Method**

On April 1, 20x1, Taylor Corporation issued $4,000,000 in 8.5 percent, five-year bonds at 98. The semiannual interest payment dates are April 1 and October 1. Prepare journal entries for the issue of the bonds by Taylor on April 1, 20x1, and the first two interest payments on October 1, 20x1, and April 1, 20x2. Use the straight-line method and ignore year-end accruals.

SE 3.

LO 3 **Journal Entries for**
LO 5 **Interest Using the**
LO 6 **Effective Interest Method**

On March 1, 20xx, River Front Freight Company sold $100,000 of its 9.5 percent, 20-year bonds at 106. The semiannual interest payment dates are March 1 and September 1. The effective interest rate is approximately 8.9 percent. The company's fiscal year ends August 31. Prepare journal entries to record the sale of the bonds on March 1, the accrual of interest and amortization of premium on August 31, and the first interest payment on September 1. Use the effective interest method to amortize the premium.

SE 4.

LO 4 **Valuing Bonds Using**
Present Value

Mine-Mart, Inc., is considering the sale of two bond issues. Choice A is a $400,000 bond issue that pays semiannual interest of $32,000 and is due in 20 years. Choice B is a $400,000 bond issue that pays semiannual interest of $30,000 and is due in 15 years. Assume that the market rate of interest for each bond is 12 percent. Calculate the amount that Mine-Mart, Inc., will receive if both bond issues occur. (Calculate the present value of each bond issue and sum.)

SE 5.

LO 3 **Journal Entries for Bond**
LO 6 **Issues**

Macrofilm Company is authorized to issue $900,000 in bonds on June 1. The bonds carry a face interest rate of 8 percent, with interest to be paid on June 1 and December 1. Prepare journal entries for the issue of the bonds under the independent assumptions that (a) the bonds are issued on September 1 at 100 and (b) the bonds are issued on June 1 at 103.

SE 6.

LO 6 **Sale of Bonds Between**
Interest Dates

Tripp Corporation sold $200,000 of 9 percent, ten-year bonds for face value on September 1, 20xx. The issue date of the bonds was May 1, 20xx. The company's fiscal year ends on December 31, and this is its only bond issue. Record the sale of the bonds on September 1 and the first semiannual interest payment on November 1, 20xx. What is the bond interest expense for the year ended December 31, 20xx?

SE 7.

LO 3 **Year-End Accrual of**
LO 5 **Bond Interest**
LO 6

On October 1, 20x1, Alexus Corporation issued $500,000 of 9 percent bonds at 96. The bonds are dated October 1 and pay interest semiannually. The market rate of interest is 10 percent, and the company's year end is December 31. Prepare the entries to record the issuance of the bonds, the accrual of the interest on December 31, 20x1, and the payment of the first semiannual interest on April 1, 20x2. Assume that the company does not use reversing entries and uses the effective interest method to amortize the bond discount.

SE 8.

LO 7 **Journal Entry for Bond**
Retirement

The Falstaf Corporation has outstanding $800,000 of 8 percent bonds callable at 104. On December 1, immediately after the payment of the semiannual interest and the amortization of the bond discount were recorded, the unamortized bond discount equaled $21,000. On that date, $480,000 of the bonds were called and retired. Prepare the entry to record the retirement of the bonds on December 1.

SE 9.

LO 7 **Journal Entry for Bond**
Conversion

The Degas Corporation has $1,000,000 of 6 percent bonds outstanding. There is $20,000 of unamortized discount remaining on the bonds after the March 1, 20x2, semiannual interest payment. The bonds are convertible at the rate of 20 shares of $10 par value common stock for each $1,000 bond. On March 1, 20x2, bondholders presented $600,000 of the bonds for conversion. Prepare the journal entry to record the conversion of the bonds.

SE 10.

LO 8 **Mortgage Payable**

Sternberg Corporation purchased a building by signing a $300,000 long-term mortgage with monthly payments of $2,400. The mortgage carries an interest rate of 8 percent. Prepare a monthly payment schedule showing the monthly payment, the interest for the month, the reduction in debt, and the unpaid balance for the first three months. (Round to the nearest dollar.)

EXERCISES

E 1.

LO 1 Interest Coverage Ratio

Compute the interest coverage ratios for 20x1 and 20x2 from the partial income statements of Treefarm Company:

	20x2	20x1
Income from operations	$23,890	$18,460
Interest expense	5,800	3,300
Income before income taxes	$18,090	$15,160
Income taxes	5,400	4,500
Net income	$12,690	$10,660

E 2.

LO 3 Journal Entries for
LO 5 Interest Using the Straight-
Line Method

Mizray Corporation issued $4,000,000 in 10.5 percent, ten-year bonds on February 1, 20x1, at 104. The semiannual interest payment dates are February 1 and August 1.

Prepare journal entries for the issue of bonds by Mizray on February 1, 20x1, and the first two interest payments on August 1, 20x1, and February 1, 20x2. Use the straight-line method and ignore year-end accruals.

E 3.

LO 3 Journal Entries for
LO 5 Interest Using the Straight-
Line Method

Collins Corporation issued $8,000,000 in 8.5 percent, five-year bonds on March 1, 20x1, at 96. The semiannual interest payment dates are March 1 and September 1.

Prepare journal entries for the issue of the bonds by Collins on March 1, 20x1, and the first two interest payments on September 1, 20x1, and March 1, 20x2. Use the straight-line method and ignore year-end accruals.

E 4.

LO 3 Journal Entries for
LO 5 Interest Using the
LO 6 Effective Interest Method

The Wooden Toy Company sold $500,000 of 9.5 percent, 20-year bonds on April 1, 20xx, at 106. The semiannual interest payment dates are April 1 and October 1. The effective interest rate is approximately 8.9 percent. The company's fiscal year ends September 30.

Prepare journal entries to record the sale of the bonds on April 1, the accrual of interest and amortization of premium on September 30, and the first interest payment on October 1. Use the effective interest method to amortize the premium.

E 5.

LO 3 Journal Entries for
LO 5 Interest Using the
LO 6 Effective Interest Method

On March 1, 20x1, the Herring Corporation issued $1,200,000 of 10 percent, five-year bonds. The semiannual interest payment dates are March 1 and September 1. Because the market rate for similar investments was 11 percent, the bonds had to be issued at a discount. The discount on the issuance of the bonds was $48,670. The company's fiscal year ends February 28.

Prepare journal entries to record the bond issue on March 1, 20x1; the payment of interest and the amortization of the discount on September 1, 20x1; the accrual of interest and the amortization of the discount on February 28, 20x2; and the payment of interest on March 1, 20x2. Use the effective interest method. (Round answers to the nearest dollar.)

E 6.

LO 4 Valuing Bonds Using
Present Value

Kitchens, Inc., is considering the sale of two bond issues. Choice A is an $800,000 bond issue that pays semiannual interest of $64,000 and is due in 20 years. Choice B is an $800,000 bond issue that pays semiannual interest of $60,000 and is due in 15 years. Assume that the market interest rate for each bond is 12 percent.

Calculate the amount that Kitchens, Inc., will receive if both bond issues are made. (Hint: Calculate the present value of each bond issue and sum.)

E 7.

LO 4 Valuing Bonds Using
Present Value

Use the present value tables in the appendix on future value and present value tables to calculate the issue price of a $1,200,000 bond issue in each of the following independent cases, assuming that interest is paid semiannually.

a. A ten-year, 8 percent bond issue; the market interest rate is 10 percent.
b. A ten-year, 8 percent bond issue; the market interest rate is 6 percent.
c. A ten-year, 10 percent bond issue; the market interest rate is 8 percent.
d. A 20-year, 10 percent bond issue; the market interest rate is 12 percent.
e. A 20-year, 10 percent bond issue; the market interest rate is 6 percent.

E 8.

LO 4 Zero Coupon Bonds

The state of Arkansas needs to raise $100,000,000 for highway repairs. Officials are considering issuing zero coupon bonds, which do not require periodic interest payments. The current market interest rate for the bonds is 10 percent. What face value of bonds must be issued to raise the needed funds, assuming the bonds will be due in 30 years and compounded annually? How would your answer change if the bonds were due in 50 years? How would both answers change if the market interest rate were 8 percent instead of 10 percent?

E 9.

LO 5 Journal Entries for
LO 6 Interest Payments Using
the Effective Interest
Method

The long-term debt section of the Garcia Corporation's balance sheet at the end of its fiscal year, December 31, 2001, was as follows:

Long-Term Liabilities		
Bonds Payable—8%, interest payable		
1/1 and 7/1, due 12/31/13	$1,000,000	
Less Unamortized Bond Discount	80,000	$920,000

Prepare the journal entries relevant to the interest payments on July 1, 2002, December 31, 2002, and January 1, 2003. Assume an effective interest rate of 10 percent.

E 10.

LO 3 Journal Entries for Bond
LO 6 Issue

Speaker Symphonics, Inc., is authorized to issue $1,800,000 in bonds on June 1. The bonds carry a face interest rate of 9 percent, which is to be paid on June 1 and December 1.

Prepare journal entries for the issue of the bonds by Speaker Symphonics, Inc., under the assumptions that (a) the bonds are issued on September 1 at 100 and (b) the bonds are issued on June 1 at 105.

E 11.

LO 6 Sale of Bonds Between
Interest Dates

Daniel Corporation sold $400,000 of 12 percent, ten-year bonds at face value on September 1, 20xx. The issue date of the bonds was May 1, 20xx.

1. Record the sale of the bonds on September 1 and the first semiannual interest payment on November 1, 20xx.

2. The company's fiscal year ends on December 31 and this is its only bond issue. What is the bond interest expense for the year ended December 31, 20xx?

E 12.

LO 3 Year-End Accrual of
LO 5 Bond Interest
LO 6

Sao Corporation issued $1,000,000 of 9 percent bonds on October 1, 20x1, at 96. The bonds are dated October 1 and pay interest semiannually. The market interest rate is 10 percent, and the company's fiscal year ends on December 31.

Prepare the entries to record the issuance of the bonds, the accrual of the interest on December 31, 20x1, and the first semiannual interest payment on April 1, 20x2. Assume the company does not use reversing entries and uses the effective interest method to amortize the bond discount.

E 13.

LO 4 Time Value of Money and
LO 7 Early Extinguishment of
Debt

Rupp, Inc., has a $1,400,000, 8 percent bond issue that was issued a number of years ago at face value. There are now ten years left on the bond issue, and the market interest rate is 16 percent. Interest is paid semiannually.

1. Using present value tables, figure the current market value of the bond issue.

2. Record the retirement of the bonds, assuming the company purchases the bonds on the open market at the calculated value.

E 14.

LO 7 Journal Entry for Bond
Retirement

The Berman Corporation has outstanding $1,600,000 of 8 percent bonds callable at 104. On September 1, immediately after recording the payment of the semiannual interest and the amortization of the discount, the unamortized bond discount equaled $42,000. On that date, $960,000 of the bonds were called and retired.

Prepare the entry to record the retirement of the bonds on September 1.

E 15.

LO 7 Journal Entry for Bond
Conversion

The Imaoka Corporation has $400,000 of 6 percent bonds outstanding. There is $20,000 of unamortized discount remaining on these bonds after the July 1, 20x8, semiannual interest payment. The bonds are convertible at the rate of 40 shares of $5 par value common stock for each $1,000 bond. On July 1, 20x8, bondholders presented $300,000 of the bonds for conversion.

Prepare the journal entry to record the conversion of the bonds.

E 16.

LO 8 Mortgage Payable

Stars Corporation purchased a building by signing a $150,000 long-term mortgage with monthly payments of $2,000. The mortgage carries an interest rate of 12 percent.

1. Prepare a monthly payment schedule showing the monthly payment, the interest for the month, the reduction in debt, and the unpaid balance for the first three months. (Round to the nearest dollar.)

2. Prepare journal entries to record the purchase and the first two monthly payments.

E 17.
LO 8 Recording Lease Obligations

Island Corporation has leased a piece of equipment that has a useful life of 12 years. The terms of the lease are $43,000 per year for 12 years. Island currently is able to borrow money at a long-term interest rate of 15 percent. (Round answers to the nearest dollar.)

1. Calculate the present value of the lease.

2. Prepare the entry to record the lease agreement.

3. Prepare the entry to record depreciation of the equipment for the first year using the straight-line method.

4. Prepare the entries to record the lease payments for the first two years.

E 18.
LO 8 Installment Notes Payable: Unequal Payments

Assume that on December 31, 20x1, $40,000 is borrowed on a 12 percent installment note, to be paid annually over four years. Prepare the entry to record the note and the first two annual payments, assuming that the principal is paid in equal annual installments and the interest on the unpaid balance accrues annually. How would your answer change if the interest rate rose to 13 percent in 20x3?

E 19.
LO 8 Installment Notes Payable: Equal Payments

Assume that on December 31, 20x1, $40,000 is borrowed on a 12 percent installment note, to be paid in equal annual payments over four years. Calculate to the nearest dollar the amount of each equal payment, using Table 4 from the appendix on future value and present value tables. Prepare a payment schedule table similar to Table 4 in the text, and record the first two annual payments.

PROBLEMS

P 1.
LO 3 Bond Transactions—
LO 5 Straight-Line Method
LO 6

Abel Corporation has $10,000,000 of 10.5 percent, 20-year bonds dated June 1, with interest payment dates of May 31 and November 30. The company's fiscal year ends on December 31. It uses the straight-line method to amortize bond premiums or discounts.

REQUIRED

1. Assume the bonds are issued at 103 on June 1. Prepare journal entries for June 1, November 30, and December 31.

2. Assume the bonds are issued at 97 on June 1. Prepare journal entries for June 1, November 30, and December 31.

3. Assume the bonds are issued at face value plus accrued interest on August 1. Prepare journal entries for August 1, November 30, and December 31.

P 2.
LO 3 Bond Transactions—
LO 5 Effective Interest
LO 6 Method

Julio Corporation has $8,000,000 of 9.5 percent, 25-year bonds dated March 1, with interest payable on March 1 and September 1. The company's fiscal year ends on November 30. It uses the effective interest method to amortize bond premiums or discounts. (Round amounts to the nearest dollar.)

REQUIRED

1. Assume the bonds are issued at 102.5 on March 1 to yield an effective interest rate of 9.2 percent. Prepare journal entries for March 1, September 1, and November 30.

2. Assume the bonds are issued at 97.5 on March 1 to yield an effective interest rate of 9.8 percent. Prepare journal entries for March 1, September 1, and November 30.

3. Assume the bonds are issued on June 1 at face value plus accrued interest. Prepare journal entries for June 1, September 1, and November 30.

P 3.
LO 3 Bonds Issued at a
LO 5 Discount and a Premium
LO 6

Waxman Corporation issued bonds twice during 20x2. A summary of the transactions involving the bonds follows.

20x2

Jan. 1 Issued $6,000,000 of 9.9 percent, ten-year bonds dated January 1, 20x2, with interest payable on June 30 and December 31. The bonds were sold at 102.6, resulting in an effective interest rate of 9.4 percent.

Mar. 1 Issued $4,000,000 of 9.2 percent, ten-year bonds dated March 1, 20x2, with interest payable March 1 and September 1. The bonds were sold at 98.2, resulting in an effective interest rate of 9.5 percent.

June 30 Paid semiannual interest on the January 1 issue and amortized the premium, using the effective interest method.

Sept. 1 Paid semiannual interest on the March 1 issue and amortized the discount, using the effective interest method.

Dec. 31 Paid semiannual interest on the January 1 issue and amortized the premium, using the effective interest method.

31 Made an end-of-year adjusting entry to accrue interest on the March 1 issue and to amortize two-thirds of the discount applicable to the second interest period.

20x3

Mar. 1 Paid semiannual interest on the March 1 issue and amortized the remainder of the discount applicable to the second interest period.

REQUIRED

Prepare journal entries to record the bond transactions. (Round amounts to the nearest dollar.)

P 4.

LO 3 Bond Interest and
LO 5 Amortization Table
LO 7 and Bond Retirements

In 20x1, the Fender Corporation was authorized to issue $60,000,000 of six-year unsecured bonds. The bonds carried a face interest rate of 9 percent, payable semiannually on June 30 and December 31. The bonds were callable at 105 any time after June 30, 20x4. All of the bonds were issued on July 1, 20x1 at 95.568, a price yielding an effective interest rate of 10 percent. On July 1, 20x4, the company called and retired half the outstanding bonds.

REQUIRED

1. Prepare a table similar to Table 1 to show the interest and amortization of the bond discount for 12 interest payment periods, using the effective interest method. (Round results to the nearest dollar.)

2. Calculate the amount of loss on early retirement of one-half of the bonds on July 1, 20x4.

P 5.

LO 3 Comprehensive
LO 5 Bond Transactions
LO 6
LO 7

The Katz Corporation, a company whose fiscal year ends on June 30, engaged in the following long-term bond transactions over a three-year period:

20x3

Nov. 1 Issued $40,000,000 of 12 percent debenture bonds at face value plus accrued interest. Interest is payable on January 31 and July 31, and the bonds are callable at 104.

20x4

Jan. 31 Made the semiannual interest payment on the 12 percent bonds.

June 30 Made the year-end accrual of interest payment on the 12 percent bonds.

July 1 Issued $20,000,000 of 10 percent, 15-year convertible bonds at 105. Interest is payable on June 30 and December 31, and each $1,000 bond is convertible into 30 shares of $10 par value common stock. The market rate of interest is 9 percent.

31 Made the semiannual interest payment on the 12 percent bonds.

Dec. 31 Made the semiannual interest payment on the 10 percent bonds and amortized the bond premium.

20x5

Jan. 31 Made the semiannual interest payment on the 12 percent bonds.

Feb. 28 Called and retired all of the 12 percent bonds, including accrued interest.

June 30 Made the semiannual interest payment on the 10 percent bonds and amortized the bond premium.

July 1 Accepted for conversion into common stock all of the 10 percent bonds.

REQUIRED Prepare journal entries to record the bond transactions, making all necessary accruals and using the effective interest method. (Round all calculations to the nearest dollar.)

ALTERNATE PROBLEMS

P 6.

LO 3 **Bond Transactions—**
LO 5 **Straight-Line Method**
LO 6

REQUIRED

Bassi Corporation has $8,000,000 of 9.5 percent, 25-year bonds dated March 1, with interest payable on March 1 and September 1. The company's fiscal year ends on November 30, and it uses the straight-line method to amortize bond premiums or discounts.

1. Assume the bonds are issued at 103.5 on March 1. Prepare journal entries for March 1, September 1, and November 30.

2. Assume the bonds are issued at 96.5 on March 1. Prepare journal entries for March 1, September 1, and November 30.

3. Assume the bonds are issued on June 1 at face value plus accrued interest. Prepare journal entries for June 1, September 1, and November 30.

P 7.

LO 3 **Bond Transactions—**
LO 5 **Effective Interest Method**
LO 6

REQUIRED

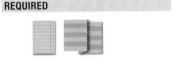

Khan Corporation has $20,000,000 of 10.5 percent, 20-year bonds dated June 1, with interest payment dates of May 31 and November 30. The company's fiscal year ends December 31. It uses the effective interest method to amortize bond premiums or discounts. (Round amounts to the nearest dollar.)

1. Assume the bonds are issued at 103 on June 1 to yield an effective interest rate of 10.1 percent. Prepare journal entries for June 1, November 30, and December 31.

2. Assume the bonds are issued at 97 on June 1 to yield an effective interest rate of 10.9 percent. Prepare journal entries for June 1, November 30, and December 31.

3. Assume the bonds are issued at face value plus accrued interest on August 1. Prepare journal entries for August 1, November 30, and December 31.

P 8.

LO 3 **Bonds Issued at a**
LO 5 **Discount and a Premium**
LO 6

Pakesh Corporation issued bonds twice during 20x1. The transactions were as follows:

20x1
Jan. 1   Issued $2,000,000 of 9.2 percent, ten-year bonds dated January 1, 20x1, with interest payable on June 30 and December 31. The bonds were sold at 98.1, resulting in an effective interest rate of 9.5 percent.

Apr. 1   Issued $4,000,000 of 9.8 percent, ten-year bonds dated April 1, 20x1, with interest payable on March 31 and September 30. The bonds were sold at 102, resulting in an effective interest rate of 9.5 percent.

June 30   Paid semiannual interest on the January 1 issue and amortized the discount, using the effective interest method.

Sept. 30   Paid semiannual interest on the April 1 issue and amortized the premium, using the effective interest method.

Dec. 31   Paid semiannual interest on the January 1 issue and amortized the discount, using the effective interest method.

      31   Made an end-of-year adjusting entry to accrue interest on the April 1 issue and to amortize half the premium applicable to the second interest period.

20x2
Mar. 31   Paid semiannual interest on the April 1 issue and amortized the premium applicable to the second half of the second interest period.

REQUIRED   Prepare journal entries to record the bond transactions. (Round amounts to the nearest dollar.)

EXPANDING YOUR CRITICAL THINKING, COMMUNICATION, AND INTERPERSONAL SKILLS

SKILLS DEVELOPMENT

Conceptual Analysis

SD 1.

LO 3 **Bond Interest Rates and Market Prices**

RJR Nabisco, Inc., is one of the largest food and tobacco companies. Among its long-term debt is a bond due in 2013 that carries a face interest rate of 9¼ percent. Recently this bond sold on the New York Stock Exchange at 113. Does this bond sell at a discount or a premium? Assuming the bond was originally issued at face value, have interest rates risen or declined since the date of issue? Do you expect the market rate of interest on this bond to be more or less than 9¼ percent? Does the current market price affect either the amount that the company pays in semiannual interest or the amount of interest expense for the same period? Explain your answers.

SD 2.

LO 5 **Nature of Zero Coupon Notes**

The Wall Street Journal reported, "Financially ailing **Trans World Airlines** has renegotiated its agreement to sell its 40 landing and takeoff slots and three gates at O'Hare International Airport to **American Airlines**." Instead of receiving a lump-sum cash payment in the amount of $162.5 million, TWA elected to receive a zero coupon note from American that would be paid off in monthly installments over a 20-year period. Since the 240 monthly payments total $500 million, TWA placed a value of $500 million on the note and indicated that the bankruptcy court would not have accepted the lower lump-sum cash payment. How does this zero coupon note differ from the zero coupon bonds described earlier in this chapter? Explain the difference between the $162.5 million cash payment and the $500 million note. Is TWA right in placing a $500 million price on the sale?[13]

SD 3.

LO 8 **Lease Financing**

Federal Express Corporation, known for overnight delivery and distribution of high-priority goods and documents throughout the world, has an extensive fleet of aircraft and vehicles. In its 1998 annual report, the company stated that it "utilizes certain aircraft, land, facilities, and equipment under capital and operating leases which expire at various dates through 2025. In addition, supplemental aircraft are leased under agreements which generally provide for cancellation upon 30 days' notice." The annual report further stated that the minimum commitments for capital leases and noncancelable operating leases for 1999 were $15,023,000 and $960,482,000, respectively.[14] What is the difference between a capital lease and an operating lease? How do the accounting procedures for the two types of leases differ? How do you interpret management's reasoning in placing some aircraft under capital leases and others under operating leases? Why do you think the management of FedEx leases most of its aircraft instead of buying them?

Ethical Dilemma

SD 4.

LO 2 **Bond Indenture and Ethical Reporting**

Celltech Corporation, a biotech company, has a $24,000,000 bond issue outstanding that has several restrictive provisions in its bond indenture. Among them are requirements that current assets exceed current liabilities by a ratio of 2 to 1 and that income

Cash Flow	CD-ROM	Communication	Critical Thinking	Ethics	General Ledger	Group Activity	Hot Links to Real Companies	International	Internet	Key Ratio	Memo	Spreadsheet

before income taxes exceed the annual interest on the bonds by a ratio of 3 to 1. If those requirements are not met, the bondholders can force the company into bankruptcy. The company is still awaiting Food and Drug Administration (FDA) approval of its new product CMZ-12, a cancer treatment drug. Management had been counting on sales of CMZ-12 this year to meet the provisions of the bond indenture. As the end of the fiscal year approaches, the company does not have sufficient current assets or income before taxes to meet the requirements. Roger Landon, the chief financial officer, proposes, "Since we can assume that FDA approval will occur early next year, I suggest we book sales and receivables from our major customers now in anticipation of next year's sales. This action will increase our current assets and our income before taxes. It is essential that we do this to save the company. Look at all the people who will be hurt if we don't do it." Is Landon's proposal acceptable accounting? Is it ethical? Who could be harmed by it? What steps might management take?

Research Activity

SD 5.

LO 3 Reading the Bond Markets

Obtain a copy of a recent issue of *The Wall Street Journal* from your school or local library. Or, if you have access to an Internet service, visit *The Wall Street Journal's* home page. In the newspaper, find Section C, "Money & Investing," and turn to the page where the New York Exchange Bonds are listed. Notice, first, the Dow Jones Bond Averages of 20 bonds, ten utilities, and ten industrials. Are the averages above or below 100? Is this a premium or a discount? Is the market interest rate above or below the face rate of the average bond? Now, identify three bonds from those listed. Choose one that sells at a discount, one that sells at a premium, and one that sells for approximately 100. For each bond, write the name of the company, the face interest rate, the year the bond is due, the current yield, and the current closing market price. (Some bonds have the letters *cv* in the Yield column. This means the bonds are convertible into common stock and the yield may not be meaningful.) For each bond, explain the relationships between the face interest rate, the current yield, and the closing price. What other factors affect the current yield of a bond? Be prepared to discuss your findings in class.

Decision-Making Practice

SD 6.

LO 1 Issuance of Long-Term
LO 2 Bonds Versus Leasing
LO 8

The *Weiss Chemical Corporation* plans to build or lease a new plant that will produce liquid fertilizer for the agricultural market. The plant is expected to cost $800,000,000 and will be located in the southwestern United States. The company's chief financial officer, Sharon Weiss, has spent the last several weeks studying different means of financing the plant. From her talks with bankers and other financiers, she has decided that there are two basic choices: The plant can be financed through the issuance of a long-term bond or through a long-term lease. Details for the two options are given below.

a. Issue $800,000,000 of 25-year, 16 percent bonds secured by the new plant. Interest on the bonds would be payable semiannually.
b. Sign a 25-year lease for an existing plant calling for lease payments of $65,400,000 on a semiannual basis.

Weiss wants to know what the effect of each choice will be on the company's financial statements. She estimates that the useful life of the plant is 25 years, at which time it is expected to have an estimated residual value of $80,000,000.

Weiss plans a meeting to discuss the alternatives. Prepare a short memorandum to her identifying the issues that should be considered in making this decision. (**Note:** You are not asked to make any calculations, discuss the factors, or recommend an action.)

FINANCIAL REPORTING AND ANALYSIS

Interpreting Financial Reports

FRA 1.

**LO 4   Valuing Bonds Using
Present Value**

REQUIRED

International Paper Company has 9 percent bonds due in 2004 (in four years) and 9 percent bonds due in 2014 (in 14 years).[15]

Using present value tables and assuming a current market interest rate of 8 percent, calculate the market value of $100,000,000 of each bond issue. Interest is paid semiannually. Will these bonds sell in the market at a premium or a discount? Explain. Also tell why there is a difference in the market value of the two issues.

FRA 2.

**LO 7   Characteristics of
Convertible Debt**

REQUIRED

Amazon.com, Inc., gained renown as an online marketplace for books, records, and other products. Its stock price has risen greatly but the company has yet to earn a profit. To support its enormous growth, the company issued $1,250,000,000 in 4¾ percent convertible notes due in 2009 at face value. Interest is payable on February 1 and August 1. The notes are convertible into common stock at a price of $156 per share, which is 27 percent above the market price of $123 for the common stock on the date of issue. The market value of Amazon.com's common stock has been quite volatile. Earlier it was $200 per share.[16]

What reasons can you suggest for Amazon.com's management choosing notes that are convertible into common stock rather than simply issuing nonconvertible notes or issuing common stock directly? Are there any disadvantages to this approach? If the price of the company's common stock returns to $200 per share, what would be the total theoretical value of the notes? If the holders of the notes were to elect to convert the notes into common stock, what would be the effect on the company's debt to equity ratio and what would be the effect on the percentage ownership of the company by other stockholders?

International Company

FRA 3.

**LO 1   Comparison of Interest
Coverage**

Japanese companies have historically relied more on debt financing and are more highly leveraged than U.S. companies. For instance, **NEC Corporation** and **Sanyo Electric Co.,** two large Japanese electronics companies, had debt to equity ratios of about 3.6 and 2.5, respectively, in 1998. From the selected data from the companies' annual reports below (in millions of yen), compute the interest coverage ratios for the two companies for the two years and comment on the riskiness of the companies and on the trends presented.

	NEC		Sanyo	
	1998	1997	1998	1997
Interest Expense	61,257	60,463	33,001	31,765
Income Before Income Taxes	90,993	121,222	38,267	41,486

Group Activity: Assign the two companies to different groups to calculate the ratios and discuss the results. Debrief by discussing the advantages and disadvantages of a debt-laden capital structure.

Toys "R" Us Annual Report

FRA 4.

LO 1   Business Practice, Long-
LO 8   Term Debt, and Leases

Refer to the Financial Statements and the Notes to Consolidated Financial Statements in the Toys "R" Us annual report and answer the following questions.

1. Is it the practice of Toys "R" Us to own or lease most of its property and equipment?

2. What proportion of total assets is financed with long-term debt? Calculate Toys "R" Us's interest coverage ratios for 1998 and 1999 and comment on the trend.

3. In what countries has Toys "R" Us incurred long-term debt? Which maturity date is farthest in the future?

4. Does Toys "R" Us lease property predominantly under capital leases or under operating leases? How much was rental expense for operating leases in 1999?

Fingraph® Financial Analyst™

FRA 5.

LO 1 **Long-Term Liabilities**
LO 2
LO 8

Select any two companies from the same industry on the Fingraph® Financial Analyst™ CD-ROM software.

1. In the annual reports for the companies you have selected, identify the long-term liabilities from the balance sheet and any reference to any long-term liabilities in the summary of significant accounting policies or notes to the financial statements. There is likely to be a separate note for each type of long-term liability. What are the most important current liabilities for each company? What are the most important long-term liabilities for each company?

2. Display and print in tabular and graphical form the Balance Sheet Analysis page. Prepare a table that compares the debt to equity and interest coverage ratios for both companies for two years.

3. Locate the statements of cash flows in the two companies' annual reports. Have the companies been increasing or decreasing their long-term debt? If increasing, what were each company's most important sources of long-term financing over the past two years? If decreasing, which liabilities are being decreased?

4. Find and read references to long-term liabilities in management's discussion and analysis in each annual report.

5. Write a one-page executive summary that highlights the most important types of long-term liabilities for these companies, identifies accounting policies for specific long-term liabilities, and compares the debt to equity and interest coverage trends of the two companies, including reference to management's assessment. Include the Fingraph® page and your table as an attachment to your report.

Internet Case

FRA 6.

LO 1 **Effect of Leases on**
LO 8 **Debt to Equity Ratio**

Go to the Needles Accounting Resource Center web site at http://college.hmco.com. Under Web links, go to the annual report at **United Airlines'** web site. Like most airlines United Airlines leases a portion of its aircraft used in daily operations. It also leases facilities at airport terminals. Within the most recent annual report disclosures, find the note disclosure on leases. Compare the dollar amount of operating leases (which are not on the balance sheet) with the total liabilities computed from the balance sheet. Does the amount of lease payments exceed the total liabilities? Compute the debt to equity ratio from the balance sheet. Discuss the impact these operating leases would have on the debt to equity ratio if these leases were reported on the balance sheet as an asset and a corresponding liability.

ENDNOTES

1. AT&T Corporation, *Annual Report*, 1998.
2. Susan Carey, "TWA Today Faces a Key Deadline on Senior Notes," *The Wall Street Journal*, March 3, 1995.
3. At the time this chapter was written, the market interest rates on corporate bonds were volatile. Therefore, the examples and problems in this chapter use a variety of interest rates to demonstrate the concepts.
4. Quentin Hardy, "Japanese Companies Need to Raise Cash, But First a Bond Market Must Be Built," *The Wall Street Journal*, October 20, 1992.
5. Quotations from *The Wall Street Journal*, May 21, 1999.
6. Bill Barnhart, "Bond Bellwether," *Chicago Tribune*, December 4, 1996.

7. A knowledge of present value concepts, as presented in the appendix on time value of money, is necessary to an understanding of this section.

8. Accounting Principles Board, *Opinion No. 21*, "Interest on Receivables and Payables" (New York: American Institute of Certified Public Accountants, 1971), par. 15.

9. *Statement of Financial Accounting Standards No. 13*, "Accounting for Leases" (Norwalk, Conn.: Financial Accounting Standards Board, 1976), par. 10.

10. Philip Morris Companies, Inc., *Annual Report*, 1998.

11. *Statement of Financial Accounting Standards No. 87*, "Employers' Accounting for Pensions" (Norwalk, Conn.: Financial Accounting Standards Board, 1985).

12. *Statement of Financial Accounting Standards No. 106*, "Employers' Accounting for Post-retirement Benefits Other Than Pensions" (Norwalk, Conn.: Financial Accounting Standards Board, 1990).

13. Stanley Ziemba, "TWA, American Revise O'Hare Gate Agreement," *The Wall Street Journal*, May 13, 1992.

14. FedEx Corporation, *Annual Report*, 1998.

15. International Paper Company, *Annual Report*, 1998.

16. Amazon.com, *Press Release*, January 28, 1999.

12

Contributed Capital

LEARNING OBJECTIVES

1 Identify and explain the management issues related to contributed capital.

2 Define start-up and organization costs and state their effects on financial reporting.

3 Identify the components of stockholders' equity.

4 Account for cash dividends.

5 Identify the characteristics of preferred stock, including the effect on distribution of dividends.

6 Account for the issuance of stock for cash and other assets.

7 Account for treasury stock.

8 Account for the exercise of stock options.

General Motors Corporation One way corporations raise new capital is by issuing stock. General Motors Corporation, a major automotive manufacturer, has issued common stock, including over $2.9 billion in a recent three-year period, as shown in the Financial Highlights from the statement of cash flows.[1]

What are some reasons General Motors' management chooses to satisfy some of its needs for new capital by issuing common stock? What are some disadvantages of this approach?

There are advantages to financing with common stock. First, financing with common stock is less risky than financing with bonds, because dividends on common stock are not paid unless the board of directors decides to pay them. In contrast, if the interest on bonds is not paid, a company can be forced into bankruptcy. Second, when a company does not pay a cash dividend, the cash generated by profitable operations can be invested in the company's operations. Third, and most important for General Motors, a company may need the proceeds of a common stock issue to improve the balance between liabilities and stockholders' equity. The company lost more than $23.5 billion in 1992, drastically reducing its stockholders' equity. However, by issuing common stock over the next several years, General Motors improved its debt to equity ratio and its credit rating.

On the other hand, issuing common stock has certain disadvantages. Unlike the interest on bonds, dividends paid on stock are not tax deductible. Furthermore, when it issues more stock, the corporation dilutes its ownership. This means that the current stockholders must yield some control to the new stockholders. It is important for accountants to understand the nature and characteristics of corporations as well as the process of accounting for a stock issue and other types of stock transactions.

Financial Highlights

(In millions of dollars)

	1999	1998	1997
Proceeds from issuing common stock	$2,005	$343	$614

Management Issues Related to Contributed Capital

OBJECTIVE

1 Identify and explain the management issues related to contributed capital

A **corporation** is defined as "a body of persons granted a charter legally recognizing them as a separate entity having its own rights, privileges, and liabilities distinct from those of its members."[2] In other words, a corporation is a legal entity separate and distinct from its owners.

VIDEO CASE

 Lotus Development Corporation

Objectives

- To become familiar with the advantages of a corporation, especially in equity financing.
- To identify the ways investors obtain return on investment in a corporation.
- To show how stock buybacks affect return on equity as a measure of profitability.

Background for the Case

The story of software giant Lotus Development Corporation is a prototype of the recent history of high-technology com-

panies. When Lotus was founded in the early 1980s, its landmark spreadsheet program Lotus 1-2-3 was an overnight sensation at corporations because of its ability to make rapid calculations based on mathematical relationships in large databases. Lotus 1-2-3 went far beyond the rudimentary spreadsheets that preceded it by incorporating a database module and graphics capability. In October 1983, investors stampeded for the company's initial public offering of 2.6 million shares at $18 per share for a total of $46.8 million. For several years the company had no real competition. By 1992, more than 11 million units of Lotus 1-2-3 had been sold, but the company was unable to solidify its position by developing any new blockbuster products. Microsoft gained on Lotus and eventually passed it with its spreadsheet program Excel. Finally, Lotus developed a hit "groupware" product called Lotus Notes, which boosts productivity by enabling co-workers to share information and work together electronically on complex tasks. The large audit firm Coopers & Lybrand (now PricewaterhouseCoopers), for example, networks more than 2,000 auditors all over the world and the knowledge of experts in various parts of the firm via Lotus Notes. Many

other big companies such as Ford, Unilever, and Citicorp (now Citigroup) are also using Lotus Notes successfully. The success of Lotus Notes attracted the notice of IBM, which had failed to develop its own groupware product. In 1995, IBM made a hostile takeover bid for Lotus and bought out the company. In fewer than 15 years, Lotus had gone from an intriguing startup to a mature company with sales of more than $1 billion and, finally, to a takeover candidate for a giant competitor.

For more information about Lotus, which is now a division of IBM, visit the company's or IBM's web site through the Needles Accounting Resource Center at: http://college.hmco.com

Required

View the video on Lotus Development Corporation that accompanies this book. As you are watching the video, take notes related to the following questions:

1. All corporations must raise equity capital in the form of common stock. In your own words, what is common stock? What is the relationship of par value to market value of the common stock? What is an initial public offering (IPO)? Why was this IPO important in Lotus's early history?

2. Investors in corporations desire to receive an adequate return on their investment. What are the ways investors can receive a return? In what way did Lotus's shareholders receive a return?

3. From 1991 to 1993, the Lotus board of directors authorized the repurchase of 7,700,000 shares of the company's approximately 44,000,000 shares. (1) What impact will the repurchase of these shares have on the investors' return? (2) What role did the takeover by IBM play in achieving an adequate return to Lotus shareholders?

4. Return on equity is a common measure of management's ability to meet the company's profitability goal. What role do common stock buybacks (purchases of treasury stock) play in the company's increasing return on equity?

The management of contributed capital is a critical component in the financing of a corporation. Important issues faced by management in the area of contributed capital are managing under the corporate form of business, using equity financing, determining dividend policies, and evaluating performance using return on equity.

Managing Under the Corporate Form of Business

Although there are fewer corporations than sole proprietorships and partnerships in the United States, the corporate form of business dominates the economy in total dollars of assets and output of goods and services. Corporations are well suited to today's trends toward large organizations, international trade, and professional management. Figure 1 illustrates the corporation's ability to raise large amounts of capital by showing the amount and sources of new funds raised by corporations over the last six years for which data are available. There were dramatic increases in the amount of funds raised after 1990. In 1997, the amount of new corporate capital was $1,291 billion, of which $1,139 billion, or 88 percent, came from new bond issues; $118 billion, or 9 percent, came from new common stock issues; and $34 billion, or 2.6 percent, came from preferred stock issues.

**Figure 1
Sources of Capital Raised
by Corporations in the
United States**

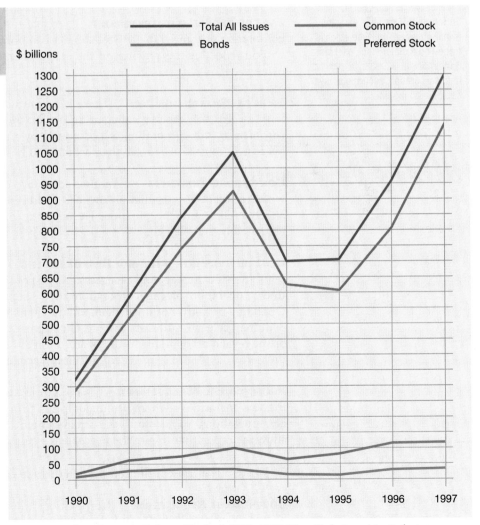

Source: Data from *Securities Industry Yearbook 1998–1999* (New York: Securities Industry Association, 1998), p. 978.

In managing the corporation, the advantages and disadvantages of this form of business must be taken into consideration. Some of the advantages of the corporation are described as follows.

SEPARATE LEGAL ENTITY   A corporation is a separate legal entity that has most of the rights of a person except those of voting and marrying. As such, a corporation can buy, sell, or own property; sue and be sued; enter into contracts; hire and fire employees; and be taxed.

LIMITED LIABILITY   Because a corporation is a separate legal entity, it is responsible for its own actions and liabilities. This means that a corporation's creditors can satisfy their claims only against the assets of the corporation, not against the personal property of the corporation's owners. Because the owners are not responsible for the corporation's debts, their liability is limited to the amount of their investment. The personal property of sole proprietors and partners, however, generally is available to creditors.

EASE OF CAPITAL GENERATION   It is fairly easy for a corporation to raise capital because shares of ownership in the business are available to a great number of potential investors for a small amount of money. As a result, a single corporation can be owned by many people.

EASE OF TRANSFER OF OWNERSHIP   A share of stock, a unit of ownership in a corporation, is transferable. A stockholder can normally buy and sell shares of stock without affecting the activities of the corporation or needing the approval of other owners.

LACK OF MUTUAL AGENCY   There is no mutual agency in the corporate form of business. If a stockholder, acting as an owner, tries to enter into a contract for the corporation, the corporation is not bound by the contract. But in a partnership, because of mutual agency, all the partners can be bound by one partner's actions.

CONTINUOUS EXISTENCE   Another advantage of the corporation's existence as a separate legal entity is that an owner's death, incapacity, or withdrawal does not affect the life of the corporation. The life of a corporation is set by its charter and regulated by state laws.

CENTRALIZED AUTHORITY AND RESPONSIBILITY   The board of directors represents the stockholders and delegates the responsibility and authority for the day-to-day operation of the corporation to a single person, usually the president. Operating power is not divided among the many owners of the business. The president may delegate authority over certain segments of the business to others, but he or she is held accountable to the board of directors. If the board is dissatisfied with the performance of the president, it can replace him or her.

PROFESSIONAL MANAGEMENT   Large corporations are owned by many people, the vast majority of whom are unequipped to make timely decisions about business operations. So, in most cases, management and ownership are separate. This allows a corporation to hire the best talent available to manage the business.

The disadvantages of the corporation include the following:

GOVERNMENT REGULATION   Corporations must meet the requirements of state laws. As "creatures of the state," corporations are subject to greater control and regulation by the state than are other forms of business. Corporations must file

Study Note: Lenders qualify a corporation for a loan as they would a person. If a corporation does not have a credit history or a good credit rating, a loan will not be granted in its name only. Others, such as the corporation's officers, will be required to co-sign the note and will therefore be personally liable.

Enrichment Note: It is easy to transfer ownership if the stock is traded on a major stock exchange. If the stock is issued by a closely held corporation, securing a buyer can take a long time.

BUSINESS FOCUS ON PRACTICE

To help with the initial issue of capital stock, called an initial public offering (IPO), a corporation often uses an underwriter—an intermediary between the corporation and the investing public. For a fee—usually less than 1 percent of the selling price—the underwriter guarantees the sale of the stock. The corporation records the amount of the net proceeds of the offering—what the public paid less the underwriter's fee, legal and printing expenses, and any other direct costs of the offering—in its capital stock and additional paid-in capital accounts. In one of the more unique IPOs, Goldman, Sachs, & Co., the renowned 130-year-old investment bank, went public in one of the largest IPOs ever of about $3.6 billion.

Enrichment Note: Some government agencies that regulate businesses are the Securities and Exchange Commission (SEC), the Occupational Safety and Health Administration (OSHA), the Federal Trade Commission (FTC), the Environmental Protection Agency (EPA), the Nuclear Regulatory Commission (NRC), the Equal Employment Opportunity Commission (EEOC), the Interstate Commerce Commission (ICC), the National Transportation Safety Board (NTSB), the Federal Aviation Administration (FAA), and the Federal Communications Commission (FCC).

many reports with the state in which they are chartered. Also, corporations that are publicly held must file reports with the Securities and Exchange Commission and with the stock exchanges. Meeting those requirements is very costly.

TAXATION A major disadvantage of the corporate form of business is **double taxation**. Because a corporation is a separate legal entity, its earnings are subject to federal and state income taxes, which may be as much as 35 percent of corporate earnings. If any of the corporation's after-tax earnings are then paid out as dividends, the earnings are taxed again as income to the stockholders. In contrast, the earnings of sole proprietorships and partnerships are taxed only once, as personal income to the owners.

LIMITED LIABILITY Above, we cited limited liability as an advantage of incorporation, but it also can be a disadvantage. Limited liability restricts the ability of a small corporation to borrow money. Because creditors can lay claim only to the assets of the corporation, they limit their loans to the level secured by those assets or ask stockholders to guarantee the loans personally.

SEPARATION OF OWNERSHIP AND CONTROL Just as limited liability can be a drawback, so can the separation of ownership and control. Sometimes management makes decisions that are not good for the corporation as a whole. Poor communication can also make it hard for stockholders to exercise control over the corporation or even to recognize that management's decisions are harmful.

Using Equity Financing

Key Point: In effect, the underwriter buys the stock from the corporation at a set price. The stock price in the secondary markets can be above or below the commitment to the corporation. Thus, the underwriter can gain or lose on the transaction and is exposed to a certain amount of risk.

A share of stock is a unit of ownership in a corporation. A **stock certificate** is issued to the owner. It shows the number of shares of the corporation's stock owned by the stockholder. Stockholders can transfer their ownership at will. When they do, they must sign their stock certificate and send it to the corporation's secretary. In large corporations that are listed on the organized stock exchanges, stockholders' records are hard to maintain. Such companies can have millions of shares of stock, thousands of which change ownership every day. Therefore, they often appoint independent registrars and transfer agents (usually banks and trust companies) to help perform the secretary's duties. The outside agents are responsible for transferring the corporation's stock, maintaining stockholders' records, preparing a list of stockholders for stockholders' meetings, and paying dividends.

When a corporation applies for a charter, the articles of incorporation specify the maximum number of shares of stock the corporation is allowed to issue. This number represents **authorized stock**. Most corporations are authorized to issue

Enrichment Note: Securing a large number of authorized shares of stock with the original articles of incorporation is wise for two reasons. First, additional shares can be offered at a later date without delay; second, additional time and money do not have to be spent amending the charter to increase the number of authorized shares.

Key Point: Par value is usually a small amount, $.01 up to $10. The amount is arbitrary and has primarily legal significance.

more shares of stock than are necessary at the time of organization, which allows for future stock issues to raise additional capital. For example, if a corporation plans to expand in the future, it will be able to sell the unissued shares of stock that were authorized in its charter. If a corporation immediately issues all of its authorized stock, it cannot issue more stock unless it applies to the state for a change in its charter.

The charter also shows the par value of the stock that has been authorized. **Par value** is an arbitrary amount assigned to each share of stock. It must be recorded in the capital stock accounts and constitutes the legal capital of a corporation. **Legal capital** equals the number of shares issued times the par value; it is the minimum amount that can be reported as contributed capital. Par value usually bears little if any relationship to the market value or book value of the shares. When a corporation is formed, a memorandum entry can be made in the general journal giving the number and description of authorized shares.

Determining Dividend Policies

A **dividend** is a distribution of a corporation's assets generated by past earnings to its stockholders. Each stockholder receives assets, usually cash, in proportion to the number of shares of stock held. The board of directors has sole authority to declare dividends, but the dividend policies are influenced by senior managers, who usually serve as members of the board. Receiving dividends from a corporation is one of the two ways stockholders can earn a return on their investment in the company. The other way is to sell their shares of stock for more than they paid for them. Investors evaluate the amount of dividends received with the ratio **dividends yield**. Dividends yield measures the current return to an investor in the form of dividends and is computed by dividing the dividends per share by the market price per share. For instance, the dividends yield (shown in Figure 2) for Abbott Laboratories, a large, successful pharmaceutical company, is computed as follows:

$$\text{Dividends Yield} = \frac{\text{Dividends per Share}}{\text{Market Price per Share}} = \frac{\$.68}{\$47.625} = 1.4\%$$

Figure 2
Stock Quotations on the New York Stock Exchange

NYSE COMPOSITE TRANSACTIONS

52 Weeks					Yld		Vol				Net
Hi	Lo	Stock	Sym	Div	%	PE	100's	Hi	Lo	Close	Chg
64¹/₁₆	32¹/₄	AT&T	T	.88	1.5	25	87587	59⁹/₁₆	58	59¹/₄	+ ¹¹/₁₆
21⁷/₈	12⁹/₁₆♦	AVX Cp	AVX	.26	1.2	44	1632	21⁷/₁₆	20⁷/₈	21	+ ¹/₁₆
80¹/₄	38¹/₄	AXA UAP	AXA	.90e	1.4	...	422	63⁷/₈	61³/₄	63³/₈	+1¹¹/₁₆
15¹/₄	1	AamesFnl	AAM	.10j	...	dd	1453	1¹¹/₁₆	1⁹/₁₆	1⁹/₁₆	− ¹/₈
23¹/₂	11¹/₈	AaronRent	RNT	.04	.2	16	652	18¹/₄	17³/₁₆	18	+ 1¹/₁₆
21	10⁹/₁₆	AaronRent A	RNTA	.04	.3	15	5	15⁵/₈	15⁵/₈	15⁵/₈	+ ¹/₈
27¹/₁₆	25⁵/₁₆	AbbeyNtl pfA		2.19	8.3	...	24	26¹/₂	26³/₈	26¹/₂	+ ¹/₁₆
53⁵/₁₆	35⁹/₁₆	AbbotLab	ABT	.68f	1.4	31	18210	48¹/₂	47⁵/₈	47⁵/₈	− ¹⁵/₁₆
101¹/₂	29¹/₂	Abercrombie A	ANF		...	40	9586	83³/₈	80¹⁵/₁₆	81⁵/₈	− ⁷/₁₆
15	7⁵/₈	Abitibi g	ABY	.40	...	...	1031	11¹/₄	11¹/₁₆	11³/₁₆	+ ³/₈
7¹⁵/₁₆	4³/₄♦	AcadiaRlty	AKR	.48	9.1	dd	74	5⁵/₁₆	5³/₁₆	5¹/₄	...
25⁵/₈	12¹/₁₆♦	Acceptlns	AIF		...	cc	247	15¹/₂	15³/₁₆	15⁷/₁₆	+ ⁷/₁₆
24⁷/₈	16¹/₂	AckrlyGp	AK	.02	.1	30	355	18¹/₄	17³/₄	18¹/₁₆	+ ³/₈
5⁷/₈	3¹⁵/₁₆	AcmeElec	ACE		...	10	35	5³/₄	5⁹/₁₆	5³/₄	− ¹/₁₆

Source: Republished with permission of *Wall Street Journal*, May 21, 1999; permission conveyed through Copyright Clearance Center, Inc.

To make available capital for European companies, a new series of exchanges are rising up around Europe. France's Nouveau Marche and Germany's Neuer Markt are two of four specialized markets set up by Europe's stock exchanges since 1996 to bring capital to cash-starved growth-stock companies. More than 160 companies have gone public via the "Euro new market" network. Unlike the United States, most of the ownership of these stocks are with individual investors, not institutional fund managers.[3]

Enrichment Note: Due to the rise in prices of stocks during the 1990s, the average dividends yield has declined and the average P/E ratio has increased.

Since the yield on corporate bonds exceeds 8 percent, the shareholders of Abbott Labs must expect some of their return to come from increases in the price of the shares. A measure of investors' confidence in a company's future is the **price/earnings (P/E) ratio**, which is calculated by dividing the market price per share by the earnings per share. The price/earnings ratio will vary as market price per share fluctuates daily and the amount of earnings per share changes. From Figure 2, the price/earnings ratio for Abbott Labs is 31 times, which was computed by using its most recent annual earnings per share, as follows:

$$\text{Price/Earnings (P/E) Ratio} = \frac{\text{Market Price per Share}}{\text{Earnings per Share}} = \frac{\$47.625}{\$1.54} = 31 \text{ times}$$

Since the market price is 31 times earnings, investors are paying what for most companies would be a high price in relation to earnings, expecting this drug company to continue its success. Caution must be taken in interpreting high P/E ratios because unusually low earnings can produce a high result.

Companies usually pay dividends to stockholders only when they have experienced profitable operations. For example, Apple Computer, Inc., paid a dividend beginning in 1987 but suspended its dividend payments in 1996 to conserve cash after large operating losses in 1995. Factors other than earnings affect the decision to pay dividends. First, the expected volatility of earnings is a factor. If a company has years of good earnings followed by years of poor earnings, the board may want to keep dividends low so as not to give a false impression of sustained high earnings. For years General Motors Corporation followed the practice of having a fairly stable dividend yield and paying a bonus dividend in especially good years. Second, the level of dividends affects cash flows. Some companies may not have the cash to pay higher dividends because operations are not generating cash at the level of earnings or because the companies are investing the cash in future operations. For instance, Abbott Labs pays a dividend of only $.68 per share in spite of earning $1.54 per share because management feels the cash generated by the earnings is better spent for other purposes, such as researching and developing new drugs that will generate revenue in the future. It is partly due to Abbott's investment in new products that stockholders are willing to pay a high price for Abbott Labs stock.

Evaluating Performance Using Return on Equity

The ratio **return on equity** is the most important ratio associated with the stockholders' equity section because it is a common measure of management's performance. For instance, when *Business Week* and *Forbes* rate companies on their success, return on equity is the major basis of this evaluation. Also, the compensation of top executives is often tied to return on equity benchmarks. This ratio is computed for Abbott Labs from information in the company's 1998 annual report, as follows:

$$\text{Return on Equity} = \frac{\text{Net Income}}{\text{Average Stockholders' Equity}}$$

$$= \frac{\$2,333,231,000}{(\$5,713,661,000 + \$4,998,677,000) \div 2}$$

$$= 43.6\%$$

> **Key Point:** A company can improve its return on equity by increasing net income or by reducing average stockholders' equity.

Abbott Labs' healthy return on equity of 43.6 percent depends, of course, on the amount of net income the company earns, but it also depends on the level of stockholders' equity. This level can be affected by management decisions. First, it depends on the amount of stock a company sells to the public. Management can keep the stockholders' equity at a minimum by financing the business with cash flows from operations and with debt instead of with stock. However, the use of debt to finance the business increases a company's risk because the interest and principal of the debt must be paid in a timely manner. In the case of common stock, dividends may be suspended if there is a cash shortage. Abbott Labs has a debt to equity ratio of over 1.4 and thus is taking advantage of the leverage provided by debt. Second, management can reduce the number of shares in the hands of the public by buying back its shares on the open market. The cost of these shares, which are called treasury stock, has the effect of reducing the amount of stockholders' equity and thereby increasing the return on equity. Many companies follow this practice instead of paying or increasing dividends because it puts money into the hands of stockholders in the form of market price appreciation without creating a commitment to higher dividends in the future. For example, during the three years ended 1998, Abbott Labs purchased its common stock at a cost of $2.7 billion.[4] Abbott Labs' stock repurchases improved the company's return on equity.

Start-up and Organization Costs

> **OBJECTIVE**
> **2** Define start-up and organization costs and state their effects on financial reporting

The costs of forming a corporation are called **start-up and organization costs**. Such costs, which are incurred before the corporation begins operations, include state incorporation fees and attorneys' fees for drawing up the articles of incorporation. They also include the cost of printing stock certificates, accountants' fees for services rendered in registering the firm's initial stock, and other expenditures necessary for forming the corporation.

> **Key Point:** Start-up and organization costs are expensed when incurred.

Theoretically, start-up and organization costs benefit the entire life of the corporation. For that reason, a case can be made for recording them as intangible assets and amortizing them over the years of the life of the corporation. However, the life of a corporation normally is not known, so accountants expense start-up and organization costs as they are incurred.[5]

Components of Stockholders' Equity

> **OBJECTIVE**
> **3** Identify the components of stockholders' equity

In a corporation's balance sheet, the owners' claims to the business are called stockholders' equity. Look at the sample stockholders' equity section of a balance sheet that follows.

Stockholders' Equity		
Contributed Capital		
Preferred Stock, $50 par value, 1,000 shares authorized, issued, and outstanding		$ 50,000
Common Stock, $5 par value, 30,000 shares authorized, 20,000 shares issued and outstanding	$100,000	
Paid-in Capital in Excess of Par Value, Common	50,000	150,000
Total Contributed Capital		$200,000
Retained Earnings		60,000
Total Stockholders' Equity		$260,000

Notice that the equity section of the corporate balance sheet is divided into two parts: (1) contributed capital and (2) retained earnings. Contributed capital represents the investments made by the stockholders in the corporation. Retained earnings are the earnings of the corporation since its inception, less any losses, dividends, or transfers to contributed capital. Retained earnings are not a pool of funds to be distributed to the stockholders; they represent, instead, earnings reinvested in the corporation.

In keeping with the convention of full disclosure, the contributed-capital part of the stockholders' equity section of the balance sheet gives a great deal of information about the corporation's stock: the kinds of stock; their par value; and the number of shares authorized, issued, and outstanding.

Common Stock

Key Point: A corporation may have more shares issued than it has outstanding because it has repurchased some shares, which are called *treasury stock.*

A corporation can issue two basic types of stock: common stock and preferred stock. If only one kind of stock is issued by the corporation, it is called **common stock**. Common stock is the company's **residual equity**. This means that all other creditors' and preferred stockholders' claims to the company's assets rank ahead of those of the common stockholders in case of liquidation. Because common stock is generally the only stock that carries voting rights, it represents the means of controlling the corporation.

The **issued stock** of a corporation is the shares sold or otherwise transferred to stockholders. For example, a corporation can be authorized to issue 500,000 shares of stock but may choose to issue only 300,000 shares when the company is organized. The holders of those 300,000 shares own 100 percent of the corporation. The remaining 200,000 shares of stock are unissued shares. No rights or privileges are associated with them until they are issued.

Outstanding stock is stock that has been issued and is still in circulation. A share of stock is not outstanding if the issuing corporation has repurchased it or if a stockholder has given it back to the company that issued it. So, a company can have more shares issued than are currently outstanding. Issued shares that are bought back and held by the corporation are called treasury stock, which we discuss in detail later in this chapter. The relationship of authorized, issued, unissued, outstanding, and treasury shares is illustrated in Figure 3.

Dividends

OBJECTIVE
4 Account for cash dividends

Dividends can be paid quarterly, semiannually, annually, or at other times decided on by the board. Most states do not allow the board to declare a dividend that

Figure 3
Relationship of Authorized, Unissued, Issued, Outstanding, and Treasury Shares

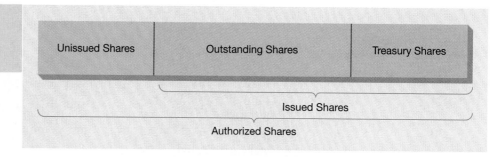

exceeds retained earnings. When a dividend that exceeds retained earnings is declared, the corporation is, in essence, returning to the stockholders part of their contributed capital. It is called a **liquidating dividend** and is usually paid when a company is going out of business or reducing its operations. Having sufficient retained earnings in itself does not justify the distribution of a dividend. If cash or other readily distributable assets are not available for distribution, the company might have to borrow money to pay a dividend—an action most boards of directors want to avoid.

There are three important dates associated with dividends. In order of occurrence, they are (1) the date of declaration, (2) the date of record, and (3) the date of payment. The **date of declaration** is the date on which the board of directors formally declares that a dividend is going to be paid. The **date of record** is the date on which ownership of the stock of a company, and therefore of the right to receive a dividend, is determined. Individuals who own the stock on the date of record will receive the dividend. Between that date and the date of payment, the stock is said to be **ex-dividend**. If one person sells the shares of stock to another, the right to the cash dividend remains with the first person; it does not transfer with the shares to the second person. The **date of payment** is the date on which the dividend is paid to the stockholders of record.

To illustrate the accounting for cash dividends, we assume that the board of directors has decided that sufficient cash is available to pay a $56,000 cash dividend to the common stockholders. The process has two steps. First, the board declares the dividend as of a certain date. Second, the dividend is paid. Assume that the dividend is declared on February 21, 20xx, for stockholders of record on March 1, 20xx, to be paid on March 11, 20xx. Here are the entries to record the declaration and payment of the cash dividend.

Enrichment Note: Some reasons that the board of directors of a corporation with sufficient cash and retained earnings might not declare a dividend include the following: the cash is needed for significant expansion; the board of directors wants to liquidate debt and improve the overall financial position of the company; there are major uncertainties threatening the corporation (such as a pending lawsuit or a possible work force strike); and the economy is poor and the board of directors decides it would be prudent to keep resources for difficult times.

Date of Declaration

A = L + OE	Feb. 21	Cash Dividends Declared	56,000	
+ −		Cash Dividends Payable		56,000
		Declaration of a cash dividend		
		to common stockholders		

Date of Record

Mar. 1 No entry is required. This date is used simply to determine the owners of the stock who will receive the dividends. After this date (starting March 2), the shares are ex-dividend.

Date of Payment

A = L + OE	Mar. 11	Cash Dividends Payable	56,000	
− −		Cash		56,000
		Payment of cash dividends		
		declared February 21		

Notice that the liability for the dividend is recorded on the date of declaration because the legal obligation to pay the dividend is established on that date. No entry is required on the date of record. The liability is liquidated, or settled, on the date of payment. The Cash Dividends Declared account is a temporary stockholders' equity account that is closed at the end of the accounting period by debiting Retained Earnings and crediting Cash Dividends Declared. Retained Earnings are thereby reduced by the total dividends declared during the period.

Some companies do not pay dividends. A company may not have any earnings. Or the cash generated by operations may need to be kept in the company for business purposes, perhaps expansion of the plant. Investors in growth companies expect a return on their investment in the form of an increase in the market value of their stock.

Preferred Stock

OBJECTIVE

5 Identify the characteristics of preferred stock, including the effect on distribution of dividends

The second kind of stock a company can issue is called **preferred stock**. Both common stock and preferred stock are sold to raise money. But investors in preferred stock have different investment goals from investors in common stock. In fact, a corporation may offer several different classes of preferred stock, each with distinctive characteristics to attract different investors. Preferred stock has preference over common stock in one or more areas. Most preferred stock has one or more of the following characteristics: preference as to dividends, preference as to assets of the business in liquidation, convertibility, and a callable option.

Key Point: Preferred stock may have many different characteristics. They are rarely exactly the same from company to company.

PREFERENCE AS TO DIVIDENDS Preferred stocks ordinarily have a preference over common stock in the receipt of dividends; that is, the holders of preferred shares must receive a certain amount of dividends before the holders of common shares can receive dividends. The amount that preferred stockholders must be paid before common stockholders can be paid is usually stated in dollars per share or as a percentage of the face value of the preferred shares. For example, a corporation can issue a preferred stock and pay an annual dividend of $4 per share, or it might issue a preferred stock at $50 par value and pay a yearly dividend of 8 percent of par value, also $4 per share.

Preferred stockholders have no guarantee of ever receiving dividends: The company must have earnings and the board of directors must declare dividends on preferred shares before any liability arises. The consequences of not declaring a dividend to preferred stockholders in the current year vary according to the exact terms under which the shares were issued. In the case of **noncumulative preferred stock**, if the board of directors fails to declare a dividend to preferred stockholders in a given year, the company is under no obligation to make up the missed dividend in future years. In the case of **cumulative preferred stock**, however, the fixed dividend amount per share accumulates from year to year, and the whole amount must be paid before any common dividends can be paid. Dividends not paid in the year they are due are called **dividends in arrears**.

Assume that a corporation has been authorized to issue 10,000 shares of $100 par value, 5 percent cumulative preferred stock, and that the shares have been issued and are outstanding. If no dividends were paid in 20x1, at the end of the year there would be preferred dividends of $50,000 (10,000 shares × $100 × .05 = $50,000) in arrears. If dividends are paid in 20x2, the preferred stockholders' dividends in arrears plus the 20x2 preferred dividends must be paid before any dividends on common stock can be paid.

Dividends in arrears are not recognized as liabilities because no liability exists until the board declares a dividend. A corporation cannot be sure it is going to make a profit. So, of course, it cannot promise dividends to stockholders. However, if a company has dividends in arrears, the amount should be reported either in the body of the financial statements or in a note. The following note appeared in a steel company's annual report.

> On January 1, 20xx, the company was in arrears by $37,851,000 ($1.25 per share) on dividends to its preferred stockholders. The company must pay all dividends in arrears to preferred stockholders before paying any dividends to common stockholders.

Suppose that on January 1, 20x1, a corporation issued 10,000 shares of $10 par, 6 percent cumulative preferred stock and 50,000 shares of common stock. The first year's operations resulted in income of only $4,000. The corporation's board of directors declared a $3,000 cash dividend to the preferred stockholders. The dividend picture at the end of 20x1 was as follows:

20x1 dividends due preferred stockholders ($100,000 × .06)	$6,000
Less 20x1 dividends declared to preferred stockholders	3,000
20x1 preferred stock dividends in arrears	$3,000

Now, suppose that in 20x2 the company earned income of $30,000 and wanted to pay dividends to both the preferred and the common stockholders. Because the preferred stock is cumulative, the corporation must pay the $3,000 in arrears on the preferred stock, plus the current year's dividends on its preferred stock, before it can distribute a dividend to the common stockholders. For example, assume that the corporation's board of directors declared a $12,000 dividend to be distributed to preferred and common stockholders. It would be distributed as follows:

20x2 declaration of dividends	$12,000
Less 20x1 preferred stock dividends in arrears	3,000
Available for 20x2 dividends	$ 9,000
Less 20x2 dividends due preferred stockholders ($100,000 × .06)	6,000
Remainder available to common stockholders	$ 3,000

And this is the journal entry when the dividend is declared:

A = L + OE				
+ −	Dec. 31	Cash Dividends Declared	12,000	
		Cash Dividends Payable		12,000
		Declaration of a $9,000 cash dividend to preferred stockholders and a $3,000 cash dividend to common stockholders		

Enrichment Note: Many companies that liquidate do not have enough assets to pay creditors. Consequently, there is nothing left for shareholders, common or preferred. Most companies that liquidate do so because business has been bad.

PREFERENCE AS TO ASSETS   Many preferred stocks have preference in terms of the assets of the corporation in the case of liquidation. If the corporation's existence is terminated, the preferred stockholders have a right to receive the par value of their stock or a larger stated liquidation value per share before the common stockholders receive any share of the company's assets. This preference can also include any dividends in arrears owed to the preferred stockholders.

CONVERTIBLE PREFERRED STOCK   A corporation can make its preferred stock more attractive to investors by adding convertibility. People who hold **convertible preferred stock** can exchange their shares of preferred stock for shares of the company's common stock at a ratio stated in the preferred stock contract. Convertibility appeals to investors for two reasons. First, like all preferred stock-

BUSINESS FOCUS ON PRACTICE

Preferred stock represents a flexible means of achieving goals that cannot be achieved with common stock. For example, Microsoft Corporation issued almost $1 billion in preferred stock even though the company probably did not need the cash.[6] Since Microsoft does not pay and has no plans to pay a dividend on its common stock, this preferred stock satisfies the desire of investors who want to own Microsoft stock but who want to buy stocks that pay a dividend. The preferred stock pays a fixed dividend and is convertible into common stock or convertible notes, or the company guarantees it can be redeemed at face value for cash in three years. In return for this flexibility and low risk, the possible gain of converting the preferred stock into common stock is limited to 25 to 30 percent. A Microsoft vice president says, "If you own the preferred, you get a dividend yield and downside protection, but the upside is capped."[7]

Enrichment Note: When a preferred shareholder converts to common stock, he or she gains voting rights but loses the dividend and liquidation preference. Conversion back to preferred stock is not an option.

holders, owners of convertible stock are more likely to receive regular dividends than are common stockholders. Second, if the market value of a company's common stock rises, the conversion feature allows the preferred stockholders to share in the increase. The rise in value would come either through increases in the value of the preferred stock or through conversion to common stock.

For example, suppose that a company issues 1,000 shares of 8 percent, $100 par value convertible preferred stock for $100 per share. Each share of stock can be converted into five shares of the company's common stock at any time. The market value of the common stock is now $15 per share. In the past, an owner of the common stock could expect dividends of about $1 per share per year. The owner of one share of preferred stock, on the other hand, now holds an investment that is approaching a value of $100 on the market and is more likely to receive dividends than is the owner of common stock.

Assume that in the next several years, the corporation's earnings increase, and the dividends paid to common stockholders also increase, to $3 per share. In addition, assume that the market value of a share of common stock rises from $15 to $30. Preferred stockholders can convert each of their preferred shares into five common shares and increase their dividends from $8 on each preferred share to the equivalent of $15 ($3 on each of five common shares). Furthermore, the market value of each share of preferred stock will be close to the $150 value of the five shares of common stock because each share can be converted into five shares of common stock.

CALLABLE PREFERRED STOCK   Most preferred stock is **callable preferred stock**. That is, it can be redeemed or retired at the option of the issuing corporation at a price stated in the preferred stock contract. A stockholder must surrender nonconvertible preferred stock to the corporation when asked to do so. If the preferred stock is convertible, the stockholder can either surrender the stock to the corporation or convert it into common stock when the corporation calls the stock. The *call price*, or redemption price, is usually higher than the par value of the stock. For example, a $100 par value preferred stock might be callable at $103 per share. When preferred stock is called and surrendered, the stockholder is entitled to (1) the par value of the stock, (2) the call premium, (3) any dividends in arrears, and (4) a portion of the current period's dividend, prorated by the proportion of the year to the call date.

A corporation may call its preferred stock for several reasons. First, the company may want to force conversion of the preferred stock to common stock because the cash dividend paid on the equivalent common stock is lower than the dividend paid on the preferred shares. Second, it may be possible to replace the outstanding preferred stock on the current market with a preferred stock at a lower dividend rate or with long-term debt, which can have a lower after-tax cost. Third, the company may simply be profitable enough to retire the preferred stock.

Retained Earnings

Retained earnings, the other component of stockholders' equity, represent stockholders' claims to the assets of the company resulting from profitable operations.

Accounting for Stock Issuance

OBJECTIVE

6 Account for the issuance of stock for cash and other assets

A share of capital stock may be either par or no-par. The value of par stock is stated in the corporate charter and must be printed on each share of stock. Par value can be $.10, $1, $5, $100, or any other amount established by the organizers of the corporation. The par values of common stocks tend to be lower than those of preferred stocks.

Par value is the amount per share that is entered into the corporation's capital stock accounts and that makes up the legal capital of the corporation. A corporation cannot declare a dividend that would cause stockholders' equity to fall below the legal capital of the firm. Therefore, the par value is a minimum cushion of capital that protects creditors. Any amount in excess of par value received from the issuance of stock is recorded in the Paid-in Capital in Excess of Par Value account and represents a portion of the company's contributed capital.

Key Point: Legal capital is the minimum amount that can be reported as contributed capital. For the protection of creditors, dividends cannot be declared that would reduce capital below the amount of legal capital.

No-par stock is capital stock that does not have a par value. There are several reasons for issuing stock without a par value. One is that some investors confuse par value with the market value of stock instead of recognizing it as an arbitrary figure. Another reason is that most states do not allow an original stock issue below par value and thereby limit a corporation's flexibility in obtaining capital.

No-par stock can be issued with or without a stated value. The board of directors of a corporation issuing no-par stock may be required by state law to place a **stated value** on each share of stock or may choose to do so as a matter of convenience. The stated value can be any value set by the board, although some states specify a minimum amount. The stated value can be set before or after the shares are issued if the state law is not specific.

If a company issues no-par stock without a stated value, all proceeds are recorded in the Capital Stock account. That amount becomes the corporation's legal capital unless a different amount is specified by state law. Because additional shares of the stock can be issued at different prices, the per-share credit to the Capital Stock account will not be uniform. This is a key way in which no-par stock without a stated value differs from par value stock or no-par stock with a stated value.

Key Point: When stock is issued with no par and no stated value, all proceeds represent legal capital and are recorded as capital stock. Because stock may be issued at different prices, the legal capital per share varies.

When no-par stock with a stated value is issued, the shares are recorded in the Capital Stock account at the stated value. Any amount that is received in excess of the stated value is recorded in the Paid-in Capital in Excess of Stated Value account. The amount in excess of the stated value is part of the corporation's contributed capital. However, the stated value is normally considered to be the legal capital of the corporation.

Par Value Stock

When par value stock is issued, the appropriate capital stock account (usually Common Stock or Preferred Stock) is credited for the par value regardless of whether the proceeds are more or less than the par value. For example, assume that Bradley Corporation is authorized to issue 20,000 shares of $10 par value common stock and actually issues 10,000 shares at $10 per share on January 1, 20xx. The entry to record the stock issue at par value would be as follows:

A = L + OE
+   +

Jan. 1	Cash	100,000	
	Common Stock		100,000
	Issued 10,000 shares of $10 par value common stock for $10 per share		

Cash is debited for $100,000 (10,000 shares × $10), and Common Stock is credited for an equal amount because the stock was sold for par value.

When stock is issued for a price greater than par, the proceeds in excess of par are credited to a capital account called Paid-in Capital in Excess of Par Value, Common. For example, assume that the 10,000 shares of Bradley common stock sold for $12 per share on January 1, 20xx. The entry to record the issuance of the stock at the price in excess of par value would be as follows:

A = L + OE
+   +
         +

Jan. 1	Cash	120,000	
	Common Stock		100,000
	Paid-in Capital in Excess of Par Value, Common		20,000
	Issued 10,000 shares of $10 par value common stock for $12 per share		

Key Point: Common Stock and Paid-in Capital in Excess of Par Value are separated for legal purposes. Their effect on the company's balance sheet is the same.

Cash is debited for the proceeds of $120,000 (10,000 shares × $12), and Common Stock is credited for the total par value of $100,000 (10,000 shares × $10). Paid-in Capital in Excess of Par Value, Common is credited for the difference of $20,000 (10,000 shares × $2). The amount in excess of par value is part of the corporation's contributed capital and will be included in the stockholders' equity section of the balance sheet. The stockholders' equity section for Bradley Corporation immediately following the stock issue would appear as follows:

Contributed Capital		
Common Stock, $10 par value, 20,000 shares authorized, 10,000 shares issued and outstanding	$100,000	
Paid-in Capital in Excess of Par Value, Common	20,000	
Total Contributed Capital	$120,000	
Retained Earnings	—	
Total Stockholders' Equity	$120,000	

If a corporation issues stock for less than par, an account called Discount on Capital Stock is debited for the difference. The issuance of stock at a discount rarely occurs because it is illegal in many states.

No-Par Stock

As mentioned earlier, stock can be issued without a par value. However, most states require that all or part of the proceeds from the issuance of no-par stock be designated as legal capital, which cannot be withdrawn except in liquidation. The purpose of this requirement is to protect the corporation's assets for creditors. Assume that Bradley Corporation's capital stock is no-par common and that 10,000 shares are issued on January 1, 20xx, at $15 per share. The $150,000 (10,000 shares × $15) in proceeds would be recorded as shown in the following entry.

A = L + OE
\+   \+

	Jan. 1	Cash	150,000	
		Common Stock		150,000
		Issued 10,000 shares of no-par		
		common stock for $15 per share		

Key Point: When no-par stock has a stated value, the stated value serves the same purpose as par value.

Because the stock does not have a stated or par value, all proceeds of the issue are credited to Common Stock and are part of the company's legal capital.

Most states allow the board of directors to put a stated value on no-par stock, and that value represents the corporation's legal capital. Assume that Bradley's board puts a $10 stated value on its no-par stock. The entry to record the issue of 10,000 shares of no-par common stock with a $10 stated value for $15 per share would appear as follows:

A = L + OE
\+   \+
        \+

	Jan. 1	Cash	150,000	
		Common Stock		100,000
		Paid-in Capital in Excess of		
		Stated Value, Common		50,000
		Issued 10,000 shares of no-par		
		common stock with $10 stated value		
		for $15 per share		

Notice that the legal capital credited to Common Stock is the stated value decided by the board of directors. Notice also that the account Paid-in Capital in Excess of Stated Value, Common is credited for $50,000. The $50,000 is the difference between the proceeds ($150,000) and the total stated value ($100,000). Paid-in Capital in Excess of Stated Value is presented on the balance sheet in the same way as Paid-in Capital in Excess of Par Value.

Issuance of Stock for Noncash Assets

Key Point: Even though the board of directors has the right to determine the fair market value of property that is exchanged for stock, it cannot establish the amount arbitrarily. It must do so in a prudent fashion, using all the information at its disposal.

Stock can be issued for assets or services other than cash. The problem is to determine the dollar amount that should be recorded for the exchange. The generally preferred rule is to record the transaction at the fair market value of what the corporation is giving up—in this case, the stock. If the fair market value of the stock cannot be determined, the fair market value of the assets or services received can be used. Transactions of this kind usually involve the use of stock to pay for land or buildings or for the services of attorneys and others who helped organize the company.

When there is an exchange of stock for noncash assets, the board of directors has the right to determine the fair market value of the property. Suppose that when Bradley Corporation was formed on January 1, 20xx, its attorney agreed to accept 100 shares of its $10 par value common stock for services rendered. At the time the stock was issued, its market value could not be determined. However, for similar services the attorney would have billed the company $1,500. The entry to record the noncash transaction is as follows:

A = L + OE
\+   \+
        \+

	Jan. 1	Start-up and Organization Expense	1,500	
		Common Stock		1,000
		Paid-in Capital in Excess of		
		Par Value, Common		500
		Issued 100 shares of $10 par		
		value common stock for attorney's		
		services		

Now suppose that two years later Bradley Corporation exchanged 1,000 shares of its $10 par value common stock for a piece of land. At the time of the exchange, the stock was selling on the market for $16 per share. The entry that follows records the exchange.

A = L + OE	Jan. 1	Land	16,000	
+ +		Common Stock		10,000
+		Paid-in Capital in Excess of		
		Par Value, Common		6,000
		Issued 1,000 shares of $10 par value		
		common stock with a market value		
		of $16 per share for a piece of land		

Treasury Stock

Treasury stock is capital stock, either common or preferred, that has been issued and later reacquired by the issuing company and has not subsequently been resold or retired. The company normally gets the stock back by purchasing the shares on the market.

It is common for companies to buy and hold their own stock. In a recent year, 387, or 65 percent, of six hundred large companies held treasury stock.[8] Although the purchase of treasury stock can be a severe drain on cash, a company may purchase its own stock for several reasons:

1. It may want stock to distribute to employees through stock option plans.
2. It may be trying to maintain a favorable market for its stock.
3. It may want to increase its earnings per share or stock price per share.
4. It may want to have additional shares of stock available for such activities as purchasing other companies.
5. It may want to prevent a hostile takeover.

Key Point: Treasury stock is not the same as unissued stock because treasury stock represents shares that have been issued but are no longer outstanding. Unissued shares, on the other hand, have never been in circulation.

A treasury stock purchase reduces the assets and stockholders' equity of the company. It is not considered a purchase of assets, as the purchase of shares in another company would be. Treasury stock is capital stock that has been issued but is no longer outstanding. Treasury shares can be held for an indefinite period of time, reissued, or retired. Like unissued stock, treasury stock has no rights until it is reissued. Treasury stock does not have voting rights, rights to cash dividends and stock dividends, or rights to share in assets during liquidation of the company, and it is not considered to be outstanding in the calculation of book value. However, there is one major difference between unissued shares and treasury shares: A share of stock that originally was issued at par value or greater and fully paid for, and that then was reacquired as treasury stock, can be reissued at less than par value without negative consequences.

PURCHASE OF TREASURY STOCK When treasury stock is purchased, it is normally recorded at cost. The transaction reduces both the assets and the stockholders' equity of the firm. For example, assume that on September 15 the Caprock Corporation purchases 1,000 shares of its common stock on the market at a price of $50 per share. The purchase would be recorded as follows:

A = L + OE	Sept. 15	Treasury Stock, Common	50,000	
− −		Cash		50,000
		Acquired 1,000 shares of the		
		company's common stock for		
		$50 per share		

Enrichment Note: Since treasury stock reduces equity, the return on equity will increase when treasury shares are purchased.

The treasury shares are recorded at cost. The par value, stated value, or original issue price of the stock is ignored.

The stockholders' equity section of Caprock's balance sheet (on the next page) shows the cost of the treasury stock as a deduction from the total of contributed capital and retained earnings.

Contributed Capital

Common Stock, $5 par value, 100,000 shares authorized,
30,000 shares issued, 29,000 shares outstanding $ 150,000

Paid-in Capital in Excess of Par Value, Common   30,000

Total Contributed Capital $ 180,000

Retained Earnings   900,000

Total Contributed Capital and Retained Earnings $1,080,000

Less Treasury Stock, Common (1,000 shares at cost)   50,000

Total Stockholders' Equity $1,030,000

Notice that the number of shares issued, and therefore the legal capital, has not changed, although the number of outstanding shares has decreased as a result of the transaction.

SALE OF TREASURY STOCK   Treasury shares can be sold at cost, above cost, or below cost. For example, assume that on November 15 the 1,000 treasury shares of the Caprock Corporation are sold for $50 per share. The following entry records the transaction:

A = L + OE
+   +

Nov. 15	Cash	50,000	
	Treasury Stock, Common		50,000
	Reissued 1,000 shares of treasury		
	stock for $50 per share		

> **Key Point:** Gains and losses on the reissue of treasury stock are never recognized as such. Instead, the accounts Retained Earnings and Paid-in Capital, Treasury Stock are used.

When treasury shares are sold for an amount greater than their cost, the excess of the sales price over cost should be credited to Paid-in Capital, Treasury Stock. No gain should be recorded. For example, suppose that on November 15 the 1,000 treasury shares of the Caprock Corporation are sold for $60 per share. The entry for the reissue would be as follows:

A = L + OE
+   +
       +

Nov. 15	Cash	60,000	
	Treasury Stock, Common		50,000
	Paid-in Capital, Treasury Stock		10,000
	Sale of 1,000 shares of treasury		
	stock for $60 per share; cost		
	was $50 per share		

If treasury shares are sold below their cost, the difference is deducted from Paid-in Capital, Treasury Stock. When this account does not exist or its balance is insufficient to cover the excess of cost over the reissue price, Retained Earnings absorbs the excess. No loss is recorded. For example, suppose that on September 15, the Caprock Corporation bought 1,000 shares of its common stock on the market at a price of $50 per share. The company sold 400 shares of its stock on October 15 for $60 per share and the remaining 600 shares on December 15 for $42 per share. The entries for these transactions follow:

A = L + OE
−   −

Sept. 15	Treasury Stock, Common	50,000	
	Cash		50,000
	Purchase of 1,000 shares of		
	treasury stock at $50 per share		

A = L + OE
+   +
       +

Oct. 15	Cash	24,000	
	Treasury Stock, Common		20,000
	Paid-in Capital, Treasury Stock		4,000
	Sale of 400 shares of treasury		
	stock for $60 per share; cost		
	was $50 per share		

A = L + OE	Dec. 15	Cash	25,200	
+		Paid-in Capital, Treasury Stock	4,000	
–		Retained Earnings	800	
–				
+		Treasury Stock, Common		30,000
		Sale of 600 shares of treasury		
		stock for $42 per share; cost		
		was $50 per share		

In the entry for the December 15 transaction, Retained Earnings is debited for $800 because the 600 shares were sold for $4,800 less than cost. That amount is $800 greater than the $4,000 of paid-in capital generated by the sale of the 400 shares of treasury stock on October 15.

RETIREMENT OF TREASURY STOCK　If a company determines that it will not reissue stock it has purchased, with the approval of its stockholders it can retire the stock. When shares of stock are retired, all items related to those shares are removed from the related capital accounts. When treasury stock whose acquisition price is less than the original contributed capital is retired, the difference is recognized in Paid-in Capital, Retirement of Stock. However, when the acquisition price is more than was received when the stock was first issued, the difference is a reduction in stockholders' equity and is debited to Retained Earnings. For instance, suppose that instead of selling the 1,000 shares of treasury stock it purchased for $50,000, Caprock decides to retire the shares on November 15. Assuming that the $5 par value common stock was originally issued at $6 per share, this entry records the retirement:

A = L + OE	Nov. 15	Common Stock	5,000	
–		Paid-in Capital in Excess of		
–		Par Value, Common	1,000	
–		Retained Earnings	44,000	
+		Treasury Stock, Common		50,000
		Retirement of 1,000 shares that		
		cost $50 per share and were		
		issued originally at $6 per share		

Exercising Stock Options

OBJECTIVE

8 Account for the exercise of stock options

More than 98 percent of public companies encourage the ownership of their common stock through a **stock option plan**, which is an agreement to issue stock to employees according to specified terms.[12] Under some plans, the option to purchase stock applies to all employees equally, and the stock is purchased at a price close to its market value at the time of purchase. In such situations, the stock issue is recorded in the same way as a stock issue to an outsider. If, for example, we assume that on March 30 the employees of a company purchased 2,000 shares of $10 par value common stock at the current market value of $25 per share, the entry would be as follows:

A = L + OE	Mar. 30	Cash	50,000	
+ +		Common Stock		20,000
+		Paid-in Capital in Excess of		
		Par Value, Common		30,000
		Issued 2,000 shares of $10 par		
		value common stock under		
		employee stock option plan		

In other cases, the stock option plan gives employees the right to purchase stock in the future at a fixed price. This type of plan, which is usually offered only to management personnel, both compensates and motivates management because the market value of a company's stock is tied to the company's performance. As the market value of the stock goes up, the difference between the option price and the market price grows, which increases management's compensation. On the date stock options are granted, the fair value of the options must be estimated and the amount in excess of the exercise price must be either recorded as compensation expense over the grant period or reported in the notes to the financial statements.[13] If a company chooses to record compensation expense, additional paid-in capital will increase as a result. Almost all companies report the excess of fair value over exercise price in the notes to the financial statements. The notes must include the impact on net income and earnings per share of not recording compensation expense.

If note disclosure is the preferred method of reporting compensation costs, then when an option eventually is exercised and the stock is issued, the entry is similar to the one above. For example, assume that on July 1, 20x1, a company grants its

BUSINESS FOCUS ON PRACTICE

Stock options have an earnings advantage for corporations that use them and their impact varies depending on the size of a company's options program and its industry. Specifically, the cost of options and its effect on earnings may be reported in the notes and not in the income statement as compensation expense. However, salaries and other cash bonuses are included as compensation expense and reported on the income statement. A recent study by Bears Sterns indicates that options grants would completely wipe out corporate profits and operating income at some fast growing high-tech companies, which tend to rely heavily on generous options grants to attract top talent. The effect for the high-tech industry ranged from 10 to 100 percent. However, the impact of options costs for industrial companies was much less, an average of 3 percent, because they do not have large options programs and the earnings of these firms was quite large.[14]

key management personnel the option to purchase 50,000 shares of $10 par value common stock at its then-current market value of $15 per share. Suppose that one of the firm's vice presidents exercises the option to purchase 2,000 shares on March 30, 20x2, when the market price is $25 per share. The following entry would record the issue:

A = L + OE	20x2		
+ +	Mar. 30 Cash	30,000	
+	Common Stock		20,000
	Paid-in Capital in Excess of		
	Par Value, Common		10,000
	Issued 2,000 shares of $10 par		
	value common stock under the		
	employee stock option plan		

Although the vice president has a gain of $20,000 (the $50,000 market value less the $30,000 option price), no compensation expense is recorded. Estimation of the fair value of options at the grant date is the subject of future courses. Information pertaining to employee stock option plans should be discussed in the notes to the financial statements.[15]

Chapter Review

REVIEW OF LEARNING OBJECTIVES

Ace it

1. **Identify and explain the management issues related to contributed capital.** The management of contributed capital is a critical component in the financing of a corporation, which is a legal entity separate and distinct from its owners. The issues faced by management in the area of contributed capital are forming a corporation, managing under the corporate form of business, using equity financing, determining dividend policies, and evaluating performance using return on equity.

2. **Define start-up and organization costs and state their effects on financial reporting.** The costs of organizing a corporation are recorded as expenses when they are incurred. They increase the initial loss or reduce the initial income of a corporation.

3. **Identify the components of stockholders' equity.** Stockholders' equity consists of contributed capital and retained earnings. Contributed capital includes two basic types of stock: common stock and preferred stock. When only one type of security is issued, it is common stock. Common stockholders have voting rights; they also share in the earnings of the corporation.

   Retained earnings, the other component of stockholders' equity, represents the claim of stockholders to the assets of the company resulting from profitable operations. These are earnings that have been invested in the corporation.

4. **Account for cash dividends.** The liability for payment of cash dividends arises on the date of declaration by the board of directors. The declaration is recorded with a debit to Cash Dividends Declared and a credit to Cash Dividends Payable. The date of record, on which no entry is required, establishes the stockholders who will receive the cash dividend on the date of payment. Payment is recorded with a debit to Cash Dividends Payable and a credit to Cash.

5. **Identify the characteristics of preferred stock, including the effect on distribution of dividends.** Preferred stock, like common stock, is sold to raise capital. But the investors in preferred stock have different objectives. To attract such investors, corporations usually give them a preference—in terms of receiving dividends and assets—over common stockholders. The dividend on preferred stock is generally figured first; then the remainder goes to common stock. If the preferred stock is cumulative and in arrears, the amount in arrears must be allocated to preferred stockholders before any allocation is made to common stockholders. In addition, certain preferred stock is convertible. Preferred stock is often callable at the option of the corporation.

6. **Account for the issuance of stock for cash and other assets.** A corporation's stock is normally issued for cash and other assets. The majority of states require that stock be issued at a minimum value called legal capital. Legal capital is represented by the par or stated value of the stock.

   When stock is issued for cash at par or stated value, Cash is debited and Common Stock or Preferred Stock is credited. When stock is sold at an amount greater than par or stated value, the excess is recorded in Paid-in Capital in Excess of Par or Stated Value.

   Sometimes stock is issued for noncash assets. Then, the accountant must decide how to value the stock. The general rule is to record the stock at its market value. If this value cannot be determined, the fair market value of the asset received is used to record the transaction.

7. **Account for treasury stock.** Treasury stock is stock that a company has issued and later reacquired but not resold or retired. A company may acquire its own stock to create stock option plans, maintain a favorable market for the stock, increase earnings per share, or purchase other companies. Treasury stock is similar to unissued stock in that it does not have rights until it is reissued. However, treasury stock can be resold at less than par value without penalty. The accounting treatment for treasury stock is as shown below.

Treasury Stock Transaction	Accounting Treatment
Purchase of treasury stock	Debit Treasury Stock and credit Cash for the cost of the shares.
Sale of treasury stock at the same price as the cost of the shares	Debit Cash and credit Treasury Stock for the cost of the shares.
Sale of treasury stock at an amount greater than the cost of the shares	Debit Cash for the reissue price of the shares, and credit Treasury Stock for the cost of the shares and Paid-in Capital, Treasury Stock for the excess.
Sale of treasury stock at an amount less than the cost of the shares	Debit Cash for the reissue price; debit Paid-in Capital, Treasury Stock for the difference between the reissue price and the cost of the shares; and credit Treasury Stock for the cost of the shares. If Paid-in Capital, Treasury Stock does not exist or its balance is not large enough to cover the difference, Retained Earnings should absorb the difference.

8. **Account for the exercise of stock options.** Companywide stock option plans are used to encourage employees to own a part of the company. Other plans are offered only to management personnel, both to compensate and to

motivate them. Usually, the issue of stock to employees under stock option plans is recorded like the issue of stock to any outsider.

The following concepts and terms were introduced in this chapter.

LO 1 **Authorized stock:** The maximum number of shares a corporation can issue without changing its charter with the state.

LO 5 **Callable preferred stock:** Preferred stock that can be redeemed or retired at a stated price at the option of the corporation.

LO 3 **Common stock:** Shares of stock that carry voting rights but that rank below preferred stock in terms of dividends and the distribution of assets.

LO 5 **Convertible preferred stock:** Preferred stock that can be exchanged for common stock at the option of the holder.

LO 1 **Corporation:** A separate legal entity having its own rights, privileges, and liabilities distinct from those of its owners.

LO 5 **Cumulative preferred stock:** Preferred stock on which unpaid dividends accumulate over time and must be satisfied in any given year before a dividend can be paid to common stockholders.

LO 4 **Date of declaration:** The date on which the board of directors declares a dividend.

LO 4 **Date of payment:** The date on which payment of a dividend is made.

LO 4 **Date of record:** The date on which ownership of stock for the purpose of receiving a dividend is determined.

LO 1 **Dividend:** The distribution of a corporation's assets (usually cash generated by past earnings) to its stockholders.

LO 5 **Dividends in arrears:** Past dividends on cumulative preferred stock that remain unpaid.

LO 1 **Dividends yield:** Current return to stockholders in the form of dividends; dividends per share divided by market price per share.

LO 1 **Double taxation:** The act of taxing corporate earnings twice—once as the income of the corporation and once as the dividends distributed to stockholders.

LO 4 **Ex-dividend:** A description of capital stock between the date of record and the date of payment, when the right to a dividend already declared on the stock remains with the person who sells the stock and does not transfer to the person who buys it.

LO 1 **Initial public offering (IPO):** Common stock issue of a company that is selling its stock to the public for the first time.

LO 3 **Issued stock:** The shares of stock sold or otherwise transferred to stockholders.

LO 1 **Legal capital:** The number of shares of stock issued times the par value; the minimum amount that can be reported as contributed capital.

LO 4 **Liquidating dividend:** A dividend that exceeds retained earnings; usually paid when a corporation goes out of business or reduces its operations.

LO 5 **Noncumulative preferred stock:** Preferred stock that does not oblige the issuer to make up a missed dividend in a subsequent year before paying dividends to common stockholders.

LO 6 **No-par stock:** Capital stock that does not have a par value.

LO 3 **Outstanding stock:** Stock that has been issued and is still in circulation.

LO 1 **Par value:** An arbitrary amount assigned to each share of stock; used to determine the legal capital of a corporation.

LO 5   **Preferred stock:** Stock that has preference over common stock, usually in terms of dividends and the distribution of assets.

LO 1   **Price/earnings (P/E) ratio:** A measure of confidence in a company's future; market price per share divided by earnings per share.

LO 3   **Residual equity:** The common stock of a corporation.

LO 1   **Return on equity:** A measure of management performance; net income divided by average stockholders' equity.

LO 2   **Start-up and organization costs:** The costs of forming a corporation.

LO 6   **Stated value:** A value assigned by the board of directors of a corporation to no-par stock.

LO 1   **Stock certificate:** A document issued to a stockholder indicating the number of shares of stock the stockholder owns.

LO 8   **Stock option plan:** An agreement to issue stock to employees according to specified terms.

LO 7   **Treasury stock:** Capital stock, either common or preferred, that has been issued and reacquired by the issuing company but has not been resold or retired.

LO 1   **Underwriter:** An intermediary between the corporation and the investing public who facilitates an issue of stock or other securities for a fee.

REVIEW PROBLEM

Stock Journal Entries and Stockholders' Equity

LO 1
LO 2
LO 3
LO 4
LO 5
LO 6
LO 7

The Beta Corporation was organized in 20x1 in the state of Arizona. Its charter authorized the corporation to issue 1,000,000 shares of $1 par value common stock and an additional 25,000 shares of 4 percent, $20 par value cumulative convertible preferred stock. Here are the transactions that related to the company's stock during 20x1.

Feb.   1   Issued 100,000 shares of common stock for $125,000.

     15   Issued 3,000 shares of common stock for accounting and legal services. The services were billed to the company at $3,600.

Mar. 15   Issued 120,000 shares of common stock to Edward Jackson in exchange for a building and land that had appraised values of $100,000 and $25,000, respectively.

Apr.   2   Purchased 20,000 shares of common stock for the treasury at $1.25 per share from a person who changed his mind about investing in the company.

July   1   Issued 25,000 shares of preferred stock for $500,000.

Sept. 30   Sold 10,000 of the shares in the treasury for $1.50 per share.

Dec. 31   The board declared dividends of $24,910 payable on January 15 to stockholders of record on January 8. Dividends included preferred stock cash dividends for one-half year.

For the period ended December 31, 20x1, the company reported net income of $40,000 and earnings per common share of $.15. At December 31, the market price per common share was $1.60.

REQUIRED

1. Record these transactions in journal form. Following the December 31 entry to record dividends, show dividends payable for each class of stock.

2. Prepare the stockholders' equity section of the Beta Corporation balance sheet as of December 31, 20x1. (*Hint:* Use net income and dividends to calculate retained earnings.)

3. Calculate dividends yield on common stock, price/earnings ratio of common stock, and return on equity.

ANSWER TO REVIEW PROBLEM

1. Prepare the entries in journal form.

20x1

Feb.	1	Cash	125,000	
		Common Stock		100,000
		Paid-in Capital in Excess of Par Value, Common		25,000
		Issue of 100,000 shares of $1 par value common stock for $1.25 per share		
	15	Start-up and Organization Expense	3,600	
		Common Stock		3,000
		Paid-in Capital in Excess of Par Value, Common		600
		Issue of 3,000 shares of $1 par value common stock for billed accounting and legal services of $3,600		
Mar.	15	Building	100,000	
		Land	25,000	
		Common Stock		120,000
		Paid-in Capital in Excess of Par Value, Common		5,000
		Issue of 120,000 shares of $1 par value common stock for a building and land appraised at $100,000 and $25,000, respectively		
Apr.	2	Treasury Stock, Common	25,000	
		Cash		25,000
		Purchase of 20,000 shares of common stock for the treasury at $1.25 per share		
July	1	Cash	500,000	
		Preferred Stock		500,000
		Issue of 25,000 shares of $20 par value preferred stock for $20 per share		
Sept.	30	Cash	15,000	
		Treasury Stock, Common		12,500
		Paid-in Capital, Treasury Stock		2,500
		Sale of 10,000 shares of treasury stock at $1.50 per share; original cost was $1.25 per share		
Dec.	31	Cash Dividends Declared	24,910	
		Cash Dividends Payable		24,910
		Declaration of a $24,910 cash dividend to preferred and common stockholders		

Total dividend	$24,910
Less preferred stock cash dividend	
$500,000 × .04 × 6/12	10,000
Common stock cash dividend	$14,910

2. Prepare the stockholders' equity section of the balance sheet.

Beta Corporation
Balance Sheet
December 31, 20x1

Stockholders' Equity

Contributed Capital		
Preferred Stock, 4% cumulative convertible, $20 par value, 25,000 shares authorized, issued, and outstanding		$500,000
Common Stock, $1 par value, 1,000,000 shares authorized, 223,000 shares issued, and 213,000 shares outstanding	$223,000	
Paid-in Capital in Excess of Par Value, Common	30,600	
Paid-in Capital, Treasury Stock	2,500	256,100
Total Contributed Capital		$756,100
Retained Earnings		15,090*
Total Contributed Capital and Retained Earnings		$771,190
Less Treasury Stock, Common (10,000 shares, at cost)		12,500
Total Stockholders' Equity		$758,690

*Retained Earnings = $40,000 − $24,910 = $15,090.

3. Calculate dividends yield on common stock, price/earnings ratio of common stock, and return on equity.

$$\text{Dividends per Share} = \$14,910 \text{ Common Stock Dividend} \div 213,000 \text{ Common Shares Outstanding} = \$.07$$

$$\text{Dividends Yield} = \frac{\text{Dividends per Share}}{\text{Market Price per Share}} = \frac{\$.07}{\$1.60} = 4.4\%$$

$$\text{Price/Earnings (P/E) Ratio} = \frac{\text{Market Price per Share}}{\text{Earnings per Share}} = \frac{\$1.60}{\$.15} = 10.7 \text{ times}$$

The opening balance of stockholders' equity on February 1, 20x1, was $125,000.

$$\text{Return on Equity} = \frac{\text{Net Income}}{\text{Average Stockholders' Equity}}$$

$$= \frac{\$40,000}{(\$758,690 + \$125,000) \div 2}$$

$$= 9.1\%$$

Chapter Assignments

QUESTIONS

1. What are the issues related to contributed capital facing management?
2. Identify and explain several advantages of the corporate form of business.

3. Identify and explain several disadvantages of the corporate form of business.

4. What is dividends yield, and what do investors learn from it?

5. What is the price/earnings (P/E) ratio, and what does it measure?

6. What are the start-up and organization costs of a corporation?

7. What is the proper accounting treatment of start-up and organization costs?

8. What is the legal capital of a corporation, and what is its significance?

9. Describe the significance of the following dates as they relate to dividends: (a) date of declaration, (b) date of record, and (c) date of payment.

10. Explain the accounting treatment of cash dividends.

11. What are dividends in arrears, and how should they be disclosed in the financial statements?

12. Define the terms *cumulative, convertible,* and *callable* as they apply to preferred stock.

13. How is the value of stock determined when stock is issued for noncash assets?

14. Define *treasury stock* and explain why a company would purchase its own stock.

15. What is the proper classification of the following accounts on the balance sheet? Indicate whether stockholders' equity accounts are contributed capital, retained earnings, or contra stockholders' equity. (a) Common Stock; (b) Treasury Stock; (c) Paid-in Capital, Treasury Stock; (d) Paid-in Capital in Excess of Par Value, Common; (e) Paid-in Capital in Excess of Stated Value, Common; and (f) Retained Earnings.

16. What is a stock option plan and why does a company have one?

SHORT EXERCISES

SE 1.

LO 1 Management Issues

Indicate whether each of the actions below is related to (a) forming a corporation, (b) managing under the corporate form of business, (c) using equity financing, (d) determining dividend policies, or (e) evaluating performance using return on equity.

1. Considering whether to make a distribution to stockholders

2. Controlling day-to-day operations not necessarily by the owners

3. Determining whether to issue preferred or common stock

4. Compensating management based on the company's meeting or exceeding the targeted return on equity

5. Issuing shares (not to exceed the maximum of authorized shares)

6. Transferring shares from one owner to another without the approval of other owners

7. Deciding who will be the officers and board of directors

SE 2.

LO 1 Advantages and Disadvantages of a Corporation

Identify whether each of the following characteristics is an advantage or a disadvantage of the corporate form of business.

1. Ease of transfer of ownership

2. Taxation

3. Separate legal entity

4. Lack of mutual agency

5. Government regulation

6. Continuous existence

SE 3.

LO 2 Effect of Start-up and Organization Costs

At the beginning of 20x1, Matson Company incurred two start-up and organization costs: (1) attorney's fees with a market value of $5,000, paid with 3,000 shares of $1 par value common stock, and (2) incorporation fees paid to the state of $3,000. Calculate total start-up and organization costs. What will be the effect of these costs on the balance sheet and income statement?

LO 3 Stockholders' Equity

SE 4. Prepare the stockholders' equity section of Lincoln Corporation's balance sheet from the following accounts and balances on December 31, 20xx.

Account	Balance Debit	Balance Credit
Common Stock, $10 par value, 60,000 shares authorized, 40,000 shares issued, and 39,000 shares outstanding		$400,000
Paid-in Capital in Excess of Par Value, Common		200,000
Retained Earnings		30,000
Treasury Stock, Common (1,000 shares, at cost)	$15,000	

LO 4 Cash Dividends

SE 5. Blancone Corporation has authorized 100,000 shares of $1 par value common stock, of which 80,000 are issued and 70,000 are outstanding. On May 15, the board of directors declared a cash dividend of $.10 per share payable on June 15 to stockholders of record on June 1. Prepare the entries, as necessary, for each of the three dates.

LO 5 Preferred Stock Dividends with Dividends in Arrears

SE 6. The Vergennes Corporation has 1,000 shares of its $100, 8 percent cumulative preferred stock outstanding and 20,000 shares of its $1 par value common stock outstanding. In its first three years of operation, the board of directors of Vergennes Corporation paid cash dividends as follows: 20x1, none; 20x2, $20,000; and 20x3, $40,000.

Determine the total cash dividends and dividends per share paid to the preferred and common stockholders during each of the three years.

LO 6 Issuance of Stock

SE 7. Ferrisburg Company is authorized to issue 100,000 shares of common stock. The company sold 5,000 shares at $12 per share. Prepare journal entries to record the sale of stock for cash under each of the following independent alternatives: (1) The stock has a par value of $5, and (2) the stock has no par value but a stated value of $1 per share.

LO 6 Issuance of Stock for Noncash Assets

SE 8. Borneo Corporation issued 8,000 shares of its $1 par value common stock in exchange for some land. The land had a fair market value of $50,000.

Prepare the journal entries necessary to record the issuance of the stock for the land under each of the following independent conditions: (1) The stock was selling for $7 per share on the day of the transaction, and (2) management attempted to place a value on the common stock but could not do so.

LO 7 Treasury Stock Transactions

SE 9. Prepare the journal entries necessary to record the following stock transactions of the Lemner Company during 20xx.

Oct. 1 Purchased 1,000 shares of its own $2 par value common stock for $20, the current market price.
   17 Sold 250 shares of treasury stock purchased on Oct. 1 for $25 per share.
   21 Sold 400 shares of treasury stock purchased on Oct. 1 for $18 per share.

LO 7 Retirement of Treasury Stock

SE 10. On October 28, 20xx, the Lemner Company (**SE 9**) retired the remaining 350 shares of treasury stock. The shares were originally issued at $5 per share. Prepare the necessary journal entry.

LO 8 Exercise of Stock Options

SE 11. On June 6, Winston Leno exercised his option to purchase 10,000 shares of Plunkett Company $1 par value common stock at an option price of $4. The market price per share was $4 on the grant date and $18 on the exercise date. Record the transaction on Plunkett's books.

EXERCISES

E 1.

LO 1 **Dividends Yield and Price/Earnings Ratio**

In 20x1, Caps Corporation earned $2.20 per share and paid a dividend of $1.00 per share. At year end, the price of its stock was $33 per share. Calculate the dividends yield and the price/earnings ratio.

E 2.

LO 3 **Stockholders' Equity**
LO 7

The accounts and balances below were taken from the records of Hagor Corporation on December 31, 20xx.

Account	Balance	
	Debit	Credit
Preferred Stock, $100 par value, 9% cumulative, 20,000 shares authorized, 12,000 shares issued and outstanding		$1,200,000
Common Stock, $12 par value, 90,000 shares authorized, 60,000 shares issued, and 57,000 shares outstanding		720,000
Paid-in Capital in Excess of Par Value, Common		388,000
Retained Earnings		46,000
Treasury Stock, Common (3,000 shares, at cost)	$60,000	

Prepare a stockholders' equity section for Hagor Corporation's balance sheet.

E 3.

LO 3 **Characteristics of**
LO 5 **Common and Preferred Stock**

Indicate whether each characteristic listed below is more closely associated with common stock (C) or preferred stock (P).

1. Often receives dividends at a set rate
2. Is considered the residual equity of a company
3. Can be callable
4. Can be convertible
5. More likely to have dividends that vary in amount from year to year
6. Can be entitled to receive dividends not paid in past years
7. Likely to have full voting rights
8. Receives assets first in liquidation
9. Generally receives dividends before other classes of stock

E 4.

LO 3 **Stock Journal Entries and**
LO 6 **Stockholders' Equity**

The Prada Hospital Supply Corporation was organized in 20xx. The company was authorized to issue 100,000 shares of no-par common stock with a stated value of $5 per share, and 20,000 shares of $100 par value, 6 percent noncumulative preferred stock. On March 1 the company issued 60,000 shares of its common stock for $15 per share and 8,000 shares of its preferred stock for $100 per share.

1. Prepare the journal entries to record the issuance of the stock.
2. Prepare the company's stockholders' equity section of the balance sheet immediately after the common and preferred stock was issued.

E 5.

LO 4 **Cash Dividends**

Cardosa Corporation has secured authorization from the state for 200,000 shares of $10 par value common stock. There are 160,000 shares issued and 140,000 shares outstanding. On June 5, the board of directors declared a $.50 per share cash dividend to be paid on June 25 to stockholders of record on June 15. Prepare the journal entries necessary to record these events.

E 6.

LO 4 **Cash Dividends**
LO 7

Bodi Corporation has 500,000 authorized shares of $1 par value common stock, of which 400,000 are issued, including 40,000 shares of treasury stock. On October 15, the board of directors declared a cash dividend of $.25 per share payable on November 15 to stockholders of record on November 1. Prepare the entries, as necessary, for each of the three dates.

LO 5 Cash Dividends with Dividends in Arrears

E 7. The Hachiya Corporation has 10,000 shares of its $100 par value, 7 percent cumulative preferred stock outstanding, and 50,000 shares of its $1 par value common stock outstanding. In its first four years of operation, the board of directors of Hachiya Corporation paid cash dividends as follows: 20x1, none; 20x2, $120,000; 20x3, $140,000; 20x4, $140,000.

Determine the dividends per share and total cash dividends paid to the preferred and common stockholders during each of the four years.

LO 5 Preferred and Common Cash Dividends

E 8. The McCay Corporation pays dividends at the end of each year. The dividends paid for 20x1, 20x2, and 20x3 were $80,000, $60,000, and $180,000, respectively.

Calculate the total amount of dividends paid each year to the common and preferred stockholders if each of the following capital structures is assumed: (1) 20,000 shares of $100 par, 6 percent noncumulative preferred stock and 60,000 shares of $10 par common stock. (2) 10,000 shares of $100 par, 7 percent cumulative preferred stock and 60,000 shares of $10 par common stock. There were no dividends in arrears at the beginning of 20x1.

LO 6 Issuance of Stock

E 9. Seong Company is authorized to issue 200,000 shares of common stock. On August 1, the company issued 10,000 shares at $25 per share. Prepare journal entries to record the issuance of stock for cash under each of the following independent alternatives:

1. The stock has a par value of $25.
2. The stock has a par value of $10.
3. The stock has no par value.
4. The stock has a stated value of $1 per share.

LO 6 Issuance of Stock for Noncash Assets

E 10. On July 1, 20xx, Whitesides, a new corporation, issued 20,000 shares of its common stock for a corporate headquarters building. The building has a fair market value of $600,000 and a book value of $400,000. Because the corporation is new, it is not possible to establish a market value for the common stock.

Record the issuance of stock for the building, assuming the following conditions: (1) the par value of the stock is $10 per share; (2) the stock is no-par stock; and (3) the stock has a stated value of $4 per share.

LO 7 Treasury Stock Transactions

E 11. Prepare the journal entries necessary to record the following stock transactions of the Skoglund Company during 20xx.

May 5 Purchased 400 shares of its own $2 par value common stock for $20 per share, the current market price.
17 Sold 150 shares of treasury stock purchased on May 5 for $22 per share.
21 Sold 100 shares of treasury stock purchased on May 5 for $20 per share.
28 Sold the remaining 150 shares of treasury stock purchased on May 5 for $19 per share.

LO 7 Treasury Stock Transactions Including Retirement

E 12. Prepare the journal entries necessary to record the following stock transactions of Vazquez Corporation, which represent all treasury stock transactions entered into by the company.

June 1 Purchased 2,000 shares of its own $30 par value common stock for $70 per share, the current market price.
10 Sold 500 shares of treasury stock purchased on June 1 for $80 per share.
20 Sold 700 shares of treasury stock purchased on June 1 for $58 per share.
30 Retired the remaining shares purchased on June 1. The original issue price was $42 per share.

LO 8 Grant and Exercise of Stock Options

E 13. On January 1, 20x3, Ho-Young Wang received an option to purchase 10,000 shares of $1 par value common stock at the January 1, 20x3, market price of $13 per share. The fair market value of the options on the date of grant was $16 per share, and the options expire on December 31, 20x3. Record the entry to recognize compensation expense for 20x3 and describe the alternative method of reporting in the notes to the financial statements. Ho-Young Wang exercised her options on November 30, 20x3. Record the issuance of stock.

PROBLEMS

P 1.

REQUIRED

Sussex Corporation began operations on September 1, 20xx. The corporation's charter authorized 300,000 shares of $8 par value common stock. Sussex Corporation engaged in the following transactions during its first quarter:

Sept. 1   Issued 50,000 shares of common stock, $500,000.
      1   Paid an attorney $32,000 to help start up and organize the corporation and obtain the corporate charter from the state.
Oct. 2   Issued 80,000 shares of common stock, $960,000.
Nov. 30   The board of directors declared a cash dividend of $.40 per share to be paid on December 15 to stockholders of record on December 10.

1. Prepare journal entries to record the first-quarter transactions shown above.

2. Prepare the stockholders' equity section of Sussex Corporation's November 30, 20xx, balance sheet. Net income for the quarter was $80,000.

P 2.

REQUIRED

The DeMeo Corporation had both common stock and preferred stock outstanding from 20x2 through 20x4. Information about each stock for the three years is as follows:

Type	Par Value	Shares Outstanding	Other
Preferred	$100	40,000	7% cumulative
Common	20	600,000	

The company paid $140,000, $800,000, and $1,100,000 in dividends for 20x2 through 20x4, respectively. The market price per common share was $15 and $17 per share at year-end 20x3 and 20x4, respectively.

1. Determine the dividends per share and total dividends paid to the common and preferred stockholders each year.

2. Repeat the computations performed in **1,** with the assumption that the preferred stock was noncumulative.

3. Calculate the 20x3 and 20x4 dividends yield for common stock using dividends per share computed in **2.**

P 3.

REQUIRED

The Spivy Corporation was involved in the following treasury stock transactions during 20x1:

a. Purchased 80,000 shares of its $1 par value common stock at $2.50 per share.
b. Purchased 16,000 shares of its common stock at $2.80 per share.
c. Sold 44,000 shares purchased in **a** for $131,000.
d. Sold the other 36,000 shares purchased in **a** for $72,000.
e. Sold 6,000 of the remaining shares of treasury stock for $1.60 per share.
f. Retired all the remaining shares of treasury stock. All shares originally were issued at $1.50 per share.

Record the treasury stock transactions in journal form.

P 4.

Kokaly Plastics Corporation was chartered in the state of Massachusetts. The company was authorized to issue 20,000 shares of $100 par value, 6 percent preferred stock and 100,000 shares of no-par common stock. The common stock has a $2 stated value. The stock-related transactions for the quarter ended October 31, 20xx, were as follows:

Aug. 3   Issued 10,000 shares of common stock for $120,000 worth of services rendered in organizing and chartering the corporation.
     15   Issued 16,000 shares of common stock for land, which had an asking price of $200,000. The common stock had a market value of $12 per share.
     22   Issued 10,000 shares of preferred stock for $1,000,000.
Oct. 4   Issued 10,000 shares of common stock for $120,000.
     10   Purchased 5,000 shares of common stock for the treasury for $13,000.
     15   Declared a quarterly cash dividend on the outstanding preferred stock and $.10 per share on common stock outstanding, payable on October 31 to stockholders of record on October 25.
     25   Date of record for cash dividends.
     31   Paid cash dividends.

1. Record transactions for the quarter ended October 31, 20xx, in journal form.

2. Prepare the stockholders' equity section of the company's balance sheet as of October 31, 20xx. Net income for the quarter was $46,000.

LO 2 Comprehensive
LO 3 Stockholders' Equity
LO 4 Transactions and
LO 5 T Accounts
LO 6
LO 7
LO 8

P 5. In January 20xx, the Jones Corporation was organized and authorized to issue 2,000,000 shares of no-par common stock and 50,000 shares of 5 percent, $50 par value, noncumulative preferred stock. The stock-related transactions for the first year's operations follow.

Jan. 19 Sold 15,000 shares of the common stock for $31,500. State law requires a minimum of $1 stated value per share.

21 Issued 5,000 shares of common stock to attorneys and accountants for services valued at $11,000 and provided during the organization of the corporation.

Feb. 7 Issued 30,000 shares of common stock for a building that had an appraised value of $78,000.

Mar. 22 Purchased 10,000 shares of common stock for the treasury at $3 per share.

July 15 Issued 5,000 shares of common stock to employees under a stock option plan that allows any employee to buy shares at the current market price, which today is $3 per share.

Aug. 1 Sold 2,500 shares of treasury stock for $4 per share.

Sept. 1 Declared a cash dividend of $.15 per common share to be paid on September 25 to stockholders of record on September 15.

15 Cash dividends date of record.

25 Paid cash dividends to stockholders of record on September 15.

Oct. 30 Issued 4,000 shares of common stock for a piece of land. The stock was selling for $3 per share, and the land had a fair market value of $12,000.

Dec. 15 Issued 2,200 shares of preferred stock for $50 per share.

1. Record the above transactions in T accounts. Prepare T accounts for Cash; Land; Building; Start-up and Organization Expense; Cash Dividends Payable; Preferred Stock; Common Stock; Paid-in Capital in Excess of Stated Value, Common; Paid-in Capital, Treasury Stock; Retained Earnings; Treasury Stock, Common; and Cash Dividends Declared.

2. Prepare the stockholders' equity section of Jones Corporation's balance sheet as of December 31, 20xx. Net income earned during the year was $100,000.

ALTERNATE PROBLEMS

LO 2 Start-up and
LO 3 Organization Costs,
LO 4 Stock and Dividend
LO 6 Journal Entries, and
Stockholders' Equity

P 6. On March 1, 20xx, Carmel Corporation began operations with a charter from the state that authorized 100,000 shares of $4 par value common stock. Over the next quarter, the firm engaged in the following transactions:

Mar. 1 Issued 30,000 shares of common stock, $200,000.

2 Paid fees associated with obtaining the charter and starting up and organizing the corporation, $24,000.

Apr. 10 Issued 13,000 shares of common stock, $130,000.

May 31 The board of directors declared a $.20 per share cash dividend to be paid on June 15 to shareholders of record on June 10.

1. Record the transactions indicated above in journal form.

2. Prepare the stockholders' equity section of Carmel Corporation's balance sheet on May 31, 20xx. Net income earned during the first quarter, $30,000.

LO 1 Preferred and Common
LO 5 Stock Dividends and
Dividends Yield

P 7. The Clockwork Corporation had the following stock outstanding from 20x1 through 20x4.

Preferred stock: $100 par value, 8 percent cumulative, 10,000 shares authorized, issued, and outstanding

Common stock: $10 par value, 200,000 shares authorized, issued, and outstanding.

The company paid $60,000, $60,000, $188,000, and $260,000 in dividends during 20x1, 20x2, 20x3, and 20x4, respectively. The market price per common share was $7.25 and $8.00 per share at year end 20x3 and 20x4, respectively.

REQUIRED

1. Determine the dividends per share and the total dividends paid to common stock-holders and preferred stockholders in 20x1, 20x2, 20x3, and 20x4.

2. Perform the same computations, with the assumption that the preferred stock was noncumulative.

3. Calculate the 20x3 and 20x4 dividends yield for common stock, using the dividends per share computed in **2.**

P 8.

LO 2 Comprehensive
LO 3 Stockholders' Equity
LO 4 Transactions
LO 5
LO 6
LO 7

Vanowski, Inc., was organized and authorized to issue 10,000 shares of $100 par value, 9 percent preferred stock and 100,000 shares of no-par, $5 stated value common stock on July 1, 20xx. Stock-related transactions for Vanowski were as follows:

July	1	Issued 20,000 shares of common stock at $11 per share.
	1	Issued 1,000 shares of common stock at $11 per share for services rendered in connection with the organization of the company.
	2	Issued 2,000 shares of preferred stock at par value for cash.
	10	Issued 5,000 shares of common stock for land on which the asking price was $70,000. Market value of the stock was $12. Management wishes to record the land at full market value of the stock.
Aug.	2	Purchased 3,000 shares of common stock for the treasury at $13 per share.
	10	Declared a cash dividend for one month on the outstanding preferred stock and $.02 per share on common stock outstanding, payable on August 22 to stockholders of record on August 12.
	12	Date of record for cash dividends.
	22	Paid cash dividends.

REQUIRED

1. Record the transactions in journal form.

2. Prepare the stockholders' equity section of the balance sheet as it would appear on August 31, 20xx. Net income for July and August was $25,000.

EXPANDING YOUR CRITICAL THINKING, COMMUNICATION, AND INTERPERSONAL SKILLS

SKILLS DEVELOPMENT

Conceptual Analysis

SD 1.

LO 1 Reasons for Issuing
LO 3 Common Stock

In a recent year, *Safeway, Inc.,* one of the United States' largest grocery chains, issued 19,750,000 shares of common stock for $52[11]/16 for a total of $1,040,578,125.[16] As a large, profitable company, Safeway could have raised this significant amount of money by issuing long-term bonds. What are some advantages of issuing common stock as opposed to bonds? What are some disadvantages?

SD 2.

LO 5 Reasons for Issuing
Preferred Stock

Preferred stock is a hybrid security that has some of the characteristics of stock and some of the characteristics of bonds. Historically, preferred stock has not been a popular means of financing. In the last few years, however, it has become more attractive to companies and individual investors alike, and investors are buying large amounts because of high yields. Large preferred stock issues have been made by banks such as *Chase Manhattan, Citibank, Republic New York,* and *Wells Fargo,* as well as other companies. The dividends yields on these stocks are over 9 percent, higher than the interest rates on comparable bonds.[17] Especially popular are preferred equity redemption

| Cash Flow | CD-ROM | Communication | Critical Thinking | Ethics | General Ledger | Group Activity | Hot Links to Real Companies | International | Internet | Key Ratio | Memo | Spreadsheet |

convertible stocks, or PERCs, which are automatically convertible into common stock after three years if the company does not redeem or call them first and retire them. What reasons can you give for the popularity of preferred stock, and of PERCs in particular, when the tax-deductible interest on bonds is less costly? Discuss both the company's and the investor's standpoints.

SD 3.

LO 7 Purposes of Treasury Stock

Many companies in recent years have bought back their common stock. For example, *IBM,* with large cash holdings, has spent almost $27 billion over five years buying back its stock. What are the reasons that companies buy back their own shares? What is the effect of common stock share buybacks on earnings per share, return on equity, return on assets, debt to equity, and the current ratio?

Ethical Dilemma

SD 4.

LO 1 Ethics of Incorporating an Accounting Firm

Traditionally, accounting firms have organized as partnerships or as professional corporations, a form of corporation that in many ways resembles a partnership. In recent years, some accounting firms have had large judgments imposed upon them as a result of lawsuits by investors who lost money when they invested in companies the firms have audited that went bankrupt. Because of the increased risk of large losses from malpractice suits, accounting firms are allowed to incorporate as long as they maintain a minimum level of partners' capital and carry malpractice insurance. Some accounting practitioners feel that incorporating would be a violation of their responsibility to the public. What features of the corporate form of business would be most advantageous to the partners of an accounting firm? Do you think it is a violation of the public trust for an accounting firm to incorporate?

Research Activity

SD 5.

LO 1 Comparison of
LO 3 Stockholders' Equity
LO 4 Characteristics
LO 5
LO 6
LO 8

Select the annual reports of three corporations using either your library or the Fingraph® Financial Analyst™ CD-ROM software that accompanies this text. You can choose them from the same industry or at random, at the direction of your instructor. (**Note:** You may be asked to use these companies again in the Research Activities in later chapters.) Prepare a table with a column for each corporation. Then answer the following questions for each corporation: Does the corporation have preferred stock? If so, what are the par value and the indicated dividend, and is the preferred stock cumulative or convertible? Is the common stock par value or no-par? What is the par value or stated value? What cash dividends, if any, were paid in the past year? What is the dividends yield? From the notes to the financial statements, determine whether the company has an employee stock option plan. What are some of its provisions? What is the return on equity? Be prepared to discuss the characteristics of the stocks and dividends for your selected companies in class.

Decision-Making Practice

SD 6.

LO 1 Analysis of Alternative
LO 3 Financing Methods

Companies offering services to the computer technology industry are growing quickly. Participating in this growth, *Northeast Servotech Corporation* has expanded rapidly in recent years. Because of its profitability, the company has been able to grow without obtaining external financing. This fact is reflected in its current balance sheet, which contains no long-term debt. The liability and stockholders' equity sections of the balance sheet on March 31, 20xx, are shown at the top of the next page.

The company now has the opportunity to double its size by purchasing the operations of a rival company for $4,000,000. If the purchase goes through, Northeast Servotech will become the top company in its specialized industry in the northeastern part of the country. The problem for management is how to finance the purchase. After much study and discussion with bankers and underwriters, management has prepared three financing alternatives to present to the board of directors, which must authorize the purchase and the financing.

Alternative A: The company could issue $4,000,000 of long-term debt. Given the company's financial rating and the current market rates, management believes the company will have to pay an interest rate of 12 percent on the debt.

Northeast Servotech Corporation
Balance Sheet
March 31, 20xx

Liabilities

Current Liabilities	$ 500,000

Stockholders' Equity

Common Stock, $10 par value, 500,000 shares authorized, 100,000 shares issued and outstanding	$1,000,000	
Paid-in Capital in Excess of Par Value, Common	1,800,000	
Retained Earnings	1,700,000	
Total Stockholders' Equity		4,500,000
Total Liabilities and Stockholders' Equity		**$5,000,000**

Alternative B: The company could issue 40,000 shares of 8 percent, $100 par value preferred stock.

Alternative C: The company could issue 100,000 additional shares of $10 par value common stock at $40 per share.

Management explains to the board that the interest on the long-term debt is tax-deductible and that the applicable income tax rate is 40 percent. The board members know that a dividend of $.80 per share of common stock was paid last year, up from $.60 and $.40 per share in the two years before that. The board has had a policy of regular increases in dividends of $.20 per share. The board feels that each of the three financing alternatives is feasible and now wants to study the financial effects of each alternative.

1. Prepare a schedule to show how the liabilities and stockholders' equity sections of Northeast Servotech's balance sheet would look under each alternative, and compute the debt to equity ratio (total liabilities ÷ total stockholders' equity) for each.

2. Compute and compare the cash needed to pay the interest or dividends for each kind of new financing net of income taxes in the first year.

3. How might the cash needed to pay for the financing change in future years under each alternative?

4. Prepare a memorandum to the board of directors that evaluates the alternatives in order of preference based on cash flow effects, giving arguments for and against each one.

Group Activity: Assign the alternatives to different groups to analyze and present to the class as the "board of directors."

FINANCIAL REPORTING AND ANALYSIS

Interpreting Financial Reports

FRA 1.

LO 1 **Effect of Stock Issue**
LO 3
LO 6

Netscape Communications Corporation, a leading provider of software, applications, and tools that link people and information over networks, the Internet, and the World Wide Web, is one of the great success stories of the Internet age. Netscape only went public with an IPO in June 1995 and issued shares at a price of $14 per share. On November 14, 1996, Netscape announced a common stock issue in an ad in *The Wall Street Journal:*

6,440,000 Shares
NETSCAPE
Common Stock
Price $53¾ a share

If Netscape sold all these shares at the offering price of $53.75, the net proceeds before issue costs would be $346.15 million.

A portion of the stockholders' equity section of the balance sheet adapted from Netscape's 1995 annual report is shown below.

	1995	1994
	(in thousands)	
Common Stock, $.0001 par value, 200,000,000 shares authorized, 12,003,594 shares in 1994 and 81,063,158 shares in 1995 issued and outstanding	$ 8	$ 1
Additional Paid-in Capital	196,749	18,215
Accumulated Deficit	(16,314)	(12,873)

REQUIRED

1. Assume the net proceeds from the sale of 6,440,000 shares at $53.75 were $342.6 million after issue costs. Record the stock issuance on Netscape's accounting records in journal form.

2. Prepare the portion of the stockholders' equity section of the balance sheet shown above after the issue of the common stock, based on the information given. Round all answers to the nearest thousand.

3. Based on your answer in **2,** did Netscape have to increase its authorized shares to undertake this stock issue?

4. What amount per share did Netscape receive and how much did Netscape's underwriters receive to help in issuing the stock if investors paid $53.75 per share? What do the underwriters do to earn their fee?

FRA 2.
LO 5 Effect of the Omission of Preferred Dividends

US Airways had indefinitely deferred the quarterly dividend on its $358 million of cumulative convertible 9¼ percent preferred stock.[18] According to a US Airways spokesperson, the company did not want to "continue to pay a dividend while the company is losing money." Others interpreted the action as "an indication of a cash crisis situation."

At the time, *Berkshire Hathaway,* the large company run by Warren Buffett and the owner of the preferred stock, was not happy, but US Airways was able to turn around, become profitable, and return to paying its cumulative dividends on preferred stock. Mr. Buffett was able to convert the preferred stock into 9.24 million common shares of US Airways' common stock at $38.74 per share at a time when the market value had risen to $62.[19]

What is cumulative convertible preferred stock? Why is the omission of dividends on those shares a drastic action? What is the impact on profitability and liquidity? Why did financing using preferred stock instead of long-term bonds probably save the company from bankruptcy? What was Berkshire Hathaway's gain on its investment at the time of the conversion?

International Company

FRA 3.
LO 3 Stockholders' Equity
LO 4 and Dividends

Roche Group is a giant Swiss pharmaceutical company. Its stockholders' equity below shows how little importance common stock, called share capital, typically plays in the financing of Swiss companies.[20]

	1998	1997
Shareholders' Equity (in millions of Swiss Francs)		
Share Capital	160	160
Retained Earnings	21,655	17,979
Total Shareholders' Equity	21,815	18,139

When Swiss companies need financing, they often rely on debt financing from large Swiss banks and from other debt markets. With only 160 million Swiss francs in share capital, Roche has had few stock issues in its history. This amount compares to over 18 billion Swiss francs in liabilities. Also, Roche has been enormously profitable, having built up retained earnings of more than 20 billion Swiss francs over the years. The company also pays a good dividend that totaled 716 million Swiss francs in 1998. Record in journal form the declaration and issue of dividends in 1998. Assuming that dividends and net income were the only factors that affected retained earnings during 1998, how much did Roche earn in 1998 in U.S. dollars (use an exchange rate of 1.4 Swiss francs to the dollar)?

Toys "R" Us Annual Report

FRA 4.

LO 1 **Stockholders' Equity**
LO 3
LO 7
LO 8

Refer to the Toys "R" Us annual report to answer the following questions.

1. What type of capital stock does Toys "R" Us have? What is the par value? How many shares are authorized, issued, and outstanding at the end of 1999?

2. What is the dividends yield for Toys "R" Us and its relationship to the investors' total return? Does the company rely mostly on stock or on earnings for its stockholders' equity?

3. From the statement of stockholders' equity how has management's policy with regard to treasury stock changed over the past three years? What favorable effects did the stock buybacks in the first two years have and how were the treasury shares used in the third year?

4. Does the company have a stock option plan? To whom do the stock options apply? Do employees have significant stock options? Given the market price of the stock shown in the report, do these options represent significant value to the employees?

5. Calculate and discuss the price/earnings ratio and return on equity for 1998 and 1999. The average share price for the fourth quarter was $30 and $18 for 1998 and 1999, respectively.

Fingraph® Financial Analyst™

FRA 5.

LO 1 **Comparison**
LO 3 **Analysis of**
LO 7 **Stockholders' Equity**
LO 8

Select any two companies from the same industry in the Fingraph® Financial Analyst™ CD-ROM software.

1. In the annual reports for the companies you have selected, identify the stockholders' equity section of the balance sheet and reference to any stockholders' equity accounts in the summary of significant accounting policies or notes to the financial statements. Do the companies have more than one kind of capital stock? What are the characteristics of each type of capital stock? Do the companies have treasury stock? Do the companies have an employee stock option plan?

2. Find the earnings per share and dividends per share in the annual reports for both companies. Also, find in the financial section of your local paper the current market prices of the companies' common stock. Prepare a table that summarizes this information and also shows the price/earnings ratio and the dividends yield.

3. Locate the statements of cash flows in the two companies' annual reports. Has the company issued capital stock or repurchased its stock in the last three years?

4. Find and read references to capital stock in management's discussion and analysis in each annual report.

5. Write a one-page executive summary that highlights the types of capital stock for these companies, significance of treasury stock, employee stock option plan, and compares the price/earnings ratio and the dividends yield trends of the two companies, including reference to management's assessment. Include your table as an attachment to your report.

Internet Case

FRA 6.
LO 1 **Comparison of Financing of**
LO 4 **Internet Companies**
LO 5
LO 6
LO 7
LO 8

Many Internet start-up companies have gone public in recent years. These companies are generally unprofitable and require a great deal of cash to finance expansion. They also reward their employees with stock options. Choose any two of the following Internet companies: *Amazon.com, Yahoo, eBay Inc., Netscape,* and *America Online (AOL)*. Go to the Needles Accounting Resource Center web site at http://college.hmco.com. Find companies under web links and go to the web sites for the two companies you have selected. In the latest annual report for each of the companies, look at the financing activities section of the statement of cash flows for the last three years. How have your two companies financed their businesses? Have they issued stock or long-term debt? Have they purchased treasury stock, paid dividends, or issued stock under stock option plans? Are the companies profitable (see net income or earnings at the top of the statement)? Are your findings in line with your expectations about these young Internet companies? Find each company's stock price, either on the Web (many companies have it on their homepage) or in the newspaper, and compare it to the average issue price of that company's past stock issues. Summarize your findings and conclusions.

ENDNOTES

1. General Motors Corporation, *Annual Report*, 1999.
2. Copyright © 1996 by Houghton Mifflin Company. Adapted and reprinted by permission from *The American Heritage Dictionary of the English Language*, Third Edition.
3. Suzanne McGee, "Europe's New Markets for IPOs of Growth Start-Ups Fly High," *The Wall Street Journal*, February 22, 1999.
4. Abbott Laboratories, *Annual Report*, 1998.
5. *Statement of Position No. 98-5*, "Report on the Costs of Start up Activities" (New York: American Institute of Certified Public Accountants, 1998).
6. Microsoft Corporation, Inc., *Annual Report*, 1997.
7. G. Christian Hill, "Microsoft Plans Preferred Issue of $750 Million," *The Wall Street Journal*, December 3, 1996.
8. American Institute of Certified Public Accountants, *Accounting Trends & Techniques* (New York: AICPA, 1998), p. 285.
9. The Coca-Cola Company, *Annual Report*, 1996 and 1998.
10. IBM Corporation, *Annual Report*, 1996 and 1998.
11. Fred P. Bleakley, "Management Problem: Reinvest High Profits or Please Institutions?" *The Wall Street Journal*, October 16, 1995.
12. American Institute of Certified Public Accountants, *Accounting Trends & Techniques* (New York: AICPA, 1998), p. 346.
13. *Statement of Accounting Standards No. 123*, "Accounting for Stock-Based Compensation" (Norwalk, Conn.: Financial Accounting Standards Board, 1995).
14. Elizabeth MacDonald, "Options' Effect on Earnings Sparks Debate," *The Wall Street Journal*, May 13, 1999.
15. Stock options are discussed here in the context of employee compensation. They can also be important features of complex corporate capitalization arrangements.
16. Announcement, *The Wall Street Journal*, February 19, 1999, p. C19.
17. Tom Herman, "Preferreds' Rich Yields Blind Some Investors to Risks," *The Wall Street Journal*, March 24, 1992.
18. Stanley Ziemba, "USAir Defers Dividends on Preferred Stock," *Chicago Tribune*, September 30, 1994.
19. Susan Carey, "US Airways to Redeem Preferred Owned by Berkshire Hathaway," *The Wall Street Journal*, February 4, 1998.
20. Roche Group, *Annual Report*, 1998.

Expanded Presentation and Analysis of Accounting Information

Because business organizations today are so complex, expanded forms of financial statements are needed to present financial information in a way that a company's operations can be fully understood. **Part Four** deals with these expanded financial statements, how to interpret and analyze them, and the effects of international operations and long-term investments.

Chapter 13 The Corporate Income Statement and the Statement of Stockholders' Equity focuses on these two important financial statements, with an emphasis on specific items that may appear in them. Assessment of a company's quality of earnings opens the chapter. In addition, retained earnings, stock dividends, stock splits, and book value per share are covered in this chapter.

Chapter 14 The Statement of Cash Flows presents the statement and explains the changes in cash flows from operating, investing, and financing activities of a business. Emphasis is placed on analyzing a company's cash-generating ability and its free cash flow. The indirect approach is used to compute net cash flows from operating activities, but the direct approach is presented as a supplemental objective.

Chapter 15 Financial Statement Analysis explains the objectives and techniques of financial statement analysis from the standpoint of the financial analyst. It summarizes all the ratios presented thus far in the book, using a comprehensive financial analysis of Sun Microsystems Inc.

Chapter 16 International Accounting and Long-Term Investments addresses two areas of relevance to most corporations in today's complex and global environment. The first is international accounting, including the effects of changing rates of exchange for foreign currencies and of diverse international accounting standards on the interpretations of financial statements. The second is accounting for investments by one company in the capital stock or bonds of another, including consolidated financial statements.

13

The Corporate Income Statement and the Statement of Stockholders' Equity

DECISION POINT: A USER'S FOCUS

Monsanto Company Monsanto Company, a producer of agricultural biotechnology and seed products as well as pharmaceuticals and other life science products, has been undergoing significant transformation over the past five years. Interpreting the company's performance is not always easy. For instance, consider Monsanto's performance for the five-year period 1994 through 1998, as measured by earnings per share.[1] Income (loss) from Continuing Operations has steadily decreased since 1995, but Net Income (Loss) has shown more variation. Someone who does not know the structure and use of corporate income statements may be confused by the apparent contradiction of these numbers. What's the explanation?

Financial Highlights

(Per share)

	1998	1997	1996	1995	1994
Income (loss) from continuing operations	($.41)	$.48	$.69	$ .79	$ .78
Net income (loss)	($.41)	$.77	$.64	$1.27	$1.06

Earnings per share is the "bottom line" that many investors look at to judge the success or failure of a company. However, just looking at the bottom line may be misleading. The corporate income statement includes a number of infrequent increases and decreases, more or less at the discretion of management, that will result in the variation exhibited for Monsanto. For the most recent three years, Monsanto took one-time special charges related to new companies acquired and restructuring charges. Without these charges, income (loss) from continuing operations would have been $.93, $1.23, and $1.12 per share. Net income per share for 1994 through 1997 was also affected by operations that Monsanto discontinued each year. Knowledge of issues involving quality of earnings and the components of corporate income statements is essential to understanding and analyzing the operations of companies like Monsanto.

Key Point: It is important to know which items included in earnings are recurring and which are one-time items. Earnings from continuing operations before nonrecurring items give a good signal about future results. In assessing the company's future earnings potential, nonrecurring items are excluded because they are not expected to continue.

Performance Measurement: Quality of Earnings Issues

Current and expected earnings are important factors to consider in evaluating a company's performance and analyzing its prospects. In fact, a survey of two thousand members of the Association for Investment Management and Research indicated that the two most important economic indicators in evaluating common stocks were expected changes in earnings per share and expected return on equity.[2] Net income is a key component of both measures. Because of the importance of net income, or the "bottom line," in measuring a company's prospects, there is significant interest in evaluating the quality of the net income figure, or the **quality of earnings**. The quality of a company's earnings refers to the substance of earnings and their sustainability into future accounting periods and may be affected by (1) the accounting methods and estimates the company's management chooses and (2) the nature of nonoperating items on the income statement.

Choice of Accounting Methods and Estimates

Key Point: Two companies in the same industry could have comparable earnings quantity but not comparable earnings quality. In order to assess the quality of reported earnings, one must know the methods and estimates used to compute income. GAAP allows several choices of methods and estimates, all yielding different results.

Choices of accounting methods and estimates affect a firm's operating income. To assure proper matching of revenues and expenses, accounting requires cost allocations and estimates of data that will not be known with certainty until some future date. For example, accountants estimate the useful life of assets when they are acquired. However, technological obsolescence could shorten the expected useful life, or excellent maintenance and repairs could lengthen it. The actual useful life will not be known with certainty until some future date. The choice of estimate affects both current and future operating income.

Because there is considerable latitude in the choice of estimates, management and other financial statement users must be aware of the impact of accounting estimates on reported operating income. Estimates include percentage of uncollectible accounts receivable, sales returns, useful life, residual or salvage value, total units of production, total recoverable units of natural resource, amortization period, expected warranty claims, and expected environmental cleanup costs.

These estimates are not all equally important to every firm. The relative importance of each estimate depends on the industry in which the firm operates. For example, the estimate of uncollectible receivables for a credit card firm, such as American Express, or a financial services firm, such as Bank of America, can have a material impact on earnings, but the choice of useful life may be less important because depreciable assets represent only a small percentage of total assets. Toys "R" Us has very few receivables, but it has substantial investment in depreciable assets; thus choice of useful life and residual value are much more important than uncollectible accounts receivable.

The choice of methods also affects a firm's operating income. Generally accepted accounting methods include uncollectible receivable methods (net sales or aging of accounts receivable), inventory methods [last-in, first-out (LIFO), first-in, first-out (FIFO), or average cost], depreciation methods (accelerated, production, or straight-line), and revenue recognition methods. These methods are designed to match revenues and expenses. Costs are allocated based on a determination of the benefits to the current period (expenses) versus the benefits to future periods (assets). The expenses are estimates, and the period or periods benefited cannot be demonstrated conclusively. The estimates are also subjective, because in practice it is hard to justify one method of estimation over another.

For these reasons, management, the accountant, and the financial statement user need to understand the possible effects of different accounting procedures on net income and financial position. Some methods and estimates are more conservative than others because they tend to produce a lower net income in the current period. For example, suppose that two companies have similar operations, but one uses FIFO for inventory costing and straight-line (SL) for computing depreciation, whereas the other uses LIFO for inventory costing and double-declining-balance (DDB) for computing depreciation. The income statements of the two companies might appear as follows:

	FIFO and SL	LIFO and DDB
Net Sales	$500,000	$500,000
Goods Available for Sale	$300,000	$300,000
Less Ending Inventory	60,000	50,000
Cost of Goods Sold	$240,000	$250,000
Gross Margin	$260,000	$250,000
Less: Depreciation Expense	$ 40,000	$ 80,000
Other Expenses	170,000	170,000
Total Operating Expenses	$210,000	$250,000
Operating Income	$ 50,000	$ 0

The operating income for the firm using LIFO and DDB is lower because, in periods of rising prices, the LIFO inventory costing method produces a higher cost of goods sold, and, in the early years of an asset's useful life, accelerated depreciation yields a higher depreciation expense. The result is lower operating income. However, future operating income is expected to be higher.

The $50,000 difference in operating income stems only from the differences in accounting methods. Differences in the estimated lives and residual values of the plant assets could lead to an even greater variation. In practice, of course, differences in net income occur for many reasons, but the user must be aware of the discrepancies that can occur as a result of the accounting methods chosen by management. In general, an accounting method or estimate that results in lower current earnings is considered to produce a better quality of operating income.

The existence of such alternatives could cause problems in the interpretation of financial statements were it not for the conventions of full disclosure and consistency. Full disclosure requires that management explain the significant accounting policies used in preparing the financial statements in a note to the statements.

Enrichment Note: Management is responsible for the content of financial statements. Financial statements report on the performance of management. When a group is responsible for reporting on its own activity, usually the best or most favorable position will be reported.

Consistency requires that the same accounting procedures be followed from year to year. If a change in procedure is made, the nature of the change and its monetary effect must be explained in a note.

Nature of Nonoperating Items

The corporate income statement consists of several components, as shown in Exhibit 1. The top of the statement presents income from current ongoing operations, called income from continuing operations. The lower part of the statement can contain such nonoperating items as discontinued operations, extraordinary gains and losses, and effects of accounting changes. Those items may drastically affect the bottom line, or net income, of the company. In fact, in Exhibit 1, earnings per common share associated with continuing operations were $2.81, but net income per share was $3.35, or 19.2 percent higher.

For practical reasons, the calculations of trends and ratios are based on the assumption that net income and other components are comparable from year to year and from company to company. However, in making interpretations, the astute analyst will always look beyond the ratios to the quality of the components. For example, restructuring charges, if they are large enough, can make a company's

Exhibit 1
A Corporate Income Statement

Junction Corporation
Income Statement
For the Year Ended December 31, 20xx

Revenues		$925,000
Less Costs and Expenses		500,000
Income from Continuing Operations Before Taxes		$425,000
Income Taxes Expense		144,500
Income from Continuing Operations		$280,500
Discontinued Operations		
Income from Operations of Discontinued Segment		
(net of taxes, $35,000)	$90,000	
Loss on Disposal of Segment (net of taxes, $42,000)	(73,000)	17,000
Income Before Extraordinary Items and		
Cumulative Effect of Accounting Change		$297,500
Extraordinary Gain (net of taxes, $17,000)		43,000
Subtotal		$340,500
Cumulative Effect of a Change in Accounting		
Principle (net of taxes, $5,000)		(6,000)
Net Income		$334,500
Earnings per Common Share:		
Income from Continuing Operations		$ 2.81
Discontinued Operations (net of taxes)		.17
Income Before Extraordinary Items and		
Cumulative Effect of Accounting Change		$ 2.98
Extraordinary Gain (net of taxes)		.43
Cumulative Effect of Accounting Change (net of taxes)		(.06)
Net Income		$ 3.35

Enrichment Note: Discontinued operations, extraordinary items, and cumulative effects of a change in accounting principle are more likely to occur in large, public corporations. A knowledge of these items is important when analyzing the financial results of such companies. These items do not occur as frequently in small, private business corporations.

Key Point: Discontinued operations, extraordinary gains and losses, and the cumulative effect of a change in accounting principle must appear as separate items below income from continuing operations. They are all shown net of taxes.

BUSINESS FOCUS ON ETHICS

External users of financial statements depend on management's honesty and openness in disclosing factual information about a company. In the vast majority of cases, management's reports are reliable, but on occasion, employees (called *whistle-blowers*) may publicly disclose wrongdoing on the part of their company. For example, after the internal audit chief of W. R. Grace, a chemical company, was fired, he made known to the SEC his concerns of deliberate deferral of reporting of income by W. R. Grace. The goal was to show growth in earnings within the targeted range of 20–24 percent, which analysts were expecting. Later the company reversed the deferral of income to offset poor operating results. The SEC is currently investigating W. R. Grace for fraudulently manipulated earnings.[4]

return on equity look better. In a recent year, Boeing Company, an aircraft manufacturer, took charges of $4 billion resulting in a loss of $178 million. The effect of this charge reduced equity by almost 20 percent. Return on equity should increase next period.[5] Although such write-offs reduce a company's net worth, they usually do not affect current cash flows or operations and in most cases are ignored by analysts assessing current performance.

In some cases, a company may boost income by including one-time gains. For example, Sears, Roebuck and Co., a multi-line retailer providing a wide array of merchandise and services, used a gain from the change of an accounting principle to bolster its net income by $136 million or $.35 per share in 1997. Without the gain, earnings per share (EPS) actually decreased, from $3.12 to $2.92, not increased as Sears originally reported.[6] The quality of Sears's earnings is in fact lower than it might appear on the surface. Unless analysts are prepared to go beyond the "bottom line" in analyzing and interpreting financial reports, they can come to the wrong conclusions.

The Corporate Income Statement

OBJECTIVE

2 Prepare a corporate income statement

Study Note: Both single-step and multistep income statements are commonly used in corporate annual reports. Whichever format is used, the income statement must be all-inclusive.

Accounting organizations have not specified the format of the income statement because they have considered flexibility more important than a standard format. Either the single-step or the multistep form can be used. However, the accounting profession has taken the position that income for a period should be all-inclusive, **comprehensive income**, which is different from net income.[7] Comprehensive income is the change in a company's equity during a period from sources other than owners and includes net income, change in unrealized investment gains and losses, and other items affecting equity. Since 1998, companies began reporting comprehensive income and its components as a separate financial statement, or as part of another financial statement. Net income or loss for a period includes all revenues, expenses, gains, and losses over the period, except for prior period adjustments. As a result, several items must be added to the income statement, among them discontinued operations, extraordinary items, and accounting changes. The Financial Accounting Standards Board has proposed adding goodwill amortization to this list, moving it down from income from operations. In addition, earnings per share figures must be disclosed. Exhibit 1 illustrated a corporate income statement and the required disclosures. The following sections discuss the components of the corporate income statement, beginning with income taxes expense.

Income Taxes Expense

OBJECTIVE
3 Show the relationships among income taxes expense, deferred income taxes, and net of taxes

Corporations determine their taxable income (the amount on which taxes are paid) by subtracting allowable business deductions from includable gross income. The federal tax laws determine which business expenses may be deducted and which cannot be deducted from taxable gross income.[8]

The tax rates that apply to a corporation's taxable income are shown in Table 1. A corporation with taxable income of $70,000 would have a federal income tax liability of $12,500: $7,500 (the tax on the first $50,000 of taxable income) plus $5,000 (25 percent of the $20,000 earned in excess of $50,000).

Income taxes expense is the expense recognized in the accounting records on an accrual basis that applies to income from continuing operations. This expense may or may not equal the amount of taxes actually paid by the corporation and recorded as income taxes payable in the current period. The amount payable is determined from taxable income, which is measured according to the rules and regulations of the income tax code.

Enrichment Note: Most people think it is illegal to keep accounting records on a different basis from income tax records. They don't realize that it is normal because the Internal Revenue Code and GAAP often do not agree. To work with two conflicting sets of guidelines, the accountant must keep two sets of records.

For the sake of convenience, most small businesses keep their accounting records on the same basis as their tax records, so that the income taxes expense on the income statement equals the income taxes liability to be paid to the Internal Revenue Service (IRS). This practice is acceptable when there is no material difference between the income on an accounting basis and the income on an income tax basis. However, the purpose of accounting is to determine net income in accordance with generally accepted accounting principles, not to determine taxable income and tax liability.

Management has an incentive to use methods that minimize the firm's tax liability, but accountants, who are bound by accrual accounting and the materiality concept, cannot let tax procedures dictate their method of preparing financial statements if the result would be misleading. As a consequence, there can be a material difference between accounting and taxable incomes, especially in larger businesses. This discrepancy can result from differences in the timing of the recognition of revenues and expenses under the two accounting methods. Some possible variations are shown below.

	Accounting Method	Tax Method
Expense recognition	Accrual or deferral	At time of expenditure
Accounts receivable	Allowance	Direct charge-off
Inventories	Average cost	FIFO
Depreciation	Straight-line	Modified Accelerated Cost Recovery System

Deferred Income Taxes

Key Point: The discrepancy between GAAP-based tax expense and Internal Revenue Code-based tax liability produces the need for the Deferred Income Taxes account.

Accounting for the difference between income taxes expense based on accounting income and the actual income taxes payable based on taxable income is accomplished by a technique called **income tax allocation**. The amount by which income taxes expense differs from income taxes payable is reconciled in an account called **Deferred Income Taxes**. For example, Junction Corporation shows income taxes expense of $144,500 on its income statement but has actual income taxes payable to the IRS of $92,000. The entry that follows is to record the estimated income taxes expense applicable to income from continuing operations using the income tax allocation procedure.

Table 1. Tax Rate Schedule for Corporations, 2000*

Taxable Income		Tax Liability	
Over	But Not Over		Of the Amount Over
—	$ 50,000	0 + 15%	—
$ 50,000	75,000	$ 7,500 + 25%	$ 50,000
75,000	100,000	13,750 + 34%	75,000
100,000	335,000	22,250 + 39%	100,000
335,000	10,000,000	113,900 + 34%	335,000
10,000,000	15,000,000	3,400,000 + 35%	10,000,000
15,000,000	18,333,333	5,150,000 + 38%	15,000,000
18,333,333	—	6,416,667 + 35%	18,333,333

*Tax rates are subject to change by Congress.

Enrichment Note: The federal income tax is progressive. That is, the rate increases as taxable income increases.

$A = L + OE$
$\quad + \quad -$
$\quad +$

Dec. 31	Income Taxes Expense	144,500	
	Income Taxes Payable		92,000
	Deferred Income Taxes		52,500
	To record estimated current and deferred income taxes		

In other years, it is possible for Income Taxes Payable to exceed Income Taxes Expense, in which case the same entry is made except that Deferred Income Taxes is debited.

The Financial Accounting Standards Board has issued specific rules for recording, measuring, and classifying deferred income taxes.[9] Deferred income taxes are recognized for the estimated future tax effects resulting from temporary differences in the valuation of assets, liabilities, equity, revenues, expenses, gains, and losses for tax and financial reporting purposes. Temporary differences include revenues and expenses or gains and losses that are included in taxable income before or after they are included in financial income. In other words, the recognition point for revenues, expenses, gains, and losses is not the same for tax and financial reporting. For example, advance payments for goods and services, such as magazine subscriptions, are not recognized in financial income until the product is shipped, but for tax purposes they are usually recognized as revenue when cash is received. The result is that taxes paid exceed tax expense, which creates a deferred income tax asset (or prepaid taxes).

Study Note: Deferred Income Taxes is classified as a liability when it has a credit balance and as an asset when it has a debit balance. It is further classified as either current or long-term depending on when it is expected to reverse.

Classification of deferred income taxes as current or noncurrent depends on the classification of the related asset or liability that created the temporary difference. For example, the deferred income tax asset mentioned above would be classified as current if unearned subscription revenue is classified as a current liability. On the other hand, the temporary difference arising from depreciation is related to a long-term depreciable asset. Therefore, the resulting deferred income tax would be classified as long-term. However, if a temporary difference isn't related to an asset or liability, then it is classified as current or noncurrent based on its expected date of reversal. Temporary differences and the classification of deferred income taxes that results are covered in depth in more advanced courses.

Each year, the balance of the Deferred Income Taxes account is evaluated to determine whether it still accurately represents the expected asset or liability in light of legislated changes in income tax laws and regulations. If changes have occurred, an adjusting entry to bring the account balance into line with current laws is required. For example, a decrease in corporate income tax rates, like the one that occurred in 1987, means that a company with deferred income tax liabilities will pay less in taxes in future years than the amount indicated by the credit balance of its Deferred Income Taxes account. As a result, the company would debit Deferred Income Taxes to reduce the liability and credit Gain from Reduction in Income Tax Rates. This credit increases the reported income on the income statement. If the tax rate increases in future years, a loss would be recorded and the deferred income tax liability would be increased.

In any given year, the amount a company pays in income taxes is determined by subtracting (or adding, as the case may be) the deferred income taxes for that year, as reported in the notes to the financial statements, from (or to) income taxes expense, which is reported in the financial statements. In subsequent years, the amount of deferred income taxes can vary based on changes in tax laws and rates.

Some understanding of the importance of deferred income taxes to financial reporting can be gained from studying a survey of the financial statements of 600 large companies. About 67 percent reported deferred income taxes with a credit balance in the long-term liability section of the balance sheet.[10]

Net of Taxes

The phrase **net of taxes**, as used in Exhibit 1, means that the effect of applicable taxes (usually income taxes) has been considered in determining the overall effect of an item on the financial statements. The phrase is used on the corporate income statement when a company has items that must be disclosed in a separate section. Each such item should be reported net of the applicable income taxes to avoid distorting the income taxes expense associated with ongoing operations and the resulting net operating income.

For example, assume that a corporation with operating income before taxes of $120,000 has a total tax expense of $66,000 and that the total income includes a gain of $100,000 on which a tax of $30,000 is due. Also assume that the gain is not part of normal operations and must be disclosed separately on the income statement as an extraordinary item (explained later). This is how the tax expense would be reported on the income statement:

Operating Income Before Taxes	$120,000
Income Taxes Expense	36,000
Income Before Extraordinary Item	$ 84,000
Extraordinary Gain (net of taxes, $30,000)	70,000
Net Income	$154,000

If all the tax expense were deducted from operating income before taxes, both the income before extraordinary item and the extraordinary gain would be distorted.

A company follows the same procedure in the case of an extraordinary loss. For example, assume the same facts as before except that the total tax expense is only $6,000 because of a $100,000 extraordinary loss. The result is a $30,000 tax savings, as shown below.

Operating Income Before Taxes	$120,000
Income Taxes Expense	36,000
Income Before Extraordinary Item	$ 84,000
Extraordinary Loss (net of taxes, $30,000)	(70,000)
Net Income	$ 14,000

In Exhibit 1, the total of the income tax items is $149,500. That amount is allocated among five statement components, as follows:

Income taxes expense on income from continuing operations	$144,500
Income tax on income from a discontinued segment	35,000
Income tax savings on the loss on the disposal of the segment	(42,000)
Income tax on the extraordinary gain	17,000
Income tax savings on the cumulative effect of a change in accounting principle	(5,000)
Total income taxes expense	$149,500

Discontinued Operations

OBJECTIVE

4 Describe the disclosure on the income statement of discontinued operations, extraordinary items, and accounting changes

Large companies in the United States usually have many **segments**. A segment may be a separate major line of business or serve a separate class of customer. For example, a company that makes heavy drilling equipment may also have another line of business, such as the manufacture of mobile homes. A large company may discontinue or otherwise dispose of certain segments of its business that do not fit its future plans or are not profitable. **Discontinued operations** are segments of a business that are no longer part of its ongoing operations. Generally accepted accounting principles require that gains and losses from discontinued operations be reported separately on the income statement. Such separation makes it easier to evaluate the ongoing activities of the business.

In Exhibit 1, the disclosure of discontinued operations has two parts. One part shows that after the date of the decision to discontinue, the income from operations of the segment that has been disposed of was $90,000 (net of $35,000 taxes). The other part shows that the loss from the disposal of the segment was $73,000 (net of $42,000 tax savings). Computation of the gains or losses is covered in more advanced accounting courses. The disclosure has been described, however, to give a complete view of the corporate income statement.

Extraordinary Items

Key Point: To qualify as extraordinary, an event must be unusual (not in the ordinary course of business) and must not be expected to occur again in the foreseeable future. Occasionally, judgment must be exercised when it is not clear whether an event meets these two criteria.

The Accounting Principles Board, in its *Opinion No. 30*, defines **extraordinary items** as "events or transactions that are distinguished by their unusual nature *and* by the infrequency of their occurrence."[11] Unusual and infrequent occurrences are explained in the opinion as follows:

> Unusual Nature—the underlying event or transaction should possess a high degree of abnormality and be of a type clearly unrelated to, or only incidentally related to, the ordinary and typical activities of the entity, taking into account the environment in which the entity operates.

> Infrequency of Occurrence—the underlying event or transaction should be of a type that would not reasonably be expected to recur in the foreseeable future, taking into account the environment in which the entity operates.[12]

If an item is both unusual and infrequent (and material in amount), it should be reported separately from continuing operations on the income statement. The disclosure allows readers to identify gains or losses in income that would not be expected to happen again soon. Items usually treated as extraordinary include (1) an uninsured loss from flood, earthquake, fire, or theft; (2) a gain or loss resulting from the passage of a new law; (3) the expropriation (taking) of property by a foreign government; and (4) a gain or loss from the early retirement of debt. Gains or losses from extraordinary items should be reported on the income statement after discontinued operations. And they should be shown net of applicable taxes. In a recent year, 64 (11 percent) of 600 large companies reported extraordinary items on their income statements.[13] In Exhibit 1, the extraordinary gain was $43,000 after applicable taxes of $17,000.

Accounting Changes

Consistency, which is one of the basic conventions of accounting, means that companies must apply the same accounting principles from year to year. However, a company is allowed to make accounting changes if current procedures are incorrect or inappropriate. For example, a change from the FIFO to the LIFO inventory method can be made if there is adequate justification for the change. Adequate justification usually means that if the change occurs, the financial statements will better show the financial activities of the company. A company's desire to lower the amount of income taxes it pays is not considered adequate justification for an accounting change. If justification does exist and an accounting change is made, generally accepted accounting principles require the disclosure of the change in the financial statements.

The **cumulative effect of an accounting change** is the effect that the new accounting principle would have had on net income in prior periods if it had been applied instead of the old principle. This effect is shown on the income statement immediately after extraordinary items.[14] For example, assume that in the five years prior to 20xx, Junction Corporation had used the straight-line method to depreciate its machinery. This year, the company retroactively changed to the double-declining-balance method of depreciation. The controller computed the cumulative effect of the change in depreciation charges (net of taxes) as $6,000, as shown below.

Cumulative, 5-year double-declining-balance depreciation	$29,000
Less cumulative, 5-year straight-line depreciation	18,000
Before tax effect	$11,000
Income tax savings	5,000
Cumulative effect of accounting change	$ 6,000

Relevant information about the accounting change is shown in the notes to the financial statements. The change results in $11,000 of depreciation expense for prior years being deducted in the current year, in addition to the current year's depreciation costs included in the $500,000 costs and expenses section of the income statement. This expense must be shown in the current year's income statement as a reduction in income (see Exhibit 1). In 1997, 95, or 16 percent, of 600 large companies reported changes in accounting procedures.[15] Further study of accounting changes is left to more advanced accounting courses.

Earnings per Share

Readers of financial statements use earnings per share information to judge a company's performance and to compare it with the performance of other companies. Because such information is so important, the Accounting Principles Board concluded that earnings per share of common stock should be presented on the face of the income statement.[16] As shown in Exhibit 1, the information is usually disclosed just below the net income.

An earnings per share amount is always shown for (1) income from continuing operations, (2) income before extraordinary items and the cumulative effect of accounting changes, (3) the cumulative effect of accounting changes, and (4) net income. If the statement shows a gain or loss from discontinued operations or a gain or loss on extraordinary items, earnings per share amounts can also be presented for them. The per share data below from the income statement of Minnesota Mining and Manufacturing Company (3M) show why it is a good idea to study the components of earnings per share.[17]

Financial Highlights

	Years ended December 31		
	1998	1997	1996
Earnings per share—Basic:			
Continuing operations	$3.01	$5.14	$3.63
Discontinued operations	—	—	.02
Extraordinary loss	(.10)	—	—
Net income	$2.91	$5.14	$3.65

Note that net income was influenced by special items in 1998 and 1996. In 1998, an extraordinary loss decreased income from continuing operations by $.10 per share to a basic net income of $2.91 per share; in 1996, discontinued operations increased net income per share by $.02. In 1997, the company had no special items; thus, 100 percent of 3M's basic earnings per share were attributable to continuing operations.

Basic earnings per share is net income applicable to common stock divided by the weighted-average number of common shares outstanding. To compute this figure, one must determine if during the year the number of common shares outstanding changed, and if the company paid preferred stock dividends.

When a company has only common stock and has the same number of shares outstanding throughout the year, the earnings per share computation is simple. From Exhibit 1, we know that Junction Corporation reported net income of $334,500. Assume that the company had 100,000 shares of common stock outstanding for the entire year. The earnings per share of common stock is computed as follows:

$$\text{Earnings per Share} = \frac{\$334,500}{100,000 \text{ shares}} = \$3.35 \text{ per share}$$

If the number of shares outstanding changes during the year, it is necessary to figure the weighted-average number of shares outstanding for the year. Suppose that Junction Corporation had the following amounts of common shares outstanding during various periods of the year: January–March, 100,000 shares; April–September, 120,000 shares; and October–December, 130,000 shares. The weighted-average number of common shares outstanding and basic earnings per share would be found this way:

100,000 shares $\times$ $\frac{1}{4}$ year	25,000
120,000 shares $\times$ $\frac{1}{2}$ year	60,000
130,000 shares $\times$ $\frac{1}{4}$ year	32,500
Weighted-average common shares outstanding	117,500

$$\text{Basic Earnings per Share} = \frac{\text{Net Income}}{\text{Weighted-Average Common Shares Outstanding}}$$

$$= \frac{\$334,500}{117,500 \text{ shares}} = \$2.85 \text{ per share}$$

If a company has nonconvertible preferred stock outstanding, the dividend for that stock must be subtracted from net income before earnings per share for common stock are computed. Suppose that Junction Corporation has preferred stock on which the annual dividend is $23,500. Earnings per share on common stock would be $2.65 [($334,500 − $23,500) ÷ 117,500 shares].

Companies with a capital structure in which there are no bonds, stocks, or stock options that could be converted into common stock are said to have a **simple capital structure**. The earnings per share for these companies is computed as shown on the previous page. Some companies, however, have a **complex capital structure**, which includes exercisable stock options or convertible stocks and bonds. Those convertible securities have the potential of diluting the earnings per share of common stock. *Potential dilution* means that a stockholder's proportionate share of ownership in a company could be reduced through the conversion of stocks or bonds or the exercise of stock options, which would increase the total shares outstanding.

For example, suppose that a person owns 10,000 shares of a company, which equals 2 percent of the outstanding shares of 500,000. Now, suppose that holders of convertible bonds convert the bonds into 100,000 shares of stock. The person's 10,000 shares would then equal only 1.67 percent (10,000 ÷ 600,000) of the outstanding shares. In addition, the added shares outstanding would lower earnings per share and would most likely lower market price per share.

> **Key Point:** A company with potentially dilutive securities (such as convertible preferred stock or bonds) has a complex capital structure and must present two earnings per share figures—basic and diluted. The latter figure is the more conservative of the two.

Because stock options and convertible preferred stocks or bonds have the potential to dilute earnings per share, they are referred to as **potentially dilutive securities**. When a company has a complex capital structure, it must report two earnings per share figures: basic earnings per share and diluted earnings per share.[18] **Diluted earnings per share** are calculated by adding all potentially dilutive securities to the denominator of the basic earnings per share calculation. This figure shows stockholders the maximum potential effect of dilution of their ownership position in the company.

The computation of diluted earnings per share is a complex process and is reserved for more advanced courses.

The Statement of Stockholders' Equity

> **OBJECTIVE**
> **6** Prepare a statement of stockholders' equity

> **Enrichment Note:** The majority of annual reports contain a statement of stockholders' equity because it discloses far more than a statement of retained earnings.

The **statement of stockholders' equity**, also called the *statement of changes in stockholders' equity*, summarizes the changes in the components of the stockholders' equity section of the balance sheet. More and more companies are using this statement in place of the statement of retained earnings because it reveals much more about the year's stockholders' equity transactions. In the statement of stockholders' equity in Exhibit 2, for example, the first line shows the beginning balance of each account in the stockholders' equity section. Each subsequent line discloses the effects of transactions on those accounts. It is possible to determine from the statement that during 20x1 Tri-State Corporation issued 5,000 shares of common stock for $250,000, had a conversion of $100,000 of preferred stock into common stock, declared and issued a 10 percent stock dividend on common stock, had a net purchase of treasury shares of $24,000, earned net income of $270,000, and paid cash dividends on both preferred and common stock. The ending balances of the accounts are presented at the bottom of the statement. Those accounts and balances make up the stockholders' equity section of Tri-State's balance sheet on December 31, 20x1, as shown in Exhibit 3.

Exhibit 2
A Statement of Stockholders' Equity

Tri-State Corporation
Statement of Stockholders' Equity
For the Year Ended December 31, 20x1

	Preferred Stock $100 Par Value 8% Convertible	Common Stock $10 Par Value	Paid-in Capital in Excess of Par Value, Common	Retained Earnings	Treasury Stock	Total
Balance, December 31, 20x0	$400,000	$300,000	$300,000	$600,000	—	$1,600,000
Issuance of 5,000 Shares of Common Stock		50,000	200,000			250,000
Conversion of 1,000 Shares of Preferred Stock into 3,000 Shares of Common Stock	(100,000)	30,000	70,000			—
10 Percent Stock Dividend on Common Stock, 3,800 Shares		38,000	152,000	(190,000)		—
Purchase of 500 Shares of Treasury Stock					($24,000)	(24,000)
Net Income				270,000		270,000
Cash Dividends						
Preferred Stock				(24,000)		(24,000)
Common Stock				(47,600)		(47,600)
Balance, December 31, 20x1	$300,000	$418,000	$722,000	$608,400	($24,000)	$2,024,400

Exhibit 3
Stockholders' Equity Section of a Balance Sheet

Key Point: The ending balances on the statement of stockholders' equity are transferred to the stockholders' equity section of the balance sheet.

Tri-State Corporation
Stockholders' Equity
December 31, 20x1

Contributed Capital		
Preferred Stock, $100 par value, 8% convertible, 10,000 shares authorized, 3,000 shares issued and outstanding		$ 300,000
Common Stock, $10 par value, 100,000 shares authorized, 41,800 shares issued, 41,300 shares outstanding	$418,000	
Paid-in Capital in Excess of Par Value, Common	722,000	1,140,000
Total Contributed Capital		$1,440,000
Retained Earnings		608,400
Total Contributed Capital and Retained Earnings		$2,048,400
Less Treasury Stock, Common (500 shares, at cost)		24,000
Total Stockholders' Equity		$2,024,400

Retained Earnings

Notice that in Exhibit 2 the Retained Earnings column has the same components as the statement of retained earnings. The **retained earnings** of a company are the part of stockholders' equity that represents stockholders' claims to assets arising from the earnings of the business. Retained earnings equal a company's profits since the date of its inception, less any losses, dividends to stockholders, or transfers to contributed capital.

It is important to remember that retained earnings are not the assets themselves. The existence of retained earnings means that assets generated by profitable operations have been kept in the company to help it grow or to meet other business needs. A credit balance in Retained Earnings is *not* directly associated with a specific amount of cash or designated assets. Rather, such a balance means that assets as a whole have been increased.

Retained Earnings can carry a debit balance. Generally, this happens when a company's dividends and subsequent losses are greater than its accumulated profits from operations. In such a case, the firm is said to have a **deficit** (debit balance) in Retained Earnings. A deficit is shown in the stockholders' equity section of the balance sheet as a deduction from contributed capital.

A corporation may be required or may want to restrict all or a portion of its retained earnings. A **restriction on retained earnings** means that dividends can be declared only to the extent of the *unrestricted* retained earnings. The following are several reasons a company might restrict retained earnings.

1. *A contractual agreement.* For example, bond indentures may place a limitation on the dividends the company can pay.

2. *State law.* Many states do not allow a corporation to distribute dividends or purchase treasury stock if doing so reduces equity below a minimum level because this would impair the legal capital of the company.

3. *Voluntary action by the board of directors.* Often a board decides to retain assets in the business for future needs. For example, the company may be planning to build a new plant and may want to show that dividends will be limited to save enough money for the building. A company might also restrict retained earnings to show a possible future loss of assets resulting from a lawsuit.

A restriction on retained earnings does not change the total retained earnings or stockholders' equity of the company. It simply divides retained earnings into two

Key Point: In accounting, a deficit is a negative (debit) balance in Retained Earnings. It is not the same thing as a net loss, which reflects the performance in just one accounting period.

Key Point: The statement of stockholders' equity is a labeled calculation of the change in each stockholders' equity account over the period.

BUSINESS FOCUS ON INTERNATIONAL

Restrictions on retained earnings, called *reserves*, are much more common in some foreign countries than in the United States. In Sweden, for instance, reserves are used to respond to fluctuations in the economy. The Swedish tax code allows companies to set up contingency reserves for the purpose of maintaining financial stability. Appropriations to those reserves reduce taxable income and income taxes. The reserves become taxable when they are reversed, but they are available to absorb losses should they occur. For example, Skandia Group, a large Swedish insurance company, reported a net income of only SK1,242 million in 1998, less than half the result of SK3,402 million in 1997. An examination of its statement of stockholders' equity shows a transfer of SK1,277 million to restricted reserves in 1997, a good year, but restricted reserves of SK588 million were transferred back to unrestricted reserves in 1998, a less successful year. Skandia also increased its dividends in 1998 to SK384 million and still had SK12.6 billion in restricted reserves.[19]

parts: restricted and unrestricted. The unrestricted amount represents earnings kept in the business that the company can use for dividends and other purposes. Also, the restriction of retained earnings does not restrict cash or other assets in any way. It simply explains to the readers of the financial statements that a certain amount of assets generated by earnings will remain in the business for the purpose stated. It is still management's job to make sure that there is enough cash or assets on hand to fulfill the purpose. Also, the removal of a restriction does not necessarily mean that the board of directors is then able to declare a dividend.

The most common way to disclose restricted retained earnings is by reference to a note to the financial statements. For example:

Retained Earnings (Note 15) $900,000

> Note 15:
> Because of plans to expand the capacity of the company's clothing division, the board of directors has restricted retained earnings available for dividends by $300,000.

Stock Dividends

A **stock dividend** is a proportional distribution of shares of a corporation's stock to its shareholders. A stock dividend does not change the firm's assets and liabilities because there is no distribution of assets, as there is when a cash dividend is distributed. A board of directors may declare a stock dividend for several reasons:

1. It may want to give stockholders some evidence of the company's success without paying a cash dividend, which would affect working capital.

2. It may seek to reduce the stock's market price by increasing the number of shares outstanding, although this goal is more often met by a stock split.

3. It may want to make a nontaxable distribution to stockholders. Stock dividends that meet certain conditions are not considered income, so they are not taxed.

4. It may wish to increase the company's permanent capital by transferring an amount from retained earnings to contributed capital.

The total stockholders' equity is not affected by a stock dividend. The effect of a stock dividend is to transfer a dollar amount from retained earnings to the contributed capital section on the date of declaration. The amount transferred is the fair market value (usually, the market price) of the additional shares to be issued. The laws of most states specify the minimum value of each share transferred under a stock dividend, which is normally the minimum legal capital (par or stated value). However, generally accepted accounting principles state that market value reflects the economic effect of small stock distributions (less than 20 to 25 percent of a company's outstanding common stock) better than par or stated value does. For this reason, market price should be used to account for small stock dividends.[20]

To illustrate the accounting for a stock dividend, let us assume that Caprock Corporation has the following stockholders' equity structure.

Contributed Capital	
Common Stock, $5 par value, 100,000 shares authorized, 30,000 shares issued and outstanding	$ 150,000
Paid-in Capital in Excess of Par Value, Common	30,000
Total Contributed Capital	$ 180,000
Retained Earnings	900,000
Total Stockholders' Equity	$1,080,000

Suppose that the board of directors declares a 10 percent stock dividend on February 24, distributable on March 31 to stockholders of record on March 15, and that the market price of the stock on February 24 is $20 per share. The entries to record the declaration and distribution of the stock dividend are shown below.

Date of Declaration

A = L + OE
−
+
+

Feb. 24	Stock Dividends Declared	60,000	
	Common Stock Distributable		15,000
	Paid-in Capital in Excess of Par		
	Value, Common		45,000

Declared a 10% stock dividend on common stock, distributable on March 31 to stockholders of record on March 15:
30,000 shares × .10 = 3,000 shares
3,000 shares × $20/share = $60,000
3,000 shares × $5/share = $15,000

Key Point: For a small stock dividend, the portion of retained earnings transferred is determined by multiplying the number of shares to be distributed by the stock's market price on the date of declaration.

Date of Record

Mar. 15 No entry required.

Date of Distribution

A = L + OE
−
+

Mar. 31	Common Stock Distributable	15,000	
	Common Stock		15,000

Distribution of a stock dividend of 3,000 shares

Key Point: The declaration of a stock dividend results in a reshuffling of stockholders' equity. That is, a portion of retained earnings is converted (by closing the Stock Dividends Declared account) into contributed capital. Total stockholders' equity is not affected. Retained earnings are transferred at the time of the recording (date of declaration) and not at the closing of the Stock Dividends Declared account.

Key Point: Common Stock Distributable is a contributed capital (stockholders' equity) account, not a liability. When the shares are issued, this account is converted into Common Stock.

The effect of this stock dividend is to permanently transfer the market value of the stock, $60,000, from retained earnings to contributed capital and to increase the number of shares outstanding by 3,000. The Stock Dividends Declared account is used to record the total amount of the stock dividend. Retained Earnings is reduced by the amount of the stock dividend when the Stock Dividends Declared account is closed to Retained Earnings at the end of the accounting period. Common Stock Distributable is credited for the par value of the stock to be distributed (3,000 × $5 = $15,000).

In addition, when the market value is greater than the par value of the stock, Paid-in Capital in Excess of Par Value, Common must be credited for the amount by which the market value exceeds the par value. In this case, the total market value of the stock dividend ($60,000) exceeds the total par value ($15,000) by $45,000. No entry is required on the date of record. On the distribution date, the common stock is issued by debiting Common Stock Distributable and crediting Common Stock for the par value of the stock ($15,000).

Common Stock Distributable is not a liability account because there is no obligation to distribute cash or other assets. The obligation is to distribute additional shares of capital stock. If financial statements are prepared between the date of declaration and the date of distribution, Common Stock Distributable should be reported as part of contributed capital.

Contributed Capital		
Common Stock, $5 par value, 100,000 shares		
authorized, 30,000 shares issued and outstanding		$ 150,000
Common Stock Distributable, 3,000 shares		15,000
Paid-in Capital in Excess of Par Value, Common		75,000
Total Contributed Capital		$ 240,000
Retained Earnings		840,000
Total Stockholders' Equity		$1,080,000

Three points can be made from this example. First, the total stockholders' equity is the same before and after the stock dividend. Second, the assets of the corporation are not reduced as in the case of a cash dividend. Third, the proportionate ownership in the corporation of any individual stockholder is the same before and after the stock dividend. To illustrate these points, assume that a stockholder owns 1,000 shares before the stock dividend. After the 10 percent stock dividend is distributed, this stockholder would own 1,100 shares, as illustrated below.

Stockholders' Equity	Before Dividend	After Dividend
Common Stock	$ 150,000	$ 165,000
Paid-in Capital in Excess of Par Value, Common	30,000	75,000
Total Contributed Capital	$ 180,000	$ 240,000
Retained Earnings	900,000	840,000
Total Stockholders' Equity	$1,080,000	$1,080,000
Shares Outstanding	30,000	33,000
Stockholders' Equity per Share	$ 36.00	$ 32.73

Stockholders' Investment

Shares owned	1,000	1,100
Shares outstanding	30,000	33,000
Percentage of ownership	3⅓%	3⅓%
Proportionate investment ($1,080,000 × .03⅓)	$36,000	$36,000

Both before and after the stock dividend, the stockholders' equity totals $1,080,000 and the stockholder owns 3⅓ percent of the company. The proportionate investment (stockholders' equity times percentage ownership) remains at $36,000.

All stock dividends have an effect on the market price of a company's stock. But some stock dividends are so large that they have a material effect. For example, a 50 percent stock dividend would cause the market price of the stock to drop about 33 percent because the increase is now one-third of shares outstanding. The AICPA has decided that large stock dividends, those greater than 20 to 25 percent, should be accounted for by transferring the par or stated value of the stock on the date of declaration from retained earnings to contributed capital.[21]

Key Point: When a large (greater than 20 to 25 percent) stock dividend is declared, the transfer from retained earnings is based on the stock's par or stated value, not on its market value.

Stock Splits

Key Point: Earnings per share are reduced by stock splits and stock dividends because the number of shares has increased. Cash dividends have no effect on earnings per share.

A **stock split** occurs when a corporation increases the number of issued shares of stock and reduces the par or stated value proportionally. A company may plan a stock split when it wants to lower the stock's market value per share and increase the demand for the stock at this lower price. This action may be necessary if the market value per share has become so high that it hinders the trading of the stock or if the company wants to signal to the market its success in achieving its operating goals. For example, the action of The Gillette Company in a recent year in declaring a 2-for-1 stock split and raising its cash dividend achieved these strategic objectives. These actions were viewed positively by the market by pushing the share price to $106 from an earlier share price of $77. After the stock split, the number of shares outstanding doubled, thereby cutting the share price in half and also the dividend per share. Importantly, each stockholder's total wealth is unchanged as a result of the stock split.

To illustrate a stock split, suppose that Caprock Corporation has 30,000 shares of $5.00 par value stock outstanding. The market value is $70.00 per share. The

Enrichment Note: Stock splits greater than 2 for 1 are unusual. Splits such as 3 for 2 or 4 for 3 are far more common. On occasion, companies whose stock sells for a very low price will perform a reverse stock split, which reduces the number of shares and increases the market price.

corporation plans a 2-for-1 split. This split will lower the par value to $2.50 and increase the number of shares outstanding to 60,000. A stockholder who previously owned 400 shares of the $5.00 par stock would own 800 shares of the $2.50 par stock after the split. When a stock split occurs, the market value tends to fall in proportion to the increase in outstanding shares of stock. For example, a 2-for-1 stock split would cause the price of the stock to drop by approximately 50 percent, to about $35.00. It would also halve earnings per share and cash dividends per share (if the board does not increase the dividend). The lower price and the increase in shares tend to promote the buying and selling of shares.

A stock split does not increase the number of shares authorized. Nor does it change the balances in the stockholders' equity section of the balance sheet. It simply changes the par value and the number of shares issued, both shares outstanding and shares held as treasury stock. Therefore, an entry is not necessary. However, it is appropriate to document the change by making a memorandum entry in the general journal.

July 15   The 30,000 shares of $5 par value common stock that are issued and outstanding were split 2 for 1, resulting in 60,000 shares of $2.50 par value common stock issued and outstanding.

The change for the Caprock Corporation is as follows:

Before Stock Split (from page 607)

Contributed Capital	
Common Stock, $5 par value, 100,000 shares authorized, 30,000 shares issued and outstanding	$ 150,000
Paid-in Capital in Excess of Par Value, Common	30,000
Total Contributed Capital	$ 180,000
Retained Earnings	900,000
Total Stockholders' Equity	$1,080,000

After Stock Split

Contributed Capital	
Common Stock, $2.50 par value, 100,000 shares authorized, 60,000 shares issued and outstanding	$ 150,000
Paid-in Capital in Excess of Par Value, Common	30,000
Total Contributed Capital	$ 180,000
Retained Earnings	900,000
Total Stockholders' Equity	$1,080,000

Key Point: A stock split affects only the common stock calculation. In this case, there are twice as many shares after the split, but par value is now half of what it was.

Key Point: As long as the newly outstanding shares do not exceed the previously authorized shares, permission from the state is not needed for a stock split.

Although the amount of stockholders' equity per share would be half as much, each stockholder's proportionate interest in the company would remain the same.

If the number of split shares will exceed the number of authorized shares, the board of directors must secure state and stockholders' approval before it can issue additional shares.

Book Value

OBJECTIVE

8 Calculate book value per share

The word *value* is associated with shares of stock in several ways. Par value or stated value is set when the stock is authorized and establishes the legal capital of a company. Neither par value nor stated value has any relationship to a stock's book

BUSINESS FOCUS ON PRACTICE

Although book value per share often bears little relationship to market value per share, some investors use the relationship between the two as a rough indicator of the relative value of the stock. For example, in early 1991, the stock of Chrysler Corporation had a book value per share of $31 and a market value per share of $14. By 1996, the book value had climbed to about $40 per share but the market value per share had risen much more, to $67 per share. Other factors being equal, investors were more optimistic about Chrysler's prospects in 1996 than they were in 1991.

Key Point: Book value per share represents the equity of one share of stock in the net assets (assets minus liabilities) of a corporation. It can apply to both common and preferred stock.

value or market value. The **book value** of a company's stock represents the total assets of the company less its liabilities. It is simply the stockholders' equity of the company or, to look at it another way, the company's net assets. The **book value per share**, therefore, represents the equity of the owner of one share of stock in the net assets of the corporation. That value, of course, does not necessarily equal the amount the shareholder would receive if the company were sold or liquidated. It differs in most cases because assets are usually recorded at historical cost, not at the current value at which they could be sold.

To determine the book value per share when a company has only common stock outstanding, divide the total stockholders' equity by the total common shares outstanding. In computing the shares outstanding, common stock distributable is included. Treasury stock (shares previously issued and now held by the company), however, is not included. For example, suppose that Caprock Corporation has total stockholders' equity of $1,030,000 and 29,000 shares outstanding after recording the purchase of treasury shares. The book value per share of Caprock's common stock is $35.52 ($1,030,000 ÷ 29,000 shares).

If a company has both preferred and common stock, the determination of book value per share is not so simple. The general rule is that the call value (or par value, if a call value is not specified) of the preferred stock plus any dividends in arrears is subtracted from total stockholders' equity to determine the equity pertaining to common stock. As an illustration, refer to the stockholders' equity section of Tri-State Corporation's balance sheet in Exhibit 3. Assuming that there are no dividends in arrears and that the preferred stock is callable at $105, the equity pertaining to common stock is calculated as follows:

Total stockholders' equity	$2,024,400
Less equity allocated to preferred shareholders (3,000 shares × $105)	315,000
Equity pertaining to common shareholders	$1,709,400

There are 41,300 shares of common stock outstanding (41,800 shares issued less 500 shares of treasury stock). The book values per share are computed as follows:

Preferred Stock: $315,000 ÷ 3,000 shares = $105 per share
Common Stock: $1,709,400 ÷ 41,300 shares = $41.39 per share

If we assume the same facts except that the preferred stock is 8 percent cumulative and that one year of dividends is in arrears, the stockholders' equity would be allocated as follows:

Total stockholders' equity		$2,024,400
Less: Call value of outstanding preferred shares	$315,000	
Dividends in arrears ($300,000 × .08)	24,000	
Equity allocated to preferred shareholders		339,000
Equity pertaining to common shareholders		$1,685,400

The book values per share are then as follows:

Preferred Stock: $339,000 ÷ 3,000 shares = $113 per share
Common Stock: $1,685,400 ÷ 41,300 shares = $40.81 per share

Undeclared preferred dividends fall into arrears on the last day of the fiscal year (the date when the financial statements are prepared). Also, dividends in arrears do not apply to unissued preferred stock.

Chapter Review

REVIEW OF LEARNING OBJECTIVES

Ace it

1. **Identify the issues related to evaluating the quality of a company's earnings.** Current and prospective net income is an important component in many ratios used to evaluate a company. The user should recognize that the quality of reported net income can be influenced by certain choices made by management. First, management exercises judgment in choosing the accounting methods and estimates that are used in computing net income. Second, discontinued operations, extraordinary gains or losses, and changes in accounting methods may affect net income positively or negatively.

2. **Prepare a corporate income statement.** The corporate income statement shows comprehensive income—all revenues, expenses, gains, and losses for the accounting period, except for prior period adjustments. The top part of the corporate income statement includes all revenues, costs and expenses, and income taxes that pertain to continuing operations. The bottom part of the statement contains any or all of the following: discontinued operations, extraordinary items, and accounting changes. Earnings per share data should be shown at the bottom of the statement, below net income.

3. **Show the relationships among income taxes expense, deferred income taxes, and net of taxes.** Income taxes expense is the taxes applicable to income from operations on an accrual basis. Income tax allocation is necessary when differences between accrual-based accounting income and taxable income cause a material difference between income taxes expense as shown on the income statement and actual income tax liability. The difference between income taxes expense and income taxes payable is debited or credited to an account called Deferred Income Taxes. *Net of taxes* is a phrase used to indicate that the effect of taxes has been considered when showing an item on the income statement.

4. **Describe the disclosure on the income statement of discontinued operations, extraordinary items, and accounting changes.** Because of their unusual nature, a gain or loss on discontinued operations and on extraordinary items, and the cumulative effect of accounting changes must be disclosed on the income statement separately from continuing operations and net of income taxes. Relevant information about any accounting change is shown in the notes to the financial statements.

5. **Compute earnings per share.** Stockholders and other readers of financial statements use earnings per share data to evaluate a company's performance and to compare it with the performance of other companies. Therefore, earnings per share data are presented on the face of the income statement. The amounts are computed by dividing the income applicable to common stock by the number of common shares outstanding for the year. If the number of shares outstanding has varied during the year, then the weighted-average number of common shares outstanding should be used in the computation. When the company has a complex capital structure, both basic and diluted earnings per share must be disclosed on the face of the income statement.

6. **Prepare a statement of stockholders' equity.** A statement of stockholders' equity shows changes over the period in each component of the stockholders' equity section of the balance sheet. This statement reveals much more about the transactions that affect stockholders' equity than does the statement of retained earnings.

7. **Account for stock dividends and stock splits.** A stock dividend is a proportional distribution of shares of a corporation's stock to the company's stockholders. Here is a summary of the key dates and accounting treatment of stock dividends.

Key Date	Stock Dividend
Date of declaration	Debit Stock Dividends Declared for the market value of the stock to be distributed (if it is a small stock dividend), and credit Common Stock Distributable for the stock's par value and Paid-in Capital in Excess of Par Value, Common for the excess of the market value over the stock's par value.
Date of record	No entry.
Date of distribution	Debit Common Stock Distributable and credit Common Stock for the par value of the stock that has been distributed.

A stock split is usually undertaken to reduce the market value of a company's stock and improve the demand for the stock. Because there is normally a decrease in the par value of the stock in proportion to the number of additional shares issued, a stock split has no effect on the dollar amounts in the stockholders' equity accounts. The split should be recorded in the general journal by a memorandum entry only.

8. **Calculate book value per share.** Book value per share is the stockholders' equity per share. It is calculated by dividing stockholders' equity by the number of common shares outstanding plus shares distributable. When a company has both preferred and common stock, the call or par value of the preferred stock plus any dividends in arrears is deducted from total stockholders' equity before dividing by the common shares outstanding.

REVIEW OF CONCEPTS AND TERMINOLOGY

The following concepts and terms were introduced in this chapter.

LO 5 **Basic earnings per share:** The net income applicable to common stock divided by the weighted-average number of common shares outstanding.

LO 8 **Book value:** The total assets of a company less its liabilities; stockholders' equity.

LO 8 **Book value per share:** The equity of the owner of one share of stock in the net assets of the corporation.

LO 5 **Complex capital structure:** A capital structure that includes convertible preferred stocks or bonds, or stock options that can be converted into common stock.

LO 2 **Comprehensive income:** The change in a company's equity during a period from sources other than owners; it includes net income, changes in unrealized investment gains and losses, and other items affecting equity.

LO 4 **Cumulative effect of an accounting change:** The effect that a different accounting principle would have had on the net income of prior periods if it had been used instead of the old principle.

LO 3 **Deferred Income Taxes:** The account used to record the difference between the Income Taxes Expense and Income Taxes Payable accounts.

LO 6 **Deficit:** A debit balance in the Retained Earnings account.

LO 5 **Diluted earnings per share:** The net income applicable to common stock divided by the sum of the weighted-average number of common shares outstanding plus potentially dilutive securities.

LO 4 **Discontinued operations:** Segments of a business that are no longer part of its ongoing operations.

LO 4 **Extraordinary items:** Events or transactions that are both unusual in nature and infrequent in occurrence.

LO 3 **Income tax allocation:** An accounting method used to accrue income taxes expense on the basis of accounting income whenever there are differences between accounting and taxable income.

LO 3 **Net of taxes:** Taking into account the effect of applicable taxes (usually income taxes) on an item in order to determine the overall effect of the item on the income statement.

LO 5 **Potentially dilutive securities:** Stock options and convertible preferred stocks or bonds, which have the potential to dilute earnings per share.

LO 1 **Quality of earnings:** The substance of earnings and their sustainability into future accounting periods.

LO 6 **Restriction on retained earnings:** The required or voluntary identification of a portion of retained earnings that cannot be used to declare dividends.

LO 6 **Retained earnings:** Stockholders' claims to assets arising from the earnings of the business; the accumulated earnings of a corporation from its inception, minus any losses, dividends, or transfers to contributed capital.

LO 4 **Segments:** Distinct parts of business operations, such as lines of business or classes of customer.

LO 5 **Simple capital structure:** A capital structure in which there are no stocks, bonds, or stock options that can be converted into common stock.

LO 6 **Statement of stockholders' equity:** A financial statement that summarizes changes in the components of the stockholders' equity section of the balance sheet; also called *statement of changes in stockholders' equity.*

LO 7 **Stock dividend:** A proportional distribution of shares of a corporation's stock to its stockholders.

LO 7 **Stock split:** An increase in the number of outstanding shares of stock accompanied by a proportionate reduction in the par or stated value.

REVIEW PROBLEM

Comprehensive Stockholders' Equity Transactions

LO 6
LO 7
LO 8

The stockholders' equity of the Szatkowski Company on June 30, 20x1, is shown below.

Contributed Capital	
Common Stock, no par value, $6 stated value, 1,000,000 shares authorized, 250,000 shares issued and outstanding	$1,500,000
Paid-in Capital in Excess of Stated Value, Common	820,000
Total Contributed Capital	$2,320,000
Retained Earnings	970,000
Total Stockholders' Equity	$3,290,000

Stockholders' equity transactions for the next fiscal year were as follows:

a. The board of directors declared a 2-for-1 stock split.
b. The board of directors obtained authorization to issue 50,000 shares of $100 par value, 6 percent noncumulative preferred stock, callable at $104.
c. Issued 12,000 shares of common stock for a building appraised at $96,000.
d. Purchased 8,000 shares of the company's common stock for $64,000.

e. Issued 20,000 shares of preferred stock for $100 per share.
f. Sold 5,000 shares of treasury stock for $35,000.
g. Declared cash dividends of $6 per share on preferred stock and $.20 per share on common stock.
h. Date of record.
i. Paid the preferred and common stock cash dividends.
j. Declared a 10 percent stock dividend on common stock. The market value was $10 per share. The stock dividend is distributable after the end of the fiscal year.
k. Closed Net Income for the year, $340,000.
l. Closed the Cash Dividends Declared and Stock Dividends Declared accounts to Retained Earnings.

Because of a loan agreement, the company is not allowed to reduce retained earnings below $100,000. The board of directors determined that this restriction should be disclosed in the notes to the financial statements.

1. Record the preceding transactions in journal form.
2. Prepare the stockholders' equity section of the company's balance sheet on June 30, 20x2, including appropriate disclosure of the restriction on retained earnings.
3. Compute the book values per share of common stock on June 30, 20x1 and 20x2, and of preferred stock on June 30, 20x2, using end-of-year shares outstanding.

ANSWER TO REVIEW PROBLEM

1. Prepare the entries in journal form.
   a. Memorandum entry: 2-for-1 stock split, common, resulting in 500,000 shares issued and outstanding of no par value common stock with a stated value of $3

   b. No entry required.

c. Building	96,000	
Common Stock		36,000
Paid-in Capital in Excess of Stated Value, Common		60,000
Issued 12,000 shares of common stock for a building appraised at $96,000		
d. Treasury Stock, Common	64,000	
Cash		64,000
Purchased 8,000 shares of common stock for the treasury for $8 per share		
e. Cash	2,000,000	
Preferred Stock		2,000,000
Issued 20,000 shares of $100 par value preferred stock at $100 per share		
f. Cash	35,000	
Retained Earnings	5,000	
Treasury Stock, Common		40,000
Sold 5,000 shares of treasury stock for $35,000, originally purchased for $8 per share		
g. Cash Dividends Declared	221,800	
Cash Dividends Payable		221,800
Declaration of cash dividends of $6 per share on 20,000 shares of preferred stock and $.20 per share on 509,000 shares of common stock:		

$$
\begin{array}{ll}
20,000 \times \$6 & = \$120,000 \\
509,000 \times \$.20 = & \underline{101,800} \\
& \underline{\underline{\$221,800}}
\end{array}
$$

h. No entry required.

i. Cash Dividends Payable	221,800	
Cash		221,800

Paid cash dividends to preferred and common stockholders

j. Stock Dividends Declared	509,000	
Common Stock Distributable		152,700
Paid-in Capital in Excess of Stated Value, Common		356,300

Declaration of a 50,900-share stock dividend (509,000 × .10) on $3 stated value common stock at a market value of $509,000 (50,900 × $10)

k. Income Summary	340,000	
Retained Earnings		340,000

To close the Income Summary account to Retained Earnings

l. Retained Earnings	730,800	
Cash Dividends Declared		221,800
Stock Dividends Declared		509,000

To close the Cash Dividends Declared and Stock Dividends Declared accounts to Retained Earnings

2. Prepare the stockholders' equity section of the balance sheet.

Szatkowski Company
Stockholders' Equity
June 30, 20x2

Contributed Capital		
Preferred Stock, $100 par value, 6% noncumulative, 50,000 shares authorized, 20,000 shares issued and outstanding		$2,000,000
Common Stock, no par value, $3 stated value, 1,000,000 shares authorized, 512,000 shares issued, 509,000 shares outstanding	$1,536,000	
Common Stock Distributable, 50,900 shares	152,700	
Paid-in Capital in Excess of Stated Value, Common	1,236,300	2,925,000
Total Contributed Capital		$4,925,000
Retained Earnings (Note x)		574,200
Total Contributed Capital and Retained Earnings		$5,499,200
Less Treasury Stock, Common (3,000 shares, at cost)		24,000
Total Stockholders' Equity		$5,475,200

Note x: The board of directors has restricted retained earnings available for dividends by the amount of $100,000 as required under a loan agreement.

3. Compute the book values.

June 30, 20x1
  Common Stock: $3,290,000 ÷ 250,000 shares = $13.16 per share
June 30, 20x2
  Preferred Stock: Call price of $104 per share equals book value per share
  Common Stock:
    ($5,475,200 − $2,080,000) ÷ (509,000 shares + 50,900 shares) =
    $3,395,200 ÷ 559,900 shares = $6.06 per share

Chapter Assignments

BUILDING YOUR KNOWLEDGE FOUNDATION

QUESTIONS

1. What is quality of earnings, and what are two ways in which quality of earnings can be affected?

2. Why would the reader of financial statements be interested in management's choice of accounting methods and estimates? Give an example.

3. In the first quarter of 1994, AT&T, the giant telecommunications company, reported a net loss because it reduced its income by $1.3 billion, or $.96 per share, as a result of changing its method of accounting for disability and severance payments. Without this charge, the company would have earned $1.15 billion, or $.85 per share. Where on the corporate income statement do you find the effects of changes in accounting principles? As an analyst, how would you treat this accounting change?

4. "Accounting income should be geared to the concept of taxable income because the public understands that concept." Comment on this statement, and tell why income tax allocation is necessary.

5. Nabisco had about $1.3 billion of deferred income taxes in 1996, equal to about 11 percent of total liabilities. This percentage has risen or remained steady for many years. Given management's desire to put off the payment of taxes as long as possible, the long-term growth of the economy and inflation, and the definition of a liability (probable future sacrifice of economic benefits arising from present obligations), make an argument for not accounting for deferred income taxes.

6. Why should a gain or loss on discontinued operations be disclosed separately on the income statement?

7. Explain the two major criteria for extraordinary items. How should extraordinary items be disclosed in the financial statements?

8. When an accounting change occurs, what disclosures must be made in the financial statements?

9. How are earnings per share disclosed in the financial statements?

10. When does a company have a simple capital structure? A complex capital structure?

11. What is the difference between basic and diluted earnings per share?

12. What is the difference between the statement of stockholders' equity and the stockholders' equity section of the balance sheet?

13. When does a company have a deficit in retained earnings?

14. Explain how the accounting treatment of stock dividends differs from that of cash dividends.

15. What is the difference between a stock dividend and a stock split? What is the effect of each on the capital structure of the corporation?

16. Would you expect a corporation's book value per share to equal its market value per share? Why or why not?

SHORT EXERCISES

SE 1.

LO 1   Quality of Earnings

Each of the following items is a quality of earnings issue. Indicate whether the item is (a) an accounting method, (b) an accounting estimate, or (c) a nonoperating item. For any item for which the answer is (a) or (b), indicate which alternative is usually the more conservative choice.

1. LIFO versus FIFO
2. Extraordinary loss
3. Ten-year useful life versus fifteen-year useful life
4. Effect of change in accounting principle
5. Straight-line versus accelerated method
6. Discontinued operations
7. Immediate write-off versus amortization
8. Increase in percentage of uncollectible accounts versus a decrease

SE 2.
LO 2 Corporate Income Statement

Assume that Griswold Company's chief financial officer gave you the following information: Net Sales, $720,000; Cost of Goods Sold, $350,000; Loss from Discontinued Operations (net of income tax benefit of $70,000), $200,000; Loss on Disposal of Discontinued Operations (net of income tax benefit of $16,000), $50,000; Operating Expenses, $130,000; Income Taxes Expense on Continuing Operations, $100,000. From this information, prepare the company's income statement for the year ended June 30, 20xx. (Ignore earnings per share information.)

SE 3.
LO 3 Use of Corporate Income Tax Rate Schedule

Using the corporate tax rate schedule in Table 1, compute the income tax liability for taxable income of (1) $400,000 and (2) $20,000,000.

SE 4.
LO 5 Earnings per Share

During 20x1, Jimmo Corporation reported a net income of $669,200. On January 1, Jimmo had 360,000 shares of common stock outstanding. The company issued an additional 240,000 shares of common stock on August 1. In 20x1, the company had a simple capital structure. During 20x2, there were no transactions involving common stock, and the company reported net income of $870,000. Determine the weighted-average number of common shares outstanding for 20x1 and 20x2. Also, compute earnings per share for 20x1 and 20x2.

SE 5.
LO 6 Statement of Stockholders' Equity

Refer to the statement of stockholders' equity for Tri-State Corporation in Exhibit 2 to answer the following questions: (1) At what price per share were the 5,000 shares of common stock sold? (2) What was the conversion price per share of the common stock? (3) At what price was the common stock selling on the date of the stock dividend? (4) At what price per share was the treasury stock purchased?

SE 6.
LO 6 Effects of Stockholders'
LO 7 Equity Actions

Tell whether each of the following actions will increase, decrease, or have no effect on total assets, total liabilities, and total stockholders' equity.

1. Declaration of a stock dividend
2. Declaration of a cash dividend
3. Stock split
4. Restriction of retained earnings
5. Purchase of treasury stock

SE 7.
LO 6 Restriction of Retained Earnings

Swift Company has a lawsuit filed against it. The board took action to restrict retained earnings in the amount of $2,500,000 on May 31, 20x1, pending the outcome of the suit. On May 31, the company had retained earnings of $3,725,000. Show how the restriction on retained earnings would be disclosed as a note to the financial statements.

SE 8.
LO 7 Stock Dividends

On February 15, Green Mountain Corporation's board of directors declared a 2 percent stock dividend applicable to the outstanding shares of its $10 par value common stock, of which 200,000 shares are authorized, 130,000 are issued, and 20,000 are held in the treasury. The stock dividend was distributable on March 15 to stockholders of record on March 1. On February 15, the market value of the common stock was $15 per share. On March 30, the board of directors declared a $.50 per share cash dividend. No other stock transactions have occurred. Record the necessary transactions on February 15, March 1, March 15, and March 30.

SE 9.
LO 7 Stock Split

On August 10, the board of directors of Symula International declared a 3-for-1 stock split of its $9 par value common stock, of which 800,000 shares were authorized and 250,000 were issued and outstanding. The market value on that date was $60 per share. On the same date, the balance of Paid-in Capital in Excess of Par Value, Common was $6,000,000, and the balance of Retained Earnings was $6,500,000. Prepare the stockholders' equity section of the company's balance sheet after the stock split. What journal entry, if any, is needed to record the stock split?

SE 10.
LO 8 Book Value for Preferred and Common Stock

Given the stockholders' equity section of the Talmage Corporation's balance sheet shown on the next page, what is the book value per share for both the preferred and the common stock?

Contributed Capital
Preferred Stock, $100 par value, 8 percent
cumulative, 10,000 shares authorized,
500 shares issued and outstanding* $ 50,000
Common Stock, $10 par value, 100,000 shares
authorized, 40,000 shares issued and
outstanding $400,000
Paid-in Capital in Excess of Par Value, Common   516,000   916,000

Total Contributed Capital $ 966,000
Retained Earnings   275,000

Total Stockholders' Equity $1,241,000

*The preferred stock is callable at $104 per share, and one year's dividends are in arrears.

EXERCISES

E 1.

**LO 1 Effect of Alternative
Accounting Methods**

At the end of its first year of operations, a company calculated its ending merchandise inventory according to three different accounting methods, as follows: FIFO, $95,000; average-cost, $90,000; LIFO, $86,000. If the average-cost method is used by the company, net income for the year would be $34,000.

1. Determine net income if the FIFO method is used.
2. Determine net income if the LIFO method is used.
3. Which method is more conservative?
4. Will the consistency convention be violated if the company chooses to use the LIFO method?
5. Does the full-disclosure convention require disclosure of the inventory method selected by management in the financial statements?

E 2.

**LO 2 Corporate Income
Statement**

Assume that the Abbey Furniture Company's chief financial officer gave you the following information: Net Sales, $1,900,000; Cost of Goods Sold, $1,050,000; Extraordinary Gain (net of income taxes of $3,500), $12,500; Loss from Discontinued Operations (net of income tax benefit of $30,000), $50,000; Loss on Disposal of Discontinued Operations (net of income tax benefit of $13,000), $35,000; Selling Expenses, $50,000; Administrative Expenses, $40,000; Income Taxes Expense on Continuing Operations, $300,000.

From this information, prepare the company's income statement for the year ended June 30, 20xx. (Ignore earnings per share information.)

E 3.

**LO 2 Corporate Income
LO 3 Statement
LO 4
LO 5**

The following items are components on the income statement of Burda Corporation for the year ended December 31, 20x1:

Sales	$500,000
Cost of Goods Sold	(275,000)
Operating Expenses	(112,500)
Total Income Taxes Expense for Period	(82,350)
Income from Operations of a Discontinued Segment	80,000
Gain on Disposal of Segment	70,000
Extraordinary Gain on Retirement of Bonds	36,000
Cumulative Effect of a Change in Accounting Principle	(24,000)
Net Income	$192,150
Earnings per Share	$.96

Recast the 20x1 income statement in proper multistep form, including allocating income taxes to appropriate items (assume a 30 percent income tax rate) and showing earnings per share figures (200,000 shares outstanding).

Using the corporate tax rate schedule in Table 1, compute the income tax liability for the following situations:

Situation	Taxable Income
A	$ 70,000
B	85,000
C	320,000

The Cohn Corporation reported the following accounting income before income taxes, income taxes expense, and net income for 20x2 and 20x3:

	20x2	20x3
Income before income taxes	$280,000	$280,000
Income taxes expense	88,300	88,300
Net income	$191,700	$191,700

Also, on the balance sheet, deferred income taxes liability increased by $38,400 in 20x2 and decreased by $18,800 in 20x3.

1. How much did Cohn Corporation actually pay in income taxes for 20x2 and 20x3?
2. Prepare entries in journal form to record income taxes expense for 20x2 and 20x3.

During 20x1, the De La Haza Corporation reported a net income of $1,529,500. On January 1, De La Haza had 700,000 shares of common stock outstanding. The company issued an additional 420,000 shares of common stock on October 1. In 20x1, the company had a simple capital structure. During 20x2, there were no transactions involving common stock, and the company reported net income of $2,016,000.

1. Determine the weighted-average number of common shares outstanding each year.
2. Compute earnings per share for each year.

The board of directors of the Edelen Company has approved plans to acquire another company during the coming year. The acquisition should cost approximately $550,000. The board took action to restrict retained earnings of the company in the amount of $550,000 on July 17, 20x1. On July 31, the company had retained earnings of $975,000. Show how the restriction on retained earnings can be disclosed as a note to the financial statements.

The stockholders' equity section of Farhad Corporation's balance sheet on December 31, 20x2, appears as follows:

Contributed Capital
   Common Stock, $2 par value, 500,000 shares
      authorized, 400,000 shares issued and outstanding $ 800,000
      Paid-in Capital in Excess of Par Value, Common   1,200,000
   Total Contributed Capital $2,000,000
Retained Earnings   4,200,000
Total Stockholders' Equity $6,200,000

Prepare a statement of stockholders' equity for the year ended December 31, 20x3, assuming the following transactions occurred in sequence during 20x3:

a. Issued 10,000 shares of $100 par value, 9 percent cumulative preferred stock at par after obtaining authorization from the state.
b. Issued 40,000 shares of common stock in connection with the conversion of bonds having a carrying value of $600,000.
c. Declared and issued a 2 percent common stock dividend. The market value on the date of declaration was $14 per share.
d. Purchased 10,000 shares of common stock for the treasury at a cost of $16 per share.
e. Earned net income of $460,000.
f. Declared and paid the full year's dividend on preferred stock and a dividend of $.40 per share on common stock outstanding at the end of the year.

LO 7 Journal Entries: Stock Dividends

E 9. The Garonski Company has 30,000 shares of its $1 par value common stock outstanding. Record the following transactions as they relate to the company's common stock:

July 17 Declared a 10 percent stock dividend on common stock to be distributed on August 10 to stockholders of record on July 31. Market value of the stock was $5 per share on this date.

31 Record date.

Aug. 10 Distributed the stock dividend declared on July 17.

Sept. 1 Declared a $.50 per share cash dividend on common stock to be paid on September 16 to stockholders of record on September 10.

LO 7 Stock Split

E 10. The Hao Company currently has 500,000 shares of $1 par value common stock authorized with 200,000 shares outstanding. The board of directors declared a 2-for-1 split on May 15, when the market value of the common stock was $2.50 per share. The Retained Earnings balance on May 15 was $700,000. Paid-in Capital in Excess of Par Value, Common on this date was $20,000.

Prepare the stockholders' equity section of the company's balance sheet before and after the stock split. What entry, if any, would be necessary to record the stock split?

LO 7 Stock Split

E 11. On January 15, the board of directors of Imhoff International declared a 3-for-1 stock split of its $12 par value common stock, of which 800,000 shares were authorized and 200,000 were issued and outstanding. The market value on that date was $45 per share. On the same date, the balance of Paid-in Capital in Excess of Par Value, Common was $4,000,000, and the balance of Retained Earnings was $8,000,000.

Prepare the stockholders' equity section of the company's balance sheet before and after the stock split. What entry, if any, is needed to record the stock split?

LO 8 Book Value for Preferred and Common Stock

E 12. Below is the stockholders' equity section of the Tri-Town Corporation's balance sheet.

Contributed Capital		
Preferred Stock, $100 per share, 6 percent cumulative, 10,000 shares authorized, 200 shares issued and outstanding*		$ 20,000
Common Stock, $5 par value, 100,000 shares authorized, 10,000 shares issued, 9,000 shares outstanding	$50,000	
Paid-in Capital in Excess of Par Value, Common	28,000	78,000
Total Contributed Capital		$ 98,000
Retained Earnings		95,000
Total Contributed Capital and Retained Earnings		$193,000
Less Treasury Stock, Common (1,000 shares at cost)		15,000
Total Stockholders' Equity		$178,000

*The preferred stock is callable at $105 per share, and one year's dividends are in arrears.

Determine the book value per share for both the preferred and the common stock.

PROBLEMS

LO 1 Effect of Alternative Accounting Methods

P 1. Zalme Company began operations this year. At the beginning of 20xx, the company purchased plant assets of $900,000, with an estimated useful life of ten years and no salvage value. During the year, the company had net sales of $1,300,000, salaries expense of $200,000, and other expenses of $80,000, excluding depreciation. In addition, Zalme Company purchased inventory as follows:

January 15	400 units at $400	$160,000
March 20	200 units at $408	81,600
June 15	800 units at $416	332,800
September 18	600 units at $412	247,200
December 9	300 units at $420	126,000
Total	2,300 units	$947,600

At the end of the year, a physical inventory disclosed 500 units still on hand. The managers of Zalme Company know they have a choice of accounting methods, but are unsure how those methods will affect net income. They have heard of the FIFO and LIFO inventory methods and the straight-line and double-declining-balance depreciation methods. Ignore income taxes.

REQUIRED

1. Prepare two income statements for Zalme Company, one using the FIFO and straight-line methods, the other using the LIFO and double-declining-balance methods.

2. Prepare a schedule accounting for the difference in the two net income figures obtained in **1**.

3. What effect does the choice of accounting method have on Zalme's inventory turnover? What conclusions can you draw?

4. How does the choice of accounting methods affect Zalme's return on assets? Assume the company's only assets are cash of $80,000, inventory, and plant assets. Use year-end balances to compute the ratios. Is your evaluation of Zalme's profitability affected by the choice of accounting methods?

P 2.

LO 2 Corporate Income
LO 3 Statement
LO 4
LO 5

Income statement information for the Sim Corporation during 20x1 is as follows:

a. Administrative expenses, $220,000.
b. Cost of goods sold, $880,000.
c. Cumulative effect of a change in inventory methods that decreased income (net of taxes, $56,000), $120,000.
d. Extraordinary loss from a storm (net of taxes, $20,000), $40,000.
e. Income taxes expense, continuing operations, $84,000.
f. Net sales, $1,780,000.
g. Selling expenses, $380,000.

REQUIRED

Prepare Sim Corporation's income statement for 20x1, including earnings per share, assuming a weighted average of 200,000 shares of common stock outstanding for 20x1.

P 3.

LO 2 Corporate Income
LO 3 Statement and
LO 4 Evaluation of
LO 5 Business Operations

During 20x3 Dasbol Corporation engaged in a number of complex transactions to restructure the business—selling off a division, retiring bonds, and changing accounting methods. The company has always issued a simple single-step income statement, and the accountant has accordingly prepared the December 31 year-end income statements for 20x2 and 20x3, as shown below.

Dasbol Corporation Income Statements For the Years Ended December 31, 20x3 and 20x2		
	20x3	**20x2**
Net Sales	$1,000,000	$1,200,000
Cost of Goods Sold	(550,000)	(600,000)
Operating Expenses	(225,000)	(150,000)
Income Taxes Expense	(164,700)	(135,000)
Income from Operations of a Discontinued Segment	160,000	
Gain on Disposal of Discontinued Segment	140,000	
Extraordinary Gain on Retirement of Bonds	72,000	
Cumulative Effect of a Change in Accounting Principle	(48,000)	
Net Income	$ 384,300	$ 315,000
Earnings per share	$ 1.92	$ 1.58

The president of the company, Joseph Dasbol, is pleased to see that both net income and earnings per share increased by 22 percent from 20x2 to 20x3 and intends to announce to the stockholders that the restructuring is a success.

REQUIRED

1. Recast the 20x3 and 20x2 income statements in proper multistep form, including allocating income taxes to appropriate items (assume a 30 percent income tax rate) and showing earnings per share figures (200,000 shares outstanding).

2. What is your assessment of the restructuring plan and business operations in 20x3?

P 4.

LO 6 Stock Dividend and Stock
LO 7 Split Transactions and
Stockholders' Equity

The stockholders' equity section of the balance sheet of Pittman Corporation as of December 31, 20x4, was as follows:

Contributed Capital	
Common Stock, $4 par value, 500,000 shares authorized,	
200,000 shares issued and outstanding	$ 800,000
Paid-in Capital in Excess of Par Value, Common	1,000,000
Total Contributed Capital	$1,800,000
Retained Earnings	1,200,000
Total Stockholders' Equity	$3,000,000

The following transactions occurred in 20x5 for Pittman Corporation:

Feb. 28 The board of directors declared a 10 percent stock dividend to stockholders of record on March 25 to be distributed on April 5. The market value on this date is $16.

Mar. 25 Date of record for stock dividend.

Apr. 5 Issued stock dividend.

Aug. 3 Declared a 2-for-1 stock split.

Nov. 20 Purchased 18,000 shares of the company's common stock at $8 per share for the treasury.

Dec. 31 Declared a 5 percent stock dividend to stockholders of record on January 25 to be distributed on February 5. The market value per share was $9.

REQUIRED

1. Record the transactions for Pittman Corporation in T accounts.

2. Prepare the stockholders' equity section of the company's balance sheet as of December 31, 20x5. Assume net income for 20x5 is $108,000.

P 5.

LO 6 Dividends and Stock
LO 7 Split Transactions and
Stockholders' Equity

The stockholders' equity section of the Rigby Moving and Storage Company's balance sheet as of December 31, 20x2, was as follows:

Contributed Capital	
Common Stock, $2 par value, 3,000,000 shares	
authorized, 500,000 shares issued and outstanding	$1,000,000
Paid-in Capital in Excess of Par Value, Common	400,000
Total Contributed Capital	$1,400,000
Retained Earnings	1,080,000
Total Stockholders' Equity	$2,480,000

The company engaged in the following stockholders' equity transactions during 20x3:

Mar. 5 Declared a $.40 per share cash dividend to be paid on April 6 to stockholders of record on March 20.

20 Date of record.

Apr. 6 Paid the cash dividend.

June 17 Declared a 10 percent stock dividend to be distributed August 17 to stockholders of record on August 5. The market value of the stock was $14 per share.

Aug. 5 Date of record.

17 Distributed the stock dividend.

Oct. 2 Split its stock 3 for 1.

Dec. 27 Declared a cash dividend of $.20 payable January 27, 20x4, to stockholders of record on January 14, 20x4.

On December 9, the board of directors restricted retained earnings for a pending law-suit in the amount of $200,000. The restriction should be shown in the notes to the firm's financial statements.

REQUIRED

1. Record the 20x3 transactions in journal form.

2. Prepare the stockholders' equity section of the company's balance sheet as of December 31, 20x3, with an appropriate disclosure of the restriction on retained earnings. Assume net income for the year is $400,000.

P 6.

LO 6 Comprehensive
LO 7 Stockholders' Equity
LO 8 Transactions

On December 31, 20x1, the stockholders' equity section of the Toczycki Company's balance sheet appeared as follows:

Contributed Capital	
Common Stock, $8 par value, 200,000 shares authorized,	
60,000 shares issued and outstanding	$ 480,000
Paid-in Capital in Excess of Par Value, Common	1,280,000
Total Contributed Capital	$1,760,000
Retained Earnings	824,000
Total Stockholders' Equity	$2,584,000

The following are selected transactions involving stockholders' equity in 20x2: On January 4, the board of directors obtained authorization for 20,000 shares of $40 par value noncumulative preferred stock that carried an indicated dividend rate of $4 per share and was callable at $42 per share. On January 14, the company sold 12,000 shares of the preferred stock at $40 per share and issued another 2,000 in exchange for a building valued at $80,000. On March 8, the board of directors declared a 2-for-1 stock split on the common stock. On April 20, after the stock split, the company purchased 3,000 shares of common stock for the treasury at an average price of $12 per share; 1,000 of these shares subsequently were sold on May 4 at an average price of $16 per share. On July 15, the board of directors declared a cash dividend of $4 per share on the preferred stock and $.40 per share on the common stock. The date of record was July 25. The dividends were paid on August 15. The board of directors declared a 15 percent stock dividend on November 28, when the common stock was selling for $20. The record date for the stock dividend was December 15, and the dividend was to be distributed on January 5. The board of directors noted that note disclosure must be made of a bank loan agreement that requires minimum retained earnings. No cash dividends can be declared or paid if retained earnings fall below $100,000.

REQUIRED

1. Record the above transactions in journal form.

2. Prepare the stockholders' equity section of the company's balance sheet as of December 31, 20x2, including an appropriate disclosure of the restrictions on retained earnings. Net loss for 20x2 was $218,000. (**Hint:** Use T accounts to keep track of transactions.)

3. Compute the book value per share for preferred and common stock (including common stock distributable) on December 31, 20x1 and 20x2, using end-of-year shares outstanding.

ALTERNATE PROBLEMS

P 7.

LO 2 Corporate Income
LO 3 Statement
LO 4
LO 5

Information concerning operations of the Norris Weather Gear Corporation during 20xx is as follows:

a. Administrative expenses, $180,000.
b. Cost of goods sold, $840,000.
c. Cumulative effect of an accounting change in depreciation methods that increased income (net of taxes, $40,000), $84,000.
d. Extraordinary loss from an earthquake (net of taxes, $72,000), $120,000.
e. Sales (net), $1,800,000.
f. Selling expenses, $160,000.
g. Income taxes expense applicable to continuing operations, $210,000.

REQUIRED

Prepare the corporation's income statement for the year ended December 31, 20xx, including earnings per share information. Assume a weighted average of 100,000 common shares outstanding during the year.

P 8.

LO 6 Stock Dividend and Stock
LO 7 Split Transactions and
Stockholders' Equity

The stockholders' equity section of Waterbury Linen Mills, Inc., as of December 31, 20x2, was as follows:

Contributed Capital
  Common Stock, $3 par value, 500,000 shares
    authorized, 40,000 shares issued and outstanding $120,000
  Paid-in Capital in Excess of Par Value, Common   37,500

  Total Contributed Capital $157,500
Retained Earnings   120,000

Total Stockholders' Equity $277,500

A review of the stockholders' equity records of Waterbury Linen Mills, Inc., disclosed the following transactions during 20x3.

Mar. 25 The board of directors declared a 5 percent stock dividend to stockholders of record on April 20 to be distributed on May 1. The market value of the common stock was $21 per share.
Apr. 20 Date of record for the stock dividend.
May 1 Issued the stock dividend.
Sept. 10 Declared a 3-for-1 stock split.
Dec. 15 Declared a 10 percent stock dividend to stockholders of record on January 15 to be distributed on February 15. The market price on this date is $9 per share.

REQUIRED

1. Record the transactions for Waterbury Linen Mills, Inc., in T accounts.
2. Prepare the stockholders' equity section of the company's balance sheet as of December 31, 20x3. Assume net income for 20x3 is $247,000.

P 9.

LO 6 Dividends and Stock
LO 7 Split Transactions and
Stockholders' Equity

The balance sheet of the O'Connor Woolen Company disclosed the following stockholders' equity as of September 30, 20x1:

Contributed Capital
  Common Stock, $4 par value, 1,000,000 shares
    authorized, 300,000 shares issued and outstanding $1,200,000
  Paid-in Capital in Excess of Par Value, Common   740,000

  Total Contributed Capital $1,940,000
Retained Earnings   700,000

Total Stockholders' Equity $2,640,000

The following stockholders' equity transactions were completed during the next fiscal year in the order presented:

20x1
Dec. 17 Declared a 10 percent stock dividend to be distributed January 20 to stockholders of record on January 1. The market value per share on the date of declaration was $8.

20x2
Jan. 1 Date of record.
     20 Distributed the stock dividend.
Apr. 14 Declared a $.50 per share cash dividend. The cash dividend is payable May 15 to stockholders of record on May 1.
May 1 Date of record.
     15 Paid the cash dividend.
June 17 Split its stock 2 for 1.
Sept. 15 Declared a cash dividend of $.30 per share payable October 10 to stockholders of record October 1.

On September 14, the board of directors restricted retained earnings for plant expansion in the amount of $300,000. The restriction should be shown in the notes to the financial statements.

REQUIRED

1. Record the above transactions in journal form.

2. Prepare the stockholders' equity section of the company's balance sheet as of September 30, 20x2, with an appropriate disclosure of the restriction of retained earnings. Assume net income for the year is $300,000.

EXPANDING YOUR CRITICAL THINKING, COMMUNICATION, AND INTERPERSONAL SKILLS

SKILLS DEVELOPMENT

Conceptual Analysis

LO 1 Classic Quality of
LO 4 Earnings

SD 1. On Tuesday, January 19, 1988, *International Business Machines Corp. (IBM),* the world's largest computer manufacturer, reported greatly increased earnings for the fourth quarter of 1987. Despite this reported gain in earnings, the price of IBM's stock on the New York Stock Exchange declined by $6 per share to $111.75. In sympathy with this move, most other technology stocks also declined.[22]

IBM's fourth-quarter net earnings rose from $1.39 billion, or $2.28 a share, to $2.08 billion, or $3.47 a share, an increase of 49.6 percent and 52.2 percent over the year-earlier period. Management declared that these results demonstrated the effectiveness of IBM's efforts to become more competitive and that, despite the economic uncertainties of 1988, the company was planning for growth.

The apparent cause of the stock price decline was that the huge increase in income could be traced to nonrecurring gains. Investment analysts pointed out that IBM's high earnings stemmed primarily from factors such as a lower tax rate. Despite most analysts' expectations of a tax rate between 40 and 42 percent, IBM's rate was a low 36.4 percent, down from the previous year's 45.3 percent.

In addition, analysts were disappointed in IBM's revenue growth. Revenues within the United States were down, and much of the growth in revenues came through favorable currency translations, increases that might not be repeated. In fact, some estimates of the fourth-quarter earnings attributed $.50 per share to currency translations and another $.25 to tax-rate changes.

Other factors contributing to the rise in earnings were one-time transactions, such as the sale of Intel Corporation stock and bond redemptions, along with a corporate stock buyback program that reduced the amount of stock outstanding in the fourth quarter by 7.4 million shares.

The analysts were concerned about the quality of IBM's earnings. Identify four quality of earnings issues reported in the case and the analysts' concern about each. In percentage terms, what is the impact of the currency changes on fourth-quarter earnings? Comment on management's assessment of IBM's performance. Do you agree with management? (Optional question: What has IBM's subsequent performance been?) Be prepared to discuss your answers to the questions in class.

LO 2 Interpretation of
LO 4 Corporate Income Statement

SD 2. *General Motors* is a major automotive manufacturing company with supporting financing and insurance operations. The independent auditors' report indicates that the company has changed some of its accounting principles as follows:[23]

Cash Flow

CD-ROM

Communication

Critical Thinking

Ethics

General Ledger

Group Activity

Hot Links to Real Companies

International

Internet

Key Ratio

Memo

Spreadsheet

As discussed in Note 1 to the financial statements, effective January 1, 1995, the Corporation changed its method of accounting for sales to daily rental car companies (EITF No. 95). Also as discussed in Note 1 and 4 to the financial statements, respectively, effective January 1, 1994, the Corporation changed its method of accounting for postemployment benefits (SFAS No. 112) and certain investments in debt and equity securities (SFAS No. 115).

The latter change had no impact on the income statement. Further, the notes reveal that on June 7, 1996, General Motors split off its Electronic Data Systems operations, which were reported as discontinued operations. Because the discontinued operation was split off and not sold, there was no gain or loss on the transaction. The accounting changes and discontinued operations disclosed on the company's income statement were as follows:

	1996	1995	1994
Income from continuing operations	$4,589	$5,404	$4,296
Income (loss) from discontinued operations (Note 2)	(5)	105	349
Cumulative effect of accounting changes (Note 1)	—	(52)	(751)
Net Income	$4,584	$5,457	$3,894
Earnings per share (Note 20)			
$1-2/3 par value from continuing operations	$6.07	$7.14	$5.74
Income (loss) from discontinued operations (Note 2)	(0.01)	0.14	0.46
Cumulative effect of accounting changes (Note 1)	—	(0.07)	(1.05)
Net earnings attributable to $1-2/3 par value	$ 6.06	$ 7.21	$ 5.15

1. Identify the amounts in the partial income statement for each item mentioned in the independent auditors' report.

2. Define discontinued operations. Why are discontinued operations shown separately on the income statement?

3. Define the cumulative effect of changes in accounting principles. Were the changes here instigated by management, or were they mandated by outside authorities? If mandated, by whom?

4. Why are several figures given for earnings per common share? Which earnings (loss) per common share figure would you say is most relevant to future operations? Why is it the most relevant?

Ethical Dilemma

SD 3.
LO 7 Ethics and Stock Dividends

For twenty years **Bass Products Corporation,** a public corporation, has followed the practice of paying a cash dividend every quarter and has promoted itself to investors as a stable, reliable company. Recent competition from Asian companies has negatively affected its earnings and cash flows. As a result, Sandra Bass, president of the company, is proposing that the board of directors declare a stock dividend of 5 percent this year instead of a cash dividend. She says, "This will maintain our consecutive dividend record and will not require any cash outflow." What is the difference between a cash dividend and a stock dividend? Why does a corporation usually distribute either kind of dividend, and how does each affect the financial statements? Is the action proposed by Bass ethical?

SD 4.
LO 1 Effect of Alternative
LO 5 Accounting Methods on
Executive Compensation

At the beginning of 20x1, Ted Lazzerini retired as president and principal stockholder in **Tedtronics Corporation,** a successful producer of personal computer equipment. As an incentive to the new management, Lazzerini supported the board of directors' new executive compensation plan, which provides cash bonuses to key executives for years in which the company's earnings per share equal or exceed the current dividends per share of $2.00, plus a $.20 per share increase in dividends for each future year. Thus, for management to receive the bonuses, the company must earn per-share income of $2.00 the first year, $2.20 the second, $2.40 the third, and so forth. Since Lazzerini owns 500,000 of the 1,000,000 common shares outstanding, the dividend income will provide for his retirement years. He is also protected against inflation by the regular increase in dividends. Earnings and dividends per share for the first three years of operation under the new management follow.

	20x3	20x2	20x1
Earnings per share	$2.50	$2.50	$2.50
Dividends per share	2.40	2.20	2.00

During this time, management earned bonuses totaling more than $1 million under the compensation plan. Lazzerini, who had taken no active part on the board of directors, began to worry about the unchanging level of earnings and decided to study the company's annual report more carefully. The notes to the annual report revealed the following information:

a. Management changed from the LIFO inventory method to the FIFO method in 20x1. The effect of the change was to decrease cost of goods sold by $200,000 in 20x1, $300,000 in 20x2, and $400,000 in 20x3.

b. Management changed from the double-declining-balance accelerated depreciation method to the straight-line method in 20x2. The effect of this change was to decrease depreciation by $400,000 in 20x2 and by $500,000 in 20x3.

c. In 20x3, management increased the estimated useful life of intangible assets from five to ten years. The effect of this change was to decrease amortization expense by $100,000 in 20x3.

1. Compute earnings per share for each year according to the accounting methods in use at the beginning of 20x1. (Use common shares outstanding.)

2. Is the action of the executives ethical? Have the executives earned their bonuses? What serious effect has the compensation package apparently had on the net assets of Tedtronics Corporation? How could Lazzerini have protected himself from what has happened?

Research Activity

SD 5.

LO 2 Corporate Income
LO 3 Statement, Statement of
LO 4 Stockholders' Equity, and
LO 6 Book Value
LO 7
LO 8

Select the annual reports of three corporations, using one or more of the following sources: your library, the Fingraph® Financial Analyst™ CD-ROM software that accompanies this text, or the Needles Accounting Resource Center Web site at http://college.hmco.com. You may choose companies from the same industry or at random, at the direction of your instructor. (If you completed the related research activity in the chapter on contributed capital, use the same three companies.) Prepare a table with a column for each corporation. Then, for any year covered by the balance sheet, the statement of stockholders' equity, and the income statement, answer the following questions: Does the company own treasury stock? Was any treasury stock bought or retired? Did the company declare a stock dividend or a stock split? What other transactions appear in the statement of stockholders' equity? Has the company deferred any income taxes? Were there any discontinued operations, extraordinary items, or accounting changes? Compute the book value per common share for the company. In *The Wall Street Journal* or the financial section of another daily newspaper, find the current market price of each company's common stock and compare it to the book value you computed. Should there be any relationship between the two values? Be prepared to discuss your answers to these questions in class.

Decision-Making Practice

SD 6.

LO 6 Analyzing Effects of
LO 7 Stockholders' Equity
LO 8 Transactions

Metzger Steel Corporation (MSC) is a small specialty steel manufacturer located in northern Alabama that has been owned by the Metzger family for several generations. Arnold Metzger is a major shareholder in MSC by virtue of his having inherited 200,000 shares of common stock in the company. Arnold has not shown much interest in the business because of his enthusiasm for archaeology, which takes him to far parts of the world. However, when he received the minutes of the last board of directors meeting, he questioned a number of transactions involving stockholders' equity. He asks you, as a person with a knowledge of accounting, to help him interpret the effect of these transactions on his interest in MSC.

You begin by examining the stockholders' equity section of MSC's December 31, 20x1, balance sheet.

Metzger Steel Corporation Stockholders' Equity December 31, 20x1	
Contributed Capital	
Common Stock, $10 par value, 5,000,000 shares authorized, 1,000,000 shares issued and outstanding	$10,000,000
Paid-in Capital in Excess of Par Value, Common	25,000,000
Total Contributed Capital	$35,000,000
Retained Earnings	20,000,000
Total Stockholders' Equity	$55,000,000

Then you read the relevant parts of the minutes of the December 15, 20x2, meeting of the firm's board of directors:

Item A: The president reported the following transactions involving the company's stock during the last quarter.

October 15. Sold 500,000 shares of authorized common stock through the investment banking firm of T.R. Kendall at a net price of $50 per share.

November 1. Purchased 100,000 shares for the corporate treasury from Lucy Metzger at a price of $55 per share.

Item B: The board declared a 2-for-1 stock split (accomplished by halving the par value and doubling each stockholder's shares), followed by a 10 percent stock dividend. The board then declared a cash dividend of $2 per share on the resulting shares. Cash dividends are declared on outstanding shares and shares distributable. All these transactions are applicable to stockholders of record on December 20 and are payable on January 10. The market value of MSC stock on the board meeting date after the stock split was estimated to be $30.

Item C: The chief financial officer stated that he expected the company to report net income for the year of $4,000,000.

1. Prepare a stockholders' equity section of MSC's balance sheet as of December 31, 20x2, that reflects the transactions above. (**Hint:** Use T accounts to analyze the transactions. Also, use a T account in order to keep track of the shares of common stock outstanding.)

2. Write a memorandum to Arnold Metzger that shows the book value per share and Metzger's percentage of ownership at the beginning and end of the year. Explain the difference and state whether Metzger's position has improved during the year. Tell why or why not and state how Metzger may be able to maintain his percentage of ownership.

FINANCIAL REPORTING AND ANALYSIS

Interpreting Financial Reports

FRA 1.

LO 1 **Quality of Earnings,**
LO 8 **Book Value, and Stock Price**

For several years, *International Business Machines Corp. (IBM)* has come under heavy criticism for repeated write-offs and restructuring charges that have lowered earnings. For example, in July 1993 IBM took a pretax $8.9 billion write-off for personnel retrenchment. The company also took a one-time pretax $1.84 billion charge in the third quarter of 1995 for purchased research and development in its acquisition of Lotus Development Corporation. In December 1995, IBM announced that it expected to take a pretax $800 million fourth-quarter charge to reflect new closings and cut-backs that were to take place over the next year. In 1996 IBM took a one-time pretax charge of $435 million for purchased research and development in its acquisition of Tivoli and Object Technology International, Inc. With the absence of one-time charges behind it, IBM earnings have improved in 1997 and 1998. Recently, one analyst following IBM has raised a potentially serious issue of IBM earnings quality as it relates to its revenue recognition policy from its service contracts. Service contracts are IBM's fastest growing revenue source but it is also a lower gross margin business. "Accounting for profits on service contracts is tricky and subject to considerable leeway. IBM won't say, for example, what percent of total contract earnings it books each year."[24] IBM earnings per share have risen faster than net income due to share repurchases. From 1995 through 1997, IBM will have bought 181 million common shares reducing its common equity by about 15 percent.

REQUIRED

1. How do write-offs and restructuring charges relate to the quality of earnings?

2. While analysts often exclude nonrecurring items such as write-offs from their analyses, what reasons would you give for including them in an analysis of IBM?

3. Explain how IBM's earnings per share are growing faster than its net income.

FRA 2.
LO 6 Interpretation of Statement of Stockholders' Equity

The consolidated statement of stockholders' equity for *Jackson Electronics, Inc.*, a manufacturer of a broad line of electrical components, appears as presented below.

Jackson Electronics, Inc.
Consolidated Statement of Stockholders' Equity
(in thousands)

	Preferred Stock	Common Stock	Paid-in Capital in Excess of Par Value, Common	Retained Earnings	Treasury Stock, Common	Total
Balance at September 30, 20x1	$2,756	$3,902	$14,149	$119,312	($ 942)	$139,177
Year Ended September 30, 20x2						
Net income	—	—	—	18,753	—	18,753
Redemption and retirement of Preferred Stock (27,560 shares)	(2,756)	—	—	—	—	(2,756)
Stock options exercised (89,000 shares)	—	89	847	—	—	936
Purchases of Common Stock for treasury (501,412 shares)	—	—	—	—	(12,552)	(12,552)
Issuance of Common Stock (148,000 shares) in exchange for convertible subordinated debentures	—	148	3,635	—	—	3,783
Issuance of Common Stock (715,000 shares) for cash	—	715	24,535	—	—	25,250
Issuance of 500,000 shares of Common Stock in exchange for investment in Electrix Company shares	—	500	17,263	—	—	17,763
Cash dividends—Common Stock ($.80 per share)	—	—	—	(3,086)	—	(3,086)
Balance at September 30, 20x2	$ —	$5,354	$60,429	$134,979	($13,494)	$187,268

REQUIRED

Jackson Electronics, Inc.'s statement of stockholders' equity has eight summary transactions. Show that you understand this statement by preparing an entry in journal form with an explanation for each. In each case, if applicable, determine the average price per common share. Sometimes you will also have to make assumptions about an offsetting part of the entry. For example, assume that debentures (long-term bonds) are recorded at face value and that employees pay cash for stock purchased under Jackson Electronics, Inc.'s employee incentive plans.

Group Activity: Assign each transaction to a different group to develop the entry and present the explanation to the class.

FRA 3.

LO 3 Analysis of Income Taxes from Annual Report

In its 1998 annual report, ***The Washington Post Company,*** a newspaper publishing and television broadcasting company based in Washington, D.C., provided the following data about its current and deferred income tax provisions (in millions):[25]

	1998	
	Current	Deferred
U.S. Federal	$200.9	$20.4
Foreign	1.2	.3
State	21.7	6.3
	$223.8	$27.0

REQUIRED

1. What was the 1998 income taxes expense? Record in journal form the overall income tax liability for 1998, using income tax allocation procedures.

2. In the long-term liability section of the balance sheet, The Washington Post Company shows deferred income taxes of $83.7 million in 1998 versus $31.3 million in 1997. This shows an increase in the amount of deferred income taxes. How do such deferred income taxes arise? What would cause deferred income taxes to increase? Give an example of this process. Given the definition of a liability, do you see a potential problem with the company's classifying deferred income taxes as a liability?

International Company

FRA 4.

LO 6 Restriction of Retained Earnings

In some countries, including Japan, the availability of retained earnings for the payment of dividends is restricted. The following disclosure appeared in the annual report of ***Yamaha Motor Company, Ltd.,*** the Japanese motorcycle manufacturer.[26]

> The Commercial Code of Japan provides that an amount not less than 10 percent of the total of cash dividends and bonuses [paid] to directors and corporate auditors be appropriated as a legal reserve until such reserve equals 25 percent of stated capital. The legal reserve may be used to reduce a deficit or may be transferred to stated capital, but is not available as dividends.

Stated capital is equivalent to common stock. For Yamaha, this legal reserve amounted to ¥3.4 billion, or $26.5 million. How does this practice differ from that in the United States? Why do you think it is government policy in Japan? Do you think it is a good idea?

Toys "R" Us Annual Report

FRA 5.

LO 2 Corporate Income
LO 4 Statement, Statement of
LO 6 Stockholders' Equity, and
LO 8 Book Value per Share

Refer to the Toys "R" Us annual report to answer the following questions.

1. Does Toys "R" Us have discontinued operations, extraordinary items, or cumulative changes in accounting principles? Would you say the income statement for Toys "R" Us is relatively simple or relatively complex?

2. What transactions most commonly affect the stockholders' equity section of the balance sheet of Toys "R" Us? Examine the statement of stockholders' equity.

3. Compute the book value of Toys "R" Us stock in 1999 and 1998 and compare it to the market price. What interpretation do you place on these relationships?

Fingraph® Financial Analyst™

FRA 6.

LO 1 Stockholders' Equity
LO 2 Analysis
LO 4
LO 5
LO 6
LO 7
LO 8

Choose any two companies from the same industry in the Fingraph® Financial Analyst™ CD-ROM software.

1. In the annual reports for the companies you have selected, identify the corporate income statement and its summary of significant accounting policies, usually the first note to the financial statements. Did the companies report any discontinued operations, extraordinary items, or accounting changes? What percentage impact did these items have on earnings per share? Summarize the methods and estimates each company uses in a table. If the company changed its accounting methods, was the change the result of a new accounting standard or a voluntary choice by management? Evaluate the quality of earnings for each company.

2. Did the companies report a statement of stockholders' equity or summarize the changes in stockholders' equity in the notes only? Did the companies declare any stock dividends or stock splits? Calculate book value per common share.

3. Find in the financial section of your local paper the current market prices of the companies' common stock. Discuss the difference between market price per share and book value per share.

4. Find and read references to earnings per share in management's discussion and analysis in each annual report.

5. Write a one-page executive summary that highlights the quality of earnings for these companies, the relationship of book value and market value, and the existence or absence of stock splits or dividends, including reference to management's assessment. Include your table as an attachment to your report.

Internet Case

FRA 7.

LO 2 Comparison of
LO 5 Comprehensive Income
LO 6 Disclosures

Reporting comprehensive income by public companies is a recent requirement. No specific guidelines were stated for how this amount and its components are disclosed. Choose two companies in the same industry from the Needles Accounting Resource Center at http://college.hmco.com. Using companies under web links, go to the annual reports on the web sites for the two companies you have selected. In the latest annual report, look at the financial statements. How have your two companies reported comprehensive income—as a part of the income statement, a part of stockholders' equity, or a separate statement? What items cause there to be a difference between net income and comprehensive income? Is comprehensive income greater or less than net income? Is comprehensive income more volatile than net income? Which measure of income is used to compute basic earnings per share?

ENDNOTES

1. Monsanto Company, *Annual Report*, 1998.
2. Cited in *The Week in Review* (Deloitte Haskins & Sells), February 28, 1985.
3. "Up to the Minute, Down to the Wire," *Twentieth Century Mutual Funds Newsletter*, 1996.
4. Ann Davis, "SEC Case Claims Profit Management by Grace," *The Wall Street Journal*, April 7, 1999.
5. Bernard Condon, "Pick a Number, Any Number," *Forbes*, March 23, 1998.
6. Sears, Roebuck and Co., *Annual Report*, 1997.
7. *Statement of Financial Accounting Standards No. 130*, "Reporting Comprehensive Income" (Norwalk, Conn.: Financial Accounting Standards Board, 1997).
8. Rules for calculating and reporting taxable income in specialized industries such as banking, insurance, mutual funds, and cooperatives are highly technical and may vary significantly from those discussed in this chapter.
9. *Statement of Financial Accounting Standards No. 109*, "Accounting for Income Taxes" (Norwalk, Conn.: Financial Accounting Standards Board, 1992).
10. American Institute of Certified Public Accountants, *Accounting Trends & Techniques* (New York: American Institute of Certified Public Accountants, 1998), p. 262.
11. Accounting Principles Board, *Opinion No. 30*, "Reporting the Results of Operations" (New York: American Institute of Certified Public Accountants, 1973), par. 20.

12. Ibid.
13. American Institute of Certified Public Accountants, *Accounting Trends & Techniques* (New York: American Institute of Certified Public Accountants, 1998), p. 397.
14. Accounting Principles Board, *Opinion No. 20*, "Accounting Changes" (New York: American Institute of Certified Public Accountants, 1971), par. 20.
15. American Institute of Certified Public Accountants, *Accounting Trends & Techniques* (New York: American Institute of Certified Public Accountants, 1998), p. 554.
16. Accounting Principles Board, *Opinion No. 15*, "Earnings per Share" (New York: American Institute of Certified Public Accountants, 1969), par. 12.
17. Minnesota Mining and Manufacturing Company, *Annual Report*, 1998.
18. *Statement of Financial Accounting Standards No. 128*, "Earnings per Share and the Disclosure of Information About Capital Structure" (Norwalk, Conn.: Financial Accounting Standards Board, 1997).
19. Skandia Group, *Annual Report*, 1998.
20. *Accounting Research Bulletin No. 43* (New York: American Institute of Certified Public Accountants, 1953), chap. 7, sec. B, par. 10.
21. Ibid., par. 13.
22. "Technology Firms Post Strong Earnings But Stock Prices Decline Sharply," *The Wall Street Journal*, January 21, 1988; Donald R. Seace, "Industrials Plunge 57.2 Points—Technology Stocks' Woes Cited," *The Wall Street Journal*, January 21, 1988.
23. Adapted from General Motors, *Annual Report*, 1996.
24. Gretchen Morgenson, "Less than Meets the Eye," *Forbes*, December 29, 1997.
25. The Washington Post Company, *Annual Report*, 1998.
26. Yamaha Motor Company, Ltd., *Annual Report*, 1998.

14

The Statement of Cash Flows

LEARNING OBJECTIVES

1 Describe the statement of cash flows, and define *cash* and *cash equivalents*.

2 State the principal purposes and uses of the statement of cash flows.

3 Identify the principal components of the classifications of cash flows, and state the significance of noncash investing and financing transactions.

4 Analyze the statement of cash flows.

5 Use the indirect method to determine cash flows from operating activities.

6 Determine cash flows from (a) investing activities and (b) financing activities.

7 Use the indirect method to prepare a statement of cash flows.

SUPPLEMENTAL OBJECTIVES

8 Prepare a work sheet for the statement of cash flows.

9 Use the direct method to determine cash flows from operating activities and prepare a statement of cash flows.

DECISION POINT: A USER'S FOCUS

Marriott International, Inc.
Marriott International, Inc., is a world leader in lodging and contract services. The balance sheet, income statement, and statement of stockholders' equity presented in the company's annual report give an excellent picture of management's philosophy and performance.

Those three financial statements are essential to the evaluation of a company, but they do not tell the entire story. Some information that they do not contain is presented in a fourth statement, the statement of cash flows, as shown in the Financial Highlights on the next page.[1] This statement shows how much cash was generated by the company's operations during the past three years and how much was used in or came from investing and financing activities. Marriott feels that maintaining adequate cash flows is important to the future of the company. In fact, Marriott's emphasis on cash flows is reflected in its executive compensation plan for its chief executive officer and senior executive officers. A review of the plan indicates that a measure of cash flows, at the firm or business group level, is the financial measure given the highest weight in determining compensation. Why would Marriott emphasize cash flows to such an extent?

Strong cash flows are essential to management's key goal of liquidity. If cash flows exceed the amount needed for operations and expansion, the company will not have to borrow additional funds. The excess cash flows will be available to reduce the company's debt and improve its financial position by lowering its debt to equity ratio. Another reason for the emphasis on cash flows may be the belief that strong cash flows from operations create shareholder value or increase the market value of the company's stock.

The statement of cash flows demonstrates management's commitments for the company in ways that are not readily apparent in the other financial statements. For example, the statement of cash flows can show whether management's focus is on the short term or the long term. This statement is required by the FASB[2] and satisfies the FASB's long-held position that a primary objective of financial statements is to provide investors and creditors with information about a company's cash flows.[3]

Key Point: The statement of cash flows helps financial statement users answer many questions that cannot be answered readily by referring to the other three financial statements. It fills the gaps by disclosing a business's inflows and outflows of cash, categorized by activity, during the period.

Financial Highlights: Consolidated Statement of Cash Flows

Marriott International, Inc., and Subsidiaries

Fiscal years ended January 1, 1999, January 2, 1998, and January 3, 1997	1998	1997	1996
		(In millions)	
Operating Activities			
Net income	$ 390	$ 324	$270
Adjustments to reconcile to cash provided by operations:			
Depreciation and amortization	140	126	89
Income taxes	76	64	69
Timeshare activity, net	28	(118)	(95)
Other	(22)	88	61
Working capital changes:			
Accounts receivable	(104)	(190)	18
Inventories	15	(3)	(17)
Other current assets	(16)	(15)	11
Accounts payable and accruals	98	266	90
Cash provided by operations	605	542	496
Investing Activities			
Capital expenditures	(937)	(520)	(293)
Acquisitions	(48)	(859)	(307)
Dispositions of property and equipment	332	571	65
Loans to Host Marriott Corporation	(48)	(95)	(89)
Loan repayments from Host Marriott Corporation	169	47	296
Other	(192)	(190)	(160)
Cash used in investing activities	(724)	(1,046)	(488)
Financing Activities			
Issuance of long-term debt	1,294	16	—
Repayment of long-term debt	(473)	(15)	(133)
Issuance of convertible subordinated debt	—	—	288
Issuance of common stock	15	—	—
Dividends paid	(37)	—	—
Purchase of treasury stock	(398)	—	—
Advances (to) from Old Marriott	(100)	576	(132)
Cash provided by (used in) financing activities	301	577	23
Increase/(Decrease) in Cash and Equivalents	182	73	31
Cash and Equivalents, beginning of year	208	135	104
Cash and Equivalents, end of year	$ 390	$ 208	$135

Overview of the Statement of Cash Flows

The **statement of cash flows** shows how a company's operating, investing, and financing activities have affected cash during an accounting period. It explains the net increase (or decrease) in cash during the accounting period. For purposes of preparing this statement, **cash** is defined to include both cash and cash equivalents. **Cash equivalents** are defined by the FASB as short-term, highly liquid investments, including money market accounts, commercial paper, and U.S. Treasury bills. A company maintains cash equivalents to earn interest on cash that would otherwise remain unused temporarily. Suppose, for example, that a company has $1,000,000 that it will not need for 30 days. To earn a return on this amount, the company may place the cash in an account that earns interest (such as a money market account); it may loan the cash to another corporation by purchasing that corporation's short-term notes (commercial paper); or it may purchase a short-term obligation of the U.S. government (Treasury bills). In this context, short-term refers to original maturities of 90 days or less. Since cash and cash

VIDEO CASE

 ## Ben & Jerry's Homemade, Inc.

Objectives

- To state the purposes of the statement of cash flows.
- To identify the three components of the statement of cash flows.
- To identify the reasons why cash flows from operating activities usually differs from net income.
- To understand the importance of cash flows from investing and financing activities.

Background for the Case

Ben & Jerry's Homemade, Inc., produces a wide variety of super-premium ice cream, ice cream novelties, and low

 fat ice cream, yogurt, and sorbet, using Vermont dairy products and high-quality all-natural ingredients. Ben & Jerry's products are distributed nationwide and in selected foreign countries in supermarkets, grocery stores, convenience stores, franchised and company-owned Ben & Jerry's Scoop shops, restaurants, and other venues.

Started with $12,000 in 1978 in a renovated gas station in Burlington, Vermont, Ben & Jerry's has stood out in the corporate world for its iconoclastic approach to business.

For example, the company donates a large share of its profits to charity and to support dairy farmers in Vermont. It has also committed to using milk and cream that have not been treated with synthetic hormones.

In recent years, this attitude of social activism has clashed with the needs of a modern corporation to produce a net income that will satisfy investors and increase shareholder value. As a result, Ben & Jerry's became a candidate for takeover by the giant Dutch company Unilever. Unilever, a company with many well-known brands, saw the possibility of using Ben & Jerry's strong brand recognition to increase its cash flows and net income.

For more information about Ben & Jerry's Homemade, Inc., visit the company's web site through the Needles Accounting Resource Center at:

http://college.hmco.com

Required

1. What are the purposes and three main components of the statement of cash flows?

2. What is the most important amount in the statement of cash flows and why?

3. What is the relationship of cash flows from operating activities to net income for Ben & Jerry's and how do you account for the difference?

4. What are the principal investing and financing activities for Ben & Jerry's?

equivalents are considered the same, transfers between the Cash account and cash equivalents are not treated as cash receipts or cash payments. In effect, cash equivalents are combined with the Cash account on the statement of cash flows.

Cash equivalents should not be confused with short-term investments or marketable securities, which are not combined with the Cash account on the statement of cash flows. Purchases of marketable securities are treated as cash outflows and sales of marketable securities as cash inflows on the statement of cash flows. In this chapter, cash will be assumed to include cash and cash equivalents.

Purposes of the Statement of Cash Flows

OBJECTIVE

2 State the principal purposes and uses of the statement of cash flows

The primary purpose of the statement of cash flows is to provide information about a company's cash receipts and cash payments during an accounting period. A secondary purpose of the statement is to provide information about a company's operating, investing, and financing activities during the accounting period. Some information about those activities may be inferred by examining other financial statements, but it is on the statement of cash flows that all the transactions affecting cash are summarized.

Internal and External Uses of the Statement of Cash Flows

Key Point: Management uses the statement of cash flows to make various investing and financing decisions. Investors and creditors, on the other hand, use the statement primarily to assess cash flow prospects.

The statement of cash flows is useful internally to management and externally to investors and creditors. Management uses the statement to assess liquidity, to determine dividend policy, and to evaluate the effects of major policy decisions involving investments and financing. In other words, management may use the statement to determine if short-term financing is needed to pay current liabilities, to decide whether to raise or lower dividends, and to plan for investing and financing needs.

Investors and creditors will find the statement useful in assessing the company's ability to manage cash flows, to generate positive future cash flows, to pay its liabilities, to pay dividends and interest, and to anticipate its need for additional financing. Also, they may use the statement to explain the differences between net income on the income statement and the net cash flows generated from operations. In addition, the statement shows both the cash and the noncash effects of investing and financing activities during the accounting period.

Classification of Cash Flows

OBJECTIVE

3 Identify the principal components of the classifications of cash flows, and state the significance of noncash investing and financing transactions

The statement of cash flows classifies cash receipts and cash payments into the categories of operating, investing, and financing activities. The components of these activities are illustrated in Figure 1 and summarized below.

1. **Operating activities** include the cash effects of transactions and other events that enter into the determination of net income. Included in this category as cash inflows are cash receipts from customers for goods and services, interest and dividends received on loans and investments, and sales of trading securities. Included as cash outflows are cash payments for wages, goods and services, expenses, interest, taxes, and purchases of trading securities. In effect, the income statement is changed from an accrual to a cash basis.

2. **Investing activities** include the acquiring and selling of long-term assets, the acquiring and selling of marketable securities other than trading securities or cash equivalents, and the making and collecting of loans. Cash inflows include the cash received from selling long-term assets and marketable securities and from collecting loans. Cash outflows include the cash expended for purchases of long-term assets and marketable securities and the cash loaned to borrowers.

Key Point: Operating activities arise from the day-to-day sale of goods and services, investing activities involve long-term assets and investments, and financing activities deal with stockholders' equity accounts and debt (borrowing).

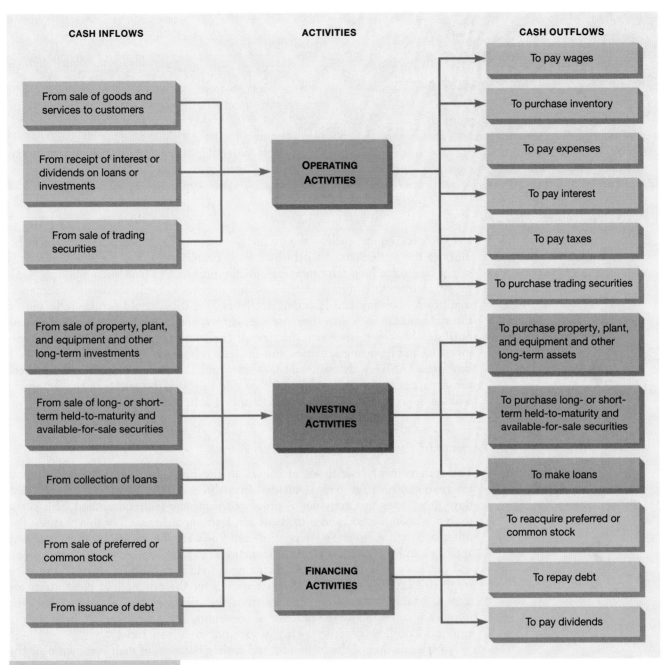

Figure 1
Classification of Cash Inflows and Cash Outflows

3. **Financing activities** include obtaining resources from or returning resources to owners and providing them with a return on their investment, and obtaining resources from creditors and repaying the amounts borrowed or otherwise settling the obligations. Cash inflows include the proceeds from issues of stocks and from short-term and long-term borrowing. Cash outflows include the repayments of loans (excluding interest) and payments to owners, including cash dividends. Treasury stock transactions are also considered financing activities. Repayments of accounts payable or accrued liabilities are not considered repayments of loans under financing activities, but are classified as cash outflows under operating activities.

A company will occasionally engage in significant **noncash investing and financing transactions** involving only long-term assets, long-term liabilities, or

BUSINESS FOCUS ON INTERNATIONAL

Despite the importance of the statement of cash flows in assessing the liquidity of companies in the United States, considerable variation in its use and format has existed in other countries. For example, the principal directives related to financial reporting for the European Union do not address the statement of cash flows. In many countries, the statement shows the change in working capital instead of the change in cash and cash equivalents. However, international accounting standards require the statement of cash flows, and international financial markets expect it to be presented. As a result, most multinational companies include the statement in their financial reports.

stockholders' equity, such as the exchange of a long-term asset for a long-term liability or the settlement of a debt by issuing capital stock. For instance, a company might take out a long-term mortgage for the purchase of land and a building. Or it might convert long-term bonds into common stock. Such transactions represent significant investing and financing activities, but they would not be reflected on the statement of cash flows because they do not involve either cash inflows or cash outflows. However, since one purpose of the statement of cash flows is to show investing and financing activities, and since such transactions will affect future cash flows, the FASB has determined that they should be disclosed in a separate schedule as part of the statement of cash flows. In this way, the reader of the statement will see the company's investing and financing activities more clearly.

Format of the Statement of Cash Flows

The statement of cash flows, as shown in the Financial Highlights for Marriott International on page 636, is divided into three sections. The first section, cash flows from operating activities, is presented using the indirect method. This is the most common method and is explained in learning objective 5 of this chapter. The other two sections of the statement of cash flows are the cash flows from investing activities and the cash flows from financing activities. The individual cash inflows and outflows from investing and financing activities are shown separately in their respective categories. Normally, cash outflows for the purchase of plant assets are shown separately from cash inflows from the disposal of plant assets. However, some companies follow the practice of combining these two lines to show the net amount of outflow, because the inflows are not usually material.

A reconciliation of the beginning and ending balances of cash is shown near the bottom of the statement. It shows that Marriott International had a net increase in cash of $182 million in 1998, which together with the beginning balance of $208 million results in $390 million of cash and cash equivalents on hand at the end of the year.

Analyzing the Statement of Cash Flows

OBJECTIVE
4 Analyze the statement of cash flows

Like the other financial statements, the statement of cash flows can be analyzed to reveal significant relationships. Two areas analysts examine when studying a company are cash-generating efficiency and free cash flow.

Cash-Generating Efficiency

Cash-generating efficiency is the ability of a company to generate cash from its current or continuing operations. Three ratios are helpful in measuring cash-generating efficiency: cash flow yield, cash flows to sales, and cash flows to assets. These ratios are computed and discussed below for Marriott International for 1998.[4] Data for the computations are obtained from the Financial Highlights for Marriott International on page 636 and below; all dollar amounts used to compute the ratios are stated in millions.

Cash flow yield is the ratio of net cash flows from operating activities to net income, as follows:

$$\text{Cash Flow Yield} = \frac{\text{Net Cash Flows from Operating Activities}}{\text{Net Income}}$$

$$= \frac{\$605}{\$390}$$

$$= 1.6 \text{ times}$$

Marriott International provides a good cash flow yield of 1.6 times; that is, operating activities are generating about 60 percent more cash flow than net income. If special items, such as discontinued operations, appear on the income statement and are material, income from continuing operations should be used as the denominator.

Financial Highlights for Marriott International

(In millions of dollars)

	1998	1997	1996
Net Sales	$7,968	$7,236	$5,738
Total Assets	6,233	5,161	3,765

Cash flows to sales is the ratio of net cash flows from operating activities to sales.

$$\text{Cash Flows to Sales} = \frac{\text{Net Cash Flows from Operating Activities}}{\text{Net Sales}}$$

$$= \frac{\$605}{\$7,968}$$

$$= 7.6\%$$

Marriott generates cash flows to sales of 7.6 percent. The company generated a positive but relatively small percentage of net cash from sales.

Cash flows to assets is the ratio of net cash flows from operating activities to average total assets, as follows:

$$\text{Cash Flows to Assets} = \frac{\text{Net Cash Flows from Operating Activities}}{\text{Average Total Assets}}$$

$$= \frac{\$605}{(\$6,233 + \$5,161) \div 2}$$

$$= 10.6\%$$

The cash flows to assets is higher than cash flows to sales because Marriott has a good asset turnover ratio (sales ÷ average total assets) of about 1.4 times. Cash flows to sales and cash flows to assets are closely related to the profitability measures profit margin and return on assets. They exceed those measures by the amount of the cash flow yield ratio because cash flow yield is the ratio of net cash flows from operating activities to net income.

Although Marriott's cash flow yield and cash flows to assets are relatively good, its efficiency at generating cash flows from operating activities, as measured by cash flows to sales, could be improved.

Free Cash Flow

It would seem logical for the analysis to move along to investing and financing activities. For example, in 1998 there is a net cash outflow of $724 million in the investing activities section, which could indicate that the company is expanding. However, that figure mixes capital expenditures for plant assets, which reflect management's expansion of operations, with the acquisition of hotel chains and loans to and repayments from Host Marriott Corporation. Also, cash flows from financing activities provided $301 million, but that figure combines financing activities associated with long-term debt and stocks with dividends paid to stockholders. While something can be learned by looking at those broad categories, many analysts find it more informative to go beyond them and focus on a computation called free cash flow.

Key Point: Free cash flow should be interpreted in light of the company's overall need for cash. For instance, the purchase of treasury stock will also reduce the amount of cash that is free for operating uses.

Free cash flow is the amount of cash that remains after deducting the funds the company must commit to continue operating at its planned level. The commitments must cover current or continuing operations, interest, income taxes, dividends, and net capital expenditures. Cash requirements for current or continuing operations, interest, and income taxes must be paid or the company's creditors and the government can take legal action. Although the payment of dividends is not strictly required, dividends normally represent a commitment to stockholders. If these payments are reduced or eliminated, stockholders will be unhappy and the price of the company's stock will fall. Net capital expenditures represent management's plans for the future.

If free cash flow is positive, it means that the company has met all of its planned cash commitments and has cash available to reduce debt or expand. A negative free cash flow means that the company will have to sell investments, borrow money, or issue stock in the short term to continue at its planned levels. If free cash flow remains negative for several years, a company may not be able to raise cash by issuing stock or bonds.

Since cash commitments for current or continuing operations, interest, and income taxes are incorporated in cash flows from current operations, free cash flow for Marriott is computed as follows (in millions):

Free Cash Flow = Net Cash Flows from Operating Activities − Dividends
− Purchases of Plant Assets + Sales of Plant Assets

= $605 − $37 − $937 + $332

= −$37

Purchases and sales of plant assets appear in the investing activities section of the statement of cash flows. Marriott reports both capital expenditures and dispositions of property and equipment. Dividends are found in the financing activities section. Marriott has negative free cash flow of $37 million due primarily to the large expansion of plant assets. The financing activities section shows how the company overcame the negative free cash flow. The company repaid long-term debt of $473 million while issuing new debt of $1,294 million. Marriott also issued common stock in the amount of $15 million and purchased treasury stock for $398 million. The result is that financing activities were a positive $301 million.

BUSINESS FOCUS ON PRACTICE

Because the statement of cash flows has been around for only a decade, no generally accepted analyses have yet been developed. For example, the term *free cash flow* is commonly used in the business press, but there is no agreement on its definition. An article in *Forbes* defines free cash flow as "cash available after paying out capital expenditures and dividends, *but before taxes and interest*"[5] [emphasis added]. In *The Wall Street Journal,* free cash flow was defined as "operating income less maintenance-level capital expenditures."[6] The definition with which we are most in agreement is the one used in *Business Week,* which is net cash flows from operating activities less net capital expenditures and dividends. This "measures truly discretionary funds—company money that an owner could pocket without harming the business."[7]

Cash flows can vary from year to year, so it is best to look at trends in cash flow measures over several years when analyzing a company's cash flows. Marriott's cash flow yield has shown little variation over the past three years. Management sums up in the annual report:

Cash from Operations
The company's operating cash flow is stable, and typically does not fluctuate widely within an economic cycle.[8]

The Indirect Method of Preparing the Statement of Cash Flows

OBJECTIVE

5 Use the indirect method to determine cash flows from operating activities

To demonstrate the preparation of the statement of cash flows, we will work through an example step by step. The data for this example are presented in Exhibits 1 and 2. Those two exhibits present Ryan Corporation's balance sheets for December 31, 20x1 and 20x0, and its 20x1 income statement. Since the changes in the balance sheet accounts will be used for analysis, those changes are shown in Exhibit 1. Whether the change in each account is an increase or a decrease is also shown. In addition, Exhibit 2 contains data about transactions that affected noncurrent accounts. Those transactions would be identified by the company's accountants from the records.

There are four steps in preparing the statement of cash flows:

1. Determine cash flows from operating activities.
2. Determine cash flows from investing activities.
3. Determine cash flows from financing activities.
4. Use the information obtained in the first three steps to compile the statement of cash flows.

Determining Cash Flows from Operating Activities

The first step in preparing the statement of cash flows is to determine cash flows from operating activities. The income statement indicates a business's success or failure in earning an income from its operating activities, but it does not reflect the inflow and outflow of cash from those activities. The reason is that the income statement is prepared on an accrual basis. Revenues are recorded even though the

Ryan Corporation
Comparative Balance Sheets
December 31, 20x1 and 20x0

	20x1	20x0	Change	Increase or Decrease
Assets				
Current Assets				
Cash	$ 46,000	$ 15,000	$ 31,000	Increase
Accounts Receivable (net)	47,000	55,000	(8,000)	Decrease
Inventory	144,000	110,000	34,000	Increase
Prepaid Expenses	1,000	5,000	(4,000)	Decrease
Total Current Assets	$238,000	$185,000	$ 53,000	
Investments Available for Sale	$115,000	$127,000	($ 12,000)	Decrease
Plant Assets				
Plant Assets	$715,000	$505,000	$210,000	Increase
Accumulated Depreciation	(103,000)	(68,000)	(35,000)	Increase
Total Plant Assets	$612,000	$437,000	$175,000	
Total Assets	$965,000	$749,000	$216,000	
Liabilities				
Current Liabilities				
Accounts Payable	$ 50,000	$ 43,000	$ 7,000	Increase
Accrued Liabilities	12,000	9,000	3,000	Increase
Income Taxes Payable	3,000	5,000	(2,000)	Decrease
Total Current Liabilities	$ 65,000	$ 57,000	$ 8,000	
Long-Term Liabilities				
Bonds Payable	295,000	245,000	50,000	Increase
Total Liabilities	$360,000	$302,000	$ 58,000	
Stockholders' Equity				
Common Stock, $5 par value	$276,000	$200,000	$ 76,000	Increase
Paid-in Capital in Excess of Par Value, Common	189,000	115,000	74,000	Increase
Retained Earnings	140,000	132,000	8,000	Increase
Total Stockholders' Equity	$605,000	$447,000	$158,000	
Total Liabilities and Stockholders' Equity	$965,000	$749,000	$216,000	

Exhibit 1
Comparative Balance Sheets with Changes in Accounts Indicated for Ryan Corporation

cash for them may not have been received, and expenses are recorded even though the cash for them may not have been expended. As a result, to arrive at cash flows from operations, the figures on the income statement must be converted from an accrual basis to a cash basis.

There are two methods of converting the income statement from an accrual basis to a cash basis: the direct method and the indirect method. Under the **direct method**, each item on the income statement is adjusted from the accrual basis to the cash basis. The result is a statement that begins with cash receipts from sales

Exhibit 2
Income Statement and Other Information on Noncurrent Accounts for Ryan Corporation

Ryan Corporation
Income Statement
For the Year Ended December 31, 20x1

Net Sales		$698,000
Cost of Goods Sold		520,000
Gross Margin		$178,000
Operating Expenses (including Depreciation Expense of $37,000)		147,000
Operating Income		$ 31,000
Other Income (Expenses)		
Interest Expense	($23,000)	
Interest Income	6,000	
Gain on Sale of Investments	12,000	
Loss on Sale of Plant Assets	(3,000)	(8,000)
Income Before Income Taxes		$ 23,000
Income Taxes		7,000
Net Income		$ 16,000

Other transactions affecting noncurrent accounts during 20x1:

1. Purchased investments in the amount of $78,000.
2. Sold investments for $102,000 that cost $90,000.
3. Purchased plant assets in the amount of $120,000.
4. Sold plant assets that cost $10,000 with accumulated depreciation of $2,000 for $5,000.
5. Issued $100,000 of bonds at face value in a noncash exchange for plant assets.
6. Repaid $50,000 of bonds at face value at maturity.
7. Issued 15,200 shares of $5 par value common stock for $150,000.
8. Paid cash dividends in the amount of $8,000.

Key Point: The direct and indirect methods relate only to the operating activities section of the statement of cash flows. They are both acceptable for financial reporting purposes.

Key Point: The direct and indirect methods will always produce the same net figure. The direct method, however, is more easily understood by the average reader because it results in a more straightforward presentation of operating cash flows than does the indirect method.

and interest and deducts cash payments for purchases, operating expenses, interest payments, and income taxes to arrive at net cash flows from operating activities. The **indirect method**, on the other hand, does not require the individual adjustment of each item on the income statement, but lists only those adjustments necessary to convert net income to cash flows from operations. Because the indirect method is more common, it will be used to illustrate the conversion of the income statement to a cash basis in the sections that follow. The direct method is presented in a supplemental objective at the end of the chapter.

BUSINESS FOCUS ON PRACTICE

The direct method and the indirect method of determining cash flows from operating activities produce the same results. If the direct method is used, a reconciliation of net income to net cash flows from operating activities must be provided in a separate schedule. The

FASB recommends, but does not require, the direct method, but a survey of large companies showed that an overwhelming majority, 98 percent, chose to use the indirect method.[9] The reasons for choosing the indirect method vary, but chief financial officers tend to prefer it because it is easier and less expensive to implement. Also, with the required reconciliation under the direct method, the same information is provided as under the indirect method.

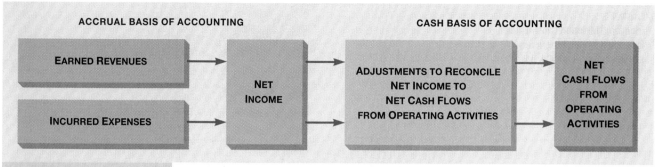

ACCRUAL BASIS OF ACCOUNTING   CASH BASIS OF ACCOUNTING

Figure 2
Indirect Method of
Determining Net Cash Flows
from Operating Activities

Key Point: The indirect method begins with net income and adjusts up or down to produce net cash flows from operating activities.

Key Point: Operating expenses on the income statement include depreciation expense, which does not require a cash outlay.

The indirect method, as illustrated in Figure 2, focuses on items from the income statement that must be adjusted to reconcile net income to net cash flows from operating activities. The items that require attention are those that affect net income but not net cash flows from operating activities, such as depreciation and amortization, gains and losses, and changes in the balances of current asset and current liability accounts. The reconciliation of Ryan Corporation's net income to net cash flows from operating activities is shown in Exhibit 3. Each adjustment is discussed in the following sections.

DEPRECIATION   Cash payments for plant assets, intangibles, and natural resources occur when the assets are purchased and are reflected as investing activities on the statement of cash flows at that time. When depreciation expense, amortization expense, and depletion expense appear on the income statement, they simply indicate allocations of the costs of the original purchases to the current accounting period; they do not affect net cash flows in the current period. The amount of such expenses can usually be found by referring to the income statement or a note to the financial statements.

For Ryan Corporation, the income statement reveals depreciation expense of $37,000, which would have been recorded as follows:

A = L + OE	Depreciation Expense	37,000
− −	Accumulated Depreciation		37,000
To record annual depreciation on plant assets		

Study Note: It is possible to earn a profit yet realize a negative cash flow from operating activities. Similarly, it is possible to suffer a net loss yet realize a positive cash flow from operating activities.

The recording of depreciation involved no outlay of cash. Thus, because cash flow was not affected, an adjustment for depreciation is needed to increase net income by the amount of depreciation recorded.

Study Note: Gains and losses by themselves do not represent cash flows; they are merely bookkeeping adjustments. For example, when a long-term asset is sold, it is the *proceeds* (cash received), not the gain or loss, that constitute cash flow.

GAINS AND LOSSES   Gains and losses that appear on the income statement also do not affect cash flows from operating activities and need to be removed from this section of the statement of cash flows. The cash receipts generated from the disposal of the assets that resulted in the gains or losses are shown in the investing section of the statement of cash flows. Thus, gains and losses are removed from net income (preventing double counting) to reconcile net income to cash flows from operating activities. For example, on the income statement, Ryan Corporation showed a $12,000 gain on the sale of investments, and this is subtracted from net income to reconcile net income to net cash flows from operating activities. Also, Ryan Corporation showed a $3,000 loss on the sale of plant assets, and this is added to net income to reconcile net income to net cash flows from operating activities.

CHANGES IN CURRENT ASSETS   Decreases in current assets other than cash have positive effects on cash flows, and increases in current assets have negative

Exhibit 3
Schedule of Cash Flows from Operating Activities: Indirect Method

Ryan Corporation
Schedule of Cash Flows from Operating Activities
For the Year Ended December 31, 20x1

Cash Flows from Operating Activities

Net Income		$16,000
Adjustments to Reconcile Net Income to Net Cash Flows from Operating Activities		
Depreciation	$37,000	
Gain on Sale of Investments	(12,000)	
Loss on Sale of Plant Assets	3,000	
Changes in Current Assets and Current Liabilities		
Decrease in Accounts Receivable	8,000	
Increase in Inventory	(34,000)	
Decrease in Prepaid Expenses	4,000	
Increase in Accounts Payable	7,000	
Increase in Accrued Liabilities	3,000	
Decrease in Income Taxes Payable	(2,000)	14,000
Net Cash Flows from Operating Activities		$30,000

Study Note: A decrease in a current asset frees up invested cash, thereby increasing cash flow. An increase in a current asset consumes cash, thereby decreasing cash flow.

effects on cash flows. For example, refer to the balance sheets and income statement for Ryan Corporation in Exhibits 1 and 2. Note that net sales in 20x1 were $698,000 and that Accounts Receivable decreased by $8,000. Thus, cash received from sales was $706,000, calculated as follows:

$$\$706,000 = \$698,000 + \$8,000$$

Collections were $8,000 more than sales recorded for the year. This relationship may be illustrated as follows:

Accounts Receivable

Sales to Customers	Beg. Bal.	55,000	706,000 ⟶	Cash Receipts from Customers
	⟶	698,000		
	End. Bal.	47,000		

Thus, to reconcile net income to net cash flows from operating activities, the $8,000 decrease in Accounts Receivable is added to net income.

Inventory may be analyzed in the same way. For example, Exhibit 1 shows that Inventory increased by $34,000 from 20x0 to 20x1. This means that Ryan Corporation expended $34,000 more in cash for purchases than was included in cost of goods sold on the income statement. As a result of this expenditure, net income is higher than the net cash flows from operating activities, so $34,000 must be deducted from net income.

Using the same logic, the decrease of $4,000 in Prepaid Expenses is added to net income to reconcile net income to net cash flows from operations.

Study Note: An increase in a current liability represents a postponement of a cash payment, which frees up cash and increases cash flow in the current period. A decrease in current liabilities consumes cash, thereby decreasing cash flow.

CHANGES IN CURRENT LIABILITIES Changes in current liabilities have the opposite effects on cash flows from those of changes in current assets. Increases in current liabilities are added to net income, and decreases in current liabilities are deducted from net income to reconcile net income to net cash flows from operating activities. For example, note from Exhibit 1 that Ryan Corporation had a $7,000 increase in Accounts Payable from 20x0 to 20x1. This means that Ryan

Corporation paid $7,000 less to creditors than what appears as purchases on the income statement. This relationship may be visualized as follows:

Accounts Payable

Cash Payments to Suppliers ← 547,000	Beg. Bal.	43,000
		554,000* ← Purchases
	End. Bal.	**50,000**

*Purchases = Cost of Goods Sold ($520,000) + Increase in Inventory ($34,000).

As a result, $7,000 is added to net income to reconcile net income to net cash flows from operating activities.

Using this same logic, the increase of $3,000 in Accrued Liabilities is added to net income and the decrease of $2,000 in Income Taxes Payable is deducted from net income to reconcile net income to net cash flows from operating activities.

SCHEDULE OF CASH FLOWS FROM OPERATING ACTIVITIES In summary, Exhibit 3 shows that by using the indirect method, net income of $16,000 has been adjusted by reconciling items totaling $14,000 to arrive at net cash flows from operating activities of $30,000. This means that although net income was $16,000, Ryan Corporation actually had net cash flows available from operating activities of $30,000 to use for purchasing assets, reducing debts, or paying dividends.

SUMMARY OF ADJUSTMENTS The effects of items on the income statement that do not affect cash flows may be summarized as follows:

	Add to or Deduct from Net Income
Depreciation Expense	Add
Amortization Expense	Add
Depletion Expense	Add
Losses	Add
Gains	Deduct

The adjustments for increases and decreases in current assets and current liabilities may be summarized as follows.

	Add to Net Income	Deduct from Net Income
Current Assets		
Accounts Receivable (net)	Decrease	Increase
Inventory	Decrease	Increase
Prepaid Expenses	Decrease	Increase
Current Liabilities		
Accounts Payable	Increase	Decrease
Accrued Liabilities	Increase	Decrease
Income Taxes Payable	Increase	Decrease

Determining Cash Flows from Investing Activities

OBJECTIVE

6a Determine cash flows from investing activities

The second step in preparing the statement of cash flows is to determine cash flows from investing activities. Each account involving cash receipts and cash payments from investing activities is examined individually. The objective is to explain the change in each account balance from one year to the next.

Investing activities center on the long-term assets shown on the balance sheet, but they also include transactions affecting short-term investments from the current assets section of the balance sheet and investment gains and losses from the income statement. The balance sheets in Exhibit 1 show that Ryan Corporation has long-term assets of investments and plant assets, but no short-term investments. The income statement in Exhibit 2 shows that Ryan has investment-related items in the form of a gain on the sale of investments and a loss on the sale of plant assets. The schedule at the bottom of Exhibit 2 lists the following five items pertaining to investing activities in 20x1:

1. Purchased investments in the amount of $78,000.
2. Sold investments for $102,000 that cost $90,000.
3. Purchased plant assets in the amount of $120,000.
4. Sold plant assets that cost $10,000 with accumulated depreciation of $2,000 for $5,000.
5. Issued $100,000 of bonds at face value in a noncash exchange for plant assets.

The following paragraphs analyze the accounts related to investing activities to determine their effects on Ryan Corporation's cash flows.

INVESTMENTS The objective here is to explain the corporation's $12,000 decrease in investments, all of which are classified as available-for-sale securities. This is accomplished by analyzing the increases and decreases in the Investments account to determine the effects on the Cash account. Purchases increase investments, and sales decrease investments. Item 1 in Ryan's list of investing activities shows purchases of $78,000 during 20x1. The transaction is recorded as follows:

A = L + OE	Investments	78,000	
+	Cash		78,000
–	Purchase of investments		

The entry shows that the effect of this transaction is a $78,000 decrease in cash flows.

Item 2 in the list shows a sale of investments for $102,000 that cost $90,000, which results in a gain of $12,000. This transaction was recorded as follows:

A = L + OE	Cash	102,000	
+ +	Investments		90,000
–	Gain on Sale of Investments		12,000
	Sale of investments for a gain		

The effect of this transaction is a $102,000 increase in cash flows. Note that the gain on sale of investments is included in the $102,000. This is the reason it was excluded earlier in computing cash flows from operations. If it had been included in that section, it would have been counted twice.

The $12,000 decrease in the Investments account during 20x1 has now been explained, as seen in the following T account.

Investments			
Beg. Bal.	127,000	Sales	90,000
Purchases	78,000		
End. Bal.	115,000		

The cash flow effects from these transactions are shown in the Cash Flows from Investing Activities section on the statement of cash flows as follows:

Purchase of Investments	($ 78,000)
Sale of Investments	102,000

Notice that purchases and sales are listed separately as cash outflows and cash inflows to give readers of the statement a complete view of investing activity. Some companies prefer to combine them into a single net amount.

If Ryan Corporation had short-term investments or marketable securities, the analysis of cash flows would be the same.

PLANT ASSETS   In the case of plant assets, it is necessary to explain the changes in both the asset account and the related accumulated depreciation account. According to Exhibit 1, Plant Assets increased by $210,000 and Accumulated Depreciation increased by $35,000. Purchases increase plant assets, and sales decrease plant assets. Accumulated depreciation is increased by the amount of depreciation expense and decreased by the removal of the accumulated depreciation associated with plant assets that are sold. Three items listed in Exhibit 2 affect plant assets. Item **3** in the list on the previous page indicates that Ryan Corporation purchased plant assets totaling $120,000 during 20x1, as shown by the following entry:

A = L + OE	Plant Assets	120,000	
+	Cash		120,000
−	Purchase of plant assets		

This transaction results in a cash outflow of $120,000.

Item **4** states that Ryan Corporation took plant assets that had cost $10,000 and had accumulated depreciation of $2,000, and sold them for $5,000, which resulted in a loss of $3,000. The entry to record this transaction is as follows:

A = L + OE	Cash	5,000	
+ −	Accumulated Depreciation	2,000	
+	Loss on Sale of Plant Assets	3,000	
−	Plant Assets		10,000
	Sale of plant assets at a loss		

Key Point: Even though a loss was suffered on the sale, a positive cash flow of $5,000 was realized and will be reported in the investing activities section of the statement. When the indirect approach is used, the loss must be eliminated with an "add-back" to net income.

Note that in this transaction the positive cash flow is equal to the amount of cash received, or $5,000. The loss on the sale of plant assets is included here and excluded from the operating activities section by adjusting net income for the amount of the loss. The amount of a loss or gain on the sale of an asset is determined by the amount of cash received and does not represent a cash outflow or inflow.

The disclosure of these two transactions in the investing activities section of the statement of cash flows is as follows:

Purchase of Plant Assets	($120,000)
Sale of Plant Assets	5,000

As with investments, cash outflows and cash inflows are not combined here, but are sometimes combined into a single net amount.

Item **5** on the list of Ryan's investing activities is a noncash exchange that affects two long-term accounts, Plant Assets and Bonds Payable. It was recorded as follows:

A = L + OE	Plant Assets	100,000	
+ +	Bonds Payable		100,000
	Issued bonds at face value for plant assets		

Although this transaction does not involve an inflow or outflow of cash, it is a significant transaction involving both an investing activity (the purchase of plant assets) and a financing activity (the issue of bonds payable). Because one purpose of the statement of cash flows is to show important investing and financing activities, the transaction is listed in a separate schedule, either at the bottom of the statement of cash flows or accompanying the statement, as follows:

Schedule of Noncash Investing and Financing Transactions

Issue of Bonds Payable for Plant Assets $100,000

Through our analysis of the preceding transactions and the depreciation expense for plant assets of $37,000, all the changes in the plant assets accounts have now been accounted for, as shown in the following T accounts:

Plant Assets

Beg. Bal.	505,000	Sale	10,000
Cash Purchase	120,000		
Noncash Purchase	100,000		
End. Bal.	715,000		

Accumulated Depreciation

Sale	2,000	Beg. Bal.	68,000
		Dep. Exp.	37,000
		End. Bal.	103,000

If the balance sheet had included specific plant asset accounts, such as Buildings and Equipment and their related accumulated depreciation accounts, or other long-term asset accounts, such as intangibles or natural resources, the analysis would have been the same.

Determining Cash Flows from Financing Activities

OBJECTIVE

6b Determine cash flows from financing activities

Key Point: Financing activities involve stockholders' equity accounts and short- and long-term borrowings. Because dividends paid involve retained earnings, they are appropriately included in this category.

The third step in preparing the statement of cash flows is to determine cash flows from financing activities. The procedure is similar to the analysis of investing activities, including treatment of related gains or losses. The only difference is that the accounts to be analyzed are the short-term borrowings, long-term liabilities, and stockholders' equity accounts. Cash dividends from the statement of stockholders' equity must also be considered. Since Ryan Corporation does not have short-term borrowings, only long-term liabilities and stockholders' equity accounts are considered here. The following items from Exhibit 2 pertain to Ryan Corporation's financing activities in 20x1:

5. Issued $100,000 of bonds at face value in a noncash exchange for plant assets.
6. Repaid $50,000 of bonds at face value at maturity.
7. Issued 15,200 shares of $5 par value common stock for $150,000.
8. Paid cash dividends in the amount of $8,000.

BONDS PAYABLE Exhibit 1 shows that Bonds Payable increased by $50,000 in 20x1. This account is affected by items **5** and **6**. Item **5** was analyzed in connection with plant assets. It is reported on the schedule of noncash investing and financing transactions (see Exhibit 4 on page 653), but it must be remembered here in preparing the T account for Bonds Payable. Item **6** results in a cash outflow, which can be seen in the following transaction.

A = L + OE
– –

Bonds Payable	50,000	
Cash		50,000
Repayment of bonds at face value		
at maturity		

This cash outflow is shown in the financing activities section of the statement of cash flows as follows:

Repayment of Bonds ($50,000)

From these transactions, the change in the Bonds Payable account can be explained as follows:

Bonds Payable

Repayment	50,000	Beg. Bal.	245,000
		Noncash Issue	100,000
		End. Bal.	295,000

If Ryan Corporation had notes payable, either short-term or long-term, the analysis would be the same.

COMMON STOCK   As with plant assets, related stockholders' equity accounts should be analyzed together. For example, Paid-in Capital in Excess of Par Value, Common should be examined with Common Stock. In 20x1 Ryan Corporation's Common Stock account increased by $76,000 and Paid-in Capital in Excess of Par Value, Common increased by $74,000. Those increases are explained by item **7,** which states that Ryan Corporation issued 15,200 shares of stock for $150,000. The entry to record the cash inflow was as follows:

A = L + OE
 +   +
       +

Cash	150,000	
Common Stock		76,000
Paid-in Capital in Excess of Par Value, Common		74,000
Issued 15,200 shares of $5 par value common stock		

Study Note: The purchase of treasury stock would also qualify as a financing activity, but would appear as a cash outflow.

The cash inflow is shown in the financing activities section of the statement of cash flows as follows:

Issue of Common Stock $150,000

The analysis of this transaction is all that is needed to explain the changes in the two accounts during 20x1, as follows:

Common Stock			**Paid-in Capital in Excess of Par Value, Common**	
	Beg. Bal. 200,000			Beg. Bal. 115,000
	Issue 76,000			Issue 74,000
	End. Bal. 276,000			End. Bal. 189,000

RETAINED EARNINGS   At this point in the analysis, several items that affect retained earnings have already been dealt with. For instance, in the case of Ryan Corporation, net income was used as part of the analysis of cash flows from operating activities. The only other item affecting the retained earnings of Ryan Corporation is the payment of $8,000 in cash dividends (item 8 on the list on page 651), as reflected by the following transaction.

A = L + OE
 −   −

Retained Earnings	8,000	
Cash		8,000
Cash dividends for 20x1		

Ryan Corporation would have declared the dividend before paying it and therefore would have debited the Cash Dividends Declared account instead of Retained Earnings, but after paying the dividend and closing the Cash Dividends Declared

Exhibit 4
Statement of Cash Flows:
Indirect Method

Ryan Corporation
Statement of Cash Flows
For the Year Ended December 31, 20x1

Cash Flows from Operating Activities

Net Income		$ 16,000
Adjustments to Reconcile Net Income to Net		
Cash Flows from Operating Activities		
Depreciation	$ 37,000	
Gain on Sale of Investments	(12,000)	
Loss on Sale of Plant Assets	3,000	
Changes in Current Assets and Current Liabilities		
Decrease in Accounts Receivable	8,000	
Increase in Inventory	(34,000)	
Decrease in Prepaid Expenses	4,000	
Increase in Accounts Payable	7,000	
Increase in Accrued Liabilities	3,000	
Decrease in Income Taxes Payable	(2,000)	14,000
Net Cash Flows from Operating Activities		$ 30,000
Cash Flows from Investing Activities		
Purchase of Investments	($ 78,000)	
Sale of Investments	102,000	
Purchase of Plant Assets	(120,000)	
Sale of Plant Assets	5,000	
Net Cash Flows from Investing Activities		(91,000)
Cash Flows from Financing Activities		
Repayment of Bonds	($ 50,000)	
Issue of Common Stock	150,000	
Dividends Paid	(8,000)	
Net Cash Flows from Financing Activities		92,000
Net Increase (Decrease) in Cash		$ 31,000
Cash at Beginning of Year		15,000
Cash at End of Year		$ 46,000
Schedule of Noncash Investing and Financing Transactions		
Issue of Bonds Payable for Plant Assets		$100,000

account to Retained Earnings, the effect is as shown. Cash dividends are displayed in the financing activities section of the statement of cash flows:

Dividends Paid ($8,000)

Key Point: It is dividends paid, not dividends declared, that appear on the statement of cash flows.

The following T account shows the change in the Retained Earnings account.

Retained Earnings

Dividends	8,000	Beg. Bal.	132,000
		Net Income	16,000
		End. Bal.	140,000

Compiling the Statement of Cash Flows

OBJECTIVE

7 Use the indirect method to prepare a statement of cash flows

At this point in the analysis, all income statement items have been analyzed, all balance sheet changes have been explained, and all additional information has been taken into account. The resulting information may now be assembled into a statement of cash flows for Ryan Corporation, as presented in Exhibit 4 on the previous page. The Schedule of Noncash Investing and Financing Transactions is presented at the bottom of the statement.

Preparing the Work Sheet

SUPPLEMENTAL OBJECTIVE

8 Prepare a work sheet for the statement of cash flows

To assist in preparing the statement of cash flows for more complex companies, accountants have developed a work sheet approach. The work sheet approach uses the indirect method of determining cash flows from operating activities because of its basis in changes in the balance sheet accounts.

Procedures in Preparing the Work Sheet

Key Point: A statement of cash flows work sheet is especially helpful in complex business situations. The work sheet takes the indirect approach.

The work sheet for Ryan Corporation is presented in Exhibit 5. The work sheet has four columns, labeled as follows:

Column A: Description

Column B: Account balances for the end of the prior year (20x0)

Column C: Analysis of transactions for the current year

Column D: Account balances for the end of the current year (20x1)

Five steps are followed in preparing the work sheet. As you read each one, refer to Exhibit 5.

1. Enter the account names from the balance sheets (Exhibit 1) in column A. Note that all accounts with debit balances are listed first, followed by all accounts with credit balances.

2. Enter the account balances for 20x0 in column B and the account balances for 20x1 in column D. In each column, total the debits and the credits. The total debits should equal the total credits in each column. (This is a check of whether all accounts were correctly transferred from the balance sheets.)

3. Below the data entered in step **2,** insert the headings Cash Flows from Operating Activities, Cash Flows from Investing Activities, and Cash Flows from Financing Activities, leaving several lines of space between each one. As you do the analysis in step **4,** write the results in the appropriate categories.

4. Analyze the changes in each balance sheet account, using information from both the income statement (see Exhibit 2) and other transactions affecting noncurrent accounts during 20x1. (The procedures for this analysis are presented in the next section.) Enter the results in the debit and credit columns. Identify each item with a letter. On the first line, identify the change in cash with an (x). In a complex situation, these letters will refer to a list of explanations on another working paper.

5. When all the changes in the balance sheet accounts have been explained, add the debit and credit columns in both the top and the bottom portions of column C. The debit and credit columns in the top portion should equal each other. They should *not* be equal in the bottom portion. If no errors have been

Exhibit 5
Work Sheet for the Statement of Cash Flows

Ryan Corporation
Work Sheet for Statement of Cash Flows
For the Year Ended December 31, 20x1

Description	Account Balances 12/31/x0	Analysis of Transactions Debit		Analysis of Transactions Credit		Account Balances 12/31/x1
Debits						
Cash	15,000	(x)	31,000			46,000
Accounts Receivable (net)	55,000			(b)	8,000	47,000
Inventory	110,000	(c)	34,000			144,000
Prepaid Expenses	5,000			(d)	4,000	1,000
Investments Available for Sale	127,000	(h)	78,000	(i)	90,000	115,000
Plant Assets	505,000	(j)	120,000	(k)	10,000	715,000
		(l)	100,000			
Total Debits	817,000					1,068,000
Credits						
Accumulated Depreciation	68,000	(k)	2,000	(m)	37,000	103,000
Accounts Payable	43,000			(e)	7,000	50,000
Accrued Liabilities	9,000			(f)	3,000	12,000
Income Taxes Payable	5,000	(g)	2,000			3,000
Bonds Payable	245,000	(n)	50,000	(l)	100,000	295,000
Common Stock	200,000			(o)	76,000	276,000
Paid-in Capital	115,000			(o)	74,000	189,000
Retained Earnings	132,000	(p)	8,000	(a)	16,000	140,000
Total Credits	817,000		425,000		425,000	1,068,000
Cash Flows from Operating Activities						
Net Income		(a)	16,000			
Decrease in Accounts Receivable		(b)	8,000			
Increase in Inventory				(c)	34,000	
Decrease in Prepaid Expenses		(d)	4,000			
Increase in Accounts Payable		(e)	7,000			
Increase in Accrued Liabilities		(f)	3,000			
Decrease in Income Taxes Payable				(g)	2,000	
Gain on Sale of Investments				(i)	12,000	
Loss on Sale of Plant Assets		(k)	3,000			
Depreciation Expense		(m)	37,000			
Cash Flows from Investing Activities						
Purchase of Investments				(h)	78,000	
Sale of Investments		(i)	102,000			
Purchase of Plant Assets				(j)	120,000	
Sale of Plant Assets		(k)	5,000			
Cash Flows from Financing Activities						
Repayment of Bonds				(n)	50,000	
Issue of Common Stock		(o)	150,000			
Dividends Paid				(p)	8,000	
			335,000		304,000	
Net Increase in Cash				(x)	31,000	
			335,000		335,000	

made, the difference between columns in the bottom portion should equal the increase or decrease in the Cash account, identified with an (x) on the first line of the work sheet. Add this difference to the lesser of the two columns, and identify it as either an increase or a decrease in cash. Label the change with an (x) and compare it with the change in Cash on the first line of the work sheet, also labeled (x). The amounts should be equal, as they are in Exhibit 5, where the net increase in cash is $31,000. Also, the new totals from the debit and credit columns should be equal.

Study Note: The work sheet would handle a net decrease in cash in the opposite way—as a credit at the top of the work sheet and as a debit to balance at the bottom.

When the work sheet is complete, the statement of cash flows may be prepared using the information in the lower half of the work sheet.

Analyzing the Changes in Balance Sheet Accounts

The most important step in preparing the work sheet is the analysis of the changes in the balance sheet accounts (step **4**). Although a number of transactions and reclassifications must be analyzed and recorded, the overall procedure is systematic and not overly complicated. It is as follows:

1. Record net income.
2. Account for changes in current assets and current liabilities.
3. Use the information about other transactions to account for changes in non-current accounts.
4. Reclassify any other income and expense items not already dealt with.

In the following explanations, the identification letters refer to the corresponding transactions and reclassifications on the work sheet.

Key Point: Retained Earnings is analyzed on the work sheet through net income and dividends paid.

a. NET INCOME Net income results in an increase in Retained Earnings (entry **a**). Under the indirect method, it is the starting point for determining cash flows from operating activities. Under this method, additions and deductions are made to net income to arrive at cash flows from operating activities.

b–g. CHANGES IN CURRENT ASSETS AND CURRENT LIABILITIES Entries **b** to **g** record the effects on cash flows of the changes in current assets and current liabilities. In each case, there is a debit or credit to the current asset or current liability to account for the change from year to year and a corresponding debit or credit in the operating activities section of the work sheet. For example, work sheet entry **b** records the decrease in Accounts Receivable as a credit (decrease) to Accounts Receivable and as a debit in the operating activities section because the decrease has a positive effect on cash flows. Work sheet entries **c–g** reflect the effects on cash flows from operating activities of the changes in the other current assets and current liabilities. As you study these entries, note how the effects of each entry on cash flows are automatically determined by debits or credits reflecting changes in the balance sheet accounts.

h–i. INVESTMENTS Among the other transactions affecting noncurrent accounts during 20x1 (see Exhibit 2 on page 645), two pertain to investments. One is the purchase for $78,000, and the other is the sale at $102,000. The purchase (entry **h**) is recorded on the work sheet as a cash flow in the investing activities section. Note that instead of a credit to Cash, a credit entry with the appropriate designation is made in the appropriate section in the lower half of the work sheet. The sale transaction (entry **i**) is more complicated because it involves a gain that appears

Study Note: Even though the gain on sale in **i** and the loss on sale in **k** are identified with the operating activities section, they do not represent cash flows.

on the income statement and is included in net income. This entry records the cash inflow in the investing activities section, accounts for the remaining difference in the Investments account, and removes the gain on sale of investments from net income.

j–m. Plant Assets and Accumulated Depreciation

The four transactions that affect plant assets and the related accumulated depreciation are the purchase of plant assets, the sale of plant assets at a loss, the noncash exchange of bonds for plant assets, and the depreciation expense for the year. Because these transactions may appear complicated, it is important to work through them systematically when preparing the work sheet. First, the purchase of plant assets for $120,000 is entered (entry **j**) in the same way the purchase of investments was entered in entry **h.** Second, the sale of plant assets is similar to the sale of investments, except that a loss is involved. The cash inflow from this transaction is $5,000. The rest of the entry is necessary in order to add the loss back into net income in the operating activities section of the statement of cash flows (since it was deducted to arrive at net income and no cash outflow resulted) and to record the effects on plant assets and accumulated depreciation.

Key Point: A noncash investing and financing transaction, such as the one here, is entered on the work sheet as a debit and credit to balance sheet accounts. No cash flow activity is identified.

The third transaction (entry **l**) is the noncash issue of bonds for the purchase of plant assets. Note that this transaction does not affect Cash. Still, it needs to be recorded because the objective is to account for all changes in the balance sheet accounts. It is listed at the end of the statement of cash flows (Exhibit 4) in the schedule of noncash investing and financing transactions.

At this point, the increase of $210,000 ($715,000 − $505,000) in plant assets has been explained by the two purchases less the sale ($120,000 + $100,000 − $10,000 = $210,000), but the change in Accumulated Depreciation has not been completely explained. The depreciation expense for the year needs to be entered (entry **m**). The debit is to the operating activities section of the work sheet because, as explained earlier in the chapter, no current cash outflow is required for depreciation expense. The effect of this debit is to add the amount for depreciation expense back into net income. The $35,000 increase in Accumulated Depreciation has now been explained by the sale transaction and the depreciation expense (−$2,000 + $37,000 = $35,000).

Study Note: It is depreciation expense, not accumulated depreciation, that appears on the statement of cash flows and is identified here with the operating activities section.

n. Bonds Payable

Part of the change in Bonds Payable was explained in entry **l** when a noncash transaction, a $100,000 issue of bonds in exchange for plant assets, was entered. All that remains to be entered is the repayment (entry **n**).

o. Common Stock and Paid-in Capital in Excess of Par Value, Common

One transaction affects both these accounts. It is an issue of 15,200 shares of $5 par value common stock for a total of $150,000 (entry **o**).

p. Retained Earnings

Part of the change in Retained Earnings was recognized when net income was entered (entry **a**). The only remaining effect to be recognized is the $8,000 in cash dividends paid during the year (entry **p**).

Study Note: Cash is identified with the letter x because its entry on the work sheet is different in nature from all the others. That is, the change in cash equals the net effect on cash of entries **a** through **p**. It therefore acts as a balancing figure.

x. Cash

The final step is to total the debit and credit columns in the top and bottom portions of the work sheet and then to enter the net change in cash at the bottom of the work sheet. The columns in the upper half equal $425,000. In the lower half, the debit column totals $335,000 and the credit column totals $304,000. The credit difference of $31,000 (entry **x**) equals the debit change in cash on the first line of the work sheet.

The Direct Method of Preparing the Statement of Cash Flows

SUPPLEMENTAL OBJECTIVE

9 Use the direct method to determine cash flows from operating activities and prepare a statement of cash flows

To this point in the chapter, the indirect method of preparing the statement of cash flows has been used. In this section, the direct method is presented.

Determining Cash Flows from Operating Activities

The principal difference between the indirect and the direct methods appears in the cash flows from operating activities section of the statement of cash flows. As you have seen, the indirect method starts with net income from the income statement and converts it to net cash flows from operating activities by adding or subtracting items that do not affect net cash flows. The direct method takes a different approach. It converts each item on the income statement to its cash equivalent, as illustrated in Figure 3. For instance, sales are converted to cash receipts from sales, and purchases are converted to cash payments for purchases. Exhibit 6 shows the schedule of cash flows from operating activities under the direct method for Ryan Corporation. The conversion of the components of Ryan Corporation's income statement to those figures is explained in the following paragraphs.

CASH RECEIPTS FROM SALES Sales result in a positive cash flow for a company. Cash sales are direct cash inflows. Credit sales are not, because they are originally recorded as accounts receivable. When they are collected, they become cash inflows. You cannot, however, assume that credit sales are automatically inflows of cash, because the collections of accounts receivable in any one accounting period are not likely to equal credit sales. Receivables may be uncollectible, sales from a prior period may be collected in the current period, or sales from the current period may be collected in the next period. For example, if accounts receivable increase from one accounting period to the next, cash receipts from sales will not be as great as sales. On the other hand, if accounts receivable decrease from one accounting period to the next, cash receipts from sales will exceed sales.

The relationships among sales, changes in accounts receivable, and cash receipts from sales are reflected in the following formula:

$$\text{Cash Receipts from Sales} = \text{Sales} \begin{cases} + \text{ Decrease in Accounts Receivable} \\ \qquad\qquad\quad \text{or} \\ - \text{ Increase in Accounts Receivable} \end{cases}$$

Refer to the balance sheets and income statement for Ryan Corporation in Exhibits 1 and 2. Note that sales were $698,000 in 20x1 and that accounts receivable

> **Study Note:** A decrease in accounts receivable during the period occurs when more has been collected than realized in accrual-based sales. The decrease, therefore, must be added to (or an increase subtracted from) sales to produce cash receipts from sales.

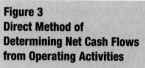

Figure 3
Direct Method of Determining Net Cash Flows from Operating Activities

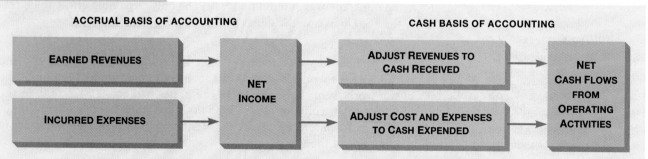

Exhibit 6
Schedule of Cash Flows from Operating Activities: Direct Method

Ryan Corporation
Schedule of Cash Flows from Operating Activities
For the Year Ended December 31, 20x1

Cash Flows from Operating Activities			
Cash Receipts from			
Sales		$706,000	
Interest Received		6,000	$712,000
Cash Payments for			
Purchases		$547,000	
Operating Expenses		103,000	
Interest		23,000	
Income Taxes		9,000	682,000
Net Cash Flows from Operating Activities			$ 30,000

decreased by $8,000. Thus, cash received from sales is $706,000:

$$\$706,000 = \$698,000 + \$8,000$$

Collections were $8,000 more than sales recorded for the year.

CASH RECEIPTS FROM INTEREST AND DIVIDENDS   Although interest and dividends received are most closely associated with investment activity and are often called investment income, the FASB has decided to classify the cash received from these items as operating activities. To simplify the examples in this text, it is assumed that interest income equals interest received and that dividend income equals dividends received. Thus, based on Exhibit 2, interest received by Ryan Corporation is assumed to equal $6,000, which is the amount of interest income.

CASH PAYMENTS FOR PURCHASES   Cost of goods sold (from the income statement) must be adjusted for changes in two balance sheet accounts to arrive at cash payments for purchases. First, cost of goods sold must be adjusted for changes in inventory to arrive at net purchases. Then, net purchases must be adjusted for the change in accounts payable to arrive at cash payments for purchases. If inventory has increased from one accounting period to another, net purchases will be greater than cost of goods sold because net purchases during the period have exceeded the dollar amount of the items sold during the period. If inventory has decreased, net purchases will be less than cost of goods sold. Conversely, if accounts payable have increased, cash payments for purchases will be less than net purchases; if accounts payable have decreased, cash payments for purchases will be greater than net purchases.

Study Note: A decrease in accounts payable during the period occurs when more has been paid for goods than has been purchased. The decrease, therefore, must be added to (or an increase subtracted from) cost of goods sold, along with an adjustment for the change in inventory, to produce cash payments for purchases.

These relationships may be stated in equation form as follows:

$$\text{Cash Payments for Purchases} = \text{Cost of Goods Sold} \begin{Bmatrix} + \text{ Increase in Inventory} \\ \text{or} \\ - \text{ Decrease in Inventory} \end{Bmatrix} \begin{Bmatrix} + \text{ Decrease in Accounts Payable} \\ \text{or} \\ - \text{ Increase in Accounts Payable} \end{Bmatrix}$$

From Exhibits 1 and 2, cost of goods sold is $520,000, inventory increased by $34,000, and accounts payable increased by $7,000. Thus, cash payments for purchases is $547,000, as the following calculation shows:

$$\$547,000 = \$520,000 + 34,000 - \$7,000$$

In this example, Ryan Corporation purchased $34,000 more inventory than it sold and paid out $7,000 less in cash than it made in purchases. The net result is that cash payments for purchases exceeded cost of goods sold by $27,000 ($547,000 − $520,000).

CASH PAYMENTS FOR OPERATING EXPENSES   Just as cost of goods sold does not represent the amount of cash paid for purchases during an accounting period, operating expenses do not match the amount of cash paid to employees, suppliers, and others for goods and services. Three adjustments must be made to operating expenses to arrive at the cash outflows. The first adjustment is for changes in prepaid expenses, such as prepaid insurance or prepaid rent. If prepaid assets increase during the accounting period, more cash will have been paid out than appears on the income statement as expenses. If prepaid assets decrease, the expenses shown on the income statement will exceed the cash spent.

The second adjustment is for changes in liabilities resulting from accrued expenses, such as wages payable and payroll taxes payable. If accrued liabilities increase during the accounting period, operating expenses on the income statement will exceed the cash spent. And if accrued liabilities decrease, operating expenses will fall short of cash spent.

The third adjustment is made because certain expenses do not require a current outlay of cash; those expenses must be subtracted from operating expenses to arrive at cash payments for operating expenses. The most common expenses in this category are depreciation expense, amortization expense, and depletion expense. For example, Ryan Corporation recorded 20x1 depreciation expense of $37,000. No cash payment was made in this transaction. Therefore, to the extent that operating expenses include depreciation and similar items, an adjustment is needed to reduce operating expenses to the amount of cash expended.

The three adjustments to operating expenses are summarized in the equations that follow.

> **Key Point:** Depreciation, amortization, and depletion must be subtracted from operating expenses when computing cash payments for operating expenses because they are legitimate accrual-based expenses. However, they do not represent cash disbursements; they are merely *paper* allocations of cost. They must be eliminated in converting from an accrual to a cash basis.

$$\text{Cash Payments for Operating Expenses} = \text{Operating Expenses} \begin{cases} + \text{ Increase in Prepaid Expenses} \\ \text{or} \\ - \text{ Decrease in Prepaid Expenses} \end{cases} \begin{cases} + \text{ Decrease in Accrued Liabilities} \\ \text{or} \\ - \text{ Increase in Accrued Liabilities} \end{cases} \begin{cases} - \text{ Depreciation and Other Noncash Expenses} \end{cases}$$

According to Exhibits 1 and 2, Ryan's operating expenses (including depreciation of $37,000) were $147,000, prepaid expenses decreased by $4,000, and accrued liabilities increased by $3,000. As a result, Ryan Corporation's cash payments for operating expenses are $103,000, computed as follows:

$$\$103,000 = \$147,000 - \$4,000 - \$3,000 - \$37,000$$

If there are prepaid expenses and accrued liabilities that are *not* related to specific operating expenses, they are not included in these computations. One example is income taxes payable, which is the accrued liability related to income taxes expense. The cash payment for income taxes will be discussed shortly.

CASH PAYMENTS FOR INTEREST   The FASB classifies cash payments for interest as operating activities, although some authorities argue that they should be considered financing activities because of their association with loans incurred to finance the business. The FASB feels that interest expense is a cost of operating a business, and this is the position followed in this text. Also, for the sake of simplicity, all examples in this text assume that interest payments are equal to interest expense on the income statement. Thus, based on Exhibit 2, Ryan Corporation's interest payments are assumed to be $23,000 in 20x1.

CASH PAYMENTS FOR INCOME TAXES The amount of income taxes expense that appears on the income statement rarely equals the amount of income taxes actually paid during the year. To determine cash payments for income taxes, income taxes (from the income statement) are adjusted by the change in Income Taxes Payable. If Income Taxes Payable increased during the accounting period, cash payments for taxes will be less than the expense shown on the income statement. If Income Taxes Payable decreased, cash payments for taxes will exceed income taxes on the income statement. In other words, the following equation is applicable:

$$\begin{matrix} \text{Cash Payments} \\ \text{for Income Taxes} \end{matrix} = \begin{matrix} \text{Income} \\ \text{Taxes} \end{matrix} \begin{cases} + \text{ Decrease in Income Taxes Payable} \\ \quad\quad\quad\quad \text{or} \\ - \text{ Increase in Income Taxes Payable} \end{cases}$$

> **Study Note:** A decrease in Income Taxes Payable during the year occurs when more has been paid than recorded as accrual-based Income Taxes Expense. The decrease therefore must be added to (or an increase subtracted from) Income Taxes Expense to obtain cash payments for income taxes.

In 20x1, Ryan Corporation showed income taxes of $7,000 on its income statement and a decrease of $2,000 in Income Taxes Payable on its balance sheets (see Exhibits 1 and 2). As a result, cash payments for income taxes during 20x1 were $9,000, calculated as follows:

$$\$9,000 = \$7,000 + \$2,000$$

Compiling the Statement of Cash Flows

The Ryan Corporation's statement of cash flows under the direct method is presented in Exhibit 7. The only differences between that statement of cash flows and the one based on the indirect method shown in Exhibit 4 occur in the first and last sections. The middle sections, which present cash flows from investing activities and financing activities, net increases or decreases in cash, and the schedule of noncash investing and financing activities, are the same under both methods.

The first section of the statement in Exhibit 7 shows the net cash flows from operating activities on a direct basis, as presented in Exhibit 6. The last section is the same as the cash flows from operating activities section of the statement of cash flows under the indirect method (see Exhibit 4 on page 653). The FASB believes that when the direct method is used, a schedule must be provided that reconciles net income to net cash flows from operating activities. Thus, the statement of cash flows under the direct method includes a section that accommodates the main difference between it and the indirect method.

Exhibit 7
Statement of Cash Flows:
Direct Method

Ryan Corporation
Statement of Cash Flows
For the Year Ended December 31, 20x1

Cash Flows from Operating Activities

Cash Receipts from		
Sales	$706,000	
Interest Received	6,000	$712,000
Cash Payments for		
Purchases	$547,000	
Operating Expenses	103,000	
Interest	23,000	
Income Taxes	9,000	682,000
Net Cash Flows from Operating Activities		$ 30,000

Cash Flows from Investing Activities

Purchase of Investments	($ 78,000)	
Sale of Investments	102,000	
Purchase of Plant Assets	(120,000)	
Sale of Plant Assets	5,000	
Net Cash Flows from Investing Activities		(91,000)

Cash Flows from Financing Activities

Repayment of Bonds	($ 50,000)	
Issue of Common Stock	150,000	
Dividends Paid	(8,000)	
Net Cash Flows from Financing Activities		92,000

Net Increase (Decrease) in Cash		$ 31,000
Cash at Beginning of Year		15,000
Cash at End of Year		$ 46,000

Schedule of Noncash Investing and Financing Transactions

Issue of Bonds Payable for Plant Assets	$100,000

Reconciliation of Net Income to Net Cash Flows from Operating Activities

Net Income		$ 16,000
Adjustments to Reconcile Net Income to Net		
Cash Flows from Operating Activities		
Depreciation	$ 37,000	
Gain on Sale of Investments	(12,000)	
Loss on Sale of Plant Assets	3,000	
Changes in Current Assets and Current Liabilities		
Decrease in Accounts Receivable	8,000	
Increase in Inventory	(34,000)	
Decrease in Prepaid Expenses	4,000	
Increase in Accounts Payable	7,000	
Increase in Accrued Liabilities	3,000	
Decrease in Income Taxes Payable	(2,000)	14,000
Net Cash Flows from Operating Activities		$ 30,000

Key Point: When the direct method is used, a supplemental reconciliation of net income to net cash flows from operating activities must also be presented.

Chapter Review

REVIEW OF LEARNING OBJECTIVES

Ace *it*

1. **Describe the statement of cash flows, and define** *cash* **and** *cash equivalents.* The statement of cash flows explains the changes in cash and cash equivalents from one accounting period to the next by showing cash inflows and cash outflows from the operating, investing, and financing activities of a company for an accounting period. For purposes of preparing the statement of cash flows, *cash* is defined to include cash and cash equivalents. *Cash equivalents* are short-term (90 days or less), highly liquid investments, including money market accounts, commercial paper, and U.S. Treasury bills.

2. **State the principal purposes and uses of the statement of cash flows.** The primary purpose of the statement of cash flows is to provide information about a company's cash receipts and cash payments during an accounting period. Its secondary purpose is to provide information about a company's operating, investing, and financing activities. The statement is useful to management as well as to investors and creditors in assessing the liquidity of a business, including its ability to generate future cash flows and to pay debts and dividends.

3. **Identify the principal components of the classifications of cash flows, and state the significance of noncash investing and financing transactions.** Cash flows may be classified as stemming from (1) operating activities, which include the cash effects of transactions and other events that enter into the determination of net income; (2) investing activities, which include the acquiring and selling of long- and short-term marketable securities and property, plant, and equipment, and the making and collecting of loans, excluding interest; or (3) financing activities, which include the obtaining and returning or repaying of resources, excluding interest, to owners and creditors. Noncash investing and financing transactions are also important because they are exchanges of assets and/or liabilities that are of interest to investors and creditors when evaluating the financing and investing activities of a business.

4. **Analyze the statement of cash flows.** In analyzing a company's statement of cash flows, analysts tend to focus on cash-generating efficiency and free cash flow. Cash-generating efficiency is a company's ability to generate cash from its current or continuing operations. Three ratios used in measuring cash-generating efficiency are cash flow yield, cash flows to sales, and cash flows to assets. Free cash flow is the cash that remains after deducting funds a company must commit to continue operating at its planned level. Such commitments must cover current or continuing operations, interest, income taxes, dividends, and net capital expenditures.

5. **Use the indirect method to determine cash flows from operating activities.** Under the indirect method, net income is adjusted for all noncash effects and for items that need to be converted from an accrual to a cash basis to arrive at a cash flow basis, as follows:

Cash Flows from Operating Activities		
Net Income		xxx
Adjustments to Reconcile Net Income to Net Cash Flows from Operating Activities		
(List of individual items)	xxx	xxx
Net Cash Flows from Operating Activities		xxx

6. **Determine cash flows from (a) investing activities and (b) financing activities.** Cash flows from investing activities are determined by identifying the cash flow effects of the transactions that affect each account relevant to investing activities. Such accounts include all long-term assets and short-term marketable securities. The same procedure is followed for financing activities, except that the accounts involved are short-term borrowings, long-term liabilities, and stockholders' equity. The effects of gains and losses reported on the income statement must also be considered. After the changes in the balance sheet accounts from one accounting period to the next have been explained, all the cash flow effects should have been identified.

7. **Use the indirect method to prepare a statement of cash flows.** The statement of cash flows lists cash flows from operating activities, investing activities, and financing activities, in that order. The sections on investing and financing activities are prepared by examining individual accounts involving cash receipts and cash payments from investing and financing activities to explain year-to-year changes in the account balances. Significant noncash transactions are included in a schedule of noncash investing and financing transactions that accompanies the statement of cash flows.

8. **Prepare a work sheet for the statement of cash flows.** A work sheet is useful in preparing the statement of cash flows for complex companies. The basic procedures are to analyze the changes in the balance sheet accounts for their effects on cash flows (in the top portion of the work sheet) and to classify those effects according to the format of the statement of cash flows (in the lower portion of the work sheet). When all changes in the balance sheet accounts have been explained and entered on the work sheet, the change in the Cash account will also be explained, and all necessary information will be available to prepare the statement of cash flows. The work sheet approach lends itself to the indirect method of preparing the statement of cash flows.

9. **Use the direct method to determine cash flows from operating activities and prepare a statement of cash flows.** The principal difference between a statement of cash flows prepared under the direct method and one prepared under the indirect method appears in the cash flows from operating activities section. Instead of beginning with net income and making additions and subtractions, as is done with the indirect method, the direct method converts each item on the income statement to its cash equivalent by adjusting for changes in the related current asset or current liability accounts and for other items such as depreciation. The rest of the statement of cash flows is the same under the direct method, except that a schedule that reconciles net income to net cash flows from operating activities must be included.

REVIEW OF CONCEPTS AND TERMINOLOGY

The following concepts and terms were introduced in this chapter.

LO 1 **Cash:** For purposes of the statement of cash flows, both cash and cash equivalents.

LO 1 **Cash equivalents:** Short-term (90 days or less), highly liquid investments, including money market accounts, commercial paper, and U.S. Treasury bills.

LO 4 **Cash flows to assets:** The ratio of net cash flows from operating activities to average total assets.

LO 4 **Cash flows to sales:** The ratio of net cash flows from operating activities to sales.

LO 4 **Cash flow yield:** The ratio of net cash flows from operating activities to net income.

LO 4 **Cash-generating efficiency:** The ability of a company to generate cash from its current or continuing operations.

LO 5 **Direct method:** The procedure for converting the income statement from an accrual basis to a cash basis by separately adjusting each item on the income statement.

LO 3 **Financing activities:** Business activities that involve obtaining resources from or returning resources to owners and providing them with a return on their investment, and obtaining resources from creditors and repaying any amounts borrowed or otherwise settling the obligations.

LO 4 **Free cash flow:** The amount of cash that remains after deducting the funds a company must commit to continue operating at its planned level; net cash flows from operating activities minus dividends paid minus net capital expenditures.

LO 5 **Indirect method:** The procedure for converting the income statement from an accrual basis to a cash basis by adjusting net income for items that do not affect cash flows, including depreciation, amortization, depletion, gains, losses, and changes in current assets and current liabilities.

LO 3 **Investing activities:** Business activities that involve the acquiring and selling of long-term assets, the acquiring and selling of marketable securities other than trading securities or cash equivalents, and the making and collecting of loans.

LO 3 **Noncash investing and financing transactions:** Significant investing and financing transactions that do not involve an actual cash inflow or outflow but involve only long-term assets, long-term liabilities, or stockholders' equity, such as the exchange of a long-term asset for a long-term liability or the settlement of a debt by issuing capital stock.

LO 3 **Operating activities:** Business activities that involve the cash effects of transactions and other events that enter into the determination of net income.

LO 1 **Statement of cash flows:** A primary financial statement that shows how a company's operating, investing, and financing activities have affected cash during an accounting period.

REVIEW PROBLEM

LO 4
LO 5
LO 6
LO 7
SO 9

The Statement of Cash Flows

The 20x2 income statement for Northwest Corporation is presented below and the comparative balance sheets for the years 20x2 and 20x1 are shown on the next page.

Northwest Corporation
Income Statement
For the Year Ended December 31, 20x2

Net Sales		$1,650,000
Cost of Goods Sold		920,000
Gross Margin		$ 730,000
Operating Expenses (including Depreciation Expense of $12,000 on Buildings and $23,100 on Equipment, and Amortization Expense of $4,800)		470,000
Operating Income		$ 260,000
Other Income (Expenses)		
Interest Expense	($55,000)	
Dividend Income	3,400	
Gain on Sale of Investments	12,500	
Loss on Disposal of Equipment	(2,300)	(41,400)
Income Before Income Taxes		$ 218,600
Income Taxes		52,200
Net Income		$ 166,400

Northwest Corporation
Comparative Balance Sheets
December 31, 20x2 and 20x1

	20x2	20x1	Change	Increase or Decrease
Assets				
Cash	$ 115,850	$ 121,850	($ 6,000)	Decrease
Accounts Receivable (net)	296,000	314,500	(18,500)	Decrease
Inventory	322,000	301,000	21,000	Increase
Prepaid Expenses	7,800	5,800	2,000	Increase
Long-Term Investments	36,000	86,000	(50,000)	Decrease
Land	150,000	125,000	25,000	Increase
Buildings	462,000	462,000	—	—
Accumulated Depreciation, Buildings	(91,000)	(79,000)	(12,000)	Increase
Equipment	159,730	167,230	(7,500)	Decrease
Accumulated Depreciation, Equipment	(43,400)	(45,600)	2,200	Decrease
Intangible Assets	19,200	24,000	(4,800)	Decrease
Total Assets	$1,434,180	$1,482,780	($ 48,600)	
Liabilities and Stockholders' Equity				
Accounts Payable	$ 133,750	$ 233,750	($100,000)	Decrease
Notes Payable (current)	75,700	145,700	(70,000)	Decrease
Accrued Liabilities	5,000	—	5,000	Increase
Income Taxes Payable	20,000	—	20,000	Increase
Bonds Payable	210,000	310,000	(100,000)	Decrease
Mortgage Payable	330,000	350,000	(20,000)	Decrease
Common Stock, $10 par value	360,000	300,000	60,000	Increase
Paid-in Capital in Excess of Par Value	90,000	50,000	40,000	Increase
Retained Earnings	209,730	93,330	116,400	Increase
Total Liabilities and Stockholders' Equity	$1,434,180	$1,482,780	($ 48,600)	

The following additional information was taken from the company's records:

a. Long-term investments (available-for-sale securities) that cost $70,000 were sold at a gain of $12,500; additional long-term investments were made in the amount of $20,000.

b. Five acres of land were purchased for $25,000 to build a parking lot.

c. Equipment that cost $37,500 with accumulated depreciation of $25,300 was sold at a loss of $2,300; new equipment costing $30,000 was purchased.

d. Notes payable in the amount of $100,000 were repaid; an additional $30,000 was borrowed by signing notes payable.

e. Bonds payable in the amount of $100,000 were converted into 6,000 shares of common stock.

f. The Mortgage Payable account was reduced by $20,000 during the year.

g. Cash dividends declared and paid were $50,000.

REQUIRED

1. Prepare a schedule of cash flows from operating activities using the (a) indirect method and (b) direct method.

2. Prepare a statement of cash flows using the indirect method.

3. Compute cash flow yield, cash flows to sales, cash flows to assets, and free cash flow for 20x2.

ANSWER TO REVIEW PROBLEM

1. (a) Prepare a schedule of cash flows from operating activities using the indirect method.

Northwest Corporation
Schedule of Cash Flows from Operating Activities
For the Year Ended December 31, 20x2

Cash Flows from Operating Activities		
Net Income		$166,400
Adjustments to Reconcile Net Income to		
Net Cash Flows from Operating Activities		
Depreciation Expense, Buildings	$ 12,000	
Depreciation Expense, Equipment	23,100	
Amortization Expense, Intangible Assets	4,800	
Gain on Sale of Investments	(12,500)	
Loss on Disposal of Equipment	2,300	
Changes in Current Assets		
and Current Liabilities		
Decrease in Accounts Receivable	18,500	
Increase in Inventory	(21,000)	
Increase in Prepaid Expenses	(2,000)	
Decrease in Accounts Payable	(100,000)	
Increase in Accrued Liabilities	5,000	
Increase in Income Taxes Payable	20,000	(49,800)
Net Cash Flows from Operating Activities		$116,600

1. (b) Prepare a schedule of cash flows from operating activities using the direct method.

Northwest Corporation
Schedule of Cash Flows from Operating Activities
For the Year Ended December 31, 20x2

Cash Flows from Operating Activities		
Cash Receipts from		
Sales	$1,668,500[1]	
Dividends Received	3,400	$1,671,900
Cash Payments for		
Purchases	$1,041,000[2]	
Operating Expenses	427,100[3]	
Interest	55,000	
Income Taxes	32,200[4]	1,555,300
Net Cash Flows from Operating Activities		$ 116,600

1. $1,650,000 + $18,500 = $1,668,500
2. $920,000 + $21,000 + $100,000 = $1,041,000
3. $470,000 + $2,000 − $5,000 − ($12,000 + $23,100 + $4,800) = $427,100
4. $52,200 − $20,000 = $32,200

2. Prepare a statement of cash flows using the indirect method.

Northwest Corporation
Statement of Cash Flows
For the Year Ended December 31, 20x2

Cash Flows from Operating Activities

Net Income		$166,400
Adjustments to Reconcile Net Income to		
Net Cash Flows from Operating Activities		
Depreciation Expense, Buildings	$ 12,000	
Depreciation Expense, Equipment	23,100	
Amortization Expense, Intangible Assets	4,800	
Gain on Sale of Investments	(12,500)	
Loss on Disposal of Equipment	2,300	
Changes in Current Assets and		
Current Liabilities		
Decrease in Accounts Receivable	18,500	
Increase in Inventory	(21,000)	
Increase in Prepaid Expenses	(2,000)	
Decrease in Accounts Payable	(100,000)	
Increase in Accrued Liabilities	5,000	
Increase in Income Taxes Payable	20,000	(49,800)
Net Cash Flows from Operating Activities		$116,600

Cash Flows from Investing Activities

Sale of Long-Term Investments	$ 82,500[1]	
Purchase of Long-Term Investments	(20,000)	
Purchase of Land	(25,000)	
Sale of Equipment	9,900[2]	
Purchase of Equipment	(30,000)	
Net Cash Flows from Investing Activities		17,400

Cash Flows from Financing Activities

Repayment of Notes Payable	($100,000)	
Issuance of Notes Payable	30,000	
Reduction in Mortgage	(20,000)	
Dividends Paid	(50,000)	
Net Cash Flows from Financing Activities		(140,000)

Net Increase (Decrease) in Cash		($ 6,000)
Cash at Beginning of Year		121,850
Cash at End of Year		$115,850

Schedule of Noncash Investing and Financing Transactions

Conversion of Bonds Payable into Common Stock	$100,000

1. $70,000 + $12,500 (gain) = $82,500
2. $37,500 − $25,300 = $12,200 (book value) − $2,300 (loss) = $9,900

3. Compute cash flow yield, cash flows to sales, cash flows to assets, and free cash flow for 20x2.

$$\text{Cash Flow Yield} = \frac{\$116,600}{\$166,400} = .7 \text{ times}$$

$$\text{Cash Flows to Sales} = \frac{\$116,600}{\$1,650,000} = 7.1\%$$

$$\text{Cash Flows to Assets} = \frac{\$116,600}{(\$1,434,180 + \$1,482,780) \div 2} = 8.0\%$$

$$\text{Free Cash Flow} = \$116,600 - \$50,000 - \$25,000 - \$30,000 + \$9,900$$
$$= \$21,500$$

Chapter Assignments

**BUILDING YOUR
KNOWLEDGE
FOUNDATION**

QUESTIONS

1. In the statement of cash flows, what is the term *cash* understood to include?

2. To earn a return on cash on hand during 20x3, Sallas Corporation transferred $45,000 from its checking account to a money market account, purchased a $25,000 Treasury bill, and invested $35,000 in common stocks. How will each of these transactions affect the statement of cash flows?

3. What are the purposes of the statement of cash flows?

4. Why is the statement of cash flows needed when most of the information in it is available from a company's comparative balance sheets and income statement?

5. What are the three classifications of cash flows? Give some examples of each.

6. Why is it important to disclose certain noncash transactions? How should they be disclosed?

7. Define *cash-generating efficiency* and identify three ratios that measure cash-generating efficiency.

8. Define *free cash flow* and identify its components. What does it mean to have a positive or a negative free cash flow?

9. What are the essential differences between the direct method and the indirect method of determining cash flows from operations?

10. In determining net cash flows from operating activities (assuming the indirect method is used), what are the effects on cash generated from the following items: (a) an increase in accounts receivable, (b) a decrease in inventory, (c) an increase in accounts payable, (d) a decrease in wages payable, (e) depreciation expense, and (f) amortization of patents?

11. Cell-Borne Corporation had a net loss of $12,000 in 20x1 but had positive cash flows from operations of $9,000. What conditions may have caused this situation?

12. What is the proper treatment on the statement of cash flows of a transaction in which a building that cost $50,000 with accumulated depreciation of $32,000 is sold at a loss of $5,000?

13. What is the proper treatment on the statement of cash flows of (a) a transaction in which buildings and land are purchased by the issuance of a mortgage for $234,000 and (b) a conversion of $50,000 in bonds payable into 2,500 shares of $6 par value common stock?

14. Why is the work sheet approach considered to be more compatible with the indirect method than with the direct method of determining cash flows from operations?

15. Assuming in each of the following independent cases that only one transaction occurred, what transactions would be likely to cause (a) a decrease in investments and (b) an increase in common stock? How would each case be treated on the work sheet for the statement of cash flows?

16. Glen Corporation has the following other income and expense items: interest expense, $12,000; interest income, $3,000; dividend income, $5,000; and loss on the retirement of bonds, $6,000. Where does each of these items appear on or affect the statement of cash flows, assuming the direct method is used?

SHORT EXERCISES

SE 1.
LO 3 Classification of Cash Flow Transactions

Tosca Corporation engaged in the transactions below. Identify each as (a) an operating activity, (b) an investing activity, (c) a financing activity, (d) a noncash transaction, or (e) none of the above.

1. Sold land for a gain.
2. Declared and paid a cash dividend.
3. Paid interest.
4. Issued common stock for plant assets.
5. Issued preferred stock.
6. Borrowed cash on a bank loan.

SE 2.
LO 4 Cash-Generating Efficiency Ratios and Free Cash Flow

In 20x2, Wu Corporation had year-end assets of $550,000, net sales of $790,000, net income of $90,000, net cash flows from operating activities of $180,000, purchases of plant assets of $120,000, sales of plant assets of $20,000, and paid dividends of $40,000. In 20x1, year-end assets were $500,000. Calculate the cash-generating efficiency ratios of cash flow yield, cash flows to sales, and cash flows to assets. Also calculate free cash flow.

SE 3.
LO 4 Cash Flow Efficiency and Free Cash Flow

Examine the cash flow measures in part **3** of the review problem on pages 668–669. Discuss the meaning of these ratios.

SE 4.
LO 5 Computing Cash Flows from Operating Activities: Indirect Method

Specialty Products Corporation had a net income of $33,000 during 20x1. During the year, the company had depreciation expense of $14,000. Accounts receivable increased by $11,000, and accounts payable increased by $5,000. Those were the company's only current assets and current liabilities. Use the indirect method to determine net cash flows from operating activities.

SE 5.
LO 5 Computing Cash Flows from Operating Activities: Indirect Method

During 20x1, Ayzarian Corporation had a net income of $72,000. Included on the income statement was depreciation expense of $8,000 and amortization expense of $900. During the year, accounts receivable decreased by $4,100, inventories increased by $2,700, prepaid expenses decreased by $500, accounts payable decreased by $7,000, and accrued liabilities decreased by $850. Use the indirect method to determine net cash flows from operating activities.

SE 6.
LO 6 Cash Flows from Investing Activities and Noncash Transactions

During 20x1, Rhode Island Company purchased land for $750,000. It paid $250,000 in cash and signed a $500,000 mortgage for the rest. The company also sold a building that had originally cost $180,000, on which it had $140,000 of accumulated depreciation, for $190,000 cash and a gain of $150,000. Prepare the cash flows from investing activities and schedule of noncash investing and financing transactions sections of the statement of cash flows.

SE 7.
LO 6 Cash Flows from Financing Activities

During 20x1, South Carolina Company issued $1,000,000 in long-term bonds at 96, repaid $150,000 of bonds at face value, paid interest of $80,000, and paid dividends of $50,000. Prepare the cash flows from the financing activities section of the statement of cash flows.

SE 8.
LO 7 Identifying Components of the Statement of Cash Flows

Assuming the indirect method is used to prepare the statement of cash flows, tell whether each item below would appear (a) in cash flows from operating activities, (b) in cash flows from investing activities, (c) in cash flows from financing activities, (d) in the schedule of noncash investing and financing transactions, or (e) not on the statement of cash flows at all.

1. Dividends paid
2. Cash receipts from sales
3. Decrease in accounts receivable
4. Sale of plant assets

5. Gain on sale of investment
6. Issue of stock for plant assets
7. Issue of common stock
8. Net income

SE 9.

SO 9 Cash Receipts from Sales and Cash Payments for Purchases: Direct Method

During 20x2, Nebraska Wheat Company, a marketer of whole-grain products, had sales of $426,500. The ending balance of Accounts Receivable was $127,400 in 20x1 and $96,200 in 20x2. Also, during 20x2, Nebraska Wheat Company had cost of goods sold of $294,200. The ending balance of inventory was $36,400 in 20x1 and $44,800 in 20x2. The ending balance of Accounts Payable was $28,100 in 20x1 and $25,900 in 20x2. Using the direct method, calculate cash receipts from sales and cash payments for purchases in 20x2.

SE 10.

SO 9 Cash Payments for Operating Expenses and Income Taxes: Direct Method

During 20x2, Nebraska Wheat Company had operating expenses of $79,000 and income taxes expense of $12,500. Depreciation expense of $20,000 for 20x2 was included in operating expenses. The ending balance of Prepaid Expenses was $3,600 in 20x1 and $2,300 in 20x2. The ending balance of Accrued Liabilities (excluding Income Taxes Payable) was $3,000 in 20x1 and $2,000 in 20x2. The ending balance of Income Taxes Payable was $4,100 in 20x1 and $3,500 in 20x2. Calculate cash payments for operating expenses and income taxes in 20x2 using the direct method.

EXERCISES

E 1.

**LO 1 Classification of Cash
LO 3 Flow Transactions**

Smelt Corporation engaged in the following transactions. Identify each as (a) an operating activity, (b) an investing activity, (c) a financing activity, (d) a noncash transaction, or (e) not on the statement of cash flows. (Assume the indirect method.)

1. Declared and paid a cash dividend.
2. Purchased a long-term investment.
3. Received cash from customers.
4. Paid interest.
5. Sold equipment at a loss.
6. Issued long-term bonds for plant assets.
7. Received dividends on securities held.
8. Issued common stock.
9. Declared and issued a stock dividend.
10. Repaid notes payable.
11. Paid employees their wages.
12. Purchased a 60-day Treasury bill.
13. Purchased land.

E 2.

LO 4 Cash-Generating Efficiency Ratios and Free Cash Flow

In 20x5, Wicker Corporation had year-end assets of $4,800,000, net sales of $6,600,000, net income of $560,000, net cash flows from operating activities of $780,000, dividends of $240,000, and net capital expenditures of $820,000. In 20x4, year-end assets were $4,200,000. Calculate the cash-generating efficiency ratios of cash flow yield, cash flows to sales, and cash flows to assets. Also calculate free cash flow.

E 3.

LO 5 Cash Flows from Operating Activities: Indirect Method

The condensed single-step income statement for the year ended December 31, 20x2, of Green Fields Chem Company, a distributor of farm fertilizers and herbicides, appears as follows:

Sales		$6,500,000
Less: Cost of Goods Sold	$3,800,000	
Operating Expenses (including depreciation of $410,000)	1,900,000	
Income Taxes	200,000	5,900,000
Net Income		$ 600,000

Selected accounts from the company's balance sheets for 20x2 and 20x1 are as follows:

	20x2	20x1
Accounts Receivable	$1,200,000	$850,000
Inventory	420,000	510,000
Prepaid Expenses	130,000	90,000
Accounts Payable	480,000	360,000
Accrued Liabilities	30,000	50,000
Income Taxes Payable	70,000	60,000

Present in good form a schedule of cash flows from operating activities using the indirect method.

E 4.

LO 5 Computing Cash Flows from Operating Activities: Indirect Method

During 20x1, Boulevard Corporation had a net income of $41,000. Included on the income statement was depreciation expense of $2,300 and amortization expense of $300. During the year, accounts receivable increased by $3,400, inventories decreased by $1,900, prepaid expenses decreased by $200, accounts payable increased by $5,000, and accrued liabilities decreased by $450. Determine net cash flows from operating activities using the indirect method.

E 5.

LO 5 Preparing a Schedule of Cash Flows from Operating Activities: Indirect Method

For the year ended June 30, 20xx, net income for Norris Corporation was $7,400. The following is additional information: (a) Depreciation expense was $2,000; (b) accounts receivable increased by $4,400 during the year; (c) inventories increased by $7,000, and accounts payable increased by $14,000 during the year; (d) prepaid rent decreased by $1,400, and salaries payable increased by $1,000; and (e) income taxes payable decreased by $600 during the year. Use the indirect method to prepare a schedule of cash flows from operating activities.

E 6.

LO 6 Computing Cash Flows from Investing Activities: Investments

Wix Company's T account for long-term available-for-sale investments at the end of 20x3 is as follows:

Investments			
Beg. Bal.	38,500	Sales	39,000
Purchases	58,000		
End. Bal.	57,500		

In addition, Wix's income statement shows a loss on the sale of investments of $6,500. Compute the amounts to be shown as cash flows from investing activities and show how they are to appear in the statement of cash flows.

E 7.

LO 6 Computing Cash Flows from Investing Activities: Plant Assets

The T accounts for plant assets and accumulated depreciation for Wix Company at the end of 20x3 are as follows:

Plant Assets					Accumulated Depreciation			
Beg. Bal.	65,000	Disposals	23,000		Disposals	14,700	Beg. Bal.	34,500
Purchases	33,600						Depreciation	10,200
End. Bal.	75,600						End. Bal.	30,000

In addition, Wix Company's income statement shows a gain on sale of plant assets of $4,400. Compute the amounts to be shown as cash flows from investing activities and show how they are to appear on the statement of cash flows.

E 8.

LO 6 Determining Cash Flows from Investing and Financing Activities

All transactions involving Notes Payable and related accounts engaged in by Wix Company during 20x3 are as follows:

Cash	18,000	
Notes Payable		18,000
Bank loan		
Patent	30,000	
Notes Payable		30,000
Purchase of patent by issuing note payable		

Notes Payable	5,000	
Interest Expense	500	
Cash		5,500

Repayment of note payable at maturity

Determine the amounts of the transactions affecting financing activities and show how they are to appear on the statement of cash flows for 20x3.

E 9.

LO 7 Preparing the Statement of Cash Flows: Indirect Method

Tham Corporation's 20x2 income statement and its comparative balance sheets for June 30, 20x2 and 20x1, follow.

Tham Corporation
Income Statement
For the Year Ended June 30, 20x2

Sales	$468,000
Cost of Goods Sold	312,000
Gross Margin	$156,000
Operating Expenses	90,000
Operating Income	$ 66,000
Interest Expense	5,600
Income Before Income Taxes	$ 60,400
Income Taxes	24,600
Net Income	$ 35,800

Tham Corporation
Comparative Balance Sheets
June 30, 20x2 and 20x1

	20x2	20x1
Assets		
Cash	$139,800	$ 25,000
Accounts Receivable (net)	42,000	52,000
Inventory	86,800	96,800
Prepaid Expenses	6,400	5,200
Furniture	110,000	120,000
Accumulated Depreciation, Furniture	(18,000)	(10,000)
Total Assets	$367,000	$289,000
Liabilities and Stockholders' Equity		
Accounts Payable	$ 26,000	$ 28,000
Income Taxes Payable	2,400	3,600
Notes Payable (long-term)	74,000	70,000
Common Stock, $10 par value	230,000	180,000
Retained Earnings	34,600	7,400
Total Liabilities and Stockholders' Equity	$367,000	$289,000

Additional information: (a) Issued $44,000 note payable for purchase of furniture; (b) sold furniture that cost $54,000 with accumulated depreciation of $30,600 at carrying value; (c) recorded depreciation on the furniture during the year, $38,600; (d) repaid a note in the amount of $40,000; (e) issued $50,000 of common stock at par value; and (f) declared and paid dividends of $8,600. Without using a work sheet, prepare a statement of cash flows for 20x2 using the indirect method.

E 10.

LO 7 Preparing a Work Sheet
SO 8 for the Statement of Cash
Flows: Indirect Method

Using the information in **E 9,** prepare a work sheet for the statement of cash flows for Tham Corporation for 20x2. From the work sheet, prepare a statement of cash flows using the indirect method.

E 11.

SO 9 Computing Cash Flows
from Operating Activities:
Direct Method

Vlieg Corporation engaged in the following transactions in 20x2. Using the direct method, compute the various cash flows from operating activities as required.

a. During 20x2, Vlieg Corporation had cash sales of $41,300 and sales on credit of $123,000. During the same year, accounts receivable decreased by $18,000. Determine the cash receipts from sales during 20x2.

b. During 20x2, Vlieg Corporation's cost of goods sold was $119,000. During the same year, merchandise inventory increased by $12,500 and accounts payable decreased by $4,300. Determine the cash payments for purchases during 20x2.

c. During 20x2, Vlieg Corporation had operating expenses of $45,000, including depreciation of $15,600. Also during 20x2, related prepaid expenses decreased by $3,100 and relevant accrued liabilities increased by $1,200. Determine the cash payments for operating expenses to suppliers of goods and services during 20x2.

d. Vlieg Corporation's income taxes expense for 20x2 was $4,300. Income taxes payable decreased by $230 that year. Determine the cash payments for income taxes during 20x2.

E 12.

SO 9 Preparing a Schedule of
Cash Flows from Operating
Activities: Direct Method

The income statement for the Vasquez Corporation follows.

Vasquez Corporation
Income Statement
For the Year Ended June 30, 20xx

Sales		$122,000
Cost of Goods Sold		60,000
Gross Margin		$ 62,000
Operating Expenses		
Salaries Expense	$32,000	
Rent Expense	16,800	
Depreciation Expense	2,000	50,800
Income Before Income Taxes		$ 11,200
Income Taxes		2,400
Net Income		$ 8,800

Additional information: (a) Accounts receivable increased by $4,400 during the year; (b) inventories increased by $7,000, and accounts payable increased by $14,000 during the year; (c) prepaid rent decreased by $1,400, while salaries payable increased by $1,000; and (d) income taxes payable decreased by $600 during the year. Using the direct method, prepare a schedule of cash flows from operating activities as illustrated in Exhibit 6.

PROBLEMS

LO 1   Classification of
LO 3   Transactions

P 1.   Analyze each transaction below and place X's in the appropriate columns to indicate its classification and its effect on cash flows using the indirect method.

	Cash Flow Classification				Effect on Cash		
Transaction	Operating Activity	Investing Activity	Financing Activity	Noncash Transaction	Increase	Decrease	No Effect
1. Earned a net income.							
2. Declared and paid cash dividend.							
3. Issued stock for cash.							
4. Retired long-term debt by issuing stock.							
5. Paid accounts payable.							
6. Purchased inventory with cash.							
7. Purchased a one-year insurance policy with cash.							
8. Purchased a long-term investment with cash.							
9. Sold trading securities at a gain.							
10. Sold a machine at a loss.							
11. Retired fully depreciated equipment.							
12. Paid interest on debt.							
13. Purchased available-for-sale securities (long-term).							
14. Received dividend income.							
15. Received cash on account.							
16. Converted bonds to common stock.							
17. Purchased 90-day Treasury bill.							

LO 4   The Statement of Cash
LO 7   Flows: Indirect Method

P 2.   The comparative balance sheets for Sharma Fabrics, Inc., for December 31, 20x3 and 20x2, appear on the next page. Additional information about Sharma Fabrics's operations during 20x3 is as follows: (a) net income, $56,000; (b) building and equipment depreciation expense amounts, $30,000 and $6,000, respectively; (c) equipment that cost $27,000 with accumulated depreciation of $25,000 sold at a gain of $10,600; (d) equipment purchases, $25,000; (e) patent amortization, $6,000; purchase of patent, $2,000; (f) funds borrowed by issuing notes payable, $50,000; notes payable repaid, $30,000; (g) land and building purchased for $324,000 by signing a mortgage for the total cost; (h) 3,000 shares of $20 par value common stock issued for a total of $100,000; and (i) paid cash dividend, $18,000.

REQUIRED

1. Using the indirect method, prepare a statement of cash flows for Sharma Fabrics, Inc. (Do not use a work sheet.)

2. Why did Sharma Fabrics have an increase in cash of $134,400 when it recorded net income of $56,000? Discuss and interpret.

3. Compute and assess cash flow yield and free cash flow for 20x3.

Sharma Fabrics, Inc. Comparative Balance Sheets December 31, 20x3 and 20x2		
	20x3	**20x2**
Assets		
Cash	$189,120	$ 54,720
Accounts Receivable (net)	204,860	150,860
Inventory	225,780	275,780
Prepaid Expenses	—	40,000
Land	50,000	—
Building	274,000	—
Accumulated Depreciation, Building	(30,000)	—
Equipment	66,000	68,000
Accumulated Depreciation, Equipment	(29,000)	(48,000)
Patents	8,000	12,000
Total Assets	$958,760	$553,360
Liabilities and Stockholders' Equity		
Accounts Payable	$ 21,500	$ 73,500
Notes Payable	20,000	—
Accrued Liabilities (current)	—	24,600
Mortgage Payable	324,000	—
Common Stock, $20 par value	360,000	300,000
Paid-in Capital in Excess of Par Value	114,400	74,400
Retained Earnings	118,860	80,860
Total Liabilities and Stockholders' Equity	$958,760	$553,360

P 3.
LO 4 Statement of Cash Flows:
LO 7 Indirect Method

The comparative balance sheets for Karidis Ceramics, Inc., for December 31, 20x3 and 20x2, appear on the next page. The following is additional information about Karidis Ceramics' operations during 20x3: (a) net income was $96,000; (b) building and equipment depreciation expense amounts were $80,000 and $60,000, respectively; (c) intangible assets were amortized in the amount of $20,000; (d) investments in the amount of $116,000 were purchased; (e) investments were sold for $150,000, on which a gain of $34,000 was recorded; (f) the company issued $240,000 in long-term bonds at face value; (g) a small warehouse building with the accompanying land was purchased through the issue of a $320,000 mortgage; (h) the company paid $40,000 to reduce mortgage payable during 20x3; (i) the company borrowed funds in the amount of $60,000 by issuing notes payable and repaid notes payable in the amount of $180,000; and (j) cash dividends in the amount of $36,000 were declared and paid.

REQUIRED

1. Using the indirect method, prepare a statement of cash flows for Karidis Ceramics. (Do not use a work sheet.)

2. Why did Karidis Ceramics experience a decrease in cash in a year in which it had a net income of $96,000? Discuss and interpret.

3. Compute and assess cash flow yield and free cash flow for 20x3.

Karidis Ceramics, Inc.
Comparative Balance Sheets
December 31, 20x3 and 20x2

	20x3	20x2
Assets		
Cash	$ 277,600	$ 305,600
Accounts Receivable (net)	738,800	758,800
Inventory	960,000	800,000
Prepaid Expenses	14,800	26,800
Long-Term Investments	440,000	440,000
Land	361,200	321,200
Building	1,200,000	920,000
Accumulated Depreciation, Building	(240,000)	(160,000)
Equipment	480,000	480,000
Accumulated Depreciation, Equipment	(116,000)	(56,000)
Intangible Assets	20,000	40,000
Total Assets	$4,136,400	$3,876,400
Liabilities and Stockholders' Equity		
Accounts Payable	$ 470,800	$ 660,800
Notes Payable (current)	40,000	160,000
Accrued Liabilities	10,800	20,800
Mortgage Payable	1,080,000	800,000
Bonds Payable	1,000,000	760,000
Common Stock	1,200,000	1,200,000
Paid-in Capital in Excess of Par Value	80,000	80,000
Retained Earnings	254,800	194,800
Total Liabilities and Stockholders' Equity	$4,136,400	$3,876,400

P 4.

LO 4 The Work Sheet and the
LO 7 Statement of Cash Flows:
SO 8 Indirect Method

Use the information for Karidis Ceramics, Inc., given in **P 3,** to complete the following requirements.

REQUIRED

1. Prepare a work sheet for the statement of cash flows for Karidis Ceramics, Inc.
2. Answer requirements **1, 2,** and **3** in **P 3** if that problem was not assigned.

P 5.

SO 9 Cash Flows from Operating
Activities: Direct Method

The income statement for Tanucci Clothing Store is at the top of the next page. The following is additional information: (a) other sales and administrative expenses include depreciation expense of $104,000 and amortization expense of $36,000; (b) accrued liabilities for salaries were $24,000 less than the previous year, and prepaid expenses were $40,000 more than the previous year; and (c) during the year accounts receivable (net) increased by $288,000, accounts payable increased by $228,000, and income taxes payable decreased by $14,400.

REQUIRED

Using the direct method, prepare a schedule of cash flows from operating activities as illustrated in Exhibit 6.

Tanucci Clothing Store Income Statement For the Year Ended June 30, 20xx		
Net Sales		$4,900,000
Cost of Goods Sold		
Beginning Inventory	$1,240,000	
Net Cost of Purchases	3,040,000	
Goods Available for Sale	$4,280,000	
Ending Inventory	1,400,000	
Cost of Goods Sold		2,880,000
Gross Margin		$2,020,000
Operating Expenses		
Sales and Administrative Salaries Expense	$1,112,000	
Other Sales and Administrative Expenses	624,000	
Total Operating Expenses		1,736,000
Income Before Income Taxes		$ 284,000
Income Taxes		78,000
Net Income		$ 206,000

P 6.

LO 4 Statement of Cash Flows:
SO 9 Direct Method

Flanders Corporation's 20x2 income statement and its comparative balance sheets as of June 30, 20x2 and 20x1, appear as follows:

Flanders Corporation Income Statement For the Year Ended June 30, 20x2		
Sales		$2,081,800
Cost of Goods Sold		1,312,600
Gross Margin		$ 769,200
Operating Expenses (including Depreciation Expense of $120,000)		378,400
Income from Operations		$ 390,800
Other Income (Expenses)		
Loss on Disposal of Equipment	($ 8,000)	
Interest Expense	(75,200)	(83,200)
Income Before Income Taxes		$ 307,600
Income Taxes		68,400
Net Income		$ 239,200

Flanders Corporation
Comparative Balance Sheets
June 30, 20x2 and 20x1

	20x2	20x1
Assets		
Cash	$ 334,000	$ 40,000
Accounts Receivable (net)	200,000	240,000
Inventory	360,000	440,000
Prepaid Expenses	1,200	2,000
Property, Plant, and Equipment	1,256,000	1,104,000
Accumulated Depreciation, Property, Plant, and Equipment	(366,000)	(280,000)
Total Assets	$1,785,200	$1,546,000
Liabilities and Stockholders' Equity		
Accounts Payable	$ 128,000	$ 84,000
Notes Payable (due in 90 days)	60,000	160,000
Income Taxes Payable	52,000	36,000
Mortgage Payable	720,000	560,000
Common Stock, $5 par value	400,000	400,000
Retained Earnings	425,200	306,000
Total Liabilities and Stockholders' Equity	$1,785,200	$1,546,000

The following is additional information about 20x2: (a) equipment that cost $48,000 with accumulated depreciation of $34,000 was sold at a loss of $8,000; (b) land and building were purchased in the amount of $200,000 through an increase of $200,000 in the mortgage payable; (c) a $40,000 payment was made on the mortgage; (d) the notes were repaid, but the company borrowed an additional $60,000 through the issuance of a new note payable; and (e) a $120,000 cash dividend was declared and paid.

REQUIRED

1. Use the direct method to prepare a statement of cash flows. Include a supporting schedule of noncash investing and financing transactions. Do not use a work sheet, and do not include a reconciliation of net income to net cash flows from operating activities.

2. What are the primary reasons for Flanders Corporation's large increase in cash from 20x1 to 20x2?

3. Compute and assess cash flow yield and free cash flow for 20x2.

ALTERNATE PROBLEMS

LO 1 **Classification of**
LO 3 **Transactions**

P 7. Analyze each transaction below and place X's in the appropriate columns to indicate its classification and its effect on cash flows using the indirect method.

Transaction	Cash Flow Classification				Effect on Cash		
	Operating Activity	Investing Activity	Financing Activity	Noncash Transaction	Increase	Decrease	No Effect
1. Incurred a net loss.							
2. Declared and issued a stock dividend.							
3. Paid a cash dividend.							
4. Collected accounts receivable.							
5. Purchased inventory with cash.							
6. Retired long-term debt with cash.							
7. Sold available-for-sale securities at a loss.							
8. Issued stock for equipment.							
9. Purchased a one-year insurance policy with cash.							
10. Purchased treasury stock with cash.							
11. Retired a fully depreciated truck (no gain or loss).							
12. Paid interest on note.							
13. Received cash dividend on investment.							
14. Sold treasury stock.							
15. Paid income taxes.							
16. Transferred cash to money market account.							
17. Purchased land and building with a mortgage.							

LO 4 **The Statement of Cash**
LO 7 **Flows: Indirect Method**

P 8. O'Brien Corporation's comparative balance sheets as of December 31, 20x2 and 20x1, and its income statement for the year ended December 31, 20x2, are on the next page. The following is additional information about 20x2: (a) furniture and fixtures that cost $17,800 with accumulated depreciation of $14,400 were sold at a gain of $3,500; (b) furniture and fixtures were purchased in the amount of $19,800; (c) a $10,000 note payable was paid and $20,000 was borrowed on a new note; (d) bonds payable in the amount of $50,000 were converted into 2,000 shares of common stock; and (e) $3,000 in cash dividends were declared and paid.

REQUIRED

1. Using the indirect method, prepare a statement of cash flows. Include a supporting schedule of noncash investing and financing transactions. (Do not use a work sheet.)

2. What are the primary reasons for O'Brien Corporation's large increase in cash from 20x1 to 20x2, despite its low net income?

3. Compute and assess cash flow yield and free cash flow for 20x2.

O'Brien Corporation
Comparative Balance Sheets
December 31, 20x2 and 20x1

	20x2	20x1
Assets		
Cash	$ 82,400	$ 25,000
Accounts Receivable (net)	82,600	100,000
Inventory	175,000	225,000
Prepaid Rent	1,000	1,500
Furniture and Fixtures	74,000	72,000
Accumulated Depreciation, Furniture and Fixtures	(21,000)	(12,000)
Total Assets	$394,000	$411,500
Liabilities and Stockholders' Equity		
Accounts Payable	$ 71,700	$100,200
Income Taxes Payable	700	2,200
Notes Payable (long-term)	20,000	10,000
Bonds Payable	50,000	100,000
Common Stock, $10 par value	120,000	100,000
Paid-in Capital in Excess of Par Value	90,720	60,720
Retained Earnings	40,880	38,380
Total Liabilities and Stockholders' Equity	$394,000	$411,500

O'Brien Corporation
Income Statement
For the Year Ended December 31, 20x2

Net Sales		$804,500
Cost of Goods Sold		563,900
Gross Margin		$240,600
Operating Expenses (including Depreciation Expense of $23,400)		224,700
Income from Operations		$ 15,900
Other Income (Expenses)		
Gain on Disposal of Furniture and Fixtures	$ 3,500	
Interest Expense	(11,600)	(8,100)
Income Before Income Taxes		$ 7,800
Income Taxes		2,300
Net Income		$ 5,500

P 9.

LO 4 The Work Sheet and the
LO 7 Statement of Cash Flows:
SO 8 Indirect Method

Use the information for O'Brien Corporation given in **P 8** to answer the following requirements.

REQUIRED

1. Prepare a work sheet to gather information for the preparation of the statement of cash flows.
2. Answer requirements **1, 2,** and **3** in **P 8** if that problem was not assigned.

EXPANDING YOUR CRITICAL THINKING, COMMUNICATION, AND INTERPERSONAL SKILLS

SKILLS DEVELOPMENT

Conceptual Analysis

LO 5 Direct Versus Indirect
SO 9 Method

SD 1. *Collins Industries, Inc.,* a manufacturing company, uses the direct method of presenting cash flows from operating activities in its statement of cash flows. As noted in the text, most companies use the indirect method.[10] Explain the difference between the direct and indirect methods of presenting cash flows from operating activities. Then choose either the direct or the indirect method and tell why it is the best way of presenting cash flows from operations. Be prepared to discuss your opinion in class.

Ethical Dilemma

LO 3 Ethics and Cash Flow
Classifications

SD 2. *Chemical Waste Treatment, Inc.,* is a fast-growing company that disposes of chemical wastes. The company has an $800,000 line of credit at its bank. One section in the loan agreement says that the ratio of cash flows from operations to interest expense must exceed 3.0. If this ratio falls below 3.0, the company must reduce the balance outstanding on its line of credit to one-half the total line if the funds borrowed against the line of credit exceed that amount. After the end of the fiscal year, the controller informs the president: "We will not meet the ratio requirements on our line of credit in 20x2 because interest expense was $1.2 million and cash flows from operations were $3.2 million. Also, we have borrowed 100 percent of our line of credit. We do not have the cash to reduce the credit line by $400,000." The president says, "This is a serious situation. To pay our ongoing bills, we need our bank to increase our line of credit, not decrease it. What can we do?" "Do you recall the $500,000 two-year note payable for equipment?" replied the controller. "It is now classified as 'Proceeds from Notes Payable' in cash flows provided from financing activities in the statement of cash flows. If we move it to cash flows from operations and call it 'Increase in Payables,' it would increase cash flows from operations to $3.7 million and put us over the limit." "Well, do it," ordered the president. "It surely doesn't make any difference where it is on the statement. It is an increase in both places. It would be much worse for our company in the long term if we failed to meet this ratio requirement." What is your opinion of the president's reasoning? Is the president's order ethical? Who benefits and who is harmed if the controller follows the president's order? What are management's alternatives? What would you do?

Research Activity

LO 3 Basic Research Skills
LO 4

SD 3. Select the annual reports of three corporations, using one or more of the following sources: your library or the Fingraph® Financial Analyst™ CD-ROM software that accompanies this text. You may choose them from the same industry or at random, at the direction of your instructor. (If you did a related exercise in a previous chapter, use the same three companies.) Prepare a table with a column for each corporation. Then, for any year covered by the statement of cash flows, answer the following questions: Does the company use the direct or the indirect approach? Is net income more or less

---

| Cash Flow | CD-ROM | Communication | Critical Thinking | Ethics | General Ledger | Group Activity | Hot Links to Real Companies | International | Internet | Key Ratio | Memo | Spreadsheet |

than net cash flows from operating activities? What are the major causes of differences between net income and net cash flows from operating activities? Compute cash flow efficiency ratios and free cash flow. Does the dividend appear secure? Did the company make significant capital expenditures during the year? How were the expenditures financed? Do you notice anything unusual about the investing and financing activities of your companies? Do the investing and financing activities provide any insights into management's plan for each company? If so, what are they? Be prepared to discuss your findings in class.

Decision-Making Practice

SD 4.

LO 4 Analysis of Cash Flow
LO 7 Difficulty

May Hashimi, president of *Hashimi Print Gallery, Inc.,* is examining the following income statement, which has just been handed to her by her accountant, Lou Klein, CPA.

Hashimi Print Gallery, Inc. Income Statement For the Year Ended December 31, 20x2	
Net Sales	$884,000
Cost of Goods Sold	508,000
Gross Margin	$376,000
Operating Expenses (including Depreciation Expense of $20,000)	204,000
Operating Income	$172,000
Interest Expense	24,000
Income Before Income Taxes	$148,000
Income Taxes	28,000
Net Income	$120,000

After looking at the statement, Hashimi said to Klein, "Lou, the statement seems to be well done, but what I need to know is why I don't have enough cash to pay my bills this month. You show that I earned $120,000 in 20x2, but I have only $24,000 in the bank. I know I bought a building on a mortgage and paid a cash dividend of $48,000, but what else is going on?" Klein replied, "To answer your question, we have to look at comparative balance sheets and prepare another type of statement. Take a look at these balance sheets." The statements handed to Hashimi are on the next page.

1. To what statement is Klein referring? From the information given, prepare the additional statement using the indirect method.
2. Hashimi Print Gallery, Inc., has a cash problem despite profitable operations. Why?

	20x2	20x1

Hashimi Print Gallery, Inc.
Comparative Balance Sheets
December 31, 20x2 and 20x1

Assets

	20x2	20x1
Cash	$ 24,000	$ 40,000
Accounts Receivable (net)	178,000	146,000
Inventory	240,000	180,000
Prepaid Expenses	10,000	14,000
Building	400,000	—
Accumulated Depreciation	(20,000)	—
Total Assets	$832,000	$380,000

Liabilities and Stockholders' Equity

	20x2	20x1
Accounts Payable	$ 74,000	$ 96,000
Income Taxes Payable	6,000	4,000
Mortgage Payable	400,000	—
Common Stock	200,000	200,000
Retained Earnings	152,000	80,000
Total Liabilities and Stockholders' Equity	$832,000	$380,000

FINANCIAL REPORTING AND ANALYSIS

Interpreting Financial Reports

FRA 1.

LO 4   Cash-Generating Efficiency and Free Cash Flow

The statement of cash flows for **Tandy Corporation,** the owner of Radio Shack and other retail store chains, appears on the next page. For the two years shown, compute the cash-generating efficiency ratios of cash flow yield, cash flows to sales, and cash flows to assets. Also compute free cash flow for the two years. Assume that you report to an investment analyst who has asked you to analyze Tandy's statement of cash flows for 1997 and 1998. Prepare a memorandum to the investment analyst that assesses Tandy's cash-generating efficiency and evaluates its available free cash flow in light of its financing activities. Are there any special operating circumstances that should be taken into consideration? Refer to your computations and to Tandy's Statement of Cash Flows as attachments. The following data come from Tandy's annual report (in thousands):[11]

	1998	1997	1996
Net Sales	$4,787.9	$5,372.2	$6,285.5
Total Assets	1,993.6	2,317.5	2,583.4

Tandy Corporation
Statement of Cash Flows
For the Years Ended December 31, 1998 and 1997

(In millions)	1998	1997
Cash flows from operating activities:		
Net income (loss)	$ 61.3	$186.9
Adjustments to reconcile net income (loss) to net cash provided by operating activities:		
Restricted stock awards	82.6	—
Provision for loss on sale of Computer City	108.2	—
Depreciation and amortization	99.0	97.2
Impairment of long-lived assets	—	—
Provision for restructuring cost and other charges	—	—
Deferred income taxes and other items	(4.0)	106.0
Provision for credit losses and bad debts	12.5	2.6
Changes in operating assets and liabilities:		
Receivables	(36.7)	(5.9)
Inventories	85.6	163.8
Other current assets	17.7	(20.7)
Accounts payable, accrued expenses and income taxes	(11.4)	(209.6)
Net cash provided by operating activities	414.8	320.3
Investing activities:		
Additions to property, plant and equipment	(131.5)	(118.4)
Proceeds from sale of property, plant and equipment	6.7	12.7
Proceeds from sale of Computer City	36.5	—
Proceeds from sale of AST common stock	—	23.8
Payment received on AST note	—	—
Payment received on InterTAN note	—	20.9
Other investing activities	(4.7)	(2.9)
Net cash used by investing activities	(93.0)	(63.9)
Financing activities:		
Purchases of treasury stock	(337.4)	(425.6)
Proceeds from sale of common stock put options	0.3	—
Sale of treasury stock to employee stock plans	35.4	35.2
Proceeds from exercise of stock options	22.4	15.5
Dividends paid	(44.8)	(48.2)
Changes in short-term borrowings, net	(44.9)	43.6
Additions to long-term borrowings	45.7	149.8
Repayments of long-term borrowings	(39.9)	(42.3)
Net cash used by financing activities	(363.2)	(272.0)
Decrease in cash and cash equivalents	(41.4)	(15.6)
Cash and cash equivalents, beginning of period	105.9	121.5
Cash and cash equivalents, end of period	$ 64.5	$105.9

International Company

FRA 2.
LO 4 **Comparison of Cash Flow Generation Ratios**

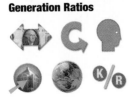

The following data pertain to two of Japan's most well-known and successful companies[12] (numbers are in billions of yen):

	Sony Corporation		Canon, Inc.	
	1998	1997	1998	1997
Net sales	¥6,425	¥5,384	¥2,826	¥2,761
Net income	222	140	110	119
Average total assets	6,041	5,363	2,792	2,740
Net cash flows from operating activities	612	723	247	153
Dividends	22	19	16	14
Net capital expenditures	356	283	194	162

Calculate the cash flow yield, cash flows to sales, cash flows to assets, and free cash flow for the two years for each company. Which company is most efficient in generating cash flow? Which company has the best year-to-year trend? Which company most likely will need external financing?

Toys "R" Us Annual Report

FRA 3.
LO 4 **Analysis of the Statement of Cash Flows**

Refer to the statement of cash flows in the Toys "R" Us annual report to answer the following questions:

1. Does Toys "R" Us use the direct or the indirect method of reporting cash flows from operating activities? Other than net earnings, what are the most important factors affecting cash flows from operating activities? Explain the trend of each.

2. Based on the cash flows from investing activities, would you say that Toys "R" Us is a contracting or an expanding company?

3. Calculate the cash flow yield, cash flows to sales, cash flows to assets, and free cash flow for the last three years for Toys "R" Us. How would you evaluate the company's cash-generating efficiency? Does Toys "R" Us need external financing? If so, where has it come from?

Fingraph® Financial Analyst™

FRA 4.
LO 3 **Cash Flow Analysis**
LO 4

Choose any two companies from the same industry in the Fingraph® Financial Analyst™ CD-ROM software.

1. In the annual reports for the companies you have selected, identify the statement of cash flows. Do the companies use the direct or indirect form of the statement?

2. Display and print in tabular and graphical form the Statement of Cash Flows: Operating Activities Analysis page. Prepare a table that compares the cash flow yield, cash flows to sales, and cash flows to assets for both companies for two years. Are the ratios moving in the same or opposite directions? Study the operating activities sections of the statements to determine the main causes of differences between the net income and cash flows from operations. How do the companies compare?

3. Display and print in tabular and graphical form the Statement of Cash Flows: Investing and Financing Activities Analysis page. Prepare a table that compares the free cash flow for both companies for two years. How do the companies compare? Are the companies growing or contracting? Study the investing and financing activities sections of the statements to determine the main causes of differences between the companies.

4. Find and read references to cash flows in the liquidity analysis section of management's discussion and analysis in each annual report.

5. Write a one-page executive summary that reports your findings from parts **1–4**, including your assessment of the companies' comparative liquidity. Include the Fingraph® pages and your tables as attachments to your report.

Internet Case

LO 4   Follow-up Analysis of Cash Flows

Go to the Needles Accounting Resource Center at http://college.hmco.com. Within companies under web links, go to the annual report on the web site for **Marriott International, Inc.** Find the financial statements including the statement of cash flows. Compare Marriott's cash flow performance for the most recent year with the 1998 statement at the beginning of this chapter by (1) identifying major changes in operating, investing, and financing activities, (2) reading management's financial review of cash flows, and (3) calculating the cash flow ratios (cash flow yield, cash flows to sales, cash flows to assets, and free cash flow) for the most recent year. Be prepared to discuss your conclusions in class.

ENDNOTES

1. Marriott International, Inc., *Annual Report*, 1998.
2. *Statement of Financial Accounting Standards No. 95*, "Statement of Cash Flows" (Norwalk, Conn.: Financial Accounting Standards Board, 1987).
3. *Statement of Financial Accounting Concepts No. 1*, "Objectives of Financial Reporting for Business Enterprises" (Norwalk, Conn.: Financial Accounting Standards Board, 1978), par. 37–39.
4. Marriott International, Inc., *Annual Report*, 1998.
5. Gary Slutsker, "Look at the Birdie and Say: 'Cash Flow,' " *Forbes*, October 25, 1993.
6. Jonathan Clements, "Yacktman Fund Is Bloodied but Unbowed," *The Wall Street Journal*, November 8, 1993.
7. Jeffrey Laderman, "Earnings, Schmearnings—Look at the Cash," *Business Week*, July 24, 1989.
8. Marriott International, Inc., *Annual Report*, 1998.
9. American Institute of Certified Public Accountants, *Accounting Trends & Techniques* (New York: AICPA, 1998), p. 485.
10. American Institute of Certified Public Accountants, *Accounting Trends & Techniques* (New York: AICPA, 1998), p. 485.
11. Tandy Corporation, *Annual Report*, 1998.
12. Sony Corporation, *Annual Report*, 1998; and Canon, Inc., *Annual Report*, 1998.

15

Financial Statement Analysis

LEARNING OBJECTIVES

1 Describe and discuss the objectives of financial statement analysis.

2 Describe and discuss the standards for financial statement analysis.

3 State the sources of information for financial statement analysis.

4 Apply horizontal analysis, trend analysis, and vertical analysis to financial statements.

5 Apply ratio analysis to financial statements in a comprehensive evaluation of a company's financial situation.

Moody's Investors Service, Inc. Moody's Investors Service, Inc., rates the bonds and other indebtedness of companies on the basis of safety—that is, the likelihood of repayment. Investors rely on this service when making investments in bonds and other long-term company debt. For instance, Moody's recently upgraded its assessment of AnnTaylor Stores, Inc., from B2 to B3.[1] AnnTaylor is a well-known chain of women's apparel retailing stores. This is just below an A rating, which is the top category. On what basis would Moody's decide to upgrade or lower the bond rating of a company?

Moody's said that the improved rating was due to "improved balance sheet measures" and "significantly lower debt and interest obligations in the near term." This improvement stems from "AnnTaylor's operating measures [that] have [shown] an improving trend in recent years." AnnTaylor did not rate an A rating because of "the volatility inherent in apparel retailing. . . . A change in customer sentiment, fashion, or changes in management philosophy could result in overstocking and declines in profitability and operating cash flow."

This case demonstrates several features of the evaluation of a company's financial prospects. First, the analysis is rooted in the financial statements (for example, financial position, profits, and cash flows). Second, it is directed toward the future (for example, expected lower debt and interest). Third, the operating environment must be taken into consideration (for example, volatility in the industry). Fourth, judgment is involved.

Enrichment Note: A bond-rating reevaluation is often triggered by poor earnings performance.

Objectives of Financial Statement Analysis

OBJECTIVE

1 Describe and discuss the objectives of financial statement analysis

Financial statement analysis comprises all the techniques employed by users of financial statements to show important relationships in the financial statements. Users of financial statements fall into two broad categories: internal and external. Management is the main internal user. However, because the people who run a company have inside information on operations, other techniques are available to them. The main focus here is on the external users of financial statements and the analytical techniques they employ.

Creditors make loans in the form of trade accounts, notes, or bonds. They expect them to be repaid according to specified terms and receive interest on the notes and bonds payable. Investors buy capital stock, from which they hope to receive dividends and an increase in value. Both groups face risks. The creditor faces the risk that the debtor will fail to pay back the loan. The investor faces the risks that dividends will be reduced or not paid and that the market price of the stock will drop. For both groups, the goal is to achieve a return that makes up for the risk. In general, the greater the risk taken, the greater the return required as compensation.

Any one loan or any one investment can turn out badly. As a result, most creditors and investors put their funds into a **portfolio** or a group of loans or investments. The portfolio allows them to average both the returns and the risks. Nevertheless, individual decisions about the loans and stock in the portfolio must still be made. It is in making those individual decisions that financial statement analysis is most useful. Creditors and investors use financial statement analysis in two general ways: (1) to judge past performance and current position and (2) to judge future potential and the risk connected with that potential.

Assessment of Past Performance and Current Position

Key Point: Past performance is a measure of relative certainty, whereas trends and projections are surrounded with varying degrees of uncertainty.

Past performance is often a good indicator of future performance. Therefore, an investor or creditor looks at the trend of past sales, expenses, net income, cash flow, and return on investment not only as a means for judging management's past performance but also as a possible indicator of future performance. In addition, an analysis of current position will tell, for example, what assets the business owns and what liabilities must be paid. It will also tell what the cash position is, how much debt the company has in relation to equity, and what levels of inventories and receivables exist. Knowing a company's past performance and current position is often important in achieving the second general objective of financial analysis.

Assessment of Future Potential and Related Risk

Study Note: Some basic considerations associated with projections are not projecting results for activities that fall outside the range of the predicting data and determining whether the environment has changed since the predicting data were generated.

Information about the past and present is useful only to the extent that it bears on decisions about the future. An investor judges the potential earning ability of a company because that ability will affect the market price of the company's stock and the amount of dividends the company will pay. A creditor judges the potential debt-paying ability of the company.

The riskiness of an investment or loan depends on how easy it is to predict future profitability or liquidity. If an investor can predict with confidence that a company's earnings per share will be between $2.50 and $2.60 in the next year, the investment is less risky than if the earnings per share are expected to fall between $2.00 and $3.00. For example, the potential associated with an investment in an established and stable electric utility, or a loan to it, is relatively easy to predict on the basis of the company's past performance and current position. The potential associated with a small microcomputer manufacturer, on the other hand, may be much harder to predict. For this reason, the investment in or loan to the electric utility carries less risk than the investment in or loan to the small microcomputer company.

Often, in return for taking a greater risk, an investor in the microcomputer company will demand a higher expected return (increase in market price plus dividends) than will an investor in the utility company. Also, a creditor of the microcomputer company will demand a higher interest rate and possibly more assurance of repayment (a secured loan, for instance) than a creditor of the utility company. The higher interest rate reimburses the creditor for assuming a higher risk.

Standards for Financial Statement Analysis

OBJECTIVE

2 Describe and discuss the standards for financial statement analysis

When analyzing financial statements, decision makers must judge whether the relationships they have found are favorable or unfavorable. Three commonly used standards of comparison are (1) rule-of-thumb measures, (2) past performance of the company, and (3) industry norms.

Rule-of-Thumb Measures

Many financial analysts, investors, and lenders employ ideal, or rule-of-thumb, measures for key financial ratios. For example, it has long been thought that a current ratio (current assets divided by current liabilities) of 2:1 is acceptable. The credit-rating firm of Dun & Bradstreet, in its *Industry Norms and Key Business Ratios*, offers such rules of thumb as the following:

Enrichment Note: Rules of thumb evolve and change as the environment changes. Not long ago, a higher current ratio than today's was considered satisfactory.

Current debt to tangible net worth   Ordinarily, a business begins to pile up trouble when this relationship exceeds 80%.

Inventory to net working capital   Ordinarily, this relationship should not exceed 80%.

Although such measures may suggest areas that need further investigation, there is no proof that the specified levels are the best for any company. A company with a current ratio higher than 2:1 may have a poor credit policy (resulting in accounts receivable being too large), too much inventory, or poor cash management. Another company may have a ratio that is lower than 2:1 as a result of excellent management in all three of those areas. Thus, rule-of-thumb measures must be used with great care.

Past Performance of the Company

An improvement over rule-of-thumb measures is the comparison of financial measures or ratios of the same company over a period of time. This standard will give the analyst at least some basis for judging whether the measure or ratio is getting better or worse. It may also be helpful in showing possible future trends. However, since trends reverse at times, such projections must be made with care. Another problem with trend analysis is that the past may not be a useful measure of adequacy. In other words, past performance may not be enough to meet present needs. For example, even if return on total investment improved from 3 percent one year to 4 percent the next, the 4 percent return may in fact not be adequate.

Industry Norms

One way of making up for the limitations of using past performance as a standard is to use industry norms. Such norms will tell how the company being analyzed compares with the average of other companies in the same industry. For example, suppose that other companies in an industry have an average rate of return on total investment of 8 percent. In such a case, 3 and 4 percent returns are probably not adequate. Industry norms can also be used to judge trends. Suppose that a company's profit margin dropped from 12 to 10 percent because of a downward turn in the economy. A finding that other companies in the same industry had experienced an average drop in profit margin from 12 to 4 percent would indicate that the first company being analyzed did relatively well. Sometimes, instead of industry averages, data for the industry leader or a specific competitor are used for analysis.

There are three limitations to using industry norms as standards. First, two companies that seem to be in the same industry may not be strictly comparable. Consider two companies in the oil industry. One company may be purchasing oil products and marketing them through service stations. The other, an international company, may discover, produce, refine, and market its own oil products. The operations of these two companies cannot be compared because they are different.

> **Key Point:** Each segment represents an investment that is evaluated and reviewed frequently by the home office or parent company. The segment can remain an active investment or be replaced by a more attractive one.

Second, most large companies today operate in more than one industry. Some of these **diversified companies**, or *conglomerates*, operate in many unrelated industries. The individual segments of a diversified company generally have different rates of profitability and different degrees of risk. In analyzing the consolidated financial statements of such companies, it is often impossible to use industry norms as standards. There are simply no other companies that are similar enough. A requirement by the Financial Accounting Standards Board, presented in *Statement No. 131*, provides a partial solution to this problem. It states that diversified companies must report segment profit or loss, certain revenue and expense items, and segment assets for each of their operating segments. Depending on how the company is organized for resource allocation in assessing performance, segment information may be reported for operations in different industries or in different geographical areas, or for major customers.[2]

An example of segment reporting may be found in Exhibit 1. Goodyear Tire & Rubber Co. is a well-known tire company but it also has significant engineered products and chemical products divisions. The selected data on sales, income, and assets for these segments shown in Exhibit 1 allows the analyst to compute important profitability performance measures such as profit margin, asset turnover, and return on assets for each segment and compare them to their respective industry. For the tire segment, the exposure to various geographic areas is also disclosed.

The third limitation of industry norms is that companies in the same industry with similar operations may use different acceptable accounting procedures. That is, different methods may be used to value inventories, or different methods may be used to depreciate similar assets. Even so, if little information about a company's prior performance is available, industry norms probably offer the best available standards for judging current performance—as long as they are used with care.

Sources of Information

OBJECTIVE

3 State the sources of information for financial statement analysis

The external analyst is often limited to using publicly available information about a company. The major sources of information about publicly held corporations are reports published by the company, SEC reports, business periodicals, and credit and investment advisory services.

(In millions)	1998	1997	1996
Exhibit 1 **Selected Segment Information for Goodyear Tire & Rubber Co.**			
Sales			
North American Tire	$ 6,235.2	$ 6,207.5	$ 6,123.8
Europe Tire	2,911.0	2,927.2	2,869.6
Latin American Tire	1,245.6	1,413.4	1,368.5
Asia Tire	501.8	666.9	736.2
Total Tires	10,893.6	11,215.0	11,098.1
Engineered Products	1,279.3	1,324.0	1,269.4
Chemical Products	970.8	1,089.1	1,152.7
Total Segment Sales	13,143.7	13,628.1	13,520.2
Income			
North American Tire	$ 378.6	$ 382.5	$ 316.2
Europe Tire	302.1	269.1	299.8
Latin American Tire	186.1	233.5	226.8
Asia Tire	7.5	58.6	70.2
Total Tires	874.3	943.7	913.0
Engineered Products	111.8	130.1	118.5
Chemical Products	139.6	128.3	136.2
Total Segment Income (EBIT)	1,125.7	1,202.1	1,167.7
Assets			
North American Tire	$ 3,944.6	$ 3,596.6	$ 3,443.5
Europe Tire	2,588.1	2,123.4	1,923.4
Latin American Tire	993.8	979.5	859.7
Asia Tire	744.0	522.3	655.8
Total Tires	8,270.5	7,221.8	6,882.4
Engineered Products	678.9	630.3	568.2
Chemical Products	576.5	541.0	566.6
Total Segment Assets	9,525.9	8,393.1	8,017.2

Source: Goodyear Tire & Rubber Co., *Annual Report,* 1998.

Reports Published by the Company

Key Point: Since published financial statements represent a major source of information for financial analysis, it is important to understand the content of the annual report.

The annual report of a publicly held corporation is an important source of financial information. The main parts of an annual report are (1) management's analysis of the past year's operations, (2) the financial statements, (3) the notes to the statements, including the principal accounting procedures used by the company, (4) the auditors' report, and (5) a summary of operations for a five- or ten-year period. Most publicly held companies also publish **interim financial statements** each quarter. Those reports present limited information in the form of condensed financial statements, which need not be subjected to a full audit by the independent auditor. The interim statements are watched closely by the financial community for early signs of important changes in a company's earnings trend.

SEC Reports

Publicly held corporations must file annual reports, quarterly reports, and current reports with the Securities and Exchange Commission (SEC). All such reports are available to the public at a small charge. The SEC calls for a standard form for the annual report (Form 10-K) that contains more information than the published annual report. For that reason, Form 10-K is a valuable source of information. It is available free of charge to stockholders of the company. The quarterly report (Form 10-Q) presents important facts about interim financial performance. The current report (Form 8-K) must be filed within a few days of the date of certain significant events, such as the sale or purchase of a division of the company or a change in auditors. This report is often the first indicator of important changes that may affect the company's financial performance in the future. Many company reports that are filed with the Securities and Exchange Commission are now available on the Internet at http://www.sec.gov/edgarhp.htm.

Business Periodicals and Credit and Investment Advisory Services

Financial analysts must keep up with current events in the financial world. Probably the best source of financial news is *The Wall Street Journal*, which is published every business day and is the most complete financial newspaper in the United States. Some helpful magazines, published every week or every two weeks, are *Forbes*, *Barron's*, *Fortune*, and the *Financial Times*.

 For further details about the financial history of companies, the publications of such services as Moody's Investors Service, Inc., and Standard & Poor's are useful. Data on industry norms, average ratios and relationships, and credit ratings are available from such agencies as The Dun & Bradstreet Corp. In its *Industry Norms and Key Business Ratios*, Dun & Bradstreet offers an annual analysis giving 14 ratios for each of 125 industry groups, classified as retailing, wholesaling, manufacturing, and construction. *Annual Statement Studies*, published by Robert Morris Associates, presents many facts and ratios for 223 different industries. A number of private services are also available for a yearly fee.

An example of specialized financial reporting that is readily available to the public is Moody's *Handbook of Dividend Achievers*, which profiles companies that have increased their dividends consistently over the past ten years. A sample listing from that publication—for PepsiCo Inc.—is shown in Exhibit 2. A wealth of information about the company is summarized on one page: the market action of its stock; summaries of its business operations, recent developments, and prospects;

BUSINESS FOCUS ON TECHNOLOGY

Performance reports and other financial information, stock quotes, reference data, and news about companies and markets are available instantaneously to individuals on the Internet through such services as CompuServe, America Online, Yahoo, and Wall Street Journal Interactive Edition. The Internet is an international web of computer-driven communications systems that links tens of millions of homes and businesses through telephone, cable, and computer networks. Combined with the services of brokers like Charles Schwab & Co., Inc., that allow customers to use their own computers to buy and sell stock and other securities, individuals have access to resources equivalent to those used by many professional analysts.

Exhibit 2
Sample Listing from Moody's *Handbook of Dividend Achievers*

PEPSICO INC.

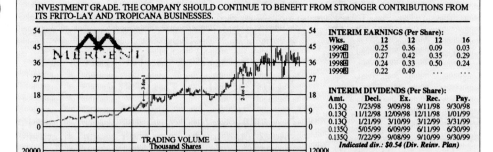

EXCH.	SYM.	REC. PRICE	P/E RATIO	YLD.	MKT. CAP.	RANGE (52-WK.)	'98 Y/E PR.	DIV. ACH.
NYSE	PEP	$34\frac{1}{8}$ (8/31/99)	23.5	1.6%	$50.20 bill.	$42\frac{9}{16}$ - 28	$40\frac{7}{8}$	27 yrs.

INVESTMENT GRADE. THE COMPANY SHOULD CONTINUE TO BENEFIT FROM STRONGER CONTRIBUTIONS FROM ITS FRITO-LAY AND TROPICANA BUSINESSES.

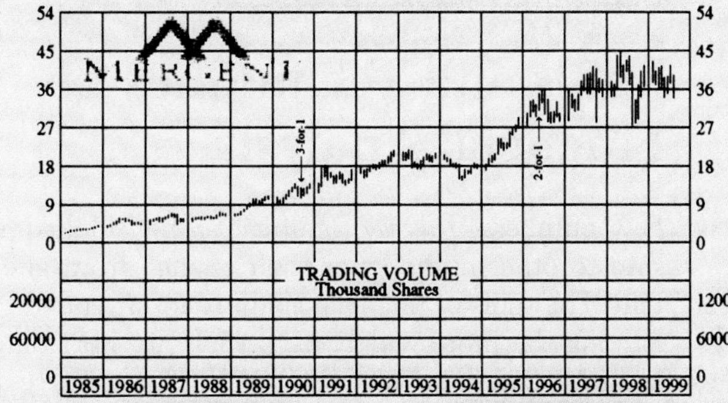

*7 YEAR PRICE SCORE 84.6 *12 MONTH PRICE SCORE 95.6
*NYSE COMPOSITE INDEX=100

INTERIM EARNINGS (Per Share):

Wks.	12	12	12	16
1996 [2]	0.25	0.36	0.09	0.03
1997 [1]	0.27	0.42	0.35	0.29
1998 [4]	0.24	0.33	0.50	0.24
1999 [5]	0.22	0.49	...	...

INTERIM DIVIDENDS (Per Share):

Amt.	Decl.	Ex.	Rec.	Pay.
0.13Q	7/23/98	9/09/98	9/11/98	9/30/98
0.13Q	11/12/98	12/09/98	12/11/98	1/01/99
0.13Q	1/21/99	3/10/99	3/12/99	3/31/99
0.135Q	5/05/99	6/09/99	6/11/99	6/30/99
0.135Q	7/22/99	9/08/99	9/10/99	9/30/99

Indicated div.: $0.54 (Div. Reinv. Plan)

CAPITALIZATION (12/26/98):

	($000)	(%)
Long-Term Debt	4,028,000	32.4
Deferred Income Tax	2,003,000	16.1
Common & Surplus	6,401,000	51.5
Total	12,432,000	100.0

BUSINESS:

PepsiCo Inc. operates on a worldwide basis within the soft drinks, juice and snack-foods businesses. The beverages segment, which accounted for 48% of sales in 1998 (35% of operating profit), manufactures concentrates, and markets PEPSI-COLA, DIET PEPSI, MOUNTAIN DEW, MUG, ALL SPORT BODY QUENCHER, AQUAFINA, SLICE and allied brands worldwide, and 7-UP internationally. This segment also operates soft drink bottling businesses principally in the United States. The juice segment, 3% (2%), includes Tropicana Products, Inc., which manufactures and sells its products under trademarks such as TROPICANA PURE PREMIUM, and TROPICANA SEASON'S BEST. Snack Foods, 49% (63%), manufactures and markets snack chips through Frito-Lay Inc. Well-known brands include: DORITOS, RUFFLES and LAYS. On 10/6/97, the Company spun off its Restaurant unit, TRICON Global Restaurants.

RECENT DEVELOPMENTS:

For the 12 weeks ended 6/12/99, net income climbed 50.4% to $743.0 million from $494.0 million in the corresponding quarter a year earlier. Results for the 1999 quarter include an after-tax credit of $270.0 million from the sale of shares by The Pepsi Bottling Group and the merger of bottling franchises with the Whitman Corporation. Total net sales slipped 5.2% to $4.98 billion from $5.26 billion. Net sales from Pepsi-Cola rose 2.9% to $1.25 billion, while Frito-Lay group sales improved 5.1% to $2.74 billion. Tropicana sales were up 11.7% to $533.0 million.

PROSPECTS:

The increase in retail prices for carbonated soft drinks should enhance the profitability of the Pepsi bottling system, and ultimately benefit equity income. However, the higher retail prices may result in slower volume growth and lower contributions from Pepsi-Cola North America in the upcoming quarter. Nevertheless, PEP expects continued strong results, propelled by contributions from Frito-Lay and Tropicana. Meanwhile, the Company is continuing with its three-year, $3.00 billion stock buyback program. As of 9/2/99, PEP had repurchase about 27.0 million of its shares at an aggregate of $986.0 million, and expects to purchase an additional $500.0 million by the end of 1999.

ANNUAL FINANCIAL DATA:

FISCAL YEAR	TOT. REVS. ($mill.)	NET INC. ($mill.)	TOT. ASSETS ($mill.)	OPER. PROFIT %	NET PROFIT %	RET. ON EQUITY %	RET. ON ASSETS %	CURR. RATIO	EARN. PER SH. $	CASH FL. PER SH. $	TANG. BK. VAL. $	DIV. PER SH. $	PRICE RANGE	AVG. P/E RATIO	AVG. YIELD %
12/26/98	22,348.0	[4] 1,993.0	22,660.0	11.6	8.9	31.1	8.8	0.6	[4] 1.31	2.12	...	0.51	$44\frac{13}{16}$ - $27\frac{9}{16}$	27.6	1.4
12/27/97	20,917.0	[1] 1,491.0	20,101.0	12.7	7.1	21.5	7.4	1.5	[1] 0.95	1.65	0.72	0.48	$41\frac{5}{16}$ - $28\frac{1}{4}$	36.6	1.4
12/28/96	31,645.0	[2] 1,149.0	24,512.0	8.0	3.6	17.3	4.7	1.0	[2] 0.72	1.79	...	0.43	$35\frac{7}{8}$ - $27\frac{1}{4}$	43.8	1.4
12/30/95	30,421.0	[2] 1,606.0	25,432.0	9.8	5.3	22.0	6.3	1.1	[2] 1.00	2.08	...	0.38	$29\frac{3}{8}$ - $16\frac{15}{16}$	23.2	1.6
12/31/94	28,472.4	[3] 1,784.0	24,792.0	11.2	6.3	26.0	7.2	1.0	[3] 1.11	2.09	...	0.34	$20\frac{9}{16}$ - $14\frac{5}{8}$	15.8	1.9
12/25/93	25,020.7	1,754.5	23,705.8	11.6	7.0	27.7	7.4	0.8	0.98	1.97	...	0.29	$21\frac{13}{16}$ - $17\frac{1}{4}$	19.9	1.5
12/26/92	21,970.0	[3] 1,301.7	20,951.2	10.8	5.9	24.3	6.2	1.1	[3] 0.81	1.56	...	0.25	$21\frac{11}{16}$ - $15\frac{1}{4}$	22.9	1.4
12/28/91	19,607.9	[2] 1,080.2	18,775.1	10.8	5.5	19.5	5.8	1.2	[2] 0.68	1.32	...	0.22	$18\frac{1}{4}$ - $11\frac{3}{4}$	22.2	1.5
12/29/90	17,802.7	1,090.6	17,143.4	11.5	6.1	22.2	6.4	0.9	0.69	1.24	...	0.18	$13\frac{15}{16}$ - 9	16.7	1.6
12/30/89	15,242.4	[2] 901.4	15,126.7	11.7	5.9	23.2	6.0	1.0	[2] 0.57	1.05	...	0.15	10 - $6\frac{5}{16}$	15.3	1.8

Statistics are as originally reported. Adj. for 2-for-1 stk. split, 5/96 & 9/90 [1] Incls. non-recurr. chrgs. $290.0 million; bef. disc. oper. gain $651.0 mill. [2] Incls. non-recurr. chrgs. 1/31/96, $716.0 mill.; non-cash chrg. 12/31/95, $520.0 mill.; chrg. 12/31/91, $119.0 mill.; credit 12/31/89, $1.8 mill.; chrg. 12/31/88, $16.3 mill. [3] Bef. acctg. change chrg. 12/31/94: $32.0 mill.; chrg. 12/31/92: $927.4 mill. [4] Incl. one-time chrg. of $288.0 mill. [5] Incls. an after-tax credit of $270.0 mill.

OFFICERS:
R. A. Enrico, Chmn., C.E.O.
K. M. von der Heyden, Vice-Chmn.
M. D. White, Sr. V.P., C.F.O.
S. S. Reinemund, Pres., C.O.O.

INVESTOR CONTACT: M. D. Moore, (914) 253-3035

PRINCIPAL OFFICE: 700 Anderson Hill Rd., Purchase, NY 10577-1444

TELEPHONE NUMBER: (914) 253-2000
FAX: (914) 253-2070
WEB: www.pepsico.com

NO. OF EMPLOYEES: 150,000 (approx.)

SHAREHOLDERS: 230,000 (approx.)

ANNUAL MEETING: In May

INCORPORATED: NC, Dec., 1986

INSTITUTIONAL HOLDINGS:
No. of Institutions: 936
Shares Held: 855,366,658
% Held: 57.9

INDUSTRY: Bottled and canned soft drinks (SIC: 2086)

TRANSFER AGENT(S): BankBoston, N.A., Boston, MA

Source: From Moody's *Handbook of Dividend Achievers.* Copyright © 1999. Reprinted by permission of Mergent, Inc.

earnings and dividend data; annual financial data for the past six or seven years; and other information. From the data contained in those summaries, it is possible to do many of the trend analyses and calculate the ratios explained in this chapter.

Tools and Techniques of Financial Analysis

OBJECTIVE

4 Apply horizontal analysis, trend analysis, and vertical analysis to financial statements

Few numbers are very significant when looked at individually. It is their relationship to other numbers or their change from one period to another that is important. The tools of financial analysis are intended to show relationships and changes. Among the more widely used tools are horizontal analysis, trend analysis, vertical analysis, and ratio analysis. To illustrate these tools, a comprehensive financial analysis of Sun Microsystems, Inc., is performed. Sun Microsystems was formed in 1982 and has emerged as a global leader in network computing. The company developed many of the core networking technologies that today are the basis of the Internet and corporate intranets, including the widely adopted Java technology.

Horizontal Analysis

Generally accepted accounting principles require the presentation of comparative financial statements that give financial information for the current year and the previous year. A common starting point for studying such statements is **horizontal analysis**, which begins with the computation of changes from the previous year to the current year in both dollar amounts and percentages. The percentage change must be computed to relate the size of the change to the size of the dollar amounts involved. A change of $1 million in sales is not as impressive as a change of $1 million in net income, because sales is a larger amount than net income.

Exhibits 3 and 4 present the comparative balance sheets and income statements, respectively, for Sun Microsystems, Inc., with the dollar and percentage changes shown. The percentage change is computed as follows:

$$\text{Percentage Change} = 100 \times \left(\frac{\text{Amount of Change}}{\text{Base Year Amount}} \right)$$

Enrichment Note: Traditional horizontal analysis presents trends in terms of nominal dollars. Advanced analysis might adjust data over several time periods to remove any inflation effect or price-level changes.

The **base year** in any set of data is always the first year being studied. For example, from 1998 to 1999, Sun Microsystems' total current assets increased by $1,969 million, from approximately $4,148 million to $6,116 million, or by 47.5 percent. This is computed as follows:

$$\text{Percentage Change} = 100 \times \left(\frac{\$1,969 \text{ million}}{\$4,148 \text{ million}} \right) = 47.5\%$$

An examination of the components of current assets in the comparative balance sheets shows the changes from 1998 to 1999. All current assets categories except inventories increased. It is important to consider both the dollar amount of the increase as well as the percentage increase. For example, accounts receivable increased 23.9 percent compared with a similar 29.6 percent increase in other current assets. However, the dollar increase in accounts receivable is more than five times the dollar increase in other current assets ($441 million versus $84 million). There was a corresponding increase in total current liabilities of $1,104 million or 52.0 percent. Total assets increased $2,709 million or 47.4 percent, which included an increase of $308 million or 23.7 percent in net property, plant, and equipment.

Exhibit 3
Comparative Balance Sheets with Horizontal Analysis

Sun Microsystems, Inc.
Consolidated Balance Sheets
June 30, 1999 and 1998

(In thousands)	1999	1998	Increase (Decrease) Amount	Percentage
Assets				
Current Assets				
Cash and Cash Equivalents	$1,088,972	$ 822,267	$ 266,705	32.4
Short-Term Investments	1,576,079	476,185	1,099,894	231.0
Accounts Receivable, Net of Allowances of $338,771 in 1999 and $235,563 in 1998	2,286,911	1,845,765	441,146	23.9
Inventories	307,873	346,446	(38,573)	(11.1)
Deferred Tax Assets	487,150	371,841	115,309	31.0
Other Current Assets	369,365	285,021	84,344	29.6
Total Current Assets	$6,116,350	$4,147,525	$1,968,825	47.5
Property, Plant, and Equipment	$2,871,348	$2,257,228	$ 614,120	27.2
Accumulated Depreciation and Amortization	(1,262,427)	(956,616)	(305,811)	32.0
Net Property, Plant, and Equipment	$1,608,921	$1,300,612	$ 308,309	23.7
Other Assets, Net	695,081	262,925	432,156	164.4
Total Assets	$8,420,352	$5,711,062	$2,709,290	47.4
Liabilities and Stockholders' Equity				
Current Liabilities				
Short-Term Borrowings	$ 1,646	$ 7,169	$ (5,523)	(77.0)
Accounts Payable	753,838	495,603	258,235	52.1
Accrued Payroll-Related Liabilities	520,068	315,929	204,139	64.6
Accrued Liabilities and Other	1,126,497	810,562	315,935	39.0
Deferred Service Revenues	422,115	264,967	157,148	59.3
Income Taxes Payable	402,813	188,641	214,172	113.5
Note Payable	—	40,000	(40,000)	(100.0)
Total Current Liabilities	$3,226,977	$2,122,871	$1,104,106	52.0
Deferred Income Taxes and Other Obligations	381,595	74,563	307,032	411.8
Stockholders' Equity	4,811,780	3,513,628	1,298,152	36.9
Total Liabilities and Stockholders' Equity	$8,420,352	$5,711,062	$2,709,290	47.4

Source: Sun Microsystems, Inc., *Annual Report*, 1999.

Total stockholders' equity increased by $1,298 million or 36.9 percent. All of this shows Sun Microsystems to be a rapidly growing company.

From the income statements in Exhibit 4, the most important result is that net revenues increased by $1,935 million or 19.8 percent, whereas operating income increased by $392 million or 34.6 percent and net income increased by $268 million or 35.2 percent. These extremely positive results were achieved in part because net revenues grew faster (19.8 percent) than total costs and expenses (17.8 percent).

Exhibit 4
Comparative Income Statements with Horizontal Analysis

			Increase (Decrease)	
(In thousands, except per share amounts)	1999	1998	Amount	Percentage
Net Revenues	$11,726,297	$9,790,840	$1,935,457	19.8
Costs and Expenses				
Cost of Sales	$ 5,648,360	$4,693,336	$ 955,024	20.3
Research and Development	1,262,517	1,013,782	248,735	24.5
Selling, General and Administrative	3,172,955	2,777,264	395,691	14.2
Purchased In-Process Research				
and Development	120,700	176,384	(55,684)	(31.6)
Total Costs and Expenses	$10,204,532	$8,660,766	$1,543,766	17.8
Operating Income	1,521,765	1,130,074	391,691	34.7
Interest Income	84,599	47,663	36,936	77.5
Interest Expense	(675)	(1,571)	(896)	(57.0)
Income Before Income Taxes	$ 1,605,689	$1,176,166	$ 429,523	36.5
Provision for Income Taxes	574,355	413,304	161,051	39.0
Net Income	$ 1,031,334	$ 762,862	$ 268,472	35.2
Net Income per Common Share—Basic	$ 1.35	$ 1.02	$ .33	32.4
Net Income per Common Share—Diluted	$ 1.27	$ .97	$ .30	30.9
Shares Used in the Calculation of Net Income				
per Common Share—Basic	765,853	747,456	18,397	2.5
Shares Used in the Calculation of Net Income				
per Common Share—Diluted	814,241	788,548	25,693	3.3

Sun Microsystems, Inc.
Consolidated Income Statements
For the Years Ended June 30, 1999 and 1998

Source: Sun Microsystems, Inc., *Annual Report*, 1999.

Exhibit 5
Trend Analysis

Sun Microsystems, Inc.
Net Revenues and Operating Income
Trend Analysis

	1999	1998	1997	1996	1995
Dollar Values					
(in millions)					
Net Revenues	$11,726	$9,791	$8,598	$7,095	$5,902
Operating Income	1,522	1,130	1,027	675	500
Trend Analysis					
(in percentages)					
Net Revenues	198.7	165.9	145.7	120.2	100.0
Operating Income	304.4	226.0	205.4	135.0	100.0

Source: Sun Microsystems, Inc., *Annual Report*, 1999.

Figure 1
Trend Analysis Presented Graphically for Sun Microsystems, Inc.

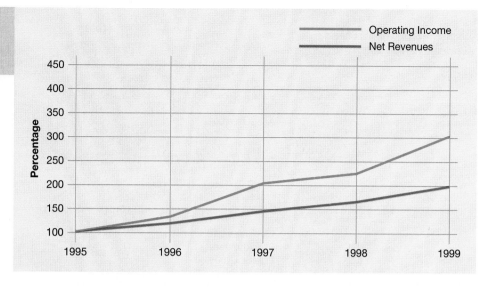

Trend Analysis

A variation of horizontal analysis is **trend analysis**, in which percentage changes are calculated for several successive years instead of for two years. Trend analysis, with its long-run view, is important because it may point to basic changes in the nature of a business. In addition to comparative financial statements, most companies present a summary of operations and data about other key indicators for five or more years. Net revenues and operating income from Sun Microsystems' summary of operations together with a trend analysis are presented in Exhibit 5.

Trend analysis uses an **index number** to show changes in related items over a period of time. For index numbers, the base year is equal to 100 percent. Other years are measured in relation to that amount. For example, the 1999 index for net revenues was figured as follows (dollar amounts in millions):

$$\text{Index} = 100 \times \left(\frac{\text{Index Year Amount}}{\text{Base Year Amount}} \right) = 100 \times \left(\frac{\$11{,}726}{\$5{,}902} \right) = 198.7$$

A study of the trend analysis in Exhibit 5 clearly shows that operating income has grown faster than net revenues at Sun Microsystems. However, both net revenues and operating income have shown increases every year. These trends may be seen visually in Figure 1.

Enrichment Note: Trend analysis is usually done for a five-year period to reflect the general five-year economic cycle that affects the U.S. economy. Cycles of other lengths exist and are tracked by the National Bureau of Economic Research. Trend analysis needs to use the appropriate cycle time to cover the complete cycle's impact on the business being studied.

Vertical Analysis

In **vertical analysis**, percentages are used to show the relationship of the different parts to a total in a single statement. The accountant sets a total figure in the statement equal to 100 percent and computes each component's percentage of that total. (The figure would be total assets or total liabilities and stockholders' equity on the balance sheet, and net revenues or net sales on the income statement.) The resulting statement of percentages is called a **common-size statement**. Common-size balance sheets and common-size income statements for Sun Microsystems are shown in pie-chart form in Figures 2 and 3, and in financial statement form in Exhibits 6 and 7.

Vertical analysis is useful for comparing the importance of specific components in the operation of a business. Also, comparative common-size statements can be

Figure 2
Common-Size Balance Sheets Presented Graphically

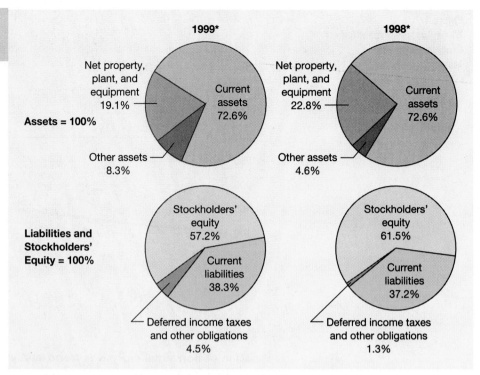

* Rounding causes some additions not to total precisely.

Key Point: Because percentages look identical in their presentation, it is important to discern what base amount is used when a percentage describes an item. For example, inventory may be 50 percent of *total current assets* but only 10 percent of *total assets*.

used to identify important changes in the components from one year to the next. For Sun Microsystems, the composition of assets in Exhibit 6, illustrated in Figure 2, shifted from net property, plant, and equipment toward other assets, whereas liabilities and stockholders' equity showed a small shift to total liabilities from stockholders' equity. The main conclusion to be drawn from this analysis of Sun Microsystems is that current assets and current liabilities make up a large portion of the company and that the company's financial structure has few long-term liabilities.

Figure 3
Common-Size Income Statements Presented Graphically

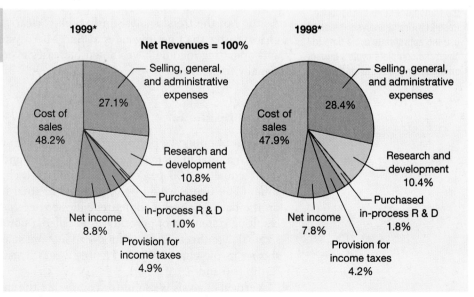

* Rounding causes some additions not to total precisely.
Note: Interest and gains are not presented.

**Sun Microsystems, Inc.
Common-Size Balance Sheets
June 30, 1999 and 1998**

	1999*	1998*
Assets		
Current Assets	72.6%	72.6%
Net Property, Plant, and Equipment	19.1	22.8
Other Assets, Net	8.3	4.6
Total Assets	100.0%	100.0%
Liabilities and Stockholders' Equity		
Current Liabilities	38.3%	37.2%
Deferred Income Taxes and Other Obligations	4.5	1.3
Total Liabilities	42.8%	38.5%
Total Stockholders' Equity	57.2	61.5
Total Liabilities and Stockholders' Equity	100.0%	100.0%

*Amounts do not precisely total 100 percent in all cases due to rounding.
Source: Sun Microsystems, Inc., *Annual Report*, 1999.

**Sun Microsystems, Inc.
Common-Size Income Statements
For the Years Ended June 30, 1999 and 1998**

	1999*	1998*
Net Revenues	100.0%	100.0%
Costs and Expenses		
Cost of Sales	48.2%	47.9%
Research and Development	10.8	10.4
Selling, General and Administrative	27.1	28.9
Purchased In-Process R&D	1.0	1.8
Total Costs and Expenses	87.0%	88.5%
Operating Income	13.0%	11.5%
Interest, Net	.7	.5
Income Before Income Taxes	13.7%	12.0%
Provision for Income Taxes	4.9	4.2
Net Income	8.8%	7.8%

*Rounding causes some additions and subtractions not to total precisely.
Source: Sun Microsystems, Inc., *Annual Report*, 1999.

The common-size income statements in Exhibit 7, illustrated in Figure 3, show that Sun Microsystems reduced its selling, general and administrative expenses from 1998 to 1999 by 1.3 percent of revenues (28.4% − 27.1%). This reduction contributed to an increase in operating income as a percentage of net revenues of 1.5 percent (13.0% − 11.5%).

Parenthetical Note: Common-size statements can be used to compare characteristics of firms reporting in different currencies.

Common-size statements are often used to make comparisons between companies. They allow an analyst to compare the operating and financing characteristics of two companies of different size in the same industry. For example, the analyst might want to compare Sun Microsystems with other companies in terms of percentage of total assets financed by debt or in terms of selling, general, and administrative expenses as a percentage of net revenues. Common-size statements would show those and other relationships.

Ratio Analysis

Ratio analysis is an important way to state meaningful relationships between the components of the financial statements. To be most meaningful, the interpretation of ratios must include a study of the underlying data. Ratios are guides or shortcuts that are useful in evaluating a company's financial position and operations and making comparisons with results in previous years or with other companies. The primary purpose of ratios is to point out areas needing further investigation. They should be used in connection with a general understanding of the company and its environment. Ratios may be expressed in several ways. For example, a ratio of net income of $100,000 to sales of $1,000,000 may be stated as (1) net income is 1/10 or 10 percent of sales; (2) the ratio of sales to net income is 10 to 1 (10:1), or sales are 10 times net income; or (3) for every dollar of sales, the company has an average net income of 10 cents.

Comprehensive Illustration of Ratio Analysis

OBJECTIVE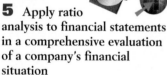
5 Apply ratio analysis to financial statements in a comprehensive evaluation of a company's financial situation

The management's discussion and analysis section of Sun Microsystems' annual report states, "The company's financial condition strengthened as of fiscal 1999 year end when compared with fiscal 1998."[3] To verify this statement, a comprehensive ratio analysis is used to compare Sun Microsystems' performance for the years 1998 and 1999 with regard to the following objectives: (1) liquidity, (2) profitability, (3) long-term solvency, (4) cash flow adequacy, and (5) market strength. Most data for the analyses come from the financial statements presented in Exhibits 3 and 4. Other data are presented as needed.

Evaluating Liquidity

Liquidity is a company's ability to pay bills when they are due and to meet unexpected needs for cash. All the ratios that relate to liquidity involve working capital or some part of it, because it is out of working capital that debts are paid. The objective of liquidity is also closely related to the cash flow ratios.

The liquidity ratios from 1998 to 1999 for Sun Microsystems are presented in Exhibit 8. The **current ratio** and the **quick ratio** are measures of short-term debt-paying ability. The principal difference between the two is that the numerator of

Exhibit 8
Liquidity Ratios of Sun Microsystems, Inc.

(Dollar amounts in thousands)	1999	1998

Current ratio: Measure of short-term debt-paying ability

$$\frac{\text{Current Assets}}{\text{Current Liabilities}} \quad \frac{\$6{,}116{,}350}{\$3{,}226{,}977} = 1.9 \text{ times} \qquad \frac{\$4{,}147{,}525}{\$2{,}122{,}871} = 2.0 \text{ times}$$

Quick ratio: Measure of short-term debt-paying ability

$$\frac{\text{Cash + Marketable}}{\text{Securities + Receivables}} \quad \frac{\$1{,}088{,}972 + \$1{,}576{,}079 + \$2{,}286{,}911}{\$3{,}226{,}977} \qquad \frac{\$822{,}267 + \$476{,}185 + \$1{,}845{,}765}{\$2{,}122{,}871}$$

$$= \frac{\$4{,}951{,}962}{\$3{,}226{,}977} = 1.5 \text{ times} \qquad = \frac{\$3{,}144{,}217}{\$2{,}122{,}871} = 1.5 \text{ times}$$

Receivable turnover: Measure of relative size of accounts receivable balance and effectiveness of credit policies

$$\frac{\text{Net Sales}}{\text{Average Accounts Receivable*}} \quad \frac{\$11{,}726{,}297}{(\$2{,}286{,}911 + \$1{,}845{,}765) \div 2} \qquad \frac{\$9{,}790{,}840}{(\$1{,}845{,}765 + \$1{,}666{,}523) \div 2}$$

$$= \frac{\$11{,}726{,}297}{\$2{,}066{,}338} = 5.7 \text{ times} \qquad = \frac{\$9{,}790{,}840}{\$1{,}756{,}144} = 5.6 \text{ times}$$

Average days' sales uncollected: Measure of average time taken to collect receivables

$$\frac{\text{Days in Year}}{\text{Receivable Turnover}} \quad \frac{365 \text{ days}}{5.7 \text{ times}} = 64.0 \text{ days} \qquad \frac{365 \text{ days}}{5.6 \text{ times}} = 65.2 \text{ days}$$

Inventory turnover: Measure of relative size of inventory

$$\frac{\text{Cost of Goods Sold}}{\text{Average Inventory*}} \quad \frac{\$5{,}648{,}360}{(\$307{,}873 + \$346{,}446) \div 2} \qquad \frac{\$4{,}693{,}336}{(\$346{,}446 + \$437{,}978) \div 2}$$

$$= \frac{\$5{,}648{,}360}{\$327{,}160} = 17.3 \text{ times} \qquad = \frac{\$4{,}693{,}336}{\$392{,}212} = 12.0 \text{ times}$$

Average days' inventory on hand: Measure of average days taken to sell inventory

$$\frac{\text{Days in Year}}{\text{Inventory Turnover}} \quad \frac{365 \text{ days}}{17.3 \text{ times}} = 21.1 \text{ days} \qquad \frac{365 \text{ days}}{12.0 \text{ times}} = 30.4 \text{ days}$$

Payables turnover: Measure of relative size of accounts payable

$$\frac{\text{Cost of Goods Sold +/-}}{\text{Change in Inventory*}} \quad \frac{\$5{,}648{,}360 - \$38{,}573}{(\$753{,}838 + \$495{,}603) \div 2} \qquad \frac{\$4{,}693{,}336 - \$91{,}532}{(\$495{,}603 + \$468{,}912) \div 2}$$
$$\text{Average Accounts Payable*} \quad = 9.0 \text{ times} \qquad = 9.5 \text{ times}$$

Average days' payable: Measure of average days to pay accounts payable

$$\frac{\text{Days in Year}}{\text{Payables Turnover}} \quad = \frac{365 \text{ days}}{9.0 \text{ times}} = 40.6 \text{ days} \qquad = \frac{365 \text{ days}}{9.5 \text{ times}} = 38.3 \text{ days}$$

*1997 figures are derived from the statement of cash flows in Sun Microsystems' annual report.
Source: Sun Microsystems, Inc., *Annual Report*, 1999.

Key Point: When comparing company ratios to published ratios, be aware that publishers often redefine the contents of the ratios. While the general content is similar, variations occur. Be sure to evaluate exactly what information a published source says it uses to calculate its ratios.

the current ratio includes inventories and prepaid expenses. Inventories take longer to convert to cash than do the current assets included in the numerator of the quick ratio. Both ratios remained almost constant from 1998 to 1999. The current ratio was 2.0 times in 1998 and 1.9 times in 1999 and the quick ratio was 1.5 times in both years. The primary reason for the consistent results is that current assets and current liabilities grew at similar rates.

Analysis of two major components of current assets, receivables and inventory, shows improving trends. The relative size of the accounts receivable and the effectiveness of credit policies are measured by the **receivable turnover**, which rose from 5.6 times in 1998 to 5.7 times in 1999. The related ratio of **average days' sales uncollected** decreased by about one day, from 65.2 days in 1998 to 64.0 days in 1999. The major change in this category of ratios is in the inventory turnover. The **inventory turnover**, which measures the relative size of inventories, improved. Inventory turnover increased from 12.0 times in 1998 to 17.3 times in 1999. This results in a favorable decrease in **average days' inventory on hand** from 30.4 days in 1998 to 21.1 days in 1999. When taken together, this means that Sun Microsystems' **operating cycle**, or the time it takes to sell products and collect for them, decreased from 95.6 days in 1998 (65.2 days + 30.4 days) to 85.1 days in 1999 (64.0 days + 21.1 days). Related to the operating cycle is the number of days the company takes to pay its accounts payable. The **payables turnover** decreased from 9.5 times in 1998 to 9.0 times in 1999. This results in average days' payable of 38.3 days in 1998 and 40.6 days in 1999. Thus, if the **average days' payable** is subtracted from the operating cycle, the days of financing required are 97.3 days in 1998 and 44.5 days in 1999, a significant improvement. Overall Sun Microsystems' liquidity remains strong.

Evaluating Profitability

Key Point: Profit often is expressed in many different ways in accounting literature. Examples are income before income taxes, income after income taxes, and net operating income. If students are aware of the content of net income data in profitability ratios, they will draw appropriate conclusions about the results of ratio computation.

The objective of profitability relates to a company's ability to earn a satisfactory income so that investors and stockholders will continue to provide capital to the company. A company's profitability is also closely linked to its liquidity because earnings ultimately produce cash flow. For this reason, evaluating profitability is important to both investors and creditors. The profitability ratios of Sun Microsystems, Inc., are shown in Exhibit 9.

Profit margin, which measures the net income produced by each dollar of sales, increased from 7.8 to 8.8 percent, and **asset turnover**, which measures how efficiently assets are used to produce sales, decreased from 1.9 to 1.7 times. The result is stable overall earning power of the company, or **return on assets**, of 14.7 percent in 1998 and 14.6 percent in 1999. These relationships are illustrated in the computations that follow.

BUSINESS FOCUS ON PRACTICE

Efforts to link management's compensation to the company's performance measures and to the creation of shareholder wealth are increasing. One such measure compares the return on assets to the company's cost of debt and equity capital. If the return on assets exceeds the cost of financing the assets with debt and equity, then management is indeed creating value for the shareholders. Coca-Cola calls this excess *economic profit*. In 1998 Coca-Cola reported economic profits of $2.48 billion with its stock price tracking the growth and decline of these economic profits.

Exhibit 9
Profitability Ratios of Sun Microsystems, Inc.

(Dollar amounts in thousands)	1999	1998

Profit margin: Measure of net income produced by each dollar of sales

$$\frac{\text{Net Income*}}{\text{Net Sales}} \qquad \frac{\$1,031,334}{\$11,726,297} = 8.8\% \qquad \frac{\$762,862}{\$9,790,840} = 7.8\%$$

Asset turnover: Measure of how efficiently assets are used to produce sales

$$\frac{\text{Net Sales}}{\text{Average Total Assets}^\dagger} \qquad \frac{\$11,726,297}{(\$8,420,352 + \$5,711,062) \div 2} \qquad \frac{\$9,790,840}{(\$5,711,062 + \$4,697,274) \div 2}$$

$$= \frac{\$11,726,297}{\$7,065,707} = 1.7 \text{ times} \qquad = \frac{\$9,790,840}{\$5,204,168} = 1.9 \text{ times}$$

Return on assets: Measure of overall earning power or profitability

$$\frac{\text{Net Income}}{\text{Average Total Assets}^\dagger} \qquad \frac{\$1,031,334}{\$7,065,707} = 14.6\% \qquad \frac{\$762,862}{\$5,204,168} = 14.7\%$$

Return on equity: Measure of the profitability of stockholders' investments

$$\frac{\text{Net Income}}{\text{Average Stockholders' Equity}^\dagger} \qquad \frac{\$1,031,334}{(\$4,811,780 + \$3,513,628) \div 2} \qquad \frac{\$762,862}{(\$3,513,628 + \$2,741,937) \div 2}$$

$$= \frac{\$1,031,334}{\$4,162,704} = 24.8\% \qquad = \frac{\$762,862}{\$3,127,783} = 24.4\%$$

*In comparing companies in an industry, some analysts use income before income taxes as the numerator to eliminate the effect of differing tax rates among firms.
†1997 figures are from the eleven-year financial history or the statements of stockholders' equity in Sun Microsystems' annual report.
Source: Sun Microsystems, Inc., *Annual Report,* 1999.

Enrichment Note: In both asset turnover and return on assets, the analysis is improved if only productive assets are used in the calculations. For example, unfinished new plant construction or investments in obsolete or nonoperating plants could be removed from the asset base to give a better picture of the productivity of assets.

Profit Margin		Asset Turnover		Return on Assets
$\dfrac{\text{Net Income}}{\text{Net Sales}}$	×	$\dfrac{\text{Net Sales}}{\text{Average Total Assets}}$	=	$\dfrac{\text{Net Income}}{\text{Average Total Assets}}$
1998 7.8%	×	1.9	=	14.8%
1999 8.8%	×	1.7	=	15.0%

The small difference in the two sets of return on assets figures results from the rounding of the ratios used in the above computation. Finally, the profitability of stockholders' investments, or **return on equity**, was also relatively stable at 24.4 percent in 1998 and 24.8 percent in 1999.

Evaluating Long-Term Solvency

Long-term solvency has to do with a company's ability to survive for many years. The aim of long-term solvency analysis is to detect early signs that a company is on the road to bankruptcy. Studies have indicated that accounting ratios can show as much as five years in advance that a company may fail.[4] Declining profitability and liquidity ratios are key indicators of possible business failure. Two other ratios that analysts often consider when assessing long-term solvency are debt to equity and interest coverage. Long-term solvency ratios are shown in Exhibit 10.

Exhibit 10
Long-Term Solvency Ratios of Sun Microsystems, Inc.

(Dollar amounts in thousands)	1999	1998

Debt to equity ratio: Measure of capital structure and leverage

$$\frac{\text{Total Liabilities}}{\text{Stockholders' Equity}} \qquad \frac{\$3,608,572}{\$4,811,780} = .7 \text{ times} \qquad \frac{\$2,197,434}{\$3,513,628} = .6 \text{ times}$$

Interest coverage ratio: Measure of creditors' protection from default on interest payments

$$\frac{\text{Income Before Income Taxes + Interest Expense}}{\text{Interest Expense}} \qquad \frac{\$1,605,689 + \$675}{\$675} \qquad \frac{\$1,176,166 + \$1,571}{\$1,571}$$
$$= 2,379.8 \text{ times} \qquad = 749.7 \text{ times}$$

Source: Sun Microsystems, Inc., *Annual Report*, 1999.

Key Point: Liquidity is a firm's ability to meet its current obligations, whereas solvency is a firm's ability to meet its maturing obligations as they become due, without losing the ability to continue operations.

Increasing amounts of debt in a company's capital structure mean that the company is becoming more heavily leveraged. This condition negatively affects long-term solvency because it represents increasing legal obligations to pay interest periodically and the principal at maturity. Failure to make those payments can result in bankruptcy. The **debt to equity ratio** measures capital structure and leverage by showing the amount of a company's assets provided by creditors in relation to the amount provided by stockholders. Sun Microsystems' debt to equity ratio was only .6 times in 1998 and .7 times in 1999. It is noteworthy to recall from Exhibit 3 that the company has primarily short-term debt and little long-term debt and that the company has ample current assets as reflected by the current ratio and the quick ratio. All of these are positive factors for the company's long-term solvency. As to the future, "The Company believes the level of financial resources is a significant competitive factor in its industry, and it may choose at any time to raise additional capital through debt or equity financing to strengthen its financial position, facilitate growth, and provide the Company with additional flexibility to take advantage of business opportunities that may arise."[5]

If debt is risky, why have any? The answer is that the level of debt is a matter of balance. Despite its riskiness, debt is a flexible means of financing certain business operations. Sun Microsystems is using debt to finance what management plans to be a temporary increase in inventory. The interest paid on that debt is deductible for income tax purposes, whereas dividends on stock are not. Because debt usually carries a fixed interest charge, the cost of financing can be limited and leverage can be used to advantage. If the company is able to earn a return on assets greater than the cost of interest, it makes an overall profit.[6] However, the company runs the risk of not earning a return on assets equal to the cost of financing those assets, thereby incurring a loss.

Enrichment Note: Because of innovative financing plans and other means of acquiring assets, a beneficial modern-day ratio is the fixed charges ratio. This ratio includes interest, lease payments, and all other fixed obligations that must be met through earnings.

The **interest coverage ratio** measures the degree of protection creditors have from a default on interest payments. Because of its small amount of long-term debt, Sun Microsystems has large interest coverage ratios of 749.7 times in 1998 and 2,379.8 times in 1999. Interest coverage is not a problem for the company.

Evaluating Cash Flow Adequacy

Because cash flows are needed to pay debts when they are due, cash flow measures are closely related to the objectives of liquidity and long-term solvency. Sun Microsystems' cash flow adequacy ratios are presented in Exhibit 11. By all meas-

Exhibit 11
Cash Flow Adequacy Ratios of Sun Microsystems, Inc.

(Dollar amounts in thousands)	1999	1998
Cash flow yield: Measure of a company's ability to generate operating cash flows in relation to net income		

$$\frac{\text{Net Cash Flows from Operating Activities*}}{\text{Net Income}} \qquad \frac{\$2,516,857}{\$1,031,334} = 2.4 \text{ times} \qquad \frac{\$1,526,512}{\$762,862} = 2.0 \text{ times}$$

Cash flows to sales: Measure of the ability of sales to generate operating cash flows

$$\frac{\text{Net Cash Flows from Operating Activities*}}{\text{Net Sales}} \qquad \frac{\$2,516,857}{\$11,726,297} = 21.5\% \qquad \frac{\$1,526,512}{\$9,790,840} = 15.6\%$$

Cash flows to assets: Measure of the ability of assets to generate operating cash flows

$$\frac{\text{Net Cash Flows from Operating Activities*}}{\text{Average Total Assets}^{\dagger}} \qquad \frac{\$2,516,857}{(\$8,420,352 + \$5,711,062) \div 2} \qquad \frac{\$1,526,512}{(\$5,711,062 + \$4,697,274) \div 2}$$

$$= \frac{\$2,516,857}{\$7,065,707} = 35.6\% \qquad = \frac{\$1,526,512}{\$5,204,168} = 29.3\%$$

Free cash flow: Measure of cash generated or cash deficiency after providing for commitments

Net Cash Flows from Operating Activities* − Dividends − Net Capital Expenditures*	$2,516,897 − $0 − $738,707 = $1,778,190	$1,526,512 − $0 − $830,143 = $696,369

*These figures are from the statements of cash flows in Sun Microsystems' annual report.
†The 1997 figure is from the 11-year financial history in Sun Microsystems' annual report.
Source: Sun Microsystems, Inc., *Annual Report*, 1999.

ures, the company's ability to generate positive operating cash flows showed improvement from 1998 to 1999. Key to those increases is the fact that net cash flows from operating activities had a large increase, from $1,526 million in 1998 to $2,517 million in 1999, while net income, net sales, and average total assets increased by lesser percentages. **Cash flow yield**, or the relationship of cash flows from operating activities to net income, increased from 2.0 to 2.4. **Cash flows to sales**, or the ability of sales to generate operating cash flows, increased from 15.6 percent to 21.5 percent. **Cash flows to assets**, or the ability of assets to generate operating cash flows, increased from 29.3 percent to 35.6 percent.

Free cash flow, the cash generated after providing for commitments, also increased and remains very positive primarily because capital expenditures were increased by a smaller amount than the increase in net cash flows from operating activities and because the company pays no dividends. Management's comment with regard to cash flows in the future is, "The Company believes that the liquidity provided by existing cash and short-term investment balances and the borrowing arrangements . . . will provide sufficient capital to meet the Company's capital requirements through fiscal 2000."[7]

Evaluating Market Strength

The market price of a company's stock is of interest to the analyst because it represents what investors as a whole think of the company at a point in time. Market

Exhibit 12
Market Strength Ratios of Sun Microsystems, Inc.

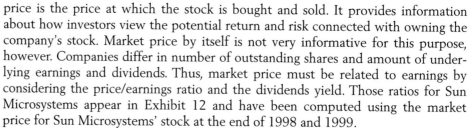

	1999	1998
Price/earnings ratio: **Measure of investor confidence in a company**		
$\dfrac{\text{Market Price per Share*}}{\text{Earnings per Share}}$	$\dfrac{\$68.875}{\$1.27} = 54.2 \text{ times}$	$\dfrac{\$43.4375}{\$.97} = 44.8 \text{ times}$
Dividends yield: **Measure of the current return to an investor in a stock**		
$\dfrac{\text{Dividends per Share}}{\text{Market Price per Share}}$	Sun Microsystems does not pay a dividend.	

*Market price is from Sun Microsystems' annual report.
Source: Sun Microsystems, Inc., *Annual Report,* 1999.

price is the price at which the stock is bought and sold. It provides information about how investors view the potential return and risk connected with owning the company's stock. Market price by itself is not very informative for this purpose, however. Companies differ in number of outstanding shares and amount of underlying earnings and dividends. Thus, market price must be related to earnings by considering the price/earnings ratio and the dividends yield. Those ratios for Sun Microsystems appear in Exhibit 12 and have been computed using the market price for Sun Microsystems' stock at the end of 1998 and 1999.

The **price/earnings (P/E) ratio**, which measures investor confidence in a company, is the ratio of the market price per share to earnings per share. The P/E ratio is useful in comparing the relative values placed on the earnings of different companies and in comparing the value placed on a company's shares in relation to the overall market. With a lower P/E ratio, the investor obtains more underlying earnings per dollar invested. However, Sun Microsystems' P/E ratio increased from 44.8 times in 1998 to 54.2 times in 1999. In effect, investors probably believe that earnings per share will increase in future years. It signals confidence by investors in Sun Microsystems. The **dividends yield** measures a stock's current return to an investor in the form of dividends. Because Sun Microsystems pays no dividend, it may be concluded that investors expect their return from owning the company's stock to come from increases in its market value.

Summary of the Financial Analysis of Sun Microsystems, Inc.

This ratio analysis clearly shows that Sun Microsystems' financial condition is strong, as measured by its liquidity, long-term solvency, and cash flow adequacy ratios. The company's profitability is excellent and was stable from 1998 to 1999, as measured by its profitability ratios. This performance has been rewarded by a higher market price per share.

Chapter Review

1. Describe and discuss the objectives of financial statement analysis. Creditors and investors, as well as managers, use financial statement analysis to judge the past performance and current position of a company, and also to judge its future potential and the risk associated with it. Creditors use the information gained from their analysis to make reliable loans that will be repaid with interest. Investors use the information to make investments that will provide a return that is worth the risk.

2. Describe and discuss the standards for financial statement analysis. Three commonly used standards for financial statement analysis are rule-of-thumb measures, the company's past performance, and industry norms. Rule-of-thumb measures are weak because of the lack of evidence that they can be widely applied. The past performance of a company can offer a guideline for measuring improvement but is not helpful in judging performance relative to other companies. Although the use of industry norms overcomes this last problem, its disadvantage is that firms are not always comparable, even in the same industry.

3. State the sources of information for financial statement analysis. The main sources of information about publicly held corporations are company-published reports, such as annual reports and interim financial statements; SEC reports; business periodicals; and credit and investment advisory services.

4. Apply horizontal analysis, trend analysis, and vertical analysis to financial statements. Horizontal analysis involves the computation of changes in both dollar amounts and percentages from year to year. Trend analysis is an extension of horizontal analysis in that percentage changes are calculated for several years. The changes are usually computed by setting a base year equal to 100 and calculating the results for subsequent years as percentages of that base year. Vertical analysis uses percentages to show the relationship of the component parts to a total in a single statement. The resulting financial statements, which are expressed entirely in percentages, are called common-size statements.

5. Apply ratio analysis to financial statements in a comprehensive evaluation of a company's financial situation. A comprehensive ratio analysis includes the evaluation of a company's liquidity, profitability, long-term solvency, cash flow adequacy, and market strength. The ratios for measuring these characteristics are found in Exhibits 8 to 12.

The following concepts and terms were introduced in this chapter.

LO 5 **Asset turnover:** Net sales divided by average total assets. Used to measure how efficiently assets are used to produce sales.

LO 5 **Average days' inventory on hand:** Days in the year divided by inventory turnover. Shows the average number of days taken to sell inventory.

LO 5 **Average days' payable:** Days in year divided by payables turnover. Used to measure days to pay accounts payable.

LO 5 **Average days' sales uncollected:** Days in the year divided by receivable turnover. Shows the speed at which receivables are turned over—literally, the number of days, on average, that a company must wait to receive payment for credit sales.

LO 4 **Base year:** In financial analysis, the first year to be considered in any set of data.

LO 5   **Cash flows to assets:** Net cash flows from operating activities divided by average total assets. Used to measure the ability of assets to generate operating cash flows.

LO 5   **Cash flows to sales:** Net cash flows from operating activities divided by net sales. Used to measure the ability of sales to generate operating cash flows.

LO 5   **Cash flow yield:** Net cash flows from operating activities divided by net income. Used to measure the ability of a company to generate operating cash flows in relation to net income.

LO 4   **Common-size statement:** A financial statement in which the components of a total figure are stated in terms of percentages of that total.

LO 5   **Current ratio:** Current assets divided by current liabilities. Used as an indicator of a company's liquidity and short-term debt-paying ability.

LO 5   **Debt to equity ratio:** Total liabilities divided by stockholders' equity. Used to measure the relationship of debt financing to equity financing, or the extent to which a company is leveraged.

LO 2   **Diversified companies:** Companies that operate in more than one industry; also called *conglomerates*.

LO 5   **Dividends yield:** Dividends per share divided by market price per share. Used as a measure of the current return to an investor in a stock.

LO 1   **Financial statement analysis:** All the techniques used to show important relationships among amounts in financial statements.

LO 5   **Free cash flow:** Net cash flows from operating activities minus dividends minus net capital expenditures. Used to measure cash generated after providing for commitments.

LO 4   **Horizontal analysis:** A technique for analyzing financial statements that involves the computation of changes in both dollar amounts and percentages from the previous to the current year.

LO 4   **Index number:** In trend analysis, a number from which changes in related items over a period of time are measured. Calculated by setting the base year equal to 100 percent.

LO 5   **Interest coverage ratio:** Income before income taxes plus interest expense divided by interest expense. Used as a measure of the degree of protection creditors have from a default on interest payments.

LO 3   **Interim financial statements:** Financial statements issued for a period of less than one year, usually a quarter or a month.

LO 5   **Inventory turnover:** The cost of goods sold divided by average inventory. Used to measure the relative size of inventory.

LO 5   **Operating cycle:** The time it takes to sell products and collect for them; average days' inventory on hand plus average days' sales uncollected.

LO 5   **Payables turnover:** Cost of goods sold plus or minus change in inventory divided by average accounts payable. Used to measure relative size of accounts payable.

LO 1   **Portfolio:** A group of loans or investments designed to average the returns and risks of a creditor or investor.

LO 5   **Price/earnings (P/E) ratio:** Market price per share divided by earnings per share. Used as a measure of investor confidence in a company and as a means of comparing values among stocks.

LO 5   **Profit margin:** Net income divided by net sales. Used to measure the percentage of each revenue dollar that contributes to net income.

LO 5   **Quick ratio:** The more liquid current assets—cash, marketable securities or short-term investments, and receivables—divided by current liabilities. Used as a measure of short-term debt-paying ability.

LO 4   **Ratio analysis:** A technique of financial analysis in which meaningful relationships are shown between the components of the financial statements.

LO 5   **Receivable turnover:** Net sales divided by average accounts receivable. Used as a measure of the relative size of a company's accounts receivable and the success of its credit and collection policies; shows how many times, on average, receivables were turned into cash during the period.

LO 5   **Return on assets:** Net income divided by average total assets. Used to measure the amount earned on each dollar of assets invested. A measure of overall earning power, or profitability.

LO 5   **Return on equity:** Net income divided by average stockholders' equity. Used to measure how much income was earned on each dollar invested by stockholders.

LO 4   **Trend analysis:** A type of horizontal analysis in which percentage changes are calculated for several successive years instead of for two years.

LO 4   **Vertical analysis:** A technique for analyzing financial statements that uses percentages to show the relationships of the different parts to the total in a single statement.

REVIEW PROBLEM

LO 5

Comparative Analysis of Two Companies

Maggie Washington is considering an investment in one of two fast-food restaurant chains because she believes the trend toward eating out more often will continue. Her choices have been narrowed to Quik Burger and Big Steak, whose balance sheets and income statements appear below and on the next page.

Balance Sheets
December 31, 20xx
(in thousands)

	Quik Burger	Big Steak
Assets		
Cash	$ 2,000	$ 4,500
Accounts Receivable (net)	2,000	6,500
Inventory	2,000	5,000
Property, Plant, and Equipment (net)	20,000	35,000
Other Assets	4,000	5,000
Total Assets	$30,000	$56,000
Liabilities and Stockholders' Equity		
Accounts Payable	$ 2,500	$ 3,000
Notes Payable	1,500	4,000
Bonds Payable	10,000	30,000
Common Stock, $1 par value	1,000	3,000
Paid-in Capital in Excess of Par Value, Common	9,000	9,000
Retained Earnings	6,000	7,000
Total Liabilities and Stockholders' Equity	$30,000	$56,000

Income Statements For the Year Ended December 31, 20xx (in thousands, except per share amounts)		
	Quik Burger	**Big Steak**
Net Sales	$53,000	$86,000
Costs and Expenses		
Cost of Goods Sold	$37,000	$61,000
Selling Expenses	7,000	10,000
Administrative Expenses	4,000	5,000
Total Costs and Expenses	$48,000	$76,000
Income from Operations	$ 5,000	$10,000
Interest Expense	1,400	3,200
Income Before Income Taxes	$ 3,600	$ 6,800
Income Taxes	1,800	3,400
Net Income	$ 1,800	$ 3,400
Earnings per Share	$ 1.80	$ 1.13

The statements of cash flows show that net cash flows from operations were $2,200,000 for Quik Burger and $3,000,000 for Big Steak. Net capital expenditures were $2,100,000 for Quik Burger and $1,800,000 for Big Steak. Dividends of $500,000 were paid by Quik Burger and $600,000 by Big Steak. The market prices of the stocks of Quik Burger and Big Steak were $30 and $20, respectively. Financial information pertaining to prior years is not readily available to Maggie Washington. Assume that all notes payable are current liabilities and that all bonds payable are long-term liabilities.

REQUIRED

Conduct a comprehensive ratio analysis of Quik Burger and Big Steak and compare the results. The analysis should be performed using the following steps (use end-of-year balances for averages, assume no change in inventory, and round all ratios and percentages to one decimal place):

1. Prepare an analysis of liquidity.
2. Prepare an analysis of profitability.
3. Prepare an analysis of long-term solvency.
4. Prepare an analysis of cash flow adequacy.

5. Prepare an analysis of market strength.
6. Indicate in the last column the company that apparently had the more favorable ratio in each case. (Consider differences of .1 or less to be neutral.)
7. In what ways would having access to prior years' information aid this analysis?

ANSWER TO REVIEW PROBLEM

K/R

Ratio Name	Quik Burger	Big Steak	6. Company with More Favorable Ratio*
1. Liquidity analysis			
a. Current ratio	$\dfrac{\$2,000 + \$2,000 + \$2,000}{\$2,500 + \$1,500}$ $= \dfrac{\$6,000}{\$4,000} = 1.5$ times	$\dfrac{\$4,500 + \$6,500 + \$5,000}{\$3,000 + \$4,000}$ $= \dfrac{\$16,000}{\$7,000} = 2.3$ times	Big Steak
b. Quick ratio	$\dfrac{\$2,000 + \$2,000}{\$2,500 + \$1,500}$ $= \dfrac{\$4,000}{\$4,000} = 1.0$ times	$\dfrac{\$4,500 + \$6,500}{\$3,000 + \$4,000}$ $= \dfrac{\$11,000}{\$7,000} = 1.6$ times	Big Steak
c. Receivable turnover	$\dfrac{\$53,000}{\$2,000} = 26.5$ times	$\dfrac{\$86,000}{\$6,500} = 13.2$ times	Quik Burger
d. Average days' sales uncollected	$\dfrac{365}{26.5} = 13.8$ days	$\dfrac{365}{13.2} = 27.7$ days	Quik Burger
e. Inventory turnover	$\dfrac{\$37,000}{\$2,000} = 18.5$ times	$\dfrac{\$61,000}{\$5,000} = 12.2$ times	Quik Burger
f. Average days' inventory on hand	$\dfrac{365}{18.5} = 19.7$ days	$\dfrac{365}{12.2} = 29.9$ days	Quik Burger
g. Payables turnover	$\dfrac{\$37,000 + 0}{\$2,500} = 14.8$ times	$\dfrac{\$61,000 + 0}{\$3,000} = 20.3$ times	Big Steak
h. Average days' payable	$\dfrac{365}{14.8} = 24.7$ days	$\dfrac{365}{20.3} = 18.0$ days	Big Steak
2. Profitability analysis			
a. Profit margin	$\dfrac{\$1,800}{\$53,000} = 3.4\%$	$\dfrac{\$3,400}{\$86,000} = 4.0\%$	Big Steak
b. Asset turnover	$\dfrac{\$53,000}{\$30,000} = 1.8$ times	$\dfrac{\$86,000}{\$56,000} = 1.5$ times	Quik Burger
c. Return on assets	$\dfrac{\$1,800}{\$30,000} = 6.0\%$	$\dfrac{\$3,400}{\$56,000} = 6.1\%$	Neutral
d. Return on equity	$\dfrac{\$1,800}{\$1,000 + \$9,000 + \$6,000}$ $= \dfrac{\$1,800}{\$16,000} = 11.3\%$	$\dfrac{\$3,400}{\$3,000 + \$9,000 + \$7,000}$ $= \dfrac{\$3,400}{\$19,000} = 17.9\%$	Big Steak

*This analysis indicates the company with the apparently more favorable ratio. Class discussion may focus on conditions under which different conclusions may be drawn.

Ratio Name	Quik Burger	Big Steak	6. Company with More Favorable Ratio*
3. Long-term solvency analysis			
a. Debt to equity ratio	$\dfrac{\$2,500 + \$1,500 + \$10,000}{\$1,000 + \$9,000 + \$6,000}$ $= \dfrac{\$14,000}{\$16,000} = .9$ times	$\dfrac{\$3,000 + \$4,000 + \$30,000}{\$3,000 + \$9,000 + \$7,000}$ $= \dfrac{\$37,000}{\$19,000} = 1.9$ times	Quik Burger
b. Interest coverage ratio	$\dfrac{\$3,600 + \$1,400}{\$1,400}$ $= \dfrac{\$5,000}{\$1,400} = 3.6$ times	$\dfrac{\$6,800 + \$3,200}{\$3,200}$ $= \dfrac{\$10,000}{\$3,200} = 3.1$ times	Quik Burger
4. Cash flow adequacy analysis			
a. Cash flow yield	$\dfrac{\$2,200}{\$1,800} = 1.2$ times	$\dfrac{\$3,000}{\$3,400} = .9$ times	Quik Burger
b. Cash flows to sales	$\dfrac{\$2,200}{\$53,000} = 4.2\%$	$\dfrac{\$3,000}{\$86,000} = 3.5\%$	Quik Burger
c. Cash flows to assets	$\dfrac{\$2,200}{\$30,000} = 7.3\%$	$\dfrac{\$3,000}{\$56,000} = 5.4\%$	Quik Burger
d. Free cash flow	$\$2,200 - \$500 - \$2,100$ $= (400)$	$\$3,000 - \$600 - \$1,800$ $= \$600$	Big Steak
5. Market strength analysis			
a. Price/earnings ratio	$\dfrac{\$30}{\$1.80} = 16.7$ times	$\dfrac{\$20}{\$1.13} = 17.7$ times	Big Steak
b. Dividends yield	$\dfrac{\$500,000/1,000,000}{\$30} = 1.7\%$	$\dfrac{\$600,000/3,000,000}{\$20} = 1.0\%$	Quik Burger

*This analysis indicates the company with the apparently more favorable ratio. Class discussion may focus on conditions under which different conclusions may be drawn.

7. **Usefulness of prior years' information**
   Prior years' information would be helpful in two ways. First, turnover, return, and cash flows to assets ratios could be based on average amounts. Second, a trend analysis could be performed for each company.

Chapter Assignments

BUILDING YOUR KNOWLEDGE FOUNDATION

QUESTIONS

1. What are the differences and similarities in the objectives of investors and creditors in using financial statement analysis?
2. What role does risk play in making loans and investments?
3. What standards of comparison are commonly used to evaluate financial statements, and what are their relative merits?
4. Why would a financial analyst compare the ratios of Steelco, a steel company, with the ratios of other companies in the steel industry? What factors might invalidate such a comparison?

5. Where may an investor look for information about a publicly held company in which he or she is thinking of investing?

6. Why would an investor want to see both horizontal and trend analyses of a company's financial statements?

7. What does the following sentence mean: "Based on 1990 equaling 100, net income increased from 240 in 1997 to 260 in 1998"?

8. What is the difference between horizontal and vertical analysis?

9. What is the purpose of ratio analysis?

10. Under what circumstances would a current ratio of 3:1 be good? Under what circumstances would it be bad?

11. In a period of high interest rates, why are receivable turnover and inventory turnover especially important?

12. The following statements were made on page 35 of the November 6, 1978, issue of *Fortune* magazine: "Supermarket executives are beginning to look back with some nostalgia on the days when the standard profit margin was 1 percent of sales. Last year the industry overall margin came to a thin 0.72 percent." How could a supermarket earn a satisfactory return on assets with such a small profit margin?

13. Company A and Company B both have net incomes of $1,000,000. Is it possible to say that these companies are equally successful? Why or why not?

14. Circo Company has a return on assets of 12 percent and a debt to equity ratio of .5. Would you expect return on equity to be more or less than 12 percent?

15. What amount is common to all cash flow adequacy ratios? To what other groups of ratios are the cash flow adequacy ratios most closely related?

16. The market price of Company J's stock is the same as that of Company Q's. How might you determine whether investors are equally confident about the future of these companies?

SHORT EXERCISES

SE 1.

LO 1   Objectives and Standards
LO 2   of Financial Statement
**   Analysis**

Indicate whether each of the following items is (a) an objective or (b) a standard of comparison of financial statement analysis.

1. Industry norms
2. Assessment of the company's past performance
3. The company's past performance
4. Assessment of future potential and related risk
5. Rule-of-thumb measures

SE 2.

LO 3   Sources of Information

For each piece of information listed below, indicate whether the *best* source would be (a) reports published by the company, (b) SEC reports, (c) business periodicals, or (d) credit and investment advisory services.

1. Current market value of a company's stock
2. Management's analysis of the past year's operations
3. Objective assessment of a company's financial performance
4. Most complete body of financial disclosures
5. Current events affecting the company

SE 3.

LO 4   Trend Analysis

Using 2000 as the base year, prepare a trend analysis for the following data, and tell whether the results suggest a favorable or unfavorable trend. (Round your answers to one decimal place.)

	20x2	20x1	20x0
Net sales	$158,000	$136,000	$112,000
Accounts receivable (net)	43,000	32,000	21,000

LO 4 **Horizontal Analysis**

SE 4. Compute the amount and percentage changes for the income statements that appear below, and comment on the changes from 20x0 to 20x1. (Round the percentage changes to one decimal place.)

	20x1	20x0
SiteWorks, Inc. Comparative Income Statements For the Years Ended December 31, 20x1 and 20x0		
Net Sales	$180,000	$145,000
Cost of Goods Sold	112,000	88,000
Gross Margin	$ 68,000	$ 57,000
Operating Expenses	40,000	30,000
Operating Income	$ 28,000	$ 27,000
Interest Expense	7,000	5,000
Income Before Income Taxes	$ 21,000	$ 22,000
Income Taxes	7,000	8,000
Net Income	$ 14,000	$ 14,000
Earnings per Share	$ 1.40	$ 1.40

LO 4 **Vertical Analysis**

SE 5. Express the comparative balance sheets that follow as common-size statements, and comment on the changes from 20x0 to 20x1. (Round computations to one decimal place.)

	20x1	20x0
SiteWorks, Inc. Comparative Balance Sheets December 31, 20x1 and 20x0		
Assets		
Current Assets	$ 24,000	$ 20,000
Property, Plant, and Equipment (net)	130,000	100,000
Total Assets	$154,000	$120,000
Liabilities and Stockholders' Equity		
Current Liabilities	$ 18,000	$ 22,000
Long-Term Liabilities	90,000	60,000
Stockholders' Equity	46,000	38,000
Total Liabilities and Stockholders' Equity	$154,000	$120,000

LO 5 **Liquidity Analysis**

SE 6. Using the information for SiteWorks, Inc., in SE 4 and SE 5, compute the current ratio, quick ratio, receivable turnover, average days' sales uncollected, inventory turnover, average days' inventory on hand, payables turnover, and average days' payable for 20x0 and 20x1. Inventories were $4,000 in 19x9, $5,000 in 20x0, and $7,000 in 20x1. Accounts Receivable were $6,000 in 19x9, $8,000 in 20x0, and $10,000 in 20x1. Accounts Payable were $9,000 in 19x9, $10,000 in 20x0, and $12,000 in 20x1. There were no marketable securities or prepaid assets. Comment on the results. (Round computations to one decimal place.)

SE 7.
LO 5 Profitability Analysis

Using the information for SiteWorks, Inc., in **SE 4** and **SE 5**, compute the profit margin, asset turnover, return on assets, and return on equity for 20x0 and 20x1. In 19x9, total assets were $100,000 and total stockholders' equity was $30,000. Comment on the results. (Round computations to one decimal place.)

SE 8.
LO 5 Long-Term Solvency Analysis

Using the information for SiteWorks, Inc., in **SE 4** and **SE 5**, compute the debt to equity and interest coverage ratios for 20x0 and 20x1. Comment on the results. (Round computations to one decimal place.)

SE 9.
LO 5 Cash Flow Adequacy Analysis

Using the information for SiteWorks, Inc., in **SE 4, SE 5,** and **SE 7,** compute the cash flow yield, cash flows to sales, cash flows to assets, and free cash flow for 20x0 and 20x1. Net cash flows from operating activities were $21,000 in 20x0 and $16,000 in 20x1. Net capital expenditures were $30,000 in 20x0 and $40,000 in 20x1. Cash dividends were $6,000 in both years. Comment on the results. (Round computations to one decimal place.)

SE 10.
LO 5 Market Strength Analysis

Using the information for SiteWorks, Inc., in **SE 4, SE 5,** and **SE 9,** compute the price/earnings and dividends yield ratios for 20x0 and 20x1. The company had 10,000 shares of common stock outstanding in both years. The price of SiteWorks' common stock was $30 in 20x0 and $20 in 20x1. Comment on the results. (Round computations to one decimal place.)

EXERCISES

E 1.
LO 1 Objectives, Standards,
LO 2 and Sources of
LO 3 Information for Financial
Statement Analysis

Identify each of the following as (a) an objective of financial statement analysis, (b) a standard for financial statement analysis, or (c) a source of information for financial statement analysis:

1. Average ratios of other companies in the same industry
2. Assessment of the future potential of an investment
3. Interim financial statements

4. Past ratios of the company
5. SEC Form 10-K
6. Assessment of risk
7. A company's annual report

E 2.
LO 4 Horizontal Analysis

Compute the amount and percentage changes for the following balance sheets, and comment on the changes from 20x1 to 20x2. (Round the percentage changes to one decimal place.)

Fodor Company Comparative Balance Sheets December 31, 20x2 and 20x1		
	20x2	20x1
Assets		
Current Assets	$ 37,200	$ 25,600
Property, Plant, and Equipment (net)	218,928	194,400
Total Assets	$256,128	$220,000
Liabilities and Stockholders' Equity		
Current Liabilities	$ 22,400	$ 6,400
Long-Term Liabilities	70,000	80,000
Stockholders' Equity	163,728	133,600
Total Liabilities and Stockholders' Equity	$256,128	$220,000

LO 4   Trend Analysis

E 3. Using 20x1 as the base year, prepare a trend analysis of the following data, and tell whether the situation shown by the trends is favorable or unfavorable. (Round your answers to one decimal place.)

	20x5	20x4	20x3	20x2	20x1
Net sales	$25,520	$23,980	$24,200	$22,880	$22,000
Cost of goods sold	17,220	15,400	15,540	14,700	14,000
General and administrative expenses	5,280	5,184	5,088	4,896	4,800
Operating income	3,020	3,396	3,572	3,284	3,200

LO 4   Vertical Analysis

E 4. Express the comparative income statements that follow as common-size statements, and comment on the changes from 20x1 to 20x2. (Round computations to one decimal place.)

Fodor Company Comparative Income Statements For the Years Ended December 31, 20x2 and 20x1		
	20x2	**20x1**
Net Sales	$424,000	$368,000
Cost of Goods Sold	254,400	239,200
Gross Margin	$169,600	$128,800
Selling Expenses	$106,000	$ 73,600
General Expenses	50,880	36,800
Total Operating Expenses	$156,880	$110,400
Net Operating Income	$ 12,720	$ 18,400

LO 5   Liquidity Analysis

E 5. Partial comparative balance sheet and income statement information for Road Company follows.

	20x2	20x1
Cash	$ 6,800	$ 5,200
Marketable Securities	3,600	8,600
Accounts Receivable (net)	22,400	17,800
Inventory	27,200	24,800
Total Current Assets	$ 60,000	$ 56,400
Accounts Payable	$ 20,000	$ 14,100
Net Sales	$161,280	$110,360
Cost of Goods Sold	108,800	101,680
Gross Margin	$ 52,480	$ 8,680

The year-end balances for Accounts Receivable and Inventory were $16,200 and $25,600, respectively, in 20x0. Accounts Payable was $15,300 in 20x0 and is the only current liability. Compute the current ratio, quick ratio, receivable turnover, average days' sales uncollected, inventory turnover, average days' inventory on hand, payables turnover, and average days' payable for each year. (Round computations to one decimal place.) Comment on the change in the company's liquidity position including operating cycle and required days of financing from 20x1 to 20x2.

E 6.
LO 5 Turnover Analysis

Davis FormalWear Shop has been in business for four years. Because the company has recently had a cash flow problem, management wonders whether there is a problem with receivables or inventories. Here are selected figures from the company's financial statements (in thousands):

	20x4	20x3	20x2	20x1
Net sales	$288	$224	$192	$160
Cost of goods sold	180	144	120	96
Accounts receivable (net)	48	40	32	24
Merchandise inventory	56	44	32	20
Accounts payable	25	20	15	10

Compute receivable turnover, inventory turnover, and payables turnover for each of the four years, and comment on the results relative to the cash flow problem that Davis Formal Wear Shop has been experiencing. Merchandise inventory was $22,000, accounts receivable was $22,000 and accounts payable was $8,000 in 20x0. Round computations to one decimal place.

E 7.
LO 5 Profitability Analysis

At year end, Jareau Company had total assets of $640,000 in 20x0, $680,000 in 20x1, and $760,000 in 20x2. Its debt to equity ratio was .67 in all three years. In 20x1, the company had net income of $77,112 on revenues of $1,224,000. In 20x2, the company had net income of $98,952 on revenues of $1,596,000. Compute the profit margin, asset turnover, return on assets, and return on equity for 20x1 and 20x2. Comment on the apparent cause of the increase or decrease in profitability. (Round the percentages and other ratios to one decimal place.)

E 8.
LO 5 Long-Term Solvency and Market Strength Ratios

An investor is considering investing in the long-term bonds and common stock of Companies F and G. Both companies operate in the same industry. In addition, both companies pay a dividend per share of $4, and a yield of 10 percent on their long-term bonds. Other data for the two companies follow:

	Company F	Company G
Total assets	$2,400,000	$1,080,000
Total liabilities	1,080,000	594,000
Income before income taxes	288,000	129,600
Interest expense	97,200	53,460
Earnings per share	3.20	5.00
Market price of common stock	40	47.50

Compute the debt to equity, interest coverage, price/earnings (P/E), and dividends yield ratios, and comment on the results. (Round computations to one decimal place.)

E 9.
LO 5 Cash Flow Adequacy Analysis

Using the data below, taken from the financial statements of Wong, Inc., compute the cash flow yield, cash flows to sales, cash flows to assets, and free cash flow. (Round computations to one decimal place.)

Net sales	$6,400,000
Net income	704,000
Net cash flows from operating activities	912,000
Total assets, beginning of year	5,780,000
Total assets, end of year	6,240,000
Cash dividends	240,000
Net capital expenditures	596,000

PROBLEMS

LO 4 **Horizontal and Vertical Analysis**

P 1. The condensed comparative income statements and balance sheets of Sanborn Corporation follow. All figures are given in thousands of dollars.

	Sanborn Corporation Comparative Income Statements For the Years Ended December 31, 20x2 and 20x1	
	20x2	**20x1**
Net Sales	$3,276,800	$3,146,400
Cost of Goods Sold	2,088,800	2,008,400
Gross Margin	$1,188,000	$1,138,000
Operating Expenses		
Selling Expenses	$ 476,800	$ 518,000
Administrative Expenses	447,200	423,200
Total Operating Expenses	$ 924,000	$ 941,200
Income from Operations	$ 264,000	$ 196,800
Interest Expense	65,600	39,200
Income Before Income Taxes	$ 198,400	$ 157,600
Income Taxes	62,400	56,800
Net Income	$ 136,000	$ 100,800
Earnings per Share	$ 3.40	$ 2.52

	Sanborn Corporation Comparative Balance Sheets December 31, 20x2 and 20x1	
	20x2	**20x1**
Assets		
Cash	$ 81,200	$ 40,800
Accounts Receivable (net)	235,600	229,200
Inventory	574,800	594,800
Property, Plant, and Equipment (net)	750,000	720,000
Total Assets	$1,641,600	$1,584,800
Liabilities and Stockholders' Equity		
Accounts Payable	$ 267,600	$ 477,200
Notes Payable (short-term)	200,000	400,000
Bonds Payable	400,000	—
Common Stock, $10 par value	400,000	400,000
Retained Earnings	374,000	307,600
Total Liabilities and Stockholders' Equity	$1,641,600	$1,584,800

Perform the following analyses. Round all ratios and percentages to one decimal place.

1. Prepare schedules showing the amount and percentage changes from 20x1 to 20x2 for Sanborn's comparative income statements and balance sheets.

2. Prepare common-size income statements and balance sheets for 20x1 and 20x2.

3. Comment on the results in **1** and **2** by identifying favorable and unfavorable changes in the components and composition of the statements.

P 2.

LO 5 **Analyzing the Effects of Transactions on Ratios**

Koz Corporation engaged in the transactions listed in the first column of the following table. Opposite each transaction is a ratio and space to indicate the effect of each transaction on the ratio.

Transaction	Ratio	Effect Increase	Effect Decrease	Effect None
a. Sold merchandise on account.	Current ratio			
b. Sold merchandise on account.	Inventory turnover			
c. Collected on accounts receivable.	Quick ratio			
d. Wrote off an uncollectible account.	Receivable turnover			
e. Paid on accounts payable.	Current ratio			
f. Declared cash dividend.	Return on equity			
g. Incurred advertising expense.	Profit margin			
h. Issued stock dividend.	Debt to equity ratio			
i. Issued bond payable.	Asset turnover			
j. Accrued interest expense.	Current ratio			
k. Paid previously declared cash dividend.	Dividends yield			
l. Purchased treasury stock.	Return on assets			
m. Recorded depreciation expense.	Cash flow yield			

Place an X in the appropriate column to show whether the transaction increased, decreased, or had no effect on the indicated ratio.

P 3.

LO 5 **Ratio Analysis**

Additional data (in thousands of dollars) for Sanborn Corporation in 20x2 and 20x1 follow. This information should be used in conjunction with the data in **P 1.**

	20x2	20x1
Net cash flows from operating activities	($196,000)	$144,000
Net capital expenditures	$40,000	$65,000
Dividends paid	$44,000	$34,400
Number of common shares	40,000,000	40,000,000
Market price per share	$18	$30

Selected balances (in thousands of dollars) at the end of 20x0 were Accounts Receivable (net), $206,800; Inventory, $547,200; Total Assets, $1,465,600; Accounts Payable, $386,600; and Stockholders' Equity, $641,200. All of Sanborn's notes payable were current liabilities; all of the bonds payable were long-term liabilities.

Perform the following analyses. Round all answers to one decimal place, and consider changes of .1 or less to be neutral. After making the calculations, indicate whether each ratio improved or deteriorated from 20x1 to 20x2 by writing *F* for favorable or *U* for unfavorable.

1. Prepare a liquidity analysis by calculating for each year the (a) current ratio, (b) quick ratio, (c) receivable turnover, (d) average days' sales uncollected, (e) inventory turnover, (f) average days' inventory on hand, (g) payables turnover, and (h) average days' payable.

2. Prepare a profitability analysis by calculating for each year the (a) profit margin, (b) asset turnover, (c) return on assets, and (d) return on equity.

3. Prepare a long-term solvency analysis by calculating for each year the (a) debt to equity ratio and (b) interest coverage ratio.

4. Prepare a cash flow adequacy analysis by calculating for each year the (a) cash flow yield, (b) cash flows to sales, (c) cash flows to assets, and (d) free cash flow.

5. Prepare a market strength analysis by calculating for each year the (a) price/earnings ratio and (b) dividends yield.

P 4.

LO 5   Comprehensive Ratio Analysis of Two Companies

Ginger Adair is considering an investment in the common stock of a chain of retail department stores. She has narrowed her choice to two retail companies, Lewis Corporation and Ramsey Corporation, whose income statements and balance sheets are shown below and at the top of the next page. During the year, Lewis Corporation paid a total of $100,000 in dividends. The market price per share of its stock is currently $60. In comparison, Ramsey Corporation paid a total of $228,000 in dividends, and the current market price of its stock is $76 per share. Lewis Corporation had net cash flows from operations of $543,000 and net capital expenditures of $1,250,000. Ramsey Corporation had net cash flows from operations of $985,000 and net capital expenditures of $2,100,000. Information for prior years is not readily available. Assume that all notes payable are current liabilities and all bonds payable are long-term liabilities and that there is no change in inventory.

	Lewis Corporation	Ramsey Corporation
Assets		
Cash	$ 160,000	$ 384,800
Marketable Securities	406,800	169,200
Accounts Receivable (net)	1,105,600	1,970,800
Inventories	1,259,600	2,506,800
Prepaid Expenses	108,800	228,000
Property, Plant, and Equipment (net)	5,827,200	13,104,000
Intangibles and Other Assets	1,106,400	289,600
Total Assets	$9,974,400	$18,653,200
Liabilities and Stockholders' Equity		
Accounts Payable	$ 688,000	$ 1,145,200
Notes Payable	300,000	800,000
Income Taxes Payable	100,400	146,800
Bonds Payable	4,000,000	4,000,000
Common Stock, $20 par value	2,000,000	1,200,000
Paid-in Capital in Excess of Par Value, Common	1,219,600	7,137,200
Retained Earnings	1,666,400	4,224,000
Total Liabilities and Stockholders' Equity	$9,974,400	$18,653,200

REQUIRED

Conduct a comprehensive ratio analysis for each company, using the available information. Compare the results. Round percentages and ratios to one decimal place, and consider changes of .1 or less to be indeterminate.

1. Prepare an analysis of liquidity by calculating for each company the (a) current ratio, (b) quick ratio, (c) receivable turnover, (d) average days' sales uncollected, (e) inventory turnover, (f) average days' inventory on hand, (g) payables turnover, and (h) average days' payable.

	Lewis Corporation	Ramsey Corporation
Net Sales	$25,120,000	$50,420,000
Costs and Expenses		
Cost of Goods Sold	$12,284,000	$29,668,000
Selling Expenses	9,645,200	14,216,400
Administrative Expenses	1,972,000	4,868,000
Total Costs and Expenses	$23,901,200	$48,752,400
Income from Operations	$ 1,218,800	$ 1,667,600
Interest Expense	388,000	456,000
Income Before Income Taxes	$ 830,800	$ 1,211,600
Income Taxes	400,000	600,000
Net Income	$ 430,800	$ 611,600
Earnings per Share	$ 4.31	$ 10.19

2. Prepare an analysis of profitability by calculating for each company the (a) profit margin, (b) asset turnover, (c) return on assets, and (d) return on equity.

3. Prepare an analysis of long-term solvency by calculating for each company the (a) debt to equity ratio and (b) interest coverage ratio.

4. Prepare an analysis of cash flow adequacy by calculating for each company the (a) cash flow yield, (b) cash flows to sales, (c) cash flows to assets, and (d) free cash flow.

5. Prepare an analysis of market strength by calculating for each company the (a) price/earnings ratio and (b) dividends yield.

6. Indicate in the right-hand column which company had the more favorable ratio in each case.

7. How could the analysis be improved if information from prior years were available?

ALTERNATE PROBLEMS

P 5.

LO 5   Analyzing the Effects of Transactions on Ratios

Benson Corporation, a clothing retailer, engaged in the transactions listed in the first column of the table below. Opposite each transaction is a ratio and space to mark the effect of each transaction on the ratio.

		Effect		
Transaction	Ratio	Increase	Decrease	None
a. Issued common stock for cash.	Asset turnover			
b. Declared cash dividend.	Current ratio			
c. Sold treasury stock.	Return on equity			
d. Borrowed cash by issuing note payable.	Debt to equity ratio			
e. Paid salaries expense.	Inventory turnover			
f. Purchased merchandise for cash.	Current ratio			
g. Sold equipment for cash.	Receivable turnover			
h. Sold merchandise on account.	Quick ratio			
i. Paid current portion of long-term debt.	Return on assets			
j. Gave sales discount.	Profit margin			
k. Purchased marketable securities for cash.	Quick ratio			
l. Declared 5% stock dividend.	Current ratio			
m. Purchased a building.	Free cash flow			

Place an *X* in the appropriate column to show whether the transaction increased, decreased, or had no effect on the indicated ratio.

LO 5   Ratio Analysis

P 6. The condensed comparative income statements and balance sheets of Basie Corporation appear below. All figures are given in thousands of dollars, except earnings per share.

Basie Corporation Comparative Income Statements For the Years Ended December 31, 20x2 and 20x1		
	20x2	**20x1**
Net Sales	$800,400	$742,600
Cost of Goods Sold	454,100	396,200
Gross Margin	$346,300	$346,400
Operating Expenses		
Selling Expenses	$130,100	$104,600
Administrative Expenses	140,300	115,500
Total Operating Expenses	$270,400	$220,100
Income from Operations	$ 75,900	$126,300
Interest Expense	25,000	20,000
Income Before Income Taxes	$ 50,900	$106,300
Income Taxes	14,000	35,000
Net Income	$ 36,900	$ 71,300
Earnings per Share	$ 1.23	$ 2.38

Basie Corporation Comparative Balance Sheets December 31, 20x2 and 20x1		
	20x2	**20x1**
Assets		
Cash	$ 31,100	$ 27,200
Accounts Receivable (net)	72,500	42,700
Inventory	122,600	107,800
Property, Plant, and Equipment (net)	577,700	507,500
Total Assets	$803,900	$685,200
Liabilities and Stockholders' Equity		
Accounts Payable	$104,700	$ 72,300
Notes Payable (due in less than one year)	50,000	50,000
Bonds Payable	200,000	110,000
Common Stock—$10 par value	300,000	300,000
Retained Earnings	149,200	152,900
Total Liabilities and Stockholders' Equity	$803,900	$685,200

Additional data for Basie Corporation in 20x2 and 20x1 follow.

	20x2	20x1
Net Cash Flows from Operating Activities	$64,000	$99,000
Net Capital Expenditures	$119,000	$38,000
Dividends Paid	$31,400	$35,000
Number of Common Shares	30,000	30,000
Market Price per Share	$40	$60

Balances of selected accounts at the end of 20x0 were Accounts Receivable (net), $52,700; Inventory, $99,400; Accounts Payable, $64,800; Total Assets, $647,800; and Stockholders' Equity, $376,600. All of the bonds payable were long-term liabilities.

REQUIRED

Perform the following analyses. Round percentages and ratios to one decimal place, and consider changes of .1 or less to be neutral. After making the calculations, indicate whether each ratio had a favorable (F) or unfavorable (U) change from 20x1 to 20x2.

1. Conduct a liquidity analysis by calculating for each year the (a) current ratio, (b) quick ratio, (c) receivable turnover, (d) average days' sales uncollected, (e) inventory turnover, (f) average days' inventory on hand, (g) payables turnover, and (h) average days' payable.

2. Conduct a profitability analysis by calculating for each year the (a) profit margin, (b) asset turnover, (c) return on assets, and (d) return on equity.

3. Conduct a long-term solvency analysis by calculating for each year the (a) debt to equity ratio and (b) interest coverage ratio.

4. Conduct a cash flow adequacy analysis by calculating for each year the (a) cash flow yield, (b) cash flows to sales, (c) cash flows to assets, and (d) free cash flow.

5. Conduct a market strength analysis by calculating for each year the (a) price/earnings ratio and (b) dividends yield.

EXPANDING YOUR CRITICAL THINKING, COMMUNICATION, AND INTERPERSONAL SKILLS

SKILLS DEVELOPMENT

Conceptual Analysis

SD 1.

LO 2 **Standards for Financial**
LO 5 **Analysis**

Helene Curtis, a well-known, publicly owned corporation, became a take-over candidate and sold out in the 1990s after years of poor profit performance. "By almost any standard, Chicago-based Helene Curtis rates as one of America's worst-managed personal care companies. In recent years its return on equity has hovered between 10% and 13%, well below the industry average of 18% to 19%. Net profit margins of 2% to 3% are half that of competitors. . . . As a result, while leading names like Revlon and Avon are trading at three and four times book value, Curtis trades at less than two-thirds book value."[8] Considering that many companies in other industries are happy with a return on equity of 10 percent to 13 percent, why is this analysis so critical of Curtis's performance? Assuming that Curtis could double its profit margin, what other

| Cash Flow | CD-ROM | Communication | Critical Thinking | Ethics | General Ledger | Group Activity | Hot Links to Real Companies | International | Internet | Key Ratio | Memo | Spreadsheet |

information would be necessary to project the resulting return on stockholders' investment? Why are Revlon's and Avon's stocks trading for more than Curtis's? Be prepared to discuss your answers to these questions in class.

SD 2.
LO 3   Using Segment Information

Refer to Exhibit 1, which shows the segment information of **Goodyear Tire & Rubber Company.** In what business segments does Goodyear operate? What is the relative size of the business segments in terms of sales and total segment income in the most recent year? Which segment is most profitable in terms of the performance measure return on assets? In the tires segment, which region of the world is largest and which is most profitable in terms of return on assets?

SD 3.
LO 3   Use of Investors Service

Refer to Exhibit 2, which contains the **PepsiCo Inc.,** listing in Moody's *Handbook of Dividend Achievers.* Assume that an investor has asked you to assess PepsiCo's recent history and prospects. Write a memorandum to the investor that addresses the following points:

1. PepsiCo's earnings history. (What generally has been the relationship between PepsiCo's return on assets and its return on equity over the years 1989 to 1998? What does this tell you about the way the company is financed? What figures back up your conclusion?)

2. The trend of PepsiCo's stock price and price/earnings ratio for the ten years shown.

3. PepsiCo's prospects, including developments that are likely to affect the future of the company.

Ethical Dilemma

SD 4.
LO 3   Management of Earnings

Management of most companies is very sensitive to the fact that analysts watch key performance measures such as meeting earnings targets. A slight weakening of analysts' confidence can severely affect the price of a company's stock. The Securities and Exchange Commission (SEC) has been cracking down on the management of earnings to achieve financial goals by targeting companies for review. For instance, the SEC filed a complaint against **W. R. Grace & Co.** for releasing $1.5 million from reserves into earnings in order to meet earnings targets. Grace officials say that the amount is immaterial and that it is in accord with accounting rules to book an immaterial item. (It was about 1.5 percent of net income.) The SEC, on the other hand, argues that it is a matter of principle: "Does anyone think that it's acceptable to intentionally book an error for the purpose of making earnings targets?" But some think such action on the part of the SEC will harm confidence in the companies.[9] Do you think it is unethical for a company's management to increase earnings periodically through the use of one-time transactions, such as adjustments of reserves or sale of assets, on which it has a profit?

Research Activity

SD 5.
LO 3   Use of Investors Services

Find *Moody's Investors Service* or *Standard & Poor's Industry Guide* in your library. Locate the reports on three corporations. You may choose the corporations at random or choose them from the same industry, if directed to do so by your instructor. (If you did a related exercise in a previous chapter, use the same three companies.) Write a summary of what you learned about each company's financial performance, including what measures of performance were mentioned in the write-ups, and its prospects for the future, and be prepared to discuss your findings in class.

Decision-Making Practice

SD 6.
LO 4   Effect of One-Time Item
LO 5   on Loan Decision

Apple a Day, Inc., and *Unforgettable Edibles, Inc.,* both operate food catering businesses in the metropolitan area. Their customers include *Fortune* 500 companies, regional firms, and individuals. The two firms reported similar profit margins for the current year, and both determine bonuses for managers based on reaching a target profit margin and return on equity. Each firm has submitted a loan request to you as a loan officer for City National Bank.

	Apple a Day	Unforgettable Edibles
Net Sales	$625,348	$717,900
Cost of Goods Sold	225,125	287,080
Gross Margin	$400,223	$430,820
Operating Expenses	281,300	371,565
Operating Income	$118,923	$ 59,255
Gain on Sale of Real Estate		81,923
Interest Expense	(9,333)	(15,338)
Income Before Income Taxes	$109,590	$125,840
Income Taxes	25,990	29,525
Net Income	$ 83,600	$ 96,315
Average Stockholders' Equity	$312,700	$390,560

1. Perform a vertical analysis and prepare a common-size income statement for each firm. Compute profit margin and return on equity.

2. Discuss these results, the bonus plan for management, and loan considerations. Make a recommendation as to which company is a better risk for receiving the loan.

FINANCIAL REPORTING AND ANALYSIS

Interpreting Financial Reports

FRA 1.

LO 4 Trend Analysis

H. J. Heinz Company is a global company engaged in several lines of business, including food service, infant foods, condiments, pet foods, tuna, and weight control food products. Below is a five-year summary of operations and other related data for Heinz.[10]

Five-Year Summary of Operations and Other Related Data H. J. Heinz Company and Subsidiaries					
	1998	1997	1996	1995	1994
	(Dollars in thousands, except per share data)				
Summary of Operations					
Sales	$9,209,284	$9,397,007	$9,112,265	$8,086,794	$7,046,738
Cost of products sold	5,711,213	6,385,091	5,775,357	5,119,597	4,381,745
Interest expense	258,616	274,746	277,411	210,585	149,243
Provision for income taxes	453,415	177,193	364,342	346,982	319,442
Net income	801,566	301,871	659,319	591,025	602,944
Other Related Data					
Dividends paid: Common	452,966	416,923	381,871	345,358	325,887
Total assets	8,023,421	8,437,787	8,623,691	8,247,188	6,381,146
Total debt	5,806,905	5,997,366	3,363,828	3,401,076	2,166,703
Shareholders' equity	2,216,516	2,440,921	2,706,757	2,472,869	2,338,551

REQUIRED

Prepare a trend analysis for Heinz with 1994 as the base year and discuss the results. Identify important trends and tell whether the trends are favorable or unfavorable. Discuss significant relationships among the trends.

International Company

FRA 2.
LO 5 Comparison of International Company Operating Cycles

Ratio analysis enables one to compare the performance of companies whose financial statements are presented in different currencies. For instance, selected 1998 data for two large pharmaceutical companies—one American, *Pfizer, Inc.,* and one Swiss, *Roche*—are presented below (in millions):[11]

	Pfizer, Inc. (U.S.)	Roche (Swiss)
Net Sales	$13,544	SF24,662
Cost of Goods Sold	2,094	7,901
Accounts Receivable	2,914	4,535
Inventories	1,828	5,389
Accounts Payable	971	2,088

Accounts receivable in 1997 were $2,220 for Pfizer and SF4,405 for Roche. Inventories in 1997 were $1,461 for Pfizer and SF5,601 for Roche. Accounts payable in 1997 were $962 for Pfizer and SF2,048 for Roche.

For each company calculate the receivable, inventory, and payables turnovers and the respective days associated with each. Then determine the operating cycle for each company and the days of financing required for current operations. Compare the results.

Group Activity: Divide class into groups to make the calculations. Assign half of the groups each company. Compare results and discuss as a class.

Toys "R" Us Annual Report

FRA 3.
LO 5 Comprehensive Ratio Analysis

Refer to the Toys "R" Us annual report, and conduct a comprehensive ratio analysis that compares data from 1999 and 1998. If you have been computing ratios for Toys "R" Us in previous chapters, you may prepare a table that summarizes the ratios for 1999 and 1998 and show calculations only for the ratios not previously calculated. If this is the first time you are doing a ratio analysis for Toys "R" Us, show all your computations. In either case, after each group of ratios, comment on the performance of Toys "R" Us. Round your calculations to one decimal place. Prepare and comment on the following categories of ratios:

Liquidity analysis: Current ratio, quick ratio, receivable turnover, average days' sales uncollected, inventory turnover, average days' inventory on hand, payables turnover, and average days' payable (Accounts Receivable, Inventory, and Accounts Payable were [in millions] $135, $2,199, and $1,346, respectively, in 1997.)

Profitability analysis: Profit margin, asset turnover, return on assets, and return on equity (Comment on the effect of the restructuring in 1998 on the company's profitability.)

Long-term solvency analysis: Debt to equity ratio and interest coverage ratio

Cash flow adequacy analysis: Cash flow yield, cash flows to sales, cash flows to assets, and free cash flow

Market strength analysis: Price/earnings ratio and dividends yield

Fingraph® Financial Analyst™

FRA 4.
LO 5 Comprehensive Financial Statement Analysis

Choose any company in the Fingraph® Financial Analyst™ CD-ROM software database.

1. Display and print for the company you have selected the following pages:
   a. Balance Sheet Analysis
   b. Current Assets and Current Liabilities Analysis
   c. Liquidity and Asset Utilization Analysis
   d. Income from Operations Analysis
   e. Statement of Cash Flows: Operating Activities Analysis
   f. Statement of Cash Flows: Investing and Financing Activities Analysis
   g. Market Strength Analysis

2. Prepare an executive summary that describes the financial condition and performance of your company for the past two years. Attach the pages you printed above in support of your analysis.

Internet Case

FRA 5.

LO 2 **Use of Investors Service**
LO 3

Go to the Needles Accounting Resource Center at http://college.hmco.com. Under web resources, go to the web site for *Moody's Investors Service.* Click on "ratings" which will show revisions of debt ratings issued by Moody's in the past few days. Choose a rating that has been upgraded or downgraded and read the short press announcement related to it. What reasons does Moody's give for the change in rating? What is Moody's assessment of the future of the company or institution? What financial performance measures are mentioned in the article? Summarize your findings on paper and be prepared to share them in class.

ENDNOTES

1. Moody's Investors Service, "Moody's Assigns B3 to Ann Taylor's Debt," www.moody.com, June 1, 1999.
2. *Statement of Financial Accounting Standards No. 131*, "Segment Disclosures" (Norwalk, Conn.: Financial Accounting Standards Board, 1997).
3. Sun Microsystems, Inc., *Annual Report*, 1999.
4. William H. Beaver, "Alternative Accounting Measures as Indicators of Failure," *Accounting Review*, January 1968; and Edward Altman, "Financial Ratios, Discriminant Analysis and the Prediction of Corporate Bankruptcy," *Journal of Finance*, September 1968.
5. Sun Microsystems, Inc., "Management's Discussion and Analysis," *Annual Report*, 1999.
6. In addition, there are advantages to being a debtor in periods of inflation because the debt, which is fixed in dollar amount, may be repaid with cheaper dollars.
7. Sun Microsystems, Inc., "Management's Discussion and Analysis," *Annual Report*, 1999.
8. *Forbes*, November 13, 1978, p. 154.
9. Elizabeth MacDonald, "Firms Say SEC Earnings Scrutiny Goes Too Far," *The Wall Street Journal*, February 1, 1999.
10. H. J. Heinz Company, *Annual Report*, 1998.
11. Pfizer, Inc., *Annual Report*, 1998; and Roche Group, *Annual Report*, 1998.

16

International Accounting and Long-Term Investments

LEARNING OBJECTIVES

1 Define *exchange rate* and record transactions that are affected by changes in foreign exchange rates.

2 Describe the restatement of a foreign subsidiary's financial statements in U.S. dollars.

3 Describe the progress toward international accounting standards.

4 Identify the classifications of long-term investments in bonds and stocks.

5 Apply the cost adjusted to market method and the equity method as appropriate in accounting for long-term investments.

6 Explain when to prepare consolidated financial statements, and describe the uses of such statements.

7 Prepare the consolidated balance sheet at acquisition date for a purchase at (a) book value and (b) other than book value.

8 Prepare a consolidated income statement.

Daimler-Benz AG & Chrysler Corporation

The last several years have been notable for the number of giant mergers, especially of American companies with European companies. One notable example is the purchase of Chrysler Corporation by Daimler-Benz AG, the maker of Mercedes-Benz automobiles, at a price of more than $40 billion. This combination produces one of the largest automobile companies in the world. What reasons would lie behind these mergers and what role does accounting play in them?

The overall reason for these mergers is that European countries are aligning their companies' operations with the strategic realities of a changed world. With the development of the European Union, and with it the Euro or common currency among most European countries, European companies must take a world-view. For Daimler-Benz, it means expanding its product line to serve people at all income levels, rather than just those with the highest income. It also means expanding Daimler-Benz's reach in the world's largest market, the United States. The purchase of Chrysler fulfills both these needs. Accounting plays a part by reflecting the effects of transactions in different currencies and recording the financial combination of the companies. How this is done affects the future performance of the merged company and thus has financial consequences. This chapter addresses these consequences as reflected by international accounting and long-term investments.

Key Point: When both parties to a transaction deal in the same currency, no foreign currency problem exists. When the parties deal in different currencies, however, the fluctuating exchange rates create a need for special accounting procedures.

International Accounting

As businesses grow, they naturally look for new sources of supply and new markets in other countries. Today, it is common for businesses, called **multinational** or **transnational corporations**, to operate in more than one country, and many of them operate throughout the world. Table 1 shows the extent of the foreign business of four of the largest U.S. corporations. IBM, for example, has operations in 80 countries and receives almost 60 percent of its sales from outside the United States. Other industrial countries, such as Switzerland, France, Germany, Great Britain, the Netherlands, and Japan, have also given rise to numerous worldwide corporations. For example, 98 percent of the sales of Nestlé, the large Swiss food company, are made outside Switzerland. Examples of companies that receive more than half of their sales from outside their home countries are Michelin, the French tire maker; Unilever, the British/Netherlands consumer products company; and Sony, the Japanese electronics company. More than five hundred companies are listed on at least one stock exchange outside their home country.

> **Key Point:** Foreign investment in U.S. companies is widespread, as is U.S. investment in foreign companies.

In addition, sophisticated investors no longer restrict their investment activities to domestic securities markets. Many Americans invest in foreign securities markets, and non-Americans invest heavily in the stock market in the United States. Figure 1 shows that from 1980 to 1997, the total value of securities traded on the world's stock markets has increased over eighteenfold, with the U.S. share of the pie declining from 55 to 52 percent. Emerging markets in the rest of the world have increased from 16 percent to 26 percent.

Foreign business transactions have two major effects on accounting. First, most sales or purchases of goods and services in other countries involve different currencies. Thus, one currency needs to be translated into another, using exchange rates.[1] An **exchange rate** is the value of one currency in terms of another. For example, an English company purchasing goods from a U.S. company and paying in U.S. dollars must exchange British pounds for U.S. dollars before making payment. In effect, currencies are goods that can be bought and sold. Table 2 lists the exchange rates of several currencies in terms of dollars. It shows the exchange rate for the British pound as $1.64 per pound on a particular date. Like the price of any good or service,

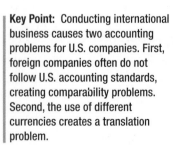

Figure 1
Value of Securities Traded on the World's Stock Markets

> **Key Point:** Conducting international business causes two accounting problems for U.S. companies. First, foreign companies often do not follow U.S. accounting standards, creating comparability problems. Second, the use of different currencies creates a translation problem.

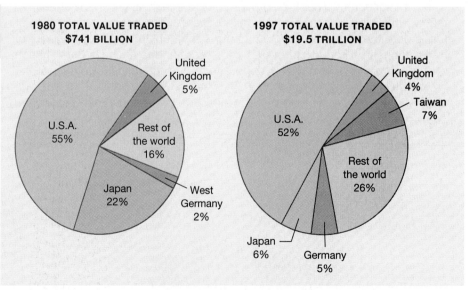

1980 TOTAL VALUE TRADED $741 BILLION

- United Kingdom 5%
- U.S.A. 55%
- Rest of the world 16%
- Japan 22%
- West Germany 2%

1997 TOTAL VALUE TRADED $19.5 TRILLION

- United Kingdom 4%
- Taiwan 7%
- U.S.A. 52%
- Rest of the world 26%
- Japan 6%
- Germany 5%

Source: International Finance Corporation, *Emerging Stock Markets Factbook,* © 1998.

Table 1. Extent of Foreign Revenues for Selected U.S. Companies

Company	Foreign Revenues (millions)	Total Revenues (millions)	Foreign Revenues (percentage)
Exxon	$80,708	$100,697	80.1
IBM	46,364	81,667	56.8
Ford	43,819	144,416	30.3
General Motors	40,918	132,863	30.8

Source: "The 100 Largest U.S. Multinationals," *Forbes*, July 27, 1999. Reprinted by permission of *Forbes* Magazine © 1999 Forbes.

Table 2. Partial Listing of Foreign Exchange Rates

Country	Price in $ U.S.	Country	Price in $ U.S.
Britain (pound)	1.64	Hong Kong (dollar)	.13
Canada (dollar)	.66	Italy (lira)	.0006
Europe (euro)	1.13	Japan (yen)	.009
France (franc)	.172	Mexico (peso)	.10
Germany (mark)	.978	Taiwan (dollar)	.03

Source: Data from *The Wall Street Journal*, February 2, 1999.

these prices change daily according to supply and demand for the currencies. Accounting for these price changes in recording foreign transactions and preparing financial statements for foreign subsidiaries is discussed in the next two sections.

The second major effect of international business on accounting is that financial standards differ from country to country, which makes it difficult to compare companies from different countries. The obstacles to achieving comparability and some of the progress in solving the problem are discussed later in this chapter.

Accounting for Transactions in Foreign Currencies

Among the first activities of an expanding company in the international market are the buying and selling of goods and services. For example, a U.S. maker of precision tools may expand by selling its product to foreign customers. Or it might lower its product cost by buying a less expensive part from a source in another country. In previous chapters, all transactions were recorded in dollars, and it was assumed that the dollar is a uniform measure in the same way that the inch and the centimeter are. But in the international marketplace, a transaction may take place in Japanese yen, British pounds, or some other currency. The values of these currencies in relation to the dollar rise and fall daily. If there is a delay between the date of sale or purchase and the date of receipt or payment of cash, the amount of cash involved may be different from that originally agreed upon due to changing exchange rates.

Key Point: A U.S. company must use dollars to record sales and purchases in its records.

FOREIGN SALES   When a domestic company sells merchandise abroad, it may bill either in its own country's currency or in the foreign currency. If the billing and the subsequent payment are both in the domestic currency, no accounting problem arises. For example, assume that the precision toolmaker sells $160,000 worth of tools to a British company and bills the British company in dollars. The entry to record the sale and receipt is familiar:

Date of Sale

A = L + OE
+   +

| Accounts Receivable, British company | 160,000 | |
| Sales | | 160,000 |

Date of Receipt

A = L + OE
+
−

| Cash | 160,000 | |
| Accounts Receivable, British company | | 160,000 |

Key Point: Exchange gains and losses occur when there is a timing difference between sale and receipt and a change in the exchange rate occurs. The larger the time span, the more likely it is that a difference will occur.

However, if the U.S. company bills the British company in British pounds and accepts payment in pounds, the U.S. company may incur an **exchange gain or loss**. A gain or loss will occur if the exchange rate between dollars and pounds changes between the date of sale and the date of receipt. Since gains and losses tend to offset one another, a single account is used during the year to accumulate the activity. The net exchange gain or loss is reported on the income statement. For example, assume that the sale of $160,000 above was billed as £100,000, reflecting an exchange rate of 1.60 (that is, $1.60 per pound) on the sale date. Now assume that by the date of receipt, the exchange rate has fallen to 1.50. The entries to record the transactions follow:

Date of Sale

A = L + OE
+   +

Accounts Receivable, British company	160,000	
Sales		160,000
£100,000 × $1.60 = $160,000		

Date of Receipt

A = L + OE
+   −
−

Cash	150,000	
Exchange Gain or Loss	10,000	
Accounts Receivable, British company		160,000
£100,000 × $1.50 = $150,000		

The U.S. company has incurred an exchange loss of $10,000 because it agreed to accept a fixed number of British pounds in payment, and the value of each pound dropped before the payment was made. Had the value of the pound in relation to the dollar increased, the U.S. company would have made an exchange gain.

FOREIGN PURCHASES   Purchases are the opposite of sales. The same logic applies to them, except that the relationship of exchange gains and losses to changes in exchange rates is reversed. For example, assume that the maker of precision tools purchases $15,000 of a certain part from a Japanese supplier. If the purchase and subsequent payment are made in U.S. dollars, no accounting problem arises.

Date of Purchase

A = L + OE
+   −

| Purchases | 15,000 | |
| Accounts Payable, Japanese company | | 15,000 |

Date of Payment

A = L + OE
−   −

| Accounts Payable, Japanese company | 15,000 | |
| Cash | | 15,000 |

However, the Japanese company may bill the U.S. company in yen and be paid in yen. If so, the U.S. company will incur an exchange gain or loss if the exchange rate changes between the date of purchase and the date of payment. For example, assume that the transaction is for 2,500,000 yen and the exchange rates on the dates of purchase and payment are $.0090 and $.0085 per yen, respectively. The entries follow.

Date of Purchase

A = L + OE	Purchases	22,500	
+ −	Accounts Payable, Japanese company		22,500
	¥2,500,000 × $.0090 = $22,500		

Date of Payment

A = L + OE	Accounts Payable, Japanese company	22,500	
− − +	Exchange Gain or Loss		1,250
	Cash		21,250
	¥2,500,000 × $.0085 = $21,250		

In this case the U.S. company received an exchange gain of $1,250 because it agreed to pay a fixed ¥2,500,000, and between the dates of purchase and receipt or payment the exchange value of the yen decreased in relation to the dollar.

REALIZED VERSUS UNREALIZED EXCHANGE GAIN OR LOSS   The preceding illustration dealt with completed transactions (in the sense that payment was completed). In each case, the exchange gain or loss was recognized on the date of receipt or payment. If financial statements are prepared between the sale or purchase and the subsequent receipt or payment, and exchange rates have changed, there will be unrealized gains or losses. The Financial Accounting Standards Board, in its *Statement No. 52*, requires that exchange gains and losses "shall be included in determining net income for the period in which the exchange rate changes."[2] The requirement includes interim (quarterly) statements and applies whether or not a transaction is complete.

This ruling has caused much debate. Critics charge that it gives too much weight to fleeting changes in exchange rates, causing random changes in earnings that hide long-run trends. Others believe that the use of current exchange rates to value receivables and payables as of the balance sheet date is a major step toward economic reality (current values). To illustrate, we will use the preceding case, in which a U.S. company buys parts from a Japanese supplier. We will assume that the transaction has not been completed by the balance sheet date, when the exchange rate is $.0080 per yen:

Key Point: Cash flows are not affected by unrealized exchange gains and losses. The cash effect is ultimately determined when the transactions are complete and exchange gains or losses are realized.

	Date	Exchange Rate ($ per Yen)
Date of purchase	Dec. 1	.0090
Balance sheet date	Dec. 31	.0080
Date of payment	Feb. 1	.0085

The accounting effects of the unrealized gain are as follows:

	Dec. 1	Dec. 31	Feb. 1
Purchase recorded in U.S. dollars (billed as ¥2,500,000)	$22,500	$22,500	$22,500
Dollars to be paid to equal ¥2,500,000 (¥2,500,000 × exchange rate)	22,500	20,000	21,250
Unrealized gain (or loss)	—	$ 2,500	
Realized gain (or loss)			$ 1,250

A = L + OE + −	Dec. 1	Purchases	22,500	
		Accounts Payable, Japanese company		22,500
A = L + OE − +	Dec. 31	Accounts Payable, Japanese company	2,500	
		Exchange Gain or Loss		2,500
A = L + OE − − −	Feb. 1	Accounts Payable, Japanese company	20,000	
		Exchange Gain or Loss	1,250	
		Cash		21,250

In this case, the original sale was billed in yen by the Japanese company. Following the rules of *Statement No. 52*, an exchange gain of $2,500 is recorded on December 31, and an exchange loss of $1,250 is recorded on February 1. Even though these large fluctuations do not affect the net exchange gain of $1,250 for the whole transaction, the effect on each year's income statements may be important.

Restatement of Foreign Subsidiary Financial Statements

OBJECTIVE
2 Describe the restatement of a foreign subsidiary's financial statements in U.S. dollars

Growing companies often expand by setting up or buying foreign subsidiaries. If a foreign subsidiary is more than 50 percent owned and the parent company exercises control, then the foreign subsidiary should be included in the consolidated financial statements (see the discussion of parent and subsidiary companies later in this chapter). The consolidation procedure is the same as that for domestic subsidiaries, except that the statements of the foreign subsidiary must be restated in the reporting currency before consolidation takes place. The **reporting currency** is the currency in which the consolidated financial statements are presented. Clearly, it makes no sense to combine the assets of a Mexican subsidiary stated in pesos with the assets of the U.S. parent company stated in dollars. Most U.S. companies present their financial statements in U.S. dollars, so the following discussion assumes that the U.S. dollar is the reporting currency used.[3]

Key Point: Restatements are necessary because financial statements in the different currencies must be consolidated.

Restatement is the stating of one currency in terms of another. The method of restatement depends on the foreign subsidiary's functional currency. The **functional currency** is the currency of the place where the subsidiary carries on most of its business. Generally, it is the currency in which a company earns and spends its cash. The functional currency to be used depends on the kind of foreign operation in which the subsidiary takes part.

There are two broad types of foreign operation. Type I includes those that are fairly self-contained and integrated within a certain country or economy. Type II includes those that are mainly a direct and integral part or extension of the parent company's operations. As a general rule, Type I subsidiaries use the currency of the country in which they are located, and Type II subsidiaries use the currency of the parent company. If the parent company is a U.S. company, the functional currency of a Type I subsidiary will be the currency of the country in which the subsidiary carries on its business, and the functional currency of a Type II subsidiary will be the U.S. dollar. *Statement No. 52* makes an exception when a Type I subsidiary operates in a country in which there is hyperinflation (as a rule of thumb, more than 100 percent cumulative inflation over three years), such as Brazil or Argentina. In such a case, the subsidiary is treated as a Type II subsidiary, with the functional currency being the U.S. dollar. Restatements in these situations do not affect cash flows because they are done simply for the convenience of preparing consolidated statements.

The Search for Comparability of International Accounting Standards

International investors need to compare the financial position and results of operations of companies from different countries. At present, however, few standards of

BUSINESS FOCUS ON INTERNATIONAL

Many foreign companies that do business in the United States have started showing in the notes to the financial statements the major differences between income in their own country and income calculated under U.S. GAAP. For instance, the Financial Highlights table that is presented here is adapted from the annual report of Glaxo Wellcome, the large British pharmaceutical company.[4] Accounting for intangibles, such as brand names, trademarks, and goodwill, presents major differences between British and U.S. GAAP. For example, brand names that are carried as assets must be written off over time as amortization costs in the United States but not in the United Kingdom. Purchased goodwill may be written off against stockholders' equity in the United Kingdom but

must be capitalized and amortized in the United States. Also, timing of the recognition of property transactions and one-time charges such as restructurings can cause significant differences. The United Kingdom does not normally require deferred taxation accounting, as is required in the United States. These disclosures are very helpful in calculating profitability ratios for Glaxo Wellcome and comparing them with those of U.S. companies.

Financial Highlights

(In millions of pounds)

	1998	1997
Income attributable to shareholders under U.K. GAAP	**1,836**	1,850
U.S. GAAP adjustments:		
Capitalised interest	**6**	4
Computer software	**(29)**	—
Amortisation of goodwill	**(557)**	(554)
Amortisation of intangible assets	**(269)**	(326)
Purchased stock	**—**	—
Pensions	**41**	35
Deferred taxation	**46**	(31)
Stock-based compensation	**(59)**	(26)
Net income under U.S. GAAP	**1,015**	952

OBJECTIVE

3 Describe the progress toward international accounting standards

accounting are recognized worldwide.[5] For example, the LIFO method of valuing inventory is the most popular in the United States, but it is not acceptable in most European countries. As another example, historical cost is strictly followed in Germany, replacement cost is used by some companies in the Netherlands, and a mixed system, allowing lower of cost or market in some cases, is used in the United States and England. Even the formats of financial statements differ from country to country. In England and France, for example, the order in which the balance sheets are presented is almost the reverse of that in the United States. In those countries, property, plant, and equipment is the first listing in the assets section.

A number of major problems stand in the way of setting international standards.[6] One is that accountants and users of accounting information have not been able to agree on the goals of financial statements. Some other problems are differences in the way the accounting profession has developed in various countries, differences in the laws regulating companies, and differences in government and other requirements. Further difficulties are created by differences among countries in the basic economic factors affecting financial reporting, inconsistencies in practices recommended by the accounting profession in different countries, and the influence of tax laws on financial reporting.

Enhancement Note: The two most important sets of accounting standards are U.S. GAAP and IASC IASs. Which of these two will ultimately prevail as the world standard is yet to be determined.

Probably the best hopes for finding areas of agreement among all the different countries are the International Accounting Standards Committee (IASC) and the International Federation of Accountants (IFAC). The IASC, formed in 1973, has representatives from more than one hundred professional accountancy bodies from over 70 countries.

The role of the IASC is to contribute to the development and adoption of accounting principles that are relevant, balanced, and comparable throughout the world by formulating and publicizing accounting standards and encouraging their observance in the presentation of financial statements.[7] The standards issued by the IASC are generally followed by large multinational companies that are clients of international accounting firms. The IASC has been especially helpful to companies in developing economies that do not have the financial history or resources to develop accounting standards. The IASC is currently engaged in a major project to improve financial reporting worldwide by introducing a set of international accounting standards that will be acceptable to the world's securities regulators, such as the SEC in the United States. If successful, the effort should make it easier for companies to raise equity capital and list their stocks in other countries.

The IFAC, formed in 1977, also includes most of the world's accountancy organizations. It fully supports the work of the IASC and recognizes the IASC as the sole body having responsibility and authority to issue pronouncements on international accounting standards. The IFAC's objective is to develop international guidelines for auditing, ethics, education, and management accounting.

In Europe, attempts are also being made to harmonize accounting standards. The European Community has issued a directive (4th) requiring certain minimum and uniform reporting and disclosure standards for financial statements. Other directives deal with uniform rules for preparing consolidated financial statements (7th) and qualifications of auditors (8th). In recent years, the European Community has paid considerable attention to the comparability of financial reporting as the organization moves toward the goal of a single European market.

The road to international harmony is a difficult one. However, there is reason for optimism because an increasing number of countries are recognizing the appropriateness of international accounting standards in international trade and commerce.

Long-Term Investments

OBJECTIVE

4 Identify the classifications of long-term investments in bonds and stocks

One corporation may invest in another corporation by purchasing bonds or stocks. These investments may be either short term or long term. In this section, we are concerned with long-term investments.

Long-Term Investments in Bonds

Like all investments, investments in bonds are recorded at cost, which is the price of the bonds plus the broker's commission. When bonds are purchased between interest payment dates, the purchaser must also pay an amount equal to the interest that has accrued on the bonds since the last interest payment date. Then, on the next interest payment date, the purchaser receives an interest payment for the whole period. The payment for accrued interest should be recorded as a debit to Interest Income, which will be offset by a credit to Interest Income when the semiannual interest is received.

Key Point: The fair value of bonds is closely related to interest rates. An increase in interest rates lowers the fair value of bonds and vice versa.

Subsequent accounting for a corporation's long-term bond investments depends on the classification of the bonds. If the company may at some point decide to sell the bonds, they are classified as **available-for-sale securities**. If the company plans to hold the bonds until they are paid off on their maturity date, they are considered **held-to-maturity securities**. Except in industries like insurance and banking, it is unusual for companies to buy the bonds of other companies with the express purpose of holding them until they mature, which can be in 10 to 30 years. Therefore, most firms classify long-term bond investments as available-for-

sale securities. Such bonds are subsequently accounted for at fair value, much like equity or stock investments are. Fair value is usually the market value. When bonds are intended to be held to maturity, which is rare, they are accounted for not at fair value but at cost, adjusted for the amortization of their discount or premium. The procedure is similar to accounting for long-term bond liabilities, except that separate accounts for discounts and premiums are not used.

Long-Term Investments in Stock

All long-term investments in stocks are recorded at cost, in accordance with generally accepted accounting principles. The treatment of the investment in the accounting records after the initial purchase depends on the extent to which the investing company can exercise significant influence or control over the operating and financial policies of the other company.

The Accounting Principles Board defined the important terms *significant influence* and *control* in its *Opinion No. 18*. **Significant influence** is the ability to affect the operating and financial policies of the company whose shares are owned, even though the investor holds 50 percent or less of the voting stock. Ability to influence a company may be shown by representation on the board of directors, participation in policy making, material transactions between the companies, exchange of managerial personnel, and technological dependency. For the sake of uniformity, the APB decided that unless there is proof to the contrary, an investment of 20 percent or more of the voting stock should be presumed to confer significant influence. An investment of less than 20 percent of the voting stock would not confer significant influence.[10]

Control is defined as the ability of the investing company to decide the operating and financial policies of the other company. Control is said to exist when the investing company owns more than 50 percent of the voting stock of the company in which it has invested.

Thus, in the absence of information to the contrary, a noninfluential and noncontrolling investment would be less than 20 percent ownership. An influential but noncontrolling investment would be 20 to 50 percent ownership. And a controlling investment would be more than 50 percent ownership. The accounting treatment differs for each kind of investment.

Key Point: Influence and control are related specifically to equity holdings, not debt holdings.

NONINFLUENTIAL AND NONCONTROLLING INVESTMENT Available-for-sale securities are debt or equity securities that are not classified as trading or held-to-maturity securities. When equity securities are involved, the further criterion is that they be noninfluential and noncontrolling investments of less than 20 percent of the voting stock. The Financial Accounting Standards Board requires a **cost adjusted to market method** for accounting for available-for-sale securities. Under this method, available-for-sale securities must be recorded initially at cost and thereafter adjusted periodically through the use of an allowance account to reflect changes in the market value.[11]

OBJECTIVE

5 Apply the cost adjusted to market method and the equity method as appropriate in accounting for long-term investments

Available-for-sale securities are classified as long term if management intends to hold them for more than one year. When accounting for long-term available-for sale securities, the unrealized gain or loss resulting from the adjustment is not reported on the income statement, but is reported as a special item in the stockholders' equity section of the balance sheet and in comprehensive income disclosure.

At the end of each accounting period, the total cost and the total market value of these long-term stock investments must be determined. If the total market value is less than the total cost, the difference must be credited to a contra-asset account called Allowance to Adjust Long-Term Investments to Market. Because of the long-term nature of the investment, the debit part of the entry, which represents a decrease in value below cost, is treated as a temporary decrease and does not appear as a loss on the income statement. It is shown in a contra-stockholders' equity account called Unrealized Loss on Long-Term Investments. Thus, both of these accounts are balance sheet accounts. If the market value exceeds the cost, the allowance account is added to Long-Term Investments and the unrealized gain appears as an addition to stockholders' equity.[12]

When long-term investments in stock are sold, the difference between the sale price and what the stock cost is recorded and reported as a realized gain or loss on the income statement. Dividend income from such investments is recorded by a debit to Cash and a credit to Dividend Income.

For example, assume the following facts about the long-term stock investments of Coleman Corporation:

Key Point: On April 1, 20x1, a *change in policy* requires the sale. This points out that intent is often the only difference between long-term investments and short-term investments.

June 1, 20x0   Paid cash for the following long-term investments: 10,000 shares of Durbin Corporation common stock (representing 2 percent of outstanding stock) at $25 per share; 5,000 shares of Kotes Corporation common stock (representing 3 percent of outstanding stock) at $15 per share.

Dec. 31, 20x0   Quoted market prices at year end: Durbin common stock, $21; Kotes common stock, $17.

Apr. 1, 20x1   Change in policy required sale of 2,000 shares of Durbin Corporation common stock at $23.

July 1, 20x1   Received cash dividend from Kotes Corporation equal to $.20 per share.

Dec. 31, 20x1   Quoted market prices at year end: Durbin common stock, $24; Kotes common stock, $13.

Entries to record these transactions follow.

Investment

20x0

A = L + OE
+
–

June 1   Long-Term Investments ... 325,000

Cash ... 325,000

Investments in Durbin common stock (10,000 shares × $25 = $250,000) and Kotes common stock (5,000 shares × $15 = $75,000)

Year-End Adjustment

20x0

A = L + OE
–   –

Dec. 31   Unrealized Loss on Long-Term Investments ... 30,000

Allowance to Adjust Long-Term Investments to Market ... 30,000

To record reduction of long-term investment to market

Company	Shares	Market Price	Total Market	Total Cost
Durbin	10,000	$21	$210,000	$250,000
Kotes	5,000	17	85,000	75,000
			$295,000	$325,000

Key Point: *Total* cost and *total* market or fair value are used to determine the adjustment.

Total Cost − Total Market Value = $325,000 − $295,000 = $30,000

Sale

20x1

A = L + OE
+   –
–

Apr. 1   Cash ... 46,000

Loss on Sale of Investments ... 4,000

Long-Term Investments ... 50,000

Sale of 2,000 shares of Durbin common stock

2,000 × $23 = $46,000

2,000 × $25 = 50,000

Loss $ 4,000

Dividend Received

20x1

A = L + OE
+   +

July 1   Cash ... 1,000

Dividend Income ... 1,000

Receipt of cash dividend from Kotes stock

5,000 × $.20 = $1,000

Year-End Adjustment

20x1

A = L + OE
+   +

Dec. 31   Allowance to Adjust Long-Term Investments to Market ... 12,000

Unrealized Loss on Long-Term Investments ... 12,000

To record the adjustment in long-term investment so it is reported at market

The adjustment equals the previous balance ($30,000 from the December 31, 20x0, entry) minus the new balance ($18,000), or $12,000. The new balance of $18,000 is the difference at the present time between the total market value and the total cost of all investments. It is figured as follows:

Company	Shares	Market Price	Total Market	Total Cost
Durbin	8,000	$24	$192,000	$200,000
Kotes	5,000	13	65,000	75,000
			$257,000	$275,000

Total Cost − Total Market Value = $275,000 − $257,000 = $18,000

The Allowance to Adjust Long-Term Investments to Market and the Unrealized Loss on Long-Term Investments are reciprocal contra accounts, each with the same dollar balance, as can be shown by the effects of these transactions on the T accounts:

Contra-Asset Account				**Contra-Stockholders' Equity Account**			
Allowance to Adjust Long-Term Investments to Market				**Unrealized Loss on Long-Term Investments**			
20x1	12,000	20x0	30,000	20x0	30,000	20x1	12,000
		Bal. 20x1	18,000	Bal. 20x1	18,000		

The Allowance account reduces long-term investments by the amount by which the cost of the investments exceeds market; the Unrealized Loss account reduces stockholders' equity by a similar amount. The opposite effects will exist if market value exceeds cost, resulting in an unrealized gain.

INFLUENTIAL BUT NONCONTROLLING INVESTMENT   As we have seen, ownership of 20 percent or more of a company's voting stock is considered sufficient to influence the operations of that corporation. When this is the case, the investment in the stock of the influenced company should be accounted for using the **equity method**. The equity method presumes that an investment of 20 percent or more is more than a passive investment, and that therefore the investing company should share proportionately in the success or failure of the investee company. The three main features of this method are as follows:

1. The investor records the original purchase of the stock at cost.
2. The investor records its share of the investee's periodic net income as an increase in the Investment account, with a corresponding credit to an income account. In like manner, the investor records its share of the investee's periodic loss as a decrease in the Investment account, with a corresponding debit to a loss account.
3. When the investor receives a cash dividend, the asset account Cash is increased and the Investment account is decreased.

To illustrate the equity method of accounting, we will assume the following facts about an investment by Vassor Corporation. On January 1 of the current year, Vassor Corporation acquired 40 percent of the voting common stock of Block Corporation for $180,000. With this share of ownership, Vassor Corporation can exert significant influence over the operations of Block Corporation. During the year, Block Corporation reported net income of $80,000 and paid cash dividends of $20,000. The entries that follow are to record these transactions by Vassor Corporation.

Investment

$A = L + OE$
$+$
$-$

Investment in Block Corporation	180,000	
Cash		180,000
Investment in Block Corporation common stock		

Recognition of Income

$A = L + OE$
$+$ $+$

Investment in Block Corporation	32,000	
Income, Block Corporation Investment		32,000
Recognition of 40% of income reported		
by Block Corporation		
40% × $80,000 = $32,000		

Receipt of Cash Dividend

$A = L + OE$
$+$
$-$

Cash	8,000	
Investment in Block Corporation		8,000
Cash dividend from Block Corporation		
40% × $20,000 = $8,000		

Study Point: Under the equity method, dividends received are credited to the Investment account because the dividends represent a return of or decrease in the investment in Block Corporation.

The balance of the Investment in Block Corporation account after these transactions is $204,000, as shown here:

Investment in Block Corporation

Investment	180,000	Dividend received	8,000
Share of income	32,000		
Balance	204,000		

Enrichment Note: Parents and subsidiaries are separate legal entities even though they combine their financial reports at year end.

CONTROLLING INVESTMENT   In some cases, an investor who owns less than 50 percent of the voting stock of a company may exercise such powerful influence that for all practical purposes the investor controls the policies of the other company. Nevertheless, ownership of more than 50 percent of the voting stock is required for accounting recognition of control. When a controlling interest is owned, a parent-subsidiary relationship is said to exist. The investing company is known as the **parent company**, the other company as the **subsidiary**. Because the two corporations are separate legal entities, each prepares separate financial statements. However, owing to their special relationship, they are viewed for public financial reporting purposes as a single economic entity. For this reason, they must combine their financial statements into a single set of statements called **consolidated financial statements**.

BUSINESS FOCUS ON PRACTICE

The purchase of one company by another is an extremely significant transaction not only for the companies involved but for the economy as a whole. Corporate buyouts set a record of $1.6 trillion in 1998. The three largest buyouts were as follows:[13]

Buyer	Seller	Dollar Value (billions)
Exxon	Mobil	$86.4
Travelers Group	Citicorp	72.6
SBC Communication	Ameritech	72.4

These consolidations represent a trend toward larger and more concentrated business. They also represent significant accounting challenges. This buyout activity has continued through 1999 and into 2000.

Table 3. Accounting Treatments of Long-Term Investments in Stock

Level of Ownership	Percentage of Ownership	Accounting Treatment
Noninfluential and noncontrolling	Less than 20%	Cost initially; investment adjusted subsequent to purchase for changes in market value.
Influential but noncontrolling	Between 20% and 50%	Equity method; investment valued subsequently at cost plus investor's share of income (or minus investor's share of loss) minus dividends received.
Controlling	More than 50%	Financial statements consolidated.

Accounting for consolidated financial statements is very complex. It is usually the subject of an advanced accounting course. However, most large public corporations have subsidiaries and must prepare consolidated financial statements. It is therefore important to have some understanding of accounting for consolidations.

The proper accounting treatments for long-term investments in stock are summarized in Table 3.

Consolidated Financial Statements

OBJECTIVE

6 Explain when to prepare consolidated financial statements, and describe the uses of such statements

Most major corporations find it convenient for economic, legal, tax, or other reasons to operate in parent-subsidiary relationships. When we speak of a large company such as Ford, IBM, or Texas Instruments, we generally think of the parent company, not of its many subsidiaries. When considering investment in one of these firms, however, the investor wants a clear financial picture of the total economic entity. The main purpose of consolidated financial statements is to give such a view of the parent and subsidiary firms by treating them as if they were one company. On a consolidated balance sheet, the Inventory account includes the inventory held by the parent and all its subsidiaries. Similarly, on the consolidated income statement, the Sales account is the total revenue from sales by the parent and all its subsidiaries. This overview helps management and stockholders of the parent company judge the company's progress in meeting its goals. Long-term creditors of the parent also find consolidated statements useful because of their interest in the long-range financial health of the company.

The Financial Accounting Standards Board ruled that, effective in 1988, all subsidiaries in which the parent owns a controlling interest (more than 50 percent) must be consolidated with the parent for financial reporting purposes.[14] As a result, with few exceptions, the financial statements of all majority-owned subsidiaries must now be consolidated with the parent company's financial statements for external reporting purposes. Some companies, such as General Electric

Company, present separate statements for their finance subsidiaries in their annual report in addition to the consolidated statements.

Methods of Accounting for Business Combinations

Key Point: Business combinations are recorded by using either the purchase method or the pooling of interests method, depending upon whether certain criteria have been met. The discussions that follow focus on the purchase method.

Interests in subsidiary companies may be acquired by paying cash; issuing long-term bonds, other debt, or common or preferred stock; or working out some combination of these forms of payment, such as exchanging shares of the parent's own unissued capital stock for the outstanding shares of the subsidiary's capital stock. For parent-subsidiary relationships that arise when cash is paid or debt or preferred stock is issued, it is mandatory to use the purchase method, which is explained below. For simplicity, our illustrations assume payment in cash. In the special case of establishing a parent-subsidiary relationship through an exchange of common stock, the pooling of interests method may be appropriate. The FASB has proposed rules that would eliminate most companies' use of the pooling of interest method.

Consolidated Balance Sheet

Key Point: The parent and the subsidiary each maintain individual accounting records as separate entities. Work sheet eliminations remove only duplications that occur in consolidation and the effects of intercompany transactions.

In preparing consolidated financial statements under the **purchase method**, similar accounts from the separate statements of the parent and the subsidiaries are combined. Some accounts result from transactions between the parent and the subsidiary. Examples are debt owed by one of the entities to the other and sales and purchases between the two entities. When considering the group of companies as a single business, it is not appropriate to include these accounts in the group financial statements; the purchases and sales are only transfers between different parts of the business, and the payables and receivables do not represent amounts due to or receivable from outside parties. For this reason, it is important that certain **eliminations** be made. These eliminations avoid the duplication of accounts and reflect the financial position and operations from the standpoint of a single entity. Eliminations appear only on the work sheets used in preparing consolidated financial statements. They are never shown in the accounting records of either the parent or the subsidiary. There are no consolidated journals or ledgers.

Another good example of accounts that result from transactions between the two entities is the Investment in Subsidiary account on the parent's balance sheet and in the stockholders' equity section of the subsidiary. When the balance sheets of the two companies are combined, these accounts must be eliminated to avoid duplicating these items in the consolidated financial statements.

To illustrate the preparation of a consolidated balance sheet under the purchase method, we will use the balance sheets below for Parent and Subsidiary companies.

Accounts	Parent Company	Subsidiary Company
Cash	$100,000	$25,000
Other Assets	760,000	60,000
Total Assets	$860,000	$85,000
Liabilities	$ 60,000	$10,000
Common Stock, $10 par value	600,000	55,000
Retained Earnings	200,000	20,000
Total Liabilities and Stockholders' Equity	$860,000	$85,000

100 Percent Purchase at Book Value Suppose that Parent Company purchases 100 percent of the stock of Subsidiary Company for an amount exactly equal to Subsidiary's book value. The book value of Subsidiary Company is $75,000 ($85,000 − $10,000). Parent Company would record the purchase as shown below:

A = L + OE
+
−

Investment in Subsidiary Company	75,000	
Cash		75,000
Purchase of 100 percent of Subsidiary Company at book value		

OBJECTIVE

7a Prepare the consolidated balance sheet at acquisition date for a purchase at book value

It is helpful to use a work sheet like the one shown in Exhibit 1 in preparing consolidated financial statements. Note that the balance of Parent Company's Cash account is now $25,000 and that Investment in Subsidiary Company is shown as an asset in Parent Company's balance sheet, reflecting the purchase of the subsidiary. In order to prepare a consolidated balance sheet, it is necessary to eliminate the investment in the subsidiary. This procedure is shown by elimination entry 1 in Exhibit 1. This elimination entry accomplishes two things. First, it eliminates the double counting that would take place when the net assets of the two companies are combined. Second, it eliminates the stockholders' equity section of Subsidiary Company.

The theory underlying consolidated financial statements is that parent and subsidiary are a single entity. The stockholders' equity section of the consolidated balance sheet is the same as that of Parent Company. So after eliminating the Investment in Subsidiary Company account and the stockholders' equity of the

Exhibit 1
Work Sheet for Preparation of Consolidated Balance Sheet

Parent and Subsidiary Companies
Work Sheet for Consolidated Balance Sheet
As of Acquisition Date

Accounts	Balance Sheet, Parent Company	Balance Sheet, Subsidiary Company	Eliminations Debit	Eliminations Credit	Consolidated Balance Sheet
Cash	25,000	25,000			50,000
Investment in Subsidiary Company	75,000			(1) 75,000	
Other Assets	760,000	60,000			820,000
Total Assets	860,000	85,000			870,000
Liabilities	60,000	10,000			70,000
Common Stock, $10 par value	600,000	55,000	(1) 55,000		600,000
Retained Earnings	200,000	20,000	(1) 20,000		200,000
Total Liabilities and Stockholders' Equity	860,000	85,000	75,000	75,000	870,000

(1) Elimination of intercompany investment.

subsidiary, we can take the information from the right-hand column in Exhibit 1 and present it in the following form:

Parent and Subsidiary Companies Consolidated Balance Sheet As of Acquisition Date			
Cash	$ 50,000	Liabilities	$ 70,000
Other Assets	820,000	Common Stock, $10 par value	600,000
		Retained Earnings	200,000
		Total Liabilities and Stockholders' Equity	
Total Assets	$870,000	Stockholders' Equity	$870,000

LESS THAN 100 PERCENT PURCHASE AT BOOK VALUE A parent company does not have to purchase 100 percent of a subsidiary to control it. If it purchases more than 50 percent of the voting stock of the subsidiary company, it will have legal control. In the consolidated financial statements, therefore, the total assets and liabilities of the subsidiary are combined with the assets and liabilities of the parent. However, it is still necessary to account for the interests of those stockholders of the subsidiary company who own less than 50 percent of the voting stock. These are the minority stockholders, and their **minority interest** must appear on the consolidated balance sheet as an amount equal to their percentage of ownership times the net assets of the subsidiary.

Suppose that the same Parent Company buys, for $67,500, only 90 percent of Subsidiary Company's voting stock. In this case, the portion of the company purchased has a book value of $67,500 (90% × $75,000). The work sheet used for preparing the consolidated balance sheet appears in Exhibit 2. The elimination is made in the same way as in the case above, except that the minority interest must be accounted for. All of the Investment in Subsidiary Company ($67,500) is eliminated against all of Subsidiary Company's stockholders' equity ($75,000). The difference ($7,500, or 10% × $75,000) is set as minority interest.

> **Key Point:** When the elimination entry is made, all of the subsidiary's stockholders' equity is eliminated. The percentage not owned by the parent company is assigned to minority interest.

There are two ways to classify minority interest on the consolidated balance sheet. One is to place it between long-term liabilities and stockholders' equity. The other is to consider the stockholders' equity section as consisting of (1) minority interest and (2) Parent Company's stockholders' equity, as shown here:

Minority Interest	$ 7,500
Common Stock, $10 par value	600,000
Retained Earnings	200,000
Total Stockholders' Equity	$807,500

PURCHASE AT MORE OR LESS THAN BOOK VALUE The purchase price of a business depends on many factors, such as the current market price, the relative strength of the buyer's and seller's bargaining positions, and the prospects for future earnings. Thus, it is only by chance that the purchase price of a subsidiary will equal the book value of the subsidiary's equity. Usually, it will not. For example, a parent company may pay more than the book value of a subsidiary to purchase a controlling interest if the assets of the subsidiary are understated. In that

OBJECTIVE

7b Prepare the consolidated balance sheet at acquisition date for a purchase at other than book value

| | Parent and Subsidiary Companies Work Sheet for Consolidated Balance Sheet As of Acquisition Date | | | | |
| | | | | | |

Accounts	Balance Sheet, Parent Company	Balance Sheet, Subsidiary Company	Eliminations Debit	Eliminations Credit	Consolidated Balance Sheet
Cash	32,500	25,000			57,500
Investment in Subsidiary Company	67,500			(1) 67,500	
Other Assets	760,000	60,000			820,000
Total Assets	860,000	85,000			877,500
Liabilities	60,000	10,000			70,000
Common Stock, $10 par value	600,000	55,000	(1) 55,000		600,000
Retained Earnings	200,000	20,000	(1) 20,000		200,000
Minority Interest				(1) 7,500	7,500
Total Liabilities and Stockholders' Equity	860,000	85,000	75,000	75,000	877,500

(1) Elimination of intercompany investment. Minority interest equals 10 percent of subsidiary's stockholders' equity.

case, the recorded historical cost less depreciation of the subsidiary's assets may not reflect current market values. The parent may also pay more than book value if the subsidiary has something that the parent wants, such as an important technical process, a new and different product, or a new market. On the other hand, the parent may pay less than book value for its share of the subsidiary's stock if the subsidiary's assets are not worth their depreciated cost. Or the subsidiary may have suffered heavy losses, causing its stock to sell at rather low prices.

The Accounting Principles Board has provided the following guidelines for consolidating a purchased subsidiary and its parent when the parent pays more than book value for its investment in the subsidiary:

Key Point: Regardless of the circumstances, the Investment in Subsidiary Company account must be eliminated completely and should not appear on the consolidated balance sheet.

First, all identifiable assets acquired . . . and liabilities assumed in a business combination . . . should be assigned a portion of the cost of the acquired company, normally equal to their fair values at date of acquisition.

Second, the excess of the cost of the acquired company over the sum of the amounts assigned to identifiable assets acquired less liabilities assumed should be recorded as goodwill.[15]

To illustrate the application of these principles, we will assume that Parent Company purchases 100 percent of Subsidiary Company's voting stock for $92,500, or $17,500 more than book value. Parent Company considers $10,000 of the $17,500 to be due to the increased value of Subsidiary's other assets and $7,500 of the $17,500 to be due to the overall strength that Subsidiary Company would add to Parent Company's organization. The work sheet used for preparing

Exhibit 3
Work Sheet Showing Elimination When Purchase Cost Is Greater Than Book Value

Parent and Subsidiary Companies
Work Sheet for Consolidated Balance Sheet
As of Acquisition Date

Accounts	Balance Sheet, Parent Company	Balance Sheet, Subsidiary Company	Eliminations Debit	Eliminations Credit	Consolidated Balance Sheet
Cash	7,500	25,000			32,500
Investment in Subsidiary Company	92,500			(1) 92,500	
Other Assets	760,000	60,000	(1) 10,000		830,000
Goodwill			(1) 7,500		7,500
Total Assets	860,000	85,000			870,000
Liabilities	60,000	10,000			70,000
Common Stock, $10 par value	600,000	55,000	(1) 55,000		600,000
Retained Earnings	200,000	20,000	(1) 20,000		200,000
Total Liabilities and Stockholders' Equity	860,000	85,000	92,500	92,500	870,000

(1) Elimination of intercompany investment. Excess of cost over book value ($92,500 − $75,000 = $17,500) is allocated to Other Assets ($10,000) and to Goodwill ($7,500).

Key Point: Goodwill is recorded in financial records when the purchase price of a business exceeds the fair market value of the net assets purchased.

Key Point: In these examples, neither company has goodwill on its balance sheet, but goodwill is "created" when consolidated statements are prepared.

the consolidated balance sheet appears in Exhibit 3. All of the Investment in Subsidiary Company ($92,500) has been eliminated against all of Subsidiary Company's stockholders' equity ($75,000). The excess of cost over book value ($17,500) has been debited in the amounts of $10,000 to Other Assets and $7,500 to a new account called **Goodwill**, or *Goodwill from Consolidation*.

The amount of goodwill is determined as follows:

Cost of investment in subsidiary	$92,500
Book value of subsidiary	75,000
Excess of cost over book value	$17,500
Portion of excess attributable to undervalued long-term assets of subsidiary	10,000
Portion of excess attributable to goodwill	$ 7,500

On the consolidated balance sheet, Goodwill appears as an asset representing the portion of the excess of the cost of the investment over book value that cannot be allocated to any specific asset. Other Assets appears on the consolidated balance sheet at the combined total of $830,000 ($760,000 + $60,000 + $10,000).

When the parent pays less than book value for its investment in the subsidiary, Accounting Principles Board *Opinion No. 16*, paragraph 87, requires that the excess of book value over cost of the investment be used to lower the carrying value of the subsidiary's long-term assets. The reasoning behind this is that market values of long-lived assets (other than marketable securities) are among the least reliable of estimates, since a ready market does not usually exist for such assets. In other words, the APB advises against using negative goodwill, except in very special cases.

The amortization of goodwill subsequent to the acquisition is covered in the chapter on long-term assets.

INTERCOMPANY RECEIVABLES AND PAYABLES If either the parent or the subsidiary company owes money to the other, there will be a receivable on the creditor company's individual balance sheet and a payable on the debtor company's individual balance sheet. When a consolidated balance sheet is prepared, both the receivable and the payable should be eliminated because, from the viewpoint of the consolidated entity, neither the asset nor the liability exists. In other words, it does not make sense for a company to owe money to itself. The eliminating entry would be made on the work sheet by debiting the payable and crediting the receivable for the amount of the intercompany loan.

The Consolidated Income Statement

OBJECTIVE

8 Prepare a consolidated income statement

The consolidated income statement for a consolidated entity is prepared by combining the revenues and expenses of the parent and subsidiary companies. The procedure is the same as that for preparing a consolidated balance sheet. That is, intercompany transactions are eliminated to prevent double counting of revenues and expenses. Several intercompany transactions affect the consolidated income statement. They are: (1) sales and purchases of goods and services between parent and subsidiary (purchases for the buying company and sales for the selling company); (2) income and expenses related to loans, receivables, or bond indebtedness between parent and subsidiary; and (3) other income and expenses from intercompany transactions.

To illustrate the eliminating entries, we will assume the following transactions between a parent and its wholly owned subsidiary. Parent Company made sales of $120,000 in goods to Subsidiary Company, which in turn sold all the goods to others. Subsidiary Company paid Parent Company $2,000 interest on a loan from the parent.

Key Point: Intercompany sales or purchases are not revenues or expenses to the consolidated entity. They are only paper transactions to provide for an exchange between affiliates. True revenues and expenses occur only when transactions are with parties *external* to the firm.

The work sheet in Exhibit 4 shows how to prepare a consolidated income statement. The purpose of the eliminating entries is to treat the two companies as a single entity. Thus, it is important to include in Sales only those sales made to outsiders and to include in Cost of Goods Sold only those purchases made from outsiders. This goal is met with the first eliminating entry, which eliminates the $120,000 of intercompany sales and purchases by a debit of that amount to Sales and a credit of that amount to Cost of Goods Sold. As a result, only sales to outsiders ($510,000) and purchases from outsiders ($240,000) are included in the Consolidated Income Statement column. The intercompany interest income and expense are eliminated by a debit to Other Revenues and a credit to Other Expenses.

Other Consolidated Financial Statements

Public corporations also prepare consolidated statements of stockholders' equity and consolidated statements of cash flows. For examples of these statements, see the financial statements in the Toys "R" Us, Inc., annual report.

Exhibit 4
Work Sheet Showing Eliminations for Preparing a Consolidated Income Statement

Exhibit 4
Work Sheet Showing Eliminations for Preparing a Consolidated Income Statement

Parent and Subsidiary Companies
Work Sheet for Consolidated Income Statement
For the Year Ended December 31, 20xx

Accounts	Income Statement, Parent Company	Income Statement, Subsidiary Company	Eliminations		Consolidated Income Statement
			Debit	Credit	
Sales	430,000	200,000	(1) 120,000		510,000
Other Revenues	60,000	10,000	(2) 2,000		68,000
Total Revenues	490,000	210,000			578,000
Cost of Goods Sold	210,000	150,000		(1) 120,000	240,000
Other Expenses	140,000	50,000		(2) 2,000	188,000
Total Costs and Expenses	350,000	200,000			428,000
Net Income	140,000	10,000	122,000	122,000	150,000

(1) Elimination of intercompany sales and purchases.
(2) Elimination of intercompany interest income and interest expense.

Chapter Review

REVIEW OF LEARNING OBJECTIVES

Ace it

1. **Define *exchange rate* and record transactions that are affected by changes in foreign exchange rates.** An *exchange rate* is the value of one currency stated in terms of another. A domestic company may make sales or purchases abroad in either its own country's currency or a foreign currency. If a transaction (sale or purchase) and its resolution (receipt or payment) are made in the domestic currency, no accounting problem arises. However, if the transaction and its resolution are made in a foreign currency and the exchange rate changes between the time of the transaction and its resolution, an exchange gain or loss will occur and should be recorded.

2. **Describe the restatement of a foreign subsidiary's financial statements in U.S. dollars.** Foreign financial statements are converted to U.S. dollars by multiplying the appropriate exchange rates by the amounts in the foreign financial statements. In general, the rates that apply depend on whether the subsidiary is separate and self-contained (Type I) or an integral part of the parent company (Type II).

3. **Describe the progress toward international accounting standards.** There has been some progress toward establishing international accounting standards, especially through the efforts of the International Accounting Standards

Committee and the International Federation of Accountants. However, there still are serious inconsistencies in financial reporting among countries. These inconsistencies make the comparison of financial statements from different countries difficult.

4. Identify the classifications of long-term investments in bonds and stocks. Long-term investments in bonds fall into two categories. First, bond investments classified as available-for-sale are recorded at cost and subsequently accounted for at fair value. Second, bond investments classified as held-to-maturity are accounted for at the amortized cost.

Long-term stock investments fall into three categories. First are noninfluential and noncontrolling investments, which represent less than 20 percent ownership. Second are influential but noncontrolling investments, which represent 20 percent to 50 percent ownership. Third are controlling interest investments, which represent more than 50 percent ownership.

5. Apply the cost adjusted to market method and the equity method as appropriate in accounting for long-term investments. The cost adjusted to market method is used to account for noninfluential and noncontrolling investments in stock. Under this method, investments are initially recorded at cost and then adjusted to market value based on overall portfolio valuations. The equity method is used to account for influential but noncontrolling investments. Under this method, the investment is initially recorded at cost and then adjusted for the investor's share of the investee's net income or loss and subsequent dividends.

6. Explain when to prepare consolidated financial statements, and describe the uses of such statements. The FASB requires that consolidated financial statements be prepared when an investing company has legal and effective control over another company. Control exists when the parent company owns more than 50 percent of the voting stock of the subsidiary company. Consolidated financial statements are useful to investors and others because they treat the parent company and its subsidiaries realistically, as an integrated economic unit.

7. Prepare the consolidated balance sheet at acquisition date for a purchase at (a) book value and (b) other than book value. At the date of acquisition, a work sheet entry is made to eliminate the investment from the parent company's financial statements and the stockholders' equity section of the subsidiary's financial statements. The assets and liabilities of the two companies are combined. If the parent owns less than 100 percent of the subsidiary, minority interest equal to the percentage of the subsidiary owned by minority stockholders multiplied by the stockholders' equity in the subsidiary will appear on the consolidated balance sheet. If the cost of the parent's investment in the subsidiary is greater than the subsidiary's book value, on the balance sheet, an amount equal to the excess of cost over book value will be allocated to undervalued subsidiary assets and to goodwill. If the cost of the parent's investment in the subsidiary is less than book value, the excess of book value over cost should be used to reduce the book value of the long-term assets (other than long-term marketable securities) of the subsidiary.

8. Prepare a consolidated income statement. When consolidated income statements are prepared, intercompany sales, purchases, interest income, interest expense, and other income and expenses from intercompany transactions must be eliminated to avoid double counting of these items.

The following concepts and terms were introduced in this chapter.

LO 4   **Available-for-sale securities:** Investments held by a company that it may at some point decide to sell.

LO 5   **Consolidated financial statements:** Financial statements that reflect the combined operations of a parent company and its subsidiaries.

LO 4   **Control:** The ability of an investing company to decide the operating and financial policies of another company through ownership of more than 50 percent of that other company's voting stock.

LO 5   **Cost adjusted to market method:** A method of accounting for available-for-sale securities at cost adjusted for changes in the market value of the securities.

LO 6   **Eliminations:** Entries made on consolidation work sheets to eliminate transactions between parent and subsidiary companies.

LO 5   **Equity method:** The method of accounting for long-term investments in which the investor records its share of the investee's periodic net income or loss as an increase or decrease in the Investment account and dividends as a decrease in the Investment account. Used when the investing company exercises significant influence over the other company.

LO 1   **Exchange gain or loss:** A gain or loss due to exchange rate fluctuation that is reported on the income statement.

LO 1   **Exchange rate:** The value of one currency in terms of another.

LO 2   **Functional currency:** The currency of the place where a subsidiary carries on most of its business.

LO 7   **Goodwill (*goodwill from consolidation*):** The amount paid for a subsidiary that exceeds the fair value of the subsidiary's assets less its liabilities.

LO 4   **Held-to-maturity securities:** Investments in debt securities that a company expects to hold until their maturity date.

LO 4   **Insider trading:** The practice of buying or selling shares of a publicly held company based on information that has not yet been made available to the public.

LO 7   **Minority interest:** The amount recorded on a consolidated balance sheet that represents the holdings of stockholders who own less than 50 percent of the voting stock of a subsidiary.

LO 1   **Multinational (transnational) corporations:** Companies that operate in more than one country.

LO 5   **Parent company:** An investing company that owns a controlling interest in another company.

LO 6   **Purchase method:** A method of accounting for parent-subsidiary relationships in which similar accounts from separate statements are combined. Used when the investing company owns more than 50 percent of a subsidiary.

LO 2   **Reporting currency:** The currency in which consolidated financial statements are presented.

LO 2   **Restatement:** The stating of one currency in terms of another.

LO 4   **Significant influence:** The ability of an investing company to affect the operating and financial policies of another company, even though the investor holds 50 percent or less of the voting stock.

LO 5   **Subsidiary:** An investee company in which a controlling interest is owned by another company.

Consolidated Balance Sheet: Less than 100 Percent Ownership

In a cash transaction, Taylor Company purchased 90 percent of the outstanding stock of Schumacher Company for $763,200 on June 30, 20xx. Directly after the acquisition, separate balance sheets of the companies appeared as follows:

	Taylor Company	Schumacher Company
Assets		
Cash	$ 400,000	$ 48,000
Accounts Receivable	650,000	240,000
Inventory	1,000,000	520,000
Investment in Schumacher Company	763,200	—
Plant and Equipment (net)	1,500,000	880,000
Other Assets	50,000	160,000
Total Assets	$4,363,200	$1,848,000
Liabilities and Stockholders' Equity		
Accounts Payable	$ 800,000	$ 400,000
Long-Term Debt	1,000,000	600,000
Common Stock, $5 par value	2,000,000	800,000
Retained Earnings	563,200	48,000
Total Liabilities and Stockholders' Equity	$4,363,200	$1,848,000

Additional information: (a) Schumacher Company's other assets represent a long-term investment in Taylor Company's long-term debt. The debt was purchased for an amount equal to Taylor's carrying value of the debt. (b) Taylor Company owes Schumacher Company $100,000 for services rendered.

Prepare a work sheet for preparing a consolidated balance sheet as of the acquisition date.

ANSWER TO REVIEW PROBLEM

Taylor and Schumacher Companies
Work Sheet for Consolidated Balance Sheet
June 30, 20xx

Accounts	Balance Sheet, Taylor Company	Balance Sheet, Schumacher Company	Eliminations Debit	Eliminations Credit	Consolidated Balance Sheet
Cash	400,000	48,000			448,000
Accounts Receivable	650,000	240,000		(3) 100,000	790,000
Inventory	1,000,000	520,000			1,520,000
Investment in					
Schumacher Company	763,200			(1) 763,200	
Plant and Equipment (net)	1,500,000	880,000			2,380,000
Other Assets	50,000	160,000		(2) 160,000	50,000
Total Assets	4,363,200	1,848,000			5,188,000
Accounts Payable	800,000	400,000	(3) 100,000		1,100,000
Long-Term Debt	1,000,000	600,000	(2) 160,000		1,440,000
Common Stock,					
$5 par value	2,000,000	800,000	(1) 800,000		2,000,000
Retained Earnings	563,200	48,000	(1) 48,000		563,200
Minority Interest				(1) 84,800	84,800
Total Liabilities and Stockholders' Equity	4,363,200	1,848,000	1,108,000	1,108,000	5,188,000

(1) Elimination of intercompany investment. Minority interest equals 10 percent of Schumacher Company's stockholders' equity [10% × ($800,000 + $48,000) = $84,800].
(2) Elimination of intercompany long-term debt.
(3) Elimination of intercompany receivables and payables.

Chapter Assignments

BUILDING YOUR KNOWLEDGE FOUNDATION

QUESTIONS

1. What does it mean to say that the exchange rate for the French franc in terms of the U.S. dollar is .15? If a bottle of French perfume costs 200 francs, how much will it cost in dollars?

2. If an American firm does business with a German firm and all their transactions take place in German marks, which firm may incur exchange gains or losses, and why?

3. What is the difference between a functional currency and a reporting currency?

4. If you as an investor were trying to evaluate the relative performance of General Motors, Volkswagen, and Toyota Motors from their published financial statements, what problems might you encounter (other than a language problem)?

5. What are some of the obstacles to uniform international accounting standards, and what efforts are being made to overcome them?

6. Why are the concepts of significant influence and control important in accounting for long-term investments?

7. For each of the following categories of long-term investments, briefly describe the applicable percentage of ownership and accounting treatment: (a) noninfluential and noncontrolling investment, (b) influential but noncontrolling investment, and (c) controlling investment.

8. What is meant by a parent-subsidiary relationship?

9. Would the stockholders of American Home Products Corporation be more interested in the consolidated financial statements of the overall company than in the statements of its many subsidiaries? Explain.

10. The 2000 annual report for Merchant Corporation included the following statement in its Summary of Significant Accounting Policies: "*Principles applied in consolidation.*—Majority-owned subsidiaries are consolidated, except for leasing and finance companies and those subsidiaries not considered to be material." What standard does this practice violate, and why?

11. Also in Merchant's annual report, in the Summary of Significant Accounting Policies, was the following statement: "*Investments.*—Investments in companies in which Merchant has significant influence in management are on the equity basis." What is the equity basis of accounting for investments, and why did Merchant use it in this case?

12. Why should intercompany receivables, payables, sales, and purchases be eliminated in the preparation of consolidated financial statements?

13. The following item appears on Merchant's consolidated balance sheet: "Minority Interest—$50,000." Explain how this item arose and where you would expect to find it on the consolidated balance sheet.

14. Why may the price paid to acquire a controlling interest in a subsidiary company exceed the subsidiary's book value?

15. The following item also appears on Merchant's consolidated balance sheet: "Goodwill from Consolidation—$70,000." Explain how this item arose and where you would expect to find it on the consolidated balance sheet.

16. Subsidiary Corporation has a book value of $100,000, of which Parent Corporation purchases 100 percent for $115,000. None of the excess of cost over book value is attributed to tangible assets. What is the amount of goodwill from consolidation?

17. Subsidiary Corporation, a wholly-owned subsidiary, has total sales of $500,000, $100,000 of which were made to Parent Corporation. Parent Corporation has total sales of $1,000,000, including sales of all items purchased from Subsidiary Corporation. What is the amount of sales on the consolidated income statement?

SHORT EXERCISES

SE 1.
LO 1 Recording Sales: Fluctuating Exchange Rate

Prepare an entry to record a sale by a U.S. company on account on September 12 in the amount of DM 420,000 to a German company. Also, record the subsequent collection in full in marks on October 12. On September 12 the exchange rate was $.60 per mark, and on October 12 it was $.50 per mark.

SE 2.
LO 1 Recording Purchases: Fluctuating Exchange Rate

Prepare an entry to record a purchase by a U.S. company on account on September 12 in the amount of DM 420,000 from a German company. Also, record the subsequent payment in full in marks on October 12. On September 12 the exchange rate was $.60 per mark, and on October 12 it was $.50 per mark.

SE 3.
LO 5 Cost Adjusted to Market Method

At December 31, 20x1, the market value of The Cedar Deck Company's portfolio of long-term available-for-sale securities was $320,000. The cost of these securities was $285,000. Prepare the entry to adjust the portfolio to market at year end, assuming that the company did not have any long-term investments prior to 20x1.

SE 4.

LO 5 Cost Adjusted to Market Method

Refer to your answer to **SE 3** and assume that at December 31, 20x2, the cost of The Cedar Deck Company's portfolio of long-term available-for-sale securities was $640,000 and that its market value was $600,000. Prepare the entry to record the 20x2 year-end adjustment.

SE 5.

LO 5 Equity Method

Sturchio Company owns 30 percent of Raymond Company. In 20x1, Raymond Company earned $120,000 and paid $80,000 in dividends. Prepare journal entries for Sturchio Company's records on December 31 to reflect this information. Assume that the dividends are received on December 31.

SE 6.

LO 5 Methods of Accounting
LO 6 for Long-Term Investments

For each of the investments listed below, tell which of the following methods should be used for external financial reporting: (a) cost adjusted to market method, (b) equity method, (c) consolidation of parent and subsidiary financial statements.

1. 49 percent investment in Motir Corporation
2. 51 percent investment in Saris Corporation
3. 5 percent investment in Ransor Corporation

SE 7.

LO 7 Purchase of 100 Percent at Book Value

Maple House Corporation buys 100 percent ownership of Winter Sweets Corporation for $50,000. At the time of the purchase, Winter Sweets' stockholders' equity consists of $10,000 in common stock and $40,000 in retained earnings, and Maple House's stockholders' equity consists of $100,000 in common stock and $200,000 in retained earnings. After the purchase, what would be the amount, if any, of the following accounts on the consolidated balance sheet: Goodwill, Minority Interest, Common Stock, and Retained Earnings?

SE 8.

LO 7 Purchase of Less Than 100 Percent at Book Value

Assume the same facts as in **SE 7** except that the purchase was 80 percent of Winter Sweets Corporation for $40,000. After the purchase, what would be the amount, if any, of the following accounts on the consolidated balance sheet: Goodwill, Minority Interest, Common Stock, and Retained Earnings?

SE 9.

LO 7 Purchase of 100 Percent at More Than Book Value

Assume the same facts as in **SE 7** except that the purchase of 100 percent of Winter Sweets Corporation was for $60,000. After the purchase, what would be the amount, if any, of the following accounts on the consolidated balance sheet: Goodwill, Minority Interest, Common Stock, and Retained Earnings? Assume that the fair value of Winter Sweets' net assets equals their book value.

SE 10.

LO 7 Intercompany
LO 8 Transactions

T Company owns 100 percent of C Company. Some of the separate accounts from the balance sheets and income statements for T Company and C Company appear below:

	T Company	C Company
Accounts Receivable	$ 230,000	$150,000
Accounts Payable	180,000	90,000
Sales	1,200,000	890,000
Cost of Goods Sold	710,000	540,000

What would be the combined amount of each of the above accounts on the consolidated financial statements assuming the following additional information: (a) C Company sold to T Company merchandise at cost in the amount of $270,000; (b) all of the merchandise sold by C Company to T Company had been resold by T Company to customers, but it still owes C Company $60,000 for the merchandise.

EXERCISES

E 1.

LO 1 Recording International Transactions: Fluctuating Exchange Rate

Cleveland Corporation purchased a special-purpose machine from Leipzig Corporation on credit for DM 50,000. At the date of purchase, the exchange rate was $.55 per mark. On the date of the payment, which was made in marks, the value of the mark had increased to $.60.

Prepare journal entries to record the purchase and payment in Cleveland Corporation's accounting records.

E 2.

LO 1 **Recording International Transactions**

U.S. Corporation made a sale on account to U.K. Company on November 15 in the amount of £300,000. Payment was to be made in British pounds on February 15. U.S. Corporation's fiscal year is the same as the calendar year. The British pound was worth $1.70 on November 15, $1.58 on December 31, and $1.78 on February 15.

Prepare journal entries to record the sale, year-end adjustment, and collection on U.S. Corporation's books.

E 3.

LO 5 **Long-Term Investments**

Laslow Corporation has the following portfolio of long-term available-for-sale securities at year end:

Company	Percentage of Voting Stock Held	Cost	Year-End Market Value
A Corporation	4	$160,000	$190,000
B Corporation	12	750,000	550,000
C Corporation	5	60,000	110,000
Total		$970,000	$850,000

The Unrealized Loss on Long-Term Investments account and the Allowance to Adjust Long-Term Investments to Market account each currently have a balance of $80,000 from the last accounting period. Prepare the year-end adjustment to reflect the above information.

E 4.

LO 4 **Long-Term Investments:**
LO 5 **Cost Adjusted to Market and Equity Methods**

On January 1, Kelley Corporation purchased, as long-term investments, 8 percent of the voting stock of Wexler Corporation for $500,000 and 45 percent of the voting stock of Pati Corporation for $2 million. During the year, Wexler Corporation had earnings of $200,000 and paid dividends of $80,000. Pati Corporation had earnings of $600,000 and paid dividends of $400,000. The market value of neither investment changed during the year. Which of these investments should be accounted for using the cost adjusted to market method? Which using the equity method? At what amount should each investment be carried on the balance sheet at year end? Give a reason for each choice.

E 5.

LO 5 **Long-Term Investments: Equity Method**

On January 1, 20xx, Cszick Corporation acquired 40 percent of the voting stock of Antonio Corporation, an amount sufficient to exercise significant influence over Antonio Corporation's activities, for $2,400,000 in cash. On December 31, Cszick determined that Antonio paid dividends of $400,000 but incurred a net loss of $200,000 for 20xx. Prepare journal entries in Cszick Corporation's records to reflect this information.

E 6.

LO 5 **Methods of Accounting**
LO 6 **for Long-Term Investments**

Diversified Corporation has the following long-term investments:

1. 60 percent of the common stock of Down Corporation
2. 13 percent of the common stock of West Lake, Inc.
3. 50 percent of the nonvoting preferred stock of Invole Corporation
4. 100 percent of the common stock of its financing subsidiary, DCF, Inc.
5. 35 percent of the common stock of the French company Maison de Boutaine
6. 70 percent of the common stock of the Canadian company Alberta Mining Company

For each of these investments, tell which of the following methods should be used for external financial reporting, and why.

a. Cost adjusted to market method
b. Equity method
c. Consolidation of parent and subsidiary financial statements

E 7.

LO 7 **Elimination Entry for a Purchase at Book Value**

The Telon Manufacturing Company purchased 100 percent of the common stock of the Reed Manufacturing Company for $300,000. Reed's stockholders' equity included common stock of $200,000 and retained earnings of $100,000. Prepare the eliminating entry in journal form that would appear on the work sheet for consolidating the balance sheets of these two entities as of the acquisition date.

E 8.

LO 7 Elimination Entry and Minority Interest

The stockholders' equity section of the Gleason Corporation's balance sheet appeared as follows on December 31:

Common Stock, $10 par value, 40,000 shares authorized and issued	$400,000
Retained Earnings	48,000
Total Stockholders' Equity	$448,000

Assume that Asuto Manufacturing Company owns 80 percent of the voting stock of Gleason Corporation and paid $11.20 for each share. In journal form, prepare the entry (including minority interest) to eliminate Asuto's investment and Gleason's stockholders' equity that would appear on the work sheet used in preparing the consolidated balance sheet for the two firms.

E 9.

LO 7 Consolidated Balance Sheet with Goodwill

On September 1, 20x1, S Company purchased 100 percent of the voting stock of T Company for $960,000 in cash. The separate condensed balance sheets immediately after the purchase follow:

	S Company	T Company
Other Assets	$2,206,000	$1,089,000
Investment in T Company	960,000	—
Total Assets	$3,166,000	$1,089,000
Liabilities	$ 871,000	$ 189,000
Common Stock, $1 par value	1,000,000	300,000
Retained Earnings	1,295,000	600,000
Total Liabilities and Stockholders' Equity	$3,166,000	$1,089,000

Prepare a work sheet for preparing the consolidated balance sheet immediately after S Company acquired control of T Company. Assume that any excess cost of the investment in the subsidiary over book value is attributable to goodwill from consolidation.

E 10.

LO 8 Preparation of Consolidated Income Statement

Saxe Company has owned 100 percent of Nepo Company since 20x0. The income statements of these two companies for the year ended December 31, 20x1, follow.

	Saxe Company	Nepo Company
Net Sales	$3,000,000	$1,200,000
Cost of Goods Sold	1,500,000	800,000
Gross Margin	$1,500,000	$ 400,000
Less: Selling Expenses	$ 500,000	$ 100,000
General and Administrative Expenses	600,000	200,000
Total Operating Expenses	$1,100,000	$ 300,000
Income from Operations	$ 400,000	$ 100,000
Other Income	120,000	—
Net Income	$ 520,000	$ 100,000

Additional information: (a) Nepo Company purchased $560,000 of inventory from Saxe Company, which had been sold to Nepo Company customers by the end of the year. (b) Nepo Company leased its building from Saxe Company for $120,000 per year.

Prepare a consolidated income statement work sheet for the two companies for the year ended December 31, 20x1. Ignore income taxes.

PROBLEMS

P 1.
LO 1 International Transactions

High Valley Company, whose year end is June 30, engaged in the following international transactions (exchange rates in parentheses):

May 15 Purchased goods from a Japanese firm for $110,000; terms n/10 in U.S. dollars (yen = $.0080).

17 Sold goods to a German company for $165,000; terms n/30 in marks (mark = $.55).

21 Purchased goods from a Mexican company for $120,000; terms n/30 in pesos (peso = $.10).

25 Paid for the goods purchased on May 15 (yen = $.0085).

31 Sold goods to an Italian firm for $200,000; terms n/60 in lire (lira = $.0005).

June 5 Sold goods to a British firm for $56,000; terms n/10 in U.S. dollars (pound = $1.30).

7 Purchased goods from a Japanese firm for $221,000; terms n/30 in yen (yen = $.0085).

15 Received payment for the sale made on June 5 (pound = $1.80).

16 Received payment for the sale made on May 17 (mark = $.60).

17 Purchased goods from a French firm for $66,000; terms n/30 in U.S. dollars (franc = $.16).

20 Paid for the goods purchased on May 21 (peso = $.09).

22 Sold goods to a British firm for $108,000; terms n/30 in pounds (pound = $1.80).

30 Made year-end adjusting entries for incomplete foreign exchange transactions (franc = $.17; peso = $.09; mark = $.60; lira = $.0003; pound = $1.70; yen = $.0090).

July 7 Paid for the goods purchased on June 7 (yen = $.0085).

19 Paid for the goods purchased on June 17 (franc = $.15).

22 Received payment for the goods sold on June 22 (pound = $1.60).

30 Received payment for the goods sold on May 31 (lira = $.0004).

REQUIRED

Prepare entries in journal form for these transactions.

P 2.
LO 5 Long-Term Investment Transactions

Red Bud Corporation made the following transactions in its Long-Term Investments account over a two-year period:

20x0

Apr. 1 Purchased with cash 20,000 shares of Season Company stock for $152 per share.

June 1 Purchased with cash 15,000 shares of Abbado Corporation stock for $72 per share.

Sept. 1 Received a $1 per share dividend from Season Company.

Nov. 1 Purchased with cash 25,000 shares of Frankel Corporation stock for $110 per share.

Dec. 31 Market values per share of shares held in the Long-Term Investments account were as follows: Season Company, $140; Abbado Corporation, $32; and Frankel Corporation, $122.

20x1

Feb. 1 Because of unfavorable prospects for Abbado Corporation, Abbado stock was sold for cash at $40 per share.

May 1 Purchased with cash 10,000 shares of Schulian Corporation for $224 per share.

Sept. 1 Received $2 per share dividend from Season Company.

Dec. 31 Market values per share of shares held in the Long-Term Investments account were as follows: Season Company, $160; Frankel Corporation, $140; and Schulian Corporation, $200.

REQUIRED

Prepare entries to record these transactions in the Red Bud Corporation records. Assume that all investments represent less than 20 percent of the voting stock of the company whose stock was acquired.

P 3.

LO 5 **Long-Term Investments:**
Equity Method

The Modi Company owns 40 percent of the voting stock of the Vivanco Company. The Investment account for this company on the Modi Company's balance sheet had a balance of $600,000 on January 1, 20xx. During 20xx, the Vivanco Company reported the following quarterly earnings and dividends paid:

Quarter	Earnings	Dividends Paid
1	$ 80,000	$ 40,000
2	60,000	40,000
3	160,000	40,000
4	(40,000)	40,000
	$260,000	$160,000

The Modi Company exercises a significant influence over the operations of the Vivanco Company and therefore uses the equity method to account for its investment.

REQUIRED

1. Prepare the entries in journal form that the Modi Company must make each quarter in accounting for its investment in the Vivanco Company.

2. Prepare a T account for the investment in common stock of the Vivanco Company. Enter the beginning balance, relevant portions of the entries made in **1,** and the ending balance.

P 4.

LO 7 **Consolidated Balance Sheet:**
n 100 Percent
ip

In a cash transaction, Geis Company purchased 70 percent of the outstanding stock of Vo Company for $593,600 cash on June 30, 20xx. Immediately after the acquisition, the separate balance sheets of the companies appeared as shown below.

	Geis Company	Vo Company
Assets		
Cash	$ 320,000	$ 48,000
Accounts Receivable	520,000	240,000
Inventory	800,000	520,000
Investment in Vo Company	593,600	—
Property, Plant, and Equipment (net)	1,200,000	880,000
Other Assets	40,000	160,000
Total Assets	$3,473,600	$1,848,000
Liabilities and Stockholders' Equity		
Accounts Payable	$ 640,000	$ 400,000
Long-Term Debt	800,000	600,000
Common Stock, $10 par value	1,600,000	800,000
Retained Earnings	433,600	48,000
Total Liabilities and Stockholders' Equity	$3,473,600	$1,848,000

Additional information: (a) Vo Company's other assets represent a long-term investment in Geis Company's long-term debt. The debt was purchased for an amount equal to Geis's carrying value of the debt. (b) Geis Company owes Vo Company $80,000 for services rendered.

REQUIRED

Prepare a work sheet for preparing a consolidated balance sheet as of the acquisition date.

P 5.
LO 7 Consolidated Balance Sheet: Cost Exceeding Book Value

The balance sheets of Sabzaal and Joseph Companies as of December 31, 20xx, are as follows.

	Sabzaal Company	Joseph Company
Assets		
Cash	$ 120,000	$ 80,000
Accounts Receivable	200,000	60,000
Investment in Joseph Company	700,000	—
Property, Plant, and Equipment (net)	200,000	360,000
Total Assets	$1,220,000	$500,000
Liabilities and Stockholders' Equity		
Accounts Payable	$ 220,000	$ 60,000
Common Stock, $20 par value	800,000	400,000
Retained Earnings	200,000	40,000
Total Liabilities and Stockholders' Equity	$1,220,000	$500,000

REQUIRED

Prepare a consolidated balance sheet work sheet for the Sabzaal and Joseph Companies. Assume that the Sabzaal Company purchased 100 percent of Joseph's common stock for $700,000 immediately prior to December 31, 20xx. Also assume that $160,000 of the excess of cost over book value is attributable to the increased value of Joseph Company's property, plant, and equipment. The rest of the excess is considered by the Sabzaal Company to be goodwill.

ALTERNATE PROBLEMS

P 6.
LO 5 Long-Term Investments Transactions

On January 2, 20x0, the Healey Company made several long-term investments in the voting stock of various companies. It purchased 10,000 shares of Zweig at $4.00 a share, 15,000 shares of Kamb at $6.00 a share, and 6,000 shares of Rodriguez at $9.00 a share. Each investment represents less than 20 percent of the voting stock of the company. The remaining securities transactions of Healey during 20x0 were as follows:

May 5	Purchased with cash 6,000 shares of Drennan stock for $6.00 per share. This investment represents less than 20 percent of the Drennan voting stock.
July 16	Sold the 10,000 shares of Zweig stock for $3.60 per share.
Sept. 30	Purchased with cash 5,000 additional shares of Kamb for $6.40 per share. This investment still represents less than 20 percent of the voting stock.
Dec. 31	The market values per share of the stock in the Long-Term Investments account were as follows: Kamb, $6.50; Rodriguez, $8.00; and Drennan, $4.00.

Healey's transactions in securities during 20x1 were as follows:

Feb. 1	Received a cash dividend from Kamb of $.20 per share.
July 15	Sold the 6,000 Rodriguez shares for $8.00 per share.
Aug. 1	Received a cash dividend from Kamb of $.20 per share.
Sept. 10	Purchased 3,000 shares of Parmet for $14.00 per share. This investment represents less than 20 percent of the voting stock of the company.
Dec. 31	The market values per share of the stock in the Long-Term Investments account were as follows: Kamb, $6.50; Drennan, $5.00; and Parmet, $13.00.

REQUIRED

Prepare the journal entries to record all of Healey Company's transactions in long-term investments during 20x0 and 20x1.

LO 5 **Long-Term Investments: Equity Method**

P 7. Rylander Corporation owns 35 percent of the voting stock of Waters Corporation. The Investment account on the books of Rylander Corporation as of January 1, 20xx, was $720,000. During 20xx, Waters Corporation reported the following quarterly earnings and dividends:

Quarter	Earnings	Dividends Paid
1	$160,000	$100,000
2	240,000	100,000
3	120,000	100,000
4	(80,000)	100,000
	$440,000	$400,000

Because of the percentage of voting shares Rylander owns, it can exercise significant influence over the operations of Waters Corporation. Therefore, Rylander Corporation must account for the investment using the equity method.

REQUIRED

1. Prepare the entries in journal form that Rylander Corporation must make each quarter to record its share of earnings and dividends.

2. Prepare a T account for Rylander Corporation's investment in Waters, and enter the beginning balance, the relevant entries from **1**, and the ending balance.

EXPANDING YOUR CRITICAL THINKING, COMMUNICATION, AND INTERPERSONAL SKILLS

SKILLS DEVELOPMENT

Conceptual Analysis

LO 1 **Effect of Change in Exchange Rate**

SD 1. *Compagnie Générale des Etablissements Michelin,* the famous French maker of Michelin tires, is one of the world's largest tiremakers. The company also owns the former U.S. tiremaker Uniroyal Goodrich Tire Company. In recent years, Michelin's sales, or exports, of tires made in France and exported to the United States have been enhanced by a relatively strong dollar. Explain why a strong dollar would lead to an increase in Michelin's sales. Why are sales of Uniroyal Goodrich in the United States not relevant to a discussion of the effects of a strong dollar?

LO 1 **Effects of Changes in Exchange Rates**

SD 2. *Japan Air Lines,* one of the world's top-ranking airlines, has an extensive global network of passenger and cargo services. The company engages in sales and purchase transactions throughout the world. At the end of the year, it will have receivables and payables in many currencies that must be translated into yen for preparation of its consolidated financial statements. The company's annual report notes that these receivables and payables are translated at the applicable year-end rates. What will be the financial effects (exchange gain or loss) under each of the following independent assumptions about changes in the exchange rates since the transactions that gave rise to the receivables or payables occurred? (1) Receivables exceed payables, and on average the yen has risen relative to other currencies. (2) Receivables exceed payables, and on average the yen has fallen relative to other currencies. (3) Payables exceed receivables, and on average the yen has risen relative to other currencies. (4) Payables exceed receivables, and on average the yen has fallen relative to other currencies. Suggest some ways in which Japan Air Lines can minimize the effects of the fluctuations in exchange rates as they relate to receivables and payables.

| Cash Flow | CD-ROM | Communication | Critical Thinking | Ethics | General Ledger | Group Activity | Hot Links to Real Companies | International | Internet | Key Ratio | Memo | Spreadsheet |

Ethical Dilemma

Refer to the Business Focus on Ethics box on page 739 in the chapter to answer the following questions:

1. What is meant by the phrase "insider trading"?
2. Why do you think insider trading is unethical and illegal in the United States and now in Germany?
3. Why do you think insider trading is an allowable practice in some other countries?
4. Do you think the prohibition of insider trading in the United States is the correct approach? Why or why not?

Group Activity: Divide the class into groups to discuss the above questions. Also, ask the groups to consider why what is considered ethical differs from country to country. Debrief in class.

Research Activity

Go to the section of the library where recent issues of *The Wall Street Journal* are located. From the index on the front page of Section C, "Money & Investing," find the page number of "foreign exchange." In the "Currency Trading" portion of that page, find a table entitled "Exchange Rates." This table shows the exchange rates of the currencies of about 50 countries with the U.S. dollar. Choose the currency of any country in which you are interested. Write down the value of that currency in U.S. dollar equivalents for one day in the first week of each month for the past six months, as reported in *The Wall Street Journal.* Prepare a chart that shows the variation in exchange rate for this currency over this time period. Assuming that you run a company that exports goods to the country you chose, would you find the change in exchange rate over the past six months favorable or unfavorable? Assuming that you run a company that imports goods from the country you chose, would you find the change in exchange rate over the past six months favorable or unfavorable? Explain your answers and tell what business practices you would follow to offset any adverse effects of exchange rate fluctuations. Be prepared to discuss your results in class.

Decision-Making Practice

Gulf Coast Corporation is a successful oil and gas exploration business in the southwestern part of the United States. At the beginning of 20xx, the company made investments in three companies that perform services in the oil and gas industry. The details of each of these investments are presented in the next three paragraphs.

Gulf Coast purchased 100,000 shares of Marsh Service Corporation at a cost of $16 per share. Marsh has 1.5 million shares outstanding, and during 20xx paid dividends of $.80 per share on earnings of $1.60 per share. At the end of the year, Marsh's shares were selling for $24 per share.

Gulf Coast also purchased 2 million shares of Crescent Drilling Company at $8 per share. Crescent has 10 million shares outstanding. In 20xx, Crescent paid a dividend of $.40 per share on earnings of $.80 per share. During the current year the president of Gulf Coast was appointed to the board of directors of Crescent. At the end of the year, Crescent's stock was selling for $12 per share.

In another action, Gulf Coast purchased 1 million of Logan Oil Field Supplies Company's 5 million outstanding shares at $12 per share. The president of Gulf Coast sought membership on the board of directors of Logan but was rebuffed by Logan's board when shareholders representing a majority of Logan's outstanding stock stated that they did not want to be associated with Gulf Coast. Logan paid a dividend of $.80 per share and reported a net income of only $.40 per share for the year. By the end of the year, the price of its stock had dropped to $4 per share.

1. What principal factors must you consider in order to determine how to account for Gulf Coast's investments? Should they be shown on the balance sheet as short-term or long-term investments? What factors affect this decision?

2. For each of the three investments, make entries in journal form for each of the following: (a) initial investment, (b) receipt of cash dividend, and (c) recognition of income (if appropriate).

3. What adjusting entry (if any) is required at the end of the year?

4. Assuming that Gulf Coast's investment in Logan is sold after the first of the year for $6 per share, what journal entry would be made? Assuming no other transactions and that the market value of the remaining investment in Marsh held by Gulf Coast exceeds cost by $2,400,000 at the end of the second year, what adjusting entry (if any) would be required?

FINANCIAL REPORTING AND ANALYSIS

Interpreting Financial Reports

FRA 1.

LO 6 Effects of Consolidating
LO 7 Finance Subsidiaries

Metropolitan Stores Corporation is one of the largest owners of discount appliance stores in the United States. It owns Highway Superstores, among several other discount chains. The company has a wholly owned finance subsidiary to finance its accounts receivable. Condensed balance sheets for Metropolitan Stores and its finance subsidiary (in millions) are shown below.[16] The fiscal year ends January 31.

	Metropolitan Stores Corporation	Finance Subsidiary
Assets		
Current Assets (except Accounts Receivable)	$ 866	$ 1
Accounts Receivable (net)	293	869
Property, Equipment, and Other Assets	933	—
Investment in Finance Subsidiary	143	—
Total Assets	$2,235	$870
Liabilities and Stockholders' Equity		
Current Liabilities	$ 717	$ 10
Long-Term Liabilities	859	717
Stockholders' Equity	659	143
Total Liabilities and Stockholders' Equity	$2,235	$870

Total sales to customers were $4 billion. The Financial Accounting Standards Board's *Statement No. 94* requires all majority-owned subsidiaries to be consolidated in the parent company's financial statements. Metropolitan's management believes that it is misleading to consolidate the finance subsidiary because it distorts the real operations of the company. You are asked to assess the effects of the statement on Metropolitan Stores' financial position.

REQUIRED

1. Prepare a consolidated balance sheet for Metropolitan Stores Corporation and its finance subsidiary.

2. Demonstrate the effects of FASB *Statement No. 94* by computing the following ratios for Metropolitan Stores before and after the consolidation in **1**: receivable turnover, average days' sales uncollected, and debt to equity (use year-end balances).

3. What are some of the other ratios that will be affected by the implementation of FASB *Statement No. 94*? Does consolidation assist investors and creditors in assessing the risk of investing in Metropolitan Stores' securities or loaning the company money? Relate your answer to your calculations in **2**. What do you think of management's position?

International Company

FRA 2.

LO 3 **Differences Between U.S. and U.K. Accounting Principles**

Cable and Wireless, plc, is a major global communications company that provides business networks and mobile communications in Europe, the Caribbean, and Asia. This United Kingdom company publishes its financial statements in accordance with generally accepted accounting principles (GAAP) in the United Kingdom but includes in its annual report a very interesting summary of the differences that would result if selected financial data were presented in accordance with GAAP in the United States, as shown below (in millions).[17]

Effect of Differences	Per U.K. GAAP		Per U.S. GAAP	
	1999 £m	1998 £m	1999 £m	1998 £m
Net income (as below)	908	1,288	670	1,288
Stockholders' equity	4,571	2,964	6,624	5,145

	1999 £m	1998 £m
Net income as reported under U.K. GAAP	908	1,288
U.S. GAAP adjustments:		
Amortisation of goodwill	(158)	(92)
Goodwill written off in respect of sale of investments	6	10
Partial depreciation	(11)	—
Equity accounting	(53)	—
Capitalisation of interest	(11)	(16)
Deferred tax—full provision	44	(31)
—reconciling items	(5)	9
Pension costs	21	(4)
Customer acquisition costs	(16)	—
Restructuring costs	—	(20)
Cumulative exchange loss on sale of investments	(37)	—
Gain on sale of subsidiary undertaking	—	138
Other	(38)	(5)
Minority interest	20	11
Net income	670	1,288

Assume that an investment analyst has asked you to evaluate Cable and Wireless's profitability. Prepare a memorandum that shows the calculation of return on equity for 1998 and 1999 under U.K. GAAP and U.S. GAAP, using year-end amounts. Indicate which country's GAAP shows better results. Explain the role of goodwill and intangibles in this difference. (**Hint:** Recall that purchased goodwill is shown as an asset and is amortized on the income statement in the United States, whereas it is deducted from stockholders' equity and does not appear on the income statement in the United Kingdom.) Identify two other important differences in accounting principles between U.K. GAAP and U.S. GAAP. Also, comment on whether accounting principles appear to be more conservative under U.K. GAAP or U.S. GAAP.

Toys "R" Us Annual Report

FRA 3.

LO 1 **Effects of Foreign**
LO 2 **Exchange**

Refer to the Toys "R" Us annual report to answer the following questions. From the note to the financial statements on segments, what percentage of Toys "R" Us sales are international? In a note to the financial statements, management indicates that the company has borrowed money in Japanese yen. Would a strong or a weak dollar have a favorable effect on international sales? Does the same conclusion hold for the money borrowed in Japanese yen?

Fingraph® Financial Analyst™

FRA 4.

LO 4 **Long-Term Investments**
LO 5 **Analysis**

Select any two companies from the same industry on the Fingraph® Financial Analyst™ CD-ROM software.

1. In the annual reports for the companies you have selected, identify the balance sheet accounts and notes to the financial statements associated with long-term investments. What type of long-term investments does each company have? Are the investments valued at cost or market? What is the difference between cost and market value? Did the companies report unrealized gains and losses on their investments? Summarize in a table the types of investments, how they are valued, and the amount of cost and market value and unrealized gains and losses.

2. Identify the income statements for the companies you selected. Did the companies report any interest or dividend income? If so, what are these amounts? An examination of the notes may be necessary.

3. Write a one-page executive summary that highlights the types of long-term investments and their valuation, and the impact on net income in the current year, including reference to management's assessment. Include your table as an attachment to your report.

Internet Case

FRA 5.

LO 4 **Comparison of Two Recent**
LO 6 **Acquisitions**

Mergers and acquisitions are in the news almost every day. Go to the Needles Accounting Resource Center at http://college.hmco.com. Under Web Resources, go to the web site for *MSNBC.* Scan the headlines for the past few days to locate two articles related to one company purchasing or making an offer to purchase another company. Read the articles and summarize the nature of the actual or proposed acquisition. What are the names of the companies? What industry are they in? What is the dollar amount of the acquisition? How will the acquisition be paid for—through cash, stock, or a combination? In what ways are the acquisitions similar? How are they different? Be prepared to present your findings in class.

ENDNOTES

1. At the time this chapter was written, exchange rates were fluctuating rapidly. Thus, the examples, exercises, and problems in this book use exchange rates in the general range for the countries involved.
2. *Statement of Financial Accounting Standards No. 52,* "Foreign Currency Translation" (Norwalk, Conn.: Financial Accounting Standards Board, 1981), par. 15.
3. This section is based on the requirements of *Statement of Financial Accounting Standards No. 52,* "Foreign Currency Translation" (Norwalk, Conn.: Financial Accounting Standards Board, 1981).
4. Glaxo Wellcome, *Annual Report,* 1998.
5. *Financial Reporting: An International Survey* (New York: Price Waterhouse, May 1995).
6. *International Accounting and Auditing Trends* (Princeton, N.J.: CIFAP Publications, 5th ed., 1996).
7. "International Accounting Standards Committee Objectives and Procedures," *Professional Standards* (New York: American Institute of Certified Public Accountants, 1988), Volume B, Section 9000, par. 24–27.
8. Greg Steinmetz and Cacilie Rohwedder, "SAP Insider Probe Points to Reforms Needed in Germany," *The Wall Street Journal,* May 8, 1997.
9. John J. Keller, "Ameritech, GE Plan $472 Million Data Venture," *The Wall Street Journal,* December 21, 1993.

10. The Financial Accounting Standards Board points out in its *Interpretation No. 35* (May 1981) that although the presumption of significant influence applies when 20 percent or more of the voting stock is held, the rule is not a rigid one. All relevant facts and circumstances should be examined in each case to find out whether or not significant influence exists. For example, the FASB notes five circumstances that may remove the element of significant influence: (1) The company files a lawsuit against the investor or complains to a government agency; (2) the investor tries and fails to become a director; (3) the investor agrees not to increase its holdings; (4) the company is operated by a small group that ignores the investor's wishes; (5) the investor tries and fails to obtain additional information from the company that is not available to other stockholders.

11. *Statement of Financial Accounting Standards No. 115*, "Accounting for Certain Investments in Debt and Equity Securities" (Norwalk, Conn.: Financial Accounting Standards Board, 1993).

12. If the decrease in value is deemed permanent, a different procedure is followed to record the decline in market value of the long-term investment. A loss account that appears on the income statement is debited instead of the Unrealized Loss account.

13. "The Year's Biggest Deals," *Business Week*, January 11, 1999.

14. *Statement of Financial Accounting Standards No. 94*, "Consolidation of All Majority-Owned Subsidiaries" (Norwalk, Conn.: Financial Accounting Standards Board, 1987).

15. Accounting Principles Board, *Opinion No. 16*, "Business Combinations" (New York: Accounting Principles Board, 1970), par. 87.

16. Metropolitan Stores Corporation, *Annual Report*, 1997.

17. Cable and Wireless, plc, *Annual Report*, 1996.

APPENDIX A

The Merchandising Work Sheet and Closing Entries

This appendix shows how the work sheet and closing entries are prepared for merchandising companies. The work sheet for a merchandising company is basically the same as that for a service business, except that it includes the additional accounts that are needed to handle merchandising transactions. The treatment of these new accounts differs depending on whether a company uses the periodic or the perpetual inventory system.

The Periodic Inventory System

The new accounts for a merchandising company using the periodic inventory system generally include Sales, Sales Returns and Allowances, Sales Discounts, Purchases, Purchases Returns and Allowances, Purchases Discounts, Freight In, and Merchandise Inventory. Except for Merchandise Inventory, these accounts are treated in much the same way as revenue and expense accounts for a service company. They are transferred to the Income Summary account in the closing process. On the work sheet, they are extended to the Income Statement columns.

Merchandise Inventory requires special treatment under the periodic inventory system because purchases of merchandise are accumulated in the Purchases account. No entries are made to the Merchandise Inventory account during the accounting period. Its balance at the end of the period, before adjusting and closing entries, is the same as it was at the beginning of the period. Thus, its balance at this point represents beginning merchandise inventory. Remember also that the cost of goods sold is determined by adding beginning merchandise inventory to net cost of purchases and then subtracting ending merchandise inventory. The objectives of handling merchandise inventory in the closing entries at the end of the period are to (1) remove the beginning balance from the Merchandise Inventory account, (2) enter the ending balance into the Merchandise Inventory account, and (3) enter the beginning inventory as a debit and the ending inventory as a credit to the Income Summary account to calculate net income. Using the figures for the Fenwick Fashions Corporation example in the chapter on accounting for merchandising operations, the T accounts below show how these objectives can be met:

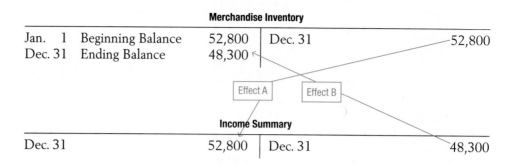

Merchandise Inventory

Jan. 1	Beginning Balance	52,800	Dec. 31	52,800
Dec. 31	Ending Balance	48,300		

Effect A   Effect B

Income Summary

Dec. 31	52,800	Dec. 31	48,300

In this example, merchandise inventory was $52,800 at the beginning of the year and $48,300 at the end of the year. Effect A removes the $52,800 from Merchandise Inventory, leaving a zero balance, and transfers it to Income Summary. In Income Summary, the $52,800 is in effect added to net purchases because, like expenses, the balance of the Purchases account is debited to Income Summary in a closing entry. Effect B establishes the ending balance of Merchandise Inventory, $48,300, and enters it as a credit in the Income Summary account. The credit entry in Income Summary has the effect of deducting the ending inventory from goods available for sale because both purchases and beginning inventory are entered on the debit side. In other words, beginning merchandise inventory and purchases are debits to Income Summary, and ending merchandise inventory is a credit to Income Summary.

The work sheet for Fenwick Fashions Corporation is shown in Exhibit 1 and is discussed below.

TRIAL BALANCE COLUMNS The first step in the preparation of the work sheet is to enter the balances from the ledger accounts into the Trial Balance columns. You are already familiar with this procedure.

ADJUSTMENTS COLUMNS The adjusting entries for Fenwick Fashions Corporation are entered in the Adjustments columns in the same way that they were for service companies. No adjusting entry is made for merchandise inventory. After the adjusting entries are entered on the work sheet, the columns are totaled to prove that total debits equal total credits.

OMISSION OF ADJUSTED TRIAL BALANCE COLUMNS These two columns, which appeared in the work sheet for a service company, can be omitted. They are optional and are used when there are many adjusting entries to record. When only a few adjusting entries are required, as is the case for Fenwick Fashions Corporation, these columns are not necessary and may be omitted to save time.

INCOME STATEMENT AND BALANCE SHEET COLUMNS After the Trial Balance columns have been totaled, the adjustments entered, and the equality of the columns proved, the balances are extended to the Income Statement and Balance Sheet columns. Again, begin with the Cash account at the top of the work sheet and move sequentially down the work sheet, one account at a time, entering each account balance in the correct Income Statement or Balance Sheet column.

The "problem" extension here is in the Merchandise Inventory row. The beginning inventory balance of $52,800 (which is already in the trial balance) is extended to the debit column of the Income Statement columns, as shown in Exhibit 1. This

Exhibit 1
Work Sheet for Fenwick Fashions Corporation: Periodic Inventory System

Fenwick Fashions Corporation
Work Sheet
For the Year Ended December 31, 20xx

Account Name	Trial Balance		Adjustments		Income Statement		Balance Sheet	
	Debit	Credit	Debit	Credit	Debit	Credit	Debit	Credit
Cash	29,410						29,410	
Accounts Receivable	42,400						42,400	
Merchandise Inventory	52,800				52,800	48,300	48,300	
Prepaid Insurance	17,400			(a) 5,800			11,600	
Store Supplies	2,600			(b) 1,540			1,060	
Office Supplies	1,840			(c) 1,204			636	
Land	4,500						4,500	
Building	20,260						20,260	
Accumulated Depreciation, Building		5,650		(d) 2,600				8,250
Office Equipment	8,600						8,600	
Accumulated Depreciation, Office Equipment		2,800		(e) 2,200				5,000
Accounts Payable		25,683						25,683
Common Stock		50,000						50,000
Retained Earnings		68,352						68,352
Dividends	20,000						20,000	
Sales		246,350				246,350		
Sales Returns and Allowances	2,750				2,750			
Sales Discounts	4,275				4,275			
Purchases	126,400				126,400			
Purchases Returns and Allowances		5,640				5,640		
Purchases Discounts		2,136				2,136		
Freight In	8,236				8,236			
Sales Salaries Expense	22,500				22,500			
Freight Out Expense	5,740				5,740			
Advertising Expense	10,000				10,000			
Office Salaries Expense	26,900				26,900			
	406,611	406,611						
Insurance Expense, Selling			(a) 1,600		1,600			
Insurance Expense, General			(a) 4,200		4,200			
Store Supplies Expense			(b) 1,540		1,540			
Office Supplies Expense			(c) 1,204		1,204			
Depreciation Expense, Building			(d) 2,600		2,600			
Depreciation Expense, Office Equipment			(e) 2,200		2,200			
Income Taxes Expense			(f) 5,000		5,000			
Income Taxes Payable				(f) 5,000				5,000
			18,344	18,344	277,945	302,426	186,766	162,285
Net Income					24,481			24,481
					302,426	302,426	186,766	186,766

procedure has the effect of adding beginning inventory to net purchases because the Purchases account is also in the debit column of the Income Statement columns. The ending inventory balance of $48,300 (which is determined by the physical inventory and is not in the trial balance) is then inserted in the credit column of the Income Statement columns. This procedure has the effect of subtracting the ending inventory from goods available for sale in order to calculate the cost of goods sold. Finally, the ending merchandise inventory ($48,300) is inserted in the debit side of the Balance Sheet columns because it will appear on the balance sheet.

After all the items have been extended into the correct columns, the four columns are totaled. The net income or net loss is the difference between the debit and credit Income Statement columns. In this case, Fenwick Fashions Corporation has earned a net income of $24,481, which is extended to the credit side of the Balance Sheet columns. The four columns are then added to prove that total debits equal total credits.

ADJUSTING ENTRIES   The adjusting entries from the work sheet are now entered into the general journal and posted to the ledger, as they would be in a service company. Under the closing entry method, there is no difference in this procedure between a service company and a merchandising company.

CLOSING ENTRIES   The closing entries for Fenwick Fashions Corporation are shown in Exhibit 2. Notice that Merchandise Inventory is credited for the amount of beginning inventory ($52,800) in the first entry and debited for the amount of the ending inventory ($48,300) in the second entry. Otherwise, these closing entries are very similar to those for a service company except that the merchandising accounts also must be closed to Income Summary. All income statement accounts with debit balances, including the merchandising accounts of Sales Returns and Allowances, Sales Discounts, Purchases, and Freight In, and beginning Merchandise Inventory are credited in the first entry. The total of these accounts ($277,945) equals the total of the debit column in the Income Statement columns of the work sheet. All income statement accounts with credit balances—Sales, Purchases Returns and Allowances, and Purchases Discounts—and ending Merchandise Inventory are debited in the second entry. The total of these accounts ($302,426) equals the total of the Income Statement credit column in the work sheet. The third and fourth entries are used to close the Income Summary account and transfer net income to Retained Earnings, and to close the Dividends account to Retained Earnings.

The Perpetual Inventory System

Under the perpetual inventory system, the Merchandise Inventory account is up to date at the end of the accounting period and therefore is not involved in the closing process. The reason for this is that purchases of merchandise are recorded directly in the Merchandise Inventory account and costs are transferred from the Merchandise Inventory account to the Cost of Goods Sold account as merchandise is sold. The work sheet for Fenwick Fashions Corporation, assuming the company uses the perpetual inventory system, is shown in Exhibit 3 on page 774. Note that the ending merchandise inventory is $48,300 in both the Trial Balance and the Balance Sheet columns.

Exhibit 2
Closing Entries for a Merchandising Concern: Periodic Inventory System

		General Journal			Page 10
Date		Description	Post. Ref.	Debit	Credit
20xx Dec.	31	*Closing entries:*			
		Income Summary		277,945	
		Merchandise Inventory			52,800
		Sales Returns and Allowances			2,750
		Sales Discounts			4,275
		Purchases			126,400
		Freight In			8,236
		Sales Salaries Expense			22,500
		Freight Out Expense			5,740
		Advertising Expense			10,000
		Office Salaries Expense			26,900
		Insurance Expense, Selling			1,600
		Insurance Expense, General			4,200
		Store Supplies Expense			1,540
		Office Supplies Expense			1,204
		Depreciation Expense, Building			2,600
		Depreciation Expense, Office Equipment			2,200
		Income Taxes Expense			5,000
		To close temporary expense and revenue accounts with debit balances and to remove the beginning inventory			
	31	Merchandise Inventory		48,300	
		Sales		246,350	
		Purchases Returns and Allowances		5,640	
		Purchases Discounts		2,136	
		Income Summary			302,426
		To close temporary expense and revenue accounts with credit balances and to establish the ending inventory			
	31	Income Summary		24,481	
		Retained Earnings			24,481
		To close the Income Summary account			
	31	Retained Earnings		20,000	
		Dividends			20,000
		To close the Dividends account			

Exhibit 3
Work Sheet for Fenwick Fashions Corporation: Perpetual Inventory System

Fenwick Fashions Corporation
Work Sheet
For the Year Ended December 31, 20xx

Account Name	Trial Balance Debit	Trial Balance Credit	Adjustments Debit	Adjustments Credit	Income Statement Debit	Income Statement Credit	Balance Sheet Debit	Balance Sheet Credit
Cash	29,410						29,410	
Accounts Receivable	42,400						42,400	
Merchandise Inventory	48,300						48,300	
Prepaid Insurance	17,400			(a) 5,800			11,600	
Store Supplies	2,600			(b) 1,540			1,060	
Office Supplies	1,840			(c) 1,204			636	
Land	4,500						4,500	
Building	20,260						20,260	
Accumulated Depreciation, Building		5,650		(d) 2,600				8,250
Office Equipment	8,600						8,600	
Accumulated Depreciation, Office Equipment		2,800		(e) 2,200				5,000
Accounts Payable		25,683						25,683
Common Stock		50,000						50,000
Retained Earnings		68,352						68,352
Dividends	20,000						20,000	
Sales		246,350				246,350		
Sales Returns and Allowances	2,750				2,750			
Sales Discounts	4,275				4,275			
Cost of Goods Sold	123,124				123,124			
Freight In	8,236				8,236			
Sales Salaries Expense	22,500				22,500			
Freight Out Expense	5,740				5,740			
Advertising Expense	10,000				10,000			
Office Salaries Expense	26,900				26,900			
	398,835	398,835						
Insurance Expense, Selling			(a) 1,600		1,600			
Insurance Expense, General			(a) 4,200		4,200			
Store Supplies Expense			(b) 1,540		1,540			
Office Supplies Expense			(c) 1,204		1,204			
Depreciation Expense, Building			(d) 2,600		2,600			
Depreciation Expense, Office Equipment			(e) 2,200		2,200			
Income Taxes Expense			(f) 5,000		5,000			
Income Taxes Payable				(f) 5,000				5,000
			18,344	18,344	221,869	246,350	186,766	162,285
Net Income					24,481			24,481
					246,350	246,350	186,766	186,766

Exhibit 4	General Journal				Page 10
Closing Entries for a Merchandising Concern: Perpetual Inventory System	Date	Description	Post. Ref.	Debit	Credit
	20xx Dec. 31	*Closing entries:* Income Summary		221,869	
		Sales Returns and Allowances			2,750
		Sales Discounts			4,275
		Cost of Goods Sold			123,124
		Freight In			8,236
		Sales Salaries Expense			22,500
		Freight Out Expense			5,740
		Advertising Expense			10,000
		Office Salaries Expense			26,900
		Insurance Expense, Selling			1,600
		Insurance Expense, General			4,200
		Store Supplies Expense			1,540
		Office Supplies Expense			1,204
		Depreciation Expense, Building			2,600
		Depreciation Expense, Office Equipment			2,200
		Income Taxes Expense			5,000

		To close temporary expense
		  and revenue accounts
		  with debit balances			

	31	Sales		246,350	
		Income Summary			246,350

		To close temporary
		  revenue account
		  with credit balance			

	31	Income Summary		24,481	
		Retained Earnings			24,481
		To close the Income Summary account			
	31	Retained Earnings		20,000	
		Dividends			20,000
		To close the Dividends account			

The closing entries for Fenwick Fashions Corporation, assuming that the perpetual inventory system is used, are shown in Exhibit 4. The Cost of Goods Sold account is closed to Income Summary along with the expense accounts because it has a debit balance. There are no entries to the Merchandise Inventory account. There is no Purchases Returns and Allowances account under the perpetual inventory system. Also, Freight In is accounted for separately but is combined with Cost of Goods Sold on the income statement.

PROBLEMS

P 1.

Work Sheet, Financial Statements, and Closing Entries for a Merchandising Company: Periodic Inventory System

The trial balance shown below was taken from the ledger of Drake Music Store, Inc., at the end of its annual accounting period.

Drake Music Store, Inc.		
Trial Balance		
November 30, 20x2		
Cash	$ 18,075	
Accounts Receivable	27,840	
Merchandise Inventory	88,350	
Store Supplies	5,733	
Prepaid Insurance	4,800	
Store Equipment	111,600	
Accumulated Depreciation, Store Equipment		$ 46,800
Accounts Payable		36,900
Common Stock		30,000
Retained Earnings		95,982
Dividends	36,000	
Sales		306,750
Sales Returns and Allowances	2,961	
Purchases	189,600	
Purchases Returns and Allowances		58,965
Purchases Discounts		4,068
Freight In	6,783	
Sales Salaries Expense	64,050	
Rent Expense	10,800	
Other Selling Expenses	7,842	
Utilities Expense	5,031	
	$579,465	$579,465

REQUIRED

1. Enter the trial balance on a work sheet, and complete the work sheet using the following information: ending merchandise inventory, $99,681; ending store supplies inventory, $912; unexpired prepaid insurance, $600; estimated depreciation on store equipment, $12,900; sales salaries payable, $240; accrued utilities expense, $450; and estimated income taxes expense, $15,000.

2. Prepare an income statement, a statement of retained earnings, and a balance sheet. Sales Salaries Expense; Other Selling Expenses; Store Supplies Expense; and Depreciation Expense, Store Equipment are all selling expenses.

3. From the work sheet, prepare the closing entries.

P 2.

Work Sheet, Financial Statements, and Closing Entries for a Merchandising Company: Perpetual Inventory System

The year-end trial balance shown at the top of the next page was taken from the ledger of Turpin Party Costumes Corporation at the end of its annual accounting period on June 30, 20x2.

Turpin Party Costumes Corporation
Trial Balance
June 30, 20x2

Cash	$ 7,050	
Accounts Receivable	24,830	
Merchandise Inventory	88,900	
Store Supplies	3,800	
Prepaid Insurance	4,800	
Store Equipment	151,300	
Accumulated Depreciation, Store Equipment		$ 25,500
Accounts Payable		38,950
Common Stock		50,000
Retained Earnings		111,350
Dividends	24,000	
Sales		475,250
Sales Returns and Allowances	4,690	
Cost of Goods Sold	231,840	
Freight In	10,400	
Sales Salaries Expense	64,600	
Rent Expense	48,000	
Other Selling Expenses	32,910	
Utilities Expense	3,930	
	$701,050	$701,050

REQUIRED

1. Enter the trial balance on a work sheet, and complete the work sheet using the following information: (a) ending store supplies inventory, $550; (b) expired insurance, $2,400; (c) estimated depreciation on store equipment, $5,000; (d) sales salaries payable, $650; (e) accrued utilities expense, $100; and (f) estimated income taxes expense, $20,000.

2. Prepare an income statement, a statement of retained earnings, and a balance sheet. Sales Salaries Expense; Other Selling Expenses; Store Supplies Expense; and Depreciation Expense, Store Equipment are to be considered selling expenses.

3. From the work sheet, prepare closing entries.

APPENDIX B

Special-Purpose Journals

Special-purpose journals achieve efficiency, economy, and control by providing a separate place to record common, similar transactions. In addition, although manual special-purpose journals are used by companies that have not yet computerized their systems, the concepts underlying special-purpose journals also underlie the programs that drive computerized general ledger accounting systems.

Most business transactions—90 to 95 percent—fall into one of four categories. Each kind of transaction can be recorded in a special-purpose journal:

Transaction	Special-Purpose Journal	Posting Abbreviation
Sale of merchandise on credit	Sales journal	S
Purchase on credit	Purchases journal	P
Receipt of cash	Cash receipts journal	CR
Disbursement of cash	Cash payments journal	CP

The general journal is used to record transactions that do not fall into any of these special categories. (The posting abbreviation used is **J.**)

Using special-purpose journals greatly reduces the work involved in entering and posting transactions. For example, instead of posting every debit and credit for each transaction, in most cases only column totals—the sum of many transactions—are posted. In addition, labor can be divided, with each journal assigned to a different employee. This division of labor is important in establishing good internal control.

Sales Journal

The *sales journal* is designed to handle all credit sales. Cash sales are recorded in the cash receipts journal. Exhibit 1 illustrates a page from a typical sales journal. Six sales transactions involving five customers are recorded in this sales journal.

Notice how the sales journal saves time:

1. Only one line is needed to record each transaction. Each entry consists of a debit to a customer in Accounts Receivable. The corresponding credit to Sales is understood.

2. The account names do not have to be written out because each entry automatically is debited to Accounts Receivable and credited to Sales.

Exhibit 1
Sales Journal and Related Ledger Accounts

	Sales Journal			Page 1
Date	Account Debited	Invoice Number	Post. Ref.	Amount (Debit/Credit Accounts Receivable/ Sales)
July 1	Peter Clark	721	✓	750
5	Georgetta Jones	722	✓	500
8	Eugene Cumberland	723	✓	335
12	Maxwell Gertz	724	✓	1,165
18	Peter Clark	725	✓	1,225
25	Michael Powers	726	✓	975
				4,950
				(114/411)

Post total at **end of month**.

Accounts Receivable						114	Sales					411
				Balance							Balance	
Date	Post. Ref.	Debit	Credit	Debit	Credit		Date	Post. Ref.	Debit	Credit	Debit	Credit
July 31	S1	4,950		4,950			July 31	S1		4,950		4,950

3. No explanations are necessary because the function of the special-purpose journal is to record just one type of transaction. Only credit sales are recorded in the sales journal. Sales for cash are recorded in the cash receipts journal.

4. Only one amount—the total credit sales for the month—has to be posted. It is posted twice: once as a debit to Accounts Receivable and once as a credit to Sales. You can see the time this saves in Exhibit 1, with just six transactions. Imagine the time saved when there are hundreds of sales transactions.

CONTROLLING ACCOUNTS AND SUBSIDIARY LEDGERS   Every entry in the sales journal represents a debit to a customer's account in Accounts Receivable. In previous chapters, we've posted all of these transactions to Accounts Receivable. However, a single entry in Accounts Receivable does not tell us how much each customer has bought and paid for or how much each customer still owes. In practice, almost all companies that sell to customers on credit keep an individual accounts receivable record for each customer. If the company has 6,000 credit customers, there are 6,000 accounts receivable. To include all these accounts in the general ledger with the other asset, liability, and stockholders' equity accounts would make it very bulky. Consequently, most companies take the individual customers' accounts out of the general ledger and place them in a separate ledger, called a *subsidiary ledger*. In the accounts receivable subsidiary ledger, customers' accounts are filed either alphabetically or numerically (if account numbers are used).

When a company puts its individual customers' accounts in an accounts receivable subsidiary ledger, it still must maintain an Accounts Receivable account in the general ledger. The Accounts Receivable account "controls" the subsidiary ledger and is called a *controlling account,* or *control account.* It controls in the sense that the total of the individual account balances in the subsidiary ledger must equal the balance in the controlling account. The balance of this account on the balance sheet date appears as Accounts Receivable on the balance sheet. In transactions that involve accounts receivable, such as credit sales, entries must be posted to the individual customers' accounts every day. Postings to the controlling account in the

Exhibit 2

Relationship of Sales Journal, General Ledger, and Accounts Receivable Subsidiary Ledger and the Posting Procedure

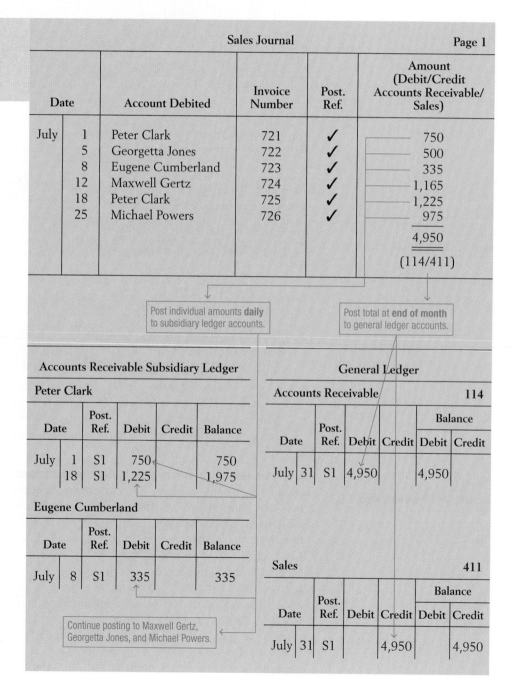

general ledger are made at least once a month. If a wrong amount has been posted, the sum of all the customers' account balances in the subsidiary accounts receivable ledger will not equal the balance of the Accounts Receivable controlling account in the general ledger. When these amounts do not match, the accountant knows there is an error to find and correct.

Exhibit 2 shows how controlling accounts work. The single controlling account in the general ledger summarizes all the individual accounts in the subsidiary ledger. Most companies use an accounts payable subsidiary ledger as well.

SUMMARY OF THE SALES JOURNAL PROCEDURE Exhibit 2 illustrates the procedure for using a sales journal:

1. Enter each sales invoice in the sales journal on a single line. Record the date, the customer's name, the invoice number, and the amount. No column is needed for the terms if the terms on all sales are the same.

2. At the end of each day, post each individual sale to the customer's account in the accounts receivable subsidiary ledger. As each sale is posted, place a checkmark (or customer account number, if used) in the Post. Ref. (posting reference) column of the sales journal to indicate that it has been posted. In the Post. Ref. column of each customer's account, place an **S** and the sales journal page number (**S1** means Sales Journal—Page 1) to indicate the source of the entry.

3. At the end of the month, sum the Amount column in the sales journal to determine the total credit sales, and post the total to the general ledger accounts (debit Accounts Receivable and credit Sales). Place the numbers of the accounts debited and credited beneath the total in the sales journal to indicate that this step has been completed. In the general ledger, indicate the source of the entry in the Post. Ref. column of each account.

4. Verify the accuracy of the posting by adding the account balances of the accounts receivable subsidiary ledger and matching the total with the Accounts Receivable controlling account balance in the general ledger. You can do this by listing the accounts in a schedule of accounts receivable, like the one shown in Exhibit 3, in the order in which the accounts are maintained. This step is performed after collections on account in the cash receipts journal have been posted.

Exhibit 3 Schedule of Accounts Receivable	Mitchell's Used Car Sales Schedule of Accounts Receivable July 31, 20xx	
	Peter Clark	$1,975
	Eugene Cumberland	335
	Maxwell Gertz	1,165
	Georgetta Jones	500
	Michael Powers	975
	Total Accounts Receivable	$4,950

Exhibit 4
Section of a Sales Journal with
a Column for Sales Taxes

| | | | | Debit | Credits | |
| | Sales Journal | | | | | Page 2 |
Date	Account Debited	Invoice Number	Post. Ref.	Accounts Receivable	Sales Taxes Payable	Sales
Aug. 1	Ralph P. Hake	727	✓	206	6	200

SALES TAXES Other columns, such as a column for credit terms, can be added to the sales journal. Many cities and states require retailers to collect a sales tax from their customers and periodically remit the total collected to the city or state. In this case, an additional column is needed in the sales journal to record the credit to Sales Taxes Payable on credit sales. The form of the entry is shown in Exhibit 4.

Purchases Journal

The *purchases journal* is used to record purchases on credit. It can take the form of either a single-column journal or a multicolumn journal. In the single-column journal, shown in Exhibit 5, only credit purchases of merchandise for resale to customers are recorded. This kind of transaction is recorded with a debit to Purchases and a credit to Accounts Payable. When the single-column purchases journal is used, credit purchases of items other than merchandise are recorded in the general journal. Cash purchases are never recorded in the purchases journal; they are recorded in the cash payments journal, which we explain later.

Like the Accounts Receivable account, the Accounts Payable account in the general ledger is used by most companies as a controlling account. So that the company knows how much it owes each supplier, it keeps a separate account for each supplier in an accounts payable subsidiary ledger.

The procedure for using the purchases journal is much like that for using the sales journal:

1. Enter each purchase invoice in the purchases journal on a single line. Record the date, the supplier's name, the invoice date, the terms (if given), and the amount. It is not necessary to record the shipping terms in the terms column because they do not affect the payment date.

2. At the end of each day, post each individual purchase to the supplier's account in the accounts payable subsidiary ledger. As each purchase is posted, place a checkmark in the Post. Ref. column of the purchases journal to show that it has been posted. Also place a **P** and the page number in the purchases journal (**P1** stands for Purchases Journal—Page 1) in the Post. Ref. column of each supplier's account to show the source of the entry.

3. At the end of the month, sum the Amount column, and post the total to the general ledger accounts (a debit to Purchases and a credit to Accounts Payable). Place the numbers of the accounts debited and credited beneath the totals in the purchases journal to show that this step has been carried out. In

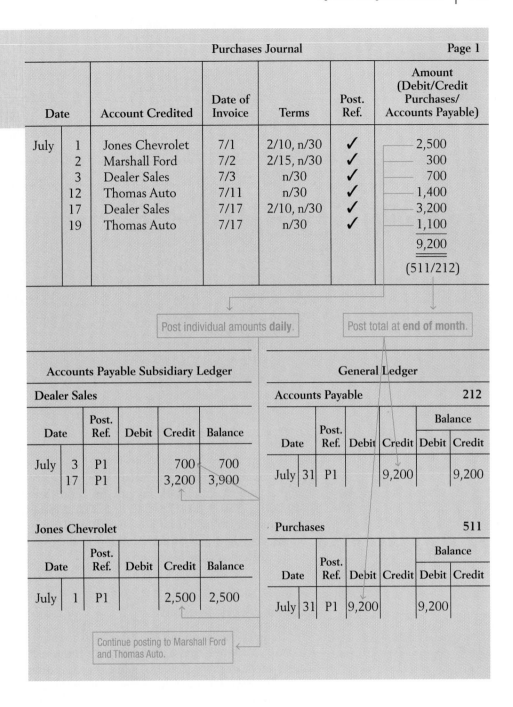

Exhibit 5

Relationship of Single-Column Purchases Journal to the General Ledger and the Accounts Payable Subsidiary Ledger

Purchases Journal   Page 1

Date		Account Credited	Date of Invoice	Terms	Post. Ref.	Amount (Debit/Credit Purchases/ Accounts Payable)
July	1	Jones Chevrolet	7/1	2/10, n/30	✓	2,500
	2	Marshall Ford	7/2	2/15, n/30	✓	300
	3	Dealer Sales	7/3	n/30	✓	700
	12	Thomas Auto	7/11	n/30	✓	1,400
	17	Dealer Sales	7/17	2/10, n/30	✓	3,200
	19	Thomas Auto	7/17	n/30	✓	1,100
						9,200
						(511/212)

Post individual amounts **daily**.   Post total at **end of month**.

Accounts Payable Subsidiary Ledger

Dealer Sales

Date		Post. Ref.	Debit	Credit	Balance
July	3	P1		700	700
	17	P1		3,200	3,900

Jones Chevrolet

Date		Post. Ref.	Debit	Credit	Balance
July	1	P1		2,500	2,500

Continue posting to Marshall Ford and Thomas Auto.

General Ledger

Accounts Payable   212

Date		Post. Ref.	Debit	Credit	Balance Debit	Balance Credit
July	31	P1		9,200		9,200

Purchases   511

Date		Post. Ref.	Debit	Credit	Balance Debit	Balance Credit
July	31	P1	9,200		9,200	

the general ledger, indicate the source of the entry in the Post. Ref. column of each account.

4. Check the accuracy of the posting by adding the balances of the accounts payable subsidiary ledger accounts and matching the total with the balance of the Accounts Payable controlling account in the general ledger. This step can be done by preparing a schedule of accounts payable from the subsidiary ledger.

The single-column purchases journal can be expanded to record credit purchases of items other than merchandise by adding separate debit columns for other

Exhibit 6
A Multicolumn Purchases Journal

						Credit			Debits				
											Other Accounts		
Date		Account Credited	Date of Invoice	Terms	Post. Ref.	Accounts Payable	Purchases	Freight In	Store Supplies	Office Supplies	Account	Post. Ref.	Amount
July	1	Jones Chevrolet	7/1	2/10, n/30	✓	2,500	2,500						
	2	Marshall Ford	7/2	2/15, n/30	✓	300	300						
	2	Shelby Car Delivery	7/2	n/30	✓	50		50					
	3	Dealer Sales	7/3	n/30	✓	700	700						
	12	Thomas Auto	7/11	n/30	✓	1,400	1,400						
	17	Dealer Sales	7/17	2/10, n/30	✓	3,200	3,200						
	19	Thomas Auto	7/17	n/30	✓	1,100	1,100						
	25	Osborne Supply	7/21	n/10	✓	187			145	42			
	28	Auto Supply	7/28	n/10	✓	200					Parts	120	200
						9,637	9,200	50	145	42			200
						(212)	(511)	(514)	(132)	(133)			(✓)

Purchases Journal   *Page 1*

accounts that are used often. For example, the multicolumn purchases journal in Exhibit 6 has columns for Freight In, Store Supplies, Office Supplies, and Other Accounts. Here, the total credits to Accounts Payable ($9,637) equal the total debits to Purchases, Freight In, Store Supplies, Office Supplies, and Parts ($9,200 + $50 + $145 + $42 + $200). Again, the individual transactions in the Accounts Payable column are posted regularly to the accounts payable subsidiary ledger, and the totals of each column in the purchases journal are posted monthly to the correct general ledger accounts.

Cash Receipts Journal

All transactions involving receipts of cash are recorded in the *cash receipts journal.* Examples of these transactions are cash from cash sales, cash from credit customers in payment of their accounts, and cash from other sources. The cash receipts journal must have several columns because, although all cash receipts are alike in that they require a debit to Cash, they are different in that they require a variety of credit entries. The Other Accounts column is used to record credits to accounts not specifically represented by a column. The account numbers are entered in the Post. Ref. column, and the amounts are posted daily to the appropriate account in the general ledger.

The cash receipts journal shown in Exhibit 7 has three debit columns and three credit columns. The three debit columns are as follows:

1. *Cash* Each entry must have an amount in this column because each transaction must be a receipt of cash.

2. *Sales Discounts* This company allows a 2 percent discount for prompt payment. Therefore, it is useful to have a column for sales discounts. Notice that

Exhibit 7
Relationship of the Cash Receipts Journal to the General Ledger and the Accounts Receivable Subsidiary Ledger

Cash Receipts Journal — Page 1

| | | | Debits | | | Credits | | |
| | | | | | | | | |
Date	Account Debited/Credited	Post. Ref.	Cash	Sales Discounts	Other Accounts	Accounts Receivable	Sales	Other Accounts
July 1	Common Stock	311	20,000					20,000
5	Sales		1,200				1,200	
8	Georgetta Jones	✔	490	10		500		
13	Sales		1,400				1,400	
16	Peter Clark	✔	750			750		
19	Sales		1,000				1,000	
20	Equipment	151	500					500
24	Notes Payable	213	5,000					5,000
26	Sales		1,600				1,600	
28	Peter Clark	✔	588	12		600		
			32,528	22		1,850	5,200	25,500
			(111)	(412)		(114)	(411)	(✔)

> Post individual amounts in Accounts Receivable Subsidiary Ledger column **daily**.

> Post totals at **end of month**.

> Post individual amounts in Other Accounts column **daily**.

> Total not posted.

General Ledger

Cash — 111

Date	Post. Ref.	Debit	Credit	Balance Debit	Balance Credit
July 31	CR1	32,528		32,528	

Accounts Receivable — 114

Date	Post. Ref.	Debit	Credit	Balance Debit	Balance Credit
July 31	S1	4,950		4,950	
31	CR1		1,850	3,100	

Equipment — 151

Date	Post. Ref.	Debit	Credit	Balance Debit	Balance Credit
Bal.				500	
July 20	CR1		500	—	

Accounts Receivable Subsidiary Ledger

Peter Clark

Date	Post. Ref.	Debit	Credit	Balance
July 1	S1	750		750
16	CR1		750	—
18	S1	1,225		1,225
28	CR1		600	625

Georgetta Jones

Date	Post. Ref.	Debit	Credit	Balance
July 5	S1	500		500
8	CR1		500	—

> Continue posting to Notes Payable and Common Stock.

> Continue posting to Sales and Sales Discounts.

in the transactions of July 8 and 28, the debits to Cash and Sales Discounts equal the credits to Accounts Receivable.

3. *Other Accounts* The Other Accounts column (sometimes called *Sundry Accounts*) is used for transactions that involve both a debit to Cash and a debit to some account other than Sales Discounts.

These are the credit columns:

1. *Accounts Receivable* This column is used to record collections on account from customers. The name of the customer is written in the Account Debited/Credited column so that the payment can be entered in the corresponding account in the accounts receivable subsidiary ledger. Posting to the individual accounts receivable accounts is usually done daily so that each customer's account balance is up to date.

2. *Sales* This column is used to record all cash sales during the month. Retail firms that use cash registers would make an entry at the end of each day for the total sales from each cash register for that day. The debit, of course, is in the Cash debit column.

3. *Other Accounts* This column is used for the credit portion of any entry that is neither a cash collection from accounts receivable nor a cash sale. The name of the account to be credited is indicated in the Account Debited/Credited column. For example, the transactions of July 1, 20, and 24 involve credits to accounts other than Accounts Receivable or Sales. These individual postings should be done daily (or weekly if there are just a few of them). If a company finds that it consistently is crediting a certain account in the Other Accounts column, it can add another credit column to the cash receipts journal for that particular account.

The procedure for posting the cash receipts journal, as shown in Exhibit 7, is as follows:

1. Post the transactions in the Accounts Receivable column daily to the individual accounts in the accounts receivable subsidiary ledger. The amount credited to the customer's account is the same as that credited to Accounts Receivable. A checkmark in the Post. Ref. column of the cash receipts journal indicates that the amount has been posted, and a **CR1** (Cash Receipts Journal—Page 1) in the Post. Ref. column of each subsidiary ledger account indicates the source of the entry.

2. Post the debits/credits in the Other Accounts columns daily, or at convenient short intervals during the month, to the general ledger accounts. Write the account number in the Post. Ref. column of the cash receipts journal as the individual items are posted to indicate that the posting has been done, and write **CR1** in the Post. Ref. column of the general ledger account to indicate the source of the entry.

3. At the end of the month, total the columns in the cash receipts journal. The sum of the Debits column totals must equal the sum of the Credits column totals:

Debits Column Totals		Credits Column Totals	
Cash	$32,528	Accounts Receivable	$ 1,850
Sales Discounts	22	Sales	5,200
Other Accounts	0	Other Accounts	25,500
Total Debits	$32,550	Total Credits	$32,550

This step is called *crossfooting.*

4. Post the Debits column totals as follows:
   a. *Cash*   Posted as a debit to the Cash account.
   b. *Sales Discounts*   Posted as a debit to the Sales Discounts account.
5. Post the Credits column totals as follows:
   a. *Accounts Receivable*   Posted as a credit to the Accounts Receivable controlling account.
   b. *Sales*   Posted as a credit to the Sales account.
6. Write the account numbers below each column in the cash receipts journal as they are posted to indicate that this step has been completed. A **CR1** is written in the Post. Ref. column of each account in the general ledger to indicate the source of the entry.
7. Notice that the Other Accounts column totals are not posted because each entry was posted separately when the transaction occurred. The individual accounts were posted in step **2**. Place a checkmark at the bottom of each column to show that postings in that column have been made and that the total is not posted.

Cash Payments Journal

All transactions involving payments of cash are recorded in the *cash payments journal* (also called the *cash disbursements journal*). Examples of these transactions are cash purchases and payments of obligations resulting from earlier purchases on credit. The form of the cash payments journal is much like that of the cash receipts journal.

The cash payments journal shown in Exhibit 8 has three credit columns and two debit columns. The credit columns for the cash payments journal are as follows:

1. *Cash*   Each entry must have an amount in this column because each transaction must involve a payment of cash.
2. *Purchases Discounts*   When purchases discounts are taken, they are recorded in this column.
3. *Other Accounts*   This column is used to record credits to accounts other than Cash or Purchases Discounts. Notice that the July 31 transaction shows a purchase of Land for $15,000, with a check for $5,000 and a note payable for $10,000.

The debit columns are as follows:

1. *Accounts Payable*   This column is used to record payments to suppliers that have extended credit to the company. Each supplier's name is written in the Payee column so that the payment can be entered in his or her account in the accounts payable subsidiary ledger.
2. *Other Accounts*   Cash can be expended for many reasons. Therefore, an Other Accounts or Sundry Accounts column is needed in the cash payments journal. The title of the account to be debited is written in the Account Credited/Debited column, and the amount is entered in the Other Accounts debit column. If a company finds that a particular account appears often in the Other Accounts column, it can add another debit column to the cash payments journal.

The procedure for posting the cash payments journal, shown in Exhibit 8, is as follows:

1. Daily post the transactions in the Accounts Payable column to each individual account in the accounts payable subsidiary ledger. Place a checkmark in the

Exhibit 8
Relationship of the Cash Payments Journal to the General Ledger and the Accounts Payable Subsidiary Ledger

Cash Payments Journal
Page 1

Date	Ck. No.	Payee	Account Credited/Debited	Post. Ref.	Credits — Cash	Credits — Purchases Discounts	Credits — Other Accounts	Debits — Accounts Payable	Debits — Other Accounts
July 2	101	Sondra Tidmore	Purchases	511	400				400
6	102	Daily Journal	Advertising Expense	612	200				200
8	103	Siviglia Agency	Rent Expense	631	250				250
11	104	Jones Chevrolet		✓	2,450	50		2,500	
16	105	Charles Kuntz	Salaries Expense	611	600				600
17	106	Marshall Ford		✓	294	6		300	
24	107	Grabow & Co.	Prepaid Insurance	119	480				480
27	108	Dealer Sales		✓	3,136	64		3,200	
30	109	A&B Equipment Company	Office Equipment Service Equipment	144 146	900				400 500
31	110	Burns Real Estate	Notes Payable Land	213 141	5,000		10,000		15,000
					13,710	120	10,000	6,000	17,830
					(111)	(512)	(✓)	(212)	(✓)

Post individual amounts in Other Accounts column **daily**.

Post individual amounts in Accounts Payable Subsidiary Ledger column **daily**.

Post totals at **end of month**.

Totals not posted.

General Ledger

Cash 111

Date	Post. Ref.	Debit	Credit	Balance Debit	Balance Credit
July 31	CR1	32,528		32,528	
31	CP1		13,710	18,818	

Prepaid Insurance 119

Date	Post. Ref.	Debit	Credit	Balance Debit	Balance Credit
July 24	CP1	480		480	

Continue posting to Land, Office Equipment, Service Equipment, Notes Payable, Purchases, Salaries Expense, Advertising Expense, and Rent Expense.

Continue posting to Purchases Discounts and Accounts Payable.

Accounts Payable Subsidiary Ledger

Dealer Sales

Date	Post. Ref.	Debit	Credit	Balance
July 3	P1		700	700
17	P1		3,200	3,900
27	CP1	3,200		700

Jones Chevrolet

Date	Post. Ref.	Debit	Credit	Balance
July 1	P1		2,500	2,500
11	CP1	2,500		—

Marshall Ford

Date	Post. Ref.	Debit	Credit	Balance
July 2	P1		300	300
17	CP1	300		—

Post. Ref. column of the cash payments journal to indicate that the posting has been made.

2. Post the debits/credits in the Other Accounts debit/credit columns to the general ledger daily or at convenient short intervals during the month. Write the account number in the Post. Ref. column of the cash payments journal as the individual items are posted to indicate that the posting has been completed and **CP1** (Cash Payments Journal—Page 1) in the Post. Ref. column of each general ledger account.

3. At the end of the month, the columns are footed and crossfooted. That is, the sum of the Credits column totals must equal the sum of the Debits column totals, as follows:

Credits Column Totals		Debits Column Totals	
Cash	$13,710	Accounts Payable	$ 6,000
Purchases Discounts	120	Other Accounts	17,830
Other Accounts	10,000		
Total Credits	$23,830	Total Debits	$23,830

4. At the end of the month, post the column totals for Cash, Purchases Discounts, and Accounts Payable to their respective accounts in the general ledger. Write the account number below each column in the cash payments journal as it is posted to indicate that this step has been completed and **CP1** in the Post. Ref. column of each general ledger account. Place a checkmark under the total of each Other Accounts column in the cash payments journal to indicate that the postings in the column have been made and that the total is not posted.

General Journal

Adjusting and closing entries are recorded in the general journal. Also, transactions that do not involve sales, purchases, cash receipts, or cash payments should be recorded in the general journal. Usually, there are only a few of these transactions. Two examples of entries that do not fit in a special-purpose journal are a return of merchandise bought on account and an allowance from a supplier for credit.

These entries are shown in Exhibit 9. Notice that the entries include a debit or a credit to a controlling account (Accounts Payable or Accounts Receivable). The

Exhibit 9
Transactions Recorded in the General Journal

		General Journal			Page 1
Date		Description	Post. Ref.	Debit	Credit
July	25	Accounts Payable, Thomas Auto	212/✓	1,400	
		Purchases Returns and Allowances	513		1,400
		Returned used car for credit; invoice date: 7/11			
	26	Sales Returns and Allowances	413	35	
		Accounts Receivable, Maxwell Gertz	114/✓		35
		Allowance for faulty tire			

name of the customer or supplier also is given here. When this kind of debit or credit is made to a controlling account in the general ledger, the entry must be posted twice: once to the controlling account and once to the individual account in the subsidiary ledger. This procedure keeps the subsidiary ledger equal to the controlling account. Notice that the July 26 transaction is posted by a debit to Sales Returns and Allowances in the general ledger (shown by the account number 413), a credit to the Accounts Receivable controlling account in the general ledger (account number 114), and a credit to the Maxwell Gertz account in the accounts receivable subsidiary ledger (checkmark).

PROBLEMS

P 1.

Cash Receipts and Cash Payments Journals

The items below detail all cash transactions by Hashim Company for the month of July. The company uses multicolumn cash receipts and cash payments journals similar to those illustrated in this appendix.

July 1 The owner, Aneesa Hashim, invested $50,000 cash and $24,000 in equipment in the business in exchange for common stock.
2 Paid rent to Duke Agency, $600, with check no. 75.
3 Cash sales, $2,200.
6 Purchased store equipment for $5,000 from Fodorel Company, with check no. 76.
7 Purchased merchandise for cash, $6,500, from Bogacz Company, with check no. 77.
8 Paid Maloney Company invoice, $1,800, less 2 percent discount, with check no. 78 (assume that a payable has already been recorded).
9 Paid advertising bill, $350, to WOSU, with check no. 79.
10 Cash sales, $3,910.
12 Received $800 on account from S. Ton.
13 Purchased used truck for cash, $3,520, from Welsh Company, with check no. 80.
19 Received $4,180 from Harbor Company, in settlement of a $4,000 note plus interest.
20 Received $1,078 ($1,100 less $22 cash discount) from Su Kye.
21 Declared and paid Hashim a dividend, $2,000, by issuing check no. 81.
23 Paid Dolor Company invoice, $2,500, less 2 percent discount, with check no. 82.
26 Paid Woods Company for freight on merchandise received, $60, with check no. 83.
27 Cash sales, $4,800.
28 Paid P. Fish monthly salary, $1,400, with check no. 84.
31 Purchased land from R. Lev for $20,000, paying $5,000 with check no. 85 and signing a note payable for $15,000.

REQUIRED

1. Enter the preceding transactions in the cash receipts and cash payments journals.

2. Foot and crossfoot the journals.

P 2.

Purchases and General Journals

The following items represent the credit transactions for Cohan Company during the month of August. The company uses a multicolumn purchases journal and a general journal similar to those illustrated in this appendix.

Aug. 2 Purchased merchandise from Preston Company, $1,400.
5 Purchased truck to be used in the business from Montez Company, $8,000.
8 Purchased office supplies from Healey Company, $400.
12 Purchased filing cabinets from Healey Company, $550.
14 Purchased merchandise, $1,400, and store supplies, $200, from Robbs Company.
17 Purchased store supplies from Preston Company, $100, and office supplies from Wilmot Company, $50.

Aug. 20 Purchased merchandise from Robbs Company, $1,472.

24 Purchased merchandise from Preston Company, $2,452; the $2,452 invoice total included shipping charges, $232.

26 Purchased office supplies from Healey Company, $150.

29 Purchased merchandise from Robbs Company, $290.

30 Returned defective merchandise purchased from Robbs Company on August 20 for full credit, $432.

REQUIRED

1. Enter the preceding transactions in the purchases journal and the general journal. Assume that all terms are n/30 and that invoice dates are the same as the transaction dates. Use Page 1 for all references.

2. Foot and crossfoot the purchases journal.

3. Open the following general ledger accounts: Store Supplies (116), Office Supplies (117), Trucks (142), Office Equipment (144), Accounts Payable (211), Purchases (511), Purchases Returns and Allowances (512), and Freight In (513). Open accounts payable subsidiary ledger accounts as needed. Post from the journals to the ledger accounts.

P 3.

Comprehensive Use of Special-Purpose Journals

During October, Pineda Refrigeration Company completed the following transactions:

Oct. 1 Received merchandise from Tark Company, $5,000, invoice dated September 29, terms 2/10, n/30, FOB shipping point.

3 Issued check no. 230 to Walters Realtors for October rent, $4,000.

4 Received merchandise from La Rock Manufacturing, $10,800, invoice dated October 1, terms 2/10, n/30, FOB shipping point.

6 Issued check no. 231 to Rabbit Company for repairs, $1,120.

7 Received $800 credit memorandum pertaining to October 4 shipment from La Rock Manufacturing for return of unsatisfactory merchandise.

8 Issued check no. 232 to Emerald Company for freight charges on October 1 and October 4 shipments, $368.

9 Sold merchandise to R. Kuldip, $2,000, terms 1/10, n/30, invoice no. 725.

10 Issued check no. 233 to Tark Company for full payment less discount.

11 Sold merchandise to A. Imoto for $2,500, terms 1/10, n/30, invoice no. 726.

12 Issued check no. 234 to La Rock Manufacturing for balance of account less discount.

13 Purchased advertising on credit from WRRT, invoice dated October 13, $900, terms n/20.

15 Issued credit memorandum to A. Imoto for $100 for merchandise returned.

16 Cash sales for the first half of the month, $19,340. (To shorten this problem, cash sales are recorded only twice a month instead of daily, as they would be in actual practice.)

17 Sold merchandise to N. Floy, $1,400, terms 1/10, n/30, invoice no. 727.

18 Received check from R. Kuldip for October 9 sale less discount.

19 Received check from A. Imoto for balance of account less discount.

20 Received merchandise from Tark Company, $5,600, invoice dated October 19, terms 2/10, n/30, FOB shipping point.

21 Received freight bill from Summers Company for merchandise received on October 20, invoice dated October 19, $1,140, terms n/5.

22 Issued check no. 235 for advertising purchase of October 13.

24 Received merchandise from La Rock Manufacturing, $7,200, invoice dated October 23, terms 2/10, n/30, FOB shipping point.

25 Issued check no. 236 for freight charge of October 21.

26 Sold merchandise to R. Kuldip, $1,600, terms 1/10, n/30, invoice no. 728.

28 Received credit memorandum from La Rock Manufacturing for defective merchandise received October 24, $600.

29 Issued check no. 237 to Western Company for purchase of office equipment, $700.

30 Issued check no. 238 to Tark Company for half of October 20 purchase less discount.

Oct. 30   Received check in full from N. Floy, no discount allowed.
     31   Cash sales for the last half of the month, $23,120.
     31   Issued check no. 239, payable to Payroll Account, for monthly sales salaries, $8,600.

REQUIRED

1. Prepare a sales journal, a multicolumn purchases journal, a cash receipts journal, a cash payments journal, and a general journal for Pineda Refrigeration Company similar to the ones illustrated in this appendix. Use Page 1 for all journal references.

2. Open the following general ledger accounts: Cash (111), Accounts Receivable (112), Office Equipment (141), Accounts Payable (211), Sales (411), Sales Discounts (412), Sales Returns and Allowances (413), Purchases (511), Purchases Discounts (512), Purchases Returns and Allowances (513), Freight In (514), Sales Salaries Expense (521), Advertising Expense (522), Rent Expense (531), and Repairs Expense (532).

3. Open the following accounts receivable subsidiary ledger accounts: N. Floy, A. Imoto, and R. Kuldip.

4. Open the following accounts payable subsidiary ledger accounts: La Rock Manufacturing, Summers Company, Tark Company, and WRRT.

5. Enter the transactions in the journals and post as appropriate.

6. Foot and crossfoot the journals, and make the end-of-month postings.

7. Prepare a trial balance of the general ledger and prove the control balances of Accounts Receivable and Accounts Payable by preparing schedules of accounts receivable and accounts payable.

APPENDIX C

Accounting for Unincorporated Businesses

The corporate form of business organization has been assumed up to this point. In this appendix, the focus is on sole proprietorships and partnerships.

Accounting for Sole Proprietorships

A *sole proprietorship* is a business owned by one person. This business form gives the individual a means of controlling the business apart from his or her personal interests. Legally, however, the proprietorship is the same economic unit as the individual. The individual business owner receives all the profits or losses and is liable for all the obligations of the proprietorship. Proprietorships represent the largest number of businesses in the United States, but typically they are the smallest in size. The life of a proprietorship ends when the owner wishes it to or at the owner's death or incapacity.

When someone invests in his or her own company, the amount of the investment is recorded in a capital account. For example, the entry to record the initial investment of $10,000 by Clara Hooper in her new mail-order business would be a debit to the Cash account for $10,000 and a credit to the Clara Hooper, Capital account for $10,000.

During the period, Clara will probably withdraw assets from the business for personal living expenses. Since legally there is no separation between the owner and the sole proprietorship, it is not necessary to make a formal declaration of a withdrawal, as would be required in the case of corporate dividends. The withdrawal of $500 by Clara is recorded as a debit to the Clara Hooper, Withdrawals account for $500 and a credit to the Cash account for $500.

Revenue and expense accounts are closed out to Income Summary in the same way for sole proprietorships as they are for corporations. Income Summary, however, is closed to the Capital account instead of to Retained Earnings. For example, the closing entries that follow assume a net income of $1,000 and withdrawals of $500.

Income Summary	1,000	
Clara Hooper, Capital		1,000
To close Income Summary in		
a sole proprietorship		
Clara Hooper, Capital	500	
Clara Hooper, Withdrawals		500
To close Withdrawals		

Accounting for Partnerships

The Uniform Partnership Act, which has been adopted by a majority of the states, defines a *partnership* as "an association of two or more persons to carry on as co-owners of a business for profit." Normally, partnerships are formed when owners of small businesses wish to combine capital or managerial talents for some common business purpose. Partnerships are treated as separate entities in accounting. They differ in many ways from the other forms of business. The next few paragraphs describe some of the important characteristics of a partnership.

VOLUNTARY ASSOCIATION   A partnership is a voluntary association of individuals rather than a legal entity in itself. Therefore, a partner is responsible under the law for his or her partners' business actions within the scope of the partnership. A partner also has unlimited liability for the debts of the partnership. Because of these potential liabilities, an individual must be allowed to choose the people who join the partnership.

PARTNERSHIP AGREEMENT   A partnership is easy to form. Two or more competent people simply agree to be partners in some common business purpose. This agreement is known as a *partnership agreement*. The partnership agreement does not have to be in writing; however, it is good business practice to have a written document that clearly states the details of the partnership. The contract should describe the name, location, and purpose of the business; the partners and their respective duties; the investments of each partner; the methods for distributing income and losses; and procedures for the admission and withdrawal of partners, the withdrawal of assets allowed each partner, and the liquidation (termination) of the business.

LIMITED LIFE   Because a partnership is formed by a contract between partners, it has a *limited life*: Anything that ends the contract dissolves the partnership. A partnership is dissolved when (1) a new partner is admitted, (2) a partner withdraws, (3) a partner goes bankrupt, (4) a partner is incapacitated (to the point at which he or she cannot perform as obligated), (5) a partner retires, (6) a partner dies, or (7) the terms set out in the partnership agreement come to pass (for example, when a major project is completed). The partnership agreement can be written to cover each of these situations, allowing the partnership to continue legally.

MUTUAL AGENCY   Each partner is an agent of the partnership within the scope of the business. Because of this *mutual agency*, any partner can bind the partnership to a business agreement as long as he or she acts within the scope of the company's normal operations. For example, a partner in a used-car business can bind the partnership through the purchase or sale of used cars. But this partner cannot bind the partnership to a contract for buying men's clothing or any other goods that are not related to the used-car business.

UNLIMITED LIABILITY Each partner has personal *unlimited liability* for all the debts of the partnership. If a partnership is in poor financial condition and cannot pay its debts, the creditors first must satisfy their claims from the assets of the partnership. If the assets of the business are not enough to pay all debts, the creditors can seek payment from the personal assets of each partner. If a partner's personal assets are used up before the debts are paid, the creditors can claim additional assets from the remaining partners who are able to pay. Each partner, then, could be required by law to pay all the debts of the partnership.

CO-OWNERSHIP OF PARTNERSHIP PROPERTY When individuals invest property in a partnership, they give up the right to their separate use of the property. The property becomes an asset of the partnership and is owned jointly by all the partners.

PARTICIPATION IN PARTNERSHIP INCOME Each partner has the right to share in the company's income and the responsibility to share in its losses. The partnership agreement should state the method of distributing income and losses to each partner. If the agreement describes how income should be shared but does not mention losses, losses are distributed in the same way as income. If the partners fail to describe the method of income and loss distribution in the partnership agreement, the law states that income and losses must be shared equally.

Accounting for Partners' Equity

The owners' equity of a partnership is called *partners' equity*. In accounting for partners' equity, it is necessary to maintain separate Capital and Withdrawals accounts for each partner and to divide the income and losses of the company among the partners. In the partners' equity section of the balance sheet, the balance of each partner's Capital account is listed separately:

Liabilities and Partners' Equity

Total Liabilities		$28,000
Partners' Equity		
Desmond, Capital	$25,000	
Frank, Capital	34,000	
Total Partners' Equity		59,000
Total Liabilities and Partners' Equity		$87,000

Each partner invests cash, other assets, or a combination in the partnership according to the partnership agreement. Noncash assets should be valued at their fair market value on the date they are transferred to the partnership. The assets invested by a partner are debited to the proper account, and the total amount is credited to the partner's Capital account.

To show how partners' investments are recorded, let's assume that Jerry Adcock and Rose Villa have agreed to combine their capital and equipment in a partnership to operate a jewelry store. According to their partnership agreement, Adcock will invest $28,000 cash and $47,000 of equipment, and the partnership will assume a note payable on the equipment of $10,000. The general journal entry to record one partner's initial investment is as follows:

20x1
July 1   Cash   28,000
          Equipment   47,000
              Note Payable   10,000
              Jerry Adcock, Capital   65,000
                  Initial investment of Jerry
                  Adcock in Adcock and Villa

Distribution of Partnership Income and Losses

A partnership's income and losses can be distributed according to whatever method the partners specify in the partnership agreement. If a partnership agreement does not mention the distribution of income and losses, the law requires that they be shared equally by all partners. Also, if a partnership agreement mentions only the distribution of income, the law requires that losses be distributed in the same ratio as income.

The income of a partnership normally has three components: (1) return to the partners for the use of their capital (called *interest on partners' capital*), (2) compensation for direct services the partners have rendered (partners' salaries), and (3) other income for any special characteristics individual partners may bring to the partnership or risks they may take. The breakdown of total income into its three components helps clarify how much each partner has contributed to the firm.

Several ways for partners to share income are (1) by stated ratios, (2) by capital balance ratios, and (3) by salaries to the partners and interest on partners' capital, with the remaining income shared according to stated ratios. *Salaries* and *interest* here are not *salaries expense* or *interest expense* in the ordinary sense of the terms. They do not affect the amount of reported net income. Instead, they refer to ways of determining each partner's share of net income or loss on the basis of time spent and money invested in the partnership.

STATED RATIOS   One method of distributing income and losses is to give each partner a stated ratio of the total income or loss. If each partner is making an equal contribution to the firm, each can assume the same share of income and losses. It is important to understand that an equal contribution to the firm does not necessarily mean an equal capital investment in the firm. One partner may be devoting more time and talent to the firm, whereas the second partner may make a larger capital investment. And, if the partners contribute unequally to the firm, unequal stated ratios—60 percent and 40 percent, perhaps—can be appropriate. Let's assume that Adcock and Villa had a net income last year of $140,000. The computation of each partner's share of the income and the journal entry to show the distribution based on these ratios are as follows:

Adcock ($140,000 × .60)	$ 84,000
Villa ($140,000 × .40)	56,000
Net income	$140,000

20x2
June 30   Income Summary   140,000
          Jerry Adcock, Capital   84,000
          Rose Villa, Capital   56,000
            Distribution of income for the year
            to the partners' Capital accounts

CAPITAL BALANCE RATIOS   If invested capital produces the most income for the partnership, then income and losses may be distributed according to *capital balance*. One way of distributing income and losses here is to use a ratio based on each partner's capital balance at the beginning of the year. For example, suppose that at the start of the fiscal year, July 1, 20x1, Jerry Adcock, Capital showed a $65,000 balance and Rose Villa, Capital showed a $60,000 balance. The total partners' equity in the firm, then, was $125,000 ($65,000 + $60,000). Each partner's capital balance at the beginning of the year divided by the total partners' equity at the beginning of the year is that partner's beginning capital balance ratio:

	Beginning Capital Balance	Beginning Capital Balance Ratio
Jerry Adcock	$ 65,000	65 ÷ 125 = .52 = 52%
Rose Villa	60,000	60 ÷ 125 = .48 = 48%
	$125,000	

The income that each partner should receive when distribution is based on beginning capital balance ratios is figured by multiplying the total income by each partner's capital ratio. If we assume that income for the year was $140,000, Jerry Adcock's share of that income was $72,800, and Rose Villa's share was $67,200:

Jerry Adcock	$140,000 × .52 = $ 72,800
Rose Villa	$140,000 × .48 = 67,200
	= $140,000

SALARIES, INTEREST, AND STATED RATIOS   Partners generally do not contribute equally to a firm. To make up for unequal contributions, a partnership agreement can allow for partners' salaries, interest on partners' capital balances, or a combination of both in the distribution of income. Again, salaries and interest of this kind are not deducted as expenses before the partnership income is determined. They represent a method of arriving at an equitable distribution of income or loss.

Salaries allow for differences in the services that partners provide the business. However, they do not take into account differences in invested capital. To allow for capital differences, in addition to salary, each partner can receive a stated interest on his or her invested capital. Suppose that Jerry Adcock and Rose Villa agree to receive annual salaries of $8,000 for Adcock and $7,000 for Villa, as well as 10 percent interest on their beginning capital balances, and to share any remaining income equally. The calculations for Adcock and Villa, if we assume income of $140,000, are shown at the top of the next page.

| | Income of Partner | | Income |
	Adcock	Villa	Distributed
Total Income for Distribution			$140,000
Distribution of Salaries			
Adcock	$ 8,000		
Villa		$ 7,000	(15,000)
Remaining Income After Salaries			$125,000
Distribution of Interest			
Adcock ($65,000 × .10)	6,500		
Villa ($60,000 × .10)		6,000	(12,500)
Remaining Income After Salaries and Interest			$112,500
Equal Distribution of Remaining Income			
Adcock ($112,500 × .50)	56,250		
Villa ($112,500 × .50)		56,250	(112,500)
Remaining Income			—
Income of Partners	$70,750	$69,250	$140,000

If the partnership agreement allows for the distribution of salaries or interest or both, the amounts must be allocated to the partners even if profits are not enough to cover the salaries and interest. In fact, even if the company has a loss, these allocations still must be made. The negative balance or loss after the allocation of salaries and interest must be distributed according to the stated ratio in the partnership agreement, or equally if the agreement does not mention a ratio.

For example, let's assume that Adcock and Villa agreed to the following conditions, with much higher annual salaries, for the distribution of income and losses:

	Salaries	Interest	Beginning Capital Balance
Adcock	$70,000	10 percent of beginning	$65,000
Villa	60,000	capital balances	60,000

The income for the first year of operation was $140,000. The computation for the distribution of the income and loss is shown at the top of the next page.

Dissolution of a Partnership

Dissolution of a partnership occurs whenever there is a change in the original association of partners. When a partnership is dissolved, the partners lose their authority to continue the business as a going concern. This does not mean that the business operation necessarily is ended or interrupted, but it does mean—from a legal and accounting standpoint—that the separate entity ceases to exist. The remaining partners can act for the partnership in finishing the affairs of the business or in forming a new partnership that will be a new accounting entity. The dissolution of a partnership takes place through, among other events, the admission of a new partner, the withdrawal of a partner, or the death of a partner.

	Income of Partner		Income
	Adcock	Villa	Distributed
Total Income for Distribution			$140,000
Distribution of Salaries			
Adcock	$70,000		
Villa		$60,000	(130,000)
Remaining Income After Salaries			$ 10,000
Distribution of Interest			
Adcock ($65,000 × .10)	6,500		
Villa ($60,000 × .10)		6,000	(12,500)
Negative Balance After Salaries			
and Interest			($ 2,500)
Equal Distribution of Negative			
Balance*			
Adcock ($2,500 × .50)	(1,250)		
Villa ($2,500 × .50)		(1,250)	2,500
Remaining Income			—
Income of Partners	$75,250	$64,750	$140,000

*Notice that the negative balance is distributed equally because the agreement does not indicate how income and losses should be distributed after salaries and interest are paid.

ADMISSION OF A NEW PARTNER   The admission of a new partner dissolves the old partnership because a new association has been formed. Dissolving the old partnership and creating a new one require the consent of all the old partners and the ratification of a new partnership agreement. An individual can be admitted into a business in one of two ways: (1) by purchasing an interest in the partnership from one or more of the original partners or (2) by investing assets in the partnership.

PURCHASING AN INTEREST FROM A PARTNER   When an individual is admitted to a firm by purchasing an interest from an old partner, each partner must agree to the change. The transaction is a personal one between the old and new partners, but the interest purchased must be transferred from the Capital account of the selling partner to the Capital account of the new partner.

Suppose that Jerry Adcock decides to sell his interest, assumed to be $70,000, in Adcock and Villa to Richard Davis for $100,000 on August 31, 20x3, and that Rose Villa agrees to the sale. The entry to record the sale on the partnership books looks like this:

```
20x3
Aug. 31   Jerry Adcock, Capital                    70,000
              Richard Davis, Capital                        70,000
                  Transfer of Jerry Adcock's equity
                  to Richard Davis
```

Notice that the entry records the book value of the equity, not the amount Davis pays. The amount Davis pays is a personal matter between him and Adcock.

INVESTING ASSETS IN A PARTNERSHIP   When a new partner is admitted through an investment in the partnership, both the assets and the partners' equity in the firm increase. Why is this so? Because the assets the new partner invests become partnership assets, and as partnership assets increase, partners' equity increases as well.

For example, assume that Richard Davis wants to invest $75,000 for a one-third interest in the partnership of Adcock and Villa. The Capital accounts of Jerry Adcock and Rose Villa are assumed to be $70,000 and $80,000, respectively. The assets of the firm are valued correctly. So, the partners agree to sell Davis a one-third interest in the firm for $75,000. Davis's $75,000 investment equals a one-third interest in the firm after the investment is added to the previously existing capital of the partnership:

Jerry Adcock, Capital	$ 70,000
Rose Villa, Capital	80,000
Davis's investment	75,000
Total capital after Davis's investment	$225,000
One-third interest = $225,000 ÷ 3 =	$ 75,000

The journal entry to record Davis's investment is as follows:

20x3			
Aug. 31	Cash	75,000	
	Richard Davis, Capital		75,000
	Admission of Richard Davis for a		
	one-third interest in the company		

BONUS TO THE OLD PARTNERS   Sometimes a partnership may be so profitable or otherwise advantageous that a new investor is willing to pay more than the actual dollar interest that he or she receives in the partnership. Suppose an individual pays $100,000 for an $80,000 interest in a partnership. The $20,000 excess of the payment over the interest purchased is a *bonus* to the original partners. The bonus must be distributed to the original partners according to the partnership agreement. When the agreement does not cover the distribution of bonuses, it should be distributed to the original partners in accordance with the method of distributing income and losses.

Assume that the Adcock and Villa Company has operated for several years and that the partners' capital balances and the stated ratios for distribution of income and loss are as follows:

Partners	Capital Balances	Stated Ratios
Adcock	$160,000	55%
Villa	140,000	45%
	$300,000	100%

Richard Davis wants to join the firm. He offers to invest $100,000 on December 1 for a one-fifth interest in the business and income. The original partners agree to the offer. This is the computation of the bonus to the original partners:

Partners' equity in the original partnership	$300,000
Cash investment by Richard Davis	100,000
Partners' equity in the new partnership	$400,000
Partners' equity assigned to Richard Davis	
($400,000 × ⅕)	$ 80,000

Bonus to the original partners

Investment by Richard Davis	$100,000	
Less equity assigned to Richard Davis	80,000	$ 20,000

Distribution of bonus to original partners

Jerry Adcock ($20,000 × .55)	$ 11,000	
Rose Villa ($20,000 × .45)	9,000	$ 20,000

And this is the journal entry that records Davis's admission to the partnership:

20x3			
Dec. 1	Cash	100,000	
	Jerry Adcock, Capital		11,000
	Rose Villa, Capital		9,000
	Richard Davis, Capital		80,000
	Investment by Richard Davis for a one-fifth interest in the firm, and the bonus distributed to the original partners		

BONUS TO THE NEW PARTNER   There are several reasons why a partnership might want a new partner. A firm in financial trouble might need additional cash. Or the original partners, wanting to expand the firm's markets, might need more capital than they themselves can provide. Also, the partners might know a person who would bring a unique talent to the firm. Under these conditions, a new partner could be admitted to the partnership with the understanding that part of the original partners' capital will be transferred (credited) to the new partner's Capital account as a bonus.

WITHDRAWAL OF A PARTNER   Generally, a partner has the right to withdraw from a partnership in accord with legal requirements. However, to avoid disputes when a partner does decide to withdraw or retire from the firm, the partnership agreement should describe the procedures to be followed. The agreement should specify (1) whether or not an audit will be performed, (2) how the assets will be reappraised, (3) how a bonus will be determined, and (4) by what method the withdrawing partner will be paid.

There are several ways in which an individual can withdraw from a partnership. A partner can (1) sell his or her interest to another partner with the consent of the remaining partners, (2) sell his or her interest to an outsider with the consent of the remaining partners, (3) withdraw assets equal to his or her capital balance, (4) withdraw assets that are less than his or her capital balance (in this case, the remaining partners receive a bonus), or (5) withdraw assets that are greater than his or her capital balance (in this case, the withdrawing partner receives a bonus). Bonuses are allocated in a manner similar to those that arise when a new partner is admitted.

DEATH OF A PARTNER   When a partner dies, the partnership is dissolved because the original association has changed. The partnership agreement should state the actions to be taken. Normally, the books are closed and financial statements prepared. These actions are necessary to determine the capital balance of each partner on the date of the death. The agreement also may indicate whether an audit should be conducted, assets appraised, and a bonus recorded, as well as the procedures for settling with the deceased partner's heirs. The remaining partners may purchase the deceased's equity, sell it to outsiders, or deliver certain business assets to the estate. If the firm intends to continue, a new partnership must be formed.

Liquidation of a Partnership

Liquidation of a partnership is the process of ending the business, of selling enough assets to pay the partnership's liabilities and distributing any remaining assets among the partners. Liquidation is a special form of dissolution. When a partnership is liquidated, the business will not continue. As the assets of the business are sold, any gain or loss should be distributed to the partners according to the stated ratios. As cash becomes available, it must be applied first to outside creditors, then to partners' loans, and finally to the partners' capital balances. Any deficits in partners' capital accounts must be made up from personal assets.

PROBLEMS

P 1.

Partnership Formation and Distribution of Income

In January 20x1, Steve Shaw and Don Noria agreed to produce and sell chocolate candies. Shaw contributed $240,000 in cash to the business. Noria contributed the building and equipment, valued at $220,000 and $140,000, respectively. The partnership had an income of $84,000 during 20x1 but was less successful during 20x2, when income was only $40,000.

REQUIRED

1. Prepare the journal entry to record the investment of both partners in the partnership.
2. Determine the share of income for each partner in 20x1 and 20x2 under each of the following conditions: (a) The partners agreed to share income equally. (b) The partners failed to agree on an income-sharing arrangement. (c) The partners agreed to share income according to the ratio of their original investments. (d) The partners agreed to share income by allowing interest of 10 percent on their original investments and dividing the remainder equally. (e) The partners agreed to share income by allowing salaries of $40,000 for Shaw and $28,000 for Noria, and dividing the remainder equally. (f) The partners agreed to share income by paying salaries of $40,000 to Shaw and $28,000 to Noria, allowing interest of 9 percent on their original investments, and dividing the remainder equally.

P 2.

Admission and Withdrawal of a Partner

Sula, Mary, and Kinesha are partners in Champion Woodwork Company. Their capital balances as of July 31, 20x4, are as follows:

Sula, Capital	Mary, Capital	Kinesha, Capital
45,000	15,000	30,000

Each partner has agreed to admit Angela to the partnership.

REQUIRED

Prepare the journal entries to record Angela's admission to or Sula's withdrawal from the partnership under each of the following independent conditions: (a) Angela pays Sula $12,500 for 20 percent of Sula's interest in the partnership. (b) Angela invests $20,000 cash in the partnership and receives an interest equal to her investment. (c) Angela invests $30,000 cash in the partnership for a 20 percent interest in the business. A bonus is to be recorded for the original partners on the basis of their capital balances. (d) Angela invests $30,000 cash in the partnership for a 40 percent interest in the business. The original partners give Angela a bonus according to the ratio of their capital balances on July 31, 20x4. (e) Sula withdraws from the partnership, taking $52,500. The excess of withdrawn assets over Sula's partnership interest is distributed according to the balances of the Capital accounts. (f) Sula withdraws by selling her interest directly to Angela for $60,000.

APPENDIX D

Future Value and Present Value Tables

Table 1 provides the multipliers necessary to compute the future value of a *single* cash deposit made at the *beginning* of year 1. Three factors must be known before the future value can be computed: (1) the time period in years, (2) the stated annual rate of interest to be earned, and (3) the dollar amount invested or deposited.

EXAMPLE—TABLE 1 Determine the future value of $5,000 deposited now that will earn 9 percent interest compounded annually for five years. From Table 1, the necessary multiplier for five years at 9 percent is 1.539, and the answer is

$$\$5,000 \times 1.539 = \$7,695$$

Where r is the interest rate and n is the number of periods, the factor values for Table 1 are

$$\text{FV factor} = (1 + r)^n$$

Situations requiring the use of Table 2 are similar to those requiring Table 1 except that Table 2 is used to compute the future value of a *series* of *equal* annual deposits at the end of each period.

Table 1. Future Value of $1 After a Given Number of Time Periods

Periods	1%	2%	3%	4%	5%	6%	7%	8%	9%	10%	12%	14%	15%
1	1.010	1.020	1.030	1.040	1.050	1.060	1.070	1.080	1.090	1.100	1.120	1.140	1.150
2	1.020	1.040	1.061	1.082	1.103	1.124	1.145	1.166	1.188	1.210	1.254	1.300	1.323
3	1.030	1.061	1.093	1.125	1.158	1.191	1.225	1.260	1.295	1.331	1.405	1.482	1.521
4	1.041	1.082	1.126	1.170	1.216	1.262	1.311	1.360	1.412	1.464	1.574	1.689	1.749
5	1.051	1.104	1.159	1.217	1.276	1.338	1.403	1.469	1.539	1.611	1.762	1.925	2.011
6	1.062	1.126	1.194	1.265	1.340	1.419	1.501	1.587	1.677	1.772	1.974	2.195	2.313
7	1.072	1.149	1.230	1.316	1.407	1.504	1.606	1.714	1.828	1.949	2.211	2.502	2.660
8	1.083	1.172	1.267	1.369	1.477	1.594	1.718	1.851	1.993	2.144	2.476	2.853	3.059
9	1.094	1.195	1.305	1.423	1.551	1.689	1.838	1.999	2.172	2.358	2.773	3.252	3.518
10	1.105	1.219	1.344	1.480	1.629	1.791	1.967	2.159	2.367	2.594	3.106	3.707	4.046
11	1.116	1.243	1.384	1.539	1.710	1.898	2.105	2.332	2.580	2.853	3.479	4.226	4.652
12	1.127	1.268	1.426	1.601	1.796	2.012	2.252	2.518	2.813	3.138	3.896	4.818	5.350
13	1.138	1.294	1.469	1.665	1.886	2.133	2.410	2.720	3.066	3.452	4.363	5.492	6.153
14	1.149	1.319	1.513	1.732	1.980	2.261	2.579	2.937	3.342	3.798	4.887	6.261	7.076
15	1.161	1.346	1.558	1.801	2.079	2.397	2.759	3.172	3.642	4.177	5.474	7.138	8.137
16	1.173	1.373	1.605	1.873	2.183	2.540	2.952	3.426	3.970	4.595	6.130	8.137	9.358
17	1.184	1.400	1.653	1.948	2.292	2.693	3.159	3.700	4.328	5.054	6.866	9.276	10.760
18	1.196	1.428	1.702	2.026	2.407	2.854	3.380	3.996	4.717	5.560	7.690	10.580	12.380
19	1.208	1.457	1.754	2.107	2.527	3.026	3.617	4.316	5.142	6.116	8.613	12.060	14.230
20	1.220	1.486	1.806	2.191	2.653	3.207	3.870	4.661	5.604	6.728	9.646	13.740	16.370
21	1.232	1.516	1.860	2.279	2.786	3.400	4.141	5.034	6.109	7.400	10.800	15.670	18.820
22	1.245	1.546	1.916	2.370	2.925	3.604	4.430	5.437	6.659	8.140	12.100	17.860	21.640
23	1.257	1.577	1.974	2.465	3.072	3.820	4.741	5.871	7.258	8.954	13.550	20.360	24.890
24	1.270	1.608	2.033	2.563	3.225	4.049	5.072	6.341	7.911	9.850	15.180	23.210	28.630
25	1.282	1.641	2.094	2.666	3.386	4.292	5.427	6.848	8.623	10.830	17.000	26.460	32.920
26	1.295	1.673	2.157	2.772	3.556	4.549	5.807	7.396	9.399	11.920	19.040	30.170	37.860
27	1.308	1.707	2.221	2.883	3.733	4.822	6.214	7.988	10.250	13.110	21.320	34.390	43.540
28	1.321	1.741	2.288	2.999	3.920	5.112	6.649	8.627	11.170	14.420	23.880	39.200	50.070
29	1.335	1.776	2.357	3.119	4.116	5.418	7.114	9.317	12.170	15.860	26.750	44.690	57.580
30	1.348	1.811	2.427	3.243	4.322	5.743	7.612	10.060	13.270	17.450	29.960	50.950	66.210
40	1.489	2.208	3.262	4.801	7.040	10.290	14.970	21.720	31.410	45.260	93.050	188.900	267.900
50	1.645	2.692	4.384	7.107	11.470	18.420	29.460	46.900	74.360	117.400	289.000	700.200	1,084.000

Table 2. Future Value of $1 Paid in Each Period for a Given Number of Time Periods

Periods	1%	2%	3%	4%	5%	6%	7%	8%	9%	10%	12%	14%	15%
1	1.000	1.000	1.000	1.000	1.000	1.000	1.000	1.000	1.000	1.000	1.000	1.000	1.000
2	2.010	2.020	2.030	2.040	2.050	2.060	2.070	2.080	2.090	2.100	2.120	2.140	2.150
3	3.030	3.060	3.091	3.122	3.153	3.184	3.215	3.246	3.278	3.310	3.374	3.440	3.473
4	4.060	4.122	4.184	4.246	4.310	4.375	4.440	4.506	4.573	4.641	4.779	4.921	4.993
5	5.101	5.204	5.309	5.416	5.526	5.637	5.751	5.867	5.985	6.105	6.353	6.610	6.742
6	6.152	6.308	6.468	6.633	6.802	6.975	7.153	7.336	7.523	7.716	8.115	8.536	8.754
7	7.214	7.434	7.662	7.898	8.142	8.394	8.654	8.923	9.200	9.487	10.090	10.730	11.070
8	8.286	8.583	8.892	9.214	9.549	9.897	10.260	10.640	11.030	11.440	12.300	13.230	13.730
9	9.369	9.755	10.160	10.580	11.030	11.490	11.980	12.490	13.020	13.580	14.780	16.090	16.790
10	10.460	10.950	11.460	12.010	12.580	13.180	13.820	14.490	15.190	15.940	17.550	19.340	20.300
11	11.570	12.170	12.810	13.490	14.210	14.970	15.780	16.650	17.560	18.530	20.650	23.040	24.350
12	12.680	13.410	14.190	15.030	15.920	16.870	17.890	18.980	20.140	21.380	24.130	27.270	29.000
13	13.810	14.680	15.620	16.630	17.710	18.880	20.140	21.500	22.950	24.520	28.030	32.090	34.350
14	14.950	15.970	17.090	18.290	19.600	21.020	22.550	24.210	26.020	27.980	32.390	37.580	40.500
15	16.100	17.290	18.600	20.020	21.580	23.280	25.130	27.150	29.360	31.770	37.280	43.840	47.580
16	17.260	18.640	20.160	21.820	23.660	25.670	27.890	30.320	33.000	35.950	42.750	50.980	55.720
17	18.430	20.010	21.760	23.700	25.840	28.210	30.840	33.750	36.970	40.540	48.880	59.120	65.080
18	19.610	21.410	23.410	25.650	28.130	30.910	34.000	37.450	41.300	45.600	55.750	68.390	75.840
19	20.810	22.840	25.120	27.670	30.540	33.760	37.380	41.450	46.020	51.160	63.440	78.970	88.210
20	22.020	24.300	26.870	29.780	33.070	36.790	41.000	45.760	51.160	57.280	72.050	91.020	102.400
21	23.240	25.780	28.680	31.970	35.720	39.990	44.870	50.420	56.760	64.000	81.700	104.800	118.800
22	24.470	27.300	30.540	34.250	38.510	43.390	49.010	55.460	62.870	71.400	92.500	120.400	137.600
23	25.720	28.850	32.450	36.620	41.430	47.000	53.440	60.890	69.530	79.540	104.600	138.300	159.300
24	26.970	30.420	34.430	39.080	44.500	50.820	58.180	66.760	76.790	88.500	118.200	158.700	184.200
25	28.240	32.030	36.460	41.650	47.730	54.860	63.250	73.110	84.700	98.350	133.300	181.900	212.800
26	29.530	33.670	38.550	44.310	51.110	59.160	68.680	79.950	93.320	109.200	150.300	208.300	245.700
27	30.820	35.340	40.710	47.080	54.670	63.710	74.480	87.350	102.700	121.100	169.400	238.500	283.600
28	32.130	37.050	42.930	49.970	58.400	68.530	80.700	95.340	113.000	134.200	190.700	272.900	327.100
29	33.450	38.790	45.220	52.970	62.320	73.640	87.350	104.000	124.100	148.600	214.600	312.100	377.200
30	34.780	40.570	47.580	56.080	66.440	79.060	94.460	113.300	136.300	164.500	241.300	356.800	434.700
40	48.890	60.400	75.400	95.030	120.800	154.800	199.600	259.100	337.900	442.600	767.100	1,342.000	1,779.000
50	64.460	84.580	112.800	152.700	209.300	290.300	406.500	573.800	815.100	1,164.000	2,400.000	4,995.000	7,218.000

EXAMPLE—TABLE 2   What will be the future value at the end of 30 years if $1,000 is deposited each year on January 1, beginning in one year, assuming 12 percent interest compounded annually? The required multiplier from Table 2 is 241.3, and the answer is

$$\$1,000 \times 241.3 = \$241,300$$

The factor values for Table 2 are

$$\text{FVa factor} = \frac{(1 + r)^n - 1}{r}$$

Table 3. Present Value of $1 to Be Received at the End of a Given Number of Time Periods

Periods	1%	2%	3%	4%	5%	6%	7%	8%	9%	10%	12%
1	0.990	0.980	0.971	0.962	0.952	0.943	0.935	0.926	0.917	0.909	0.893
2	0.980	0.961	0.943	0.925	0.907	0.890	0.873	0.857	0.842	0.826	0.797
3	0.971	0.942	0.915	0.889	0.864	0.840	0.816	0.794	0.772	0.751	0.712
4	0.961	0.924	0.888	0.855	0.823	0.792	0.763	0.735	0.708	0.683	0.636
5	0.951	0.906	0.883	0.822	0.784	0.747	0.713	0.681	0.650	0.621	0.567
6	0.942	0.888	0.837	0.790	0.746	0.705	0.666	0.630	0.596	0.564	0.507
7	0.933	0.871	0.813	0.760	0.711	0.665	0.623	0.583	0.547	0.513	0.452
8	0.923	0.853	0.789	0.731	0.677	0.627	0.582	0.540	0.502	0.467	0.404
9	0.914	0.837	0.766	0.703	0.645	0.592	0.544	0.500	0.460	0.424	0.361
10	0.905	0.820	0.744	0.676	0.614	0.558	0.508	0.463	0.422	0.386	0.322
11	0.896	0.804	0.722	0.650	0.585	0.527	0.475	0.429	0.388	0.350	0.287
12	0.887	0.788	0.701	0.625	0.557	0.497	0.444	0.397	0.356	0.319	0.257
13	0.879	0.773	0.681	0.601	0.530	0.469	0.415	0.368	0.326	0.290	0.229
14	0.870	0.758	0.661	0.577	0.505	0.442	0.388	0.340	0.299	0.263	0.205
15	0.861	0.743	0.642	0.555	0.481	0.417	0.362	0.315	0.275	0.239	0.183
16	0.853	0.728	0.623	0.534	0.458	0.394	0.339	0.292	0.252	0.218	0.163
17	0.844	0.714	0.605	0.513	0.436	0.371	0.317	0.270	0.231	0.198	0.146
18	0.836	0.700	0.587	0.494	0.416	0.350	0.296	0.250	0.212	0.180	0.130
19	0.828	0.686	0.570	0.475	0.396	0.331	0.277	0.232	0.194	0.164	0.116
20	0.820	0.673	0.554	0.456	0.377	0.312	0.258	0.215	0.178	0.149	0.104
21	0.811	0.660	0.538	0.439	0.359	0.294	0.242	0.199	0.164	0.135	0.093
22	0.803	0.647	0.522	0.422	0.342	0.278	0.226	0.184	0.150	0.123	0.083
23	0.795	0.634	0.507	0.406	0.326	0.262	0.211	0.170	0.138	0.112	0.074
24	0.788	0.622	0.492	0.390	0.310	0.247	0.197	0.158	0.126	0.102	0.066
25	0.780	0.610	0.478	0.375	0.295	0.233	0.184	0.146	0.116	0.092	0.059
26	0.772	0.598	0.464	0.361	0.281	0.220	0.172	0.135	0.106	0.084	0.053
27	0.764	0.586	0.450	0.347	0.268	0.207	0.161	0.125	0.098	0.076	0.047
28	0.757	0.574	0.437	0.333	0.255	0.196	0.150	0.116	0.090	0.069	0.042
29	0.749	0.563	0.424	0.321	0.243	0.185	0.141	0.107	0.082	0.063	0.037
30	0.742	0.552	0.412	0.308	0.231	0.174	0.131	0.099	0.075	0.057	0.033
40	0.672	0.453	0.307	0.208	0.142	0.097	0.067	0.046	0.032	0.022	0.011
50	0.608	0.372	0.228	0.141	0.087	0.054	0.034	0.021	0.013	0.009	0.003

Table 3 is used to compute the value today of a single amount of cash to be received sometime in the future. To use Table 3, you must first know: (1) the time period in years until funds will be received, (2) the stated annual rate of interest, and (3) the dollar amount to be received at the end of the time period.

EXAMPLE—TABLE 3   What is the present value of $30,000 to be received 25 years from now, assuming a 14 percent interest rate? From Table 3, the required multiplier is .038, and the answer is

$$\$30,000 \times .038 = \$1,140$$

14%	15%	16%	18%	20%	25%	30%	35%	40%	45%	50%	Periods
0.877	0.870	0.862	0.847	0.833	0.800	0.769	0.741	0.714	0.690	0.667	1
0.769	0.756	0.743	0.718	0.694	0.640	0.592	0.549	0.510	0.476	0.444	2
0.675	0.658	0.641	0.609	0.579	0.512	0.455	0.406	0.364	0.328	0.296	3
0.592	0.572	0.552	0.516	0.482	0.410	0.350	0.301	0.260	0.226	0.198	4
0.519	0.497	0.476	0.437	0.402	0.328	0.269	0.223	0.186	0.156	0.132	5
0.456	0.432	0.410	0.370	0.335	0.262	0.207	0.165	0.133	0.108	0.088	6
0.400	0.376	0.354	0.314	0.279	0.210	0.159	0.122	0.095	0.074	0.059	7
0.351	0.327	0.305	0.266	0.233	0.168	0.123	0.091	0.068	0.051	0.039	8
0.308	0.284	0.263	0.225	0.194	0.134	0.094	0.067	0.048	0.035	0.026	9
0.270	0.247	0.227	0.191	0.162	0.107	0.073	0.050	0.035	0.024	0.017	10
0.237	0.215	0.195	0.162	0.135	0.086	0.056	0.037	0.025	0.017	0.012	11
0.208	0.187	0.168	0.137	0.112	0.069	0.043	0.027	0.018	0.012	0.008	12
0.182	0.163	0.145	0.116	0.093	0.055	0.033	0.020	0.013	0.008	0.005	13
0.160	0.141	0.125	0.099	0.078	0.044	0.025	0.015	0.009	0.006	0.003	14
0.140	0.123	0.108	0.084	0.065	0.035	0.020	0.011	0.006	0.004	0.002	15
0.123	0.107	0.093	0.071	0.054	0.028	0.015	0.008	0.005	0.003	0.002	16
0.108	0.093	0.080	0.060	0.045	0.023	0.012	0.006	0.003	0.002	0.001	17
0.095	0.081	0.069	0.051	0.038	0.018	0.009	0.005	0.002	0.001	0.001	18
0.083	0.070	0.060	0.043	0.031	0.014	0.007	0.003	0.002	0.001		19
0.073	0.061	0.051	0.037	0.026	0.012	0.005	0.002	0.001	0.001		20
0.064	0.053	0.044	0.031	0.022	0.009	0.004	0.002	0.001			21
0.056	0.046	0.038	0.026	0.018	0.007	0.003	0.001	0.001			22
0.049	0.040	0.033	0.022	0.015	0.006	0.002	0.001				23
0.043	0.035	0.028	0.019	0.013	0.005	0.002	0.001				24
0.038	0.030	0.024	0.016	0.010	0.004	0.001	0.001				25
0.033	0.026	0.021	0.014	0.009	0.003	0.001					26
0.029	0.023	0.018	0.011	0.007	0.002	0.001					27
0.026	0.020	0.016	0.010	0.006	0.002	0.001					28
0.022	0.017	0.014	0.008	0.005	0.002						29
0.020	0.015	0.012	0.007	0.004	0.001						30
0.005	0.004	0.003	0.001	0.001							40
0.001	0.001	0.001									50

The factor values for Table 3 are

$$\text{PV factor} = (1 + r)^{-n}$$

Table 3 is the reciprocal of Table 1.

Table 4 is used to compute the present value of a *series* of *equal* annual cash flows.

EXAMPLE—TABLE 4   Arthur Howard won a contest on January 1, 2002, in which the prize was $30,000, the money was payable in 15 annual installments of $2,000 every December 31, beginning in 2002. Assuming a 9 percent interest rate, what is

Table 4. Present Value of $1 Received Each Period for a Given Number of Time Periods

Periods	1%	2%	3%	4%	5%	6%	7%	8%	9%	10%	12%
1	0.990	0.980	0.971	0.962	0.952	0.943	0.935	0.926	0.917	0.909	0.893
2	1.970	1.942	1.913	1.886	1.859	1.833	1.808	1.783	1.759	1.736	1.690
3	2.941	2.884	2.829	2.775	2.723	2.673	2.624	2.577	2.531	2.487	2.402
4	3.902	3.808	3.717	3.630	3.546	3.465	3.387	3.312	3.240	3.170	3.037
5	4.853	4.713	4.580	4.452	4.329	4.212	4.100	3.993	3.890	3.791	3.605
6	5.795	5.601	5.417	5.242	5.076	4.917	4.767	4.623	4.486	4.355	4.111
7	6.728	6.472	6.230	6.002	5.786	5.582	5.389	5.206	5.033	4.868	4.564
8	7.652	7.325	7.020	6.733	6.463	6.210	5.971	5.747	5.535	5.335	4.968
9	8.566	8.162	7.786	7.435	7.108	6.802	6.515	6.247	5.995	5.759	5.328
10	9.471	8.983	8.530	8.111	7.722	7.360	7.024	6.710	6.418	6.145	5.650
11	10.368	9.787	9.253	8.760	8.306	7.887	7.499	7.139	6.805	6.495	5.938
12	11.255	10.575	9.954	9.385	8.863	8.384	7.943	7.536	7.161	6.814	6.194
13	12.134	11.348	10.635	9.986	9.394	8.853	8.358	7.904	7.487	7.103	6.424
14	13.004	12.106	11.296	10.563	9.899	9.295	8.745	8.244	7.786	7.367	6.628
15	13.865	12.849	11.938	11.118	10.380	9.712	9.108	8.559	8.061	7.606	6.811
16	14.718	13.578	12.561	11.652	10.838	10.106	9.447	8.851	8.313	7.824	6.974
17	15.562	14.292	13.166	12.166	11.274	10.477	9.763	9.122	8.544	8.022	7.120
18	16.398	14.992	13.754	12.659	11.690	10.828	10.059	9.372	8.756	8.201	7.250
19	17.226	15.678	14.324	13.134	12.085	11.158	10.336	9.604	8.950	8.365	7.366
20	18.046	16.351	14.878	13.590	12.462	11.470	10.594	9.818	9.129	8.514	7.469
21	18.857	17.011	15.415	14.029	12.821	11.764	10.836	10.017	9.292	8.649	7.562
22	19.660	17.658	15.937	14.451	13.163	12.042	11.061	10.201	9.442	8.772	7.645
23	20.456	18.292	16.444	14.857	13.489	12.303	11.272	10.371	9.580	8.883	7.718
24	21.243	18.914	16.936	15.247	13.799	12.550	11.469	10.529	9.707	8.985	7.784
25	22.023	19.523	17.413	15.622	14.094	12.783	11.654	10.675	9.823	9.077	7.843
26	22.795	20.121	17.877	15.983	14.375	13.003	11.826	10.810	9.929	9.161	7.896
27	23.560	20.707	18.327	16.330	14.643	13.211	11.987	10.935	10.027	9.237	7.943
28	24.316	21.281	18.764	16.663	14.898	13.406	12.137	11.051	10.116	9.307	7.984
29	25.066	21.844	19.189	16.984	15.141	13.591	12.278	11.158	10.198	9.370	8.022
30	25.808	22.396	19.600	17.292	15.373	13.765	12.409	11.258	10.274	9.427	8.055
40	32.835	27.355	23.115	19.793	17.159	15.046	13.332	11.925	10.757	9.779	8.244
50	39.196	31.424	25.730	21.482	18.256	15.762	13.801	12.234	10.962	9.915	8.305

the present value of Mr. Howard's prize on January 1, 2002? From Table 4, the required multiplier is 8.061, and the answer is:

$$\$2,000 \times 8.061 = \$16,122$$

The factor values for Table 4 are

$$\text{PVa factor} = \frac{1 - (1 + r)^{-n}}{r}$$

Table 4 is the columnar sum of Table 3. Table 4 applies to *ordinary annuities,* in which the first cash flow occurs one time period beyond the date for which the present value is to be computed.

14%	15%	16%	18%	20%	25%	30%	35%	40%	45%	50%	Periods
0.877	0.870	0.862	0.847	0.833	0.800	0.769	0.741	0.714	0.690	0.667	1
1.647	1.626	1.605	1.566	1.528	1.440	1.361	1.289	1.224	1.165	1.111	2
2.322	2.283	2.246	2.174	2.106	1.952	1.816	1.696	1.589	1.493	1.407	3
2.914	2.855	2.798	2.690	2.589	2.362	2.166	1.997	1.849	1.720	1.605	4
3.433	3.352	3.274	3.127	2.991	2.689	2.436	2.220	2.035	1.876	1.737	5
3.889	3.784	3.685	3.498	3.326	2.951	2.643	2.385	2.168	1.983	1.824	6
4.288	4.160	4.039	3.812	3.605	3.161	2.802	2.508	2.263	2.057	1.883	7
4.639	4.487	4.344	4.078	3.837	3.329	2.925	2.598	2.331	2.109	1.922	8
4.946	4.772	4.607	4.303	4.031	3.463	3.019	2.665	2.379	2.144	1.948	9
5.216	5.019	4.833	4.494	4.192	3.571	3.092	2.715	2.414	2.168	1.965	10
5.453	5.234	5.029	4.656	4.327	3.656	3.147	2.752	2.438	2.185	1.977	11
5.660	5.421	5.197	4.793	4.439	3.725	3.190	2.779	2.456	2.197	1.985	12
5.842	5.583	5.342	4.910	4.533	3.780	3.223	2.799	2.469	2.204	1.990	13
6.002	5.724	5.468	5.008	4.611	3.824	3.249	2.814	2.478	2.210	1.993	14
6.142	5.847	5.575	5.092	4.675	3.859	3.268	2.825	2.484	2.214	1.995	15
6.265	5.954	5.669	5.162	4.730	3.887	3.283	2.834	2.489	2.216	1.997	16
6.373	6.047	5.749	5.222	4.775	3.910	3.295	2.840	2.492	2.218	1.998	17
6.467	6.128	5.818	5.273	4.812	3.928	3.304	2.844	2.494	2.219	1.999	18
6.550	6.198	5.877	5.316	4.844	3.942	3.311	2.848	2.496	2.220	1.999	19
6.623	6.259	5.929	5.353	4.870	3.954	3.316	2.850	2.497	2.221	1.999	20
6.687	6.312	5.973	5.384	4.891	3.963	3.320	2.852	2.498	2.221	2.000	21
6.743	6.359	6.011	5.410	4.909	3.970	3.323	2.853	2.498	2.222	2.000	22
6.792	6.399	6.044	5.432	4.925	3.976	3.325	2.854	2.499	2.222	2.000	23
6.835	6.434	6.073	5.451	4.937	3.981	3.327	2.855	2.499	2.222	2.000	24
6.873	6.464	6.097	5.467	4.948	3.985	3.329	2.856	2.499	2.222	2.000	25
6.906	6.491	6.118	5.480	4.956	3.988	3.330	2.856	2.500	2.222	2.000	26
6.935	6.514	6.136	5.492	4.964	3.990	3.331	2.856	2.500	2.222	2.000	27
6.961	6.534	6.152	5.502	4.970	3.992	3.331	2.857	2.500	2.222	2.000	28
6.983	6.551	6.166	5.510	4.975	3.994	3.332	2.857	2.500	2.222	2.000	29
7.003	6.566	6.177	5.517	4.979	3.995	3.332	2.857	2.500	2.222	2.000	30
7.105	6.642	6.234	5.548	4.997	3.999	3.333	2.857	2.500	2.222	2.000	40
7.133	6.661	6.246	5.554	4.999	4.000	3.333	2.857	2.500	2.222	2.000	50

An *annuity due* is a series of equal cash flows for N time periods, but the first payment occurs immediately. The present value of the first payment equals the face value of the cash flow; Table 4 then is used to measure the present value of N − 1 remaining cash flows.

EXAMPLE—TABLE 4　Determine the present value on January 1, 2002, of 20 lease payments; each payment of $10,000 is due on January 1, beginning in 2002. Assume an interest rate of 8 percent.

Present value = Immediate payment + $\begin{cases} \text{Present value of 19 subsequent} \\ \text{payments at 8\%} \end{cases}$

= $10,000 + ($10,000 × 9.604) = $106,040

Company Name Index

Subject Index

Print and Electronic Supplements

For Instructors

Instructor's Solutions Manual. The manual contains answers to all text exercises, financial analysis cases, problems, and skills development cases.

Electronic Solutions. This resource, which contains solutions from the printed Instructor's Solutions Manual, allows instructors to manipulate the numbers in the classroom or to distribute solutions electronically.

Course Manual. Filled with practical advice and teaching tips, this helpful manual includes a discussion of recent changes in accounting information, chapter-by-chapter instructional materials, and review quizzes.

Test Bank with Achievement Test Masters and Answers. This test bank provides more than 3,000 true-false, multiple choice, short essay, and critical-thinking questions, as well as exercises and problems.

Computerized Test Bank. This Windows-based supplement allows instructors to create tests based on any combination of questions in the *Test Bank*.

Teaching Transparency Masters. This booklet contains figures, tables, exhibits, and learning objectives from the text, as well as supplementary material from outside the text.

Solutions Transparencies. More than 1,000 transparencies provide solutions for every exercise problem, alternate problem, and case in the text, including appendices.

PowerPoint Classroom Presentation Slides. This lecture system offers 50–60 slides per chapter. The slides contain classroom presentation materials, discussion questions, figures, exhibits, and tables.

Video Cases. These videos accompany the in-text cases and provide real-world opportunities to reinforce key terms and concepts.

Business Bulletin Videos. These videos present four 10-minute segments about real companies facing accounting issues.

For Students

Study Guide. Designed to help students improve their course performance, the Study Guide is divided into five sections: "Reviewing the Chapter," "Self-Test," "Testing Students' Knowledge," "Applying Your Knowledge," and "Answers."

Working Papers for Exercises and Problems. The Working Papers provide the appropriate forms for solving computational exercises and problems from the text.

NEW! Ready Notes. PowerPoint slides are provided in a printed format, with space for in-class note taking.

Windows General Ledger Software. This general ledger program is designed to function as a commercial package, and contains preliminary data for selected problems in the text.

Excel Templates. This program contains templates for all Problems and Alternate Problems in the text. Using it, students learn both accounting and the basic skills required for spreadsheet applications.

NEW! Houghton Mifflin Brief Accounting Dictionary. Compiled by the same team that creates the American Heritage Dictionary, this supplement is designed to help students understand accounting terminology.

Soft-Tec Practice Case. This practice case, which can be solved either manually or on a computer, involves a one-month accounting cycle for a wholesale software merchandiser operating as a corporation.

General Mills, Inc. Annual Report Financial Decision Case. This decision case, which includes a real company's annual report, introduces students to the ways financial accounting information is used in real-world circumstances.